Mass Media Law

20th Edition

Clay Calvert
University of Florida

Dan V. Kozlowski
Saint Louis University

Derigan Silver
University of Denver

Mc
Graw
Hill
Education

MASS MEDIA LAW, TWENTIETH EDITION

Published by McGraw-Hill Education, 2 Penn Plaza, New York, NY 10121. Copyright © 2018 by McGraw-Hill Education. All rights reserved. Printed in the United States of America. Previous editions © 2015, 2013, and 2011. No part of this publication may be reproduced or distributed in any form or by any means, or stored in a database or retrieval system, without the prior written consent of McGraw-Hill Education, including, but not limited to, in any network or other electronic storage or transmission, or broadcast for distance learning.

Some ancillaries, including electronic and print components, may not be available to customers outside the United States.

This book is printed on acid-free paper.

1 2 3 4 5 6 7 8 9 LCR 21 20 19 18 17

ISBN 978-1-259-91390-7
MHID 1-259-91390-2

Portfolio Manager: *Jamie Laferrera*
Product Developer: *Alexander Preiss*
Senior Marketing Manager: *Laura Young*
Content Project Managers: *Ryan Warczynski, Samantha Donisi-Hamm, Sandra Schnee*
Senior Buyer: *Sandy Ludovissy*
Lead Content Licensing Specialist: *Carrie Burger*
Cover Image: *©wellphoto/Shutterstock RF*
Compositor: *MPS Limited*

All credits appearing on page or at the end of the book are considered to be an extension of the copyright page.

The Internet addresses listed in the text were accurate at the time of publication. The inclusion of a Web site does not indicate an endorsement by the authors or McGraw-Hill Education, and McGraw-Hill Education does not guarantee the accuracy of the information presented at these sites.

mheducation.com/highered

CONTENTS

Contents

9 Gathering Information: Records and Meetings   323

10 Protection of News Sources/Contempt Power   387

11 Free Press–Fair Trial: Trial-Level Remedies and Restrictive Orders ———— 429

12 Free Press–Fair Trial: Closed Judicial Proceedings ———— 455

13 Regulation of Obscene and Other Erotic Material ———— 483

16 Telecommunications Regulation _____ 611

PREFACE

Today, perhaps more than ever, it is vital for college students in the United States to understand the principles of media law and the First Amendment freedoms of speech, press and assembly. Shortly before this preface was drafted, the nation's president labeled journalists at ABC, CBS, NBC, CNN and *The New York Times* "the enemy of the American people." What's more, terms such as "fake news" and "alternative facts" were taking on controversial lives of their own. And at least 15 states had bills pending in their legislatures in 2017 that threatened to reduce the ability of citizens to engage in protests, thus not only jeopardizing free speech but also "the right of the people peaceably to assemble."

It thus is fitting that the 20th edition of this textbook sees two new co-authors who bring fresh perspectives, renewed energy and scholarly expertise to the topics spanning all 16 chapters. It simply wouldn't be possible for any one person alone to replace outgoing author Don Pember. This edition thus brings with it both Dan Kozlowski of Saint Louis University and Derigan Silver of the University of Denver. They have extensive backgrounds in teaching and writing about a wide range of media law topics. Their new voices, coupled with the continuing guidance and authorship of Clay Calvert, hopefully make the 20th edition of *Mass Media Law* timely, relevant and helpful to undergraduates across the communication fields of advertising, journalism, media studies, public relations and telecommunications.

Although updating this edition began as an attempt to keep real-life examples fresh and lively, it quickly became apparent that so much had happened in media law (and continues to happen) that a more thorough rewrite was needed. First, the text changes its approach to Internet and new(er) communication law. Rather than continually devoting separate sections to address media law and the Internet, chapters now generally integrate discussions of how the law applies to the Internet throughout the book. So much of media law today involves the Web—meaning that so much of each chapter in this book now necessarily involves the Web.

In addition, the 20th edition has updated information, examples and cases in every chapter. The last few years of media law have been very active, with courts regularly facing new cases and issues. In addition to a wide number of new examples, such as the recent privacy case involving Hulk Hogan and the defamation suit against *Rolling Stone* magazine filed by a dean at the University of Virginia, the book features new material on the right to record police officers in public settings, on net neutrality, on the FCC's regulation of indecency, on laws concerning information gathering with drones, a new section on Internet defamation by anonymous third-party posters, updates on recent changes to the Freedom of Information Act (FOIA) and new information about trademark law in our chapter on intellectual property, among other updates.

In light of the lack of recent obscenity prosecutions in the United States, as well as comments from some reviewers and users of the book that they don't cover obscenity during class and to reduce pages where possible, we have significantly streamlined

Chapter 13. The key rules and tests regarding obscenity, child pornography and the zoning of sexually oriented businesses, however, remain and have been updated where needed.

Mc Graw Hill Education connect®

The 20th edition of *Mass Media Law* is now available online with Connect, McGraw-Hill Education's integrated assignment and assessment platform. Connect also offers Smart-Book for the new edition, which is the first adaptive reading experience proven to improve grades and help students study more effectively. All of the title's Web site and ancillary content is also available through Connect, including:

- A full Test Bank of multiple-choice questions that test students on central concepts and ideas in each chapter.
- An Instructor's Manual for each chapter with full chapter outlines, sample test questions and discussion topics.
- Lecture Slides for instructor use in class and downloadable RAP forms.

McGraw-Hill Connect® is a highly reliable, easy-to-use homework and learning management solution that utilizes learning science and award-winning adaptive tools to improve student results.

Homework and Adaptive Learning

- Connect's assignments help students contextualize what they've learned through application, so they can better understand the material and think critically.
- Connect will create a personalized study path customized to individual student needs through SmartBook®.
- SmartBook helps students study more efficiently by delivering an interactive reading experience through adaptive highlighting and review.

Connect's Impact on Retention Rates, Pass Rates, and Average Exam Scores

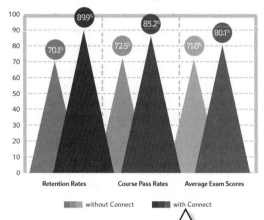

	Retention Rates	Course Pass Rates	Average Exam Scores

■ without Connect   ■ with Connect

Values shown: 70.1%, 89.9%, 72.5%, 85.2%, 71.0%, 80.1%

Over **7 billion questions** have been answered, making McGraw-Hill Education products more intelligent, reliable, and precise.

Using **Connect** improves retention rates by **19.8%**, passing rates by **12.7%, and** exam scores by **9.1%.**

73% of instructors who use **Connect** require it; instructor satisfaction **increases** by 28% when **Connect** is required.

Quality Content and Learning Resources

- Connect content is authored by the world's best subject matter experts, and is available to your class through a simple and intuitive interface.
- The Connect eBook makes it easy for students to access their reading material on smartphones and tablets. They can study on the go and don't need Internet access to use the eBook as a reference, with full functionality.
- Multimedia content such as videos, simulations, and games drive student engagement and critical thinking skills.

Robust Analytics and Reporting

- Connect Insight® generates easy-to-read reports on individual students, the class as a whole, and on specific assignments.

- The Connect Insight dashboard delivers data on performance, study behavior, and effort. Instructors can quickly identify students who struggle and focus on material that the class has yet to master.

- Connect automatically grades assignments and quizzes, providing easy-to-read reports on individual and class performance.

©Hero Images/Getty Images

Impact on Final Course Grade Distribution

without Connect		with Connect
22.9%	A	31.0%
27.4%	B	34.3%
22.9%	C	18.7%
11.5%	D	6.1%
15.4%	F	9.9%

More students earn **As** and **Bs** when they use **Connect**.

Trusted Service and Support

- Connect integrates with your LMS to provide single sign-on and automatic syncing of grades. Integration with Blackboard®, D2L®, and Canvas also provides automatic syncing of the course calendar and assignment-level linking.

- Connect offers comprehensive service, support, and training throughout every phase of your implementation.

- If you're looking for some guidance on how to use Connect, or want to learn tips and tricks from super users, you can find tutorials as you work. Our Digital Faculty Consultants and Student Ambassadors offer insight into how to achieve the results you want with Connect.

ACKNOWLEDGMENTS

Clay Calvert thanks both Dan Kozlowski and Derigan Silver for enthusiastically and energetically taking on the massive endeavor that it is co-authoring a textbook. He also thanks his undergraduates in the College of Journalism and Communications at the University of Florida for their feedback on the book. Finally, Clay Calvert thanks Berl Brechner for his continuing support of the Marion B. Brechner First Amendment Project and other initiatives in the College of Journalism and Communications.

Dan Kozlowski is grateful that Clay Calvert invited him to join the book as a co-author. Clay is a giant in the field of media law, and Dan appreciates the guidance Clay has provided both throughout the writing of this edition and also throughout Dan's academic career in general. Dan also thanks Derigan Silver for his feedback and his sense of humor as they worked together on this project. And Dan thanks his wife and two daughters for being awesome and for helping to keep him level-headed.

Derigan Silver thanks Clay Calvert for inviting him to be a co-author of the book and for providing mentorship and advice for a number of years. He also thanks Dan for his feedback and inspiration throughout this project. He would also like to thank his students at the University of Denver for their interesting and engaging questions, comments and concerns. Finally, he thanks his wife, Alison, for putting up with him.

We would also like to thank those instructors who reviewed our book and gave us their valuable input. It is much appreciated. They are: Betsy Emmons, Samford University; Dr. Felisa B. Kaplan, NY Institute of Technology; and David Shipley, Samford University.

Finally, all three authors greatly appreciate the support of McGraw-Hill and the multiple individuals there who assisted with the publishing of this book.

IMPORTANT NEW, EXPANDED OR UPDATED MATERIAL

Chapter 1

- New examples of equity law, including a restraining order against a South Carolina reporter and an injunction barring speakers from repeating defamatory comments
- New case illustrating the void for vagueness doctrine
- Discussion of a 2016 North Carolina Supreme Court decision striking down a cyberbullying statute as overbroad

Chapter 2

- New examples of self-censorship, including major U.S. news outlets not publishing cartoons depicting the Prophet Muhammad in 2015 and ESPN's firing of Curt Schilling in 2016
- New discussion about Milo Yiannopoulos' college campus visits and community censorship

Chapter 3

- Multiple new examples of high school censorship involving newspapers, T-shirts and Confederate flag imagery
- New discussion of the 2015 case *Bell* v. *Itawamba County School Board* involving punishment of a student for posting a profanity-laced rap recording online
- New examples of efforts to ban books in public schools and libraries
- New discussion of a 2016 appellate court case striking down a state law banning "ballot selfies" because the law failed intermediate scrutiny
- New content on the U.S. Supreme Court's *McCullen* v. *Coakley* decision regarding abortion protests
- New discussion of the U.S. Supreme Court's *Elonis* v. *United States* decision regarding social media, rap music and true threats
- New section on net neutrality, with a particular focus on the FCC's 2015 Open Internet Order

Chapter 4

- New discussion of Communications Decency Act Section 230 and libel by anonymous third-party posters
- New section about defamation on social media sites such as Twitter and Facebook

Chapter 5

- New section on "involuntary limited-purpose public figures"
- New material on the Consumer Review Fairness Act affecting "gag clauses" in contracts

Chapter 6

- New material on the "self-defense privilege"
- New discussion of criminal libel

Chapter 7

- New discussion of Lindsay Lohan's lawsuit against Rockstar Games and Take Two Interactive over a character in "Grand Theft Auto V"
- New section on intrusion by drones
- New section on an appropriation case involving the videogame "Madden NFL"

Chapter 8

- Discussion of *The New York Times'* publication of part of Donald Trump's 1995 income tax returns
- Discussion of *Hulk Hogan* v. *Gawker*
- New material on secret-recording cases

Chapter 9

- Updates on media access to executions and information about execution drugs
- New section on journalists arrested for covering Dakota Access Pipeline protests and the inauguration of President Donald Trump
- New section on government officials using private text messages and e-mail accounts

Chapter 10

- New discussion of the appellate court decision in *U.S.* v. *Sterling*
- Updated discussion of *Convertino* v. *U.S. Department of Justice*, where an appellate court ruling seemed to give journalists another weapon to protect source confidentiality
- New section addressing the Department of Justice's revised guidelines for when and how a federal prosecuting attorney can subpoena a reporter

Chapter 11

- New discussion of the U.S. Supreme Court's decision in *U.S.* v. *Skilling* and when a change of venue is appropriate
- New discussion about importance of news media intervening when judges close courtrooms

Chapter 12

- New section on social media use by lawyers, reporters, jurors and others
- Updates on state and federal rules dealing with microblogging from courtrooms
- New material about the U.S. Judicial Conference's pilot project evaluating effects of cameras in trial courtrooms

Chapter 13

- New examples of convictions for distributing and possessing child pornography via the Internet and smartphones
- New content on the U.S. Supreme Court's 2017 *Packingham* v. *North Carolina* decision regarding the online speech rights of sex offenders

Chapter 14

- Expanded discussion of trademark law
- New content on the Trademark Dilution Revision Act of 2006
- New section on the U.S. Supreme Court case *Lee* v. *Tam* dealing with disparaging trademarks
- New section on the copyright case of *Star Athletica* v. *Varsity Brands*
- New material on parody, satire and trademark law focusing on *Cariou* v. *Prince*

Chapter 15

- New discussion of the FTC's antitrust case against the Staples, Inc., and Office Depot merger

- New discussion of the U.S. Supreme Court's *Lexmark International, Inc. v. Static Control Components* decision regarding standing to file Lanham Act claims
- New content on the Lanham Act case between Dannon and General Mills against Chobani involving an injunction over Chobani's ads for Greek yogurt
- Updated material on controversies involving Backpage.com, including whether the site should have immunity under the Communications Decency Act Section 230

Chapter 16

- New discussion of the 2016 appellate court ruling in *Prometheus Radio Project* v. *FCC* regarding ownership restrictions
- New content regarding the U.S. Supreme Court's ruling against Aereo in *ABC, Inc.* v. *Aereo*
- Updated discussion of the FCC's regulation of broadcast indecency, including its $325,000 fine against a Virginia TV station in 2015

CHAPTER 1

The American Legal System

©McGraw-Hill Education/Jill Braaten

Before studying media law, one needs a general background in law and the judicial system. In the United States, as in most societies, law is a basic part of existence, as necessary for the survival of civilization as are economic and political systems, the mass media, cultural achievement and the family.

This chapter has two purposes: to acquaint you with the law and to outline the legal system in the United States. While not designed to be a comprehensive course in law and the judicial system, it provides a sufficient introduction to understand the next 15 chapters.

The chapter opens with a discussion of the law, considering the most important sources of the law in the United States, and it moves on to the judicial system, including both the federal and state court systems. A summary of judicial review and a brief outline of how both criminal and civil lawsuits start and proceed through the courts are included in the discussion of the judicial system.

> **FIVE SOURCES OF LAW**
>
> 1. Common law
> 2. Equity law
> 3. Statutory law
> 4. Constitutional law (federal and state)
> 5. Executive orders and administrative rules

SOURCES OF THE LAW

There are many definitions of law. Some say law is any social norm or any organized method of settling disputes. Most writers insist it is more complex, that some system of sanctions and remedies is required for a genuine legal system. John Austin, a 19th-century English jurist, defined law as definite rules of human conduct with appropriate sanctions for their enforcement. He added that both the rules and the sanctions must be prescribed by duly constituted human authority.[1] Roscoe Pound, an American legal scholar, suggested that law is social engineering—the attempt to order the way people behave. For the purposes of this book, it is helpful to consider law to be a set of rules that attempt to guide human conduct and a set of formal, governmental sanctions that are applied when those rules are violated.

What is the source of American law? There are several major sources of the law in the United States: the U.S. Constitution and state constitutions; common law; the law of equity; statutory law; and the rulings of various executives, such as the president and mayors and governors, and administrative bodies and agencies. Historically, we trace American law to Great Britain. As colonizers of much of the North American continent, the British supplied Americans with an outline for both a legal system and a judicial system. In fact, because of the many similarities between British and American law, many people consider the Anglo-American legal system to be a single entity. Today, our federal Constitution is the supreme law of the land. Yet when each of these sources of law is considered separately, it is more useful to begin with the earliest source of Anglo-American law, the common law.

COMMON LAW

Common law,* which developed in England during the 200 years after the Norman Conquest in the 11th century, is one of the great legacies of the British people to colonial America. During those two centuries, the crude mosaic of Anglo-Saxon customs was replaced by a single system of law worked out by jurists and judges. The system of law became common throughout England; it became common law. It was also called common

---

* Terms in boldfaced type are defined in the glossary.
1. Abraham, *Judicial Process.*

law to distinguish it from the ecclesiastical (church) law prevalent at the time. Initially, the customs of the people were used by the king's courts as the foundation of the law, disputes were resolved according to community custom, and governmental sanction was applied to enforce the resolution. As such, common law was, and still is, considered "discovered law."

As legal problems became more complex and as the law began to be professionally administered (the first lawyers appeared during this era, and eventually professional judges), it became clear that common law reflected not so much the custom of the land as the custom of the court—or more properly, the custom of judges. While judges continued to look to the past to discover how other courts decided a case when given similar facts (precedent is discussed in a moment), many times judges were forced to create the law themselves. Common law thus sometimes is known as judge-made law.

Common law thus sometimes is known as judge-made law.

Common law is an inductive system in which a legal rule and legal standards are arrived at after consideration of many cases involving similar facts. In contrast, in a deductive system of law, which is common in many other nations, the rules are expounded first and then the court decides the legal situation under the existing rule. The ability of common law to adapt to change is directly responsible for its longevity.

Fundamental to common law is the concept that judges should look to the past and follow court precedents.* The Latin expression for the concept is this: "Stare decisis et non quieta movere" (to stand by past decisions and not disturb things at rest). **Stare decisis** is the key phrase: Let the decision stand. A judge should resolve current problems in the same manner as similar problems were resolved in the past. Put differently, a judge will look to a prior case opinion to guide his or her analysis and decision in a current case. Following precedent is beneficial as it builds predictability and consistency into the law—which in turn fosters judicial legitimacy. Courts may be perceived as more legitimate in the public's eye if they are predictable and consistent in their decision-making process.

Stare decisis is the key phrase: Let the decision stand.

The Role of Precedent

At first glance one would think that the law never changes in a system that continually looks to the past. Suppose that the first few rulings in a line of cases were bad decisions. Are courts saddled with bad law forever? The answer is no. While following **precedent** is desired (many people say that certainty in the law is more important than justice), it is not always the proper way to proceed. To protect the integrity of common law, judges developed means of coping with bad law and new situations in which the application of old law would result in injustice.

Imagine that the newspaper in your hometown publishes a picture and story about a 12-year-old girl who gave birth to a 7-pound son in a local hospital. The mother and father do not like the publicity and sue the newspaper for invasion of privacy. The attorney for the parents finds a precedent, *Barber* v. *Time*,[2] in which a Missouri court ruled that to photograph a patient in a hospital room against her will and then to publish that picture in a newsmagazine is an **invasion of privacy.**

---

*Appellate courts (see page 18) often render decisions that decide only the particular case and do not establish binding precedent. Courts refer to these as "unpublished decisions." In some jurisdictions it is unlawful for a lawyer to cite these rulings in legal papers submitted in later cases.
2. 159 S.W. 2d 291 (1942).

> ## FOUR OPTIONS FOR HANDLING PRECEDENT
>
> 1. Accept/Follow
> 2. Modify/Update
> 3. Distinguish
> 4. Overrule

Does the existence of this precedent mean that the young couple will automatically win this lawsuit? Must the court follow and adopt the *Barber* decision? The answer to both questions is no. For one thing, there may be other cases in which courts have ruled that publishing such a picture is not an invasion of privacy. In fact, in 1956 in the case of *Meetze* v. *AP*[3] a South Carolina court made such a ruling. But for the moment assume that *Barber* v. *Time* is the only precedent. Is the court bound by this precedent? No. The court has several options concerning the 1942 decision.

First, it can *accept* the precedent as law and rule that the newspaper has invaded the privacy of the couple by publishing the picture and story about the birth of their child. When a court accepts a prior court ruling as precedent, it is adopting it and following it for guidance. Second, the court can *modify*, or change, the 1942 precedent by arguing that *Barber* v. *Time* was decided more than 75 years ago when people were more sensitive about going to a hospital, since a stay there was often considered to reflect badly on a patient. Today hospitalization is no longer a sensitive matter to most people. Therefore, a rule of law restricting the publication of a picture of a hospital patient is unrealistic, unless the picture is in bad taste or needlessly embarrasses the patient. Then the publication may be an invasion of privacy. In our imaginary case, then, the decision turns on what kind of picture and story the newspaper published: a pleasant picture that flattered the couple or one that mocked and embarrassed them? If the court rules in this manner, it *modifies* the 1942 precedent, making it correspond to what the judge perceives to be contemporary sensibilities and circumstances.

As a third option the court can decide that *Barber* v. *Time* provides an important precedent for a plaintiff hospitalized because of an unusual disease—as Dorothy Barber's was—but that in the case before the court, the plaintiff was hospitalized to give birth to a baby, a different situation: Giving birth is a voluntary status; catching a disease is not. Because the two cases present different problems, they are really different cases. Hence, the *Barber* v. *Time* precedent does not apply. This practice is called *distinguishing the precedent from the current case,* a very common action. In brief, a court can distinguish a prior case (and therefore choose not to accept it and not to follow it) because it involves either different facts or different issues from the current case.

Finally, the court can *overrule* the precedent. When a court overrules precedent, it declares the prior decision wrong and thus no longer the law. Courts generally overrule prior opinions as bad law only when there are changes in:

---

3. 95 S.E. 2d 606 (1956).

1. factual knowledge and circumstances;
2. social mores and values; and/or
3. judges/justices on the court.

For instance, in 2003 the U.S. Supreme Court in *Lawrence* v. *Texas*[4] overruled its 1986 opinion called *Bowers* v. *Hardwick*[5] that had upheld a Georgia anti-sodomy statute prohibiting certain sexual acts between consenting gay adults. By 2003, American society increasingly accepted homosexuality (evidenced then by both the dwindling number of states that prohibited the conduct referenced in *Bowers* and by at least two Supreme Court rulings subsequent to *Bowers* but before *Lawrence* that were favorable to gay rights and thus eroded *Bowers'* strength). There also was growing recognition that consenting adults, regardless of sexual orientation, should possess the constitutional, personal liberty to engage in private sexual conduct of their choosing. Furthermore, six of the nine justices on the Supreme Court had changed from 1986 to 2003. Thus, 17 years after *Bowers* was decided, there were changes in social values, legal sentiment and the court's composition. The Supreme Court in *Lawrence* therefore struck down a Texas anti-sodomy statute similar to the Georgia one it had upheld in *Bowers*. It thus overruled *Bowers*. Justice Anthony Kennedy noted that although "the doctrine of stare decisis is essential to the respect accorded to the judgments of the court and to the stability of the law," it "is not, however, an inexorable command." In the hypothetical case involving the 12-year-old girl who gave birth, the only courts that can overrule the Missouri Supreme Court's opinion in *Barber* v. *Time* are the Missouri Supreme Court and the U.S. Supreme Court.

In 2010, a closely divided Supreme Court in *Citizens United* v. *Federal Elections Commission* overruled a 1990 opinion called *Austin* v. *Michigan State Chamber of Commerce*. The Court in *Austin* had upheld a Michigan law banning corporations from spending money from their own treasury funds in order to create their own ads in support of, or in opposition to, any candidate in elections for state office. By 2010, the composition of the Court had shifted over 20 years and the five conservative-leaning justices (Kennedy, John Roberts, Antonin Scalia, Samuel Alito and Clarence Thomas) in *Citizens United* voted to overrule *Austin* in the process of declaring unconstitutional a federal law that prohibited corporations and unions from using their general treasury funds to make independent expenditures for speech expressly advocating for the election or defeat of a candidate for public office. In reaching this conclusion, Justice Kennedy wrote for the majority about the importance of protecting political speech, regardless of who the speaker is (a corporation, a union or the common citizen), and he concluded "that stare decisis does not compel the continued acceptance of *Austin*. The Government may regulate corporate political speech through disclaimer and disclosure requirements, but it may not suppress that speech altogether."

Obviously, the preceding discussion oversimplifies the judicial process. Rarely is a court confronted with only a single precedent. Indeed, as attorneys would put it, there may be several prior cases that are "on point" or may apply as precedent. And whether or not precedent is binding on a court is often an issue. For example, decisions by the

---

4. 539 U.S. 558 (2003).
5. 478 U.S. 186 (1986).

Supreme Court of the United States regarding the U.S. Constitution and federal laws are binding on all federal and state courts. Decisions by the U.S. Court of Appeals on federal matters are binding only on other lower federal and state courts in that circuit or region. (See pages 27–29 for a discussion of the circuits.) The supreme court of any state is the final authority on the meaning of the constitution and laws of that state, and its rulings on these matters are binding on all state and *federal* courts in that state. Matters are more complicated when federal courts interpret state laws. State courts can accept or reject these interpretations in most instances. Because mass media law is so heavily affected by the First Amendment, state judges frequently look outside their borders to precedents developed by the federal courts. A state court ruling on a question involving the First Amendment guarantees of free speech and press will be substantially guided by federal court precedents on the same subject.

Lawyers and law professors often debate how important precedent really is when a court makes a decision. Some have suggested a "hunch theory" of jurisprudence: A judge decides a case based on a gut feeling of what is right and wrong and then seeks out precedents to support the decision.

Finding Common-Law Cases

Common law is not specifically written down someplace for all to see and use. It is instead contained in hundreds of thousands of decisions handed down by courts over the centuries. Many attempts have been made to summarize the law. Sir Edward Coke compiled and analyzed the precedents of common law in the early 17th century. Sir William Blackstone later expanded Coke's work in the monumental *Commentaries on the Law of England*. More recently, in such works as the massive *Restatement of the Law, Second, of Torts,* the task was again undertaken, but on a narrower scale.

Courts began to record their decisions centuries ago. These decisions are called "opinions" in legal parlance. The modern concept of fully reporting written decisions of all courts probably began in 1785 with the publication of the first British Term Reports.

While scholars and lawyers still uncover common law using the case-by-case method, it is fairly easy today to locate the appropriate cases through a simple system of citation. The cases of a single court (such as the U.S. Supreme Court or the federal district courts) are collected in a single **case reporter** (such as the "United States Reports" or the "Federal Supplement"). The cases are collected chronologically and fill many volumes. Each case collected has its individual **citation,** or identification number, which reflects the name of the reporter in which the case can be found, the volume of that reporter, and the page on which the case begins (Figure 1.1). For example, the citation for the decision in *Adderly* v. *Florida* (a freedom-of-speech case) is 385 U.S. 39 (1966). The letters in the middle (U.S.) indicate that the case is in the "United States Reports," the official government reporter for cases decided by the Supreme Court of the United States. The number 385 refers to the specific volume of the "United States Reports" in which the case is found. The second number (39) gives the page on which the case appears. Finally, 1966 provides the year in which the case was decided. So, *Adderly* v. *Florida* can be found on page 39 of volume 385 of the "United States Reports."

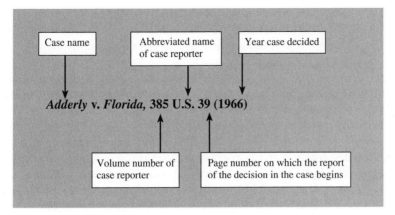

FIGURE 1.1

Reading a case citation.

Computers affected the legal community in many ways. Court opinions are now available via a variety of online services. For instance, two legal databases attorneys often use and that frequently are available free to students at colleges and universities are LexisNexis and Westlaw. These databases provide access to court opinions, statutory law (see pages 9–11) and law journal articles. In most jurisdictions, lawyers may file documents electronically with the court.

If you have the correct citation, you can easily find any case you seek. Locating all citations of the cases apropos to a particular problem—such as a libel suit—is a different matter and is a technique taught in law schools. A great many legal encyclopedias, digests, compilations of common law, books and articles are used by lawyers to track down the names and citations of the appropriate cases.

> **TYPICAL REMEDIES IN EQUITY LAW**
>
> 1. Temporary restraining order (TRO)
> 2. Preliminary injunction
> 3. Permanent injunction

EQUITY LAW

Equity is another kind of judge-made law. The distinction today between common law and equity law has blurred. The cases are heard by the same judges in the same courtrooms. Differences in procedures and remedies are all that is left to distinguish these two categories of the law. Separate consideration of common law and equity leads to a better understanding of both, however. Equity was originally a supplement to the common law and developed side by side with common law.

The rules and procedures under equity are far more flexible than those under common law. Equity really begins where common law leaves off. Equity suits are never tried before a jury. Rulings come in the form of **judicial decrees,** not in judgments of yes or no. Decisions in equity are (and were) discretionary on the part of judges. And despite the fact that precedents are also relied upon in the law of equity, judges are free to do what they think is right and fair in a specific case.

Equity provides another advantage for troubled litigants—the restraining order. While the typical remedy in a civil lawsuit in common law is **damages** (money), equity allows a judge to issue orders that can either be preventive (prohibiting a party from engaging in a potential behavior it is considering) or remedial (compelling a party to stop doing something it currently is doing). Individuals who can demonstrate that they are in peril or are about to suffer a serious irremediable wrong can usually gain a legal writ such as an injunction or a restraining order to stop someone from doing something. Generally, a court issues a temporary restraining order or preliminary injunction until it can hear arguments from both parties in the dispute and decide whether an injunction should be made permanent.

For instance, in January 2015 a South Carolina judge issued a temporary restraining order (TRO) preventing a small-town newspaper reporter in that state from publishing the contents of a diary belonging to the widow of James Brown, the famous singer known as the "Godfather of Soul." In the midst of an ongoing legal battle over Brown's estate, the reporter received an anonymous package containing the diary of Brown's widow. The diary, which had been sealed by a court, contained entries that seemed to suggest that the widow might not have actually been legally married to Brown. The reporter posted some passages from the diary to Facebook, but the widow then went to court and persuaded a lower-court judge that she "may suffer irreparable harm" if the reporter was not restrained from publishing any more of the diary's contents. Such injunctions—even TROs, which are brief in time, as the word "temporary" suggests—stopping the dissemination of truthful speech about a newsworthy matter presumptively violate the First Amendment (see Chapter 2 regarding prior restraints). The reporter's lawyers thus appealed the order, and the South Carolina Supreme Court vacated the TRO, ruling that it "clearly violates" the First Amendment and "will not be upheld by this Court."

On the other hand, equitable remedies in the form of injunctions are more likely to be granted in copyright cases where the plaintiff can demonstrate the defendant is selling copyrighted material owned by the plaintiff (see Chapter 14 regarding copyright). Universal Studios, which owns the movie rights to the "Fifty Shades of Grey" book series, sought an injunction in 2013 against an adult-movie company called Smash Pictures to stop the distribution of a movie called "Fifty Shades of Grey: A XXX Adaptation." While parodies that make fun of or comment on the original work often are protected against copyright claims, this porn parody copied many lines from the book nearly verbatim and simply claimed to be a hard-core version of the book. The case ultimately settled, with Smash Pictures consenting to a permanent injunction prohibiting the distribution of its parody.

Ultimately, a party seeks an equitable remedy (a restraining order or injunction) if there is a real threat of a direct, immediate and irreparable injury for which monetary damages won't provide sufficient compensation.

**YOU CAN'T SAY THAT AGAIN!:
ENJOINING DEFAMATION**

As discussed in Chapters 4, 5 and 6, when a speaker publishes something defamatory about another person—a false statement of fact that damages that person's reputation—the traditional legal recourse in the United States is a lawsuit for defamation, with the defamed party receiving monetary damages from the defendant. But as Professor David Ardia has argued, over the past decade, the Internet has brought increased attention to the adequacy of monetary damages as the only remedy for defamation. Today, defamation cases are increasingly arising from online speech, with plaintiffs claiming speech published by bloggers or users of social media defames them. Rather than seek monetary damages to compensate themselves or to punish the defendants, some of the plaintiffs in these cases have instead sought to have the speech stopped altogether using injunctions. Alarmingly, some courts have been increasingly willing to grant injunctions that bar—or forbid—speakers from repeating their defamatory comments.

For instance, a district court in Indiana issued a permanent injunction that would have prevented an Indiana man and a former religious sister from repeating blog comments they had made in what amounted to an online smear campaign. The blog comments came in the midst of a dispute over who was entitled to the documents and artifacts of a religious sister who had experienced a series of apparitions of the Virgin Mary. The particulars of the case were messy, but, ultimately, the district court permanently enjoined the defendants from repeating several specific comments—even though the jury had not ruled that those specific comments were defamatory—as well as "any similar statements that contain the same sort of allegations or inferences, in any manner or forum."

On appeal, the Seventh Circuit U.S. Court of Appeals struck down the injunction as unconstitutional in December 2015. In *McCarthy* v. *Fuller*, the Seventh Circuit said the injunction was a "patent violation of the First Amendment" because it was "so broad and vague" that it threatened to silence the defendants completely. Although this particular injunction was poorly crafted and thus problematic, the court left open the question of whether defamation could *ever* be enjoined. More cases like this will likely appear in the near future.

STATUTORY LAW

While common law sometimes is referred to as discovered or judge-made law, the third great source of laws in the United States today is created by elected legislative bodies at the local, state and federal levels and is known as statutory law.

Several important characteristics of statutory law are best understood by contrasting them with common law. First, **statutes** tend to deal with problems affecting society or large groups of people, in contrast to common law, which usually deals with smaller, individual problems. (Some common-law rulings affect large groups of people, but this occurrence is rare.) It should also be noted in this connection the importance of not confusing common law with constitutional law. Certainly when judges interpret a constitution, they make policy that affects us all. However, it should be kept in mind that a constitution is a legislative document voted on by the people and is not discovered law or judge-made law.

Second, statutory law can anticipate problems, and common law cannot. For example, a state legislature can pass a statute that prohibits publication of the school records of a student without prior consent of the student. Under common law the problem cannot be resolved until a student's record has been published in a newspaper or transmitted over the Internet and the student brings action against the publisher to recover damages for the injury incurred.

The criminal laws in the United States are all statutory laws.

Third, the criminal laws in the United States are all statutory laws—common-law crimes no longer exist in this country and have not since 1812. Common-law rules are not precise enough to provide the kind of notice needed to protect a criminal defendant's right to due process of law.

Fourth, statutory law is collected in codes and law books, instead of in reports as is common law. When a bill is adopted by the legislative branch and approved by the executive branch, it becomes law and is integrated into the proper section of a municipal code, a state code or whatever. However, this does not mean that some very important statutory law cannot be found in the case reporters.

Passage of a law is rarely the final word. Courts become involved in determining what that law means. Although a properly constructed statute sometimes needs little interpretation by the courts, judges are frequently called upon to rule on the exact meaning of ambiguous phrases and words. The resulting process of judicial interpretation is called **statutory construction** and is very important. Even the simplest kind of statement often needs interpretation. For example, a statute that declares "*it is illegal to distribute a violent video game to minors*" is fraught with ambiguities that a court must construe and resolve in order to determine if it violates the First Amendment speech rights of video game creators and players (see pages 68–74 regarding regulation of video games). What type of content, for instance, falls within the meaning of the word "violent" as it is used in this statute? How young must a person be in order to be considered a "minor" under the law? Does the term "distribute" mean to sell a video game, to rent a video game or to give it away for free? Finally, because games are played in arcades, on computers and via consoles, just what precisely is a "video" game under the statute?

Usually a legislature leaves a trail to help a judge find out what the law means. When judges rule on the meaning of a statute, they are supposed to determine what the legislature meant when it passed the law (the legislative intent), not what they think the law should mean. Minutes of committee hearings in which the law was discussed, legislative staff reports and reports of debate on the floor can all be used to determine legislative intent. Therefore, when lawyers deal with statutes, they frequently search the case reporters to find out how the courts interpreted a law in which they are interested.

> ### ATTACKING THE CONSTITUTIONALITY OF STATUTES: FACIAL CHALLENGES VERSUS AS-APPLIED CHALLENGES
>
> There are two primary ways to argue that a statute violates the First Amendment right of free speech: (1) by attacking problems with its wording, terms and language (known as a facial attack); or (2) by attacking problems with its actual application to a particular factual scenario (known as an as-applied attack). A facial attack tests a law's constitutionality based on its text (its words and language), but does not consider the facts or circumstances of a particular case. For instance, a challenge to a statute based on the ground that it is either overbroad or unduly vague in its use of language (both the overbreadth doctrine and the void for vagueness doctrine are described in the next few pages of this chapter) are examples of facial challenges. In contrast, an as-applied attack does not contend that a law is unconstitutional because of how it is written, but because of how it actually applies to a particular person or particular group of people under specific factual circumstances that allegedly deprive the person of a First Amendment right. In general, as-applied challenges are the preferred method for attacking a statute. As Justice Samuel Alito wrote in 2010 in *United States* v. *Stevens*,[6] "the 'strong medicine' of overbreadth invalidation need not and generally should not be administered when the statute under attack is unconstitutional as applied to the challenger before the court." Ultimately, however, as Justice Anthony Kennedy wrote in 2010 in *Citizens United* v. *Federal Elections Commission*[7] (see pages 136–139 describing this case in the unit "The First Amendment and Election Campaigns"), "the distinction between facial and as-applied challenges is not so well defined that it has some automatic effect or that it must always control the pleadings and disposition in every case involving a constitutional challenge."

CONSTITUTIONAL LAW

Great Britain lacks a written **constitution.** The United States, in contrast, has a written constitution, and it is an important source of our law. In fact, there are many constitutions in this country: the federal Constitution, state constitutions, city charters and so forth. All these documents accomplish the same ends. First, they provide the plan for the establishment and organization of the government. Next, they outline the duties, responsibilities and powers of the various elements of government. Finally, they usually guarantee certain basic rights to the people, such as freedom of speech and freedom to peaceably assemble.

Legislative bodies may enact statutes rather easily by a majority vote. It is far more difficult to adopt or change a constitution. State constitutions are approved or changed by a direct vote of the people. It is even more difficult to change the federal Constitution. An amendment may be proposed by a vote of two-thirds of the members of both the U.S. House of Representatives and the Senate. Alternatively, two-thirds of the state

6. 559 U.S. 460 (2010).
7. 558 U.S. 310 (2010).

legislatures can call for a constitutional convention for proposing amendments. Once proposed, amendments must be approved either by three-fourths of the state legislatures or by three-fourths of the constitutional conventions called in all the states. Congress decides which method of ratification or approval is to be used. Because the people have an unusually direct voice in the approval and change of a constitution, constitutions are considered the most important source of U.S. law.

The U.S. Constitution is the supreme law of the land.

One Supreme Court justice described a constitution as a kind of yardstick against which all the other actions of government must be measured to determine whether the actions are permissible. The U.S. Constitution is the supreme law of the land. Any law or other constitution that conflicts with the U.S. Constitution is unenforceable. A state constitution plays the same role for a state: A statute passed by the Michigan legislature and signed by the governor of that state is clearly unenforceable if it conflicts with the Michigan Constitution. And so it goes for all levels of constitutions.

Constitutions tend to be short and, at the federal level and in most states, infrequently amended. Consequently, changes in the language of a constitution are uncommon. But a considerable amount of constitutional law is nevertheless developed by the courts, which are asked to determine the meaning of provisions in the documents and to decide whether other laws or government actions violate constitutional provisions. Hence, the case reporters are repositories for the constitutional law that governs the nation.

Twenty-seven amendments are appended to the U.S. Constitution. The first 10 are known as the Bill of Rights and guarantee certain basic human rights to all citizens. Included in the First Amendment to the U.S. Constitution are freedom of speech and press, rights you will understand more fully in future chapters.

The federal Constitution and the 50 state constitutions are very important when considering media law problems. All 51 of these charters contain provisions, in one form or another, that guarantee freedom of speech and freedom of the press.

The scope of protection for speech and press afforded by any given state constitution thus may be broader than that bestowed by the First Amendment.

Importantly, state constitutions can give more and greater rights to their citizens than are provided under the U.S. Constitution; they cannot, however, reduce or roll back rights given by the federal Constitution. The scope of protection for speech and press afforded by any given state constitution thus may be broader than that bestowed by the First Amendment to the U.S. Constitution. For instance, whereas obscene speech is not protected by the First Amendment (see Chapter 13), the Oregon Supreme Court held in 1987 that obscene expression is protected in that state under Article I, Section 8 of the Oregon Constitution.[8] A lawyer challenging a state statute that allegedly restricts any form of speech therefore is wise to argue before a court that the statute in question violates either or both the First Amendment and the relevant state's constitutional provision protecting expression. Consequently, any government action that affects in any way the freedom of individuals or mass media to speak or publish or broadcast must be measured against the constitutional guarantees of freedom of expression.

---

8. *Oregon* v. *Henry*, 302 Ore. 510 (1987). Article I, Section 8 of the Oregon Constitution provides that "no law shall be passed restraining the free expression of opinion, or restricting the right to speak, write, or print freely on any subject whatever; but every person shall be responsible for the abuse of this right." A 1996 ballot measure, drafted in part in response to the *Henry* opinion and that would have amended Article I, Section 8 so as not to protect obscenity, narrowly failed when put before Oregon voters.

There are several reasons why a law limiting speaking or publishing might be declared unconstitutional. The law might be a direct restriction on speech or press that is protected by the First Amendment. For example, an order by a Nebraska judge that prohibited the press from publishing certain information about a pending murder trial was considered a direct restriction on freedom of the press (see *Nebraska Press Association* v. *Stuart*,[9] Chapter 11).

A criminal obscenity statute or another kind of criminal law might be declared unconstitutional because it is too vague. Under the **void for vagueness doctrine,** a law will be declared unconstitutional and struck down if a person of reasonable and ordinary intelligence would not be able to tell, from looking at its terms, what speech is allowed and what speech is prohibited. Put differently, people of ordinary intelligence should not have to guess at a statute's meaning. As the U.S. Supreme Court wrote in 2012 in a broadcast indecency case called *FCC* v. *Fox Television Stations, Inc.* (see Chapter 16 for more on both broadcast indecency and this case), "a fundamental principle in our legal system is that laws which regulate persons or entities must give fair notice of conduct that is forbidden or required." The Court added that "this requirement of clarity in regulation . . . requires the invalidation of laws that are impermissibly vague." Vague laws are problematic because they

- don't provide fair notice of what speech is permitted; and
- can be enforced unfairly and discriminatorily because they give too much discretion (due to the vague terms) to those who enforce them (police and judges).

For instance, in September 2016 a district court judge in Florida blocked enforcement of a Florida law that required convicted sex offenders in the state to register all of their "internet identifiers." Failing to register their "internet identifiers" amounted to a crime. The plaintiffs challenging the law said that they were confused about what counted as an "internet identifier" and that they would forgo speech on the Internet if the law took effect rather than risk being punished. In *Doe* v. *Swearingen,* Judge Robert Hinkle agreed and said the definition of "internet identifier" in the law was "hopelessly vague" and "chills speech protected by the First Amendment." The judge said the law's definition of the term, arguably already broader than ordinary usage of "internet identifier" to begin with, started by "saying what the term 'includes, but is not limited to.'" That phrasing in effect gave the term "internet identifier" an "unlimited description," the judge wrote, leaving sex offenders "guessing at what must be disclosed."

A statute might also be declared unconstitutional because it violates what is known as the **overbreadth doctrine.** A law is overbroad if it does not aim only at problems within the allowable area of legitimate government control but also sweeps within its ambit or scope other activities that constitute an exercise of protected expression. For instance, in 2010 the U.S. Supreme Court in *United States* v. *Stevens*[10] declared as unconstitutionally overbroad a federal statute that criminalized the commercial creation, sale or possession of certain depictions of animal cruelty. The statute defined a depiction of

9. 427 U.S. 539 (1976).
10. 559 U.S. 460 (2010).

animal cruelty as one "in which a living animal is intentionally maimed, mutilated, tortured, wounded or killed," provided that such conduct is illegal under a federal or state law where the creation, sale or possession of the depiction occurs. In holding the law overbroad, Chief Justice John Roberts wrote that it "create[s] a criminal prohibition of alarming breadth. To begin with, the text of the statute's ban on a 'depiction of animal cruelty' nowhere requires that the depicted conduct be cruel. That text applies to 'any . . . depiction' in which 'a living animal is intentionally maimed, mutilated, tortured, wounded, or killed.' . . . [M]aimed, mutilated, [and] tortured' convey cruelty, but 'wounded' or 'killed' do not suggest any such limitation."

The overbreadth doctrine was used in 2016 by the North Carolina Supreme Court to declare unconstitutional a cyberbullying law that made it a crime "for any person to use a computer or computer network to . . . [p]ost or encourage others to post on the Internet private, personal, or sexual information pertaining to a minor" "[w]ith the intent to intimidate or torment a minor." In *State of North Carolina* v. *Bishop,* the state Supreme Court said that it was "undisputed" that protecting children from online bullying was a compelling governmental interest. But the law swept up far more protected speech than was necessary to serve that interest, the court ruled. For instance, the law criminalized posting "personal" information, and the state suggested personal meant "[o]f or relating to a particular person," a definition the court called "especially sweeping." As the court wrote, "Such an interpretation would essentially criminalize posting *any* information about *any* specific minor if done with the requisite intent."

HONK IF YOU LOVE FREE SPEECH AND HATE OVERBROAD LAWS

In 2011, the Supreme Court of Washington state declared unconstitutionally overbroad a Snohomish County ordinance that prohibited honking a car horn for a purpose other than public safety or originating from an officially sanctioned parade or public event. The case of *Washington* v. *Immelt*[11] involved Helen Immelt, who intentionally sounded a car horn at length in front of a neighbor's house in the early morning hours because she was mad at the neighbor. Does honking a horn constitute speech? The Supreme Court of Washington invoked the symbolic speech doctrine (see pages 48–49) and found that "conduct such as horn honking may rise to the level of speech when the actor intends to communicate a message and the message can be understood in context." Examples of horn honking as speech, the court wrote, include "a driver of a carpool vehicle who toots a horn to let a coworker know it is time to go, a driver who enthusiastically responds to a sign that says 'honk if you support our troops,' wedding guests who celebrate nuptials by sounding their horns, and a motorist who honks a horn in support of an individual picketing on a street corner."

In striking down the ordinance, the court wrote that "a law is overbroad if it 'sweeps within its prohibitions' a substantial amount of constitutionally

---

11. 267 P.3d 305 (Wash. 2011).

protected conduct." Although emphasizing that "local governments maintain a legitimate interest in protecting residents from excessive and unwelcome noise," the Snohomish ordinance simply went too far because it "prohibits a wide swath of expressive conduct in order to protect against a narrow category of public disturbances," such as all of the examples noted earlier. The court suggested that a better and more narrowly written ordinance—one confined, perhaps, to horn honking intended to annoy or harass—might be constitutional.

EXECUTIVE ORDERS AND ADMINISTRATIVE RULES

The final source of American law has two streams. First are orders issued by elected officers of government, often called executive orders. Second are rules generated by the administrative agencies of government, at the federal, state and local levels.

Government executives—the U.S. president, governors, mayors, county executives, village presidents—all have more or less power to issue rules of law, sometimes referred to as executive orders or declarations. This power is normally defined by the constitution or the charter that establishes the office, and it varies widely from city to city or state to state. In some instances the individual has fairly broad powers; in others the power is sharply confined. For instance, in 2016 former President Barack Obama issued an executive order establishing the Federal Privacy Council to serve as "the principal interagency forum to improve the government privacy practices of agencies and entities acting on their behalf." Such declarations are possible so long as they are properly within the delegated powers held by the executive. An order from an executive who exceeds his or her power can be overturned by the legislature (the mayor's order can be changed or vacated by the city council, for example) or by a court. Such overstepping by a president would violate the separation of powers among the legislative, judicial and executive branches of government.

A more substantial part of U.S. law is generated by myriad administrative agencies that exist in the nation today, agencies that first began to develop in the latter part of the 19th century. By that time in the country's history, Congress was being asked to resolve questions going far beyond such matters as budgets, wars, treaties and the like. Technology created new kinds of problems for Congress to resolve. Many such issues were complex and required specialized knowledge and expertise that the representatives and senators lacked and could not easily acquire, had they wanted to. Specialized federal administrative agencies were therefore created to deal with these problems.

Hundreds of such agencies now exist at both federal and state levels. Each agency undertakes to deal with a specific set of problems too technical or too large for the legislative branch to handle. Perhaps the most relevant **administrative agency** for purposes of media law, along with the Federal Trade Commission (FTC; see Chapter 15), is the Federal Communications Commission (FCC), created by Congress in 1934. It regulates broadcasting and other telecommunication in the United States, a job that Congress has attempted only sporadically. Its members must be citizens of the United States and are appointed by the president. The single stipulation is that at any one time no more than three of the five individuals on the commission can be from the same political party. The Senate must confirm the appointments.

Congress has sketched the framework for the regulation of broadcasting in the Federal Communications Act of 1934 and subsequent amendments to this statute. This legislation is used by the FCC as its basic regulatory guidelines. But the agency generates much law on its own as it interprets the congressional mandates, and uses its considerable authority to generate rules and regulations. Today, the FCC is involved with issues ranging from net neutrality (see Chapter 3) to indecency on broadcast television (see Chapter 16).

But courts have limited power to review decisions made by administrative agencies.

People dissatisfied with an action by an agency can attempt to have it modified by asking the legislative body that created and funds the agency—Congress, for example, when considering the FCC—to change or overturn the action. In the 1980s when the FTC made several aggressive pro-consumer rulings, Congress voided these actions because members disagreed with the extent of the rulings. More commonly the actions of an agency will be challenged in the courts. But courts have limited power to review decisions made by administrative agencies and can overturn such a ruling in only these limited circumstances:

1. If the original act that established the commission or agency is unconstitutional.
2. If the commission or agency exceeds its authority.
3. If the commission or agency violates its own rules.
4. If there is no evidentiary basis whatsoever to support the ruling.

The reason for these limitations is simple: These agencies were created to bring expert knowledge to bear on complex problems, and the entire purpose for their creation would be defeated if judges with no special expertise in a given area could reverse an agency ruling merely because they had a different solution to a problem.

The case reporters contain some law created by the administrative agencies, but the reports that these agencies themselves publish contain much more such law. Today, you can look up recent opinions and rulings of both the FCC and FTC at their respective Web sites, located at http://www.fcc.gov and http://www.ftc.gov.

There are other sources of American law, but the sources just discussed—common law, law of equity, statutory law, constitutional law, executive orders and rules and regulations by administrative agencies—are the most important and are of most concern in this book. First Amendment problems fall under the purview of constitutional law. Libel and invasion of privacy are matters generally dealt with by common law and equity law. Obscenity laws in this country are statutory provisions (although this fact is frequently obscured by the hundreds of court cases in which judges attempt to define the meaning of obscenity). And of course the regulation of broadcasting and advertising falls primarily under the jurisdiction of administrative agencies.

SUMMARY There are several important sources of American law. Common law is the oldest source of our law, having developed in England more than 700 years ago. Fundamental to common law is the concept that judges should look to the past and follow earlier court rulings, called precedents. Stare decisis (let the decision stand) is a key concept. But judges have developed the means to change or adapt common law by modifying, distinguishing or overruling precedent case law. Common law, a type of judge-made law, is not written in a law book but is collected in volumes of case reporters that contain the decisions, known as opinions, handed down by courts. Each case is given its own legal identity through a system of numbered citations.

Equity law is the second source of American law. The rules and procedures of equity are far more flexible than those of common law and permit a judge (equity cases are never heard before a jury) to fashion a solution to unique or unusual problems. A court is permitted under equity law to restrain an individual or a corporation or even a government from taking an action by issuing a judicial decree such as an injunction. Under common law a court can attempt to compensate the injured party only for the damage that results from the action.

A great volume of law is generated by legislative bodies. This legislation, called statutory law, is the third important source of American law. All criminal laws are statutes. Statutes usually deal with problems that affect great numbers of people, and statutes can anticipate problems, whereas common law cannot. Statutes are collected in codes or statute books. Courts become involved when they are called on to interpret the meaning of the words and phrases contained in a statute, a process known as statutory construction.

Constitutions, the fourth source of law, take precedence over all other American law. The U.S. Constitution is the supreme law of the land. A state constitution actually can provide more rights to citizens of a state than the U.S. Constitution, but it cannot reduce or limit U.S. constitutional rights. Other laws, whether they spring from common law, equity, legislative bodies or administrative agencies, cannot conflict with the provisions of the Constitution. Courts interpret the meaning of the provisions of our constitutions (one federal and 50 state constitutions) and through this process often make these seemingly rigid legal prescriptions adaptable to contemporary problems.

Executives (presidents and governors) can issue orders that carry the force of law. And there are thousands of administrative agencies, boards and commissions in the nation that produce rules and regulations. This administrative law usually deals with technical and complicated matters requiring levels of expertise that members of traditional legislative bodies do not normally possess. Members of these agencies and commissions are usually appointed by presidents or by governors or mayors, and the agencies are supervised and funded by legislative bodies. Their tasks are narrowly defined, and their rulings, while they carry the force of law, can always be appealed.

THE JUDICIAL SYSTEM

This section introduces the court system in the United States. Since the judicial branch of our three-part government is the field on which most of the battles involving communications law are fought, an understanding of the judicial system is essential.

It is technically improper to talk about the American judicial system. There are 52 different judicial systems in the United States, one for the federal government and one for each of the 50 states, plus the District of Columbia. While each system is somewhat different from the others, the similarities among the 52 systems are much more important than the differences. Each of the systems is divided into two distinct sets of courts—trial courts and appellate courts. Each judicial system is established by a constitution, federal or state. In each system the courts act as the third branch of a triumvirate of government: a legislative branch, which makes the law; an executive branch, which enforces the law; and a judicial branch, which interprets the law.

FACTS VERSUS THE LAW

Common to all judicial systems is the distinction between trial courts and appellate courts. Each level of court has its own function: Basically, **trial courts** are fact-finding courts and **appellate courts** are law-reviewing courts. Trial courts are the courts of first instance, the place where nearly all cases begin. Juries sometimes sit in trial courts (a trial held before a judge and without a jury is known as a bench trial) but never in appellate courts. Trial courts are empowered to consider both the facts and the law in a case. Appellate courts normally consider only the law. The difference between facts and law is significant. The facts are what happened. The law is what should be done because of the facts.

The facts are what happened. The law is what should be done because of the facts.

The difference between facts and law can be emphasized by looking at an imaginary libel suit that might result if the *River City Sentinel* published a story about costs at the Sandridge Hospital, a privately owned medical facility.

Ineffective Medications Given to Ill, Injured
SANDRIDGE HOSPITAL OVERCHARGING PATIENTS ON PHARMACY COSTS

Scores of patients at the Sandridge Hospital have been given ineffective medications, a three-week investigation at the hospital has revealed. In addition, many of those patients were overcharged for the medicine they received.

The *Sentinel* has learned that many of the prescription drugs sold to patients at the hospital had been kept beyond the manufacturer's recommended storage period.

Many drugs stored in the pharmacy (as late as Friday) had expiration dates as old as six months ago. Drug manufacturers have told the *Sentinel* that medication used beyond the expiration date, which is stamped clearly on most packages, may not have the potency or curative effects that fresher pharmaceuticals have.

Hospital representatives deny giving patients any of the expired drugs, but sources at the hospital say it is impossible for administrators to guarantee that none of the dated drugs were sold to patients.

In addition, the investigation by the *Sentinel* revealed that patients who were sold medications manufactured by Chaos Pharmaceuticals were charged on the basis of 2017 price lists despite the fact that the company lowered prices significantly in 2018.

The Sandridge Hospital sues the newspaper for libel. When the case gets to court, the first thing that must be done is to establish what the facts are—what happened. The hospital and the newspaper each will present evidence, witnesses and arguments to support its version of the facts. Several issues have to be resolved. In addition to the general questions of whether the story has been published and whether the hospital has been identified in the story, the hospital will have to supply evidence that its reputation has been injured, that the story is false and that the newspaper staff has been extremely careless or negligent in the publication of the report. The newspaper will seek to defend itself by attempting to document the story or raise the defense that the report was privileged in some way. Or the newspaper may argue that even if the story is mistaken, it was the result of an innocent error; the newspaper staff was not negligent when it wrote and published the story.

All this testimony and evidence establishes the factual record—what actually took place at the hospital and in preparation of the story. When there is conflicting evidence, the jury decides whom to believe (in the absence of a jury, the judge makes the decision). Suppose the hospital is able to prove by documents that pharmacists in fact had removed the dated medicine from their shelves and stored it to return to the manufacturers. Further, the hospital can show that while it did accidentally overcharge some patients for Chaos products, it quickly refunded the excess charge to these patients. Finally, attorneys for the hospital demonstrate that the story was prepared by an untrained stringer for the newspaper who used but a single source—a pharmacist who had been fired by Sandridge for using drugs while on the job—to prepare the story and failed to relate to readers the substance of the evidence (which the reporter had when the story was published) presented by the hospital in court. In such a case, a court would likely rule that the hospital had carried its burden of proof and that no legitimate defense exists for the newspaper. Therefore, the hospital wins the suit. If the newspaper is unhappy with the verdict, it can appeal.

In an appeal, the appellate court does not establish a new factual record. No more testimony is taken. No more witnesses are called. The factual record established by the jury or judge at the trial stands. The appellate court has the power in some kinds of cases (libel suits that involve constitutional issues, for example) to examine whether the trial court properly considered the facts in the case. But normally it is the task of the appellate court to determine whether the law has been applied properly in light of the facts established at the trial. Perhaps the appellate court might rule that even with the documentary evidence the hospital presented in court, this evidence failed to prove that the news story was false. Perhaps the judge erred in allowing certain testimony into evidence or refused to allow a certain witness to testify. Or maybe the trial court judge gave the jury the wrong set of instructions for libel. That would be a clear error of law. Nevertheless, in reaching an opinion the appellate court considers only the law; the factual record established at the trial stands.

The appellate court does not establish a new factual record. No more testimony is taken.

What if new evidence is found or a previously unknown witness comes forth to testify? If the appellate court believes that the new evidence is important, it can order a new trial. However, the court itself does not hear the evidence. These facts are developed at a new trial.

There are other differences between the roles and procedures of trial and appellate courts. Juries are never used by appellate courts; a jury may be used in a trial court proceeding. The judge normally sits alone at a trial; appeals are heard by a panel of judges, usually three or more. Cases always begin at the trial level and then proceed to the appellate level. Although the appellate courts appear to have the last word in a legal dispute, that is not always the case. Usually cases are returned to the trial court for resolution with instructions from the appeals court to the trial judge to decide the case, keeping this or that factor in mind. This is called remanding the case to the trial court. In such a case the trial judge can often do what he or she wants.

In the discussion that follows, the federal court system and its methods of operating are considered first, and then some general observations about state court systems are given, based on the discussion of the federal system.

THE FEDERAL COURT SYSTEM

Congress has the authority to abolish every federal court in the land, save the Supreme Court of the United States. The U.S. Constitution calls for but a single federal court, the Supreme Court. Article III, Section 1 states: "The judicial power of the United States shall be vested in one Supreme Court." The Constitution also gives Congress the right to establish inferior courts if it deems these courts to be necessary. And Congress has, of course, established a fairly complex system of courts to complement the Supreme Court.

The jurisdiction of the federal courts is also outlined in Article III of the Constitution. The jurisdiction of a court is its legal right to exercise its authority. Briefly, federal courts can hear the following cases:

1. Cases that arise under the U.S. Constitution, U.S. law and U.S. treaties
2. Cases that involve ambassadors and ministers, duly accredited, of foreign countries
3. Cases that involve admiralty and maritime law
4. Cases that involve controversies when the United States is a party to the suit
5. Cases that involve controversies between two or more states
6. Cases that involve controversies between a state and a citizen of another state (the 11th Amendment to the Constitution requires that a state give its permission before it can be sued)
7. Cases that involve controversies between citizens of different states

While special federal courts have jurisdiction that goes beyond this broad outline, these are the circumstances in which a federal court may normally exercise its authority. Of the seven categories, Categories 1 (known as federal question jurisdiction) and 7 (known as diversity jurisdiction) account for most of the cases tried in federal court. For example, disputes that involve violations of the myriad federal laws and disputes that involve constitutional rights such as the First Amendment are heard in federal courts under federal question jurisdiction. Disputes between citizens of different states—a diversity of citizenship matter—are heard in federal courts provided that the amount at stake is more than $75,000. It is very common, for example, for libel suits and invasion-of-privacy suits against publishing companies to start in federal courts rather than in state courts. If a citizen of Arizona is libeled by the *Los Angeles Times*, the case will very likely be tried in a federal court in the state of Arizona rather than in a state court in either Arizona or California. Arizona law will be applied. The case will most often be heard where the legal wrong, in this case the injury to reputation by libel, occurs.

The Supreme Court

The Supreme Court of the United States is the oldest federal court, having operated since 1789. The Constitution does not establish the number of justices who sit on the high court. That task is left to Congress. Since 1869 the Supreme Court has comprised the chief justice of the United States and eight associate justices. (Note the title: not chief justice of the Supreme Court, but chief justice of the United States.) In 2017, the chief justice was John Roberts, who was nominated by former President George W. Bush and became just the 17th chief justice in the court's history in 2005. The first Hispanic to take the oath of office as an associate justice was Sonia Sotomayor in 2009; it also marked the first time that an oath-taking ceremony at the Supreme Court was open to broadcast coverage.

Since 1869, the Supreme Court has comprised the chief justice of the United States and eight associate justices.

Shortly after taking office in 2017, President Donald Trump nominated Neil Gorsuch to the U.S. Supreme Court to fill the position vacated by the death of conservative-leaning Justice Antonin Scalia in February 2016. This put the nomination in the hands of the U.S. Senate, which must give its "advice and consent" on any Supreme Court nominee. Gorsuch had been serving as a federal judge on the 10th U.S. Circuit Court of Appeals. The Republican-controlled Senate ultimately confirmed Gorsuch's nomination later in 2017 by a vote of 54–45 that closely divided along party lines. Gorsuch, who was only 49 years old at the time of his confirmation, could serve on the court for decades.

The Supreme Court exercises both original and appellate jurisdictions. Under its **original jurisdiction,** which is established in the Constitution, the Supreme Court is the first court to hear a case and acts much like a trial court. The Supreme Court has original jurisdiction in disputes between two or more states, with these scenarios typically involving battles over land or water rights. In brief, original jurisdiction is for the resolution of claims between and among the states, not claims by private entities within states. Sometimes the justices will hold a hearing to ascertain the facts; more commonly they will appoint what is called a special master to discern the facts and make recommendations. For example, in 2016 the Supreme Court declined to exercise its original jurisdiction authority over a proposed lawsuit by the states of Nebraska and Oklahoma against their neighboring state of Colorado. Nebraska and Oklahoma alleged that a 2012 amendment to the Colorado constitution that legalized the recreational use of marijuana in the Centennial State violated federal anti-drug laws and resulted in increased drug trafficking and transportation in their own states. By refusing to exercise original jurisdiction over the dispute, the Supreme Court essentially rejected the claims of Nebraska and Oklahoma.

The primary task of the Supreme Court is as an appellate tribunal, hearing cases already decided by lower federal and state courts of last resort. The appellate jurisdiction of the Supreme Court is established by Congress, not by the Constitution. A case will come before the Supreme Court of the United States for review in one of two principal ways: on a direct appeal or by way of a writ of certiorari. The certification process is a third way for a case to get to the high court, but this process is rarely used today.

In some instances a litigant has an apparent right, guaranteed by federal statute, to appeal a case to the Supreme Court. This is called **direct appeal.** For example, if a federal appeals court declares that a state statute violates the U.S. Constitution or conflicts with a federal law, the state has a right to appeal this decision to the Supreme Court. But this is only an apparent right, because since 1928 the Supreme Court has had the right to reject such an appeal "for want of a substantial federal question." This is another way of the court saying, "We think this is a trivial matter." Almost 90 percent of all appeals that come to the Supreme Court via the direct appeal process are rejected.

The much more common way for a case to reach the nation's high court is via a **writ of certiorari.** No one has the right to such a writ. It is a discretionary order issued by the court when it feels that an important legal question has been raised. Litigants using both the federal court system and the various state court systems can seek a writ of certiorari. The most important requirement that must be met before the court will even consider issuing a writ is that a petitioner first exhaust all other legal remedies. Although there are a few exceptions, this generally means that if a case begins in a federal district court (the trial-level court), the **petitioner** must first seek a review by a U.S. Court of Appeals before bidding for a writ of certiorari. The writ can be sought if the Court of Appeals refuses to hear the case or sustains the verdict against the petitioner. All other legal remedies have then been exhausted. In state court systems every legal appeal possible must be made within the state before seeking a review by the U.S. Supreme Court. This usually means going through a trial court, an intermediate appeals court and finally the state supreme court.

When the Supreme Court grants a writ of certiorari, it is ordering the lower court to send the records to the high court for review. Any litigant can petition the court to grant a writ, and the high court receives more than 7,500 petitions each year (a year for the Supreme Court is known as a term, with a new term starting on the first Monday in October and lasting usually through late June of the following year). Each request is considered by the entire nine-member court. If four justices think the petition has merit, the writ will be granted. This is called the **rule of four.** But the court rejects the vast majority of petitions it receives. Recently only 75 to 80 cases a year are accepted. Workload is the key factor. Certain important issues must be decided each term, and the justices do not have the time to consider thoroughly most cases for which an appeal is sought.

During the Supreme Court's 2015 term, which ran from October 2015 though June 2016, the Court considered only 63 cases that were fully briefed and argued before it. That is the lowest number in many decades, due in part to the death of Justice Antonin Scalia in February 2016 that left the Court rendering several four-to-four tied decisions. Such four-to-four rulings simply affirm the lower-court ruling below rather than break new ground. As legal scholar Erwin Chemerinsky wrote in the *ABA Journal*, it "was the year that the law did not change. It is hard to remember a Supreme Court term where the decisions did less to change the law."

The Supreme Court is more likely to hear a case if there is a **split of authority** (a disagreement among the lower courts) on a particular issue. In other words, if one federal appellate court concludes that Law A is not constitutional, but a different federal appellate court finds that Law A is constitutional, that would be a split of authority, and the high court might take the case so as to provide uniformity across the nation on Law A.

One final point: The Supreme Court of the United States is not as interested in making certain that justice has been served as it is in making certain that the law is developing properly. A petitioner seeking redress through the high court may have a completely valid argument that a lower court has ignored an important precedent in ruling against him or her. But if the law on this point has been established, the Supreme Court is very likely to reject the petition and instead use this time to examine and decide a new or emerging legal issue.

LEARNING MORE ABOUT THE U.S. SUPREME COURT

To find out more about the U.S. Supreme Court, ranging from its history to biographies of the nine current justices to its docket and recent opinions, you can visit the high court's official Web site at http://www.supremecourt.gov and peruse its many links. In addition, the Legal Information Institute at Cornell University Law School has an excellent online database at https://www.law.cornell.edu /supct/supremes.htm that features a wealth of information about the high court, its justices and its decisions.

Hearing a Case The operation of the Supreme Court is unique in many ways, but by gaining an understanding of how the high court does its business, a reader will also gain an understanding of how most appellate courts function.

Once the Supreme Court agrees to hear a case, the heaviest burden falls upon the attorneys for the competing parties. The oral argument—the presentation made by the attorneys to the members of the court—will be scheduled. The parties (their attorneys) are expected to submit what are called **legal briefs**—their written legal arguments—for the members of the court to study before the oral hearing. The party that has taken the appeal to the Supreme Court—the **appellant**—must provide the high court with a complete record of the lower-court proceedings: the transcripts from the trial, the rulings by the lower courts and other relevant material.

Arguing a matter all the way to the Supreme Court takes a long time, often as long as five years (sometimes longer) from initiation of the suit until the court gives its ruling. James Hill brought suit in New York in 1953 against Time, Inc., for invasion of privacy. The U.S. Supreme Court made the final ruling in the case in 1967 (*Time, Inc.* v. *Hill*).[12] Even at that the matter would not have ended had Hill decided to go back to trial, which the Supreme Court said he must do if he wanted to collect damages. He chose not to.

After the nine justices study the briefs (or at least summaries provided by their law clerks), the **oral argument** is held. Attorneys are strictly limited as to how much they may say. Each side is given a brief amount of time, usually no more than 30 minutes to an hour, to present its arguments. The attorneys often are interrupted by the justices, who ask them questions and pose hypothetical situations. One current justice, Clarence Thomas, is known for not asking questions, but most of the justices verbally

---

12. 385 U.S. 374 (1967).

spar in collegial fashion with attorneys to test and challenge their arguments. There are no witnesses who testify before the Supreme Court—only the attorneys who argue the case. You can listen to oral arguments in many recent Supreme Court cases online at The Oyez Project Web site at http://www.oyez.org. In important cases, "friends of the court" (**amici curiae**) are allowed to present briefs and to participate for 30 minutes in the oral arguments. For example, the American Civil Liberties Union often seeks the friend status in important civil rights cases. Likewise, the Reporters Committee for Freedom of the Press (http://www.rcfp.org) may file a friend-of-the-court brief in cases affecting journalists' rights, even though it is not a party in the cases. In a nutshell, a friend-of-the-court is not a party to the case but holds a vested interest or concern with its outcome.

Deciding a Case After oral argument (which occurs in open court with visitors welcome), the members of the high court move behind closed doors to undertake their deliberations. No one is allowed in the discussion room except members of the court itself—no clerks, no bailiffs, no secretaries. The discussion, which often is held several days after the arguments are completed, is opened by the chief justice. Discussion time is limited, and by being the first speaker the chief justice is in a position to set the agenda, so to speak, for each case—to raise what he or she thinks are the key issues. Next to speak is the justice with the most seniority, and after him or her, the next most senior justice. The court will have many items or cases to dispose of during one conference or discussion day; consequently, brevity is valued. Each justice has just a few moments to state his or her thoughts on the matter. After discussion, a tentative vote is taken and recorded by each justice in a small, hinged, lockable docket book. In the voting procedure the junior justice votes first; the chief justice, last.

TYPES OF SUPREME COURT OPINIONS

1. Opinion of the court (majority opinion)
2. Concurring opinion
3. Dissenting opinion (minority opinion)
4. Plurality opinion
5. Per curiam opinion (unsigned opinion)
6. Memorandum order

Under the U.S. legal system, which is based so heavily on the concept of court participation in developing and interpreting the law, a simple yes-or-no answer to any legal question is hardly sufficient. More important than the vote, for the law if not for the **litigant,** are the reasons for the decision. Therefore the Supreme Court and all courts that deal with questions of law prepare what are called **opinions,** in which the reasons, or rationale, for the decision are given. One of the justices voting in the majority is asked to write what is called the **court's opinion.** If the chief justice is in the majority, he or she selects the author of the opinion. If not, the senior associate justice in the majority makes the assignment. Self-selection is always an option.

Opinion writing is difficult. Getting five or six or seven justices to agree to yes or no is one thing; getting them to agree on why they say yes or no is something else. The opinion must therefore be carefully constructed. After it is drafted, it is circulated among all court members, who make suggestions or even draft their own opinions. The opinion writer may incorporate as many of these ideas as possible into the opinion to retain its majority backing. Although all this is done in secret, historians have learned that rarely do court opinions reflect solely the work of the writer. They are more often a brokered conglomeration of paragraphs, pages and sentences from the opinions of several justices.

A justice in agreement with the majority who cannot be convinced to join in backing the court's opinion has the option of writing what is called a **concurring opinion.** A justice who writes a concurring opinion may agree with the outcome of the decision, but does so for reasons different from those expressed in the majority opinion. Or the concurring justice may want to emphasize a specific point not addressed in the majority opinion.

A justice who writes a concurring opinion may agree with the outcome of the decision, but does so for reasons different from those expressed in the majority opinion.

Justices who disagree with the majority can also write an opinion, either individually or as a group, called a **dissenting opinion.** Dissenting opinions are very important. Sometimes, after the court has made a decision, it becomes clear that the decision was not proper. The issue thus may be litigated again by other parties who use the arguments in the dissenting opinion as the basis for a legal claim. If enough time passes, if the composition of the court changes sufficiently or if the court members change their minds, the high court can swing to the views of the original dissenters.

An opinion in which five justices cannot agree on a single majority opinion—there is no opinion of the court—but that is joined by more justices than any other opinion in the case is known as a **plurality opinion.** For instance, imagine that four justices agree with a particular outcome in a case for reason A. Two other justices may also agree with that same outcome, but for reason B, while three other justices do not agree with the outcome at all. In this split of 4-2-3 among the justices, the four-justice opinion constitutes the plurality. This was precisely the result in a 2012 U.S. Supreme Court decision called *United States* v. *Alvarez* in which the Court declared unconstitutional, in violation of the First Amendment right of free speech, the Stolen Valor Act. The Stolen Valor Act made it a crime to falsely claim to have won a Congressional Medal of Honor (see pages 66–67 discussing the Stolen Valor Act in more detail). Four of the nine justices concluded that the Stolen Valor Act violated the freedom of speech because it did not pass constitutional muster under the **strict scrutiny** standard of review (see pages 72–73 discussing strict scrutiny), while two justices declared the law violated the freedom of speech because it did not pass the **intermediate scrutiny** standard of review (see pages 114–118 discussing intermediate scrutiny). In other words, six total justices found the law was unconstitutional, but four did so for one reason and two did so for a different reason. Finally, three justices in *Alvarez* dissented because they found the Stolen Valor Act was perfectly acceptable and they would have upheld it.

Finally, it is possible for a justice to concur with the majority in part and to dissent in part as well. That is, the justice may agree with some of the things the majority says but disagree with other aspects of the ruling. Such splits thwart the orderly development of the law. They often leave lawyers and other interested parties at a loss when trying to predict how the court might respond in the next similar case that comes along.

The Supreme Court can dispose of a case in two other ways. A **per curiam** (by the court) **opinion** can be prepared. This is an unsigned opinion drafted by one or more members of the majority and published as the court's opinion. Per curiam opinions are not common, but neither are they rare. For instance, the U.S. Supreme Court issued a two-paragraph per curiam opinion—such brevity is another common characteristic of per curiam opinions—in a 2012 case called *American Tradition Partnership, Inc.* v. *Bullock*.[13] In *Bullock*, the Court reversed a decision by the Montana Supreme Court that had upheld a state statute restricting corporate expenditures supporting or opposing candidates and political parties. The per curiam opinion found the Montana law violated the court's 2010 precedent on this issue from *Citizens United* v. *Federal Elections Commission* (see both earlier this chapter and pages 136–139 for more on *Citizens United*). Four justices filed a similarly short dissent. The names of the four dissenting justices (all members of the Court's so-called liberal wing) appeared on the case, however, thus indicating that the unsigned or anonymous per curiam opinion must have been written by one of the five other justices from the Court's so-called conservative wing. This is another important aspect of per curiam opinions—while per curiam decisions themselves are not attributed to any specific justice, concurring and dissenting opinions are signed by identified justices.

Finally, the high court can dispose of a case with a **memorandum order**—that is, it just announces the vote without giving an opinion. Or the order cites an earlier Supreme Court decision as the reason for affirming or reversing a lower-court ruling. In cases with little legal importance and in cases in which the issues were really resolved earlier, the court saves a good deal of time by just announcing its decision.

One final matter in regard to voting remains for consideration: What happens in case of a tie vote? When all nine members of the court are present, a tie vote is technically impossible. However, if there is a vacancy on the court, only eight justices hear a case. Even when the court is full, a particular justice may disqualify himself or herself from hearing a case. As discussed earlier, when a vote ends in a tie, the decision of the lower court is affirmed. No opinion is written. It is as if the Supreme Court had never heard the case.

During the circulation of an opinion, justices have the opportunity to change their vote. The number and membership in the majority may shift. It is not impossible for the majority to become the minority if one of the dissenters writes a particularly powerful dissent that attracts support from members originally opposed to his or her opinion. This event is probably very rare. Nevertheless, a vote of the court is not final until it is announced on decision day, or opinion day. The authors of the various opinions—court opinions, concurrences and dissents—publicly read or summarize their views. Printed copies of these documents are handed out to the parties involved and to the press, and are quickly available online.

Courts have no real way to enforce decisions and must depend on other government agencies for enforcement of their rulings. The job normally falls to the executive

13. 132 S. Ct. 2490 (2012).

branch. If perchance the president decides not to enforce a Supreme Court ruling, no legal force exists to compel the president to do so.

At the same time, there is one force that usually works to see that court decisions are carried out: It is that vague force called public opinion or what political scientists call "legitimacy." Most people believe in the judicial process; they have faith that what the courts do is probably right. This does not mean that they always agree with court decisions, but they do agree that the proper way to settle disputes is through the judicial process. Jurists help engender this spirit or philosophy by acting in a temperate manner. The Supreme Court, for example, has developed means that permit it to avoid having to answer highly controversial questions in which an unpopular decision could weaken its perceived legitimacy. The justices might call the dispute a political question, a **nonjusticiable matter,** or they may refuse to hear a case on other grounds. When the members of the court sense that the public is ready to accept a ruling, they may take on a controversial issue. School desegregation is a good example. In 1954 the Supreme Court ruled in *Brown* v. *Board of Education*[14] that segregated public schools violated the U.S. Constitution. The foundation for this ruling had been laid by a decade of less momentous desegregation decisions and executive actions. By 1954 the nation was prepared for the ruling, and it was generally accepted, even in many parts of the South. The legitimacy of a court's decisions, then, often rests upon prudent use of the judicial power.

People believe in the judicial process; they have faith that what the courts do is probably right.

Other Federal Courts

The Supreme Court of the United States is the most visible, perhaps the most glamorous (if that word is appropriate), of the federal courts. But it is not the only federal court nor even the busiest. There are two lower echelons of federal courts, plus various special courts, within the federal system. These special courts, such as the U.S. Court of Military Appeals, U.S. Tax Court and so forth, were created by Congress to handle special kinds of problems.

Most federal cases begin and end in one of the 94 U.S. District Courts located across the nation, in Puerto Rico and in various U.S. territories. In 2017, the district courts were staffed with 677 authorized judgeships (in 2017, however, there were more than 100 vacancies at the district court level), a figure that Congress can vote to increase or decrease. In addition to these authorized U.S. District Court judges (known as "Article III" judges), by 2017 there were more than 530 federal magistrate judges. Federal magistrate judges are appointed for eight-year terms by a federal district court to handle some matters (initial proceedings in criminal cases, for instance) and certain cases delegated to them by the district court judges or with the consent of the parties (magistrate judges cannot, however, preside over felony criminal trials).

District courts are the trial courts of the federal court system, hearing both civil and criminal matters. Each state has at least one federal district court, with more populous states divided into two or more districts, leading to the total of 94 U.S. judicial districts. Pennsylvania, for instance, has three districts (western, middle and eastern), as does Florida (northern, middle and southern).

14. 347 U.S. 483 (1954).

At the intermediate appellate level in the federal judiciary there are 13 circuits of the U.S. Court of Appeals, with 179 authorized judgeships in 2017 (twenty of those appellate judgeships were vacant in 2017). These courts were created by the Federal Judiciary Act of 1789. Until 1948 these courts were called circuit courts of appeal, a reflection of the early years of the republic when the justices of the Supreme Court "rode the circuit" and presided at the courts-of-appeal hearings. While the title circuit courts of appeal is officially gone, the nation is still divided into 11 numbered circuits, each of which is served by one court (see Figure 1.2).

The 12th and 13th circuits are unnumbered. One is the court of appeals for the District of Columbia. This is a very busy court because it hears most of the appeals from decisions made by federal administrative agencies. The 13th is the court of appeals for the Federal Circuit, a court created by Congress in 1982 to handle special kinds of appeals. This court is specially empowered to hear appeals from patent and trademark decisions of U.S. District Courts and other federal agencies such as the Board of Patent Appeals. It also hears appeals from rulings by the U.S. Claims Court, the U.S. Court of International Trade, the U.S. International Trade Commission, the Merit Systems Protection Board and from a handful of other special kinds of rulings. Congress established this court to try to develop a uniform, reliable and predictable body of law in each of these very special fields.

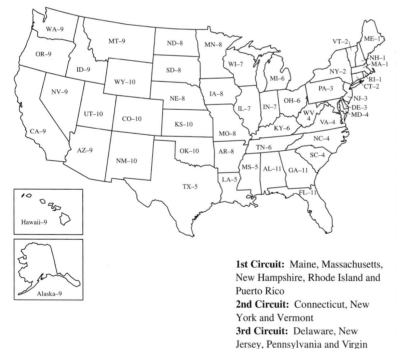

4th Circuit: Maryland, North Carolina, South Carolina, Virginia and West Virginia
5th Circuit: Mississippi, Louisiana and Texas
6th Circuit: Kentucky, Michigan, Ohio and Tennessee
7th Circuit: Illinois, Indiana and Wisconsin
8th Circuit: Arkansas, Iowa, Minnesota, Missouri, Nebraska, North Dakota and South Dakota
9th Circuit: Alaska, Arizona, California, Hawaii, Idaho, Montana, Nevada, Oregon, Washington, Guam and Northern Mariana Islands
10th Circuit: Colorado, Kansas, New Mexico, Oklahoma, Utah and Wyoming
11th Circuit: Alabama, Florida, Georgia and the Canal Zone

1st Circuit: Maine, Massachusetts, New Hampshire, Rhode Island and Puerto Rico
2nd Circuit: Connecticut, New York and Vermont
3rd Circuit: Delaware, New Jersey, Pennsylvania and Virgin Islands

FIGURE 1.2

Circuits 1 through 11 comprise the 50 states and the multiple U.S. territories.

The 12 regional federal courts of appeal (the 11 numbered circuits, plus the District of Columbia circuit) hear appeals from the federal district courts located within them, as well as appeals from decisions of federal administrative agencies. The courts are the last stop for 95 percent of all cases in the federal system. The number of appellate judges in each circuit varies, depending upon geographic size and caseload. The 9th U.S. Circuit Court of Appeals, which sweeps up nine western states as well as the Territory of Guam and the Commonwealth of the Northern Mariana Islands, is the largest and busiest circuit. There occasionally are moves to break up the 9th Circuit, which is perceived as too large (and too liberal by some conservatives). Typically, a panel of three judges will hear a case. In unusual cases, a larger panel of judges, usually 11, will hear the appeal. When this happens, the court is said to be **sitting en banc.** A litigant who loses an appeal heard by a three-judge panel can ask for a rehearing by the entire court. This request is not often granted.

The *ABA Journal* recently awarded the 6th U.S. Circuit Court of Appeals with the somewhat dubious distinction of becoming the most overruled appellate court in the country, edging out the 9th Circuit. During a seven-year stretch, the U.S. Supreme Court overruled slightly more than 81 percent of the 6th Circuit opinions that it considered. Put differently, about four out of every five of the 6th Circuit opinions that the Supreme Court considered were reversed. The 6th Circuit includes the states of Kentucky, Michigan, Ohio and Tennessee.

Federal Judges

All federal judges, other than magistrate judges, are appointed for life terms under Article III of the U.S. Constitution by the president, with the advice and consent of the Senate. The only way a federal judge can be removed is by **impeachment.** Eleven federal judges have been impeached: Seven were found guilty by the Senate, and the other four were acquitted. Impeachment and trial is a long process and one rarely undertaken.

Political affiliation plays a distinct part in the appointment of federal judges. Democratic presidents usually appoint Democratic judges, and Republican presidents appoint Republican judges. Nevertheless, it is expected that nominees to the federal bench be competent jurists. This is especially true for appointees to the U.S. Court of Appeals and to the Supreme Court. The Senate must confirm all appointments to the federal courts, a normally perfunctory act in the case of lower-court judges. More careful scrutiny is given nominees to the appellate courts.

The appointment process now is of great public interest, as the current justices appear in many people's eyes to be narrowly divided along ideological and political lines. Justice Anthony Kennedy today is the pivotal swing vote on the high court that parties arguing before it hope to capture. In fact, while John Roberts is the chief justice, many people nonetheless referred in 2017 to the Supreme Court as "the Kennedy Court."

The president appoints the members of the high court with the "advice and consent" of the U.S. Senate. When the White House and the Senate are both in the hands of the same party, Republicans or Democrats, this appointment process will usually proceed smoothly. But when the White House and Senate are not controlled by the same party, bitter fights over future justices can occur, with a president sometimes struggling or even failing to gain the advice and consent of the Senate over a given appointee.

In addition to having replaced the seat vacated by Justice Antonin Scalia's death, President Donald Trump may well have the opportunity to nominate three more justices to the nation's high court during his first term. That's because in late 2017, Justice Ruth Bader Ginsburg was 84 years old, Justice Anthony Kennedy was 81, and Justice Stephen Breyer was 79. Given their ages, these justices might either retire or pass away while Trump is in office. Battles over confirmation are sure to be contentious, as Trump has the power to shape the direction of the court for decades to come.

Presidents and senators alike have discovered that the individual who is nominated is not always the one who spends the remainder of his or her lifetime on the court. Justices and judges appointed to the bench for life sometimes change. Perhaps they are affected by their colleagues. Or maybe it is because they are largely removed from the political and social pressures faced by others in public life. For whatever reasons, men and women appointed to the bench sometimes modify their philosophy. For instance, current Justice Kennedy was appointed by Republican President Ronald Reagan in 1988, but now has alienated cultural conservatives by writing decisions that legalized same-sex marriage and that declared unconstitutional a law against virtual child pornography (see Chapter 13).

THE STATE COURT SYSTEM

The constitution of each of the 50 states either establishes a court system in that state or authorizes the legislature to do so. The court system in each of the 50 states is somewhat different from the court system in all the other states. There are, however, more similarities than differences among the 50 states.

Trial courts are the base of each judicial system. At the lowest level are usually what are called courts of limited jurisdiction. Some of these courts have special functions, such as a traffic court, which is set up to hear cases involving violations of the motor-vehicle code. Some of these courts are limited to hearing cases of relative unimportance, such as trials of persons charged with misdemeanors, or minor crimes, or civil suits in which the damages sought fall below a small amount of money (a so-called small claims court). The court may be a municipal court set up to hear cases involving violations of the city code. Whatever the court, the judges in these courts have limited jurisdiction and deal with a limited category of problems.

Above the lower-level courts normally exist trial courts of general jurisdiction similar to the federal district courts. These courts are sometimes county courts and sometimes state courts, but whichever they are, they handle nearly all criminal and civil matters. They are primarily courts of original jurisdiction; that is, they are the first courts to hear a case. However, on occasion they act as a kind of appellate court when the decisions of the courts of limited jurisdiction are challenged. When that happens, the case is retried in the trial court—the court does not simply review the law. This proceeding is called hearing a case **de novo.**

A **jury** is most likely to be found in the trial court of general jurisdiction. It is also the court in which most civil suits for libel and invasion of privacy are commenced (provided the state court has jurisdiction), in which prosecution for violating state obscenity laws starts and in which many other media-related matters begin.

Above this court may be one or two levels of appellate courts. Every state has a supreme court, although some states do not call it that. In New York, for example, it is called the Court of Appeals, but it is the high court in the state, the court of last resort.* Formerly, a supreme court was the only appellate court in most states. As legal business increased and the number of appeals mounted, the need for an intermediate appellate court became evident. Therefore, in nearly all states there is an intermediate court, usually called the court of appeals. This is the court where most appeals end. In some states it is a single court with three or more judges. More often, numerous divisions within the appellate court serve various geographic regions, each division having three or more judges. Since every litigant is normally guaranteed at least one appeal, this intermediate court takes much of the pressure off the high court of the state. Rarely do individuals appeal beyond the intermediate level.

State courts of appeals tend to operate in much the same fashion as the U.S. Court of Appeals, with cases being heard by small groups of judges, usually three at a time.

Cases not involving federal questions go no further than the high court in a state, usually called the supreme court. This court—usually a seven- or nine-member body—is the final authority regarding the construction of state laws and interpretation of the state constitution. Not even the Supreme Court of the United States can tell a state supreme court what that state's constitution means.

Not even the Supreme Court of the United States can tell a state supreme court what that state's constitution means.

State court judges are frequently elected. Normally the process is nonpartisan, but because they are elected and must stand for re-election periodically, state court judges are generally a bit more politically active than their federal counterparts. Nearly half the states in the nation use a kind of compromise system that includes both appointment and election. The compromise is designed to minimize political influence and initially select qualified candidates but still retain an element of popular control. The plans are named after the states that pioneered them, the **California Plan** and the **Missouri Plan.**

JUDICIAL REVIEW

One of the most important powers of courts (and at one time one of the most controversial) is the power of **judicial review**—that is, the right of any court to declare any law or official governmental action invalid because it violates a constitutional provision. We usually think of this right in terms of the U.S. Constitution. However, a state court can declare an act of its legislature to be invalid because the act conflicts with a provision of the state constitution. Theoretically, any court can exercise this power. The Circuit Court of Lapeer County, Mich., can rule that the Environmental Protection Act of 1972 is unconstitutional because it deprives citizens of their property without due process of law, something guaranteed by the Fifth Amendment to the federal Constitution. But this action isn't likely to happen, because a higher court would quickly overturn such a ruling. In fact, it is rather unusual for any court—even the U.S. Supreme Court—to invalidate a state or federal law on grounds that it violates the Constitution. Judicial review is therefore not a power that the courts use excessively. A judicial maxim states: When a court has a choice of two or more ways in which to interpret a statute, the court should always interpret the statute in such a way that it is constitutional.

* To further confuse matters, the trial court of general jurisdiction in New York is called the Supreme Court. This is a fact with which avid "Law & Order" fans should already be familiar.

Judicial review is extremely important when matters concerning regulations of mass media are considered. Because the First Amendment prohibits laws that abridge freedom of press and speech, each new measure passed by Congress, by state legislatures and even by city councils and township boards must be measured by the yardstick of the First Amendment. Courts have the right, in fact have the duty, to nullify laws and executive actions and administrative rulings that do not meet the standards of the First Amendment. While many lawyers and legal scholars rarely consider constitutional principles in their work and rarely seek judicial review of a statute, attorneys who represent newspapers, magazines, broadcasting stations and movie theaters constantly deal with constitutional issues, primarily those of the First Amendment. The remainder of this book will illustrate the obvious fact that judicial review, a concept at the very heart of American democracy, plays an important role in maintaining the freedom of the American press, even though the power is not explicitly included in the Constitution.

SUMMARY

There are 52 different judicial systems in the nation: one federal system, one for the District of Columbia and one for each of the 50 states. Courts within each of these systems are divided into two general classes—trial courts and appellate courts. In any lawsuit both the facts and the law must be considered. The facts or the factual record is an account of what happened to prompt the dispute. The law is what should be done to resolve the dispute. Trial courts determine the facts in the case; then the judge applies the law. Appellate courts, using the factual record established by the trial court, determine whether the law was properly applied by the lower court and whether proper judicial procedures were followed. Trial courts exercise original jurisdiction almost exclusively; that is, they are the first courts to hear a case. Trial courts have very little discretion over which cases they will and will not hear. Appellate courts exercise appellate jurisdiction almost exclusively; that is, they review the work done by the lower courts when decisions are appealed. Whereas the intermediate appellate courts (i.e., courts of appeals; the appellate division) have limited discretion in the selection of cases, the high courts (supreme courts) in the states and the nation generally have the power to select the cases they wish to review.

Federal courts include the Supreme Court of the United States, the U.S. Courts of Appeals, the U.S. District Courts and several specialized tribunals. These courts have jurisdiction in all cases that involve the U.S. Constitution, U.S. law and U.S. treaties; in disputes between citizens of different states; and in several less important instances. In each state there are trial-level courts and a court of last resort, usually called the supreme court. In about half the states there are intermediate appellate courts as well. State courts generally have jurisdiction in all disputes between citizens of their state that involve the state constitution or state law.

Judicial review is the power of a court to declare a statute, regulation or executive action to be a violation of the Constitution and thus invalid. Because the First Amendment to the U.S. Constitution guarantees the rights of freedom of speech and press, all government actions that relate to the communication of ideas and information face potential scrutiny by courts to determine their validity.

LAWSUITS

The final topic is lawsuits. To the layperson, the United States appears to be awash in lawsuits. This notion can probably be blamed on the increased attention the press has given legal matters. Courts are fairly easy to cover, and stories about lawsuits are commonly published and broadcast.

This is not to say that we are not a highly litigious people. Backlogs in the courts are evidence of this. Going to court today is no longer a novelty but a common business or personal practice for a growing number of Americans. And too many of these lawsuits involve silly or trivial legal claims. In the end, the public pays a substantial price for all this litigation, through higher federal and state taxes to build and maintain courthouses and money to pay the salaries of those who work in the judiciary, and through higher insurance costs on everything from automobiles to protection from libel suits.

The material that follows is a simplified description of how a lawsuit proceeds. The picture is stripped of a great deal of the procedural activity that so often lengthens the lawsuit and keeps attorneys busy.

The party who commences or brings a civil lawsuit is called the **plaintiff.** The party against whom the suit is brought is called the **defendant.** In a libel suit the person who has been libeled is the plaintiff and is the one who starts the suit against the defendant—the newspaper, television station or blog. A civil suit is usually a dispute between two private parties. The government offers its good offices—the courts—to settle the matter. A government can bring a civil suit such as an antitrust action against someone, and an individual can bring a civil action against the government. But normally a civil suit is between private parties. (In a criminal action, the government always initiates the action.)

To start a civil suit the plaintiff first picks the proper court, one that has jurisdiction in the case. Then the plaintiff typically files a **civil complaint** with the court clerk. This complaint, or **pleading,** is a statement of the allegations against the defendant and the remedy that is sought, typically money damages. The complaint will also include:

1. A statement of the relevant facts upon which the plaintiff is suing
2. The legal theory or theories (known as causes of action) upon which the plaintiff is suing (libel, for instance, is a cause of action or legal theory)
3. A request for a remedy or relief (typically, the plaintiff requests monetary damages in a civil lawsuit, although equitable relief also can be sought in some instances)

The plaintiff then serves the defendant with the complaint to answer these allegations. The plaintiff may later amend his or her pleadings in the case. After the complaint is filed, a hearing is scheduled by the court.

If the defendant fails to answer the allegations, he or she normally loses the suit by default. Usually, however, the defendant will respond and prepare his or her own set of pleadings, which constitute an answer to the plaintiff's allegations. If there is little disagreement at this point about the facts—what happened—and that a wrong has been committed, the plaintiff and the defendant might settle their differences out of court. The defendant might say, "I guess I did libel you in this article, and I really don't have a very good defense. You asked for $100,000 in damages; would you settle for $50,000 and keep this out of court?" The plaintiff might very well answer yes, because a court trial is costly and takes a long time, and the plaintiff can also end up losing the case. Smart lawyers try to keep their clients out of court and settle matters in somebody's office. The overwhelming majority of cases, in fact, never go to trial.

If there is disagreement, the case is likely to continue. One common response to a complaint is for the defendant to file in court and to serve the plaintiff with an **answer.** An answer typically denies most of the facts and all of the allegations in the complaint; it may also assert various defenses to the plaintiff's complaint. Another typical move for the defendant to make at this point is to file a motion to dismiss, or a **demurrer.** In such a motion the defendant says this to the court: "I admit that I did everything the plaintiff says I did. On June 5, 2017, I did publish an article in which she was called a socialist. But, Your Honor, it is not libelous to call someone a socialist." The plea made then is that even if everything the plaintiff asserts is true, the defendant did nothing that was legally wrong. The law cannot help the plaintiff. The court might grant the motion, in which case the plaintiff can appeal. Or the court might refuse to grant the motion, in which case the defendant can appeal. If the motion to dismiss is ultimately rejected by all the courts up and down the line, a trial is then held. It is fair play for the defendant at that time to dispute the plaintiff's statement of the facts; in other words to deny, for example, that his newspaper published the article containing the alleged libel.

Before the trial is held, the judge may schedule a conference between both parties in an effort to settle the matter or to narrow the issues so that the trial can be shorter and less costly. If the effort to settle the dispute fails, the lawsuit goes forward. Either party could ask for a **summary judgment,** which is a way of ending a case before trial. The party moving for summary judgment is trying to avoid the cost and time of a trial by asserting that both parties agree to the facts of the case, and, based on those facts, the outcome of the trial is obvious. With no factual issues to be sorted out at trial, this makes it possible for the judge to decide the case on the basis of the law. The judge can then rule that the law dictates that one party must win and the other must lose. If the facts are disputed, though, the case can proceed and be tried before either a jury or only a judge. Note that both sides must waive the right to a jury trial. In this event, the judge becomes both the fact finder and the lawgiver, a situation known as a bench trial. Now, suppose that the case is heard by a jury. After all the testimony is given, all the evidence is presented and all the arguments are made, the judge instructs the jury in the law. Instructions are often long and complex, despite attempts by judges to simplify them. **Judicial instructions** guide the jury in determining guilt or innocence if certain facts are found to be true. The judge will say that if the jury finds that X is true and Y is true and Z is true, then it must find for the plaintiff, but if the jury finds that X is not true, but that R is true, then it must find for the defendant.

In a civil lawsuit, the burden is on the plaintiff to prove her case by a preponderance of the evidence. This simply means that it is more likely than not that the defendant should be held liable (greater than 50 percent chance that the plaintiff's argument is true). Notice here the use of the term "liable." A defendant who loses a civil case is found liable (the term "guilty" applies only in criminal cases).

After deliberation, the jury presents its **verdict,** the action by the jury. The judge then announces the **judgment of the court.** This is the decision of the court. The judge is not always bound by the jury verdict. If he or she feels that the jury verdict is unfair or unreasonable, the judge can reverse it and rule for the other party. This rarely happens.

If either party is unhappy with the decision, an appeal can be taken. At that time the legal designations may change. The person seeking the appeal becomes the *appellant,* or petitioner. The other party becomes the **appellee,** or **respondent.** The name of the party initiating the action is usually listed first in the name of the case. For example: Smith sues Jones for libel. The case name is *Smith* v. *Jones.* Jones loses and takes an appeal. At that point in most jurisdictions Jones becomes the party initiating the action and the case becomes *Jones* v. *Smith.* This change in designations often confuses novices in their attempt to trace a case from trial to final appeal. If Jones wins the appeal and Smith decides to appeal to a higher court, the case again becomes *Smith* v. *Jones.* In more and more jurisdictions today, however, the case name remains the same throughout the appeal process. This is an effort by the judiciary to relieve some of the confusion wrought by this constant shifting of party names within the case name. In California, for example, the case of *Smith* v. *Jones* remains *Smith* v. *Jones* through the entire life of that case.

The end result of a successful civil suit is usually the awarding of money damages. Sometimes the amount of damages is guided by the law, as in a suit for infringement of copyright in which the law provides that a losing defendant pay the plaintiff the amount of money he or she might have made if the infringement had not occurred, or at least a set number of dollars. But most of the time the damages are determined by how much the plaintiff seeks, how much the plaintiff can prove he or she lost and how much the jury thinks the plaintiff deserves. It is not a very scientific means of determining the dollar amount.

A **criminal prosecution,** or **criminal action,** is like a civil suit in many ways. The procedures are more formal, elaborate and involve the machinery of the state to a greater extent. The state brings the charges, usually through the county or state prosecutor. The defendant can be apprehended either before or after the charges are brought. In the federal system people must be **indicted** by a **grand jury,** a panel of 16 to 23 citizens, before they can be charged with a serious crime. But most states do not use grand juries in that fashion, and the law provides that it is sufficient that the prosecutor issue an **information,** a formal accusation. After being charged, the defendant is arraigned. An **arraignment** is the formal reading of the charge. It is at the arraignment that the defendant makes a formal plea of guilty or not guilty. If the plea is guilty, the judge gives the verdict of the court and passes sentence, but usually not immediately, for presentencing reports and other procedures must be undertaken. If the plea is not guilty, a trial is scheduled.

Some state judicial systems have an intermediate step called a preliminary hearing or preliminary examination. The preliminary hearing is held in a court below the trial court, such as a municipal court, and the state has the responsibility of presenting enough evidence to convince the court—only a judge—that a crime has been committed and that there is sufficient evidence to believe that the defendant might possibly be involved. Today it is also not uncommon that **pretrial hearings** on a variety of matters precede the trial.

If a criminal case does go to trial, the burden is on the prosecution (the government) to prove its case beyond a reasonable doubt. This is a much higher burden of proof than the civil case standard of a preponderance of the evidence.

In both a civil suit and a criminal case, the result of the trial is not enforced until the final appeal is exhausted. That is, a money judgment is not paid in civil suits until defendants exhaust all their appeals. The same is true in a criminal case. Imprisonment or payment of a fine is not always required until the final appeal. If the defendant is dangerous or if there is some question that the defendant might not surrender when the final appeal is completed, bail can be required. Bail is money given to the court to ensure appearance in court.

SUMMARY There are two basic kinds of lawsuits—civil suits and criminal prosecutions or actions. A civil suit is normally a dispute between two private parties in which the government offers its courts to resolve the dispute. The person who initiates the civil suit is the plaintiff; the person at whom the suit is aimed is the defendant. A plaintiff who wins a civil suit is normally awarded money damages.

A criminal case is normally an action in which the state brings charges against a private individual, who is called the defendant. A defendant who loses a criminal case can be assessed a fine, jailed or, in extreme cases, executed. A jury can be used in both civil and criminal cases. The jury becomes the fact finder and renders a verdict in a case. But the judge issues the judgment in the case. In a civil suit, a judge can reject any jury verdict and rule in exactly the opposite fashion, finding for either plaintiff or defendant if the judge feels the jury has made a serious error in judgment. Either side can appeal the judgment of the court. In a criminal case the judge can take the case away from the jury and order a dismissal, but nothing can be done about an acquittal, even an incredible acquittal. While a guilty defendant may appeal the judgment, the state is prohibited from appealing an acquittal.

BIBLIOGRAPHY

Abraham, Henry J. *The Judicial Process.* 7th ed. New York: Oxford University Press, 1998.

Ardia, David S. "Freedom of Speech, Defamation, and Injunctions." *William & Mary Law Review* 55 (2013): 1.

Pound, Roscoe. *The Development of the Constitutional Guarantees of Liberty.* New Haven, Conn.: Yale University Press, 1957.

CHAPTER 2

The First Amendment

THE MEANING OF FREEDOM

The First Amendment is the wellspring for nearly all U.S. laws on freedom of speech and press. The amendment, adopted in 1791 as part of the Bill of Rights, is only 45 words, but court decisions during the past two-plus centuries have added substantial meaning to this basic outline. This chapter explores the evolution of freedom of expression, outlines the adoption of the First Amendment, and examines the development of some elements of the fundamental meaning of free speech and press.

HISTORICAL DEVELOPMENT

Free expression is not exclusively an American idea. It traces back to Socrates and Plato. The concept developed more fully during the past 400 years. The modern history of freedom of the press began in England during the 16th and 17th centuries as printing developed. Today the most indelible embodiment of the concept is the First Amendment to the U.S. Constitution, forged in the last half of the 18th century by individuals who built upon their memory of earlier experiences and unchanged in its wording today. To understand the meaning of freedom of the press and speech, it is necessary to understand the meaning of censorship. That's because, when viewed from a negative position, freedom of expression can be simply defined as the absence of censorship or a freedom from government control.

FREEDOM OF THE PRESS IN ENGLAND

When William Caxton set up the first British printing press in 1476, his printing pursuits were restricted only by his imagination and ability. There were no laws governing what he could not print—he was completely free. For more than five centuries, the British and Americans have attempted to regain the freedom that Caxton enjoyed, for shortly after he started publishing, the British Crown began to regulate printing presses in England. Printing developed during a period of religious struggle in Europe, and it soon became an important tool in that struggle. Printing presses made communication with hundreds of people fairly easy and thus gave considerable power to small groups or individuals who owned or could use a press.

The British government realized that unrestricted publication and printing could dilute its power. Information is a potent tool in any society, and those who control the flow and content of information exercise considerable power. The printing press broke the Crown's monopoly of the flow of information, and therefore control of printing was essential.

Between 1476 and 1776 the British used several means to limit or restrict the press in England. **Seditious libel** laws were used to punish those who criticized the government or the Crown, and it did not matter whether the criticism was truthful or not. The press also suffered under **licensing** or **prior restraint** laws, which required printers to obtain prior approval from the government or the church before printing their handbills, pamphlets or newspapers. Printers were often required to deposit with the government large sums of money called **bonds.** This money was forfeited if material appeared that the government felt should not have been published. And the printer was forced to post another bond before printing could be resumed. The British also granted special patents and monopolies to certain printers in exchange for their cooperation in printing only acceptable works and in helping the Crown ferret out other printers who broke the publication laws.

As ideas about democracy spread throughout Europe, it became harder and harder for the government to limit freedom of expression.

British control of the press during these 300 years was generally successful, but did not go unchallenged. As ideas about democracy spread throughout Europe, it became harder and harder for the government to limit freedom of expression. The power of the printing press in spreading ideas quickly to masses of people greatly helped foster the democratic spirit. Although British law regulated American printers as well during the colonial era, regulation of the press in North America was never as successful as it was in Great Britain.

FREEDOM OF THE PRESS IN COLONIAL AMERICA

There were laws in the United States restricting freedom of the press for almost 30 years before the first newspaper was published. As early as 1662, statutes in Massachusetts made it a crime to publish anything without first getting prior approval from the government, 28 years before Benjamin Harris published the first—and last—edition of *Publick Occurrences*. The second and all subsequent issues were banned because Harris had failed to get permission to publish the first edition, which contained material construed to be critical of British policy in the colonies, as well as a report that scandalized the Massachusetts clergy because it said the French king took immoral liberties with a married woman (not his wife).

Despite this inauspicious beginning, American colonists had a much easier time getting their views into print (and staying out of jail) than did their counterparts in England. There was censorship, but American juries were reluctant to convict printers prosecuted by the colonial authorities. The colonial governments were less efficient than the government in England.

The British attempted to use licensing, taxes and sedition laws to control American printers and publishers. Licensing, which ended in England in 1695, lasted until the mid-1720s in the American colonies. Benjamin Franklin's older brother James was jailed in 1722 for failing to get prior government approval for publishing his *New England Courant*. The unpopular government move failed to daunt the older Franklin, and licensing eventually ended in the colonies as well. The taxes levied against the press, most of which were genuine attempts to raise revenues, were nevertheless seen as censorship by American printers and resulted in growing hostility toward Parliament and the Crown. Most publishers refused to buy the tax stamps, and there was little retribution by the British.

The most famous case of government censorship in the American colonies was the seditious libel trial of immigrant printer John Peter Zenger, who found himself involved in a vicious political battle between leading colonial politicians in New York. Zenger published the *New York Weekly Journal,* a newspaper sponsored by Lewis Morris and James Alexander, political opponents of the unpopular colonial governor, William Cosby. Zenger was jailed in November 1734 after his newspaper published several stinging attacks on Cosby, who surmised that by jailing the printer—one of only two working in New York—he could silence his critics. There is little doubt that Zenger was guilty under 18th-century British sedition law. But his attorneys, including the renowned criminal lawyer Andrew Hamilton, were able to convince the jury that no man should be imprisoned or fined for publishing criticism of the government that was both truthful and fair. Jurors simply ignored the law and acquitted Zenger. It was an early example of what today is called **jury nullification**—the power of a jury in a criminal case to ignore (and thereby to "nullify") a law and to return a verdict (typically a not guilty verdict) according to its conscience. While certainly controversial and relatively rare, jury nullification can be seen as an essential part of the legislative process because a law that is repeatedly nullified by juries probably should be revised or discarded by the legislative body that created it.

The verdict in the Zenger case was a great political triumph but did nothing to change the law of seditious libel. In other words, the case did not set an important legal precedent. But the revolt of the American jurors did force colonial authorities to

The most famous case of government censorship in the American colonies was the seditious libel trial of immigrant printer John Peter Zenger.

©Bettman/Contributor/Getty Images

reconsider the use of sedition law as a means of controlling the press. Although a few sedition prosecutions were initiated after 1735, there is no record of a successful prosecution in the colonial courts after the Zenger case. The case received widespread publicity both in North America and in England, and the outcome played an important role in galvanizing public sentiment against this kind of government censorship.

The Zenger trial today is part of American journalism mythology, but it doesn't represent the end of British attempts to control the press in the American colonies. Rather than haul printers and editors before jurors hostile to the state, the government instead hauled them before colonial legislatures and assemblies hostile to journalists. The charge was not sedition, but breach of parliamentary privilege or contempt of the assembly. There was no distinct separation of powers then, and the legislative body could order printers to appear, question, convict and punish them. Printers and publishers were thus still being jailed and fined for publications previously considered seditious.

Despite these potent sanctions occasionally levied against publishers and printers, the press of this era was remarkably robust. Researchers who have painstakingly read the newspapers, pamphlets and handbills produced in the last half of the 18th century are struck by the seeming lack of concern for government censorship. Historian Leonard Levy notes in his book *Emergence of a Free Press* the seeming paradox uncovered by scholars who seek to understand the meaning of freedom of expression during that era.[1] "To one [a scholar] whose prime concern was law and theory, a legacy of suppression [of the press] came into focus; to one who looks at newspaper judgments on public men

---

1. Levy, *Emergence of a Free Press.*

and measures, the revolutionary controversy spurred an expanding legacy of liberty," he wrote. What Levy suggests is that while the law and legal pronouncements from jurists and legislatures suggest a fairly rigid control of the press, in fact journalists and other publishers tended to ignore the law and suffered little retribution.

But the appearance of such freedom can be deceptive, as political scientist John Roche points out in his book *Shadow and Substance,*[2] for the community often exerted tremendous, and sometimes extralegal, pressure on anyone who expressed an unpopular idea. The belief of many people that freedom was the hallmark of society in America ignores history, Roche argues. In colonial America the people simply did not understand that freedom of thought and expression meant freedom for the other person also, particularly for the person with hated ideas. Roche points out that colonial America was an open society dotted with closed enclaves—villages and towns and cities—in which citizens generally shared similar beliefs about religion and government and so forth. Citizens could hold any belief they chose and could espouse that belief, but personal safety depended on the people in a community agreeing with a speaker or writer. If they didn't, the speaker then kept quiet—an early example of self-censorship or what scholars today call a "chilling effect" on speech—or moved to another enclave where the people shared those ideas. While there was much diversity of thought in the colonies, there was often little diversity of belief within individual towns and cities, according to Roche.

The belief of many people that freedom was the hallmark of society in America ignores history.

The propaganda war that preceded the Revolution is a classic example of the situation. In Boston, the patriots argued vigorously for the right to print what they wanted in their newspapers, even criticism of the government. Freedom of expression was their right, a God-given right, a natural right, a right of all British subjects. Many people, however, did not favor revolution or even separation from England. Yet it was extremely difficult for them to publish such pro-British sentiments in many American cities after 1770. Printers who published such ideas in newspapers and handbills did so at their peril. In cities like Boston the printers were attacked, their shops were wrecked and their papers were destroyed. Freedom of the press was a concept with limited utility in many communities for colonists who opposed revolution once the patriots had moved the populace to their side.

Community Censorship, Then and Now

The plight of the pro-British printer in Boston in the 1770s is not a unique chapter in American history. Today such community censorship still exists—and in some instances is growing.

Community censorship does not mean censorship or punishment imposed by the government, but rather the silencing of speech by private people or business entities, often as a result of pressure exerted by political activists, public interest groups and economic stakeholders. It amounts to self-censorship, not government censorship. For example, in 2016 Pittsburgh TV station WTAE fired anchor Wendy Bell after a public outcry based on a Facebook message Bell posted that many perceived as racist against black males. Following a mass shooting near Pittsburgh, Bell posted, "You needn't be a

2. Roche, *Shadow and Substance*.

criminal profiler to draw a mental sketch of the killers who broke so many hearts . . . they are young black men, likely in their teens or early 20s. They have multiple siblings from multiple fathers and their mothers work multiple jobs." Groups such as the Pittsburgh Black Media Federation and publications such as *Very Smart Brothas* loudly protested Bell's remarks, and WTAE later fired her. This is not government censorship because the Federal Communications Commission (the government) did not fire Bell. Rather, it is community censorship or self-censorship because a private entity (WTAE) fired Bell in the face of public protests about Bell's remarks.

COMMUNITY CENSORSHIP AND COUNTRY MUSIC: THE DIXIE CHICKS WEREN'T THE FIRST TO RUFFLE FEATHERS

In 2003, many country music radio stations across the country decided not to play songs by the Dixie Chicks after the group's lead singer, Natalie Maines, made derogatory remarks about then President George W. Bush during a concert in England. A documentary called "Shut Up and Sing" ultimately was made about the incident. But they weren't the first "chicks" to experience community censorship in the world of country music. In the 1970s, a number of country music radio stations refused to play Loretta Lynn's song "The Pill" because its subject matter (birth control) was considered too risqué and because it depicted a woman as being happy because she finally went on the pill after having babies year after year. For instance, "The Pill" contains the following lyrics: "All these years I've stayed at home while you had all your fun, and every year that's gone by another baby's come. There's gonna be some changes made right here on Nursery Hill. You've set this chicken your last time 'cause now I've got the pill." In fact, the song was actually recorded in 1972, but even Lynn's record label refused to release it until 1975. Another Lynn song, "Rated X," also was boycotted by some country stations because it portrayed the double standards that divorced women face. For example, one lyric from "Rated X" is "women all look at you like you're bad and the men all hope you are." In 2016, the 83-year-old Lynn was still going strong, releasing her 54th studio album, "Full Circle."

It is very important to remember here that the First Amendment protects only against government censorship. The First Amendment thus does not apply or protect speech when a company like Facebook adopts a policy of censorship. In fact, in 2016 Facebook made it clear in its "Statement of Rights and Responsibilities" that users should "not post content that: is hate speech, threatening, or pornographic; incites violence; or contains nudity or graphic or gratuitous violence" and that users should "not bully, intimidate, or harass any user." Similarly, the First Amendment does not apply when Twitter censors and terminates accounts that support the terrorist organization known as ISIS.

Self-censorship occurred in 2015 when several major U.S. media organizations chose not to publish controversial cartoons depicting the Prophet Muhammad. The cartoons had appeared in *Charlie Hebdo,* a satirical French magazine. Many Muslims consider any image of the Prophet Muhammad to be offensive. In January 2015, gunmen claiming to be affiliated with Al-Qaeda stormed into *Charlie Hebdo's* office in Paris and killed 12 people, including four prominent cartoonists. In reporting on the killings, U.S. media organizations such as *The New York Times,* CNN and NBC News chose to describe the cartoons at the center of the controversy rather than show them on air or publish them in print. CNN's president said at the time, "Journalistically, every bone says we want to use and should use [the cartoons]." But, he said, "as managers, protecting and taking care of the safety of our employees around the world is more important right now."

Sometimes self-censorship occurs for other reasons. For instance, after the December 2012 shooting at Sandy Hook Elementary School in Connecticut, Paramount Pictures delayed by about one week the release of "Jack Reacher," a violent movie starring Tom Cruise. A statement by Paramount said the decision came "out of honor and respect for the families of the victims whose lives were senselessly taken." The Hollywood premiere of Quentin Tarantino's violent "Django Unchained" also was delayed after Sandy Hook. Perhaps even more famously, the movie "Gangster Squad" not only was delayed in its release following the July 2012 movie-theater shooting in Aurora, Colorado, but a scene from the movie depicting a fictional shooting inside Grauman's Chinese Theatre in Hollywood was edited out.

In April 2016, ESPN fired Curt Schilling, the former Boston Red Sox pitcher and a prominent baseball analyst on ESPN, for an offensive social media post involving which restroom transgender people are allowed to use. On his Facebook wall, Schilling shared a meme that depicted an overweight man wearing a wig and women's clothing but with exposed breasts. Text to the right of the man read: "LET HIM IN! to the restroom with your daughter or else you're a narrow-minded, judgmental, unloving racist bigot who needs to die." Schilling shared that meme and added this commentary: "A man is a man no matter what they call themselves. I don't care what they are, who they sleep with, men's room was designed for the penis, women's not so much. Now you need laws telling us differently? Pathetic." Schilling's post immediately drew criticism. The next day, ESPN issued a statement that said it was "an inclusive company" and that Schilling's conduct was "unacceptable."

Sometimes a word itself becomes the subject of community censorship. For instance, use of the word "retard" in 2010 became fodder for such censorship after White House Chief of Staff Rahm Emanuel uttered it to describe the strategies of some activists during the contentious debate on health-care reform. Then Rush Limbaugh used it. That, in turn, got Sarah Palin (her son Trig has Down syndrome) into the mix to object to the word's usage, and a Web site (http://www.r-word.org) actually was created by the Special Olympics to "eliminate the demeaning use of the r-word." Joe Jonas of the Jonas Brothers even taped a public service announcement urging people to visit the Web site and to take a pledge to stop saying "retard."

It is important to understand that the First Amendment does not protect against community censorship. It protects only against censorship by government officials and government entities. Students at some private universities have attempted to block the appearances of right-wing speakers with whom they disagree. For instance, a case of community censorship at the university level occurred in 2016 when conservative speaker Milo Yiannopoulos, a self-proclaimed "supervillain on the Internet," was shut down by protesters at DePaul University. Yiannopoulos had been invited to speak by DePaul's College Republicans. According to the DePaul student newspaper's coverage of the event, "a group of protesters stormed the stage and interrupted Yiannopoulos, riling up the crowd. One of the protesters . . . ran up on stage about 15 minutes after Yiannopoulos began speaking. [The protester] stormed the stage with a whistle and yelled 'this man's an idiot!' while members in the crowd yelled 'get a job!'" That protester was then joined onstage by other students, "and the noise from the crowd and the protesters drowned out Yiannopoulos." In a statement released after the event, DePaul's president apologized to the College Republicans. But when the College Republicans wanted to invite Yiannopoulos back for a second speech, school officials refused, claiming in an e-mail that Yiannopoulos' "inflammatory" speech and behavior during his first appearance contributed to a "hostile environment" on campus and that the school would not be able to "provide the security that would be required for such an event." Other instances of community censorship at private universities occurred in 2017.

But such instances of nongovernmental community censorship also run in the opposite political direction, as when *The New York Times'* Chris Hedges, "a war correspondent who sharply criticized the war in Iraq, had to cut his speech short after he was repeatedly interrupted by boos and his microphone was unplugged twice" during a commencement address at Rockford College in Illinois.[3] This and the incident at DePaul are examples of what attorneys sometimes call a **heckler's veto**—when a crowd or audience's reaction to a speech or message is allowed to control and silence that speech or message. Courts have made it clear that the existence of a hostile audience, standing alone, has never been sufficient to sustain a denial of or punishment for the exercise of First Amendment rights. In other words, the government must come to the defense of the speaker, not the heckler.

When such censorship occurs on public university campuses, of course, it does raise First Amendment concerns and is no longer just community censorship. For instance, in 2016 the Young America's Foundation (YAF) student chapter at California State University at Los Angeles invited conservative writer Ben Shapiro to campus, with some funding for the event provided by student government. Various people criticized the event, though, prompting the university president to postpone Shapiro's visit "for a later date, so that we can arrange for him to appear as part of a group of speakers with differing viewpoints on diversity." But after Shapiro vowed to show up for his scheduled visit anyway, and after YAF threatened legal action if he wasn't allowed to speak, the president reversed his position, and Shapiro spoke on campus as planned.

Public malaise about such conditions is dangerous. No individual's freedom is secure unless the freedom of all is ensured. This last point—that the freedom of speech must be ensured for *all* people, not simply those on one side of the political spectrum—is critical. As Nadine Strossen, president of the American Civil Liberties Union, told one of the authors of this textbook, "the notion of neutrality is key. You cannot have freedom of speech only for ideas that you like and people that you like."[4] Those who would engage in community censorship because they don't like what someone has to say would be wise to remember this principle of viewpoint neutrality embodied in the freedom of speech.

3. Young, "The Tyranny of Hecklers."
4. Richards and Calvert, "Nadine Strossen and Freedom of Expression," 202.

SUMMARY

Freedom of the press, part of the great Anglo-American legal tradition, is a right won only through many hard-fought battles. The British discovered the power of the press in the early 16th century and devised numerous schemes to restrict publication. Criticism of the government, called seditious libel, was outlawed. Licensing or prior censorship was also common. In addition, the Crown for many years used an elaborate system of patents and monopolies to control printing in England.

While under British law for more than 100 years, American colonists enjoyed somewhat more freedom of expression than did their counterparts in England. Censorship laws existed before the first printing press arrived in North America, but they were enforced erratically or not at all. Licensing ended in the colonies in the 1720s. There were several trials for sedition in the colonies, but the acquittal of John Peter Zenger in 1735 by a recalcitrant jury ended that threat. Colonial legislatures and assemblies then attempted to punish dissident printers by using their contempt power. By the time the American colonists began to build their own governments in the 1770s and 1780s, they had the history of a 300-year struggle for freedom of expression on which to build.

Today, community censorship and self-censorship are common problems in the United States and are often as problematic as government censorship.

THE FIRST AMENDMENT

In 1781, even before the end of the Revolutionary War, the new nation adopted its first constitution, the Articles of Confederation. The Articles provided for a loose-knit confederation of the 13 colonies, or states, in which the central or federal government had little power. The Articles reflected the spirit of the Declaration of Independence, adopted five years earlier, which ranked the rights of individuals higher than the needs of a government to organize and operate a cohesive community. The Articles of Confederation did not contain a guarantee of freedom of expression. In fact, it had no bill of rights of any kind. The individuals who drafted this constitution did not believe such guarantees were necessary. Guarantees of freedom of expression were already part of the constitutions of most of the 13 states.

But the system of government created by the Articles of Confederation did not work very well. In the summer of 1787, 12 of the 13 states sent a total of 55 delegates to Philadelphia to revise or amend the Articles, to make fundamental changes in the structure of the government.

THE NEW CONSTITUTION

It was a remarkable group of men; perhaps no such group has gathered before or since. The members were merchants, planters and professionals. None were full-time politicians. These men were members of the economic, social and intellectual aristocracy of their states. They shared a common education centered on history, political philosophy and science. Some spent months preparing for the meeting—studying the governments of past nations. Whereas some members came to modify the Articles of Confederation, many others knew that a new constitution was needed. In the end that is what they produced, a new governmental charter. The charter was far different from the Articles in that it gave vast powers to a central government. The states remained supreme in some matters, but in other matters they relinquished their sovereignty to the new federal government.

No official record of the convention was kept. The delegates deliberated behind closed doors as they drafted the new charter. However, some personal records remain. We know, for example, that inclusion of a bill of rights was not discussed until the last days of the convention. The Constitution was drafted in such a way as not to infringe on state bills of rights. When the meeting was in its final week, George Mason of Virginia indicated his desire that "the plan be prefaced with a Bill of Rights. . . . It would give great quiet to the people," he said, "and with the aid of the state declarations, a bill might be prepared in a few hours." Few joined Mason's call. Only one delegate, Roger Sherman of Connecticut, spoke against the suggestion. He said he favored protecting the rights of the people when it was necessary, but in this case there was no need. "The state declarations of rights are not repealed by this Constitution; and being in force are sufficient." The states, voting as units, unanimously opposed Mason's plan. While the Virginian later attempted to add a bill of rights in a piecemeal fashion, the Constitution emerged from the convention and was placed before the people for ratification without a bill of rights.

The new Constitution was not without opposition. The struggle for its adoption was hard fought. The failure to include a bill of rights in the document was a telling complaint raised against the new document. Even Thomas Jefferson, who was in France, lamented, in a letter to his friend James Madison, the lack of a guarantee of political rights in the charter. When the states finally voted on the new Constitution, it was approved, but only after supporters in several states had promised to petition the First Congress to add a bill of rights.

James Madison was elected from Virginia to the House of Representatives, defeating James Monroe only after promising his constituents to work in the First Congress toward adoption of a declaration of human rights. When Congress convened, Madison worked to keep his promise. He first proposed that the new legislature incorporate a bill of rights into the body of the Constitution, but the idea was later dropped. That the Congress would adopt the declaration was not a foregone conclusion. There was much opposition, but after several months, 12 amendments were finally approved by both houses and sent to the states for ratification. Madison's original amendment dealing with freedom of expression states: "The people shall not be deprived or abridged of their right to speak, to write or to publish their sentiments and freedom of the press, as one of the great bulwarks of liberty, shall be inviolable." Congressional committees changed the wording several times, and the section guaranteeing freedom of expression was merged with the amendment guaranteeing freedom of religion and freedom of assembly. The final version is the one we know today:

> *Congress shall make no law respecting an establishment of religion, or prohibiting the free exercise thereof; or abridging the freedom of speech, or of the press; or the right of the people peaceably to assemble, and to petition the Government for a redress of grievances.*

Historical myth tells us that because the amendment occurs first in the Bill of Rights it was considered the most important right.

The concept of the "first freedom" is discussed often. Historical myth tells us that because the amendment occurs first in the Bill of Rights it was considered the most important right. In fact, in the Bill of Rights presented to the states for ratification, the amendment was listed third. Amendments 1 and 2 were defeated and did not become part of the Constitution.

Passage of Amendments 3 through 12 did not occur without struggle. Not until two years after being transmitted to the states for approval did a sufficient number of states adopt the amendments for them to become part of the Constitution. Connecticut, Georgia and Massachusetts did not ratify the Bill of Rights until 1941, a kind of token gesture on the 150th anniversary of its constitutional adoption. In 1791 approval by these states was not needed, since only three-fourths of the former colonies needed to agree to the measures.

DO YOU KNOW WHAT THE FIRST AMENDMENT SAYS? MANY AMERICANS HAVE NO CLUE

A 2016 survey of more than 1,000 adults nationwide conducted on behalf of the Newseum Institute found that 39 percent of Americans could not name any of the rights guaranteed by the First Amendment. Furthermore, in a bad sign for journalists, only 11 percent knew that the First Amendment protects a free press. On the other hand, 54 percent of adults surveyed knew that the First Amendment protects free speech. As for the least known First Amendment freedom, it was the right to petition the government for a redress of grievances—only 2 percent of those surveyed could name it. The complete report, titled "The 2016 State of the First Amendment," is available at http://www.newseuminstitute.org/wp-content /uploads/2016/06/FAC_SOFA16_report.pdf.

FREEDOM OF EXPRESSION IN THE 18TH CENTURY

What did the First Amendment mean to the people who supported its ratification? Technically, the definition of freedom of the press approved by the nation when the First Amendment was ratified in 1791 is what is guaranteed today. To enlarge or narrow that definition requires another vote of the people, a constitutional amendment. This notion is referred to today as "original intent" of the Constitution; that is, if we knew the meaning intended by the framers of the First Amendment, then we would know what it means today.

Most people today consider this notion misguided. The nation has changed dramatically in 227 years. Television, radio, film and the Internet did not exist in 1791. Does this mean that the guarantees of the First Amendment should not apply to these mass media? Of course not. Our Constitution has survived more than two centuries because the Supreme Court of the United States, our final arbiter on the meaning of the Constitution, has helped adapt it to changing times.

Still, it is important that we respect the document that was adopted more than two centuries ago. If we stray too far from its original meaning, the document may become meaningless; there will be no rules of government. The Constitution will mean only what those in power say it means. Thus the judicial philosophy of historicism, despite what professor

Rodney Smolla correctly calls "the obstinate illusiveness of original intent in the free speech area,"[5] remains an important consideration for some judges and justices. For instance, Justice Clarence Thomas on the U.S. Supreme Court often uses historicism/originalism. "The experience of the framers will never give us precise answers to modern conflicts," Smolla writes, "but it will give us a sense of how deeply free speech was cherished, at least as an abstract value."[6]

What was the legal or judicial definition of the First Amendment in 1791? Surprisingly, that is not an easy question to answer. The records of the period carry mixed messages. There was no authoritative definition of freedom of the press and freedom of speech rendered by a body like the Supreme Court. And even the words used by people of that era may have meant something different from what they mean in the 21st century. Most everyone agrees that freedom of expression meant at least the right to be free from prior restraint or licensing. Sir William Blackstone, a British legal scholar, published a major summary of common law between 1765 and 1769. In *Commentaries on the Law of England,* Blackstone defined freedom of expression as "laying no previous restraints upon publication." Today we call this no prior censorship or no prior restraint. Many scholars argue that freedom of expression surely meant more than simply no prior censorship, that it also protected people from punishment *after publication* or, as First Amendment scholars might put it, from subsequent punishments. In other words, the First Amendment also precluded prosecutions for seditious libel. After all, they argue, one of the reasons for the American Revolution was to rid the nation of the hated British sedition laws.

Most everyone agrees that freedom of expression meant at least the right to be free from prior restraint or licensing.

The truth is that we don't know what freedom of the press meant to American citizens in the 1790s. The written residue of the period reveals only a partial story. It's very likely that it meant something a little different to different people, just as it does today. Even those individuals who drafted the Bill of Rights probably held somewhat different views on the meaning of the First Amendment.

WHAT IS "SPEECH" ANYWAY?

The word "speech" in the First Amendment sometimes (but not always) encompasses and includes *conduct*, not simply what we might think of as *pure speech*, such as the written, printed or spoken word or image. Under the **symbolic speech doctrine,** courts treat conduct, such as burning a flag in political protest at a rally, as speech if two elements—one focusing on the actor, the other on the audience—are satisfied:

1. *Actor:* The person engaging in the conduct must intend to convey a particular or specific message with his or her conduct.
2. *Audience:* There must be a great likelihood, under the surrounding circumstances in which the conduct takes place, that some people who witness it will reasonably understand the particular message that was intended by the actor.

---

5. Smolla, *Free Speech in an Open Society,* 28.
6. Ibid., 39.

Under the two-part symbolic speech doctrine, burning an American flag in one's own backyard, when no one else is around and in an effort to stay warm during a snowstorm, does not constitute speech. On the other hand, the U.S. Supreme Court has recognized that burning the flag outside of a political convention in the midst of a protest or rally may be speech. The court has held that nude dancing in a strip club is a form of symbolic speech (see Chapter 13); there's an intent to convey an erotic, sexual message, and there is a clear likelihood (judging by the tips, if nothing else) that the message will be understood as intended. When 50-year-old John E. Brennan went through a pat-down security search at the Portland International Airport in April 2012, a Transportation Security Administration official suspected that he was carrying nitrates. For Brennan, a frequent flier who earlier had refused to go through a TSA full-body scanner, the implicit accusation that he was a terrorist was, as the Associated Press reported, the last straw. Brennan quickly stripped completely naked and, after about five minutes, was arrested and later charged with indecent exposure. But in July 2012, Multnomah County (Oregon) Circuit Court Judge David Rees dismissed the charge, finding that Brennan's act of nudity was one of symbolic protest and therefore constituted speech protected by the First Amendment. "It is the speech itself that the state is seeking to punish, and that it cannot do," Judge Rees declared. Indeed, Brennan said that since the TSA's body scanners can see what one looks like naked, he was simply upping the ante by completely disrobing.

FREEDOM OF EXPRESSION TODAY

If we are not certain what the First Amendment meant in 1791, do we know what it means today? More or less. The First Amendment means today what the Supreme Court of the United States says it means.

The First Amendment means today what the Supreme Court of the United States says it means.

The Supreme Court is a collection of nine justices. Consequently, at any given time there can be nine different definitions of freedom of expression. This has never happened—at least not on important issues. What has happened is that groups of justices have subscribed to various theoretical positions regarding the meaning of the First Amendment. These ideas on the meaning of the First Amendment help justices shape their vote on a question regarding freedom of expression. These ideas have changed since 1919 when the First Amendment first came under serious scrutiny by the Supreme Court.

Legal theories are sometimes difficult to handle. Judge Learned Hand, the most important judge *never* to have served on the U.S. Supreme Court, referred to the propagation of legal theory as "shoveling smoke." With such cautions in mind, here are seven important First Amendment theories or strategies to help judges develop a practical definition of freedom of expression.

SEVEN FIRST AMENDMENT THEORIES

1. Absolutist theory
2. Ad hoc balancing theory
3. Preferred position balancing theory
4. Meiklejohnian theory
5. Marketplace of ideas theory
6. Access theory
7. Self-realization theory

Absolutist Theory.   Some argue that the First Amendment presents an absolute or complete barrier to government censorship. When the First Amendment declares that "no law" shall abridge freedom of expression, the framers of the Constitution meant *no law*. This is the essence of **absolutist theory.** The government cannot censor the press for any reason. There are no exceptions, no caveats, no qualifications.

A majority of the Supreme Court never has adopted an absolutist position.

Few have subscribed to this notion wholeheartedly. A majority of the Supreme Court *never* has adopted an absolutist position. In fact, as this book later illustrates, the Supreme Court has held that several types of speech fall outside the scope of First Amendment protection and thus can be abridged without violating the freedoms of speech or press. As Justice Anthony Kennedy wrote in 2002, "[t]he freedom of speech has its limits; it does not embrace certain categories of speech, including defamation, incitement, obscenity, and pornography produced with real children."[7] Other categories of speech also fall outside the ambit of First Amendment protection, including fighting words (see pages 127–130) and true threats of violence.[8]

In 2010, however, the U.S. Supreme Court refused to carve out another unprotected category of speech in *United States* v. *Stevens*[9] when it held unconstitutional a federal law that criminalized the commercial creation, sale or possession of certain depictions of animal cruelty (the statute did not address the underlying conduct of cruelty to animals, but only the visual portrayals of such conduct in photographs and videos, thus making it a First Amendment speech issue). The ostensible goal of the law was to target so-called crush videos in which women slowly crush to death small animals, like hamsters and chicks, while wearing high-heeled shoes, sometimes while talking to the animals in a kind of dominatrix patter over the squeals of the animals. While recognizing that the prohibition of animal cruelty itself has a long history in American law, the prohibition of speech depicting it does not. In other words, there is a key difference between the underlying conduct of animal cruelty (which is punishable as a crime) and the speech products that depict it, which receive First Amendment protection.

---

7. *Ashcroft* v. *Free Speech Coalition,* 535 U.S. 234, 245–46 (2002).
8. *Watts* v. *U.S.,* 394 U.S. 705, 708 (1969).
9. 559 U.S. 460 (2010).

PROFANITY, CIVILITY & FREEDOM OF EXPRESSION: SWEARING IN PUBLIC PLACES

In June 2012, the town of Middleborough, Massachusetts, adopted an ordinance (a form of statutory law) allowing police to issue civil fines of $20 to people who publicly accost others with spoken profanity. Does the First Amendment guarantee of free speech protect a person's right to swear on public property? The answer is: it depends, and this helps to illustrate the principle that free speech is not absolutely protected.

For example, if the profanity is used in a face-to-face, personally abusive manner that might provoke an immediate violent reaction by the person it targets, then it probably is not protected because it likely falls within one of the few unprotected categories of speech—fighting words (see pages 127–130 on fighting words). On the other hand, laws targeting profanity often are fraught with vagueness issues—how exactly does one define profanity (see page 13 regarding the void for vagueness doctrine)?

In 2002, for instance, an appellate court in *Michigan* v. *Boomer* struck down as unconstitutionally vague a state law which dated back to 1897 and provided that "[a]ny person who shall use any indecent, immoral, obscene, vulgar or insulting language in the presence or hearing of any woman or child shall be guilty of a misdemeanor." The appellate court observed that "it is far from obvious what the reasonable adult considers to be indecent, immoral, vulgar, or insulting." In addition to vagueness issues, if the profanity is imbued with a political message ("Fuck healthcare reform and higher taxes"), it stands a better chance of being protected, as when the U.S. Supreme Court in 1971 protected a man's right to wear a jacket emblazoned with the message "Fuck the Draft" during the Vietnam War in *Cohen* v. *California*.

On the other hand, using the f-bomb in a public court and directing it toward a judge is not protected by the First Amendment, as the 4th U.S. Circuit Court of Appeals held in 2012 in *United States* v. *Peoples*. In that case, Robert Peoples was held in contempt after he told a clerk while inside a courtroom, "Tell Judge Currie [to] get the fuck off all my cases. I started to tell her something there. I started to tell her ass something today." In ruling against Peoples, the 4th Circuit observed that "courts repeatedly have found that offensive words directed at the court may form the basis for a contempt charge." The appellate court concluded that "Peoples' profane language in Judge Currie's courtroom constituted intentional misbehavior that obstructed the administration of justice."

The bottom line is that with rights come responsibilities, and while swearing in some public settings may be protected, a little self-censorship in the name of civility and respect for others in the vicinity probably is a very good thing.

Ad Hoc Balancing Theory. Freedom of speech and press are two of a number of important human rights we value in this nation. These rights often conflict. When conflict occurs, it is the responsibility of the court to balance the freedom of expression with other values. For example, the government must maintain the military to protect the security of the nation.

To function, the military must maintain secrecy about many of its weapons, plans and movements. Imagine that the press seeks to publish information about a secret weapons system. The right to freedom of expression must be balanced with the need for secrecy in the military.

This theory is called *ad hoc* balancing because the scales are erected anew in every case; the meaning of the freedom of expression is determined solely on a case-by-case basis. Freedom of the press might outweigh the need for the government to keep secret the design of its new rifle, but the need for secrecy about a new fighter plane might take precedence over freedom of expression.

Ad hoc balancing is really not a theory; it is a strategy. Developing a definition of freedom of expression on a case-by-case basis leads to uncertainty. Under ad hoc balancing we will never know what the First Amendment means except as it relates to a specific, narrow problem (e.g., the right to publish information about a new army rifle). If citizens cannot reasonably predict whether a particular kind of expression might be protected or prohibited, they will have the tendency to play it safe and keep silent. This is known as a "chilling effect" on speech. This will limit the rights of expression of all persons. Also, ad hoc balancing relies too heavily in its final determination on the personal biases of the judge or justices who decide a case. Ad hoc balancing is rarely invoked as a strategy today except by judges unfamiliar with First Amendment law.

Preferred Position Balancing Theory. The Supreme Court has held in numerous rulings that some constitutional freedoms, principally those guaranteed by the First Amendment, are fundamental to a free society and consequently are entitled to more judicial protection than other constitutional values are.[10] Freedom of expression is essential to permit the operation of the political process and to permit citizens to protest when government infringes on their constitutionally protected prerogatives. The Fourth Amendment guarantee of freedom from illegal search and seizure surely has diminished value if citizens who suffer from such unconstitutional searches cannot protest such actions. Freedom of expression does not trump all other rights. Courts, for example, have attempted to balance the rights of free speech and press with the constitutionally guaranteed right of a fair trial. On the other hand, courts have consistently ruled that freedom of expression takes precedence over the right to personal privacy and the right to reputation, neither of which is explicitly guaranteed by the Bill of Rights.

Giving freedom of expression a preferred position *presumes* that government action that limits free speech and free press to protect other interests is usually unconstitutional. This presumption forces the government to bear the burden of proof in any legal action challenging the censorship. The city, county, state or federal government must prove to the court that its censorship is, in fact, justified and is not a violation of the First Amendment. Were it not for this presumption, the persons whose expression was limited would be forced to convince a court that they had a constitutional right to speak or publish. This difference sounds minor, but in a lawsuit this presumption means a great deal.

10. See *U.S.* v. *Carolene Products,* 304 U.S. 144 (1938); and *Palko* v. *Connecticut,* 302 U.S. 319 (1937). See also *Abrams* v. *U.S.,* 250 U.S. 616 (1919).

While this theory retains some of the negative features of ad hoc balancing, by tilting the scales in favor of freedom of expression, it adds somewhat more certainty to our definition of freedom of expression. By basing this balancing strategy on a philosophical foundation (the maintenance of all rights is dependent on free exercise of speech and press), it becomes easier to build a case in favor of the broad interpretation of freedom of expression under the First Amendment.

Meiklejohnian Theory. Philosopher and educator Alexander Meiklejohn presented a rather complex set of ideas about freedom of expression in the late 1940s.[11] Meiklejohn argued that freedom of expression is a means to an end. That end is successful self-government or, as Meiklejohn put it, "the voting of wise decisions." Freedom of speech and press are protected in the Constitution so that our system of democracy can function, and that is the only reason they are protected. Expression that relates to the self-governing process must be protected absolutely by the First Amendment. There can be no government interference with such expression. Expression that does not relate to the self-governing process is not protected absolutely by the First Amendment. The value or worth of such speech must be balanced by the courts against other rights and values. Meiklejohnian theory thus represents a hierarchical approach to First Amendment theory, with political speech placed at the top of this hierarchy.

Expression that relates to the self-governing process must be protected absolutely by the First Amendment.

Critics of this theory argue that it is not always clear whether expression pertains to self-government (public speech) or to other interests (private speech). Although not providing the specific definition sought by critics, Meiklejohn argued that a broad range of speech is essential to successful self-government. He included speech related to education (history, political science, geography, etc.), science, literature and many other topics. This theory has been embraced by some members of the Supreme Court of the United States, most notably former Justice William Brennan. American libel law was radically changed when Brennan led the Supreme Court to give First Amendment protection to people who have defamed government officials or others who attempt to lead public policy, a purely Meiklejohnian approach to the problem.

Marketplace of Ideas Theory. The marketplace of ideas theory embodies what First Amendment scholar Daniel Farber calls "the truth-seeking rationale for free expression."[12] Although the theory can be traced back to the work of John Milton and John Stuart Mill, it was U.S. Supreme Court Justice Oliver Wendell Holmes Jr. who introduced the marketplace rationale for protecting speech to First Amendment case law in 1919. In his dissent in *Abrams* v. *United States,*[13] Holmes famously wrote:

> But when men have realized that time has upset many fighting faiths, they may come to believe even more than they believe the very foundations of their own conduct that the ultimate good desired is better reached by free trade in ideas—that the best test of truth is the power of the thought to get itself accepted in the competition of the market, and that truth is the only ground upon which their wishes safely can be carried out.[14]

11. Meiklejohn, *Free Speech*.
12. Farber, *The First Amendment,* 4.
13. 250 U.S. 616 (1919).
14. 250 U.S. 616, 630 (Holmes, J., dissenting).

Today, the economics-based marketplace metaphor "consistently dominates the Supreme Court's discussion of freedom of speech."[15] For instance, Justice Stephen Breyer wrote in a 2015 case called *Reed* v. *Town of Gilbert* that "whenever government disfavors one kind of speech, it places that speech at a disadvantage, potentially interfering with the *free marketplace of ideas*."[16]

The marketplace theory, however, is often criticized by scholars. Common condemnations are that much shoddy speech, such as hate speech (see pages 127–135), circulates in the marketplace of ideas despite its lack of value and that access to the marketplace is *not* equal for everyone. In particular, those having the most economic resources (today, large conglomerates such as Comcast, News Corp. and Gannett) are able to own and to control the mass media and, in turn, to dominate the marketplace of ideas. Nonetheless, professor Martin Redish observes that "over the years, it has not been uncommon for scholars or jurists to analogize the right of free expression to a marketplace in which contrasting ideas compete for acceptance among a consuming public."[17] The premise of this idealistically free and fair competition of ideas is that truth will be discovered or, at the very least, conceptions of the truth will be tested and challenged.[18]

The premise of this idealistically free and fair competition of ideas is that truth will be discovered.

Access Theory. A.J. Liebling wrote that freedom of the press belongs to the man who owns one. What he meant was that a constitutional guarantee of freedom of expression had little meaning if a citizen did not have the economic means to exercise this right. Owners of magazines, newspapers and broadcasting stations could take advantage of the promises of the First Amendment, whereas the average person lacked this ability. Put differently, access to the metaphorical marketplace of ideas is *not* equal for all, but is skewed in favor of those with the most economic resources. What Liebling wrote is true today, although the evolution of the Internet has at least given millions more Americans the opportunity to share their ideas as bloggers and tweeters with a wider audience than was accessible in the past. Still, the audience for the vast majority of Web sites is small compared with the number of people reached by a television network, national magazine or even a metropolitan newspaper.

In the mid-1960s some legal scholars, most notably professor Jerome Barron, former dean of the National Law Center at George Washington University, argued that the promise of the First Amendment was unfulfilled for most Americans because they lacked the means to exercise their right to freedom of the press.[19] To make the guarantees of the First Amendment meaningful, newspapers, magazines and broadcasting stations should open their pages and studios to the ideas and opinions of their readers and listeners and viewers. If the press will not do this voluntarily, the obligation falls upon the government to force such access to the press. The access theory thus can be seen as a remedy to correct some of the flaws of the marketplace of ideas theory described earlier.

The access theory thus can be seen as a remedy to correct some of the flaws of the marketplace of ideas theory.

The Supreme Court unanimously rejected the access theory in 1974 in *Miami Herald* v. *Tornillo*.[20] Chief Justice Warren Burger, writing for the court, said that the choice of material

15. Baker, *Human Liberty,* 7.
16. 135 S. Ct. 2218, 2234 (2015) (Breyer, J., concurring in the judgment).
17. Redish and Kaludis, "The Right of Expressive Access," 1083.
18. Chemerinsky, *Constitutional Law,* 753.
19. Barron, "Access to the Press."
20. 418 U.S. 241 (1974).

to go into a newspaper and the decisions made as to content and treatment of public issues and public officials are decisions that must be made by the editors. The First Amendment does not give the government the right to force a newspaper to publish the views or ideas of a citizen. The *Tornillo* case sounded the death for this access theory for print media.

At the same time that federal courts were rejecting the access theory as it applied to the printed press, many courts were embracing these notions to justify the regulation of American radio and television. In 1969 the Supreme Court ruled in *Red Lion Broadcasting* v. *FCC*[21] that "[i]t is the right of the public to receive suitable access to social, political, esthetic, moral, and other ideas and experiences, which is crucial here." The apparent contradiction in accepting the access theory for broadcast media but rejecting its application to the printed press was based on what many broadcasters regarded as an ill-conceived notion of differences in the two media forms. There could be an unlimited number of voices in the printed press, it was argued, but technological limits in the electromagnetic broadcast spectrum controlled the number of radio and television stations that could broadcast, and the government was required to protect the public interest in the case of the latter. The flaw in this assumption, the broadcasters argued, was that it failed to take into account 20th-century (and now 21st-century) economic limits that sharply curtailed the number of printing presses.

Self-Realization/Self-Fulfillment Theory. While the primary goal of Meiklejohnian theory is successful self-government and the main objective of the marketplace theory is discovery of the truth, it may be that speech is important to an individual *regardless* of its impact on politics or its benefit to society at large. For instance, transcribing one's thoughts in a private diary or a personal journal can be beneficial to the writer, even though no one else ever will (at least the writer hopes!) read them. Speech, in other words, can be inherently valuable to a person regardless of its effect on others—it can be an end in itself. An individual who wears a shirt with the name of his or her favorite political candidate on it may not change anyone else's vote or influence discovery of the truth, yet the shirt-wearer is realizing and expressing his or her own identity through speech.

Speech is important to an individual regardless of its impact on politics or its benefit to society at large.

SUMMARY

The nation's first constitution, the Articles of Confederation, did not contain a guarantee of freedom of speech and press, but nearly all state constitutions provided for a guarantee of such rights. Citizens insisted that a written declaration of rights be included in the Constitution of 1787, and a guarantee of freedom of expression was a part of the Bill of Rights that was added to the national charter in 1791.

There is a debate over the meaning of the First Amendment when it was drafted and approved in the late 18th century. Some people argue that it was intended to block both prior censorship and prosecution for seditious libel. Others argue that it was intended to prohibit only prior censorship. We will never know what the guarantee of free expression meant to the people who drafted it, but it is a good bet they had a variety of interpretations of the First Amendment.

21. 395 U.S. 367 (1969).

The meaning of the First Amendment today is largely determined by the Supreme Court of the United States. Jurists use legal theories to guide them in determining the meaning of the constitutional guarantee that "Congress shall make no law abridging freedom of speech or of the press." Seven such theories are (1) absolutist theory, (2) ad hoc balancing theory, (3) preferred position balancing theory, (4) Meiklejohnian theory, (5) marketplace of ideas theory, (6) access theory and (7) self-realization theory.

THE MEANING OF FREEDOM

The struggle since 1791 to define the meaning of freedom of expression has involved a variety of issues. Two topics are at the heart of this struggle: the power of the state to limit criticism or published attacks on the government and the power of the government to forbid the publication of ideas or information it believes to be harmful. Each of these classic battles is considered in the remainder of this chapter.

SEDITIOUS LIBEL AND THE RIGHT TO CRITICIZE THE GOVERNMENT

The essence of a democracy is participation by citizens in the process of government. This participation involves selecting leaders through the electoral process. Popular participation also includes examination of government and public officials to determine their fitness for serving the people. The 2016 presidential campaign, for instance, included often caustic criticism of candidates ranging from eventual winner Donald Trump to Bernie Sanders. Discussion, criticism and suggestion all play a part in the orderly transition of governments and elected leaders. The right to speak and print, then, is inherent in a nation governed by popularly elected rulers.

The right to criticize and oppose the government is central to our political philosophy in the United States. The Supreme Court has ruled, for example, that the First Amendment protects both the right to burn the American flag as a form of political protest[22] and the right to wear a jacket with the words "Fuck the Draft" in a public courthouse during the Vietnam War.[23] But even today it is not always possible to criticize the government or to advocate political change without suffering government reprisals.

---

22. *Texas* v. *Johnson,* 491 U.S. 397 (1989). Flag mutilation statutes remain controversial today. Citing the 1989 ruling in *Johnson* as precedent, the Attorney General of Nebraska in 2010 issued a memorandum giving his opinion that a Cornhusker state statute was unconstitutional. His opinion that the law violated the First Amendment allowed a federal judge to issue a permanent injunction banning its enforcement in a case brought by members of the Westboro Baptist Church. The now-enjoined Nebraska law provided that "a person commits the offense of mutilating a flag if such person intentionally casts contempt or ridicule upon a flag by mutilating, defacing, defiling, burning, or trampling upon such flag." Nebraska Rev. Stat. § 28-928 (2010).
23. *Cohen* v. *California,* 403 U.S. 15 (1971).

GIVING THE MIDDLE FINGER GESTURE TO COPS: PROTECTED POLITICAL SPEECH?

Is there a First Amendment right to give the middle finger gesture to police? The answer is yes (but the authors don't recommend you test the law!). In November 2012, the town of Orem City, Utah, agreed that Seth Dame should not have been detained and should not have been cited for disorderly conduct after he "flipped the bird" at a police officer in a passing car back in June 2010. Acting on Dame's behalf, the ACLU of Utah obtained $2,500 in damages for Dame and $2,500 in attorneys' fees to cover its own work on his behalf. As John Mejia, legal director of the ACLU of Utah, explained in a press release announcing the settlement, "various courts have concluded that using your middle finger to express discontent or frustration is expressive conduct protected by the First Amendment." The gesture itself constitutes speech under the **symbolic speech doctrine** described earlier in this chapter. The case also illustrates that speech that merely offends people generally is protected by the First Amendment. On the other hand, giving the middle-finger gesture to a person who is *not* a law enforcement officer in the process of a face-to-face and heated dispute might fall outside the scope of First Amendment protection under the **fighting words doctrine** described later in Chapter 3.

BLASPHEMY AND COUNTERSPEECH: HOW AMERICAN VALUES DON'T TRANSLATE WORLDWIDE

In September 2016, police in Pakistan arrested a 16-year-old Christian teenager on blasphemy charges after he "liked" a picture deemed "inappropriate" on Facebook of the Kaaba in Mecca, which is one of the holiest sites in Islam. The Associated Press reported that a senior police official said he made the arrest after being alerted of the Facebook post by a Muslim man who found the picture insulting and sacrilegious. Under Pakistan's blasphemy laws, insulting Islam can result in a death sentence. The AP reported that in 2015 in Pakistan, a Christian couple was beaten to death and their bodies were burned for allegedly desecrating the Quran.

In the United States, the First Amendment clearly prevents the government from punishing blasphemous speech—even if some people find the speech offensive or disagreeable. As the U.S. Supreme Court wrote in 1989 in *Texas* v. *Johnson* when protecting the right to burn an American flag as a form of political speech, "If there is a bedrock principle underlying the First Amendment, it is that the government may not prohibit the expression of an idea simply because society finds the idea itself offensive or disagreeable."

Another fundamental First Amendment value is that the remedy for speech that offends us or with which we disagree is not censorship, violence or murder, but rather to add more speech to the marketplace of ideas to counteract or contradict the disagreeable speech. This is known as the doctrine of **counterspeech**. It is captured by the following statement from Justice Louis Brandeis in 1927 in *Whitney* v. *California*: "If there be time to expose through discussion the falsehood and fallacies, to avert the evil by the processes of education, the remedy to be applied is more speech, not enforced silence. Only an emergency can justify repression."

Other countries with little or no history of protection for free speech engrained in either their cultures or constitutions don't easily understand such American values. In many countries, any form of political or religious dissent simply is not tolerated. A 38-nation Pew Research Center survey conducted in 2015 found that Americans were among the most supportive of free speech and the right to use the Internet without government censorship. The survey also showed that Americans are much more tolerant of *offensive* speech than people in other nations.

In 2006, the federal government launched the first treason case since World War II, targeting California-born Adam Gadahn. The case was based largely on five propaganda videos for Al Qaeda calling for the death of Americans in which Gadahn allegedly appeared and/or translated the words (i.e., he did the voiceovers) of Osama bin Laden's terrorist network. In one video Gadahn called on U.S. citizens to "escape from the unbelieving army and join the winning side," while in another he referred to the events of Sept. 11, 2001, as "the blessed raids on New York and Washington." In 2015, Gadahn was killed by a U.S. drone strike in Pakistan and thus a trial for treason never took place. The case would have pitted the First Amendment right of speech against the U.S. Constitution's seldom-used treason provision (Art. III, Sect. 3), which states that "treason against the United States, shall consist only in levying war against them, or in adhering to their enemies, giving them aid and comfort." As this chapter later describes in its discussion of *Brandenburg* v. *Ohio*, the abstract advocacy of violence is protected by the First Amendment while the direct incitement of imminent lawless action that is likely to occur is not protected (see page 66).

ALIEN AND SEDITION ACTS

The United States wasn't even 10 years old when its resolve in protecting free expression was first tested. Intense rivalry between President John Adams' Federalist party and Thomas Jefferson's Republican or Jeffersonian party, coupled with the fear that the growing violence in the French Revolution might spread to this country, led to the adoption by the Federalist-dominated Congress of a series of highly repressive measures known as the **Alien and Sedition Acts of 1798**.[24] The sedition law forbade false, scandalous and malicious publications against the U.S. government, Congress and the president. The new law also punished persons who sought to stir up sedition

24. Smith, *Freedom's Fetters*.

	CRITICAL DATES IN THE HISTORY OF SEDITION LAW IN THE UNITED STATES
1735	Acquittal of John Peter Zenger
1791	Adoption of First Amendment
1798	Alien and Sedition Acts of 1798
1917	Espionage Act
1918	Sedition Act
1919	Clear and present danger test enunciated
1927	Brandeis sedition test in *Whitney* v. *California*
1940	Smith Act adopted
1951	Smith Act ruled constitutional
1957	Scope of Smith Act greatly narrowed
1969	*Brandenburg* v. *Ohio* substantially curbs sedition prosecutions

or urged resistance to federal laws. Punishment was a fine of as much as $2,000 and a jail term of up to two years. This latter statute was aimed at the Jeffersonian political newspapers, many of which were relentless in attacks on President Adams and his government.

There were 15 prosecutions under this law. Among those prosecuted were editors of eight Jeffersonian newspapers, including some of the leading papers in the nation. Imagine the federal government bringing sedition charges today against the editors of *The New York Times*, *Washington Post* and *Chicago Tribune*. Also prosecuted was a Republican member of Congress. The so-called seditious libel that was the basis for the criminal charges was usually petty and hardly threatened our admittedly youthful government. But Federalist judges heard most of the cases and convictions were common.

Far from inhibiting dissent, the laws succeeded only in provoking dissension among many of President Adams' supporters. Many argue that Adams lost his bid for re-election in 1800 largely because of public dissatisfaction with his attempt to muzzle his critics. The constitutionality of the laws was never tested before the full Supreme Court, but three members of the court heard Sedition Act cases while they were on the circuit. The constitutionality of the provisions was sustained by these justices. The Sedition Act expired in 1801, and newly elected President Thomas Jefferson pardoned all people convicted under it, while Congress eventually repaid most of the fines. This was the nation's first peacetime sedition law, and it left such a bad taste that another peacetime sedition law was not passed until 1940.

Most historians of freedom of expression in the United States focus on two eras in the 19th century during which censorship was not uncommon: the abolitionist period and the Civil War. A wide range of government actions, especially in the South, were aimed at shutting down the abolitionist press in the years between 1830 and 1860. And both the U.S. government and the Confederate States government censored the press during the Civil War. But in his book *Free Speech in Its Forgotten Years* author David M. Rabban argues that there were also extensive censorship efforts in the latter half of the 19th century against radical labor unionists, anarchists, birth control advocates and other so-called freethinkers. And there was little meaningful public debate about such activities. "In the decades before World War I," Rabban wrote, "Americans generally needed to experience repression of views they shared before formulating a theory of free speech that extended to ideas they opposed."[25]

The issue of political dissent did not enter the national debate again until the end of the 1800s, when hundreds of thousands of Americans began to understand that democracy and capitalism were not going to bring them the prosperity promised as an American birthright. Thousands were attracted to radical political movements such as socialism and anarchism, movements that were considered by most in the mainstream to be foreign to the United States. Revolution arose as a specter in the minds of millions of Americans. Hundreds of laws were passed by states and cities across the nation to try to limit this kind of political dissent. War broke out in Europe in 1914; the United States joined the conflict three years later. This pushed the nation over the edge, and anything that remained of our national tolerance toward political dissent and criticism of the government and economic system vanished. At both the state and the federal level, government struck out at those who sought to criticize or suggest radical change.

SEDITION IN WORLD WAR I

Suppression of freedom of expression reached a higher level during World War I than at any other time in our history.

Suppression of freedom of expression reached a higher level during World War I than at any other time in our history.[26] Government prosecutions during the Vietnam War, for example, were minor compared with government action between 1918 and 1920. Vigilante groups were active as well, persecuting when the government failed to prosecute.

Two federal laws were passed to deal with persons who opposed the war and U.S. participation in it. In 1917 the **Espionage Act** was approved by Congress and signed by President Woodrow Wilson. The measure dealt primarily with espionage problems, but some parts were aimed expressly at dissent and opposition to the war. The law provided that it was a crime to willfully convey a false report with the intent to interfere with the war effort. It was a crime to cause or attempt to cause insubordination, disloyalty, mutiny or refusal of duty in the armed forces. It also was a crime to willfully obstruct the recruiting or enlistment service of the United States. Punishment was a fine of not more than $10,000 or a jail term of not more than 20 years. The law also provided that material violating the law could not be mailed.

In 1918 the **Sedition Act,** an amendment to the Espionage Act, was passed, making it a crime to attempt to obstruct the recruiting service. It was criminal to utter or print or write or publish disloyal or profane language that was intended to cause contempt of, or scorn for, the federal government, the Constitution, the flag or the uniform of the armed forces. Penalties for violation of the law were imprisonment for as long as 20 years or a

---

25. Rabban, *Free Speech.*
26. See Peterson and Fite, *Opponents of War.*

fine of $10,000 or both. Approximately 2,000 people were prosecuted under these espionage and sedition laws, and nearly 900 were convicted.

In addition the U.S. Post Office Department censored thousands of newspapers, books and pamphlets. Some publications lost their right to the government-subsidized second-class mailing rates and were forced to use the costly first-class rates or find other means of distribution. Entire issues of magazines were held up and never delivered, on the grounds that they violated the law (or what the postmaster general believed to be the law). Finally, the states were not content with allowing the federal government to deal with dissenters, and most adopted sedition statutes, laws against **criminal syndicalism,** laws that prohibited the display of a red flag or a black flag, and so forth.

Political repression in the United States did not end with the termination of fighting in Europe. The government was still suspicious of the millions of European immigrants in the nation and frightened by the organized political efforts of socialist and communist groups. As the Depression hit the nation, first in the farm belt in the 1920s, and then in the rest of the nation by the next decade, labor unrest mushroomed. Hundreds of so-called agitators were arrested and charged under state and federal laws. Demonstrations were broken up; aliens were detained and threatened with deportation.

But what about the First Amendment? What happened to freedom of expression? The constitutional guarantees of freedom of speech and press were of limited value during this era. The legal meaning of freedom of expression had developed little in the preceding 125 years. There had been few cases and almost no important rulings before 1920. The words of the First Amendment—"Congress shall make no law"—are not nearly as important as the meaning attached to them. And that meaning was only then beginning to develop through court rulings that resulted from the thousands of prosecutions for sedition and other such crimes between 1917 and the mid-1930s.

Nearly 95 years after it became law, the Sedition Act of 1917 was back in the news in 2011 when the federal government considered whether to prosecute Julian Assange, the founder of Wikileaks, for disclosing hundreds of thousands of leaked, classified government documents on the Internet. For instance, Senator Dianne Feinstein (D.–Cal.) called for his prosecution, claiming Assange intentionally harmed the United States by releasing information related to the national defense that could be used against the country. If such a prosecution were to proceed, it would put the aging Sedition Act to a high-technology test that never could have been imagined when it was adopted. By August 2017, Assange had not been indicted in the United States, though in April 2017 news organizations reported that the Department of Justice was still considering charges against him.

THE SMITH ACT

Congress adopted the nation's second peacetime sedition law in 1940 when it ratified the **Smith Act,** a measure making it a crime to advocate the violent overthrow of the government, to conspire to advocate the violent overthrow of the government, to organize a group that advocated the violent overthrow of the government, or to be a member of a group that advocated the violent overthrow of the government.[27] The law was aimed directly at the Communist Party of the United States. While a small group of Trotskyites

27. Pember, "The Smith Act," 1.

(members of the Socialist Workers Party) were prosecuted and convicted under the Smith Act in 1943, no Communist was indicted under the law until 1948 when many of the nation's top Communist Party leaders were charged with advocating the violent overthrow of the government. All were convicted after a nine-month trial and their appeals were denied. In a 7-2 ruling in 1951, the Supreme Court of the United States rejected the defendants' arguments that the Smith Act violated the First Amendment.[28]

Government prosecutions persisted during the early 1950s. But then, in a surprising reversal of its earlier position, the Supreme Court in 1957 overturned the convictions of West Coast Communist Party leaders.[29] Justice John Marshall Harlan wrote for the 5-2 majority that government evidence showed that the defendants had advocated the violent overthrow of the government but only as an abstract doctrine, and this was not sufficient to sustain a conviction. Instead there must be evidence that proved the defendants advocated actual *action* aimed at the forcible overthrow of the government. This added burden of proof levied against the government prosecutors made it extremely difficult to use the Smith Act against the Communists, and prosecutions dwindled. The number of prosecutions diminished for other reasons as well, however. The times had changed. The Cold War was not as intense. Americans looked at the Soviet Union and the Communists with a bit less fear. In fact, political scientist John Roche has remarked with only a slight wink that it was the dues paid to the party by FBI undercover agents that kept the organization economically solvent in the mid-to-late 1950s.

With the practical demise of the Smith Act, sedition has not been a serious threat against dissent for nearly 50 years. No sedition cases were filed against Vietnam War protesters, and the last time the Supreme Court heard an appeal in a sedition case was in 1969 when it overturned the conviction of a Ku Klux Klan leader (*Brandenburg* v. *Ohio*).[30] The federal government has filed sedition charges several times in recent years against alleged white supremacists, neo-Nazis and others on the fringe of the right wing. Whereas juries have been willing to convict such individuals of bombing, bank robbery and even racketeering, the defendants have been acquitted of sedition. The federal government had greater success in the 1990s using a Civil War–era sedition statute to prosecute Muslim militants who bombed the World Trade Center in New York City in 1993. Sheikh Omar Abdel Rahman and nine of his followers were found guilty of violating a 140-year-old law that makes it a crime to "conspire to overthrow, or put down, or to destroy by force the Government of the United States." Although the government could not prove that Abdel Rahman actually participated in the bombing, federal prosecutors argued that his exhortations to his followers amounted to directing a violent conspiracy. The sheikh's attorneys argued that his pronouncements were protected by the First Amendment. In August 1999 the 2nd U.S. Circuit Court of Appeals disagreed, noting that the Bill of Rights does not protect an individual who uses a public speech to commit crimes. Abdel Rahman's speeches were not simply the expression of ideas; "in some instances they constituted the crime of conspiracy to wage war against the United States," the court ruled. "Words of this nature," the three-judge panel wrote, "ones that instruct, solicit, or persuade others to commit crimes

28. *Dennis* v. *U.S.*, 341 U.S. 494 (1951).
29. *Yates* v. *U.S.*, 354 U.S. 298 (1957).
30. 395 U.S. 444 (1969).

of violence—violate the law and may be properly prosecuted regardless of whether they are uttered in private, or in a public place."[31] In the wake of the terror attacks on Sept. 11, 2001, federal prosecutors in New York said they were looking into the possibility that the attacks included a seditious conspiracy to levy war against the United States. This accusation means that individuals suspected of playing a part in the attacks could be charged under the same seditious conspiracy statute that was used against the previously convicted Trade Center bombers. No such charges were filed. Also, the USA Patriot Act, which was passed as a part of the anti-terrorism bill adopted in 2001, defines terrorism as any "attempt to intimidate or coerce a civilian population" or change "the policy of the government by intimidation or coercion." Some civil libertarians argue that this definition could include some kinds of political dissent and that it closely resembles what traditionally has been called sedition.

Another controversial section of the Patriot Act that pits free speech against the war on terror makes it a crime to provide "expert advice or assistance" to terrorists. In 2004, a federal jury acquitted a Saudi-born computer doctoral student at the University of Moscow, Sami Omar Al-Hussayen, of charges under this provision that he spread terrorism by "designing websites and posting messages on the Internet to recruit and raise funds for terrorist missions in Chechnya and Israel. His attorneys argued that he was being prosecuted for expressing views protected by the First Amendment."[32] Georgetown University law professor David Cole remarked after the verdict that it was a "case where the government sought to criminalize pure speech and was resoundingly defeated."

The Espionage Act of 1917 (see page 60) was resuscitated in 2006 when a federal judge allowed charges to proceed under it against two former lobbyists for the American Israel Public Affairs Committee—known by the acronym AIPAC—who allegedly obtained classified U.S. defense information and then communicated it to both Israeli officials and journalists.[33] The defendants in *United States* v. *Rosen*, neither of whom was either a government employee or a spy, contested the constitutionality of the Espionage Act on, among other things, free speech grounds. Judge T.S. Ellis III noted that their "First Amendment challenge exposes the inherent tension between the government transparency so essential to a democratic society and the government's equally compelling need to protect from disclosure information that could be used by those who wish this nation harm." Although the judge rejected the government's argument "for a categorical rule that Espionage Act prosecutions are immune from First Amendment scrutiny," he nonetheless stressed the government was seeking to punish the disclosure of information that could threaten national security. Ellis concluded "the Constitution permits the government to prosecute . . . [a person] for the disclosure of information relating to the national defense when that person knew that the information is the type which could be used to threaten the nation's security, and that person acted in bad faith, *i.e.,* with reason to believe the disclosure could harm the United States or aid a foreign government." Although upholding the Espionage Act and allowing the case to continue, Ellis suggested Congress revisit the aging act's provisions to ensure they reflect "contemporary views about the appropriate balance between our nation's security and our citizens' ability to engage in public debate about the United States' conduct." In May 2009 federal

31. *U.S.* v. *Rahman,* 189 F. 3d 88 (1999).
32. Schmitt, "Acquittal in Internet Terrorism Case."
33. *U.S.* v. *Rosen,* 445 F. Supp. 2d 602 (E.D. Va. 2006).

prosecutors gave up and asked the judge to dismiss the case, citing the inevitable disclosure of classified information that would occur at trial.

DEFINING THE LIMITS OF FREEDOM OF EXPRESSION

The first time the Supreme Court of the United States seriously considered whether a prosecution for sedition violated the First Amendment was in 1919. The Philadelphia Socialist Party authorized Charles Schenck, the general secretary of the organization, to publish 15,000 leaflets protesting against U.S. involvement in World War I. The pamphlet described the war as a cold-blooded and ruthless adventure propagated in the interest of the chosen few of Wall Street and urged young men to resist the draft. Schenck and other party members were arrested, tried and convicted for violating the Espionage Act (see page 60). The case was appealed to the Supreme Court, with the Socialists asserting that they had been denied their First Amendment rights of freedom of speech and press. Justice Oliver Wendell Holmes penned the court's opinion and rejected the First Amendment argument. In ordinary times, he said, such pamphlets might have been harmless and protected by the First Amendment. "But the character of every act depends upon the circumstances in which it is done. . . . The question in every case is whether the words used, are used in such circumstances and are of such a nature as to create a clear and present danger that they will bring about the substantive evils that Congress has a right to prevent. It is a question of proximity and degree."[34]

"The question in every case is whether the words used . . . create a clear and present danger that they will bring about the substantive evils that Congress has a right to prevent."

How can prosecutions for sedition be reconciled with freedom of expression? According to the Holmes test, Congress has the right to outlaw certain kinds of conduct that might be harmful to the nation. In some instances, words, through speeches or pamphlets, can push people to undertake acts that violate the laws passed by Congress. In such cases publishers or speakers can be punished without infringing on their First Amendment freedoms. How close must the connection be between the advocacy of the speaker or publisher and the forbidden conduct? Holmes said that the words must create a "clear" (unmistakable? certain?) and "present" (immediate? close?) danger.

In rejecting Schenck's appeal, the high court ruled that these 15,000 seemingly innocuous pamphlets posed a real threat to the legitimate right of Congress to successfully conduct the war. To many American liberals, this notion seemed farfetched, and Holmes was publicly criticized for the ruling. But the magic words "clear and present danger" stuck like glue on American sedition law. Holmes changed his mind about his test in less than six months and broke with the majority of the high court to outline a somewhat more liberal definition of freedom of expression in a ruling on the Sedition Act in the fall of 1919.[35] But the majority of the court continued to use the Holmes test to reject First Amendment appeals.

Justice Louis Brandeis attempted to fashion a more useful application of the clear and present danger test in 1927, but his definition of "clear and present danger" was confined to a concurring opinion in the case of *Whitney* v. *California*.[36] The state of California prosecuted Anita Whitney, a 64-year-old philanthropist. She was charged with violating

34. *Schenck* v. *U.S.,* 249 U.S. 47 (1919).
35. *Abrams* v. *U.S.,* 250 U.S. 616 (1919).
36. 274 U.S. 357 (1927).

the state's Criminal Syndicalism Act after she attended a meeting of the Communist Labor Party. She was not an active member in the party and during the convention had worked against proposals made by others that the party dedicate itself to gaining power through revolution and general strikes in which workers would seize power by violent means. But the state contended that the Communist Labor Party was formed to teach criminal syndicalism, and as a member to the party she participated in the crime. After her conviction she appealed to the Supreme Court.

Justice Edward Sanford wrote the court's opinion and ruled that California had not violated Whitney's First Amendment rights. The jurist said it was inappropriate to even apply the clear and present danger test. He noted that in *Schenck* and other cases, the statutes under which prosecution occurred forbade specific actions, such as interference with the draft. The clear and present danger test was then used to judge whether the words used by the defendant presented a clear and present danger that the forbidden action might occur. In this case, Sanford noted, the California law forbade specific words—the advocacy of violence to bring about political change. The Holmes test was therefore inapplicable. In addition, the law was neither unreasonable nor unwarranted.

Justice Brandeis concurred, but only because the constitutional issue of freedom of expression had not been raised sufficiently at the trial to make it an issue in the appeal. (If a legal issue is not raised during a trial, it is often impossible for an appellate court to later consider the matter.) Brandeis disagreed sharply with the majority regarding the limits of free expression. In doing so, he added flesh and bones to Holmes' clear and present danger test. Looking to *Schenck,* the justice noted that the court had agreed there must be a clear and imminent danger of a substantive evil that the state has the right to prevent before an interference with speech is allowed. He described what he believed to be the requisite danger:

> To justify suppression of free speech there must be reasonable ground to fear that serious evil will result if free speech is practiced. There must be reasonable ground to believe that the danger apprehended is imminent. There must be reasonable ground to believe that the evil to be prevented is a serious one. . . . In order to support a finding of clear and present danger it must be shown either that immediate serious violence was to be expected or was advocated, or that the past conduct furnished reason to believe that such advocacy was then contemplated.[37]

Brandeis concluded that if there is time to expose through discussion the falsehoods and fallacies, to avert the evil by the process of education, the remedy to be applied is more speech, not enforced silence. Put differently, Brandeis believed that **counterspeech** is the ideal, self-help remedy (i.e., adding more speech to the marketplace of ideas in order to counterargue), not censorship.

The next major ruling in which the high court attempted to reconcile sedition law and the First Amendment came in 1951 in the case of *Dennis* v. *U.S.*[38] Eleven Communist Party members had been convicted of advocating the violent overthrow of the government, a violation of the Smith Act. Chief Justice Vinson, who wrote the opinion for the court, used a variation of the clear and present danger test enunciated by Holmes in the *Schenck* case.

37. *Whitney v. California,* 274 U.S. 357 (1927).
38. 341 U.S. 494 (1951).

He called it a clear and probable danger test. "In each case [courts] must ask whether the gravity of the 'evil' discounted by its improbability, justifies such invasion of free speech as is necessary to avoid the danger," Vinson wrote, quoting a lower-court opinion written by Judge Learned Hand. The test went only slightly beyond the original Holmes test, and the court ruled that the defendants' First Amendment rights had not been violated.

It has been about 50 years since the Supreme Court heard the case of *Brandenburg* v. *Ohio* and made its last and probably best attempt to resolve the apparent contradiction between sedition law and freedom of expression. A leader of the Ku Klux Klan was prosecuted and convicted of violating an Ohio sedition law for stating: "We're not a revengent [revengeful] organization, but if our President, our Congress, our Supreme Court, continues to suppress the white Caucasian race, it's possible there might have to be some revengeance [revenge] taken." In reversing the conviction, the high court said the law must distinguish between the abstract advocacy of ideas and the incitement to unlawful conduct. "The constitutional guarantees of free speech and free press do not permit a state to forbid or proscribe advocacy of the use of force or of law violation except *where such advocacy is directed to inciting or producing imminent lawless action and is likely to incite or produce such actions.*"[39]

This test, which represents the current version of Justice Holmes' old clear and present danger standard, can be broken down into four components. First, the word "directed" represents an intent requirement on the part of the speaker: Did the speaker actually intend for his or her words to incite lawless action? Second, the word "imminent" indicates that the time between the speech in question and the lawless action must be very close or proximate. Third, the conduct itself must be "lawless action," requiring that there be a criminal statute forbidding or punishing the underlying action that is allegedly advocated. Finally, the word "likely" represents a probability requirement—that the lawless action must be substantially likely to occur and not merely a speculative result of the speech. All four of these elements must be proven before the speech can be considered outside the scope of First Amendment protection.

> *"The constitutional guarantees of free speech and free press do not permit a state to forbid or proscribe advocacy of the use of force or of law violation except where such advocacy is directed to inciting or producing imminent lawless action and is likely to incite or produce such actions."*

A LIMITED FIRST AMENDMENT RIGHT TO LIE: MEDALS OF HONOR AND *UNITED STATES* V. *ALVAREZ*

In a June 2012 **plurality opinion** (see page 25 regarding plurality opinions), the U.S. Supreme Court declared unconstitutional in *United States* v. *Alvarez*[40] part of a federal law called the Stolen Valor Act, which made it a crime to lie about having won a Congressional Medal of Honor.

The act was so poorly drafted and overbroad (see pages 13–14 regarding the **overbreadth doctrine**) that it made it a crime to falsely claim to have earned such a medal, regardless of whether anyone was actually injured by the lie and irrespective of whether the lie was made for the purpose of material gain. The act, in other words, applied to false statements made at any time, in any place and to any person, even if made merely in whispered conversations in one's home.

---

39. 395 U.S. 444 (1969) (emphasis added).
40. 132 S. Ct. 2537 (2012).

In announcing the judgment of the Court, Justice Anthony Kennedy wrote for the plurality that while some categories of speech, such as fighting words (see pages 127–130) and obscenity (see Chapter 13), fall completely outside the scope of First Amendment protection, there is no such "general exception to the First Amendment for false statements" because, as the Court has observed in areas such as defamation (see Chapters 4, 5 and 6) "some false statements are inevitable if there is to be an open and vigorous expression of views in public and private conversation." Rejecting the Obama administration's defense of the law, Kennedy opined that "the Court has never endorsed the categorical rule the Government advances: that false statements receive no First Amendment protection. Our prior decisions have not confronted a measure, like the Stolen Valor Act, that targets falsity and nothing more."

The last part of that quotation—*falsity and nothing more*"—is very important. Some lies are not protected by the First Amendment. For instance, perjury under oath, fraud, defamation and lies integral to committing criminal conduct are not safeguarded by the First Amendment. In all of those instances, a tangible injury is caused by the lie and the laws are drafted much more narrowly than the provision of the Stolen Valor Act at issue in *Alvarez*. In defamation law, for instance, the false statements must be the kind that harm the reputation of an individual (see Chapter 4) or deter others from associating or dealing with that individual. Likewise, perjury applies to lies made under oath and then only when the lies are material (i.e., important). False statements made as the result of honest mistakes or inadvertence, however, do not constitute perjury.

The bottom line? There is no general exception to First Amendment protection for all false statements and lies in general. Some kinds of lies are not protected by the First Amendment and thus can still be punished, especially when they are intended to procure a material benefit. For instance, in August 2012—just two months after the *Alvarez* decision—the U.S. Court of Appeals for the 4th Circuit upheld a Virginia statute that prohibits individuals from falsely assuming or pretending to be a law enforcement officer. Among other things, the 4th Circuit in *United States* v. *Chappell* noted that "no Justice [in *Alvarez*] thought it advisable to drape a broad cloak of constitutional protection over actionable fraud, identity theft, or the impersonation of law enforcement officers." In *Chappell*, the defendant had lied to an officer for the material purpose of avoiding a speeding ticket.

Furthermore, as Chapters 4, 5 and 6 make abundantly clear, false statements that harm a person's reputation can result in massive civil liability under defamation law. In addition, in response to the Court's *Alvarez* ruling, the Pentagon announced in July 2012 that it would create a searchable and publicly accessible database of military valor awards and medals that anyone could use to verify who really has won such awards and medals. Such a database amounts to a great example of counterspeech to unmask a lie. Rather than censoring the lie, we add more speech to the marketplace of ideas—in this case, a database of medal winners—to counteract the lie.

Subsequent to *Alvarez*, Congress passed and former President Obama signed into law the Stolen Valor Act of 2013. The new law imposes criminal sanctions only if one lies about winning a medal with the "intent to obtain money, property, or other tangible benefit." It thus is more narrowly tailored than the law at issue in Alvarez.

The legal theory behind the law of sedition was outlined previously; if someone publishes something that incites another person to do something illegal, the publisher of the incitement can be punished. While charges of sedition are rarely filed today, it is not uncommon for private persons to sue the mass media on the grounds that something that was published or recorded or exhibited incited a third person to commit an illegal act. These cases are similar to sedition prosecutions in many ways, and the constitutional shield developed by the courts that protects the mass media against convictions for sedition is applied in these cases as well.

Real-Life Violence: Blaming Movies, Video Games and Books

In 2016, a 16-year-old boy named Eldon Samuel III of Coeur D'Alene, Idaho, was found guilty of killing his father and younger brother. Part of Samuel's defense was that he claimed to have been influenced by "The Walking Dead" video game series and zombie movies. Should the makers of "The Walking Dead" be held civilly liable for the deaths of Samuel's father and brother?

WHAT WERE THEY THINKING?
WHEN RADIO CONTESTS GO WRONG

Sometimes members of the media simply do stupid things that scream out for liability and for which the First Amendment provides no defense. For instance, a jury in Sacramento in 2009 awarded more than $16 million to the family of Jennifer Lea Strange after she died of water intoxication while participating in a local radio station's contest, "Hold Your Wee for a Wii." The contest required drinking massive amounts of water without going to the bathroom during a three-hour period in order to win a Wii video game. The jury held the local owners of the station, KDND, liable for wrongful death under basic negligence principles by creating a foreseeable risk of harm that caused Strange's death. It wasn't the first time a radio contest urging listeners to take part in risky behavior resulted in liability. In *Weirum* v. *RKO General, Inc.*,[41] the Supreme Court of California ruled in 1975 in favor of the plaintiffs in another wrongful death case, this one involving a contest that urged drivers near Los Angeles to be the first to locate the station's disc jockey, who was driving on a freeway. Two listeners were chasing the DJ at nearly 80 miles per hour when one collided with and killed the driver of another car. In ruling against the station, the court reasoned that "the risk of a high speed automobile chase is the risk of death or serious injury. Obviously, neither the entertainment afforded by the contest nor its commercial rewards can justify the creation of such a grave risk."

---

41. 539 P.2d 36 (Cal. 1975).

Mark Wahlberg, James Madio, Leonardo DiCaprio and Patrick McGaw, in a scene from "The Basketball Diaries," which was the focus of a lawsuit in 2002.

©*New Line Cinema/Getty Images*

Courts are frequently asked to rule in wrongful death, negligence and product liability lawsuits whether a media artifact like a film or video game played some part in inciting the actual perpetrator of the crime to commit illegal acts. To determine liability in such cases, courts often use the *Brandenburg* test for incitement to violence just outlined in this chapter. For example, in 2002 the 6th U.S. Court of Appeals ruled that the producers of the film "The Basketball Diaries," the makers of several video games and some Internet content providers were not liable in a lawsuit brought by the parents of students who were killed and wounded when teenager Michael Carneal went on a shooting rampage in the lobby of Heath High School in Paducah, Ky. The plaintiffs argued, among other things, that Carneal had watched the film, which depicts a student daydreaming about killing a teacher and several classmates. "We find it is simply too far a leap from shooting characters on a video screen (an activity undertaken by millions) to shooting people in a classroom (an activity undertaken by a handful, at most) for Carneal's activities to have been reasonably foreseeable to the manufacturers of the media Carneal played and viewed," the court ruled. The material in this case falls far short of the standard required by *Brandenburg,* the judges added.[42] Why did they reach this conclusion? First and foremost, the movie was not "directed" to cause violence. As the appellate court wrote

---

42. *James* v. *Meow Media Inc.,* 300 F. 3d 683 (6th Cir. 2002).

in *James* v. *Meow Media*, "while the defendants in this case may not have exercised exquisite care regarding the persuasive power of the violent material that they disseminated, they certainly did not 'intend' to produce violent actions by the consumers, as is required by the *Brandenburg* test." In addition, the appellate court reasoned that "it is a long leap from the proposition that Carneal's actions were foreseeable to the *Brandenburg* requirement that the violent content was 'likely' to cause Carneal to behave this way."

SHOULD SNAPCHAT BE HELD LIABLE FOR TRAFFIC ACCIDENTS?

An 18-year-old driving with three friends crashed into a vehicle driven by a Georgia man, leaving him with severe injuries. The man spent five weeks in an intensive-care unit, where he was treated for traumatic brain injury.

In April 2016, the man filed suit against the driver, accusing her of recklessly using Snapchat while driving over 100 miles per hour and slamming into his vehicle. The lawsuit alleged that the driver was using a Snapchat lens that clocked the speed of vehicles, which encouraged her to push her car to higher speeds. The man also sued Snapchat, accusing the company of negligence.

While a lawsuit against the driver might have merit, the lawsuit against Snapchat was dismissed in early 2017. Under basic negligence principles, Snapchat was not the direct or proximate cause of the injuries sustained by the plaintiff. The real cause was the 18-year-old driver.

It is very difficult for a plaintiff ever to prove the intent ("directed") prong of the *Brandenburg* test against the media. The media simply don't intend for violence to occur as a result of viewing, playing or reading their products. Rather, the typical intent is to entertain and to make a profit! But of course, there are exceptions to the rule.

In 1996 the families of Mildred and Trevor Horn and Janice Saunders filed a wrongful death suit against Paladin Enterprises and its president, Peter Lund. The company published a book titled *Hit Man: A Technical Manual for Independent Contractors*. Lawrence Horn hired James Perry to kill his ex-wife, their 8-year-old quadriplegic son and the son's nurse to gain access to the proceeds of a medical malpractice settlement. Both Perry and Horn were arrested and convicted of the murders; Perry was sentenced to death, Horn to life in prison. The plaintiffs contended that Perry used the Paladin publication as an instruction manual for the killings. A U.S. District Court in Maryland ruled in August 1996 that the book was protected by the First Amendment. "However loathsome one characterizes the publication, 'Hit Man' simply does not fall within the parameters of any recognized exceptions to the First Amendment principles of freedom of speech." The book failed to cross the line between permissible advocacy and impermissible incitation to crime or violence, Judge Williams wrote.[43]

Fifteen months later the 4th U.S. Circuit Court of Appeals reversed the lower-court ruling. The defendant had agreed to a stipulation in the case that stated Paladin provided its assistance to Perry with both the knowledge and the intent that the book would immediately be used by criminals and would-be criminals in the solicitation, planning and commission of murder and murder for hire. The court said the book was not an example of abstract advocacy but a form of aiding and abetting a crime. The book "methodically and comprehensively prepares and steels its audience to specific criminal conduct through exhaustively detailed instructions on planning, commission and concealment of criminal conduct," the panel ruled. There is no First Amendment protection for such a publication. The court noted that this case was unique and should not be read as expanding the potential liability of publishers and broadcasters when third parties copy or mimic a crime or other act contained in a news report or a film or a television program.[44] An appeal to the U.S. Supreme Court was denied, and the case was returned to the U.S. District Court for trial. In May 1999 Paladin Press settled the case out of court. In spite of this case, the stringent requirements of the *Brandenburg* test make it difficult, bordering on impossible, for a plaintiff to win a lawsuit that alleges a play or book or song or movie was responsible for causing someone's illegal acts. The case law is highly one-sided in this regard.

"TO CATCH A PREDATOR": MEDIA LIABILITY FOR SUICIDE AND EMOTIONAL DISTRESS?

In 2006, Louis William Conradt Jr. took his own life, just as police were about to arrest him at home for allegedly soliciting sex from a minor on the Internet. In fact, there was no minor but rather a decoy that was part of a sting orchestrated by the TV show "NBC Dateline," along with a group called Perverted Justice, as part of the show's sensationalistic "To Catch a Predator" series. But when Conradt never went to the "sting" house to meet the supposed minor, NBC took its cameras and crew to Conradt's residence, along with a SWAT team and local police in Murphy, Texas, who had an arrest warrant. Apparently unable to face the humiliation and public spectacle, Conradt killed himself. His sister, Patricia Conradt, sued for more than $100 million, alleging that "NBC Dateline" was responsible for her brother's death. In 2008, in *Conradt* v. *NBC Universal*, 536 F. Supp. 2d 380 (S.D. N.Y. 2008), Judge Denny Chin refused to dismiss the lawsuit, reasoning that if the allegations in Patricia Conradt's amended complaint were true, "a reasonable jury could find that NBC crossed the line from responsible

---

43. *Rice* v. *Paladin Enterprises Inc.,* 940 F. Supp. 836 (1996).
44. *Rice* v. *Paladin Enterprises Inc.,* 128 F. 3d 233 (1997).

journalism to irresponsible and reckless intrusion into law enforcement" and that "NBC created a substantial risk of suicide or other harm." He added that the complaint stated facts sufficient to render plausible the claims the suicide was foreseeable and that "NBC acted with deliberate indifference and in a manner that would shock one's conscience." Rather than going to trial, NBC settled the case for an undisclosed sum. The dispute suggests that journalists should take caution when they stage news and, in the process, cross the line separating news reporting from news making.

"To Catch a Predator" was back in court in 2011 when a judge denied NBC's motion to dismiss a lawsuit for intentional infliction of emotional distress (see Chapter 5 regarding intentional infliction of emotional distress). The lawsuit was filed by a man who claimed his arrest in a "sting house" was staged to create drama, sensationalism and humiliation. Writing in *Tiwari* v. *NBC Universal, Inc.*,[45] U.S. District Judge Edward Chen found that "a reasonable jury could find that it wasn't necessary for police to arrest Tiwari in a sensational way, or film him being restrained in handcuffs during his detention and interview with police." In *Tiwari*, NBC worked hand-in-hand with police in Petaluma, California, providing them with purported chatroom logs and other recordings it had received from Perverted Justice. Judge Chen wrote that if NBC "direct[ed] the police to arrest Mr. Tiwari in a dramatic fashion with guns raised when there was no basis for such an approach, that act alone might be found outrageous." He added that "the bottom line is that the alleged sensationalization of the news could be deemed outrageous—beyond the common bounds of decency—by a reasonable jury, particularly if this was done for no legitimate law enforcement purpose."

Because of the success of "Grand Theft Auto," "Mortal Kombat" and "Resident Evil," video games depicting violent images and storylines are under scrutiny today by lawmakers who believe the games cause real-life violence and/or psychologically harm kids who play them. School shootings often are blamed on games ("Doom" was blamed, in part, for the tragedy at Columbine in 1999). Several states (California, Illinois, Louisiana, Michigan, Minnesota, Oklahoma and Washington) and municipalities (St. Louis County, Mo., and Indianapolis, Ind.) adopted statutes to limit minors' access to violent video games by either prohibiting their sale or rental to minors or by fining kids who buy them. All of these laws, however, were enjoined as unconstitutional by federal courts, thus stopping their enforcement. Here's why.

First, because video games have stories and plots, they are considered speech products and receive First Amendment protection. Thus, in order to justify regulation of them based upon their content (here, violent content), the **strict scrutiny** standard of judicial review must be satisfied. In particular, a state or municipality must prove both that it has a compelling interest (an interest of the highest order) that justifies the games' regulation,

45. 2011 U.S. Dist. LEXIS 123362 (N.D. Cal. Oct. 25, 2011).

and that the regulation restricts no more speech than absolutely necessary to serve that allegedly compelling interest (the law is narrowly tailored). By early 2011, all courts that had considered the issue found the social science evidence offered by the states and municipalities named previously to be lacking and insufficient to prove that playing violent video games either causes minors to commit violence or harms them psychologically. In other words, social science evidence failed to demonstrate a compelling interest. Second, laws targeting video games often are declared unconstitutional because they fail to clearly define "violence." As noted earlier (see page 13), a statute will be declared unconstitutional under the void for vagueness doctrine if people of reasonable and ordinary intelligence cannot discern, from looking at its terms, what speech is allowed and what speech is prohibited. Some states have used vague terms like "inappropriate violence" and "ultra-violent video games" in their laws.

Perhaps the final nail in the coffin of video game statutes was pounded in by the United States Supreme Court in 2011. That's when a seven-justice majority of the Court in *Brown* v. *Entertainment Merchants Association* struck down a California statute that prohibited the sale or rental of "violent video games" to minors and required their packages to carry an "18" warning label.[46]

Although the majority opinion authored by Justice Antonin Scalia broke little new ground, it reinforced the tall wall of lower-court precedent that was erected during the previous decade against similar statutes across the country. It also buttressed a key point in all of First Amendment law about protecting offensive speech, when Scalia wrote that "disgust is not a valid basis for restricting expression."

In *Brown*, the majority of the Supreme Court deemed California's effort to create a new category of unprotected expression (namely, violent content aimed at minors) "unprecedented and mistaken." In the process, Justice Scalia refused to extend the Court's variable obscenity (see Chapter 13) jurisprudence of *Ginsberg* v. *New York* beyond the confines of sexually explicit speech.

Applying the strict scrutiny standard noted above, Scalia determined that the social science offered by California was insufficient to prove a compelling interest necessary to support the statute.

Pointing out the critical difference between causation and correlation, Scalia observed that the studies offered by California "show at best some correlation between exposure to violent entertainment and minuscule real-world effects, such as children's feeling more aggressive or making louder noises in the few minutes after playing a violent game than after playing a nonviolent game."

Scalia also focused on the underinclusive nature of the statute in terms of serving California's interest in protecting minors from the supposed deleterious effects of violent media content. "California has (wisely) declined to restrict Saturday morning cartoons, the sale of games rated for young children, or the distribution of pictures of guns. The consequence is that its regulation is wildly underinclusive when judged against its asserted justification, which in our view is alone enough to defeat it," Scalia wrote.

Furthermore, Scalia lauded the video game industry's voluntary ratings system, noting that it "does much to ensure that minors cannot purchase seriously violent games

46. 564 U.S. 786 (2011).

on their own, and that parents who care about the matter can readily evaluate the games their children bring home."

Despite the Supreme Court's ruling in *Brown*, violent video games are likely to continue to draw the attention of lawmakers for years to come. A 2015 report by the American Psychological Association added fuel to the fire, finding that "research demonstrates a consistent relation between violent video game use and increases in aggressive behavior, aggressive cognitions and aggressive affect, and decreases in prosocial behavior, empathy and sensitivity to aggression." Yet, the report also pointed out that "no single risk factor consistently leads a person to act aggressively or violently."

A widely publicized case involving the application of the *Brandenburg* test involved Web postings by anti-abortion activists that branded doctors who performed abortions as "baby butchers." The postings were prepared by the American Coalition of Life Activists. They included dossiers—so-called Nuremberg files (a reference to the war crimes trials held after the Second World War)—on abortion rights supporters, including doctors, clinic employees, politicians and judges. The group said the files could be used to conduct Nuremberg-like war crime trials in "perfectly legal courts once the tide of this nation's opinion turns against the wanton slaughter of God's children." On the site the names of murdered abortion supporters were struck through and the names of those wounded were grayed out. A Planned Parenthood affiliate in Oregon sued, claiming that the material constituted threats against the persons named. A jury agreed and awarded more than $100 million in actual and punitive damages. A panel of the 9th U.S. Court of Appeals overturned this verdict in 2001. The court said the postings may have made it more likely that third parties would commit violent acts against the physicians, but they did not constitute a direct threat from the anti-abortion activists against the doctors.[47] The plaintiffs petitioned for a rehearing by the court and 14 months later, in a 6-5 vote, the court changed its ruling, declaring that there was no First Amendment protection for the Web postings. "While advocating violence is protected," wrote Judge Pamela Ann Rymer, "threatening a person with violence is not." She noted that three abortion providers had been murdered after similar "wanted posters" had circulated regarding them. By the time the posters at issue were published, the poster format had acquired currency as a death threat for abortion providers, she added. The postings connote something they do not literally say, Judge Rymer wrote, yet both the actor and the recipient get the message.[48] The Supreme Court denied a petition to review the case.

The Gitlow *Ruling and the Incorporation Doctrine*

The First Amendment provides that "Congress" shall make no law abridging the freedoms of speech and press. Read literally, this language ("Congress") indicates the amendment prohibits actions by only the U.S. Congress; the First Amendment's terms say nothing about actions by state or local governments. Thus it would seem the First Amendment

---

47. *Planned Parenthood at Columbia/Willamette, Inc.* v. *American Coalition of Life Activists,* 244 F. 3d 1007 (2001).
48. *Planned Parenthood of the Columbia/Willamette, Inc.* v. *American Coalition of Life Activists,* 290 F. 3d 1058 (2002).

does not prevent or prohibit state or local government officials or entities from abridging or restricting people's speech and press rights.

That indeed was the case until a 1925 U.S. Supreme Court opinion called *Gitlow* v. *New York*[49] in which, for the first time, the nation's high court held that the term "Congress" in the First Amendment was not so narrowly limited in scope to the U.S. Congress or actions by the federal government. The case involved the prosecution, under a New York state criminal anarchy law, of a socialist named Benjamin Gitlow for printing a document called *The Left Wing Manifesto*. Initially it appeared the First Amendment was irrelevant because it was a New York state law under which Gitlow was prosecuted, not an act of Congress.

But the U.S. Supreme Court concluded differently, writing that "we may and do assume that freedom of speech and of the press—which are protected by the First Amendment from abridgment by Congress—are among the fundamental personal rights and 'liberties' protected by the due process clause of the Fourteenth Amendment from impairment by the States." What the high court did in *Gitlow*, in brief, was to link the First Amendment with the 14th Amendment and, in particular, with the due process clause of the 14th Amendment, which provides that "*no state*" shall "deprive any person of life, *liberty*, or property, without due process of law [emphasis added]." Notice that the 14th Amendment dictates what states cannot do; it restricts the power of states. The *Gitlow* court then, essentially, read into (incorporated into) the 14th Amendment's term "liberty" the freedoms of speech and press explicitly found in the First Amendment.

The importance of the ruling in *Gitlow* is that the high court acknowledged that the Bill of Rights places limitations on the actions of states and local governments as well as on the federal government. *Gitlow* states that freedom of speech is protected by the 14th Amendment. This is known as the incorporation doctrine: The free speech and free press clauses of the First Amendment have been "incorporated" through the 14th Amendment due process clause as fundamental liberties to apply to state and local government entities and officials, not just to "Congress." Today, most rights in the Bill of Rights are protected via the 14th Amendment from interference by states and cities as well as the federal government. The importance of the *Gitlow* case cannot be underestimated. It marked the beginning of attainment of a full measure of civil liberties for the citizens of the nation.

SUMMARY

Within eight years of the passage of the First Amendment, the nation adopted its first (and most wide-ranging) sedition laws, the Alien and Sedition Acts of 1798. Many leading political editors and politicians were prosecuted under the laws, which made it a crime to criticize both the president and the national government. While the Supreme Court never heard arguments regarding the constitutionality of the laws, several justices presided at sedition act trials and refused to sustain a constitutional objection to the laws. The public hated the measures. John Adams was voted out of office in 1800 and was replaced by his political opponent and target of the sedition laws, Thomas Jefferson. The

49. 268 U.S. 652 (1925).

laws left such a bad taste that the federal government did not pass another sedition law until World War I, 117 years later.

Sedition prosecutions in the period from 1915 to 1925 were the most vicious in the nation's history as war protesters, socialists, anarchists and other political dissidents became the target of government repression. It was during this era that the Supreme Court began to interpret the meaning of the First Amendment. In a series of rulings stemming from the World War I cases, the high court fashioned what is known as the clear and present danger test to measure state and federal laws and protests and other expressions against the First Amendment. In 1925 the court ruled that the guarantees of freedom of speech apply to actions taken by all governments—that freedom of speech under the First Amendment protects individuals from censorship by all levels of government, not just from actions by the federal government. This pronouncement in *Gitlow* v. *New York* opened the door to a much broader protection of freedom of expression in the nation.

The Supreme Court made its last important attempt to reconcile the First Amendment and the law of sedition in 1969 when it ruled in *Brandenburg* v. *Ohio* that advocacy of unlawful conduct is protected by the Constitution unless it is directed toward inciting or producing imminent lawless action and is likely to incite or produce such action.

PRIOR RESTRAINT

The great compiler of the British law, William Blackstone, defined freedom of the press in the 1760s as freedom from "previous restraint," or prior restraint. Most agree the guarantees of free speech and press enshrined in the First Amendment were intended to bar the government from exercising prior restraint. Despite the weight of such authority, media in the United States today still face instances of prepublication censorship.

Prior restraint comes in many different forms.

Prior restraint comes in many different forms. Most obvious are instances in which the government insists on giving prior approval before something may be published or broadcast, or simply bans the publication or broadcast of specific kinds of material. There are examples of these varieties in this chapter and the next. Similar kinds of prior restraint occur when the courts forbid the publication of certain kinds of material before a trial (see Chapters 11 and 12) or when a court issues an order forbidding the publication of material that might constitute an invasion of privacy (Chapters 7 and 8).

As discussed in Chapter 1, in terms of nongovernmental efforts to restrain allegedly libelous statements (see Chapters 4, 5 and 6 regarding libel), the traditional principle in U.S. law is that courts will not issue an injunction stopping the publication of an allegedly libelous statement before it occurs. Thus, if you believe a newspaper next week is going to print something false about you that will harm your reputation, you will not be able to obtain a prior restraint from a court stopping in advance its publication. The preferred remedy in American libel law, instead, is to allow the allegedly libelous statement to be published and then to sue for monetary damages. In other words, a subsequent punishment of speech is the traditional remedy. Once a statement has been judicially determined after a trial to be false and libelous, however, then some courts have allowed an injunction prohibiting the defendant in the case from repeating the same statement that has been held to be libelous.[50]

Prior restraints affecting information uploaded to the Internet are generally ineffective because once information is posted on one Web site, it can be copied on multiple mirror sites and cached forever. Nonetheless, some courts still issue prior restraints affecting information posted on the Internet.

For instance, a Florida trial court judge in December 2015 ordered the *Palm Beach Post* to remove from its Web site transcripts of taped jailhouse phone conversations involving a notorious jailhouse snitch named Frederick Cobia, who was secretly working for the State Attorney's Office in getting the dirt on other inmates. The transcripts had been posted on the newspaper's Web site for nearly two months when the judge ordered them removed, citing Cobia's "right to privacy." By that time, however, a prior restraint against the *Palm Beach Post* would be ineffective because other Web sites already had the information. That is an important point: Courts generally will not grant prior restraints if they will not be effective in preventing the alleged harm or injury (in this case, an alleged harm to Cobia's privacy).

In January 2016, a Florida appellate court in *Palm Beach Newspapers* v. *State of Florida*[51] threw out the trial court judge's order. How did the appellate court reach this conclusion? Initially, it cited the general rule that "a prior restraint on publication, or censorship of information that has already been published, is presumptively unconstitutional under the First Amendment." It then reasoned that: (1) the *Post* had lawfully obtained the transcripts from the public defender's office; (2) "Florida law is well-settled that a jail inmate has no reasonable expectation of privacy in his telephone conversations," and (3) "the trial court's order was ineffectual. By the time the court entered its order, the full transcripts of Cobia's conversations had been available on the *Post's* website and in the open court file for over a month." The appellate court thus concluded "that the *Post's* publication of the transcripts is protected by the First Amendment."

Prior restraints also occur when a federal, state or local ordinance requires individuals or groups to first obtain a permit before engaging in protected speech like holding a rally, picket or march. As described later in Chapter 3, however, such ordinances are permissible in some cases if they meet the requirements of a content-neutral time, place and manner restriction.

But there are subtler forms of prior restraint as well. For example, many states have laws aimed at discouraging convicted criminals from profiting from their crimes by making money from books or films that detail their exploits (see pages 123–125). These are called Son of Sam laws because the first state statute enacted was aimed at stopping a notorious New York serial murderer, David Berkowitz, nicknamed the Son of Sam, from earning money by selling an account of his rampage. Such laws are permissible, but broadly worded statutes have been ruled to be a prior restraint because they may stop the convicted felon from expressing his or her views on a variety of subjects. And some courts have considered laws that limit how or how much a political candidate can

---

50. *Balboa Island Village Inn, Inc.* v. *Lemen*, 40 Cal. 4th 1141 (2007).
51. 183 So. 3d 480 (Fla. Dist. Ct. App. 2016).

spend during an election campaign to be prior censorship as well (see pages 136–139). The discussion in this chapter focuses on the most blatant kind of prior restraint, direct government restrictions on expression.

Before studying some key prior restraint cases involving the government, some rules are important to understand:

1. Prior restraints on speech by the government are presumptively unconstitutional. The burden falls on the government to prove in court that a prior restraint is justified.

2. The government's burden is high, with courts often requiring it to prove there is a compelling interest or an interest of the highest order justifying the restraint.

3. The scope of any prior restraint (how broadly the restraint is drafted and how much speech is restrained) must be very narrow, so as not to stop publication of any more speech than actually is necessary to effectively serve the government's allegedly compelling interests.

4. Speech that falls outside the scope of First Amendment protection (obscenity, child pornography and false advertising, for instance) can be restrained by the government, but only after a judicial proceeding in which a court has determined that the speech indeed is not protected. Thus, if a particular issue of a sexually explicit magazine like *Hustler* has been found by a court to be obscene (see Chapter 13), then all future sales of the exact same issue may be restrained in the area within that court's jurisdiction.

PRIOR RESTRAINTS ON GOVERNMENT EMPLOYEES: SIGNING AWAY ONE'S FIRST AMENDMENT RIGHTS

Can the Central Intelligence Agency stop its former spies from publishing classified information in books about their undercover work? Yes. In *Plame Wilson* v. *Central Intelligence Agency*[52], the 2nd U.S. Circuit Court of Appeals ruled in 2009 that the CIA could stop Valerie Plame Wilson, a former covert operative, from publishing certain information relating to her service with the agency prior to 2002. Plame Wilson signed a secrecy agreement when she joined the CIA pledging not to disclose in any manner classified information obtained during the course of her employment. She also signed a pledge requiring her to submit for prepublication review by the CIA all information and materials, including works of fiction, that contained any mention of intelligence data or activities, as well as classified information. The 2nd Circuit began its analysis of the case by noting that when a government employee voluntarily assumes a duty of confidentiality, governmental restrictions on disclosure are not subject to the same stringent standards that would apply to restrictions on unwilling members of the general public. The decision against Plame Wilson follows the U.S. Supreme Court's

---

52. 586 F.3d 171 (2d Cir. 2009).

1980 precedent in *Snepp* v. *United States* in which it rejected a First Amendment challenge to the CIA's enforcement of its secrecy agreement with former employee Frank Snepp, who had published a book about CIA activities in South Vietnam without submitting his manuscript for prepublication CIA review. A requirement of prepublication review is, of course, a prior restraint on speech because the government gets to review and approve the speech before it can be published.

It is more than just CIA agents, of course, who are subject to nondisclosure agreements as government employees. This was evident in 2012 when several members of the secretive Navy SEAL Team 6 were punished for disclosing classified information regarding the raid that killed Osama Bin Laden. Jeh Johnson, general counsel of the Defense Department, explained in a letter to former Navy SEAL Matt Bissonnette, who wrote a book called *No Easy Day* about the raid, that the nondisclosure agreement he signed "remains in force even after you left the active duty Navy." The letter added that "in the judgment of the Department of Defense, you are in material breach and violation of the nondisclosure agreements you signed. Further public dissemination of your book will aggravate your breach and violation of your agreements." In August 2016, Bissonnette agreed to pay back the proceeds he earned from the book's publication—nearly $6.7 million—as part of a deal to end the government's investigation into his use of unapproved materials in the book and during several speaking engagements.

NEAR v. *MINNESOTA*

The Supreme Court did not directly consider the constitutionality of prior restraint until more than a decade after it had decided its first major sedition case. In 1931, in *Near* v. *Minnesota*,[53] the high court struck an important blow for freedom of expression.

City and county officials in Minneapolis, Minn., brought a legal action against Jay M. Near and Howard Guilford, publishers of the *Saturday Press*, a small weekly newspaper. Near and Guilford were self-proclaimed reformers whose ostensible purpose was to clean up city and county government in Minneapolis. In their attacks on corruption in city government, they used language that was far from temperate and defamed some of the town's leading government officials. Near and Guilford charged that Jewish gangsters were in control of gambling, bootlegging and racketeering in the city and that city government and its law enforcement agencies did not perform their duties energetically. They repeated these charges over and over in a highly inflammatory manner.[54]

Minnesota had a statute that empowered a court to declare any obscene, lewd, lascivious, malicious, scandalous or defamatory publication a public nuisance. When such a publication was deemed a public nuisance, the court issued an injunction against future publication or distribution. Violation of the injunction resulted in punishment for contempt of court.

53. 283 U.S. 697 (1931).
54. Friendly, *Minnesota Rag.*

In 1927 county attorney Floyd Olson initiated an action against the *Saturday Press*. A district court declared the newspaper a public nuisance and "perpetually enjoined" publication of the *Saturday Press*. The only way either Near or Guilford would be able to publish the newspaper again was to convince the court that their newspaper would remain free of objectionable material. In 1928 the Minnesota Supreme Court upheld the constitutionality of the law, declaring that under its broad police power the state can regulate public nuisances, including defamatory and scandalous newspapers.

The case then went to the U.S. Supreme Court, which reversed the ruling by the state Supreme Court. The nuisance statute was declared unconstitutional. Chief Justice Charles Evans Hughes wrote the opinion for the court in the 5-4 ruling, saying that the statute in question was not designed to redress wrongs to individuals attacked by the newspaper. Instead, the statute was directed at suppressing the *Saturday Press* once and for all. The object of the law, Hughes wrote, was not punishment but censorship—not only of a single issue, but also of all future issues—which is not consistent with the traditional concept of freedom of the press. That is, the statute constituted prior restraint, and prior restraint is clearly a violation of the First Amendment.

The object of the law, Hughes wrote, was not punishment but censorship—not only of a single issue, but also of all future issues—which is not consistent with the traditional concept of freedom of the press.

One maxim in the law holds that when a judge writes an opinion for a court, he or she should stick to the problem at hand and not wander off and talk about matters that do not really concern the specific issue before the court. Such remarks are considered **dicta,** or words that do not really apply to the case. These words, these dicta, are never considered an important part of the ruling in the case. Chief Justice Hughes' opinion in *Near* v. *Minnesota* contains a good deal of dicta.

In this case Hughes wrote that the prior restraint of the *Saturday Press* was unconstitutional, but in some circumstances, he added, prior restraint might be permissible. In what kinds of circumstances? The government can constitutionally stop publication of obscenity, material that incites people to acts of violence, and certain kinds of materials during wartime. (It is entirely probable that the chief justice was forced to make these qualifying statements in order to hold his slim five-person majority in the ruling.) Hughes admitted, on the other hand, that defining freedom of the press as only the freedom from prior restraint is equally wrong, for in many cases punishment after publication (i.e., subsequent punishment) imposes effective censorship upon the freedom of expression.

Near v. *Minnesota* stands for the proposition that under American law prior censorship is permitted only in very unusual circumstances; it is the exception, not the rule. Courts have reinforced this interpretation many times since 1931. Despite this considerable litigation, there remains an incomplete understanding of the kinds of circumstances in which prior restraint might be acceptable under the First Amendment, as the following cases illustrate.

PENTAGON PAPERS CASE

Another important, well-known Supreme Court ruling on prior restraints came in 1971 and addressed the federal government's ability to stop publication of stolen, classified information that it contended jeopardized national security during the war in Vietnam. This is the famous Pentagon Papers decision.[55] The case began in the summer of 1971

---

55. *New York Times* v. *U.S.*, 403 U.S. 713 (1971).

when *The New York Times*, followed by the *Washington Post* and a handful of other newspapers, began publishing a series of articles based on pilfered copies of a top-secret 47-volume government study officially titled "History of the United States Decision-Making Process on Vietnam Policy." The day after the initial article on the so-called Pentagon Papers appeared, Attorney General John Mitchell asked *The New York Times* to stop publication of the material. When the *Times'* publisher refused, the government went to court to get an injunction to force the newspaper to stop the series. A temporary restraining order was granted as the case wound its way to the Supreme Court. The government also sought to impose a similar injunction on the *Washington Post* after it began to publish reports based on the same material.

At first the government argued that the publication of this material violated federal espionage statutes. When that assertion did not satisfy the lower federal courts, the government argued that the president had inherent power under his constitutional mandate to conduct foreign affairs to protect the national security, which includes the right to classify documents secret and top secret. Publication of this material by the newspapers was unauthorized disclosure of such material and should be stopped. This argument did not satisfy the courts either, and by the time the case came before the Supreme Court, the government argument was that publication of these papers might result in irreparable harm to the nation and its ability to conduct foreign affairs. The *Times* and the *Post* made two arguments. First, they said that the classification system is a sham, that people in the government declassify documents almost at will when they want to sway public opinion or influence a reporter's story. Second, the press argued that an injunction against the continued publication of this material violated the First Amendment. Interestingly, the newspapers did not argue that under all circumstances prior restraint is in conflict with the First Amendment. Defense attorney Alexander Bickel argued that under some circumstances prior restraint is acceptable—for example, when the publication of a document has a direct link with a grave event that is immediate and visible. Apparently, both newspapers decided a victory in that immediate case was far more important than to establish a definitive, long-lasting constitutional principle. They therefore concentrated on winning the case, acknowledging that in future cases prior restraint might be permissible.[56]

On June 30 the high court ruled 6-3 in favor of *The New York Times* and the *Washington Post* and refused to block the publication of the Pentagon Papers. But the ruling was hardly the kind that strengthened the First Amendment. In a very short per curiam opinion, the majority said that in a case involving the prior restraint of a publication, the government bears a heavy burden to justify such a restraint. In this case the government failed to show the court why such a restraint should be imposed on the two newspapers. In other words, the government failed to justify its request for the permanent restraining order.

The decision in the case rested on the preferred position First Amendment theory or doctrine (see pages 52–53). The ban on publication was *presumed* to be an unconstitutional infringement on the First Amendment. The government had to prove that the ban was needed to protect the nation in some manner. If such evidence could be adduced, the court would strike the balance in favor of the government and uphold the

---

56. Pember, "The Pentagon Papers," 403.

ban on the publication of the articles. But in this case the government simply failed to show why its request for an injunction was vital to the national interest. Consequently, the high court denied the government's request for a ban on the publication of the Pentagon Papers on the grounds that such a prohibition was a violation of the First Amendment. The court did not say that in all similar cases an injunction would violate the First Amendment. It merely said that the government had not shown why the injunction was needed, why it was not a violation of the freedom of the press.

What many people initially called the case of the century ended in a First Amendment fizzle.

What many people initially called the case of the century ended in a First Amendment fizzle. The press won the day; the Pentagon Papers were published. But a majority of the court had not ruled that such prior restraint was unconstitutional—only that the government had failed to meet the heavy burden of showing such restraint was necessary in this case.

PROGRESSIVE MAGAZINE CASE

In a rare case in which national security concerns were found by a federal court to merit a prior restraint, a federal judge in 1979 in *United States* v. *Progressive*[57] issued a preliminary injunction stopping publication of a magazine article that specified "with particularity the three key concepts necessary to construct a hydrogen weapon." The judge determined the article included information "not found in the public realm" and that its publication "would likely cause a direct, immediate and irreparable injury to this nation."

The decision, however, is of little precedential value, as it was the opinion of only one federal district court judge, not an appellate court. Before the decision worked its way up the appellate court ladder, a newspaper in Wisconsin published the same information, thus rendering moot the case against the publishers of the *Progressive* magazine. We will never know if the prior restraint would have been sustained by an appellate court.

UNITED STATES v. *BELL*

Prior restraint speech cases need not always involve national security interests (the Pentagon Papers case and *United States* v. *Progressive*) or vociferous attacks against public officials (*Near* v. *Minnesota*). Indeed, in some instances the government may seek a prior restraint against an individual in order to stop the dissemination of false or fraudulent speech that subverts federal laws. That happened in 2005 when a federal appellate court in *United States* v. *Bell*[58] upheld a permanent injunction barring Thurston Paul Bell from promoting and selling unlawful tax advice. Bell, as the court put it, was a "professional tax protester who ran a business and a Web site selling bogus strategies to clients endeavoring to avoid paying taxes." Bell's Web site, the court wrote, "invited visitors to violate the tax code, and sold them materials instructing them how to do so." The federal government sought and won a district court injunction stopping Bell from engaging in false, deceptive or misleading commercial speech relating to any "abusive tax shelter, plan or arrangement that incites taxpayers to attempt to violate

57. 486 F. Supp. 5 (W.D. Wisc. 1979).
58. 414 F. 3d 474 (3d Cir. 2005).

the internal revenue laws or unlawfully evade the assessment or collection of their federal tax liabilities or unlawfully claim improper tax refunds."

The 3rd U.S. Circuit Court of Appeals in *Bell* began its analysis by noting that "permanent injunctions like the one here are 'classic examples of prior restraints' on speech." The appellate court then cited the Pentagon Papers case described earlier in this chapter for the proposition that "prior restraints are generally presumed unconstitutional." But the appellate court then wrote, citing *Near* v. *Minnesota*, that prior restraints "may be permissible depending on the type of speech at issue."

In this case, the appellate court determined that the general principle of First Amendment law that prior restraints bear a heavy presumption against their constitutional validity "does not apply to restrictions on unprotected speech, including false or unlawful commercial speech" (see Chapter 15 regarding commercial speech). The court thus affirmed the injunction restraining Bell's false commercial speech. The outcome suggests that when speech falls completely outside the scope of the First Amendment protection of speech, a government-requested restraint against its dissemination may be permissible.

SUMMARY

While virtually all American legal scholars agree that the adoption of the First Amendment in 1791 was designed to abolish prior restraint in this nation, prior restraint still exists. A reason it still exists is the 1931 Supreme Court ruling in *Near* v. *Minnesota* in which Chief Justice Charles Evans Hughes ruled that although prior restraint is unacceptable in most instances, there are times when it must be tolerated if the republic is to survive. Protecting the security of the nation is one of those instances cited by Hughes. In the past quarter century in two important cases, the press has been stopped from publishing material the courts believed to be too sensitive. Although the Supreme Court finally permitted *The New York Times* and the *Washington Post* to publish the so-called Pentagon Papers, the newspapers were blocked for two weeks from printing this material. And in the end the high court merely ruled that the government had failed to make its case, not that the newspapers had a First Amendment right under any circumstance to publish this history of the Vietnam War. Eight years later the *Progressive* magazine was enjoined from publishing an article about thermonuclear weapons. Only the publication of the same material by a small newspaper in Wisconsin thwarted the government's efforts to permanently stop publication of this article in the *Progressive*.

BIBLIOGRAPHY

Alexander, James. *A Brief Narrative on the Case and Trial of John Peter Zenger.* Edited by Stanley N. Katz. Cambridge: Harvard University Press, 1963.

Baker, C. Edwin. *Human Liberty and Freedom of Speech.* New York: Oxford University Press, 1989.

Barron, Jerome. "Access to the Press—A New First Amendment Right." *Harvard Law Review* 80 (1967): 1641.

Chemerinsky, Erwin. *Constitutional Law: Principles and Policies.* 2nd ed. New York: Aspen, 2002.

Farber, Daniel A. *The First Amendment.* 2nd ed. New York: Foundation Press, 2003.

Friendly, Fred. *Minnesota Rag.* New York: Random House, 1981.

Levy, Leonard. *Emergence of a Free Press.* New York: Oxford University Press, 1985.

Meiklejohn, Alexander. *Free Speech and Its Relation to Self-Government.* New York: Harper & Brothers, 1948.

Pember, Don R. "The Pentagon Papers: More Questions Than Answers." *Journalism Quarterly* 48 (1971): 403.

———. "The Smith Act as a Restraint on the Press." *Journalism Monographs* 10 (1969): 1.

Peterson, H.C., and Gilbert Fite. *Opponents of War, 1917–1918.* Seattle: University of Washington Press, 1957.

Rabban, David M. *Free Speech in Its Forgotten Years.* Cambridge, United Kingdom: Cambridge University Press, 1997.

Redish, Martin H., and Kirk J. Kaludis. "The Right of Expressive Access in First Amendment Theory." *Northwestern University Law Review* 93 (1999): 1083.

Richards, Robert D., and Clay Calvert. "Nadine Strossen and Freedom of Expression." *George Mason University Civil Rights Law Journal* 13 (2003): 185.

Roche, John P. *Shadow and Substance.* New York: Macmillan, 1964.

Schmitt, Richard B. "Acquittal in Internet Terrorism Case Is a Defeat for Patriot Act." *Los Angeles Times,* 11 June 2004, A20.

Smith, James M. *Freedom's Fetters.* Ithaca, N.Y.: Cornell University Press, 1956.

Smolla, Rodney. *Free Speech in an Open Society.* New York: Knopf, 1992.

Wike, Richard. "Americans More Tolerant of Offensive Speech Than Others in the World." Pew Research Center, 12 October 2016, http://www.pewresearch.org/fact-tank/2016/10/12/americans-more-tolerant-of-offensive-speech-than-others-in-the-world/.

Young, Cathy. "The Tyranny of Hecklers." *The Boston Globe,* 2 June 2003, A13.

The First Amendment

CONTEMPORARY PROBLEMS

This chapter examines a wide range of contemporary topics affecting the freedom of expression, starting with the First Amendment rights of public school and university students. As you'll discover, students at public high schools do possess some First Amendment rights, but those rights are not the same as the rights of adults. You also will learn about topics including book banning, hate speech and freedom of expression on the Internet, among other issues. Ultimately, you will find out that each of these areas has its own set of unique issues, rules and court rulings.

THE FIRST AMENDMENT IN SCHOOLS

Censorship of school newspapers is a serious First Amendment issue in America today. For instance, in 2015 the principal at Fauquier High School in Warrenton, Va., told a student reporter that she couldn't publish an article in the student newspaper about students "dabbing," which involves smoking concentrated marijuana. Sensing that dabbing was gaining popularity in her school, the student reporter told *The Washington Post* that she wanted to write a story about it because "I was just interested in exactly what it was and exactly what the effects of it were. I wanted my peers to know what they were doing." But her principal forbade her from publishing the piece, telling her he was concerned that students reading the article would "be exposed to a new and dangerous drug without adult guidance." The student appealed the principal's decision to the school superintendent, but he backed the principal because he, too, worried the article "unintentionally promotes and encourages illegal and unhealthy activity." But the saga didn't end there. After the editor of an online news outlet in Fauquier saw an editorial the student reporter had written in the student newspaper describing the censorship, he decided to publish her original story online. The online editor said the article about dabbing was "a good story that deserved publication" and that he didn't perceive it as being dangerous. The student's story thus ultimately reached a much wider audience than it would have in the student newspaper—it had more than 11,000 unique visitors on the online news outlet, *Fauquier Now*, within the first 10 days of its publication.

Students at Harrisonville High School in Harrisonville, Mo., also clashed with their principal in 2015. The student newspaper wanted to report on the recent resignation of the district's superintendent, but the principal at the school told the newspaper staff that he would need to review any article about the resignation first before he would let the newspaper publish it. The principal's demand to review the article before publication is a good example of a prior restraint on speech, which was discussed in Chapter 2. The principal told the *Kansas City Star* newspaper that the students could face punishment if they published an article without his permission. "I wouldn't expel them, but there would be consequences," Principal Andy Campbell said. "The paper here at school is mine to control."

And in 2016, a censorship battle at Steinmetz College Prep, a public school in Chicago, resulted in a threat from the school principal to eliminate the school newspaper entirely. Student reporters for the school's paper, the *Steinmetz Star* (which is the alma mater of *Playboy* editor-in-chief Hugh Hefner), said they spent weeks working on an article about a change in the school bell schedule that pushed the school start time back an hour. Their reporting included data from a survey students conducted about the change. The newspaper's adviser said the principal had never withheld an article in the past—but he did this time. The principal, Stephen Ngo, decided to postpone the article's publication until a later edition so that students could "address some things that were missing," according to the Student Press Law Center. Ngo met with the newspaper staff to explain his decision, but a student reporter who was there said the meeting was "useless" and that, in her view, Ngo never provided a clear reason why he was censoring the article. Frustrated with the meeting and with

Ngo's decision, that student decided instead to publish the story on her personal blog. That prompted Ngo to email school counselors and tell them the journalism program would be eliminated—though Ngo later walked back the email and said the program would continue. The bell schedule article did eventually run in the January–February edition of the paper.

Not only does school censorship deprive students and others of information they should rightfully see, but when practiced in the schools, censorship can take on the aura of being good policy, the right thing for the government to do. School, after all, is where students are taught the difference between right and wrong, and where they learn about the freedoms Americans enjoy under their Constitution.

CENSORSHIP OF EXPRESSION IN PUBLIC HIGH SCHOOLS

For centuries, students were presumed to have few constitutional rights. They were regarded as second-class people and were told it was better to be seen and not heard. Parents were, and still are, given wide latitude in controlling the behavior of their offspring, and when these young people moved into schools or other public institutions, the government had the right to exercise a kind of parental control over them: *in loco parentis,* in the place of a parent. During the social upheaval of the 1960s and 1970s, students began to assert their constitutional rights, and in several important decisions the federal courts acknowledged these claims. In 1969, in the case of *Tinker* v. *Des Moines Independent Community School District,* the Supreme Court ruled that students in the public schools do not shed at the schoolhouse gate their constitutional rights to freedom of speech or expression.

During the social upheaval of the 1960s and 1970s, students began to assert their constitutional rights, and in several important decisions the federal courts acknowledged these claims.

On December 16, 1966, Christopher Eckhardt, 16, and Mary Beth Tinker, 13, went to school wearing homemade black armbands, replete with peace signs, to protest the war in Vietnam. Mary Beth's brother John, 15, wore a similar armband the following day. All three were suspended from school after they refused requests by school officials to remove the armbands. School administrators feared that wearing the armbands might provoke violence among the students, most of whom supported the war in Vietnam. The students appealed to the courts to overturn their suspensions. Three years later, the Supreme Court held that students have a First Amendment right to express their opinions on even controversial subjects like the war in Vietnam if they do so "without materially and substantially interfering with the requirements of appropriate discipline in the operation of the school and without colliding with the rights of others."[1] In ruling in favor of the Tinker children and Eckhardt, the Supreme Court added that an "undifferentiated fear or apprehension of disturbance is not enough to overcome the right to freedom of expression" in public schools. The Court concluded that, in this case, the "record does not demonstrate any facts which might reasonably have led school authorities [in Des Moines] to forecast substantial disruption of or material interference with school activities, and no disturbances or disorders on the school premises in fact occurred."

1. *Tinker* v. *Des Moines Independent Community School District,* 393 U.S. 503 (1969).

This is the T-shirt Bretton Barber wore to school that sparked a federal lawsuit.

©*McGraw-Hill Education/photographer, Mark Dierker*

The *Tinker* standard applies not only to students in public high schools, but also all the way down to students in public elementary schools. As the 3rd U.S. Circuit Court of Appeals wrote in a 2013 opinion involving a fifth-grader called *K.A.* v. *Pocono Mountain School District,* "the *Tinker* test has the requisite flexibility to accommodate the age-related developmental, educational, and disciplinary concerns of elementary school students."

The *Tinker* standard played a key role in the 2003 federal district court opinion in *Barber* v. *Dearborn Public Schools.*[2] The case arose from a dispute in Dearborn, Mich. That city boasts, the court noted, "the largest concentration of Arabs anywhere in the world outside of the Middle East" and "approximately 31.4% of Dearborn High's students are Arab." Many of these residents reportedly fled Iraq to escape the regime of the now deceased former dictator, Saddam Hussein. It was in this environment on Feb. 17, 2003—just before the launch of the U.S. military offensive in Iraq—that Bretton Barber, then a high school junior, wore a T-shirt labeling President George W. Bush an "International Terrorist" in order "to express his feelings about President Bush's foreign policies and the imminent war in Iraq." Barber went through the first three class periods of the day without having anyone mention the shirt. It was during the lunch period, however, that one student (and one student only) complained to an assistant principal about Barber's political fashion statement. That student was upset because he had a relative in the military being sent to Iraq and at least one of his family members served in each of the country's prior wars. Barber soon was

---

2. 286 F. Supp. 2d 847 (E.D. Mich. 2003).

asked to remove the T-shirt—he was wearing a different shirt underneath it—or turn it inside out. Refusing to take either option, Barber called his father and went home from school that day. Shortly thereafter, he filed a federal lawsuit against the school district.

Judge Patrick J. Duggan faced the issue of whether the school violated Barber's First Amendment right to free speech and political expression when it prohibited him from wearing the anti-Bush T-shirt. He first held that Barber's case was controlled by the U.S. Supreme Court's 1969 opinion in *Tinker* that upheld the right of students to wear black armbands to school to protest the Vietnam War. Duggan thus decided that Barber's case was not guided by the high court's more recent decisions in either the sexually offensive, captive-audience expression case of *Bethel School District* v. *Fraser*[3] (see page 97–98) or the school-sponsored newspaper case of *Hazelwood School District* v. *Kuhlmeier*[4] (see pages 92–96). Barber's situation, in brief, was much more factually similar to *Tinker* than it was to either *Bethel* or *Hazelwood,* thus allowing the judge to distinguish the latter two cases.

Applying the *Tinker* precedent, Judge Duggan reasoned that the school officials' "decision to ban Barber's shirt only can withstand constitutional scrutiny if they show that the T-shirt caused a substantial disruption of or material interference with school activities or created more than an unsubstantiated fear or apprehension of such a disruption or interference." The judge found that only one student and one teacher had expressed negative opinions about the shirt and that there was "no evidence that the T-shirt created any disturbance or disruption in Barber's morning classes, in the hallway between classes or between Barber's third hour class and his lunch period, or during the first twenty-five minutes of the lunch period."

As for the school officials' argument that the continued wearing of the shirt might cause trouble in the future, given the ethnic composition of the student body and the imminence of war, Judge Duggan found that "even if the majority or a large number of Dearborn High's Arab students are Iraqi, nothing in the present record suggests that these students were or would be offended by Barber's shirt which conveys a view about President Bush. More importantly, there is nothing in the record before this Court to indicate that those students, or any students at Dearborn High, might respond to the T-shirt in a way that would disrupt or interfere with the school environment." He added that "it is improper and most likely detrimental to our society for government officials, particularly school officials, to assume that members of a particular ethnic group will have monolithic views on a subject and will be unable to control those views."

Comparing the situation in Barber's case with the Vietnam War protest scenario at issue in the *Tinker* case, Judge Duggan wrote: "[C]learly the tension between students who support and those who oppose President Bush's decision to invade Iraq is no greater than the tension that existed during the United States' involvement in Vietnam between

3. 478 U.S. 675 (1986).
4. 484 U.S. 260 (1988).

supporters of the war and war-protesters." The judge added that "students benefit when school officials provide an environment where they can openly express their diverging viewpoints and when they learn to tolerate the opinions of others." Judge Duggan thus ruled in favor of Bretton Barber.

PUNISHING STUDENTS FOR DISPLAYING THEIR "SEXUALITY" ON T-SHIRTS: VIEWPOINT-BASED DISCRIMINATION AGAINST SPEECH?

A high school student in Manteca, Calif., sued school administrators after she was sent home from school for refusing to change out of a T-shirt that said, "Nobody knows I'm a lesbian." Most people at the school actually *did* know the student's sexual orientation; the student, Taylor Victor, had come out the year before and wore the shirt ironically, saying in a blog post that it "made me laugh because pretty much everyone knows I'm a lesbian." But a teacher who noticed Victor wearing the shirt sent her to speak with the school's vice principal, who told her to change her shirt "on the grounds that she was not allowed to display her 'sexuality' on clothing." He later said the shirt violated the school's dress code because it was "disruptive." Another administrator at the school apparently also told her the shirt was "promoting sex" and an "open invitation to sex."

The student sued, and in February 2016, she reached a settlement with the school district. Under the terms of the settlement, the district agreed to let Victor wear her shirt to school. The district also agreed to change its dress code to clarify that students "will not be prohibited from wearing clothing, jewelry or personal items that express self-identification with, or support for, individuals or groups on the basis of ... disability, gender, gender identity, gender expression, nationality, race or ethnicity, religion or sexual orientation." The settlement also stipulated that the district was required to retain a consultant to provide training about student free speech rights to all district administrators. Linnea Nelson, the American Civil Liberties Union lawyer who represented Victor in her suit, told the *Los Angeles Times*, "Students don't leave their rights to free speech at the schoolhouse gates. At the end of the day, the law on this is very clear, that public schools can't censor the personal beliefs of students just because they think it might be controversial."

In a rather remarkable T-shirt censorship case, a federal judge in 2011 upheld under the *Tinker* standard a California school's decision to prohibit the wearing by students of T-shirts bearing the American flag on May 5. May 5 is the date of a Mexican holiday known as Cinco de Mayo. The judge in *Dariano* v. *Morgan Hill Unified School District*[5] determined

---

5. 822 F. Supp. 2d 1037 (N.D. Cal. 2011), *affirmed*, 767 F. 3d 764 (9th Cir. 2014), cert. den., 135 S. Ct. 1700 (2015).

that wearing American flag shirts on that specific day might lead to a substantial disruption of the educational atmosphere. He cited "a context of ongoing racial tension and gang violence within the school" and noted that the ban was implemented "after a near-violent altercation had erupted during the prior Cinco de Mayo over the display of an American flag." Based upon this history of racial trouble at Live Oak High School, the judge concluded that "school officials [could] reasonably forecast that Plaintiffs' clothing could cause a substantial disruption with school activities."

The *Dariano* decision tracks a long line of cases in which courts allow schools to prohibit students from wearing confederate flag symbols if there is a recent history of racial tension and trouble within a school. In 2012, the *Dariano* students who found their American-flag adorned clothing censored appealed to the 9th U.S. Circuit Court of Appeals. They argued in their brief that "without exception, the celebration of the American flag should be protected no less than its desecration. Indeed, it is a poor lesson in American civics to ban the American flag as a polarizing racist pariah when competing symbols of nationhood are at issue." In 2014, the 9th Circuit affirmed the 2011 ruling in favor of the school district, concluding that school officials could "reasonably forecast substantial disruption or violence." The U.S. Supreme Court declined to hear the case in 2015.

The legacy of *Tinker* has largely failed to live up to the Court's bold language in the case. Although *Tinker*'s material-and-substantial interference or disruption standard remains good law and has never been overruled, many lower courts attempt to factually distinguish *Tinker* in student-speech cases to avoid applying its precedent. It is a major problem for students' speech rights that has grown worse after the tragedy at Columbine High School in Littleton, Colo., in 1999. Judges remain extremely sensitive to the legacy of Columbine and other school shootings and, in turn, give great deference to school administrators and principals and are loathe to question their judgment about when speech might reasonably lead to a substantial and material disruption of the educational process or interference with the rights of other students.

The killing of 20 elementary school students in December 2012 in Newtown, Connecticut, spawned another crackdown on student speech referencing violence. For instance, a high school senior named Courtni Webb was suspended from her charter school in the San Francisco Unified School District shortly after the Newtown tragedy for writing a poem about it. The poem included the lines "I understand the killings in Connecticut. I know why he pulled the trigger" and "Why are we oppressed by a dysfunctional community of haters and blamers?" In an interview with a reporter from KGO-TV, Webb said the poem was "just talking about society and how I understand why things like that incident happened." She said writing poetry was therapeutic for her. California Education Code Section 48907 makes it clear that "pupils of the public schools, *including charter schools,* shall have the right to exercise freedom of speech and of the press" (emphasis added).

While *Tinker* applies today in cases involving student speech that occur on school grounds and that are neither school sponsored nor sexually lewd, vulgar or profane, or advocate illegal drug use, a very different legal standard applies when the speech is sponsored by the school, such as a school newspaper that is part of the curriculum. The standard in this latter situation was created by the Supreme Court in 1988 in *Hazelwood School District* v. *Kuhlmeier*,[6] and it is discussed next.

BANNING CONFEDERATE FLAG CLOTHING AT SCHOOL: THE *TINKER* ANALYSIS APPLIES

In September 2015, more than 20 students were suspended from Christiansburg High School in southwestern Virginia for peacefully wearing clothing emblazoned with the Confederate battle flag. Is such censorship permissible? It all depends on whether there has been a recent history of racial violence or racial trouble at the school. If there has been a history of racial trouble at the school, then the censorship is likely permissible. That's because school officials would have reasonable grounds to predict and forecast that the wearing of such clothing will cause a substantial and material disruption of the educational environment, under *Tinker*. On the other hand, if there is no recent history of racial trouble at the school in question, then such banning of Confederate battle flag clothing is likely unconstitutional. In the Christiansburg High School case, *The Washington Post* reported that Confederate flag symbols had been banned at the school for more than a dozen years, dating back to 2002 after a series of racially motivated fights between students. Was that too far in the past to reasonably predict trouble in 2015 when the students were suspended from Christiansburg High School? What do you think?

The Hazelwood *Case*

In 1983 the principal at Hazelwood East High School near St. Louis censored the school newspaper by completely removing two pages that contained articles about teen pregnancy and the impact of parents' divorce on children. The articles on pregnancy included personal interviews with three Hazelwood students (whose names were not used) about how they were affected by their unwanted pregnancies. There was also information about birth control in the story. The story on divorce quoted students—again not identified—about the problems they had suffered when their mothers and fathers had split up. The censorship of the articles was defended on the grounds of privacy and editorial balance. School officials said they were concerned that the identity of the three girls who agreed to anonymously discuss their pregnancies might nevertheless become known. School officials said they acted to protect the privacy of students and parents in the story on divorce as well. In addition, the principal said the latter story was unbalanced, giving the views of only the students. In 1988 the Supreme Court ruled that the censorship was permissible under the First Amendment.[7]

It is important to note that this ruling involved censorship of a high school newspaper that was published as a part of the school curriculum. The court strongly suggested

6. 484 U.S. 260 (1988).
7. *Hazelwood School District* v. *Kuhlmeier,* 484 U.S. 260 (1988).

the ruling would not necessarily apply to a high school paper published as an extracurricular activity where any student might contribute stories. Justice Byron White, author of the court's opinion, noted specifically in a footnote that the court did not at that time have to decide whether its ruling might also be applied to school-sponsored college and university newspapers.

The Supreme Court refused to apply the *Tinker* standard by distinguishing the *Hazelwood* case from the earlier ruling. The *Tinker* ruling, Justice White said in the 5-3 decision, deals with the right of educators to silence a student's personal expression that happens to occur on school property. *Hazelwood* concerns the authority of educators over school-sponsored publications. "Educators are entitled to exercise greater control over this second form of student expression to assure that participants learn whatever lessons the activity is designed to teach, that readers or listeners are not exposed to material that may be inappropriate for their level of maturity, and that the views of individual speakers are not erroneously attributed to the school," he wrote. Educators do not offend the First Amendment by exercising editorial control over the style and content of student speech in school-sponsored publications as long as their actions are reasonably related to "legitimate pedagogical concerns." This means school officials could censor out material they found "ungrammatical, poorly written, inadequately researched, biased or prejudiced, vulgar or profane, or unsuitable for immature audiences." Justice White stressed at one point in the ruling that the education of the nation's youth is primarily the responsibility of parents, teachers and state and local school officials, not federal judges. Only when the decision to censor has "no valid educational purpose" is the First Amendment directly and sharply involved.

Educators do not offend the First Amendment by exercising editorial control over the style and content of student speech in school-sponsored publications as long as their actions are reasonably related to "legitimate pedagogical concerns."

SATIRE, SWASTIKAS AND HIGH SCHOOL PLAYS: A GLARING OMISSION IN 2016 FROM "THE PRODUCERS"

Mel Brooks' Tony Award-winning musical "The Producers" satirizes Nazis and features a play-within-a-play called "Springtime for Hitler." Part of the set for that scene typically includes several huge banners featuring swastikas. But when Tappan Zee High School in New York produced the play in 2016, the large swastika-emblazoned banners went missing. That's because the school district's superintendent ordered them removed, apparently failing to understand the humorous context in which they were used. "There is no context in a public high school where a swastika is appropriate," the superintendent told a WCBS television reporter. He did, however, allow much smaller swastikas on the armbands of several of the student thespians.

Is such censorship permissible? Because "The Producers" was put on as a school-sponsored play and was directed by a faculty member, the rule from *Hazelwood* would apply to determine if the censorship violated the First Amendment. Applying *Hazelwood*, a court would need to ask, "Was the censorship reasonably related to legitimate pedagogical concerns?" No lawsuit in this instance was filed, however, but the political correctness and interference with artistic freedom is nonetheless disturbing.

It is not only stories about sexual behavior or violence that can provoke school administrators to censor student publications. School officials frequently seek to block the publication of stories that will make school administrators or teachers appear to be foolish or incompetent or lacking judgment.

There are only a few rare instances in which courts have held that school administrators have gone too far and violated the rights of student-journalists under *Hazelwood*'s expansive "legitimate pedagogical concerns" standard. One such case of a First Amendment violation involved the censorship of an article in the Utica High School *Arrow* in Utica, Mich. The student-authored article in question reported on a lawsuit filed against the Utica Community Schools (UCS) by two local residents, Joanne and Rey Frances, who lived next door to the UCS bus depot. The Frances' lawsuit claimed injuries and illnesses allegedly caused by breathing in the diesel fumes emitted by the UCS's idling buses each school day. A local newspaper had already covered the story about the lawsuit before student Katherine "Katy" Dean researched and wrote an article about the situation for her school newspaper, the *Arrow*. The *Arrow* is an officially sponsored publication of the UCS and, as part of the high school's curriculum for which students receive credit and grades, operates under the direction of a faculty adviser. The faculty adviser, however, does not regulate the subjects covered by students, but instead merely provides advice on which stories to run. She also reviews, criticizes and checks the grammar contained in articles. The *Arrow*'s staff of student journalists controls the content of the monthly paper, is responsible for major editorial decisions without significant administrative intervention and typically does not submit its content to school administrators for prepublication review.

The article written by Dean was balanced and accurate, and it correctly reported that school district officials declined to comment on the lawsuit. One day before the article was scheduled to go to press, however, UCS administrators ordered that it be removed from the *Arrow*, citing so-called journalistic defects and "inaccuracies" (for instance, the UCS administration did not like the fact that Dean's article accurately attributed scientific data to a story in *USA Today*—apparently it was not a credible source in the minds of the school officials—and the fact that a draft of the story used pseudonyms for the Frances' real names). The American Civil Liberties Union filed a lawsuit on behalf of Dean, claiming the censorship violated Dean's First Amendment rights under *Hazelwood*.[8]

In 2004 U.S. District Court Judge Arthur Tarnow applied the *Hazelwood* legitimate-pedagogical-concerns standard and ruled in favor of Dean and against the school. The judge called the school's censorship and suppression of the article "unconstitutional," adding that the school's "explanation that the article was deleted for legitimate educational purposes such as bias and factual inaccuracy is wholly lacking in credibility in light of the evidence in the record."[9] Judge Tarnow distinguished the *Arrow* article about the lawsuit from the censored content in the *Hazelwood* case that dealt with teen pregnancy and divorce. He observed that Katy Dean's article about the bus-fumes lawsuit did not raise any privacy concerns since a local paper had already addressed the lawsuit, and it did not contain any sexual "frank talk" and thus could not reasonably be perceived as being unsuitable for immature audiences. Beyond such critical distinctions, Judge

---

8. *Dean* v. *Utica Community Schools,* 345 F. Supp. 2d 799 (E.D. Mich. 2004).
9. *Associated Press,* "Utica Schools."

Tarnow found the article to be fair and balanced, noting that Dean's story "sets forth the conflicting viewpoints on the health effects of diesel fumes, and concludes that the link between diesel fumes and cancer is not fully established." Finally Tarnow noted that the story contained no serious grammatical errors and that "Dean's article properly and accurately attributes its quotations to their sources. The article qualifies any statement made by its sources. The article does not present the author's own conclusions on unknown facts." Judge Tarnow thus concluded that "Katy Dean had a right to publish an article concerning the Frances' side of the lawsuit so long as it accurately reported the Frances' side of the lawsuit."

In addition to holding that the school's actions against Dean violated the *Hazelwood* standard, Judge Tarnow ruled that the censorship of her article violated the more general but important First Amendment rule against **viewpoint-based discrimination.** In support of this holding, Judge Tarnow noted that the UCS attorney "conceded that Dean's article would not have been removed from the Arrow if it had explicitly taken the district's side with respect to the Frances' lawsuit against UCS." This is the essence of viewpoint-based discrimination: The government (in this case, the school district) restricts and restrains one side of a debate but not the other. For instance, in 2012 a federal judge in *ACLU* v. *Conti* held that the state of North Carolina's "offering of a Choose Life license plate in the absence of a pro-choice plate constitutes viewpoint discrimination in violation of the First Amendment." More simply put, the government should remain neutral in the marketplace of ideas (see pages 53–54 regarding the marketplace of ideas) and not favor one side of a debate over the other. By acknowledging that the school would have allowed Katy Dean to print an article that favored the UCS's position in the lawsuit filed against it by the Franceses, the UCS attorney essentially admitted the viewpoint-based discrimination that drove it to censor Dean's story.

The case of *Dean* v. *Utica Community Schools* should stand as a stark reminder to overzealous and censorious high school administrators that there are limits, even under the *Hazelwood* legitimate-pedagogical-concern standard, to censorship of the student press.

High school journalism remains vigorous in many schools. And the legislatures in a handful of states, including California, Colorado, Arkansas, Illinois, Iowa, Maryland, Massachusetts, Nevada, North Dakota, Oregon, Rhode Island, Vermont and Kansas, have passed statutes granting student-journalists in those states a fuller measure of freedom of expression than was granted by the Supreme Court in *Hazelwood.* For instance, Oregon's anti-*Hazelwood* statute, enacted in 2007, provides that student-journalists "have the right to exercise freedom of speech and of the press in school-sponsored media, whether or not the media are supported financially by the school or by use of school facilities or are produced in conjunction with a high school class" and that "student journalists are responsible for determining the news, opinion and feature content of school-sponsored media," subject only to the substantial-and-material disruption limitations articulated by the U.S. Supreme Court in *Tinker* (rather than to the *Hazelwood* standard) and general rules of libel and privacy laws.[10]

The question, "In what ways can a high school newspaper be censored?" cannot be answered until two other questions are. First, is the newspaper published at a public or private high school? Constitutional protections have substantially less meaning at private

---

10. Oregon Revised Statutes § 336.477 (2009).

schools. The First Amendment is not considered an impediment at private high schools or private colleges and universities. A newspaper at a private school can be censored in just about any way imaginable. There is, however, one minor exception to this general rule. In particular, California has a statute known as the "Leonard Law" that applies First Amendment standards to private, secular high schools and to secondary schools; these private schools, in other words, are forbidden from violating students' First Amendment rights.[11] Although California is the only state to have such a law extending First Amendment rights to private school students, there is nothing to prevent legislative bodies in other states from drafting and approving similar legislation in the future.

The next question to ask when focusing on public schools is, "What kind of newspaper is it?" Three kinds of publications are possible:

- A school-sponsored newspaper, generally defined as a paper that uses the school's name and resources, has a faculty adviser and serves as a tool to teach knowledge or skills. Typically this kind of newspaper is produced as part of a journalism class.
- An unsupervised or student-controlled newspaper produced on the school's campus as an extracurricular activity.
- A student newspaper produced and distributed off campus.

The *Hazelwood* ruling spoke only to the first kind of newspaper. This type of paper can be most heavily censored. Most authorities agree that school officials have less power to censor the second kind of publication, and no power to censor the third kind of newspaper, unless students attempt to distribute it on campus. School administrators can ban the on-campus distribution of material produced elsewhere, and this authority provides them with a kind of informal censorship power if students seek to circulate the material on school property.

**STUDENT SPEECH RIGHTS ON THE WEB:
THE ISSUE THE SUPREME COURT MUST ADDRESS**

When students use their home computers, outside school and on their own time, to post Internet content that ridicules their teachers, administrators or classmates, can schools punish them without violating the First Amendment right of free speech? As of late 2017, the U.S. Supreme Court had not ruled on this issue, and lower courts were split on whether schools should have jurisdiction over such off-campus-created student expression. Only one thing appears fairly clear today: If a student who creates the off-campus, Internet-posted speech later downloads it or accesses it at school and shows it to other students while on campus, then the

---

11. California Education Code § 48950 (providing in relevant part that "school districts operating one or more high schools and private secondary schools shall not make or enforce any rule subjecting any high school pupil to disciplinary sanctions solely on the basis of conduct that is speech or other communication that, when engaged in outside of the campus, is protected from governmental restriction by the First Amendment to the United States Constitution").

school has jurisdiction and the *Tinker* standard typically applies. But some courts have held that schools can punish student-authors even if they never download the speech in school.

For instance, the 5th U.S. Circuit Court of Appeals ruled in 2015 that school officials did not violate the First Amendment speech rights of student Taylor Bell when they punished him for posting on Facebook and YouTube a profanity-laced rap recording. The rap, which Bell created while off campus and without using any school resources, accused two coaches at Itawamba Agricultural High School in Mississippi of sexually harassing several girls at the school. Rapping under the name T-Bizzle, Bell rapped, among other things, that one coach "took some girls in the locker room in PE / cut off the lights / you motherfucking freak / fucking with the youngins / because your pimpin game weak." The rap added, with violent overtones, that "you fucking with the wrong one / going to get a pistol down your mouth / Boww." Bell said he created the rap to call attention to the alleged sexual harassment.

In ruling for the school and against Bell, however, the 5th Circuit in *Bell* v. *Itawamba County School Board*[12] found that the rule from *Tinker* applied to the case because Bell intentionally directed the rap at the school community. Applying *Tinker*, the 5th Circuit concluded that "a substantial disruption reasonably could have been forecast" by school officials because the "rap pertained directly to events occurring at school, identified the two teachers by name, and was understood by one to threaten his safety and by neutral, third parties as threatening."

In late 2015, Taylor Bell filed a petition for a writ of certiorari asking the U.S. Supreme Court to hear his case. The Supreme Court, however, denied the petition in 2016, thus failing to clarify whether, in fact, school officials should have jurisdiction over student speech created off campus and during non-school hours.

The bottom line, as of late 2017, is that an increasing number of courts (although not all) are concluding that: 1) a public school *does* have jurisdiction to punish its students for their off-campus created speech posted online *if* the speech is directed at or otherwise targets other students or school officials; and 2) *Tinker*'s substantial-and-material disruption standard supplies the correct test for determining if punishment in any given case is justified.

The **Bethel** *Case*

In addition to the tests created in the *Tinker* and *Hazelwood* rulings, the U.S. Supreme Court prior to 2007 had considered the speech rights of public high school students in one other case. In particular, the court held in 1986 in *Bethel School District* v. *Fraser*[13] that officials at Bethel High School in Pierce County, Wash., did not violate the free-speech rights of student Matthew Fraser when they suspended him for making a sexually suggestive speech nominating a classmate for student government at an assembly packed

12. 799 F. 3d 379 (5th Cir. 2015), cert. den., 194 L. Ed. 2d 240 (2016).
13. 478 U.S. 675 (1986).

with 600 students. Although he did not use profanity, the sexual innuendos were clear to some students in the audience who "hooted and yelled" (other students, conversely, were "bewildered and embarrassed") when Fraser said:

> Jeff Kuhlman is a man who takes his point and pounds it in. If necessary, he'll take an issue and nail it to the wall. He doesn't attack things in spurts—he drives hard, pushing and pushing until finally—he succeeds. Jeff is a man who will go to the very end—even the climax, for each and every one of you.

In rejecting Fraser's First Amendment argument, the majority of the Supreme Court refused to apply the *Tinker* substantial-and-material-disruption standard, noting what it called a "marked distinction between the political 'message' of the armbands in *Tinker* and the sexual content" of Fraser's talk, as well as the fact that the speech in *Tinker* was "passive expression" (it was an armband) while Fraser's speech was actively spoken to a captive audience of students gathered for the assembly. Having thus distinguished *Tinker*, the court in *Fraser* held that schools can punish students who use "offensively lewd and indecent speech" that is "unrelated to any political viewpoint" because

- such expression "would undermine the school's basic educational mission";
- "it is a highly appropriate function of public school education to prohibit the use of vulgar and offensive terms in public discourse"; and
- society has an interest "in teaching students the boundaries of socially appropriate behavior."

In addition to these rationales for allowing the school's punishment of Matthew Fraser, the majority reasoned that "by glorifying male sexuality, and in its verbal content, the speech was acutely insulting to teenage girl students."

The bottom line is that, prior to 2007, there was a trilogy of Supreme Court cases (*Tinker*, *Hazelwood* and *Bethel*), each with its own rules and guidelines, that public schools may use to squelch the speech rights of students. They are summarized in the following box.

THREE KEY SCHOOL-SPEECH CASES PRIOR TO 2007

1. *Tinker:* School officials may regulate speech that they reasonably believe will materially and substantially disrupt or interfere with classwork, educational activities and/or discipline.
2. *Hazelwood:* Schools may regulate speech that is school sponsored and/or that is part of the school curriculum, so long as the censorship is reasonably related to legitimate pedagogical (i.e., teaching and learning) concerns.
3. *Bethel:* Schools may regulate sexually offensive speech that is lewd, vulgar or indecent (they also can regulate obscene speech since it is without any First Amendment protection [see Chapter 13]; *Fraser*'s language about speech that "would undermine the school's basic educational mission" also is used successfully by some schools to ban images and ads for drugs, tobacco and alcohol).

In reality, many student-speech cases do not fit squarely into any of the three Supreme Court precedents described in the box. For instance, a case may be a hybrid of political content and drug-related imagery (a T-shirt showing a pot leaf and the accompanying message, "Vote Yes on Proposition 42: Legalize Marijuana"). Lower courts in these situations are forced to try to find the precedent that comes the closest, factually speaking, to the issue at hand.

"I ♥ BOOBIES! (KEEP A BREAST)": MAKING A FEDERAL CASE OVER BRACELETS

In 2013, several federal courts considered if public schools could lawfully ban students from wearing breast cancer awareness bracelets bearing the slogan "I ♥ Boobies! (Keep A Breast)." Some schools asserted authority to ban the bracelets under the Supreme Court's precedent in *Bethel School District* v. *Fraser*, arguing that the word "boobies" is sexually lewd and vulgar. They added that the phrase "I ♥ Boobies!" is an impermissible double entendre about sexual attraction to breasts.

Students, however, countered that the entire message is far more political, providing an effective, yet fun, way of raising awareness of breast cancer. In other words, they argued that "boobies" is not lewd or vulgar when used in conjunction with the other words on the bracelets. They thus claimed the First Amendment protected wearing the bracelets to school.

The 3rd U.S. Circuit Court of Appeals concluded in August 2013 in *B.H.* v. *Easton Area School District* that students had a First Amendment right to wear the bracelets, finding that "the bracelets here are not plainly lewd" under *Fraser* and adding that the school district "failed to show that the bracelets threatened to substantially disrupt the school under *Tinker*." In 2014, the U.S. Supreme Court rejected the school's petition for a writ of certiorari, thus leaving the students' victory and the 3rd Circuit's ruling intact. Should the age of the students—middle schoolers rather than high schoolers—make a difference in how the court decides the case? What do you think about the ban on such bracelets in public schools?

The Morse *Case*

In 2007, the U.S. Supreme Court heard a student-speech case called *Morse* v. *Frederick*. In this dispute, known as the "Bong Hits 4 Jesus" case, the 9th U.S. Circuit Court of Appeals ruled in 2006 that the First Amendment protected a student's right to unfurl, while standing on a sidewalk across the street from his high school as an Olympic torch relay passed by, a banner emblazoned with that drug-related catchphrase.[14] The students at Juneau-Douglas High School in Alaska had permission to be on the sidewalk during the relay and were under teacher supervision. While student Joseph Frederick claimed the "Bong Hits 4 Jesus" language was meaningless, funny and done in order to get on television, Principal Deborah Morse did not find it amusing and considered it a pro-drug message in conflict with the school's "basic educational mission to promote a healthy, drug-free life style." Frederick's banner was taken down and he was suspended for 10 days.

14. *Frederick v. Morse*, 439 F. 3d 1114 (9th Cir. 2006).

In ruling for Frederick, the 9th Circuit applied the *Tinker* standard. Noting there was no substantial and material disruption of educational activities caused by Frederick's banner, the 9th Circuit focused on the fact that the school conceded the banner "was censored only because it conflicted with the school's 'mission' of discouraging drug use."

The school petitioned the U.S. Supreme Court to hear the case and to reverse the 9th Circuit's opinion. The school was represented by Ken Starr, the former independent counsel who investigated Bill Clinton's affair with Monica Lewinsky. Starr asked the nation's high court to consider the following question:

> *Whether the First Amendment allows public schools to prohibit students from displaying messages promoting the use of illegal substances at school-sponsored, faculty-supervised events.*

The Supreme Court ruled in 2007, holding that the First Amendment rights of Joseph Frederick were not violated. Writing for a five-member majority of the court, Chief Justice John Roberts explained that "schools may take steps to safeguard those entrusted to their care from speech that can reasonably be regarded as encouraging illegal drug use. We conclude that the school officials in this case did not violate the First Amendment by confiscating the pro-drug banner and suspending the student responsible for it." Roberts rejected the idea that the banner constituted political speech, writing that "this is plainly not a case about political debate over the criminalization of drug use or possession."[15] The long-term impact of this decision in *Morse* remains to be seen, but the ruling itself was very narrow and limited. It is important to note that the court in *Morse* did not overrule *Tinker*, *Hazelwood* or *Bethel*; those decisions remain intact. The *Morse* opinion is limited in scope to nonpolitical speech that advocates or celebrates the use of illegal drugs.

Unfortunately for advocates of student-speech rights, some courts are stretching the Supreme Court's ruling in *Morse* far beyond its narrow facts about nonpolitical speech advocating illegal drug use. Just six months after *Morse*, the 5th U.S. Circuit Court of Appeals interpreted *Morse* to stand for a broad, pro-censorship principle—that "speech advocating a harm that is demonstrably grave and that derives that gravity from the 'special danger' to the physical safety of students arising from the school environment is unprotected."[16] The 5th Circuit held in *Ponce* v. *Socorro Independent School District* that a "*Morse* analysis is appropriate"—rather than the traditional and more rigorous substantial-and-material disruption standard from the high court's ruling in *Tinker*—when the student speech at issue "threatens a Columbine-style attack on a school." As the 5th Circuit wrote in holding that *Morse* can be used to squelch and punish not just speech that advocates illegal drug use, but also student speech that threatens mass violence:

> If school administrators are permitted to prohibit student speech that advocates illegal drug use because "illegal drug use presents a grave and in many ways unique threat to the physical safety of students" . . . then it defies logical extrapolation to hold school administrators to a stricter standard with respect to speech that gravely and uniquely threatens violence, including massive deaths, to the school population as a whole.

15. *Morse* v. *Frederick*, 551 U.S. 393 (2007).
16. *Ponce* v. *Socorro Independent School District*, 508 F. 3d 765, 770 (5th Cir. 2007).

CENSORSHIP OF COLLEGE NEWSPAPERS

The Supreme Court in *Hazelwood* did not decide whether its "reasonably related to legitimate pedagogical concerns" test applied to college newspapers. In fact, it wrote, "We need not now decide whether the same degree of deference is appropriate with respect to school-sponsored expressive activities at the college and university level." Since then, two federal appellate court decisions have addressed censorship by university officials of student-run publications:

- *Kincaid* v. *Gibson*[17]
- *Hosty* v. *Carter*[18]

The first case suggests that the federal courts are reluctant to expand the censorial powers of college administrators via *Hazelwood*. In 2001 the 6th U.S. Court of Appeals ruled that when administrators at Kentucky State University refused to permit the distribution of the school's yearbook because they didn't approve of its content and the color of its cover, they violated the First Amendment rights of the students at the school. But the 10-3 ruling was based largely on the fact that the creation of the yearbook was not a classroom activity in which students are assigned a grade. The yearbook was a designated public forum (see pages 118–119) created by the university to exist in an atmosphere of free and responsible discussion and intellectual exploration, the court said. What the school officials did was clearly censorship. "There is little if any difference between hiding from public view the words and pictures students use to portray their college experience, and forcing students to publish a state-sponsored script. In either case, the government alters student expression by obliterating it," Judge R. Guy Cole wrote. But in reality, the court had merely distinguished the production of the yearbook from the classroom-generated newspaper in *Hazelwood*.

A more disturbing, disappointing and important federal appellate court decision affecting the college press was handed down in 2005 in *Hosty* v. *Carter*. The *Hosty* case centered on demands by university administrators in 2000 for prior review and approval—a classic prior restraint on speech, in other words—of the *Innovator*, the student-run newspaper at Governors State University, located south of Chicago. The *Innovator* had previously published articles under the byline of student Margaret Hosty that were critical of a school official, sparking the confrontation.

A major issue in the resulting lawsuit was whether the legitimate-pedagogical-concerns standard articulated by the U.S. Supreme Court in the *Hazelwood* case for controlling the censorship of school-sponsored, high school newspapers that are part of the curriculum is also applicable to college newspapers.

In *Hosty*, the student-journalist plaintiffs argued that *Hazelwood*'s legitimate-pedagogical-concerns standard was never made applicable to the college press, and they contended that university administrators cannot ever insist that student newspapers be submitted for review and approval. But by a 7-4 vote, the U.S. 7th Circuit Court of Appeals rejected these contentions and rebuffed the idea that there is a bright-line difference

17. 236 F. 3d 342 (6th Cir. 2001).
18. 412 F. 3d 731 (7th Cir. 2005), cert. den., 126 S. Ct. 1330 (2006).

between high school and college newspapers. The 7th Circuit wrote that the Supreme Court's footnote in *Hazelwood* "does not even hint at the possibility of an on/off switch: high school papers reviewable, college papers not reviewable." It added that "whether *some* review is possible depends on the answer to the public-forum question, which does not (automatically) vary with the speakers' age." The key in *Hosty*, then, was whether the student newspaper constituted a public forum. Whether a particular physical venue or location constitutes a public forum for purposes of First Amendment speech protection is discussed later in this chapter (see pages 118–123). Writing for the seven-judge majority in *Hosty*, Judge Frank Easterbrook articulated a rule that "speech at a non-public forum, and underwritten at public expense, may be open to reasonable regulation even at the college level."

Thus, for the majority of the 7th Circuit, "*Hazelwood*'s first question therefore remains our principal question as well: was the reporter a speaker in a public forum (no censorship allowed?) or did the University either create a non-public forum or publish the paper itself (a closed forum where content may be supervised)?" This meant that the appellate court had to examine the status of the particular student newspaper at issue in *Hosty*, namely the *Innovator*, to determine whether or not it was a public forum. The court noted that if the *Innovator* "operated in a public forum, the University could not vet its contents." The appellate court, unfortunately, held that it was not possible on the record in front of it to determine what kind of forum Governors State University had established with the *Innovator*. The court did, however, provide some guidance on this for the future, noting among other things that

- while "being part of the curriculum may be a *sufficient* condition of a non-public forum, it is not a *necessary* condition. Extracurricular activities may be outside any public forum . . . without also falling outside all university governance [emphasis added]." In other words, just because a college newspaper is an extracurricular activity and not part of the curriculum does not mean that it necessarily escapes all university control or regulation; and
- "a school may declare the pages of the student newspaper open for expression and thus disable itself from engaging in viewpoint or content discrimination while the terms on which the forum operates remain unaltered."

Another important factor in the public forum determination of a university newspaper is whether the university underwrote and subsidized the newspaper without any strings attached or, conversely, whether it "hedge[d] the funding with controls that left the University itself as the newspaper's publisher."

What does all of this mean for college newspapers? First, it's important to remember that the decision is binding in only the three states that comprise the 7th Circuit Court of Appeals—Illinois, Indiana and Wisconsin (see page 28 for a map of the federal appellate court circuits). Second, many college newspapers, such as the *Alligator* at the University of Florida, are independent of the universities that their student-journalists attend and are not directly funded by the university. In an official press release on the *Hosty* decision, Mark Goodman, former executive director of the Student Press Law Center that had filed a friend-of-the-court brief in the case, stated:

As a practical matter, most college student newspapers are going to be considered designated public forums and entitled to the strongest First Amendment protection because that's the way they've been operating for decades. But this decision gives college administrators ammunition to argue that many traditionally independent student activities are subject to school censorship.

In 2006, California became the first state to pass so-called anti-*Hosty* legislation after the U.S. Supreme Court refused earlier that year to hear the *Hosty* case. California's law prohibits state public university officials from making and enforcing rules "subjecting any student to disciplinary sanction solely on the basis of conduct that is speech or other communication that, when engaged in outside a campus of those institutions, is protected from governmental restriction by the First Amendment."[19] In brief, the law prohibits prior restraints and censorship by university administrators (officials, for instance, in the University of California and California State University systems) of public college and university newspapers. This, in turn, means that the *Hazelwood* rule cannot apply to the public collegiate press in California; instead, college newspapers in the Golden State must be treated like real-world professional newspapers such as the *Los Angeles Times* and the *San Francisco Chronicle*.

Some courts, unfortunately, still apply *Hazelwood*'s "reasonably related to legitimate pedagogical concerns" standard in university settings. For instance, in 2012 the 6th U.S. Circuit Court of Appeals in *Ward* v. *Polite*[20] considered whether Eastern Michigan University had violated the First Amendment rights of graduate student Julea Ward. Ward claimed she was expelled from the university's counseling program because some professors objected to her expression of her religious viewpoints and beliefs. In holding that *Hazelwood* supplied the proper standard to determine if Ward's free-speech rights were violated, the 6th Circuit acknowledged that *Hazelwood* stemmed from a high school case, but it then added that *Hazelwood* "works for students who have graduated from high school. The key word is student. *Hazelwood* respects the latitude educational institutions—at any level—must have to further legitimate curricular objectives. All educators must be able 'to assure that participants learn whatever lessons the activity is designed to teach.'" The appellate court added that "[n]othing in *Hazelwood* suggests a stop-go distinction between student speech at the high school and university levels, and we decline to create one." The *Ward* decision is binding only in the 6th Circuit, which includes the states of Kentucky, Michigan, Ohio and Tennessee.

Problems for College Journalists

What kinds of censorship problems affect the college press? Getting access to information is one problem. Student-journalists often have difficulty gaining access to reports on faculty performance, student government meetings and school disciplinary hearings. It is not uncommon for a college to reject the criminal prosecution of a student apprehended for a minor crime, and instead punish the student through a disciplinary proceeding. The criminal trial would be open to the public and the press; disciplinary hearings are routinely closed. Hence, no bad publicity for the school. Campus administrators have even

19. California Education Code § 66301. Illinois adopted a similar law in 2007.
20. 667 F.3d 727 (6th Cir. 2012).

attempted to bar all reporters from access to university police reports, citing the Family Educational Rights and Privacy Act (FERPA; see Chapter 9), which limits the public access to most student records. School officials have argued—unsuccessfully—that crime reports that name students as victims, perpetrators or even witnesses are educational records and hence inaccessible under this law. If the press can't see the official police reports, stories about the incident generally won't be written. The courts have rejected this interpretation of the law.[21]

For instance, in 2016 the attorney general of Kentucky criticized the University of Kentucky for refusing to hand over documents both to UK's student-run newspaper and then to the attorney general himself. The newspaper, the *Kentucky Kernel*, submitted an open-records request to the university for records related to graduate students' sexual harassment accusations against a faculty member at the school. The university denied the request. When the newspaper appealed the university's denial to the attorney general, he requested copies of the documents in order to substantiate the university's decision. But, citing FERPA, the university denied his request too and "unlawfully withheld the requested documents," the attorney general wrote in a motion he filed seeking a court order to force the university to turn over the documents to his office. UK then sued the newspaper in an attempt to overturn the attorney general's ruling. In early 2017, a state court in Kentucky ruled in favor of the school. The newspaper, with the support of the attorney general, vowed to appeal the decision.

In another example, in 2016 a Florida trial court ruled against the University of Central Florida in its battle to keep documents out of the hands of a student news outlet. *The Knight News* had requested from the university unredacted student government association budget records, including payments made to student government officers that came from student activity fees. The judge in the case rejected the university's argument that those records could be withheld as "education records" under FERPA. "If a student or parent requested that student's records as intended by FERPA, it is almost certain that that student or parent would not receive a copy of the requested Budget forms and Database records merely because the subject student's name appeared somewhere in those documents," Judge John Jordan wrote in his opinion. A Florida appeals court upheld Judge Jordan's ruling in June 2017.

Under a federal law called the Clery Act (named for a Lehigh University student raped and killed in her dorm in 1986), all colleges and universities that participate in federal student-aid programs are required to give timely warnings of campus crimes that represent a threat to the safety of students and/or employees and to make public their campus security policies. The law also mandates that colleges and universities collect data and statistics on a number of specific crimes and then report that information to the campus community on an annual basis. These data obviously can help student-journalists in reporting on problems on their campuses. One major problem with the law is that it does not define what constitutes a timely warning. In light of shooting tragedies in recent years at Virginia Tech and Northern Illinois University, such warnings are of obvious

---

21. See *Student Press Law Center* v. *Alexander,* 778 F. Supp. 1227 (1991); and *Ohio ex rel The Miami Student* v. *Miami University,* 79 Ohio St. 3d 168 (1997).

importance. Due in part to these terrible events, the Clery Act was amended in 2008 to require campus authorities "to immediately notify the campus community upon the confirmation of a significant emergency or dangerous situation involving an immediate threat to the health or safety of students or staff occurring on the campus."

A FAILURE TO TIMELY WARN OF DANGER: THE VIRGINIA TECH MASSACRE

Seung-Hui Cho, a student at Virginia Tech University in Blacksburg, Va., shot and killed two students in a dormitory at 7:15 in the morning on April 16, 2007. Campus police quickly discovered the shooting at 7:24 a.m. Cho, however, remained on the loose, and he continued his on-campus rampage, ultimately killing 32 students before taking his own life. Virginia Tech officials took more than two hours before they finally sent an e-mail at 9:26 a.m. warning students, faculty and staff about the shootings.

More than three years later, the U.S. Department of Education concluded that Virginia Tech failed to adequately warn students that day and violated the Clery Act. The report, released in December 2010, found that "the warnings that were issued by the University were not prepared or disseminated in a manner to give clear and timely notice of the threat to the health and safety of campus community members" and, to make matters even worse, that "Virginia Tech did not follow its own policy for the issuance of timely warnings as published in its annual campus security reports."

In April 2014, after a protracted battle with the U.S. Department of Education and seven years after the campus shooting, Virginia Tech paid a fine of $32,500, thus closing the case against it. The $32,500 total included $27,500 for failing to timely warn and $5,000 for incorrectly stating warning policies.

In 2013, the Department of Education fined Yale University $165,000 under the Clery Act for, among other things, failing to report four forcible sex offenses, dating back to 2001 and 2002, in its annual campus crime statistics. An April 2013 letter to Yale President Richard Levin from the DOE stated that although Yale corrected its reports in 2004 after being notified of the problem, "the correction of violations does not diminish the seriousness of not correctly reporting these incidents at the time they occurred." While Yale is a private institution, it nonetheless participates in federal student-aid programs and thus is subject to the Clery Act.

In 2011, the U.S. Department of Education opened a massive investigation into Penn State's compliance with the Clery Act in light of the sexual abuse scandal at Pennsylvania State University focusing on accusations against former assistant football coach and convicted child molester Jerry Sandusky. The investigation looked at the university's compliance from 1998 to 2011 because the allegations of abuse covered that 14-year span. In November 2016, Penn State agreed to pay a record $2.4 million fine for failing to comply with the Clery Act. According to the U.S. Department of Education, the fine covered 11 serious findings of Clery Act noncompliance related to the university's handling of Sandusky's crimes as well as the university's long-standing failure to comply with federal requirements on campus safety and substance abuse. Interestingly, only $27,500 of the fine directly stemmed from the Sandusky matter. Failure to properly classify reported incidents and disclose crime statistics from 2008-2011 resulted in the bulk of the fine ($2,167,500).

In June 2012, Education Secretary Duncan ordered Tarleton State University, a public institution of higher education in Texas, to pay $110,000 for failing to report three forcible sex offenses and a robbery. Each of the four violations individually cost the university $27,500. Duncan furthermore asked an administrative law judge to determine the amount of a possible additional fine for 70 nonviolent crimes that also went unreported. Ultimately, Tarleton State University agreed to pay a total fine of $123,500 in July 2012 to settle the matter with the Department of Education.

In October 2012, the Department of Education increased the maximum fine for a single instance of a violation of the Clery Act to $35,000 (up from the $27,500 established in 2002) to adjust for inflation.

HOW MUCH CRIME OCCURS ON YOUR CAMPUS?

Student journalists (as well as anyone else) can locate data about crime on their campus by visiting a Web site hosted by the Office of Postsecondary Education of the U.S. Department of Education. The Web site, known as the Campus Security Data Analysis Cutting Tool, is a clearinghouse for data collected under the Clery Act. You can find it at http://ope.ed.gov/security.

The theft of all the issues of a single edition of a newspaper by those who disagree with the material published in the paper is a problem on some campuses. Campus police usually claim they are powerless to pursue the thieves, since, because the student newspapers are free, no law has been broken.

And therein lies the problem of quite literally stealing "free" speech: How can one steal something if it is free? In fact, only three states—California, Colorado and Maryland—have statutes specifically aimed to penalize the theft of free newspapers. California's law provides that a person can be fined $250 on a first offense for taking more than 25 copies of a free or complimentary newspaper if done so with the intent to "deprive others of the opportunity to read or enjoy the newspaper."[22]

Because only three states have statutes targeting the theft of free newspapers, incidents of newspaper theft on college campuses are rampant today. The SPLC tracks and describes the incidents from a link on its Web site at http://www.splc.org/page/newspaper-theft-resources and provides a helpful "Newspaper Theft Checklist" of strategies and advice for college newspaper journalists at http://www.splc.org/page/newspaper-theft-checklist.

---

22. California Penal Code § 490.7 (2009).

For instance, the SPLC reported that hundreds of copies of student newspapers were stolen at universities in Florida, Massachusetts and Oregon after a string of thefts took place in March 2016. In one example, Florida Atlantic University's student newspaper, the *University Press*, had reported on a sexual assault that allegedly occurred at a party near campus the previous year. The article explored the party's connections to Greek life on campus. The paper's editor-in-chief reported that within hours of the paper's distribution, nearly 300 issues of the paper had been trashed, and by the next morning, nearly 700 issues had been taken out of bins and thrown away. When a photographer on staff witnessed two women throwing away an issue, he snapped their picture. One of the women grabbed his arm and told him that her "sorority sisters would beat him up" if he didn't delete the photo. The editor-in-chief, Emily Bloch, told the SPLC that she considered the thefts a form of censorship, but that the actions wouldn't deter the paper from reporting on contentious issues in the future. "If anything, what happened will make us pursue controversial stories more fiercely," she said.

One month earlier, in February 2016, more than 4,000 copies of the student newspaper went missing at Coastal Carolina University. The Feb. 24 issue of the paper had incorrectly reported that a fraternity chapter on campus was under investigation for sexual assault and hazing. The paper later issued a correction clarifying that the university had suspended the chapter due to complaints of hazing but that the university did not investigate the fraternity for sexual assault. After the Feb. 24 issue was published, though, the paper's editor-in-chief told the SPLC that the staff noticed that papers had been cleaned out from newspaper stands at various buildings on campus. The editor-in-chief estimated the cost of the missing papers to be between $3,000 and $4,500. The university's department of public safety identified one man involved in taking the newspapers and was pursuing two others.

Finally, attempts to censor college newspapers indirectly, by reducing or even ending their funding, have generally failed. In 1983 the 8th U.S. Court of Appeals handed down an important ruling that still represents the state of the law,[23] more than 30 years later. The case began in the late 1970s when the University of Minnesota *Daily* published a year-end edition containing content that, according to one university faculty member, offended Third World students, blacks, Jews, feminists, gays, lesbians and Christians.[24] In the wake of complaints from students and off-campus readers, the university regents embarked on a plan to cut the funding for the newspaper. The plan was to allow students to decide whether or not to contribute $2 each semester to fund the newspaper. The $2 fee had automatically gone to the newspaper in the past. Two university review committees advised the regents the plan was a bad idea, but it was adopted nevertheless. Before the vote many of the regents publicly stated they favored the plan because students should not be forced to support a newspaper that was "sacrilegious and vulgar."

A lawsuit followed the decision, and the appellate court ruled the move by the regents violated the First Amendment. A reduction in or even the elimination of fees is certainly permissible, the court said, so long as it is not done for the wrong reasons. But there was ample evidence in this case, the court said, that the reduction was

23. *Stanley* v. *McGrath,* 719 F. 2d 279 (1983).
24. Gillmor, "The Fragile First."

enacted to punish the newspaper. As such it was an attempt at censorship. The court cited the negative comments about the newspaper by the regents during consideration of the plan, as well as the fact that the change was not made at other University of Minnesota campuses (which are governed by the same board of regents), only the Twin Cities campus, home of the offending newspaper, as evidence of the punitive nature of the new policy. "Reducing the revenues available to the newspaper is therefore forbidden by the First Amendment," the court concluded.

In June 2016, a satirical student newspaper at the University of California, San Diego, sued the school, claiming the student council there violated the paper's First Amendment rights by eliminating funding for student print media on campus. According to the Student Press Law Center, the newspaper, called *The Koala*, is "known for its offensive and vulgar mockery of issues like ethnicity, religion, rape, and people with illnesses and disabilities." In November 2015, the paper published an article that used several racial slurs and mocked students' desire for safe spaces on campus. Two days later, administrators issued a statement condemning the paper, and that same day the student council voted to cut funding for all student print media outlets on campus. The paper sued, represented by the ACLU, arguing that the defunding was motivated by disagreement with the paper's content. The legal director of the ACLU of San Diego said in a statement, "However offensive and outrageous *The Koala* may be, its authors are writing about topical issues of public concern. No matter how offended I may be, it is still much worse to give government the power to decide what speech to censor. Once granted, that power will inevitably stifle protest and dissent." But in March 2017, a district court judge in California dismissed the lawsuit, ruling that the student council did not violate the First Amendment since all print media outlets were defunded, not just *The Koala*. The ACLU of San Diego said *The Koala* planned to appeal the decision.

Alcohol Advertisements and the College Press

In 1996, Pennsylvania adopted a law known as Act 199. The law prohibited the paid dissemination of alcoholic beverage advertising in college newspapers.[25] After Act 199 became law, the Pennsylvania Liquor Control Board issued an advisory notice clarifying how the law applied to universities and the collegiate press. The notice stated:

> Advertisements which indicate the availability and/or price of alcoholic beverages may not be contained in publications published by, for and in behalf of any educational institutions. Universities are considered educational institutions under this section. Thus, an advertisement in a college newspaper or a college football program announcing beverages would not be permissible.

What does this statement mean? Under this law, an advertisement paid for by a local bar in State College, Pa., and placed in the student newspaper at the Pennsylvania State University, the *Daily Collegian*, that described the availability and/or price of beer at the bar during happy hours would not be permissible. The student newspaper at the University of Pittsburgh, the *Pitt News*, decided to challenge the law on First Amendment grounds because the *Pitt News*, like the *Daily Collegian*, had received a substantial

25. 47 Pennsylvania Statutes Annotated § 4-498 (2004).

portion of its advertising revenue from alcoholic beverage ads prior to the enactment of Act 199. But in 1998 alone, the *Pitt News* lost $17,000 in advertising revenue because of the law.

Pennsylvania, in contrast, argued that the law was necessary to curb both underage drinking (although many college students and all faculty are of at least the legal drinking age of 21) and binge drinking/alcohol abuse. The theory on the latter interest apparently was that if students didn't know where the cheap beer was being served because they couldn't find advertisements for it in college newspapers, then they wouldn't drink as much.

In 2004, however, the U.S. Court of Appeals for the 3rd Circuit held in *Pitt News* v. *Pappert* that Act 199 violated the First Amendment rights of the *Pitt News* and, by implication, other college newspapers in Pennsylvania.[26] The appellate court ruled that the law was "an impermissible restriction on commercial speech" (see Chapter 15 and the *Central Hudson* test for commercial speech) and that it was presumptively unconstitutional because it targeted a too narrow segment of the media—newspapers affiliated with colleges and universities—and thus conflicted with U.S. Supreme Court precedent on taxation of the press. The appellate court observed that Pennsylvania "has not pointed to any evidence that eliminating ads in this narrow sector [of the media] will do any good. Even if Pitt students do not see alcoholic beverage ads in the Pitt News, they will still be exposed to a torrent of beer ads on television and the radio, and they will still see alcoholic beverage ads in other publications, including the other free weekly Pittsburgh papers that are displayed on campus together with the *Pitt News*." The appellate court added that "in contending that underage and abusive drinking will fall if alcoholic beverage ads are eliminated from just those media affiliated with educational institutions, the Commonwealth relies on nothing more than 'speculation' and 'conjecture.'" The court suggested that rather than restricting the First Amendment speech and press rights of college newspapers, the "most direct way to combat underage and abusive drinking by college students is the enforcement of the alcoholic beverage control laws on college campuses."

Nearly a decade later, the 4th U.S. Circuit Court of Appeals in 2013 declared unconstitutional a very similar Virginia statute in *Educational Media Co.* v. *Insley*.[27] The Virginia statute barred college newspapers in the Old Dominion State from running alcohol advertisements. The Virginia Alcoholic Beverage Control Board claimed the law was necessary "to combat underage and abusive college drinking."

Just as the 3rd Circuit did in Pennsylvania in the *Pitt News* case described above, the 4th Circuit in *Insley* concluded that Virginia's statute imposed an unconstitutional burden on truthful commercial speech under the *Central Hudson* test (again, see Chapter 15 and the *Central Hudson* test for commercial speech). Specifically, the 4th Circuit determined the statute was not narrowly tailored under the last part of the *Central Hudson* test because the statute "prohibits large numbers of adults who are 21 years of age or older from receiving truthful information about a product that they are legally allowed to consume." In other words, there was not a "reasonable

---

26. *Pitt News v. Pappert*, 379 F. 3d 96 (3d Cir. 2004).
27. 731 F. 3d 291 (4th Cir. 2013).

fit" between the twin goals of combating underage and abusive drinking, on the one hand, and the sweep or reach of the statute, on the other. In brief, while the goal of combating underage drinking was substantial and important (and thus satisfied this aspect of the *Central Hudson* test), the statute kept many readers of lawful drinking age in the dark about truthful information (and thus failed the "reasonable fit" requirement of *Central Hudson*).

BOOK BANNING

In 2013, the Thomas Jefferson Center for the Protection of Free Expression gave a "Muzzle Award" for censorship to the Annville-Cleona School Board in Pennsylvania. Why? Because the board, as the Jefferson Center explained, removed an award-winning children's picture storybook called *The Dirty Cowboy* from its elementary school library after one student's parents complained. The parents apparently objected to colorful illustrations depicting a cowboy's efforts to reclaim his clothes after they were taken away by a dog as the cowboy bathed in a river. Although the cowboy is depicted without his clothes, the book shows no nudity, as the illustrations cleverly obscure his genitalia with items such as a boot and a flock of birds.

In 2016, a teacher in Lebanon, Ky., fought to keep John Green's *Looking for Alaska*, a coming-of-age work of fiction, in the curriculum of her high school senior-level English class. Although Green's best-selling novel has won literary awards, the American Library Association (ALA) reported that it led the ALA's list of most frequently challenged books in 2015 and was on the list again in 2016. The book has been banned from assigned classroom reading lists in several schools, with charges that it is sexually explicit, contains offensive language and is unsuitable for high school audiences. In Lebanon, the teacher sent home a permission slip, giving parents the option, if they wanted, to keep their child from reading the book; those students would be assigned an alternative book instead. One parent chose that option, but that parent evidently also thought that other students shouldn't be reading Green's novel too, so she filed a complaint, alleging that *Looking for Alaska* would tempt students "to experiment with pornography, sex, drugs, alcohol and profanity." The teacher, buoyed by support from groups such as the National Coalition Against Censorship's Kids' Right to Read Project, American Booksellers for Free Expression, the Association of American Publishers and the National Council of Teachers of English, challenged the complaint, and a school review committee ultimately voted that she could keep the book in her curriculum.

In 2015, *The Curious Incident of the Dog in the Night-Time*, Mark Haddon's award-winning book about a 15-year-old autistic child who investigates the death of a neighbor's dog, was pulled as a summer reading assignment at Lincoln High School in Tallahassee, Fla. The principal had received complaints about the book's language, which includes profanity and "taking God's name in vain." For instance, one parent who complained told the *Tallahassee Democrat*, "I am not interested in having books banned. But to have that language and to take the name of Christ in vain—I don't go for that," she said. "As a Christian, and as a female, I was offended ... I know it's not realistic to pretend bad words don't exist, but it is my responsibility as a parent to make sure that my daughter knows what is right or wrong."

As noted, the American Library Association keeps tabs on what it calls the "most challenged" books in the United States. The ALA defines a challenged book as one against which a formal, written complaint has been filed with a library or school requesting it be removed due to content or appropriateness. Among the 10 most challenged books in the United States in 2016—in addition to *Looking for Alaska*—were modern titles such as *This One Summer, I Am Jazz* and *George*. Overall, the ALA's Office for Intellectual Freedom received 323 reports of attempts to remove or restrict materials from school curricula and library bookshelves in 2016.

When it comes to removing books from public school libraries, the only U.S. Supreme Court opinion on point is an aging 1982 case called *Board of Education* v. *Pico*.[28] Unfortunately, there was no majority opinion in *Pico* (there were seven separate opinions) as the Court addressed the issue of whether a school board could constitutionally remove from a public school library books by the likes of Kurt Vonnegut and Langston Hughes that it characterized as "Anti-American, Anti-Christian, Anti-Sem[i]tic, and just plain filthy." There was, however, a plurality opinion (see page 25) holding that "local school boards may not remove books from school library shelves simply because they dislike the ideas contained in those books and seek by their removal to 'prescribe what shall be orthodox in politics, nationalism, religion, or other matters of opinion.'" The plurality opinion noted that school boards

> rightly possess significant discretion to determine the content of their school libraries. But that discretion may not be exercised in a narrowly partisan or political manner. If a Democratic school board, motivated by party affiliation, ordered the removal of all books written by or in favor of Republicans, few would doubt that the order violated the constitutional rights of the students denied access to those books. . . . Our Constitution does not permit the official suppression of ideas. Thus whether [the school board's] removal of books from their school libraries denied [students'] their First Amendment rights depends upon the motivation behind [the school board's] actions.

In contrast to unconstitutional justifications for removing books from school libraries based upon dislike of the ideas and political viewpoints in them, the plurality wrote that it would be okay to remove books if done so "based solely upon the 'educational suitability' of the books in question" or if the books were "pervasively vulgar." The court thus suggested that motivation of a school board in removing a book is key in determining whether its removal violates the First Amendment rights of minors to access the ideas in the book.

The guidelines from *Pico* were applied in 2006 by a federal court in Florida in *ACLU of Florida* v. *Miami-Dade County School Board*.[29] The dispute centered not on pervasive vulgarity, but on the removal from school libraries of particular books, targeting children from 4 to 8 years old, about Cuba and life in that island nation. The school removed the books after a parent complained they were "untruthful" and portrayed "a life in Cuba that does not exist." As U.S. District Court Judge Alan S. Gold wrote, the "heart of the argument is that the Cuba books omit the harsh truth about totalitarian life in Communist Cuba."

28. 457 U.S. 853 (1982).
29. 439 F. Supp. 2d 1242 (S.D. Fla. 2006).

In ruling against the school board and in ordering it to immediately replace the Cuba books, the judge wrote that "[s]ignificant weight must be given to the board's failure to consider, much less adopt, the recommendations of the two previous committees, and that of the school superintendent, to leave the Cuba books on the library shelves because they were educationally suitable." Recall that in *Pico* the Supreme Court wrote that school boards could legitimately remove books from libraries if they did so based upon concerns about "educational suitability." This case, however, was different, as Judge Gold reasoned:

> The majority of the Miami-Dade County School Board members intended by their removal of the books to deny schoolchildren access to ideas or points-of-view with which the school officials disagreed, and that this intent was the decisive factor in their removal decision. In so acting, the School Board abused its discretion in a manner that violated the transcendent imperatives of the First Amendment.

In 2009, however, the 11th U.S. Circuit Court of Appeals reversed Judge Gold's opinion with a split 2-1 decision and, in so doing, it allowed the school board to remove the contested book, *Vamos a Cuba*, from its libraries.[30] The two-judge majority initially noted there was no majority opinion in the Supreme Court's *Pico* ruling, and thus it observed that "the question of what standard applies to school library book removal decisions is unresolved" and "we have no need to resolve it here." But in ruling in favor of the school board, the 11th Circuit majority adopted the school board's position that its motive for removing the book was not based on any improper political reasons or the book's political viewpoint, but rather was due to legitimate pedagogical concerns (akin to *Hazelwood*, page 92) about factual inaccuracies and critical omissions. The majority wrote that "whatever else it prohibits, the First Amendment does not forbid a school board from removing a book because it contains factual inaccuracies, whether they be of commission or omission. There is no constitutional right to have books containing misstatements of objective facts shelved in a school library." This was the situation with *Vamos a Cuba*. The majority found:

> The book did not tell the truth. It made life in Cuba under Castro appear more favorable than every expert who testified for either side at the hearing knows it to be, more favorable than the State Department knows it to be, more favorable than the district court knows it to be, and more favorable than we know it to be. Once you find, as we have, that the book presents a false picture of life in Cuba, one that misleadingly fails to mention the deprivations and hardships the people there endure, the argument that the [school] board acted for ideological reasons collapses on itself.

There was a strenuous dissent by Judge Charles R. Wilson, who wrote that "the school board's claim that *Vamos a Cuba* is grossly inaccurate is simply a pretense for viewpoint suppression, rather than the genuine reason for its removal. The record supports the district court's determination that the book was not removed for a legitimate pedagogical reason." The Supreme Court declined to hear the case, thus leaving the 11th Circuit's pro-censorship opinion intact.

---

30. *ACLU of Florida* v. *Miami-Dade County School Board*, 557 F. 3d 1177 (11th Cir. 2009), cert. den., 558 U.S. 1023.

Four U.S. Supreme Court decisions—*Tinker, Hazelwood, Bethel* and *Morse*—provide the legal tests for determining the free-speech rights of students in public schools. Each of the four cases features its own rule and applies to a particular situation. School officials have abused *Hazelwood*'s "reasonably related to legitimate pedagogical concerns" standard when it comes to censoring student newspapers produced as part of the school curriculum. A new problem not addressed in these four cases is school censorship of speech created by students off campus, on their own computers and posted on the Internet. The impact of the court's 2007 ruling in *Morse* remains to be seen, but the scope of the *Morse* ruling is very narrow.

Two federal appellate court cases—*Kincaid* and *Hosty*—address censorship of college newspapers. Another problem college papers face today is theft by disgruntled students. Alcohol ads pose an additional issue for some college newspapers, as some states have attempted to regulate them.

Book banning and removal from public school libraries is a problem today.

SUMMARY

TIME, PLACE AND MANNER RESTRICTIONS

Most attempts by the government to use prior censorship are based on the content of the material it seeks to censor. But the government can also base its attempts at prior censorship on other factors—specifically, the time, the place or the manner of the communication. There would certainly be few content-based objections to an individual presenting a speech on how to grow mushrooms. But the government (as well as citizens) would surely object if the speaker wanted to give the speech while standing in the middle of Main Street, or on a sidewalk at 2 a.m. in a residential neighborhood. These are called **time, place and manner restrictions or rules.**

But the government can also base its attempts at prior censorship on other factors—specifically, the time, the place or the manner of the communication.

FUNERAL PROTESTS AND TIME, PLACE AND MANNER REGULATIONS: TARGETING THE WESTBORO BAPTIST CHURCH?

The topic of time, place and manner regulations is of particular importance today in measuring the constitutionality of the increasing number of funeral protest laws adopted across the country at the federal, state and local levels. For instance, former President Obama in 2012 signed a bill amending two federal statutes (18 U.S.C. § 1388 and 38 U.S.C. § 2413) to now prohibit protests and demonstrations within 300 feet of any funeral, memorial service or ceremony held for a member or former member of the Armed Forces. The prohibition begins two hours before such a funeral or service and concludes two hours afterward. In other words, the law restricts both the time (a two-hour buffer zone) and place (a 300-foot buffer zone) of speech near funerals.

By 2017, more than 40 states had adopted funeral-picketing statutes. Like the federal statutes described above, these laws typically involve both time and distance buffer zones. Several of these statutes have been challenged—sometimes successfully—as unconstitutional violations of the First Amendment right of free speech. Key questions in these state-law cases are whether: 1) the statutes are content based or content neutral; 2) the time periods, such as prohibiting protests starting two hours before a funeral and lasting until two hours after a funeral, are too extensive; and 3) whether the physical reach of buffer zones, such as keeping people 300 or 500 feet away from a funeral, is a reasonable distance. For example, Florida Statute Section 871.015, which took effect in 2014 and still exists today, provides that "a person may not knowingly engage in protest activities or knowingly cause protest activities to occur within 500 feet of the property line of a residence, cemetery, funeral home, house of worship, or other location during or within 1 hour before or 1 hour after the conducting of a funeral or burial at that place." It is a first-degree misdemeanor to violate this Florida law.

Measures such as this often are adopted because of the tactics of the members of the Westboro Baptist Church, who protest near funerals of U.S. soldiers killed in battle in order to convey their belief that the soldiers' deaths represent God's punishment for American tolerance of homosexuality. That said, however, it is possible to craft the language in such a funeral protest ordinance in a content-neutral way that applies to all picketing and protesting, regardless of the messages being conveyed.

Such rules generate no serious First Amendment problems so long as they meet a set of criteria the courts have developed. This set of criteria is sometimes referred to as the **intermediate scrutiny** standard of judicial review.

1. **The rule must be neutral as to content, or what the courts call content neutral, both on its face and in the manner in which it is applied.** A rule that is content neutral is applied the same way to all communications, regardless of what is said or printed. In other words, a law cannot permit the distribution of flyers promoting the construction of a new stadium, but restrict persons from handing out material in favor of tearing down a viaduct. A viable time, place and manner rule must be content neutral. In 2000 the Supreme Court ruled that a Colorado law that made it unlawful for any person within 100 feet of the entrance to a health care facility to approach within 8 feet of another person to pass out a handbill or a leaflet, display a sign or engage in "oral protest, education or counseling" was content neutral. The statute prohibited unwanted approaches to all medical facilities in the state, *regardless* of the message the speaker was attempting to communicate, the court said.[31]

   The 9th U.S. Court of Appeals ruled that a Las Vegas ordinance that banned the distribution of commercial leaflets along Las Vegas Boulevard, commonly known as Las Vegas Strip, was not content neutral because it didn't apply to persons handing out other kinds of leaflets as well.[32] An ordinance

31. *Hill* v. *Colorado*, 530 U.S. 703 (2000).
32. *S.O.C.* v. *Clark County, Nevada*, 152 F. 3d 1136 (1998).

like this that is not content neutral is considered a content-based law and is subject to the much more rigorous **strict scrutiny** standard of judicial review that requires the government to prove a compelling interest—not simply a substantial interest—and that the statute restricts no more speech than is absolutely necessary to serve the allegedly compelling interest (see pages 72–73).

Sometimes a restriction will appear to be content neutral but is not because it gives far too much discretion to the officials who are assigned to administer it. For instance, in September 2015 a federal judge in California forced the city of San Francisco to approve a parade permit application filed by two political activists for "body freedom"—a cause that includes advocating for rights to public nudity. The activists wanted to hold a public march on San Francisco city streets to protest the enactment and enforcement of a municipal ordinance regulating public nudity. Believing their march came within the definition of a "parade" under another municipal ordinance, the activists applied for a parade permit. But the police chief denied the application, explaining that because the activists expected 100 or fewer participants, their march could only be carried out on city sidewalks, not streets. The activists sued. In ruling against the city in *Davis* v. *City and County of San Francisco*, Judge Richard Seeborg wrote, "[T]he City is arguing, in effect, that the ordinance delegates to the Chief of Police discretion to conclude that a particular proposed expressive march is too small to be entitled to use of the streets, and thus can instead be relegated to the sidewalks. The City is unable, however, to point to *any* provisions in the text of the ordinance expressly assigning such discretion to the Chief or providing standards under which it is to be exercised." Judge Seeborg said the lack of any guideposts in the law that would constrain an official from approving only speech he or she liked could not be "overlooked."

Just because a statute restricts the noise or sound level of speech does not necessarily mean that it is content neutral. It is only a content-neutral statute if *all* noises—all messages, all sounds, regardless of topic or subject matter—are treated equally. For instance, in 2012 the Supreme Court of Florida held in *Florida* v. *Catalano*[33] that a state statute that prohibited playing car stereos at a sound level "plainly audible at a distance of 25 feet or more" away was a content-based law. Why? Because the Florida statute carved out an exemption from this rule for "motor vehicles used for business or political purposes, which in the normal course of conducting such business use soundmaking devices." As the Supreme Court of Florida wrote in explaining how this exemption made the law content based rather than content neutral, "business and political vehicles may amplify commercial or political speech at any volume, whereas an individual traversing the highways for pleasure would be issued a citation for listening to any type of sound, whether it is religious advocacy or music, too loudly. Thus, this statute is content based because it does not apply equally to music, political speech and advertising." As a content-based law, the Florida statute was subject to the much more rigorous

---

33. 104 So. 3d 1069 (Fla. 2012).

strict scrutiny standard of review (see pages 72–73 regarding strict scrutiny) and ultimately was declared unconstitutional.

2. **The law must not constitute a complete ban on a kind of communication.** There must be ample alternative means of accomplishing this communication. In the 1980s several states sought to ban the polling of voters outside voting booths. The polling was conducted by the news media for several reasons, including an attempt to find out what kinds of people (age, political affiliation, occupation, etc.) voted for which candidates. Many of these statutes were struck down at least in part, the courts ruled, because the press could not ask these questions at any other place or in any other manner and expect to get the same data. The ban on exit polling, then, constituted a complete ban on the kinds of questions reporters sought to ask.

GUIDELINES FOR TIME, PLACE AND MANNER RESTRICTIONS

1. Rules must be content neutral.
2. Rules must not constitute a complete ban on communication.
3. Rules must be justified by a substantial state interest.
4. Rules must be narrowly tailored.

---

3. **The state must articulate a substantial interest to justify this restraint on speech.** A ban against using loudspeakers to communicate a political message after 10 p.m. could surely be justified on the grounds that most people are trying to sleep at that time. A ban against passing out literature and soliciting money in the passageways between an airport terminal and the boarding ramps could also be justified by the state, which wants to keep these busy areas clear for passengers hurrying to board airplanes.[34] But attempts by the government to ban distribution of handbills on city streets because many people throw them away and cause a litter problem are typically rejected.[35] The state interest in keeping the streets clean can be accomplished by an anti-litter law. At times communities have attempted to raise aesthetic reasons to justify limiting or banning newspaper boxes. Some courts refuse to allow these concerns alone to justify limits on First Amendment freedoms, usually noting that many other common objects on the streets (telephone poles, trash cans, fire hydrants, street signs) are also eyesores.[36] Other courts have ruled that aesthetic considerations can be included in a community's justification for limits.[37] If the community can demonstrate a strong rationale for its aesthetic

---

34. See, for example, *International Society for Krishna Consciousness* v. *Wolke,* 453 F. Supp. 869 (1978).
35. *Schneider* v. *New Jersey,* 308 U.S. 147 (1939); and *Miller* v. *Laramie,* 880 P. 2d 594 (1994).
36. See *Providence Journal* v. *Newport,* 665 F. Supp. 107 (1987); and *Multimedia Publishing Co. of South Carolina, Inc.* v. *Greenville-Spartanburg Airport District,* 991 F. 2d 154 (1993).
37. See *Gold Coast Publications, Inc.* v. *Corrigan,* 42 F. 3d 1336 (1995); and *Honolulu Weekly Inc.* v. *Harris,* 298 F. 3d 1037 (2002).

concerns, even a total ban on the placement of racks in a specific area might be acceptable. In 1996 the 1st U.S. Court of Appeals permitted the city of Boston to completely ban news racks from the public streets of a historic district of the city, where the architectural commission was trying to restore the area to what it looked like hundreds of years earlier.[38]

In addition to asserting a substantial interest, the state is required to bring evidence to court to prove its case. Southwest Texas State University in San Marcos attempted to restrict the distribution of a small community newspaper on its campus. It told the 5th U.S. Circuit Court of Appeals that it sought such restrictions in order to preserve the academic environment and the security of the campus, protect privacy on campus, control traffic, preserve the appearance of the campus, prevent fraud and deception and eliminate unnecessary expenses. These were all laudable goals, but the court said the university presented no evidence to support the notion that restricting the sale of these newspapers to a few vending machines or direct delivery to subscribers on campus would accomplish these goals. "[T]he burden is on the defendants [university] to show affirmatively that their restriction is narrowly tailored to protect the identified interests. Defendants failed to carry this burden," the court ruled.[39]

4. **The law must be narrowly tailored so that it furthers the state interest that justifies it, but does not restrain more expression than is actually required to further this interest.** "A regulation is narrowly tailored when it does not burden substantially more speech than is necessary to further the government's legitimate interests."[40] Officials in the city of Sylvania, Ga., believed they had a litter problem. The *Penny-Saver*, a weekly free newspaper, was thrown on the lawn or driveway of each residence in the city. Often residents just left the paper where it fell. These unclaimed papers were unsightly and sometimes wound up on the street or in the gutter. The city adopted an ordinance that made it illegal to distribute free, printed material in yards, on driveways or on porches. The publisher of the *Penny-Saver* sued, claiming the new law was a violation of the First Amendment. The Georgia Supreme Court agreed, rejecting the city's argument that this was a proper time, place and manner rule. The ordinance was certainly content neutral, but it was not narrowly tailored. The law blocked the distribution of the *Penny-Saver* but also barred political candidates from leaving literature on doorsteps, stopped many religious solicitors who hand out material and blocked scores of others from passing out pamphlets door-to-door. In addition, the court ruled, the problem could be solved in other ways that do not offend the First Amendment. The city could require either the *Penny-Saver* publisher or the city residents to retrieve the unclaimed papers or could punish the publisher for papers that end up in the ditch or on the street.[41]

---

38. *Globe Newspaper Company* v. *Beacon Hill Architectural Commission,* 100 F. 3d 175 (1996).
39. *Hays County Guardian* v. *Supple,* 969 F. 2d 111 (1992).
40. *Ward* v. *Rock Against Racism,* 491 U.S. 781 (1989).
41. *Statesboro Publishing Company* v. *City of Sylvania,* 516 S.E. 2d 296 (1999); see also *Houston Chronicle* v. *Houston,* 630 S.W. 2d 444 (1982); and *Denver Publishing Co.* v. *Aurora,* 896 P. 2d 306 (1995).

The 2016 appellate court decision in *Rideout* v. *Gardner* provides another example of a law that failed intermediate scrutiny because it was not narrowly tailored. A New Hampshire law barred citizens in that state from taking "ballot selfies"—where voters take pictures of their marked ballots and then share those pictures on social media. The state maintained the law prevented new technology from facilitating future vote buying and voter coercion. Three plaintiffs challenged the law, including Andrew Langlois. Frustrated by the Republican candidates running for U.S. Senate in New Hampshire, Langlois instead wrote in the name of his recently deceased dog, "Akira," and took a photograph of his ballot. When he returned home, he posted the ballot selfie on Facebook and wrote: "Because all of the candidates SUCK, I did a write-in of Akira." An investigator from the New Hampshire Attorney General's Office called him and informed him he was under investigation for violating the law against ballot selfies.

The 1st U.S. Circuit Court of Appeals struck down the law as unconstitutional. The court said it did not need to decide definitively whether the law in question was content based or content neutral because, even assuming it was content neutral, the law failed intermediate scrutiny for not being narrowly tailored. The court said that "at least two different reasons" showed that New Hampshire did not adequately tailor its solution (the law barring ballot selfies) to the potential problem (vote buying and voter coercion) that it perceived. "First, the prohibition on ballot selfies reaches and curtails the speech rights of all voters, not just those motivated to cast a particular vote for illegal reasons." The state was "trying to prevent a much smaller hypothetical pool of voters who, New Hampshire fears, may try to sell their votes." But the First Circuit said no vote-selling market had emerged. Second, the court said, New Hampshire "has not demonstrated that other state and federal laws prohibiting vote corruption are not already adequate to the justifications it has identified." In other words, the state has other remedies to outlaw actual coercion or vote buying. Ballot selfies have taken on "a special communicative value," the court said, allowing voters to express support for a candidate. The First Circuit thus concluded, "New Hampshire may not impose such a broad restriction on speech by banning ballot selfies in order to combat an unsubstantiated and hypothetical danger."

A law can be declared invalid if it fails to pass any of these four criteria. The manner in which courts apply the intermediate scrutiny test—how rigorously they employ it, how much deference they grant to asserted legislative interests and even whether they choose to use a different test—often depends on the nature of the specific location where the law in question applies.

FORUM ANALYSIS

Courts have identified four kinds of forums:

Traditional Public Forum: Traditional public forums are public places that have by long tradition been devoted to assembly and speeches, places like street corners, public parks, public sidewalks or a plaza in front of city hall. The highest level of First Amendment protection is given to expression occurring in traditional public forums.

Designated Public Forum: Designated public forums are places created by the government to be used for expressive activities, among other things. A city-owned auditorium, a fairgrounds, a community meeting hall and even a student newspaper intended to be open for use by all students are examples of designated public forums. It is clear today that "the government must have an affirmative intent to create a public forum in order for a designated public forum to arise."[42] Intent may be determined by three factors:

1. Explicit expressions of intent
2. Actual policy and history of practice in using the property
3. Natural compatibility of the property with the expressive activity

For instance, in 2006 a federal appellate court in *Bowman* v. *White*[43] held that three specific areas on the University of Arkansas at Fayetteville campus were designated public forums: the Union Mall (an outdoor area in the center of campus near the library composed of grassy mounds surrounded by sidewalks and walkways, benches and potted trees and plants); the Peace Fountain (a metallic tower structure, also located in the center of the campus, with a fountain at the base); and an area outside a major campus dining hall. In concluding these areas were designated public forums, the court reasoned that

> [the] tradition of free expression within specific parts of universities, the University's practice of permitting speech at these locations, and the University's past practice of permitting both University Entities and Non-University Entities to speak at these locations on campus demonstrate that the University deliberately fosters an environment that permits speech.

Although a government entity is not required either to create or to maintain indefinitely a designated public forum (i.e., a designated public forum can be closed if the government wishes to do so), once it creates a designated public forum and chooses to keep it open, it "is bound by the same rules that govern traditional forums."[44] This means that a time, place and manner regulation in both a traditional public forum and a designated public forum must survive and pass the four-part intermediate scrutiny standard just described,[45] whereas a content-based restriction must pass the more stringent strict scrutiny standard of review (see pages 72–73) and thus is more likely to be held invalid and unconstitutional.

Public Property That Is Not a Public Forum: Some kinds of public property not considered to be public forums are obvious—prisons and military bases, for example. The Supreme Court has stated that a nonpublic forum consists of "[p]ublic property which is not by tradition or designation a forum for public communication."[46] Law professors

---

42. *Ridley* v. *Massachusetts Bay Transportation Authority*, 390 F. 3d 65 (1st Cir. 2004).
43. 444 F. 3d 967 (8th Cir. 2006). See also *Hays County Guardian* v. *Supple*, 969 F. 2d 111, 117 (5th Cir. 1992), which found certain outdoor areas at Southwest Texas State University to be a designated public forum, designated for the speech of students.
44. Weaver and Lively, *Understanding the First Amendment*, 118.
45. See *Wells* v. *City and County of Denver*, 257 F. 3d 1132, 1147 (10th Cir. 2001), which wrote that "a content-neutral restriction in a traditional or designated public forum is subject to review as a regulation on the time, place, and manner of speech."
46. *Perry Education Association* v. *Perry Local Educators' Association*, 460 U.S. 37, 46 (1983).

Russell Weaver and Donald Lively observe that courts have identified a number of places as nonpublic forums including:

- Postal service mailboxes
- Utility poles
- Airport terminals
- Political candidate debates on public television[47]

In addition to these examples, a court in 2010 held that Hawaii's unencumbered beaches (beaches not set aside for any specific purpose and not otherwise leased or permitted) are nonpublic forums for purposes of the First Amendment. The court wrote that "nothing in the record demonstrates or indicates that all Hawaii unencumbered State beaches have traditionally been places for the free exchange of ideas generally."[48]

In (and on) such places and venues, the government has much greater power to regulate and restrict speech, and thus "regulation of speech in a nonpublic forum is subject to less demanding judicial scrutiny."[49] Regulations on speech activities in nonpublic forums will be upheld and allowed as long as they are reasonable and viewpoint neutral (see page 95 discussing viewpoint-based discrimination and page 44 discussing viewpoint neutrality). The latter requirement entails "not just that a government refrain from explicit viewpoint discrimination, but also that it provide adequate safeguards to protect against the improper exclusion of viewpoints."[50]

Unconstitutional viewpoint-based discrimination in a nonpublic forum is illustrated by a 2010 case called *Nieto* v. *Flatau*[51] in which officials at Camp Lejeune Marine Corps Base prohibited Jesse Nieto from displaying a bumper sticker with the message "ISLAM = TERRORISM" on his car that he drove to work on the base. Nieto's youngest son had been killed when the USS Cole was bombed by Islamic terrorists. Camp Lejeune had a policy prohibiting the display of "extremist, indecent, sexist or racist" messages on motor vehicles on the base. Observing that military bases are not public forums for First Amendment purposes and that the government is entitled to great deference in restricting speech on them, U.S. District Judge Malcolm Howard restated the rule that the government may enact restrictions on speech in nonpublic forums, provided those restrictions are reasonable and not viewpoint-based. The problem for Camp Lejeune was that it freely allowed the display of bumper stickers with pro-Islam messages including "Islam is Love" and "Islam is Peace" but it prohibited Nieto's anti-Islam message of "ISLAM = TERRORISM" on his car. That is viewpoint-based discrimination because the military discriminated against Nieto's speech based upon his particular viewpoint on Islam. The judge also noted that the mere fact that some people may be highly offended by Nieto's bumper sticker is not a sufficient reason for banning it.

47. Weaver and Lively, *Understanding the First Amendment*, 120.
48. *Kaahumanu* v. *Hawaii*, 685 F. Supp. 2d 1140 (D. Haw. 2010).
49. *Faith Center Church Evangelistic Ministries* v. *Glover*, 462 F. 3d 1194, 1203 (9th Cir. 2006).
50. *Child Evangelism Fellowship of Maryland* v. *Montgomery County Public Schools*, 457 F. 3d 376, 384 (4th Cir. 2006).
51. 715 F. Supp. 2d 650 (E.D. N.C. 2010).

In 2016 a federal appellate court in *NAACP* v. *City of Philadelphia*[52] held that a ban on noncommercial ads at the city's international airport was unconstitutional because it was not a reasonable restriction of speech in a nonpublic forum. The city had long accepted paid advertisements that were posted in display cases and on screens throughout the airport. But when the National Association for the Advancement of Colored People (NAACP) submitted an ad that read, "Welcome to America, home to 5% of the world's people & 25% of the world's prisoners. Let's build a better America together," the city rejected it based on what it said was an informal practice of only accepting ads that proposed a commercial transaction. After the NAACP sued, the city adopted a written policy that crystallized the informal practice. The policy barred ads that do not "propose a commercial transaction," though it made an exception for ads that promote subjects such as Philadelphia tourism, city initiatives, air service and use of the airport. The city said the policy helped further its goals of maximizing revenue and avoiding controversy. In August 2016, the 3rd U.S. Circuit Court of Appeals ruled the policy was unreasonable and violated the First Amendment. The court said the city offered no evidence to support the contention that the policy helped it maximize revenue. Moreover, the court found that the city also failed to justify the avoidance-of-controversy rationale. The court noted that, elsewhere in the airport, travelers were exposed to TV broadcasting shows and commercials containing a wide variety of noncommercial content. The court wrote, "For instance, the NAACP submitted pictures of the Airport's televisions that show content related to a gubernatorial election in Virginia, the war on drugs, the Confederate flag, and a piece of anti-discrimination legislation." The court thus concluded that the airport exposes travelers "to an onslaught of non-commercial content outside of its advertising space without any suggestion that doing so is inconsistent with the environment it seeks to foster."

Private Property: Owners of private property, which includes everything from a backyard patio to a giant shopping mall, are free to regulate who uses their property for expressive activity. There are no First Amendment guarantees of freedom of expression on private property.

The problem of dealing with distribution of materials at privately owned shopping centers has been a troubling one. In 1968, in *Amalgamated Food Employees Local 590* v. *Logan Valley Plaza*,[53] the Supreme Court ruled that the shopping center was the functional equivalent of a town's business district and permitted informational picketing by persons who had a grievance against one of the stores in the shopping center. Four years later in *Lloyd Corp.* v. *Tanner*,[54] the court ruled that a shopping center can prohibit the distribution of handbills on its property when the action is unrelated to the shopping center operation. Protesters against nuclear power, for example, could not use the shopping center as a forum. People protesting against the policies of one of the stores in the center, however, could use the center to distribute materials.

In 1976 the Supreme Court recognized the distinctions it had drawn between the rules in the *Logan Valley* case and the rules in the *Lloyd Corp.* case for what they were—

52. 834 F. 3d 435 (3rd Cir. 2016).
53. 391 U.S. 308 (1968).
54. 407 U.S. 551 (1972).

restrictions based on content. The distribution of messages of one kind was permitted, while the distribution of messages about something else was banned. In *Hudgens* v. *NLRB*,[55] the high court ruled that if, in fact, the shopping center is the functional equivalent of a municipal street, then restrictions based on content cannot stand. But rather than open the shopping center to the distribution of all kinds of material, *Logan Valley* was overruled, and the court announced that "only when . . . property has taken all the attributes of a town" can property be treated as public. Distribution of materials at private shopping centers can be prohibited.

Just because the First Amendment does not include within its protection of freedom of expression the right to circulate material at a privately owned shopping center does not mean that such distribution might not be protected by legislation or by a state constitution. That is exactly what happened in California. In 1974 in the city of Campbell, Calif., a group of high school students took a card table, some leaflets and unsigned petition forms to the popular Pruneyard Shopping Center. The students were angered by a recent anti-Israel U.N. resolution and sought to hand out literature and collect signatures for a petition to send to the president and Congress. The shopping center did not allow anyone to hand out literature, speak or gather petition signatures, and the students were quickly chased off the property by a security guard. The students filed suit in court, and in 1979 the California Supreme Court ruled that the rights of freedom of speech and petitioning are protected under the California Constitution, even in private shopping centers, as long as they are "reasonably exercised."[56] The shopping center owners appealed the ruling to the U.S. Supreme Court, arguing that the high court's ruling in *Lloyd Corp.* v. *Tanner* prohibited the states from going further in the protection of personal liberties than the federal government. But six of the nine justices disagreed, ruling that a state is free to adopt in its own constitution individual liberties more expansive than those conferred by the federal Constitution.[57]

A state is free to adopt in its own constitution individual liberties more expansive than those conferred by the federal Constitution.

Although the California Supreme Court held in the Pruneyard Shopping Center dispute that the speech clause of the California Constitution protected expression in a privately owned shopping center (subject to the owner's reasonable time, place and manner restrictions), subsequent decisions by lower-level appellate courts in California have distinguished between large, Pruneyard-type shopping centers (Pruneyard itself consisted of 21 acres, with 65 shops, 10 restaurants and a cinema) and large, individual retail stores, even though those stores are located within a larger retail development. These cases have held that the entrance areas and aprons of such large retail stores are not public forums. For instance, a California appellate court ruled in 2010 that the entrance to Foods Co., a large warehouse grocery store located in Sacramento in a retail development, was not a public forum.[58] The store has only one customer entrance, consisting of a sidewalk or apron extending out about 15 feet to a driving lane that separates the apron from the parking lot. The entrance area is about 31 feet wide. The appellate court added that the entrance way neither was designed to be nor was presented to the public as a

55. 424 U.S. 507 (1976).
56. *Robins* v. *Pruneyard Shopping Center,* 592 P. 2d 341 (Cal. 1979).
57. *Pruneyard Shopping Center* v. *Robins,* 447 U.S. 74 (1980).
58. *Ralphs Grocery Co.* v. *United Food & Commercial Workers Union Local 8,* 186 Cal. App. 4th 1078 (2010).

public meeting place. It noted that because the area was a private forum, its owner could "selectively permit speech or prohibit speech."

Courts in many states (Washington, Colorado, New Jersey, Oregon, New York and others) have interpreted their state constitutions as providing broader free-speech and press rights than those provided by the First Amendment to the U.S. Constitution. This trend becomes particularly noticeable when the federal courts narrow the meaning of the First Amendment.

SUMMARY

The prior restraint of expression is permissible under what are known as time, place and manner regulations. That is, the government can impose reasonable regulations about when, where and how individuals or groups may communicate with other people. In order to be constitutional, time, place and manner restraints must meet certain criteria:

1. The regulation must be content neutral; that is, application of the rule should not depend on the content of the communication.
2. The regulation must serve a substantial governmental interest, and the government must justify the rule by explicitly demonstrating this interest.
3. There cannot be total prohibition of the communication. The speakers or publishers must have reasonable alternative means of presenting their ideas or information to the public.
4. The rules cannot be broader than they need to be to serve the governmental interest. For example, the government cannot stop the distribution of literature on all public streets if it only seeks to stop the problem of congestion on public streets that carry heavy traffic.

OTHER PRIOR RESTRAINTS

Major issues regarding prior restraint have been outlined in the previous pages. Yet each year other instances of prior restraint are challenged in the courts, and frequently the Supreme Court is called on to resolve the issue. Here is a brief outline of some of these issues.

SON OF SAM LAWS

Americans have always been interested in crime and criminals. But in recent decades our desire to know more about this sordid side of contemporary life has spawned books and television programs about killers, rapists, robbers, hijackers and their victims. Indeed, it is often jokingly said of those accused of high-profile crimes that when they are captured they are more eager to contact an agent than a defense attorney. Efforts have been made by government to stop felons from receiving money that might be earned by selling stories about their crimes. Many civil libertarians say this is a prior censorship. The laws in question, which have been adopted in one form or another by about 40 states and the federal government, are called "Son of Sam" laws after a serial killer in New York who was dubbed that name by the press. Before the Son of Sam (David Berkowitz) was caught, reports circulated that the press was offering to pay for the rights to his story. The New York legislature responded to those reports by passing a law that permits the state to seize and hold for five years all the money earned by an individual from the sale of his or her story of crime. The money is supposed to be used to compensate the victims of the crimes caused by the felon. The criminal/author collects what is left in the fund after five years.

Two separate challenges to the New York law were mounted in the late 1980s and early 1990s. Simon & Schuster contested the law when it was applied against the best-selling book "Wiseguys" (the basis for the film "GoodFellas"). Career mobster Henry Hill was paid for cooperating with the book's author, Nicholas Pileggi. Macmillan Publishing Co. also challenged the validity of the law when New York sought to seize the proceeds of Jean Harris's autobiography, "Stranger in Two Worlds," because some of the material in the work was based on her trial for the murder of her lover, diet doctor Herman Tarnower.

The statute was upheld in both federal and state courts. The 2nd U.S. Circuit Court of Appeals ruled in *Simon & Schuster* v. *Fischetti*[59] that the purpose of the law was not to suppress speech but to ensure that a criminal did not profit from the exploitation of his or her crime, and that the victims of the crime are compensated for their suffering. A compelling state interest is served, and the fact that this imposes an incidental burden on the press is not sufficient to rule the law a violation of freedom of expression.

But in late 1991 the U.S. Supreme Court disagreed and in an 8-0 decision ruled that the Son of Sam law was a content-based regulation that violated the First Amendment.[60] "The statute plainly imposes a financial disincentive only on a particular form of content," wrote Justice Sandra Day O'Connor. In order for such a law to pass constitutional muster, the state must show that it is necessary to serve a compelling state interest and that the law is narrowly constructed to achieve that end. The members of the high court agreed that the state has a compelling interest in ensuring that criminals do not profit from their crimes, but this law goes far beyond that goal; it is not narrowly drawn. The statute applies to works on any subject provided they express the author's thoughts or recollections about his or her crime, however tangentially or incidentally, Justice O'Connor noted. The statute could just as easily be applied to "The Autobiography of Malcolm X" or Thoreau's "Civil Disobedience" or the "Confessions of St. Augustine," she added. While Justice O'Connor specifically noted that this ruling was not necessarily aimed at similar laws in other states because they might be different, the decision has forced substantial changes in most of the existing laws. In Massachusetts, however, the Supreme Judicial Court of that commonwealth approved a probationary scheme that had clear earmarks of a Son of Sam law. Katherine Power, a 1970s radical who participated in a bank robbery in which a police officer was killed, pleaded guilty to her crimes and a trial court ordered the defendant to serve 20 years' probation. Attached to the probation sentence was a provision that Power could not in any way profit from the sale of her

---

59. 916 F. 2d 777 (1990).

60. *Simon & Schuster, Inc.* v. *New York Crime Victims Board,* 502 U.S. 105 (1991); see also *Bouchard* v. *Price,* 694 A. 2d 670 (1998) and *Keenan* v. *Superior Court,* 40 P. 3d 718 (2002) in which courts in Rhode Island and California struck down similar laws.

story to the news media during those 20 years. Power appealed the provision, citing the First Amendment and the Supreme Court ruling in *Simon & Schuster*. The Massachusetts high court rejected this appeal, arguing that a specific condition of probation (which frequently restricts a probationer's fundamental rights) is not the same as a Son of Sam law, which is a statute of general applicability.[61] So, are Son of Sam laws constitutional? They certainly can be, but most of the current laws are not narrowly tailored in such a way as to pass muster. Because the laws are content-based statutes, the state has to first demonstrate that a compelling state interest is at stake and then prove that the law does not bar more speech than is necessary to further that interest.

Although courts are likely to find that two different compelling interests justify these laws (compensating victims of crimes and preventing criminal profiteering), they also are likely to declare the laws not narrowly tailored because most Son of Sam laws regulate more speech than is necessary to serve these twin interests. For instance, in 2004, the Supreme Court of Nevada in *Seres* v. *Lerner* struck down that state's law that allowed felony victims to recover from the felon any monetary proceeds the felon might generate from published materials substantially related to the offense.[62] The high court of Nevada held the law unconstitutional because it "allows recovery of proceeds from works that include expression both related and unrelated to the crime, imposing a disincentive to engage in public discourse and non-exploitative discussion of it." A nonexploitative discussion might include such things as the writer (the felon) warning about the consequences of crime, describing life behind bars and urging others not to commit the same acts.

PRIOR RESTRAINT AND PROTESTS

Two 1994 decisions by the Supreme Court focus on the prior restraint of those seeking to demonstrate or protest. In June the Supreme Court unanimously ruled that cities may not bar residents from posting signs on their own property. Margaret Gilleo had challenged the Ladue, Mo., ordinance by posting an 8-by-11-inch sign in a window of her house protesting the Persian Gulf War. The lower courts ruled that the ban on residential signs was flawed because the city did not ban signs on commercial property; the law favored one kind of speech over another. But the Supreme Court struck down the ordinance in a broader fashion, ruling that the posting of signs on residential property is "a venerable means of communication that is both unique and important. A special respect for individual liberty in the home has long been part of our culture and law," wrote Justice John Paul Stevens. "Most Americans would be understandably dismayed, given that tradition, to learn that it was illegal to display from their window an 8-by-11-inch sign expressing their political views," he added.[63]

Yard signs carrying political messages still cause trouble today. For instance, in November 2010 the town of Valley Center, Kan., was ordered by a judge to pay $8,000 to Jarrod West. Why? The town had stopped him from posting a sign in his yard complaining about drainage problems in his neighborhood. The sign said, "Dear Valley Center, I did not buy Lake Front Property! Fix this problem. This is what I pay taxes

61. *Massachusetts* v. *Power,* 420 Mass. 410 (1995).
62. 102 P. 3d 91 (Nev. 2004).
63. *City of Ladue* v. *Gilleo,* 512 U.S. 43 (1994).

for." Valley Center responded by charging West with criminal defamation, and it took the intervention of a local American Civil Liberties Union on West's behalf for him to prevail. It was a classic case of government censorship of a political message with which it disagreed.

In another 1994 ruling involving the right to protest, the high court upheld a Florida state court injunction that established a 36-foot buffer zone between an abortion clinic in Melbourne, Fla., and anti-abortion protesters.[64] The buffer zone, or ban on picketing, was designed to keep protesters away from the entrance to the clinic, the parking lot and the public right-of-way. Chief Justice Rehnquist, who wrote the 6-3 ruling, said the ban "burdens no more speech than is necessary to accomplish the governmental interest at stake." The court did strike down, however, a 300-foot buffer zone within which protesters could not make uninvited approaches to patients and employees, as well as a buffer zone the same size around the houses of clinic doctors and staff members. The chief justice said a smaller zone or restriction on the size and duration of demonstrations would be constitutional.*

DEFENDING SPEECH OUTSIDE OF ABORTION CLINICS

In the 2014 ruling in *McCullen* v. *Coakley*, the Supreme Court struck down a Massachusetts law that made it a crime to stand on a public road or sidewalk within 35 feet of a reproductive health care facility. The petitioners in the case were individuals who attempt to engage women approaching abortion clinics in "sidewalk counseling," which involves offering information about alternatives to abortion and help pursuing those options. The petitioners claimed that the 35-foot buffer zone hindered their counseling efforts.

All nine justices on the Court found the law violated the First Amendment—though the justices disagreed (largely along political lines) about whether the law was content neutral or content based. Chief Justice Roberts sided with the Court's four liberal justices to strike down the law as a content-neutral restriction that failed intermediate scrutiny because it wasn't narrowly tailored. Roberts' majority opinion noted that the buffer zones "impose serious burdens on petitioner's speech" by carving out "a significant portion of the adjacent public sidewalks, pushing petitioners well back from the clinics' entrances and driveways." Moreover, the Court found the law burdened "substantially more speech than necessary." The Court said the state's interests—ensuring public safety outside abortion clinics, preventing harassment and intimidation of patients and clinic staff and combating deliberate obstruction of clinic entrances—could be addressed with

---

* In 2003 the Supreme Court refused to permit two abortion clinics and the National Organization for Women to use the federal Racketeer Influenced and Corrupt Organizations Act (RICO) when they sued anti-abortion activists who disrupted and blockaded abortion clinics in Chicago in the 1990s. The high court said the protests did not constitute extortion, a crime that might make the RICO law applicable. *Scheidler* v. *National Organization for Women*, 537 U.S. 393 (2003). The court implied that it was inappropriate to use the federal racketeering law as a weapon against political protests.
64. *Madsen* v. *Women's Health Center*, 512 U.S. 753 (1994).

a variety of other approaches the state had not yet tried that wouldn't categorically ban individuals "from areas historically open for speech and debate." The Court's conservative justices (other than Roberts) agreed the law was unconstitutional, but they argued it was a content-based law, aimed at restricting the speech of abortion protesters, and should have been reviewed under strict scrutiny.

In 1995 the Supreme Court struck down an Ohio law (and for all intents and purposes laws in almost every other state in the nation) that prohibited the distribution of anonymous election campaign literature. Margaret McIntyre had circulated leaflets opposing an upcoming school levy, but failed to include her name and address on the campaign literature as required by law. She was fined $100. The state argued the statute was needed to identify those responsible for fraud, false advertising and libel, but seven members of the high court said the law was an unconstitutional limitation on political expression. "Under our constitution, anonymous pamphleteering is not a pernicious, fraudulent practice, but an honorable tradition of advocacy and of dissent," wrote Justice John Paul Stevens for the majority. "Anonymity is a shield from the tyranny of the majority." Stevens said anonymity might in fact shield fraudulent conduct, but our society "accords greater weight to the value of free speech than to the dangers of its misuse."[65]

SUMMARY

A wide variety of legal issues relate to prior restraint. In recent years the Supreme Court of the United States has voided a statute aimed at denying criminals the right to earn profits from books or films about their crimes and voided a city ordinance that barred residents from putting signs on their front lawns or in their windows. At the same time, the high court has permitted limited restrictions aimed at those seeking to protest abortion at a clinic in Florida but struck down a broader law that restricted abortion protesters in Massachusetts.

HATE SPEECH/FIGHTING WORDS

Hate speech—words written or spoken that attack individuals or groups because of their race, ethnic background, religion, gender or sexual orientation—is a controversial but not altogether uncommon aspect of contemporary American life. Few people openly acknowledge a value in such speech, but there is a considerable debate over what to do about it. How do you balance the need to protect the sensibilities of members of the community with the right to speak and publish freely, a right guaranteed by the First Amendment?

The Supreme Court endeavored to balance these issues more than 70 years ago when it ruled that those who print such invective in newspapers or broadcast them on the radio or paint them on walls or fences are generally protected by the Constitution, but those who utter the same words in a face-to-face confrontation do not enjoy similar

65. *McIntyre v. Ohio Elections Commission*, 514 U.S. 334 (1995).

protection. The case involved a man named Chaplinsky, who was a member of the Jehovah's Witness religious sect. Face-to-face proselytization or confrontation is a part of the religious practice of the members of this sect. Chaplinsky attracted a hostile crowd as he attempted to distribute religious pamphlets in Rochester, N.H. When a city marshal intervened, Chaplinsky called the officer a "God-damned racketeer" and a "damned fascist." The Jehovah's Witness was tried and convicted of violating a state law that forbids offensive or derisive speech or name-calling in public. The Supreme Court affirmed the conviction by a 9-0 vote. In his opinion for the court Justice Frank Murphy outlined what has become known as the **fighting words doctrine:**

"There are certain well-defined and narrowly limited classes of speech, the prevention and punishment of which have never been thought to raise any constitutional problems."

> There are certain well-defined and narrowly limited classes of speech, the prevention and punishment of which have never been thought to raise any constitutional problems. These include . . . fighting words—those which by their very utterance inflict injury or tend to incite an immediate breach of the peace. It has been well observed that such utterances are no essential part of any exposition of ideas, and are of such slight social value as a step to the truth that any benefit that may be derived from them is clearly outweighed by the social interest in order and morality.[66]

Fighting words may be prohibited, then, so long as the statutes are carefully drawn and do not permit the application of the law to protected speech. Also, the fighting words must be used in a personal, face-to-face encounter—a true verbal assault. The Supreme Court emphasized this latter point in 1972 when it ruled that laws prohibiting fighting words be limited to words "that have a direct tendency to cause acts of violence by the person to whom, individually, the remark is addressed."[67] It is important to note that the high court has given states permission to restrict so-called fighting words because their utterance could result in a breach of the peace, a fight, a riot; not because they insult or offend or harm the person at whom they are aimed. Finally, there is not an official list of words that are always classified by courts as "fighting words." Whether any given word amounts to a "fighting word" depends on the context of how it is used and to whom it is addressed.

PROTECTING THE SPEECH OF THE WESTBORO BAPTIST CHURCH: THE SUPREME COURT'S 2011 RULING

In 2011, the U.S. Supreme Court issued a ruling in *Snyder* v. *Phelps*[68] that protected what many people would consider hate speech. Members of the Westboro Baptist Church (WBC) believe that God hates the United States for its tolerance of homosexuality and, in turn, punishes the country by killing American soldiers. WBC members expressed these views near the funeral for Marine Lance Corporal Matthew Snyder, who was killed in Iraq in the line of duty, by carrying signs with anti-gay and anti-military messages such as "Thank God for Dead Soldiers,"

---

66. *Chaplinsky* v. *New Hampshire*, 315 U.S. 568 (1942).
67. *Gooding* v. *Wilson*, 405 U.S. 518 (1972).
68. 562 U.S. 443 (2011).

"Semper Fi Fags" and "God Hates Fags." The WBC protestors stood on public property about 1,000 feet away from the funeral where they had been told to stand by local police.

Albert Snyder, the father of Matthew Snyder, sued the members of the church for intentional infliction of emotional distress (see Chapter 5) and intrusion into seclusion (see Chapter 7). The WBC, however, argued that the First Amendment protected its right to engage in such speech. An eight-justice majority of the U.S. Supreme Court agreed with the WBC, basing its decision on several grounds.

First, the Court held that the speech in question, although offensive, dealt with matters of public concern, including "the political and moral conduct of the United States and its citizens, the fate of our Nation, homosexuality in the military, and scandals involving the Catholic clergy." Second, the Court reasoned that "the church members had the right to be where they were," as "the picketing was conducted under police supervision some 1,000 feet from the church, out of the sight of those at the church. The protest was not unruly; there was no shouting, profanity, or violence." Finally, the Court concluded by observing that "speech is powerful. It can stir people to action, move them to tears of both joy and sorrow, and—as it did here—inflict great pain. On the facts before us, we cannot react to that pain by punishing the speaker. As a Nation we have chosen a different course—to protect even speech on public issues to ensure that we do not stifle public debate."

The lone dissenter was Justice Samuel Alito. He wrote that "our profound national commitment to free and open debate is not a license for the vicious verbal assault that occurred in this case. . . . Mr. Snyder wanted what is surely the right of any parent who experiences such an incalculable loss: to bury his son in peace."

See pages 113–114 for another controversy involving the WBC.

Does swearing at members of a government committee to express frustration with their actions (or lack thereof) constitute fighting words? The 10th U.S. Circuit Court of Appeals addressed this question in 2011 in *Klen* v. *City of Loveland*.[69] Plaintiffs Edward and Stephen Klen were building contractors upset at what they perceived to be unreasonable, deliberate delays over the issuing of permits by officials in the city of Loveland, Colo. On multiple occasions, the Klens used profane language and insults out of frustration when discussing the permit delays with city officials. They said such things as "when the hell are you going to get your shit together in this department?"; "[w]here is our damn permit?"; and "what kind of idiot are you, if you can't even run your own goddamned department?"

In concluding that this language did not constitute fighting words, the 10th Circuit reasoned that "although the Klens used less-than-polite epithets in delivering their message, and occasionally even employed insulting terms to describe city officials,

69. 661 F.3d 498 (10th Cir. 2011).

there is no indication that their words were accompanied by provocative gestures or threats. Nor did their use of vulgar or offensive language necessarily make their outbursts fighting words." The appellate court added that the Klens were not trying to provoke a fight but were trying to "express ideas—chiefly that City building department officials were incompetent and were taking too long in processing plaintiffs' application for a building permit." The decision illustrates the key point that offensive speech is not necessarily the same thing as fighting words.

On the other hand, a 2012 decision by an appellate court in *Kansas* v. *Meadors*[70] illustrates that swearing sometimes can amount to fighting words, particularly when an unfriendly tension already exists between the individuals involved. In *Meadors*, those individuals were a divorced couple who shared custody of their children. While the woman was dropping off the kids at her ex-husband's house, the ex-husband "began to berate her by yelling, 'I hate you, you F'ing cunt. I hate you bitch. I'm going to get you.' He was approaching the vehicle, yelling, pointing and displaying his middle finger." The woman "testified it was very traumatic for her and the children," and she called the police. Her ex-husband continued to yell profanities after the officer arrived and told him not to do so. The ex-husband was arrested on disorderly conduct charges but claimed his speech was protected by the First Amendment. Under these circumstances, however, the court ruled his language constituted unprotected fighting words. Importantly, the court noted that a threat of violence is *not* required for speech to constitute fighting words. Instead, "a threat is merely another factor to be considered by the courts when determining whether the words spoken were fighting words."

Very few types of speech . . . fall completely outside the scope of First Amendment protection.

Another key point here is that legislators must be very precise when they try to carve out statutory exceptions for categories of speech they believe should not be protected by the First Amendment. Very few types of speech, in fact, fall completely outside the scope of First Amendment protection, according to the U.S. Supreme Court; unprotected categories include (1) child pornography involving real minors, as well as obscenity (see Chapter 13); (2) fighting words under *Chaplinsky*, described here; (3) incitement to violence under *Brandenburg* v. *Ohio* (see Chapter 2); (4) certain types of libelous statements (see Chapters 4, 5 and 6); and (5) advertising that is false, misleading or about an unlawful product or service (see Chapter 15).

INTERNET-POSTED THREATS AGAINST THE PRESIDENT: A COLLEGE STUDENT LEARNS THE HARD WAY

"If anyone going to UM [University of Miami] to see Obama today, get ur phones out and record. Cause at any moment im gonna put a bullet through his head and u don't wanna miss that? Youtube!"

That was the message Joaquin Serrapio, a student at Miami-Dade College, posted on his Facebook page in 2012. It proved highly problematic when the Secret

---

70. 268 P.3d 12 (Kan. 2012).

Service discovered it. Serrapio was sentenced later that year to four months of home confinement, three years of probation and ordered to perform 250 hours of community service for posting both it and another message threatening then-President Barack Obama. A federal statute (18 U.S.C. § 871) makes it a crime to communicate "any threat to take the life of, to kidnap, or to inflict bodily harm upon the President of the United States, the President-elect, the Vice President or other officer next in the order of succession to the office of President of the United States." During sentencing, U.S. District Judge Marcia Cooke offered this simple yet sage piece of advice: "I want to make clear that people have the right to criticize our government, but the critique should not threaten peoples' lives."

Hate speech is one thing, but what about symbolic acts that attempt to communicate the same kinds of messages, burning a cross on someone's lawn, for example? The Supreme Court faced this question in 1992 when it struck down a St. Paul, Minn., ordinance that forbade the display of a burning cross or a Nazi swastika or any writing or picture that "arouses the anger, alarm or resentment in others on the basis of race, color, creed, religion or gender." Minnesota courts had approved the law, saying the phrase "arouses anger, alarm or resentment in others" was another way of saying "fighting words." But the statute violated the First Amendment, the high court said, because it was content based—that is, it only applied to fighting words that insult or provoke violence on the basis of race, color, creed or gender. What about fighting words used to express hostility toward someone because of their political affiliation, or their membership in a union or the place where they were born? Justice Antonin Scalia asked. The city has chosen to punish the use of certain kinds of fighting words, but not others, he said. The majority of the court agreed that cross burning was a reprehensible act, but contended there were other laws that could be used to stop such terroristic threats that did not implicate the First Amendment, such as trespass or criminal damage to property. Eleven years later the high court revisited the issue in a case involving Virginia's law against cross burning and ruled that a state could proscribe cross burning without infringing on First Amendment freedoms, so long as the state made it a crime to burn a cross *with the purpose to intimidate the victim.* The intimidation factor is the key, Justice Sandra Day O'Connor wrote. The state would have to prove that the cross burner intended to intimidate the victim; the threat could not be inferred simply because a cross was burned on the victim's lawn.[71]

The opinion in this second cross-burning case highlights another category of speech (a category distinct from both fighting words in *Chaplinsky* and incitement to violence in *Brandenburg*) that is not protected by the First Amendment—**true threats** of violence. As defined by Justice O'Connor in the Virginia cross-burning case, true threats are "those statements where the speaker means to communicate a serious expression of an intent to commit an act of unlawful violence to a particular individual or group of individuals." She added that "intimidation in the constitutionally proscribable sense of the word is a type of true threat, where a speaker directs a threat to a person or group

---

71. *Virginia* v. *Black,* 538 U.S. 343 (2003).

of persons with the intent of placing the victim in fear of bodily harm or death." On the other hand, "political hyperbole" is not a true threat.

SOCIAL MEDIA AND TRUE THREATS

What counts as a true threat of violence in an Internet age filled with social media such as Twitter, YouTube and Facebook?

In 2015, the Supreme Court addressed that question in the case of *Elonis* v. *United States*. Anthony Elonis was sentenced to 44 months in jail for Facebook postings that he said were merely rap lyrics, inspired in part by rapper Eminem. One such post, written about his estranged wife who had obtained a protection from abuse (PFA) order against him, read:

> Fold up your PFA and put it in your pocket
> Is it thick enough to stop a bullet?
> Try to enforce an Order
> That was improperly granted in the first place
> Me thinks the judge needs an education on true threat jurisprudence.

In another example of his violent-themed posts, this one about a female FBI agent who had interviewed Elonis about prior postings, Elonis wrote:

> You know your shit's ridiculous
> when you have the FBI knockin' at yo' door
> Little Agent Lady stood so close
> Took all the strength I had not to turn the bitch ghost
> Pull my knife, flick my wrist, and slit her throat
> Leave her bleedin' from her jugular in the arms of her partner.

For those posts, and others, Elonis was prosecuted under a federal statute—18 U.S.C. § 875(c)—that makes it a crime to transmit in interstate commerce "any communication containing any threat . . . to injure" another person. The 3rd U.S. Circuit Court of Appeals upheld his conviction, ruling that Elonis' subjective intent—whether or not he actually intended to threaten anyone—did not matter. What mattered instead, the 3rd Circuit ruled, was that Elonis intended to communicate a message for others to see and that a reasonable person could interpret his speech as threatening.

Elonis appealed, arguing that the First Amendment protected his posts and that the intent of the *speaker* (in this case him) should matter in deciding if speech amounts to a true threat. In June 2015, the Supreme Court reversed the 3rd Circuit's ruling and remanded the case, but without resolving the key First Amendment issue. In its opinion, the Court instead only addressed the statutory grounds for Elonis' conviction. Premising his conviction under 18 U.S.C. § 875(c) solely on how his posts would be viewed by a reasonable person, the Court ruled, was inconsistent with the conventional requirement under criminal law that a criminal needs to have "awareness of some wrongdoing." So on statutory grounds (i.e., the application of the specific law under which Elonis was convicted), the Court reversed and remanded the case. We still don't know today then whether the *First Amendment* requires consideration of the subjective intent of the speaker in a true threats analysis. The Court's opinion in *Elonis* is an example of the judicial principle of constitutional avoidance in action. Constitutional avoidance holds that if the Court can resolve a case on statutory grounds without ever reaching the constitutional issue, then it should do so. The Roberts Court often employs that principle.

The *Elonis* case has continued. On remand from the Supreme Court, in October 2016, the 3rd U.S. Circuit Court of Appeals ruled that, even had a jury considered Elonis' intent, no jury would have doubted that Elonis knew his lyrics would intimidate his targets.

Sometimes there is a right way to market one's book, and sometimes there is a wrong way. This is a case involving the latter. To drum up publicity for his self-published book *Anthrax: Shock and Awe Terror*, Marc McMain Keyser mailed about 120 envelopes to news outlets, elected officials and businesses like Starbucks and McDonalds. The envelopes included materials touting the book. So far so good. What was the problem?

Keyser also included in each envelope a white sugar packet "with the sugar markings covered by a label stating 'Anthrax' in large letters, 'Sample' in smaller letters and an orange and black biohazard symbol." Keyser was convicted on two counts of mailing threatening communications and three "hoax" counts for communicating false or misleading information regarding the presence of a biological weapon. Keyser, however, argued that the First Amendment protected his speech.

In 2012, the 9th U.S. Circuit Court of Appeals rejected Keyser's free-speech argument in *United States* v. *Keyser*. As for the threats counts, the appellate court observed that "a reasonable person would understand that a recipient would perceive a packet of powder with the word 'Anthrax' and a biohazard symbol printed on it as a threat. A reasonable person would also understand that the word 'sample' would not alleviate that concern—if read and processed at all, the word would likely indicate a small amount of the actual substance." As for the hoax counts, the court held the First Amendment did not protect Keyser because "false and misleading information indicating an act of terrorism is not a simple lie. Instead, it tends to incite a tangible negative response. Here, law enforcement and emergency workers responded to the mailings as potential acts of terror, arriving with hazardous materials units, evacuating buildings, sending the samples off to a laboratory for tests and devoting resources to investigating the source of the mailings."

Today, many states are adopting anti-cyberbullying statutes, using language from the true threats doctrine to sweep up this growing problem. Whether such laws are constitutional will be sorted out by courts throughout the rest of this decade (see page 14 for an example of a cyberbullying law that was struck down). But the reality is that adoption of such laws is not likely to deter a teenager from bullying another teenager in cyberspace.

The efforts to control hate speech in the past three decades have focused particularly on public schools and universities. More than 300 colleges promulgated speech codes in the 1980s and early 1990s, but after several court rulings against such policies, most school policies were either abandoned or simply unenforced.[72] The courts tended to follow the principles from *Chaplinsky* and *Gooding* that limit prosecution of such hate speech to face-to-face encounters that could result in physical injury or provoke violent acts.

A policy drafted by the school board in State College, Pa., was declared unconstitutional by a federal appeals court because it was vague and overbroad and would punish students for "simple acts of teasing and name calling." A lawsuit against the policy was filed on behalf of two students who said they feared they would be punished if they expressed their religious belief that homosexuality is a sin. The district defined harassment as verbal or physical conduct based on race, sex, national origin, sexual orientation or other personal characteristics that has the effect of creating an intimidating or hostile environment. Examples of such harassment included jokes, name-calling, graffiti and innuendo as well as making fun of a student's clothing, social skills or surname. The appeals court agreed that preventing actual discrimination in school was a legitimate, even compelling, government interest. But the school district's policy was simply overbroad, prohibiting a substantial amount of speech that would not constitute actionable harassment under either federal or state law.[73] The government cannot prohibit invectives or epithets that simply injure someone's feelings or are merely rude or discourteous. The Pennsylvania ruling mirrors other similar decisions throughout the nation that pose a real dilemma for school administrators and legislators who are seeking to reduce the verbal aggressiveness common on many school yards.

The government cannot prohibit invectives or epithets that simply injure someone's feelings or are merely rude or discourteous.

At the college level, the difference between unprotected harassment and protected expression that merely offends was clarified by the Office of Civil Rights (OCR) of the U.S. Department of Education in a July 28, 2003, memorandum. That memorandum provides that harassment

> must include something beyond the mere expression of views, words, symbols or thoughts that some person finds offensive. Under OCR's standard, the conduct must also be considered sufficiently serious to deny or limit a student's ability to participate in or benefit from the educational program. Thus, OCR's standards require the conduct be evaluated from the perspective of a reasonable person in the alleged victim's position, considering all the circumstances, including the alleged victim's age.

This statement is important because many public universities today have policies that, although they are no longer called or referred to as speech codes, nonetheless restrict students' expressive rights. A Philadelphia-based organization called the Foundation for Individual Rights in Education (FIRE) aggressively challenges such policies while it simultaneously defends college students' rights of free speech. FIRE keeps tabs on these policies online in its Speech Codes Database at https://www.thefire.org/spotlight/ and encourages students to come forward with instances of campus censorship.

---

72. See, for example, *John Doe* v. *University of Michigan,* 721 F. Supp. 852 (1989); and *UWM Post* v. *Board of Regents of the University of Wisconsin,* 774 F. Supp. 1163 (1991).
73. *Saxe* v. *State College Area School District,* 240 F. 3d 200 (2001).

University speech codes are still litigated today and, almost inevitably, are declared unconstitutional. For example, in 2010 a federal district court in Texas ruled that restrictions on symbolic speech at Tarrant County College were unconstitutional. Members of the group Students for Concealed Carry on Campus wanted to stage an "empty-holster protest," where they would wear empty holsters during their normal campus activities to symbolize that they were unarmed and potentially defenseless in the case of a school shooting. School officials said the empty holsters would not be allowed. In *Smith* v. *Tarrant County College District,* Judge Terry Means ruled that the school's reliance on a policy barring "disruptive activities" to justify its ban on the protest violated the First Amendment because school officials "failed to show that the disruptive-activities provision of the student handbook furthers the important interests on which they rely to justify it."[74] The court also ruled that the school's prohibition on "cosponsorship," which prohibited students from engaging in speech activities on campus when that speech or event was associated with an off-campus person or organization, was unconstitutional. That "sweeping" ban, Judge Means wrote, "broadly prohibits any speech by students that involves an off-campus organization in almost any conceivable way."

In 2008, the 3rd U.S. Circuit Court of Appeals held that Temple University's sexual harassment policy (notice it was not called a speech code) was unconstitutionally overbroad in the scope of the speech it restricted (see pages 13–14 regarding the overbreadth doctrine).[75] In ruling against Temple, the appellate court in *DeJohn* v. *Temple University* observed that "overbroad harassment policies can suppress or even chill core protected speech, and are susceptible to selective application amounting to content-based or viewpoint discrimination." In language incredibly favorable to the First Amendment freedom of speech, the court wrote that "discussion by adult students in a college classroom should not be restricted." Importantly, the court distinguished between high schools and colleges when it comes to restricting speech, writing "that Temple's administrators are granted *less leeway* in regulating student speech than are public elementary or high school administrators." Temple's policy was flawed, in part, because it punished individuals for the intent of their speech, even if the speech caused no harm.

FIRE has identified another disturbing trend on college campuses: charging student groups who bring controversial speakers to campus exorbitant "security fees" for police protection. For instance, FIRE reported that three times in 2016 DePaul University imposed fees on student organizations engaging in "controversial" expression. In September 2016, the student group the DePaul Socialists was forced to pay hundreds of dollars for security guards to be present at their informational student meeting, even though the group did not want security guards there. According to a FIRE article titled "DePaul Continues to Impose 'Speech Tax' on Student Expression," DePaul administrators said the event was "potentially controversial" and told the students that if they did not agree to pay for the security guards, then they would not be able to hold the event. In response, FIRE wrote a letter to university officials, encouraging the university to "live up to its promises of free speech and cease charging student organizations for security based on the content of their expression."

74. 694 F. Supp. 2d 610 (N.D. Tex. 2010).

75. *DeJohn* v. *Temple University*, 537 F. 3d 301 (3d Cir. 2008).

SUMMARY   Hate speech is not a new problem in America, but courts now are being called on to determine just how far the state may go in limiting what people say and write about other people when their language is abusive or includes racial, ethnic or religious invective. In the early 1940s the Supreme Court ruled that so-called fighting words could be prohibited, but these words have come to mean face-to-face invective or insults that are likely to result in a violent response on the part of the victim. The high court voided a St. Paul, Minn., ordinance that punished such abusive speech because, the court said, the law did not ban all fighting words, merely some kinds of fighting words (i.e., racial or religious invective) that the community believed were improper. The decision in this case has sharply limited attempts by state universities and colleges and public schools to use speech codes to discourage hate speech or other politically incorrect comments or publications.

THE FIRST AMENDMENT AND ELECTION CAMPAIGNS

The First Amendment is clearly implicated in any election campaign. Candidates give speeches, publish advertising, hand out leaflets and undertake a variety of other activities that clearly fall within the ambit of constitutional protection. But since the mid-1970s the First Amendment and political campaigns have intersected in another way as well. Attempts by Congress and other legislative bodies to regulate the flow of money in political campaigns have been consistently challenged as infringing on the right of freedom of expression.

Campaign reform laws tend to fall into one of two categories: those that limit how much candidates and their supporters can spend on the election, and those that limit how much money people can contribute to candidates and political parties. The courts have tended to find more serious First Amendment problems with the laws that limit spending than the laws that limit contributions, although this is not always the case.

A Supreme Court opinion on point is a 2006 decision, *Randall v. Sorrell*.[76] At issue was a Vermont campaign-finance statute limiting both the amounts that candidates for state office could spend on their campaigns (expenditure limitations) and the amounts that individuals, organizations and political parties could contribute to those campaigns (contribution limitations). For instance, a candidate for governor could spend no more than $300,000 during a two-year general election cycle, while a candidate for lieutenant governor could spend an even lower maximum of $100,000 (under the statute, the figures could be adjusted upward slightly for inflation). Vermont also had the most strict campaign contribution limits in the nation, including a $400 cap that any single individual could contribute to the campaign of a candidate for statewide office (governor, lieutenant governor, etc.) during a two-year general election cycle and a $200 cap for contributions to state legislators.

76. 548 U.S. 230 (2006).

In 2006, the nation's high court declared both the expenditure and contribution limits in Vermont "inconsistent with the First Amendment." It noted that "well-established precedent makes clear that the expenditure limits violate the First Amendment." The precedent referred to was the 1976 decision in *Buckley* v. *Valeo*[77] in which the court first adopted, in the context of the Federal Election Campaign Act of 1971, the dichotomy between expenditure limits and contribution limits. In *Buckley*, the court upheld a $1,000 per election limit on individual contributions and reasoned that contribution limits are permissible in order to prevent "corruption and the appearance of corruption."[78] The court in *Buckley*, however, held that this same interest was not sufficient to justify limits on expenditures by candidates and, instead, reasoned that expenditure caps are not permissible because they "necessarily reduce the quantity of expression by restricting the number of issues discussed, the depth of their exploration, and the size of the audience reached."

As for Vermont's contribution limits, a majority of the justices found they were "well below the limits this court upheld in *Buckley*," noting that "in terms of real dollars (i.e., adjusting for inflation), [Vermont's limit] on individual contributions to a campaign for governor is slightly more than one-twentieth of the limit on contributions to campaigns for federal office before the Court in *Buckley*." The court concluded in *Randall* that Vermont's contribution limits were simply "too restrictive," threatened "to inhibit effective advocacy by those who seek election, particularly challengers," and imposed burdens on the First Amendment right of expression that were "disproportionately severe" to advancing the goals of preventing actual corruption and the appearance of corruption. The court, however, did not identify a precise dollar amount limitation that would be permissible on contributions.

The bottom line from Supreme Court decisions stretching from *Buckley* through *Randall* is that expenditure limits imposed on candidates violate free-expression rights of candidates for public office, while contribution limits imposed on donors are permissible unless, as was the case in *Randall*, they become so restrictive and limiting that they prevent more expression than is needed to serve the interests of preventing corruption and its appearance. The decision in *Randall* was seen by some as "a defeat for liberal reformers who wanted to lessen the impact of money in politics."[79] Both cases, however, involved splintered decisions among the justices, suggesting that the still-valid dichotomy between expenditure limits (not permissible) and contributions (permissible if not too low) is tenuous and may change if the court's composition shifts significantly. In fact, only three justices in *Randall* firmly endorsed the continued use of the *Buckley* dichotomy.

Other recent issues affecting the intersection of money, speech and politics involve challenges to the Bipartisan Campaign Reform Act (BCRA) of 2002 that, among other things, makes it a federal crime for any corporation to broadcast, shortly before an election, any ads that name a federal candidate for elected office and that target the electorate.

---

77. 424 U.S. 1 (1976).
78. Subsequent to *Buckley*, the court also upheld a $1,075 limit on contributions to candidates for Missouri state auditor in *Nixon* v. *Shrink Missouri Government PAC*, 528 U.S. 377 (2000).
79. Savage, "Kennedy Moves Front and Center."

In 2008, the Supreme Court in *Davis* v. *Federal Election Commission* struck down as unconstitutional a portion of the BCRA called the Millionaire's Amendment.[80] The provision stated that if a candidate for the U.S. House of Representatives spent more than $350,000 of his or her own personal funds running for office, then that candidate's opponent was exempt from the normal, strict limits on contributions that can be received from individual donors (the 2008 contribution cap on a donor to a candidate for Congress was $2,300 during a two-year election cycle) and could instead receive three times the normal amount. The self-financing candidate (the one spending more than $350,000), however, was still subject to the normal limits on donor contributions. In brief, if a wealthy candidate spent too much of his or her own money (more than $350,000), then his or her opponent was cut a break from the normal contribution limits while the wealthy candidate was not. In declaring that the Millionaire's Amendment impermissibly burdened the First Amendment right of a wealthy, self-financing candidate "to spend his own money for campaign speech" by imposing asymmetrical contribution limits, Justice Samuel Alito wrote for the five-justice majority that "we have never upheld the constitutionality of a law that imposes different contribution limits for candidates who are competing against each other." The majority rejected the idea that leveling the playing field for candidates of different wealth justified the provision.

In 2010, the Supreme Court declared unconstitutional in *Citizens United* v. *Federal Elections Commission*[81] a federal law that prohibited corporations (both for-profit and nonprofit advocacy corporations) and unions from using their general treasury funds to pay for ads expressly advocating for the election or defeat of a candidate or for similar electioneering communications made within 30 days of a primary or 60 days of a general election. In reaching the conclusion that this statute violated the free-speech rights of corporations, a five-justice majority concluded that the First Amendment "generally prohibits the suppression of political speech based on the speaker's identity." The decision, which centered on a documentary that was sponsored by a nonprofit corporation and that was highly critical of Hillary Clinton, reinforced the twin principles that: (1) corporations have First Amendment speech rights; and (2) political speech—even that paid for by corporations—is at the core of the First Amendment. Writing for the majority, Justice Anthony Kennedy reasoned that "speech restrictions based on the identity of the speaker are all too often simply a means to control content." The Court left in place, however, rules imposed upon corporations that spend such money that require them to disclose and report it. The decision in *Citizens United* overruled the precedent from the 1990 ruling in *Austin* v. *Michigan State Chamber of Commerce*[82] that had held that political speech may be banned based on the speaker's corporate identity (see pages 3–6 regarding stare decisis and overruling precedent).

The aftermath of *Citizens United* saw a rise in so-called Super PACs (political action committees), such as the conservative-leaning Restore Our Future and the liberal-slanting

---

80. 554 U.S. 724 (2008).
81. 558 U.S. 310 (2010). The documentary, "Hillary: The Movie," was released during the 2008 Democratic presidential primaries in which Hillary Clinton was competing against Barack Obama and John Edwards.
82. 494 U.S. 652 (1990).

Priorities USA Action, raising and spending vast sums of money on advertisements during the 2012 election-year cycle. Priorities USA Action, for instance, stated on its Web site in June 2012, "We are committed to the reelection of President Obama and setting the record straight when there are misleading attacks against him and other progressive leaders," while Restore Our Future called Mitt Romney "the Republican candidate that can put our country back on the right path and the only one who can defeat Barack Obama."

The Supreme Court, however, narrowly rejected an opportunity in 2012 to reconsider its controversial *Citizens United* opinion when it issued a **per curiam opinion** in *American Tradition Partnership, Inc.* v. *Bullock*.[83] The case involved a century-old Montana statute prohibiting corporations from spending money "in connection with a candidate or a political committee that supports or opposes a candidate or a political party." The Supreme Court of Montana had upheld the law in 2011—one year after *Citizens United* was decided—because it concluded that independent expenditures by corporations had, in fact, caused actual corruption or given the appearance of corruption in the Big Sky state. The five conservative-leaning justices on the U.S. Supreme Court, however, found that *Citizens United* involved "a similar federal law" and that Montana, in an effort to defend its law, had failed to meaningfully distinguish it from that in *Citizens United*. In doing so, the majority overruled the Supreme Court of Montana and struck down the state law for violating the ruling in *Citizens United*. The four liberal-leaning justices at the time—Ruth Bader Ginsburg, Stephen Breyer, Sonia Sotomayor and Elena Kagan—dissented. Justice Breyer wrote for the dissenters that "Montana's experience, like considerable experience elsewhere since the Court's decision in *Citizens United,* casts grave doubt on the Court's supposition that independent expenditures do not corrupt or appear to do so."

SUMMARY

Efforts to reform the expensive American electoral process seem to be gaining momentum in the early part of the 21st century, but under the Constitution there is only so much that the law can do. The Supreme Court has ruled that while it is permissible to place a limit on how much money one person or business can donate to a campaign, it may be a violation of the First Amendment to place a limit on how much a candidate may spend. Because the presentation of campaign messages via the mass media is so much a part of the current electoral process and because sending such messages costs money, campaign spending is tied closely to freedom of speech and press and is protected by the First Amendment, the court has ruled.

THE FIRST AMENDMENT AND THE INFORMATION SUPERHIGHWAY

The First Amendment was drafted and approved in the late 18th century, a time when newspapers, magazines, books and handbills comprised the press that was intended to be protected by the constitutional provision. As each new mass medium

83. 132 S. Ct. 2490 (2012).

has emerged—radio, motion pictures, over-the-air television, cable television and so forth—the courts have had to define the scope of First Amendment protection appropriate to that medium. And so it is with the Internet, computer-mediated communication. The next 13 chapters of this book contain references to laws regarding libel, invasion of privacy, access to information, obscenity, copyright and advertising, and they contain references to how these laws are being applied to computer-mediated communication. These emerging rules have in no small part been dictated by decisions by the federal courts that speak to the general question of the application of the First Amendment to the Internet. The next few pages focus on this general question.

How the government regulates a message communicated by any medium is generally determined by the content of that particular message. A plea to burn down city hall and kill the mayor is sedition; a call to vote the mayor out of office is not. Calling Mary Smith a thief is libelous; calling Mary Smith a good student is not. The law is applied, then, based on what the message says. But in some instances the regulation of a message is based on more than the content of the message; it is also influenced by the kind of medium through which the message is transmitted. As some have stated, there is a medium-specific First Amendment jurisprudence in the United States, meaning that the scope and amount of protection that speech receives will be influenced by the nature of the medium on which it is conveyed.

At least four categories of traditional communications media were in common use when the Internet first burst onto the scene, and even today each is regulated somewhat differently by the law. The printed press—newspapers, magazines, books and pamphlets—enjoys the greatest freedom of all mass media from government regulation. The over-the-air broadcast media—television and radio—enjoy the least amount of freedom from government censorship. Cable television is somewhere between these two, enjoying more freedom than broadcasting but somewhat less than print. Few limits are placed on the messages transmitted via the telephone, and those that are must be very narrowly drawn.[84] There are some ifs, ands or buts in this simple outline, but it is an accurate summary of the hierarchy of mass media when measured by First Amendment freedom.

Why is the printed press allotted the most protection by the First Amendment? There are no physical limits on the number of newspapers and magazines or handbills that can be published. (Economic limits are another matter, but one not considered by the courts in this context.) Since the founding of the Republic in 1789, the printed press has traditionally been free. The receiver must generally take an active role in purchasing a book or a magazine or newspaper. Young people must have the economic wherewithal to buy a newspaper or magazine, and then have the literacy skills to read it.

It is just as obvious why broadcast media have fared the poorest in First Amendment protection. There is an actual physical limit on the number of radio and television channels that exist. All but a very few are in use. Since not everyone who wants such a channel can have one, it is up to the government to select who gets these scarce broadcast frequencies and to make certain those who use the frequencies serve the interests of all listeners and viewers. Because of spectrum scarcity and other reasons, broadcasting has been regulated nearly since its inception. It has no tradition of freedom. All the receiver

---

84. *Sable Communications v. FCC,* 492 U.S. 115 (1989).

must do to listen to the radio or watch television is to flick a switch. Even children who don't know how to read can do this; radio and television are easily accessible to children.

Cable television and telephones fit somewhere in between. There is potentially an unlimited capacity for messages to be transmitted by each medium. Both have been historically regulated, but not to the extent that broadcasting has been regulated. Although a receiver can watch a cable television channel as easily as he or she can watch an over-the-air channel, the receiver must take a far more active role by subscribing to a cable system. Although this action may seem like a trivial distinction, the courts have made much of it. Judges have presumed that the people who subscribe to cable television should know what they will receive. Federal law mandates that cable television companies provide safeguards (called cable locks) for parents who want to shield their children from violent or erotic programming.* Such screening technology is only now coming into use for over-the-air television. The use of a telephone also requires a more active role by the receiver than simply switching on a radio or television set.

GOOGLE AND CENSORSHIP REQUESTS ACROSS THE GLOBE

In 2010, Google launched a Web site devoted to documenting the number of requests it received from government entities across the globe for the removal of content or the disclosure of user data. Removal requests seek the removal of content from Google search results or from another Google product, including YouTube, while data requests seek information about Google user accounts or products. According to the site, Google received more than 8,000 requests to remove content from government agencies around the world in 2015. The Web site is located at http://www.google.com/governmentrequests.

Where do computer-mediated communication systems fit into this hierarchy? In 1997 the Supreme Court ruled that communication via the Internet deserves the highest level of First Amendment protection, protection comparable to that given to print newspapers, magazines and books.[85] The high court made this decision as it ruled that the central provisions of the 1996 Communications Decency Act that restricted the transmission of indecent material over the Internet violated the U.S. Constitution. Recognizing that each medium of communication may present its own constitutional problems, Justice John Paul Stevens wrote that the members of the high court could find no basis in past decisions for "qualifying the level of First Amendment scrutiny that should be applied to this medium [the Internet]."

The court rejected the notion prevalent among those in Congress who voted for the Communications Decency Act that communication via the Internet should be treated in

---

* But in U.S. v. *Playboy Entertainment Group, Inc.,* 529 U.S. 803 (2000), the Supreme Court suggested that cable television enjoys the full protection of the First Amendment. This notion has yet to be fleshed out by the court.

85. *Reno* v. *American Civil Liberties Union,* 521 U.S. 844 (1997).

the same manner as communication via over-the-air radio and television. The court said that the scarcity of frequencies that had long justified the regulation of broadcasting did not apply in the case of the Internet, which, it said, can hardly be considered a "scarce" expressive commodity.

The importance of this ruling cannot be overestimated. Not only did the court strike down a restrictive federal law that was certain to retard the growth of computer-mediated communication, it ruled that any other governmental agency that seeks to regulate communication via the information superhighway must treat this medium in the same manner it would treat a print newspaper or book.

NET NEUTRALITY

The potential of the Internet as "vast democratic fora" and a "new marketplace of ideas"—terms used by Justice Stevens to describe it back in 1997 in *Reno* v. *ACLU*—is seriously jeopardized by the possibility that the companies controlling broadband access to the Internet will block, degrade and otherwise discriminate against some types of Internet content, services and applications. Put differently, the danger exists that those who provide on-ramps to the Internet will harm the open and nondiscriminatory nature of the medium. Interest groups such as Public Knowledge[86] thus advocate the concept of *net neutrality*, a relatively abstract term suggesting that Internet service providers should treat all traffic and content similarly and that they should not charge more money for or block access to faster services. More simply put, as the *San Francisco Chronicle* described it, net neutrality is "the idea that traffic on the Internet should flow as democratically as possible."[87]

Net neutrality raises important First Amendment issues for all Internet users, including the right to receive speech (including a diversity of ideas) and the right to access information. The statutes and regulations adopted by Congress and the Federal Communications Commission (FCC) today will largely determine whether net neutrality remains a reality or whether the Internet will someday be treated more like cable, where the cable system provider charges different rates for different content and services. As media merge (possibly changing the nature of the medium-specific First Amendment jurisprudence adopted by the Supreme Court) and as cable operators and phone companies compete for control over the on-ramps to the Internet, the First Amendment rights of all citizens are placed in the balance.

The issue of net neutrality heated up in 2008 after allegations that Comcast, a major opponent of government action mandating network neutrality, was restricting and interfering with Internet access to the flow of content, such as video clips, songs and software files, on a file-sharing service called BitTorrent.[88] Such a discriminatory practice by a service provider like Comcast, which provides broadband Internet access over cable lines,

---

86. The organization describes itself as a Washington, D.C.–based "advocacy group working to defend your rights in the emerging digital culture." See http://www.publicknowledge.org.
87. Abate and Kopytoff, "Are Internet Toll Roads Ahead?"
88. Kang, "FCC Head Says Action Possible on Web Limits"; *Associated Press*, "FCC Poised to Punish Comcast for Traffic Blocking."

that targets the use of a particular peer-to-peer application is precisely what advocates of net neutrality fear.

The fight over net neutrality has raged on. In March 2015, the FCC released an Open Internet Order meant, it said, to "enact strong, sustainable rules ... to protect the open Internet and ensure that Americans reap the economic, social, and civic benefits of an open Internet today and into the future." In the order, the FCC reclassified broadband Internet service as a telecommunications service, subject to common carrier regulation under Title II of the Communications Act of 1934. In effect, the FCC classified the Internet as a public utility, with the goal of ensuring an open Internet for all content.

The FCC's order banned three specific practices that it said invariably harm the principle of an open Internet: blocking, throttling and paid prioritization.

1. No blocking. The FCC said consumers who subscribe to broadband Internet service "must get what they have paid for—access to all (lawful) destinations on the Internet." Therefore, the FCC's order mandated that Internet service providers "shall not block lawful content, applications, services, or non-harmful devices."

2. No throttling. The FCC's order also included a ban on throttling, or degrading, access to the Internet. Such throttling would involve a broadband Internet service provider slowing down access to a site, service or application. If throttling were allowed, the FCC said, such "gamesmanship" could effectively avoid the no-blocking rule by rendering an application effectively unusable.

3. No paid prioritization. The FCC said paid prioritization occurs "when a broadband provider accepts payment (monetary or otherwise) to manage its network in a way that benefits particular content applications, services, or devices." Those sorts of agreements would create a "fast lane" on the Internet where some content is privileged (and accessible more quickly) than others. The FCC's order banned the practice.

These rules applied to both fixed and mobile broadband Internet service. The FCC's order also required enhanced transparency, so that "consumers are fully informed about the Internet access they are purchasing" and so that sites, such as Amazon, "have the information they need to understand whether their services will work as advertised." The order required that broadband Internet service providers must disclose promotional rates, all fees and surcharges, and all data caps or data allowances. The order also required specific notification to consumers if a "network practice" is likely to significantly affect their Internet use.

The FCC passed the order along party lines, with the three Democratic commissioners on the FCC voting for the order and the two Republican commissioners voting against it (and issuing strongly worded dissents). The order frustrated broadband Internet service providers (ISPs), who have fought against rules that mandate net neutrality. The ISPs argue, among other things, that they should be able to charge a service such as Netflix—which one report found accounts for more than a third of all downstream Internet bandwidth during peak periods—higher preferred-access fees.

Three separate groups of petitioners, consisting primarily of broadband providers and their associations, challenged the order. But in June 2016 the U.S. Circuit Court of

Appeals for the District of Columbia ruled in favor of the FCC. In *United States Telecom Association* v. *FCC*,[89] the D.C. Circuit upheld, by a 2-1 vote, the FCC's net neutrality rules as well as its classification of broadband Internet access as a public utility. An appeal of the decision is likely. Moreover, under the Trump administration, the majority of the FCC commissioners are now Republicans (under Obama, three of the five were Democrats), and the Republican commissioners have indicated that they hope to roll back the net neutrality efforts launched when the Democrats had a majority on the FCC. In May 2017, the FCC—now chaired by Ajit Pai, a Republican who was appointed FCC chairman by President Trump—voted to start the process of reversing the 2015 order's classification of the Internet as a telecommunications service. That May 2017 vote initiated a period where the public could comment on the proposed reversal. So the issue is far from settled.

BIBLIOGRAPHY

Abate, Tom, and Verne Kopytoff. "Are Internet Toll Roads Ahead?" *San Francisco Chronicle*, 7 February 2006, C1.

Associated Press. "FCC Poised to Punish Comcast for Traffic Blocking." 26 July 2008.

——. "U.S. Judge Says Utica Schools Illegally Censored Prep Paper." 13 October 2004.

Gillmor, Donald. "The Fragile 'First.'" *Hamline Law Review* 8 (1985): 277.

Kang, Cecilia. "FCC Head Says Action Possible on Web Limits." *Washington Post*, 26 February 2008, D1.

Savage, David G. "Kennedy Moves Front and Center on Court." *Los Angeles Times*, 2 July 2006.

Weaver, Russell L., and Donald E. Lively. *Understanding the First Amendment*. Newark, N.J.: LexisNexis.

89. 825 F.3d 674 (D.C. Cir. 2016).

Libel

ESTABLISHING A CASE

The law of libel is centuries old. Its roots in this country spring directly from the British common law. Throughout most of this nation's history the states were left to fashion their own libel laws. But since the mid-1960s, the U.S. Supreme Court has "federalized" basic elements of defamation law, obligating the states to keep their rules and regulations within boundaries defined by the First Amendment. This development has transformed what was a fairly simple aspect of American law into a legal thicket. In this first of three chapters about defamation, some basic dimensions of this common tort action are characterized and the requirements that have been placed on the plaintiff to establish a cause of action for libel are outlined.

THE LIBEL LANDSCAPE

Defamation, or libel, is a **tort,** or a civil wrong. It is the most common legal problem faced by people who work in the mass media, and often the most troublesome. Allegations of libel are the basis of about two-thirds of all lawsuits filed against mass media defendants in any given year. In simple terms, **libel** is the publication or broadcast of any false statement of fact that injures somone's reputation.

Anyone who speaks, publishes (including material on the Internet) or broadcasts anything can become the target of a defamation action. Libel can lurk in a news story or editorial, a press release, a company newsletter, advertising copy, letters to the editor, a tweet, a Facebook post or even oral statements made publicly.[1] The mainstream mass media face the vast majority of libel suits, and that is why most of the cases cited in the three subsequent chapters tend to involve lawsuits against newspapers, radio and television stations, magazines and books and the growing number of information-oriented sites on the Internet. Traditional principles of libel law apply uniformly in all libel cases, regardless of the medium used to communicate the allegedly defamatory words or pictures. But media in what we might call the public or mainstream press, such as newspapers, magazines, broadcast stations and online sites, enjoy some First Amendment protections that may not accrue to those who publish defamation in a company newsletter or press release, a personal blog or a posting on Facebook or Twitter.

DAMAGE CLAIMS

Plaintiffs often seek large amounts of money in libel cases against media defendants. For example, in 2015 a dean of students at the University of Virginia named Nicole Eramo sued *Rolling Stone* magazine for $7.5 million in compensatory damages over a now debunked 2014 story called "A Rape on Campus." Eramo contended the article, which *Rolling Stone* later retracted, portrayed her as the "chief villain" in not supporting or helping a woman named "Jackie," who claimed she was gang raped at a University of Virginia fraternity. A jury eventually awarded Eramo $3 million after a two-week trial. Also in 2016, a North Carolina jury awarded Beth Desmond, an agent with the North Carolina Bureau of Investigation, $1.5 million in compensatory damages and $7.5 million in punitive damages in a defamation suit against *The News & Observer* and reporter Mandy Locke. The award was so large it exceeded the state's legal cap limit on punitive damages. That year also saw Mike McQueary, the former Penn State assistant football coach and whistleblower in the Jerry Sandusky case, awarded $7.3 million by a jury in his defamation suit against the university. And sometimes plaintiffs want even more money. In 2016, for example, a Nashville district attorney named Glenn Funk sued

---

1. See, for example, *Troy Group, Inc.* v. *Tilson*, 364 F. Supp. 2d 1149 (2005) for a suit based on an e-mail; *600 West 115th Street Corp.* v. *von Gotfeld*, 80 N.Y. 2d 130 (1992) for a case based on a comment made at a public meeting, and *Gordon & Holmes* v. *Courtney Love*, No. B256367, Court of Appeals. Cal. Feb. 1, 2016, for a case based on a tweet made by musician and actress Courtney Love.

©AP Photo/Steve Helber

Nicole Eramo, a former dean at the University of Virginia, won a $3 million judgment in a defamation suit against Rolling Stone magazine and the author of the story, "A Rape on Campus." Rather than appeal the case, Rolling Stone reached a confidential settlement with Eramo in April 2017.

Scripps Media, the owner of WTVF-NewsChannel 5, for $200 million over an investigative story that suggested Funk tried to blackmail a defendant and attempted to solicit a bribe. Not to be outdone, in late 2016, Burke Ramsey, the brother of JonBenet Ramsey, sued CBS, a production company and a host of contributors for the whopping sum of $750 million. Ramsey alleged that the "gist" of the September 2016 program "The Case of: JonBenet Ramsey" was that he killed his sister in 1996. In 2008, JonBenet's family, including Burke, were officially cleared of wrongdoing in the case by the Boulder, Colorado, district attorney.

As the next few pages indicate, such cases often cost media defendants huge sums of money to defend in terms of legal fees and litigation costs. Additionally, litigation frequently stretches on for years. And while many libel cases ultimately are thrown out, dismissed or settled before trial, if a case does reach a jury, plaintiffs often win enormous damage awards (see the gray-shaded text box on page 149 entitled "Taking the Media to Trial"). Even when those awards later are reduced or tossed out on appeal, as they often are, that does not reduce the time and expense of fighting the cases.

TIME AND MONEY

All lawsuits take time to resolve. Some libel suits take many years. The Knight-Ridder Company settled a libel suit in 1996 brought by a former Philadelphia prosecuting attorney. The case began 23 years earlier. Consumers Union, the publisher of *Consumer Reports*, settled a libel suit in 2004 that had been brought by the Suzuki Motor Corporation. The case began in 1996.[2] Although these cases aren't necessarily typical, protracted litigation is always a threat in a defamation action because of the complex nature of libel law. And while the case goes on, the defense lawyers remain on the job, racking up billable hours. Additionally, successfully defending a newspaper or broadcasting network in a libel suit requires the work of talented attorneys. Defending a libel suit is far more

2. Hakim, "Suzuki Resolves a Dispute."

complicated than writing a will or seeking damages for an automobile accident. Fees of $500 per hour for attorneys are not unusual.

TIME AND THE LAW

The likelihood of defamatory material being published or broadcast today is extraordinarily high, given the volume of words and pictures transmitted and posted online by the media. The editing process in the mainstream press has been diluted due to budget cutbacks. The time traditional media have to make decisions regarding the liability inherent in publishing a story has been compressed. Where 20 years ago multiple editors might have looked at a story, there is simply not time for that to occur today given the rush to get the story not only in tomorrow's edition or on tonight's newscast, but immediately online.

Libel law is among the most tangled areas of American law. It is filled with many poorly defined amorphous concepts. Although libel is based on traditional common law, it is infused with statutory and constitutional elements. The vast majority of American judges will never hear a libel case, no matter how many years they sit on the bench. And most lawyers have never considered the topic since two or three days of lectures in a torts class in law school. Jurors—laypeople who have little or no experience with any aspect of the law—are usually even more in the dark. Mistakes are often made at trials; wrong decisions are handed down. Errors can be corrected on appeal—and usually are. But this takes time and costs money for the defendant newspaper or broadcasting station.

Lawyers who represent the press usually follow a similar strategy: First, try to have the case dismissed before it goes to trial. Failing that, offer to settle the case. Most of the time this can save money. (The cost of settling a case can often be much lower than the legal costs involved in a trial.) A settlement before a trial also makes sense because, according to Media Law Resource Center (MLRC) research, the odds are better than 50-50 that the press will lose the case if it goes before a jury. Why? Well, some libel plaintiffs have actually been wronged and deserve to win their case. But there are other reasons as well.

■ As noted, the law is complex and errors are sometimes made by jurors and judges.

■ Important libel defenses are anchored in the First Amendment, an abstract concept to many people. A juror can often see damage to a person's reputation much more clearly than the theoretical value inherent in freedom of the press.

■ The mass media today are not held in high regard by a great many people in the nation. A lot of people don't like the press. A libel trial can provide an opportunity for a juror to express his or her frustrations with the press by awarding damages to a plaintiff. Attorney Thomas D. Yannucci, who represents libel plaintiffs, called the jury box the mass media's Achilles' heel. "If you take it to the jury, the ordinary citizen begins [the trial] thinking the media is unfair."[3]

---

3. Moscov, "Truth, Justice and the American Tort," 22.

TAKING THE MEDIA TO TRIAL: FACTS, FIGURES AND TRENDS

The Media Law Resource Center in April 2016 issued a report describing the results of trials against media defendants for libel, privacy and related claims from 1980 through 2015. Here are key findings.

- From 1980 through 2015, media defendants won only 251 of 606 trial verdicts (slightly more than 40 percent). However, *after trial* (on appeal and during post-trial motions), media defendants won 56 percent of tried cases, with plaintiffs recovering nothing. In fact, only about 19 percent of damage awards to plaintiffs fully stood up after trial. As the MLRC report concluded, plaintiff "damage awards dropped 86.2% from the amount awarded at trial to the amount awarded after post-trial motions and appeals, not counting amounts that may have been obtained in settlements."

- From 1980 through 2015, the average trial damage award to plaintiffs was a whopping $2.82 million, while the median award was $310,000. After post-trial motions and appeals filed by media defendants, however, the size of the average award fell to just under $700,000 while the median dropped to $115,000.

- The number of cases reaching trial against media defendants has steadily declined. In 2015, in fact, there was only one trial against a media defendant. It was a libel case called *Mitre* v. *HBO* stemming from a 2008 segment of "Real Sports with Bryant Gumbel" about the use of child labor in the manufacture of soccer balls. Mitre, a soccer ball manufacturer, lost the case before a jury in New York.

The bottom line seems clear: While plaintiffs may do well against media defendants when a case actually reaches trial, the amounts juries award often either are completely thrown out or are significantly reduced on appeal or post-trial motions. But regardless of the ultimate outcome, it costs media organizations vast sums of money and time to defend and litigate these cases.

THE LAWSUIT AS A WEAPON

In the typical libel suit the injured party, or the plaintiff, initiates the lawsuit to (1) repair any damage to reputation and (2) collect money damages to compensate for the harm to reputation. To reach either of these ends, the plaintiff must either win a settlement or a court case. In the last last 35 years, however, a different kind of libel action has emerged. In these cases the plaintiff is far more interested in blocking the defendant from publishing further harmful comments than winning damages.

Legal authorities call these kinds of libel suits Strategic Lawsuits Against Public Participation, or SLAPP suits.[4]

Imagine these situations:

- Ted Spiker is upset about the quality of work performed at his house by a local carpet company, Carpet Masters. Spiker thus posts a negative review on Yelp! that says "Carpet Masters? Worst. Service. Ever." Carpet Masters sues Spiker for libel, claiming his review is false and hurts its business.
- Community activist Sarah Newman sends a letter to the editor in which she says she opposes the city's proposal to rezone a large land parcel to permit construction of a 350-unit apartment complex. She writes that "Stang Development Company has in the past failed in its other development to live up to promises that it will include a substantial number of low-income units in the building." Stang sues for libel.
- Comments made in a consumer affairs segment of a television news broadcast suggest that the dealer of small mobile homes is misinforming its customers who buy the homes. The dealer tells the buyers they will be permitted to install these small trailers on the property that contains their existing homes. County zoning rules prohibit such installation. The mobile home dealer sues the station for libel.

In all three cases, the lawsuits were initiated to block the defendants from making further critical comments about the plaintiff. It is not important for the plaintiff to win these cases; most don't expect to. But by forcing their critics to mount a costly defense, they hope to silence these critics. It is one thing for individuals to speak their mind; another to hire lawyers to mount a libel defense.

The legal system has devised a means to thwart such lawsuits by passing laws that permit a court to expedite a judicial review of the plaintiff's allegations. Rather than sending the dispute to trial, so-called anti-SLAPP statutes, or what are sometimes called Citizen Participation Acts, permit the defendant to ask a judge to dismiss the complaint immediately. While the statutes vary in details, all require the judge to undertake a two-step examination of the complaint.

First, the defendant must convince the court the challenged activity arose from a constitutionally protected activity, one that focused on a matter of public interest; that the defendant was using his or her basic First Amendment rights. If the court agrees with the defendant, then the plaintiff must convince the court that he, she or it has brought forth a legally sufficient claim. That is, there is sufficient evidence that the plaintiff will likely win any libel suit that occurs. At this point the court will consider whether the plaintiff can establish facts to meet its burden of proof, and whether there are defenses that would likely defeat the libel suit. If the activity is constitutionally protected, and the plaintiff fails to bring forth sufficient evidence to sustain a suit, the judge will dismiss the complaint immediately.

About 30 states now have anti-SLAPP statutes. In 2016, a subcommittee of the House Judiciary Committee held hearings on a federal anti-SLAPP statute, the SPEAK FREE Act. As of 2017, however, there was no federal anti-SLAPP statute. As of 2017, only California, Washington, Texas, the District of Columbia, Illinois, Indiana and Louisiana

4. See Pring, "SLAPPs"; Pring and Canan, "Strategic Lawsuits"; and Dill, "Libel Law Doesn't Work."

had expansive statutes that cover statements made outside a governmental setting. The strongest statutes are those that protect speech that occurs in any forum and address matters that range from government to economic concerns. California courts have included comments made in the press within the protection of the anti-SLAPP laws, and the state court of appeals ruled in late 2011 that even a feature film, the movie "Bruno," a purported documentary with Sacha Baron Cohen that raised public issues, was protected by the state's statute. This ruling went far beyond the scope of most state laws.[5]

RESOLVING THE PROBLEM

Going to court in a libel action is rarely a happy experience for any of the participants. Plaintiffs are rarely gratified. Lawyers' fees can take as much as 50 percent of their winnings. The typical case takes several years to litigate, years during which their lives are disrupted. Two-thirds of the plaintiffs questioned by researchers in the massive Iowa Libel Research Project said they were dissatisfied with their litigation experience.[6] The press isn't happy either. Defense costs and damage awards cut into revenues. Reporters and editors are immobilized for long periods of time. Publicity about the lawsuit only reinforces the negative attitudes many people have about the news media.

Going to court in a libel action is rarely a happy experience for any of the participants.

An important question to ask is this: Are there better ways to resolve legitimate disputes between a mass medium and an injured party? Is going to court, or even threatening to go to court, the only solution? Newspapers, broadcasting stations, magazines and others often have been reluctant to publish or broadcast corrections, retractions or apologies. Few people like to admit they were wrong, especially in a public forum. But three-fourths of the plaintiffs interviewed for the Iowa Libel Research Project just discussed said they would not have filed a lawsuit if the news medium had published or broadcast a correction or retraction. The publication of such corrections has become more common in the past two decades. Undoubtedly this has helped defuse many disputes that might otherwise have ended up in court.

Laws have been adopted in about 30 states that reward the press for publishing a correction or retraction. These retraction statutes typically cap or limit the types of damages a plaintiff can recover if a defendant makes a timely retraction or correction. These laws are discussed in greater depth on pages 243–244.

Libel is the most common and often the most troublesome problem faced by people who work in the mass media. It usually takes a great deal of money to successfully defend a libel suit. Damage claims are sometimes outrageous, and occasionally damage awards are extremely high and have little to do with the harm caused by the defamation. The law is very complicated, and mistakes made by judges and juries have to be rectified by lengthy and costly appeals. Some plaintiffs attempt to use the law to harass or punish defendants rather than simply repair a damaged reputation, but many states have attempted to block these so-called SLAPP suits with legislation.

SUMMARY

---

5. *Olson* v. *Cohen,* Cal. Ct. of Apps., No. 13 221956 (9/12/11).
6. Bezanson, Cranberg, and Soloski, *Libel Law and the Press.*

LAW OF DEFAMATION

The law of defamation can be traced back several centuries. Initially, the law was an attempt by government to establish a forum for persons involved in a dispute brought about by an insult or by what we today call a defamatory remark. One man called another a robber and a villain. The injured party sought to avenge his damaged reputation. A fight or duel of some kind was often the only means of gaining vengeance before the development of libel law. It was obvious that fights and duels were not satisfactory ways to settle such disputes, so government offered to help solve these problems. Slowly the law of defamation evolved.

Parts of the law of libel do not concern those who work in mass communications. For example, elements of libel deal with allegations contained in private communications, a letter from one person to another, a job recommendation from a former employer to a prospective employer or private communications between ordinary individuals. This chapter focuses on public communications—material that is published or broadcast via the mass media, using that term in its broadest sense to include advertising, company magazines, trade association newsletters, press releases, the Internet, material posted on social media and so on. Similarly, because newspapers, broadcasting stations, magazines and the like tend to focus on material considered to be of public concern, courts often treat them differently from nonmedia defendants. Unless otherwise stated, it can be presumed the discussion in this text focuses on the rights and responsibilities of media defendants.

Additionally, it must be remembered that libel law is essentially state law. It is possible to describe the dimensions of the law in broad terms that transcend state boundaries, and that is what this text attempts to do. But important variations exist in the law from state to state, as will be demonstrated in Chapter 5 in the discussion of fault requirements. It is important for students to focus on the specific elements of the law in their states after gaining an understanding of the general boundaries of the law.

The law of defamation includes both **libel** (written defamation) and **slander** (oral defamation). One hundred and fifty years ago these two kinds of defamation were treated differently by the courts. Written defamation was considered a more serious offense because it lasted longer, was more widely circulated and was planned or more purposeful (as opposed to a spoken comment made in the heat of anger). Therefore the law treated libel more harshly. The coming of radio, television, film and other forms of electronic media in which spoken communication could be recorded and retained, circulated as widely or more widely than a newspaper or handbill, and was often written down in a script before it was spoken, forced changes in the law. While the law in some states still distinguishes between libel and slander, in most states the two are treated alike. A more meaningful distinction today is between published communication, which includes printed matter, radio, television, film, the Internet and so on, and purely spoken, interpersonal conversation. All published communication is treated today as libel.

ELEMENTS OF LIBEL

Defamation is any communication that holds a person up to contempt, hatred, ridicule or scorn.

Defamation can be defined as a false statement of fact about the plaintiff that is communicated by the defendant to a third party (one person *other than* the defendant and the plaintiff must receive the allegedly defamatory statement) and that harms the plaintiff's reputation. The plaintiff in a defamation suit can be either a person or a business.

Reputational harm to the plaintiff is the key injury with which defamation law is concerned. A reputation is reflected in how others treat or act toward a person or a business. Reputational harm therefore is different from the internal emotional distress a person might feel after reading something false and negative about himself, although many states today allow for recovery of both reputational harm and emotional distress in defamation cases.

A person's reputation is harmed when a false, factual assertion causes the person to be hated, scorned, ridiculed, shunned or avoided, or injures the person in his occupation or profession. A business's reputation, in turn, is harmed when customers patronize it less after a false factual assertion about it is made.

For example, a high school teacher who is falsely accused by a parent in front of the principal of having sex with a student has a potentially great defamation lawsuit against the parent. Why? Because there is a false factual assertion (that the teacher is having sex with a student) about the teacher (the plaintiff) that was communicated to a third party (the principal) by the defendant (the parent) that injures the teacher in his occupation. The teacher's defamation suit would be for slander if the parent spoke those words to the principal. It would be for libel if the parent conveyed them in writing, such as a letter, to the principal. Most states treat communications via the Internet as libel.

Similarly, a restaurant that is falsely accused in a newspaper review of having rats in its kitchen (a false factual assertion) has an excellent potential defamation lawsuit against the newspaper *and* the person who wrote the review because the restaurant's revenue likely decreased after the review was published (i.e., communicated to third-party readers). There will be more to come in Chapter 6 about the key, but sometimes slippery, distinction between factual assertions (there are rats in the kitchen) and statements of opinion (the restaurant has horrible service), which are generally protected.

What if a person has such a low or terrible reputation to start with *before* a defamatory message is communicated by the defendant? Some states recognize a very limited class of individuals known as libel-proof plaintiffs. These are people who, essentially, cannot be harmed by any false statements because they have no good reputation to start with and thus cannot maintain an action for defamation. Their reputations are so poor to begin with that statements about them do not harm their reputation. Courts, however, typically limit libel-proof plaintiffs only to people who have been convicted of very serious criminal offenses, such as felonies like murder and rape. Simply being unlikeable or a jerk does not make a person a libel-proof plaintiff.

Whether a statement conveys a defamatory meaning—a meaning, in other words, that would harm a person's reputation—ultimately depends on how a community responds to it. The general rule in the United States is that a statement conveys a defamatory meaning if it would harm a person's reputation in the eyes of "a substantial and respectable minority" of the community. Courts often apply some variation of this benchmark, such as a "considerable and respectable segment in the community" formulation.

Any living person can bring a civil action for libel. In the United States, deceased individuals can't sue for libel. Common law bars suits by the relatives of someone who has died on behalf of the deceased. Note, however, that if a living person is defamed, brings suit and then dies before the matter is settled by the court, it is possible in some states that have what are called **survival statutes** for relatives to continue to pursue the lawsuit.[7] A business corporation can sue for libel. So can a nonprofit corporation, if it can show that it has lost public support and contributions because of the defamation. Cities, counties, agencies of government and governments in general cannot bring a civil libel suit. This question was decided years ago and is settled law.[8]

One important key to understanding any lawsuit is to understand the concept of the burden of proof. Which party must prove what? While this point sounds trivial to many laypeople, it is a very significant element in a lawsuit. Remember, under our adversarial legal system, the court only evaluates and analyzes the material brought before it by the adversaries. Judges and juries don't go out and look for evidence themselves. So the matter of who must bring the evidence before the court is critical. If a plaintiff, for example, is required to prove a specific element in a case and fails to bring sufficient evidence before the court to convince the judge or jury, the plaintiff loses the case.

In a libel case, the plaintiff bears the initial burden of proof. He or she must establish five separate elements of the case in order to have any chance of winning.

TO WIN A LIBEL SUIT A PLAINTIFF MUST PROVE:

1. The libel was published.
2. Words were of and concerning the plaintiff.
3. Material is defamatory.
4. Material is false.
5. Defendant was at fault.

Each of the five elements in this box is outlined in detail shortly. Items 4 and 5 are sometimes only required if the plaintiff is suing a mass media defendant. These elements are fairly recent additions to the law of libel, and despite significant amounts of litigation, all the courts have not yet fully resolved the question of how far they should be extended.[9] Fault is discussed in Chapter 5.

PUBLICATION

Before the law recognizes a statement or comment as a civil libel, the statement must be published. Under the law, **publication** means that one person, in addition to the source of the libel and the person who is defamed, sees or hears the defamatory material. Just one person is all it takes. But isn't this a contradiction to what was written on page 153 that a significant number of persons must believe that the plaintiff's reputation has been harmed before he or she can collect damages? Here it is stated that only a single person must see or hear the libel for publication to take place. Two different concepts are being discussed.

---

7. See *MacDonald* v. *Time*, 554 F. Supp. 1053 (1983); *Canino* v. *New York News*, 475 A. 2d 528 (1984); and *Coppinger* v. *Schantag*, 34 M.L.R. 1141 (2006).
8. *City of Chicago* v. *Tribune Publishing Co.*, 139 N.E. 2d 86 (1923).
9. See *Columbia Sussex* v. *Hay*, 627 S.W. 2d 270 (1981); *Mutafis* v. *Erie Insurance Exchange*, 775 F. 2d 593 (1985); and *Philadelphia Newspapers* v. *Hepps*, 475 U.S. 767 (1986).

The first is publication. The plaintiff has to show that at least one other person saw the libelous material or the court will not allow the lawsuit to proceed. No publication, no lawsuit. Assume the plaintiff can show all five elements needed—publication, identification, defamation, falsity and fault—and the publisher of the libel fails to raise a workable defense. The plaintiff wins the case. Then comes the assessment of damages. At this point, the plaintiff must show that the false statement that was published lowered his or her reputation among a significant number of the right-thinking people in the community. If the plaintiff cannot show this, the victory is a moral one at best. No damages will be awarded. It is even possible that the court might rule that the words are not defamatory if they don't lower the plaintiff's reputation in the eyes of a significant number of persons.

The question of publication is largely academic when the mass media are sued. If something is in a newspaper or on television or transmitted over the Internet, the court will presume that a third party has seen or heard the matter.[10]

Republication of a libel can also result in a successful libel suit. Under the common law of libel, a person who repeats a libel is also responsible for the damage caused by the libelous statement. For example, in 2010, lawyers for *The Anniston Star* newspaper tried to argue that the newspaper could not be sued for accurately reporting rumors that were being spread in town. The Alabama Court of Civil Appeals ruled the rumor was simply gossip and the newspaper never examined whether it was truthful or not. Repeating a libelous statement accurately is subject to the same liability as one who published it originally.[11] However, this doctrine is limited by several factors.

First, the republication rule is typically limited to situations where the publisher controls the content. Media companies are responsible for the republication of libelous statements because employees are responsible for writing and editing the content of the communication. So-called common carriers such as telephone companies, libraries, bookstores, newsstands and others who provide content but do not edit it are not typically liable for the defamatory content they distribute. Network-affiliated television stations are not responsible for defamatory content in the programming they transmit for the networks either. Like bookstores, they do not edit this material and are thus regarded as vendors.

Second, in the United States every distribution of a libelous statement does not constitute a separate publication. Under the "single publication rule," a libel plaintiff may only sue once. The single publication rule also applies to text and videos on the Internet. Plaintiffs may sue in one jurisdiction even if a defamatory statement published on the Internet was accessible in every state. In addition, content being continuously available on a Web site does not constitute a "republication" each time it is viewed by a third party.

Third, as discussed below, under federal statutory law, operators of Web sites, blogs, online bulletin boards and discussion groups are not considered publishers and are thus not liable for statements posted on their sites by third parties. This is true even if the Web site's operator attempts to edit or screen material for defamatory content. In addition, courts have held that providing a hyperlink to a publication is not a republication. For example, in Kentucky, a federal court was asked whether it was a republication when a Web site referenced or provided a link to a defamatory article. The site did not include the articles or the defamatory charges contained in the article, but told users where they

10. *Hornby* v. *Hunter*, 385 S.W. 2d 473 (1964).
11. *Little* v. *Consolidated Pub. Co.*, 38 M.L.R. 2569 (2010).

could find the article on the Internet. The court ruled that providing a link to defamatory content was not a "republication." The court noted, a hyperlink is "simply a new means for accessing . . . an article" and not a new publication.[12]

You are also liable for repeating a defamatory statement that comes from a source. This includes journalists who accurately quote a source or media organizations that publish or broadcast defamatory advertisements. Some people mistakenly believe that attributing a libel to a third party will shield them from a lawsuit, but this is one of the great myths of American journalism. For example, most good reporters know that it is libelous to label someone a murderer. But a remarkably high percentage of professionals erroneously believe you can label someone a murderer, as long as you attribute the statement to a third party. "Jones killed his wife" is obviously defamatory. So is "Jones killed his wife, according to neighbor Ned Block." The media organization has simply republished Block's original libel of Jones. (Because the reporter apparently quoted a source for the allegation of murder, the plaintiff might find it more difficult to prove the required fault element. While that could doom Mr. Jones' libel in the long run, it doesn't change the fact that the allegation—attributed or not—is the republication of a libel.) Because of the republication rule, nearly everyone in the chain of production of a news story is technically liable in a lawsuit.

Some people mistakenly believe that attributing a libel to a third party will shield them from a lawsuit, but this is one of the great myths of American journalism.

Libel on the Internet

The great bulk of the law of libel that is outlined in this chapter and Chapters 5 and 6 applies to defamation that is transmitted via the Internet. Courts regard communication on the Web the same way they regard material published in newspapers, magazines or books. Two issues have arisen, however, that have forced the courts and Congress to consider the relationship between libel and the Internet. The first has to do with the status of online service providers (OSPs) in the transmission of a libel; the second has to do with jurisdiction.

There are many contexts in which a libel might be published on the Internet. A defamatory message might be sent to every person who logs on to an OSP's computers. Libelous material might be contained in a database that is viewed or downloaded by a user. Defamatory content also may appear in postings and comments made by readers in a Web site's comments section.

If the OSP is the author or creator of the libelous message, it will be regarded as the publisher of the material in a libel suit and be treated as a newspaper publisher is treated. It is liable for the defamatory publication and can be sued for libel.

More commonly, however, the OSP merely transmits what another party has posted on the system as an e-mail or a message on a bulletin board or on a Web site. In this case the system operator will be regarded as a vendor or distributor rather than a publisher. Section 230 of the Communications Decency Act, enacted in 1996 in an attempt to encourage "interactive computer services" to restrict the flow of objectionable content, provides a "safe harbor" for OSPs from liability for material posted by third parties. Section 230 states, "No provider or user of an interactive computer service shall be treated as the publisher or speaker of any information provided by another information content provider."[13] The law

---

12. *Salyer* v. *Southern Poverty Law Center Inc.,* 701 F. Supp. 2d 912, 916–18 (W.D. Ky. 2009).
13. U.S.C. 230 (1996).

was passed to ensure that by editing material on the Internet, an OSP could not be held liable under the republication rule. In 1995, a New York court held that Prodigy, an OSP that was editing out offensive language and using a moderator to enforce content provisions, was liable for its user's posts.[14] To encourage interactive computer services to make efforts to control indecency on the Internet, Congress provided OSPs with immunity from libel suits. After all, if policing content had made Prodigy libel for defamatory content posted by a third party, few providers would want to exercise editorial control over content.

Section 230 defines "an interactive computer service" as "an information service, system, or access software provider that provides or enables computer access by multiple users to a computer server, including specifically a service or system that provides access to the Internet and such systems operated or services offered by libraries or educational institutions."[15] An OSP is protected from defamatory statements made by other information content providers, or "any person or entity that is responsible, in whole or in part, for the creation or development of information provided through the Internet or any other interactive computer service."[16]

Although Section 230 attempts to distinguish between OSPs and content providers, the law has been applied broadly to a wide number of Web sites. Section 230 has been applied to interactive Web sites, forums, listservs and blogs. Here are some examples:

- The 9th U.S. Court of Appeals ruled that the immunity applied even if the OSP operator selected and lightly edited the defamatory comment.[17]
- Section 230 immunized Internet-book vendor Amazon.com from liability when it was sued by an author for including readers' comments on its Web site that were critical of the author's work.[18]
- A Web site operator who refused to remove allegedly defamatory matter from its site, even after the author of the material asked that it be removed, was immune from liability. The plaintiff argued that by refusing to remove the material, the Web site operator had adopted the content of the message as its own. The federal court disagreed.[19]
- A TV station that permitted its Web site visitors to post comments following an article about the arrest of a former news anchor on felony drug charges did not contribute to the contents of the comments. Hence, it was a distributor, not a publisher.[20] Thus it is clear that online newspapers, magazines and other Internet content providers are immune from liability for content created and posted by others.

14. *Stratton Oakmont, Inc.* v. *Prodigy Services Co.,* 1995 WL323710 (N.Y. Sup. Ct. 1995).
15. U.S.C. 230(f)(2).
16. U.S.C. 230(f)(3).
17. *Batzel* v. *Smith,* 333 F. 3d 1018 (2003).
18. *Schneider* v. *Amazon.com Inc.,* 31 P. 3d 37 (2001). See also *Universal Communications Systems Inc.* v. *Lycos Inc.,* 35 M.L.R. 1417 (2007), where the U.S. Court of Appeals ruled that the defendant, which operates a financial message board, was an online service provider for purposes of the law.
19. *Globe Royalties Ltd.* v. *Xcentric Ventures LLC,* 544 F. Supp. 929 (2008). See also *Barnes* v. *Yahoo! Inc.,* 37 M.L.R. 1705 (2009), where the U.S. 9th Circuit Court of Appeals ruled the CDA shielded Yahoo! from a claim that it negligently failed to remove content posted by a third party on an online message board.
20. *Miles* v. *Raycom Media Inc.,* S.D. Miss., No. 09-713, 8/26/2010.

What if a Web site operator encourages a third party to submit content that is tortuous or unlawful? Not a lot of court decisions have dealt with this question. In 2008 the 9th U.S. Court of Appeals ruled that if a site operator encourages illegal content, or designs a Web site that requires users to post illegal content, it would lose its CDA immunity.[21] In 2013, numerous commentators questioned the future of Section 230 when a federal jury awarded $338,000 to a former Cincinnati Bengals cheerleader for postings made by a third party to thedirty.com. In 2012, the trial judge in the case ruled that thedirty.com was not protected by Section 230, a decision that was initially upheld on appeal.[22] The judge ruled there was evidence the site encouraged the development of the offensive content. However, in 2014, the 6th Circuit Court of Appeals ruled thedirty.com was protected under Section 230 because the Web site did not materially contribute to the statements posted on the site about the former cheerleader.[23]

The bottom line is simply this: An online service provider is immune from a defamation suit for transmitting defamatory matter created by a third party, unless the Web site operator has in some way participated in the creation of the illegal content, or has designed the Web site in such a way that requires users who wish to post material to input illegal content.

Another issue that arises with Internet content is related to jurisdiction. Libel laws in the United States often make it very difficult for public figures and public officials to win in this country. But the libel laws of many other countries make it much easier for these individuals to prevail in libel suits. In response to what some have called "libel tourism"— traveling to a foreign venue to file a defamation action that would not succeed in this country—U.S. governments have attacked the problem. At least two states, New York and Illinois, have enacted legislation that prohibits courts in those jurisdictions from enforcing overseas judgments. A British court could still rule against a U.S. defendant, but the plaintiff would not be able to use American courts to enforce the ruling. In 2010 Congress passed legislation that prohibits the domestic enforcement of foreign libel judgments against U.S. persons where the judgments are inconsistent with First Amendment protections built into American law. The so-called SPEECH Act (Securing the Protection of Our Enduring and Established Constitutional Heritage Act) was signed by President Barack Obama in 2010. In brief, plaintiffs may win large verdicts in libel cases overseas, but the SPEECH Act makes it impossible to recover or collect the money in the United States if the laws of the other country are not as protective of speech as they are in the United States.

Can parties in a lawsuit force an OSP or Web site operator to reveal the names of people who post anonymous messages on the Web? Because Web sites are protected from lawsuits related to posts by third parties under Section 230, an interesting problem arises when these Web sites are asked to reveal the identity of anonymous third-party posters. In 2009, for instance, fashion model and former *Vogue* cover girl Liskula Cohen filed a motion against Google and Blogger.com to compel them in a defamation suit to reveal the identity of the person who anonymously posted comments on a blog calling her a "skank," a "ho" and "other defamatory statements concerning her appearance, hygiene

21. *Fair Housing Council of San Fernando Valley* v. *Roommates.com*, 36 M.L.R. 1545 (2008).
22. *Jones* v. *Dirty World Entertainment Recordings, LLC.*, 840 F. Supp. 2d 1008 (2012), appeal dismissed, No. 12-5133 (6th Cir. May 9, 2012).
23. *Jones* v. *Dirty World Entertainment Recording, LLC.* 755 F. 3d 398 (6th Cir. 2014).

and sexual conduct."[24] Judge Joan A. Madden ruled in favor of Cohen and held that Google and/or its Blogger.com subsidiary had to reveal to the former model the identity of the anonymous blogger (via the IP and e-mail address) who posted the defamatory comments about her at http://skanksnyc.blogspot.com. Cohen then discovered the blogger was a female acquaintance she knew from parties and restaurants.

The problem gained widespread media attention in 2008 when a now-defunct Web site called JuicyCampus.com, which boasted the motto "Always Anonymous . . . Always Juicy" and later "C'mon. Give Us the Juice," became known for allowing college students to anonymously post gossip about fellow students that was sometimes offensive, homophobic and/or defamatory.[25] Or imagine that someone creates a fake Facebook profile about you that says defamatory things and you want to unmask its creator. Can you find out who created the fake profile and posted defamatory content about you?

The answer is yes, sometimes, if certain steps are met. State courts across the country are grappling with the issue of anonymous postings and when to allow those harmed by them to force the OSP or host in question to disclose the poster's identity. In particular, they are attempting to accommodate competing interests, namely, the judicially recognized First Amendment right to engage in anonymous speech (see Chapter 3 regarding prior restraints and protests) versus compensating those harmed by anonymous Internet speech that is defamatory or otherwise unlawful, such as the disclosure of proprietary information like trade secrets. The First Amendment right to engage in anonymous speech is not absolute; it may be overcome in some situations. Determining when, however, is tricky. As a California appellate court wrote in 2008 in a case involving allegedly defamatory postings on a Yahoo! message board and in which the plaintiff sought the identity of the poster of those comments, "the proper focus . . . should be on providing an injured party a means of redress without compromising the legitimate right of the Internet user to communicate freely with others."[26]

A New Jersey appellate court ruled that a subpoena to ascertain the identity of anonymous Internet posters in a libel case should not be issued unless the plaintiff could first make a prima facie case for libel.[27] The court outlined a four-part test it said lower courts should follow that is known as the Dendrite test:

- The plaintiff must first make an effort to notify the anonymous poster that he or she is the subject of an application for disclosure.
- The plaintiff must identify and set forth the allegedly defamatory statements.
- The plaintiff must provide sufficient evidence to support each element of the cause of action, including the harm that has allegedly been incurred.
- The court must then balance the defendant's right to anonymous speech under the First Amendment (see Chapter 3) against the strength of the plaintiff's case and the necessity of disclosure to allow the plaintiff to proceed properly.

24. Gregorian, "Model Snared in Ugly Web."
25. At least two states in 2008 investigated whether JuicyCampus was engaging in possible fraud by failing to follow its own terms-of-use agreement by allowing defamatory messages to be posted. In February 2009 JuicyCampus was shut down by its founder, Matt Ivester, who denied the closure was related to potential legal liability problems but rather that it was based on economic and advertising issues.
26. *Krinsky* v. *Doe 6*, 159 Cal. App. 4th 1154, 1167 (Cal. Ct. App. 2008).
27. *Dendrite International Inc.* v. *Doe*, 775 A. 2d 756 (N.J. Super. Ct. 2001).

In the New Jersey case the unidentified posters were named as defendants in the lawsuit. A federal court in Washington state fashioned a somewhat similar rule in a suit in which the anonymous posters were not a party in the lawsuit. It said the subpoena would not be issued unless the information sought went to a core claim made by the plaintiff or the defense, the information was directly or materially relevant to the case and the party seeking the identities had demonstrated that the information was unavailable from other sources.[28]

UNMAKING ANONYMOUS POSTERS OF DEFAMATORY CONTENT

"A whole Boat load of money is missing and Tina won't let anyone see the books. Doesn't she make her living as a bookkeeper? Did you just see where Idaho is high on the list for embezzlement? Not that any of that is related or anything."

Those were some of the damning and possibly defamatory comments posted in 2012 on a blog by a person who identified herself only as "almostinnocentbystander." The "Tina" mentioned in the comments was Tina Jacobson, chair of the Kootenai County Republican Central Committee, and she filed a defamation lawsuit against the unknown poster as a so-called Doe Defendant. When a plaintiff sues an anonymous defendant, the term "Doe" is used in a case name as a placeholder for the name of the actual defendant when the name is later discovered.[29]

The blog where the statements about Jacobson were posted was called Huckleberries Online. It was (and still is) operated by the *Spokesman-Review*, a newspaper serving the area surrounding Spokane, Washington, including nearby Kootenai County, Idaho, where Tina Jacobson lived.

The key legal issue facing the court was whether Tina Jacobson could obtain a court order requiring the *Spokesman-Review* to disclose the identity of "almostinnocentbystander" so that Jacobson could proceed with her lawsuit. The answer was yes, and the *Spokesman-Review* revealed that the poster was a woman named Linda Cook.

How did District Judge John Patrick Luster reach his decision to force the *Spokesman-Review* to unmask Cook and reveal her identity? He initially observed that while the First Amendment protects anonymous speech, such protections are not absolute. Judge Luster applied a modified version of the so-called Dendrite and Cahill standards. Based on these tests, Luster found Jacobson had a solid defamation action against the poster that would survive summary judgment. In addition, when balancing the poster's First Amendment right of free speech against Jacobson's interest in being compensated for reputational harm, Judge Luster concluded that the "necessity of almostinnocentbystander's identity to the plaintiff's case outweighs the defendant's right to anonymous free speech in this case." He thus ordered the owners of the *Spokesman-Review* to give to Jacobson "any document establishing the identity, email address, and IP addresses of 'almostinnocentbystander,' as identified on the Huckleberries Online blog." This is an increasingly common "unmasking" scenario across the United States today, and it proves that people's expectations of online anonymity are often wrong.

---

28. *Doe* v. *2TheMart.com Inc.,* 140 F. Supp. 2d 1088 (W.D. Wash. 2001).
29. Memorandum Opinion and Order, *Jacobson* v. *Doe*, Case No. CV-12-3098 (Idaho Dist. Ct. July 10, 2012).

In a 2005 opinion called *Doe* v. *Cahill* based on statements posted on a blog, the Supreme Court of Delaware held that "the summary judgment standard is the appropriate test by which to strike the balance between a defamation plaintiff's right to protect his reputation and a defendant's right to exercise free speech anonymously."[30] What does this mean? The court called it a "modified" two-part version of the Dendrite test. In particular, the plaintiff must 1) make reasonable efforts to notify the defendant (the anonymous poster) that he or she is the subject of a subpoena or application for an order of disclosure; and 2) provide sufficient evidence to support and sustain each and every element of the plaintiff's cause of action versus the defendant (in this case, defamation) against a motion for summary judgment.

While different courts have used different versions of these two tests, today, the bottom line is fairly clear: 1) the right to online anonymity is not absolute and courts do have the power to force Web site operators and interactive computer services to reveal the IP and e-mail addresses of otherwise anonymous posters; and 2) most courts apply some version or variation of either the Dendrite or Cahill test to determine if such "unmasking" of anonymous posters is justified in a given case.

IDENTIFICATION

The second element in a libel suit is **identification:** The injured party must show the court that the allegedly defamatory statement is "of and concerning him, her, or it." Failing to do this, the plaintiff will lose the suit. A tax preparer named Timothy Hanks sued a television station that had broadcast a story about unscrupulous tax preparers. The story recounted the story of a taxpayer who said that a business called Reliable Tax had made an error on his return that cost him money. Hanks was not mentioned or alluded to in the story. A U.S. District Court ruled in 2012 that while a corporation can receive damages if it is defamed, no employee or stockholder of the business is so entitled. Not even the president of the company, which Hanks was. Since he was not mentioned in the story, the court ruled the negative remarks were not "of and concerning" him.[31] The plaintiff must be identified. Not every reader or viewer needs to know to whom the libel refers. But certainly more than one or two people must be able to recognize the plaintiff as the subject of the derogatory remark. Libel authorities disagree on how many people must be able to identify the subject of the remark. But remember, to win damages the plaintiff must prove that his or her reputation has been lowered in the eyes of a significant minority of the members of the community. If only a handful of people can recognize the plaintiff, it is doubtful that he or she can prove sufficient harm to win damages.

Identification can occur in several ways. A plaintiff may be explicitly named. Or the defendant can use a similar name that suggests the plaintiff's actual name. The producers of the television show "Hard Copy" were sued for using the name Sweepstakes Clearing House when they aired a story on sweepstakes scams. Sweepstakes Clearing House is a made-up name, but there is a company called Sweepstakes Clearinghouse and its owners sued. The Texas Court of Appeals reversed the summary judgment

---

30. *Doe* v. *Cahill,* 884 A. 2d 451 (Del. 2005).
31. *Hanks* v. *Wavy Broadcasting LLC,* 40 M.L.R. 1424 (2012).

granted the defendant and ruled that a publication is "of and concerning" the plaintiff if persons who knew or were acquainted with the plaintiff believed that the libelous material referred to the plaintiff.[32] The individual can be described, for example, as the host of the quiz show "Jeopardy" or the city's superintendent of public works. A picture or a drawing, even without a caption, can be sufficient if the likeness is recognizable. Even descriptive circumstances can sometimes point the finger at someone. In 1991 a young woman, after attending a party, was abducted as she was standing outside a house near the University of Pennsylvania campus. She said she was raped by her abductor. A local television station reported the attack, including comments by a police officer who cast some doubts on the victim's story. The young woman claimed these comments defamed her. The station did not use the victim's name, but described her as a female Bryn Mawr student (Bryn Mawr is a small college near the University of Pennsylvania that enrolls less than 1,500 undergraduates) who had been raped on a certain day, that she lived in a dorm at Bryn Mawr, that she drove a Nissan, and that she had attended a party at the University of Pennsylvania shortly before her abduction. The station claimed that broadcasting these facts did not constitute identification. But a U.S. District Court disagreed, noting the small school environment at Bryn Mawr. "In this type of environment, it would not be surprising if some people could identify the plaintiff from the information supplied in the broadcast."[33] In fact, the plaintiff presented affidavits from students attesting to the fact that the story of her rape had spread rapidly across campus after the broadcast.

If a libelous statement does not make an explicit identification, then the plaintiff must somehow prove that the defamatory words refer to him or her. In some cases, plaintiffs have successfully sued for libel based on fictional characters.

The Illinois Supreme Court held the publishers of *Seventeen* magazine liable for publishing a short story labeled fiction that described as a slut a girl identified only as "Bryson." The author of the story, Lucy Logsdon, a native of southern Illinois, wrote a first-person narrative that recounts a conflict she said she had with a high school classmate. The classmate in the short story bore a slight physical resemblance to the plaintiff, Kimberly Bryson, who had attended high school with Logsdon. The court said that third persons familiar with both the plaintiff and the defendant would understand that the story was referring to the plaintiff despite the fiction label.[34] In 2008, a New York trial court was faced with a so-called libel-in-fiction case when an attorney sued the producer of the popular television series "Law and Order" for telecasting an ostensibly fictional episode about a Brooklyn judge who was accused of accepting bribes from an attorney. There had been a widely publicized case in New York City in which a judge was accused of taking bribes from a divorce lawyer. Both the fictional TV lawyer and the real-life lawyer were about the same age and bore a physical resemblance to one another. The producers of the TV show petitioned the court to dismiss the case, but the court rejected the request. Given the context in which the TV show was presented, and the extensive media coverage of the actual scandal, "there is a reasonable likelihood that the ordinary

32. *Allied Marketing Group Inc.* v. *Paramount Pictures Corp.*, 111 S.W. 3d 168 (2003).
33. *Weinstein* v. *Bullock*, 827 F. Supp. 1193 (1994).
34. *Bryson* v. *News America Publications Inc.*, 672 N.E. 2d 1207 (1996).

viewer, unacquainted with Batra [the real-life lawyer] personally, could understand Patel's [the TV lawyer] corruption to be the truth about Batra," the court said.[35] In March 2011, however, the California Court of Appeals ruled that the creators of "CSI: Crime Scene Investigation" could not be sued for libel for an episode that aired in February 2009. The episode featured married real estate agents in Los Angeles. In the episode, the wife's death "may have occurred during kinky sex in which she was handcuffed to the bed." Married real estate agents Scott and Melinda Tamkin sued, alleging that the fictional married real estate couple were their likeness because one of the writers for the show had been shown property by the Tamkins and used their names as "placeholders" in early versions of the script. Although the Tamkins names were not used, the characters on the show had similar characteristics, financial difficulties and marital problems. The court ruled that a reasonable person would not understand that the fictional representations were "of and concerning" the Tamkins. Therefore, the representations could not be the basis for a libel suit.[36]

Journalists face somewhat of a conundrum today regarding identification. Traditionally, reporters have been taught to include full identification when writing or talking about someone: John Smith, 36, of 1234 Boone Street, a carpenter. This information will separate this John Smith from any other person with the same name. But the issue of privacy is of great concern today, and many people don't want their ages or addresses in the newspaper or broadcast on television. Some news organizations now permit less than complete identification in sensitive situations. The reporter should always get complete identification for the subject of a news story, if only to confirm that he or she is writing about the correct person. Newspaper or broadcast station policy will determine how much of this information is used.

The reporter should always get complete identification for the subject of a news story, if only to confirm that he or she is writing about the correct person.

Group Identification

Can an individual who is not specifically identified in a libelous communication successfully prove identification by arguing that he or she is a member of a group or organization that was named in the communication?

The first consideration is the size of the group. Although persons who are part of a large group are usually not able to prove identification, in some situations members of a small group may be able to prove they have been identified by reference to the group as a whole. The courts have not come up with a magic number in this regard. Under the group libel rule, large groups, such as all college professors, could not sue for libel based on statements such as, "All college professors are lazy and most are unqualified to teach." However, members of smaller groups might be able to sue depending on the size of the group and the language used. The smaller the group, the more likely it is that a statement identifies members of the group. Courts also consider if the statement is about "all" or "most" members of a small group. In 2009 three members of the St. Regis Mohawk Tribe sued *The New York Post* after the newspaper published an editorial opposing a proposal to let the tribe operate a gambling casino. The *Post* said the casino "amounts to a criminal

35. *Batra* v. *Wolf,* 36 M.L.R. 1592 (2008).
36. *Tamkin* v. *CBS Broad. Inc.*, 122 Cal. Rptr. 3d 264 (Ct. App. 2011).

enterprise." The three plaintiffs were members of the tribal council, but the editorial did not name any individual. The court noted that there were 2,700 members in the tribe, a group far too large to satisfy the requirements of identification. Even accepting the arguments that the statements were directed against the governing body, no statements that tribal council members individually were corrupt or promoting a criminal enterprise were published, the court said.[37]

Courts will look at the circumstances as well as the number in the group. Care is especially appropriate if only a small number of the defamed group live in the community. If the charge is made that all astrologers are frauds and there is only one astrologer in the community, the remark can be dangerous. The plaintiff could convince a sympathetic jury that the comment was aimed at him, and that he has been severely harmed by the remark. While there is no definitive size or "magic number," in an oft-cited example, the Oklahoma Supreme Court ruled a magazine article that said team "members" of a university football team used an amphetamine nasal spray to increase aggressiveness libeled all 60 members of the team. Although the article did not name any team member by name or position, a jury awarded fullback Dennis Morris $75,000, an award held up on appeal by the Oklahoma Supreme Court.[38]

DEFAMATION

The third element in the plaintiff's case focuses on the words themselves. There are two kinds of defamatory words. The first kind, typically called "libel per se," consists of words that are libelous on their face, words that obviously can damage the reputation of any person. Words like "thief," "cheat" and "traitor" are libelous per se—there is no question that they are defamatory.

The second kind of words, usually called "libel per quod," are innocent on their face and become defamatory only if the reader or viewer knows other facts. To say that Duane Arnold married Jennifer Carter appears safe enough. But if the reader knows that Arnold is already married to another woman, the statement accuses Arnold of bigamy. And that is a libelous accusation.

The distinction between these two kinds of words was once more important than it is today. At one time plaintiffs had to prove they were specifically harmed by the words in the second category. Damage was presumed from the words in the first category. All plaintiffs today must prove they were damaged by the publication of the libel. Still, in many jurisdictions, courts have erected significant barriers that make it more difficult for persons who sue for libel per quod to win their case than persons who sue for words that are clearly defamatory on their face.

The law does not contain a list of words that are defamatory. What is considered defamatory will vary by location *and* change over time. In each case a court must examine the particular words or phrase or paragraph and decide whether these words lower the individual's reputation among a significant number of so-called right-thinking people in the community. Sometimes a precedent or many precedents will exist. Numerous cases, for example, establish that stating a woman is unchaste is libelous. But sometimes precedents

37. *Lazore v. NYP Holdings Inc.*, 876 NY52d 59 (2009).
38. *Fawcett Publications, Inc. v. Morris*, 377 P.2d 42 (Okla.).

aren't always that useful. Times change; the meanings of words change. Describing someone as a slacker today might be unkind, but hardly libelous. But during World War I the term "slacker" was used to identify a draft dodger and was certainly defamatory.

At a libel trial, a judge and jury are supposed to consider the words in light of their ordinary meaning unless the evidence is persuasive that the defendant meant something else when the statement was published. Deciding if a statement is defamatory is a two-step process. First, the judge must decide if the statement is capable of being defamatory as a matter of law. Second, the judge will decide as a matter of law whether particular words are capable of conveying a defamatory meaning. The court will ask whether a reasonable person would regard this as a defamatory comment.

Legally, a communication is defamatory if it harms an individual's reputation in the eyes of a "substantial and respectable minority" of a community. If only a small group of individuals would find a statement defamatory, that is not enough to be actionable. What constitutes a "substantial and respectable" minority of a community depends on a judge's presumptions about a community's values.

Peter Damon was an Army reservist who lost his arms while fighting in Iraq. He was interviewed on NBC television and told reporter Brian Williams "the pain is like my hands are being crushed in a vice." Medication, he said, made the pain more tolerable. Damon added that despite his injuries and the injuries to others, he and other wounded servicemen and women were not anti-war; they stood behind the war effort. Filmmaker Michael Moore used a portion of Damon's remarks about his pain in his anti-war film, "Farenheit 9/11." He did not, however, include the comments about Damon's support of the war. Damon sued, arguing that by including any of his comments in the film, it falsely portrayed him as endorsing Moore's attack on the war and President Bush. The 1st U.S. Court of Appeals rejected this argument, ruling that there was no way that a reasonable viewer could construe Damon's limited remarks about his injuries as supporting Moore's attack on the war and the president.[39]

If the judge rules that the words *are capable* of a defamatory meaning, the fact finder—the jury, if there is one, or the judge—then must determine whether the words *in fact convey* a defamatory meaning. For example, when the superintendent of the sewer department for the small town of Abington, Mass., was terminated because he allegedly used town computers for personal business, he sued the local newspaper for stories about his firing. Town officials said they found pictures of nude and scantily clad women and other sexually suggestive subject matter on the computers. The newspaper reported that "pornography" was found on the computers. The Massachusetts Court of Appeals ruled that, as a matter of law, charges that the plaintiff had stored "pornography" on the town computers would be defamatory. But it said a jury would have to decide whether the images stored on the computers were really "pornography," as that term is commonly understood.[40]

Innuendo as opposed to a flat assertion can be defamatory. Read the following actual news item from the *Boston Record*:

Innuendo as opposed to a flat assertion can be defamatory.

> The Veterans Hospital here suspected that 39-year-old George M. Perry of North Truro, whose death is being probed by federal and state authorities, was suffering from chronic arsenic poisoning.

39. *Damon v. Moore* 520 F. 3d 98 (2008).
40. *Howell v. Enterprise Publishing Co.*, 893 N.E. 2d 1270 (2008).

> State police said the body of Perry, and of his brother, Arthur, who is buried near him, would probably be exhumed from St. Peter's Cemetery in Provincetown.
>
> George Perry died in the VA hospital last June 9, forty-eight hours after his tenth admission there. . . . His brother, who lived in Connecticut and spent two days here during George's funeral, died approximately a month later. About two months later, in September, George's mother-in-law, seventy-four-year-old Mrs. Mary F. Mott, who had come to live with her daughter, died too. Her remains were cremated.

While the story lacked a good deal in journalistic clarity, it didn't take a terribly insightful reader to understand what the reporter was trying to suggest. Mrs. Perry murdered her husband, her brother-in-law and her mother. The insinuations are that Arthur died after visiting the plaintiff's home and that the mother had "died too." Isn't it too bad that her remains were cremated? This story cost the Hearst Corporation, publishers of the *Boston Record*, $25,000.[41]

A libel suit cannot be based on an isolated phrase wrenched out of context. The article as a whole must be considered. A story about baseball's legendary base stealer, Ricky Henderson, might contain the sentence "Henderson might be the best thief of all time," referring to his prowess as a base-stealer. Henderson cannot sue on the basis of that single sentence. The story itself makes it clear the kind of thievery the writer is discussing. Nevertheless, a libelous remark in a headline—even though it is cleared up in the story that follows—may be the basis for a libel suit.

One week after O.J. Simpson was acquitted of the criminal charge of murdering his wife and her companion, the *National Examiner* carried a headline on its cover, "Cops Think Kato Did It—He fears they will want him for perjury, pals say." The story appeared on page 17 and carried the headline, "Kato Kaelin. . . . Cops Think He Did It." The story said the police were trying to prove that when Kaelin testified at Simpson's trial, he lied under oath, that he committed perjury. In his libel suit Kaelin argued that the headlines for the story suggested he was a suspect in the murders. Attorneys for the *National Examiner* said no, that was not what was intended. The word "it" meant perjury. Judges on the 9th U.S. Circuit Court of Appeals ruled that under California law the meaning of the publication must be measured by the effect it would have on the mind of the average reader, and in this case it was highly likely that an average, reasonable reader might conclude that the word "it" referred to murder.[42] Kaelin and the *Examiner* settled this suit in October 1999.

In 2014, the *New York Post* settled a high-profile defamation case involving its coverage of the April 2013 Boston Marathon terrorist bombing. The lawsuit stemmed from the paper's infamous "Bag Men" cover of two people—16-year-old Salaheddin Barhoum and 24-year-old Yassine Zaimi—holding bags while attending the marathon. The case was settled after the trial judge refused to dismiss the case. Barhoum and Zaimi were not suspects in the bombings, but the *Post's* use of the phrase "Bag Men" and the subhead "Feds seek this duo pictured at Boston Marathon" implied they were suspects.

---

41. *Perry v. Hearst Corp.*, 334 F. 2d 800 (1964).
42. *Kaelin v. Globe Communications Corp.*, 162 F. 3d 1036 (1998).

©ZUMA Press, Inc./Alamy Stock Photo

The New York Post *settled a lawsuit over the April 18, 2013 cover of the* Post. *The cover featured a photo of two men near the site of the Boston Marathon bombing, with the headline, Bag Men: Feds seek this duo pictured at Boston Marathon*

Although the *Post* argued a reasonable reader would only conclude that authorities were looking to speak with Barhoum and Zaimi and would not conclude they were suspects, the trial judge held otherwise. The judge wrote, "[A] reasonable reader could construe the publication as expressly saying that law enforcement personnel were seeking not only to identify [Barhoum and Zaimi], but also to find them, and as implying that the plaintiffs were the bombers, or at least investigators [suspected they were the bombers]."[43]

In 2016, a William Rembis sued Fox News for more than $10 million after the cable news network published an Associated Press article about him and posted pictures of Rembis and his wife on their Web site under the heading "Sex Crimes." The article stated Rembis and his wife had been investigated by child welfare services in New Jersey, Michigan and Texas and stated the couple was accused of neglect. The story, however, did not involve any sex crimes.[44] In another 2016 case, Leah Manzari, more popularly known as "Danni Ashe" or the "most downloaded woman on the Internet," sued Associated Newspapers over an article that appeared in the *Daily Mail*. In 2013, the *Daily Mail* published an article headlined, "Porn industry shuts down with immediate effect after 'female performer' tests positive for HIV." The publication used a picture of Manzari despite the fact she wasn't the 'female performer' referenced in the article.[45] These cases stand as examples of why individuals working in the media must be careful when they use images unrelated to the stories they write. As the judge in the Manzari case wrote, "A picture is worth a thousand words. A photograph, especially when coupled with text, can convey a powerful message: in this case a potentially defamatory one." In addition to defamation claims, the careless use of pictures can also lead to trouble for appropriation for public relations and advertising professionals if the pictures are used without permission for "commercial purposes," an issue discussed later.

43. *Barhoum* v. *NYP Holdings, Inc.,* Superior Court Civil Actions No. 13-2062 (Mar. 5, 2014).
44. *Rembis* v. *Fox News Network, LLC,* Case. No. 5:16-cv-00242-C (N.D.T. Oct. 28, 2016).
45. *Manzari* v. *Associated Newspapers, Ltd.,* No. 2:13-cv-06830-GW-PJW (9th Cir. 2016).

Factual assertions can obviously be the basis of a libel suit. Can a statement of opinion be defamatory? Well, that depends. If the question is, Can an opinion lower someone's reputation? which is the definition of defamation, the answer is yes, an opinion can be defamatory. But if the question is, Can a defamatory opinion be the basis for a libel suit? The answer is probably no. American courts have ruled on numerous occasions that pure opinion is protected by the First Amendment.[46] A plaintiff cannot successfully sue for libel based on a statement that is pure opinion. Why? Because pure opinion cannot be proved to be true or false—it is simply an opinion. For example, "I think Brenda Baylor is a stupid jerk." Even though this comment might lower Brenda's reputation in the eyes of the community, how can you prove or disprove that someone is a stupid jerk? Without proof of falsity, the libel suit fails. So pure opinion is not a problem. But unfortunately, courts frequently have a difficult time determining what is and what is not pure opinion. Clearly, an opinion statement that contains a false fact can be libelous because of the false fact. "I think Brenda Baylor is a stupid jerk. You know, she scored only 150 on her SAT test." The second sentence is a factual assertion and if it is false, it could surely support a claim of libel. In addition, simply including the phrase "In my opinion" does not automatically convert a factual statement into opinion. But other kinds of statements are not so clear. "Emissions from the Acme Smelter are harming the environment." Is that a statement of fact or an opinion? Some people might believe that any emission from a smokestack harms the environment. But Acme might be in full compliance with Environmental Protection Agency rules and will argue its emissions are safe. So it depends. This topic is explored more fully on pages 229–236. Suffice to say for this discussion, opinion statements can harm a person's reputation and are therefore defamatory. But if such statements are free of false and libelous facts, they usually cannot sustain a defamation lawsuit.

Although there is no space in this text for a catalog of defamatory words, an outline of the most common categories of problem words, words to which writers and editors need to pay special attention, is feasible.

Crime

Imputations of criminal behavior are responsible for a great many libel suits. Saying someone has done something illegal—from jaywalking to murder—is libelous. The use of the word "alleged" in these cases is often of little help. The meaning of the word "alleged" is "to be declared or asserted to be as described." An alleged murderer is someone who has been declared or asserted to be a murderer. But by whom? If the state has charged Jones with murder, the state has alleged that he is a murderer. If that is the case, a reporter should say so: "Jones, who has been charged with murder" rather than simply, "the alleged murderer Jones." But if Jones is merely being questioned in connection with the murder, he is not an alleged murderer, he is an alleged suspect. To call him an alleged murderer is inaccurate and libelous. The best guide for the reporter is this: Report what you know to be true. If Jones is being questioned as a suspect, say that. If police consider him a suspect, say that.

---

46. See, for example, *Milkovich v. Lorain Journal Co.*, 110 S. Ct. 2695 (1991).

Sexual References

Statements that a woman is unchaste, is sleeping with a man to whom she is not married, has been raped or is just promiscuous can be defamatory. A 2003 issue of *Boston Magazine* carried a story titled "The Mating Habits of the Suburban High School Teenager." The thrust of the article was that teenagers in the Boston area have become more sexually promiscuous in the last decade. The article was illustrated with a photograph of Stacey Stanton and four other teenagers. In small type on the first page of the article was the following disclaimer:

> The photos on these pages are from an award-winning five-year project on teen sexuality taken by photo journalist Dan Habib. The individuals pictured are unrelated to the people or events described in this story. The names of the teenagers interviewed for this story have been changed.

Stanton sued for libel, alleging that by juxtaposing her photo and the text in the article, the magazine insinuated that she was engaged in the promiscuous behavior described in the article. The trial court ruled against the plaintiff, saying that the disclaimer negated this interpretation. But the 1st U.S. Court of Appeals reversed this ruling, saying that the type in the disclaimer was so small that it might be overlooked by readers, or a reader might just look at the first sentence, describing where the photos came from, and ignore the second and third sentences. The lawsuit was allowed to proceed. And a U.S. District Court ruled in 2006 that allegations that a woman was using her position in the media to meet and engage in sexual relations with powerful and prestigious men to advance her career and social status was defamatory.[47]

The law traditionally has been less protective of men in this regard, but there are indications that this might be changing. A young male model sued the publishers of gay and lesbian publications for including his photo in advertising for "Lust," a collection of photographs of naked, sexually aroused men engaged in explicit sex acts. The defendant was alone in the photo and was clothed from the waist down, but he argued that the use of the photo in advertising for such a publication suggests that he is sexually promiscuous. The defendants tried to argue that even if the use of the photo did imply sexual promiscuity, this was not a defamatory statement when made about a man rather than a woman. The Appellate Division of the New York Supreme Court disagreed, stating that "the notion that while the imputation of sexual immorality to a woman is defamatory per se, but is not so with respect to a man, has no place in modern jurisprudence. Such a distinction, having its basis in gender-based classification, would violate constitutional precepts."[48]

Comments about other kinds of sexual behavior are also sensitive, but as Americans seem to be developing a more open mind regarding sexual behavior, the law is changing. Thirty years ago any allegation that a man was gay or a woman was a lesbian was defamatory per se.[49] There are surely courts that would still abide by that rule today. But many courts have taken a different position. A federal court in Massachusetts ruled in mid-2004 that an accusation that an individual is gay no longer imputes

---

47. *Stanton* v. *Metro Corp.*, 438 F. 3d 119 (2006); and *Benz* v. *Washington Newspaper Publishing Co. LLC,* 34 M.L.R. 2368 (2006).

48. *Rejent* v. *Liberation Publications, Inc.*, 197 A. 2d 240 (1994).

49. *Gray* v. *Press Communications LLC*, 775 A. 2d 678 (2001).

criminal conduct and, therefore, cannot be the basis for a claim of libel per se. The plaintiff in the case argued that some people in the community believe that homosexuals are less reputable than heterosexuals and cited laws against gay marriage to support his case. The court rejected this argument, noting that in the past, statements misidentifying whites as blacks were also considered defamatory, but not so today.[50] In 2012 the Appellate Division of the New York Supreme Court ruled that statements falsely describing someone as a lesbian, gay or bisexual were not defamatory.[51] The majority of recent cases have found that false allegations of homosexuality are not per se defamatory, although it is possible that the term is capable of a defamatory meaning and thus requires proof of damages. For example, in 2009 the U.S. District Court for the Southern District of New York rejected a claim from Howard K. Stern, a former companion of the late model/celebrity/socialite Anna Nicole Smith, that being called gay was defamatory per se under New York law. Stern sued over a book that suggested he had oral sex with another man at a party and appeared in pornographic videos having sex with other men. Citing changing public opinion, the decriminalization of sodomy, and the movement to legalize gay marriage, the judge in the case found that being falsely called a homosexual was no longer libelous on its face.[52]

Personal Habits

Material about the personal habits of an individual need to be carefully screened. To raise questions about an individual's honesty, integrity or financial responsibility can be dangerous. Comments about consumption of alcohol or drugs can also cause problems. Libel law has traditionally protected people from false assertions that they have a contagious disease. Such an allegation can cause friends and acquaintances to shun the supposed victim because they don't want to be infected by the disease themselves. This is not a common libel problem today. But it is a problem to suggest that someone suffers from a medical condition that implies, for example, sexual promiscuity or unsavory behavior on the part of the victim. The Nebraska Supreme Court in 1990 sustained a jury award of $23,350 to a Springfield, Neb., man who was falsely accused of having AIDS. This was a slander suit; it resulted when a prominent woman in a small town began spreading rumors about the plaintiff.[53] Finally, comments about an individual's personal religious faith ("She doesn't live up to the teachings of her church"), patriotism or political activities have also generated libel actions.

Ridicule

A person can be libeled by ridicule. Not all humorous stories about someone are necessarily defamatory; only those in which the subject of the story is made to appear "uncommonly foolish" tend to be dangerous. Newspapers are commonly victimized by false

---

50. *Albright* v. *Morton*, 321 F. Supp. 2d 130 (2004). See also *Donovan* v. *Fiumara*, 114 N.C. App. 524 (1994); *Miles* v. *National Enquirer*, 38 F. Supp. 2d 1226 (1999); and *Amrak Productions Inc.* v. *Morton*, 33 M.L.R. 1891 (2005).
51. *Yonaty* v. *Mincolla*, 40 M.L.R. 2014 (2012).
52. *Stern* v. *Cosby*, 645 F. Supp. 2d 258 (S.D.N.Y. 2009).
53. Robbins, "Spring Field Journal; A Rumor of AIDS, A Slander Award."

obituaries. At times the "deceased" has brought a libel suit in response to such a publication, but the courts have consistently ruled that to say someone has died is not defamatory; it does not lower that person's reputation. But once a New England newspaper ridiculed a man by saying he was so thrifty that he built his own casket and dug his own grave. This story made the man appear to be foolish or unnatural.[54]

Business Reputation

Libel law probably goes furthest in protecting people in their business and occupations. Any comment that injures people's ability to conduct a business, harms them in their job or makes it more difficult for them to pursue their occupation is generally defamatory. And businesspeople are generally more likely to sue. They tend to be more acquainted with law and more comfortable initiating a legal suit.

Corporations that believe their credit has been damaged or their reputation has been harmed can sue for this injury. The list of kinds of defamatory accusations is long. Assertions that a company is involved in illegal business or that it fails to pay its bills on time or that it deliberately manufactures unsafe products or that it is trying to break a union are all libelous. A suggestion that the proprietor of a public business encourages rowdy behavior, or tolerates fighting or permits drug deals to be made may also be libelous. In these cases the story reflects on the behavior of the owner and would be libelous.

Criticism of a Product

Criticism of a product falls into a different legal category, called "disparagement of property." Such criticism is often called **trade libel,** but it is not really libel at all. Trade libel, or product disparagement, focuses on the product itself. "Viking Runabout automobiles continually stall during a rainstorm." That is an attack on the product. A libel of a business tends to focus on the alleged failings of the people who operate the business. "Viking Runabout automobiles continually stall during a rainstorm. The manufacturer, in order to save a few dollars, did not shield the electrical system properly and water leaks in at alarming levels, causing a short circuit." This is an attack on the company as well as the product.

Many states also have adopted statutes aimed at protecting the reputations of specific kinds of businesses. Banks and insurance companies in many jurisdictions are shielded by special statutes designed to protect them from attacks on their fiscal integrity. In recent years many states have adopted statutes that outlaw publication of intentional lies about the fruits and vegetables grown in the state. These so-called "veggie libel laws" generally give farmers and growers a cause of action to sue anyone who makes a statement about the health risks of a particular food product that is not based on "verifiable fact or scientific or other reliable evidence."

Talk show producer and host Oprah Winfrey was sued in 1998 by Texas cattle ranchers under that state's False Disparagement of Perishable Food Products Act. A guest on Winfrey's talk show had alleged that thousands of head of U.S. cattle were infected with bovine spongiform encephalopathy, the so-called mad cow disease, prompting the talk

---

54. *Powers v. Durgin-Snow Publishing Co.*, 144 A. 2d 294 (1958).

show host to declare that she was giving up eating hamburgers. Cattle prices dropped precipitously after the broadcast, and the ranchers sought millions of dollars in damages. Experts who viewed the case as the first important test of the constitutionality of the veggie hate laws were disappointed when U.S. District Judge Mary Lou Robinson ruled that the case could not proceed under the Texas law because the plaintiffs had not proved that cattle are "perishable food" as defined by the statute, or that "knowingly false" statements had been made, a requirement under the Texas law.[55] The 5th U.S. Circuit Court of Appeals affirmed the lower-court decision, but solely on the grounds that no knowingly false statements had been made about the cattle.[56] Similarly, in 2016, the North American Olive Oil Association filed a lawsuit in Georgia against Oprah's protege, Dr. Mehmet Oz. According to Georgia law, food libel occurs when someone states that a perishable food product is not safe for consumption without reliable scientific inquiry, facts or data. Oz was sued for stating "[A] shocking 80 percent of the extra virgin olive oil that you buy every day in your supermarket isn't the real deal. It may even be fake."[57]

FALSITY

The fourth requirement the plaintiff must meet to sustain a libel suit is proof of falsity. But as previously noted, not every plaintiff must meet this requirement.

The world of libel plaintiffs is divided into two groups, public people and private people. A public person is a government official, an elected officer, someone who is leading a public crusade, a prominent entertainer, a visible religious or business leader. A private person is someone who is not a public person. As you will soon see, the law makes it far more difficult for a public person, as opposed to a private person, to win a libel suit.

In every instance a public-person plaintiff must prove that the libelous remarks are not truthful. But the Supreme Court has ruled that a private-person plaintiff must prove the falsity of the libelous statements only when the subject of the statement is a matter of public concern.[58] What is a matter of public concern? The U.S. Supreme Court has never defined "matters of public concern" although the phrase appears in a wide variety of cases, including cases involving speech by government employees, intentional infliction of emotional distress and false light invasion of privacy, as well as others. The Court has said that whether a statement dealt with a matter of public concern must be determined on the basis of the statement's "content, form and context."[59] Not a very clear definition.

In *Snyder* v. *Phelps*,[60] a case involving the tort of intentional infliction of emotional distress, the Court attempted to explain the concept in greater detail. After writing that "the boundaries of the public concern test are not well defined," Chief Justice John Roberts nonetheless set out to articulate some principles. Roberts stated that speech is a matter of public concern when it relates to any political, social or other concern to the

55. *Texas Beef Group* v. *Winfrey*, 11 F. Supp. 2d 858 (1998).
56. *Texas Beef Group* v. *Winfrey*, 201 F. 3d 680 (2000).
57. Bentley, "Virgin or not? TV's Dr. Oz faces Georgia lawsuit over olive oil claims."
58. *Philadelphia Newspapers, Inc.* v. *Hepps*, 475 U.S. 767 (1986).
59. *Dun & Bradstreet* v. *Greenmoss*, 472 U.S. 749 (1985).
60. 562 U.S. 443 (2011).

community, when it is the subject of legitimate news interest or general interest or when the speech has value to the public. Private speech, on the other hand, "concerns no public issue."

Over time, courts will undoubtedly flesh out the definition of a "matter of public concern." It could be argued that the definition should be broadly based and include most of what is published in newspapers and magazines, and what is aired on television or radio. However, we are now in an era of what might be called micro-media, vast numbers of Internet sites aimed not at large and diverse audiences, but tiny groups of users. Would the argument apply to these media as well as to a blogger who reaches only a few hundred like-minded individuals? Who knows.

Most plaintiffs, then, must prove that the defamatory material is false. In those few instances when a private person sues for a story that is not a matter of public concern, the defendant must prove that the material is truthful. How does one prove falsity or truth?

The first rule of proving truth or falsity is that the evidence presented in court must go to the heart of the libelous charge. The proof must be direct and explicit. If there is conflicting evidence, the fact finder—the judge or the jury—will decide who is telling the truth. Every word of a defamatory charge need not be truthful, only the part that carries the gist or the sting of the libel. To be protected, a defamatory statement does not have to be absolutely accurate in every aspect. Minor flaws are not actionable, so long as the statement was "substantially true." Mistakes in a statement that do not harm a plaintiff's reputation cannot be the subject of a defamation suit.

The first rule of proving truth or falsity is that the evidence presented in court must go to the heart of the libelous charge.

For example, if a journalist reports that Bill Williams was convicted of stealing $1 million when, in fact, Williams was convicted of stealing $950,000, the statement is substantially true. The statement is substantially true because the "gist" or "sting" of the defamatory statement is true. The statement that Williams was convicted of stealing a large amount of money is accurate. The statement that caused the harm was that Williams stole a lot of money.

A man was filmed fighting with another inmate in a prison and was identified in a TV broadcast as a member of the Aryan Brotherhood, a white prison gang and crime syndicate in the United States. The plaintiff sued the broadcasters, arguing that the allegation was false. But the court rejected the argument, noting that while the plaintiff technically was not a member of the Brotherhood, he was a member of Mexikanemi, a gang affiliated with the Aryan Brotherhood. The allegation was therefore substantially true.[61]

Courts give libel defendants considerable leeway when evaluating the truth or falsity of a statement. But not all errors will be tolerated. At times even what might be regarded as a detail will result in a verdict for the plaintiff if it can be proved to be false. A firefighter in Des Moines, Iowa, was fired because, fire officials said, he had failed to pass a written emergency medical technician exam, a requirement to hold the job. The fire chief told reporters that the man had a reading problem. Despite undergoing tutoring at taxpayers' expense, he was still capable of reading at only the third-grade level. The defendants asked that the case be dismissed because it was substantially true. But the court refused, and the Iowa Supreme Court affirmed this decision. There were two errors

---

61. *Bustos* v. *United States,* 38 M.L.R. 1747 (2010).

in the story, perhaps only details, but they carried a libelous sting. First, the firefighter had himself paid a substantial portion of the cost of the tutoring. More important, tests showed he read at a level comparable with the lower one-third of community college students, not a third-grader. The story was not substantially true.[62]

Reporters must also remember that a jury in a libel suit will determine the truth or falsity of a story based on what the story said, not what the reporter meant. ABC was sued by the maker of a garbage recycling machine. Lundell Manufacturing sold the $3 million machine to a county in Georgia. After using the machine for a year or so, some people in the county said that the new machine had not solved the garbage problem. An ABC "World News Tonight" story included these comments:

> In this south Georgia county of tobacco farms and pecan groves taxpayers are angry that they are stuck with a three million dollar debt for this garbage recycling machine that they never approved and does not work.

Network attorneys argued that the reporter meant that the machine does not work in the larger sense, that it doesn't solve the county's garbage problem. But a jury agreed with the plaintiff instead and said that they interpreted the comment to mean that the garbage recycling machine did not work, that it was defective. In 1996 the 8th U.S. Circuit Court of Appeals upheld the more than $1 million jury award and ruled that a jury could conclude that the network's statement about the machine was false.[63]

How does the court evaluate the truth of the charge? The jury does this with guidance from the judge. The jurors are presented with both the libelous untruthful statement about the plaintiff and the truth about the plaintiff. The untruthful statement will leave a certain impression about the plaintiff in the jurors' minds. Does learning the truthful statement change that impression? For example, a television station refers to Hal Jones as a wife beater. Jurors gain an impression of Jones based on that statement. In truth, Jones struck his wife only once, during an argument, after she threw a coffee pot at him. Does the truth leave a different impression of Jones in the jurors' minds? One court said that "a workable test of truth is whether the libel as published would have a different effect on the mind of the reader from that which the pleaded truth would have produced."[64]

Even if a story contains nothing but truthful statements it still might be regarded as false if important facts are left out and the story leaves a false impression.

Even if a story contains nothing but truthful statements it still might be regarded as false if important facts are left out and the story leaves a false impression. Some courts have called this defamation by implication. A South Carolina driver accidentally struck and injured the police chief of Eastover, S.C. She pleaded guilty to driving too fast for road conditions. A year later the police chief died and in two stories the newspaper repeated the account of the traffic accident, adding that the woman would not face additional charges despite the chief's death. Everything in both stories was true, but the newspaper did not report that the police chief died from cancer. Readers could easily conclude that he had died from injuries sustained in the accident, and this would be false, the South Carolina Court of Appeals concluded.[65] In 2007 the Iowa Supreme Court said that defamation by implication was recognized in that state. However, a year earlier

---

62. *Jones v. Palmer Communications, Inc.,* 440 N.W. 2d 884 (1989).
63. *Lundell Manufacturing Co. v. ABC Inc.,* 98 F. 3d 351 (1996).
64. *Fleckstein v. Friedman,* 195 N.E. 537 (1934).
65. *Richardson v. State-Record Co.,* 499 S.E. 2d 822 (1998).

the Ohio Court of Appeals ruled false innuendo emanating from accurate statements—defamation by implication—was not actionable under Ohio libel law.[66] The Washington Court of Appeals ruled the same way in 2010.[67]

Remember, truth and accuracy are not always the same thing. Correctly quoting someone or accurately reporting what someone else has said does not necessarily constitute publishing a truthful statement. Imagine that John Smith tells a reporter that the police chief changes arrest records of certain prisoners to simplify their getting bail and winning acquittal. This charge, attributed to John Smith, is contained in the reporter's story, which is subsequently published. The police chief sues for libel. It is not sufficient for the reporter to prove merely that the statement in the story was an accurate account of what Smith said. Even if the reporter's story contained an exact duplicate of Smith's charge, truth can be sustained only by proving the substance of the charge, that the police chief has altered arrest records. It is the truth of the libelous charge that is at issue, not merely the accuracy of the quote in the story. Accuracy, then, is not always the same thing as truth.

The initial burden in the libel suit rests with the plaintiff, who must prove five important elements: that the defamation was published, that it was of and concerning the plaintiff, that the words were defamatory, that the allegations were false and that the defendant was at fault in causing this legal harm. The first four elements have been discussed in this chapter. Proving fault, the most complicated of the five elements, is the subject of Chapter 5.

SUMMARY

A plaintiff in a libel suit must first prove that the defamatory material was published; that is, that one additional person besides the plaintiff and the defendant has seen the material. The plaintiff must next show that the libel is of and concerning him or her. An individual can be identified for purposes of a libel suit by a name, nickname, photograph or even through a report of circumstances. Statements made about a very large group of people cannot be used as the basis for a libel suit for a single member of that group. However, if the group is smaller, individual members of the group may be able to sue for comments made about the entire group. The plaintiff must also prove that the words in the offensive statement are defamatory, that they lower his or her reputation. The most common kinds of defamatory statements contain allegations about criminal acts or sexual impropriety, include comments about personal habits or characteristics or reflect on the plaintiff's patriotism, political beliefs or competence and qualifications in a business or occupation. Corporations or other businesses can be defamed, and the manufacturer of a product can sue, with great difficulty, for product disparagement. In lawsuits against the mass media the plaintiff normally must prove that the damaging statements are false. The evidence presented in court must go to the heart of the libelous charge; the gist or sting of the libel must be false. Minor errors, unless they relate directly to the gist of the libel, will not usually result in a finding of falsity. The test of falsity is whether the proven truth leaves a different impression of the plaintiff in the minds of the jury than the impression created by the defamatory falsehood.

66. *Stevens* v. *Iowa Newspapers Inc.*, 35 M.L.R. 1385 (2007); and *Stohlman* v. *WJW-TV, Inc.*, 35 M.L.R. 1103 (2006).
67. *Yeakey* v. *Hearst Communications Inc.*, 234 P. 3d 332 (2010).

BIBLIOGRAPHY

American Law Institute. *Restatement of the Law of Torts*. 2nd ed. Philadelphia: American Law Institute, 1975.

Bezanson, Randall P., Gilbert Cranberg, and John Soloski. *Libel Law and the Press*. New York: The Free Press, 1987.

Gregorian, Dareh. "Ex-Vogue Model Snared in Ugly Web," *New York Post*, January 6, 2009.

Hakim, Danny. "Suzuki Resolves a Dispute with a Consumer Magazine." *The New York Times*, 9 June 2004, C6.

Media Law Resource Center. MLRC 2005 Report on Trials and Damages. Bulletin 2015 No. 1 (February 2015).

Moscov, Jim. "Truth, Justice and the American Tort." *Editor & Publisher*, 27 November 2000, 16.

Pring, George. "SLAPPs: Strategic Lawsuits Against Public Participation." *Pace Environmental Law Review*, Fall 1989, 8.

Pring, George, and Penelope Canan. "Strategic Lawsuits Against Public Participation." *Social Problems* 35 (1988): 506.

Prosser, William L. *Handbook of the Law of Torts*. St. Paul, Minn.: West Publishing, 1963.

Rosalind Bentley, "Virgin or not? TV's Dr. Oz faces Georgia lawsuit over olive oil claims," *Atlanta Constitution Journal*, 30 November 2016.

William Robbins, "Springfield Journal; A Rumor of AIDS, a Slander Award." The New York Times, 23 July 1990.

CHAPTER 5

Libel

PROOF OF FAULT

©McGraw-Hill Education/Jill Braaten

In 1964, for the first time, the U.S. Supreme Court ruled that a libel plaintiff was required to show proof a defendant had been at fault when the defamatory material was published. Until that time, civil libel law had been governed by the doctrine of strict liability. Under this doctrine, a libel defendant was responsible for harming a plaintiff regardless of how cautious and careful he or she had been in preparing and publishing or broadcasting the story. This ruling changed the face of libel law. What had been a relatively simple tort became complex when it was infused with

First Amendment considerations. This chapter outlines the two basic considerations relevant to fault:

Who is the plaintiff?

How was the story or material processed or prepared?

NEW YORK TIMES CO. v. SULLIVAN

A difficult and often violent struggle for civil rights took place in much of the Deep South in the late 1950s and early 1960s. Blacks, often accompanied by white civil rights workers, engaged in nonviolent civil disobedience to challenge a wide range of voting, accommodation and education laws that had left them as second-class citizens. Network television news was still in its early adolescence in this era; NBC and CBS carried only 15 minutes of news each night. There were no cable news organizations such as CNN, MSNBC or Fox News to provide 24-hour coverage. The story of the civil rights movement was carried throughout the nation via a handful of prestigious and frequently liberal newspapers, especially *The New York Times*. Segregationist leaders in the South hated these newspapers, which each day carried stories and pictures of another peaceful civil rights protest that had been met with violence or some other illegal act by government officials or by angry southern citizens.

On March 29, 1960, the *Times* carried a full-page editorial-advertisement titled "Heed Their Rising Voices." The ad was placed by an ad hoc coalition of civil rights leaders called the "Committee to Defend Martin Luther King and the Struggle for Freedom in the South." The ad leveled charges against public officials in the South who, the committee contended, had used violence and illegal tactics to quell the peaceful civil rights struggle. The basic thrust of the charges contained in the advertisement was true; but the ad, was filled with small, factual errors.* Several public officials in Alabama sued the newspaper. The first case to go to trial was brought by Montgomery, Ala., police commissioner L.B. Sullivan, who sought $500,000 in damages for false and defamatory statements about the conduct of the Montgomery police department.† Sullivan was never named in the ad, but contended that comments about the behavior of the Montgomery police reflected on him. A trial court ruled on behalf of Sullivan, and his $500,000 damage award was upheld by the Alabama Supreme Court. This was despite the fact that only 35 copies of the offending issue of *The New York Times* were circulated in Montgomery County.

The U.S. Supreme Court reversed the decision, ruling that Sullivan could not recover damages in this case unless he proved that *The New York Times* published the false and defamatory advertisement either knowing it was false or that the paper exhibited reckless disregard for the truth when it printed the material.[1] That is, the Montgomery police

---

* For example, the ad claimed that when students at Alabama State College staged a protest, armed police "ringed" the campus. Police were at the protest, but they did not ring the campus. When students refused to register for classes as a protest, the dining hall was padlocked, the ad claimed. In fact, only a small number of students without valid meal tickets were turned away from the dining hall.

† Compared with the multimillion-dollar damage awards sought today, $500,000 doesn't sound like much. But it was a staggering amount half a century ago.

1. *New York Times Co. v. Sullivan*, 376 U.S. 254 (1964).

Associate Justice William Brennan, the author of the Supreme Court decision in New York Times Co. v. Sullivan *in 1964 and many other notable First Amendment rulings.*

commissioner had to prove the newspaper had published the ad with knowledge of its falsity or that the persons who published the ad (both the members of the committee and the members of the newspaper's staff) had been extraordinarily careless by not examining the charges made in the statement much more carefully (reckless disregard for the truth). Justice William Brennan labeled these two elements **"actual malice"**; proof of knowledge of falsity or proof of reckless disregard for the truth was proof of actual malice. The language in the court's opinion extended the ruling in this case to all people whom the court called **public officials.** All public officials who sought to win a libel suit based on defamatory allegations about how they did their jobs or whether they were fit to hold those jobs henceforth would have to prove actual malice. Before examining the various elements in this new libel standard, let's look briefly at the rationale Brennan and his colleagues used to support this fundamental change in the law.

THE RATIONALE FOR THE RULING

▮ **Stripped of its civil libel cover, this case was clearly one of seditious libel.** A government official was criticized for the way he handled his public office. The newspaper was punished for publishing this criticism. The issues that generated the court ruling and the penalty for the newspaper were really not much different from what occurred in prosecutions under the Alien and Sedition Acts of 1798 and the Espionage and Sedition Acts of 1917 and 1918. Rulings by the Supreme Court had sharply limited the government's power to use seditious libel to punish those who criticize it (see pages 56–68). What Sullivan and his co-plaintiffs were attempting to do was to resurrect sedition law via a civil libel action.

■ **The nation has a profound and long-standing national commitment to the principle that debate on public issues should be uninhibited, robust and wide open.** Debate on public issues is a fundamental part of the democratic process. All citizens are encouraged to take part in this debate. In the heat of any discussion it is inevitable that erroneous statements will be made by the participants. Many people will be fearful of taking part in the debate if they think they might be sued for libel if they make a misstatement that harms someone's reputation. Whatever is added to the field of libel, wrote Justice Brennan, is taken away from the field of free debate. Freedom of expression, Brennan noted, needs breathing space to survive, and actual malice supplies that breathing space by protecting false statements unless they were published by the defendant who knew they were false or acted with reckless disregard toward their veracity.[2]

■ **When public officials like Sullivan take a government post, they must expect that their work will be closely scrutinized and even criticized by the people they serve.** Officers of government have ample means to rebut this criticism. They usually have easy access to the press to deny allegations made against them, to give their side of the story, and to even verbally attack their critics. This kind of speech is also a part of the important debate within a democracy. Police commissioner Sullivan could have easily talked to reporters in Montgomery if he sought to publish the truth. Instead, he chose to punish *The New York Times*.

Freedom of expression, Brennan noted, needs breathing space to survive.

The actual malice rule imposed on the law of libel by the Supreme Court was already a part of the law in a handful of states prior to the 1964 ruling in *New York Times Co.* v. *Sullivan*. In the wake of the *Sullivan* decision, all state and federal courts had to follow this rule. By the end of the decade, the Supreme Court had extended the actual malice rule to people called **public figures.** People outside government frequently try to lead public debate on important issues. These people should not be any more immune to criticism and complaints than government officials, the court rationalized.[3] Public figures also need to prove actual malice in order to win a libel suit. Finally, in 1974, the high court added the final element to the libel fault rule when it declared that even private persons, persons who are not part of government or who have not tried to influence public opinion, must prove that the mass medium was at fault when the libel was published or broadcast.[4] The state courts were given some freedom in this ruling to determine just what kind of fault the private party suing a mass medium must prove. Under the First Amendment, the private-person plaintiff at least must prove that the mass media defendant failed to

2. *New York Times Co.* v. *Sullivan*, 376 U.S. 254 (1964).
3. *Curtis Publishing Co.* v. *Butts*, 388 U.S. 130 (1967).
4. *Gertz* v. *Robert Welch, Inc.*, 418 U.S. 323 (1974).

exercise reasonable care in preparing and transmitting the story, or was **negligent,** the high court said. But a state could ask that these plaintiffs prove even more to sustain their libel suits, the court added. The issue of the level of fault that the plaintiff must prove will be discussed in the second half of this chapter (see pages 198–208).*

Several words have been used in the past few pages that beg for fuller explanation. Who is a public official? Who is a public figure? How do you define negligence? How do you define actual malice? The next section of this chapter attempts to add flesh to these bones, to make these legal concepts come more alive. Before moving to that, let's briefly summarize the basic rules of fault.

1. Private persons who sue the media for defamation must at least prove that the material was published through negligence. Negligence is defined in the law as the failure to exercise reasonable care.

2. Individuals who are either public officials or public figures for purposes of a libel suit have to prove that the defendant exhibited actual malice when the material was published. Actual malice is defined in the law as publishing with the knowledge that the libelous assertion is false, or with reckless disregard for whether it is true or false.

PUBLIC PERSONS VERSUS PRIVATE PERSONS

All libel plaintiffs who sue the mass media must prove that the defendant in the case was at fault, that the publication or broadcast of the libelous material was not simply the result of an innocent error. Public officials and public figures must prove a higher level of fault than do private individuals. But who are public officials and public figures in the eyes of the law? Before exploring this issue a brief caution is warranted. One of the problems in the law of libel is that courts have taken perfectly good words that most of us use daily and have attached a slightly different meaning to these words. Students need to exercise caution because of this. Most of us could probably agree on a general definition of a public figure, for example. But in libel law these words mean something different. What we need to remember is the legal definition of these words, not the common everyday definition.

WHO IS A PUBLIC OFFICIAL?

Two questions must be asked to determine whether a libel plaintiff should be considered a public official:

1. Who is this plaintiff—what kind of government job does he or she have? What is the **job description?**
2. What was the allegedly libelous story about? What is the **nature of the story?**

We will consider these questions separately.

* In 2006 Britain's highest court, the Law Lords, ruled that journalists in that nation have added protections in libel actions brought by public figures, as long as their reporting is responsible and in the public interest. This was the first time a European nation adopted a *Sullivan*-like libel rule. In 2009 the Canadian Supreme Court handed down two decisions that also expanded protection for journalists who are responsible in reporting on issues of public interest. Austen, "Canadian Rulings."

Job Description

The kind of government job a person holds is one key to determining who is and who is not a public official for purposes of libel law. Let's start with three general rules:

1. Any person who is elected to public office, to even the most lowly public office, qualifies as a public official.
2. Individuals who are appointed to or hired for government jobs *may qualify* as public persons in a libel action. It depends on the nature of the job.
3. But not everyone who works for the government will be regarded as a public official.

Determining if a nonelected government employee should be considered a public official in a libel action is often troublesome for the courts. What lawyers like to call a bright-line rule doesn't exist. (When courts consistently rule the same way on a legal question, lawyers often say a bright-line rule has been established. If, for example, in every instance the courts rule that a school teacher or a public works supervisor is a public official, this would be considered a bright-line rule.) Nevertheless, the Supreme Court has provided some useful guidance for the lower courts.

The Supreme Court has said:

> It is clear that the "public official" designation applies at the very least to those among the hierarchy of government employees *who have or appear to have to the public a substantial responsibility for or control over the conduct of governmental affairs.*[5]

Justice Brennan added that when a position in government has such apparent importance that the public has an independent interest in the qualifications and performance of the person who holds it, beyond the general public interest in the qualifications and performance of all government employees, the person in that position qualifies as a public official. While Brennan's remarks are fairly clear, let's try to translate a bit. Citizens are concerned that everyone who works for the government—from the clerk at the welfare office to the crossing guard outside the school to the person who reads the water meter—does his or her job efficiently and correctly. But some government employees have jobs that include responsibilities that go far beyond the responsibilities of the average government employee: people like the head of the city's welfare department, the individual in charge of school safety programs and the supervisor of the city water department. We have a special interest in their qualifications and how well they do their jobs. These people are likely to be counted as public officials.

Here are some examples of cases in which the public official designation has been an issue.

■ A timber management and contracting officer in the Eldorado National Forest in California was deemed to be a public official by a U.S. Court of Appeals.

---

5. *Rosenblatt v. Baer*, 383 U.S. 75 (1966) [emphasis added].

The appellate court said that his role in management of the sale of U.S. resources clearly marked him as one who had substantial responsibility for the administration of government matters.[6]

∎ An assistant superintendent of schools in a New York school district sued a newspaper for reporting that she had been convicted of misuse of school funds, which was incorrect. In her job, she supervised school principals and department heads, prepared curriculum proposals and had a role in determining what teachers got tenure. The New York Supreme Court ruled she was a public official because she had or appeared to have substantial responsibility over the operation of the school district.[7]

∎ The Ohio Court of Appeals ruled that the chief of the criminal section of a city law department was a public official because of his responsibilities and the importance of his position in the eyes of the public.[8]

∎ A junior state social worker was ruled to be a public official because her job carried with it "duties and responsibilities affecting the lives, liberty, money or property of a citizen that may enhance or disrupt his enjoyment of life."[9] Public school teachers and police officers are also frequently determined to be public officials because they deal daily with the welfare or safety of people in the community.[10]

∎ In Washington state the administrator of a motor pool for a small county was declared to be a public official because he had the power to spend county funds without his supervisors' approval.[11]

∎ The secretary and chief examiner of the Public Safety Civil Service Commission in Seattle was a public official, a federal court ruled, because she supervised other employees, managed the application process for people seeking employment with both the police and fire departments and supervised the testing process for all these applicants.[12]

∎ The city manager of a small Texas town was ruled to be a public official because she "wielded substantial responsibility for or control over the conduct of public affairs."[13]

The context in which the defamation occurs is often important. A planner with a state geological survey office might not normally hold a position that invites public scrutiny. But if this person is appointed by the governor to conduct a study of the feasibility of constructing a hazardous waste dump site near the state capital, this special assignment brings with it closer public scrutiny. In such a case a person who was not a public official might suddenly become one in terms of libel law.

6. *Baumback* v. *American Broadcasting Cos.*, 26 M.L.R. 2138 (1998).

7. *Silverman* v. *Newsday Inc.*, 38 M.L.R. 1613 (2010).

8. *Scaccia* v. *Dayton Newspapers Inc.*, 30 M.L.R. 1172 (2001).

9. *Press* v. *Verran*, 589 S.W. 2d 435 (1978).

10. See, for example, *Soke* v. *The Plain Dealer*, 69 Ohio St. 3d 395 (1994); and *Clark* v. *Clark*, 21 M.L.R. 1650 (1993).

11. *Clawson* v. *Longview Publishing Co.*, 589 P. 2d 1223 (1979).

12. *Harris* v. *City of Seattle*, 315 F. Supp. 2d 1105 (2004).

13. *Sparks* v. *Reneau Publishing Inc.*, 35 M.L.R. 2185 (2007).

SUMMARY   To summarize, some of the criteria for determining when a nonelected government employee is a public official include:

- The level of responsibility the individual has. In other words, how important is the job?
- The kind of responsibility the person has. Police officers, teachers and social workers may be lower-level employees, but the way they do their jobs can have an important and immediate impact on people's lives.
- Does the individual have the authority to spend public money independently, without supervision?

What is the nature of the person's job? The head of a task force to reorganize city employee health benefits and the head of the city's anti-terrorism task force might supervise the same number of workers, earn the same salary and be at the same city management level. But it is likely that the public will take a far greater interest in the qualifications of the anti-terrorism task force supervisor and the way she does her job than in the qualifications and competency of the person heading the employee benefits task force.

The Nature of the Story

Who the person is—the kind of job he or she holds—is an important criterion. But it is only half the test. Equally important is the nature of the story. What was the defamatory content about? Whether proof of actual malice will be required depends upon the focus of the libelous statement. If the statement concerns (1) *the manner in which the plaintiff conducts himself or herself in office—in other words, the way he or she does the job*—or (2) *the plaintiff's general fitness to hold that job*, then the plaintiff carries the burden of proving actual malice.

The first criterion relates to the plaintiff's official duties and focuses on matters directly related to public responsibilities. For example, in the Seattle Civil Service Commission case noted earlier, the allegations against the chief examiner focused on a trip she took to Las Vegas to attend a black public administrators conference. The television station said she spent little time in seminars and workshops during the trip, but considerable time at the gaming tables. The court ruled that the strong nexus between her position and the alleged false statements meant that the story directly related to the way she conducted herself on the job.[14]

But remember that public officials have private lives and not everything a government employee does in public necessarily relates to his or her official conduct. Dr. Lazelle Michaelis was the coroner of Otter Tail County, Minn., a position of substantial responsibility. She was also a private physician employed by a medical association. Because of her expertise in pathology she occasionally, as a favor, performed autopsies for

14. *Harris v. City of Seattle*, 315 F. Supp. 2d 1223 (2004).

the coroner in neighboring Becker County. A controversy developed when a television station reported that Michaelis concluded that the death of a young woman in Becker County was a suicide. Claiming her reputation was damaged by the publicity, she sued CBS broadcasting station WCCO for libel. The station argued that because Michaelis was the coroner in Otter Tail County she was a public official, obligated to prove actual malice. The court disagreed, saying that when Michaelis performed the autopsy in Becker County she was acting as a private doctor; she was paid by the medical association for which she worked. Her position in Otter Tail County had no relevance in this case.[15]

The second element in this test—the plaintiff's general fitness to hold office—is much broader and can even relate to a public official's private life or personal habits. For example, the fact that the fire chief's personal financial affairs are in considerable disarray probably doesn't have much to do with how well she performs her job as fire chief. But a city treasurer who has problems with personal finances could be a different story. This might suggest the treasurer is not fit to manage the city's financial affairs. The decision whether a particular allegation reflects on a public official's fitness to hold the job will necessarily be a subjective one. And it is complicated by the fact that courts, in making this determination, seem to use an elastic standard that relates to the importance of the plaintiff's job. It seems that almost anything about the personal life of the president of the United States is considered a measure of his or her fitness to hold that office. But the courts are unwilling to say the same thing about lower government officials. And the lower you go on the totem pole of public officeholders, the more the courts seem willing to rule that stories about private life have little to do with being a public official for purposes of a libel suit. It is incumbent on any journalist preparing a story on a public official's private life to demonstrate within the story just how these revelations affect the government officer's official responsibilities. This, in itself, could thwart a lawsuit.

ALL-PURPOSE PUBLIC FIGURES

Individuals deemed to be public figures must also prove actual malice when suing for libel. The Supreme Court has said that there are two kinds of public figures: all-purpose public figures and limited-purpose public figures. It was Justice Lewis Powell who established these twin categories in his opinion in *Gertz* v. *Welch*.[16] All-purpose public figures are those persons who "occupy positions of such pervasive power and influence that they are deemed public figures for all purposes." The Court has also said there is a very rare subcategory of individuals called involuntary limited-purpose public figures.

TYPES OF PUBLIC FIGURES

1. All-purpose public figures
2. Voluntary limited-purpose public figures
3. Involuntary limited-purpose public figures

---

15. *Michaelis* v. *CBS, Inc.*, 119 F. 3d 697 (1997).
16. 418 U.S. 323 (1974).

While Justice Powell's description of an all-purpose public figure sounds simple enough, this is a category of libel plaintiffs that most courts have had difficulty identifying. Do the criteria relate to power or fame? Sometimes the powerful have little public recognition. Name the presidents of the 10 largest U.S. corporations—powerful individuals, but hardly widely known. For example, in the late 1980s, federal judges refused to classify William Tavoulareas, the president of Mobil Oil, one of the nation's largest companies, as a public figure, saying that such a person must be so well known that his or her name is a household word. On the other hand, the famous often have little real power. People like Kim Kardashian or Taylor Swift come to mind. So who is an all-purpose public figure?

Surprisingly, perhaps, there haven't been a lot of other cases that have legally defined an all-purpose public figure. In many cases, the plaintiff himself or herself who agrees to the designation as an all-purpose public figure.[17] Why would a plaintiff agree to such a designation since it certainly makes it more difficult to win a libel action? Most likely they want to exaggerate their prominence in the public eye to support a higher damage claim. Then again, a lot of performers, sports stars and other celebrities have very large egos that need constant care and feeding.

Typically, all-purpose public figures have fame and notoriety or pervasive power and influence on a national level. Everyone, everywhere knows about them. But others may enjoy such power and influence strictly on a local level. Everyone in a specific town or region or state knows about them. These people can be deemed all-purpose public figures as well. Consider the woman who lives in a community of 6,500 people. She was formerly the mayor, has served on the school board in the past and has been a perennial choice for president of the parent-teacher association. She is the president of the largest real estate company in town, is a director on the board of the local bank and owns the local pharmacy and dry cleaners. She is active in numerous service clubs, is a leader in various civic projects and is instantly recognizable on the street by the town's residents. Her family founded the town 150 years earlier. If she is libeled in a community newspaper whose circulation remains almost exclusively in the community, it could be argued persuasively that this woman is an all-purpose public figure in the community. (See *Steere* v. *Cupp*,[18] in which the Kansas Supreme Court ruled such an individual was a total, or all-purpose, public figure.)

But some courts have rejected the notion that because someone is well known in a community, this automatically makes him or her an all-purpose public figure. A television reporter in Utah sued the station where she had worked for making false statements about why she was fired. The station argued she was an all-purpose public figure. She had reported stories for the station for three years, done promotional spots and appeared at special events for the station. One could speculate that a large percentage of people in the community could recognize the plaintiff, Holly Wayment. At least that is what the trial court surmised. But the Utah Supreme Court rejected the ruling that she was an all-purpose public figure. There was no evidence presented that she wielded any particular social or political influence or even proof that the news show on

---

17. See *Masson* v. *New Yorker Magazine, Inc.*, 881 F. 2d 1452 (1989), for example.
18. 602 P. 2d 1267 (1979).

which she appeared was widely watched. "If we accept these facts as sufficient evidence of general fame in the local community, any reporter would qualify as an all-purpose public figure," the court said.[19]

What if the defamatory material circulates outside the local community, as well, to people who may not be familiar with the plaintiff? This question arose in 1985 in a libel suit by business executive George Martin against the *Chariho Times* in Rhode Island. Martin was clearly well known in the village of Shannock, where he owned and had developed a considerable amount of property over a period of 15 years. The *Times* was widely read by the 300 residents of the village, and a trial court ruled that Martin was a local all-purpose public figure. On appeal Martin argued that the newspaper had 3,000 subscribers, a far larger readership than just among the village residents by whom he was so well known. The Rhode Island Supreme Court, noting that Martin's fame had spread beyond the Shannock village limits, agreed with the lower court and added that "very few individuals will be known to all subscribers or purchasers of any publication."[20]

LIMITED-PURPOSE PUBLIC FIGURES

Individuals in the second category of public figures outlined by Justice Powell in the *Gertz* decision are called limited-purpose public figures. Limited-purpose public figures are individuals who ". . . have thrust themselves to the forefront of particular public controversies in order to influence the resolution of the issues involved."[21] This kind of libel plaintiff is regarded as a public person for a discrete part of his or her life, usually because of something this person has done to try to influence public opinion on a public issue. Between 1974 and 1979 the Supreme Court made four attempts to try to flesh out the definition of a limited-purpose public figure. From these four decisions three elements of a definition emerged. These elements form a base upon which other courts have erected their own definitions of limited-purpose public figures. Here are the elements:

Limited-purpose public figures are individuals who ". . . have thrust themselves to the forefront of particular public controversies in order to influence the resolution of the issues involved."

- **A public controversy must exist before the publication or broadcast of the libelous matter. The outcome of this controversy must have an impact on individuals beyond those directly involved in the dispute. As one court noted, "A public controversy is not simply a matter of interest to the public; it must be a real dispute, the outcome of which affects the general public or some segment of it in an appreciable way."[22]**
- **The plaintiff must have voluntarily participated in this controversy. The press cannot generate a controversy and then pull the plaintiff into the fray.**
- **The plaintiff must take a role in trying to influence public opinion regarding the controversy. In *Gertz*, the Court put a great deal of emphasis on the plaintiff's access to media and whether that access was used in an effort to affect the outcome of the controversy.**

19. *Wayment v. Clear Channel Broadcasting*, 116 P. 3d 271 (2005).
20. *Martin v. Wilson Publishing*, 497 A. 2d 322 (1985).
21. *Gertz v. Welch*, 418 U.S. 323 (1974).
22. *Eric Waldbaum, Appellant, v. Fairchild Publications, Inc.*, 627 F. 2d 1287 (D.C. Cir. 1980)

Now let's look briefly at the four rulings to see how these elements emerged.

In the first case the plaintiff was Elmer Gertz, a well-known civil rights attorney. A police officer shot and killed a young man, and a serious controversy erupted in Chicago as authorities tried to determine what had happened. The officer was ultimately tried and convicted of murder. Gertz was retained by the family of the dead man to bring a civil action against the officer and the city. He played no part in the criminal investigation that resulted in the trial and conviction of the police officer. An extreme right-wing organization called the John Birch Society made outrageous charges against Gertz in a publication and he sued for libel. Was he a limited-purpose public figure?

The Supreme Court said no. The public controversy was about the murder of an innocent man by a police officer, and his subsequent trial and conviction. Gertz was at the periphery of this controversy, and he made no attempt to influence public opinion in this matter. He had a limited role as an attorney who represented the family in their attempt to win damages because of the death.[23]

The plaintiff in the second case was a young Florida socialite named Mary Alice Firestone. She and her husband, Russell Firestone, a member of the Firestone tire family, sued each other for divorce. She contended she was libeled by *Time* magazine when it inadvertently labeled her an adulteress in a short article in the magazine. Mary Alice Firestone was widely known in the community as a member of the elite Palm Beach Society, an active member of the so-called sporting set. She was also aggressive in meeting with reporters on an almost daily basis to give her side of the story. When she sued, attorneys for *Time* argued she was a public figure who must prove actual malice. The Supreme Court disagreed.

Mary Alice Firestone, the Court wrote, did not assume any *"role of especial prominence"* in the affairs of society, other than Palm Beach society. And she did not volunteer to participate in the controversy that resulted from the divorce action. She was forced by law to go to court to dissolve her marriage.[24]

In 1979 the high court decided two more cases. Ilya Wolston was the prototype private citizen. Unfortunately, he was the nephew of Myra and Jack Soble, two well-publicized American communists who were arrested during the Red Scare of the 1950s and charged with spying. Wolston lived in Washington, D.C., at the time, and after he was interviewed by the FBI he was ordered on several occasions to testify before a federal grand jury in New York. He grew weary of the harassment and after several grand jury appearances ignored a subpoena. He was held in contempt of court and was sentenced to three years' probation. Fifteen news stories were published about Wolston and his grand jury appearances and one nonappearance. But after all the investigation, the government failed to discover any information that linked Wolston to communist activities.

Fifteen years later a book published by the *Reader's Digest* identified Wolston as a Soviet agent. When he sued for libel, the publisher argued that because he was called to testify before a grand jury, because he was held in contempt of court and

23. Ibid.
24. *Time, Inc.* v. *Firestone*, 424 U.S. 448 (1976).

because this episode was reported in the press, Wolston was a limited-purpose public figure. The Supreme Court disagreed. Wolston did not voluntarily inject himself into any controversy; he was pulled in as the government pursued him because of his relationship with the Sobles. In the mid-1950s there was a legitimate public controversy over Soviet espionage in the United States, but Wolston had little if anything to do with that controversy and he made no effort to influence public opinion about any controversy.[25]

In the final case, the high court decided that the research director of a public mental health hospital in Michigan was not a limited-purpose public figure. The plaintiff had applied for and received about $500,000 in federal grants to conduct research on animal aggression. Each month, William Proxmire, a United States senator from Wisconsin whom some regarded as the "fiscal conscience" of the Senate, awarded a federal agency or a federal official what he called "The Golden Fleece" award, because Proxmire believed he or she or it wasted taxpayer money. Proxmire regarded Hutchinson's research as inconsequential if not silly and gave a Golden Fleece award to the agencies that had been funding his studies for the previous seven years and made derogatory comments about Hutchinson as well. The researcher sued for libel.

The Court ruled that Hutchinson played no part in the broad general controversy over how tax dollars are spent. Nor did he try to influence public opinion about this matter—all he did was apply for research grants to sustain his work. Simply taking public money to undertake research is not enough to make a person like Hutchinson into a public figure.[26]

LOWER-COURT RULINGS

Deciding who is and who is not a limited-purpose public figure is one of the most subjective decisions courts must make in applying the law of libel. It is not surprising then that, despite the guidance from the Supreme Court, differences in this definition exist among the lower courts.

THE THREE FACTORS LOWER COURTS CONSIDER TO DETERMINE IF A PLAINTIFF IS A LIMITED-PURPOSE PUBLIC FIGURE

1. Is the subject matter of the defamatory statement a pre-existing public controversy?
2. Did the plaintiff voluntarily inject himself or herself into the controversy in a significant way?
3. Did he or she try to affect the outcome or influence public opinion about the public controversy?

---

25. *Wolston v. Reader's Digest*, 443 U.S. 157 (1979).
26. *Hutchinson v. Proxmire*, 443 U.S. 111 (1979).

A limited-purpose public figure must voluntarily become involved in a pre-existing public controversy in an attempt to influence the resolution of the controversy. A few lower courts have viewed the "voluntary participation" element of the criteria in a more liberal fashion. The Pennsylvania Supreme Court noted in 2007 that "some courts have held that a controversy may be created by a plaintiff's own activities."[27] A criminal rarely seeks to attract attention; yet some courts have said that by committing a criminal act an individual can legitimately expect to draw the kind of public attention that fosters a definition of a public figure. Lower courts typically hold that voluntary entry into the public eye is a prerequisite for public figure status. But there is disagreement among the courts as well. In March 1998 a U.S. District Court in Connecticut ruled that the wife of a physician who had continuing legal problems was a public figure. The doctor, on probation for five years because of charges of incompetence, was arrested and charged with 20 counts of fraud. "Despite the fact that plaintiff has not sought a public role, she has been thrust into the role of a public figure by virtue of her marriage to Dr. Zupnik—who clearly is a public figure."[28] Three months later the Appellate Division of the New York Supreme Court ruled that the ex-husband of prominent television celebrity Joan Lunden was not a public figure simply because he was married for many years to the co-host of ABC's "Good Morning America." The *Globe* tabloid had suggested that prior to the divorce, while the couple was separated, Lunden's husband had an affair with a prostitute. "Plaintiff is not famous in his own right and his marriage to Lunden certainly did not bestow upon him the sort of fame that is necessary to be considered a general public figure."[29]

An interesting case involving five broadcasts by CBS news over 18 months demonstrates how courting media attention can transform a plaintiff into a limited-purpose public figure. In 2009, the U.S. District Court for New Mexico heard a case involving Lillian Anaya, an employee of the Los Alamos National Laboratory (LANL) who was accused of using a government purchase card to buy a customized souped-up Ford Mustang. Based on a press release by LANL, the media began to investigate the alleged Mustang purchase and other irregularities in 2002. CBS aired five separate broadcasts on the investigation between November 2002 and April 2004. Initially after CBS named Anaya, she avoided media contact and refused interviews. When she later became the focus of CBS's reports, however, she sought media coverage to combat the bad publicity being generated. When Anaya sued for defamation, CBS argued that she was a limited-purpose public figure because she had injected herself voluntarily into the public controversy over wasteful and fraudulent government spending. The court ruled that because Anaya had not injected herself into the controversy or sought media attention between November 2002 and February 2003, she was not a limited-purpose public figure when CBS's first three broadcasts on the issue aired during that time. However, because Anaya began to court the press in a "concerted effort to publicize exonerating evidence" in June 2003, she became a public figure for broadcasts aired in October 2003 and April 2004.[30]

---

27. See *Clardy* v. *The Cowles Pub. Co.*, 912 P. 2d 1078 (1996); and *Carr* v. *Forbes*, 259 F. 3d 273 (2001).
28. *American Future Systems Inc.* v. *Better Business Bureau of Eastern Pennsylvania*, 923 A. 2d 389 (2007).
29. *Krauss* v. *Globe International Inc.*, 674 N.Y.S. 2d 662 (1998).
30. *Anaya* v. *CBS Broadcasting*, 626 F. Supp. 1158 (2009).

The Nature of the Controversy

The kind of controversy that generated the libel is an obviously important factor in determining whether a plaintiff is a limited-purpose public figure. Unfortunately, because the Supreme Court has never fully articulated what constitutes a public controversy, lower courts have had difficulty applying the concept and use different approaches. In 1994 in a decision that echoed earlier Supreme Court rulings, the 4th U.S. Circuit Court of Appeals declared that "a public controversy is a dispute that in fact has received public attention because its ramifications will be felt by persons who are not direct participants."[31] This is the same standard applied by the Georgia Supreme Court when it ruled that a group of plastic surgeons who were involved in a fight with other physicians over what kinds of medical specialists were qualified to perform plastic surgery were not public figures. This was a dispute that affected only members of the medical community, not the general public.[32] Courts do not always provide a great deal of analysis as to why a matter might be a public controversy. In 2000, a federal district court ruled that lobbying in Washington, D.C., was a public controversy because from "the early 1980s onward there has been a tide of concern and criticism about Washington lobbying."[33] In 2011, a federal court held that a documentary film that depicted the treatment of Haitian laborers on sugarcane plantations in the Dominican Republic related to a public controversy with little explanation.[34] In 2011, in the Anaya case discussed earlier, the court wrote that the issues in question—fraud and the mismanagement of government resources—was a public controversy. Although the court wrote that not every controversy was automatically a "public controversy," the court held that the misuse and mismanagement of funds at a major government facility was the sort of public controversy referred to in *Gertz* without explaining why. In 2013, in a case involving a profile of art appraiser and authenticator Peter Paul Biro that appeared in *The New Yorker* magazine, the U.S. Court of Appeals for a federal court ruled that statements about art and art authenticity addressed a public controversy.[35] In 2010, a court determined that statements by Oprah Winfrey about the headmistress of the Oprah Winfrey Leadership Academy for Girls, a private academy opened by Winfrey in South Africa, were related to two public controversies. First, the court determined that whether a public-private institution employing "a novel and innovative approach to providing a high-caliber education to girls from disadvantaged backgrounds" would succeed was a public controversy. Second, the court determined that statements related to abuse of students by "Dorm Parents" at the Academy was also a legitimate public controversy.[36]

Many courts have repeatedly ruled that the mass media cannot generate a controversy and then, when a libel suit is filed, label the people they pulled into that controversy as public figures. A radio station in Brunswick, Ga., tried this ploy after it broadcast rumors that a local musician had murdered his girlfriend, who was the mother of his child. Travis Riddle had achieved a small degree of notoriety in Brunswick. He performed

The kind of controversy that generated the libel is an obviously important factor in determining whether a plaintiff is a limited-purpose public figure.

31. *Foretich* v. *Capital Cities/ABC, Inc.*, 37 F. 3d 1541 (1994).
32. *Georgia Society of Plastic Surgeons* v. *Anderson*, 363 S.E. 2d 710 (1987).
33. *Gray* v. *St. Martin's Press, Inc.* 221 F. 3d 243 (D.N.H. 2000).
34. *Felipe Lluberes & Juan Lluberes* v. *Uncommon Productions, LLC,* 663 F. 3d 6 (D. Mass. 2011).
35. *Biro* v. *Conde Nast,* 963 F. Supp. 2d 255 (S.D.N.Y. 2013).
36. *Mzamane* v. *Winfrey,* 693 F. Supp. 2d 442 (E.D.P. 2010).

at local rap concerts, appeared once in a segment on MTV, self-produced a CD that sold fairly well in the area and was the subject of at least one newspaper article. But testimony revealed most of the staff at the radio station had never heard of him prior to the lawsuit. One of the DJs at the station began receiving calls one day accusing Riddle of murder and aired some of these callers. Riddle, who at the time was working as a banquet server in Atlanta, sued for libel. The station claimed he was a public figure.

The Georgia Court of Appeals asked the question, What was the controversy in this case? The accusations of murder generated a controversy, the defendant argued. But Riddle was never named as a suspect in a murder investigation. In fact, there was no murder. His girlfriend had merely disappeared for a few days. Her disappearance might have been newsworthy, but it was never publicized. But even then, if this generated a controversy, it was an issue that affected only her family and friends. This would not have been a public controversy. A jury awarded Riddle $100,000.[37]

The Plaintiff's Role

Once a court has ruled that a legitimate controversy existed it must then determine what role the plaintiff played in the controversy. This is a more difficult question. Was the plaintiff actually involved in the controversy that gave rise to the defamation? Or was he or she simply on the periphery? Was the participation voluntary or was the plaintiff drawn into the controversy by the mass media? Because no two cases are exactly alike, and because the answers to the questions raised above often involve subjective judgments, it is not surprising to find contradictory rulings among the courts in cases in which the facts seem somewhat similar. But this should stand as a warning to those who think the law is made up of a set of specific rules that are applied in exactly the same fashion in every case. This rarely happens, and perhaps never will, unless the human judges and jurors are replaced by computers. Let's look at a few cases to explore how various courts have dealt with the matter of the role of the plaintiff in the controversy.

There is a sharp difference of opinion in the United States on the role women should play in combat. Carey D. Lohrenz was one of the first two women who became Navy combat pilots. She was assigned as an F-14 pilot on a Navy aircraft carrier. The controversy heated up when the other female combat pilot died when her aircraft malfunctioned as she attempted a carrier landing. At this point, some people began attacking both the idea of allowing women to fly high-performance combat aircraft and Lohrenz herself, saying she was incompetent and unqualified. She sued for libel.

The defense argued that because of the controversy over whether women should be allowed to fly fighter aircraft, Lohrenz, a female combat pilot, was a public figure for purposes of this issue. But Lohrenz's attorney argued that she had not taken any part in this controversy—she simply trained as a naval aviator, chose to fly jets and accepted her assignment as a combat pilot when the opportunity presented itself. She certainly did not publicly participate in the debate over the wisdom of this change in policy.

The U.S. Court of Appeals sided with the defense. The court ruled that when Lohrenz *chose* to become a Navy aviator and when she *chose* to accept the assignment as an F-14 pilot,

---

37. *Riddle v. Golden Isle Broadcasting LLC*, 621 S.E. 2d 822 (2005); 36 M.L.R. 2084 (2008).

she should have realized she was becoming embroiled in the controversy over the role to be played by women in combat. She attained a special prominence in the dispute when she suited up to fly a Navy warplane, assuming a "central role in the controversy."[38]

In 1999 a Georgia court ruled that Richard Jewell was a public figure for purposes of his libel suit against Cox Enterprises Inc., publisher of the *Atlanta Journal-Constitution*. Jewell, a former deputy sheriff, discovered a bomb in a knapsack in a park during the 1996 Summer Olympic Games in Atlanta and then herded spectators out of the area before the device exploded. One person was killed, 11 others were injured. After the incident, Jewell gave about a dozen interviews to local and national media about the bombing and about park security in general. While Jewell was regarded as a hero at first, later law enforcement officials focused on him as a suspect in the bombing. Although Jewell was eventually cleared, he sued the Atlanta newspapers for comments published while he was the prime suspect in the case. The court ruled that Jewell was a public person because he voluntarily stepped into the controversy by giving the interviews to the press. At the time the statements were made by the newspapers, he was not simply defending himself from the accusations. "It is beyond argument," the court ruled, "that plaintiff did not reject any role in the debate, was a prominent figure in the coverage of the controversy, and, whatever his reticence regarding his media appearances, encountered them voluntarily."[39]

A controversy arose in a small community in western Kentucky when a radiologist was fired at a regional medical center following complaints from former patients and a doctor who worked at the same facility. Extensive publicity accompanied the doctor's termination, and ultimately he sued the local newspaper for libel, among other things. The newspaper argued that because of the controversy in the community, and the attending publicity, the physician was a limited-purpose public figure. But a federal court disagreed, ruling that the radiologist had not injected himself into the controversy. He was pulled into the fray when he was terminated, the court said. Also, he did not act in a manner designed to attain publicity; nor did he have unusual access to the media.[40]

Contradictory decisions like these are often confusing, even to lawyers who specialize in libel law. They are evidence of two things: first, that the law of libel is still evolving, as it has during the past several centuries; and second, as noted in Chapter 4, that libel is still basically state law. While the constitutionalization of the tort has added some consistency to the development of the libel law, state judges still have considerable room to shape their own law.

BUSINESSES AS PUBLIC FIGURES

Businesses and corporations can sue for libel; they can also be classified as public figures for purposes of a libel suit. Surely if a business attempts to lead public opinion during a controversy over an important public issue, it could be categorized as a limited-purpose public figure. For example, General Motors could be classified as a limited-purpose

Businesses and corporations can sue for libel; they can also be classified as public figures for purposes of a libel suit.

38. *Lohrenz* v. *Donnelly*, 350 F. 3d 1272 (2003). The Supreme Court refused in 2004 to review this decision.
39. *Jewell* v. *Cox Enterprises Inc.*, 27 M.L.R. 2370 (1999), aff'd *Atlanta Journal-Constitution* v. *Jewell*, Ga. Ct. App., 29 M.L.R. 2537 (2001). In 2005 Eric E. Rudolph, who had bombed abortion clinics and a gay bar, admitted the Olympic bombing as well. Richard Jewell died on August 29, 2007.
40. *Trover* v. *Paxton Medical Group*, 36 M.L.R. 1241 (2007).

public figure if it was libeled as it attempted to lead public opinion against government-imposed automobile emission standards. But businesses have been regarded as public figures based on other criteria as well, criteria hammered out over the past two decades.

STANDARDS USED TO DETERMINE WHETHER A BUSINESS IS A PUBLIC FIGURE

▌ Did the business use a highly unusual advertising or promotional scheme to draw attention to itself?

▌ Is the business well known to the average person in the area where it has a presence?

▌ Is the business regulated by the government?

▌ Did the libelous comment about the business focus on a matter of public concern?

▌ Has the business undergone frequent and intense scrutiny by the media?

The Ohio Court of Appeals ruled in 2006 that two adult entertainment clubs that featured nude or partially nude dancing were public figures. The court said the clubs had been in the news for 10 years due to licensing matters and opposition from people in the area during zoning hearings.[41]

Normal advertising will not generally establish the level of notoriety required to turn a business into a public figure. In 2014, the Thomas M. Cooley Law School sued a law firm, Kurzon Strauss, LLP, for $17 million over statements that criticized law schools for over-enrolling students and contended that law students could not pay back their student loans. The 6th U.S. Circuit Court of Appeals ruled that the law school was a limited-purpose public figure because it had voluntarily issued a report on the topics, publicly responded to the controversy in the media and used its Web site, advertisements, recruiting materials, written publications and career services presentations to disseminate its message.[42] However, even a spirited, but typical, comparative advertising campaign between U.S. Healthcare Inc. and Blue Cross in Pennsylvania did not propel either company into the public-figure status, according to the 3rd U.S. Circuit Court of Appeals.[43]

Two court rulings in the 1990s, including one by the 5th U.S. Circuit Court of Appeals, have provided additional criteria that might be applied when determining whether a business is a public figure for purposes of a libel suit. In *Snead* v. *Redland Aggregates, Ltd.*, the court of appeals ruled that the notoriety of a business to the average person in the relevant geographical area (the area in which the libel is circulated), the public prominence of the business because it manufactures widely known consumer

---

41. *Total Exposure.com, Ltd.* v. *Miami Valley Broadcasting Corp.*, 34 M.L.R. 1880 (2006).
42. *Thomas M. Cooley Law School* v. *Kurzon Strauss LLP,* 759 F.3d 522 (6th Cir. 2014).
43. *U.S. Healthcare, Inc.* v. *Blue Cross of Greater Philadelphia*, 898 F. 2d 914 (1990).

goods and the frequency and intensity of media scrutiny of the business are all factors that need to be considered when a court makes a determination about the public-figure status of a business.[44] Also to be considered, the court said, is whether the libelous speech involves a matter of public or private concern. In this case the court ruled that a British firm that quarried sand, gravel and crushed stone was not a public figure. And a U.S. District Court in Pennsylvania ruled that a business's relative access to the media and the manner in which the risk of defamation came upon the business (i.e., the context of the dispute that generated the libel) must be considered when deciding whether a business was a public figure or not.[45] While the criteria in both these decisions lack precision, these rulings indicate that some courts seem willing to consider the public-figure status of businesses in a broader light.

As noted by the 5th U.S. Circuit Court of Appeals in the *Snead* decision, generalizations that have some value when determining the public or private status of an individual don't work well when applied to a business. Most courts seem more comfortable approaching the problem on a case-by-case basis. The lack of clear standards is an important reason journalists should be cautious when communicating about businesses, even those that have a high visibility in the community.

PUBLIC PERSONS OVER TIME

If someone is a public person (public official or public figure) today, will he or she still be regarded as a public figure 20 years from now? Yes, but only in regard to the issues or matters that generated the public-person status today. If Foster Pierson is a public figure today because he is at the forefront of a fight against a gun control initiative on the ballot in Indiana, he will still be regarded as a public figure in any story published or broadcast in the future regarding this initiative battle. Similarly, a woman who retires to private life after being mayor of Houston will still be regarded as a public person if she sues for libel for a story published 25 years from now that focuses on her conduct while she was mayor.

The 10th U.S. Court of Appeals ruled in 2002 that the former associate deputy director of the Federal Bureau of Investigation was a public person for the purposes of a libel suit based on a book about the Oklahoma City bombing in 1995. Oliver Revell was retired from the FBI when the book was published, but the court ruled that this was immaterial. That

> the person defamed no longer holds the same position does not by itself strip him of this status as a public official for constitutional purposes. If the defamatory remarks relate to his conduct while he was a public official and the manner in which he performed his responsibilities is still a matter of public interest, he remains a public official within the meaning of *New York Times*.[46]

A U.S. District Court ruled that a U.S. Secret Service agent who saved the life of President Gerald Ford in 1975 must still be regarded as a public person for purposes of a libel

---

44. 998 F. 2d 1325 (1993).
45. *Rust Evader Corp.* v. *Plain Dealer Publishing Co.*, 21 M.L.R. 2189 (1993).
46. *Revell* v. *Hoffman*, 309 F. 3d 1228 (2002). See also *Newsom* v. *Henry*, 443 So. 2d 817 (1984); and *Contemporary Mission* v. *New York Times*, 665 F. Supp. 248 (1987), 842 F. 2d 612 (1988).

suit based on a story broadcast in 1992 about the attempted assassination.[47] Two attempts were made on Ford's life in September 1975. Agent Larry Buendorf deflected the arm of assailant Lynette "Squeaky" Fromme on Sept. 5, 1975, and saved the life of President Ford while he was visiting Sacramento, Calif. Two weeks later a private citizen, Oliver Sipple, pushed away the arm of assailant Sara Jane Moore as she attempted to shoot the president when he was in San Francisco. This second incident became a major issue in the Bay Area when newspaper columnist Herb Caen speculated in print that the White House had not thanked Sipple for his heroic act because he was a homosexual. Sipple was gay, but sued the newspaper for invasion of privacy.[48] (See page 298 for more on this case.) Researchers at National Public Radio got the two incidents mixed up, and commentator Daniel Schorr, in a report on how the press tramples on the privacy of public people, said it was revealed after he saved the president's life that agent Buendorf was a homosexual. The court ruled that Buendorf would have to prove actual malice to win his libel suit, something he was unable to do.[49] But in 1997 the Arkansas Supreme Court ruled that J. Michael Fitzhugh, a former federal prosecutor, was not a public person for purposes of a libel action he brought against the *Arkansas Democrat-Gazette*. The newspaper published a story that federal prosecutor Robert Fiske Jr. was about to initiate the first prosecution in the Whitewater investigation. Two men, Charles Matthews and Eugene Fitzhugh, were the defendants in the case. The newspaper ran what it thought were pictures of the pair. The Matthews photo was correct, but the *Democrat-Gazette* mistakenly published a photo of J. Michael Fitzhugh instead of a picture of Eugene Fitzhugh. The newspaper argued that because the plaintiff had been a federal prosecutor for eight years—clearly a public official during those years—he surely should be considered a public person for the purposes of this lawsuit. The court disagreed, ruling that while J. Michael Fitzhugh was and still is a public person for any story relating to his work as a federal prosecutor, he was not a public person for stories about matters outside that realm, including the Whitewater investigation. The simple error cost the newspaper $50,000 in damages.[50]

INVOLUNTARY PUBLIC FIGURES

In *Gertz*, the Supreme Court also stated that there may be an "exceedingly rare" category of public figures: involuntary public figures. **Involuntary public figures** are people who are drawn into public controversies rather than those who have thrust themselves into a public controversy voluntarily. While the court did not provide a definitive definition of an involuntary public figure, typically individuals who have been drawn into a controversy through unforeseen or unintended circumstances are considered to be involuntary public figures. Although the court wrote that involuntary public figures would be "exceedingly rare," some lower courts have found individuals to be involuntary public figures under specific situations. An involuntary public figure might not intentionally or purposefully seek attention. Rather, that person might have obtained the public's

---

47. *Buendorf* v. *National Public Radio, Inc.*, 822 F. Supp. 6 (1993).

48. *Sipple* v. *Chronicle Publishing Co.*, 154 Cal. App. 3d 1040 (1984).

49. *Buendorf* v. *National Public Radio, Inc.*, 822 F. Supp. 6 (1993).

50. *Little Rock Newspapers* v. *Fitzhugh*, 954 S.W. 2d 187 (1997).

attention unintentionally or without deliberate action. The person might have access to the media but did not necessarily voluntarily enter into a public controversy. Unfortunately, courts have been inconsistent in how they define involuntary public figures. In addition, some courts confuse the matter even more by finding there is no such thing as an involuntary public figure. In addition, while the Supreme Court hypothetically wrote that a plaintiff could be an involuntary public figure, the court itself has never specifically recognized a plaintiff as one.

PRIVATE PERSONS

In a libel action, if the plaintiff does not meet the definition of a public official, an all-purpose public figure, or a limited-purpose public figure, the court will regard the individual as a private person. This designation means the plaintiff will not be required to prove that the defendant lied or exhibited reckless disregard for the truth in publishing the libel. The plaintiff in most jurisdictions will have to demonstrate only that the defendant failed to exercise reasonable care in preparing and publishing the defamatory material. There are, however, a few exceptions to this rule. In Alaska, Colorado, Indiana and New Jersey, private-person plaintiffs must prove actual malice in cases involving matters of public concern.[51] In New York, private persons must prove a higher standard than simple negligence, but do not need to prove actual malice.[52] Gross negligence is a higher degree of fault than simple negligence, but a lesser degree of fault than actual malice. To find out the rule in your state, locate the most recent state supreme court ruling on libel. Within the text of this decision there is very likely to be a reference to the level of fault required by private-person plaintiffs.

Under the fault requirement all individuals who sue a mass medium for libel must prove that the defendant was somehow at fault in publishing the defamatory material and that the publication (or broadcast) did not result from an innocent error.

SUMMARY

What the courts call a public person must normally prove that the defendant acted with actual malice in publishing the libel; that is, the defendant knew the material was false but still published it or exhibited reckless disregard for the truth. What the courts define as private persons must prove at least that the defendant acted negligently, that is, in such a way as to create an unreasonable risk of harm. The courts have ruled that there are four kinds of public persons:

I. *Public officials:* Individuals who work for a government in a position of authority, who have substantial control over the conduct of governmental affairs, and whose position in government invites independent public scrutiny beyond the general public interest in the qualifications and performance of all government employees. Libelous comments must focus on the plaintiff's official conduct (the manner in which the plaintiff conducts his or her job) or on the plaintiff's general fitness to hold public office.

51. John McCrory & Robert Bernius, "Constitutional Privilege in Libel Law."
52. *Chapadeau v. Utica Observer-Dispatch, Inc.,* 341 N.E. 2d 569 (1975).

II. *All-purpose public figures:* People who occupy positions of persuasive power and influence in the nation or in a community, who are usually exposed to constant media attention.

III. *Voluntary limited-purpose public figures:* Individuals who voluntarily inject themselves into an important public controversy in order to influence public opinion regarding the resolution of that controversy. The key elements are these:

a. Public controversy, the resolution of which must affect more people than simply the participants. The outcome must have an impact on people in a community.

b. Plaintiffs who voluntarily thrust themselves into this controversy. An individual who has been drawn involuntarily into a controversy created by someone else (such as the press) will not usually be considered a limited-purpose public figure.

c. Plaintiffs who attempt to influence the outcome of the controversy, to shape public opinion on the subject. This implies that a plaintiff has some access to the mass media to participate in the public discussion surrounding the controversy.

IV. *Involuntary limited-purpose public figures:* Those rare individuals who have involuntarily entered into a public controversy. These individuals have access to the media to participate in the discussion surrounding the controversy but did not voluntarily seek out this access.

Using a variety of criteria, courts have ruled that businesses can be deemed public figures in a libel suit. Individuals who become public persons remain public persons throughout their lives with regard to stories published or broadcast that relate to incidents or events that occurred while they were public persons.

THE MEANING OF FAULT

Negligence = Failure to exercise ordinary or reasonable care
Actual malice = Knowledge of falsity or reckless disregard for the truth

NEGLIGENCE

"Negligence" is a term that has been commonly used in tort law for centuries, but has been applied to libel law only since 1974. In simple terms, **negligence** implies the failure to exercise ordinary care. In deciding whether to adopt the negligence or the stricter actual malice fault requirements, state courts are providing their own definitions of the standard. Washington state adopted a "reasonable care" standard. Defendants are considered negligent if they do not exercise reasonable care in determining whether a statement is false or will create a false impression.[53] The Tennessee Supreme Court has adopted a "reasonably prudent person test": What would a reasonably prudent person have done or not have done in the same circumstance? Would a reasonably prudent reporter have checked the truth of a story more fully? Would such a reporter have waited a day or so to get more information? Would a reasonably prudent reporter have worked harder in trying to reach the plaintiff before publishing the charges?[54] In Arizona, negligence has been defined as conduct that creates unreasonable risk of harm. "It is the failure to use that amount of care which a reasonably prudent person would use under like circumstances," the Arizona Supreme Court ruled.[55]

Some of the more common reasons a defendant might be found negligent are these:

- **Reliance on an untrustworthy source**
- **Not reading or misreading pertinent documents**
- **Failure to check with an obvious source, perhaps the subject of the story**
- **Carelessness in editing and news handling**

The question the court will always ask is, **Did the reporter make a good faith effort to determine the truth or falsity of the matter?**

Did the reporter make a good faith effort to determine the truth or falsity of the matter?

Courts will often scrutinize the source of the reporter's story when deciding whether or not there was negligence. After a reporter relied on a source whom police described as being an unreliable informant, and even the reporter admitted in court that he had found some of his source's information to be incorrect, the Massachusetts Supreme Judicial Court ruled that a jury might find negligence in such a case.[56] But a superior court in New Jersey ruled in 2003 that when a criminal suspect was misidentified in a news story there was no negligence, because the reporter had gotten the wrong name from both the police and an assistant prosecutor.[57] And the courts have consistently ruled that a newspaper or broadcast station is not negligent when it relies on reports received from the Associated Press, Reuters or other legitimate news services.[58]

Reportorial techniques,[59] are often scrutinized when a plaintiff asserts that a news medium has been negligent. But courts do not expect superhuman efforts from journalists, only general competence. The *San Antonio Express-News* was sued for libel when it inadvertently ran the wrong picture with a story it published on a woman convicted of prostitution, selling a child into prostitution and drug-related offenses. The plaintiff, who had the same name as the woman described in the *Express-News* story, had also been convicted of selling a child into prostitution, but was clearly not the woman described in the newspaper. Was there negligence in this case? The reporter had seven years of experience

53. *Taskett* v. *King Broadcasting Co.*, 546 P. 2d 81 (1976).
54. *Memphis Publishing Co.* v. *Nichols*, 569 S.W. 2d 412 (1978).
55. *Peagler* v. *Phoenix Newspapers*, 547 P. 2d 1074 (1976).
56. *Jones* v. *Taibbi*, 512 N.E. 2d 260 (1987).
57. *Yeager* v. *Daily Record*, 32 M.L.R. 1667 (2003).
58. *Appleby* v. *Daily Hampshire*, 395 Mass. 2 (1985); *McKinney* v. *Avery Journal, Inc.*, 393 S.E. 2d 295 (1990); and *Cole* v. *Star Tribune*, 26 M.L.R. 2415 (1998).
59. Sometimes referred to as "the wire service defense."

covering the courthouse and had spent six months researching the series of articles on the Texas Department of Correction's parole system. She had submitted a request to the county sheriff's office for a mug shot of the woman who was the subject of the story. The request included the woman's name, date of birth and Department of Corrections identification number. The sheriff's office gave her the wrong photo. The plaintiff insisted that the reporter failed to verify that she had the correct photo and that the reporter should have checked with the woman's mother to make certain the correct photo was being used. The court disagreed. "The issue was not what Fox [the reporter] could have done to avoid the mistake. It is whether she acted reasonably; that is, as a reasonable reporter under similar circumstances would have acted." The court said there was no negligence in this case.[60]

The definition of the term "negligence" will undoubtedly vary from state to state and possibly from judge to judge within a state. It is going to be some time before any kind of broad, consistently applied guidelines emerge. It is unlikely the Supreme Court will be of any help in this matter as it appears to be the intention of the court to leave the matter to the states.

There are, however, a few practical guidelines journalists and bloggers should follow to avoid liability. Being thorough, fair, accurate, carefully attributing sources and quotes, using photos that correspond to the story you are writing and not using ambiguous phrases that could libel someone through innuendo will minimize claims of negligence. In addition, using reliable sources will decrease the likelihood you publish false information. You should also always seek comments from the subject of your statements to give them an opportunity to respond to any allegedly defamatory statements. While nothing will completely reduce your liability, following professional norms and practices will help.

ACTUAL MALICE

Defining actual malice is somewhat easier than defining who is and who is not a public figure or public official, but it still presents judges with problems. In *New York Times Co.* v. *Sullivan*,[61] Justice Brennan defined **actual malice** as "knowledge of falsity or reckless disregard of whether the material was false or not." The two parts of this definition should be considered separately.

Knowledge of Falsity

"Knowledge of falsity" is a fancy way of saying "lie." If the defendant lied and the plaintiff can prove it, actual malice has then been shown. In 1969 Barry Goldwater was able to convince a federal court that political gadfly Ralph Ginzburg published known falsehoods about him during the 1964 presidential campaign in a "psychobiography" carried in Ginzburg's *Fact Magazine*. Ginzburg sent questionnaires to hundreds of psychiatrists, asking them to analyze Goldwater's mental condition. Ginzburg published only those responses that agreed with the magazine's predisposition that Goldwater was mentally ill

---

60. *Garza* v. *The Hearst Corporation*, 23 M.L.R. 1733 (1995). See also *Martinez* v. *WTVG Inc.*, 35 M.L.R. 2176 (2007).
61. 376 U.S. 254 (1964).

and changed the responses on other questionnaires to reflect this point of view. Proof of this conduct, plus other evidence, led the court to conclude that Ginzburg had published the defamatory material with knowledge of its falsity.[62]

Quotations are a part of most news stories, and they can pose an interesting problem for a court when libel is alleged. Two kinds of quotes might appear in a story. Statements that are enclosed within quote marks are called direct quotes and are supposed to represent an exact (or as close as possible) copy of what the subject said. But reporters also use what are called indirect quotes. These represent the substance of what the subject said, but not necessarily his or her exact words. Imagine that Sen. Maria Fernandez tells a reporter "We need to increase the size of the U.S. Army."

Direct quote: "We need to increase the size of the U.S. Army," Sen. Maria Fernandez said.

Indirect quote: Sen. Maria Fernandez said she believed the nation needs a larger army.

A legal question that can arise is this: If a journalist changes the words that were uttered by a subject, but still puts them inside quote marks, implying this is exactly what the subject said, can these be used as evidence of knowledge of falsity, actual malice? The Supreme Court confronted this question 20 years ago when a psychoanalyst named Jeffrey Masson sued *New Yorker* magazine and writer Janet Malcolm. Malcolm had interviewed Masson for more than 40 hours and wrote a long article about him, an article that was later republished as a book. Masson objected to many of the comments attributed to him as direct quotes, claiming that Malcolm had changed his words, that she had fabricated the statements. The quoted statements made him look foolish, he said, and he sued for defamation. Masson stipulated that he was a public figure, so he had to prove actual malice. He argued that changing his words in the direct quotes was evidence of knowledge of falsity.

A lower court agreed with the psychoanalyst, but the Supreme Court reversed this decision in a 7-2 ruling. The court ruled that readers do presume that words contained within quotation marks are a verbatim reproduction of what the subject said. Nevertheless, Justice Anthony Kennedy wrote, to demand that the press meet such a high standard is unrealistic. "If every alteration [of a quote] constituted the falsity required to prove actual malice, the practice of journalism, which the First Amendment is designed to protect, would require a radical change. . . . We conclude that a deliberate alteration of the words uttered by a plaintiff does not equate with knowledge of falsity . . . unless the alteration results in a *material change* [emphasis added] in the meaning conveyed by the statement."[63] The case was sent back for a trial in a lower court, but Masson was unable to convince a jury that Malcolm had knowledge of falsity when she wrote the story, and lost the case. An appellate court affirmed this verdict.

Reporters should strive to make certain direct quotes contain good copy of what a subject said, despite the leeway granted by the high court. But anyone who has worked as a journalist for even a short time knows it is often a real challenge to write down a speaker's exact words. People can talk a lot faster than a reporter can write. Indirect quotes are a useful substitute.

62. *Goldwater* v. *Ginzburg*, 414 F. 2d 324 (1969).
63. *Masson* v. *The New Yorker, Inc.*, 111 S. Ct. 2419 (1991).

In a similar vein the Texas Supreme Court in 2005 ruled that it is not evidence of knowledge of falsity simply to show that a headline on a news story paraphrases the remarks of a speaker and is not a verbatim recitation of what the speaker said. The court said two questions must be answered: Would a reasonable reader believe these were the actual words of the speaker? And did the paraphrased comment alter the meaning of what the speaker actually said? If a reasonable reader would understand that this was a paraphrase or interpretation of what the speaker said, and not a recitation of the exact remark attributed to him or her, there can be no finding of actual malice.

Finally, if a headline says one thing, but the story says something else, is this always evidence of knowledge of falsity? The plaintiff will argue the defendant should have known that either the headline or the story was wrong—knowledge of falsity. But courts usually look beyond the obvious in such cases. A headline in the *Nutley Sun* said that two local men were arrested for stock fraud. The story said two men had been charged in a Securities and Exchange Commission civil complaint. The men were never arrested. The New Jersey Supreme Court ruled that just because the story said one thing and the headline something else, this was not evidence that the editors entertained serious doubts as to the statement in the headline. The discrepancy between the two was surely sloppy journalism, but the editor had been harried in getting the paper out. The fact the two items carried a different message was not evidence of knowledge of falsity.[64]

Reckless Disregard for the Truth

Proof that the defendant failed to investigate a charge that later turns out to be false is not in and of itself sufficient evidence to prove actual malice.

Reckless disregard for the truth is a bit more difficult to define. In 1964 the Supreme Court said that reckless disregard could be shown by proving that the defendant had "a high degree of awareness of [the] probable falsity" of the defamatory material when it was published.[65] Four years later the Supreme Court said that in order to show reckless disregard for the truth, the plaintiff must bring forth "sufficient evidence to permit the conclusion that the defendant in fact entertained serious doubts as to the truth of his publication."[66] Proof that the defendant failed to investigate a charge that later turns out to be false is not in and of itself sufficient evidence to prove actual malice.

RECKLESS DISREGARD

A high degree of awareness of the probable falsity of the defamatory material when it was published

or

Sufficient evidence to permit the conclusion that the defendant in fact entertained serious doubts as to the truth of the publication

or

Evidence the defendant purposefully avoided the truth

---

64. *Durando* v. *Nutley Sun*, 40 M.L.R. 1461 (2012).
65. *Garrison* v. *Louisiana*, 379 U.S. 64 (1964).
66. *St. Amant* v. *Thompson*, 390 U.S. 727 (1968).

These definitions of reckless disregard are certainly useful in a theoretical sense. It is surely possible to envision a reporter or editor entertaining serious doubts about the truth of an allegation and publishing it anyway. However, neither of these definitions is terribly helpful in a practical sense. As Judge Kozinski of the 9th U.S. Circuit Court of Appeals wrote in his decision in a case involving the *National Enquirer* and Clint Eastwood, "As we have yet to see a defendant who admits to entertaining serious subjective doubt about the authenticity of an article it published, we must be guided by circumstantial evidence."[67] Six years later the Georgia Court of Appeals ruled that "Absent an admission by the defendant that he knew his material was false or that he doubted its truth, a public figure [or public official] must rely upon circumstantial evidence to prove his case."[68] Fortunately there is language in a 1967 Supreme Court ruling that has been extremely helpful to both jurists and journalists in charting a course by using such evidence. The ruling involved two cases, *Curtis Publishing Co.* v. *Butts* and *AP* v. *Walker.*[69] Justice John Marshall Harlan outlined a test in his opinion to evaluate the conduct of both defendants in these libel cases. While a few courts have rejected Harlan's criteria as a test for actual malice,[70] many courts have used it as the basis for their own definition of reckless disregard for the truth.

The two cases were joined and decided as one case. In the first case, Wally Butts, the athletic director at the University of Georgia, brought suit against the *Saturday Evening Post* for an article it published alleging that Butts and University of Alabama football coach Paul "Bear" Bryant had conspired to fix the Georgia-Alabama football game. The *Post* obtained its information from a man who said that while making a telephone call, he had accidentally overheard a phone conversation between Butts and Bryant. George Burnett, who had a criminal record, told the *Post* editors that he had taken careful notes. The story was based on Burnett's recollection of what was said.

In the other case, Major General (retired) Edwin Walker, a political conservative and segregationist from Texas, brought suit against the Associated Press and a score of publications and broadcasting stations for publishing the charge that he led a mob of white citizens against federal marshals who were attempting to preserve order at the University of Mississippi in September 1962, during the crisis over the enrollment of a black man, James Meredith. Walker was on campus during the disturbances, but did not lead a mob. The AP report was filed by a young AP correspondent on the scene.

The court ruled that in the *Butts* case the *Post* had exhibited highly unreasonable conduct in publishing the story but that in the *Walker* case no such evidence was present. In the *Butts* case, the story was not what would be called a hot news item. It was published months after the game occurred. The magazine had ample time to check the report. The source of the story was not a trained reporter, but a layman who happened to be on probation on a bad-check charge. The *Post* made no attempt to investigate the story further, to screen the game films to see if either team had made changes in accord with what Bryant and Butts supposedly discussed. None of

---

67. *Eastwood* v. *National Enquirer Inc.*, 123 F. 3d 1249 (1997).
68. *Lake Park Post, Inc.* v. *Farmer*, 264 Ga. App. 299 (2003).
69. 388 U.S. 130 (1967).
70. See, for example, *Clyburn* v. *News World Communications*, 903 F. 2d 29 (1990).

the many people supposedly with Burnett when he magically overheard this conversation were questioned by the Post. The magazine did little, then, to check the story, despite evidence presented at the trial that one or two of the editors acknowledged that Burnett's story needed careful examination. Finally, both Butts and Bryant had strong reputations for integrity. There had never even been hints of this kind of behavior in the past.

In the *Walker* case, different circumstances were present. For the AP editor back in the office who was responsible for getting the story on the wires, it was breaking news, a story that should be sent out immediately. The information was provided in the "heat of battle" by a young, but trained, reporter who in the past had given every indication of being trustworthy. All but one of the dispatches from the correspondent said the same thing: Walker led the mob. So there was internal consistency. Finally, when General Walker's previous actions and statements are considered, the story that he led a mob at Ole Miss was not terribly out of line with his prior behavior. There was nothing in the story to cause AP editors to suspect that it might be in error.

FACTORS COURTS USE TO HELP DETERMINE RECKLESS DISREGARD FOR THE TRUTH

1. *Story Timeliness:* Was the news breaking? Was it "hot" news? Was the publication of the story urgent? Or was there sufficient time or reasons to more fully check the facts in the story?
2. *Source Credibility:* How credible or reliable were the sources used? How reliable was the source of the story? Should the reporter have trusted the news source? Should the editor have trusted the reporter?
3. *Story Probability:* Was the story inherently believable or probable? Or was the story so unlikely that it cried out for further examination?

These elements form the base of most judicial definitions of reckless disregard for the truth. Two additional burdens face the plaintiff seeking to prove actual malice.

■ **The plaintiff must prove actual malice with "clear and convincing" evidence.**[71] Normally in a civil lawsuit the plaintiff must prove his or her allegations with a "preponderance of the evidence," which means that the plaintiff has more evidence than the defendant. "Clear and convincing" is a higher standard than a preponderance of the evidence, and it means that there can be little or no dispute about the evidence.
■ **The Supreme Court has instructed appellate courts to re-examine the evidence in the case to determine that the record "establishes actual malice**

71. *Gertz* v. *Robert Welch, Inc.*, 418 U.S. 323 (1974).

with convincing clarity."[72] Typically an appellate court is bound to accept the evidentiary findings of the trial court (see pages 18–20). But if the First Amendment defense applies in a libel case, the appellate court is mandated to take a close look and make certain the evidence supports the finding of malice. Allotting the appellate court such evidentiary power not only gives the defendant a second chance to win the case on the basis of the facts, but it also forces trial court judges to take extra pains when examining the facts, knowing that their work will likely be closely scrutinized in the future. The following overview of court rulings on actual malice will help illuminate both the criteria for such a finding and these two defense advantages.

Applying the Actual Malice Standard

Courts use a variety of means to try to determine whether or not the defendant acted with reckless disregard for the truth. Since, as noted earlier, few defendants admit to entertaining serious doubts about the truth of something they have published, circumstantial evidence becomes an important element in many cases. And different courts use different tests.

In sorting out claims of actual malice, courts often are forced to delve deeply into the reporting process. In July 2003 newspapers in South Carolina reported that county employees, in competition with private business, had been seen working on property belonging to Deputy County Supervisor Robert Metts. A county councilwoman named Judy Mims originated these charges. The allegations were false, and Metts, a public official, charged that the newspapers exhibited actual malice by publishing them. A trial court and state court of appeals both awarded the defendants a summary judgment because there was no evidence of actual malice. But the state Supreme Court reversed and said a jury possibly could find evidence of actual malice. In its opinion the court listed the following factors a jury should consider.

- The newspaper had a list of people who had received service from county employees and the defendant's name was not on the list.
- This was not a hot news story.
- The reporter did not attempt to contact Metts for a comment or verification.
- The reporter did not talk with Mims about how she supposedly discovered that county employees were working on Metts' property.
- The reporter was aware that Mims and Metts had an adversarial relationship.[73]

The law does not require the complete verification of a story, especially a breaking story. Two cases make this point. In 2003 the *New York Post* carried a short rewrite of a story carried on the *Los Angeles Times* wire service. The story suggested that rock music personality Ozzy Osborne's former doctor had overprescribed various drugs during the time Ozzy was featured in a reality TV series, and these left him "stoned" most of the time during the TV series. The *L.A. Times* story accurately stated the state medical

The law does not require the complete verification of a story, especially a breaking story.

---

72. *Bose Corporation* v. *Consumers Union of the United States, Inc.,* 446 U.S. 485 (1984).
73. *Metts* v. *Mims,* 37 M.L.R. 2275 (2009).

board "moved to revoke" the doctor's license. However, the *Post* story, headlined "Ozzy's Rx doc's license pulled," said the board had revoked his license.[74] The physician had a well-known detoxification practice, and had been in movies and on TV. He was a public person and would have to prove actual malice. At the trial the reporter said he did not recall writing that the license had been revoked, and thought the error might have occurred during editing. The editors testified they had no knowledge of how the mistake got into the story, that they did not investigate the claim because they thought it came from the *Times* story. It was not normal practice to check the facts in wire stories, they said.[75] The New York Court of Appeals ruled that it could find no evidence that suggested with convincing clarity the *Post* had committed actual malice and ruled in favor of the newspaper.[76]

In 2011 the Appellate Division of the New York Supreme Court ruled that there was no evidence of reckless disregard for the truth when author Tim O'Brien wrote that Donald Trump did not have a net worth of $3 to $5 billion as Trump often asserted. O'Brien wrote that "three people with direct knowledge of Donald's finances, people who had worked closely with him for years, told me his net worth was somewhere between $150 million and $250 million." Trump insisted the information was false and that O'Brien's reliance on the word of three unidentified sources was evidence of reckless disregard.

O'Brien showed the court that he had reinterviewed the three sources before he published the material; all three sources independently gave him the same information; he then verified the information with other sources; and the three sources had given him other information on other matters that proved to be accurate. There was no evidence of reckless disregard of the truth, the court ruled.[77]

In 2012, a Virginia court threw out a $3 million libel verdict against a local newspaper, finding that a local school official failed to show that the allegedly defamatory article was published with actual malice. An assistant principal at Oscar Smith High School in Chesapeake, Va., sued The *Virginian-Pilot* for libel based on the newspaper's reporting of his son's 2008 assault on Robert Bristol, the father of a classmate who is a special education student. An article in December 2009 reported that Webb's son, then a student at Great Bridge High School in Chesapeake, was not disciplined by the local school system for the assault. Although the statements were factually true, the article implied that the assistant principal obtained preferential treatment for his son and "a great injustice took place." The judge ruled that Webb, a public official, failed to prove that Louis Hansen published the defamatory statements about him with "actual malice." The judge ruled that although the only possible inference of the article was that the assistant principle secured preferential treatment for his son, this did not establish the reporter had serious doubts about what he wrote or implied, although it might be considered negligence.[78]

A 2014 case demonstrates that successful libel suits can also come from political advertisements. Iowa state Senator Rick Bertrand, a Republican, filed suit over a campaign ad claiming that Bertrand "put profit over children's health." The ad, paid for by

74. *Kipper v. NYP Holding Co.*, 37 M.L.R. 1673 (2009).
75. Ibid.
76. Ibid.
77. *Trump v. O'Brien*, 39 M.L.R. 2471 (2011).
78. *Webb v. Virginian-Pilot Media Companies, LLC*, Case No. CL10-2933 (Aug. 6, 2012).

the Iowa Democratic Party, claimed Bertrand was a "salesman for the most unethical company in the world" and that the company Bertrand had previously worked for sold a dangerous sleeping drug for children. On appeal the Iowa Supreme Court overturned the jury's verdict in favor of Bertrand and ruled that he could not prove actual malice as a matter of law. In writing the ad, Bertrand's opponent and the Iowa Democratic Party conducted research that revealed the FDA and others had criticized Bertrand's former company for selling the drug. No further investigation was done to support the implication that Bertrand himself had sold the drug. The court held there was no evidence of reckless disregard for the truth because the statements were based on reliable sources and it didn't matter that no further research had been conducted. In ruling against Bertrand, the Iowa Supreme Court wrote, "The First Amendment protects public discourse—even in the form of withering criticism of a political opponent's past dealings or associations—unless the lodged attack is clearly shown to be false and made with actual malice."[79]

Reporters and editors who attempt to rebut a charge of reckless disregard for the truth by using information they claim came from confidential sources need to be very careful. In some instances a court will simply block the efforts by the defense to even introduce such material. A federal court in Washington, D.C., ruled that *The New York Times* could not use such information in defending itself from a lawsuit by Dr. Steven J. Hatfill, a germ warfare specialist who once worked for the Army. Hatfill asserted that a column by Nicholas D. Kristof suggested he was responsible for the deadly anthrax mailings in 2001. Kristof claimed he had five sources for the allegations, but refused to identify them. Three of those sources ultimately gave Kristof permission to reveal their identities, but two remain confidential. Judge Liam O'Grady ruled that information from these sources could not be introduced at trial to substantiate the allegations in the column.[80]*

One evolving issue related to actual malice is the matter of the defendant's motivation for publishing the defamatory material. Before the ruling in *New York Times Co.* v. *Sullivan* the term "malice" was related to the question, Why did the defendant make these defamatory charges? Was it simply to inform the public of a problem or a concern, or were the charges published because the defendant didn't like the plaintiff or was angry with the plaintiff? In other words, was the publication fostered by ill will, spite or malice? The actual malice standard outlined by the Supreme Court in 1964 doesn't address why something was published or broadcast, but focuses instead on the defendant's state of mind at the time of publication regarding the truth of the story. The high court called this actual malice, to distinguish it from traditional or common-law malice.

The Supreme Court has ruled on at least two occasions that a showing by the plaintiff of ill will or spite is not sufficient to prove actual malice.[81] A Florida District Court of Appeals ruled in 2010 that even an intention to portray the plaintiff in a negative light, even if motivated by ill will or evil intent, is not sufficient to show actual malice unless

---

* In January 2007 the U.S. District Court granted the newspaper's motion for a summary judgment, ruling that Hatfi ll had failed to show evidence of actual malice. *Hatfill* v. *New York Times Co.* , 35 M.L.R. 1391
79. *Bertrand* v. *Mullin,* No. 12-0649 (May 16, 2014).
80. Lewis, "Judge's Ruling Bars The Times."
81. See *Harte-Hanks Communications Inc.* v. *Connaughton,* 109 S. Ct. 2678 (1989); and *Beckley Newspapers* v. *Hanks,* 389 U.S. 81 (1967). See also *Johnson* v. *E.W. Scripps Co.,* 31 M.L.R. 1503 (2003).

the publisher intended to *inflict harm* through knowing or reckless falsehood. Boxing promoter Don King had argued that when statements were made during an ESPN broadcast accusing him of crooked dealings, the producers were trying to put him in a bad light.[82] But state courts in Kentucky[83] and Washington[84] have ruled that evidence of ill will and spite can be used as evidence of actual malice in some circumstances. The 2nd U.S. Circuit Court of Appeals ruled in 2001 a reporter's bias against an organization could be relevant to show a purposeful avoidance of the truth (actual malice) if it were coupled with evidence of an extreme departure from standard investigative techniques.[85] But even those courts willing to hear such evidence have set a fairly high standard for the plaintiff to meet.

SUMMARY

In a lawsuit against a mass medium, a private person must prove that the defendant was at least negligent in publishing the defamatory matter. Negligence has been defined as the failure to exercise reasonable care or as acting in such a way as to create a substantial risk of harm. In some states, in certain cases private persons will be required to prove more than simple negligence. They may be required to prove gross negligence, which is a standard that implies a greater degree of carelessness on the part of the defendant. An individual who has been declared to be a public person for the purposes of a libel suit must prove actual malice. Actual malice is defined as knowledge of falsity or reckless disregard of the truth. Transmitting a story with the knowledge of its falsity means that the publishers of the story knew it was not true but still communicated it to the public. To prove reckless disregard for the truth, the plaintiff must show that the publisher of the defamation had a "high degree of awareness of the probable falsity of the material" when it was published or that the publisher in fact "entertained serious doubts about the truth of the material" before it was published. The courts have established a set of three criteria to help determine whether material was published with reckless disregard for the truth. The jurists tend to look at these factors:

1. Whether there was time to investigate the story or whether the material had to be published quickly
2. Whether the source of the information appeared to be reliable and trustworthy
3. Whether the story itself sounded probable or far-fetched

If the item was hot news, if the source was a trained journalist and if the information in the story sounded probable, it is unlikely there will be a finding of reckless disregard. However, if there was plenty of time to investigate, if the source of the material was questionable or if the information in the story sounded completely improbable, courts are more likely to permit a finding of reckless disregard for the truth.

---

82. *Don King Productions Inc.* v. *Walt Disney Co.*, 40 So. 3d 2516 (2010).
83. *Ball* v. *E.W. Scripps Co.*, 801 S.W. 2d 684 (1990).
84. *Herron* v. *King Broadcasting Co.*, 746 P. 2d 295 (1987).
85. *Church of Scientology International* v. *Behar*, 238 F. 3d 168 (2001).

INTENTIONAL INFLICTION OF EMOTIONAL DISTRESS

The tort of intentional infliction of emotional distress (IIED) first appeared in the late 19th century, but was not recognized by the "Restatement of the Law of Torts," the highly regarded synthesis of tort law published by the American Law Institute, until 1948. As noted by a federal judge in 2008, the tort was created for a limited purpose to allow recovery in those rare instances in which a defendant intentionally inflicts severe emotional distress in a manner so unusual that the victim has no other recognized theory of redress.[86] In 1965 the "Restatement" provided for the first time a definition of the tort, which has four parts:

- **The defendant's conduct was intentional or reckless.**
- **The defendant's conduct was extreme and outrageous.**
- **The defendant's conduct caused the plaintiff emotional distress.**
- **The emotional distress was severe.**[87]

What does "extreme and outrageous" conduct mean? Courts say it means conduct that goes beyond the bounds of decency and is utterly intolerable in a civilized society. This means something much more than just insults and indignities. And what does "severe" emotional distress mean? It means the distress suffered must be substantial and enduring, not merely minor and fleeting. On this element of IIED, courts also ask if a reasonable person in the position of the plaintiff would have suffered severe emotional distress. Why do they add this "reasonable person in the position of the plaintiff" require-ment? To prevent thin-skinned or so-called eggshell plaintiffs (people who are too easily offended by almost anything) from recovering damages.

What does this tort have to do with libel law? Some plaintiffs who feel blocked in their attempts to sue for libel by the First Amendment defenses erected since 1964 have sought to use IIED as an alternate legal remedy. The most notable case emerged in the 1980s. The lawsuit was prompted when *Hustler* magazine published a parody of a series of widely circu-lated ads for Campari liquor. The real Campari ads featured interviews with celebrities who discussed the first time they tasted the liquor. The printed advertisements had fairly strong sexual overtones as the subjects talked about their "first time." Although it was apparent by the end of each "interview" the celebrities were discussing the first time they had Campari, the ads played on the sexual double entendre of the general subject of "first times." The *Hustler* parody was a fictitious interview with the Rev. Jerry Falwell, an evangelical preacher who in the 1980s led a conservative political action group called The Moral Majority. Falwell described his first sexual experience as an incestuous encounter with his mother. Falwell was also characterized by the parody as a drunkard. There was a small disclaimer at the bottom of the parody, and it was listed in the table of contents as fiction.

Falwell sued the magazine for libel, invasion of privacy and intentional infliction of emotional distress. The trial judge and its publisher, Larry Flynt, dismissed the inva-sion of privacy claim, but sent the other two to the jury. Jurors rejected the libel claim on the grounds that the parody was so farfetched, no person could possibly believe that it described actual facts about Falwell. The jury did award the Baptist preacher $200,000 in damages for emotional distress.

---

86. *Conradt v. NBC Universal Inc.*, 536 F. Supp. 2d 380 (2008).
87. American Law Institute, *Restatement of the Law of Torts.*

The November 1983 issue of Hustler Magazine featured a "parody" advertisement for Campari Liqueur that contained an "interview" with Jerry Falwell. Falwell sued for invasion of privacy, libel and intentional infliction of emotional distress.

Jerry Falwell talks about his first time.*

FALWELL: My first time was in an outhouse outside Lynchburg, Virginia.

INTERVIEWER: Wasn't it a little cramped?

FALWELL: Not after I kicked the goat out.

INTERVIEWER: I see. You must tell me all about it.

FALWELL: I never *really* expected to make it with Mom, but then after she showed all the other guys in town such a good time, I figured, "What the hell!"

INTERVIEWER: But your mom? Isn't that a bit odd?

FALWELL: I don't think so. Looks don't mean that much to me in a woman.

INTERVIEWER: Go on.

FALWELL: Well, we were drunk off our God-fearing asses on Campari, ginger ale and soda—that's called a Fire and Brimstone—at the time. And Mom looked better than a Baptist whore with a $100 donation.

INTERVIEWER: Campari in the crapper with Mom . . . how interesting. Well, how was it?

FALWELL: The Campari was great, but Mom passed out before I could come.

INTERVIEWER: Did you ever try it again?

FALWELL: Sure . . .

lots of times. But not in the outhouse. Between Mom and the shit, the flies were too much to bear.

INTERVIEWER: We meant the Campari.

FALWELL: Oh, yeah. I always get sloshed before I go out to the pulpit. You don't think I could lay down all that bullshit sober, do you?

© 1983—Imported by Campari U.S.A. New York, NY 48°proof Spirit Aperitif (Liqueur)

Campari, like all liquor, was made to mix you up. It's a light, 48-proof, refreshing spirit, just mild enough to make you drink too much before you know you're schnockered. For your first time, mix it with orange juice. Or maybe some white wine. Then you won't remember anything the next morning. *Campari. The mixable that smarts.*

CAMPARI **You'll never forget your first time.**

*AD PARODY—NOT TO BE TAKEN SERIOUSLY

©LFP Publishing Group LLC

Hustler appealed the ruling, but a unanimous three-judge panel of the U.S. Court of Appeals for the 4th Circuit upheld the damage award, noting that all the proof that was needed in such a case was that the item was sufficiently outrageous as to cause emotional harm and that it was published intentionally.[88] While most journalists did not condone the *Hustler* style of parody, they nevertheless viewed the decision as a serious threat to freedom of expression. The sturdy First Amendment barrier built up to protect the mass media from libel suits brought by persons in the public eye was neatly circumvented by Falwell in this case. Because of his presence as a spokesperson for the conservative religious right in this

88. *Falwell* v. *Flynt*, 797 F. 2d 1270 (1986).

nation, Falwell would likely be considered a public figure in a libel action and be forced to prove actual malice before he could collect damages. In this suit he did not even have to show negligence. Nor did the broad First Amendment protection that is granted to statements of opinion apply outside the law of libel. In the future, individuals suing for satire or parody could avoid having to surmount the constitutional barriers in libel law by instead filing an action for intentional infliction of emotional distress.

Hustler appealed to the Supreme Court and in 1988, in a unanimous ruling, the high court reversed the appellate court ruling. Chief Justice Rehnquist, noting that most people would see the *Hustler* parody as gross and repugnant, nevertheless rejected Falwell's argument that because he was seeking damages for severe emotional distress rather than reputational harm, a standard different from that applied in libel should apply. "Were we to hold otherwise," the chief justice wrote, "there can be little doubt that political cartoonists and satirists would be subjected to damages awarded without any showing that their work falsely defamed its subject." Rehnquist added:

> The appeal of the political cartoon or caricature is often based on exploration of unfortunate physical traits or politically embarrassing events—an exploration often calculated to injure the feelings of the subject of the portrayal. The art of the cartoonist is often not reasoned or evenhanded, but slashing and one-sided.[89]

Falwell contended it was making a mockery of serious political cartoons to compare them to the *Hustler* parody, which was truly outrageous. The law should protect even public figures from such outrageous caricatures. Rehnquist disagreed, noting the outrageousness standard of liability would not work.

> "Outrageousness" in the area of political and social discourse has an inherent subjectiveness about it which would allow a jury to impose liability on the basis of jurors' tastes and views or perhaps on the basis of their dislike of a particular expression.[90]

The Court ruled that in order for a public figure or public official to win an emotional distress claim, it would be necessary to prove three things:

1. That the parody or satire amounted to statement of fact, not an opinion.
2. That it was a false statement of fact.
3. That the person who drew the cartoon or wrote the article knew it was false, or exhibited reckless disregard for the truth or falsity of the material. In other words, proof of actual malice is necessary.

Typical of many of the IIED cases that have been filed is a lawsuit from Florida. The 2-year-old child of a woman named Melinda Duckett was reported missing. CNN's Nancy Grace, a former prosecutor, interviewed Duckett by telephone for use on her nightly cable broadcast. During the interview Grace verbally attacked Duckett, intimating that she had killed her own child. Just before the interview was aired on CNN, Duckett killed herself. CNN telecast the interview anyway, and rebroadcast it several

89. *Hustler Magazine v. Falwell*, 485 U.S. 46 (1988).
90. Ibid.

times thereafter. The family sued for IIED/wrongful death. It claimed the interview was solicited by Grace under false pretenses, and was used merely to increase the ratings of the cable show. The federal court denied CNN's motion to dismiss the case, noting that the plaintiffs had correctly alleged all the needed elements of an IIED action. A trial would be needed. The judge noted that there had been very few IIED cases in Florida where damages had been awarded and affirmed, but added that courts have tended to find that conduct that would normally be merely insulting or careless can become "outrageous" if it follows the death of a family member. In 2009 Grace reached a settlement with the Duckett estate in which she agreed to establish a $200,000 trust dedicated to finding Duckett's missing son.[91]

SUMMARY

The intentional infliction of emotional distress is a new tort and punishes a wide range of conduct, including the publication or broadcast of material that is outrageous and causes severe emotional distress. Courts have made it extremely difficult for plaintiffs to win such suits by placing a substantial burden of proof on the injured party. The Supreme Court added to this burden in 1988 when it ruled that public-person plaintiffs would have to show actual malice as well to win their lawsuits.

BIBLIOGRAPHY

American Law Institute. *Restatement of the Law of Torts*. 2nd ed. Philadelphia: American Law Institute, 1975.

Ashley, Paul. *Say It Safely*. 5th ed. Seattle: University of Washington Press, 1976.

Austen, Ian. "Canadian Rulings Revise Law on Libel." *The New York Times*, 23 December 2009, A12.

Barron, Jerome, and C. Thomas Dienes. *Handbook of Free Speech and Free Press*. Boston: Little, Brown, 1979.

Lewis, Anthony. *Make No Law*. New York: Random House, 1991.

Lewis, Neil A. "Judge's Ruling Bars The Times From Using Sources' Information in Defense Against Suit." *The New York Times*, 17 November 2006, A12.

McCrory, John & Robert Bernius. "Constitutional Privilege in Libel Law." 1 Communications Law 1997.

Prosser, William L. *Handbook of the Law of Torts*. St. Paul, Minn.: West Publishing, 1963.

Smolla, Rodney A. *Suing the Press*. New York: Oxford University Press, 1986.

——. "Dun & Bradstreet, Hepps, and Liberty Lobby: A New Analytic Primer on the Future Course of Defamation." *Georgetown Law Journal* 75 (1987): 1519.

Stonecipher, Harry, and Don Sneed. "A Survey of the Professional Person as Libel Plaintiff." *Arkansas Law Review* 46 (1993): 303.

91. *Estate of Duckett* v. *Cable News Network, LLP*, 36 M.L.R. 2210 (2008).

CHAPTER 6

Libel

DEFENSES AND DAMAGES

©McGraw-Hill Education/Jill Braaten

Libel defenses are centuries old. Most grew out of common law, but today many defenses are contained in state statutes. Before the mid-1960s, when the Supreme Court began to add substantial new First Amendment burdens upon libel plaintiffs, defenses were the primary means of warding off a defamation lawsuit. Most plaintiffs today lose because they can't meet the required fault standard (actual malice or negligence), but defenses remain important. Not only can a libel defense protect a defendant, it also can stop a plaintiff's case quickly, saving the publication or broadcasting outlet both time and money. Citing an appropriate defense, a defendant can ask a judge to dismiss a case before trial. Such a dismissal is called a summary judgment. The judge may issue such a ruling if he or she does not think the plaintiff can prove what is required, as outlined in Chapters 4 and 5, or believes the defendant had a legal right (a defense) to publish or broadcast the defamatory material. Libel defenses are the primary subject of this chapter. Following this material is a brief outline of both civil libel damages and criminal libel.

SUMMARY JUDGMENT/STATUTE OF LIMITATIONS

The **summary judgment** is one of the best friends a media libel defendant has. About three-fourths of media requests for a summary judgment are granted by the courts. If the defendant's request for such a judgment is granted by the court, the case ends without a trial. Trials cost a lot of money, and the press has not established a good track record for winning cases sent to a jury. Here is a brief outline of what happens in the summary judgment procedure.

After the plaintiffs have made their initial written allegations to the court, but before the trial begins, the defendants can argue that the lawsuit should be dismissed either because the plaintiff has failed to establish what is necessary to sustain the libel suit (publication, identification, defamation, falsity and the requisite level of fault) or because there is a legal defense that blocks a successful lawsuit. Under the summary judgment process, discussed in Chapter 1, as it considers this motion by the defense, the court is obligated to look at the plaintiff's allegation in the most favorable possible way. And if there is any dispute regarding facts (which would be settled at a subsequent trial), it must be for now resolved in favor of the plaintiff. If, having considered these factors, the court determines that a reasonable juror, acting reasonably, could not find for the plaintiff, then the motion for summary judgment will be granted.[1] The plaintiff can also ask for a summary judgment, arguing there is no possible way a jury could find for the defendant.

Imagine that Laura Parker, the editor of a small newsletter, the *Iowa Consumer News*, publishes a story that accuses Argot Farms, a giant corporate grain producer, of selling corn to cereal makers that has been labeled as adulterated and unfit for human consumption by the U.S. Department of Agriculture. For many years Argot has portrayed itself in television advertising as an environmentally friendly and responsible corporation. Argot sues for libel, claiming that the story is false. Parker asks the court for a summary judgment and makes two arguments to support her request:

1. The story is true and therefore the case should be dismissed.
2. Argot Farms, because of its heavy television advertising, is a public figure. Therefore it must have proof of actual malice to win its case. It has made no allegations regarding actual malice, only charges of simple negligence on Parker's part.

1. See, for example, *Nader* v. *DeToledano*, 408 A. 2d 31 (1979).

Argot Farms asks the court to deny the motion for a summary judgment and makes the following three arguments:

1. It is not a public figure, simply a business trying to win customers through normal advertising. Therefore it must only show negligence.
2. The story is false.
3. Parker got the information for her story from an unreliable source.

In ruling on Parker's motion for a summary judgment the court must assume that the facts, as stated by Argot Farms, are true; the story is false and the information is from an unreliable source. If the case later goes to trial, both these "facts" will be examined through the presentation of evidence. Regardless of how the trial court judge rules, the side that loses could appeal the ruling to an appellate court.

The Supreme Court has given both trial and appellate courts wide latitude in granting summary judgments in libel cases, especially in suits brought by public persons. In 1986 the justices said that federal courts must grant a summary judgment in favor of the media defendants in cases involving actual malice unless the plaintiffs can demonstrate that they will be able to offer a jury clear and convincing evidence of actual malice.[2] Some trial judges had been hesitant about granting summary judgments because they believed that proof of actual malice calls the defendant's state of mind into question, which is a matter better considered at trial. But judges who force a trial even in the face of a weak libel claim are playing into the hands of those litigants who like to use the law to harass the press.

The Supreme Court has given both trial and appellate courts wide latitude in granting summary judgments in libel cases.

STATUTE OF LIMITATIONS

For nearly all crimes and civil actions, there is a **statute of limitations.** As the name suggests, these represent the limitations on the time period the prosecution or a plaintiff has for filing suit. Courts do not like stale legal claims because memories fade and evidence is lost or destroyed. Prosecution for most crimes except homicide and kidnapping must be started within a specified period of time. For example, in many states if prosecution is not started within seven years after an armed robbery is committed, the robber cannot be brought to trial. He or she is home free.

The duration of the statute of limitations for libel actions differs from state to state, from one to three years (Figure 6.1).* In most states the duration is one or two years; this means the libel suit must be started within one or two years following the date of publication of the offending material. Courts have had to decide the date of publication for the various mass media. The consensus is:

▮ **Newspapers:** The date of publication for newspapers is the date that appears on the newspaper.
▮ **Radio and television:** The date of publication is the date on which the material is broadcast or telecast.

2. *Anderson* v. *Liberty Lobby,* 477 U.S. 242 (1986).
* Most courts that have considered the question have ruled the statute of limitations for libel actions applies as well to invasion-of-privacy suits. See, for example, *Christoff* v. *Nestle USA Inc.*, 152 Cal. App. 4th 1439 (2007); *Pierce* v. *Clarion Ledger,* 34 M.L.R. 1275 (2006); and *Chaker* v. *Crogan,* 33 M.L.R. 2569 (2005).

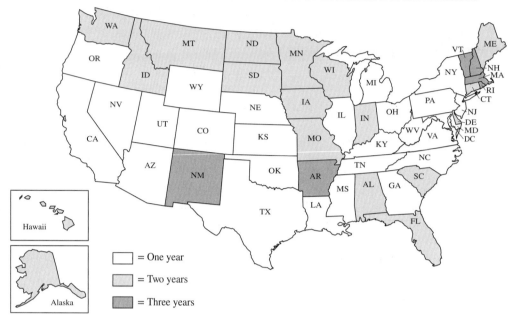

MAP SHOWING DURATION OF STATUTE OF LIMITATIONS IN LIBEL ACTIONS

☐ = One year

▨ = Two years

▩ = Three years

FIGURE 6.1

Plaintiffs must file libel suits before the statute of limitations expires. This chart indicates the duration of this filing period in the 50 states.

- **Magazines:** The date of publication is the date on which the magazine is distributed to a substantial portion of the public, regardless of the date printed on the cover of the magazine.[3] The date printed on the cover rarely coincides with the date the magazine is distributed; for example, the October issue of a magazine is usually distributed in September or even August.
- **Internet:** The date of publication is the date the material is first posted on the Web.

What if one or a few copies of the offending material are redistributed or republished after the initial publication date? If the material is altered or revised before it is republished, the statute of limitations is restarted.[4] Many states have adopted "the single publication rule." This rule says that the entire edition of a newspaper or magazine is

3. *Printon Inc.* v. *McGraw-Hill Inc.,* 35 F. Supp. 2d 1325 (1998). See also *MacDonald* v. *Time,* 554 F. Supp. 1053 (1983); *Wildmon* v. *Hustler,* 508 F. Supp. 87 (1980); *Bradford* v. *American Media Operations, Inc.,* 882 F. Supp. 1508 (1995); and *Williamson* v. *New Times Inc.,* 980 S.W. 2d 706 (1998).

4. *Firth* v. *New York,* 747 N.Y.S. 2d 69 (2002); *Van Buskirk* v. *New York Times,* 325 F. 3d 87 (2003); *Mitan* v. *Davis,* W.D. Ky., Civil Action No. 3:00 CV-841-5, 2/3/03; *McCandliss* v. *Cox Enterprises Inc.,* 593 S.E. 2d 856 (2004); and *Traditional Cat Ass'n* v. *Gilbreath,* Cal. Ct. App. No. D041421, 5/6/04. In some states, if the offending material is republished in a different edition of a newspaper, or is posted by the newspaper on its Web site, this constitutes a separate publication. See *Rivera* v. *NYP Holdings Inc.,* 35 M.L.R. 2127 (2007). And some states have not adopted the single publication rule. See *Taub* v. *McClatchy Newspapers Inc.,* 35 M.L.R. 2179 (2007), for example.

a single publication, and isolated republication of the material months or years later does not constitute a republication. The March 1, 2017, edition of the Richmond Beach *Examiner* is a single publication. The statute of limitations for anything contained in that edition starts on that day. If a few copies of the paper are distributed weeks or months later, this does not restart the statute of limitations clock. If a TV station rebroadcasts material, however, this might restart the clock since some courts think this is a new publication intended to reach a new audience.[5]

Because material posted on the Internet is sometimes so ephemeral and easy to modify, the question of whether the single publication rule applies to a Web posting is raised frequently. For the most part the courts have said yes, it does apply. For example, in a California case a plaintiff argued that each time a defendant added anything to a Web site, this constituted a republication of all the postings on the site. The 9th U.S. Court of Appeals disagreed, ruling that unless the allegedly defamatory statement was altered or augmented or aimed at a different audience, it was not a republication.[6] Perhaps the best statement of the rationale behind these rulings came from the 3rd U.S. Court of Appeals in 2012.

> Web sites are constantly linked and updated. If each link or technical change were an act of republication, the statute of limitations would be retriggered endlessly and its effectiveness essentially eliminated.[7]

Jurisdiction

Is it possible for a plaintiff who has not filed a libel suit within the statute of limitations in his or her home state to file an action in another state that has a longer statute of limitations? The answer is yes, so long as the libel has been circulated in this other state. The Supreme Court clarified this question in two 1984 rulings, *Keeton* v. *Hustler*[8] and *Calder* v. *Jones*.[9] Kathy Keeton, a resident of New York, sued *Hustler* magazine, an Ohio corporation, for libel in the state of New Hampshire. She did this because the statutes of limitations in both New York and Ohio had already expired. She was, in other words, too late to file in those two states. New Hampshire, however, at that time had a six-year statute of limitations. *Hustler* challenged the action, arguing that the suit should be brought in New York or Ohio but not New Hampshire. Only about 15,000 copies of the 1-million-plus circulation of the magazine were sold in New Hampshire, the defendant argued. A court of appeals ruled that the plaintiff had too tenuous a contact with New Hampshire to permit the assertion of personal jurisdiction in that state, but the Supreme Court unanimously reversed the ruling. *Hustler's* regular circulation of magazines in New Hampshire was sufficient to support an assertion of jurisdiction in a libel action, Justice William Rehnquist wrote.[10]

---

5. *Lehman* v. *Discovery Communications Inc.,* 32 M.L.R. 2377 (2004).
6. *Yeager* v. *Bowlin,* 40 M.L.R. 2491 (2012).
7. *In re Philadelphia Newspapers, LLC.,* 3 Fd. 161 (2012).
8. 465 U.S. 770 (1984).
9. 465 U.S. 783 (1984).
10. *Keeton* v. *Hustler,* 465 U.S. 770 (1984).

The same day, the high court ruled that California courts could assume jurisdiction in a case brought by a California resident against the authors of a story that was written and published in a newspaper in Florida but circulated in California. Shirley Jones, the actress and singer who played the mother in "The Partridge Family" television show, sued two journalists for an article they wrote and edited in Florida and that was then published in the *National Enquirer*. At that time the *Enquirer* had a national circulation of about 5 million and distributed about 600,000 copies each week in California. A trial court ruled that Jones could certainly sue the publishers of the *Enquirer* in California, but not the reporters. Requiring journalists to appear in remote jurisdictions to answer for the contents of articles on which they worked could have a chilling impact on the First Amendment rights of reporters and editors, the court said. But again a unanimous Supreme Court disagreed, with Justice Rehnquist noting that the article was about a California resident who works in California. Material for the article was drawn from California sources, and the brunt of the harm to both the career and the personal reputation of the plaintiff will be suffered in California where the *Enquirer* has a huge circulation. In other words, the primary negative effect of the libel will be in California, he added. "An individual injured in California need not go to Florida to seek redress from persons who, though remaining in Florida, knowingly cause the injury in California," Rehnquist wrote. The justice said that the potential chill on protected First Amendment activity stemming from libel actions is already taken into account in the constitutional limitations on the substantive law governing such suits. "To reinforce those concerns at the jurisdictional level would be a form of double counting," he said.[11]

Jurisdiction and the Internet

These two Supreme Court rulings stand for the proposition that publishers may be sued in any jurisdiction in which they distribute even a relatively small portion of their publication—even if the plaintiff does not reside in that jurisdiction. How does this principle apply to communication on the Internet? Any message published on the Internet is conceivably accessible in any state in the nation. Can the Web site operator or publisher of the allegedly defamatory material be sued in any or every jurisdiction? Is evidence that the message was received and downloaded by residents of the jurisdiction sufficient to begin a lawsuit in that jurisdiction? Or must there be stronger ties to the jurisdiction? The Supreme Court of the United States has passed on reviewing at least three cases that involve this jurisdiction question.[12] Lower courts seem to be more or less following one of two strategies: one that broadly applies the so-called effects test from the *Calder* case, or one that applies the *Calder* test much more narrowly. Remember, in that case the Supreme Court ruled that California courts could exercise jurisdiction over journalists who resided in Florida because the article concerned California activities of a California resident and was published in a national publication that had a large circulation in

11. *Calder* v. *Jones,* 465 U.S. 783 (1984).
12. *ALS Scan Inc.* v. *Digital Services Consultants Inc.,* U.S. No. 02-483, cert. den. 1/13/03; *Griffs* v. *Luban,* U.S. No. 02-754, cert. den. 3/10/03; and *Young* v. *New Haven Advocate,* 315 F. 3d 256 (2002).

California.[13] But while the number of cases arising in the lower courts increases each year, there doesn't seem to be a "one rule fits all" test emerging.

- The Florida Supreme Court ruled in 2010 that a Washington resident who made defamatory comments about a Nevada corporation, whose principal place of business was Florida, could be sued in Florida. Several Florida residents had seen the article and responded to it. The court said the posting of defamatory comments online about a Florida company, comments that were accessible in Florida, constitutes committing a tortious act in Florida.[14]
- When an allegedly defamatory article about an Arizona corporation was placed online, the plaintiff sought to sue in an Arizona court. But a U.S. District Court ruled in 2010 that the material was not sufficiently focused on the state to generate specific jurisdiction, even if it was posted with knowledge of the company's location.[15]
- The Ohio Supreme Court said in 2010 that a Virginia resident who posted allegedly defamatory comments on several Web sites may be sued in an Ohio court, even if his comments were not aimed at an audience there. When defamatory statements are made outside of Ohio, a nonresident may be sued in Ohio courts if the purpose of the statements was to cause injury to an Ohio resident.[16]
- On the other hand, in 2011, the 10th Circuit Court of Appeals ruled that neither simply posting material to the Internet nor hosting a Web site was enough to establish jurisdiction in an Internet defamation case. An Oklahoma man sued both the operators of a Web-based forum over an e-mail that was posted on the site and the individual who posted the e-mail. The court ruled that simply because the plaintiff's reputation was harmed in Oklahoma, this was not enough to establish jurisdiction.[17]

This recounting of these somewhat contradictory rulings is not presented to confuse the reader, but to demonstrate the lack of agreement in the courts. Where the plaintiff lives, where the defendant resides, what the defendant intended, at whom the article was aimed and what the article was about are all factors the courts are raising.

One final point: Courts in Australia and Great Britain, among others, have asserted jurisdiction in cases involving allegedly defamatory Internet messages that originated in the United States. The High Court of Australia ruled that because the plaintiff lived in Australia, and because the harm from the allegedly defamatory message did not occur until it was downloaded in Australia, the courts there could exercise jurisdiction.[18] The British case involved a U.S. resident, boxing promoter Don King, who the court said had many friends and acquaintances in England. The court ruled that the publication of an Internet posting

13. 465 U.S. 783 (1984).
14. *Internet Solutions Corp.* v. *Marshall*, 38 M.L.R. 2428 (2010).
15. *Xcentric Ventures, LLC* v. *Bird*, 683 F. Supp. 2d 1068 (2010).
16. *Kauffmann Racing Equipment, LLC* v. *Roberts*, 126 Ohio St. 3d 81 (2010).
17. *Shrader* v. *Biddiner*, 315 F. 3d 1235 (10th Cir. 2011).
18. *King* v. *Lewis,* High Court of Justice, Queen's Bench Division, No. [2004] EWHC, 168 (QB), 2/6/04.

takes place when it is downloaded. Please note that when a court in a foreign nation asserts jurisdiction in a libel case, the many important First Amendment protections that apply in a case tried in the United States rarely protect a defendant tried outside this country. (See page 159 for a fuller discussion of this problem.)

SUMMARY   A libel suit must be started before the statute of limitations expires. Each state determines how long this period will be. In all states it is one, two or three years for libel. A libel suit started after the expiration of the statute of limitations will be dismissed. Jurisdiction questions in Internet-based libel suits are still being sorted out by the courts, but usually are based upon where the content of the message was aimed, where the harm was caused and where the message was downloaded.

TRUTH

The First Amendment provides defendants in libel suits considerable protection. The defendant in a lawsuit filed against a newspaper or other mass medium is well defended by the constitutional fault requirements of actual malice and negligence placed on the plaintiff. But ther-e were defenses for libel even before the ruling in *New York Times Co.* v. *Sullivan.*[19] These emerged through common law and via statutes in many states. Truth, privileged communication, fair comment, consent and right of reply all work to protect the libel defendant—no matter who he or she might be. The applicability of each of these defenses in a particular case is determined by the facts in the case: what the story is about, how the information was gained and the manner in which it was published.

Traditionally, truth has been regarded as an important libel defense that completely protected defendants in lawsuits for defamation. To use this defense, the defendant was required to prove the truth of the libelous allegations he or she published. Truth is still a defense in a libel action, but it has lost much of its importance in light of recent rulings that require most libel plaintiffs to carry the burden of proving a defamatory allegation to be false when the story focuses on a matter of public concern. In those few instances when a private-person plaintiff sues for a libelous statement that does not focus on something of public concern and therefore does not have to show the falsity of the matter as a part of proving negligence, the libel defendant can escape liability in the case by showing that the defamatory matter is true. But the defendant carries the burden of proof; truth becomes a defense. The same rules apply to proving truth that apply to proving falsity, only they are reversed. The defendant must show that the allegations are substantially true. Extraneous errors will not destroy the defense. See pages 172–175 to refresh your memory on these matters.

19. 376 U.S. 254 (1964).

PRIVILEGED COMMUNICATIONS

The people of the United States have traditionally valued robust debate as one means of discovering the truths essential to building consensus. The law takes pains to protect this debate, making sure that speakers are not unduly punished for speaking their minds. Article 1, Section 6 of the federal Constitution provides that members of Congress are immune from suits based on their remarks on the floor of either house. This protection is called a privilege. The statement in question is referred to as a privileged communication.

ABSOLUTE PRIVILEGE

Today this privilege, sometimes called the privilege of the participant, attaches to a wide variety of communications and speakers. Anyone speaking in a legislative forum—members of Congress, senators, state representatives, city council members and so forth—enjoys this privilege. In 2005, appellate courts in Colorado and Illinois ruled that the privilege applied to statements made during meetings of a county hospital board and a city council zoning committee, respectively.[20] Even the statements of witnesses at legislative hearings are privileged. But the comments must be made in the legislative forum. The Supreme Court ruled in 1979 that while a speech by a senator on the floor of the Senate would be wholly immune from a libel action, newsletters and press releases about the speech issued by the senator's office would not be protected by the privilege. Only speech that is "essential to the deliberations of the Senate" is protected, and neither newsletters to constituents nor press releases are parts of the deliberative process.[21]

Today, privilege attaches to a wide variety of communications and speakers.

Similarly, the privilege attaches to communications and documents made in judicial forums—courtrooms, grand jury rooms and so forth. Judges, lawyers, witnesses, defendants, plaintiffs and all other individuals are protected so long as the remark is uttered during the official portions of the hearing or trial and the statement or document is in some way relevant to the proceeding. An attorney in Pennsylvania filed a complaint in a lawsuit and then faxed a copy to a reporter. He was sued for libel by the person named in the complaint, who argued that when he sent the complaint to the journalist, he was publishing its defamatory allegations. The attorney argued that since the complaint was a privileged judicial document, which it is, his act of sending the complaint was also privileged. The Supreme Court of Pennsylvania disagreed, ruling that sending the document to a reporter was an extrajudicial act and was not relevant in any way to the legal proceedings.[22]

Finally, people who work in the administrative and executive branches of government enjoy the privilege as well. Official communications including reports, policy statements, even press conferences, presented by presidents, governors, mayors, department heads and others are protected. The Supreme Court of the United States ruled in 1959 that the privilege applies to any publication by government officials that is in line with the discharge of their official duties.[23] This case involved a press release issued by an official

---

20. *Wilson* v. *Meyer,* 34 M.L.R. 1906 (2005); and *Stevens* v. *Porr,* 34 M.L.R. 1086 (2005).
21. *Hutchinson* v. *Proxmire,* 443 U.S. 111 (1979). Proxmire was sued when he attacked a Michigan man in a press release critical of wasteful government spending.
22. *Bochetto* v. *Gibson,* 32 M.L.R. 2474 (2004).
23. *Barr* v. *Mateo,* 353 U.S. 171 (1959).

explaining why two federal workers were fired. The New York Court of Appeals echoed this ruling 20 years later when it said that a press release issued by an assistant attorney general concerning the investigation of a possible fund-raising scam was protected by the privilege.[24] The difference in the manner in which the courts treated the press releases by Sen. William Proxmire in a case noted previously (see page 189) and the two cases just cited stems from the different roots of the privilege. The congressional privilege stems directly from the U.S. Constitution and is limited by constitutional language that focuses on the deliberative process and lawmaking. Proxmire's remarks fell outside these boundaries. The common law and/or state statutes are the sources of all other parts of the privilege, and courts have construed this protection quite liberally.

The privilege just discussed is an **absolute privilege.** The speaker cannot be sued for defamation on the basis of such a remark. A similar kind of privilege applies also to certain kinds of private communications. Discussions between an employer and an employee are privileged; the report of a credit rating is privileged; a personnel recommendation by an employer about an employee is privileged. These kinds of private communications remain privileged so long as they are not disseminated beyond the sphere of those who need to know.

QUALIFIED PRIVILEGE

What is called **qualified privilege** goes far beyond the absolute immunity granted to speakers at public and official meetings and the conditional immunity granted to certain types of private communications. Under the qualified privilege, an individual may report what happens at an official governmental proceeding or transmit the substance of an official government report or government document and remain immune from libel even if the publication of the material defames someone. This is how the privilege is outlined in the "Restatement of the Law of Torts":

> The publication of defamatory matter concerning another in a report of any
> official proceeding or any meeting open to the public which deals with mat-
> ters of public concern is conditionally privileged if the report is accurate and
> complete, or a fair abridgment of what has occurred.[25]

Actually, this definition of the privilege in the "Restatement" is a bit conservative, as courts continually extend the protection of qualified privilege to reports of more diverse kinds of government activity. This qualified privilege is sometimes called the privilege of the reporter, as opposed to the absolute immunity noted previously, which is often referred to as the privilege of the participant. The use of the term "reporter" signifies anyone who reports on what has happened, as opposed to the journalistic meaning of the term, a newspaper or television reporter.

CRITERIA FOR APPLICATION OF QUALIFIED PRIVILEGE

- Report of a privileged proceeding or document
- A fair and accurate summary published or broadcast as a report

---

24. *Gautsche* v. *New York*, 415 N.Y.S. 2d 280 (1979).
25. American Law Institute, *Restatement of the Law of Torts.*

At the start, it is important to note that qualified privilege is a conditional privilege; that is, the privilege works as a libel defense only if certain conditions are met. First, the privilege applies only to reports of certain kinds of meetings, hearings, proceedings, reports and statements. Second, the law requires that these reports be a fair and accurate or truthful summary of what took place at the meeting or what was said in the report. The privilege is not lost even though there are allegations of actual malice against the reporter. The "Restatement of the Law of Torts" states: "The privilege exists even though the publisher himself does not believe the defamatory words he reports to be true, and even when he knows them to be false."[26] Most state courts follow this rule.[27]

The defendant bears the burden of proving that the privilege applies to the libelous material. The court determines whether the particular occasion (meeting, proceeding, report) is privilege. The jury determines whether the defendants report of the occasion is a fair and accurate report.

Before going into the details relating to the application of this defense, let's look at a brief hypothetical example. During a meeting of the Mayberry City Council, Councilman Floyd Lawson, while discussing an increase in the garbage rates for city residents, says this: "Allied Garbage Co., which supposedly gives us a good rate to pick up the trash, is run by a bunch of crooks who are intent on cheating this city and all its citizens. I mean, I read it in the newspaper. These guys are a part of organized crime." Because of the protection of the absolute privilege, the owners of Allied Garbage cannot sue Lawson. When the reporter who attended the meeting includes this comment in her story, the newspaper also is shielded from a lawsuit so long as the story is a fair and accurate summary of what Lawson said: "Councilman Floyd Lawson charged last night during a city council meeting that the owners of Allied Garbage Co. are a part of organized crime and are cheating the city."

Courts have found the privilege applies to:

- Legislative proceedings
- Judicial proceedings
- Executive actions

The privilege applies to what occurs during meetings of legislative bodies, from the U.S. Congress down to a meeting of a village council or a water district board. But courts have ruled that only what is said during the official portion of the meeting is included within the protective ambit of the defense. The privilege also applies to the reports of committee meetings of such organizations as well as to stories about petitions, complaints and other communications received by these bodies. The only requirement that must be met with regard to this aspect of the privilege is that the official body, such as a city council, must officially receive the complaint or petition before the privilege applies. The privilege usually applies to stories about the news conferences of members of a legislative body following a session, to stories about what was said during a closed meeting by the body and to stories about what was said during an informal gathering of legislators before or

---

26. American Law Institute, *Restatement of the Law of Torts*.
27. See *Solaia Technology, LLC* v. *Specialty Publishing Co.,* 34 M.L.R. 1997 (2006), for example. But see also *Freedom Communications Inc.* v. *Sotelo,* 34 M.L.R. 2207 (2006), where the Texas Court of Appeals said that actual malice would rebut the privilege.

after the regular session, especially if what is said or what occurs during these kinds of events is of great public interest.

The privilege of the reporter also applies to actions that take place in judicial forums: testimony and depositions of witnesses, arguments of attorneys, pronouncements of judges and so forth. Stories about trials, decisions, jury verdicts, court opinions, judicial orders and decrees and grand jury indictments are all protected by the privilege. In 2011 a New York Supreme Court ruled that material contained in a criminal complaint was privileged.[28] Probably the most difficult problem a reporter on the court beat has to face is what to do when a civil lawsuit is initially filed. Under our legal system a lawsuit is started when a person files a complaint with a court clerk and serves a summons on the defendant. The complaint is filled with charges, most of which are libelous. Can a reporter use that complaint as the basis for a story?

In some states a complaint that has been filed is not considered privileged until some kind of judicial action has been taken.[29] The scheduling of an appearance by the litigants may be sufficient judicial action to cloak the document with the privilege. This rule, which requires a judge to become involved in the matter before the complaint is privileged, is designed to protect an innocent party from being smeared in a news report written about a lawsuit that has been filed but then quickly withdrawn. More and more states today follow the rule that the complaint becomes privileged as soon as it has been filed with the court and a docket number has been assigned or the defendant has been issued a summons.[30] Two cautionary notes are important. A reporter should never take a lawyer's word that the lawsuit has been filed. The announcement may be a hoax to get publicity favorable to a client. A call to the courthouse is always in order. Also, ignore what the lawyer says about the case when he or she proclaims that the legal action has been filed. Normally, only comments or material contained in the formal judicial proceedings or court documents are protected by privilege.

Stories about those parts of the judicial process that are closed to the public may or may not be protected by the privilege. For example, court sessions for juveniles and divorce proceedings are frequently closed to protect the privacy of the individuals involved.[31] Some states regard these closures as important public policy and attempt to discourage publicity about such proceedings by denying the mass media the opportunity to apply the privilege if a lawsuit should result from press coverage. But this rule is changing. The 9th U.S. Circuit Court of Appeals has ruled that under California law, the press enjoyed the privilege to publish reports of proceedings in a family court that excluded the general public during its hearings.[32] And a broad reading of U.S. Supreme Court rulings in certain privacy lawsuits that were generated because of press reports of court hearings suggests that the First Amendment may place substantial limits on libel plaintiffs as well as those who are suing because of a report of a closed legal proceeding.[33]

28. *Klig* v. *Harper's Magazine Foundation,* 39 M.L.R. 1987 (2011).
29. See *Amway Corp.* v. *Procter and Gamble Co.,* 31 M.L.R. 2441 (2003), for example.
30. See *Clapp* v. *Olympic View Publishing Co., LLC,* 136 Wn. App. 1045 (2007), for example.
31. But see *Riemers* v. *Grand Forks Herald,* 32 M.L.R. 2381 (2004) for a ruling by the North Dakota Supreme Court that reports of divorce proceedings are protected by the privilege.
32. *Dorsey* v. *National Enquirer, Inc.,* 973 F. 2d 1431 (1992).
33. See *Cox Broadcasting Co.* v. *Cohn,* 420 U.S. 469 (1975); and *Florida Star* v. *B.J.F.,* 109 S. Ct. 2603 (1989).

As the evolution of the privilege proceeds, there is considerable litigation today about its application to elements in the so-called executive branch of government. Reports of the statements and proceedings conducted by mayors, department heads and other administrators and agencies, including law enforcement agencies, are usually shielded by the privilege.

The defense is generally confined to stories about speeches, reports, hearings or statements that are official in nature, things that are substantially "acts of state." The law sometimes requires officials to undertake certain actions; other times, the actions are logical extensions of their official responsibilities. Reports based on confidential reports[34] or closed hearings that focus on governmental misconduct have been protected by the privilege. In the case of the closed hearing the Massachusetts Supreme Judicial Court official government actions include those conducted behind closed doors.[35]

Reporters get volumes of information from the police and other law enforcement agencies. How much of this information is privileged? More and more each day. For decades a report that an individual has been arrested and charged with a crime has been protected by the privilege. Typically this was information contained on official police documents—called the blotter in some places, or the jail register in others. Today much more is protected. The Oklahoma Court of Civil Appeals ruled in 2010 that a police press release and press conference related to the search for a suspect were official functions of the police department and protected by the privilege.[36] Statements made to a reporter by a sheriff during an interview about an investigation were privileged, the Georgia Court of Appeals ruled in 2009.[37] The privilege can apply even if the information provided by the police is erroneous. A Florida judge wrote in 2007, "It will be inevitable that on occasion the media will publish information from government sources that turns out to be inaccurate. While this may be irritating to the subject of the newspaper or television reports, this is a small price to pay for the benefits the public receives from the privilege."[38] And in 2009 the Arkansas Supreme Court ruled that witness statements contained in case reports were protected by the privilege even though these statements should not have been released.[39]

Caution needs to be exercised here, however. The privilege surely does not apply to every statement made by every police officer on every topic. The Idaho Supreme Court refused to apply the privilege to statements that were made privately to a reporter by a police officer. The court said these statements went beyond the official police reports, which are clearly privileged documents.[40] Another note of caution. Some American courts have refused to allow the privilege defense when the document that contained the defamatory statement was not generated in the United States. In 2005, a U.S. District Court refused to allow the privilege defense to protect allegations that two Russians were involved in corrupt and criminal conduct. The court said, "the privilege is unavailable to

---

34. *Ingere* v. *ABC*, 11 M.L.R. 1227 (1984).
35. *Howell* v. *Enterprise Publishing Co.*, 455 Mass. 641 (2010).
36. *Stewart* v. *NYT Broadcast Holdings, LLC*, 240 P. 3d 772 (2010).
37. *Community Newspapers Holding Inc.* v. *King*, 682 S.E. 2d 346 (2009).
38. *Vaillcourt* v. *Media General Operations Inc.*, 36 M.L.R. 1543 (2007).
39. *Whiteside* v. *Russellville Newspapers Inc.*, 375 Ark. 245 (2009).
40. *Wiemer* v. *Rankin*, 790 P. 2d 347 (1990).

defendants in this case because it does not extend to official reports of the actions of a foreign government."[41]

The privilege is not confined to those instances of reporting official government proceedings. The Washington Supreme Court ruled that the reporting of the charges on recall petitions is privileged.[42] A federal court in Idaho ruled that the privilege applied to a story about a meeting called by citizens to protest the actions of a judge. It clearly was not an official meeting but concerned important public business, the conduct of a public official.[43] The "Restatement of the Law of Torts" says that reports of what occurs at meetings open to the public at which matters of public concern are discussed are privileged.[44] In such a circumstance, the report of a public meeting, the key element undoubtedly is the subject of debate. Was it of public concern? Was it of limited public concern? Was it a purely private matter?

NEUTRAL REPORTAGE

In 1977 the 2nd U.S. Court of Appeals created a new variety of qualified privilege called **neutral reportage**.[45] In a nutshell this privilege says that when the press reports newsworthy but defamatory allegations made by a responsible and prominent source, these reports are privileged, even if the reporter believed the allegations were false when he or she included them in the story. Very few other courts have joined the 2nd Circuit in accepting this privilege.[46] Most other courts that have been confronted with the defense have rejected it, including the Pennsylvania Supreme Court.[47] These courts have argued that neutral reportage is incompatible with previous Supreme Court rulings such as *Gertz* v. *Robert Welch Inc.*, that it is unnecessary because of other high-court rulings, or that there is simply no basis in the law to support the defense. Neutral reportage is simply not a viable defense in most jurisdictions. The few courts that have accepted this defense seem to agree that it has four distinct elements.

- ▪ The defamatory allegations must be newsworthy charges that create or are associated with a public controversy.
- ▪ The charges must be made by a responsible and prominent source.
- ▪ The charges must be reported accurately and neutrally.
- ▪ The charges must be about a public official or public figure.[48]

---

41. *Wynn* v. *Smith,* 16 P. 3d 424 (2001); and *OAO Alfa Bank* v. *Center for Public Integrity,* D.D.C., No. 00-2208 (JDB), 9/27/05.
42. *Herron* v. *Tribune Publishing Co.,* 736 P. 2d 249 (1987).
43. *Borg* v. *Borg,* 231 F. 2d 788 (1956).
44. American Law Institute, *Restatement of the Law of Torts.*
45. *Edwards* v. *National Audubon Society, Inc.,* 556 F. 2d 113 (1977), cert. den. 434 U.S. 1002 (1977).
46. See *Price* v. *Viking Penguin, Inc.,* 881 F. 2d 1426 (1989); and *Schwartz* v. *Salt Lake City Tribune* (2005).
47. See, for example, *Dickey* v. *Columbia Broadcasting System, Inc.,* 583 F. 2d 1221 (1978); *Young* v. *The Morning Journal,* 76 Ohio St. 3d 627 (1996); *Norton* v. *Glenn,* 797 A. 2d 294 (2002); aff'd 860 A. 2d 48 (2004); and *Bennett* v. *Columbia University,* 34 M.L.R. 2202 (2006).
48. See *Khawar* v. *Globe International Inc.,* 46 Cal. App. 4th 22 (1996); aff'd 79 Cal. Rptr. 2d 178 (1998).

ABUSE OF PRIVILEGE

Whether qualified privilege applies to a particular story is the first part of the test. Next, a court will ask whether the story is a fair and accurate or true report of what took place or what is contained in the record.

A court will ask whether the story is a fair and accurate or true report of what took place or what is contained in the record.

- Fair means balanced. The story should be complete and include all sides of a contentious dispute. If at a public meeting speakers both attack and defend Conrad Nagel, the story should reflect both the attack and the defense. If a court record contains both positive and negative references about the subject, the news account should contain both kinds of references as well. If a reporter writes a story about a lawsuit that has been filed against a local doctor, the story should also contain the doctor's response to the charges. There must be balance; that is the key.

- An accurate or true report means that the story should honestly reflect what is in the record, or what was said. The story doesn't have to be a verbatim account of what was said. The California Court of Appeals noted, "The privilege applies unless the differences between the facts and the manner in which they are described are of such a substantial character that they produce a different effect on the readers."[49] The story must be an accurate summary of the statement or document. If the original statement or document contains erroneous material, it will not affect the privilege. But stories that contain even seemingly small errors can lose the privilege, if the errors are such that they change the impact of the report in the minds of the average reader.

A newspaper in Ohio reported that a sergeant in the local police department was terminated because he "had sex with a woman while on the job." The woman was a female police dispatcher. An arbitration hearing was held when the officer denied the charges. The arbitration report concluded that the officer had made sexual remarks to the woman, but there was not conclusive evidence that he had ever touched her and no evidence to support the charge of having sexual relations with her. When the officer sued the newspaper for libel, the defendant argued that the story was essentially an accurate summary of the hearing report. The court disagreed. The court ruled that while there was evidence that there was some type of sexual relationship between the officer and the female officer, there was nothing in the arbitration report or a subsequent judicial review of the findings that said the officer had sexual relations with her while on the job. The story was not accurate because it did not contain the essence of the official reports.[50]

Other kinds of errors are not as important. A Spokane, Wash., newspaper was sued after it reported that a businessman had lost a $250,000 judgment in a suit brought against him by Microsoft. The software maker accused T. James Le of selling counterfeit copies of Microsoft software. There were a few minor inaccuracies in the

---

49. *Colt* v. *Freedom Communications Inc.,* 109 Cal. App. 4th 1551 (2003).
50. *Young* v. *Gannett Satellite Information Network,* 40 M.L.R. 1197 (2011).

story, which was based on a privileged court file. One statement was false. The story said that Le had sold counterfeit copies of Office Pro and Windows 95 in December 1998. Actually, he sold only copies of Windows 95 in December 1998. But the Washington Court of Appeals ruled that the error was insubstantial. "Viewed in context with the entire story, the challenged passage is substantially accurate and fair as a matter of law," the court said.[51]

The story should also be in the form of a report. If defendants fail to make it clear that they are reporting something that was said at a public meeting or repeating something that is contained in the public record, the privilege may be lost. The law says the reader should be aware that the story is a report of what happened at a public meeting or at an official hearing or is taken from the official record. These facts should be noted in the lead and in the headline if possible, as noted in the following boxed example.

AT CITY COUNCIL SESSION: MAYOR BLASTS CONTRACTOR WITH CHARGES OF FRAUD

Mayor John Smith during a city council meeting today charged the Acme Construction Company with fraudulent dealings.

The U.S. Court of Appeals for the District of Columbia Circuit ruled that qualified privilege did not apply to a magazine summary of statements contained in an official report from the National Transportation Safety Board. The report is an official record; it is clearly covered by the reporter's privilege. But the summary in the magazine gave readers no clue that the statements constituted a summary of an official document. "The challenged [defamatory] assertion is simply offered as historical fact without any particular indication of its source," the court said. The reader was left with the impression that the author of the article reached the conclusion contained in the defamatory allegations based on his own research.[52]

One last point needs to be made. Traditionally, under the common law, if even a fair and true report was published not to inform the public but because the publisher wanted to hurt the target of the defamation, the privilege could be lost. Courts called this intent to harm the plaintiff common-law malice because the publisher had a malicious intent. In most states today, even if the plaintiff is able to prove common-law malice, the privilege will still protect the publisher. But this protection is not the law everywhere. The Minnesota Court of Appeals decided in June 1999 that proof of common-law malice can defeat the privilege in that state.[53] Be forewarned.

---

51. *Alpine Industries Computers Inc.* v. *Cowles Publishing Co.,* 57 P. 3d 1178 (2002).
52. *Dameron* v. *Washingtonian,* 779 F. 2d 736 (1985); see also *Trover* v. *Kluger,* 37 M.L.R. 1165 (2008).
53. *Moreno* v. *Crookston Times Printing Co.,* 594 N.W. 2d 555 (1999).

SUMMARY

The publication of defamatory material in a report of a public meeting, legislative proceeding or legal proceeding or in a story that reflects the content of an official government report is conditionally privileged. The privilege extends to the meetings of all public bodies, to all aspects of the legal process, to reports and statements issued by members of the executive branch of government and even to nonofficial meetings of the public in which matters of public concern are discussed. Such reports cannot be the basis for a successful libel suit as long as the report presents a fair (balanced) and accurate (truthful) account of what took place at the meeting or what is contained in the record.

PROTECTION OF OPINION

The law has traditionally shielded statements of opinion from suits for defamation. Opinion is a basic part of mass media in the 21st century, with art, music, film and television reviews; political commentary; news analysis; editorials and even advertising. Opinion-filled exchanges, often heated and exaggerated, are part of the basic political and social discourse in the United States. For several centuries a common-law defense, called fair comment and criticism, was the shield used to protect opinion statements from libel suits. In the past 45 years, however, two other defenses have been added, and there is some question whether the common-law protection afforded to opinion statements by the fair comment defense is needed or viable. In the following pages we examine all three of these potential defenses.

The law has traditionally shielded statements of opinion from suits for defamation.

THE RIGHT TO LEAVE A BAD YELP REVIEW

In 2016, Congress passed and President Obama signed the Consumer Review Fairness Act. The law, which passed with bipartisan support, came after years of legal efforts to overturn so-called gag clauses in contracts. These clauses, which have been included in the fine print of sign-up forms and purchase agreements, are designed to prevent consumers from public criticism of companies.
Opponents of these clauses say they are used by businesses to stifle free speech.

Such clauses are banned under the new law. The law also prohibits businesses from imposing a penalty or fee on a client if they write a bad review. Yelp, whose users have been sued by companies over negative reviews, said the Act "gives Americans nationwide new guaranteed legal protections when it comes to sharing these honest, first-hand experiences."

Any business that violates the law will be fined up to $2,500 upon first violation and $5,000 for following violations. Consumers can receive up to $10,000 if they can prove the business acted recklessly in violating the law.

RHETORICAL HYPERBOLE

In the late 1960s, a real estate developer had engaged in negotiations with a local city council for a zoning variance on some land he owned. At the same time the developer was also negotiating with the same city council regarding another parcel of land that the city wanted him to buy. The local newspaper published articles on the bargaining and said that some people had characterized the developer's negotiating positions as "blackmail." The libel suit that followed ultimately found its way to the U.S. Supreme Court. The high court rejected the plaintiff's notion that readers would believe the developer had committed the actual crime of blackmail. "Even the most careless reader must have perceived that the word was no more than rhetorical hyperbole, a vigorous epithet used by those who considered the [developer's] negotiating position extremely unreasonable."[54]

Four years later the high court rendered a similar ruling in a case involving a dispute among postal workers. The National Association of Letter Carriers was trying to organize workers at a post office in Virginia. The monthly union newsletter included the names of those who had not yet joined the union under the heading "List of Scabs." Quoting the author Jack London, the newsletter said a scab carries a tumor of rotten principles where others have heart and is a traitor to his God, his country, his family and his class. A postal worker sued, claiming he was not a traitor. The high court cited the earlier decision in *Greenbelt* and said it was impossible to believe that any readers would have understood the newsletter to be charging the plaintiff with the criminal offense of treason. It was rhetorical hyperbole—lusty, imaginative expression.[55]

Opinion statements, then, may be defended as being unbelievable rhetoric.

Opinion statements, then, may be defended as being unbelievable rhetoric. Here are some examples of the kinds of statements courts have ruled are rhetorical hyperbole:

- Comments were made by a talk-show host that U.S. government contractors at the infamous Abu Ghraib prison in Iraq were "hired killers" and "mercenaries" who could kill without being held to account.[56]
- Charges were made by a New York City council member that a disc jockey was a "sick, racist pedophile, a child predator," and a "lunatic" who must be put behind bars and "should be terminated from the face of the earth."[57]
- In 2013, a federal district court ruled that statements made during the 2012 election cycle were protected opinion because they were part of a heated political debate. The court ruled that calling campaign contributions to Mitt Romney "dirty" or "tainted" was protected opinion because the terms were loose and not susceptible of being proven true or false.[58]

Rhetorical hyperbole is protected, then, because the language is so expansive that the reader or listener knows it is only an opinion, that it is not an assertion of fact. The tone of the language is normally the key. But in cases of satire or parody, the writer or broadcaster

---

54. *Greenbelt Publishing Ass'n, Inc.* v. *Bresler,* 398 U.S. 6 (1970).
55. *Old Dominion Branch No. 496, National Association of Letter Carriers* v. *Austin,* 418 U.S. 264 (1974); see also *Delaney* v. *International Union UAW Local 94,* 32 M.L.R. 1454 (2004).
56. *Caci Premier Technology Inc.* v. *Rhodes,* 36 M.L.R. 2121 (2008).
57. *Torain* v. *Liu,* 479 Fed. Appx. 46 (2008).
58. *Adelson* v. *Harris,* 973 F. Supp. 2d 467 (SDNY 2013).

must be certain that a reasonable reader will in fact realize that the assertions are not meant to be taken as statements of fact. And this can be a close call sometimes. In 2002 a Texas appellate court was faced with a difficult case after a Dallas alternative weekly newspaper published what was purported to be a news story but was actually a fictional satirical piece. A seventh grader in the small town of Ponder, Texas, had been held in juvenile detention for five days after he read a Halloween story to his classmates that was laced with references to drugs and violence. Local authorities said the story amounted to a threat of violence and punished the boy. A reporter for the *Dallas Observer* apparently thought the punishment was nonsense and wrote a satirical fictional story about the same Ponder judge and prosecutor. The satire said authorities locked up a first-grade girl for preparing a report on Maurice Sendak's *Where the Wild Things Are*, a popular children's book. The story described the 6-year-old as being shackled in court and quoted the prosecutor as saying he had not yet decided whether to try the child as an adult. The story mentioned the earlier case, but everything else was pure fiction. It was published under a "News" heading in the newspaper. Some readers apparently thought the story was factual, and many complaints were filed against the two public officials. The judge and prosecutor sued for libel. The newspaper sought a summary judgment, arguing that the column was rhetorical hyperbole. The trial court rejected the motion and an appellate court affirmed the refusal. The court said the story had to be viewed in the light of several years of media attention to violence in the schools. The court added that the earlier real incident occurred in Ponder and involved two of the public officials quoted in the satirical column.[59] The Texas Supreme Court reversed and granted the summary judgment, ruling that reasonable readers would not understand the story as stating actual facts. There were clues within the column that the column was fiction, the court said, noting that the judge was quoted as calling for "panic and overreaction." The story also quoted former Texas Gov. George W. Bush as stating that Maurice Sendak's book "clearly has deviant sexual overtones," and that "zero tolerance means just that. We won't tolerate anything." The court said the article did have a superficial degree of plausibility, but that is the hallmark of satire.[60] The paper won in the end, but it took about five years and undoubtedly cost a considerable sum. Satirists need to be careful.

Rhetorical hyperbole is a powerful defense, but it is not unassailable. And Web users especially must be careful. Communication on the Internet by nonprofessionals is often driven by emotion, not thought. Users often don't even think about incurring liability for the comments they post. In 2017, a New York court dismissed a lawsuit against President Donald Trump based on a tweet made while he was a candidate. In January 2016, political consultant Corey Lewandowski appeared on CNN to criticize Trump's decision to skip a primary debate on Fox News. Later, she appeared on CNN again stating she doubted Trump's claims that he intended to self-finance his presidential bid. In response, Trump tweeted that after she begged him for a job, he had "turned her down twice and she went hostile. Major loser, zero credibility." The court ruled that Trump's language was "loose, figurative, hyperbolic reference to [Lewandowski's] state of mind" and was therefore not capable of verification. Context, the court noted, was key in determining whether a statement was opinion. Trump's tweets, according to the

59. *New Times Inc.* v. *Isaacks,* 91 S.W. 3d 844 (2002).
60. *New Times Inc.* v. *Isaacks,* 32 M.L.R. 2480 (2004).

court, were typically vague and simplistic insults not worthy of serious consideration. The court wrote, that to some "truth itself has been lost in the cacophony of online and Twitter verbiage to such a degree that it seems to roll off the national consciousness like water off a duck's back."[61]

THE FIRST AMENDMENT

The Supreme Court ruled in 1991 that a statement of "pure opinion" on a matter of public concern is protected by the First Amendment.[62] A libel action based on such a statement cannot succeed. Courts across America have adopted this principle as a fundamental rule of libel law. There has been substantially less agreement, however, on how to identify a statement of "pure opinion." Chief Justice Rehnquist, the author of the 1991 ruling, said a statement of pure opinion is a statement that is incapable of being proved true or false. Pure opinion, Rehnquist said, does not assert or even imply a provably false fact.

The Supreme Court decision flowed from a case in which an Ohio sports columnist wrote that a high school wrestling coach and a school superintendent "lied" during a hearing in which they argued for the reinstatement of the wrestling team, which had been disqualified from participating in the state wrestling tournament. It's hard to know what writer Ted Diadiun really meant when he wrote his column, but after a libel suit was filed against the newspaper, the sportswriter argued that he was simply stating his opinion that the coach and the school superintendent had not been honest when they testified at the hearing.

The case meandered through state and federal courts for nearly 15 years before the Supreme Court ultimately ruled in 1991 that Diadiun's statement was an assertion of a fact, not simply an opinion. Rehnquist said the columnist would not have helped his case had he written "In my opinion, Milkovich [the coach] lied" or "I think Milkovich lied." He is still asserting a fact. He is telling readers, the chief justice said, that "I know something that leads me to believe that this man lied under oath." And this is the assertion of a fact, nothing more, nothing less. The newspaper ultimately paid $116,000 in damages to the plaintiffs. More important, perhaps, the publication spent close to a half million dollars defending itself.

It is unusual for lower courts to reject outright a principle of law enunciated by the Supreme Court, but that is what has happened in this case. The majority of lower courts in the United States that since 1991 have decided cases involving statements of opinion have indicated a dissatisfaction with the *Milkovich* standard. The consensus seems to be that defining an opinion statement using the single criterion of proving a statement true or false is far too conservative, that it would deny First Amendment protection to statements that an author intended to be opinion and that a reader or viewer would assume was opinion.

Many courts have gravitated to a different test for determining whether a remark is intended as an assertion of fact or a statement of opinion. This test includes the criterion outlined by the high court—can the statement be proved true or false—but requires the court to look at other dimensions of the published comment as well.

---

61. *Jacobus* v. *Trump*, No. 153252/16 (Jan. 9, 2017, NY Sup. Court).
62. *Milkovich* v. *Lorain Journal Co.*, 110 S. Ct. 2695 (1991).

The Ollman *Test*

In 1984 the U.S. Court of Appeals for the District of Columbia Circuit outlined a four-part test to determine whether a statement should be regarded as the assertion of a fact or as simply the speaker's or writer's opinion. The test, which emerged from the case of *Ollman* v. *Evans*,[63] is known as the *Ollman* test for obvious reasons. Here are the four elements:

- **Can the statement be proved true or false?** This is the basic test from *Milkovich*.
- **What is the common or ordinary meaning of the words?** Some words that appear to be factual assertions are more often used as statements of opinion. If you call someone a turkey, you don't really mean to suggest that the person has feathers and says gobble-gobble. Calling someone a moron doesn't normally mean that his or her IQ score is way below average.
- **What is the journalistic context of the remark?** Newspaper readers expect to find factual assertions in news stories on the front page. They don't expect to find facts in editorial columns, they expect to find opinions. NBC news anchor Brian Williams gives us the news; Rush Limbaugh gives us his opinions, no matter how he happens to word the statements.
- **What is the social context of the remark?** Certain kinds of speech are common to certain kinds of political or social settings. The audience attending a lecture by an eminent scientist on the need to vaccinate young children is expecting to hear facts. In a debate between two candidates for the legislature, the audience is prepared to hear opinion. Labor disputes, political meetings, protest rallies and other such settings usually generate high-spirited and free-wheeling commentary. People don't usually expect to hear factual assertions.

OLLMAN TEST

1. Can the statement be proved true or false?
2. What is the common or ordinary meaning of the words?
3. What is the journalistic context of the remark?
4. What is the social context of the remark?

The first important court to reject the single-criterion *Milkovich* test was the New York Court of Appeals, the high court in that state. The case, *Immuno, A.G.* v. *Moor-Jankowski*,[64] involved a scholarly scientific journal. The journal published a letter from a researcher who asserted that a plan by an Austrian pharmaceutical company to establish a laboratory in Sierra Leone that would use chimpanzees for research on hepatitis was simply a ploy to avoid the restrictions in place in western Europe and North America that prohibit the importation of the primates, which are regarded as an endangered species.

63. 750 F. 2d 970 (1984).
64. 77 N.Y. 2d 235 (1991).

The researcher, Dr. Shirley McGreal, further asserted that the plan could cause serious harm to the chimpanzee population in the region. The comments were published in a letter to the editor and were prefaced by an editorial note that identified McGreal as an animal rights advocate and stated that the company, Immuno, A.G., regarded the charges as inaccurate and reckless. The state high court said the letter was protected opinion. Under the single-criterion *Milkovich* standard, some of the statements would likely be regarded as factual assertions. But Chief Judge Judith Kaye rejected the single-criterion test, calling it a "hypertechnical" test that paid no attention to contextual matters. The defamatory matter was published in a letter to the editor, a forum where readers expect to find opinion statements. The page carried a warning that the views expressed in the letters were those of the letter writers. Judge Kaye noted that the readers of this journal were highly specialized researchers who were aware of the ongoing debate over the use of primates in medical research. The statements were protected, the court ruled, under the free press provisions of the New York state constitution.[65]

In 2010 a federal court in Virginia was faced with a libel suit not unlike the *Immuno* case. The plaintiff was Barbara Arthur, who is co-founder of the National Vaccine Information Center, an organization that is arguing that mandatory childhood vaccinations for measles, mumps and other such diseases should stop, because the vaccinations cause autism in children. The defendant was Dr. Paul Offit, a pediatrician and infectious disease specialist. Arthur writes books, serves on committees, appears on radio and TV and spends a good deal of time attacking Offit, who she says walks in lockstep with the pharmaceutical industry and demonizes caring parents. In a magazine feature story on Offit, "An Epidemic of Fear: One Man's Battle Against the Anti-Vaccine Movement," the doctor is quoted as saying Arthur's theories make him crazy: "You just want to scream because she lies." Offit added, "I'm in this for the same reason she is, I care about kids."

Arthur said the statement "she lies" was false and defamatory. The court dismissed the claim, ruling that the statement was just emphatic language, an expression of outrage, and did not suggest Arthur lacked honesty or integrity. The court added:

> Both the nature of the statement—including that it was quoting an advocate with a particular scientific viewpoint and policy position—and the statement's context—a very brief passage in a lengthy description of an on-going heated public controversy—confirms that his is a protected expression of opinion.[66]

Both a U.S. District Court and the 9th U.S. Circuit Court of Appeals have ruled that a statement published in a *New York Post* column about the late Johnnie Cochran, one of O.J. Simpson's attorneys, was protected by the First Amendment. The columnist called Cochran a "legal scoundrel" who "will say or do just about anything to win, typically at the expense of the truth." The trial court ruled that the tenor of the column and the context of the statements dictated the readers would view the remarks as opinion, not allegations of fact. The appellate court agreed.[67] And the 1st U.S. Circuit Court of Appeals ruled that statements in a biography of Robert K. Gray that said the former Republican politician and public relations practitioner had faked his closeness to

65. *Immuno, A.G. v. Moor-Jankowski,* 77 N.Y. 2d 235 (1991).
66. *Arthur v. Offit,* 38 M.L.R. 1508 (2010).
67. *Cochran v. NYP Holdings Inc.,* 27 M.L.R. 1108 (1998), aff'd 210 F. 3d 1036 (2000).

Ronald Reagan and other senior administration officials were protected opinions. "This is just the kind of subjective judgment that is only minimally about 'what happened,' but expresses instead a vague and subjective characterization of what happened," the court said.[68] Again, context was a key.

It is often important to support opinion statements with facts unless the comments are obviously simply opinions. A hotel sued a Web site that reviewed hotels after the resort hotel was included on a list of "2011 dirtiest hotels." The plaintiff complained that this was a statement of fact, but the federal court ruled that no reasonable person would confuse a ranking system, which uses consumer reviews for its ratings, for an assertion of facts.[69] Courts have also ruled that if the facts in a dispute are well known, opinion statements based on these facts don't have to be fully outlined with the opinion statements. Recently, two courts dismissed defamation suits after ruling the statements were opinions based on facts that were disclosed. The Massachusetts Supreme Judicial Court held articles published in the *Boston Herald* regarding the suicide of Brad Delp, the lead singer of the band Boston, were protected. The newspaper was sued for an article that discussed potential reasons for Delp's suicide. In ruling in favor of the newspaper, the court concluded the reasonable reader would have concluded the statements were opinion and deduction based on the disclosed facts.[70] A federal district court ruled that a *Forbes* article written by Dolia Estevez, a part-time correspondent for the Mexican media company Noticias MVS and *Forbes* contributor, was protected. Alejandra Sota Mirafuentes, a former spokesperson and advisor to former Mexican President Felipe Calderon, sued arguing she was defamed in an article titled, "The 10 Most Corrupt Mexicans of 2013." The court ruled the article was protected opinion because there was no way to determine who was "most corrupt." In addition, the decision to place Sota on the list was supported by the facts that Sota was being investigated by Mexican authorities for alleged embezzlement and trafficking and she attended Harvard's Kennedy School without a bachelor's degree. The court held that because the bases of the conclusion were fully disclosed and the article did not imply any further facts that were not disclosed, a reasonable reader would consider the conclusion to include Sota on the list to be the opinion of the author.[71]

But care must be exercised. The facts used to support the opinion must be correct. The pure opinion defense will not protect false facts contained in an opinion statement. Courts have ruled that some statements of opinion suggest the author has knowledge of defamatory facts that have not been disclosed, and these statements of what courts call mixed facts and opinion might fall outside the First Amendment protection given to pure opinion. When an executive told the *New York Post* that he had fired an employee because "she had a lousy work ethic," and that "she was the highest paid person in the company who did the least amount of work," he was suggesting he knew certain facts, unknown to the audience, that supported his opinion, facts that are detrimental (and hence defamatory) to the person about whom he is speaking, the New York Supreme Court ruled.[72]

68. *Gray* v. *St. Martin's Press, Inc.,* 221 F. 3d 243 (2000).
69. *Seaton* v. *TripAdvisor LLC,* E.D.Tenn. No. 11-549, 8/22/12.
70. *Scholz v. Boston Herald, Inc.,* No. 10-189-15 (Nov. 25, 2015).
71. *Sota Mirafuentes v. Estevez,* 2015 U.S. Dist. LEXIS 166157.
72. *Pepler* v. *Rugged Land, LLC,* 34 M.L.R. 1796 (2006).

> ## AN UNVERIFIABLE STATEMENT OF OPINION CAN LOSE ITS PROTECTION IF IT
>
> ■ implies the existence of false, defamatory but undisclosed facts,
> ■ is based on disclosed but false or incomplete facts, or
> ■ is based on erroneous assessments of accurate information.

Leaving out facts in a story can also be a problem when the defendant attempts to assert the opinion defense. It could give readers an impression of the plaintiff that was unintended by the opinion writer. A case in point was decided several years ago in Rhode Island.

A man picketing and protesting the dismissal of an employee at a YMCA branch collapsed. The president of the branch was a physician who was conducting a board meeting while protesters marched outside. When he was informed that a picketer had collapsed, he offered his assistance. He was told his help was not needed because an aid unit was expected momentarily. When the protester died, the story received widespread publicity. The press reports included criticism of the doctor for not aiding the stricken man. All the stories left out the fact that the physician had offered to help the victim. The doctor sued and argued that the stories made him appear to be indifferent, uncaring and even callous. The defendants argued that the defamatory criticisms were opinions. A jury agreed with the plaintiff, noting that by leaving out the essential fact that the doctor had offered to help, the stories implied something that was untruthful.[73] The absence of this information turned protected opinion statements into defamatory factual allegations.

FAIR COMMENT AND CRITICISM

Fair comment is a common-law defense that protects the publication of statements of opinion. It has worked satisfactorily for several centuries. But like many other elements in the law of libel, fair comment has been seriously affected by the application of First Amendment protections to libel law. With the emergence of the First Amendment privilege for statements of opinion that has been outlined in the previous section, most lawyers say it makes more sense to rely on the power of the Constitution to protect their clients as opposed to using a workable, but less powerful, common-law defense. Hence, the status of the fair comment defense is in a kind of legal limbo right now.[74] The

---

73. *Healy* v. *New England Newspapers,* 520 A. 2d 147 (1987).
74. But see *Magnusson* v. *New York Times Co.,* 32 M.L.R. 2496 (2004), where the Oklahoma Supreme Court ruled the fair comment defense was applicable in a lawsuit brought against a TV station by a physician.

hundreds of fair comment precedents remain on the books as good law, but no one seems to cite them anymore.

The use of a fair comment defense requires the court to apply a three-part test:

1. **Is the comment an opinion statement?** Courts have traditionally used a single-criterion test to answer this question: Can the statement be proved true or false?

2. **Does the defamatory comment focus on a subject of legitimate public interest?** The courts have defined legitimate public interest very broadly to include everything from cultural artifacts to religion to medicine to advertising.

3. **Is there a factual basis for the comment?** The third requirement of the three-part test is critical, for it is grounded in the legal rationale for the defense: the notion that both our democratic system of government and our culture are enhanced by the free exchange of ideas and opinions. Under this defense the facts may be outlined in the article or broadcast that contains the opinion, or, if the facts regarding a situation are so widely known, it is not necessary that they be spelled out anew for readers or viewers.

The defendant who is sued for defamatory opinion, then, may attempt to defeat the lawsuit using any or all of the three strategies just outlined. The defendant can argue that the defamatory statements are so broad, so exaggerated, that no one would regard them as factual assertions; that they are rhetorical hyperbole. The defendant may also argue that the statement is a pure opinion and protected by the Constitution. Finally, the defendant can argue that the common-law defense of fair comment provides a shield against a lawsuit.

TIPS ON AVOIDING A LIBEL SUIT BASED ON STATEMENTS OF OPINION

Journalists can take steps to avoid such a lawsuit in the first place. Mass media attorney David Utevsky suggests the following:

- When stating an opinion, try to make certain it is understood as such. But remember the words "in my opinion" don't change a statement of fact into protected opinion.
- Don't rely on journalistic context to protect you. Just because the libel appears in a review or a column or a commentary does not mean a court will always regard it as opinion.
- Clearly state and summarize the facts on which your opinion is based. Ask yourself whether you believe a court could find that these facts support your opinion about the matter.
- Make certain the facts are true. If there is a dispute about the facts, refer to both sides of the dispute when stating your opinion.

SUMMARY Statements of opinion are often immune to a successful libel action. The courts have said that rhetorical hyperbole—broad, exaggerated comments about someone or something—are obviously not assertions of fact and cannot stand as the basis for a successful libel suit. The Constitution also protects statements of opinion, but only pure opinion, according to the Supreme Court. Opinion statements that imply the assertion of falsehoods are not protected. The Supreme Court has ruled that the test to determine whether a statement is opinion or not is whether the statement may be proved false. Other courts have applied somewhat broader tests for opinion that focus on the ordinary meaning of the words and the journalistic and social context of the statement in addition to whether the statement can be proved to be false. Finally, opinion is protected by the common-law defense of fair comment.

DEFENSES AND DAMAGES

The privilege of the reporter and the defenses for opinion are not the only means at hand to thwart a libel suit. At least two other common-law defenses exist: **consent** and **right of reply.** Like fair comment, these defenses are old. Both have been used on occasion in the past with substantial success. Yet they are not universally accepted, and only rarely have they been applied in a libel suit in the last 45 years. Let's briefly examine each.

CONSENT

Many legal authorities agree that an individual cannot sue for libel if he or she consented to the publication of the defamatory material.[75] Imagine that Mary Jones, a reporter for the *River City Sentinel*, hears rumors that John Smith is a leader of organized crime. Jones visits Smith and tells him that she has heard these rumors. Then Jones asks Smith if he cares if the rumors are published in the newspaper. Smith says it is OK with him, and Jones writes and publishes the story. In this instance Smith consented to publication of the defamation. Now this event is not too likely to happen, is it? Cases of this kind of express consent are extremely rare. Courts insist that the plaintiff either knew or had a good reason to know the full extent of the defamatory statement in advance of its publication before consent can be said to exist.

But there is another kind of consent that some courts have recognized. It is called indirect or implied consent. A plaintiff can give this kind of consent in at least a couple of ways. Some courts have ruled that when an individual comments on a defamatory charge and this response is published with the charge, the injured party has given indirect consent to publish the libel.[76] The logic to this argument is simple: If the response is printed, the charge must be printed as well or the story won't make any sense. Courts have also ruled that if the plaintiff has told others of the defamatory charges against him or her, this amounts to implied consent to publication elsewhere.[77] Implied consent is constructed on

Implied consent is constructed on sound legal theory, but only a handful of courts have accepted this theory.

75. Phelps and Hamilton, *Libel;* and Sanford, *Libel and Privacy.*
76. See *Pulverman v. A.S. Abell Co.,* 228 F. 2d 797 (1956), for example.
77. *Pressley v. Continental Can Co.,* 250 S.E. 2d 676 (1978).

sound legal theory, but only a handful of courts have accepted this theory. Nevertheless, getting a comment from an individual you are about to libel is a very good idea. Giving the subject of the story a chance to reply might reveal mistakes in the story, mistakes that can be corrected before publication or broadcast. It is the fair and equitable thing to do as well.

RIGHT OF REPLY/SELF-DEFENSE

Right of reply is another secondary defense. Like consent, it has not been commonly applied in recent years. Right of reply is sometimes called "the self-defense." If an individual has been defamed, he or she may answer the defamation with a libelous communication and not be subject to a successful libel suit. The only limitation here is that the reply must approximate the original defamation in magnitude. Self-defense has this same limitation. The response cannot greatly exceed the provocation. The court will not accept a claim of self-defense if you shoot and kill someone who threw a spitwad at you.

As applied in libel law, if Joseph Adieu libels Kerry O'Shea, O'Shea has the right to respond. And if the response is defamatory, the right of reply defense will block a successful libel suit by Adieu. But scenarios like this are rare today; it is much more likely that O'Shea will forgo a reply, and simply sue Adieu. How does the right of reply defense protect the mass media, since newspapers and broadcasting stations rarely attack someone who has attacked them? Some libel authorities have argued that if the press acts as a conduit for comments carried by a party in a dispute, it can use the right of reply in defense of a lawsuit.[78] In other words, imagine Adieu libels O'Shea in a public speech. The local newspaper carries O'Shea's libelous reply in its letters to the editor column. Adieu then sues the newspaper for publishing the libel. The publication can argue the right of reply defense protects it.[79]

In "Cases and Materials on Torts," law professors Charles Gregory and Harry Kalven wrote:

> The boundaries of this privilege are not clearly established and it gives rise to questions amusingly reminiscent of those raised in connection with self-defense: How vigorous must the plaintiff's original aggression have been? Must the original attack itself have been defamatory? What if it [the original attack] is true or privileged? How much verbal force can the defendant use in reply? Can he defend third parties?[80]

In 2015, a Massachusetts judge specifically rejected the self-defense privilege. The lawsuit involved allegations and counter statements related to sexual assault allegations against actor and comedian Bill Cosby. After three women came forward to various media outlets alleging Cosby had sexually assaulted them, Cosby's lawyer, Martin Singer, responded to the comments on behalf of Cosby. The women then sued, claiming Singer's response defamed them. Among other things, Cosby's lawyers argued the plaintiff's claims should be dismissed even if they were defamatory because the statements were protected by the

---

78. See Phelps and Hamilton, *Libel.*
79. See *Fowler v. New York Herald*, 172 N.Y.S. 423 (1918).
80. Gregory and Kalven, *Cases and Materials on Torts.*

common-law privilege of self-defense. Although the case was tried in Massachusetts, the court applied the substantive law of Florida and California because the plaintiffs in the case resided in those states. The court ruled that neither California nor Florida recognize the self-defense privilege. The court noted that California courts have specifically rejected the privilege, and that while Florida courts have never explicitly rejected the privilege there was no reason to assume they would. The court wrote, "In the court's view, the absence of any indication that Florida courts would adopt this privilege, especially when they have explicitly adopted other common-law defamation privileges, establishes no basis to assume the self-defense privilege would be recognized in Florida."[81] Questions like these continue to reduce the effectiveness of the defense of a right of reply.

DAMAGES

In general, there are two broad categories of damages (or money) available in many civil lawsuits. They are: 1) **compensatory damages,** which are designed to compensate the plaintiff for injuries suffered as a result of the defendant's conduct and to make the plaintiff whole again for the injuries he or she suffered; and 2) **punitive damages,** which are designed to punish and to deter the defendant (and others like the defendant) from engaging in the same type of conduct in the future. Punitive damages thus go above and beyond compensatory damages, and they are supposed to send a message—often due to their vast size—to the defendant to never do the same thing again. Sometimes a jury may not award punitive damages (and, as discussed later, some states do not allow any punitive damages in libel cases), but when punitive damages are awarded, the plaintiff gets to keep them as a windfall, along with the compensatory damages.

Compensatory Damages

In general, there are three types of compensatory damages a libel plaintiff may be awarded: 1) **general damages** (sometimes called actual damages), which are designed to compensate for the intangible injuries of reputational harm and, in most states, emotional harm that a plaintiff might experience as a result of the publication of a defamatory statement (damages to compensate one for being shunned or avoided or exposed to hatred and ridicule, for instance, after a defamatory statement is published); 2) **special damages,** which are designed to compensate for specific, precise and identifiable monetary harms, such as lost wages, lost income or a decrease in business revenue, that a plaintiff can prove he suffered as a result of a defamatory statement; and 3) **presumed damages,** which are an old oddity in libel law that allow a plaintiff to recover damages for reputational harm without any proof of injury. Each of these three types of damages is discussed in more detail here.

The most common libel damages are called actual damages, or damages for actual injury.

General or Actual Damages

The most common libel damages are called **general damages** or **actual damages**. Plaintiffs must bring evidence to the court to show that because of the publication of the defamation

---

81. *Green* v. *Cosby,* 138 F. Sup. 3d 114 (D. Mass. 2015).

they have suffered reputational harm, which might include impairment of reputation or standing in the community, personal humiliation, or mental suffering and anguish.[82] Some of these concepts are pretty nebulous. How can mental suffering or anguish be proved in court and then measured in dollar amounts? As such, the awarding of even so-called actual damages is rarely a precise process. The plaintiff will ask for an amount that may or may not bear any relationship to the actual harm inflicted, and the court—usually the jury—will award what it thinks the plaintiff deserves, often regardless of the amount of damage inflicted. As noted in Chapter 4, juries have recently been asked to award or have awarded very large damages. If the amount is too high, the trial judge or an appellate court will frequently modify the amount of money awarded. The gross imprecision in awarding damages puts considerable pressure on both parties, but especially the defendant, to settle the case without going to trial.

Special Damages

Special damages are specific items of monetary or pecuniary loss, such as lost wages, caused by published defamatory statements. Special damages must be established in precise terms, much more precise terms than those for the actual damages just outlined. If a plaintiff can prove that he or she lost $23,567.19 because of the libel, that amount is then what the plaintiff can ask for and what will likely be awarded if he or she can convince the jury of the validity of the case. Special damages represent a specific monetary, and only monetary, loss as the result of the libel. Most plaintiffs do not seek special damages. However, in some cases special damages are all that can be sought. In trade libel, for example, the only award a plaintiff can get is special damages.

Presumed Damages

Presumed damages are damages that a plaintiff can get without proof of injury or harm. They can be larger than other types of compensatory damages. Thus, the Supreme Court has required defendants to show a higher level of fault in most cases to recover presumed damages. A public-person plaintiff or a private-person plaintiff suing for a libelous statement that focuses on a matter of public concern can only be awarded presumed damages (sometimes called general or compensatory damages) on a showing of actual malice, knowledge of falsity or reckless disregard of the truth. However, a private person suing on the basis of a libelous statement that focuses on a private matter and not a public concern need only show negligence to collect presumed damages.[83]

Punitive Damages

Lawyers frequently call **punitive damages,** or exemplary damages, the "smart money." Punitive damage awards are usually very large. As noted earlier, punitive damages are designed to punish defendants for misconduct and to warn others not to act in a similar manner.

82. See Justice Lewis Powell's opinion in *Gertz v. Robert Welch, Inc.,* 4118 U.S. 323 (1974).
83. *Dun & Bradstreet v. Greenmoss Builders,* 472 U.S. 479 (1985).

A public-person plaintiff or a private-person plaintiff suing for a libelous statement that focuses on a matter of public concern can only win punitive damages on a showing of actual malice, knowledge of falsity or reckless disregard for the truth. A private person suing for libel based on remarks made about a private matter, and not a public concern, can win punitive damages on a showing of negligence.

Punitive damages are the most onerous aspect of any libel suit, and many persons think they are grossly unfair. Punitive damages have been barred in some jurisdictions, including Louisiana, Massachusetts, Nebraska, New Hampshire, Oregon and Washington and have been limited in Colorado, Florida, Georgia, Kansas, Montana, Mississippi, North Dakota and Virginia.[84] Legislatures in other states, such as Alabama, Illinois and Indiana, have considered placing some kind of limits on punitive damages. In North Carolina, for example, punitive damages are limited to three times the amount of compensatory damages. Few, if any, legal authorities will argue that punitive damages ought to be completely abolished. They do in some instances serve a purpose. A business that consciously and aggressively sells harmful or dangerous products must be punished, most legal experts will argue. A publisher who consistently prints gross lies that shred the reputations of innocent people should suffer serious consequences. But the gargantuan size of some punitive damage awards, amounts that bear no resemblance whatsoever to the harm inflicted, has led many attorneys to argue that such awards violate the Eighth Amendment to the U.S. Constitution, which forbids the levying of excessive fines. In 1991, the U.S. Supreme Court ruled that the methods used by the courts to assess punitive damages are not "so inherently unfair as to be per se unconstitutional." But, Justice Harry Blackmun wrote for the court, "the general concerns of reasonableness and adequate guidance from the court when the case is tried to a jury properly enter into the constitutional calculus."[85] Five years later the high court overturned as "grossly excessive" an award of $2 million to an Alabama man who sued BMW for selling him, as a new car, an automobile that had been refinished to correct minor paint damage incurred in shipping. Again, the court declined to provide a specific test that should be applied at trial to guide the assessment of punitive damage awards, but offered three guideposts that could be used: the degree of reprehensibility of the defendant's conduct, the ratio between punitive and actual damages and a comparison between the punitive damage award and any criminal or civil fines that could be levied by the state for similar conduct.[86] In 2001 the high court again spoke to the problem, warning lower appellate courts that they must give "searching scrutiny" to whether a jury's punitive damage award is excessive.[87] In 2003 the high court made its sharpest attack on punitive damages when it overturned an award of $145 million that a Utah jury had given a couple who had sued State Farm insurance company. Justice Anthony Kennedy, writing for the six-person majority, said that the wealth of a defendant cannot justify an otherwise unconstitutional punitive damage award. The couple had been awarded $1 million in compensatory damages, the remaining $144 million as punitive damages. Kennedy said the ratio of

84. Dill, "Libel Law Doesn't Work."
85. *Pacific Mutual Life Insurance Co.* v. *Haslip,* 111 S. Ct. 1032 (1991).
86. Greenhouse, "Justices Reject Punitive Award."
87. Greenhouse, "Punitive Damages."

145 to 1 resulted in a damage award that was "neither reasonable nor proportionate to the wrong committed."[88]

RETRACTION STATUTES

The phrase "I demand a retraction" is common in the folklore of libel. What is a **retraction?** A retraction is both an apology and an effort to set the record straight. Let's say you blow one as an editor. You report that Jane Adams was arrested for shoplifting, and you are wrong. In your retraction you first tell readers or viewers that Jane Adams was not arrested for shoplifting, that you made a mistake. Then you might also apologize for the embarrassment caused Adams. You might even say some nice things about her. At common law a prompt and honest retraction is usually relevant to the question of whether the plaintiff's reputation was actually harmed. After all, you are attempting to reconstruct that part of her reputation that you tore down just the day before. She might have difficulty proving actual harm.

The phrase "I demand a retraction" is common in the folklore of libel.

A majority of states have some kind of retraction law, according to libel authority Bruce Sanford. Some of these laws are very comprehensive; others provide extremely limited protection. Under a typical retraction statute, a plaintiff must give the publisher an opportunity to retract the libel before a suit may be started. Most states require the retraction to be published within a fixed amount of time after the defamatory material was published, such as 20 days, and that the retraction be published in as conspicuous a place and location as the original defamatory statement. In broadcasting, this means the same hour of the original broadcast. Retraction statutes, however, do not eliminate a libel suit if a retraction is timely published. They only affect the type of damages that can be recovered. If the publisher promptly honors the request for a retraction and retracts the libelous material in a place as prominent as the place in which the libel originally appeared, the retraction will reduce, and in some instances cancel, any damage judgment the plaintiff might later seek in a lawsuit. Most states hold that a timely retraction that is published in as conspicuous a place as the original defamatory statement prevents the recovery of punitive and or general/actual damages. Plaintiffs may only recover special damages. Failure to ask for a retraction or failure to ask for a retraction in the way prescribed by the statute can result in a dismissal of the libel complaint.[89]

In at least two states, retraction statutes adopted by the legislature have been ruled unconstitutional. In both Arizona[90] and Montana,[91] the state high courts have ruled that the state constitution gives citizens the right to sue for injury to person, property or character. The retraction statute diminishes that right and is hence unconstitutional, the courts ruled.

A court in at least one state applied a retraction statute to libel published on the Internet. The Georgia Supreme Court ruled in 2002 that the state's law, which applies

---

88. *State Farm* v. *Campbell,* 538 U.S. 408 (2003); and Greenhouse, "Justices Limit."
89. *Milsap* v. *Stanford,* 139 F. 3d 902 (1998).
90. *Boswell* v. *Phoenix Newspapers,* 730 P. 2d 186 (1986).
91. *Madison* v. *Yunker,* 589 P. 2d 126 (1978).

only to punitive damages, not the right to sue, is applicable to publications occurring on the Internet. Both the trial court and the state court of appeals had ruled it did not apply to Internet publications, that it applied only to publications in the traditional media. In this case the plaintiff had failed to ask for a retraction and therefore was denied the opportunity to seek punitive damages.[92]

In 2014, the Florida Court of Appeals concluded that the "media" covered in the Florida statute aren't limited to the institutional media that have publishing as the main vehicle of publication. The court stated the question was whether the Internet site "is operated to further the free dissemination of information or disinterested and neutral commentary or editorializing as to matter of public interest."[93] Online publications that meet this definition are covered by the Florida statute, ruled the court. In 2014, the California Court of Appeals ruled that California's retraction statute did not apply to thewrap.com. Commenting on the law that was enacted in 1931 and amended in 1945, the court wrote, "Had the Legislature intended the statute to apply to defamatory material published on an online website, it could have amended the statute to say so."[94]

SUMMARY   Secondary defenses, consent and right of reply, exist and may in rare instances aid a libel defendant. To collect damages in a libel suit, plaintiffs must demonstrate to the court that there was actual harm to their reputations. These are called actual damages. If plaintiffs can demonstrate specific items of monetary loss, special damages may be awarded. Plaintiffs may also seek to win punitive damages. In many states, a timely retraction of the libel can reduce damages significantly and even lessen the likelihood of a libel suit. These rules are governed by state laws called retraction statutes.

CRIMINAL LIBEL

Criminal libel has been a part of the law of defamation for as long as the law has existed. It is a close cousin to seditious libel and civil libel. Chapters 4, 5 and the better part of this chapter have dealt with civil libel, one person suing another for defamation. **Criminal libel** is founded on the theory that sometimes it is appropriate for the state to act on behalf of the party injured by the libel and bring criminal charges against the defendant. Criminal libel has been justified traditionally with the argument that if the state fails to act, the injured party or parties may take violent action against the libeler to compensate for the damage they have suffered. The state has a substantial interest in preventing this violence from occurring.

Today, criminal libel law remains as kind of a relic of the past. But it is a relic that won't seem to go away. Florida, Idaho, Kansas, Louisiana, Michigan, Montana,

---

92. *Mathis* v. *Cannon,* 573 S.E. 2d 376 (2002).
93. *Comis* v. *Vanvoorhis* (Fla. Ct. App. Apr. 11, 2014).
94. *Theiriot* v. *The Wrapnews, Inc.* (Cal. Ct. App. Apr. 15, 2014).

New Hampshire, New Mexico and North Carolina still have criminal libel laws. In 2008 an appellate court in Washington state declared its statute unconstitutional, and the legislature repealed the law the following year.[95] During the 2014-2015 legislative session, Georgia removed the State's **criminal defamation** law. And there have been fewer than 100 criminal libel cases in the past 45 years. But seemingly every year one or two cases pop up. In 2008 two Wisconsin high school students were charged with criminal libel after assembling and posting a nude photo collage of a female classmate.

While prosecutions for criminal libel are limited, they have not disappeared. However, they frequently involve private individuals and not members of the media. In one in-depth study of criminal libel laws in Wisconsin, 37 of 61 (61%) prosecutions for criminal libel over a 16-year period in Wisconsin were "purely private quarrels." A significant number of these involved attacks by spurned ex-lovers. For example, four specifically involved the spread of HIV/AIDS rumors and one involved a fake online posting of a profile and solicitation for nontraditional sex.[96] In 2015, the International Press Institute identified several prosecutions for criminal libel.

- A former police chief in Utah was charged with criminal defamation for allegedly using the name of the current police chief to disparage Border Patrol agents.
- A Louisiana man was convicted of criminal libel for criticizing a local public official. In an unpublished e-mail to the local newspaper, he questioned the paper's lack of reporting on allegations of improper conduct by the public official.
- A New Hampshire man was accused of criminal libel for misappropriating the name of a U.S. marine when criticizing local officers and officials in letters to the local newspaper.
- A Minnesota man was accused of creating an e-mail account for his ex-girlfriend, posting a fake online profile for her and arranging meetings with strangers at her residence.[97]

Thus, while criminal libel does not receive much attention from either scholars or the media, it still exists. Despite these notable exceptions, however, authorities in most states are unwilling to take on someone else's troubles and prosecute for criminal libel so long as a civil remedy is available. A prosecutor will generally gain very little public support by taking such an action. In an age when people are murdered, robbed, raped and assaulted with alarming frequency, most voters would rather see government officers arrest and prosecute real criminals.

Criminal libel differs from civil libel in several important respects. First of all, it is possible to criminally libel the dead. The state can use a criminal libel statute to prosecute

95. *Parmelee v. O'Neal*, 36 M.L.R. 1863 (2008).
96. Pritchard, "Rethinking Criminal Libel: An Empirical Study."
97. Special Report, Criminal Libel in the United States, http://legaldb.freemedia.at/special-report
-criminal-libel-in-the-united-states/.

an individual for damaging the reputation of someone who is deceased. In some states criminal libel is tied to causing or potentially causing a breach of the peace. This charge used to be quite common. If a publication, speech or handbill so provoked the readers or listeners that violence became possible or did in fact occur, criminal libel charges might result. But in 1966 the Supreme Court ruled that basing a criminal libel charge on a breach of the peace was unconstitutional.[98] This decision was an important factor, but only one factor, in the passing of "breach of the peace" as an aspect of criminal libel. It is extremely rare for such a case to occur today.

The Supreme Court has heard one other criminal libel case since the *New York Times Co.* v. *Sullivan*[99] ruling. The court ruled in *Garrison* v. *Louisiana*[100] that when the defamation of a public official is the basis for a criminal libel suit, the state has to prove actual malice on the part of the defendant—that is, knowledge of falsity, reckless disregard for the truth or falsity of the matter. Justice Brennan wrote that the reasons that persuaded the court to rule that the First Amendment protected criticism of public officials in a civil libel suit apply with equal force in a criminal libel suit. "The constitutional guarantees of freedom of expression compel application of the same standard to the criminal remedy," he added. The Supreme Court has never answered the question of whether the actual malice rule applies to cases involving the criminal libel of private persons. Nevertheless, this ruling was a potent blow against criminal libel. Most of the state criminal libel laws that still exist fail to meet even the minimum constitutional requirements sent out by the high court in 1966.*

This ruling was a potent blow against criminal libel.

BIBLIOGRAPHY

American Law Institute. *Restatement of the Law of Torts.* 2nd ed. Philadelphia: American Law Institute, 1975.

Dill, Barbara. "Libel Law Doesn't Work, But Can It Be Fixed?" In *At What Price? Libel Law and Freedom of the Press,* by Martin London and Barbara Dill. New York: The Twentieth Century Fund Press, 1993.

Greenhouse, Linda. "For First Time Justices Reject Punitive Award." *The New York Times,* 21 May 1996, A1.

——. "Justices Limit Punitive Damages—Victory for Tort Reform." *The New York Times,* 8 April 2003, A16.

——. "Punitive Damages Must Get a Searching Review on Appeal, Justices Rule." *The New York Times,* 15 May 2001, A18.

98. 384 U.S. 195 (1966).
99. 376 U.S. 254 (1964); see also *Ivey* v. *State,* 29 M.L.R. 2089 (2001).
100. 379 U.S. 64 (1964).

* In 2004 a U.S. District Court in California struck down on First Amendment grounds a state law that made it a crime to make a false accusation against a police officer. This wasn't technically a criminal libel law, but it had many elements common to such laws. *Hamilton* v. *City of San Bernardino,* 32 M.L.R. 2594 (2004). The 9th U.S. Court of Appeals made a similar ruling on this law in 2005. See *Chaker* v. *Crogan,* 33 M.L.R. 2569 (2005). The California Supreme Court had two years earlier upheld the same statute. *People* v. *Stanistreet,* 58 P. 3d 465 (2002).

Gregory, Charles O., and Harry Kalven. *Cases and Materials on Torts.* 2nd ed. Boston: Little, Brown, 1969.

Phelps, Robert, and Douglas Hamilton. *Libel.* New York: Macmillan, 1966.

Pritchard, David. "Rethinking Criminal Libel: An Empirical Study." 14 Communication Law and Policy 3 (2009)

Prosser, William L. *Handbook of the Law of Torts.* St. Paul, Minn.: West Publishing, 1963.

Sanford, Bruce W. *Libel and Privacy.* 2nd ed. Englewood Cliffs, N.J.: Prentice-Hall Law & Business, 1993.

CHAPTER 7

Invasion of Privacy

APPROPRIATION AND INTRUSION

©McGraw-Hill Education/Jill Braaten

Invasion of privacy is a multifaceted concept that is designed to redress a variety of grievances. These include the commercial exploitation of an individual's name or likeness, the intrusion on our private domains, the public revelation of private and embarrassing facts about someone, and the libel-like publication of embarrassing false information about a person. After an initial exploration of the broader dimensions of the right to privacy, we will explore these four discrete legal areas in this chapter and in Chapter 8.

CONCEPTIONS AND SOURCES OF PRIVACY IN THE UNITED STATES

The abstract concept of the right to privacy didn't enter the American ethos until the end of the 19th and beginning of the 20th centuries.

Now, at the end of the second decade of the 21st century, there is little doubt that the privacy that still exists is in jeopardy; partly because of dramatic changes in communication technology, partly because of concerns raised after the 9/11 terrorist attacks and partly because a new generation of Americans, weaned on dozens of exhibitionist reality TV shows, seems more than willing to give away their privacy in exchange for the opportunity to participate in electronic social networking and perhaps achieve 15 minutes of Warholian fame or notoriety.

Privacy is an amorphous concept—what one generation considers private another may not, and what people consider private will vary from time to time, place to place and culture to culture. There are at least three basic conceptions of privacy:

- **Privacy of autonomy:** In this light, privacy means private and personal decision making by an autonomous individual, free from government interference and intrusion. The most controversial niche of this conception of privacy is the right of a woman to choose to have an abortion found in the U.S. Supreme Court's 1973 ruling in *Roe* v. *Wade*. More recently, the Court wrote in *Lawrence* v. *Texas* (see Chapter 1 for more on *Lawrence*) "our laws and tradition afford constitutional protection to *personal decisions* relating to marriage, procreation, contraception, family relationships, child rearing, and education." Put differently, there is a right of decisional privacy possessed by individuals (and sometimes couples and families) that should be free from undue government interference.
- **Privacy of space:** In this traditional conception of privacy, people possess a geographical or physical zone of privacy into which others may not intrude or trespass. Professor Jerry Kang refers to this as an individual's territorial solitude. The notion that a person's home is his or her castle captures the essence of this view. The legal theory described in this chapter called intrusion provides a remedy for violations of one's physical space by means such as trespass or high-tech recording of images and sounds.
- **Privacy of information:** The right of informational privacy—that there are some facts and data about oneself that should not be revealed either to or by others or that you should be able to control what other people do with information about you—is a third conception of privacy. It is particularly relevant today, as companies like Google, Facebook and Yahoo collect massive amounts of information about people—these companies, at heart, are all in the data collection business and they likely possess much information about you—that they sometimes sell to businesses, other individuals and even the government.

What all three of these conceptions of privacy have in common is the notion of control—the ability of individuals to control decisions, physical space and the flow of information. Discussions and debates about privacy thus frequently implicate other concepts such as access, secrecy and anonymity.

What are the sources of privacy law in the United States? There four primary sources of privacy rights:

- **Constitutional law:** At both the federal and state constitution levels, courts recognize privacy rights, either explicitly in the text of the constitutions or implicitly through their language. Although neither the U.S. Constitution nor the amendments to it specifically use the word "privacy," the U.S. Supreme Court has recognized an unenumerated or implied federal constitutional right to privacy residing in multiple amendments. For instance, the Fourth Amendment protects people against unreasonable searches and seizures in their homes, papers and effects, and it generally requires a warrant issued by a judge, upon a showing of probable cause by law enforcement officers, to search such places and items. Viewed in this light, the Fourth Amendment implies privacy in one's home, papers and effects. In addition, the Supreme Court has said that the term "liberty" within the Fourteenth Amendment's Due Process Clause includes certain privacy interests.

  In contrast, the constitutions of at least 10 states specifically include the word "privacy" or "private" in their texts. For instance, Article 1, Section 1 of the California Constitution provides that people have an inalienable right in "pursuing and obtaining safety, happiness and privacy." Article 1, Section 23 of the Florida Constitution, in turn, states that "every natural person has the right to be let alone and free from governmental intrusion into the person's private life except as otherwise provided herein." Hawaii makes it explicit in Article 1, Section 6 of its constitution that "the right of the people to privacy is recognized and shall not be infringed without the showing of a compelling state interest." The right of privacy thus is framed in many different ways in state constitutions.

- **Statutory law:** Many statutes at both the federal and state levels protect privacy interests. For instance, the federal Family Educational Rights and Privacy Act (FERPA) limits public access to student educational records (see Chapters 3 and 9 for more on FERPA), while the federal Health Insurance Portability and Accountability Act (HIPAA) protects the privacy of individually identifiable health information possessed by health-care providers and health plans (see Chapter 9 for more on HIPAA). The federal Children's Online Privacy Protection Act (COPPA) is designed to protect the privacy of children (and their parents) when using the Internet and other modes of digital technology (see Chapter 15 for more on COPPA). States also have statutes that protect privacy interests. In fact, as this chapter later makes clear, several states now have statutes that give heirs the right to control the publicity interests in the names and likenesses of deceased celebrities. In addition, states like Florida have adopted statutory exemptions to their public records laws in order to prevent the public disclosure autopsy images. Such exemptions protect the privacy interests of the deceased's loved ones (see Chapter 9 on "State Statutes That Limit Access to Information").

- **Common law:** This chapter and the one that follows it concentrate on three common law privacy causes of actions (legal theories of recovery): 1) appropriation/right of publicity; 2) intrusion into seclusion; and 3) public disclosure of private facts (also called publication of private information).

These common law privacy theories provide remedies to individuals for certain invasions of their privacy interests. A fourth common law privacy theory called false light is discussed in a more limited fashion in this book because it significantly overlaps with defamation law and because an increasing number of states refuse to recognize its existence. Some states, it should be noted, have adopted statutes that codify all or part of these common law privacy theories.

- **Administrative law:** Increasingly, the Federal Trade Commission (FTC) finds itself playing a front-and-center role as the nation's chief privacy policy maker and enforcer. In 2015, the FTC issued a report called "Internet of Things: Privacy and Security in a Connected World." The report is found at https://www.ftc.gov /system/files/documents/reports/federal-trade-commission-staff-report-november -2013-workshop-entitled-internet-things-privacy/150127iotrpt.pdf. In recent years, the FTC has settled claims against both Facebook, Google and Snapchat regarding alleged misrepresentations and deceptions in their privacy polices (see Chapter 15 for more on this discussion and the FTC's active role in policing privacy on the Internet). Furthermore, the FTC today is concerned about the privacy implications of facial recognition technology used by both the government and private sectors. As this indicates, technology has forced many changes in the way we consider privacy. Any reference in this book a decade ago to facial recognition technology and the FTC's concerns about it would have been unimaginable.

INVASION OF PRIVACY

Mass media have been integrally involved with the growth of the law of privacy, since the vast majority of early lawsuits were aimed at the press in one way or another. Over the past century, state legislatures and courts have fashioned legal rights that permit people who believe they have been injured to sue the mass media for infringing on their rights of privacy. The law is ragged in many ways because it is young and still developing, unlike libel law, which has existed for several centuries. And today, while concerns over the right to privacy range far beyond the behavior of the mass media, it is interesting to note that it was the intrusive newspaper reporting of the late 19th century that is the likely genesis of the law that exists today.

THE GROWTH OF PRIVACY LAWS

It wasn't until the end of the 19th century that the need for a right to privacy became a public issue in the United States. America was rapidly becoming an urban nation. The streets of many cities were clogged with poor immigrants or first-generation Americans. Big city daily newspapers used a variety of sensational schemes to attract these potential readers. Editors often played out the lives of the "rich and famous" on the pages of their newspapers, permitting their readers to vicariously enjoy wealth, status and celebrity.

It was this kind of journalism that pushed two Boston lawyers, Samuel D. Warren and Louis D. Brandeis, to use the pages of the *Harvard Law Review* to propose a legally recognized right to privacy. Warren, the scion of a prominent Boston family, urged his friend (and future Supreme Court justice) Brandeis to help him write the piece,

"The Right to Privacy."[1] The article appeared in 1890 and is the fountain from which the modern law of privacy has flowed.

The pair argued, "Instantaneous photographs and newspaper enterprise have invaded the sacred precincts of private and domestic life; and numerous mechanical devices threaten to make good the prediction that 'what is whispered in the closet shall be proclaimed from the house-tops.'" Warren and Brandeis said they were offended by the gossip in the press, which they said had overstepped in every direction the obvious bounds of propriety and decency:

> To satisfy a prurient taste the details of sexual relations are spread broadcast in the columns of the daily papers. To occupy the indolent, column upon column is filled with idle gossip, which can only be procured by intrusion upon the domestic circle. . . .
>
> The common law has always recognized a man's house as his castle, impregnable, often, even to its own officers engaged in the execution of its commands. Shall the courts thus close the front entrance to constituted authority, and open wide the back door to idle or prurient curiosity?[2]

To stop this illicit behavior, the two lawyers proposed that the courts recognize the legal right of privacy; that is, citizens should be able to go to court to stop such unwarranted intrusions and also secure money damages for the hardship they suffered from such prying and from publication of private material about them.

It was 13 years from the time the Warren and Brandeis article was first published until the first state recognized the law of privacy. The state of New York adopted a law that prohibited the commercial exploitation of an individual and called it a right to privacy. Interestingly, the right this new statute sought to safeguard was not even mentioned in the famous *Harvard Law Review* article.

The law of privacy grew slowly and sporadically over the next century. All but three states today recognize some kind of legal right to privacy. North Dakota has thus far refused to recognize the tort, and there have been no reported privacy cases in either Vermont or Wyoming.[3] Other states have rejected one or more of the four torts that constitute the modern right to privacy.* And until the European Convention on Human Rights became a part of the law in Western Europe, nations like England and France didn't recognize the invasion-of-privacy tort.†

The law of privacy grew slowly and sporadically over the next century.

Privacy law is far more idiosyncratic from state to state than is libel law. In other words, it is somewhat easier to make generalizations about libel law that reflect the law in every state or in most states than it is to make these generalizations about the law of privacy. Part of the problem is that some states have protected the right to privacy through statutes, and these often are very particular. The New York statute, for example, is quite

---

* Several states have rejected the false-light invasion-of-privacy tort, for example, because it is too much like libel. See *Jews for Jesus Inc.* v. *Rapp*, 36 M.L.R. 2540 (2008), for example.
† The Irish government has considered enacting a privacy law that included provisions that mirrored elements in U.S. laws regarding appropriation, intrusion and private facts. See Crampton, "Oops, Did It Again."
1. Warren and Brandeis, "The Right to Privacy," 220.
2. Ibid., 230.
3. Sanford, *Libel and Privacy.*

explicit about how the right to privacy is protected in that state, and some aspects of the law common in most states are not a part of the New York law.

Today the law of privacy encompasses protection for at least four separate legal wrongs. Three of these have absolutely nothing to do with the law as outlined in 1890 by Warren and Brandeis.

FOUR AREAS OF PRIVACY LAW

1. Appropriation of one's name or likeness for trade purposes
2. Intrusion upon an individual's solitude or seclusion
3. Public disclosure of private facts about an individual
4. Publishing material that puts an individual in a false light

---

The first kind of invasion of privacy is called **appropriation** and is defined as taking a person's name, picture, photograph or likeness and using it for commercial gain without permission. Appropriation is technically the only right of privacy guaranteed in some of the states that have privacy statutes. When a celebrity's name or likeness is used without his or her consent, the appropriation is said to affect the celebrity's **right of publicity**. For example, in 2016 Lindsay Lohan sued the video game maker Rockstar Games claiming the fictional character Lacey Jonas from the video game "Grand Theft Auto V" violated Lohan's right of publicity. The laws are limited to outlawing this one kind of behavior. But as a matter of fact, judicial construction of these laws has allowed them to encompass some of the other aspects of invasion of privacy as well.

Intrusion is the second type of invasion of privacy, an area of the law growing rapidly today, and is what most people think of when invasion of privacy is mentioned. Intrusion upon the solitude and into the private life of a person is prohibited. As discussed later in this chapter, the use of drones raises serious concerns about intrusion.

The third arm of the law prohibits **publication of private information**—truthful private information—about a person. What is truthful private information? Gossip, substance of private conversations and details of a private tragedy or illness have all been used as the basis of a suit. And in 2016, wrestler Hulk Hogan won a jury verdict of more than $100 million based upon Gawker's publication of a hidden-camera sex tape featuring Hogan (see Chapter 8 for more on this case).

Finally, the publication of material that places a person in a **false light** is the fourth category of the law of privacy. This category is an outgrowth of the first area of the law, appropriation, and doesn't at first glance seem like an invasion of privacy at all, but it is regarded as such by the law. Because false light overlaps significantly with libel and because a growing number of states don't look favorably upon the false-light category of privacy, it is given less space in this edition of the book than the other three areas.

The tremendous growth of communication via interactive computer systems (i.e., the Internet) has generated substantial challenges in the application of the law of privacy. The relative ease of access and use of these systems has resulted in numerous privacy problems. In March 2012, the Federal Trade Commission issued a report called "Protecting Consumer Privacy in an Era of Rapid Change: Recommendations for Business and Policy Makers." It provides a framework of recommendations and best practices for all commercial entities that collect or use consumer data that can be reasonably linked to a specific consumer, computer or other device, unless the entity collects only nonsensitive data from fewer than 5,000 consumers per year and does not share the data with third parties. Several federal laws already address some aspects of privacy, such as the Health Insurance Portability and Accountability Act (see Chapter 9). The FTC report provides that "the framework is meant to encourage best practices and is not intended to conflict with requirements of existing laws and regulations. To the extent that components of the framework exceed, but do not conflict with existing statutory requirements, entities covered by those statutes should view the framework as best practices to promote consumer privacy." A copy of the report is available at http://ftc.gov/os/2012/03/120326privacyreport.pdf.

Among the highlights is a principle called "Privacy by Design," under which the FTC calls for companies to incorporate privacy protections into their practices, such as data security, reasonable collection limits, sound retention and disposal practices and data accuracy. Other key principles are:

- **Simplified Choice for Businesses and Consumers:** Companies should give consumers the option to decide what information is shared about them, and with whom. This includes a "Do-Not-Track" mechanism that would provide a simple way for consumers to control the tracking of their online activities.
- **Greater Transparency:** Companies should disclose details about their collection and use of consumers' information, and provide consumers access to the data collected about them.

Although merely recommendations, the FTC report called on Congress to consider enacting baseline privacy legislation and it reiterated an earlier call for data security and data broker legislation. The bottom line for now is that if self-regulatory efforts continue to flounder and fail, we can expect a large wave of federal privacy statutes in the near future.

A few caveats or warnings are appropriate before each of the four aspects of privacy law is detailed. First, only people enjoy protection for their right to privacy. Corporations, labor unions, associations and so forth can protect their reputations through libel law, but they do not have a right to privacy.* (Other laws protect businesses against unfair commercial exploitation.)

The right to privacy is most easily understood if each of the four areas of the law is considered as a discrete unit. Don't try to apply the defenses that may be applicable in appropriation to publication of private information. They don't work.

---

* The Supreme Court of the United States ruled in 2011 that corporations do not enjoy a right of privacy. This case stems from the personal privacy exemption in the federal Freedom of Information Act (see Chapter 9) and does not relate directly to other statutes and common law privacy rights. AT&T attempted to invoke the privacy exemption to block the release of documents it provided to the Federal Communications Commission, documents sought by one of the company's competitors. *Federal Communications Commission* v. *AT&T*, 131 S. Ct. 1177 (2011), and Liptak, "Court Weighs Whether Corporations."

There is much about the law of privacy that defies logic. Why is putting someone in a false light considered an invasion of privacy, for example? Challenging the logic of the law serves little purpose and usually makes learning the law more difficult.

The law of privacy is young—about 128 years old if you start with the Warren and Brandeis proposal. There are a lot of legal questions that haven't been answered, or at least answered satisfactorily. Bad court decisions are abundant. With these warnings in mind, let's now turn to the privacy torts, starting with appropriation.

APPROPRIATION

It is illegal to use an individual's name or likeness for commercial or trade purposes without consent.

Appropriation is the oldest of the four privacy torts. Until recently it was the most comprehensible. Appropriation protects an individual's name or likeness from commercial exploitation. Two of the earliest privacy cases on record are good examples of how the appropriation tort is supposed to protect an individual from commercial exploitation. In 1902 young Abigail Roberson of Albany, N.Y., awoke one morning to find her picture all over town on posters advertising Franklin Mills Flour. Twenty-five thousand copies of the advertisement had been placed in stores, warehouses, saloons and other public places. Roberson said she felt embarrassed and humiliated, that she suffered greatly from this commercial exploitation and she therefore sued for invasion of privacy. But she lost her case, and the state's high court ruled that

> an examination of the authorities leads us to the conclusion that the so-called "right of privacy" has not yet found an abiding place in our jurisprudence, and, as we view it, the doctrine cannot now be incorporated without doing violence to settled principles of law by which the profession and the public have long been guided.[4]

Following this decision a great controversy arose in New York, led by newspapers and magazines, many of whom expressed outrage at the way the court had treated Roberson. The controversy settled on the state legislature, which during the following year, 1903, adopted the nation's first privacy law. The statute was very narrow; that is, it prohibited a very specific kind of conduct. Use of an individual's name or likeness without the individual's consent for advertising or trade purposes was made a minor crime. In addition to the criminal penalty, the statute allowed the injured party to seek both an injunction to stop the use of the name or picture and money damages.

Two years later Georgia became the first state to recognize the right of privacy through the common law. Paolo Pavesich, an Atlanta artist, discovered that a life insurance company had used his photograph in newspaper advertisements. Pavesich's photograph was used in a before-and-after advertisement to illustrate a contented, successful man who had bought sufficient life insurance. A testimonial statement was also ascribed

---

4. *Roberson v. Rochester Folding Box Co.,* 171 N.Y. 538 (1902).

to the artist. He sued for $25,000 and won his case before the Georgia Supreme Court, which ruled that

> the form and features of the plaintiff are his own. The defendant insurance company and its agents had no more authority to display them in public for the purpose of advertising the business . . . than they would have had to compel the plaintiff to place himself upon exhibition for this purpose.[5]

RIGHT OF PUBLICITY

The appropriation tort actually encompasses two slightly different legal causes of action. One is the right to privacy; the other is called the **right of publicity.** The differences between these two sound legalistic, but they are actually quite important.

- Traditionally, the right-to-privacy dimension of appropriation was designed to protect an individual from the *emotional damage* that can occur when a name or likeness is used for a commercial or trade purpose. Imagine how embarrassed Abigail Roberson felt the morning she awoke to find her picture on all those advertising posters. The right to publicity, on the other hand, is an attempt to remunerate individuals for the *economic harm* suffered when their name or picture is used for advertising or trade purposes, and they are not compensated for it. The proposition is a simple one: An individual's name or likeness has economic value, and using it without permission is akin to theft. But the difference between emotional harm and economic harm is sometimes easier to state than to apply.[6]
- The second distinction between the right of privacy and the right of publicity often helps resolve this question. Because the right of publicity protects a property right—the economic value in a name or likeness— normally only someone whose name or likeness has a commercial value can successfully allege a violation of his or her right of publicity. An average person—Jane Doe, for example—would likely be embarrassed to find her picture on a box of Wheaties. But it would be extremely difficult for Doe to argue in court that General Mills was actually promoting its cereal this way because kids all over America want to eat what Jane Doe eats. But kids may want to eat the same cereal that basketball player LeBron James or swimmer Michael Phelps eat. The names and pictures of these professional athletes have commercial value and would enhance the value of the cereal (or the cereal box) in the eyes of consumers. Simply put, only well-known people have a legally recognized economic value in their names or likenesses, and except in unusual cases, they are the only ones who can sue for damage to their right to publicity. The average person can only assert emotional damage in a right of privacy suit.

---

5. *Pavesich* v. *New England Mutual Life Insurance Co.,* 122 Ga. 190 (1905).
6. See *Villalovos* v. *Sundance Associates Inc.,* 31 M.L.R. 1274 (2003), for example.

■ Finally, something that has an economic value, like a house or a painting or a ring, can usually be passed on to an heir when the owner dies. Something of emotional value, like a reputation or mental health, is gone when its owner passes on. Consequently, it is possible in some states for a celebrity, sports star or some other well-known person who has died to pass on the property right in his or her name to his or her heirs. The heirs can sue for violation of the deceased's right to publicity. Lawyers say that the right of publicity is descendible. For the rest of the people, their right to privacy dies when they do.

LOHAN LEGALLY MAULED BY PITBULL? NAME-CHECKING ALONE IS NOT APPROPRIATION

The rapper Pitbull (Armando Christian Perez for those less canine inclined) includes a lyric in the 2011 hit song "Give Me Everything" that goes: *"So, I'm tiptoein' to keep flowin'/ I got it locked up like Lindsay Lohan."* Apparently no fan of Pitbull (although supposedly a big one of Red Bull), the trouble-plagued actress sued the rapper. She alleged that she did not consent to or authorize the use of her name in the song and that the use of her name thus constituted appropriation.

In February 2013, however, a federal judge in New York granted Pitbull's motion to dismiss Lohan's lawsuit. Specifically, Judge Denis R. Hurley wrote that under New York's misappropriation statute, "the use of an individual's name—even without his consent—is not prohibited . . . if that use is part of a work of art." Songs, in turn, are works of art protected by the First Amendment. Furthermore, Judge Hurley reasoned that "the fact that the song was presumably created and distributed for the purpose of making a profit does not mean that plaintiff's name was used for 'advertising' or 'purposes of trade' within the meaning" of New York's misappropriation statute. Additionally, the judge noted that the use was merely incidental, as Lohan's "name is mentioned one time in only one of 104 lines of the song." For all of these reasons, Lohan's lawsuit was easily dismissed; she was barking up the wrong legal tree.

While the legal right to privacy is about 128 years old, the notion of a right to publicity is far younger.[7] And it really has only been in the past three decades that right to publicity litigation has accelerated. There are two reasons for this. The first is the tremendous growth of the cult of celebrity in the United States and the world. Stories and pictures about entertainers, musicians, sports personalities and others overflow in the traditional mass media and online. Entire publications, television shows and Web sites are devoted to them. Second, American businesses and other organizations have seen this trend and now decorate their products, ads, promotions and so on with the likenesses and names of these celebrities. And many of these individuals believe they should be compensated

---

7. *Haelan Laboratories, Inc. v. Topps Chewing Gum,* 202 F. 2d 866 (1953).

for these uses. For example, many college athletes have brought actions against the video game maker Electronic Arts which has used their likenesses, names and other personal data without permission or payment.

AN AD IS AN AD . . . EVEN WHEN IT OFFERS CONGRATULATIONS TO MICHAEL JORDAN

In 2015, basketball legend Michael Jordan settled a lawsuit against two Chicago-area supermarket chains, Jewel Food Stores Inc. and the now-defunct Dominick's Finer Foods LLC, based on the unauthorized use of the basketball legend's likeness in a 2009 special edition of *Sports Illustrated*. The settlement followed an August 2015 trial in which Jordan won an $8.9 million jury verdict from Dominick's. The Jewel case never went to trial. While the terms of the agreement were confidential, Jordan's team was reported to be pleased with the deal.

In 2010, Jordan, widely considered the greatest basketball player of all time, sued Safeway Inc., the parent company of Jewel Food Stores, and the now-defunct Dominick's, contending the companies used his likeness without his permission to tout their brands in a special issue of *Sports Illustrated* that commemorated Jordan's entrance into the NBA Hall of Fame. Jordan argued the two chains used his name in violation of the Illinois Right of Publicity Act, the Lanham Act, the Illinois Consumer Fraud and Deceptive Trade Practices Act and the common law tort of unfair competition.

The Dominick's full-page ad featured a coupon for the chain's "Rancher's Reserve" steak below the words "Michael Jordan . . . you are a cut above" and displayed the grocer's trademarked logo and slogan colored in the Chicago Bulls' signature red, black and white.

The Jewel ad was placed on the inside back cover of the same issue and, while it offered no promotion, included a picture of the Jewel Osco logo and a nod to Jordan that played off the supermarket's logo "good things are just around the corner." The ad read, "Jewel-Osco salutes #23 on his many accomplishments as we honor a fellow Chicagoan who was 'just around the corner' for so many years."

Today there are probably as many right-to-publicity cases being litigated as right-to-privacy lawsuits. In the following discussion of the appropriation tort, the two—right of publicity and right of privacy—will be intermingled. The law is basically the same; only the damage asserted by the plaintiff in the lawsuit is different.

USE OF NAME OR LIKENESS

Courts have spent considerable time attempting to define what is or is not an illegal use of a name or likeness. In the 1970s and 1980s, most courts seemed to take a very expansive view of the concept of use. But beginning in the 1990s, some appellate courts began to narrow this definition. A summary of cases will illustrate this trend.

Everybody knows what a name is, and it is therefore unnecessary to dwell on that term. It should be noted, however, that stage names, pen names, pseudonyms and so forth count the same as real names in the eyes of the law. For example, if the name of singer Lady Gaga is used by a wig company in advertisements for its wigs without her consent, the wig company cannot successfully defend against Lady Gaga's right of publicity lawsuit because her real name is Stefani Joanne Angelina Germanotta. Only the names of people are protected under appropriation. The names of businesses, corporations, schools and other "things" are not protected under the law. However, the use of a trade name like Kodak or Crest can create other serious legal problems (see Chapter 14).

What is a likeness? A photograph of an individual is obviously a likeness. But the photo doesn't have to be a facial shot.[8] A New York court ruled it was up to a jury to decide if a photograph in a cosmetics advertisement of the back of a woman bathing in a stream could be identified as a likeness of the plaintiff, who had been secretly photographed.[9] On the other hand, another New York court ruled in 2011 that a physical fitness company called Pure Power Boot Camp did not violate the publicity rights of two of its former drill instructors when it used their images in an advertisement for Pure Power. Why? Because their backs were turned to the camera and thus they were not recognizable. As the court noted, there must be a "clear representation" of "identifying features" such that the individuals would be "recognizable from the advertisement itself."[10] A likeness can also be a sketch or a drawing.[11]

Protecting a voice might also be encompassed in a law protecting a name or likeness. In 2008 the 3rd U.S. Court of Appeals refused to dismiss a lawsuit by the son of John Facenda who sued N.F.L. Films for using his father's distinctive baritone voice in a commercial vehicle promoting the release of the video game "Madden N.F.L. 06." For years Facenda had been the voice of N.F.L. Films, a popular series of video summaries of the National Football League games. But he had never agreed to have his voice used in a commercial for the video game. The defendants used 13 seconds of his commentary from the N.F.L. Films series in the promotional TV video to underscore the degree to which the Madden video game authentically re-created the N.F.L. experience. The court said Facenda's voice had commercial value, that the N.F.L. used it for commercial purposes and that he had never consented to such a use. The case would have to go to trial.[12]

Celebrities have argued—with some success—that the protection of their likeness extends to depictions of characters they played in movies or on television. An actor named George McFarland, who as a child in the 1930s played a character called Spanky in a series of short comedies known as the "Our Gang" comedies (and later as "The Little Rascals" when they were shown on television), sued the owner of a restaurant called Spanky McFarland's. The eating establishment was filled with memorabilia from the film series. A federal appeals court ruled that it was clearly a triable issue of fact as to whether the actor had become so identified with the character that the use of the name

---

8. *Yasin* v. *Q-Boro Holdings LLC*, 38 M.L.R. 1733 (2010).
9. *Cohen* v. *Herbal Concepts*, 473 N.Y.S. 2d 426 (1989).
10. *Pure Power Fitness Camp* v. *Warrior Fitness Boot Camp*, 813 F. Supp. 2d 489 (S.D.N.Y. 2011).
11. *Ali* v. *Playgirl*, 447 F. Supp. 723 (1978).
12. *Facenda* v. *N.F.L. Films*, 36 M.L.R. 2473 (2008). The case was settled in 2009.

in a commercial venture would invoke McFarland's own image.[13] The 9th U.S. Court of Appeals reached the same conclusion when George Wendt and John Ratzenberger sued a restaurant chain for installing animatronic robots that looked like Norm Peterson and Cliff Clavin, characters played by Wendt and Ratzenberger on the long-running TV series "Cheers." The court said a performer does not lose the right to control the commercial exploitation of his or her likeness merely by portraying a fictional character in a motion picture or television series.[14] In 2009 Woody Allen agreed to a $5 million settlement in his lawsuit against American Apparel, a trendy clothing company known for its racy advertising. The apparel company used a frame from the film "Annie Hall," which depicted Allen as a Hasidic Jew, on billboards in Los Angeles and New York, and on its Web site. Allen had sought a $10 million judgment. But not all courts have followed this path. In 2008, a federal court in New York ruled that the state statute did not "extend to fictitious characters adopted or created by celebrities."[15]

"LACEY JONAS?" OR LINDSAY LOHAN?

Actress Lindsay Lohan has sued for appropriation more than once. In 2014, Lohan sued video game maker Rockstar Games and distributor Take Two Interactive over a character featured in the video game "Grand Theft Auto V." Lohan's lawsuit claimed that the character, Lacey Jonas, was based off a photograph of her taken in 2007. Despite prominent placement in the game's marketing, Jonas is a minor character in the game itself. Players in the game are tasked with enduring Jonas, a vain, vapid, demanding and self-indulgent actress, while attempting to outrun paparazzi. Lohan claimed the character, combined with cover art and promotional material, constituted an "unequivocal" use of her likeness without her permission.

The defendants initially responded by asking a court to dismiss the case, stating the lawsuit was a "legally meritless" publicity stunt and noting that Lohan had filed frivolous lawsuits in the past (such as when she attempted to sue rapper Pitbull over his lyrics, discussed earlier in this chapter). Lohan responded by filing a more detailed version of the lawsuit. The court allowed the lawsuit to move forward, ruling that Lohan's statement showed enough evidence that her right to publicity had been violated and that Rockstar did not provide sufficient evidence to prove that the character was not based on Lohan.

Eventually, however, a five-judge panel in the Manhattan Appellate Division ruled that the lawsuit was without merit. Even if Rockstar found inspiration in Lohan, the court reasoned, the "video game's unique story, characters, dialogue, and environment, combined with the player's ability to choose how to proceed in the game," rendered it a work of fiction and satire. That is, the court ruled that even if the in-game character constituted a representation of Lohan, the video game did not fall under the statutory definitions of "advertising" or "trade."

---

13. *McFarland* v. *Miller,* 14 F. 3d 912 (1994).
14. *Wendt* v. *Host International,* 125 F. 3d 800 (1997).
15. *Burck d/b/a The Naked Cowboy* v. *Mars., Inc.,* No. 08 Cir. 1330 (S.D.N.Y., June 23, 2008).

©Michael Tran/FilmMagic/Getty Images   ©Galvin Rodgers/Alamy Stock Photos

"Actress Lindsay Lohan sued the makers and distributors of Grand Theft Auto V for using her 'likeness' without permission."

Other celebrities have argued—again, sometimes successfully—that their right to publicity was violated when a business used someone who looked like or sounded like the celebrity in its advertisements. In August 2012, Old Navy reached a settlement for an undisclosed amount with Kim Kardashian over a TV commercial called "Super C-U-T-E." It featured a Kardashian lookalike named Melissa Molinaro singing while shopping her way down the aisles of an Old Navy store. Kardashian sued for millions, claiming Old Navy and its owner, The Gap, had violated her right of publicity. The complaint alleged that the ad featuring Molinaro "falsely represent[s] that Kim Kardashian sponsors, endorses, or is associated with" Old Navy and that the ad was purposefully "designed and intended to confuse, to cause mistake, and to deceive the public into believing" Kardashian appeared in it. Do your own online search for side-by-side images of Kardashian and Molinaro (perhaps best known for her stellar performance in the 2012 motion picture "Jersey Shore Shark Attack") to determine if there is a confusing resemblance.[16]

Bette Midler successfully sued the Ford Motor Company when it hired a singer who sounded almost exactly like Midler to sing one of Midler's hit songs for a soundtrack in a television advertisement. A federal appeals court ruled, "The singer manifests herself in the song. To impersonate her voice is to pirate her identity." Not every voice impersonation would necessarily be actionable, the court said. But when the distinctive voice of a widely known professional singer is deliberately imitated, this can amount to an appropriation.[17] Other performers have filed similar actions against advertisers. Will a

16. Mangan, "Lawsuit Settled Over Look-Alike."
17. *Midler* v. *Ford Motor Co.*, 849 F. 2d 460 (1988).

disclaimer protect an advertiser from an appropriation suit when a look-alike model or sound-alike singer is used? Yes, if the disclaimer is prominent. Small type at the bottom of a full-page ad will not do the trick; nor will an audio disclaimer camouflaged by music or noise in a radio or television spot.

A high-water mark (or low-water mark, depending on your point of view) in the battle by celebrities against advertisers came in 1992 when television personality Vanna White successfully sued electronics manufacturer Samsung when it published a newspaper and magazine advertisement that depicted a robot, reminiscent of C3PO of "Star Wars" fame, wearing a blond wig, evening dress and jewelry, standing next to a video board similar to the one used on "Wheel of Fortune." The ad was supposedly saying that Samsung electronic products would still be state of the art long after White had been replaced by an android. A federal court ruled that this photo was a use of White's image, and constituted an actionable appropriation.[18]

The tide favoring celebrities seems to have turned somewhat in the wake of the *White* ruling, which was widely criticized. In some important cases defense attorneys were successful in raising First Amendment issues and the courts were asked to balance the protection for freedom of expression with the protection of a celebrity's image. The 10th U.S. Court of Appeals blocked an attempt by the Major League Players Association to stop the distribution of a set of satirical baseball cards that made fun of many well-known players. The court said even though the cards used caricatures of the players, and the sale of the items was a commercial enterprise, the cards were parodies or social commentary protected by the First Amendment. "While not core political speech . . . this type of commentary on an important social institution constitutes protected expression," the court said.[19] More recently a federal court ruled that the use of Major League baseball players' names in online fantasy baseball leagues did not amount to making commercial use of a player's identity.[20]

In an important ruling in 2001 the California Supreme Court fashioned a useful test for determining when the use of a celebrity's likeness constitutes an infringement on the right of publicity, and when it is protected free expression. The test, which is known as the transformative use test, has been cited favorably by other courts.

An artist named Gary Saderup created a charcoal drawing of the Three Stooges comedy team. Making a single drawing is not a problem since the law exempts single and original works of fine art from the purview of the California statute. But Saderup went on to create lithographic prints and T-shirts that also contained the drawing and was sued by Comedy III Inc., a company that owns the rights to the Stooges. Justices on the California high court noted immediately the First Amendment implications in the issue. "Because celebrities take on public meaning, the appropriation of their likenesses may have important uses in uninhibited debate on public issues, particularly debates about culture and values," the court noted. The creative appropriation of celebrity images can

The creative appropriation of celebrity images can be an important avenue of individual expression.

18. *White* v. *Samsung Electronics America, Inc.,* 971 F. 2d 1395 (1992); rehearing den. 989 F. 2d 1512 (1992).
19. *Cardtoons* v. *Major League Baseball Players Association,* 95 F. 3d 959 (1996).
20. *C.B.C. Distribution and Marketing Inc.* v. *Major League Baseball Advanced Media L.P.,* 34 M.L.R. 2287 (2006). The Supreme Court refused to hear an appeal of this ruling. U.S. No. 07-1099 (2008).

be an important avenue of individual expression, the justices added. The importance of celebrities in society means that the right to publicity has the potential of censoring significant expression by suppressing alternative versions of celebrity images that are "iconoclastic, irrelevant, or otherwise attempt to redefine the celebrity's image." There must be a test, then, that takes these values into account, the justices went on. The court focused on what it called the transformative elements in the reproduction. If the reproduction is simply a literal translation of the celebrity's image, then the First Amendment concerns are surely minimal. But it is a different matter if the user has added other elements to the image, has significantly transformed the image into a parody, used the name in a song, lampooned the prominent person, or in some way used the celebrity's likeness as a vehicle for the expression of opinion or ideas. Then the rights of free expression take precedence over the right of the celebrity to protect his or her right to publicity. As noted above, this rule from the Three Stooges case is frequently known as the transformative use test. In this case, the court said, Saderup used a literal depiction of the Stooges for commercial gain without adding significant expression beyond his trespass on the right to publicity. He was held liable for violating the publicity rights of Comedy III Productions.[21]

In 2016, the 9th U.S. Circuit Court of Appeals rejected a First Amendment defense to right of publicity claims in a case involving the video game Madden NFL made by Electronic Arts. Released annually, every updated version of the Madden NFL video game series includes all current players for all 32 NFL teams, along with player names, team logos, colors and uniforms. Electronic Arts paid National Football Players Inc., the licensing arm of the National Football League Players Association, annual licensing fees in millions of dollars to use current players' likenesses. From 2001 through 2009, however, the annual version of Madden NFL also included popular "historic teams." Electronic Arts did not obtain a license to use the likenesses of the former players on these teams. Although the players on the historic teams were not identified by name or photograph, each was described by his position, years in the NFL, height, weight, skin tone and relative skill level in different aspects of the sport. Some of the former players on these teams sued Electronic Arts under California statutory and common law. Electronic Arts claimed its use of the former players' likeness was protected under the transformative use defense formulated by the California Supreme Court in *Comedy III Productions*. The 9th Circuit, however, ruled that the video game was not transformative. "Madden NFL replicates players' physical characteristics and allows users to manipulate them in the performance of the same activity for which they are known in real-life—playing football for an NFL team. Neither the individual players' likenesses nor the graphics and other background content are transformed," wrote the court.[22] In March 2016, the U.S. Supreme Court denied Electronic Arts' petition for a writ of certiorari.

21. *Comedy III Inc. v. Gary Saderup Inc.,* 21 P. 3d 797 (2001). The Supreme Court of the United States refused to hear an appeal of this ruling. See also *Kirby* v. *Sega of America Inc.,* 50 Cal. Rptr. 3d 607 (2006), where the California Court of Appeals used the transformative test to reject the claim of a woman who argued her likeness had been appropriated in a video game.
22. *Davis* v. *Electronic Arts,* 775 F. 3d 1172 (9th Cir. 2015).

THE HURT LOCKER OF APPROPRIATION?
A TRANSFORMATIVE MOVIE CHARACTER

"The Hurt Locker" won six Academy Awards, including best picture, in March 2010. The movie, about an elite U.S. Army bomb squad doing dangerous duty in Iraq, also spawned a lawsuit. Jeffrey Sarver, who served in Iraq as an explosive ordinance disposal technician, claimed that a central character (staff sergeant Will James) in the movie was based upon his life. He sued in *Sarver* v. *Hurt Locker, LLC* for misappropriation/right of publicity, alleging his identity and likeness were used without his consent to make "The Hurt Locker." Indeed, the movie's screenwriter, Mark Boal, was embedded with Sarver's unit in 2004 while Boal was gathering information for an article that appeared in *Playboy*. Boal also interviewed Sarver on several occasions after Sarver returned to the United States.

In 2016, the 9th U.S. Circuit Court of Appeals held that Sarver could not sue for appropriation for several reasons. First, the court noted that "The Hurt Locker" was not a commercial use. Therefore, it did not receive less First Amendment protection. Second, Sarver did not make the investment required to produce a performance of interest to the public or invest time and money to build up economic value in a marketable performance or identity. The court ruled while Sarver's story was of public interest, Sarver had not sought to attract public attention to himself. The movie that brought Sarver's story to life did not steal Sarver's "entire act" or otherwise exploit the economic value of any performance or persona he had worked to develop. Instead, the movie's writers used Sarver's life to inspire their work. The court concluded, "In sum, 'The Hurt Locker' is speech that is fully protected by the First Amendment, which safeguards the storytellers and artists who take the raw materials of life—including the stories of real individuals, ordinary or extraordinary—and transform them into art, be it articles, books, movies, or plays."[23]

The 6th U.S. Court of Appeals, citing both the *Cardtoons* and *Saderup* decisions, ruled in 2003 that artist Rick Rush did not violate Tiger Woods' right to publicity when he painted a picture of the golfer commemorating his 1997 Master's golf tournament victory. The picture featured Woods in the foreground and six other golfing greats in the background. Rush produced 250 limited edition serigraphs, which he sold for $700 each, and 5,000 smaller lithographs, which were priced at $15 each. He was sued by ETW Corporation, which holds the exclusive marketing rights to Woods, for trademark infringement and violation of the golfer's right to publicity. (The court held a person's image or likeness cannot function as a trademark. See Chapter 14 for more on trademark law.) As for the right to publicity, the court said Rush's work was creative and transformative, and this made it worthy of First Amendment protection. The substantial creative content in the work outweighed any adverse effect on ETW's market.[24]

23. *Sarver* v. *Chartier,* 813 F. 3d. 891 (9th Cir. 2016).
24. *ETW Corp.* v. *Jireh Publishing Inc.,* 332 F. 3d 915 (2003). See also Chambers, "Case of Art, Icons and Law."

©Hulton Archives/Getty Images

An important *contrary* ruling involving a celebrity since the *Saderup* case was a decision in the summer of 2006 by the Missouri Court of Appeals upholding a $15 million verdict against comic book artist Todd McFarlane. McFarlane created a Spawn comic book character named Anthony Twistelli in 1992. McFarlane changed the name of the character to Tony Twist and later told fans the character was modeled after National Hockey League player Tony Twist. Twist sued for appropriation. After nearly 10 years of litigation the appellate court rejected free speech arguments and adopted what it called a "predominant-use" test. Speech with a predominant artistic purpose is protected, while

---

COLLEGE FOOTBALL VIDEO GAMES: FORMER PLAYERS SUCCESSFULLY SUED ELECTRONIC ARTS FOR VIOLATING THEIR RIGHT OF PUBLICITY

Electronic Arts once produced a video game series called "NCAA Football." These games were popular for their realism and detail, including the use of more than 100 "virtual teams" that used real college's names, uniforms, fight songs and mascots. The virtual players, in turn, closely resembled real-life players and shared their vital and biographical information.

Former Rutgers quarterback Ryan Hart sued Electronic Arts, alleging the use of his likeness and biographical information in "NCAA Football" violated his right of publicity. Electronic Arts countered that video games are a form of speech protected by the First Amendment and that the "NCAA Football" series is artistic expression.

In 2013, the 3rd U.S. Circuit Court of Appeals ruled in *Hart* v. *Electronic Arts*[25] that the transformative use test developed in the Three Stooges case of *Saderup* (described earlier in this section) was the proper test to balance Hart's right of publicity interest against Electronic Art's interest in freedom of expression. In explaining this test, the appellate court noted that a mere literal depiction of a celebrity re-created in a different medium is not a transformative use. On the other hand, a transformative use alters the meaning behind the use of a celebrity's likeness, perhaps by lampooning, adding social commentary or placing the celebrity in a fanciful and imaginative setting.

Applying the transformative use test to the facts of *Hart*, the appellate court wrote that the issue was whether real-life quarterback Ryan Hart's identity was sufficiently transformed in the "NCAA Football" video games. Hart's "identity," the court explained, encompassed not only his visual likeness, but also his biographical data.

The court then examined the content of the video games. It determined that Hart's "avatar does closely resemble the genuine article. Not only does the digital avatar match [Hart] in terms of hair color, hair style and skin tone, but the avatar's accessories mimic those worn by [Hart] during his time as a Rutgers player. The information . . . also accurately tracks [Hart's] vital and biographical details."

Next, the court examined a critical factor—the context in which Hart's identity was used—to determine if the use was transformative. In ruling for Hart and against Electronic Arts, the court wrote that "the digital Ryan Hart does what the actual Ryan Hart did while at Rutgers: he plays college football, in digital re-creations of college football stadiums, filled with all the trappings of a college football game. This is not transformative; the various digitized sights and sounds in the video game do not alter or transform the Appellant's identity in a significant way."

The court also rejected Electronic Arts' argument that a video game player's ability to alter the avatar's appearance makes the use transformative. "Given that Hart's unaltered likeness is central to the core of the game experience, we are disinclined to credit users' ability to alter the digital avatars in our application of the transformative use test to this case," the court wrote.

The 9th U.S. Circuit Court of Appeals reached a very similar conclusion in 2013 in favor of another former college football player in *Keller* v. *Electronic Arts*. The 9th Circuit also applied the transformative use test from *Saderup*, and it found that Electronic Arts' use of former Arizona State quarterback Sam Keller's image and biographical information was not transformative. In brief, two different federal appellate courts—the 3rd and 9th Circuits—in 2013 ruled for the college players and against Electronic Arts.

In September 2013, shortly after both rulings against it in *Hart* and *Keller*, Electronic Arts announced it would stop producing the NCAA Football video game series. In 2014, Electronic Arts submitted for judicial approval a whopping $40 million settlement with the class-action plaintiffs in both *Hart* and *Keller*, along with a third case involving former UCLA basketball player Ed O'Bannon that stemmed from a college basketball video game. The settlement was approved in 2015 by a federal judge in California.

And what about the NCAA? In 2014, it paid $20 million to the plaintiffs to settle the lawsuits.

25. 717 F. 3d 141 (3d Cir. 2013).

speech with a predominant commercial purpose is not. This is a highly subjective test that had never been used by another court. The burden falls on the judge to decide what is art and what is commerce. McFarlane argued that when he first used Twist's name, he was a relatively unknown player in Canada, and therefore use of the name had no commercial benefit. The court disagreed. It was enough that McFarlane intended to create the impression that the hockey player was associated with the comic book, the court said.[26]

It's important to note that similar issues of transformative use and parody arise in copyright cases (see Chapter 14). In fact, the transformative use test fashioned in *Saderup* is largely borrowed from fair use considerations in copyright law. For instance, the 7th U.S. Circuit Court of Appeals in 2012 in *Brownmark Films* v. *Comedy Partners*[27] considered whether a "South Park" parody of a real-world viral video called "What What (In The Butt)" violated the copyright interests of the owner of that video. As the appellate court colorfully wrote, "the 'South Park' version re-creates a large portion of the original version, using the same angles, framing, dance moves and visual elements. However, the 'South Park' version stars Butters, a naïve nine-year old, in a variety of costumes drawing attention to his innocence: at various points he is dressed as a teddy bear, an astronaut and a daisy." In ruling in favor of "South Park," the court noted that the underlying purpose of the "South Park" version of the video "was to comment on and critique the social phenomenon that is the 'viral video.'" The court added that the "South Park" video "imitates viral video creation while lampooning one particularly well-known example of such a video" and that "this kind of parodic use has *obvious transformative value* [emphasis added]."

ADVERTISING AND TRADE PURPOSES

What are advertising and trade purposes? While minor differences exist among the states—especially among the states with statutes—a general guideline can be set down: Advertising or trade purposes are commercial uses; that is, someone makes money from the use. Here are examples of the kinds of actions that may be regarded as a commercial use:

1. **Use of a person's name or photograph in an *advertisement* on television, on radio, in newspapers, in magazines, on the Internet, on posters, on billboards and so forth. Rapper 50 Cent sued a Philadelphia car dealer for $1 million in 2005 for using his name in an ad for a Dodge Magnum. The ads used the slogan, "Just Like 50 Says."**

2. **Display of a person's photograph in the window of a photographer's shop to show potential customers the quality of work done by the studio.**

3. **A testimonial falsely suggesting that an individual eats the cereal or drives the automobile in question.**

4. **Use of an individual's name or likeness in a banner ad or some other commercial message on a Web site.**

5. **The use of someone's likeness or identity in a commercial entertainment vehicle like a feature film, a television situation comedy or a novel.**

26. *Doe* v. *McFarlane*, 34 M.L.R. 2057 (2006).
27. 682 F.3d 687 (7th Cir. 2012).

A 2013 decision by the Supreme Court of Georgia in *Bullard* v. *MRA Holding, LLC,* illustrates well the first of these categories. The case centered on Lindsey Bullard, who claimed the use of her photo on a box cover for a "Girls Gone Wild" video constituted misappropriation of her likeness. Back in 2000, when Bullard was just age 14 and a middle schooler, she exposed her breasts during spring break to two unknown men in a parking lot in Panama City, Fla. Although aware the men were taping her, Bullard did not know what future use they might make of the video. Ultimately, the video was sold to MRA Holding, which markets "Girls Gone Wild." A still photo of Bullard flashing was taken from the video and put on the box cover. MRA Holding blocked out Bullard's breasts and superimposed the inscription "Get Educated!" in that space. This image also appeared in TV commercials and Internet ads.

In ruling for Bullard, Georgia's high court wrote that "under the facts of this case, Bullard can be seen as endorsing the 'College Girls Gone Wild' video through the use of her image." The court rejected the notion that Bullard's consent to be videotaped amounted to consent for MRA Holding to use her image on the box cover. "The men to whom Bullard exposed her breasts never indicated to Bullard that they worked for, had any connection with, or had any intention of giving Bullard's image to, MRA for the purpose of selling 'College Girls Gone Wild' videos. Nor did Bullard have any contact with MRA to give MRA permission to use her image for that purpose," the court reasoned. Is there another problem with lack of consent in this case? As described in the next few pages, minors typically cannot consent to the use of their names or likenesses without additional permission from a parent or guardian. Having already found for Lindsey Bullard, however, the court "decline[d] to reach that issue."

The kinds of uses outlined in Example 5 pose the most complicated legal problems because of the varied circumstances involved. And courts often have difficulty sorting through these circumstances to arrive at consistent decisions. What if a producer just happens to pick the name of a real person for use in a television program? Michael Costanza sued Jerry Seinfeld and others for use of the name Costanza in the successful situation comedy. But the fictional character was named George and the plaintiff's full name or photo was never associated with the show. The similarity of the plaintiff's last name and the fictional character did not amount to an illegal appropriation, the New York court ruled.[28] In 2005, the Florida Supreme Court ruled that the state's commercial misappropriation statute did not apply to a motion picture or any other use that does not "directly" promote a product or service. The children of two of the crew members of the Andrea Gail, the fishing boat that was lost during "The Perfect Storm," sued Time Warner for using the names of the men in the feature film of the same name without permission. The fact that the motion picture was created for profit did not warrant defining the term "commercial purpose" in the statute to include a motion picture, the court said.[29] As noted earlier, the Manhattan Appellate Division ruled that Grand Theft Auto V did not fall under the statutory definitions of "advertising" or "trade." But caution should be exercised in such cases as a cause of action for false-light privacy might be generated because the events included in the film have been fictionalized in some manner (see Chapter 8).

28. *Costanza* v. *Seinfeld,* 719 N.Y.S. 2d 29 (2001).
29. *Tyne* v. *Time Warner Entertainment Co.,* 901 S. 2d 802 (2005); 33 M.L.R. 2318 (2005).

NEWS AND PUBLIC INTEREST EXCEPTION

What about this argument? A newspaper runs a photograph of John Smith on the front page after his car rolled over several times during a high-speed police pursuit. Smith sues for invasion of privacy, arguing that his picture on the front page of the newspaper attracted readers to the paper, resulted in the sale of newspapers and therefore was used for commercial or trade purposes.

More than a century ago New York courts first rejected this argument, ruling that the law was intended to punish commercial use, not the dissemination of information.[30] And since that ruling other courts have consistently rejected this claim. The U.S. Supreme Court has ruled that the fact that newspapers and books and magazines are sold for profit does not deny them the protection of liberty of expression.[31]

Asking 15 different judges what is newsworthy or what constitutes a matter of public interest could very likely result in 15 different answers. So-called reality television shows blur the line between legitimate news and entertainment. And judges can become confused. A New Jersey appellate judge noted this problem when he wrote, "It is neither feasible nor desirable to make a distinction between news for information and news for entertainment in determining the extent to which the publication is privileged." In this case several individuals who had been admitted to an emergency room at a hospital were videotaped for the television program, "Trauma: Life in the ER," which was telecast on The Learning Channel. The court ruled the program to be news.[32] In 2016, a federal court dismissed a misappropriation of likeness claim stemming from the movie "Straight Outta Compton." Gerald Heller, a highly successful music executive sued over the use of his likeness in a movie about the rise of the rap group N.W.A. Heller also sued for defamation and false-light invasion of privacy. On the misappropriation claim, the judge ruled that the public interest defense allowed "film producers to depict matters in the public arena without fear of liability." The judge wrote that the subject matter of the film—Heller's tumultuous relationship with NWA—involved a matter of public interest. The judge held that because there was "little doubt that N.W.A. has had an influence on popular culture both domestically and internationally," Heller's role in the group's rise to stardom was certainly a matter of public interest and the film's use of Heller's likeness was protected by the First Amendment.[33]

In another case a 14-year-old Florida girl posed for a series of pictures that she believed would appear in *Young and Modern*, a magazine aimed at teenage girls. The photos appeared in a 1995 edition of the publication, but not exactly in the context the young model expected. They illustrated a regularly published column called Love Crisis. In this edition a 14-year-old letter writer told the columnist she had gotten drunk at a party and had sex with three different boys. What should I do? she asked. Don't do it again, the advice columnist replied, and be sure to get tested for both sexually transmitted diseases and pregnancy. The column was headlined, "I got trashed and had sex with three guys,"

---

30. *Moser* v. *Press Publishing Co.*, 109 N.Y.S. 963 (1908); *Jeffries* v. *New York Evening Journal,* 124 N.Y.S. 780 (1910).
31. *Time, Inc.* v. *Hill,* 385 U.S. 374 (1967).
32. *Castro* v. *NYT Television,* 32 M.L.R. 2555 (2004).
33. *Heller* v. *NBC Universal,* Case No. CV-15-09631-MWF-KS (C.D.C. Mar. 30, 2016).

and three photos of the plaintiff were used to illustrate the letter. She alleged the photos were published for commercial purposes, but the New York Court of Appeals disagreed. The article was newsworthy, the court said. It was not an advertisement in disguise. The fact that a publication may have used the photos primarily to enhance the value of the magazine by increasing its circulation did not mean that the photos were used for purposes of trade.[34]

The blurring between news and entertainment is one issue. An even greater problem in privacy law is the convergence of information and marketing. The close association between advertising and the editorial content of publications or television programs raises real questions about whether a particular use should be considered an exemption to the general prohibition against a commercial use. The case described below illustrates the tension between advertising and news editorial content.

Actor Dustin Hoffman sued *Los Angeles Magazine* in 1999 for using his photo in a fashion feature called Grand Illusions. Using computer imaging technology, the magazine combined still photos of actresses and actors (both living and dead) with photos of contemporary models wearing the latest fashions by many designers who were advertisers in the magazine. But the photo feature was not an advertisement; it was editorial copy. Hoffman's picture was taken from a publicity still used to publicize the film "Tootsie," in which the actor is made up like a woman. Hoffman's face and head were attached to the body of a female model and the new photo appeared over this caption: "Dustin Hoffman isn't a drag in a butter-colored silk gown by Richard Tyler and Ralph Lauren heels." A trial court ruled that the use of the photo was for commercial purposes, but the 9th U.S. Circuit Court of Appeals disagreed. "Viewed in context the article as a whole is a combination of fashion photography, humor, and visual and verbal editorial content on classic films and famous actors. Any commercial aspects are 'inextricably entwined' with expressive elements and so they cannot be separated out 'from the fully protected whole,'" the court ruled.[35]

OTHER EXCEPTIONS

The right to publish or broadcast an individual's name or likeness for news and information purposes is a broad exception to the appropriation rule. Other courts have found other exceptions as well, but this is where the law of privacy gets a little dicey. Not all courts view the same actions as exceptions to the appropriation rule. The doctrine of incidental use, for example, is recognized in many jurisdictions and permits a fleeting or brief use of an individual's name or likeness in some kinds of commercial creations. "The doctrine of incidental use was developed," one court ruled, "to address concerns that penalizing every unauthorized use, no matter how insignificant or fleeting, of a person's name or likeness would impose undue burdens on expressive activity."[36] When Amazon.com showed the cover of a book it was selling online, the model who had posed for the cover photo sued for appropriation. The 11th U.S. Court of Appeals ruled that the online seller merely displayed the book cover in an effort to replicate the experience of a

The doctrine of incidental use, for example, is recognized in many jurisdictions and permits a fleeting or brief use of an individual's name or likeness in some kinds of commercial creations.

34. *Messenger* v. *Gruner + Jahr Printing and Publishing,* 94 N.Y. 2d 436 (2000).
35. *Hoffman* v. *Capital Cities/ABC Inc.,* 33 F. Supp. 2d 867 (1999), rev'd 255 F. 3d 1180 (2001).
36. *Preston* v. *Martin Bregman Productions, Inc.,* 765 F. Supp. 116 (1991).

physical bookstore. "It is clear that Amazon's use of book cover images is not an endorsement or promotion of any product or service, but is merely incidental to, and customary for, the business of Internet book sales," the court said.[37] Plaintiff Evelyn Candelaria appeared for three to four seconds in the documentary film "Super Size Me," an attack on fast-food eating habits. She doesn't say anything in a scene that discusses the nutritional content of McDonald's offerings and the availability of this information to the public. A court ruled her appearance was incidental.[38] But the use of legendary pilot Chuck Yeager's name in a press release touting the introduction of a new mobile phone service by Cingular might not be merely incidental, a federal court in California ruled, rejecting a motion to dismiss. The press release said, "Nearly 60 years ago the legendary test pilot Chuck Yeager broke the sound barrier and achieved MACH 1. Today, Cingular is breaking another kind of barrier with our MACH 1 and MACH 2 mobile command centers."[39]

Booth *Rule*

The *Booth* rule is closely related to the incidental use doctrine; in fact, some courts refer to it as part of that doctrine. The rule provides fairly broad protection to the mass media in most states if an individual's name or likeness is used in advertising for a particular information medium. In other words, the use of a person's name or likeness in an advertisement *for* a magazine or a newspaper or a television program is usually not regarded as an appropriation if the photograph or name has been or will be a part of the medium's news or information content.

The controversy that sparked this rule involved Academy Award–winning actress Shirley Booth.* She was photographed in Jamaica, and the picture was published in a feature story in *Holiday*, a popular travel magazine. *Holiday* then used the same picture to advertise the magazine itself. The full-page advertisement told readers that the picture was typical of the material appearing in *Holiday* magazine and urged people to advertise in the periodical or subscribe to *Holiday*. Booth did not object to her photograph in the feature story, only to its use in the subsequent advertisement. The courts, however, refused to call the use an invasion of privacy. The New York Supreme Court ruled that the maintenance of freedom of expression depends in no small part on the economic support of the press by advertisers and subscribers. And to win such support a publication or broadcasting station must be able to promote itself. Since the picture in this case was first used in an information story, its subsequent use in a promotion for the magazine was really only incidental to its original use and was merely to show the quality and content of the magazine. The picture was not used to sell spaghetti or used cars. Hence the use did not constitute an invasion of privacy.[40]

Originally it was believed that the *Booth* rule protected only the *republication* or *rebroadcast* of material previously used in the medium. Some courts still follow this rule, whereas other courts have enunciated a broader protection. For example, a U.S. District Court ruled that it is permissible for a newspaper or magazine to use previously published

---

* Booth won an Oscar as Best Actress in 1952 for her role in the film "Come Back Little Sheba."

37. *Almeida* v. *Amazon.com Inc.,* 34 M.L.R. 2118 (2006).
38. *Candelaria* v. *Spurlock,* 36 M.L.R. 2150 (2008).
39. *Yeager* v. *Cingular Wireless LLC,* 36 M.L.R. 2396 (2008); 38 M.L.R. 1183 (2009).
40. *Booth* v. *Curtis Publishing Co.,* 11 N.Y.S. 2d 907 (1962).

material in a television advertisement for the publication.[41] That is, a name or likeness that appeared in a newspaper story can be *republished* in a television advertisement for that newspaper. In 2014, publisher Condé Nast was sued over a video posted on *Vogue's* Web site. *Vogue's* April 2014 issue featured an article about the relationship between reality star Kim Kardashian and rapper Kanye West. The video contained behind-the-scenes footage of the article, and an edited version of West's song "Bound 2" was used as the background music for the video. The "hook" in "Bound 2" contains the lead vocals of Ricky Spicer, a singer in the 1970s group The Ponderosa Twins plus One. Spicer is heard at least four times throughout the song, and his voice was used substantially throughout the video, comprising approximately 44 percent of the vocals. Spicer sued Condé Nast, the publisher of *Vogue*, arguing the company knowingly used his voice on its Web site for advertising purposes and for purposes of trade and commercial benefits, without his authorization or consent. The court ruled, however, that even if the video was "an advertisement in disguise," the use was a "media source advertising its own goods" and thus protected.[42] No one yet knows just how far the courts will go in extending the *Booth* rule. The tendency, however, seems to be to expand the protection rather than restrict it.

Clearly the use of a name or photo to promote a medium cannot be an explicit or even implied endorsement of the medium. Cher won a lawsuit against *Forum* magazine after it used her photo to promote an edition of the publication. The advertisements clearly implied that the actress-singer endorsed *Forum*, which was not true. That issue of the magazine did contain an interview with Cher, but the court ruled that the advertisements went far beyond establishing the news content and quality of the publication for potential readers.[43]

Finally, the use of an individual's name or likeness in a political advertisement is not regarded as an appropriation. A campaign advertisement that says "Vote for Jones, not Smith" would not give Smith a legal right to sue for appropriation. The use of an individual's name or likeness in an issue-oriented advertisement such as "Save the Whales" or "Stop Racism" likewise would not sustain an appropriation lawsuit. A federal court ruled in 2006 that the use of two plaintiffs' pictures in an advertisement attacking the American Association of Retired Persons' supposed support of gay marriage was not an appropriation because it was not a commercial use, and addressed an issue of public concern.[44] What about the use of a name or likeness in an advertisement or promotion for a nonprofit organization in brochures or pamphlets to stimulate donations to further their community work? The 6th U.S. Circuit Court of Appeals upheld a small damage award to a child whose picture was used without permission in a direct mail solicitation by a Kentucky religious order. The Little Sisters of the Assumption Order included the photo with a letter that was sent to 125,000 homes asking for donations for the poor. The appellate court affirmed the lower court award of $100 in damages for appropriation.[45] While it's not clear how liable not-for-profit organizations would be, the simplest and best solution in these situations is to get consent from people before you use their likeness for fundraising opportunities.

---

41. *Friedan* v. *Friedan*, 414 F. Supp. 77 (1976).
42. *Spicer* v. *Condé Nast Entertainment, LLC*, 2014 N.Y. Misc. LEXIS 5156 (Dec. 3, 2014).
43. *Cher* v. *Forum International*, 692 F. 2d 634 (1982).
44. *Raymen* v. *United Senior Association Inc.*, 409 F. Supp. 2d 15 (2006).
45. *Bowling* v. *The Missionary Servants of the Most Holy Trinity*, 972 F. 2d 346 (1992).

CONSENT AS A DEFENSE

The law prohibits only the unauthorized use of a name or likeness for commercial or trade purposes. States with privacy statutes usually require that written authorization or consent be given before the use. On the other hand, consent thus does not always need to be in writing to be effective. As the 9th U.S. Circuit Court of Appeals wrote in 2012, "consent may be implicit and is to be determined objectively from the perspective of a reasonable person" and in light of things such as "the well-known and established customs of the industry" (in this particular case, the imaging license business) that used or sold the photograph.[46] But in any legal action the defendant is going to have to prove that he or she had consent to use the name or photograph. Written consent is usually uncontestable and will stand as a solid defense against an appropriation claim, even if the plaintiff argues that he or she didn't really understand what he or she was signing. When a photographer took pictures of professional tennis player Anastasia Myskina, the athlete signed a consent form, or release, permitting Condé Nast publishers to include the photos in the 2002 sports issue of *GQ* magazine. But she sued the magazine for invasion of privacy, claiming that the magazine appropriated her likeness when it used the photos in ways she did not approve of or anticipate. In its defense the magazine raised the matter of the consent form she had signed. She said she misunderstood the document she signed; English was not her first language. A federal court said her assertion—even if true—was irrelevant. When a party signs a contract, which a release is, she is bound by the terms of the contract, whether or not she understood it, whether or not she read it.[47] Attempts to convince a court that oral consent was given can be met by the plaintiff's denial, and then the fact finder will have to decide who is telling the truth. Also, oral consent can be withdrawn up to the moment of publication or broadcast.

The consent issue is most easily resolved if the subject has signed a model release similar to the one printed later this chapter. But such legal documents are not always required to establish consent. Two rulings make this point. Sam and Joseph Schifano sued the Greene County Greyhound Park, a dog racing track, for including their photo in an advertising brochure for the facility. The plaintiffs, who visited the park often, were photographed while they sat with several other persons in what is called The Winner's Circle, a section of the park that can be reserved by interested groups of spectators. There was no written consent for the use of their picture, but there was ample evidence that park officials had told the plaintiffs why they were taking the photos and gave them a chance to leave if they did not want to be in the picture. "Plaintiffs, neither by objecting nor moving, when those options were made available by park employees, consented to having their photograph taken at the Park," the Alabama Supreme Court ruled in 1993.[48]

A year later the 9th U.S. Circuit Court of Appeals handed down a similar ruling in a lawsuit involving a popular television situation comedy called "Evening Shade." Country music songwriter and performer Wood Newton sued the producers of the program because the lead character in the show, played by Burt Reynolds, was also named Wood Newton. The creator of the program, Linda Bloodworth-Thomason, grew up in the same town as the real Wood Newton, and there are some similarities between the real and fictional characters. Newton never signed a release for the use of his name, but when the program was first

---

46. *Jones v. Corbis Corp.,* 2012 U.S. App. LEXIS 14543 (9th Cir. July 16, 2012).
47. *Myskina v. Condé Nast Publications Inc.,* 33 M.L.R. 2199 (2005).
48. *Schifano v. Greene County Greyhound Park, Inc.,* 624 So. 178 (1993).

telecast he sent a letter to the producers that said, "I want you to know that I'm flattered that you are using my name, everyone who I've talked to thinks it's exciting and so do I." The lawsuit was filed many months later, after the producers of the program had rejected music that Newton had written and submitted for use on the program. "Although Newton never uttered the words 'I consent,' it is obvious that he did consent," the court ruled.[49]

MODEL RELEASE OR CONSENT FORM USED BY A PHOTOGRAPHER

For and in consideration of my engagement as a model/subject by (insert photographer's name), hereafter referred to as the photographer, on terms or fee hereinafter stated, I hereby give the photographer, his/her legal representatives, and assigns, those for whom the photographer is acting, and those acting with his/her permission, or his/her employees, the right and permission to copyright and/or use, reuse, and/or publish, and republish photographic pictures or portraits of me, or in which I may be distorted in character, or form, in conjunction with my own or a fictitious name, on reproductions thereof in color, or black and white made through any media by the photographer at his/her studio or elsewhere, for any purpose whatsoever; including the use of any printed matter in conjunction therewith.

I hereby waive any right to inspect or approve the finished photograph or advertising copy of printed matter that may be used in conjunction therewith or to the eventual use that it might be applied.

I hereby release, discharge and agree to save harmless the photographer, his/her representatives, assigns, employees or any person or persons, corporation or corporations, acting under his/her permission or authority, or any person, persons, corporation or corporations, for whom he/she might be acting, including any firm publishing and/or distributing the finished product, in whole or in part, from and against any liability as a result of any distortion, blurring, or alteration, optical illusion, or use in composite form, either intentionally or otherwise, that may occur or be produced in the taking, or processing or reproduction of the finished product, its publication or distribution of the same, even should the same subject me to ridicule, scandal, reproach, scorn, or indignity.

When Consent Might Not Work

There are times when even written consent might not work as a defense, and the media must be aware of such situations:

1. **Consent given today may not be valid in the distant future, especially if it is gratuitous oral consent.** Consent given via a written contract will normally hold up over time. But there have been instances in which courts have ruled that oral consent became invalid over time, especially if the notoriety of the person who gave the consent has increased. Imagine if Harry Carson took a picture of the kids in a local garage band, Hideous Shellfish, playing Acme guitars and bass. He says

---

49. *Newton* v. *Thomason,* 22 F. 3d 1455 (1994). But express oral or written consent is required under some state right-of-publicity statutes. See, for example, *Bosley* v. *Wildwett. Com,* 310 F. Supp. 2d 914 (2004), rev'd on other grounds, 32 M.L.R. 1641 (2004).

he will try to sell the photo to the instrument maker and the band members orally agree. But nothing comes of the deal. Fast-forward to five years later. The band has sold five million CDs. Acme now buys the picture and uses it in an advertising slogan, "Hideous Shellfish plays Acme instruments." The band sues; Harry and Acme say the group gave consent five years ago. The court very likely could rule the consent is no longer valid. Harry and Acme should have gotten reauthorization before using the photo in the ad. Written consent very likely would have held up.[50]

2. **Some people cannot give consent.** Who can't give consent? Here is a short list.

   ▪ People who are under age cannot give consent. In most states a person must be 18 to enter into a legally binding agreement. There are many cases in which teenage girls who insist they are 18 have signed consent forms permitting photographers to use their pictures, for whatever reason. When they disapprove of the use and sue, they reveal that they were only 16 when they signed the forms. Courts usually demand to see evidence that the teenager was believable when he or she lied, and ask the defendant to show proof that he or she attempted to verify the age.
   ▪ People who are mentally ill are very often unable to give consent.[51]
   ▪ People incarcerated in prisons sometimes cannot give consent.

   It is up to the defendant to be certain that the individual who signs the consent form is in fact able to legally give his or her consent. Simply showing the judge a signed consent statement will rarely carry the day in court.

3. **Consent to use a particular photograph may be lost if the photograph is substantially altered.** Years ago a prominent American fashion model signed a standard release form after a photo session giving the photographer and anyone else who came to own the pictures the right to use them in any way they chose. She gave up her right to approve of any use. The photo ended up in the hands of an advertiser that retouched it and created a rather salacious tableau. The model sued; the advertisers argued she had given consent for any use. A New York court agreed she had abandoned her rights to control the use of the original pictures, but the picture that appeared in the ad was not one of those taken by the photographer. The original photo had been substantially altered. The broad consent did not work to protect the defendants.[52] This case was decided 50 years ago when it took some work to retouch a photo. Nowadays anyone with a home computer and any one of a handful of software programs can substantially alter any photo in the blink of an eye. But just because it is easy, doesn't make it legal. Magazine editors and the providers of content for the Web must take special care. A signed consent will protect the use of only the original photo with slight retouching, not wholesale modification of the particular subject in the picture or the setting in which the subject has been photographed.[53]

50. See *McAndrews* v. *Roy*, 131 So. 2d 256 (1961); and *Welch* v. *Mr. Christmas Tree*, 57 N.Y. 2d 143 (1982).
51. *Delan* v. *CBS*, 445 N.Y.S. 2d 898 (1981).
52. *Russell* v. *Marboro Books*, 183 N.Y.S. 2d 8 (1959).
53. See, for example, *Dittner* v. *Troma*, 6 M.L.R. 1991 (1980).

LIFE AFTER DEATH: POST-MORTEM PUBLICITY RIGHTS

The right to privacy traditionally is considered a personal right that dies with the individual. But the right to publicity may live on after death. According to *Forbes Magazine*, one group of dead celebrities or "delebs" tracked by the magazine generated $363.5 million between October 2013 and October 2014, with Michael Jackson's music and publicity rights generating $140 million alone. Elvis Presley, who died in 1977, generated $55 million in the same time period.[54] New technology that has made it even easier for deceased celebrities' images to be used in a variety of ways will only increase revenue streams long after death. However, it is not always clear how states will deal with these revenues. Several states have passed statutes guaranteeing to heirs the right to protect the commercial exploitation of dead public figures for as long as 70 years in California and as short as 20 years in Virginia.* Tennessee, home of Presley, provides a celebrity's estate with an initial 10-year post-mortem right of publicity that can be extended forever if the right is continually exploited (the right is terminated only when there is a two-year period of nonuse by the estate). Thus, as long as Presley's heirs continue to exploit his name, likeness and image, they will be able to profit forever. And in at least one state, New York, the notion that an heir should be able to control such publicity has been flatly rejected. In states that recognize the right of publicity as a matter of common law, the situation is far less clear. So where a particular lawsuit is tried is usually critical to the outcome.

For instance, Vernon J. Tatum, Jr. sued the operators of the New Orleans International Airport for appropriation when an image of his late mother, Ellyna C. Tatum, appeared in a mural on the airport's walls. Ellyna Tatum was a well-known jazz singer in New Orleans who died in 1986. A Louisiana appellate court in 2012, however, dismissed the case of *Tatum* v. *New Orleans Aviation Board*, noting that the "right to privacy is a personal right that belonged only to the late Ms. Tatum. Nothing in Louisiana law, statutorily or jurisprudentially, gives Mr. Tatum [the son] the authority to assert this right on behalf on his deceased mother." Louisiana does not have a post-mortem right of publicity statute, essentially ending the case filed by the late singer's son.

Also in 2012, the Hebrew University of Jerusalem, which owns all of Albert Einstein's "literary property and rights" under his will, sued General Motors for unauthorized use of Einstein's likeness. The case involved a magazine advertisement that featured Einstein's face "digitally pasted onto a muscled physique, accompanied by the written message, 'Ideas are sexy too.'" Because it was not settled if New Jersey common law recognized a common law post-mortem right of publicity or how long that right should last, the court looked to copyright law for guidance. The court concluded that a maximum 50-year post-mortem duration would be "a reasonable middle ground" because, among other things, at the time that Einstein's rights passed to the Hebrew University in 1982, the then-existing Copyright Act suggested that a life-plus-50-years term was reasonable. The district court noted that an open-ended right of publicity or one longer than 50 years

---

* California, Florida, Indiana, Kentucky, Nebraska, Oklahoma, Tennessee, Utah and Virginia are among the states that have statutes that speak to this matter in some way.
54. Pomerantz, "Michael Jackson Tops Forbes' List of Top-Earning Dead Celebrities with $140 Million Haul."

would raise "considerable First Amendment concerns and create a potentially infinite curb on expression."[55]

The use of dead entertainment celebrities to sell products is a growing phenomenon, and in some ways makes sense. But today it is not simply dead denizens of the stage and screen whose images are protected. The images of historical figures like Martin Luther King Jr., Gen. George Patton, civil rights icon Rosa Parks, architect Frank Lloyd Wright and Babe Ruth are claimed as private property, usable only with permission for a fee. The Hebrew University of Jerusalem earned $76 million between 2006 and 2011 from companies seeking to use Einstein's image.[56]

New challenges in this area of privacy law will continue to emerge in the coming years as computer technology makes it possible to bring the images of creatures, aliens, starships and even dead celebrities to the motion picture and television screen. Using technologies pioneered by individuals like George Lucas and others, it is possible to create entire commercials and even feature films that contain the images of celebrities long since departed from this earth, images that look as real as photographs of living, breathing people. There is no doubt that the individuals who are charged with crafting the law in this realm will have to be as creative as the men and women who have generated this remarkable technology.

SUMMARY Appropriation of a person's name or likeness for commercial or trade purposes without permission is an invasion of privacy and may violate a person's right to publicity. Use of an individual's photograph, a sketch of the person, a nickname or a stage name are all considered use of a name or likeness. However, the publication of news and matters of public interest in magazines, books, newspapers and news broadcasts is not considered a trade purpose, even though the mass medium may make a profit from such publication. Consequently, people who are named or pictured in news stories or other such material cannot sue for appropriation. Also, a news medium may republish or rebroadcast news items or photographs already carried as news stories in advertising for the mass medium to establish the quality or kind of material carried by the medium.

Anyone who seeks to use the name or likeness of an individual for commercial or trade purposes should gain written consent from that person. Even written consent may be invalid as a defense if the consent was given many years before publication, if the person from whom the consent was gained cannot legally give consent or if the photograph or other material that is used is substantially altered.

Courts have also recognized what is known as the right to publicity. Right-to-publicity actions are most often instituted by well-known people who believe the unauthorized use of their name or likeness has deprived them of an opportunity to reap financial gain by selling this right to the user. In some states the right to publicity can be passed on to heirs like any other piece of property, which means that an individual's estate can control the use of his or her name and likeness after the person's death.

55. *Hebrew Univ. of Jerusalem* v. *General Motors*, LLC, 2012 U.S. Dist. LEXIS 148150 (2012).
56. Madoff, "The New Grave Robbers."

INTRUSION

It is illegal to intrude, physically or otherwise, upon the solitude, seclusion or private affairs of an individual if a reasonable person would find the manner of the intrusion to be highly offensive.

When people hear the phrase "invasion of privacy," the intrusion tort is what frequently comes to mind. Cameras with telephoto lenses, hidden microphones, snooping through records—all of these are associated with intrusion. Intrusion has a lot in common with both civil and criminal trespass (see Chapter 9 regarding trespass). It is not unusual for a plaintiff to sue for both trespass and intrusion in the same lawsuit. But the causes of action are different: Not every intrusion is a trespass, and vice versa. Google has a "Street View" map service that provides navigable views of streets in many American cities.[57] The maps are prepared by attaching panoramic cameras to cars, which are driven around photographing areas along the streets. The vehicles normally stay on the public streets, but in one case a car entered the driveway of a home in Pennsylvania. The homeowner sued for both intrusion and trespass. The 3rd U.S. Court of Appeals rejected the intrusion claim, saying the photos simply showed an external view of the home and yard, something that could be seen by any person walking or driving down the street. But when the car moved onto the driveway, it made an uninvited intentional entry onto private property: a trespass. This is a viable legal claim, the court ruled. The law governing the two legal actions is different as well. Intrusion is the focus of this section; trespass and other laws that regulate the use of hidden microphones or video cameras will be outlined in the section on news gathering in Chapter 9.

The intrusion tort differs from the other three invasion-of-privacy torts in a very important way: Intrusion cases focus exclusively on how information is gathered and collected, not on how it is reported or published. The act of gathering the material constitutes the intrusion. A successful intrusion lawsuit thus can be brought regardless of whether or not the information gathered is ever published or broadcast.

The most important legal element in an intrusion case is what the courts call "a reasonable expectation of privacy." If a court rules that a plaintiff did not enjoy a reasonable expectation of privacy when the defendant gathered or attempted to gather the information at issue, the intrusion suit will fail.

INTRUSION AND THE PRESS

An illegal intrusion can occur in myriad ways. Eavesdropping to overhear a conversation could be an intrusion. Gathering personal information from an individual's private records or computer could also be an intrusion. The use of a telephoto lens on a camera to photograph a subject might violate the law as well. *The court will ask in every case in which an intrusion is alleged whether the subject of the intrusion "enjoyed a reasonable expectation of privacy" when the information was collected.* This issue is the key to determining whether an invasion of privacy took place. A reporter who sits at a

---

57. *Boring v. Google Inc.,* 362 Fed. Appx. 273 (2010).

table in a restaurant and eavesdrops on the conversation at the next table is not committing an intrusion. If other diners can hear the conversation, the speakers did not enjoy a reasonable expectation of privacy.[58] If, however, the reporter hides in a closet in the subject's office and listens to a conversation, this would be an intrusion. Two people talking in a private office with the door closed have a reasonable expectation of privacy. Courts are sorting out when an Internet user can expect to enjoy a reasonable expectation of privacy, and the decisions have not been favorable to those who think the Web should be a secure haven. At least two lower courts have ruled that the user of an online service who participated in a chat room conversation and sent e-mail messages to other chat room participants did not have a reasonable expectation of privacy with regard to the content of these messages.[59] A federal court in Massachusetts ruled in 2002 that two employees of an insurance company did not enjoy a reasonable expectation of privacy in the content of the sexually explicit e-mail messages they sent and received at work.[60] In 2010 the Supreme Court of the United States ruled that Ontario, Calif., police sergeant Jeffry Quon did not have a reasonable expectation of privacy when the city audited text messages he had sent on a pager issued to him by the city, as long as his employers had a "legitimate work-related purpose" for inspecting communications.[61] A U.S. District Court in Maine ruled that a student lacked a reasonable expectation of privacy in files on a shared-usage university computer.[62] And the 1st U.S. Court of Appeals ruled that if e-mail messages were stored for even a millisecond on the computers of an Internet service provider that transmitted them, federal wiretap laws were not violated if employees of the provider read the messages. A company called Interloc Inc., a literary clearinghouse, made copies of the messages its subscribers sent to competitor Amazon.com. Interloc's customers were dealers in rare and out-of-print books, and while Amazon did not offer its customers out-of-print and rare books, it did help customers track down such books. The court ruled that while the wiretap law prohibits eavesdropping on messages that are not stored, it does not protect stored messages.[63]

While many questions regarding intrusion and online communications have been answered, many others have not. For example, courts have yet to rule on whether an Internet user who is sending or receiving material through a wireless connection—so-called wi-fi—enjoys a reasonable expectation of privacy. And while courts are generally in agreement that personal e-mails sent or received on a company computer are not shielded from company officials, there has been no determination whether e-mails sent on a company computer by using a personal e-mail account, such as one provided by Yahoo!, are also open to scrutiny by company officials.[64]

58. See *Simtel Communications* v. *National Broadcasting Company Inc.,* 84 Cal. Rptr. 2d 329 (1999).
59. See *U.S.* v. *Charbonneau,* 979 F. Supp. 1177 (1997); and *Pennsylvania* v. *Proetto,* Pa. Super. Ct. No. 1076 EDA 2000, 3/28/01.
60. *Garrity* v. *John Hancock Mutual Life Insurance Co.,* D. Mass., No. 00-12143-RWZ, 5/7/02.
61. *City of Ontario* v. *Quon,* 560 U.S. 746 (2010).
62. *U.S.* v. *Bunnell,* D. Me., Crim. No. 0213-B-S, 5/10/02.
63. Jewell, "Setback Seen for E-Mail Privacy."
64. Glater, "Open Secrets."

NO PRIVACY IN PUBLIC

What occurs in public is generally not regarded as being private. This sounds like a simple rule, and in some ways it is. If a girl is photographed while twerking on a street corner, she can't argue that she is in a private setting. On the other hand, what occurs between a married couple in their bedroom is certainly private (assuming, of course, that their bedroom does not have a large glass window and that people standing on a nearby public sidewalk cannot see inside). But determining what is public and what is private in situations between these two extremes often gives judges and juries difficulty. The Utah Supreme Court ruled that whether a reasonable expectation of privacy existed "depends on the exact nature of the conduct and all the surrounding circumstances."[65] The court is saying, in simple terms, it all depends. And often it is left to a jury to decide. But case law can provide guidance.

- ▮ The California Court of Appeals ruled in 2006 that it was not an intrusion into a private place when a photographer standing in a public park took a picture of a crime victim.[66]
- ▮ A federal appeals court ruled that a woman who was photographed talking with a TV producer as she stood at the front door of her home did not enjoy a reasonable expectation of privacy. The court noted she was standing in plain sight of anyone passing on the street.[67]

WHOREHOUSES, HIDDEN CAMERAS AND PRIVACY:
NO HAPPY ENDING FOR UNSUSPECTING PATRONS IN MAINE

In 2013, a judge in Maine held that patrons of a woman charged with multiple counts of prostitution at a Zumba studio that allegedly fronted as a brothel had no reasonable expectation of privacy when they were secretly filmed having sex. According to a story in the *Portland Press Herald*, Judge Nancy Mills reasoned that "these patrons may have had a subjective expectation of privacy, but I can't find an objective expectation of privacy that society would be willing to accept." In brief, people who are breaking the law cannot have a reasonable expectation of privacy in what they are doing.

Why was this issue before the judge? Maine has a video voyeurism law (Maine Revised Statutes, Title 17, Section 511) that makes it a crime to video record a person in a "private place," such as a changing room, dressing room or bathroom. Mark Strong, Sr. was charged with 46 counts of violating this statute for allegedly recording the sexual acts between the patrons and the alleged prostitute at the Zumba studio in Kennebunk. Because Judge Mills determined that patrons of brothels are not entitled to privacy therein, all of those 46 charges against Strong were dropped. The alleged prostitute, who reportedly was Strong's business partner, denied all of the charges against her.

---

65. *Jensen* v. *Sawyers,* 33 M.L.R. 2578 (2005).
66. *Deteresa* v. *American Broadcasting Co. Inc.,* 121 F. 3d 460 (1997).
67. *Savala* v. *Freedom Communications Inc.,* 34 M.L.R. 2241 (2006).

The principle that one does not have a reasonable expectation of privacy in a public place is illustrated by the 2011 federal appellate court ruling in *Spilfogel* v. *Fox Broadcasting Co.*[68] The case centered on plaintiff Arlene Spilfogel, who was filmed for an episode of the television show "COPS" without her knowledge during a traffic stop in Florida. Spilfogel was recorded by "COPS" while on a public street discussing the details of her traffic stop for running through several stop signs and driving without working tag and head lights on her vehicle. Applying Florida law, the appellate court rejected her claim for intrusion into seclusion because "the recording occurred on a public street" and "Florida law explicitly requires an intrusion into a private place." It concluded that "Spilfogel voluntarily placed herself in a public place where she did not have a reasonable expectation of privacy."

Determining whether or not there is a reasonable expectation of privacy in the workplace often causes problems for the courts. ABC sent a reporter to work as a telephone psychic at a telemarketing company in California. While there the reporter secretly photographed and tape-recorded conversations with several co-workers. The network was sued for intrusion, among other things. ABC argued that there was no legitimate expectation of privacy in the office setting because workers shared small, three-walled cubicles. Conversations could be heard by other employees. The California Supreme Court disagreed with the network, ruling that

> in an office or other workplace to which the general public does not have unfettered access employees may enjoy a limited, but legitimate expectation that their conversations and other interactions will not be secretly videotaped by undercover television reporters, even though their conversations may not have been completely private.[69]

ABC suffered another setback in 2004 when its motion for a summary judgment was denied in an intrusion case in which one of its reporter/producers had secretly taped conversations at a workshop given for aspiring actors and actresses by casting directors. By paying a fee to attend the workshops the performers got to meet and talk with casting directors, the people who play an important role in employing actors and actresses who appear in movies and on television. The workshops were a controversial issue in California, and the network did a segment on it for a "20/20" broadcast. The reporter taped not only the actual presentations during the workshop but also private conversations among the performers during breaks. Some of the performers sued. In California all parties must agree to the recording of a conversation unless it takes place at a public gathering. ABC asked that the case be dismissed, claiming the conversations took place in public spaces. The U.S. District Court ruled that even though some of their conversations could have been overheard by other students, the plaintiffs still had a reasonable expectation of privacy. They could not have expected as they talked among themselves in the corners or against the walls of the classroom, much less in the restrooms, that a reporter was covertly recording their conversations. This was not a public place.[70]

---

68. 39 M.L.R. 1977 (11th Cir. 2011).

69. *Sanders* v. *American Broadcasting Companies,* 978 P. 2d 67 (1999). Sanders received a settlement of more than $900,000 from ABC.

70. *Turnbull* v. *American Broadcasting Companies,* 32 M.L.R. 2442 (2004). However, the plaintiff lost the case at trial.

THE RIGHT TO FILM POLICE IN PUBLIC PLACES: USING YOUR SMART PHONE AS A CITIZEN JOURNALIST

Do people, including citizen journalists, have a First Amendment right to videotape and photograph the activities of police officers performing their duties in public? The U.S. Court of Appeals for the 1st Circuit considered this issue in *Glik* v. *Cunniffe*[71] in 2011. Simon Glik was arrested on the Boston Commons for using his cell phone's video camera to film several police officers arresting a man and using what Glik thought was excessive force. Glik was standing about 10 feet away from the officers.

The 1st Circuit ruled that "Glik was exercising clearly established First Amendment rights in filming the officers in a public space, and that his clearly-established Fourth Amendment rights were violated by his arrest without probable cause." In reaching this conclusion, the appellate court reasoned that "gathering information about government officials in a form that can readily be disseminated to others serves a cardinal First Amendment interest in protecting and promoting the free discussion of governmental affairs." It added that its "recognition that the First Amendment protects the filming of government officials in public spaces accords with the decisions of numerous circuit and district courts." In January 2012, the Boston Police Department sent Glik a letter acknowledging "some violations of the Boston Police Department Rules" were confirmed by an internal affairs review that showed two members of the police exercised "unreasonable judgment" when they decided to arrest Glik. More good news for Glik came in April 2012 when the City of Boston agreed to pay him $170,000 to cover damages and legal fees he incurred in fighting his arrest.

By 2017, the Court of Appeals for the 3rd Circuit wrote there was a growing consensus among courts there was a First Amendment right to record the police in public. The case involved the 2013 arrest of Rick Fields and 2012 arrest of Amanda Geraci. Fields was arrested for taking a photo with his iPhone of a large number of Philadelphia police officers breaking up a house party. Geraci, a trained legal observer, was detained by police while attempting to monitor police interactions with anti-fracking protesters outside the Pennsylvania Convention Center.

The ruling by the 3rd Circuit returned the cases to district court to hear arguments that failure to train police officers on the First Amendment right to record the police lead to the incidents. In the opinion, the 3rd Circuit noted that while the the right to record the police in public was not absolute, a right to record in similar circumstances had been established by at least five other federal appeals courts.[72]

---

71. 655 F.3d 78 (1st Cir. 2011). For a recent case regarding the audio recording of police officers in public places and a state eavesdropping statute, see *ACLU of Illinois* v. *Alvarez*, 679 F. 3d 583 (7th Cir. 2012). The 7th Circuit in *Alvarez* wrote that "the First Amendment limits the extent to which Illinois may restrict audio and audiovisual recording of utterances that occur in public."
72. Fields v. City of Philadelphia, No. 16-1650 (Jul. 7, 2017).

Another California ruling demonstrates how carefully judges will sometimes look at a situation to judge the extent of a potential intrusion. A car containing four members of the Shulman family accidentally left Interstate 10, tumbled down an embankment and came to rest upside down in a drainage ditch. Rescue apparatus arrived at the scene, including a Mercy Air helicopter with a medic and a flight nurse. Also on board was a camera operator who worked for a television production company. The photographer was accumulating footage for a television program called "On Scene: Emergency Response." Nurse Laura Carnahan was wearing a microphone that supplied the audio stream for the video. As rescue workers cut Ruth Shulman out of the car, she was comforted by Carnahan. The conversation was recorded as the photographer videotaped the rescue. Shulman was placed in the rescue helicopter, and during the flight to the hospital more video and audio material was gathered. Shulman, who ended up a paraplegic because of her injuries, sued for invasion of privacy, both intrusion and publication of private facts. The California courts dismissed the private facts claim, noting that there was tremendous public interest in what happened in this case. But the California Supreme Court said a jury could certainly find a valid intrusion claim with regard to the video and audio recordings of Shulman while she was in the rescue helicopter on the way to the hospital. But she had no reasonable expectation of privacy while she was being removed from the vehicle, which was located along a public highway.[73] In 2009, a U.S. District Court in California ruled that the press has no right of access to an accident or crime scene if the general public is excluded.[74]

Does the use of a zoom lens to photograph or videotape a person in his own backyard constitute an intrusion into seclusion when the images in question are captured from a neighbor's home? Not necessarily. It all depends on the specific facts and context of the case, as the 2011 federal court ruling in *Webb* v. *CBS Broadcasting, Inc.*[75] illustrates. In *Webb*, a reporter and a videographer for CBS news obtained permission from the neighbor of the plaintiffs (Jill and Robert Webb) to bring a video camera, which had a zoom lens, into the neighbor's home and to set up the camera in front of one of the kitchen windows on the first floor. From that vantage point, the CBS journalists were able to videotape footage of the plaintiffs near their swimming pool in their backyard. In holding that the plaintiffs did not have a reasonable expectation of privacy, the court wrote that the "backyard is visible to the naked eye from the first-floor windows of the [neighbor's] house" and that "when objects are in plain view, there is no legitimate expectation of privacy." The court also emphasized that the neighbor's house was on a hill about three to five feet higher than the plaintiffs' backyard (thus allowing the CBS journalists to peer down into the backyard) and that there was undisputed evidence that the videotape made from the neighbor's "kitchen window could have been made from the public sidewalk or public street because the . . . backyard was visible to the public from many vantage points." The Webbs thus lost their case because they simply were not in a place that a reasonable person would have believed to have been secluded.

---

73. *Shulman* v. *Group W. Productions Inc.*, 955 P. 2d 469 (1998). The case was subsequently settled out of court.
74. *Chavez* v. *City of Oakland*, 137 M.L.R. 1905 (2009).
75. 39 M.L.R. 2627 (N.D. Ill. Oct. 17, 2011).

An Illinois appellate court in 2014 reached the same conclusion in a separate lawsuit for intrusion arising from the exact same location in *Webb* but involving a different plaintiff. Specifically, in *Jacobson v. CBS Broadcasting, Inc.,*[76] plaintiff Amy Jacobson sued for intrusion based upon a videotape made of her and her two young children while they were swimming in the backyard pool. In finding that Jacobson lacked a reasonable expectation of privacy in the swimming pool, the appellate court wrote that "although the pool was surrounded by a six-foot fence, the lot lay at the bottom of an incline, which, according to undisputed expert testimony, made the property between 3 to 5 feet lower than the surrounding area." The court added that "given the layout of the property and the surrounding area, the videotape could just as easily have been shot from the public sidewalk or the grassy area behind the property." This illustrates an important point—whether a reasonable expectation of privacy requires a highly fact specific analysis.

Courts will almost always reject the argument that photographing someone in a truly public place is an invasion of privacy. But sometimes there is a fine line between taking a photograph, and harassing the subject of that photograph. Over 40 years ago the courts barred a photographer from coming within 10 yards of Jacqueline Kennedy Onassis and her children because he was, the judges decided, harassing the family with his incessant picture taking.[77] In 1996 a court in Pennsylvania issued a similar order to protect a family in the state from the intense scrutiny of reporters trying to prepare a story for the television program "Inside Story."[78] Paparazzi have been a problem in California and New York for many years. These aggressive photographers dog celebrities in hopes of getting a picture they can sell to the growing number of tabloid newspapers and magazines that focus on celebrities and the entertainment business.

California has been especially aggressive in dealing with the paparazzi. A state statute creates tort liability for physical and "constructive" invasions of privacy through photographing, videotaping or recording a person engaged in "a private, personal, or familial activity." While this law limits so-called in your face photography, it also sharply limits the use of visual (telephoto lens) or auditory enhancement devices (microphones that can pick up conversations from great distances). The law triples the damages celebrities can win from paparazzi if they are assaulted while the photos are being taken and denies the photographers any profits from the sale of pictures taken during the photographic melees.

The statute was toughened in 2010 when it abolished immunity for individuals or companies that publish the "constructive invasion of privacy" pictures taken by photographers. Penalties can be significant. Also, damages can be levied against media outlets that initially purchase photos or recordings they know were taken in violation of the statute.

In 2012, a new part of California's anti-paparazzi statute received its first judicial challenge. The case centered on a photographer named Paul Raef who allegedly drove more than 80 miles per hour and cut across multiple lanes of traffic on a Los Angeles

---

76. 19 N.E. 3d 1165 (Ill. App. Ct. 2014), app. den., 23 N.E.3d 1201 (Ill. 2015).
77. *Gallela v. Onassis,* 487 F. 2d 986 (1973), 533 F. Supp. 1076 (1982).
78. *Wolfson v. Lewis,* 924 F. Supp. 1413 (1996).

area freeway chasing a vehicle Justin Bieber was driving (a Fisker Karma for fans of the Biebs, and "the 101" for SoCal natives). Raef was the first person charged under California Vehicle Code Section 40008(a), which took effect in 2011 and makes it a misdemeanor punishable by up to $2,500 and six months in jail to violate various California safe driving laws "with the intent to capture any type of visual image, sound recording, or other physical impression of another person for a commercial purpose." Raef argued that this provision, which increases the punishment for reckless driving committed with the intent to capture an image for a commercial purpose, was unconstitutional because he claimed it narrowly targeted only members of the press. He made this argument because, in fact, laws that single out the press, or certain members of it, for special treatment are subject to heightened scrutiny by courts.

In 2015, however, a California appellate court upheld the provision in *Raef* v. *Appellate Division of Superior Court.*[79] The appellate court found that California Vehicle Code Section 40008(a) was "a law of general application that does not target speech or single out the press for special treatment." In reaching this conclusion, the court reasoned that "[o]n its face, Section 40008 is not limited to paparazzi chasing celebrities or reporters gathering news. Instead, the statute targets 'any person' who commits an enumerated traffic offense with the intent to capture the image, sound, or physical impression of 'another person' for a commercial purpose." In brief, the law was constitutional because, by its terms, it did not discriminate against the news media. In 2016, the Supreme Court of California declined to review the case, thus letting the appellate court's ruling stand and leaving California Vehicle Code Section 40008(a) in place.

In 2015, California's anti-paparazzi statute was amended and expanded once more—this time to deal with drones that might record images of celebrities flying above their property. In brief, the statute now provides for civil liability when a person knowingly enters "onto the land or *into the airspace above the land* of another person without permission." The law fails to define, however, exactly how high that protected airspace extends above one's property. This anti-drone provision was adopted after celebrities, including Kanye West and Miley Cyrus, claimed to have been "droned" by the paparazzi.

THE USE OF HIDDEN RECORDING DEVICES

The miniaturization of video and audio equipment has made it possible for anyone, including reporters, to secretly record conversations, confrontations, meetings and other happenings. Can such recording constitute an intrusion, an invasion of privacy? It is not easy to answer this question definitively.

In 1971 a U.S. Court of Appeals in California ruled that such surreptitious recording could constitute an illegal intrusion. The case was an odd one. Two reporters for *Life* magazine agreed to cooperate with Los Angeles police who sought to arrest a man who was practicing medicine without a license. Posing as man and wife, the pair went to the "doctor's" home where he conducted his practice. While A.A. Dietemann examined the woman, the man secretly photographed the procedure. At the same

---

79. 193 Cal. Rptr. 3d 159 (Cal. Ct. App. 2015), review denied, 2016 Cal. LEXIS 509 (Cal. Jan. 20, 2016).

time the conversation was secretly recorded. Police arrested Dietemann several weeks later, and following his apprehension the magazine published a story with a transcript of the recorded conversation and some of the photos taken in his home. The appellate court sustained his suit for intrusion, ruling that a homeowner should not "be required to take the risk that what is heard or seen [in his or her home] will be transmitted by photography or recording . . . to the public at large."[80] Other courts have not followed this precedent, although none of the subsequent cases involved recording or photography in a private home.

For example, in 1975 Arlyn Cassidy and several other Chicago police officers were acting as undercover agents, investigating massage parlors in the city. The owner of one massage parlor where police previously had made arrests believed he was being harassed by the officers and invited a television news camera crew to come in and secretly film an encounter between an undercover agent and a model at the parlor. The camera was set up behind a two-way mirror and was filming when officer Cassidy came in, paid $30 for deluxe lingerie modeling and subsequently arrested the girl for solicitation. Three other agents came into the room at about the same time the television news crew burst through another door, filming as they left the building. The officers sued the station for intrusion, using the *Dietemann* case as precedent.

But an Illinois appellate court ruled in favor of the journalists, distinguishing the *Dietemann* case in some important ways. First, Cassidy and the other plaintiffs were public officers acting in the line of duty as the filming took place. Second, the film crew was not in a private home but in a public business. And third, the crew was on hand at the invitation of the operator of the premises. "In our opinion," the court ruled, "no right of privacy against intrusion can be said to exist with reference to the gathering and dissemination of news concerning discharge of public duties."[81]

A Kentucky circuit court ruled that it was not an intrusion when a young woman, at the instigation of a newspaper, secretly recorded a conversation she had with an attorney in the attorney's office. After the newspaper published a transcript of the conversation, during which attorney John T. McCall proposed an unethical fee arrangement with the woman, the lawyer sued for intrusion. Again, the court distinguished *Dietemann*, noting that the woman was in McCall's office at his invitation. "A lawyer, an officer of the court, discussing a public court with a potential client, is not in seclusion within the meaning of the law," the court ruled.[82] A Kentucky appellate court subsequently upheld this ruling.[83]

Finally, a U.S. District Court in Illinois in 1994 rejected an intrusion claim made against ABC News after it had secretly photographed and recorded eye examinations at an ophthalmology clinic. The owners of the clinic sued. The court ruled that the plaintiffs in the case had alleged no damage from the recording, other than that it had been broadcast. The court also rejected the claim that the recording violated the doctor-patient privilege. That privilege, the court said, belongs to the patient, not the doctor. If the

"A lawyer, an officer of the court, discussing a public court with a potential client, is not in seclusion within the meaning of the law."

80. *Dietemann* v. *Time, Inc.,* 499 F. 2d 245 (1971).
81. *Cassidy* v. *ABC,* 377 N.E. 2d 126 (1978).
82. *McCall* v. *Courier-Journal,* 4 M.L.R. 2337 (1979).
83. *McCall* v. *Courier-Journal,* 6 M.L.R. 1112 (1980).

doctor had filmed the examination, it would have been a violation of this privilege and likely an intrusion. But when the patients authorized the recording (they were working for the network), no legal wrong occurred.

The 5th U.S. Circuit Court of Appeals upheld this ruling in early 1995. The appellate court specifically rejected the plaintiff's arguments that the 1971 *Dietemann* ruling should control in this situation. The court said Dietemann was operating out of his home, not a public place of business like the ophthalmology clinic. And Dietemann did no advertising whereas the eye clinic actively solicited the public to visit the facility.[84] Cases like those cited here have chipped away at the substance of the *Dietemann* ruling.

UNDERCOVER INTRUSIONS INTO ANIMAL FACILITIES: THE RISE OF "AG-GAG" LAWS AND THE "FARMARAZZI"

Many animal rights activists, as well as investigative news organizations, are concerned about the sometimes deplorable conditions and alleged abuse of animals at factory farms and slaughterhouses. The activists and investigative reporters sometimes try to go undercover to videotape such conditions and abuses. For such actions, they have been dubbed the "farmarazzi," a twist on the paparazzi who photograph celebrities.

In 2012, however, Iowa and Utah adopted criminal statutes known as "ag-gag" laws that make taking such undercover images much more difficult. Utah's law provides that a person is "guilty of agricultural operation interference" if the person, without the consent of the operation's owner, either "knowingly or intentionally records an image of, or sound from, the agricultural operation by leaving a recording device on the agricultural operation" or "obtains access to an agricultural operation under false pretenses."

By 2017, at least eight states had adopted some variation of an ag-gag statute.

In August 2015, a federal district court declared Idaho's ag-gag law unconstitutional for violating the First Amendment freedom of speech in *Animal Legal Defense Fund* v. *Otter*.[85] The Idaho statute created a new crime called "interference with agricultural production." Judge Lynn Winmill wrote that the statute was designed to criminalize undercover investigations of agricultural production facilities by, in part, prohibiting a person from obtaining employment at such facilities by "misrepresentation with the intent to cause economic or other injury" and by prohibiting "audio or video recordings of the conduct of an agricultural production facility's operation."

Judge Winmill found the law was a content-based restriction on speech subject to the rigorous standard of judicial review known as **strict scrutiny**. He reasoned, by ruling in favor of the Animal Legal Defense Fund that "the lies used to facilitate

84. *Desnick* v. *Capital Cities/ABC, Inc.,* 851 F. Supp. 303 (1994), aff'd *Desnick* v. *American Broadcasting Companies, Inc.,* 44 F. 3d 1345 (1995).
85. 118 F. Supp. 3d 1195 (D. Idaho 2015).

undercover investigations actually advance core First Amendment values by exposing misconduct to the public eye and facilitating dialogue on issues of considerable public interest. This type of politically-salient speech is precisely the type of speech the First Amendment was designed to protect."

In 2017, in *Animal Legal Defense Fund v. Herbert*[86] U.S. District Judge Robert Shelby ruled that Utah's ban was also unconstitutional. Shelby ruled the state failed to show the ban was intended to ensure the safety of animals and farm workers from disease or injury. Shelby noted that while the state had an interest in addressing "perceived threats to the state agricultural industry . . . [s]uppressing broad swaths of protected speech" was not the proper way to achieve these goals. Although these two cases are the first to overturn bans on filming at farms, the future of ag-gag laws is yet to be determined. The Idaho case is currently pending in the 9th Circuit.

INTRUSION BY DRONES

The rapid proliferation of unmanned aircraft systems (UAS), commonly called drones, armed with video recorders creates the potential for a large number of civil lawsuits for intrusion into seclusion. Imagine, for instance, intentionally flying about 100 feet above the ground an image-recording drone over your neighbor's fenced-in and otherwise secluded backyard swimming pool while the neighbor sunbathes nude. Many would no doubt consider such an aerial intrusion into a private location highly offensive to a reasonable person. As noted earlier in this chapter, California amended its anti-paparazzi statute in 2015 to cover invasions "into the airspace above the land of another person without permission."

By 2016, more than half of the states had adopted some form of legislation to address the use of drones, coming on top of Federal Aviation Administration regulations and requirements for drone registration. Some state laws prohibit the use of drones to hunt animals or to capture images of critical infrastructure buildings and structures, but others affect the use of drones by journalists to gather newsworthy images and thus seriously raise First Amendment concerns. These laws affect drone journalists by creating legal remedies (civil causes of actions) for individuals who are surveilled or who have their pictures taken by drones without their consent while situated on their own private property.

Imagine the backyard pool scenario above, but now consider if the drone is flown by a journalist who only briefly flies it over the nude sunbather while on the way to capture images of a roaring house fire two blocks down the street. The drone incidentally captures fleeting images of the sunbather, but only does so in the process of reaching the fire—a newsworthy event. It is doubtful that the image capture of the sunbather would be considered "highly offensive" under the intrusion cause of action because it was both fleeting and not done for a voyeuristic or deviant purpose. But might there be liability under a state drone statute?

86. Case No. 2:13-cv-00679-RJS (Jul. 7, 2017).

North Carolina's drone statute—General Statute Section 15A-300.1—prohibits the use of drones to "photograph an individual, without the individual's consent, for the purpose of publishing or otherwise publicly disseminating the photograph." But lawmakers in the Tar Heel State wisely carved out an exemption from liability under this statute for "newsgathering, newsworthy events, or events or places to which the general public is invited."

Florida, on the other hand, lacks such a newsworthiness exemption from its drone law, Florida Statute Section 934.50. That law provides that a person (including a journalist) "may not use a drone equipped with an imaging device to record an image of privately owned real property or of the owner, tenant, occupant, invitee, or licensee of such property with the intent to conduct surveillance on the individual or property captured in the image in violation of such a person's reasonable expectation of privacy without his or her written consent." The Sunshine State law creates a private civil remedy for individuals who are victims of such conduct.

Texas goes even further with its drone statutes, making it a criminal misdemeanor under Government Code Section 423.003 to use a drone to "to capture an image of an individual or privately owned real property in this state with the intent to conduct surveillance on the individual or property captured in the image." As with Florida, Texas does not provide an exemption for journalists who gather images of individuals involved in newsworthy activities on their own property.

Ultimately, the problem with the growing number of state statutes targeting drone use is that they create an uneven patchwork of laws that journalists must, quite literally when it comes to flying drones, navigate to avoid civil and criminal liability. The tort of intrusion discussed in this chapter already should provide a sufficient remedy—by itself and without the need for additional state laws—for any individual whose privacy is truly invaded in a highly offensive manner by either a drone hobbyist or a drone journalist.

INTRUSION AND THE PUBLICATION OF INFORMATION OBTAINED ILLEGALLY

Gathering information through illegal intrusions is not the way most journalists typically behave. But using information gathered illegally by others is another matter altogether, and while not a common practice, it does occur. Can a newspaper or broadcasting station or Web site operator be successfully sued for publishing or broadcasting material obtained via an illegal intrusion by a third party? The Supreme Court, echoing some older lower-court decisions, said no in a case called *Bartnicki* v. *Vopper* when asked this question.[87] The case involved the broadcast by a radio station of an audiotape recording of a cell phone conversation between two officials of a teachers' union. Not-so-veiled threats were made during the conversation against local school board members. The conversation was illegally intercepted and taped by unknown persons and then distributed to the local press. The two union officials brought suit under the federal wiretap statute, which makes it a violation for anyone to disclose the contents of an illegally intercepted communication. In the 6-3 ruling, the high court acknowledged that the case presented

---

87. *Bartnicki* v. *Vopper*, 532 U.S. 514 (2001).

a tough choice between protecting the free flow of information in society and the individual's right to privacy and the protection of private speech. Justice John Paul Stevens noted that the framers of the Constitution "surely did not foresee the advances in science that produced the conversation, the interception or the conflict" that generated the case. But while the majority of the court ruled that there was no liability in this case for broadcasting the tape, the justices said they did so only because the broadcasters in the case had played no part in intercepting or obtaining the taped conversation, and because of the public significance—not simply the newsworthiness—of the content of the conversation. The bottom line from *Bartnicki*? The press may freely publish: 1) truthful material; 2) about matters of public significance; 3) that it has lawfully obtained, even if from a source who obtained it unlawfully; 4) unless the government can demonstrate an interest of the highest order. The majority in *Bartnicki* ruled in favor of allowing the press to broadcast the illegally recorded tape, reasoning that "in this case, privacy concerns give way when balanced against the interest in publishing matters of public importance."

Previous rulings had focused on cases in which a right-to-privacy intrusion claim was made. In three separate rulings, two by U.S. Courts of Appeals[88] and a third by a Maryland state court,[89] judges found that no liability for intrusion could be assessed against the publisher of that material so long as it had been obtained innocently. In the Maryland case several former and current members of the University of Maryland basketball team sued the *Washington Evening Star* for publishing an article that revealed portions of their academic records. Somebody gave the newspaper the information. There was no evidence presented that the reporters had either personally inspected the records or asked someone else to do it. Consequently, no suit could be maintained by the athletes on the intrusion theory.*

In 2016, *The New York Times* published a portion of the then-presidential-candidate Donald Trump's 1995 income tax returns demonstrating that Trump had taken a massive deduction to avoid paying federal income taxes for 18 years. The tax returns had been unlawfully obtained by a third party and provided to *The Times*. Although some commentators suggested *The Times* had violated federal law by publishing Trump's returns, *The Times* broke no law and, even if the newspaper had broken the law, the First Amendment would have protected it. While federal law prohibits the publication of federal tax documents, *The Times* published portions of tax returns from *state* filings.

---

* In 1996 a Florida couple used a police radio scanner to eavesdrop on a conference call conversation among members of the Republican congressional leadership, who were discussing an ethics investigation about to take place. The couple recorded the conversation and gave a copy of the tape to Rep. James McDermott, D-Wash., who sent copies to the fellow members of the Ethics Committee and played the tape for reporters. One of the people whose conversations were recorded sued McDermott under the federal wiretap statute. The U.S. Court of Appeals for the District of Columbia ruled in 2006 that the First Amendment did not shield the congressman from liability under the law for disclosing the conversation to newspapers because he knew who intercepted it and that it had been illegally intercepted. The same court sitting en banc affirmed this decision in May 2007. *Boehner* v. *McDermott*, 441 F. 3d 1010 (2006); *Boehner* v. *McDermott*, 35 M.L.R. 1705 (2007); and the Supreme Court refused to hear an appeal from the ruling.

88. *Liberty Lobby* v. *Pearson*, 390 F. 2d 489 (1968); and *Pearson* v. *Dodd*, 410 F. 2d 701 (1969).
89. *Bilney* v. *Evening Star*, 406 A. 2d (1979).

Furthermore, it is highly likely that a judge would rule that the First Amendment protected the publication of the information, as the government cannot stop or punish truthful publications about matters of public concern minus a government interest of the highest order. In addition, under *Bartnicki*, *The Times* would be protected when publishing documents unlawfully obtained by a third party.

Remember, however, nothing protects a journalist who actually makes the illegal intrusion by pilfering documents or intercepting telephone conversations. And in some instances, as noted by the high court in the *Bartnicki* case, even the obvious newsworthiness of a story might be insufficient to shield a news medium that publishes the contents of illegally obtained material in direct violation of statutes such as the federal wiretap laws. Beyond just the law, ethical considerations abound as well and must be factored into the equation. Journalists whose decision to publish or broadcast is based on their often self-serving declaration of "serving the public good" will not always prevail in the 21st century.

SUMMARY

Intruding on an individual's solitude, or intrusion, can be an invasion of privacy. The legal wrong occurs as soon as the information about the individual is illegally collected. Subsequent publication of the material is not needed to establish a cause of action, and defending an intrusion by arguing that in publishing the information the defendant was serving the public interest rarely succeeds. The plaintiff carries the burden of convincing the court that when the intrusion occurred, he or she enjoyed a reasonable expectation of privacy. The general rule is that there can be no such expectation if the plaintiff was in a public place. Public streets, restaurants, even areas in private businesses normally accessible to the public are not places where an individual can reasonably expect to find privacy. The use of hidden cameras and microphones frequently prompts intrusion suits, and the courts have viewed such intrusions in various ways, depending on where the information was gathered. But in some jurisdictions the use of such devices is barred by other laws. The subsequent publication or broadcast of material obtained through an intrusion by a third party (i.e., not the publisher or broadcaster) has not been regarded as a violation of privacy law.

BIBLIOGRAPHY

Chambers, Marcia. "Case of Art, Icons and Law, with Woods in the Middle." *The New York Times,* 3 July 2002, C13.

Crampton, Thomas. "Oops, Did It Again. An Irish Bill Seeks to Protect Personal Privacy." *The New York Times,* 2 October 2006, C6.

Glater, Jonathan D. "Open Secrets." *The New York Times,* 27 June 2008, C1.

Jewell, Mark. "Setback Seen for E-Mail Privacy." *Seattle Post-Intelligencer,* 2 July 2004, C2.

Kirkpatrick, David. *The Facebook Effect.* New York: Simon and Schuster, 2010.

Liptak, Adam. "Court Weighs Whether Corporations Have Personal Property Rights." *The New York Times,* 20 January 2011, A-21.

Madoff, Ray. "The New Grave Robbers." *The New York Times*, 28 March 2011, A25.

Mangan, Timothy. "Lawsuit Settled Over Look-Alike." *Orange County Register*, 30 August 2012.

Pomerantz, Dorothy. "Michael Jackson Tops Forbes' List of Top-Earning Dead Celebrities with $140 Million Haul," *Forbes*, 15 October 2014.

Prosser, William L. "Privacy." *California Law Review* 48 (1960): 383.

Thamel, Pete. "N.C.A.A. Fails to Stop Licensing Lawsuit." *The New York Times*, 9 February 2010, B-11.

Thomas, Katie. "Image Rights vs. Free Speech in Video Game Suite." *The New York Times*, 10 November 2010, A1.

Warren, Samuel D., and Louis D. Brandeis. "The Right to Privacy." *Harvard Law Review* 4 (1890): 220.

CHAPTER 8

Invasion of Privacy

PUBLICATION OF PRIVATE INFORMATION
AND FALSE LIGHT

Giving publicity to private facts about someone's life is what provoked legal scholars Samuel D. Warren and Louis D. Brandeis to propose in 1890 that the law should protect an individual's right to privacy. Some label this gossipmongering, others describe it as legitimate journalism. Whatever it is called, it has become the stock-in-trade of a growing number of American periodicals, Web sites and television programs. And the law, as you will see in the next section, is largely ineffective in stopping it. We also explore in this chapter the strangest of the privacy torts, false-light invasion of privacy.

PUBLIC DISCLOSURE OF PRIVATE FACTS

The most common definition of the privacy tort (civil legal cause of action) known as public disclosure of private facts is the following one set forth in the Restatement (Second) of Torts and adopted by many states:

> **One who gives publicity to a matter concerning the private life of another is
> subject to liability to the other for invasion of his privacy, if the matter
> publicized is of a kind that**

a. **would be highly offensive to a reasonable person, and**

b. **is not of legitimate concern to the public.**

"Keyhole journalism" is what press critics in the late 19th century called it. The snooping, prying, gossipy, scandal-driven reporting that many of us today have come to take for granted in both the print and electronic media was just emerging at the end of the 19th century. A lot of people believed it was offensive and wanted it stopped. Attorneys Samuel Warren and Louis Brandeis even proposed a legal solution, a right of privacy, enforceable in a court of law.[1] But American courts have been less than enthusiastic in their support for such ideas. What makes this tort constitutionally suspect in the eyes of many judges and legal scholars is that it punishes the press, or whomever, for publishing truthful information that has been legally obtained. Making the press liable in such instances seems to run against basic American First Amendment tenets and a substantial body of case law. Truth, in other words, is not a defense for the media when sued for public disclosure of private facts. The best defense, instead, is that the facts disclosed are of legitimate public concern or are newsworthy. The tort applies to the publication of *non-newsworthy* private facts.

Many Americans seem to care very little about personal privacy. While declaring the press should be liable for publishing stories about the private lives of public persons, stories in the printed press, on television and on the Web are seemingly gobbled up by readers and viewers. Is there really a concern about privacy when a vast majority of Americans carry devices that can openly or surreptitiously record and photograph their friends, neighbors and even strangers? The explosive growth of social media sites where users seem willing to share the most intimate aspects of their private lives with their "friends" and even strangers seems to run counter to any stated concerns over privacy.

It is easiest to understand this aspect of the law by taking the tort apart and looking at each element separately (see boxed text). The plaintiff in a private facts case carries the burden of proving each element. Failure to convince the court of any one of these three parts of the law means the lawsuit is doomed.

In Chapter 7, the problem of gathering personal information via the Internet was explored as an intrusion. Disclosing personal information gathered via the Internet and then publishing it would fall under the publication-of-private-facts area of privacy law. As with defamation and intrusion, it is important to remember that the law applies in much the same way to online publications as it would if the information were published in a newspaper or broadcast on television.

Today, however, gathering information and disseminating it is easier than ever. It is possible in many instances to literally surf through people's lives with just a few keystrokes on a computer. In addition, news stories about leaks of personal data from companies, various data banks and other Web sources are commonplace. Internet data privacy is a growing concern and an expanding area of law. However, while the Federal Trade Commission has developed ways to protect an individual's online data[2] and have acted against companies who have exploited the information or not properly disclosed how personal information is being gathered or used, the government has done little else. Why?

1. Warren and Brandeis, "The Right to Privacy."
2. For example, the FTC has developed guidelines for dealing with online data security. See, for example, https://www.ftc.gov/tips-advice/business-center/privacy-and-security/data-security.

Members of Congress annually condemn tech companies' treatment of personal information, but despite substantial public concern, little has been done to solve the problems. Companies like Facebook, Google and Twitter all have personal representatives, usually called lobbyists, in Washington, D.C., who meet members of the Senate and House of Representatives. (Twitter does not call its representative a lobbyist, but rather an "unofficial ambassador to help politicians understand the micro blogging service."[3]) These companies are spending more and more each year on contributions to political candidates. It is not entirely correct to say the term "Internet privacy" is an oxymoron, but each year that description becomes more and more accurate. Things won't change until Americans demand a change, and as noted in Chapter 7, most Americans, who say they care about protecting privacy, often don't behave in such a way which demonstrates that. But, as noted above, it is important to remember that the privacy law applies to social media, microblogging sites and Internet publications the same way it does to more traditional publications, as the Web site Gawker discovered when it published a sex tape of professional wrestler Hulk Hogan.

BASIC ELEMENTS OF THE PUBLIC DISCLOSURE OF PRIVATE FACTS TORT

1. There must be publicity given to private facts about an individual.
2. The revelation of these facts must be highly offensive to a reasonable person.
3. The published material must not be of legitimate public concern.

PUBLICITY

The term "publicity" in privacy law means something different than the term "publication" does in libel law. In defamation, "publication" means to communicate the material to a single third party. The word "publicity" in privacy law implies far more. It means that the material is communicated to the public at large or to a great number of people, making it certain that the facts will shortly become public knowledge.[4] This kind of publicity can usually be presumed when a story is published in a newspaper, broadcast over radio or television or posted on a Web site. Simply communicating the facts to two or three people, on the other hand, does not amount to "publicity."

How would you feel if the private details of your 20-year personal relationship (one that produced a child) with a radio disc jockey—in particular, a so-called shock jock—were disclosed by the disc jockey in a series of on-air diatribes after the relationship ends? That was the factual scenario in a 2012 Florida appellate court ruling called *Doe* v. *Beasley Broadcast Group, Inc.*[5] The appellate court refused to dismiss the plaintiff's cause of action for public disclosure of private facts. The court reasoned that the plaintiff "presented evidence that the disc jockey publicly disclosed private facts about her during the subject

---

3. Swift, "Bracing for Privacy Battle."
4. See *Lowe* v. *Hearst Communications Inc.*, 34 M.L.R. 1823 (2006). In 2009 the Minnesota Court of Appeals ruled that simply posting private information on the Internet is enough to allow an invasion of privacy claim, no matter how many people see it. See http://www.rcfp.org/newsitems/index.php?i=10857.
5. 105 So.3d 1 (Fla. Dist. Ct. App. 2012).

broadcasts. She also presented evidence that as a result of the broadcasts, she suffered stress, anxiety, humiliation, and physical ailments such as a large rash and boil on her face, which left a residual scar." Such mental injuries are recoverable as damages in public disclosure of private facts lawsuits.

PRIVATE FACTS

Before a public disclosure suit can be successful, the plaintiff must demonstrate that the material publicized was indeed private. What happens in public is considered public information. When the Associated Press reported the identity of the victim of a sexual assault who testified at the sentencing hearing of the molester, the young man sued for invasion of privacy. The name was not in the court records and had not been made public before the hearing. But the testimony was given in open court. The 4th U.S. Court of Appeals ruled in favor of the news-gathering agency, saying "we cannot understand how the voluntary disclosure of information in an unrestricted, open courtroom setting could be anything but a matter of public interest."[6] One of two young women who were photographed while attending a rock concert at the Big Cypress Indian Reservation in Florida sued when her picture—showing her exposed breasts adorned with tattoos or body paint—was published in *Stuff* magazine with the caption "Their Parents Must Be Proud." She argued that because the picture was taken on privately owned land at a concert open only to ticket holders it was a private affair. The Florida Circuit Court disagreed, noting that as a matter of law and common sense, a rock concert is a public event.[7] Protecting your privacy in public is even more difficult now that everyone carries a smartphone with a camera. Some people have learned the hard way that you should act as if someone is taking photos and shooting videos of you all the time and that the footage is going to end up all over the Internet.

If a large segment of the public is already aware of supposedly intimate or personal information, it is not private. Oliver Sipple, who deflected a gun held by a woman who tried to assassinate President Gerald Ford, sued the *San Francisco Chronicle* after a columnist noted that the fact that Sipple was a homosexual was probably the reason Ford had never thanked his benefactor for his heroic act. But Sipple's suit failed, in part at least, because his sexual orientation was hardly a secret in San Francisco. A California Court of Appeals noted that Sipple routinely frequented gay bars, marched in parades with other homosexuals and openly worked for the election of homosexual political candidates, and that many gay publications had reported stories about his activities in the homosexual community. That he was a homosexual was not a private fact, the court ruled.[8]

In 2007, Robert Steinbuch, a former Congressional aide, sued Jessica Cutler, another former Congressional aide, for publishing detailed and explicit information about their sexual relations on her blog, Washingtonienne. Cutler used Steinbuch's initials "RS" when using graphic terms to describe their sex life, including details such as he "[h]as a great ass" and "likes spanking (both giving and receiving)." Steinbuch also sued Anna Marie Cox of the blog Wonkette for describing Cutler's blog contents, republishing excerpts on the Wonkette Web site and providing a hyperlink to Cutler's blog. While

6. *Doe 2* v. *Associated Press,* 331 F. 3d 417 (2003).
7. *Mayhall* v. *Dennis Stuff Inc.,* 31 M.L.R. 1567 (2002).
8. *Sipple* v. *Chronicle Publishing Co.,* 154 Cal. App. 3d 1040 (1984).

the court ruled the lawsuit against Cutler could proceed, the court dismissed the claim against Cox because she did nothing but blog about what was already public.[9]

In 2005, several Navy SEALs sued the Associated Press for publishing photographs of them posing with Iraqi captives in compromising positions. The court held the images were not private facts because the Navy SEALs were members of the military on active duty conducting wartime operations and agreed to be photographed and to have those photographs placed on the Internet.[10]

But it is an overstatement to say that if *anyone else* knows the information it is no longer a private fact. A Georgia appellate court ruled in 1994 when a television station inadvertently revealed the identity of a victim of AIDS who was being interviewed during a broadcast, the fact that the plaintiff had discussed his AIDS with friends, family and doctors did not defeat his privacy claim. The court said he could waive his right of privacy for one purpose—discussing the matter with family and physicians—and still assert it for another purpose—a television broadcast. Who knew what about the private life of the individual could be considered by a court.[11]

Information contained in documents and files that are considered public records—that is, open to public inspection—is generally not regarded as private. What if no person has ever inspected the file, but then its contents are published? It may still not be considered private. The *Idaho Statesman* in Boise was sued when it published a photo of a handwritten statement that was given to the police in 1955 during the investigation of a sex scandal. The individual who gave the statement was charged and convicted, but the statement implicated other people who were never charged in the case. The document was never part of a criminal proceeding and never made it into a public court record, but was kept for 40 years in a public criminal case file that was stored in the court clerk's office. It was discovered and published in 1995 in an article about the earlier scandal during a debate on a public initiative to limit the rights of gays in Idaho. An individual who was linked to a homosexual relationship (but never charged with a crime) in the original 40-year-old document sued for invasion of privacy. The Idaho Court of Appeals said the publication was protected because it was a part of an official criminal court file. Quoting an opinion by Justice Warren Burger from 1975, the Idaho court noted, "A responsible press is an undoubtedly desirable goal, but press responsibility is not mandated by the Constitution and like many other virtues it cannot be legislated." After two hearings the Idaho Supreme Court affirmed the lower court rulings, saying the newspaper could not be held liable for accurately reporting what was contained in a court record open to the public.[12]

If an individual tells a reporter something about himself or herself that others don't know, is that information still private? No, but what if the reporter promised not to reveal the name of the person who revealed the information? This question arose in a case in Washington state where four high school students sued the school district for invasion of privacy (among other things) because the student newspaper published detailed stories about their sex lives. The students said when they discussed the subject

9. *Steinbuch* v. *Cutler & Cox*, No. 05-0970, (D.C.D.C. May 21, 2007).
10. *Four Navy Seals* v. *Associated Press*, 413 F. Supp. 2d 1136 (S.D. Cal. 2005).
11. *Multimedia WMAZ Inc.* v. *Kubach*, 443 S.E. 2d 491 (1994).
12. *Uranga* v. *Federated Publications Inc.*, 28 M.L.R. 2265 (2000), aff'd 67 P. 3d 29 (2003).

with the student reporters, they were promised anonymity. The school district maintained that the students actually agreed to have their names included in the story. The case went to trial, and a jury found in 2010 that the story was newsworthy (see later this chapter regarding newsworthiness) and was not an invasion of privacy.[13] Written consent undoubtedly would have resolved the case more quickly. Courts have generally followed the standard that a person's consent is valid, so long as the person has the legal capacity to give it—regardless of age. The key is, according to attorneys at the Student Press Law Center, does the individual understand the consequences of revealing the information?

Naming Rape Victims

One of the most controversial issues in the private facts realm of privacy law concerns the publication of the name of a victim of a sexual assault. Two questions arise: *Can* the name or identity be legally published? And, *should* the name or identity be published? The law is clear on this matter; the ethical issue is more complicated.

Since the mid-1970s courts have consistently ruled that if the victim's name is part of a public document or proceeding, or if the press obtains it in another legal manner, it can be published without incurring liability. In 1975, in *Cox Broadcasting* v. *Cohn*, the Supreme Court ruled that a privacy action against a Georgia broadcasting station for publishing the name of a rape victim could not succeed because the victim's identity had been included in public court documents. "We are reluctant to embark on a course that would make public records generally available to the media, but forbid their publication if offensive to the sensibilities of the supposed reasonable man," Justice Byron White wrote. "Such a rule would make it very difficult for the press to inform their readers about the public business and yet stay within the law," he added.[14] Fourteen years later, in *Florida Star* v. *BJF*, the court reiterated this decision when it ruled that a privacy action could not proceed against a newspaper that inadvertently published a sexual assault victim's name it had obtained from a document that was not a public record. The document had been mistakenly given to the reporter by a police officer, and the publication violated the newspaper's own policy against publishing such information. "The fact that state officials are not required to disclose such reports does not make it unlawful for a newspaper to receive them when furnished by the government," wrote Justice Thurgood Marshall. But the justice noted that the court's ruling was a limited one. "We hold only that where a newspaper publishes truthful information which it has lawfully obtained, punishment may be imposed, if at all, only when narrowly tailored to a state interest of the highest order."[15] Since this 1989 decision, lower courts have consistently followed this course.[16] The chances, then, of the victim of a sexual assault successfully suing a newspaper or broadcast station or blogger for revealing his or her name are extremely remote, if not impossible.

But *should* the name of a rape victim be published? As a matter of fact, most publications and broadcasting stations have not routinely publicized the name of the victim

---

13. "Washington Jury Finds."
14. *Cox Broadcasting* v. *Cohn,* 420 U.S. 469 (1975).
15. 491 U.S. 524 (1989).
16. See, for example, *Macon Telegraph Publishing Co.* v. *Tatum,* 436 S.E. 2d 655 (1993); and *Star Telegram Inc.* v. *Doe,* 23 M.L.R. 2492 (1995).

of a sexual assault during the last two decades.[17] What was once a common practice even 50 years ago has been largely abandoned. But some media outlets do publish this material. Critics of this practice raise three arguments:

- Someone who is sexually assaulted becomes a victim three times: the first during the assault; the second during the interrogation by often unsympathetic police, prosecutors and defense lawyers during the investigation and the public trial; and the third when the identity is published and broadcast in the press, revealing the details of the attack to neighbors, friends, co-workers and others.
- Society often judges the rape victim to be as guilty as the rapist, and this can stigmatize the victim for many years.
- Because of the first two factors, victims who realize that their identities will be revealed frequently fail to report the crime, especially if the rape has been committed by an acquaintance. The rapist is not punished and may go on to attack another victim.

The validity of the arguments is difficult to dispute. But some journalists will publish or broadcast the victim's name regardless of the consequences. They argue that it is important for society to know the names of all crime victims. Publishing the name of a victim adds credibility to a news story, making the story more meaningful to readers or viewers. Others argue that when the press fails to publish the name of a rape victim it is treating this victim differently from the victim of a simple assault or a robbery. This reinforces the notion that rape victims are at least partly responsible for their fate, or that they are "damaged goods." "Now is the time for us to understand that keeping the hunted under wraps merely establishes her as an outcast and implies that her chances for normal social relations are doomed forevermore," said Karen DeCrow, former president of the National Organization for Women. "Pull off the veil of shame. Print the name," she added. Geneva Overholser, former editor of the *Des Moines Register*, argues that by not printing the name, the press is reinforcing the idea that rape is a different kind of attack, not a crime of brutal violence. She said that this "sour blight of prejudice is best subjected to strong sunlight."[18] Some newspapers are trying to reach a compromise on this matter by not printing the victim's name unless she or he consents to the use. Victims who fear the publicity are protected; using the names of those who don't mind undermines the myth noted by DeCrow.

HIGHLY OFFENSIVE PUBLICITY

If the determination has been made that private facts about a person's life have been given publicity, a court must then ask two more questions:

1. Would a reasonable person find the publicity given to the fact highly offensive?
2. Was the private fact that was disclosed of legitimate public concern? In other words, was the disclosed fact newsworthy?

17. Marcus and McMahon, "Limiting Disclosure," 1019.
18. Ibid.

Judges and juries are often faced with the dilemma of deciding whether the revelation of important, but offensive or embarrassing, information is an invasion of privacy. The law on this question is pretty clear: If the material is of legitimate public concern, it doesn't matter how offensive or embarrassing the revelation is. There was no invasion of privacy. Courts sometimes use the term "newsworthiness" interchangeably with the concept of "legitimate public concern." For the past 100 years courts have been extremely reluctant to fashion narrow limits on the kinds of information people need to receive. Time and time again judges have ruled that it is not only the responsibility of the press to bring important public information to the public, but also that it is the job of editors and reporters, not the courts, to decide what is and what isn't important. If there is any legitimate public interest at all in the material, the press will usually win the case, regardless of how embarrassing revelation of the material might be. This notion is more fully discussed later in this chapter.

It is the job of editors and reporters, not the courts, to decide what is and what isn't important.

Remember, the revelation of the material must be highly offensive to a reasonable person, not to someone who is overly sensitive. The test is this: would a hypothetical reasonable person who is put in the same position as the plaintiff (the person who is suing) find the publicity given to the allegedly private fact highly offensive? A reasonable person is used here because the law worries about so-called thin-skull or eggshell plaintiffs who are overly sensitive and find anything and everything offensive. Without a reasonable person standard, eggshell plaintiffs would recover damages (money) far too easily for the normal emotional bumps and bruises we encounter in every day life.[19]

Courts have typically rejected the notion that a parent or other relative can maintain a privacy suit because of stories about the death of a family member. These suits are usually built around protecting private information about the deceased: He or she was a drug user, a gang member, committed suicide and so on. But remember, the right of privacy is a personal right; the plaintiff must allege some kind of emotional harm. Someone who is dead cannot do that; the person's right of privacy ends with his or her death. But in recent years, in a discrete set of cases, plaintiffs have raised a different argument. The cases have focused on photos taken of the deceased. The relatives claimed that the circulation or distribution of such images would or did cause them serious emotional harm.

In 2004, the Supreme Court of the United States upheld the refusal of a government agency to release the death-scene photos of an aide to President Bill Clinton because family members complained that their own privacy interests would be damaged if the pictures were made public. The agency was relying on a privacy exemption in the Freedom of Information Act to support its refusal. (See Chapter 9 for a complete discussion of this ruling, *National Archives & Records Administration* v. *Favish*.)[20] But three years later, in *Showler* v. *Harper's Magazine Foundation,* the 10th U.S. Court of Appeals ruled that this Supreme Court ruling did not apply in a case where the father of a dead soldier sued for invasion of privacy when an open casket photo of his son was taken during a public funeral. The court said the 2004 ruling was inapplicable because the high court was applying a statute—the Freedom of Information Act—and not considering a cause of action for invasion of privacy.[21] This was an intrusion case, not a private facts case.

---

19. *Andren* v. *Knight-Ridder Newspapers,* 10 M.L.R. 2109 (1984).
20. *National Archives & Records Administration* v. *Favish*, 541 U.S. 157 (2004).
21. *Showler* v. *Harper's Magazine Foundation*, 35 M.L.R. 1577 (2007).

In 2009 the 3rd U.S. Court of Appeals dismissed a right of privacy suit brought by the father of a young man, who had died accidentally or committed suicide, when the photos of the body taken by a coroner found their way onto the Internet (*Werner* v. *County of Northampton*).[22] Finally, in 2010 the California Court of Appeals ruled that a trial court had erred when it dismissed an invasion of privacy suit after police officers e-mailed photos of a teenager's decapitated corpse to acquaintances. The court in *Catsouras* v. *Department of the California Highway Patrol* ruled that family members have a privacy interest in the death images of a member of the family. The court noted that since the images did not appear in any mass medium as a part of a news story, the traditional defenses in a private facts case, that the revelation was newsworthy, was in the public interest and therefore was protected by the First Amendment, did not apply in the case.[23]

Perhaps the biggest expansion in the emerging privacy-of-death jurisprudence came in 2012 when the U.S. Court of Appeals for the 9th Circuit held in *Marsh* v. *County of San Diego*[24] that the U.S. Constitution "protects a parent's right to control the physical remains, memory and images of a deceased child against unwarranted public exploitation by the government." In becoming the first federal appellate court to recognize that individuals possess a constitutional right—not merely a statutory or common law right—to control public dissemination of a family member's death images, the 9th Circuit cited favorably both *Favish* and *Catsouras* (described above). Writing for a unanimous three-judge panel, Alex Kozinski wrote that the "long-standing tradition of respecting family members' privacy in death images partakes of both types of privacy interests protected by the Fourteenth Amendment."

Marsh involved the copying and disclosure of autopsy photographs by a former deputy district attorney, who gave one photo to a newspaper and a television station. The photos depicted a two-year-old boy who had died of severe head injuries that allegedly were caused by an abusive adult. The deceased boy's mother sued, fearing the emotional harm she would suffer by seeing the images in the news media and on the Internet. Judge Kozinski reasoned that the mother's "fear is not unreasonable given the viral nature of the Internet, where she might easily stumble upon photographs of her dead son on news Web sites, blogs or social media Web sites. This intrusion into the grief of a mother over her dead son—without any legitimate governmental purpose—'shocks the conscience' and therefore violates Marsh's substantive due process right." Whether other courts follow the 9th Circuit's lead in recognizing such a constitutional privacy right over images of dead family members will be sorted out in coming years.

As for now, it must be pointed out that newsworthiness (material constituting a matter of legitimate public concern, as described in the next few pages) still provides a defense for journalists to the disclosure of such images in a public disclosure of private facts case. Furthermore, non-gruesome images of the dead may not necessarily rise to the level of offensiveness required for a plaintiff to win a public disclosure of private facts lawsuit.

Many years ago a woman with a rather unusual medical disorder—she ate constantly, but still lost weight—was admitted to a hospital. Journalists were tipped off and descended on her room, pushed past the closed door and took pictures against the patient's will. *Time* magazine ran a story about the patient, Dorothy Barber, and in it

22. *Werner* v. *County of Northhampton*, 37 M.L.R. 2592 (2009).
23. *Catsouras* v. *Department of the California Highway Patrol*, 181 Cal. App. 4th 856 (2010).
24. 680 F.3d 1148 (9th Cir. 2012).

referred to her, in inimitable *Time* style, as "the starving glutton." Barber sued and won her case. The judge said the hospital is one place people should be able to go for privacy.[25] More than the patient's expectation of privacy in a hospital room influenced the ruling, because there are several decisions in which persons in hospitals have been considered to be the subject of legitimate concern and did not therefore enjoy the right to privacy. The story about the unusual disorder was surely offensive, almost mocking. The disorder was not contagious, and the implications for the general public were minimal. The *Time* story seemed to focus on Barber almost as if she were a freak, and in doing so the revelation of this information was highly offensive to any reasonable person, the court ruled.

The South Carolina Supreme Court affirmed a jury verdict against a newspaper that, in publishing a story about teenage pregnancies, had identified a young man—a minor—as the father of an illegitimate child. The teenage mother of the baby had given the reporter the father's name. The reporter talked to the young man, who understood that the newspaper was doing a survey on teenage pregnancy. He said he was never told that his name might be used in the story. The newspaper argued that the information—including the boy's name—was of great public interest. The state Supreme Court said that was a jury question, and a jury ruled that it was not of great public interest[26] and that its publication was highly offensive.

LEGITIMATE PUBLIC CONCERN AND NEWSWORTHINESS

The previous rulings are not typical of the results of most private facts cases. Yes, there are instances when a court will rule that private facts have been published, and that the revelation of these facts is highly offensive to a reasonable person. More often than not, however, a judge or an appellate tribunal will rule that a legitimate public interest in the subject matter or the plaintiff outweighs any embarrassment the publication might have caused. Public interest trumps offensiveness. And during the past 100 years public interest has been broadly defined. Most judges set the public interest bar fairly low and focus not on what people *should* be interested in reading or hearing, but on what readers and listeners actually find interesting. The relatively narrow definition of public concern fashioned by the courts in applying the *New York Times* Co. v. *Sullivan* libel rule (see Chapter 5) has not been applied in privacy rulings. A 72-year-old case, still often cited by jurists, set the standard in this regard.

In 1937, *New Yorker* magazine published a story about a child prodigy who had failed to fulfill the promise many had predicted for him. (See box regarding William James Sidis.) The prodigy, then nearly 40, sued for invasion of privacy. A federal appeals court ruled that while the story might have embarrassed the man, the public enjoyed reading about the problems, misfortunes and troubles of their neighbors and members of the community. "When such are the mores of the community, it could be unwise for a court to bar their expression in the newspapers, books, and magazines of the day," wrote Judge Charles Clark.[27] Since that time courts have ruled that there was public interest or legitimate public concern in stories about how two lawyers used extramarital affairs they arranged in a blackmail scheme;[28] in news reports that revealed the names of two undercover police officers who were charged with,

25. *Barber* v. *Time*, 159 S.W. 2d 291 (1942).
26. *Hawkins* v. *Multimedia*, 344 S.E. 2d 145 (1986).
27. *Sidis* v. *F-R Publishing Co.*, 113 F. 2d 806 (1940).
28. *Lowe* v. *Hearst Communications Inc.*, 487 F. 3d 246 (2007).

SIDIS v. F-R PUBLISHING CO.: A CLASSIC EXAMPLE OF "LEGITIMATE PUBLIC CONCERN"

The following are excerpts from an article written by Jared L. Manley (a pen name for noted writer James Thurber) about William James Sidis. The piece was published in *New Yorker* magazine on August 14, 1937, and provoked one of the nation's most celebrated invasion-of-privacy lawsuits (*Sidis* v. *F-R Publishing Co.*).

"Where Are They Now?" "April Fool!"

"One snowy January evening in 1910 about a hundred professors and advanced students of mathematics from Harvard University gathered in a lecture hall in Cambridge, Massachusetts, to listen to a speaker by the name of William James Sidis. He had never addressed an audience before, and he was abashed and a little awkward at the start. His listeners had to attend closely, for he spoke in a small voice that did not carry well, and he punctuated his talk with nervous, shrill laughter. . . . The speaker wore black velvet knickers. He was eleven years old. . . . When it was all over, the distinguished Professor Daniel F. Comstock of Massachusetts Institute of Technology was moved to predict to reporters, who had listened in profound bewilderment, that young Sidis would grow up to be a great mathematician, a famous leader in the world of science."

(The next section of the article explains how Sidis, as a small child, had become a kind of guinea pig for his psychologist father, who used experimental techniques to educate his son when he was little more than a baby. Manley goes on to describe Sidis' education, his extreme efforts to hide from the spotlight of publicity, his series of mundane jobs and his rejection of a career in science or mathematics.)

"William James Sidis lives today, at the age of thirty-nine, in a hall bedroom of Boston's shabby south end. . . . He seems to get a great and ironic enjoyment out of leading a life of wandering irresponsibility after a childhood of scrupulous regimentation. . . . Sidis is employed now, as usual, as a clerk in a business house. He said that he never stays in one office long because his employers or fellow-workers soon find out that he is the famous boy wonder, and he can't tolerate a position after that. 'The very sight of a mathematical formula makes me physically ill,' he said."

(Manley relates that Sidis has become a passionate collector of streetcar transfers, that he enjoys the study of certain aspects of the history of Native Americans and that he is writing a treatise on floods.)

"His visitor [Manley] was emboldened, at last, to bring up the prediction, made by Professor Comstock . . . back in 1910, that the little boy who lectured that year on the fourth dimension to a gathering of learned men would grow up to be a great mathematician, a famous leader in the world of science. 'It's strange,' said William James Sidis, with a grin, 'but you know, I was born on April Fool's Day.'"

but later cleared of, sexual assault;[29] in the sterilization of an 18-year-old girl;[30] in a young man being treated for substance abuse at a hospital;[31] in a 12-year-old giving birth to a child;[32] and in the personal activities of a body surfer.[33] A New York court ruled that even a television report celebrating a warm spring day that featured video of a man and a woman walking hand in hand on Madison Avenue had legitimate public interest. The couple objected to the story because he was married to another woman, and she was engaged to be married to another man. The court said that the film explored the prevailing attitudes on romance when it showed people behaving in this fashion, a subject that was newsworthy.[34]

But the newsworthiness argument will not always carry the day. The 11th U.S. Circuit Court of Appeals ruled in 2009 that when *Hustler* magazine published the 20-year-old nude photos of a female professional wrestler named Nancy Benoit who had been murdered by her husband—also a professional wrestler—the newsworthiness defense did not shield the publication from a privacy lawsuit brought by her mother under Georgia state law. Attorneys for *Hustler* argued that because the photos accompanied a short biographical piece about the woman, they were newsworthy. The question was, did including the short biography with the pictures insulate the photos from a lawsuit? The court said no. The publication of the brief biographical story did not "ratchet otherwise personal protected photographs into the newsworthiness exception," the judges ruled.[35] The appellate court added that the decades-old nude photos of Nancy Benoit that *Hustler* published had no relationship whatsoever to what was newsworthy (her murder) and that *Hustler's* "brief biography of Benoit's life, even with its reference to her youthful pursuit of modeling, is merely incidental to its publication of her nude photographs. Therefore, the biographical piece cannot suffice to render the nude photographs newsworthy."

HULK HOGAN v. *GAWKER*:
WRESTLING WITH NEWSWORTHINESS OVER A SEX TAPE

In March 2016, Terry Gene Bollea, better known as wrestler Hulk Hogan, won a massive $140 million jury verdict ($115 million in compensatory damages and $25 million in punitive damages) in Florida against Gawker, a celebrity-gossip Web site. Bollea sued Gawker under the theory of public disclosure of private facts. He did so based on Gawker's posting of excerpts of a hidden-camera sex tape that showed Bollea having sex with Heather Clem, the then-wife of one of Bollea's best friends, a nationally syndicated radio show host known as Bubba the Love Sponge Clem. Born Todd Alan, Clem legally changed his name to "Bubba the Love Sponge" in 1999.

Bollea asserted that the sex tape was covertly made, without his knowledge or permission, by Bubba. Assuming that the contents of the tape, which was

29. *Alvardo* v. *KOB-TV*, 493 F. 3d 1210 (2007).
30. *Howard* v. *Des Moines Register*, 283 N.W. 2d 789 (1979).
31. *Carter* v. *Superior Court of San Diego County*, 30 M.L.R. 1193 (2002).
32. *Meetze* v. *AP*, 95 S.E. 2d 606 (1956).
33. *Virgil* v. *Time, Inc.*, 527 F. 2d 1122 (1975).
34. *DeGregario* v. *CBS*, 43 N.Y.S. 2d 922 (1984).
35. *Toffoloni* v. *LFP Publishing Group LLC*, 572 F. 3d 1201 (11th Cir. 2009).

Terry Bollea, aka Hulk Hogan testifies in Gawker Media Suit.
©John Pendygraft/Pool/Getty Images

shot in a private bedroom, were private, and assuming that a reasonable person in Bollea's position would find the publicity given by Gawker to the contents of the tape highly offensive, the case boiled down to one key question: Were the contents of the sex tape—the actual images of Bollea having sex—newsworthy?

The Florida jury found that the images of Bollea having sex were not newsworthy. We know that because the jury ruled for Bollea and, as noted in this chapter, a plaintiff can only win a case for public disclosure of private facts if the information or facts published are not of legitimate public concern.

Gawker argued unsuccessfully to the jury that because Bollea was a well-known celebrity and because he had openly talked about his sex life in the media (including on Howard Stern's radio show), that the contents of the tape were newsworthy. In contrast, experts for Bollea, including University of Florida journalism professor Mike Foley, argued that while the existence of a sex tape involving Bollea might be newsworthy, watching the actual contents of the tape itself was not.

In June 2016, Gawker filed a motion for a stay of execution of the judgment pending appeal. The next day, however, Gawker filed for bankruptcy protection and put itself up for sale. Gawker's assets were acquired by Univision Communications for $135 million at a bankruptcy auction in August 2016. The sale included six Gawker Web sites: Deadspin, Gizmodo, Jalopnik, Jezebel, Kotaku and Lifehacker. The sale did not include the company's flagship Web site Gawker, which was shut down. On November 2, 2016, Gawker Media and Bollea reached a $31 million settlement. Gawker also agreed to forgo its appeal, and three articles from gawker.com were taken down, including the one involving Bollea. The rest of the Gawker Media archive remains online.

Let's explore some often-asked questions about legitimate public concern, or what the courts sometimes call newsworthiness.

Does the manner in which the story is presented have an impact on whether it has legitimate public interest? In spite of the *Barber* case previously cited, sensational treatment of a story does not usually remove the protection of newsworthiness. The parents of two young children who had suffocated in an abandoned refrigerator said the sensational way the story was presented was as objectionable as the story itself. However, the court ruled that the manner in which the article was written was not relevant to whether the article was protected by the constitutional guarantees of free speech and free press—which, by the way, it was.[36] In another case a Boston newspaper published a horrible picture of an automobile accident in which the bloodied and battered body of one of the victims was clearly visible and identifiable, and the court rejected the plaintiff's claim. The Massachusetts Supreme Court noted, "Many things which are distressing or may be lacking in propriety or good taste are not actionable."[37] A woman told police she was raped by her husband while she was unconscious and did not know it had happened until she found a videotape of the incident. She gave the tape to police, who promised it would be kept confidential and used only for law enforcement purposes. The tape nevertheless found its way to a TV station, which broadcast segments of it when the husband was arrested for other, alleged sexual assaults. The woman sued for publication of private facts. But the courts rejected her lawsuit, ruling the video was related to a matter of legitimate public concern—the prosecution of her husband. The court said the sensitive nature of the video did not make it any less newsworthy.[38]

Does the law of privacy protect what are called involuntary public figures, people who are pushed into the public spotlight through no fault of their own? While the so-called involuntary public person receives enhanced protection in libel law (see Chapter 5), this protection does not normally apply in privacy actions. Eighty-three years ago the Kentucky Supreme Court ruled that although the right of privacy protected the right of a person to live his or her life in seclusion, without being subject to undesired publicity, there are times "when one, whether willing or not, becomes an actor in an occurrence of public or general interest." At this point, the court noted, the individual loses much of his or her right to privacy.[39] A Kansas court ruled that a television report about a young man who had been arrested on suspicion of burglary, but who was released later when police admitted they had arrested the wrong man, was not an invasion of privacy. The court ruled that the plaintiff was involved in a noteworthy event, and the public had a right to be informed about the event. "This was true even though his involvement therein was purely involuntary and against his will," the court said.[40] And in 1978 an Illinois court ruled that a story that reported the death of a boy from an apparent drug overdose and recounted details of his life was not an invasion of privacy. He had

---

36. *Costlow* v. *Cuismano,* 311 N.Y.S. 2d 92 (1970).
37. *Kelley* v. *Post Publishing Co.,* 327 Mass. 275 (1951).
38. *Anderson* v. *Suiters,* 499 F. 3d 1228 (2007).
39. *Jones* v. *Herald Post Co.,* 18 S.W. 2d 972 (1929).
40. *Williams* v. *KCMO Broadcasting Co.,* 472 S.W. 2d 1 (1971).

become an involuntary public figure because of his actions within the drug culture in the community. "It is not necessary for an individual to actively seek publicity in order to be found in the public eye," the court ruled.[41] These cases are consistent with how the law is applied in most instances.

Do people who are closely associated with or related to public persons also lose elements of their right to privacy? Although there have not been a lot of court decisions based on this question, the current answer seems to be yes. People whose lives intersect with famous, infamous or other newsworthy individuals also lose some of their privacy. A story published in a Utah newspaper in 1997 said hikers had found the body of a man near a dirt trail. Police said the death looked "like one of those autoerotic things." When murder charges were subsequently filed, the story was widely reported. Family members sued saying that the reports contained information that reflected upon intimate details of the marital relationship. The 10th U.S. Court of Appeals affirmed the dismissal of the complaint saying that while it was almost impossible to define the limits of the right to privacy, it did not block the revelation of information of a spouse's behavior that reflected on the marital relationship. "Any other conclusion would stretch the right to privacy beyond any reasonable limits," the court said.[42] A New York court came to a similar conclusion nine years earlier. The plaintiff's husband had secretly committed the plaintiff to a private psychiatric facility. Few of her friends and relatives knew of the commitment. Another patient at the facility, Hedda Nussbaum, had been in the national news for many months as the adoptive mother of a 6-year-old girl who had died from child abuse. A photographer secretly snapped a photo of Nussbaum while the plaintiff Pamela Howell was standing next to her. Howell was not identified in the photo that was published in a New York newspaper. She sued for invasion of privacy but lost. The court said the Nussbaum story still had considerable public interest and the only way Howell could win was to demonstrate that her photo bore no real relationship to the article and photo. But the court said she could not do this. She was in the wrong place at the wrong time, but this did not create liability.[43]

How far into a private life can the press go when discussing a newsworthy person? Courts began to enunciate guidelines for the press in cases decided in the last quarter of the 20th century. While these limits are narrow, they are nevertheless real. Two important cases illustrate this point.

In the early 1970s *Sports Illustrated* published a long article on a body surfer named Mike Virgil. At the time, body surfing was a relatively unknown sport outside the fraternity of surfers in Southern California and at other beaches. Reporter Curry Kirkpatrick asked Virgil why he seemed so willing to risk life and limb in a sport many regarded as extremely dangerous. Virgil replied that he lived his life pretty much as he practiced his sport and outlined some of his personal traits that most would regard as reckless, if not stupid (e.g., he would extinguish burning cigarettes with his mouth, dive headfirst down flights of stairs and eat live insects). When the story

---

41. *Beresky v. Teschner,* 381 N.E. 2d 979 (1978).
42. *Livsey v. Salt Lake County,* 275 F. 3d 952 (2002).
43. *Howell v. New York Post Co.,* 612 N.E. 2d 699 (1993).

appeared, Virgil sued. He agreed that his public life was fair game for the press, but the embarrassing aspects of his private life should not have been reported. The court disagreed. The appellate court ruled that the line between private and public information "is to be drawn when the publicity ceases to be the giving of information to which the public is entitled, and becomes morbid and sensational prying into the private life *for its own sake*."[44] Put differently, a morbid and sensational prying into one's life for its own sake is the opposite of newsworthiness. When a lower court applied this standard it ruled "any person reading the article would conclude that the personal facts concerning the individual were revealed in a legitimate journalistic attempt to explain his extremely daring and dangerous style of body surfing." In other words, if the magazine had published a story that described this weird man who lived in California who ate bugs and dived down stairs, it very likely would have been an invasion of privacy. But the personal details were added to a story to try to explain Virgil's public life. Although they were embarrassing, they provided important context to the story of his public persona.

What courts often look for in these kinds of cases, then, is a nexus between the admittedly private and embarrassing information and the newsworthy subject of the story. How far the press can go in reporting the private life of public persons often depends not only on what was said—how private the information is—but also on why the material was used. When an individual's public life is explained, many parts of that person's private life are of legitimate public concern.

NEWSWORTHINESS IN A NUTSHELL: FACTORS FOR LEGITIMATE PUBLIC CONCERN

Courts often consider the following three factors in determining if the private facts in question are of legitimate public concern (i.e., are newsworthy). Recall from the *Virgil* case described earlier that "a morbid and sensational prying into one's private life for its own sake" is tantamount to the opposite of what is newsworthy or of legitimate public concern.

1. The social value of the private facts that were published.
2. How deeply the disclosed private facts cut into ostensibly private affairs.
3. The extent to which the plaintiff (the individual to whom the private facts pertain) voluntarily rose to a position of public notoriety.

Ultimately, as one court observed, newsworthiness is measured along a sliding scale of competing interests: an individual's right to keep private facts from the public's gaze versus the public's right to know.

---

44. *Virgil* v. *Time, Inc.,* 527 F. 2d 1122 (1975) [emphasis added].

ETHICS AND PRIVACY

Journalists, bloggers, and other professional communicators need to remember that liability in a private facts case is usually determined by a judge or jury asking questions about some fairly elastic concepts. Was the material highly offensive to a reasonable person? Was the material of legitimate public concern? The law in this area is not carved in stone and could change as public sentiments change. If nothing else, in the long term, decisions by judges and juries usually reflect public opinion. And this is why people who work in the mass media need to begin to ask more questions as well—especially, what are the ethical implications of revealing this personal information?

When it comes to privacy, good editors agree that the feelings and sensibilities of the subject of the story should always be considered. But, at the same time, these feelings and sensibilities should never be used as a reason to deny to the public information that has legitimate public concern. The last three words are the key: *legitimate public concern*. The decision on whether to publish or broadcast a story will always be a judgment call that must be made carefully and thoughtfully. Too many journalists are reluctant to make this call. Instead, they declare that their job is to simply report the news, to pass along whatever they discover. Journalists are not supposed to make judgments, they argue. Some people call this the sewer pipe school of journalism: What goes in one end of a sewer pipe comes out the other end with little change. But today people in the mass media, and even members of their audience, know that journalists make judgments every day of the week. What stories should be covered? Who should be quoted? How should the story be played? Journalism is not now nor ever has been a purely objective activity.

It is worth noting that the ethics code of the Society of Professional Journalists (SPJ), an organization of reporters and editors, reminds reporters to "recognize that gathering and reporting information may cause harm and discomfort. Pursuit of the news is not a license for arrogance." The SPJ's ethics code also instructs journalists to "show good taste. Avoid pandering to lurid curiosity." Such ethical considerations are clearly relevant when considering whether to publish private facts.[45]

The courts and the public will continue to support the endeavors of the press in privacy actions so long as there is some assurance that journalists are willing to ask the question, Is there legitimate public concern in this story? At present, this is primarily an ethical issue. But if journalism is pursued with the kind of reckless abandon that is common today at a few media outlets, it could one day become a defining legal question as well. We must constantly remember the words of the great U.S. jurist Learned Hand. Liberty rests in the hearts and minds of the people, Hand wrote. When it dies there, no court or constitution can revive it.

RECOUNTING THE PAST

If an individual is in the public eye, revelations about his or her private life are normally fair game for the press. As noted, courts have erected an almost impenetrable defense that blocks such lawsuits. However, lawsuits by individuals who were once in the public eye, but have retreated to a quiet life of solitude out of the public spotlight, are fairly

---

45. Available online at http://www.spj.org/ethics.asp.

common. These litigants usually argue that the passing of time dims the public spotlight and that a person stripped of a right to privacy because of his or her notoriety regains at least some of that protection after an indeterminate period of time.

There are at least two kinds of cases that usually occur. The first is the simplest to describe: a news story or book or TV documentary that simply recounts the past. In other words, history. "On this day in 1990 Mary Beth Ellroy was convicted of killing her two-week-old baby and sentenced to 15 years in prison." These kinds of lawsuits are never successful. Typical is a decision by the New Jersey Supreme Court in a case involving a book that recounted a crime spree that occurred eight years earlier. Joseph Kallinger and his son were apprehended by police in 1975 after their criminal rampage that included killing, robbing and raping. In 1983 a professor of criminal justice at City University of New York published a book about Kallinger's life and crimes. One of Kallinger's victims sued, arguing that replaying this tragedy in public print was traumatic and disturbing and would be highly offensive. The court agreed with that assessment but ruled that the case failed because the facts revealed were not private but public, and "even if they were private, they are of legitimate concern to the public."[46] The lapse of time did nothing to insulate the plaintiff from such publicity. The facts were taken from the public trial record in the case, and the court noted that the Supreme Court ruling in *Cox* v. *Cohn*[47] was not limited to contemporaneous events.

The second kind of story is a bit more problematic. A report that film star Sid Feldman was accused in 1995 by his former wife of possessing child pornography is again retelling history. But the added sentence, "Today, Feldman is selling real estate in Dade County, Florida," pushes the report beyond history. Some courts have ruled that such "Where are they now" kinds of stories are permissible, so long as the report was not designed to purposely embarrass or humiliate the plaintiff.[48] But other judges are less tolerant of such publicity and will sometimes ask the question, What is the purpose of tying Feldman's current job with these accusations from the past?[49] To defend such a suit, the press needs a good answer. If Feldman were running for public office, if he ran a popular photographic studio that specialized in taking pictures of youngsters, if he were arrested today for possessing child pornography—all of these would supply the rationale for tying the past to the present. But simply reporting that he is selling real estate might not convince the court that such a story should be immune from suit.

Perhaps the most important question any journalist can ask when preparing to publish a story is, why? Why is this information being published? If there is a good reason, most judges will bend over backward to protect the press. But without a good reason, the legal terrain can get a lot more complicated.

---

46. *Romaine* v. *Kallinger,* 537 A. 2d 284 (1988).
47. 420 U.S. 469 (1975).
48. See *Kent* v. *Pittsburgh Press,* 349 F. Supp. 622 (1972); *Sidis* v. *F-R Publishing Co.,* 113 F. 2d 806 (1940); and *Bernstein* v. *NBC,* 232 F. 2d 369 (1955).
49. See, for example, *Hall* v. *Post,* 355 S.E. 2d 816 (1987).

It is an invasion of privacy to publicize private information about another person's life if the publication of this information would be embarrassing to a reasonable person and the information is not of legitimate public interest or concern. To publicize means to communicate the information to a large number of people. There is no liability for giving further publicity to information that is already considered public. The press is free, for example, to report even embarrassing and sensitive matters contained in public records. The information that is publicized must be considered offensive to a reasonable person; the law does not protect hypersensitive individuals.

Courts use many strategies to determine whether information has legitimate public concern. Stories that are of great interest have legitimate public concern. Stories about both voluntary and involuntary public figures are normally considered of legitimate public concern. When private information is published or broadcast, it is important that a connection exists between the revelation of the embarrassing private information and the newsworthy aspects of the story. Embarrassing details about a person's private life cannot be publicized simply to amuse or titillate audiences. News stories that recount past events—including embarrassing details of an individual's life—are normally protected from successful privacy suits. However, courts will usually insist on a good reason for relating these embarrassing past events to an individual's current life or work.

SUMMARY

FALSE-LIGHT INVASION OF PRIVACY

It is illegal to publicize material that places an individual in a false light if

a. **the false light in which the individual was placed would be highly offensive to a reasonable person, and**
b. **the publisher of the material was at fault when the publication was made.**

This fourth tort in the invasion-of-privacy quartet has engendered the most disputes within the law. What does this have to do with invasion of privacy? Many state courts have refused to recognize this variety of invasion of privacy. In 1998 the Minnesota Supreme Court recognized a cause of action for appropriation, private facts and intrusion, but rejected the false-light tort. Four years later the Colorado Supreme Court also refused to recognize false-light invasion of privacy. Both courts said the cause of action was largely

---

FALSE-LIGHT PRIVACY

1. Publication of material must put an individual in a false light.
2. The false light would be highly offensive to a reasonable person.
3. The publisher of the material was at fault.

---

coextensive with libel and didn't see the need to embrace both torts.[50] And in 2008 the Florida Supreme Court ruled that the state did not recognize the false-light tort for the same reason.[51]

On the other hand, the Supreme Court of Nevada in 2014 for the first time recognized the false-light cause of action.[52] In doing so, the Silver State's high court wrote that "we, like the majority of courts, conclude that a false light cause of action is necessary to fully protect privacy interests, and we now officially recognize false light invasion of privacy as a valid cause of action in connection with the other three privacy causes of action." It added that a majority of courts have found that "false light and defamation are distinct torts."

THE DANGERS OF OMITTING KEY FACTS: CREATING FALSE MEANINGS BY LEAVING OUT MATERIAL AND SELECTIVELY AMPLIFYING OTHER FACTS

Journalists can get into legal trouble for omitting key facts from stories. A Tennessee appellate court explained this principle in 2012 in *Eisenstein* v. *WTVF-TV, News Channel 5 Network*. Noting that literal truth is not a defense in false light, the court wrote that "the facts may be true in a false light claim. However, the angle from which the facts are presented, or the omission of certain material facts, results in placing the plaintiff in a false light. Literal accuracy of separate statements will not render a communication 'true' where the implication of the communication as a whole was false." The phrase "the angle from which the facts are presented" means that journalists can get into trouble by amplifying discrete information or making selective presentations of information that would cast a person in a false light. As a Pennsylvania Superior Court explained in 2012 in *Krajewski* v. *Gusoff*, "false light invasion of privacy offers redress not merely for the publication of matters that are provably false, but also for those that, although true, are selectively publicized in a manner creating a false impression." The key is whether "the scenario depicted created a false impression, even if derived from true statements."

Libel and false-light privacy are similar in some ways. At the base both involve the publication of something derogatory about the plaintiff. The practical difference between the two is that the nasty words published about the plaintiff don't have to actually be strong enough to harm a reputation to qualify for a false-light action. In other words, the plaintiff doesn't have to show the court that his reputation was harmed, only that something false was published and that this caused him to suffer

---

50. *Lake* v. *Wal-Mart Stores Inc.*, 582 N.W. 2d 231 (1998); and *Denver Publishing* v. *Bueno*, 54 P. 3d 893 (2002).
51. *Jews for Jesus Inc.* v. *Rapp*, 36 M.L.R. 2540 (2008); and *Anderson* v. *Gannett*, 36 M.L.R. 2553 (2008).
52. *Franchise Tax Board* v. *Hyatt*, 335 P. 3d 125 (Nev. 2014).

embarrassment or humiliation. But in a libel action, the plaintiff is going to have to prove harm to his or her reputation. The false-light tort was generated more than 80 years ago by judges who were trying to find a remedy for plaintiffs who alleged harm, but whose problems did not meet the specific requirements of existing privacy law. In the first recorded case a woman sued when she was pictured for six seconds selling bread on the streets of New York in a so-called documentary about the city. Because the main players in the film were actors, who had been given lines to speak, the court ruled the film was fiction or entertainment, not news, despite the fact there was no plot to the picture. (Yes, this sounds like appropriation, but the court didn't see it that way.) The false-light tort grew from that case.[53]

There are three important elements in the tort. The plaintiff must first prove that the specific allegations are false. The same rules that apply in a libel action when truth or falsity is at issue apply (see Chapter 4). The key is whether or not the words that carry the sting, that cause humiliation or embarrassment, are substantially true. Errors in details don't matter much. For example, Deangelo Bailey sued rapper Marshall Bruce Mathers III (better known as Eminem) for false-light invasion of privacy because of the lyrics in the 1999 song "Brain Damage." The supposedly autobiographical song described how Mathers was bullied when he was in school, how Bailey banged his head against a urinal, broke his nose, soaked his clothes in blood and so on. Bailey argued that there was no proof of these specific allegations, but the court said the sting in the song lyrics was that Bailey was a bully—and he had admitted that he picked on Mathers when they were younger. This amounted to substantial truth. Case dismissed.[54]

The plaintiff must also prove that the false statements are highly offensive to a reasonable person, and that the defendant was at fault in publishing this material. The definition of fault in privacy law is the same one that is applied in libel law (see Chapter 5). A false-light case can develop from a simple error made by the publisher, but there are other ways such cases arise as well. Here is a summary of the more common kinds of cases.

FICTIONALIZATION

Fictionalization is really the purposeful distortion of the truth, usually for dramatic purposes. Some of the earliest false-light cases involved radio and television dramatizations of actual news events. Because they did not know exactly what happened, and because real life is generally boring, script writers often changed these events to increase the drama. False-light suits were often a consequence of this creativity.[55] Television programming and motion pictures are filled these days with stories that supposedly represent events that really happened. Television producers even have a name for these kinds of programs—docudramas. These kinds of productions pose risks

---

53. *Blumenthal* v. *Picture Classics,* 235 App. Div. 570 (1931); aff'd 261 N.Y. 504 (1933).
54. *Bailey* v. *Mathers,* 33 M.L.R. 2053 (2005).
55. See, for example, *Strickler* v. *NBC,* 167 F. Supp. 68 (1958).

for their creators because of libel and false-light invasion-of-privacy suits. The simple way to avoid these problems is for a television or motion picture company to buy the rights to the story from the real people they plan to portray. By signing a standard contract (and accepting a few dollars in payment), the real-life characters in the story forfeit their right to sue if they are unhappy with how they are portrayed. Individuals who refuse to sign such an agreement are simply written out of the story; they don't exist as far as the video story is concerned. (And you always thought these presentations were accurate and truthful.) More and more, production companies try to avoid involving the real characters in the story and simply advertise their productions as being "based on a true story." This is shorthand for a more honest statement—"most of this story is fiction."

It was not uncommon years ago for reporters and editors at many magazines and some newspapers to try to dramatize their stories a bit by adding what they suggested was real-life dialogue or maybe some additional "facts" to their news reports.[56] Today, most of this kind of journalism is confined to supermarket tabloid newspapers, or what most would call sleazy magazines. This kind of journalism has prompted more than its share of libel and false-light privacy claims. And some of the antics that prompt these lawsuits are hard to believe. A 96-year-old Arkansas resident sued the *Sun* tabloid newspaper for using her photo to illustrate a totally fabricated story about a 101-year-old female newspaper carrier who had to give up her route because she was pregnant. Plaintiff Nellie Mitchell's photo had been published 10 years earlier in another tabloid owned by the same company in a true story about the Mountain Home, Ark., woman. But the editors at the *Sun* needed a picture to illustrate their phony story and simply used Mitchell's, undoubtedly thinking she was dead. A U.S. District Court jury awarded the elderly woman $1.5 million in damages.[57] The simple rule for writers who want to be dramatists is this: If you change the facts, change the names and don't use photos of real people.

Real names often appear in novels, feature films, TV shows or even advertisements. Oftentimes individuals will sue (normally unsuccessfully) under appropriation when this occurs (see Chapter 7 regarding appropriation). But false-light cases can result as well. In such actions the decision usually rests on whether just the name was taken, or whether the identity was taken as well. *The New York Times*, an advertising agency and the United Negro College Fund were sued for false-light invasion of privacy by Lawrence Botts Jr., a well-educated white man who complained that he and his family had been put in a false light by an ad carried in the newspaper for the educational charity. The ad depicts a fictional black man who has turned to alcohol and "wasted" his mind because he could not afford a college education. The man's name in the ad was Larry Botts. The 3rd U.S. Court of Appeals rejected the suit, saying the name in the ad was simply a John Doe, "a generic place holder for the prototypical underprivileged black youth."[58]

56. See *Acquino* v. *Bulletin Co.*, 190 Pa. Super. 528 (1959), for example.
57. *Peoples Bank & Trust Co. of Mountain Home* v. *Globe International, Inc.*, 786 F. Supp. 791 (1992). See also *Varnish* v. *Best Medium*, 405 F. 2d 608 (1968).
58. *Botts* v. *New York Times Co.*, 106 Fed. Appx. 109 (2004).

> ## DISCOVERING THE CHALLENGES OF FALSE LIGHT:
> ### *LOVINGOOD* v. *DISCOVERY COMMUNICATIONS*
>
> In 2015, the U.S. District Court for the Northern District of Alabama allowed a false-light invasion of privacy case stemming from the popular 2013 film "The Challenger Disaster" to proceed. The film chronicled the events leading up to the 1986 explosion and crash of the Challenger space shuttle that killed its seven crew members. The film depicted Judson Lovingood, a NASA engineer, testifying before the Presidential Commission investigating the disaster. In the film, the actor playing Lovingood is asked before the Commission to estimate the probability of total system failure. The actor replies that the probability is 1 in 100,000. An actor playing a member of the Commission calls this calculation "a wish" rather than an estimate and states that NASA's own engineers estimated the probability of total system failure to be close to 1 in 200. Lovingood sued, alleging he never testified before the Commission or offered any estimate of total system failure and that no NASA engineer had ever calculated total system failure. Instead, Lovingood argued that the writers and producers of the film "sacrificed the truth" in an effort to make a more dramatic film. Lovingood contended the film cast him in a false light because it suggested that NASA and Lovingood knew the fictional calculation of 1 in 200 before the Challenger disaster and chose to ignore it. The defendants in the case moved to dismiss the false-light claim, arguing that the suit should be dropped because the statements in the film were substantially true and did not concern Lovingood. Applying Alabama's definition of false-light invasion of privacy, the court ruled that the statements—that Lovingood misrepresented critical facts to the Presidential Commission and appeared to be trying to cover up details of the launch that would have saved the crew—were false and they placed Lovingood in a false light that would be highly offensive to a reasonable person.[59]

The differences between taking just a name and taking an identity can be subtle, but they are easy to grasp. Look at these hypothetical situations. Let's say that author Nora Roberts writes a novel about a popular actress who has AIDS. In the book, the actress' best friend is a short, chubby nurse named Julia Roberts. The writer has taken actress Julia Roberts' name, but not her identity. But if, in the novel, an actress who has AIDS is named Julia Roberts, if she is rather tall and thin, if she won an Academy Award, if she is married to a cinematographer named Daniel Moder and so on, then the writer has taken the identity as well as the name. How many characteristics must be the same before plaintiffs can claim their identity was taken and they were placed in a false light? Courts decide this question on a case-by-case basis.

Novels and feature films often carry a disclaimer: "This is a work of fiction. All the characters and events portrayed are fictitious. Any resemblance to real people and events is purely coincidental." Will this ward off a false-light suit? No. Although the statement has minimal value in showing the intent of the author or publisher or producer, the rule is simple: You cannot escape liability for committing a legal wrong by announcing that you

---

59. *Lovingood* v. *Discovery Communications, Inc.*, 43 Media L. Rep. 2971 (N.D. Ala. 2015).

are not liable. If you put a large sign on the top of your car that said "Stay out of my way. I am a very bad driver and if I hit someone, it is not my fault," this would not relieve you from any liability if you caused an accident. Similarly, the disclaimer that a book is a work of fiction and the characters are fictitious will not prevent a successful privacy suit if the author has obviously appropriated someone's identity and put him or her in a false light.

OTHER FALSEHOODS

Misuse of photographs, both still and video, is a common problem.

False-light privacy suits based on fictionalization are not too common today. False-light lawsuits more typically involve simple editing or writing errors, or errors in judgment. Misuse of photographs, both still and video, is a common problem. The *Saturday Evening Post* was plagued by such lawsuits in the 1940s and 1950s. For example, the magazine once published a picture of a little girl who was brushed by a speeding car in an intersection and lay crying in the street. The girl was the victim of a motorist who ignored a red traffic light, but in the magazine the editors implied that she had caused the accident herself by darting into the street between parked cars. The editors simply needed a picture to illustrate a story on pedestrian carelessness and plucked this one out of the files. The picture was totally unrelated to the story, except that both were about people being hit by cars. Eleanor Sue Leverton sued the *Post* and won. Judge Herbert F. Goodrich ruled that the picture was clearly newsworthy in connection with Eleanor's original accident.

> But the sum total of all this is that this particular plaintiff, the legitimate subject for publicity for one particular accident, now becomes a pictorial, frightful example of pedestrian carelessness. This, we think, exceeds the bounds of privilege.[60]

WJLA-TV in the nation's capital was sued in a case that graphically demonstrates how a broadcasting station or publication can and cannot use unrelated pictures to illustrate a story. The station broadcast a story on a new medical treatment for genital herpes. Unfortunately, TV news directors believe all news reports need to be illustrated with pictures because viewers won't sit still for talking heads. But stories about medical matters usually offer few opportunities for visuals. The report on herpes appeared on both the 6 p.m. and 11 p.m. newscasts. Both reports carried the same opening videotape of scores of pedestrians walking on a busy city street. Then the camera zoomed in on one woman, Linda Duncan, as she stood on a corner. Duncan turned and looked at the camera. She was clearly recognizable. On the 6 p.m. news there was no narration during the opening footage. The camera focused on the plaintiff Duncan, and then the tape cut to a picture of the reporter, who was standing on the street, and said, "For the twenty million Americans who have herpes, it's not a cure." The remainder of the story followed. But for the 11 p.m. news, the reporter's opening statement was read by the news anchor as viewers watched the opening videotape, including the close-up of Linda Duncan. A defense motion to dismiss the privacy and defamation actions was granted as it related to the 6 p.m. newscast. The court said there was not a sufficient connection between pictures of the plaintiff and the reporter's statement. But the court denied a summary judgment relating to the 11 p.m. broadcast. "The coalescing of the camera action, plaintiff's action (turning toward the camera), and the position of the passerby caused plaintiff to be the focal point on the screen. The juxtaposition of this film and commentary concerning twenty million Americans with

60. *Leverton* v. *Curtis Publishing Co.*, 192 F. 2d 974 (1951).

herpes is sufficient to support an inference that indeed the plaintiff was a victim," the court ruled. A jury should decide whether the connection was strong enough.[61]

Courts recognize that the reasonable juror is capable of distinguishing between the use of an unrelated photograph with a story that creates a false impression and one that doesn't. When the newspaper *El Diario Juarez* ran a story about an immigration officer who let truckloads of illegal immigrants come into the country, and who took money from drug traffickers in exchange for not checking trucks for drugs, it ran a photo of another officer, Christopher Houseman, to illustrate the report. The photo showed Houseman, who was not involved in the illegal activity, working a border checkpoint in uniform, with a police dog. There was a bridge in the background. The story about the suspect agent was datelined McAllen, Texas, and named a crossing bridge used by the agents. The picture of Houseman showed him working in El Paso, Texas, alongside a different bridge. The Texas Court of Appeals ruled the false-light claim filed by Houseman would not stand because a reasonable reader would recognize that the plaintiff was working in El Paso, not McAllen, and could not be the officer charged with illegal activity.[62]

Sometimes an error simply occurs, and there is little anyone can do about it. A newspaper in Oklahoma published an article concerning the death of a former local schoolteacher who had been convicted of murder and who was reportedly mentally ill. But the photo used to accompany the story was that of Frenche Colbert, who lived in Phoenix, Ariz. Colbert's picture had been sent to the newspaper years earlier when he graduated from law school. Somehow, his photo got mixed up with that of the schoolteacher. There is no question that this publication put Colbert in a false light.[63] In such cases the fault requirement is a strong defense.

A simple precaution will protect publishers and broadcasters against many false-light suits. Refrain from using unrelated photos to illustrate stories and articles. When a story is published in the employee magazine about worker carelessness as a prime cause of industrial accidents, control the impulse to pull from the files a random picture of one of the employees working on the assembly line. That employee could contend that the story and photo suggest she is careless. Similarly, don't use old photos of kids hanging around the parking lot at a local park to illustrate a news story on neighborhood complaints about drug dealing in the park. Juxtaposing the wrong pictures with the wrong words could give viewers the impression that one of these kids is selling or using drugs.

HIGHLY OFFENSIVE MATERIAL

Before a plaintiff can win a false-light case, the court must be convinced that the material that is false is highly offensive to a reasonable person. It should be noted that records contain a handful of cases where nonoffensive material was the basis for a successful false-light suit.[64] Typical of modern decisions, however, is the case of *Cibenko v. Worth Publishers*. The plaintiff was a New York–New Jersey Port Authority police officer whose photograph appeared in a college sociology text. In a section of the book titled *Selecting the Criminals*,

---

61. *Duncan v. WJLA-TV,* 10 M.L.R. 1395 (1984).
62. *Houseman v. Publicationes Paso Del Norte, S.A.,* No. 08-06-00034-CV, Aug. 23, 2007.
63. *Colbert v. World Publishing,* 747 P. 2d 286 (1987).
64. See *Molony v. Boy Comics Publishers,* 65 N.Y.S. 173 (1948); and *Spahn v. Julian Messner, Inc.,* 18 N.Y. 2d 324 (1966).

the picture depicted a white police officer (Cibenko) in a public place apparently prodding a sleeping black man with his nightstick. The caption for the picture stated:

> The social status of the offender seems to be the most significant determinant of whether a person will be arrested and convicted for an offense and of the kind of penalty that will be applied. In this picture a police officer is preventing a black male from falling asleep in a public place. Would the officer be likely to do the same if the "offender" were a well-dressed, middle-aged white person?

Officer Cibenko claimed the photograph and caption made him appear to be a racist, and this portrayal was false. A U.S. District Court in New Jersey disagreed and ruled that there was no offensive meaning attached to the photograph and caption, especially not a highly offensive meaning.[65] A U.S. District Court in Maine dismissed a suit by a man who had fallen out of the hatch of a small airplane, but managed to cling to the door rails until the pilot made an emergency landing. An article in *National Enquirer* embellished the story somewhat, adding material on what the plaintiff had thought about as he clung to the airplane. The reporter had never communicated with the accident victim and therefore could not have known what went through his mind. The court ruled that the description of physical sensations and predictable fears, though possibly exaggerated or maybe even fanciful, was not offensive to a reasonable person.[66] It is important to remember, however, that the harm in false light is different from the harm in a defamation case. In defamation, the harm comes from a loss of reputation. In a false light suit, the harm is caused by a loss of privacy or the right to be left alone.

THE FAULT REQUIREMENT

Since 1967, plaintiffs in false-light suits have been required to prove a fault requirement much like the one applied in libel cases. The case in which this fault requirement was applied to invasion of privacy was the first mass media invasion-of-privacy suit ever heard by the U.S. Supreme Court.[67] In the early 1950s the James Hill family was held captive in their home for nearly 24 hours by three escaped convicts. The fugitives were captured by police shortly after leaving the Hill home. The incident became a widely publicized story. At about the same time there were other similar hostage-takings in other parts of the United States. Author Joseph Hayes wrote a fictional account, a novel about such an occurrence called *The Desperate Hours*, which focused on a fictional four-member Hilliard family that was held hostage by three escaped convicts. The book was made into a movie and a play. Before the play "The Desperate Hours" opened on Broadway, *Life* magazine published a feature story about the drama, stating that the play was a reenactment of the ordeal suffered by the James Hill family. The actors were even taken to the home in which the Hills had lived (now vacant) and were photographed at the scene of the original captivity.

James Hill sued for invasion of privacy. He complained that the magazine had used his family's name for trade purposes and that the story put the family in a false light. *The Desperate Hours* did follow the basic outline of the Hill family ordeal, but it contained many differences. The fictional Hilliard family, for example, suffered far more physical and verbal indignities at the hands of the convicts than did the Hill family.

65. *Cibenko* v. *Worth Publishers,* 510 F. Supp. 761 (1981).
66. *Dempsey* v. *National Enquirer Inc.,* 687 F. Supp. 692 (1988).
67. *Time, Inc.* v. *Hill,* 385 U.S. 374 (1967).

The family won money damages in the New York state courts,[68] but the Supreme Court of the United States vacated the lower-court rulings and sent the case back for yet another trial. The Hill family gave up at this point, and no subsequent trial was held.

Justice William Brennan, in a 5-4 ruling, applied the same First Amendment standards he had developed in the *New York Times Co.* v. *Sullivan* libel suit to this category of invasion-of-privacy litigation (see Chapter 5). "We hold that the constitutional protections for speech and press preclude the application of the New York [privacy] statute to redress false reports of matters of public interest in the absence of proof that the defendant published the report with knowledge of its falsity or in reckless disregard of the truth."[69]

The *Time, Inc.* v. *Hill* case was decided in 1967, three years after the *Sullivan* ruling. But since 1967 the high court has substantially modified the fault requirement in libel cases. In 1974 in *Gertz* v. *Welch* the court reiterated that so-called public persons must prove actual malice to maintain a successful libel action, but added that private persons must also prove fault—at least negligence.[70] Did the high court intend that this two-part fault standard be applied to false-light invasion-of-privacy cases as well? The Supreme Court had an occasion to answer this question shortly after its ruling in *Gertz* but declined to do so. In *Cantrell* v. *Forest City Publishing Co.*,[71] a false-light invasion-of-privacy case, the high court concluded that there was sufficient evidence to show that the defendant had acted with reckless disregard for the truth. Because the defendant could prove actual malice in this case, the court said it did not have to consider whether a private-person plaintiff would have to prove only negligence to sustain the fault requirement in a false-light privacy action. "This case presents no occasion to consider whether a state may constitutionally apply a more relaxed standard of liability for a publisher or broadcaster of false statements injurious to a private individual under a false-light theory of invasion of privacy or whether the constitutional standard announced in *Time, Inc.* v. *Hill* applies to all false light cases," wrote Justice Stewart for the court.

Whether the *Gertz* variable-fault standard is applicable to false-light cases remains an open question. Most authorities tend to think that the rule of *Time, Inc.* v. *Hill*—that all plaintiffs are required to show actual malice, knowledge of falsity or reckless disregard of the truth—will stand as the law in most jurisdictions. Several factors prompt this conclusion. The Supreme Court could have changed the rules in the *Cantrell* case, but did not. The high court could have modified the *Time, Inc.* v. *Hill* rule in *Gertz,* but did not. Finally, a statement that is not defamatory is likely to be far less damaging to a plaintiff—the less harm, higher fault requirement. Some courts have taken a different point of view and ruled that private-person false-light plaintiffs must prove only negligence.[72] But most courts that have considered the matter have ruled that all false-light plaintiffs must show actual malice to recover.[73]

Whether the Gertz *variable-fault standard is applicable to false-light cases remains an open question.*

68. *Hill* v. *Hayes,* 207 N.Y.S. 2d 901 (1960), 18 App. Div. 2d 485 (1963).
69. *Time, Inc.* v. *Hill,* 385 U.S. 374 (1967).
70. 418 U.S. 323 (1974).
71. 419 U.S. 245 (1974).
72. See *Wood* v. *Hustler,* 736 F. 2d 1084 (1984); and *Crump* v. *Beckley Newspapers,* 370 S.E. 2d 70 (1984).
73. See *Dodrill* v. *Arkansas Democrat Co.,* 5 M.L.R. 1090 (1979); *McCall* v. *Courier-Journal and Louisville Times Co.,* 4 M.L.R. 2337 (1979), aff'd 6 M.L.R. 1112 (1980); *Goodrich* v. *Waterbury Republican-American Inc.,* 448 A. 2d 1317 (1987); *Colbert* v. *World Publishing Co.,* 747 P. 2d 286 (1987); *Ross* v. *Fox Television Stations Inc.,* 34 M.L.R. 1567 (2006); *Welling* v. *Weinfeld,* 113 Ohio St. 3d 464 (2007); and *Meyerkord* v. *Zipatoni Co.,* 276 S.W. 3d 319 (2008); *Miles* v. *Raycom Media Inc.,* 38 M.L.R. 2374 (2010).

Before the discussion of the right of privacy comes to an end, a few points should be reiterated. First, remember that only people have the right of privacy. Corporations, businesses and governments do not enjoy the legal right of privacy as such. Second, it is impossible to civilly libel a dead person, but a few state privacy statutes make it possible for an heir to maintain an action for invasion of privacy.

Although privacy law is not as well charted as libel law, and although there are fewer privacy cases, suits for invasion of privacy are a growing menace to journalists. If journalists stick to the job of responsibly reporting the news, they may rest assured that the chance for a successful privacy suit is slim.

SUMMARY

It is an invasion of privacy to publish false information that places an individual into what is called a false light. However, this false information must be considered offensive to a reasonable person. Also, the plaintiff must prove that the information was published negligently, with knowledge of its falsity, or with reckless disregard for the truth.

One common source of false-light privacy suits is any drama that adds fictional material to an otherwise true story. The use of fictional rather than real names in such a drama will normally preclude a successful invasion-of-privacy suit. The coincidental use of a real name in a novel or stage play will not stand as a cause of action for invasion of privacy. Most false-light cases, however, result from the publication of false information about a person in a news or feature story. Pictures of people who are not involved in the stories that the pictures are used to illustrate frequently provide false-light privacy suits.

BIBLIOGRAPHY

Marcus, Paul, and Tara L. McMahon. "Limiting Disclosure of Rape Victims' Identities." *Southern California Law Review* 64 (1991): 1019.

Prosser, William L. "Privacy." *California Law Review* 48 (1960): 383.

Swift, Mike. "Bracing for Privacy Battle." *The Seattle Times*, 21 June 2010, A7.

"Washington Jury Finds Paper's Oral Sex Articles Did Not Invade Student's Privacy." Student Press Law Center, April 22, 2010.

Warren, Samuel D., and Louis D. Brandeis. "The Right to Privacy." *Harvard Law Review* 4 (1890): 220.

CHAPTER 9

Gathering Information

RECORDS AND MEETINGS

This chapter focuses on how the law affects the efforts of reporters and ordinary citizens to gather information about what is going on in the nation and their communities. Until about 25 years ago the text focused on federal and state statutes that either permit or limit the gathering of information from government records or from meetings of government agencies. Today the law regarding news gathering is also focused on efforts by the government and others to stop the press from collecting data about a wide range of people and activities. Both topics are covered here. Additional material on access to the judicial process and judicial records is presented in Chapter 12.

Information is the lifeblood of American journalism and American politics. Until the mid-20th century there were few significant rules that defined the rights of citizens, including journalists, to gain access to the information generated and kept by the government. Reporters developed sophisticated but informal schemes with news sources in government to get the material they needed. The average citizen was shut out.

Since the 1950s state and federal governments have passed laws defining public access to records and meetings. If there was a "Golden Age of Access" to information, it was likely in the 1970s and early 1980s. Since then, there has been a growing government resistance to public (especially press) access to such materials—a resistance exacerbated by the events of Sept. 11, 2001.

Obama declared a new era of open government.

President Barack Obama vowed to change this shortly after taking office. He declared a new era of open government and asserted that when it comes to Freedom of Information Act (FOIA) requests to government agencies, there should be a clear presumption in favor of disclosure and that, in turn, disclosure should be timely.[1]

Obama's pledges of greater government openness, however, never came to fruition. For example, the Associated Press reported in 2016 that "the Obama administration set a record for the number of times its federal employees told disappointed citizens, journalists, and others that despite searching they couldn't find a single page requested under the Freedom of Information Act."[2] Furthermore, documents obtained by the Freedom of the Press Foundation under a FOIA request demonstrated that the Obama White House "worked aggressively behind the scenes to scuttle congressional reforms designed to give the public better access to information possessed by the federal government."[3] Whether the administration of Donald Trump does any better in the long run than the Obama administration in improving government transparency remains to be seen. It is, perhaps, a natural tendency for those in power to try to keep secrets affecting their administrations. Considering President Trump has referred to journalists as the "enemy of the American people" on multiple occasions and has derided the multiple leaks that come from his administration, it is unlikely he will attempt to make the federal government more transparent. In addition, moves by the

1. Memorandum for the Heads of Executive Departments and Agencies, Freedom of Information Act, Jan. 21, 2009, available online at http://www.whitehouse.gov/the_press_office/FreedomofInformationAct.
2. Bridis and Gillum, "US Gov't Sets Record for Failures to Find Files When Asked."
3. Leopold, "It Took a FOIA Lawsuit to Uncover How the Obama Administration Killed FOIA Reform."

Trump Administration to limit press conferences and ban cameras from the press conferences that are held suggest this administration will be one of the least transparent in history.

Journalists and citizen activists are often forced to go to court to assert rights they believe have been abridged by government restrictions on access to information. But rights and liberties are grounded in the law. When someone goes to court and asks for something, the first thing the judge will say is "Show me the law." So if journalists hope to use the law for assistance, they must find support in one of those sources of the law discussed in Chapter 1.

But rights and liberties are grounded in the law.

NEWS GATHERING AND THE LAW

In order for journalists to gather news, they must have access to information. While information from courts, trials and judicial proceedings is discussed in Chapter 12, there are three primary sources of law to which journalists might look to find a legal right of access to information such as documents, records, meetings and venues. Those sources of law are,

- Common law
- Constitutional law (the First Amendment to the U.S. Constitution)
- Statutory law (both state and federal statutes)

Despite the tradition of open government both in this country and in Great Britain, common law provides only bare access to government documents and to meetings of public agencies. Secrecy in England had a direct impact on how colonial legislatures conducted their business. The Constitutional Convention of 1787 in Philadelphia was conducted in secret. The public and the press had almost immediate access to sessions in the U.S. House of Representatives, but it was not until 1794 that spectators and reporters were allowed into the Senate chamber. Although today access is guaranteed to nearly all sessions of Congress, much (maybe even most) congressional business is conducted by committees that frequently meet in secret.

Common-law precedents exist that open certain public records to inspection by members of the public, but distinct limitations have been placed on this common-law right. For example, under common law a person seeking access to a record normally must have an "interest" in that record. Most often this interest must relate to some kind of litigation in which the person who seeks the record is a participant. Also, only those records "required to be kept" by state law are subject to even such limited disclosure under common law. Many important records kept by the government are not "required to be kept" by law. Hence, common law must be found wanting as an aid in the process of news gathering.

THE CONSTITUTION AND NEWS GATHERING

Does the U.S. Constitution provide any assistance to citizens who seek to scrutinize government records or attend meetings of government bodies? Surprisingly the First Amendment plays a rather insignificant role in defining the rights of citizens and journalists in the news-gathering process. The amendment was drafted in an age when news gathering was not a primary function of the press. The congressional records of the drafting and adoption of the First Amendment fail to support the notion that the protection of the news-gathering process was to be included within the scope of freedom of the press.

The First Amendment was seen as a means by which the public could confront its government, not necessarily report on its activities.[4]

The Supreme Court has explored the nexus between freedom of expression and news gathering. In a non-press-related case in 1964, the high court ruled that the constitutional right to speak and publish does not carry with it the unrestrained right to gather information.[5] Eight years later Justice Byron White, speaking for three other members of the court, said: "Nor is it suggested that news gathering does not qualify for First Amendment protection; without some protection for seeking out the news, freedom of the press could be eviscerated."[6] While some First Amendment lawyers regard this statement as supporting a constitutional right to gather information, others do not.

The high court has been asked on three occasions whether the First Amendment guarantees a journalist the unobstructed right to gather news in a prison. In each case the court said no. In *Pell* v. *Procunier*,[7] reporters in California attempted to interview specific inmates at California prisons. In *Saxbe* v. *Washington Post*,[8] reporters from that newspaper sought to interview specific inmates at federal prisons at Lewisburg, Pa., and Danbury, Conn. In both instances the press was barred from conducting the interviews. The U.S. Bureau of Prisons rule, which is similar to the California regulation, states:

> Press representatives will not be permitted to interview individual inmates.
> This rule shall apply even where the inmate requests or seeks an interview.

At issue was not access to the prison system. The press could tour and photograph prison facilities, conduct brief conversations with randomly encountered inmates and correspond with inmates through the mails. In addition, the federal rules had been interpreted to permit journalists to conduct lengthy interviews with randomly selected groups of inmates. In fact, a reporter in the *Washington Post* case did go to Lewisburg and interview a group of prisoners.

The argument of the press in both cases was that to ban interviews with specific inmates abridged the First Amendment protection afforded the news-gathering activity of a free press. The Supreme Court disagreed in a 5-4 decision in both cases. Justice Stewart wrote in the majority opinion that the press already had substantial access to the prisons and that there was no evidence that prison officials were hiding things from reporters. Stewart rejected the notion that the First Amendment gave newspeople a special right of access to the prisons. "Newsmen have no constitutional right of access to prisons or their inmates beyond that afforded the general public," the justice wrote.[9] Since members of the general public have no right to interview specific prisoners, the denial of this right to the press does not infringe on the First Amendment.

"Without some protection for seeking out the news, freedom of the press could be eviscerated."

"Newsmen have no constitutional right of access to prisons or their inmates beyond that afforded the general public."

---

4. See Rourke, *Secrecy and Publicity;* and Padover, *The Complete Madison.*
5. *Zemel* v. *Rusk,* 381 U.S. 1 (1964).
6. *Branzburg* v. *Hayes,* 408 U.S. 665 (1972).
7. 417 U.S. 817 (1974).
8. 417 U.S. 843 (1974).
9. *Pell* v. *Procunier,* 417 U.S. 817 (1974).

The high court did not disagree with the findings of the district court in the *Saxbe* case that face-to-face interviews with specific inmates are essential to accurate and effective reporting about prisoners and prisons. What the court seemed to say was that while the First Amendment guarantees freedom of expression, it does not guarantee effective and accurate reporting.

In 1978 the high court split along similar lines on a case involving press access to a county jail.[10] An inmate at the Santa Rita County, Calif., jail committed suicide in 1975. Following the death and a report by a psychiatrist that jail conditions were bad, KQED television sought permission to inspect and take pictures in the jail. Sheriff Houchins announced that the media could certainly participate in one of the six tours of the jail facility given to the public each year. However, the tours did not visit the disciplinary cells nor the portion of the jail in which the suicide had taken place. No cameras or tape recorders were allowed, but photographs of some parts of the jail were supplied by the sheriff's office.

Chief Justice Warren Burger wrote the opinion for the court in the 4-3 decision. "Neither the First Amendment nor the Fourteenth Amendment mandates a right of access to government information or sources of information within the government's control," Burger asserted. The chief justice seemed troubled by the argument of KQED that only through access to the jail could the press perform its public responsibility.

> Unarticulated but implicit in the assertion that the media access to jail is essential for an informed public debate on jail conditions is the assumption that the media personnel are the best qualified persons for the task of discovering malfeasance in public institutions. . . . The media are not a substitute for or an adjunct of government. . . . We must not confuse the role of the media with that of government.[11]

"Neither the First Amendment nor the Fourteenth Amendment mandates a right of access to government information or sources of information within the government's control."

In 1980 in a case that many commentators hailed as the beginning of a general constitutionally guaranteed "right to know," the Supreme Court ruled that the First Amendment does establish for all citizens the right to attend criminal trials.[12] (See Chapter 12 for a full discussion of this case.) But while Chief Justice Burger's opinion was quite explicit regarding the First Amendment and attendance at criminal trials, it was obscure regarding the larger constitutional right to gather news in other contexts. And the high court has done little in the past two decades to clarify its position on this question. Although it has decided a number of right-of-access cases since *Richmond Newspapers*,[13] the Supreme Court has never explicitly recognized this right outside of judicial proceedings.

The lower federal and state courts tend to mirror the rulings by the Supreme Court that reject the notion of a First Amendment right of access to information and meetings. There are, however, significant exceptions:

▪ In 2008 a federal district court reiterated the findings of other courts that "exit polling, which involves a discussion of governmental affairs and politics as well

10. *Houchins* v. *KQED*, 438 U.S. 1 (1978).
11. *Houchins* v. *KQED*, 438 U.S. 1 (1978).
12. *Richmond Newspapers* v. *Virginia*, 448 U.S. 555 (1980).
13. See, for example, *Press-Enterprise Co.* v. *Riverside Superior Court*, 464 U.S. 501 (1984).

as the media's right to gather news, is protected by the First Amendment."[14] The court noted that while content-based regulations on exit polling are impermissible, content-neutral time, place and manner regulations (see Chapter 3) may be okay depending upon how far away the media are kept from the polls.

- In direct contrast, the 3rd U.S. Circuit Court of Appeals in 2013 concluded "there is no protected First Amendment right of access to a polling place for news-gathering purposes," and the U.S. Supreme Court later decided not to hear a challenge to the 3rd Circuit's decision.[15]
- When the White House staff tried to exclude camera crews with CNN from the pool of network television photographers who cover the president, a U.S. District Court forbade the discriminatory action, noting that the First Amendment includes a "right of access to news and information concerning the operations and activities of government."[16]

Similarly, for the last 15 years, states have struggled to define the public's right of access to information about executions. Media organizations and death row inmates have sought information about drugs states use to execute inmates. In addition, media organizations have sought the right to attend executions. Some courts have agreed there is a right to attend executions. In 2002, for example, the 9th U.S. Circuit Court of Appeals held that the public enjoys "a First Amendment right of access to view executions from the moment the condemned is escorted into the execution chamber."[17] The court reasoned that access was supported because of the need for informed public debate about the death penalty. "[I]nformed public debate is the main purpose for granting a right of access to governmental proceedings," the court wrote. Precisely one decade later, the 9th Circuit reiterated its position after Idaho refused to allow witness access to the initial part of an execution procedure, namely the entry of the condemned individual into the execution chamber and the insertion of intravenous lines into his body. In 2012, in *California First Amendment Coalition* v. *Woodford*, Judge Stephen Reinhardt rebuked Idaho and wrote for a unanimous three-judge panel that "the First Amendment protects the right to witness executions in their entirety."[18] In late 2016, a U.S. District Court judge in Phoenix, Ariz., ruled that under state law, journalists and other witnesses must be allowed to see all aspects of executions by lethal injection carried out in Arizona. Under Arizona state law, executions must be witnessed by several groups of people, including officials, family members and five journalists. The law, however, was typically interpreted to only allow witnesses to view the insertion of the catheters that carry the drugs used in executions. In response to a lawsuit filed by the *Arizona Republic* and other news organizations, Judge G. Murray Snow ordered that witnesses be allowed to see

---

14. *American Broadcasting Companies, Inc.* v. *Ritchie,* 36 M.L.R. 2601 (D. Minn. 2008). See also *CBS, Inc.* v. *Smith,* 681 F. Supp. 794 (S.D. Fla. 1988) (holding that it is "clear that the conduct of exit polling and journalistic interviews are protected by the First Amendment guarantees of free speech and free press"); and *Daily Herald Co.* v. *Munro,* 838 F. 2d 380 (9th Cir. 1988) (holding that exit polling is "speech that is protected, on several levels, by the First Amendment").
15. *PG Publ'g Co.* v. *Aichele,* 705 F.3d 91 (3d Cir. 2013), *cert. denied,* 133 S. Ct. 2771 (2013).
16. *CNN* v. *ABC,* 518 F. Supp. 1238 (1981).
17. 299 F. 3d 868 (2002).
18. *Associated Press* v. *Otter,* 682 F. 3d 821 (9th Cir. 2012).

the condemned enter the execution chamber and get strapped to the gurney. Witnesses will then be allowed to watch the lethal drugs be administered from another room. The judge also permanently enjoined a provision that allowed the Arizona Corrections Director the discretion to close a curtain to block witnesses' view if an execution went poorly.[19]

The U.S. Supreme Court has declined to review cases involving death row inmates' right of access to information regarding the drugs the state will use to execute them or the qualifications of individuals who will administer the drugs. In 2016, a Missouri Circuit Judge ruled Missouri must release the names of pharmacies that have provided lethal injection drugs for executions. The case, however, concerned a state "right to know" or "sunshine law" and not the First Amendment. The court ruled the records were "public records" as defined by Missouri's Sunshine Laws and thus must be disclosed. While the law in question allowed the state to withhold the identity of persons who provided direct support for the administration of lethal gases or chemicals, pharmacies were not "persons" as defined by the law.[20] (These kinds of state laws are examined later in this chapter.) The 9th Circuit has ruled that a First Amendment right of access extends to

---

DO YOU NEED A PERMIT TO TAKE PHOTOS IN A NATIONAL PARK?

Not everyone knows it, but the Department of Interior (DOI) has regulations for commercial filming and still photography. The DOI is in charge of the National Park Service, Bureau of Land Management and the U.S. Fish and Wildlife Services. Under DOI rules, you may need a permit to film or take photos in certain locations, including national parks. In 2014, the U.S. Forest Service adopted plans to fine photographers $1,000 for taking pictures in any of the wilderness areas under its care, a total of close to 36 million acres. While the U.S. Forest Service abandoned the plan after intense scrutiny from media organizations and the public, there are still a number of things to consider when taking pictures or shooting film on federal lands. The National Park service does not require a permit for personal, noncommercial filming and photography activities within normal visitation areas and hours. However, filming outside normal visitation areas and hours and all commercial filming does require a permit. The National Park Service defines commercial filming as anything that involves the digital or film recording of a visual image or sound recording by a person, business or other entity for a market audience. This includes recordings such as those used for a documentary or educational program, television and feature films and advertisements. Commercial media coverage of breaking news may also require a permit if the activities are of such size and scope that a permit would help manage the activity to minimize damage to the park or reduce visitor use conflicts or if the activities require authorized entrance to a closed area.

---

19. *Guardian News & Media LLC* v. *Charles L. Ryan*, No. CV-14-02363-PHX-GMS (D.C.A. Dec. 21, 2016).
20. *Reporters Committee for Freedom of the Press* v. *Missouri Department of Corrections*, Case No. 14AC-CC00254 (July 15, 2015).

information about drugs used in executions and the qualifications of individuals who will administer those drugs. In 2014, based on its own decision in *California First Amendment Coalition* v. *Woodford* and the U.S. Supreme Court's decisions in cases dealing with a right of access to judicial documents (discussed in Chapter 12), there was a First Amendment right of access to information about drugs used in executions and the qualifications of individuals who would administer those drugs.[21] Other circuit courts have reached different conclusions on the issue, however. In 2014, for example, the 11th Circuit declined to find a Constitutional right of access to this information, reasoning that "[n]either the Fifth, Fourteenth, or First Amendments afford [a prisoner] the broad right to know where, how, and by whom" lethal injection drugs will be manufactured or any information about the qualifications or identity of the person or persons who will manufacture or administer the drugs.[22] The 11th Circuit reaffirmed this decision in 2016.[23]

Access to Government Officials: A Right to Interview?

Each example described so far involved a question of First Amendment access to either a place, such as a government-run prison, or to proceedings, like a government meeting or an execution, or to government documents. But what happens when a reporter simply wants access to speak with a person—namely, a government official such as a mayor or a governor—and that official has issued a "no-comment policy" and refuses to speak with specific members of the press? Is there, in other words, a First Amendment right of access for the media to conduct one-on-one interviews with government officials such that the officials cannot refuse to speak with the news media?

The answer appears to be no. In 2006 the 4th U.S. Circuit Court of Appeals held that then–Maryland Gov. Robert L. Ehrlich Jr. did not violate the First Amendment rights of two *Baltimore Sun* reporters when he issued a directive denying them interview access. In *Baltimore Sun* v. *Ehrlich*,[24] the paper claimed the no-access directive was in retaliation for what the governor believed was negative coverage and commentary by *Sun* journalists David Nitkin and Michael Olesker. The appellate court, however, held that "no actionable retaliation claim arises when a government official denies a reporter access to discretionarily afforded information or refuses to answer questions." It reasoned that the governor's response to the *Sun*'s coverage "is a pervasive feature of journalism and of journalists' interaction with government. Having access to relatively less information than other reporters on account of one's reporting is so commonplace that to allow the Sun to proceed on its retaliation claim addressing that condition would 'plant the seed of a constitutional case' in 'virtually every' interchange between public official and press."

21. *Wood* v. *Ryan*, 759 F.3d 1076 (9th Cir. 2014).
22. *Wellons* v. *Commissioner, Georgia Department of Corrections*, 754 F.3d 1260 (11th Cir. 2014).
23. *Jones* v. *Commissioner, Georgia Department of Corrections*, 812 F.3d 923 (11th Cir. 2016).
24. 437 F. 3d 410 (4th Cir. 2006). The governor's order provided in relevant part that "effective *immediately* [author's emphasis], no one in the Executive Department or Agencies is to speak with David Nitkin or Michael Olesker until further notice. Do not return calls or comply with any requests. The Governor's Press Office feels that currently both are failing to objectively report on any issue dealing with the Ehrlich-Steele Administration."

This ruling agrees with the 2005 federal district court decision in *Youngstown Publishing Co. v. McKelvey*.[25] In this case, a judge held that a no-comment policy issued in 2003 by George McKelvey, then the mayor of Youngstown, Ohio, that directed city employees not to speak with reporters from a bimonthly newspaper called the *Business Journal* did not violate the First Amendment. The judge concluded "the right of access sought by the *Business Journal* is to information not otherwise available to the public, and, therefore, is a privileged right of access above that of the general public to which no constitutional right of access applies. The no-comment policy does not impede the *Business Journal* from engaging in a constitutionally protected activity, and Plaintiffs cannot establish this element of their First Amendment retaliation claim."[26]

In 2007, however, in a slightly different scenario, a federal judge held in *Citicasters Co. v. Finkbeiner* that the mayor of Toledo, Ohio, could not exclude a specific radio reporter from attending the mayor's press conferences that are open generally to all journalists.[27] Judge James G. Carr reasoned that a press conference is a public event, in contrast to the cases of *Baltimore Sun* v. *Ehrlich* and *Youngstown Publishing Co.* v. *McKelvey* in which reporters were denied private interview access and/or direct comments to their questions. The mayor's office unsuccessfully argued that the radio personality who was denied access was not a news reporter but was an entertainer.

Viewed collectively, then, this trio of cases suggests that while government officials can refuse to grant one-on-one interview access to specific reporters and can refuse to give comments to specific members of the news media, they cannot selectively deny access to specific reporters from public press conferences that are open to all members of the news media.

The First Amendment Protection of News Gathering

The First Amendment generally provides no special protection for journalists or exemption from generally applicable laws when they gather news. Arguments that the constitutional protection of a free press allows journalists to bend or break criminal and civil laws when gathering news typically are rejected by courts.

In 1998, for example, a U.S. District Court in Maryland refused to dismiss charges of transporting and receiving child pornography against a freelance journalist who attempted to block the prosecution by arguing that he was gathering news, not child pornography. Lawrence Matthews said that law enforcement officials were too zealous in their prosecution of Internet users and that the news stories resulting from his investigation would reveal this overly aggressive official action. But the court was not moved. "It is well settled that the First Amendment does not grant the press automatic relief from laws of general application," the court said. "If law enforcement officials are doing something improper in their investigations the court does not understand how the defendant would uncover malfeasance by receiving and disseminating the materials himself."[28]

"It is well settled that the First Amendment does not grant the press automatic relief from laws of general application."

25. 2005 U.S. Dist. LEXIS 9476 (N.D. Ohio 2005).
26. 34 M.L.R. 2036 (6th Cir. 2006).
27. Permanent Injunction, *Citicasters Co. v. Finkbeiner,* Case No. 07-CV-00117 (N.D. Ohio 2007).
28. *U.S. v. Matthews,* 11 F. Supp. 2d 656 (1998). Matthews was sentenced to 18 months in prison.

In 2000, the 4th U.S. Circuit Court of Appeals affirmed the decision and rejected Matthews' assertion that the First Amendment entitled him to assert a legitimate-journalistic-purpose defense to conviction under federal child pornography laws.[29] It also rejected the friend-of-the-court argument of the Reporters Committee for Freedom of the Press that there should be a more general journalistic news-gathering exemption from those laws. The appellate court cited with approval the Supreme Court's opinion in *Branzburg* v. *Hayes* for the proposition that the First Amendment does not provide "a license on either the reporter or his news sources to violate valid criminal laws."[30]

Most reporters don't violate criminal statutes, as Matthews was charged with doing, to investigate how the police enforce those statutes. But reporters do break other laws. An overview of some of these kinds of situations will demonstrate that the courts are no more tolerant of these actions.

Trespass. **Trespass** is an intentional, unauthorized (i.e., without consent) entry onto land that is occupied or possessed by another. While consent is a defense to a claim of trespass, journalists who exceed the scope of consent by taking actions in abuse of the authorized entry or by going into places beyond where they have permission may be held liable. Reporters may face both civil liability and criminal prosecution when they trespass. It is important for journalists to remember, as one federal appellate court wrote in 1995, that "there is no journalists' privilege to trespass."[31] What's more, reporters don't have the right to trespass on private property or even government-owned property.

Reporters may face both civil liability and criminal prosecution when they trespass.

Several examples illustrate the dangers journalists being charged with criminal trespass or other generally applicable charges. Reporter Bryon Wells of the East Valley Tribune near Phoenix, Ariz., sought to interview a recently fired local police officer named Daniel Lovelace. Lovelace had been involved in a fatal shooting and was charged, at the time, with second-degree murder. Wells went through a closed but unlocked gate, posted with a "no trespassing" sign, and entered Lovelace's fenced property. The reporter walked to the front door, rang the bell and was told by the woman who answered, Lovelace's wife, to leave. Wells apparently left peacefully, but in 2004 a judge upheld Wells' conviction for misdemeanor criminal trespass—he was fined $300 and sentenced to a year of probation—based on the incident.[32] In upholding a ruling by a lower-court judge, Judge Michael D. Jones wrote that "reporters who are in violation of a criminal trespass statute are not exempt from prosecution simply because they are exercising a First Amendment right." The Arizona criminal trespass law at issue provides: "A person commits criminal trespass in the first degree by knowingly . . . entering or remaining unlawfully in a fenced residential yard."[33]

In 2014, a *Washington Post* reporter and a *Huffington Post* reporter were arrested at a restaurant and later charged with trespass and interfering with a police officer while reporting on the widely covered protests in Ferguson, Missouri. Wesley Lowery, a reporter on the *Post*'s national desk, and Ryan Reilly of the *Huffington Post*, were detained

29. *U.S.* v. *Matthews,* 209 F. 3d 338 (2000), cert. den., 531 U.S. 910 (2000).
30. 408 U.S. 665, 691 (1972).
31. *Desnick* v. *American Broadcasting Companies, Inc.,* 44 F. 3d 1345, 1351 (1995).
32. *Arizona* v. *Wells,* 2004 WL 1925617 (Ariz. Super. 2004).
33. Arizona Revised Statute § 13–1504 (2004).

in a McDonald's while covering demonstrations sparked by a white police officer fatally shooting an unarmed 18-year-old black man. Lowery was charged with trespassing on private property and interfering with a police officer's performance of his duties for refusing to leave the McDonald's after being asked to leave by a police officer. In May 2016, the charges were dropped as part of a settlement in which the reporters agreed not to sue the county over the incident.[34]

In late 2016, Amy Goodman, the host of the syndicated radio, television and Web show "Democracy Now!" faced misdemeanor charges of criminal trespass over her coverage of a protest against the $3.8 billion Dakota Access Pipeline. While that charge was dropped, the North Dakota state prosecutors' announced their intention to bring more serious charges of participating in a riot against the journalist. Goodman had planned to enter a not guilty plea, but District Judge John Grinsteiner declined to sign the charging document.[35] Journalists were also among 230 people arrested and detained in Washington, D.C., during the inauguration of President Donald Trump. The journalists were all charged with the highest level of offense under Washington D.C.'s law against rioting, which applies when there are injuries because of activity or property damage more than $5,000, although chargers were later dropped against one of the seven individuals arrested because of his status as a journalist.[36]

Not all reporters who enter private property uninvited are necessarily trespassing. Whether or not the owner or occupant of the property asks the reporter to leave is a critical factor. A woman who permitted a CBS television crew to accompany a crisis intervention team that entered her home was later unable to maintain that the visit had been a trespass, a court ruled.[37] Also, the public is invited to visit some kinds of private property, and the press is a part of the public. ABC sent a camera crew to secretly film eye examinations being given to patients at an optical business. The exams were being administered in the portion of the business that was open to customers who wandered in seeking information, medication or other services. The 7th U.S. Circuit Court of Appeals rejected a trespass action brought by the owners of the property, saying that there was no invasion in this case of any of the interests that the tort of trespass is designed to protect, namely the use and enjoyment of one's property without interference. The offices were open to anyone who sought ophthalmologic services offered by the business. The activity in the office was not disrupted; there was no invasion of anyone's private space.[38]

In a modern twist on trespass involving Google's Street View program, a federal appellate court in 2010 in *Boring* v. *Google, Inc.*[39] ruled in favor of a Pennsylvania couple who live on a private road posted with a sign reading "Private Road, No Trespassing."

34. Chokshi, "Ferguson-Related Charges Dropped against Washington Post and Huffington Post reporters."
35. McCann, "Judge Rejects Riot Charge against Amy Goodman of 'Democracy Now' Over Pipeline Protest."
36. Lux, "Journalists Face Charges in Inauguration Arrests; One Sees Charges Dropped.", The Reports Committee keeps an updated list of the status of those arrested at https://www.rcfp.org /inauguration-protest-arrests.
37. *Baugh* v. *CBS, Inc.,* 828 F. Supp. 745 (1993).
38. *Desnick* v. *American Broadcasting Companies, Inc.,* 44 F. 3d 1345 (1995).
39. 38 M.L.R. 1306 (3d Cir. 2010), cert. den., 131 S. Ct. 150 (2010).

As described by the appellate court, the Street View program "offers free access on the Internet to panoramic, navigable views of streets in and around major cities across the United States. To create the Street View program, representatives of Google attach panoramic digital cameras to passenger cars and drive around cities photographing the areas along the street." The couple sued after they discovered that Google had taken "colored imagery of their residence, including the swimming pool, from a vehicle in their residence driveway months earlier without obtaining any privacy waiver or authorization." In ruling in favor of the couple on their trespass claim, the 3rd U.S. Circuit Court of Appeals observed that "the Borings have alleged that Google entered upon their property without permission. If proven, that is a trespass, pure and simple." The U.S. Supreme Court declined to hear the case in October 2010.

Is it a trespass to photograph or film a person from above his or her home or other private property using a helicopter to get the desired images?

Is it a trespass to photograph or film a person from above his or her home or other private property using a helicopter to get the desired images? It all depends on how high the chopper passes. Television newsmagazines often try to capture images of celebrity weddings using aerial shots taken from hovering helicopters. In a slightly different twist, a news helicopter hovered for 10 minutes above the home of Gail Bevers to obtain footage for a story about the poor condition of rental properties. Bevers, who was "scared to death" by the helicopter, sued for trespass. In 2002 a Texas appellate court hearing her case observed that "one of the key facts in ascertaining whether a flight through airspace constitutes a trespass is the altitude of the aircraft."[40] The court noted that while "landowners have no right to exclude overflights above their property because airspace is part of the public domain," flights that are within the "immediate reaches of the airspace next to the land" and that also interfere substantially with the use and enjoyment of that land may constitute a trespass. In Bevers' case, the court concluded "a single ten-minute hover over her property at 300 to 400 feet does not, as a matter of law, rise to the level of 'substantial interference' with the use and enjoyment of the underlying land." The appellate court thus affirmed summary judgment for the media defendants.

The *Bevers* case takes on added importance today as journalists increasingly use drones to capture images that are taken by helicopters. The notion of an aerial trespass, in fact, has early roots in a 1946 U.S. Supreme Court decision in which the justices remarked that "if the landowner is to have full enjoyment of the land, he must have exclusive control of *the immediate reaches of the enveloping atmosphere.*"[41] Unfortunately, there is no bright-line rule regarding what constitutes the immediate reaches above a person's property. And, as described earlier in Chapter 7, journalists who use drones also face potential liability under the privacy theory of intrusion into seclusion.

What if the reporter accompanies government officials, police or firefighters onto the property? Can these government agents give permission for the press to illegally enter private property? The simple answer is no. And the courts have ruled that not only are reporters potentially liable for damages in such a case, but the law officers themselves may be at risk for bringing reporters along.

In 1999 the Supreme Court of the United States unanimously ruled that when law enforcement officers permit reporters to accompany them when they enter private

---

40. *Bevers v. Gaylord Broadcasting Co.*, 30 M.L.R. 2586, 2590 (2002).
41. *United States v. Causby*, 328 U.S. 256, 264 (1946) (emphasis added).

homes to conduct searches or arrests, the officers violate "the right of residential privacy at the core of the Fourth Amendment." Two cases found their way to the high court. The first, *Wilson* v. *Layne,* resulted when members of a joint federal and local law enforcement task force invited a *Washington Post* reporter and photographer to accompany them when they arrested fugitives in Rockville, Md., just outside the nation's capital. The other case, *Hanlon* v. *Berger,* involved agents of the U.S. Fish and Wildlife Service who invited reporters and photographers from CNN to accompany them as they searched the property of a Montana rancher for evidence that the property owner was illegally poisoning wildlife. The issue the Supreme Court focused upon was whether the government agents who brought the journalists onto the private property could be held responsible for civil rights violations; in other words, could the property owners sue the government agents for violating their Fourth Amendment rights against an illegal search? The government agents attempted to justify the invitations by arguing that such close-up coverage of their action would assist the public in understanding law enforcement problems and help the police in getting more public cooperation. "Surely the possibility of good public relations for the police is simply not enough, standing alone, to justify the ride-along intrusion into a private home," Chief Justice William Rehnquist wrote for the court. The chief justice quoted an almost 400-year-old British court ruling in supporting the high court's decision: "The house of everyone is to him as his castle and fortress, as well for his defence [*sic*] against injury and violence, for his repose." But because the law concerning media ride-alongs had not been developed when these arrests took place, the high court ruled that it would be unfair to subject the police officers in this case to money damages for their behavior. The officers could not have clearly foreseen that what they did would be a violation of the Constitution.[42]

"Surely the possibility of good public relations for the police is simply not enough, standing alone, to justify the ride-along intrusion into a private home."

In this instance the court did not rule on the matter of the liability of reporters and photographers who enter private premises with the permission of police. The *Berger* case was remanded to the 9th U.S. Circuit Court of Appeals in light of the high-court ruling regarding the liability of the police.[43] In an earlier decision before the case reached the Supreme Court, the Court of Appeals had ruled that, because of the extremely close cooperation between the journalists and the government agents who searched the Montana ranch, the television reporters and producers were actually "state actors" or "joint actors" with the wildlife agents and could be subject to the same kind of Fourth Amendment action brought against the federal officers.[44] After the Supreme Court decision, the appellate court ruled that the journalists did not enjoy the kind of qualified immunity that had shielded the government agents in the *Wilson* case, reinstated Berger's Fourth Amendment claim against the reporters, and also reversed a lower court's dismissal of claims for trespass and the intentional infliction of emotional distress against the media defendants.[45] In 2001 Paul Berger finally reached a confidential settlement agreement with CNN, bringing the case to a close for an undisclosed amount of cash.[46]

42. *Wilson* v. *Layne,* 526 U.S. 603 (1999).
43. *Hanlon* v. *Berger,* 526 U.S. 808 (1999).
44. *Berger* v. *Hanlon,* 129 F. 3d 505 (1997).
45. *Berger* v. *Hanlon,* 188 F. 3d 1155 (1999). The rancher and his wife were absolved of all felony charges, but the search was nevertheless broadcast 10 different times by CNN.
46. "CNN, Federal Government Settle Suit with Montana Rancher."

In a 2010 case called *Frederick v. Biography Channel*,[47] U.S. District Judge Milton Shadur refused to dismiss a complaint filed by two women over what the judge called a "highly disturbing" collaborative arrangement between the police in Naperville, Ill., and several media organizations, including the Biography Channel and A&E Television Networks. The media defendants worked very closely with the Naperville police to gather footage for a reality television show called "Female Forces"—including unflattering footage of the two women who filed the lawsuit, one of whom was being arrested and specifically objected to being filmed. The truly disturbing part is that after a Naperville officer detained the two women, he deliberately waited for the arrival of a camera crew that was assigned to film "Female Forces," doing so for the express purpose of having the arrest filmed for the show. In other words, rather than readily and immediately arresting one of the two women who had an outstanding warrant, the officer delayed and stalled until the cameras arrived! Observing that "a symbiotic relationship between a governmental body and a private party" (in this case, the private parties were the Biography Channel and A&E Television Networks) can transform the private party into a government actor, Judge Shadur found that there actually was a formal contract between the City of Naperville and the media defendants. The bottom line is that by acting so closely with government officials (here, the Naperville police), the media defendants were transformed into government actors. The two women thus could proceed to sue the Biography Channel and A&E Television Networks for violating their Fourth Amendment right against unreasonable searches and seizures, just as was the case in *Hanlon v. Berger*.

In a 2013 case involving a reality show called "Police Women of Broward County," a federal judge refused to dismiss a Fourth Amendment claim against the Discovery Channel when it filmed the plaintiff as he was being arrested inside a motel room during a prostitution sting. Plaintiff Jerry Byrd argued that he was never advised that he was being filmed for the show, and U.S. Judge James Cohn found that Byrd's allegation that defendants filmed him without his consent was "sufficient to state a claim for a violation of his Fourth Amendment right to be free from an unreasonable seizure."[48]

In 2014, however, the 10th U.S. Circuit Court of Appeals held that employees of the NBC Universal show "Dateline" did not violate the Fourth Amendment rights of Tyrone Clark when they surreptitiously filmed a seminar he conducted for his company, Brokers' Choice of America (BCA).[49] Clark claimed that "Dateline" employees engaged in an unreasonable search and seizure under the Fourth Amendment when they used fake insurance agent credentials supplied by Alabama law enforcement officials, who were also investigating Clark and BCA, to enter BCA's property and secretly tape the seminar. The appellate court assumed, for the sake of argument, that "Dateline" was acting as "either an agent of the Alabama officials or sufficiently engaged in concerted activity with them to meet the joint action test." Yet, the court found that the "Dateline" employees' misrepresentation of themselves as insurance agents did not violate the Fourth Amendment and was, "instead, the classic ruse of misrepresented identity."

47. 683 F. Supp. 2d 798 (N.D. Ill. 2010).
48. *Byrd v. Lamberti*, 2013 U.S. Dist. LEXIS 101327 (S.D. Fla. Jul. 19, 2013).
49. *Brokers' Choice Am. v. NBC Universal, Inc.*, 757 F. 3d 1125 (10th Cir. 2014).

The court called "it is a classic case of government agents sending willing and available operatives to obtain information freely revealed to those operatives. The fake insurance agent credentials supplied by Alabama officials fit easily into the types of deception courts have generally found permissible because it involved no coercion, express or implied." In summary, even if the "Dateline" employees were assumed to be joint actors with law enforcement, their misrepresentation was not a Fourth Amendment violation.

Reporters who want to enter private property need the permission of the occupant or the owner of the property. Police and firefighters are unable to give the press this permission. Reporters who are sent to cover demonstrations or protests that may stray onto nonpublic areas are advised to meet with the police beforehand and explain what they will be doing. They should carry full press credentials and obey all legitimate police orders. Reporters need to be careful not to interfere with police or have a verbal confrontation with officers who are attempting crowd control. Tensions run high, and the police often fear losing control of the situation.

Reporters who want to enter private property need the permission of the occupant or the owner of the property.

Student journalists sometimes face disorderly conduct charges in the line of duty. From 2015 to 2017, college campuses were regularly the scenes of mass public gatherings and protests. At the University of Missouri, for example, student videographers Tim Tai and Mark Schierbecker found themselves unexpectedly at the center of a national controversy for reporting on protests at the University of Missouri, home of the nation's oldest journalism school. Tai and Schierbecker refused to comply with demonstrators who demanded they stop shooting videos and photos in a publicly viewable location on the campus quad. The scene nearly erupted into violence when university employees supporting the protesters escalated the confrontation.

There are myriad catchall laws in most cities and states, laws like interfering with an officer in the execution of his or her duty, that might be the basis for an arrest even if a trespass is not involved. When applied to the press, these laws might be unconstitutional,[50] but such a ruling will not be made until weeks or months after the journalist has been arrested. These laws are discussed over the next several pages.

Harassment. In 1996 a federal judge in Pennsylvania took the extraordinary action of enjoining the news-gathering activities of two reporters who worked for the television infotainment program "Inside Edition." Reporters Paul Lewis and Stephen Wilson were preparing a story on the high salaries paid to corporate executives at U.S. HealthCare while the company was imposing severe cost cutting on patients. The story focused on Leonard Abramson, board chair, and Abramson's daughter and son-in-law, Nancy and Richard Wolfson, who also worked at U.S. HealthCare. The Wolfsons argued that the reporters used ambush interviews, shotgun microphones and other electronic equipment to harass them and invade their privacy after they rejected requests for on-camera interviews. The reporters went so far, the couple said, as to follow their daughter to school and to follow the entire family when they took a vacation in Florida. The Wolfsons sued the reporters for tortious stalking, harassment, trespass and invasion of privacy–intrusion upon seclusion, and asked the judge to stop the reporters from using the intrusive news-gathering techniques until a jury trial was held. The judge thought the Wolfsons would

---

50. *City of Houston v. Hill,* 482 U.S. 451 (1987).

prevail in their lawsuit against the reporters. He said that through their unreasonable surveilling, hounding and following, the two news gatherers had effectively rendered the family captive in their own home. The judge entered a preliminary injunction that barred Lewis and Wilson from any conduct, with or without the use of cameras, that invades the Wolfsons' privacy, actions including but not limited to harassing, hounding, following, intruding, frightening, terrorizing or ambushing the family.[51] In 1997, the parties reached a settlement and the judge dissolved the preliminary injunction he had issued against "Inside Edition."

In 2009 Nicole Richie obtained a three-year restraining order from a Los Angeles judge against two photographers requiring them to stay at least 50 yards away from famous-for-being-famous Richie. She blamed the two men for causing a car crash in Beverly Hills and claimed she was frightened for her safety and that of her two children.

Fraud. Fraud is a knowingly false statement of a material or significant fact that is communicated with the intent to induce the plaintiff to rely on that statement and that does, in fact, induce the plaintiff to reasonably rely upon it to the plaintiff's harm or injury. Typically we think of sellers of goods as engaging in fraud when they lie to buyers about the quality of those goods. But can journalists be held liable for fraud when they try to obtain information by telling a lie? Imagine this scenario. A newspaper editor hears well-founded rumors that a local retail business is cheating its customers. To check out this story, two newspaper reporters apply for jobs at the business to take a look at what goes on inside. The pair use false names, fake work histories and tell the business owners they are looking for work. They do not reveal they are newspaper reporters and will be spying on the other workers at the business. Are the reporters' activities legal? In 1996 a jury in North Carolina decided that ABC television journalists had committed fraud and an assortment of other legal wrongs when they lied about their backgrounds and intentions in order to get jobs at a supermarket chain the network was investigating for potential health code violations. A damage award of $5 million was later reduced to all but nothing ($2) when a U.S. Court of Appeals ruled that the behavior of the two journalists did not meet the strict legal standard for fraud required by North Carolina statutes.[52] But this high-profile case, which generated considerably more news coverage than the original ABC broadcast about the supermarket chain, brought into sharp focus the issue of reporters pretending to be people they are not in order to secretly gather news. In a different state with a different statute the fraud conviction might have been sustained. Indeed, in Minnesota just a year later, WCCO television and one of its reporters were found guilty of both fraud and trespass in a situation that mirrored the ABC case. In this instance the reporter lied about her background and her reportorial intentions when she applied for a position as a volunteer at a care facility for people with mental retardation. She secretly videotaped activities at the facility and portions of the tape were later telecast.[53]

---

51. *Wolfson* v. *Lewis*, 924 F. Supp. 1413 (1996).
52. *Food Lion Inc.* v. *Capital Cities/ABC*, 194 F. 3d 505 (1999); see also Barringer, "Appeals Court Rejects Damages."
53. *Special Force Ministries* v. *WCCO Television*, 584 N.W. 2d 789 (1998).

An issue closely related to fraud is impersonation by journalists of government officials in order to obtain information. Such impersonation is prohibited by both federal and state law and the First Amendment provides no defense. For instance, journalist Avi Lidgi was sentenced in April 2002 to one-year probation and 60 hours of community service by a federal court for posing as both a federal prosecutor and a federal judge's aide in order to obtain secret legal documents in an espionage case in Cleveland, Ohio.[54] The 27-year-old journalist agreed to plead guilty to one count of impersonating a federal official after a grand jury had indicted him on three counts and he faced up to nine years in prison.

Failure to Obey Lawful Orders. Police and fire officials at the scene of disasters, accidents and fires frequently restrict the access of the press and public to the site. Reporters must respect these rules or face charges of disorderly conduct or worse.

Sometimes it is not always clear, however, whether police orders directed at reporters are indeed lawful. In 2011 a veteran journalist for a Fox TV station in Milwaukee was arrested for "resisting and obstructing an officer" as he videotaped a house fire while standing several feet behind a perimeter that police had taped off. According to a post on the Web site of the Reporters Committee for Freedom of the Press, journalist Clint Fillinger can be heard saying on the tape after he was asked to step further back, "But the public is out here. If the public is out here, I'm allowed to be out here."[55] Fillinger and his TV station considered the request unreasonable because Fillinger was asked to move away from the scene while the general public was allowed access. Both the National Press Photographers Association and the Wisconsin News Photographers Association wrote formal letters to the chief of the Milwaukee Police Department demanding that all charges be immediately dropped. The Wake County (N.C.) District Attorney's office dropped misdemeanor charges against veteran *Charlotte Observer* reporter Tim Funk after he was arrested during a protest. In 2013, Funk was arrested while covering "Moral Monday" protests at the Raleigh General Assembly. General Assembly Police Chief Jeff Weaver said that Funk was the only reporter who failed to heed three warnings from officers asking the crowd to disperse. Funk was wearing his *Charlotte Observer* press credentials around his neck when he remained to interview a group of about 60 protesters who were peacefully waiting for arrest. Officers moved him aside before handcuffing and taking him to be arraigned on trespassing and failure to disperse charges.[56]

The First Amendment thus does not give the press special rights of access to disaster scenes or protect reporters from arrest and disorderly conduct charges when they fail to obey lawful commands of police at accident scenes. But at least three states—California, Ohio and Oregon—have statutes that carve out some (although not complete) protection for journalists gathering news in certain situations. California, for example, allows "duly authorized" members of "any news service, newspaper, or radio or television station or network" to enter areas closed by law enforcement due to a "flood, storm, fire,

---

54. "Journalist Gets Probation."
55. Lozare, "Milwaukee Photojournalist Arrested."
56. Zhang, "Charges Against Arrested N.C. Reporter Dropped."

earthquake, explosion, accident or other disaster,"[57] while Oregon provides journalists with "reasonable access" to search and rescue areas.[58]

Grand juries work behind closed doors, and courts are very sensitive when anyone attempts to elicit information from the jurors about what has taken place. Any attempt to induce grand jurors to reveal secret testimony can surely be punished by the courts.

Taping and Recording. Many other laws may directly affect news gathering. And the First Amendment does not offer a shield to reporters who violate these, either. For example, in most states and the District of Columbia, a reporter can secretly record a conversation or interview with a news source. These are known as one-party consent states, since only one party to the conversation (the journalist taping it) needs to know it is being recorded. While 38 states and the District of Columbia fall into this journalist-friendly, one-party consent category, a dozen states, including California, Pennsylvania and Florida, require reporters to obtain permission from all parties in a conversation before recording (all-party consent states).[59] These laws prohibit anyone from secretly recording a conversation face-to-face, on the telephone or almost anywhere. For instance, California Penal Code Section 632 provides that a crime is committed by anyone (including a journalist) who

> intentionally and *without the consent of all parties* [emphasis added] to a confidential communication, by means of any electronic amplifying or recording device, eavesdrops upon or records the confidential communication, whether the communication is carried on among the parties in the presence of one another or by means of a telegraph, telephone, or other device, except a radio.

California courts have held that a "confidential communication" is one in which a party to the conversation has an objectively reasonable expectation that it is not being overheard or recorded.[60] A violation occurs at the moment the recording is made, *regardless* of whether the material recorded is later published or aired.

What law applies if a person calling from a one-party consent state records a conversation with a recipient who lives in an all-party consent state? In 2006, the Supreme Court of California held in *Kearney* v. *Salomon Smith Barney* that California's all-party consent statute applied and controlled when a caller from Georgia (a one-party consent state) secretly recorded a conversation with a California resident.[61] Maryland also holds that its all-party consent law controls when out-of-state callers record conversations.[62] Journalists calling into all-party consent states are wise to get permission before taping.

---

57. California Penal Code § 409.5 (2016). See also Ohio Revised Code Annotated § 2917.13 (2016).
58. Oregon Revised Statute § 401.570 (2016).
59. The 12 all-party consent states are California, Connecticut, Florida, Illinois, Maryland, Massachusetts, Michigan, Montana, Nevada, New Hampshire, Pennsylvania and Washington.
60. *Flanagan* v. *Flanagan,* 41 P. 3d 575 (2002).
61. 39 Cal. 4th 95 (2006).
62. *Perry* v. *Maryland,* 357 Md. 37 (Md. Ct. App. 1999).

SECRET RECORDINGS, THE LA CLIPPERS AND THE LAW

In 2014, the sports world was rocked by a secret recording of racist remarks made by Los Angeles Clippers owner Donald Sterling to his girlfriend V. Tiviano. Sterling was recorded in September 2013 making the comments after Tiviano posted a picture of herself on Instagram with basketball legend and Hall of Famer Ervin "Magic" Johnson. In the recording, a voice identified as Sterling can be heard telling Tiviano, "It bothers me a lot that you want to broadcast that you're associating with black people. . . . You can sleep with [black people]. You can bring them in, you can do whatever you want, [but] the little I ask you is . . . not to bring them to my games." After *TMZ Sports* released the recording, Sterling was banned from the NBA for life and fined $2.5 million by the league. After the recording was released, Sterling's wife, Shelly, reached an agreement to sell the Clippers for $2 billion to Steve Ballmer. The NBA Board of Governors approved the sale of the Clippers to Ballmer on August 12, 2014, although Sterling sued to stop the sale. But was the recording made legally?

It is possible the recording was made illegally. But it remains unclear because the circumstances of the recording are largely unclear. The person who recorded Sterling, either Tiviano or someone else, could have been held liable under a California law that requires the consent of all parties in a private conversation for it to be recorded. The law applies only to conversations that are "truly private," however. If Sterling and Tiviano were having a quiet conversation at a Clippers game, it wouldn't be considered a "truly private" conversation. In addition, the law only applies if one intentionally records a private conversation. Accidentally recording a conversation without Sterling's knowledge would not be illegal. Finally, it remains unclear if Sterling knew he was being recorded. After the recording became public, attorneys for Tiviano stated that Sterling consented to having the conversation recorded, although this was never confirmed by Sterling or his lawyers.

Regardless of the circumstances, the recording is a reminder of the changing landscape of privacy in a digital age. As more and more of private life is played out in public where nearly everyone has immediate access to a smartphone with the ability to immediately record and widely distribute content across the Internet, the lines between public and private continue to blur.

Nearly half the states and the federal government have laws prohibiting eavesdropping. A growing number of states also have statutes that prohibit secretly taking a video recording or still photograph of a person in a location where he or she has a reasonable expectation of privacy. These laws target video voyeurs, but they impact journalists and legitimate photographers. Anyone who hopes to practice journalism without violating the law needs to know the laws in his or her particular state that relate to news gathering. There are subtle differences among the state laws, and the statutes change from time to time. Awareness of the law is the best protection a reporter can have. A good resource on taping can be found online at the Reporters Committee for Freedom of the Press Web site at http://www.rcfp.org/reporters-recording-guide.

Eavesdropping statutes often involve consideration of what constitutes a reasonable expectation of privacy in a conversation. For instance, the Michigan Supreme Court in *Bowens* v. *Ary*[63] in 2011 considered whether that state's eavesdropping statute was violated by the backstage recording of a conversation at a concert featuring performances by Dr. Dre, Snoop Dogg, Ice Cube and Eminem at Detroit's Joe Louis Arena. The conversation in question involved discussions by police officials (the plaintiffs) with concert organizers regarding whether or not a sexually explicit video could be shown before a performance by Dre and Snoop. A tape of the conversation later was featured as "exclusive backstage footage" on a tour concert DVD, and the police officials sued. Michigan's eavesdropping statute prohibits "any person who is present or who is not present during a private conversation [from] willfully us[ing] any device to eavesdrop upon the conversation without the consent of all parties thereto." The key phrase is "private conversation"—there must be a private conversation in order for the statute to be violated.

In *Bowens*, the following were crucial facts in the Michigan Supreme Court's conclusion that there was no reasonable expectation of privacy in the recorded conversation: 1) more than 400 people had backstage passes, including many members of the local and national media; 2) there were at least nine identified people in the room where the conversation was taped, plus unidentified others who were free to come and go from the room, and listen to the conversation, as they pleased; and 3) the plaintiffs who were recorded were aware that there were multiple camera crews in the vicinity, including a crew from MTV and a crew specifically hired by defendants to record backstage matters of interest. Because there was no reasonable expectation of privacy in the recorded conversations, the court ruled that Michigan's eavesdropping statute was not violated.

SUMMARY   Gaining access to government-held information is a major problem for journalists and citizens alike. The law is not always helpful. Common law offers little assistance to people attempting to inspect government records. The U.S. Constitution was drafted when news gathering was not the central role of the press. There is little evidence that the right to gather news was intended to be guaranteed by the First Amendment. Federal courts have suggested that news and information gathering is entitled to some protection under the U.S. Constitution, but they have been stingy in granting such protection. The U.S. Supreme Court has limited the rights of reporters to gather information at prisons and jails to the same rights enjoyed by other citizens. Lower courts have found broader, albeit qualified, constitutional rights of access. Courts have not permitted, however, the use of the First Amendment to immunize reporters from legal consequences that result when the law is broken while news is being gathered. Many plaintiffs find it is easier to sue the press for how the news has been gathered than for libel or invasion of privacy. Suits for trespass, fraud, misrepresentation, failure to obey lawful orders and other causes of action are common.

63. 794 N.W.2d 842 (Mich. 2011).

THE FREEDOM OF INFORMATION ACT

Neither common law nor the U.S. Constitution provides a clear and well-defined right of access to government information. Although scholars have argued that access to government information is a constitutional right and at least two international courts have declared access to government information is a human right,[64] in the United States and much of the world, access to government information is guaranteed by statutory law.[65] While government transparency has taken hold across the globe, the United States was a leader in the modern movement to pass access laws. Beginning in the early 1950s, there were concerted efforts by press and citizen lobbying groups in the United States to pass statutes that guarantee the public and press the right to inspect records and other information held by the government and to attend meetings held by public agencies. These laws now exist in almost every state. In addition, there are federal open-records and open-meetings laws. Let us look at the federal legislation first.

In 1966, after many years of hearings, testimony and work, Congress adopted the Freedom of Information Act (FOIA), which was ostensibly designed to open records and files long closed to public inspection. The documentary evidence left by Congress relating to the passage of this measure leaves little doubt that the purpose of this bill was to establish a general philosophy of the fullest possible disclosure of government-held records.

Now over 50 years old, FOIA provides a powerful tool for investigative journalists. Journalists cite public records in a fifth of their news stories, and some sources suggest journalists' use of FOIA is increasing. Thus, while the law is far from perfect, FOIA greatly contributes to journalists' ability to keep the public informed and increase its understanding of government activities.

For example, the Memphis Commercial Appeal scored a victory in 2013 using FOIA when it reached a settlement with the FBI over documents related to Ernest Withers. Withers was a famous African-American photographer who captured iconic black-and-white images of many pivotal battles in the civil rights movement in the South during the 1950s and 1960s, such as the Little Rock Central High School integration battle. It also turned out, as the newspaper discovered, that Withers was a paid FBI informant during much of this period. The newspaper entered an expensive and protracted battle with the FBI to obtain records regarding Withers' relationship with the FBI, including his informant file. The settlement came after a federal judge forced the FBI, which would neither admit nor deny Withers' service, to concede that he had been its informant.

In 2012, the *Wall Street Journal* used FOIA to uncover records related to the powers of the National Counterterrorism Center (NCTC) and the huge clash over this counterterrorism program within the Obama administration. The NCTC was given vast power by the Obama administration to examine government files on U.S. citizens for possible criminal behavior, even if there is no reason or probable cause to suspect them of any

---

64. In 2006, the Inter-American Court of Human Rights declared access to government information to be included within the human rights of free thought and freedom of expression. *Reyes* v. *Chile,* Inter-Am. Ct. H.R. (ser. C) No. 151, ¶ 77 (Sept. 19, 2006). In 2009, the European Court of Human rights did the same. *Társaság a Szabadságjogokért* v. *Hungary,* App. No. 37374/05, ¶ 39 (Apr. 14, 2009).

65. In the United States, the notable exception to this is access to court documents, which is secured via the First Amendment. This issue is addressed in Chapter 12.

wrongdoing. As the *Wall Street Journal* reported in December 2012, "the agency has new authority to keep data about innocent U.S. citizens for up to five years, and to analyze it for suspicious patterns of behavior. Previously, both were prohibited." The 2014 Pulitzer Prize–winning "Other than Honorable" series used FOIA requests to the U.S. Army to gather information about Army personnel suffering from post-traumatic stress disorder who were given so-called Chapter 10 discharges and lost their veterans benefits in lieu of facing a court-martial.[66]

In addition, any citizen, not just journalists, can make a FOIA request, and journalists routinely use information provided by nonprofit organizations, government watchdog groups and other organizations that were obtained via FOIA requests. In fact, some of the most effective requesters are well-financed nonprofits. Organizations such as the National Security Archives, the American Civil Liberties Union, the Electronic Privacy Information Center, the Electronic Frontier Foundation, the Center for Constitutional Rights, Judicial Watch and the Center for National Security Studies frequently work to disseminate information on government activities.

In 2009, for instance, the National Security Archive at George Washington University filed FOIA requests with the Department of Defense on behalf of some famous recording artists, including Pearl Jam and Trent Reznor. What did the musicians want? They sought records revealing which artists' music was being used as an interrogation technique at Guantanamo and other detention centers. Based upon previously released documents, as well as testimony of prisoners and guards about the type of loud music that was played during interrogations, the FOIA requests made specific reference to music by Nine Inch Nails, Rage Against the Machine, Red Hot Chili Peppers and Limp Bizkit. The artists filing the FOIA request were upset that their music might be used to torture detainees.

How many FOIA requests do all federal agencies receive? In fiscal year 2015, there were a total of 713,168 FOIA requests, down slightly from FY 2014, where there were 714,231 requests. Although, as discussed below, FOIA contains a 20-day deadline for an agency to respond to a request, FOIA requesters frequently face long delays. At the end of FY 2015, there was a backlog of 102,828 requests, a 35.6 percent decrease from FY 2014.*

For reporting purposes, agencies are directed to separate requests into three categories or "tracks": simple, complex and expedited. Requests that "seek a high volume of material or require additional steps to process such as the need to search for records in multiple locations" are categorized as "complex." The average processing time for "simple track requests" was 23 days. The average processing time for complex requests was 122 days. Only five agencies could process complex requests in 20 or fewer days in FY 2015. FOIA also allows you to make expedited requests for both simple and

---

66. "Other Than Honorable," *The Gazette,* available at http://cdn.csgazette.biz/soldiers/. See also, "The FOIA Files," The Sunshine in Government Initiative, http://sunshineingovernment.org/wordpress/the-foia-files/ (last visited Jul. 1, 2016) (catalog of more than 700 stories using information obtained via FOIA).

* FY 2014 had an exceptionally high number of backlogged requests. In FY 2012 there were 71,790 backlogged requests. In FY 2013 there were 95,564. In FY 2014 there were 102,828. Rather than a vast improvement over historical numbers, FY 2015 numbers seem to simply be a return to previous levels with a slight increase from FY 2013.

complex requests. In FY 2015, the average processing times for expedited requests was approximately 54 days. Some journalists have suggested these delays and failures to find records are deliberate decisions by government bureaucrats. Another explanation is that FOIA is an underfunded mandate.

In addition, FOIA requests can be costly. Under FOIA, a court *may* order federal agencies to pay reasonable attorneys' fees and other litigation costs incurred in cases in which the plaintiff (the person seeking records) has substantially prevailed. Courts, however, are not *required* to award prevailing plaintiffs attorneys' fees and litigation costs. When deciding to award fees and other costs, courts typically consider and weigh four factors. Those four factors are: (1) the public benefit resulting from FOIA disclosures in the case; (2) the commercial benefit to the prevailing plaintiff resulting from the disclosures; (3) the nature of the plaintiff's interest in the disclosed records (scholarly? journalistic? public-oriented?) and (4) whether the government's rationale for withholding the records had a reasonable basis in law or whether it simply denied the request to avoid embarrassment or to frustrate the requester.

In October 2012, a federal judge in San Francisco ordered the Department of Justice and the FBI to pay investigative journalist and author Seth Rosenfeld more than $470,000, the amount Rosenfeld spent on attorneys' fees and litigation costs in two successful and long-running lawsuits he filed against the FBI to obtain records relating to the 1960s protest movement at the University of California, Berkeley. Those documents included records demonstrating the FBI's surveillance of students and faculty and records involving Ronald Reagan's relationship with the FBI when Reagan was California governor. Considering the second factor, Judge Edward Chen noted that although Rosenfeld may have had a financial incentive in writing a book based on the records, the "mere intention to publish a book does not necessarily mean that the nature of the plaintiff's interest is purely commercial."[67]

The success of any freedom of information law, of course, depends on how the government chooses to interpret and apply the law. Upon taking office in 2009, President Barack Obama issued a memorandum suggesting his administration would bring new openness to government and, in particular, to how it responded to FOIA requests. The results of the Obama administration's approach to FOIA and other transparency issues, however, were far from stellar. Some journalists have called Obama's administration one of the most secretive in history. In 2015, for example, the Society of Professional Journalists and 52 other journalism organizations sent a letter to the White House urging an end to excessive secrecy. In addition, although the United States was the third country to adopt a law governing access to government information, today's scholars have noted FOIA's relative weakness compared to other nations' access laws. It is far too early to know how the administration of Donald Trump will respond to FOIA requests, particularly when they come from media organizations he has deemed "fake news."

Journalists were at the forefront of the effort to pass the FOIA and were intrinsically involved in crafting the legislation. In addition, journalists believe access laws are important tools, with one study showing that 97 percent of journalists believe open-records laws are important for them to fulfill their duties.[68] The law, however, has been

---

67. Kraut, "A Marathon Freedom of Information Fight."
68. Davis, "Stacked Deck Favors Government Secrecy."

highly criticized by journalists. While FOIA is failing journalists for many reasons—most notably, as discussed earlier, the long delays and processing inefficiencies associated with access requests—a key reason the law is failing journalists is because journalists simply do not use the law nearly as much as corporations and other nonmedia individuals and organizations, a fact that stands in stark contrast to the history and purpose of the law. Why don't journalists use FOIA more?

A major problem with journalists using FOIA is the way the law is written. FOIA directs federal agencies to "make records promptly available to any person." It does not provide journalists with analysis or answers to general queries and does not command government officials to research where information can be found. FOIA does not even require the government to affirmatively disclose information about what records it has. Thus, if a journalist does not know what records exist or what records to be looking for, FOIA is of little use.

Economics might also impact FOIA requests by members of the news media. As the U.S. news media has been hit with a historical decline in profits, some commentators are worried that economic constraints may limit both FOIA requests and challenges to FOIA denials.[69] Buyouts and layoffs typically affect more experienced, costly journalists, who are most likely to use FOIA. As noted above, litigating denials are both costly and time consuming, creating additional barriers to access. Only large or well-financed news organizations have the funds to support speculative investigation and provide for attorney's fees. This might be the biggest problem with the media's use of FOIA. In practice, FOIA is meaningless if the financial resources are not available to fight the time-consuming battles when requests are denied.

A final worry is that privacy concerns are keeping FOIA officials from releasing information to journalists that would be valuable in writing stories. Because journalists frequently are interested in writing about people, some journalists believe FOIA is not worth using because the government goes overboard to protect personal information. A major concern is that as government increasingly gathers personal information and better understands how much can be gleaned from that information, government officials are increasingly reluctant to share personal information with journalists. *National Archives and Records Administration* v. *Favish*,[70] a 2004 Supreme Court decision that broadly interpreted the personal privacy exemption in FOIA to include a right of familial or survivor privacy, is an example of how the concept of privacy has changed since FOIA was enacted. For these reasons, in some ways it is not surprising that commercial requesters are using FOIA more than journalists even if the law was primarily intended to benefit the news media.

Despite these problems, however, as noted at the beginning of this section, many great stories are made possible by FOIA requests and young journalists shouldn't be afraid to make public records requests at the local and federal level. Maybe your instructor will even require you to make one as part of your grade in this class!

---

69. See, e.g., Rydell, "No Money to Fight."
70. 541 U.S. 157 (2003).

RECENT FOIA REFORMS

By 2000 the vast majority of government records were created, transported and stored electronically. As computer technology replaced paper records, agencies within the federal government balked at allowing access to these electronic records. Most bureaucrats seemed to hold the opinion that the electronic records were a special class of data, outside the range of FOIA and off limits to the public.[71]

In 1996 Congress adopted an amendment to the Freedom of Information Act that requires government agencies to apply the same standards of disclosure to electronic records that they have always applied to paper documents. This includes all e-mail correspondence as well as letters or notes. The Electronic Freedom of Information Act, as codified at 5 U.S.C. § 552 and known as e-FOIA, also establishes priorities that the agencies must apply when faced with multiple requests for computer searches for records. Top priority goes to FOIA requests in which a delay would threaten the life or safety of an individual. Next in line comes the news media and others in the business of disseminating information to the public. The law also requires agencies to publish an online index of the documents they have and to make a reasonable attempt to provide documents in the requested format, that is, on tapes, diskettes, paper and so on. The law does not, however, define electronic information, instead leaving this important question to federal agencies and the courts.

What about e-mail of people working in the White House? In 2010, after a protracted legal battle that started during the Bush administration, the Obama administration issued letters to the attorneys for both the National Security Archive at George Washington University and the organization Citizens for Ethics and Responsibility in Washington outlining new procedures for capturing and preserving e-mail records for people working in the Executive Office of the president using an EmailXtender system. In 2007, whistle-blowers with knowledge of the White House computer system alleged that the unclassified White House e-mail system had not archived e-mail systematically since 2002, and that at least five million e-mail messages were missing from the period of March 2003 through October 2005.

In December 2007, President Bush signed the first major amendments to FOIA since the 1990s. The Openness Promotes Effectiveness in Our National Government Act of 2007 (OPEN Government Act) made several reforms designed to expedite processing of FOIA requests, help requesters easily obtain better information about the status of their requests and hold federal agencies more accountable if they fail to timely respond to requests. Under the act, government agencies are required to assign a tracking number for each FOIA request that will take more than 10 days to process and to establish a phone number or an Internet site to help requesters check the status of their requests. Agencies that fail to comply with the 20-day window in which to respond to a FOIA request are no longer allowed to charge any search and duplication fees related to that request unless there are "unusual or exceptional circumstances" that justify the delay. As noted above, the law also allows for the recovery of attorney fees and litigation costs for

---

71. Morrissey, "FOIA Foiled?" 29.

FOIA requesters who substantially prevail in FOIA lawsuits. The law created the Office of Government Information Services (OGIS) to serve as a FOIA ombudsperson to mediate FOIA disputes. The OGIS is charged with reviewing compliance by government agencies with FOIA's rules and making recommendations to Congress and the president on how to improve FOIA.

In 2016, President Barrack Obama signed a bill that significantly reformed and improved access to public records. Perhaps most importantly, the FOIA Improvement Act of 2016 requires that agencies operate from a presumption of openness. The law codified the "foreseeable harm" standard, meaning that even if a record falls within one of FOIA's nine exemptions, it will still be released unless it is reasonably foreseeable that disclosure will harm an interest protected by an exemption. The law also paved the way for the creation of a single online portal to accept FOIA requests for all agencies, similar to FOIAonline, which is already used by 12 agencies and offices. Unfortunately, the law did not create a deadline for the creation of the portal. Agencies are now required to put online all documents that have been requested three or more times. The law also strengthened the OGIS, permitting it to make recommendations for improving FOIA without seeking the input of other agencies. In addition, the new law limited FOIA exemption 5 (discussed later in this chapter). Under the law, the ability of agencies to withhold "deliberative process" documents—such as memoranda, letters and drafts—is now limited to 25 years. Abuse had led some journalists to refer to exemption 5 as the "withhold it because you want to exemption." Agencies must now also submit FOIA processing statistics a month earlier so they are available for Sunshine Week in March.

In early 2017, however, the FBI announced that it would revert to using fax machines and regular mail to handle the bulk of FOIA requests it receives. The FBI announced that starting March 1, 2017, it would implement a new policy and would no longer accept FOIA requests via e-mail. In addition to fax and mail requests, the FBI announced it would accept a small number of requests through an online portal, provided users agreed to a terms-of-service agreement and were willing to provide the FBI with personal information, including a phone number and a physical address. This new procedure mirrors the one used by the Central Intelligence Agency (CIA) and the Defense Advanced Research Projects Agency (DARPA), the agency responsible for advanced technology research conducted on behalf of the Pentagon.

AGENCY RECORDS

The broad outlines of the federal Freedom of Information Act, the nine areas of exempted information, and suggested ways in which a journalist or citizen can use the law are sketched out in the next few pages. One can write an open-records law in two basic ways. The first way is to declare that the following kinds of records are to be accessible for public inspection and then list the kinds of records that are open. The second way is to proclaim that all government records are open for public inspection except the following kinds of records and then list the exceptions. Congress approved the second kind of law in 1966, and it went into effect in 1967. The law has been amended several times, with substantial changes being enacted in 1974, 1976, 1986, 1996, 2002 (with the adoption of the Homeland Security Act), 2007 and 2016.

What Is an Agency?

The U.S. Freedom of Information Act gives any person access to all the records kept by all federal agencies, unless the information falls into one of nine categories of exempted material. An agency has been defined under the law as

> any executive department, military department, government corporation, government-controlled corporation or other establishment in the executive branch of government (including the executive office of the president), or any independent regulatory agency.

The law governs records held by agencies in the executive branch of government and all the independent regulatory agencies like the **Federal Trade Commission (FTC),** the Federal Aviation Agency, the Nuclear Regulatory Commission, the Social Security Administration and the Securities and Exchange Commission. The law does not cover records held by Congress or the federal courts. Some agencies associated with the executive branch of government also fall outside the purview of the law. In 1985 the U.S. Court of Appeals for the District of Columbia Circuit ruled that the Council of Economic Advisors, which works closely with the president on economic matters, is not covered by the law because it exists solely to advise and assist the president and makes no policy on its own. The agency has no regulatory power; it cannot issue rules or regulations. Although FOIA does govern some operations in the executive office of the president, the law does not reach "the president's immediate personal staff or units in the executive office whose *sole function* is to advise and assist the president," the court ruled.[72]

The law does not cover records held by Congress or the federal courts.

A couple of quasi-governmental entities raise interesting questions as to whether they are agencies subject to FOIA. The Smithsonian Institution in Washington, D.C., for instance, is not a government agency and is not subject to FOIA, even though the vast majority of its budget comes from taxpayer dollars. After financial scandals and spending problems rocked the museum, however, a bill was introduced in Congress in 2008 to make it a government agency. To address these concerns and to fend off legislation, the Smithsonian responded in November 2008 by holding what *The New York Times* described as its "first public board meeting in its 162-year history . . . as part of its new commitment to openness and accountability."[73] The Smithsonian also formally adopted in January 2009 a new policy, patterned after FOIA, to allow for the disclosure of more records.

In contrast to the Smithsonian, the U.S. Postal Service is considered a government agency and features its own FOIA Web site at http://www.usps.com/foia. Although Amtrak (the National Railroad Passenger Corporation) is a private corporation operated for profit and is not technically a government agency, it too is subject to FOIA, under

72. *Rushforth* v. *Council of Economic Advisors,* 762 F. 2d 1038 (1985).
73. Pogrebin, "At Public Board Meeting, Smithsonian Practices New Openness."

provisions of the Rail Passenger Service Act. On the other hand, the Corporation for Public Broadcasting, a private, nonprofit corporation that was created by Congress in 1967, is not subject to FOIA.

What Is a Record?

Congress did not specify the physical characteristics of a record in the Freedom of Information Act. Certainly records are paper documents, e-mail and other computer-generated material.[74] But the term "record" also includes films, tapes and even three-dimensional objects such as evidence in a criminal prosecution. The FOIA statute provides that a record includes information "maintained by an agency in any format, including an electronic format." Importantly, the OPEN Government Act of 2007 expanded the description of a record to also include information "maintained for an agency by an entity under government contract." This change is key: It means that records held by outside private contractors working for the government are subject to FOIA requests.

Records held by outside private contractors working for the government are subject to FOIA requests.

What Is an Agency Record?

"Agency" has been defined under the law; so has "record." What is an agency record? It is not, unfortunately, simply a combination of the definition of these two terms. In this case the whole, the term "agency record," involves a good deal more than the sum of its parts. Courts have established the following definition of an agency record:

If the record is either created or obtained by an agency, and the record is under agency control at the time of the FOIA request, it is very likely an agency record.

If the agency has created the document but does not possess or control it, it is not an agency record.

If the agency merely possesses the document but has not created it, it might be an agency record, or it might not. If the agency came into possession of the document as a part of its official duties, it is probably an agency record. If it just happens to have the document, it is probably not an agency record.

In 2009 U.S. District Judge Royce C. Lamberth held that White House visitor logs are public records subject to FOIA since they are under the legal "control" of a government agency, U.S. Department of Homeland Security (DHS), even if they are transferred to the White House or the Office of the Vice President and destroyed or deleted from DHS' internal files.[75] The Secret Service, which actually creates the records, is a division of DHS. Judge Lamberth also concluded that the logs do not fall within the scope of the presidential communications privilege and thus are not shielded from disclosure by FOIA Exemption 5 (see pages 355–357). In an earlier ruling in the same case,[76] he articulated

---

74. *Long v. IRS*, 596 F. 2d 362 (1979).

75. *Citizens for Responsibility and Ethics in Washington v. U.S. Department of Homeland Security*, 2009 WL 50149 (D.D.C. Jan. 9, 2009). Another recent opinion related to White House visitor logs is *Judicial Watch, Inc. v. U.S. Secret Service*, 579 F. Supp. 2d 182 (D.D.C. 2008).

76. *Citizens for Responsibility and Ethics in Washington v. U.S. Department of Homeland Security*, 527 F. Supp. 2d 76 (D.D.C. 2007).

four factors relevant in determining if an agency exercises sufficient "control" over a document to render it an "agency record":

1. The intent of the document's creator to retain or relinquish control over the records.
2. The ability of the agency to use and dispose of the record as it sees fit.
3. The extent to which agency personnel have read or relied upon the document.
4. The degree to which the document was integrated into the agency's record system or files.

The Justice Department in 2010 continued to argue in a long-running dispute with a public-interest group called Judicial Watch that White House visitor logs held by the Secret Service are not subject to disclosure under the Freedom of Information Act. In August 2013, however, the U.S. Court of Appeals for the District of Columbia ruled in *Judicial Watch* v. *Secret Service*[77] that White House logs are not agency records and thus are not subject to FOIA. It wrote that "Congress made clear that it did not want documents like the appointment calendars of the President and his close advisors to be subject to disclosure under FOIA. Granting Judicial Watch's request for certain visitors records, however, could effectively disclose the contents of those calendars."

FOIA EXEMPTIONS

A document or tape or file that has been determined to be an agency record accessible via the Freedom of Information Act may still be withheld from public inspection if it properly falls into one of the nine categories of exempted material. Please note, federal agencies *are not required* to withhold documents from disclosure simply because they are included in an exempted category.[78] The law basically says they may withhold such material. The nine exemptions outlined in the following pages are fairly specific, yet not specific enough to be free from substantial judicial interpretation. How a judge defines a word or phrase in these exemptions can result in a significant change in the meaning of the law and can lead to either expanded public access or, more likely in recent years, substantially reduced public access. We will examine each exemption separately, try to outline its meaning, and briefly explore case law that illuminates how the exemption is applied. It is important to remember that in light of the war on terror and the Trump administration's ongoing battle with journalists, it is likely that many of these exemptions will be viewed even more broadly by government agencies and the courts.

Federal agencies are not required *to* withhold documents *from disclosure simply because they are included in an exempted category.*

As noted earlier, over 500,000 FOIA requests were processed in FY 2015. Agencies released records in full 33 percent of the time, and released records in part 59 percent of the time. Just over 7 percent of requests in FY 2015 resulted in a full denial. As has been the case for many years, the FOIA's privacy exemptions, Exemption 6 and 7(C), were the most cited FOIA exemptions used in FY 2015. Over half of the exemptions cited by agencies were those two exemptions. Exemption 7(E), which protects law enforcement techniques, procedures and guidelines, was the third most used exemption.

77. 726 F. 3d 208 (D.C.C. 2013)
78. See *Chrysler Corp.* v. *Brown,* 441 U.S. 281 (1979).

> ## EXEMPTIONS TO DISCLOSURE UNDER THE FREEDOM OF INFORMATION ACT
>
> 1. National security matters
> 2. Housekeeping materials
> 3. Material exempted by statute
> 4. Trade secrets
> 5. Working papers/lawyer–client privileged materials
> 6. Personal privacy files
> 7. Law enforcement records
> 8. Financial institution materials
> 9. Geological data

National Security

Exemption 1: Matters specifically authorized under criteria established by an executive order to be kept secret in the interest of national defense or foreign policy and in fact properly classified pursuant to such an executive order. This exemption deals with a wide range of materials, but primarily with information related to national security and national defense, intelligence gathering and foreign relations. The system has a three-tier classification. Material, the release of which could reasonably be expected to damage national security, is classified as "confidential," the lowest level of classification. The "secret" classification is used to shield material that if disclosed could be expected to cause serious damage to national security. "Top secret," the highest level of classification, is reserved for material that if revealed could be expected to cause exceptionally grave damage to national security.[79]

   Although government agencies have the burden to justify nondisclosure under any FOIA exemption, courts applying Exemption 1 give substantial deference and weight to agency affidavits implicating national security. In fact, they rule in favor of the government on Exemption 1 if an agency's affidavits (1) describe justifications for nondisclosure in reasonably specific detail; (2) demonstrate the information withheld logically falls within the claimed exemption; and (3) are not contradicted by evidence in the record or by evidence of agency bad faith. Applying this test in 2006, a federal judge held that the Department of Defense was protected under Exemption 1 from disclosing photographs of past and present detainees at the U.S. facility at Guantanamo Bay, Cuba. Among other things, the judge accepted the government's claim that public disclosure of the photos "would both increase the risk of retaliation against the detainees and their families and exacerbate the detainees' fears of reprisal, thus reducing the likelihood that detainees would cooperate in intelligence-gathering efforts."[80]

79. Executive Order No. 12958, 3 C.F.R. 333 (1996).
80. *Associated Press v. U.S. Department of Defense,* 462 F. Supp. 2d 573 (S.D.N.Y. 2006).

In 2012, the 2nd Circuit ruled that reports about the CIA's use of "enhanced interrogation techniques," such as waterboarding, could be withheld under Exemption 1, even though the use of the techniques was widely known.[81] In October 2011, the ACLU submitted a FOIA request seeking information about the killings of three U.S. citizens in Yemen: Anwar al-Aulaqi; his 16-year-old son, Abdulrahman al-Aulaqi; and Samir Kahn. Over 5 years of litigation, this case was appealed to the 2nd Circuit three times. The FOIA request sought disclosure of the legal memorandum written by the Department of Justice Office of Legal Counsel that provided justifications for the targeted killing of Anwar al-Aulaqi (sometimes spelled al-Awlaki), as well as records describing the factual basis for the killings of all three Americans. The government was forced to describe targeted-killing program documents in its possession, but many other documents were not released under Exemption 1.[82] In December 2016, the 2nd Circuit ruled that no other documents must be disclosed.

Housekeeping Practices

Exemption 2: Matters related solely to the internal personnel rules and practices of an agency. In 2011 the U.S. Supreme Court ruled that Exemption 2, which protects from disclosure material that is "related solely to the internal personnel rules and practices of an agency," could not be used by the Department of the Navy to suppress the release of data and maps relating to a naval base where explosives and weapons are stored in Puget Sound, Wash. The Navy had refused to release the data, alleging that disclosure would threaten the security of the base and surrounding community. The court reasoned in *Milner* v. *Department of the Navy*[83] that, as used in Exemption 2, "an agency's 'personnel rules and practices' are its rules and practices dealing with employee relations or human resources" and that "all the rules and practices referenced in Exemption 2 share a critical feature: They concern the conditions of employment in federal agencies—such matters as hiring and firing, work rules and discipline, compensation and benefits." Thus, under what the court called the "plain meaning" of the words in Exemption 2, the maps and data requested did not qualify for withholding under that exemption. Rather than use Exemption 2, the court added, "the Government has other tools at hand to shield national security information and other sensitive materials. Most notably, Exemption 1 of FOIA prevents access to classified documents."

The 2011 ruling in *Milner* was important because it gave a very narrow reading and interpretation to Exemption 2 and put an end to the federal government using it more broadly to try to suppress disclosure of records that would significantly risk circumvention of federal agency functions. Some lower courts had adopted such an expansive interpretation (known as a "High 2" interpretation), but the high court's ruling in *Milner* specifically rejected it.

In May 2011, the Justice Department issued an extensive guidance report on how Exemption 2 should be interpreted in light of the *Milner* ruling. That report is available at http://www.justice.gov/oip/foiapost/2011foiapost15.html.

---

81. *ACLU* v. *U.S. Department of Justice,* 681 F.3d 61 (2d Cir. 2012).
82. Nos. 15-2956(L), 15-3122 (2nd Cir. 2016).
83. 131 S. Ct. 1259 (2011).

Statutory Exemption

Exemption 3: Matters specifically exempted from disclosure by statute (other than section 552b of this title), if that statute—(A) (i) requires that the matters be withheld from the public in such a manner as to leave no discretion on the issue; or (ii) establishes particular criteria for withholding or refers to particular types of matters to be withheld; and (B) if enacted after the date of enactment of the OPEN FOIA Act of 2009, specifically cites to this paragraph.

This exemption was amended in 2009 to add an extra requirement, namely the portion set forth after "**(B)**" above mandating that statutes enacted after the date of the OPEN FOIA Act of 2009 (October 28, 2009) must specifically cite to Exemption 3 of the FOIA in order to qualify under Exemption 3. The amendment thus imposes an additional hurdle for exemption for any new laws enacted today. Such statutes must satisfy both part "**(A)**" and part "**(B)**" in order to qualify for nondisclosure under Exemption 3. This exemption is designed to protect from disclosure information required or permitted to be kept secret by scores of other federal laws. A wide range of records fall under this exemption, including Census Bureau records, public utility information, trade secrets, patent applications, tax returns, bank records, veterans benefits and documents held by both the CIA and the National Security Agency.

Courts generally ask three questions when determining whether Exemption 3 applies to a specific record or document:

1. Is there a specific statute that authorizes or requires the withholding of information?
2. Does the statute designate specific kinds of information or outline specific criteria for information that may be withheld?
3. Does the record or information that is sought fall within the categories of information that may be withheld?

If all three questions are answered yes, disclosure can be legally denied.

The CIA has managed to use this exemption to almost completely shield its operations from public scrutiny.

Via congressional action and numerous court rulings the CIA has managed to use this exemption to almost completely shield its operations from public scrutiny. In 1984 Congress voted to exempt all CIA operational files from release under the Freedom of Information Act. In 1985 the Supreme Court ruled that records relating to CIA-funded research from 1952 to 1966 at 80 universities to study the effects of mind-altering substances on humans were off-limits to public inspection. A lawyer named John Sims wanted to see the names of the schools and the individuals who had participated in the research projects. The agency argued that the names were exempt from disclosure because, under a 1947 law, the names of intelligence sources cannot be disclosed by the CIA. The Supreme Court agreed and ruled that the director of the spy agency had broad authority under the 1947 National Security Act to protect all sources of information, confidential or not.[84]

---

84. *Sims* v. *CIA*, 471 U.S. 159 (1985). Sims today is a constitutional law professor at the University of the Pacific McGeorge School of Law in Sacramento, Calif.

An appellate court held the Bureau of Alcohol, Tobacco, Firearms and Explosives did not need to produce, per Exemption 3, to the City of Chicago records held in ATF databases about the sale and recovery of firearms. The court held that provisions in a 2005 federal appropriations act specifying the ATF's firearm databases were "immune from legal process" and "not . . . subject to subpoena or other discovery in any civil action" and were intended "to cut off access to the databases for any reason not related to law enforcement." Chicago wanted the records not for law enforcement but to help in a civil action it filed against gun makers and dealers for creating a public nuisance.[85]

Trade Secrets

Exemption 4: Trade secrets and commercial or financial information obtained from any person and privileged or confidential. This exemption applies only if a three-part test is satisfied: (1) The information for which the exemption is sought must be a trade secret or commercial or financial in character; (2) it must be obtained from a person; and (3) it must be privileged or confidential. Two kinds of information are exempt from disclosure under this exemption—trade secrets and financial or commercial information. The term "person" is broadly defined to sweep up not just individuals, but also partnerships, corporations and associations. The trade secret exemption has not been heavily litigated.

Companies that want to stop government agencies from releasing confidential commercial or financial information about them must prove that the release of the information will either: (1) cause them "substantial competitive harm" in their business operations; or (2) impair the government's ability to obtain such information in the future. Once a company demonstrates by letter and affidavit that the release of its confidential commercial or financial information will cause it substantial competitive harm, then the burden shifts to the government agency to explain why substantial competitive harm is not likely to result if the information is disclosed.

Working Papers/Discovery

Exemption 5: Interagency and intra-agency memorandums and letters which would not be available by law to a party other than an agency in litigation with the agency. This exemption shields two kinds of materials from disclosure. The first are best described as working papers: studies, reports, memoranda and other sorts of documents that are prepared and circulated to assist government personnel to make a final report, an agency policy or a decision of some kind. For Exemption 5 to apply to such documents used in the decision-making processes of an agency, the documents typically must be (1) predecisional (used before a decision is made by the agency); and (2) deliberative (the documents must play a direct part in the deliberative process of making recommendations and decisions). Courts thus refer to this part of Exemption 5 as the deliberative-process exemption, and they hold that it generally shields

---

85. *City of Chicago v. U.S. Department of Treasury,* 423 F. 3d 777 (7th Cir. 2005).

from disclosure records used in agency or interagency decision-making processes such as:

- recommendations
- advisory opinions
- draft documents
- proposals
- suggestions and
- other subjective documents reflecting personal opinions of the writer.

Sometimes documents generated during the deliberative process to help formulate a policy either become expressly adopted by an agency as its final policy or are incorporated into a final policy by reference to them (such as when a government agency repeatedly refers to a memorandum in order to explain its policy or when the policy cites the memorandum). The Supreme Court ruled in 1975 that Exemption 5 cannot be used to shield such documents. Once the decision has been made, the court said, public disclosure of these materials cannot damage the decision-making process.[86]

What's an example of a predecisional document used by a government agency when deliberating about a final decision? In 2013, a federal district court held in *Charles* v. *Office of the Armed Forces Medical Examiner*[87] that preliminary autopsy reports on soldiers killed in Iraq and Afghanistan fall within the scope of protection of Exemption 5. The court noted that "preliminary autopsy reports are drafts of the final autopsy reports." The court accepted the government's contention that information in a preliminary autopsy report is incomplete and often later is altered in the final autopsy report to reflect a different cause of death determination.

The second part of the exemption protects from public disclosure material that would not normally be open to inspection in a civil legal proceeding. There is something called the discovery process that is a part of all litigation. Through discovery one party is able to gain access to evidence, testimony and other kinds of material possessed by the other party. But some kinds of material are not accessible through this discovery process. When a private person consults an attorney and discusses matters relevant to a lawsuit, what is said during those conversations is confidential. The attorney-client privilege protects communications between a client and his or her attorney that are intended to be, and in fact were, kept confidential for the purpose of obtaining or providing legal assistance. It thus protects most confidential communications between government attorneys and their clients made for the purpose of obtaining or providing legal advice.

In 2001 the Supreme Court limited the scope of Exemption 5 when it said communication between a group of Native American tribes and the Bureau of Indian Affairs, a government agency that represents the United States in the nation's relationships with the tribes, was not covered by Exemption 5. The issue focused on a dispute about the allocation of water from the Klamath River Basin in Oregon and northern California. A group of irrigators filed a series of FOIA requests to see copies of correspondence between the tribes and the BIA regarding water issues. The government rejected the

---

86. *NLRB* v. *Sears, Roebuck and Company,* 421 U.S. 132 (1973).
87. 935 F. Supp. 2d 86 (D.D.C. Mar. 27, 2013).

request, claiming that because of the special relationship between the tribes and the BIA, the records should be protected under Exemption 5 in much the same way that correspondence between lawyers and clients is protected. The Supreme Court, in a unanimous ruling, rejected this argument. Justice David Souter wrote for the court that although there are surely exceptions to the general rule of public disclosure mandated by the Freedom of Information Act, these exceptions are to be applied narrowly. The court also rejected the notion that the communication between the tribes and the BIA was comparable to communication between an agency and an outside consultant, material that is sometimes regarded as interagency or intra-agency memoranda.[88]

Exemption 5 also includes an **executive privilege** doctrine related to the president, including a presidential communications privilege.[89] Details are complex, but three points are key. First, these privileges are not absolute. Second, while the "Executive Office of the President" is an agency subject to FOIA, the "Office of the President" (the president's immediate key advisers, such as the chief of staff and White House counsel, who have significant responsibility for investigating and formulating presidential advice) is not subject to FOIA. Finally, as an appellate court observed in 2004, the confines of the presidential communications privilege are construed narrowly, balancing a president's need for confidentiality and frank advice with the obligations of open government.[90]

In 2008, a federal court held that Exemption 5's presidential communications privilege protected from disclosure 68 pages of e-mails sent between officials in the White House and the Department of Justice relating to the controversial termination and dismissal of several U.S. attorneys while Alberto Gonzales was attorney general.[91] The Justice Department claimed the e-mails pertained "to matters such as responding to an upcoming Congressional hearing, formulating official responses to inquiries from outside the Executive Branch, suggesting a plan of action for the appointment of a U.S. Attorney or conferring on issues arising from such appointments, recommending revisions to documents, and planning for the hiring of new Department personnel." Such decision-making materials were protected because the presidential communications privilege sweeps up both final and postdecisional materials, as well as predeliberative ones, and it extends to the president's immediate advisers and documents not actually reviewed by the president.

As noted above, in 2016, FOIA was amended to limit Exemption 5. The ability of agencies to withhold "deliberative process" documents is now limited to 25 years.

Personal Privacy

Exemption 6: Personnel and medical files and similar files the disclosure of which would constitute a clearly unwarranted invasion of privacy. This exemption shields "personnel and medical files and similar files." Personnel files and medical files are fairly easy to identify. Courts have had more of a problem determining the nature of a "similar file." The key consideration is not the kind of file at issue, but the kind of information in the file that is the object of the FOIA request. An individual's medical and personnel files

---

88. *Department of the Interior* v. *Klamath Water Users,* 532 U.S. 1 (2001).
89. See *Judicial Watch, Inc.* v. *Department of Justice,* 365 F. 3d 1108 (D.C. Cir. 2004).
90. Ibid.
91. *Democratic National Committee* v. *Department of Justice,* 539 F. Supp. 2d 363 (D.D.C. 2008).

contain highly personal information about an individual. A file is a "similar file" if it contains this same kind of personal information.[92] Not every file that contains personal information will be considered a similar file. "The test is not merely whether the information is in some sense personal," a U.S. Court of Appeals ruled, "but whether it is of the same magnitude—as highly personal in nature—as contained in personnel or medical records."[93]

A ruling that a file is a medical or personnel or similar file does not automatically bar the release of data in the file. Establishing that the information or material sought is the kind of information protected by Exemption 6 is just the first step. The court must then determine that

1. the release of this information will constitute an invasion of personal privacy, *and*

2. this invasion of personal privacy is clearly unwarranted.

The Supreme Court made it clear in 1976 that exemption is not intended to preclude every incidental invasion of privacy, but rather "only such disclosures as constitute clearly unwarranted invasions of personal privacy."[94] The government normally carries the burden of proof that the release of the information will amount to an unwarranted invasion of privacy. But this burden is not a terribly heavy one. For example, a U.S. District Court accepted government arguments that the release of the voice communications tape-recorded aboard the space shuttle Challenger would be an unwarranted invasion of privacy.[95] The ruling was made despite the fact that a printed transcript of the tape had been previously released.

In 2008 a federal appellate court held that the privacy interests protected by Exemption 6 outweighed any public interest in releasing to the Associated Press (AP) petitions sent by John Walker Lindh, the so-called American Taliban, to the Office of the Pardon Attorney seeking to reduce his 20-year prison sentence after he pled guilty to aiding the Taliban in Afghanistan.[96] In describing the privacy interests at stake, the appellate court noted that "a Petition for Commutation of Sentence requires the applicant to provide his name, social security number, date and place of birth, criminal record, conviction information, information about any post-conviction relief sought, a detailed account of the circumstances surrounding the offense, and a detailed explanation of the reasons clemency should be granted." The court then had to address "whether Lindh's privacy interest outweighs any public interest that would be served by disclosure of the documents." Observing that the AP had presented no evidence to refute a Justice Department filing asserting that Lindh's petition had nothing to do with any alleged government misconduct, the appellate court concluded that the "AP has failed to demonstrate that disclosure of Lindh's petition would serve a cognizable public purpose such that it may not be withheld." The court also observed that the privacy concerns in Exemption 7(c), discussed later in this chapter, would prevent the disclosure of Lindh's petitions.

---

92. *State Department v. Washington Post,* 456 U.S. 595 (1982).
93. *Kurzon v. Health and Human Services,* 649 F. 2d 65 (1981).
94. *Department of the Air Force v. Rose,* 425 U.S. 352 (1976).
95. *New York Times v. NASA,* 782 F. Supp. 628 (1991).
96. *Associated Press v. Department of Justice,* 549 F. 3d 62 (2d Cir. 2008).

Law Enforcement

Exemption 7: Records or information compiled for law enforcement purposes, but only to the extent that the production of such law enforcement records or information (a) could reasonably be expected to interfere with enforcement proceedings, (b) would deprive a person of a right to a fair trial or an impartial adjudication, (c) could reasonably be expected to constitute an unwarranted invasion of personal privacy, (d) could reasonably be expected to disclose the identity of a confidential source, including a state, local or foreign agency or authority or any private institution which furnished information on a confidential basis, and, in the case of a record or information compiled by criminal law enforcement authority in the course of a criminal investigation or by an agency conducting a lawful national security intelligence investigation, information furnished by confidential source, (e) would disclose techniques and procedures for law enforcement investigations or prosecutions, or would disclose guidelines for law enforcement investigations or prosecutions if such disclosure could reasonably be expected to risk circumvention of the law, or (f) could reasonably be expected to endanger the life or physical safety of any individual.

Exemption 7 provides an agency a broad exception to the general rule of access. Like Exemption 6, Exemption 7 requires a two-tiered test in its application. The first tier or question (what lawyers and judges often call the threshold question) is this: Was the information or record sought compiled for law enforcement purposes?

If the government is unable to show that the records were compiled for law enforcement purposes, the exemption does not apply. But the courts are generally willing to grant the government wide latitude in applying this test. The key question is whether the information is being used for law enforcement purposes when the response to the FOIA inquiry is sent to the person seeking the data.

Law enforcement agencies, however, are not given carte blanche discretion to designate any record they choose as one gathered for law enforcement purposes. Seth Rosenfeld sued the Department of Justice and the FBI to gain access to records of FBI investigations of faculty, students and journalists at the University of California in the early 1960s when the so-called Free Speech Movement challenged the university administration's regulations barring political activities on campus. The federal agencies argued that the material had been gathered for the purpose of examining whether the student movement had been captured from within by communists. The U.S. Court of Appeals for the 9th Circuit agreed that although some of the material sought by Rosenfeld had indeed been gathered for legitimate law enforcement purposes, other records were gathered long after the need for such an investigation ceased to exist. The law enforcement purpose argument was only a pretext, the court said, invoked to pursue routine monitoring of many individuals and to shield the harassment of the political opponents of the FBI.[97]

Information compiled for law enforcement purposes may still be accessible under the Freedom of Information Act. The court next must determine whether the release of the material would result in one of the six consequences outlined in *a* through *f* in the exemption; for example, would the release of the information be expected to interfere with law enforcement proceedings or deprive a person of a right to a fair trial?

---

97. *Rosenfeld v. U.S. Department of Justice,* 57 F. 3d 803 (1995).

Congress amended Exemption 7 in 1986 and gave federal law enforcement agencies far broader authority to refuse FOIA requests. Courts have read the exemption in an expansive manner, giving the FBI, the Secret Service, the Drug Enforcement Administration and other federal police agencies even more legal excuses to deny access to information they possess. For example, in 1989 the Supreme Court agreed that the release of computerized arrest records (often called "rap sheets") held by the FBI could reasonably be expected to constitute an unwarranted invasion of personal privacy. The rap sheets contain information indicating arrests, indictments, acquittals, convictions and sentences on about 24 million people in the nation. Some of this material is highly sensitive, but much of it has been publicized previously when individuals were being processed by the criminal justice system. In addition, all of these data are available from state and local law enforcement agencies across the nation. The FBI has simply put together all the bits and pieces of data about an individual held by various police agencies into a single, computerized file.

MURDER, MUG SHOTS & EXEMPTION 7(C)

When Jared Lee Loughner was booked into federal custody in connection with the murder of U.S. District Judge John M. Roll and the shooting of U.S. Rep. Gabrielle Giffords in Tucson, Ariz., in 2011, multiple mug shots (booking photographs) of Loughner were taken. These federal mug shots were in addition to the one that the Pima County Sheriff's Department previously had released of Loughner and that was widely publicized showing a smirking Loughner.

Several news media outlets sought the federal mug shots under a federal FOIA request, but Loughner's attorneys filed a motion seeking an order barring the United States Marshals Service ("USMS") from releasing them, claiming their release would jeopardize Loughner's right to a fair trial under the Sixth Amendment. Loughner's attorneys argued that Exemption 7(c) prevented their release, asserting the mug shots were: (1) created for law enforcement purposes; (2) reasonably triggered individual privacy concerns; and (3) did not advance any public interest advanced by FOIA. The U.S. Attorney prosecuting Loughner supported the motion to prevent their release.

In December 2012, the USMS adopted a formal "Booking Photograph Disclosure Policy." It provides that "the USMS will not disclose booking photographs under the FOIA, regardless of where the FOIA request originated, unless USMS Office of General Counsel determines either that the requester has made the requisite showing that the public interest in the requested booking photograph outweighs the privacy interest at stake or that other factors specific to the particular FOIA request warrant processing that request consistent with existing Sixth Circuit precedent." What's the importance of this reference to the Sixth Circuit?

Although the Supreme Court has not addressed the issue, the 6th U.S. Circuit Court of Appeals in *Detroit Free Press v. Department of Justice*, 73 F. 3d 93 (6th Cir. 1996), held that, contrary to the USMS's position, booking photos must be released under certain circumstances. Recently, however, the 6th Circuit reversed course. Although a three-judge panel of the 6th Circuit ruled in August 2016 that mug shots had to be released by the Department of Justice, in July 2016 the 6th Circuit sitting en banc ruled that the Department of Justice could withhold mug shots of criminal defendants from the media. The 9-7 decision covered defendants in Ohio, Kentucky, Michigan and Tennessee and overruled the 1996 decision by the 6th Circuit. Writing for the majority, Circuit Judge Deborah Cook said the Internet gives criminal defendants a "non-trivial" privacy interest in their photos, which can stay online for years. Cook reasoned that in 1996, the court could not have understood how the Internet would change privacy rights. Cook wrote, "In 1996, this court could not have known or expected that a booking photo could haunt [an individual] for decades. Experience has taught us otherwise."[98] The 6th Circuit's decision was similar to decisions made by the 10th and 11th Circuits. It remains to be seen how the USMS will respond to the decision.

The U.S. Supreme Court held in 2004 in *National Archives & Records Administration* v. *Favish* that Exemption 7(c) prevented the release to Allan Favish of certain death-scene photographs of Vincent Foster Jr., deputy counsel to President Bill Clinton.[99] Favish wanted the photos because he questioned the government's finding that Foster's death was a suicide; he believed the government's investigations of Foster's death were "grossly incomplete and untrustworthy." Foster's family members, however, objected to the release of the photos. They contended their own personal privacy interests would be harmed by such release, and thus they argued the photos were shielded by Exemption 7(c) to secure what the Supreme Court called "their own refuge from a sensation-seeking culture for their own peace of mind and tranquility."

Exemption 7(c) prevented the release to Allan Favish of certain death-scene photographs.

In ruling for Foster's immediate relatives, the high court initially held that Exemption 7(c) permits surviving family members to assert their own privacy rights against public intrusions when it comes to death-scene images of their immediate relatives. The court then turned to whether the release of the photos would be an unwarranted intrusion on the privacy rights of those family members. Justice Anthony Kennedy wrote for the court:

> Where there is a privacy interest protected by Exemption 7(c) and the public interest being asserted is to show that responsible officials acted negligently or otherwise improperly in the performance of their duties, the requester must establish more than a bare suspicion in order to obtain disclosure. Rather, the requester [Favish] must produce evidence that would warrant a belief by a reasonable person that the alleged Government impropriety might have occurred.

The court concluded Allan Favish had not met this burden, finding that he had "not produced any evidence that would warrant a belief by a reasonable person that the alleged Government impropriety might have occurred to put the balance into play."

In 2011 a federal appellate court in *Prison Legal News* v. *Executive Office for United States Attorneys*[100] addressed whether Exemption 7(c) would prevent the release to a

98. *Detroit Free Press* v. *U.S. Department of Justice,* No. 14-1670 (6th Cir. 2016).
99. 541 U.S. 157 (2004).
100. 628 F. 3d 1243 (10th Cir. 2011).

newspaper that covers prison issues copies of certain autopsy images and a videotape taken by Bureau of Prisons (BOP) personnel that showed the mutilated body of an inmate named Joey Jesus Estrella who was savagely killed by two cellmates. The parties to the case agreed that the privacy interests at stake were those of Estrella's surviving family members.

The 10th U.S. Circuit Court of Appeals looked to the Supreme Court's ruling in *Favish* for precedent. As in *Favish*, the appellate court noted that the records sought by the Prison Legal News "unquestionably reflect death-scene images." Describing the images as "gruesome," it specified that "photographs depict close-up views of the injuries to Estrella's body and the first portion of the video prominently features Estrella's body on the floor of the prison cell." The appellate court thus characterized Estrella's family as having a "high" privacy interest in the images and video. Although the images were publicly displayed during the criminal trial of Estrella's cellmates, the appellate court still found that Estrella's family possessed a privacy interest in them because, after the trial, they were no longer publicly available and because Estrella's family members "did not take any affirmative actions to place the images in the public domain."

After recognizing the family's privacy interest, the appellate court then weighed and balanced it against the alleged public interest in the images. In particular, the *Prison Legal News* asserted that the images would: (1) "shed light on the BOP's performance of its duty to protect prisoners from violence perpetrated by other prisoners"; and (2) help the public to better understand the prosecutor's decision to seek the death penalty against Estrella's killers. The appellate court found these interests lacking, observing that the "video does not begin until Estrella has already been murdered and therefore does not depict any BOP conduct prior to Estrella's death" and that, during the trial of Estrella's killers, "the parties indicated that the length of time between the beginning of the video and the time BOP personnel extracted [Estrella's killers] from the cell is publicly known. Thus, all aspects of the video documenting BOP's response to the situation have been fully disclosed." The court added that the content of all of the images was widely reported by the news media during the trial.

The 10th Circuit thus concluded that, "to the extent any additional information can be gained by release of the actual images for replication and public dissemination, the public's interest in that incremental addition of information over what is already known is outweighed by the Estrella family's strong privacy interests in this case." It thus held that Exemption 7(c) and the family's privacy interests prevailed—the images and videotape in question would be permanently sealed. The decision reflects the lasting power and precedent of *Favish* in extending a privacy right under FOIA to family members over gruesome death-scene images of their loved ones.

Finally, it is important to note that Exemption 7 (c) applies only to people; the United States Supreme Court ruled in March 2011 in *FCC v. AT&T, Inc.*[101] that corporations do not possess "personal privacy" rights for the purposes of this exemption. In brief, only individuals, not corporations, can assert the personal privacy exemption.

In 2016, a federal court ruled that the Federal Elections Commission (FEC) could withhold a study that assessed the vulnerability of the Commission's information technology (IT) systems or e-mails related to the study, citing FOIA exemption 7(E). The Center

---

101. 131 S. Ct. 1177 (2011).

for Public Integrity requested the information in 2015, but the FEC denied the request. The court noted there was a rational "nexus" because the FEC could not carry out its law enforcement functions without a secure and reliable IT system. The judge noted the FEC's IT system contained sensitive information related to investigations, including "subpoenas, requests for information and documents, reports of investigation, and responses to Commission-issued subpoenas and requests." In addition, the court ruled there was a connection between the study and possible security risks or violations of federal law.[102] In early 2017, the same court ruled that the FBI had to provide documents to the Electronic Privacy Information Center (EPIC) related to studies the law enforcement agency has done of how its own record-keeping systems could impact personal privacy. EPIC sued the FBI in 2014, seeking copies of the FBI's "privacy impact assessments" and "privacy threshold analyses" on various bureau databases containing personal information. The FBI eventually produced about 2,200 heavily redacted pages with much of the information deleted because it might reveal sensitive law enforcement methods or techniques. U.S. District Court Judge Amit Mehta ruled the FBI had failed to demonstrate that the deleted content was compiled for law enforcement purposes. The decision was especially notable because courts generally give the term "compiled for law enforcement purposes" a very broad definition. The judge, however, also said he would give the FBI another opportunity to justify the withholdings and explaining the search process.[103]

Financial Records

Exemption 8: Matters contained in or related to examination, operating or condition reports prepared by, on behalf of or for the use of any agency responsible for the regulation and supervision of financial institutions. This is a little-used exemption that is designed to prevent the disclosure of sensitive financial reports or audits that, if made public, might undermine the public confidence in banks, trust companies, investment banking firms and other financial institutions.

In 2007 a federal court held that the U.S. Securities and Exchange Commission had successfully asserted Exemption 8 to withhold documents relating to an SEC investigation of Charles Schwab Corporation and Nucor Corporation.[104] The court initially found that the "purpose underlying Exemption 8 is to ensure financial institutions' security" and that "Congress also enacted Exemption 8 to promote communication between banks and regulating agencies." It then held that Exemption 8 protected the requested documents because they "were produced in connection with an ongoing SEC examination or investigation and provide insight into the information and entities the SEC attorneys were examining and investigating."

---

102. *Dave Levinthal, et al.* v. *FEC,* Civil No. 15-cv-01624 (D.D.C. 2016).

103. *Electronic Privacy Information Center* v. *FBI,* No. 1:14-cv-o1311 (D.D.C., 2017).

104. *Gavin* v. *Securities and Exchange Commission,* 2007 U.S. Dist. LEXIS 62252 (D. Minn. 2007). The SEC has successfully asserted Exemption 8 in other matters. See *Bloomberg* v. *Securities and Exchange Commission,* 357 F. Supp. 2d 156 (D.D.C. 2004) (holding the interests behind Exemption 8 "would undeniably be served by exempting documents summarizing a meeting at which financial institutions were encouraged to engage in a candid assessment of industry problems and discussions regarding potential self-regulatory responses").

Geological Data

Exemption 9: Geological and geophysical information and data, including maps concerning wells. People who drill oil and gas wells provide considerable information about these wells to the government. This exemption prevents speculators and other drillers from gaining access to this valuable information.

HANDLING FOIA REQUESTS

Filing a FOIA request is a relatively simple matter. The Reporters Committee for Freedom of the Press has an online request letter generator on its Web site at http://www.rcfp.org /foia. Government agencies also provide extensive online information about filing FOIA requests. For example, the U.S. Department of Justice maintains a link on its Web site at http://www.justice.gov/oip/index.html devoted to the Freedom of Information Act. The Student Press Law Center also offers a free automated open-records request letter generator that can be accessed at http://www.splc.org.

UNDERSTANDING THE 20-DAY RESPONSE TIME

The 20-day response time, which is spelled out by federal statute, is important to understand. First, the clock generally starts to run on the date on which the request is first received by the appropriate component of the agency. Second, the 20 days does not include Saturdays, Sundays and legal public holidays. Third, the agency does not need to produce the documents within 20 days, but it must make a substantive "determination" about how it will respond to the request.

For example, in 2013 the U.S. Court of Appeals for the District of Columbia held that while a government agency "need not actually produce the documents" within 20 business days, it "must at least indicate within the relevant time period the scope of the documents it will produce and the exemptions it will claim with respect to any withheld documents."[105] The court noted that within the 20-day window, "an agency must determine whether to comply with a request—that is, whether a requester will receive all the documents the requester seeks. It is not enough that, within the relevant time period, the agency simply decide to later decide."

The court added, however, that in "unusual circumstances," agencies may extend the 20-day limit to up to 30 working days by serving written notice to the requester. Circumstances justifying an extension include situations where a voluminous amount of separate and distinct records are demanded in a single request. The complete list of "unusual circumstances" is described by a federal statute (5 U.S.C. § 552(a)(6)(B)(i)). As noted above, many agencies have difficulty meeting the 20-day deadline.

Agencies are required to report to Congress each year and must include in the report a list of the materials to which access was granted and to which access was denied and the costs incurred. The OPEN Government Act of 2007 also requires that, in addition

105. *Citizens for Responsibility & Ethics in Washington* v. *FEC*, 711 F. 3d 180 (D. D.C. Apr. 2, 2013).

to reporting the median number of days required to process requests, government agencies must provide the "average number of days for the agency to respond to a request beginning on the date on which the request was received by the agency, the median number of days for the agency to respond to such requests, and the range in number of days for the agency to respond to such requests." In addition, in a way of shaming foot-dragging agencies into compliance, government agencies must now report their 10 oldest pending requests. As noted earlier, if an individual or group has to go to court to get the agency to release materials and the agency loses the case, the agency may be assessed the cost of the complainant's legal fees and court costs. FOIA allows a court to award reasonable attorney fees to a plaintiff who has "substantially prevailed" in a FOIA lawsuit against a government agency, although a court is not required to grant such fees. Agency personnel are personally responsible for granting or denying access, a requirement federal agencies object to strenuously. An employee of an agency who denies a request for information must be identified to the person who seeks the material, and if the access is denied in an arbitrary or capricious manner, the employee can be disciplined by the Civil Service Commission.

Government agencies must now report their 10 oldest pending requests.

There is no initial fee to file a FOIA request, but agencies may charge reasonable fees for searching, copying and reviewing files, depending on the particular category into which a FOIA requester falls. FOIA divides requesters into three groups for fee purposes:

1. **Commercial Requesters:** Charged for search time, processing time (costs incurred during initial review of a record to see if it must be disclosed under FOIA) and duplicating.

2. **Educational Institutions, Noncommercial Scientific Institutions and Representatives of the News Media:** Charged only for duplicating (first 100 pages free).

3. **All Other Requesters:** Charged for search time (after two free hours) and duplicating (first 100 pages free).

Anyone who seeks a fee waiver under FOIA must show that the disclosure of the information is "in the public interest because it is likely to contribute significantly to public understanding of the operations or activities of the government and is not primarily in the commercial interest of the requester." Significantly, the OPEN Government Act of 2007 broadened the definition of a "representative of the news media" exempt from document search fees to include a freelance journalist working for a news media entity "if the journalist can demonstrate a solid basis for expecting publication through that entity, whether or not the journalist is actually employed by the entity." In addition, the act made it clear that "as methods of news delivery evolve (for example, the adoption of the electronic dissemination of newspapers through telecommunications services), such alternative media shall be considered to be news-media entities."

Under an executive order signed by President George W. Bush in 2005, each federal agency must maintain a "FOIA Requester Service Center" that requesters may contact to speak with a FOIA public liaison in order to check on the status of their FOIA requests and to receive information about an agency's response. Are the FOIA service centers and liaisons useful? A 2008 report, issued by the National Security Archive (NSA), tested the centers and liaisons at different government agencies and found the experiences were generally "positive" and that "the new customer service system has made it easier to follow up on requests."[106] The report determined that of the 53 service centers called by the NSA to check on the status of a request, 44 provided "at least basic information on the pending FOIA request," such as where the request stood in the processing queue, while all 53 agencies called were able to confirm that the request in question was received. The OPEN Government Act of 2007 discussed earlier turned the establishment of FOIA public liaisons under Bush's executive order into statutory law that requires each government agency to have one or more such public liaisons that are "responsible for assisting in reducing delays, increasing transparency and understanding of the status of requests and assisting in the resolution of disputes."

This part of Chapter 9 provided an overview of the federal Freedom of Information Act. Seven excellent online resources—the first five of which are private organizations, while the final two are government agencies—related to FOIA that supply more details and information are:

- **The FOIA Project:**
  http://foiaproject.org
- **National Security Archive, George Washington University:**
  http://www.gwu.edu/~nsarchiv/nsa/foia.html
- **National Freedom of Information Center:**
  http://www.nfoic.org
- **Public Citizen Freedom of Information Clearinghouse:**
  http://www.citizen.org/publications/publicationredirect.cfm?ID=7078
- **RCFP Federal Open Government Guide:**
  http://www.rcfp.org/federal-open-government-guide
- **U.S. Department of Justice, Office of Information Policy:**
  http://www.justice.gov/oip

TIPS ON HOW TO GET RECORDS

Many old journalistic hands argue that formal FOIA requests should be a last resort. Jack Briggs, former editor of the *Tri-City* (Wash.) *Herald*, advises reporters to do the following:

- Ask informally for documents—a formal FOIA request often takes much longer.
- Look to public court records for information that takes longer to get through a FOIA request.
- Cultivate trusted sources within federal agencies.
- Follow up FOIA requests with telephone calls.
- Don't kick and scream, unless kicking and screaming is justified. And don't forget to occasionally praise the FOIA officer who helps you.

---

106. *Knight Open Government Survey 2008,* 4–5, available online at http://www.gwu.edu/~nsarchiv /NSAEBB/NSAEBB246/eo_audit.pdf.

FEDERAL OPEN-MEETINGS LAW

In 1976 Congress passed and the president signed into law the **Government in Sunshine Act,** the **federal open-meetings law.** The statute affects approximately 50 federal boards, commissions and agencies "headed by a collegial body composed of two or more individual members, a majority of whom are appointed to such position by the president with the advice and consent of the Senate." Importantly for media law students, this includes the Federal Communications Commission, and meetings of three or more of the five FCC commissioners must be open to the public. Ironically, the Government in Sunshine Act has been criticized by some as actually promoting secrecy at the FCC, with many of the real discussions and debates happening in closed-door meetings between two commissioners or in meetings between legal assistants and liaisons for the commissioners. These public bodies are required to conduct their business meetings in public. Notice of public meetings must be given one week in advance, and the agencies are required to keep careful records of what occurs at closed meetings. The law also prohibits informal communication between officials of an agency and representatives of companies and other interested persons with whom the agency does business unless this communication is recorded and made part of the public record.

Courts have strictly interpreted the requirement that the law applies only to bodies whose members are appointed by the president. In 1981 the U.S. Court of Appeals for the District of Columbia Circuit ruled that the Government in Sunshine Act did not govern meetings of the Chrysler Loan Guarantee Board, a body created by Congress to oversee federal loan guarantees for the financially troubled automaker. People who served on the board were not actually named by the president, but served because they held other federal offices (i.e., secretary of the treasury, comptroller general, chair of the Federal Reserve).[107] A board or agency must also have some independent authority to act or take action before the law applies. A U.S. Court of Appeals ruled that the law does not apply to the president's Council of Economic Advisors. The sole function of the CEA is to advise and assist the president, the court said. It has no regulatory power. It cannot fund projects, even though it may appraise them. It has no function, save advising and assisting the president. Hence, it is not subject to either the FOIA or the Government in Sunshine Act.[108] Even agencies or commissions that fall under the aegis of the law may meet behind closed doors. The 1976 law lists 10 conditions or exemptions under which closed meetings might be held. The first nine of these exemptions mirror the exemptions in the Freedom of Information Act. The 10th exemption focuses on situations in which the agency is participating in arbitration or is in the process of adjudicating or otherwise disposing of a case.

This exemption was used to block access to a meeting of the Nuclear Regulatory Commission. The NRC was discussing the reopening of the nuclear power plant at Three Mile Island in Pennsylvania. The federal district court ruled that this meeting would likely focus on the final adjudication of the federal action involving the nuclear reactor and hence could be closed to press and public.[109]

Courts have strictly interpreted the requirement that the law applies only to bodies whose members are appointed by the president.

107. *Symons v. Chrysler Corporation Loan Guarantee Board,* 670 F. 2d 238 (1981).
108. *Rushforth v. Council of Economic Advisors,* 762 F. 2d 1038 (1985).
109. *Philadelphia Newspapers v. Nuclear Regulatory Commission,* 9 M.L.R. 1843 (1983).

SUMMARY   Statutes provide public access to both federal records and meetings held by federal agencies. The federal records law, the Freedom of Information Act, makes public all records including electronic records and e-mail held by agencies within the executive branch of government and the independent regulatory commissions. Courts have given a broad meaning to the term "record" but have ruled that an agency must normally create and possess such a record before it becomes subject to FOIA. Nine categories of information are excluded from the provisions of the law. These include exemptions for national security, agency working papers, highly personal information and law enforcement files. Agencies must publish indexes of the records they hold and must permit copying of these materials. It is important to follow specific procedures when making a FOIA request to see certain records or documents.

The Government in Sunshine Act is the federal open-meetings law. This law reaches about 50 agencies in the executive branch and the regulatory commissions. Members of these organizations are not permitted to hold secret meetings unless they will discuss material that falls into one of 10 categories. These categories mirror the FOIA exemptions but also include a provision that permits closed-door meetings to discuss attempts to arbitrate or adjudicate certain cases or problems.

STATE LAWS ON MEETINGS AND RECORDS

It is not as easy to talk about access at the state level as it is at the federal level, because the discussion involves hundreds of different statutes. (Most states have multiple laws dealing with access to meetings, access to records and other access situations.) The following pages provide at best a few generalizations. Harold Cross made some of the most astute generalizations in 1953 in his pioneering book "The People's Right to Know."[110] Cross was really the first scholar to present a comprehensive report on access problems. In his book he listed four issues, or questions, common to every case of access:

1. Is the particular record or proceeding public? Many records and meetings kept or conducted by public officers in public offices are not really public at all. Much of the work of the police, though they are public officers and work in public buildings, is not open to public scrutiny.

2. Is public material public in the sense that records are open to public inspection and sessions are open to public attendance? Hearings in juvenile courts are considered public hearings for purposes of the law, but they are often not open to the public.

3. Who can view the records and who can attend the meetings open to the public? Many records, for example, might be open to specific segments of the public, but not to all segments. Automobile accident reports by police departments are open to insurance company adjusters and lawyers, but such records are not usually open to the general public.

4. When records and meetings are open to the general public and the press, will the courts provide legal remedy for citizens and reporters if access is denied?

110. Cross, *The People's Right to Know.*

The last question is probably not as important today as it was when Cross wrote his book in 1953, for at that time access to many public records and meetings in the states was based on common law. Today this fact is no longer true. Access to meetings and records is nearly always governed by statute, and these statutes usually, but not always, provide a remedy for citizens who are denied access. This provision is more widespread in open-meetings laws, which tend to be more efficient in providing access, than in open-records laws, which are still weak and vague in many jurisdictions.

STATE OPEN-MEETINGS LAWS

All 50 states have statutes that mandate open meetings, and these laws range from good to awful.

It is difficult to make generalizations about all the laws dealing with open government in all 50 states. The Reporters Committee for Freedom of the Press published an Open Government Guide. The guide is meant to serve as a complete compendium of information on every state's open records and open meetings laws. Each state's section is arranged according to a standard outline, making it easy to compare laws in various states. The guide is available at http://www.rcfp.org/open -government-guide.

One of the most important aspects of any open-meetings law is the strong sanctions that may be imposed on government officials who fail to follow the mandate of the law. Laws that provide for substantial personal fines against these individuals are generally more desirable than laws that impose only small fines or no penalties at all.

Can a state's open meetings law include criminal sanctions and punishments for government officials who violate it? The answer is yes, according the 5th U.S. Circuit Court of Appeals' 2012 ruling in *Asgeirsson* v. *Abbott*.[111] The case involved a challenge to the Texas Open Meetings Act (TOMA) brought by a number of local government officials. Like many open meetings laws, TOMA requires the meetings of governmental bodies to be open to the public. It prohibits members of governing bodies from knowingly participating in closed meetings, organizing closed meetings or closing meetings to the public. Violations are considered misdemeanors punishable by a fine of up to $500 and/or jail time ranging from one to six months. In *Asgeirsson*, the government officials claimed this violated their First Amendment speech rights by criminalizing political speech—discussions of public business—if it did not occur in an open meeting (in other words, TOMA punishes government officials when they engage in private political speech at a closed-door meeting). The 5th Circuit rejected this challenge and upheld TOMA, including the criminal sanctions for government officials who violate it. The court wrote that the law serves many substantial interests that justify it, including reducing government corruption, increasing transparency of government, fostering trust in government and ensuring that all members of a governing body may take part in the discussion of public business.

Another important part of an open-meetings law is the legislative declaration at the beginning of the law. A clear, strong statement in favor of open access to meetings

---

111. 696 F.3d 454 (5th Cir. 2012).

of government bodies can persuade a judge trying to interpret the law to side with the advocates of access rather than with the government. For example, in the state of Washington the open-meetings law begins as follows:

> The legislature finds and declares that all . . . public agencies of this state and subdivisions thereof exist to aid in the conduct of the people's business. It is the intent of this chapter that their actions be taken openly and that their deliberations be conducted openly.

State open-meetings laws are normally written in one of two ways. Some laws declare that all meetings are open, except the following. Meetings that are closed are then listed. Other state laws simply list the agencies that must hold open meetings. State legislatures are generally excluded from the provisions of their state open-meetings laws. But the issue is not quite as clear-cut as the situation at the federal level. Some state open-meetings laws do in fact cover some kinds of legislative proceedings. State open-meetings laws routinely do not include meetings of parole and pardon boards, of law enforcement agencies, of military agencies like the National Guard, of medical agencies like hospital boards and so forth.

Can a state open-meetings statute that fails to define a key term such as "meeting" nonetheless be constitutional? Yes, according to the Supreme Court of Arkansas in its December 2012 ruling in *McCutchen* v. *City of Fort Smith*.[112] The case involved the open-meetings provision of the Arkansas Freedom of Information Act (Arkansas FOIA). A key issue was whether the circulation of a memorandum by a member of the board of directors of the City of Fort Smith to other board members in advance of an official study session constituted a meeting. The memorandum expressed one board member's opinion and background information on a proposed ordinance that was to come before the board. The Supreme Court of Arkansas engaged in **statutory construction,** examining the legislative intent and history behind the purpose of the Arkansas FOIA. After doing so, the court concluded the board member's actions did not constitute a meeting and thus did not violate the Arkansas statute. It noted that "it is left to the judiciary to give effect to the intent of the legislature, and in our prior decisions construing the [Arkansas] FOIA, we have given effect to that intent." As for the absence of a statutory definition of the term "meeting," the court concluded that those challenging the constitutionality should ask the legislature—not the court—to provide a better definition. This last point illustrates the separation of powers between the legislative and judicial branches of government, with the role of the legislature being to draft laws and the role of the judiciary being to interpret them.

Most open-meetings laws provide for closed meetings, or **executive sessions,** in certain kinds of cases. Meetings at which personnel problems are discussed are an obvious example. A public airing of a teacher's personal problems could be an unwarranted invasion of privacy. The discussion of real estate transactions is another obvious example. All but 13 state open-meetings laws contain a provision that no final action can be taken at an executive session, that the board or commission must reconvene in public before a final determination can be made on any issue.

---

112. 2012 Ark. 452 (2012).

When a presiding officer of a governmental body announces at a meeting that the body is going into executive session, a reporter at the meeting should make certain of the following items:

1. The presiding officer has specified what topics will be discussed during the closed session, or why the executive session has been called.
2. A reporter who believes that a meeting is being closed improperly should formally object. He or she should ask members of the body specifically which provision in the law they are using to go into closed session. It is not inappropriate to ask for a vote of the body to make certain the required simple majority (or two-thirds majority in some states) approves of the closed session.
3. The reporter should also ask what time the closed session will end, so he or she can attend a reconvened public session.

Most open-meetings statutes require not only that meetings be open to the public, but also that the public be notified of both regular and special meetings far enough in advance that they can attend if they wish. Time requirements vary, but normally a special meeting cannot be held without an announcement a day or two in advance.

Virtually all laws provide some kind of injunctive or other civil remedy if the law is violated; almost half the statutes provide for criminal penalties if the statute is knowingly violated. In many states any action taken at a meeting that was not public, but should have been public, is null and void. The action must be taken again at a proper meeting. Most laws provide fines and short jail terms for public officers who knowingly violate the law, but prosecution is rare.

What should a reporter do when asked to leave a meeting that he or she believes should be open to the press and public? First, find out who has denied you access to the meeting and ask for the legal basis of this denial. Never leave a meeting voluntarily; but if ordered to leave, do so and contact your editor immediately. Resistance is not advised, for criminal charges may be filed against you. Whereas open-meetings laws provide a good means of access to proceedings, the reporter possesses what is probably a more powerful weapon—the power of publicity. Public officials don't like stories about secret meetings. If an agency abuses its right to meet in executive session, describe these meetings as they really are—secret sessions. A photo essay showing a meeting room door open, closing and closed, accompanied by a caption citing appropriate parts of the open-meetings law, will often get a reporter back into a proceeding faster than a court action.

Whereas open-meetings laws provide a good means of access to proceedings, the reporter possesses what is probably a more powerful weapon—the power of publicity.

OPEN-MEETINGS TIPS FOR REPORTERS

▮ Ask for the legal basis for closure.
▮ Find out who is asking that the meeting be closed and why.
▮ Never leave a meeting voluntarily, but don't resist being escorted out the door.
▮ Call your editor immediately.
▮ Use publicity as well as the law to gain access.

STATE OPEN-RECORDS LAWS

Every state in the union also has some kind of **open-records law.** The access laws either follow the federal formula—all records are open except the following—or list the kinds of records that the public does have a right to inspect.

The scope and reach of state open-records laws, which sometimes are known as public-records laws or state freedom-of-information laws, will vary from state to state. It is important to know what the law is in your state. Excellent online resources relating to state open-records laws include:

▮ **Reporters Committee for Freedom of the Press, Open Government Guide**
  https://www.rcfp.org/open-government-guide
▮ **National Freedom of Information Coalition, State FOI Laws**
  http://www.nfoic.org/state-foi-laws

In addition, there are many organizations across the country that concentrate primarily on the open-records laws of a specific state. Some of these organizations, which include both privately funded groups and government entities, have created helpful handbooks for journalists summarizing the open-records statutes and open-meetings laws in a given state. The organizations listed below are merely examples of such groups for different states:

▮ **Colorado: Colorado Freedom of Information Coalition**
  http://www.coloradofoic.org
▮ **Connecticut: Freedom of Information Commission**
  http://www.ct.gov/foi/site/default.asp
▮ **Florida: First Amendment Foundation**
  http://floridafaf.org
▮ **New York: Committee on Open Government**
  https://www.dos.ny.gov/coog/
▮ **Pennsylvania: Pennsylvania Freedom of Information Coalition**
  http://www.pafoic.org
▮ **Texas: Freedom of Information Foundation of Texas**
  http://www.foift.org

There is a growing movement to roll back access provided under state shield laws when it comes to audio recordings of 911 emergency telephone calls, especially when the caller is being attacked or the caller is otherwise in a panicked or terrified state. Critics of the release of such tapes contend they feed sensational and voyeuristic tastes, especially when the recordings are played on TV and then are uploaded to the Internet where anyone can listen to them. Access proponents, however, countered that the public needs to hear such calls to determine how effectively government agencies like law enforcement respond to such situations. This battle will continue to be played out in the coming years.

Most state laws permit inspection of records by any person.

Most state laws permit inspection of records by any person, but a few limit access to public records to residents of the state, as discussed later. The reason people want to see a record is normally considered immaterial when determining whether they can gain access to the record. The freedom of information laws provide access to records held by public agencies in the state, and normally these statutes provide a broad definition of these agencies. Normally included are state offices, departments, divisions, bureaus, boards and commissions. Records kept by local government agencies (cities, counties, villages) are also included, as are those kept by school districts, public utilities and municipal corporations. In some states these laws also apply to records held by the governor.[113] These state laws do not normally govern records kept by courts or the legislature. Frequently these branches of government have established their own policies regarding access to records. State laws follow either a liberal or conservative definition of a public record. *All records possessed by an agency* are deemed to be public records in those states with liberal definitions of a public record. But some state laws are more conservative and provide access only to those *records that are required to be kept by law.*

PRIVATE TEXT MESSAGES AND E-MAIL ACCOUNTS AND PUBLIC RECORDS

Early in 2017, it was revealed that Vice President Mike Pence used a private e-mail account for official business when he was governor of Indiana when the Indianapolis Star received 29 pages of e-mails from Pence's AOL account. The news created quite a stir as it was reminiscent, of course, of the private e-mail server Hillary Clinton used while she was secretary of state. Pence was among the many Republicans who were highly critical of Clinton for using a private e-mail server. While it is not illegal in Indiana to use a private e-mail account for work, using private e-mail to conduct government business raises questions about the public's right to access those e-mails.

A number of states have ruled the public has a right of access to e-mails and text messages about government business on private phones and e-mail accounts. For example, in 2017 in a lawsuit against the city of San Jose, the California Supreme Court ruled that government employees cannot keep the public from seeing work-related e-mails and texts sent on personal devices or through private accounts. In the unanimous decision, the court wrote that work-related communications on private devices and accounts were subject to disclosure under the California Public Records Act. "If communications sent through personal accounts were categorically excluded from CPRA, government officials could hide their most sensitive, and potentially damning, discussions in such accounts," Associate Justice Carol Corrigan wrote. The ruling applied to both top officials and lower-level city, county and state officials, and public employees. It did not apply to the California state legislature, which has its own public records policy. Many other state courts and attorney generals have made similar conclusions that official communications on personal devices are subject to public disclosure. At the federal level, in 2016, an appeals court ruled that work-related e-mails from a private account used by the White House's top science adviser were subject to disclosure under federal open-records laws.

---

113. Bush, "Access to Governors' Records," 135.

Is it permissible for one state to preclude citizens of other states from enjoying the same right of access to public records that the state affords its own citizens? Yes. That question was resolved by the U.S. Supreme Court in April 2013 in the case of *McBurney* v. *Young*.[114] At issue in *McBurney* was the Virginia Freedom of Information Act (FOIA), which provides that "all public records shall be open to inspection and copying by any citizens of the Commonwealth," but it grants no such right to non-Virginians. In other words, only Virginians can use Virginia's FOIA law. Seven other states have similar citizens-only open-records laws (Alabama, Arkansas, Delaware, Missouri, New Hampshire, New Jersey and Tennessee).

In upholding Virginia's law and rejecting a challenge brought against it by citizens of Rhode Island and California, Justice Samuel Alito wrote for a unanimous Supreme Court that "the distinction that the statute makes between citizens and noncitizens has a distinctly nonprotectionist aim. The state FOIA essentially represents a mechanism by which those who ultimately hold sovereign power (i.e., the citizens of the Commonwealth) may obtain an accounting from the public officials to whom they delegate the exercise of that power." Alito added that "the provision limiting the use of the state FOIA to Virginia citizens recognizes that Virginia taxpayers foot the bill for the fixed costs underlying recordkeeping in the Commonwealth." The Court thus concluded that Virginia's FOIA law did not violate the Privileges and Immunities Clause of the U.S. Constitution, a discussion of which is beyond the scope of this book.

All state freedom of information laws provide exemptions to disclosure. Agencies *may* withhold material that falls under an exemption in some states; agencies *must* withhold this information in other states. Six common exemptions to the state open-records laws are the following:

1. Information classified as confidential by state or federal law
2. Law enforcement and investigatory information
3. Trade secrets and commercial information
4. Preliminary departmental memorandums (working papers)
5. Personal privacy information
6. Information relating to litigation against a public body

Can state and local governments copyright certain records?

Can state and local governments copyright certain records they create and maintain in order to stop their widespread distribution under freedom of information laws? That issue arose in South Carolina in 2008 when the state's highest court in *Seago* v. *Horry County* considered whether further dissemination of public documents obtained pursuant to the South Carolina Freedom of Information Act "may be restricted where the government entity claims the information is copyright-protected under the federal copyright law."[115] The dispute centered on a company that collected electronic mapping data, including digital photographic maps, from various government entities (in this case, Horry County) and then charged customers a fee for accessing such data on its Web

---

114. 133 S. Ct. 1709 (2013).
115. 663 S.E. 2d 38 (S.C. 2008).

site. Horry County had copyrighted parts of its mapping data. In ruling in favor of the county, the Supreme Court of South Carolina held that "while public information must be granted pursuant to FOIA, a public entity may restrict further commercial distribution of the information pursuant to a copyright."

---

911 TELEPHONE RECORDINGS AND THE SOUNDS OF DEATH

There is a growing movement in some states to exempt from their open-records laws the tapes and/or transcripts of 911 emergency telephone calls. Why? Because a 911 call might include a person's dying words or terrified response as he or she is being attacked or otherwise is in a state of danger. Alabama thus amended its open-records laws in 2010 to prohibit the release of audio recordings of 911 calls unless a judge first determines that the public's interest in disclosure outweighs the privacy interest of the person making the call. The Alabama law applies only to audio recordings; transcripts of the calls are available for a "reasonable fee" to cover the costs of transcription.

Obtaining copies of state records can sometimes be an expensive proposition. For instance, the police department in Milwaukee was going to require the *Milwaukee Journal Sentinel* in 2010 to prepay more than $3,500 to fulfill the newspaper's request for certain police incident reports. The department claimed there were more than 500 such reports and that significant time needed to be spent to redact (black out) confidential information from them before they could be released. The police department was going to charge the newspaper more than $40 an hour for labor and 25 cents per page copied. Rather than pay up, the *Milwaukee Journal Sentinel* sued the Milwaukee Police Department, claiming it violated the Wisconsin Open Records Law by charging it excessive fees for the opportunity to inspect and copy the records it requested and by imposing arbitrary limits on the amount of time staff could spend complying with the newspaper's request. The Wisconsin Supreme Court unanimously ruled that information should be released to the newspaper without having to pay for the redactions.[116] Sometimes lawsuits, it seems, are necessary to bring fees down. When records are produced, the charges may be steep. While many states have recently considered charging fees for public records search, charging a fee for producing a public record isn't common, although it is certainly not unheard of. Rhode Island, for example, charges a $15-per-hour search and retrieval fee. Colorado, on the other hand, charges $30 per hour. In 2014, a West Virginia court allowed public bodies in that state to charge for search and retrieval, although the state legislature banned such fees in 2015.

Violating a state's open records law can prove very expensive for government entities. For instance, the Iowa Supreme Court in November 2011 held that the city of Riverdale, Iowa, had to pay trial attorney fees of more than $64,000 to three individuals who sought to

---

116. *Milwaukee Journal Sentinel* v. *City of Milwaukee*, No. 2011AP1112 (Wis. Sup. Court, Jun. 27, 2012).

obtain security camera videotape under Iowa's Freedom of Information Act.[117] In particular, the trio wanted to view security camera video of a confrontation between themselves and Riverdale Mayor Jeffrey Grindle over earlier records requests at the city clerk's counter. The mayor was advised in writing by the city's lead attorney that video from city hall security cameras was subject to disclosure, and the mayor even allowed a newspaper reporter to watch it. Nevertheless, the mayor refused to turn it over to the trio of citizens. That proved to be a $64,000 mistake. The Iowa Supreme Court blasted the mayor, writing that "it is untenable for Riverdale to play the video for a reporter covering the dispute between the parties and yet withhold the same video from the defendants who requested it."

THE PRIVATIZATION OF PUBLIC GOVERNMENT

One of the challenges facing the press today results from the trend of private companies taking over what has been traditionally regarded as government business. For-profit and nonprofit organizations are replacing the government in operating public schools, jails and prisons, state and local welfare agencies, and many other state services. These private agencies are not generally regarded to have the same responsibilities as public agencies to maintain open records or hold meetings in public. For instance, in 2006 the Ohio Supreme Court held in *Oriana House, Inc.* v. *Montgomery* that a private corporation called Oriana House, which contracted with Summit County, Ohio, to operate its alternative jail sentencing and rehabilitation programs, was not the "functional equivalent" of a government agency and thus was not subject to the Ohio Public Records Act.[118] By a 4-3 decision, Ohio's high court found Oriana House exempt, even though Oriana House performed duties historically left to government agencies and despite the fact that it received all of Summit County's funds for running community-based correctional facilities and programs. The majority emphasized, instead, the fact there was "no evidence . . . that any government entity controls the day-to-day operations of Oriana House" and that Oriana House was "created as a private, nonprofit corporation. It was not established by a government entity." Sadly for journalists and access advocates, the majority concluded that "a private business does not open its records to public scrutiny merely by performing services on behalf of the state or a municipal government. It ought to be difficult for someone to compel a private entity to adhere to the dictates of the Public Records Act."

Although the Ohio ruling is not access friendly, some courts have held differently in similar scenarios. For instance, a judge in Tennessee ruled in 2008 that a private prison company was the functional equivalent of a government agency and thus was subject to Tennessee's open-records law.[119] The judge found it significant that the state's constitution makes prison maintenance a state function. The private company, Corrections Corporation of America (CCA), operates more than a half-dozen detention facilities in Tennessee. In 2009 the Tennessee Court of Appeals in *Friedman* v. *Corrections Corporation of America* upheld the decision. It observed that the state could not delegate away to a private entity its responsibilities. The Tennessee Supreme Court declined in 2010 to hear CCA's appeal, thus giving a clear victory for access advocates. The Supreme Court

117. *City of Riverdale* v. *Diercks,* 806 N.W.2d 643 (Iowa 2011).
118. 854 N.E. 2d 193 (Ohio 2006).
119. *Associated Press,* "Judge: Private Prison Company Must Produce Records."

of Wisconsin held in 2008 that municipalities may not avoid liability under Wisconsin's open-records law by contracting with an independent contractor assessor for the collection and custody of its property assessment records, and by then directing any requester of those records to such an assessor.[120]

SUMMARY

All states have laws that govern access to public meetings and public records. Good state open-meetings laws have strong legislative declarations in support of public meetings, specifically define a public meeting by listing the number of members who must gather to constitute a meeting, and declare void all actions taken during a meeting that was improperly closed to the public. Most laws provide for closed sessions to discuss such matters as personnel actions, real estate transactions and litigation.

State open-records laws tend to mirror the federal law. Both state and local agencies are governed by the laws, which apply to most governmental bodies except the legislature and the courts. Most state laws govern all records kept by these agencies, but a few are applicable only to records that are required to be kept by law. Exemptions to state open-records laws include material specifically excluded by other statutes, law enforcement investigatory information, working papers and highly personal information. Most laws provide for access to the judicial system in case a request for data is rejected, but both New York and Connecticut have established commissions to act as arbiters in these matters, and Florida has adopted a constitutional amendment that governs access throughout state government. A major concern facing both journalists and the public today is the growing use of private businesses to carry out governmental functions.

LAWS THAT RESTRICT ACCESS TO INFORMATION

Just as there are laws that provide for public access to government-held documents, there are laws that specifically preclude access to government-held information. There are provisions in scores of federal laws alone that limit the right of access. Tax statutes, espionage laws, legislation on atomic energy and dozens of other kinds of laws are filled with limitations on the dissemination of information (e.g., personal information on taxes, national security questions and matters relating to nuclear weapons). But in addition to these kinds of laws, the federal government has adopted in the past four decades at least three rather broad sets of regulations regarding information held by the government. All three were adopted in the name of protecting the right to privacy. While these regulations cannot be considered here in a comprehensive sense, people who gather information for a living need to be aware of their implications.

All three were adopted in the name of protecting the right to privacy.

SCHOOL RECORDS

The Family Educational Rights and Privacy Act (FERPA), adopted in 1974 and also known as the Buckley Amendment, is a federal law designed to safeguard the privacy

120. *Wiredata, Inc. v. Village of Sussex*, 751 N.W. 2d 736 (Wisc. 2008).

of students' "education records."[121] It applies to all levels of schools (grade schools, high schools and universities) that receive funds under any program administered by the U.S. Department of Education. FERPA, in brief, affects

- *who can access education records* (defined as records "directly related to a student" that are "maintained by an educational agency or institution"); and
- *what information a school may or may not disclose* without the permission of either a student or parent.

The most recent amendments to its regulations interpreting FERPA took effect in 2009. What follows is an overview of the law.

Under FERPA, parents can inspect their child's education records until their child turns 18 or attends a school beyond the high school level. Thus, in general, parents cannot access education records of their college-attending child, unless their child grants them written permission. Exceptions, however, permit disclosure to a student's parents without consent if (1) the student is a dependent for federal tax purposes; (2) there is a health or safety emergency involving the student; or (3) if the student is under 21 and violated a law or policy concerning use or possession of alcohol or controlled substances.

FERPA impacts journalists covering colleges and universities.

FERPA impacts journalists covering colleges and universities because it generally prohibits such institutions from disclosing a student's education records, without that student's prior consent, if the records contain "personally identifiable information." Such information includes a student's name, address, date and place of birth, Social Security and student identification numbers, as well as (under the regulations that took effect in 2009) any "other information that . . . is linked or linkable to a specific student that would allow a reasonable person in the school community, who does not have personal knowledge of the relevant circumstances, to identify the student with reasonable certainty." Any and all such personally identifiable information, when located in a student's education records (for instance, a transcript or discipline report), would need to be redacted (blacked out or removed) before the records could be disclosed without permission. The names and addresses of a student's parents (including mother's maiden name) and family members also cannot be disclosed without permission.

On the other hand, FERPA allows disclosure without consent of so-called directory information (a student's name, major, address and telephone number, for instance) that might be listed in an online or hard-copy student directory. However, colleges must tell students about directory information and give them a chance to request its nondisclosure; in brief, students must have notice and opportunity to opt out of the disclosure.

Does a college student's e-mail sent to school officials complaining about an instructor constitute an "education record" within the meaning of FERPA or can the instructor find out the complaining student's name under state open records laws? In 2012, a Florida appellate court held in *Rhea* v. *District Board of Trustees of Sante Fe College* that such an e-mail is not an education record because it is not directly related to a student. Instead, it is directly related to an instructor and only tangentially related to a student, and thus the instructor has a right to discover who sent the e-mail complaining about him.

---

121. 20 U.S.C. § 1232g (2009). The Department of Education maintains a Web site devoted to FERPA, available at http://www.ed.gov/policy/gen/guid/fpco/ferpa/index.html.

Although the decision is binding precedent within one Florida appellate district only, the case illustrates the larger point that to constitute an education record under FERPA, the information in a document must be "directly related" to a student. As the Florida appellate court wrote, "[t]he e-mail focuses primarily on instructor [Darnell] Rhea's alleged teaching methods and inappropriate conduct and statements in the classroom, and only incidentally relates to the student author or to any other students in the classroom. The fundamental character of the e-mail relates directly to the instructor; the fact that it was authored by a student does not convert it into an 'education record.'"

In a portion of FERPA that is critical for student journalists reporting on campus crime, FERPA states that education records do *not* include "records maintained by a law enforcement unit of the educational agency or institution that were created by that law enforcement unit for the purpose of law enforcement." In other words, incident reports, arrest reports, parking tickets and other documents made by campus or university police are not "education records" covered by FERPA and thus they may be obtained without a student's permission.

For instance, in 2012, a North Carolina judge ruled that FERPA did not protect from disclosure information in the University of North Carolina's statements of facts and responses submitted to the NCAA and relating to impermissible benefits received by student-athletes such as plane tickets, jewelry, clothing, shoes, automobiles, payments to cover parking tickets, monetary gifts and free meals. Judge Manning opined that "This kind of behavior (impermissible benefits—nonacademic) does not relate to the classroom, test scores, grades, SAT or ACT scores, academic standing or anything else relating to a student's educational progress or discipline for violating the educational rules or honor code, all of which are clearly protected by FERPA." Victory came for the *Daily Tar Heel*, the Raleigh *News & Observer* and other news organizations in October 2012 when the University of North Carolina agreed to settle the case, produce the records Judge Manning had ordered and pay $45,000 of their legal fees.

Numerous universities, it should be noted, invoke FERPA (sometimes rightly, sometimes wrongly) to hide potentially damaging information about their athletic programs, student-athletes and even their boosters/donors. For instance, in November 2012 the *Post and Courier* newspaper reported that the College of Charleston cited FERPA when it repeatedly refused to release incident reports containing the identities of suspects (supposedly varsity baseball players) in the alleged sexual assault of a female varsity softball player. As the *Post and Courier* story noted, "the information is considered vital, as it would confirm or refute the crux of an argument presented by the alleged victim's family: that the suspects are baseball players and are being protected because of that."

FERPA is so abused that the Student Press Law Center (SPLC) keeps a running Tumblr account that documents the use of FERPA as an excuse to not release records and other "questionable uses of FERPA." In 2017, for example, East Tennessee State University (ETSU) claimed that the number of athletes treated for concussions was a FERPA-protected secret. When the *Johnson City Press* asked for the number of times football players suffered concussions during practices and games, an ETSU lawyer responded that the information fell into the education record category. The SPLC categorized this as an example of material that was clearly not protected by FERPA. The University of Minnesota Golden Gophers football team garnered national attention for a FERPA issue in 2017. The team came within hours of boycotting a postseason bowl game in protest of the disciplinary suspensions of 10 teammates. Players on the team criticized the university's lack of transparency and communication—"under the cover of student privacy," as a team spokesman put it—in explaining why Athletic Director Mark Coyle banned 10 of their teammates from playing in the Dec. 27 Holiday Bowl. The proposed boycott ended only when Minneapolis' KSTP-TV obtained and released investigative reports compiled by Minneapolis police and the university's Office of Equal Opportunity and Affirmative Action that graphically described allegations of sexual assault that led to the recommendation to expel five athletes, suspend four and put a tenth on disciplinary probation. The SPLC classified the university's initial decision to not release the documents as a "questionable use of FERPA."[122]

In 2002 the U.S. Supreme Court issued a 7-2 opinion interpreting the Family Educational Rights and Privacy Act that could help the media obtain campus crime reports and records by reducing universities' worries about being sued for violating the law. In particular, the court held that FERPA does not give students the personal right to sue their schools for releasing personal material covered by that statute.[123] The remedy for violation, the court held, is not an individual lawsuit but, as noted previously, solely the loss to schools of federal funds.

HEALTH AND MEDICAL RECORDS

In 2003 a new set of privacy rules and regulations went into effect that limit the ability of journalists to obtain information about patients in hospitals and in the custody of other health care providers. The rules, officially known as the Federal Standards for Privacy of Individually Identifiable Health Information, were enacted pursuant to the Health Insurance Portability and Accountability Act of 1996, which is commonly known by the acronym HIPAA (see later in this chapter). *The Seattle Times* wrote that "for the news media, HIPAA rules will mean that in the event of a shooting, car crash or other newsworthy event, hospitals will disclose no information unless a reporter knows the patient's name. In the past, reporters could ascertain a patient's condition in those situations without a name."[124] In a special white paper called "The Lost Stories," Jennifer LaFleur of the Reporters Committee for Freedom of the Press (RCFP) observed that "under HIPAA, hospitals may release only the name and one-word status of the patient—but only if the patient has agreed to have his or her name released and then only if the reporter has the individual's full name."[125] LaFleur added that many "journalists around the country report that police and fire departments have cited HIPAA for not disclosing accident information."

It is important to note that police and fire departments, along with other law enforcement agencies, are *not* entities covered by HIPAA. Thus HIPAA does not give the police the power or the right to keep secret information in their reports and logs about

---

122. FERPA Fact, The Student Press Law Center, http://ferpafact.tumblr.com.
123. *Gonzaga University* v. *Doe,* 536 U.S. 273 (2002).
124. Ostrom, "Privacy Rules to Limit Word on Patients."
125. LaFleur, "The Lost Stories."

accident or shooting victims. The entities covered by HIPAA, in contrast, are health plans, health care clearinghouses and health care providers.

The Department of Health and Human Services maintains a Web site devoted to HIPAA and its privacy provisions. It is located at http://www.hhs.gov/ocr/privacy/index .html and journalists seeking information from health care providers should be familiar with its myriad relevant terms and provisions. One very important statement for journalists on that Web site relates to the relationship between HIPAA and state open-records laws. It can be found on a link for frequently asked questions about state public records laws. In particular, the Web site provides that "if a state agency is not a 'covered entity' . . . it is not required to comply with the HIPAA Privacy Rule and, thus, any disclosure of information by the state agency pursuant to its state public records law would not be subject to the Privacy Rule." This makes it clear that police and fire departments, which are not covered entities, cannot hide behind HIPAA to keep information secret that is otherwise open under a state law.

Seemingly inappropriate stretches of HIPAA still occur. In 2008 a Nebraska judge cited HIPAA when denying a historical society's request for records identifying 957 people buried in graves marked only by numbers at a psychiatric institution's cemetery in Hastings, Neb., from the 1880s through the late 1950s. The records are held by the Hastings Regional Center, a health care provider. Although the burial records in question obviously related to individuals deceased for many decades and despite the general legal maxim that an individual's right to privacy dies with the individual, Adams County District Judge Terri Harder nonetheless found the records constituted "individually identifiable health information" protected from disclosure by HIPAA and that their release "would reveal that the individual[s] [were] institutionalized for a mental illness or for a condition serious enough to require institutionalization."[126]

In 2009, however, the Nebraska Supreme Court reversed the lower court's decision and allowed access to the names. It wrote that "although HIPAA prevents the release of individually identifiable medical information, it also provides for release of information when required by state law. Nebraska's public records statutes require that medical records be kept confidential, but exempt birth and death records from that requirement. Our privacy laws also apply to medical records and patient histories, but not to records of deaths. The records sought by ACHS are records of deaths and therefore are public records."[127]

THE FEDERAL PRIVACY LAW

The **Privacy Act of 1974** has two basic thrusts. First, it attempts to check the misuse of personal data obtained by the federal government, the quantity of which has, of course, reached staggering proportions. Second, the law is intended to provide access for individuals to records about themselves that are held by federal agencies. The first objective of the law could be the more troublesome to the press.

---

126. Bergman, "Unearthing An Unusual Privacy Battle."
127. *Nebraska Ex Rel Adams County Historical Society v. Kinyoun,* 765 N.W. 2d 212 (Neb. 2009).

The act requires that each federal agency limit the collection of information to that which is relevant and necessary, to collect information directly from the subject concerned when possible, and to allow individuals to review and amend their personal records and information. Also, under the act agencies are forbidden from disclosing what is called "a personally identifiable record" without the written consent of the individual to whom the record pertains. Since this section of the law is seemingly contradictory to the spirit of the federal FOIA, Congress was forced to clarify the responsibilities of federal agencies with regard to the law. A provision was added to the Privacy Act that declares that records required to be disclosed under FOIA are not subject to the provisions of the Privacy Act and consequently cannot be withheld from inspection. To the government official with control of information, however, neither the Privacy Act nor FOIA is unambiguous.

One federal appellate court recently summed up the tension between FOIA and the Privacy Act, writing that "the net effect of the interaction between the two statutes is that where the FOIA requires disclosure, the Privacy Act will not stand in its way, but where the FOIA would permit withholding under an exemption, the Privacy Act makes such withholding mandatory upon the agency."[128]

In 2012 the U.S. Supreme Court held in *Federal Aviation Administration* v. *Cooper*[129] that plaintiffs who win cases under the Privacy Act because a government agency wrongfully disclosed private information about them cannot recover monetary damages for mental or emotional distress allegedly caused by the disclosure. In an example of a court engaging in **statutory construction** (see Chapter 1), Justice Samuel Alito wrote for the majority that the term "actual damages" used within the Privacy Act is limited to proof of tangible economic and monetary losses, akin to **special damages** in defamation law addressed in Chapter 6.

How does the Privacy Act of 1974 affect journalists? When journalists receive information from confidential sources that was leaked by those sources in violation of the Privacy Act of 1974, those journalists may be subpoenaed to testify in civil actions filed by the individuals about whom the leaked information pertains. In other words, the person whose information is leaked in violation of the Privacy Act of 1974 will file a lawsuit under the act and then try to find out who leaked it by subpoenaing the journalists who received it from confidential sources.

CRIMINAL HISTORY PRIVACY LAWS

In accordance with the broad scope of the Omnibus Crime Control and Safe Streets Act of 1968, the federal Law Enforcement Assistance Administration, an agency created by the Nixon administration to help local police forces fight crime, sought to develop a national computerized record-keeping system. The system that was established permits any police department in the nation to have access to the records of virtually all other police departments.

---

128. *News-Press* v. *Department of Homeland Security,* 489 F. 3d 1173, 1189 (11th Cir. 2007).
129. 132 S. Ct. 1441 (2012).

Congressional concern about the misuse of this record system led to limitations on access to the data. Police records have always contained a considerable amount of information that is erroneous, out-of-date or private. The centralized record-keeping system presents a problem referred to by some writers as the "dossier effect." The contrast between these computerized and centrally maintained records immediately accessible across the country and those police records of the past was sharp and immediately evident: Fragmented, original-source records kept by a single police agency for a limited geographical area were not readily accessible because of their bulk and associated indexing problems. Hence, federal policy mandated that states, if they wish to participate in the national record-keeping system, adopt rules that, among other things, limit the dissemination of some criminal history nonconviction data.

The "Code of Federal Regulations" ("Criminal Justice Information Systems") defines nonconviction data as

> arrest information without disposition if an interval of one year has elapsed from the date of arrest and no active prosecution of the charge is pending, or information disclosing that the police have elected not to refer a matter to a prosecutor, or that a prosecutor has elected not to commence criminal proceedings, or that proceedings have been indefinitely postponed, as well as all acquittals and all dismissals.

As a result of the state laws, press access to criminal history records kept by the police has been virtually eliminated unless data sought are pertinent to an incident for which a person is currently being processed by the criminal justice system, are conviction records or are original records of entry, such as arrest records, that are maintained chronologically and are accessible only on that basis. Reporters can also obtain information about arrests not resulting in conviction, however, if they are aware of the specific dates of the arrests. It is hard to determine whether these laws have substantially affected the press's ability to report on the criminal justice system. A good police reporter usually can gain access to information he or she wants to see.

The ability to achieve that scrutiny is important. For example, it is possible to envision a situation in which a prosecutor is accused of favoring friends or certain ethnic or racial groups when deciding whether to prosecute arrested persons. Without access to arrest records that can be compared with prosecution records, such a charge would be difficult to investigate. People within the criminal justice system could gain access to the needed records, but history indicates that they must be prodded before they take action. And, of course, prodding is the function of the press.

STATE STATUTES THAT LIMIT ACCESS TO INFORMATION

All states have statutes that limit access to information that would otherwise be available under a freedom of information law. Washington, for example, has more than 100 different laws that govern the access to particular information. Some of these state statutes are aimed at blocking access to trade secrets; others limit access to information submitted to the state in compliance with environmental laws. In 2001, in direct response to the racetrack death of driver Dale Earnhardt at the Daytona 500 and the subsequent request for autopsy

All states have statutes that limit access to information that would otherwise be available under a freedom of information law.

photographs by the *Orlando Sentinel* and other newspapers, the Florida legislature passed a bill that makes confidential and exempt from that state's public records act photographs and videotapes of autopsies.[130] The newspapers had sought access to the photographs to determine the reasons for Earnhardt's death and, in particular, whether a particular safety device might have saved his life. In 2002 a Florida appellate court upheld the constitutionality of that statute and its retroactive application, and the Supreme Court of Florida declined to hear the case in July 2003, letting the appellate court decision stand.[131] Finally, in December 2003, the U.S. Supreme Court declined to hear the case.[132]

The Pennsylvania Supreme Court ruled in 2009 that autopsy reports are official records subject to disclosure under Pennsylvania's open records laws. The Pennsylvania high court noted, however, that trial court judges may protect autopsy reports from disclosure based on judicial discretion and necessity under appropriate circumstances, adding that "this inherent power provides trial courts with the means to limit public access to autopsy reports (or portions thereof) based on privacy or privilege concerns where warranted."[133]

Divorce is another area where some states adopt statutes limiting public access to certain records. For instance, in 2006 a California appellate court in *Burkle* v. *Burkle* struck down a state statute that allowed a party in a divorce case, upon request to a judge, to have sealed in their entirety any and all court documents referencing in any way the financial assets and liabilities of the parties getting divorced.[134] Although the court acknowledged privacy interests of divorcing parties in financial information (including the possibility of identity theft), it nonetheless found that "the First Amendment provides a right of access to court records in divorce proceedings" and held the statute was overbroad and not narrowly tailored to protect privacy interests. In particular, the statute mandated a judge to automatically seal in their entirety court pleadings relating to financial information even if they just briefly mentioned that information, rather than providing the judge with discretion to redact only those specific parts of the documents relating to financial information that actually could harm privacy interests. Courts in other states have struck down similar laws—sometimes based on a First Amendment right of access, sometimes based on a state constitutional right of access.[135]

Jon and Kate Gosselin filed for divorce where filings are secret.

In 2009, when Jon and Kate Gosselin, stars of the reality series "Jon & Kate Plus 8," filed for divorce, they did so in Montgomery County, Pa. (rather than their own Berks County), where divorce filings are automatically sealed from public view. It apparently was one of the few things in their lives they didn't want publicly exploited.

---

130. Florida Statute § 406.135 (2001).

131. *Campus Communications, Inc.* v. *Earnhardt,* 821 So. 2d 388 (2002). The Supreme Court of Florida's decision not to hear the case came in a close 4-3 vote.

132. *Campus Communications, Inc.* v. *Earnhardt,* 124 S. Ct. 821 (2003).

133. *Penn Jersey Advance, Inc.* v. *Grim,* 962 A. 2d 632 (Pa. 2009).

134. 135 Cal. App. 4th 1045 (2006). The California Supreme Court declined to hear the case. *Burkle* v. *Burkle,* 2006 Cal. LEXIS 5955 (2006).

135. See *Associated Press* v. *New Hampshire,* 153 N.H. 120 (2005), which held unconstitutional a New Hampshire law limiting access to divorce records that abrogated "entirely the public right of access to a class of court records," and emphasized that "the New Hampshire Constitution creates a public right of access to court records."

All the states and the federal government have laws that specifically exclude certain kinds of information from the public scrutiny. Some of these exclusions were noted in the discussion of Exemption 3 of the Freedom of Information Act. Today, the right to privacy has been erected as a substantial barrier to access to information held by government agencies. The federal government has adopted a law protecting the privacy of student records. Congress passed a federal privacy law, which often conflicts with the provisions of FOIA. The federal government has also insisted that states pass statutes that control access to criminal history records. Much privacy legislation has been passed by the states themselves, and today the right to privacy is being used frequently to block access to public records.

SUMMARY

BIBLIOGRAPHY

Associated Press. "Judge: Private Prison Company Must Produce Records." 29 July 2008.
———. "Judge Says Regional Center Burial Records Can Remain Sealed." 16 February 2008.
Barringer, Felicity. "Appeals Court Rejects Damages Against ABC in Food Lion Case." *The New York Times,* 21 October 1999, A1.
Bergman, Hannah. "Unearthing An Unusual Privacy Battle." The News Media and the Law, Winter 2009.
Bridis, Ted, and Gillum, Jack. "US Gov't Sets Record for Failures to Find Files When Asked." *Associated Press,* 18 (March 2016), http://bigstory.ap.org/article/697e352300 3049cdb0847ecf828afd62/us-govt-sets-record-failures-find-files-when-asked.
The Bush Administration and the News Media. Washington, D.C.: Reporters Committee for Freedom of the Press, 1992.
Bush, Ellen M. "Access to Governors' Records: State Statutes and the Use of Executive Privilege." *Journalism Quarterly* 71 (1994): 135.
Chokshi, Niraj. "Ferguson-Related Charges Dropped Against *Washington Post and Huffington Post* Reporters." *Washington Post,* 19 May 2016, available at https://www .washingtonpost.com/news/post-nation/wp/2016/05/19/ferguson-related-charges -dropped-against-washington-post-and-huffington-post-reporters/?utm_term =.5a2b186d2fc2.
The Clinton Administration and the News Media. Washington, D.C.: Reporters Committee for Freedom of the Press, 1996.
"CNN, Federal Government Settle Suit with Montana Rancher." *Associated Press,* 5 June 2001.
Cross, Harold. *The People's Right to Know.* New York: Columbia University Press, 1953.
Davis, Charles. "Stacked Deck Favors Government Secrecy." *IRE J.,* March/April 2002, 14.
Dobbs, Michael. "Records Counter a Critic of Kerry." *Washington Post,* 19 April 2004.
"Journalist Gets Probation for Posing as Federal Official." *Plain Dealer,* 13 April 2002, B2.
Knight Open Government Survey 2008. Washington, D.C.: National Security Archive at George Washington University, 2008.

LaFleur, Jennifer. *The Lost Stories: How a Steady Stream of Laws, Regulations and Judicial Decisions Have Eroded Reporting on Important Issues.* Arlington, Va.: Reporters Committee for Freedom of the Press, 2003.

Leopold, Jason. "It Took a FOIA Lawsuit to Uncover How the Obama Administration Killed FOIA Reform." *Vice News,* 9 March 2016, https://news.vice.com/article/it-took-a-foia-lawsuit-to-uncover-how-the-obama-administration-killed-foia-reform.

Lux, Emma. "Journalists Face Charges in Inauguration Arrests, One See Charges Dropped." Reporter's Committee for Freedom of the Press, 27 Jan. 2017.

Mifflin, Laurie. "Judge Slashes $5.5 Million Award to Grocery Chain for ABC Report." *The New York Times,* 30 August 1997, A1.

Morrissey, David H. "FOIA Foiled?" *Presstime,* March 1995, 29.

Ostrom, Carol M. "Privacy Rules to Limit Word on Patients." *The Seattle Times,* 13 April 2003, B1.

Pogrebin, Robin. "At Public Board Meeting, Smithsonian Practices New Openness." *The New York Times,* 18 November 2008, A13.

Rourke, Francis. *Secrecy and Publicity.* Baltimore, Md.: Johns Hopkins University Press, 1961.

Rydell, Michelle. "No Money to Fight." *Quill,* Sept.–Oct. 2009, 34.

Stewart, Potter. "Or of the Press." *Hastings Law Journal* 26 (1975): 631.

Zhang, Amy. "Charges Against Arrested N.C. Reporter Dropped." Reporters Committee for Freedom of the Press, August 14, 2013.

CHAPTER 10

Protection of News Sources/ Contempt Power

©McGraw-Hill Education/Jill Braaten

The lifeblood of journalism is information. Each day reporters gather information. It is not uncommon for people outside the news-gathering business to want the information gathered by journalists. Sometimes they merely seek copies of what has already appeared in print or over the airwaves. Sometimes they want more: information that has not been published; photos or video that have not been broadcast; the names of people who provided information to the journalists. Judges, grand juries and even legislative committees all have the power to issue subpoenas to try to force reporters to reveal this information. The first part of this chapter explores exactly how much protection the law provides to reporters who refuse to cooperate when they are presented with subpoenas and how the actions of the journalist ultimately affect what we all read, see and hear.

Anyone who refuses to submit to a court order can be punished with a citation for contempt of court, a swift judicial ruling in which the target can find himself or herself in jail in a matter of hours. This occurred several times in recent years when journalists went to jail for refusing to reveal either their confidential sources or their unpublished information.

JOURNALISTS, JAIL AND CONFIDENTIAL SOURCES

The following are some harsh occupational hazards of which aspiring journalists must be aware:

1. If you refuse to reveal, after having been subpoenaed to do so, the name of a confidential source to a grand jury investigating a potential criminal law violation, then you can be held in contempt of court, ordered to go to jail and forced to pay (along with your newspaper, TV station or Web site employer) an often steep monetary fine. For instance, former *New York Times* reporter Judith Miller spent 85 days in a Virginia detention facility in 2005 after she refused to reveal the identity of the confidential source who leaked to her the name of Valerie Plame as a covert CIA operative.

2. If you refuse to turn over your notes, photographs or videotapes after having been ordered to do so by a judge in a criminal or civil law proceeding, then you might be held in contempt, ordered to go to jail and forced to pay (along with your newspaper, TV station or Web site employer) an often steep monetary fine. For example, freelance blogger Josh Wolf spent a record-setting 226 days in jail in 2006 and 2007 after he refused, in the face of a subpoena, to turn over unaired videotape he made of a demonstration in San Francisco that damaged a police car.

If you breach a promise of confidentiality given to a source by revealing and disclosing that source's name in court, to a grand jury or simply by publishing it in the pages of your newspaper or on its Web site, then you can be sued.

3. If you breach a promise of confidentiality given to a source by revealing and disclosing that source's name in court, to a grand jury or simply by publishing it in the pages of your newspaper or on its Web site, then you can be sued by that source in a civil law proceeding for monetary damages on a theory known as promissory estoppel.

Journalists who refuse either to comply with subpoenas and court orders to reveal the identity of confidential sources or to turn over in court their notes, photographs and videotapes are forced to turn for possible protection either to legislatively created shield laws or to judicially adopted First Amendment (and sometimes common-law) privileges to try to ward off contempt orders, jail sentences and monetary fines. As this chapter makes clear, however, the mere existence of a shield law in your state or the recognition of a court-created First Amendment privilege does not guarantee that you will get off the legal hook. Thirty-nine states and the District of Columbia had adopted shield laws by August 2017, with the scope of those laws varying significantly in terms of (1) who is protected, (2) what is protected and (3) when material is protected. What is more, the U.S. Supreme Court has held that there is no First Amendment privilege for a journalist to refuse to testify before a grand jury proceeding. In civil and criminal proceedings (as compared to grand jury proceedings), lower federal appellate courts and some state courts have recognized First Amendment–based privileges, but these judicially created privileges are not absolute and may be overcome.

So why are journalists subject to subpoenas, requests for information and court orders? There are several answers.

Most journalists are efficient information gatherers. Some information they gather is not included in the newspaper stories or television reports they prepare. Sometimes the source of a story doesn't want to be named and asks the reporter to promise not to reveal his or her identity. The obvious example here is the Watergate source known only as Deep Throat until he finally came forward decades later in 2005 to reveal his identity as W. Mark Felt. Felt died in 2008 as the most famous confidential source in modern American journalism history. But reporters are not only efficient gatherers, they are excellent record keepers as well. Unreported material is often retained in notebooks and computer memories, or on videotape and audiotape. For some people this undisclosed information is important, even vital. Law enforcement officials frequently want to know what a criminal suspect told a journalist during an interview—only parts of which have been published or broadcast. Libel plaintiffs often need to know the identity of the sources used by reporters in preparation of a story in order to try to prove the story was untrue, fabricated or published with actual malice. Video recordings of a violent demonstration are often useful to police who seek to identify those who incited the violence or committed criminal acts. Hence, reporters are often asked to reveal information they have gathered but chosen not to publish or broadcast. Most of the time journalists comply with such requests. At times, however, they refuse. When this happens, those seeking this information often get a court order or **subpoena** to force the journalist to reveal the name of the news source or to disclose the confidential information. Or government agents may get a **warrant** to search a newsroom or a reporter's home to find the information they want.

In our society the press is supposed to represent a neutral entity as it gathers and publishes news and information. When the government or anyone else intrudes into the newsroom or the reporter's notebook, it compromises this neutrality. A news source who normally trusts journalists may choose not to cooperate with a reporter if government agents can learn the source's name by threatening the reporter with a court order. Television news crews will hardly be welcome at protest rallies if the demonstrators know that the government will use the film to identify and prosecute the protesters. The effectiveness of the reporter as an information gatherer may be seriously compromised if government agents or civil and criminal litigants can force journalists to reveal information they choose not to disclose. Society also may ultimately suffer because the flow of information to the public may be reduced.

So why are journalists subject to subpoenas, requests for information and court orders? There are several answers to that question.

In our society the press is supposed to represent a neutral entity as it gathers and publishes news and information.

NEWS AND NEWS SOURCES

If news and information are the lifeblood of the press, then news sources are one of the important wells from which that lifeblood springs. Journalists are often no better than the sources they cultivate. News sources come in all shapes and sizes. Occasionally their willingness to cooperate with a reporter depends on assurances from the journalist that their identity will not be revealed. Why would a news source wish to remain anonymous? There are many reasons. Often the source of a story about criminal activities has participated in criminal activities and has no desire to publicize this fact. Frequently the source of a story

Why would a news source wish to remain anonymous? There are many reasons.

about government mismanagement or dishonesty is an employee of that government agency, and revelation of his or her identity as a whistle-blower could result in loss of the job for informing the press of the errors made by the employee's superiors. Some people simply do not want to get involved in all the hassle that frequently results when an explosive story is published; by remaining anonymous they can remain out of the limelight.

Journalists have always used confidential sources and obtained information that government officials sought to uncover. The earliest reported case of a journalist's refusal to disclose his sources of information took place in 1848 when a reporter for the *New York Herald* refused to reveal to the U.S. Senate the name of the person who had given him a secret copy of the treaty the United States was negotiating to end the Mexican-American War. He was held in contempt of the Senate and jailed. A U.S. Court of Appeals denied the journalist's petition for release.[1]

The number of requests to journalists to reveal the names of sources or share confidential information with authorities escalated at the end of the 1960s and into the 1970s. The nation went through a period of great social upheaval, and the press played a significant role in documenting the confrontations between blacks and whites, between war protesters and police and between the mainstream culture and the nascent counterculture. The press was often privy to information that government officials wanted. The confidential relationship between a journalist and a news source often sparks the interest of authorities who are seeking to discover who leaked confidential information to the press.

THE COLORADO THEATER SHOOTING CASE:
THE 2013 CONTEMPT BATTLE OVER LEAKED INFORMATION
IN THE PROSECUTION OF JAMES HOLMES

In 2013, Fox News reporter Jana Winter faced possible contempt charges, including monetary fines and up to six months in jail. Why? Because Winter refused to reveal to a judge the identity of the sources who described to her the contents of a notebook that James Holmes mailed to a psychologist before allegedly killing 12 people in an Aurora, Colo., movie theater in July 2012.

Two days before Winter's story was published, the judge had issued a gag order limiting pretrial publicity in the case. Specifically, the gag order instructed both the parties to the case against Holmes and law enforcement officials to refrain from disseminating to the media information that would be substantially likely to prejudice Holmes' Sixth Amendment right to a fair trial by an impartial jury.

In her July 25, 2012, story describing the contents of Holmes' notebook, Winter identified her sources as two unnamed law enforcement officials. Winter's story quoted one source as stating there was a "notebook full of details about how he was going to kill people. There were drawings of what he was going to do in it—drawings and illustrations of the massacre." Certainly it was the type of out-of-court information that could prejudice potential jurors against Holmes.

Colorado is one of the 39 states as of August 2017 to have a shield law (see later in this chapter for more on shield laws). Colorado's shield law, however, creates

---

1. *Ex parte Nugent,* 16 Fed. Cas. 471 (1848).

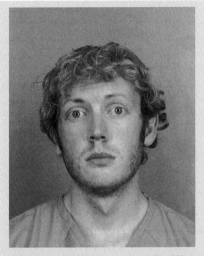

*James Holmes, who killed
12 people in a Colorado
movie theater in 2012.*

©*Photo by Arapahoe County Sheriff's Office
via Getty Images*

only a qualified or limited privilege for a journalist not to reveal his or her sources.
To overcome the privilege and force a journalist to reveal information, a person
(in this case, James Holmes) must prove three things: 1) the information sought
is directly relevant to a substantial issue involved in the case; 2) the information
sought cannot reasonably be obtained from a source other than the journalist; and
3) a strong interest of the party seeking to subpoena the journalist outweighs the
journalist's interests under the First Amendment.

Winter, who works in New York City, also asserted that New York's shield
law would protect her from revealing her confidential sources, even if Colorado's
shield law would not. New York's shield law is much stronger than Colorado's
shield law. In December 2013, New York's highest appellate court ruled for Winter
and found that she was protected by the Empire State's shield law and could
not be compelled by subpoena to testify in Colorado.[2] The court reasoned that
"as a New York reporter, Winter was aware of—and was entitled to rely on—the
absolute protection embodied in our shield law when she made the promises of
confidentiality that she now seeks to honor." It thus concluded that allowing a
New York court to issue a subpoena compelling a New York journalist like Winter
to appear as a witness in another state to give testimony was inconsistent with
New York's "public policy of the highest order" safeguarding journalistic sources.
In 2014, the U.S. Supreme Court declined to hear the case, thus leaving intact the
New York appellate court ruling.

In 2015, a jury found Holmes guilty of first-degree murder of all 12 victims,
as well as multiple counts of attempted murder for 70 others he wounded. He is
serving a life sentence in prison.

---

2. *Matter of Holmes* v. *Winter*, 3 N.E. 3d 694 (N.Y. 2013), *cert. denied*, 134 S. Ct. 266 (2014).

A journalist served with a subpoena has few options. The reporter or news organization can cooperate with those who seek the information and reveal what it is they want to know. This cooperation could damage the reporter-source relationship or threaten the image of independence fostered by most news media. The journalist can seek to have the subpoena withdrawn or attack the order in court and hope to have it quashed. Going to court can be expensive and is time-consuming. If in the end the journalist refuses to cooperate, he or she will likely be held in contempt of court. A fine and a jail sentence usually follow. So the choice for the journalist is not an easy one.

But the choice for society is difficult as well. The interests that are involved in this dilemma are basic to our system of government and political values. On one hand, it is clearly the obligation of every citizen to cooperate with the government and testify before the proper authorities. This concept was so well established by the early 18th century that it had become a maxim. John Henry Wigmore, in his classic treatise on evidence, cites the concept thus: "The public has a right to everyman's evidence."[3] The Sixth Amendment to the U.S. Constitution guarantees the right to have witnesses and to compel them to testify in our behalf. And surely this right is a valuable one, both to society and to the individual seeking to prove his or her innocence of charges of wrongdoing. The Supreme Court in 1919 wrote on the duties and rights of witnesses:

The Sixth Amendment to the U.S. Constitution guarantees the right to have witnesses and to compel them to testify in our behalf.

> [I]t is clearly recognized that the giving of testimony and the attendance upon court or grand jury in order to testify are public duties which everyone within the jurisdiction of the government is bound to perform upon being properly summoned, . . . the personal sacrifice involved is a part of the necessary contribution to the public welfare.[4]

But society benefits from information provided by the news media. When a reporter is forced to break a promise of confidentiality or is used as an arm of law enforcement investigators, it harms this flow of information. People who know things, often important things, simply won't give this information to journalists for fear of being exposed if the reporter is squeezed for the information. The fragile reporter-source relationship may be damaged.

As more and more reporters were called on to cooperate with legal authorities during the last 40 years, courts and state legislatures were asked to fashion protection for both the legal system and the press. What was needed were rules that required the reporter to share valuable information with the parties that needed it, but only in those rare circumstances when severe harm might result without this cooperation. These rules are called the reporter's privilege. Such a privilege is not a novelty in the law. A variation of this privilege is given to doctors, lawyers and members of the clergy. The reporter's privilege that emerged in the past five decades is hardly a nice, neat, legal proposition. The source of the privilege varies from jurisdiction to jurisdiction. In some places its genesis is in the U.S. or state constitution; in other places it flows from the common law or state statute. The scope of the privilege also varies from jurisdiction to jurisdiction. A reporter in Michigan may be legally immune from a certain kind of subpoena, whereas

The reporter's privilege that emerged during the past five decades is hardly a nice, neat, legal proposition.

3. Wigmore, *Anglo-American System of Evidence.*
4. *Blair* v. *U.S.,* 250 U.S. 273 (1919).

her counterpart in Ohio may not enjoy the same immunity. What follows is a general outline of the broad provisions of the privilege, focusing especially on the rights that spring from the First Amendment. To be safe a journalist should know the specific law in his or her own state. An excellent online resource for the rules of each state that is prepared by the Reporters Committee for Freedom of the Press is called "The Reporter's Privilege." It can be found on the RCFP Web site, http://www.rcfp.org/reporters-privilege, and is billed by that organization as "a complete compendium of information on the reporter's privilege—the right not to be compelled to testify or disclose sources and information in court—in each state and federal circuit."

TIPS FOR REPORTERS ON PROMISING CONFIDENTIALITY

Here are some suggestions that were given by newspaper attorney David Utevsky to reporters and writers at a seminar in Seattle.

- Do not routinely promise confidentiality as a standard interview technique.
- Avoid giving an absolute promise of confidentiality. Try to persuade the source to agree that you may reveal his or her name if you are subpoenaed.
- Do not rely exclusively on information from a confidential source. Get corroboration from a nonconfidential source or documents.
- Consider whether others (police, attorneys, etc.) will want to know the identity of the source before publishing or broadcasting the material. Will you be the only source of this information, or can they get it elsewhere?
- Consider whether you can use the information without disclosing that it was obtained from a confidential source.

Reporters should always consult with a supervisor or editor before promising anonymity to a source; if a legal action results, the journalist will have to rely on the news outlet to assist in defending the action.

THE FAILURE TO KEEP A PROMISE

Many journalists are reluctant to reveal the names of their sources because they think it would be unethical or would diminish their ability to use the source at some point in the future. About 20 years ago reporters discovered another reason to protect the identity of a source: They could be sued if they broke their promise of confidentiality.

In 1991 a five-justice majority of the U.S. Supreme Court held in *Cohen* v. *Cowles Media, Inc.*[5] that the First Amendment does not prevent a lawsuit against a journalist

---

5. 501 U.S. 663 (1991).

who breaches a promise of confidentiality to a source when the source suffers direct harm from reliance on the breached promise. In this case, a Republican political operative named Dan Cohen was given a promise of anonymity by reporters from two Minnesota papers in return for information Cohen would supply about a rival candidate for public office. The information Cohen gave turned out to be both old and insignificant, and the newspapers' editors decided the real story was not the information Cohen supplied but, instead, Cohen's own tactics in spreading dirt under the cloak of anonymity about a rival candidate. The two newspapers thus decided to reveal Cohen's name, a move that cost Cohen his job when his employer read his name and then fired him.

Upholding Cohen's right to sue the papers for their breached confidentiality promise under a legal theory called promissory estoppel, the majority held that "the First Amendment does not confer on the press a constitutional right to disregard promises that would otherwise be enforced under state law." The majority found the case was controlled by a "well-established line of decisions holding that generally applicable laws do not offend the First Amendment simply because their enforcement against the press has incidental effects on its ability to gather and report the news." This language is important for journalists to remember when gathering news: They cannot break general laws and then try to claim a First Amendment exemption from them. Recall this same maxim from the discussion in Chapter 9 of the Lawrence Matthews case involving child pornography.

Promissory estoppel is an old legal rule that was promulgated to prevent injustice when someone fails to keep a promise that he or she has made, a promise that by itself does not add up to an enforceable contract, but a promise someone else has relied on. To prevail in an action for promissory estoppel the plaintiff is usually required to show

1. *that the defendant made a clear and definite promise to the plaintiff;*
2. *that the defendant intended to induce the plaintiff's reliance on that promise;*
3. *that the plaintiff, in fact, reasonably relied on that promise to his or her detriment and harm; and*
4. *that the promise must be enforced by the court in the interests of justice to the plaintiff.*

Imagine a journalist tries to convince a lab technician at a chemical company to reveal specific information that proves that her employer is polluting a nearby stream. She is reluctant; she fears she will be fired if her cooperation with the reporter is discovered. But the reporter presses her and clearly promises that he will never, under any circumstance, reveal her name if she gives him the information. The story is published. The employee is subsequently fired after the reporter provides her name to a state legislative committee investigating the pollution. She then could bring an action for promissory estoppel. The bottom line is that if you break a promise of confidentiality to a source and the source is harmed by that breach, then you cannot rely on the First Amendment to protect you.

> **TIPS FOR REPORTERS WHEN CONFRONTED WITH A SOURCE WHO DEMANDS CONFIDENTIALITY**
>
> 1. Assume the interview is on the record unless the subject seeks anonymity.
> 2. Realize that there is no obligation to grant anonymity for information that has already been provided.
> 3. Before making any promise to a source, try to find something out about the information and where it comes from.
> 4. Talk with an editor or news director before making any promises to a source.
> 5. Keep any promise made to a source simple and easy to fulfill, and be certain both you and the source completely understand the conditions to which you have agreed.
> 6. Record any promise you make to a source.
> 7. Avoid adding material to a story that a source has already approved, or try to avoid promising the source that he or she has story approval.

CONSTITUTIONAL PROTECTION OF NEWS SOURCES

In 1972 the Supreme Court of the United States ruled, in a 5-4 decision, that there was no privilege under the First Amendment for journalists to refuse to reveal the names of confidential sources or other information when called to testify before a grand jury.[6] This ruling of more than 45 years ago in a case called *Branzburg* v. *Hayes* is the last word the nation's high court has spoken on the subject. In 2013, the 4th U.S. Circuit Court of Appeals observed in *United States* v. *Sterling* that "the *Branzburg* Court declined to treat reporters differently from all other citizens who are compelled to give evidence of criminal activity."[7] *Sterling* was a criminal espionage case involving the federal government's subpoenaing of *New York Times* reporter James Risen. The government wanted Risen to testify in the prosecution of former CIA agent Jeffrey Sterling, who allegedly leaked classified information to Risen. The 4th Circuit denied Risen, a two-time Pulitzer Prize winner, a qualified First Amendment reporter's privilege that would have shielded him from being compelled to testify in the case against Sterling. In addition to rejecting the existence of a First Amendment reporter's privilege not to testify, the 4th Circuit also refused to create or recognize a federal common-law reporter's privilege protecting confidential sources. In 2014, the U.S. Supreme Court chose not to hear Risen's appeal of the 4th Circuit's ruling, thus passing on a prime opportunity to revisit *Branzburg*.

At the same time, however, most federal courts have limited the *Branzburg* ruling to apply only to grand jury settings, and they have created, either under First Amendment

---

6. *Branzburg* v. *Hayes*, 408 U.S. 665 (1972).
7. *United States* v. *Sterling*, 724 F. 3d 482 (4th Cir. 2014), *cert. denied*, 134 S. Ct. 2696 (2014). Ultimately, the federal government in 2015 decided not to call Risen to testify.

or common-law principles, qualified (limited) protection for journalists not to testify in other, non-grand-jury settings. The following describes how it got to this point, starting with the *Branzburg* case and ruling.

The Supreme Court consolidated three similar cases in *Branzburg* to consider whether the First Amendment privileged journalists not to testify before grand juries about confidential information. One case involved Paul Branzburg, a reporter for the Louisville *Courier-Journal*. Branzburg was called to testify in 1971 about drug use in Kentucky after he wrote two stories about drugs and drug dealers in the area. In the second case, Paul Pappas, a television reporter for a Massachusetts television station, was called before a grand jury to relate what he had seen and heard when he spent three hours at a Black Panther headquarters in July 1970. Finally, *New York Times* reporter Earl Caldwell was subpoenaed to appear before a grand jury investigating the activities of the Black Panthers in Oakland, Calif. Caldwell, a black man, had gained the confidence of the leaders of the militant group and had consistently written illuminating stories about the Panthers that demonstrated an astute awareness of their activities. The decisions in the three cases are referred to collectively as the *Branzburg* ruling.

The Supreme Court fractured into three groups. Four justices, led by Byron White, who wrote the court's opinion, ruled that there was no First Amendment privilege for reporters called to testify before a grand jury. White said that although the court was sensitive to First Amendment considerations, the case did not present any such considerations. There were no prior restraints, no limitations on what the press might publish, and no order for the press to publish information it did not wish to. No penalty for publishing certain content was imposed. White wrote:

> The use of confidential sources by the press is not forbidden or restricted. . . .
>
> The sole issue before us is the obligation of reporters to respond to grand jury subpoenas as other citizens do and answer questions relevant to an investigation into the commission of crime. Citizens generally are not constitutionally immune from grand jury subpoenas; and neither the First Amendment nor other constitutional provisions protect the average citizen from the disclosing to a grand jury information that he has received in confidence.[8]

Reporters are no better than average citizens, White concluded.

The four dissenters differed sharply with the other justices. Justice William O. Douglas took the view that the First Amendment provides the press with an absolute and unqualified privilege. In any circumstance, under any condition, the reporter should be able to shield the identity of a confidential source. Justices Potter Stewart, William Brennan and Thurgood Marshall were unwilling to go as far as Douglas and instead proposed that reporters should be protected by a privilege that is qualified, not absolute. These three dissenters argued that the reporter should be able to protect the identity of the confidential source unless the government can show the following:

1. That there is a probable cause to believe that the reporter has information that is clearly relevant to a specific violation of the law

8. *Branzburg* v. *Hayes*, 408 U.S. 665 (1972).

2. That the information sought cannot be obtained by alternative means less destructive of First Amendment rights

3. That the state has a compelling and overriding interest in the information

When the government cannot fulfill all three requirements, Justice Stewart wrote for the dissenters, the journalist should not be forced to testify.

Justice Lewis Powell provided the fifth vote needed for the court to reject the notion of a constitutional privilege for reporters. But whereas Powell voted with those who could find no privilege in the First Amendment, his brief concurring opinion seemed to support the opposite proposition. "The Court does not hold that newsmen, subpoenaed to testify before a grand jury, are without constitutional rights with respect to the gathering of news or in safeguarding their sources," he wrote. No harassment of reporters will be allowed, and a balance must be struck between freedom of the press and the obligation of all citizens to give relevant testimony. "In short, the courts will be available to newsmen under circumstances where legitimate First Amendment interests require protection," Powell wrote. Two years later, in a footnote in another case, *Saxbe* v. *Washington Post,*[9] Powell emphasized that the high court's ruling in *Branzburg* was an extremely narrow one and that reporters were not without First Amendment rights to protect the identity of their sources.

LOWER-COURT RULINGS

Most lower federal courts have treated the high court's decision in *Branzburg* as the very narrow ruling that Justice Powell said it was in 1974. The *Branzburg* ruling focused on a reporter's responsibility to testify before a grand jury. And that is generally how the lower courts have applied the precedent, granting reporters a qualified right to refuse testimony in other kinds of circumstances. Note the language from the 3rd U.S. Circuit Court of Appeals in a 1979 ruling, which characterized *Branzburg* in this fashion:

Most lower federal courts have treated the high court's decision in Branzburg as the very narrow ruling that Justice Powell said it was in 1974.

> There (in *Branzburg*), the Supreme Court decided that a journalist does not have an absolute privilege under the First Amendment to refuse to appear and testify before a grand jury to answer questions relevant to an investigation of the commission of a crime. No Supreme Court case since that decision has extended the holding beyond that which was necessary to vindicate the public interest in law enforcement and ensuing effective grand jury proceedings.[10]

Not all the U.S. Courts of Appeals have looked at *Branzburg* in such an expansive manner. In 1998 a panel of judges in the 5th Circuit wrote:

> Although some courts have taken from Justice Powell's concurrence a mandate to construct a broad, qualified news reporters' privilege in criminal cases, we decline to do so. Justice Powell's separate writing only emphasizes that at a certain point, the First Amendment must protect the press from government intrusion.[11]

The court went on to require a television station to surrender the unaired portions of a videotape interview with a man accused of arson.

9. 417 U.S. 843 (1974).
10. *Riley* v. *Chester,* 612 F. 2d 708 (1979).
11. *U.S.* v. *Smith,* 135 F. 2d 363 (1998); see also *WTHR-TV* v. *Cline,* 693 N.E. 2d 1 (1998).

Similarly, the 4th Circuit in 2013 rejected an expansive reading of *Branzburg* in the *Sterling* case involving James Risen discussed earlier in this unit. The 4th Circuit wrote that "Justice Powell's concurrence in *Branzburg* simply does not allow for the recognition of a First Amendment reporter's privilege in a criminal proceeding which can only be overcome if the government satisfies the heavy burdens of the three-part, compelling-interest test." The three-part test referred to here is the same one described earlier that was articulated by the three dissenters in *Branzburg* (see pages 396–397).

Ten of 12 of the federal appellate courts have ruled that the First Amendment provides at least limited or qualified protection for reporters who are asked to testify or produce photos or other materials at hearings other than grand jury proceedings.* The 6th U.S. Circuit Court of Appeals (Kentucky, Michigan, Ohio and Tennessee) rejected this notion in 1987. "Because we conclude that acceptance of the position . . . would be tantamount to our substituting, as a holding in *Branzburg,* the dissent written by Justice Stewart, we must reject that position. . . . That portion of Justice Powell's opinion certainly does not warrant rewriting the majority opinion to grant a First Amendment testimonial privilege to news reporters," the court ruled.[12]

The 6th Circuit's refusal to recognize a qualified First Amendment privilege for reporters proved pivotal more than two decades later in 2008. That's when a federal judge in Michigan ordered David Ashenfelter, a Pulitzer Prize-winning reporter for the *Detroit Free Press,* to reveal the identity of anonymous Justice Department officials he used as sources for a negative story four years earlier about Richard Convertino, then an assistant U.S. attorney. Convertino later filed a civil lawsuit against the Justice Department for allegedly violating the federal Privacy Act (see Chapter 9) by leaking confidential and harmful information about him from his personnel file. To determine the identity of the unnamed leakers within the Justice Department, Convertino subpoenaed Ashenfelter, who refused to reveal his sources. In ruling against Ashenfelter in August 2008, Judge Robert Cleland wrote that "the Sixth Circuit has explicitly declined to recognize a qualified First Amendment privilege for reporters," and he pointed out the need for disclosure, writing that "Convertino cannot sustain his burden of proof on the Privacy Act claim without identifying Ashenfelter's source."[13] In October that year, Ashenfelter failed to show up at a deposition where he would have been questioned about his sources—a brazen move that typically triggers contempt proceedings. Ashenfelter then tried a new and somewhat novel tactic to keep silent at a December 2008 deposition: He repeatedly invoked his right against self-incrimination protected by the Fifth Amendment to the U.S. Constitution (that right might be relevant to the extent that Convertino had suggested that Ashenfelter conspired with, protected and abetted the Justice Department

---

* The 5th U.S. Circuit Court of Appeals is included among the 10 because, despite the 1998 ruling in *U.S.* v. *Smith,* judges in the circuit have ruled that a privilege exists at least for civil suits. (See, for example, *Miller* v. *Transamerican Press, Inc.,* 621 F. 2d 721 (1980).) The 1998 decision did not reject these earlier rulings, but argued that because a criminal case was at issue, a different standard should apply.

12. *Storer Communications* v. *Giovan,* 810 F. 2d 580 (1987).

13. *Convertino* v. *U.S. Department of Justice,* 2008 WL 4104347 (E.D. Mich. Aug. 28, 2008). See also *Convertino* v. *U.S. Department of Justice,* 2008 WL 4998369 (E.D. Mich. Nov. 21, 2008); *Convertino* v. *U.S. Department of Justice,* Order and Order Denying Non-Party Respondent's Emergency Order, Case No. 07-CV-13842 (E.D. Mich. Mar. 31, 2009).

leakers by refusing to reveal their identities when they broke federal laws by revealing the investigation of Convertino).

In February 2009 Ashenfelter was ordered to reappear for a deposition and to either answer Convertino's questions about the Justice Department sources or to provide evidence of the specific criminal charge underlying his Fifth Amendment objection. The battle continued until the April 2009 deposition, during which Judge Cleland ruled in favor of Ashenfelter when he asserted his Fifth Amendment right against self-incrimination after Convertino's attorney asked Ashenfelter to reveal the names of his sources. That ruling, which kept Ashenfelter from going to jail, was hailed by many observers as a victory for freedom of the press, even though it rested on the Fifth Amendment and not the First Amendment.

In July 2015, the 6th Circuit affirmed Judge Cleland's ruling in *Convertino* v. *United States Department of Justice*.[14] The court said the test for a valid invocation of the Fifth Amendment, articulated by the Supreme Court in *Hoffman* v. *United States*, is "whether the witness has reasonable cause to apprehend danger from a direct answer." And the test, the 6th Circuit ruled, "turns not on the probability or likelihood of prosecution, but rather on the possibility of prosecution." The court said that here prosecution was possible for Ashenfelter. Convertino's suit against the Department of Justice "alleges facts that if proven could implicate Ashenfelter in the commission of one or more crimes, including the allegation that federal officials illegally provided Ashenfelter with two confidential . . . documents." Even if it was unlikely that Ashenfelter *would* be prosecuted if he revealed his sources, the fact that prosecution was at least *possible* meant that his invocation of the Fifth Amendment was valid, the 6th Circuit thus concluded. "After 11 years of worry, stress and sleepless nights, I'm relieved that this legal nightmare may finally be over—at least for me," Ashenfelter said in a statement after the 6th Circuit's ruling. The *Convertino* decision seems to give journalists another weapon in their battle to keep a source's identity confidential. "In circumstances where reporters receive written government reports, the Fifth Amendment is available," said Richard Zuckerman, Ashenfelter's lawyer, in the *Detroit Free Press*.

The other federal appellate court to rule that the First Amendment does not provide protection for reporters who are asked to testify or produce photos or other materials at hearings other than grand jury proceedings was the 7th U.S. Circuit Court of Appeals. Guided by Judge Richard Posner, the 7th Circuit in *McKevitt* v. *Pallasch*[15] refused to recognize a reporter's privilege and, instead, held that "courts should simply make sure that a subpoena . . . directed to the media . . . is reasonable in the circumstances, which is the general criterion for judicial review of subpoenas." While the ultimate impact of this decision is yet unclear, one thing definitely is certain: It represents a substantial rethinking of the *Branzburg* decision by an extremely well-respected jurist. As of August 2017, 39 states had enacted a statutory protection called a **shield law** that offers reporters some (although not usually absolute) protection against being forced to reveal the identity of confidential sources. Figure 10.1 shown later in this chapter shows a map indicating which states have shield laws. Appellate courts in all of the remaining

---

14. 795 F.3d 587 (6th Cir. 2015).
15. 339 F. 3d 530 (7th Cir. 2003).

The constitutional privilege has considerable elasticity.

11 states, except for Wyoming, have recognized various kinds of constitutional and/or common-law testimonial privileges for reporters.

The constitutional privilege has considerable elasticity. Its successful application depends on several factors. What kind of proceeding is involved? The privilege is more readily granted to a journalist involved in a civil suit than to one called to testify before a grand jury. What kind of material is sought? A journalist is more likely to be protected by the privilege when the name of a confidential source is sought than when courts are seeking testimony about information that is not confidential or about events actually witnessed by the reporter. Finally, testimonial privilege derived by both federal and state courts through the Constitution or the common law is qualified by the various tests that courts have developed, tests that usually mirror the one outlined by Justice Stewart in *Branzburg.* Is the information important? Is it clearly relevant to the proceedings? Is there somewhere else to get the information? It is important to remember that without a binding Supreme Court ruling, the lower federal and state courts have been permitted to fashion their own rules; and there is distinct variance from state to state, federal circuit to federal circuit. Look to the court precedents in your region as the final authority in this matter.

Civil Cases

Courts are most likely to recognize the right of a journalist to refuse to testify in a civil action.

A reporter could be called to testify in three different kinds of court proceedings: a civil lawsuit, a criminal case or a grand jury. Courts are most likely to recognize the right of a journalist to refuse to testify in a civil action, and least likely to recognize this right if the reporter is called before a grand jury. Recognition of the privilege in civil cases came only a year after the *Branzburg* ruling, when a U.S. District Court in Washington, D.C., quashed a subpoena issued to reporters from a variety of newspapers and magazines who were thought to have materials obtained during their coverage of the Watergate break-in. The materials were sought by members of the Democratic National Committee who were suing to win damages from some of the Watergate burglars.[16] The court said that reporters had at least a qualified privilege under the First Amendment to refuse to answer such questions or provide such material. Four years later the 10th U.S. Circuit Court of Appeals ruled that filmmaker Arthur Hirsch could not be forced to reveal confidential information he had obtained in connection with a civil suit by the estate of Karen Silkwood against the Kerr-McGee Corporation.[17] Silkwood died mysteriously in an auto accident after she threatened to expose improper safety conditions at the nuclear facility at which she worked. Hirsch was preparing a documentary film on Karen Silkwood's life and death.

In a typical civil suit, the court will ask three questions.

In a typical civil suit, the court will ask three questions when deciding whether to force the reporter to testify:

1. Has the person seeking the information from the reporter—normally the plaintiff—shown that this information is of *certain relevance* in the case? It must be related to the matter before the court.

2. Does this information go to the heart of the issue before the court? That is, is it critical to the outcome of the case?

16. *Democratic National Committee* v. *McCord,* 356 F. Supp. 1394 (1973).
17. *Silkwood* v. *Kerr-McGee,* 563 F. 2d 433 (1977).

3. Can the person who wants the information show the court that there is no other alternative source for this information?

If all three questions are answered yes, the chances are good that the court will require the reporter to reveal the confidential information. How rigorously the judge applies this test often depends on the reporter's relationship to the lawsuit. If the reporter is not a party to the lawsuit but merely has information that may be of value to one or both parties, a judge typically applies the test very rigorously and normally the journalist will not be required to testify. But that is not always the case. In 1996 a federal judge in Connecticut ruled that a reporter had to testify in a securities case as to whether one of the defendants had actually made the statements that were attributed to him in a newspaper article written by the reporter.[18] The judge ruled that the testimony sought was directly relevant to the case and was unavailable from another source. The court also noted that it was not seeking information about a confidential source. If the reporter is a party in the lawsuit, either as a plaintiff or a defendant, courts are less willing to let the journalist off the hook. In these instances it is more likely, but still not common, for the court to require the reporter to cooperate.

In 2007, in Dr. Steven Hatfill's civil lawsuit against the federal government for leaking to journalists his name as the possible perpetrator who mailed anthrax-laced letters in 2001, a federal judge ordered six nonparty journalists to reveal the names of their confidential FBI and Justice Department sources that leaked Hatfill's name.[19] Although recognizing that the journalists had a qualified First Amendment–based privilege not to testify, U.S. District Court Judge Reggie B. Walton reasoned that the privilege had been overcome by Hatfill because "the actual identity of the sources will be important and quite possibly essential" to his lawsuit and because Hatfill "has exhausted all reasonable alternatives for acquiring the sources of the leaked information."

Although three of the journalists caught a break when their sources voluntarily released them from their promises of confidentiality, the Hatfill saga continued in 2008 when former *USA Today* reporter Toni Locy, as described later in this chapter, was held in contempt of court by Judge Walton and ordered to personally pay up to $5,000 a day until she revealed to Hatfill the name of her source.[20] Judge Walton prohibited Locy from accepting reimbursement from *USA Today* to satisfy the monetary sanction, although an appellate court quickly stayed the fines until it could hear the matter in full, and it later dismissed the matter as moot after Hatfill settled his case with the government for more than $5 million.[21]

Reporters far more commonly find themselves as defendants in lawsuits, typically a libel suit. Oftentimes the plaintiff seeks to know about sources the reporter used to prepare the libelous story, or where and how the reporter got information for the libelous story. Whether the court will force the reporter to testify in such instances usually depends on several factors, all of which are related to the three-part test outlined earlier. A plaintiff will often be required to show that the information held by the reporter goes

---

18. *SEC v. Seahawk Deep Ocean Technology, Inc.,* 166 F.R.D. 268 (1996).
19. *Hatfill v. Gonzales,* 505 F. Supp. 2d 33 (D.D.C. 2007).
20. *Hatfill v. Mukasey,* 539 F. Supp. 2d 96 (D.D.C. 2008).
21. *Hatfill v. Mukasey,* Order No. 08-5049 (D.C. Cir. Nov. 17, 2008).

to the very heart of the lawsuit. For example, the plaintiff may have to show that he or she cannot possibly prove negligence or actual malice (see Chapter 5 to refresh your memory on these matters) without information from the reporter.[22] Or, the court will require that the plaintiff show that the libel claim actually has merit, that it is not simply an attempt to harass the defendant.[23] Finally, the court will usually require the plaintiff to show that there is no other source for this information, that the plaintiff has exhausted all other potential means of gaining this information. In 1979 the U.S. Supreme Court ruled that it was not an infringement of the reporters' First Amendment rights for the defendant to ask reporters what they were thinking about as they prepared the libelous story.[24] Such questions may or may not involve confidential sources.

The reporter who refuses to obey a court order and give the plaintiff critical information in a libel suit surely faces a **contempt of court** charge and potentially a fine and a jail sentence. But that is not all. In a few cases when a reporter has refused to reveal his or her source for a libelous story, the court has ruled as a matter of law that no source for the story exists.[25] This declaration effectively strips away the libel defense for a newspaper or broadcasting station. In effect, the judge is saying that the reporter made up the story. This is not a common occurrence, but it certainly is a frightening one.

For instance, in the case of *Ayash* v. *Dana-Farber Cancer Institute*[26] the Supreme Judicial Court of Massachusetts in 2005 affirmed a default judgment against *The Boston Globe* in a libel suit because the newspaper failed to disclose confidential sources. In this lawsuit Dr. Lois J. Ayash of the Dana-Farber Cancer Institute alleged that *The Globe* published a series of scathing and inaccurate articles in 1995 written by reporter Richard A. Knox about Ayash's treatment of several patients who allegedly were given overdoses of a highly toxic chemotherapy drug, thereby destroying the doctor's reputation. One article even ran under the blunt (and, if false, defamatory) headline "Doctor's Orders Killed Cancer Patient" (remember from Chapter 4 and the description from the case involving Kato Kaelin that, if false, headlines can form the basis for a libel suit). During the discovery stage of the litigation, Ayash sought the identities of sources consulted by Knox before writing articles that were subsequently published in *The Globe* and that formed, at least in part, the basis of the doctor's lawsuit. At the trial court level, *The Globe* had refused to provide information that would lead to the identities of Knox's confidential sources, despite a court order to disclose their identities. Massachusetts is one of 11 states that does not have a shield law giving some protection to reporters against disclosure of confidential information (see later in this chapter). A judgment of civil contempt was entered by the trial court judge against *The Globe* and Knox and, in turn, the judge awarded a pretrial judgment against them. A jury was allowed to determine damages and it meted out a whopping $2.1 million award to Ayash.

In affirming both the default judgment and the damage award, the Massachusetts high court noted that "the Globe defendants had no special constitutional or statutory

---

22. *Cervantes* v. *Time,* 446 F. 2d 986 (1972).
23. *Senear* v. *Daily Journal-American,* 641 P. 2d 1180 (1982).
24. *Herbert* v. *Lando,* 441 U.S. 153 (1979).
25. See *Downing* v. *Monitor Publishing,* 415 A. 2d 683 (1980); and *Sierra Life* v. *Magic Valley Newspapers,* 623 P. 2d 103 (1980).
26. 822 N.E. 2d 667; 33 M.L.R. 1513 (Mass. 2005).

testimonial privilege, based on their status as a newspaper publisher or reporter, that would justify their refusal to obey the orders." It agreed with the trial court judge's determination that "the plaintiff's need for the requested information outweighed the public interest in the protection of the free flow of information to the press." The Massachusetts high court's decision affirming the award sparked renewed discussion in that state's legislature about the need to join the majority of states and adopt a shield law to protect reporters such as Richard Knox from making the uncomfortable choice between either breaching promises of confidentiality to their sources or facing entry of default judgments with potentially devastating jury awards.

Finally, the 9th U.S. Circuit Court of Appeals handed down an important ruling in 1993 when it extended the reporter's privilege in a civil suit to the authors of books as well. Typically the privilege has been granted to so-called working journalists, salaried employees of newspapers, magazines and broadcasting stations. Freelance writers like book authors were often denied the protection. The court ruled that a book author clearly had a right to invoke the First Amendment privilege.[27] "The journalist's privilege is designed to protect investigative reporting regardless of the medium used to report the news to the public," Judge William Norris wrote.

Criminal Cases

Courts have granted the First Amendment privilege to reporters quite freely in civil actions in part, at least, because there is no competing constitutional right involved. In a criminal case, however, the privilege for the reporter must be balanced against the Sixth Amendment right of the defendant to compel testimony on his or her behalf. Consequently, it is somewhat less likely that a court will permit a reporter to refuse to answer questions about the identity of a confidential source or other confidential information. Courts most often apply slight variations of the Stewart test from the *Branzburg* case (see earlier in this chapter) to determine whether the journalist will be compelled to testify.

In a criminal case, the privilege for the reporter must be balanced against the Sixth Amendment right of the defendant to compel testimony on his or her behalf.

In *U.S. v. Burke,* for example, the defendant was indicted for conspiracy in connection with a basketball point-shaving scheme at Boston College and attempted to impeach the testimony of the prosecution's chief witness, a reputed underworld figure. The defendant asked the court to subpoena the unpublished notes and drafts of *Sports Illustrated* reporter Douglas Looney, who had interviewed the witness. The U.S. Court of Appeals for the 2nd Circuit quashed the subpoena, noting that a court may order reporters to reveal confidential sources only when the information is (1) highly material and relevant, (2) necessary or critical to the defense and (3) unobtainable from other sources.[28]

In 1984 the Washington state Supreme Court ruled that an Everett (Wash.) *Herald* reporter did not have to reveal the names of several confidential sources he had used to prepare an article about alleged cult activities at an 80-acre farm near rural Snohomish, Wash. The owner of the farm, Theodore Rinaldo, had been convicted of statutory rape, assault, coercion and intimidating a witness. A year after his conviction, several persons who had testified on Rinaldo's behalf at his trial stepped forward and admitted they had committed perjury. It was during his second trial for tampering with witnesses and other offenses that

27. *Shoen* v. *Shoen,* 5 F. 3d 1289 (1993).
28. *U.S.* v. *Burke,* 700 F. 2d 70 (1983).

403

Rinaldo tried to force reporter Gary Larson to reveal the names of persons who gave the reporter information for six articles that had brought the activities at the farm to the attention of local authorities. Justice James Dolliver, speaking for the court, ruled that Rinaldo would have to show that the information was necessary or critical to his defense and that he had made a reasonable effort to get the material by other means. He could not make such a showing, and the subpoena was quashed.[29]

More recently, the First Amendment privilege came into play in a high-profile criminal case involving John Phillip Walker Lindh, the so-called American Taliban who was indicted in February 2002 after he allegedly joined certain terrorist organizations in Afghanistan to fight against American forces. Robert Young Pelton, a freelance journalist who was covering the military conflict in Afghanistan on behalf of CNN, had interviewed Lindh after Lindh was captured by U.S. troops in November 2001. Attorneys for Lindh subpoenaed Pelton to testify about the interview at a hearing on various motions they had filed to suppress evidence in the case against their client. Pelton moved to quash the subpoena on the ground that he had a First Amendment privilege against disclosure of information obtained during the news-gathering process in Afghanistan. In July 2002, however, Pelton's motion to quash was denied by a federal district court judge in Alexandria, Va.[30] The judge held that the First Amendment privilege grounded in Justice Powell's concurrence in *Branzburg* applies only "where the journalist produces some evidence of confidentiality or governmental harassment." Pelton conceded that there was no confidentiality of sources involved—Lindh was the source—and thus the judge held that "he cannot invoke any First Amendment privilege on the basis of confidentiality of sources or government harassment." Pelton, however, raised another argument that was also rejected by the court—"that the special circumstance of his role as a war correspondent in Afghanistan is a sufficient factor to trigger application of the privilege." The judge called this a "novel claim," found absolutely no case law precedent to support it and thus denied Pelton's motion to quash the subpoena. Ultimately, Lindh pleaded guilty just three days after the judge's decision to two charges of aiding the Taliban and carrying explosives and therefore Pelton never was forced to testify.

Grand Jury Proceedings

Although the qualified privilege for reporters to refuse to reveal the identities of confidential sources in civil and criminal actions has been recognized by most lower federal courts and state supreme courts that have considered the question, these same courts have routinely refused to extend the First Amendment privilege to grand jury proceedings. This refusal is true even though the grand jury's power to force disclosure is not constitutionally guaranteed, as is the criminal defendant's right to compel a witness to testify. The obvious explanation for this reluctance on the part of judges is that the single U.S. Supreme Court precedent on the question focused on grand jury testimony and in that case, *Branzburg* v. *Hayes*,[31] the high court ruled that no privilege existed.

For example, in 2001, the 5th U.S. Circuit Court of Appeals rejected an appeal from a freelance writer named Vanessa Leggett who refused to turn over research materials to

---

29. *State* v. *Rinaldo*, 684 P. 2d 608 (1984).
30. *U.S.* v. *Lindh*, 210 F. Supp. 2d 780 (E.D. Va. 2002).
31. 408 U.S. 665 (1972).

a federal grand jury in Houston. Leggett was trying to write a book about a 1997 murder that was being investigated by the Justice Department. Texas then had no shield law to protect reporters although it now does (see later in this chapter), but there was considerable doubt Leggett would have qualified for protection under the law in any case since she was a freelancer, not a staff reporter for a publication. The appellate court rejected her effort to invoke the constitutional privilege. The court said while the privilege under the First Amendment may protect a journalist's confidential sources in civil cases, its applicability is diminished in criminal cases and it reaches its nadir or lowest point in grand jury proceedings. "The public's interest in law enforcement proceedings always outweighs the media interests," the court ruled.[32] The Supreme Court declined in 2002 to hear Leggett's case.

What happens when the individual requesting the information is a special prosecutor rather than a grand jury? The 1st U.S. Circuit Court of Appeals squarely addressed this question in 2004 when it handed down its decision in *In re Special Proceedings*.[33] The appellate court, in a blow to journalists, held that "*Branzburg* governs in this case even though we are dealing with a special prosecutor rather than a grand jury," adding that "the considerations bearing on privilege are the same in both cases." The court thus refused to extend a reporter's privilege when confidential information is requested by a special prosecutor.

The case transpired in the context of an FBI investigation, called "Operation Plunder Dome," into governmental corruption in Providence, R.I. The investigation was successful, as it sent several city officials, including former Mayor Vincent "Buddy" Cianci, to prison. The First Amendment dispute involved efforts to obtain the name of a source that leaked to James Taricani, a veteran television reporter covering "Operation Plunder Dome," a copy of a secret surveillance videotape of an FBI informant handing an envelope that allegedly contained a $1,000 cash bribe to a Providence city official named Frank E. Corrente. Corrente was later convicted of bribery.

Taricani's station, the Providence NBC-affiliate WJAR-TV, aired a portion of the secret tape, and a federal judge appointed a special prosecutor to determine who leaked it to Taricani. When Taricani refused to give up his confidential source, he was hit by the judge with civil contempt and a $1,000-a-day fine. In holding that the opinion in *Branzburg*, which rejected a testimonial privilege in grand jury proceedings, also controlled cases involving special prosecutors, the 1st U.S. Circuit Court of Appeals affirmed the district court judge's civil contempt finding against Taricani. It wrote that "there is no doubt that the request to Taricani was for information highly relevant to a good faith criminal investigation" and that "reasonable efforts were made to obtain the information elsewhere." Importantly, the appellate court cited somewhat favorably Judge Posner's 2003 opinion in the *McKevitt* case (see earlier in this chapter) that was skeptical of the *Branzburg* opinion offering any protection to journalists beyond what ordinary relevance and reasonableness requirements would demand.

With the appellate court decision going against Taricani, the district court began assessing the $1,000-a-day fine against the reporter in August 2004. By early November

32. *In re Grand Jury Subpoenas,* 29 M.L.R. 2301 (2001).
33. 373 F. 3d 37 (1st Cir. 2004).

Investigative broadcast journalist Jim Taricani was sentenced to six months of home confinement in late 2004 for refusing to divulge the identity of a confidential source.

©AP Photo/Victoria Arocho

of 2004, Taricani still had not revealed his source and, in the process, he had racked up (and paid) fines of about $85,000. Recognizing the civil fine was not forcing Taricani to give up his confidential source, U.S. District Court Judge Ernest Torres then ordered Taricani tried for criminal contempt unless the reporter gave up his source. In taking this step, the judge suspended the $1,000 fine because the case was now about *criminal* contempt, not a *civil* penalty. Judge Torres soon found Taricani guilty of criminal contempt, prompting the Emmy Award-winning journalist to proclaim, "When I became a reporter 30 years ago, I never imagined that I would be put on trial and face the prospect of going to jail simply for doing my job."[34]

In December 2004, shortly before Taricani was to be sentenced for his criminal contempt conviction, an attorney named Joseph Bevilacqua Jr. came forward and admitted under oath that he was Taricani's source for the videotape. Bevilacqua had represented one of the city officials, Joseph Pannone, convicted in the corruption scandal in Providence that Taricani was investigating. Bevilacqua's admission, however, did not negate the criminal contempt conviction of journalist Taricani. On December 9, 2004, the 55-year-old Taricani was sentenced to six months of home confinement. Judge Torres chose home confinement rather than prison because of health concerns about Taricani. The judge stated from the bench, "Except for his health and history of a good record, all of the factors call for a meaningful prison sentence."[35] During his confinement, Tariacani could leave his home only for medical treatments.

Taricani ultimately was released from home confinement in April 2005 upon recommendation from his probation officer, about two months earlier than originally

34. Belluck, "Reporter Is Found Guilty."
35. Belluck, "Reporter Who Shielded Source."

scheduled. Despite the early release, the case of Jim Taricani represents a very low mark in recent years in terms of the legal protection that journalists have—or don't have—in protecting their sources. Had it not been for his fragile health, Taricani would have landed in jail for protecting his source rather than getting home confinement.

NONCONFIDENTIAL INFORMATION AND WAIVER OF THE PRIVILEGE

While U.S. courts have been willing to permit journalists to protect confidential sources and confidential information, most have been far more reluctant to protect reporters when nonconfidential information is at issue. And most subpoenas issued today to journalists are to gain access to nonconfidential information.

Typical is a ruling by the 5th U.S. Circuit Court of Appeals that said that reporters do not enjoy any privilege, qualified or otherwise, not to disclose nonconfidential information in a criminal case.[36] This ruling seems to be in line with previous court rulings. A U.S. District Court ruled in 1990 that a journalist who witnessed a beating of a criminal suspect by police had to testify on behalf of the injured party. "This court knows of no authority to support the proposition that such personal observations are privileged simply because the eyewitness is a journalist," the judge ruled.[37]

Photographers have been forced to surrender photos they have taken of building fires,[38] industrial accidents,[39] fatal auto accidents[40] or even of an individual who has filed a personal injury lawsuit against an insurance company.[41] The press has generally been unable to convince judges that it has an important interest at stake when it refuses to cooperate with those who seek nonconfidential information.

This sentiment certainly was true in 2006 when the 9th U.S. Circuit Court of Appeals denied First Amendment protection for Joshua Wolf, who videotaped a protest demonstration and refused to turn over the tape to government authorities. The appellate court wrote that "[t]he taped activities occurred entirely in public and did not occur in response to Wolf's prompting, whether by questions or recording. He simply videotaped what people did in a public place. Wolf does not claim that he filmed anything confidential nor that he promised anyone anonymity or confidentiality. Therefore, this case does not raise the usual concerns in cases involving journalists."[42]

Even when federal courts have recognized a qualified privilege to protect nonconfidential information, the scope of the privilege has been very limited. For instance, the 2nd U.S. Circuit Court of Appeals, which includes New York, Connecticut and Vermont, in 1998 "recognized a qualified privilege for nonconfidential press information," but noted that "where nonconfidential information is at stake, the showing needed

36. *U.S.* v. *Smith,* 135 F. 3d 963 (1998).
37. *Dillon* v. *San Francisco,* 748 F. Supp. 722 (1990).
38. *Marketos* v. *American Employers Insurance Co.,* 460 N.W. 2d 272 (1990).
39. *Stickels* v. *General Rental Co., Inc.,* 750 F. Supp. 729 (1990).
40. *Idaho* v. *Salsbury,* 924 P. 2d 208 (1996).
41. *Weathers* v. *American Family Mutual Insurance Co.,* 17 M.L.R. 1534 (1990).
42. *In re Grand Jury Subpoena: Joshua Wolf,* 35 M.L.R. 1207 (9th Cir. 2006).

to overcome the journalists' privilege is less demanding than for material acquired in confidence."[43]

Reporters must worry about another aspect of the privilege, the problem that through some action they may actually waive their right to refuse to testify. A case in Washington, D.C., focuses on this dilemma. Six police officers brought a $9 million lawsuit against the city and top police officials. They were disciplined by the police department after a botched 1986 drug operation that failed to net the hundreds of arrests expected. In the wake of the failed raid, *Washington Post* reporter Linda Wheeler revealed in a newspaper story that the *Post* had obtained secret plans for the raid. The six officers who were disciplined argued that leaks from high-level police officials, not from them, caused the raid to fail. And they subpoenaed Wheeler to find out where she got the plans for the operation.

The reporter refused to identify her source and was found in contempt of court. The court said that any privilege a reporter might enjoy in such an instance was waived when, in 1986, she told her husband and another man, both officers in the U.S. Park Police, the name of her confidential source. "A reporter cannot choose in 1986 to disclose her source to others . . . and then choose in 1991—as a witness in a judicial proceeding—not to make this same disclosure," wrote Judge Richard A. Levie. The District of Columbia Court of Appeals upheld this ruling.[44]

Wheeler was excused from testifying in the summer of 1991 when a mistrial was declared in the lawsuit, but a retrial was scheduled. The reporter's husband, to whom she had revealed the identity of her source, was forced to testify before the hearing was adjourned. "This could become a very effective harassment technique," said Jane Kirtley, who was then executive director of the Reporters Committee for Freedom of the Press. She suggested that a judge or attorney might say, "Well, journalists, I recognize you're covered by a shield law or a reporter's privilege, but I'm just going to bring in your spouse, your kid, your parents, your dog, anybody who's around, and see what they know."

The question of waiving a reporter-source privilege also arises in the context of state statutory shield laws addressed later in this chapter. Two recent cases involving a discussion of the possible waiver of such statutory privileges for journalists are *Flores* v. *Cooper Tire and Rubber Co.*[45] and *McGarry* v. *University of San Diego.*[46]

There is really no bright line marking when and how a reporter may in fact waive the privilege. The law is too diffuse for such a generalization. But reporters who have promised confidentiality should keep the information completely confidential.

43. *Gonzales* v. *National Broadcasting Co., Inc.,* 186 F. 3d 102 (2d Cir. 1998). A few other federal appellate courts have recognized the existence of a qualified privilege to protect information in a reporter's possession that comes from a nonconfidential source. See *U.S.* v. *LaRouche Campaign,* 841 F. 2d 1176 (1st Cir. 1988); and *Mark* v. *Shoen,* 48 F. 3d 412 (9th Cir. 1995), which held that "where information sought is not confidential, a civil litigant is entitled to requested discovery notwithstanding a valid assertion of the journalist's privilege by a nonparty only upon a showing that the requested material is: (1) unavailable despite exhaustion of all reasonable alternative sources; (2) noncumulative; and (3) clearly relevant to an important issue in the case."
44. *Wheeler* v. *Goulart,* 18 M.L.R. 2296 (1990); and *Goulart* v. *Barry,* 18 M.L.R. 2056 (1991).
45. 178 P. 3d 1176 (Ariz. 2008) (involving Arizona's shield law).
46. 154 Cal. App. 4th 97 (Cal. 2007) (involving California's shield law).

WHO IS A JOURNALIST?

An emerging problem relating to the constitutionally based journalist's privilege is, Who is a journalist?[47] When the privilege was developed in the 1970s and 1980s the definition of a journalist was relatively clear: A journalist was someone who gathered news for a news medium. In the 21st century, with the growth of interactive computer communication, virtually anyone can report the news, or what he or she might refer to as the news. Is, for instance, a blogger a journalist? Should anyone who uses the Internet to spread information be regarded as a journalist for purposes of the law? This issue has not been resolved definitively, but some courts have attempted to solve the dilemma.

Mark Madden is an irrepressible professional-wrestling commentator who "broadcast" his commentary via 900-number telephone calls. His commentaries were usually sarcastic, sometimes fanciful and always provocative. To listen to these messages callers paid $1.69 per minute. World Championship Wrestling (WCW) owns the line and paid Madden $350 per week to operate it.[48] During a commentary Madden reported that the World Wrestling Federation (WWF), the archrival of the WCW, was in serious financial difficulty. WCW and WWF were suing each other, claiming unfair competition. Madden was subpoenaed to testify about the sources for his report on WWF's financial difficulties. Madden raised the First Amendment privilege, claiming he was a journalist entitled to constitutional protection. A U.S. District Court agreed in 1997,[49] but the U.S. Court of Appeals overturned the lower-court decision in July 1998. The appellate judges said that Madden was an entertainer disseminating hype, not news.

In ruling that Madden was not a journalist, the three-judge panel from the 3rd U.S. Circuit Court of Appeals defined a journalist (for purposes of application of the privilege) in this fashion: A journalist is one

- who engages in investigative reporting;
- who gathers news; and
- who possesses the intent at the beginning of the news-gathering process to disseminate this news to the public.[50]

**INDEPENDENT GATHERING AND REPORTING:
A "CRUDE" KEY FOR DEFINING WHO IS A JOURNALIST**

In 2011, the 2nd U.S. Circuit Court of Appeals issued an opinion in *Chevron Corp.* v. *Berlinger* in which it held that individuals who try to assert a journalistic privilege in order to protect from in-court disclosure information they gathered during an investigation must prove that they, in fact, gathered that information for "purposes of *independent* reporting and commentary" [emphasis in original].

---

47. Calvert, "And You Call Yourself a Journalist?"
48. Glaberson, "Wrestling Insults."
49. *Titan Sports Inc.* v. *Turner Broadcasting Systems Inc.*, 967 F. Supp. 142 (1997).
50. *In re Madden,* 151 F. 3d 125 (1998).

> The dispute centered on the attempts of oil company Chevron to obtain outtakes from a documentary film called "Crude" by Joseph Berlinger. Berlinger asserted that he was a journalist and claimed a privilege not to give the outtakes to Chevron, which wanted them to help it in separate litigation in which it was involved. The 2nd Circuit, however, rejected Berlinger's argument and affirmed a trial court's ruling that Berlinger's making of the film was not independent but, instead, had been solicited by a private party for purposes of telling that private party's story and that Berlinger had made changes in "Crude" at the insistence of the private party. Although it noted that "a person need not be a credentialed reporter working for an established press entity to establish entitlement to the privilege," the 2nd Circuit stressed that in collecting the information in question, the person must have acted "in the role of the independent press." The bottom line is that individuals seeking a journalistic privilege should, in line with a key ethical journalistic tenet, be independent and free from conflicts of interest that compromise objective reporting.

In 2010 the Supreme Court of New Hampshire held that a Web site operated by a company called Implode, which ranks businesses in the mortgage industry and allows registered visitors to post public comments about lenders, fell within the scope of that state's recognition of a newsperson's privilege not to reveal sources. The court wrote in *Mortgage Specialists, Inc.* v. *Implode-Explode Heavy Industries, Inc.*[51] that "the fact that Implode operates a web site makes it no less a member of the press. . . . [W]e conclude that Implode's web site serves an informative function and contributes to the flow of information to the public. Thus, Implode is a reporter for purposes of the newsgathering privilege."

One of the most intriguing issues involving the question of who is a journalist, for purposes of both state shield laws (see later in this chapter) and the First Amendment journalistic privilege protection, centers on the status of bloggers. In 2006 a California appellate court concluded in *O'Grady* v. *Superior Court*[52] that the publishers of two Web sites—O'Grady's PowerPage and Apple Insider—carrying information about Apple computers and other Apple products were entitled to protection under both California's shield law as well as the First Amendment and state constitution. Apple had subpoenaed the operators of both Web sites in order to find out who leaked to them Apple's secret plans to release a particular computer device. The Web site operators argued they were acting as publishers, editors and reporters in posting the information on their sites and thus did not need to reveal the names of their sources.

By their terms, both the California shield law and state constitution protect "a publisher, editor, reporter or other person connected with or employed upon a newspaper, magazine or other periodical publication" from disclosing sources of information.[53] Notice how the precise language includes newspapers and magazines but is silent about Web sites and digital media. In holding, however, that this language protected the Web

51. 999 A. 2d 184 (N.H. 2010).
52. 139 Cal. App. 4th 1423 (2006).
53. California Evidence Code § 1070 (2007); and California Constitution, Article I, § 2.

operators of PowerPage and Apple Insider, the appellate court wrote that these sites "came into possession of, and conveyed to their readers, information those readers would find of considerable interest" and noted that "in no relevant respect do they appear to differ from a reporter or editor for a traditional business-oriented periodical who solicits or otherwise comes into possession of confidential internal information about a company." The court added that the Web sites differed from traditional news periodicals "only in their tendency, which flows directly from the advanced technology they employ, to continuously update their content." Turning to the First Amendment claim of protection, the court found "no sustainable basis to distinguish [the Web site operators] from the reporters, editors, and publishers who provide news to the public through traditional print and broadcast media," adding that they "gather, select, and prepare, for purposes of publication to a mass audience, information about current events of interest and concern to that audience." It remains to be seen how many other courts will take such a pro-journalist, pro-blogger approach (see pages 416–417 for a New Jersey ruling that held that state's shield law also protected a blogger).

TELEPHONE RECORDS

The names of confidential news sources, reporters' notes, news film and photographs are not the only records that have been sought by government agents and attorneys through the use of a subpoena. In particular, reporters' telephone records provide a trail of numbers that could reveal the identity of confidential sources.

In 2006 a federal appellate court in *New York Times Co. v. Gonzales*[54] considered a federal grand jury subpoena seeking 11 days' worth of telephone records of two *New York Times* reporters who had investigated a secret government plan to freeze the assets of two Islamic charities that allegedly funded terrorism. The subpoenas were served on the telephone service providers of *The Times* as part of an investigation to find out who leaked and disclosed without authorization to the reporters the government's plans. The good news for *The Times*' reporters was that the appellate court initially held that "whatever rights a newspaper or reporter has to refuse disclosure in response to a subpoena extends to the newspaper's or reporter's telephone records in the possession of a third party provider." The court reasoned that "the telephone is an essential tool of modern journalism and plays an integral role in the collection of information by reporters," and thus "any common law or First Amendment protection that protects the reporters also protects their third party telephone records sought by the government."

But the bad news was that the appellate court also held that whatever common-law privilege might protect reporters in such cases, it is a qualified (limited) privilege overcome on the facts of this case by the need of the government. The appellate court wrote:

> The government has a compelling interest in maintaining the secrecy of imminent asset freezes or searches lest the targets be informed and spirit away those assets or incriminating evidence. At stake in the present investigation, therefore, is not only the important principle of secrecy regarding imminent law enforcement actions but also a set of facts—informing the targets of those impending actions—that may constitute a serious obstruction of justice.

54. 459 F. 3d 160 (2d Cir. 2006).

In ordering the review of the phone records, the court added that the reporters "are the only witnesses—other than the source(s)—available to identify the conversations in question and to describe the circumstances of the leaks," and that "the reporters' actions are central to (and probably caused) the grand jury's investigation. Their evidence as to the relationship of their source(s) and the leaks themselves . . . is critical to the present investigation." The court also flatly rejected the newspaper's argument that the First Amendment protected the reporters, reasoning that the Supreme Court's precedent from *Branzburg* v. *Hayes* (see earlier this chapter) controlled (it too was a grand jury setting) and did not provide any privilege against grand jury subpoenas. The Supreme Court in 2006 refused to disturb the appellate court's decision against *The New York Times*.[55]

Nearly three decades before, a different appellate court also had dealt a blow to journalists in *Reporters Committee for Freedom of the Press* v. *American Telephone & Telegraph Co.*[56] The *Reporters Committee* case, as the appellate court in *New York Times* v. *Gonzales* interpreted it 18 years later, "suggested that journalists have no more First Amendment rights in their toll-call records in the hands of third parties than they have in records of third party airlines, hotels, or taxicabs."

SUMMARY   In recent years more and more reporters have been called to testify in legal proceedings. Often they are asked to reveal confidential information to aid police in criminal investigations, to assist in the defense of a criminal defendant or to help a libel plaintiff establish negligence or actual malice. Failure to comply with a court order can result in a citation for contempt of court. The Supreme Court of the United States ruled in 1972 that reporters were like all other citizens: They did not enjoy a First Amendment privilege that permitted them to refuse to testify before a grand jury. Despite this high-court ruling, the lower federal courts and state courts have fashioned a constitutional, common-law privilege that often protects a journalist who has been subpoenaed to testify at a legal hearing. The privilege is qualified. In many instances a court will not require a journalist to testify unless the person seeking the information held by the journalist can demonstrate that the reporter has information that is relevant to the hearing, that there is a compelling need for the disclosure of this information and that there are no alternative sources for this information.

Courts tend to apply this three-part test differently in different types of legal proceedings. Journalists are most likely to escape being forced to testify in a civil suit, especially if the reporter is not a party to the suit in some way. Reporters are more likely to be forced to testify in a criminal case, but there are numerous examples of reporters being granted a qualified privilege to escape such testimony as well. Reporters called to testify before a grand jury, however, usually are required to honor the subpoena. More and more courts are seeking journalists' testimony regarding nonconfidential information, and the law is of substantially less protective value in these cases. A U.S. court of appeals has ruled that the records of telephone calls made by journalists may also be subpoenaed to further legitimate law enforcement proceedings.

55. *New York Times Co.* v. *Gonzales,* 549 U.S. 1049 (2006).
56. 593 F. 2d 1030 (D.C. Cir. 1978).

LEGISLATIVE AND EXECUTIVE PROTECTION OF NEWS SOURCES

By 2017 all states except Wyoming provided some form of legally recognized protection, albeit in varying degrees and forms, for journalists seeking to preserve confidentiality of sources and/or information. In particular, 39 states had shield laws protecting reporters, while other states recognized a judicially created privilege rooted in one or more of three sources—the First Amendment, a state constitution or the common law. It is important to note that a state with a statutory shield law may also recognize a judicially created privilege, so a reporter in a given state may have two possible avenues of protection.

As of 2017, however, there was no federal shield law to protect reporters who are hauled before federal courts and federal grand juries. There have been several failed attempts over the past decade to adopt a federal shield law.

SHIELD LAWS

In 1896 Maryland became the first state to grant journalists a limited privilege to refuse to testify in legal proceedings. In 2011, West Virginia became the 40th state with a shield law, but on July 1, 2013, Hawaii's shield law lapsed (or "sunsetted") after lawmakers in that state failed to renew it. When Hawaii adopted its shield law in 2008, it included a provision that would allow it to expire in five years unless lawmakers renewed it. Thus, as of August 2017, 39 states had shield laws (see Figure 10.1). The District of Columbia

In 1896 Maryland became the first state to grant journalists a limited privilege to refuse to testify in legal proceedings.

SHADED STATES HAVE SHIELD LAWS

FIGURE 10.1

As of 2017, 39 states plus the District of Columbia had some form of a shield law.

Source: Agents of Discovery

also has such a law, but, again, there is no federal shield law. Shield laws are statutes, adopted by state legislative bodies, except in the case of Utah, in which that state's high court in 2008 approved and adopted a reporter's shield rule (Utah Rule of Evidence 509) governing all court proceedings in that state. The Utah rule was proposed and advocated by several journalism groups. There often is substantial variance from state to state in both the scope of protection and the definitions used in these shield laws (there is, for example, no uniform definition across the states in terms of who constitutes a journalist or reporter protected under these laws).

These laws, in more or less limited terms, outline the reporter's privilege that has been established by the state. The statutes generally establish who can use the privilege (i.e., who is a reporter?), the kinds of information the privilege protects (i.e., confidential and/or nonconfidential; sources only or sources and/or information), and any qualifications that might accrue (i.e., the privilege is waived through voluntary disclosure of other parts of the material; instances when disclosure is mandated).

For example, the Alabama shield law provides the following:

> No person engaged in, connected with, or employed on any newspaper, radio broadcasting station or television station, while engaged in a news gathering capacity shall be compelled to disclose, in any legal proceeding or trial, before any court or before a grand jury of any court, before the presiding officers of any tribunal or his agent or agents, or before any committee of the legislature, or elsewhere, the sources of any information procured or obtained by him and published in the newspaper, broadcast by any broadcasting station, or televised by any television station on which he is engaged, connected with or employed.[57]

The precise language of state shield laws is very important in determining both who and what they will and will not cover or protect. This was illustrated in 2005 in the case of *Price* v. *Time, Inc.* in which the 11th U.S. Circuit Court of Appeals held that Alabama's shield law, quoted immediately above in this section, did not apply to the magazine *Sports Illustrated*. Engaging in the process of statutory construction (see Chapter 1 on statutory law), the appellate court held that the Alabama statute's phrase "newspaper, radio broadcasting station or television station" did not cover magazines like *Sports Illustrated*. In reaching this conclusion, the appellate court followed the plain meaning rule—it gave the statutory words their ordinary meaning and did not impart its own views on the legislative language. The 11th Circuit wrote that "it seems to us plain and apparent that in common usage 'newspaper' does not mean 'newspaper and magazine.'"

FIGHTING SUBPOENAS IN COURT: THE BABY HOPE CASE

The presence of a shield law in their state doesn't always protect journalists from subpoenas ordering them to reveal their sources or work products or from having to testify in court. Shield laws typically offer privileges that are subject to exceptions—and judges can differ on when those exceptions are met. This is what happened in a case in New York state courts in 2016.

---

57. Alabama Code, 12-21-142 (2010).

Conrado Juárez was arrested for the murder of a toddler. The girl's body was found in a cooler back in 1991. No one had reported the girl missing, and for more than 20 years, her identity remained a mystery, with detectives referring to her as Baby Hope. Police finally were able to identify the 4-year-old girl as Anjélica Castillo, and they arrested Juárez as her killer in 2013. He was her older cousin.

After an all-night police interrogation, Juárez confessed to the murder on videotape. Four days later, *New York Times* reporter Frances Robles interviewed Juárez in prison. In the interview, Juárez admitted that he helped dispose of Castillo's body, but he denied he had killed her and claimed that detectives coerced him into a confession. *The New York Times* published an article based on that interview.

Prosecutors argued that, even though Juárez denied he was the killer in his conversation with Robles, he still corroborated many of the same details he had told police—which proved the confession to police was neither coerced nor fabricated. Since no scientific evidence linked Juárez to the crime, prosecutors said his statements to Robles were critical to make the case to jurors that he had told police the truth. Prosecutors thus subpoenaed Robles, compelling her to testify about her interview with Juárez. Robles challenged the subpoena.

New York's shield law provides qualified, or limited, protection for named sources in stories, which Juárez was here (in other words, he wasn't a confidential source). In such instances, the law says journalists' privileges can be overcome—forcing them to testify—if prosecutors can show the information is "highly material and relevant" as well as "critical or necessary" to prove their case. A state lower court judge agreed with prosecutors that the exception was met here, ruling that Robles' notes from and testimony about her interview with Juárez were "material, relevant and critical" to the case against him. The judge said Robles would thus be forced to testify at trial, answering questions "directly relevant to her reporting of [Juárez's] statements," and to provide her notes for an in-camera review.

The New York Times appealed that decision immediately, and in October 2016, a state appellate court reversed it. In *People* v. *Juárez*, the appellate court said "in keeping with the consistent tradition in this State of providing the broadest possible protection to the sensitive role of gathering and disseminating news of public events," it found that the government had not made a "clear and specific showing" that Robles' testimony and interview notes were "critical or necessary" to the prosecutors' case. The appellate court said Juárez's videotaped confession already included statements that were consistent with other evidence in the case.

The Times celebrated the appellate decision. "We are grateful to the court for recognizing how important this issue is not just to *The Times* and to Ms. Robles, but to journalists everywhere," said David McCraw, who is the vice president and assistant general counsel of The New York Times Company. "It's important that our reporters be allowed to give voice to people who are incarcerated, and this subpoena threatened to silence those voices."

Are individuals who post factual information and opinions on online message boards journalists for purposes of state shield laws? In 2010 a New Jersey appellate court ruled in *Too Much Media, LLC* v. *Hale*[58] that New Jersey's shield law did not cover or protect a woman who posted messages on a site called Oprano.com. The site describes itself as the "Wall Street Journal for the online adult entertainment industry." It is a forum where members read and post their thoughts on message boards regarding various subjects related to the adult entertainment industry, with the comments typically available for public viewing. New Jersey's shield law, however, applies to members of the "news media," which it defines as individuals who are "engaged on, engaged in, connected with, or employed by newspapers, magazines, press associations, news agencies, wire services, radio, television or other similar printed, photographic, mechanical or electronic means of disseminating news to the general public." It defines "news," in turn, as "any written, oral or pictorial information gathered, procured, transmitted, compiled, edited or disseminated by, or on behalf of any person engaged in, engaged on, connected with or employed by a news media and so procured or obtained while such required relationship is in effect." In rejecting the woman's contention that she should fall within these definitions, the appellate court reasoned that "it is not enough to simply self-proclaim oneself a journalist. Here, the only evidence in support of defendant's claim that she is a newsperson is her own self-serving characterization and testimony as to her intent in gathering information, which the trial court found not credible." The court added that the woman "produced no credentials or proof of affiliation with any recognized news entity, nor has she demonstrated adherence to any standard of professional responsibility regulating institutional journalism, such as editing, fact-checking or disclosure of conflicts of interest."

In June 2011, the New Jersey Supreme Court affirmed the decision that New Jersey's shield law did not apply in the case, reasoning that "we do not find that online message boards are similar to the types of news entities listed in the statute, and do not believe that the Legislature intended to provide an absolute privilege in defamation cases to people who post comments on message boards." New Jersey's high court added that "neither writing a letter to the editor nor posting a comment on an online message board establishes the connection with 'news media' required by the statute." On the other hand, the New Jersey Supreme Court made it clear that "maintaining particular credentials or adhering to professional standards of journalism—like disclosing conflicts of interest or note taking—is . . . not required by the Shield Law."

In 2013, a trial court judge held that New Jersey's shield law did protect Tina Renna, the primary writer and editor of a blog called County Watchers. The blog reports on alleged waste, corruption and mismanagement in Union County, New Jersey. At issue in the case were blog postings Renna made about the alleged misuse of county-owned power generators by 16 different Union County employees during Hurricane Sandy in October 2012. A local prosecutor subpoenaed Renna to testify before a grand jury about the alleged improper use of the generators, but Renna wanted to quash the subpoena on grounds that she was protected by New Jersey's shield law.

---

58. 993 A.2d 845 (N.J. Super. Ct. App. Div. 2010), *affirmed*, 20 A.3d 364 (N.J. 2011).

To resolve the case, Judge Karen Cassidy applied the New Jersey Supreme Court's ruling from the *Too Much Media* case just described. In ruling in favor of Renna, Judge Cassidy initially observed that "Renna and her two or three other bloggers do in fact author posts about alleged occurrences and issues related to Union County governance and politics not covered by other media sources." The fact that the quality of her writing was "not akin to that of a print news reporter" and the fact that Renna's posts sometimes devolved into "ad hominem attacks" on Union County employees did not eliminate protection under the New Jersey shield law. What was important was that Renna regularly posted stories on county meetings, ordinances and budgets. Furthermore, she followed newsgathering methods commonly employed by what Judge Cassidy called "traditional news media entities," such as talking to sources, asking questions at county meetings and using New Jersey's open records law to obtain documents.

Furthermore, the judge wrote that the fact that "Renna's organization has an official stated purpose of being a citizen watchdog and an advocate for transparency in government does not preclude this court from finding that the County Watchers blog does not also have the alternate purpose of disseminating news. Being a reporter and a citizen watchdog are not mutually exclusive." Cassidy noted that while the County Watchers blog might be biased against Union County, such bias does not affect its status as a member of the news media. "In fact, many national publications such as the Weekly Standard (conservative) and the New Republic (liberal) have a point of view, yet are considered mainstream publications employing journalists to report on newsworthy events despite their ideological bent." Judge Cassidy thus granted Renna's motion to quash the subpoena and to protect her under New Jersey's shield law.

Shield laws sometimes suffer from deficiencies. Here are some of the problems:

■ Few of the laws give a protection that exceeds, or is even equal to, that given by the constitutional privilege.

■ The laws in most of the states are significantly qualified. For example, the laws in Alaska, Louisiana, New Mexico and North Dakota can be overcome by a mere judicial determination that justice or public policy requires the privilege to yield to some other interest.[59]

■ In some states the reporter waives the privilege upon disclosure of any portion of the confidential matter.[60]

■ In other states the shield law will not apply unless there was an understanding of confidentiality between the reporter and the source.[61]

■ State shield laws often exclude freelance writers, book authors and cable television operators, as well as bloggers. For instance, Florida's shield law applies only to "professional journalists," and it excludes from this definition "book authors." Florida's shield law, however, does include "independent contractors,"

---

59. *Confidential Sources and Information.*
60. *In re Schuman,* 537 A. 2d 297 (1988).
61. *Outlet Communications, Inc.* v. *Rhode Island,* 588 A. 2d 1050 (1991).

which means it covers freelancers provided they are "regularly engaged in collecting, photographing, recording, writing, editing, reporting, or publishing news, for gain or livelihood."

- Shield laws rarely cover what a reporter witnesses, only what a reporter has been told or given. For instance, an appellate court in Maryland held in 2003 that that state's shield law did not protect reporters from complying with administrative subpoenas seeking their testimony at police department administrative hearings when those reporters personally observed and witnessed the relevant event about which their testimony was sought.[62]

- Many shield laws have loopholes that allow subpoenas of third-party records. As the Reporters Committee for Freedom of the Press reports, the laws do not account for journalists' electronic communications through phones, computers or other technologies.[63] These loopholes could thus allow the government to evade shield laws by instead subpoenaing phone companies or e-mail services to gather journalists' records—cell phone records, for instance, that would document phone numbers and dates of a journalist's communications. In October 2015, Montana became the first state to amend its law to shield journalists' electronic communications from government investigations. The amended Montana law bars the government from requesting disclosure of "privileged news media information from services that transmit electronic communications." Shield laws in three states—California, Connecticut and Maine—require government bodies to notify the media of third-party subpoenas. While those laws do not provide the absolute protection of Montana's law, requiring notification at least gives journalists the opportunity to fight the third-party subpoenas in court.

As discussed in Chapter 4, some newspaper Web sites allow readers to anonymously post comments about online stories, and sometimes those anonymous comments defame individuals. The newspapers, of course, know the IP addresses of the anonymous posters on their Web sites. Judges in Florida, Montana and Oregon ruled in 2008 that the shield laws in those three states were drafted broadly enough to protect newspapers there from giving up the IP addresses of people who anonymously post on newspapers' Web sites, at least when the comments relate to the articles that spawned the postings.[64] Whether shield laws in other states will be interpreted so broadly as to prevent the disclosure of the identity of such third-party, newspaper-Web site posters remains to be seen.

---

62. *Prince George's County, Maryland v. Hartley,* 31 M.L.R. 1679 (2003).
63. Lambert, "Stopping an End-Run Around the Reporter's Privilege."
64. Order, *Beal v. Calobrisi,* Case No. 08-Ca-1075 (Fla. Cir. Ct. Okaloosa County Oct. 9, 2008), available online at http://www.newsroomlawblog.com/uploads/file/Beal_v_Calobrisi.pdf; and Associated Press, "Judge: Shield Law Protects Anonymous Commentators."

NEWSPAPERS FIGHT BACK AGAINST ANONYMOUS FLAME THROWING ON THEIR WEB SITES

Apparently growing weary of the decidedly low-brow and often defamatory postings of anonymous people following news articles on their Web sites, several papers now are adopting policies that require individuals to log in using a Facebook account. In announcing its implementation of such a policy in February 2013, the *Miami Herald* proclaimed "that anyone who has something to say should be willing to put their name to it." Aminda Marques Gonzalez, the paper's executive editor, added that "we know the move to Facebook commenting is not a cure-all nor without controversy. Some users will find a way to create accounts using fake identities. We'll watch for that as we continue to monitor for posts that deviate from the rules of civil engagement."

The perfect shield law would likely be preferable to the First Amendment privilege; but the perfect shield law does not exist. Hence, even in those states that have a shield law, reporters frequently end up relying on the constitutional privilege.

FEDERAL GUIDELINES

As a kind of corollary to a shield law, the Department of Justice has adopted guidelines that define when and how a federal prosecuting attorney can obtain a subpoena against a working reporter.[65]

The guidelines have been around for decades, but they were revised significantly in 2014 and 2015 in response to widespread criticism the Justice Department received for arguably ignoring them.

In May 2013, it was revealed that the Justice Department had secretly seized telephone records of Associated Press reporters for more than two months the year before. In particular, the Justice Department examined records of more than 20 different phone lines (some business, some private) used by about 100 AP reporters. The Justice Department said it seized the records to try to determine, by examining the telephone numbers called, who leaked to AP reporters classified information about a failed terror plot linked to an al-Qaida affiliate in Yemen in 2012. The vast scale of the seizure of the AP's records was unprecedented. In a letter to then-Attorney General Eric Holder, Gary Pruitt, the president and CEO of the AP, argued that "there can be no possible justification for such an overbroad collection of the telephone communications of the Associated Press and its reporters." *The New York Times* characterized the Justice Department's seizure of the phone records as "a fishing expedition for sources and an effort to frighten off whistle-blowers." Also in May 2013, it was revealed that the Justice Department had searched the private e-mails of Fox News reporter James Rosen, purportedly to determine who leaked to Rosen classified information about North Korea.

65. See 28 C.F.R. § 50.10.

In response to the fiasco, then–Attorney General Holder announced that the guidelines would be revised to make them more favorable to journalists. Holder invited interested groups to comment and propose changes to the guidelines. The Reporters Committee for Freedom of the Press coordinated a proposal from a broad coalition of more than 50 media companies and journalism organizations.

The revised guidelines were released in February 2014 and then modified some again in January 2015. Holder said the revised guidelines "ensure the highest level of oversight when members of the Department [of Justice] seek to obtain information from, or records of, a member of the news media." The revised guidelines extend protections to journalists for third-party records, permitting the attorney general to authorize subpoenaing journalists' third-party communications "only after the government has made all reasonable attempts to obtain the information from alternative sources." And if the authorization is granted, the guidelines say that journalists should be given "reasonable and timely notice" before the subpoena is sent, "unless the Attorney General determines that, for compelling reasons, such notice would pose a clear and substantial threat to the integrity of the investigation, risk grave harm to national security, or present an imminent risk of death or serious bodily harm." The guidelines make clear that law enforcement tools such as subpoenas to seek information from journalists are "extraordinary measures, not standard investigatory practices." The guidelines also reinforce that the information sought from journalists must be "essential," not "peripheral" or "speculative." And the guidelines say that before granting the subpoena, the Justice Department should first negotiate with the news media in an attempt to gain the information.

NEWSROOM SEARCHES

Is a newsroom or a journalist's home protected by the First Amendment from a search by the police or federal agents?

Is a newsroom or a journalist's home protected by the First Amendment from a search by the police or federal agents? The Supreme Court of the United States refused to extend the First Amendment in such a manner in 1978.[66] Since then, however, Congress and many state legislatures have provided qualified legislative protection for premises where news and scholarship are produced. The lawsuit that resulted in the Supreme Court ruling stemmed from the political turmoil of the early 1970s, a period that generated many of the previously discussed cases regarding reporters' sources.

In April 1971 police were asked to remove student demonstrators who were occupying the administrative offices of Stanford University Hospital. When police entered the west end of the building, demonstrators poured out of the east end, and during the ensuing melee outside the building, several police officers were hurt, two seriously. The battle between the police and the students was photographed by a student, and the following day pictures of the incident were published in the *Stanford Daily* student newspaper. In an effort to discover which students had attacked the injured police officers, law enforcement officials from Santa Clara County secured a warrant for a search of the *Daily's* newsroom, hoping to find more pictures taken by the student photographer. There was no allegation that any member of the *Daily* staff was involved in the attack or other unlawful acts. No evidence was discovered during the thorough search.

66. *Zurcher v. Stanford Daily,* 436 U.S. 547 (1978).

This type of search is known as an innocent third-party search, or simply a third-party search. Police search the premises or a room for evidence relating to a crime even though there is no reason to suspect that the owner of the premises or the occupant of the room is involved in the crime that is being investigated. Such searches are not uncommon, but in the lawsuit that followed, the student newspaper argued that this kind of search threatened the freedom of the press and should not be permitted unless police officials first obtain a subpoena—which is more difficult for police to get than a simple search warrant. The subpoena process would also provide the press with notice prior to the search and allow editors and reporters to challenge the issuance of the subpoena.

The newspaper argued that the unannounced third-party search of a newsroom seriously threatened the ability of the press to gather, analyze and disseminate news. The searches could be physically disruptive for a craft in which meeting deadlines is essential. Confidential sources—fearful that some evidence that would reveal their identity might surface in such a search—would refuse to cooperate with reporters. Reporters would be deterred from keeping notes and tapes if such material could be seized in a search. All of this, and more, could have a chilling effect on the press, lawyers for the newspaper argued.

The Supreme Court, in a 5-3 ruling, disagreed with the newspaper. Justice Byron White ruled that the problem was essentially a Fourth Amendment question (i.e., was the search permissible under the Fourth Amendment?), not a First Amendment question, and that under existing law a warrant may be issued to search any property if there is reason to believe that evidence of a crime will be found. "The Fourth Amendment has itself struck the balance between privacy and public need and there is no occasion or justification for a court to revise the Amendment and strike a new balance," White wrote. He conceded that "where the materials sought to be seized may be protected by the First Amendment, the requirements of the Fourth Amendment must be applied with 'scrupulous exactitude.'" He added, "Where presumptively protected materials are sought to be seized, the warrant requirement should be administered to leave as little as possible to the discretion of the officer in the field." But Justice White rejected the notion that such unannounced searches are a threat to the freedom of the press, arguing that the framers of the Constitution were certainly aware of the struggle between the press and the Crown in the 17th and 18th centuries, when the general search warrant was a serious problem for the press. Yet the framers did not forbid the use of search warrants where the press was involved, White asserted. They obviously believed the protections of the Fourth Amendment would sufficiently protect the press.

Newsroom searches by the police, a rarity in the decades before the *Zurcher* case, suddenly became a common occurrence. Journalists sought legislative relief from this onslaught and Congress responded by adopting the Privacy Protection Act of 1980.[67] The law limits the way law officers and government agents can search for or seize materials that are in the hands of persons working for the mass media or persons who expect to publicly disseminate the material in some other manner (e.g., public speech). The statute designates two categories of material that are protected: work products and documentary materials. The law says a work product "encompasses the material

This type of search is known as an innocent third-party search.

---

67. See 42 U.S.C. §§ 2000aa–2000aa-12.

whose very creation arises out of a purpose to convey information to the public." In layperson's language, work products are reporters' notes, undeveloped film, outtakes and so forth. Documentary materials are described as "materials upon which information is formally recorded," such as government reports, manuscripts and the like. Congress based the statute on the commerce clause in the U.S. Constitution in order to extend the reach of the law to include state and local agencies as well as federal law enforcement personnel. To obtain either work products or documentary materials, law enforcement agencies must obtain a subpoena; a search warrant will not do. There are, however, exceptions to the rule. A law enforcement agency may conduct a warranted search of a newsroom to find work products in either of the following two situations:

1. When there is a probable cause to believe that the person possessing such materials has committed or is committing a criminal offense to which the materials will relate. This is known as the "suspect exception."

2. Where there is reason to believe that the immediate seizure of such materials is necessary to prevent the death of or serious harm to a person.

A search warrant may be used instead of a subpoena to obtain documentary materials if either of the two conditions just listed is met or in either of these two situations:

1. There is reason to believe that the giving of notice pursuant to gaining a subpoena would result in the destruction, alteration or concealment of such materials.

2. That such materials have not been provided in response to a court order directing compliance with a subpoena, all other legal remedies have been exhausted, and there is reason to believe that further delay in gaining the material would threaten the interests of justice.

In most instances, then, law enforcement personnel will be forced to seek a subpoena to gain access to information kept in a newsroom or a reporter's home.

The 2012 decision by the 4th U.S. Circuit Court of Appeals in *Sennett* v. *United States*,[68] however, illustrates the use of the "suspect exception" noted above for when a search warrant (rather than a subpoena) is permissible. Laura Sennett is a photojournalist who took pictures of a major disturbance at the Four Seasons Hotel in Washington, D.C., several years earlier. In particular, a group of about 16 masked individuals demonstrating during the International Monetary Fund's April 2008 meeting "entered the hotel lobby and threw firecrackers and smoke-generating pyrotechnic devices, along with paint-filled balloons, at various targets." The vandals, who also shattered a large glass window at the hotel, fled the scene before they could be arrested. A hotel security camera, however, captured images of Sennett arriving on the scene at the same time as the protesters and also showed her fleeing the hotel "with or in the same general direction as the protesters."

A law enforcement officer later identified Sennett on the hotel's surveillance video and determined through a reliable source, as well as through video footage

68. 667 F.3d 531 (4th Cir. 2012).

found on Google and Yahoo, that Sennett had attended multiple protests throughout the Washington, D.C., area. In brief, Sennett appeared to be as much of a suspect as a journalist, and the law enforcement officials obtained a warrant to search her residence believing it likely "contained evidence of suspected criminal activity that occurred during the IMF protest at the Four Seasons."

During the search of Sennett's residence, federal agents seized an external hard drive allegedly containing more than 7,000 photographs, two computers and several cameras and memory cards. Sennett sued, claiming the warrant-based search violated the Privacy Protection Act and that the agents should have obtained a subpoena. The agents, however, countered that the suspect exception applied because there was probable cause to believe that Sennett committed a criminal offense to which her photographs related.

The 4th Circuit ruled against Sennett, despite observing that she offered "a plausible, innocent explanation for her appearance on the videotape—that she was present to document what she believed would be a lawful demonstration." The appellate court reasoned that such a plausible explanation "does not negate probable cause" on the part of law enforcement officers in obtaining a search warrant. The appellate court thus affirmed the ruling of a district court judge who concluded that "a reasonable person would be warranted in believing that Sennett's role in the vandalism was to serve as the group's photographer or videographer, so that a memorialization of the event could be used to advance the group's purposes and to claim responsibility."

HOW TO RESPOND TO A SUBPOENA

What should a reporter do if he or she is subpoenaed? First, try to avoid the problem altogether. Don't give a promise of confidentiality to a source without first carefully considering whether such a promise is actually needed to get the story. Discuss the matter with an editor or the news director before agreeing to keep the name of a source confidential. Also, don't talk, even informally, with people outside the newspaper about stories in which confidential information or sources are involved. Such discussions may be ruled to constitute a waiver of the privilege you seek to assert at a later date.

What should a reporter do if he or she is subpoenaed?

But if a subpoena should arrive, the first thing to remember is that the police are not coming to your door to arrest you. The subpoena is simply an order that you have been called to appear at some type of proceeding or supply certain documents. So don't panic. Tell your editor or news director immediately. Ask to talk with your news organization's legal counsel. Don't attempt to avoid being served with the subpoena. While a reporter is under no obligation to make the job easier for the person serving the subpoena, resistance to this service may result in the subpoena being abandoned and a search warrant issued in its place. Don't ever accept a subpoena for someone else.

Ask to talk with your news organization's legal counsel.

If the subpoena requests only published material, or video that has previously been broadcast, the newspaper or broadcasting station may simply provide this material without dispute. Journalists should be familiar with their news organization's policy on retaining notes, tapes, first drafts and so on. If there is no policy, it is worthwhile to ask management to consider adopting one. Once the subpoena has been served, the material sought is considered official evidence, and if it is destroyed to avoid having to produce it, the reporter very likely will be held in contempt of court. So once you have been served, begin gathering the material together in case you have to surrender it at some later time.

If you believe that the material or names of sources should be withheld, and your news organization disagrees, it is in your interest to hire your own attorney to represent you. The company attorney is working for the company, not you. Finally, remember that the odds of being forced to give up the material or names are low. The law is, for the most part, on your side these days.

And what happens if the police improperly show up at the newsroom door with a warrant instead of the required subpoena and they begin to search your newsroom? The Reporters Committee for Freedom of the Press recommends in its "First Amendment Handbook" that "staff photographers or camera operators should record the scene. Although staff members may not impede the law enforcement officials, they are not required to assist the searchers." Today, of course, any journalist with a cell phone could photograph or record such an illegal search, thus preserving evidence for a court proceeding to declare the search invalid under the Privacy Protection Act of 1980. You also should immediately call your news organization's attorney.

SUMMARY

State legislatures and the federal government have adopted statutes and rules that offer some protection to journalists who hold confidential information sought by government agents and other individuals. Thirty-nine states and the District of Columbia have adopted shield laws, which provide a qualified privilege for reporters to refuse to testify in legal proceedings. Although these statutes can be helpful, they are not without problems. There is a lack of consistency among the state shield laws. These laws have definitional problems that permit courts to construe them very narrowly. The laws usually protect only what someone tells a reporter, not what a reporter personally sees or hears. Often courts see the statutes as legislative interference with judicial prerogatives and interpret the laws in the least useful manner. As of August 2017, there was no federal shield law to protect journalists from revealing sources and confidential information in federal court proceedings.

The Department of Justice has adopted guidelines that govern when and how federal agents may subpoena journalists and their records. The guidelines also extend protection to journalists' third-party records, limiting, for instance, when a journalist's phone records could be subpoenaed from her cell phone provider. The guidelines require federal agents to strike a balance between the public's interest in the free flow of information and effective law enforcement.

Congress passed the Privacy Protection Act of 1980 in response to a ruling by the U.S. Supreme Court that the First Amendment does not ban searches of newsrooms or reporters' homes. This act requires federal, state and local police agencies who seek a journalist's work products or other documentary materials to get a subpoena for these materials rather than seize them under the authority of a search warrant. The statute does provide exceptions to these rules. For example, premises may be searched and materials seized under a search warrant if police believe the reporter has committed a crime, if there is reason to believe someone will be harmed if the materials are not seized or if police fear the materials might be destroyed if a subpoena is sought.

THE CONTEMPT POWER

Those who work in the mass media and run afoul of judicial orders or the commands of legislative committees can quickly feel the sharp sting of a contempt citation. Reporters who refuse to respond to a subpoena, editors who criticize a judge, newspapers that refuse to pay a libel or invasion-of-privacy judgment, all of these and more can be held in contempt. For example, as discussed earlier (see page 401) former *USA Today* reporter Toni Locy was held in contempt by a federal judge in 2008 and fined $5,000 per day after she did not reveal her sources for stories connecting scientist Steven J. Hatfill to a series of anthrax-laced letters sent in late 2001.[69] Under the contempt ruling, the fines added up for every day that Locy refused to give up her sources' identity, and Locy was personally liable for paying the fines (the contempt order precluded her from accepting reimbursement from her employer or others to satisfy the monetary sanction). Hatfill had sued the federal government under the Privacy Act (see Chapter 9), claiming his privacy was violated by government employees who deliberately leaked his name to certain journalists as a person of interest in the investigation into who sent the letters. Hatfill subpoenaed Locy, as well as a number of other journalists, seeking to find out who their government sources were. Locy refused to reveal her sources, claiming she couldn't remember them. United States District Judge Reggie B. Walton rejected Locy's argument that her refusal to disclose the identity of her sources was sanctioned by either the First Amendment or a common-law privilege she requested that Walton recognize. Locy escaped paying a steep contempt fine, however, when the government agreed later in 2008 to pay Hatfill $5.8 million to settle his case before an appellate court could rule on the merits of Hatfill's efforts to force Locy to testify. In November 2008 a three-judge panel of the U.S. Circuit Court of Appeals for the District of Columbia vacated Judge Walton's contempt order and dismissed the case as moot due to the settlement. Judge Walton then issued a one-page order in February 2009 accepting the appellate court's ruling and vacating his own earlier contempt decision. Despite the settlement and tossing out of the contempt order, however, Hatfill still wanted Locy to pay his hefty legal fees sustained during the period of time when she refused to give up her sources.

In a case with a colorful set of facts, in June 2016 a federal judge in New Jersey found Girls Gone Wild founder Joe Francis in contempt of court and ordered him to pay more than $3 million for disregarding orders in a defamation suit. Ashley Dupre, who later gained fame as former New York Governor Eliot Spitzer's call girl, was filmed dressed in a towel, and at one point, holding a driver's license on camera in one of Francis' films—but the license was not hers. It instead belonged to Amber Arpaio, who was not involved in the filming at all. Arpaio sued Francis for defamation. But after Francis was unreachable for a deposition—purportedly having moved to Mexico—the judge found him in contempt of court, ordered him to turn over a valid address and said the court may issue an arrest warrant if he failed to comply.

69. *Hatfill* v. *Mukasey,* 539 F. Supp. 2d 96 (D.D.C. 2008). An appellate court stayed the contempt fine while the case was on appeal. *Hatfill* v. *Mukasey,* 2008 U.S. App. LEXIS 5755 (D.C. Cir. Mar. 11, 2008).

KINDS OF CONTEMPT

Varieties of contempt are recognized through common law, and efforts have been made to label these varieties. But these efforts have been unsatisfactory; there is frequently disagreement among courts about what kinds of behavior constitute what kinds of contempt. No attempt will be made to resolve these discrepancies in this book. It is sufficient to note that judges use the contempt power for two purposes:

A court can use the contempt power to protect the rights of a litigant in a legal dispute. A reporter who refuses to reveal the name of a source critical to the defense of a person charged with larceny could endanger the person's right to a fair trial. The contempt power can be used to force the reporter to testify. Similarly, a broadcasting station that refuses to pay the plaintiff a judgment after losing a libel case endangers the right of the injured party to repair his or her reputation. Again, the contempt power can be used to force the broadcaster to pay the judgment.

The contempt power can be used to vindicate the law, the authority of the court or the power of the judge. A defendant who refuses to stop talking during a trial or an attorney who continually ignores judicial warnings against talking to reporters about the merits of the case can be punished with a contempt citation. So can a writer who carelessly and aggressively criticizes a court ruling in a newspaper editorial.

Judges who use the contempt power to protect the rights of litigants usually impose an indeterminate sentence against the target of the contempt. That is, a judge can jail a reporter until he or she is willing to reveal the name of the critical source. Or the court can fine the broadcaster a specific amount each day until the civil judgment is paid. The punishment is used to coerce the target of the citation to take some action.

Judges who use the contempt power to vindicate the law, the authority of the court or the power of the judge will generally impose a determinate sentence—that is, a specific fine ($25,000) or jail sentence (30 days in jail). Here the sentence is strictly punishment; no coercion is implied.

Contempt and the Press

The contempt power is broad and touches all manner of persons who run afoul of a judge. Journalists are among those at jeopardy. What kinds of situations are most likely to result in contempt problems for the press? To list a few:

1. Failure to pay a judgment in a libel or invasion-of-privacy case.
2. Failure to obey a court order. The judge rules that no photos may be taken in the courtroom, or orders reporters not to publish stories about certain aspects of a case. If these orders are disobeyed, a contempt citation may result.
3. Refusal of a journalist to disclose the identity of a source or to testify in court or before a grand jury.
4. Critical commentary about the court. This might be an editorial critical of the court or a cartoon mocking the judge. Contempt citations have been issued to punish the press in such cases.
5. Tampering with a jury. A reporter tries to talk with jurors during a trial, asking questions about their views on the defendant's innocence or guilt.

These situations are some of the more common ways that members of the press might become involved in a contempt problem, although the list is by no means exhaustive.

COLLATERAL BAR RULE

When a journalist violates a court order, a contempt citation is probably forthcoming. But what if the court order appears to be illegal or unconstitutional on its face? Can a journalist still be held in contempt of court for violating such an order? The answer to that important question is maybe, for there is no clear resolution of this matter at present. The legal concept involved is called the **collateral bar rule,** a rule that requires that all court orders, even those that appear to be unconstitutional and are later deemed to be unconstitutional by an appellate court, must still be obeyed until they are overturned. The collateral bar rule states that a person who violates a court order cannot collaterally challenge the order's constitutionality as a defense to the contempt charge. Instead, that person must obey the order and hope to get it overturned on appeal. While this rule has been rarely invoked against the press, a U.S. Court of Appeals ruling from 1972 stands as a stark reminder of its meaning. In that case reporters Gibbs Adams and Larry Dickinson of the Baton Rouge (La.) *Morning Advocate* and *State Times* ignored what they believed was an unconstitutional court order forbidding them from publishing information about what took place in an open federal court hearing. The pair, who were each fined $300, appealed the order and the 5th U.S. Circuit Court of Appeals ruled that the trial judge's actions were clearly unconstitutional. At the same time, the court upheld the contempt citations, ruling that a person may not, with impunity, violate a court order that later turns out to be invalid.[70]

While this rule, sometimes called the *Dickinson rule,* seems grossly unfair, there is a logic to it. The court system would cease to operate as it does if people had a choice of whether or not to obey a court order. Without the power to coerce behavior, judges would be unable to discharge their duties and responsibilities, and courts would become mere boards of arbitration that issue advisory opinions. The judge who wrote the opinion in the *Dickinson* case probably spoke for many jurists when he wrote, "Newsmen are citizens too. They too may sometimes have to wait."

While this rule, sometimes called the Dickinson rule, *seems grossly unfair, there is a logic to it.*

Only one important collateral bar case involving the press has occurred since this 1972 ruling. In this case a federal judge in Rhode Island found the *Providence Journal* and its editor, Charles Hauser, in contempt of court for violating the judge's order forbidding the publication of any information that had been obtained by the government from an illegal FBI wiretap. The 1st U.S. Circuit Court of Appeals ruled that the trial judge's order was transparently invalid and could not serve as a basis for a contempt citation. The appellate court added, however, that in the future publishers and broadcasters should first try to get an appellate review before violating a court order.[71] With the 5th Circuit and the 1st Circuit somewhat in disagreement about this matter, the Supreme Court agreed to hear an appeal. But after reading briefs and hearing arguments, the members of the high court dismissed the appeal because the special prosecutor who handled the appeal for the government had failed to obtain proper authorization from the Solicitor General of the United States to petition for a writ of certiorari. At the federal level, then,

---

70. *U.S. v. Dickinson,* 465 F. 2d 496 (1972).
71. *In re Providence Journal,* 820 F. 2d 1354 (1987).

the issue remains unresolved. But courts in Washington and Illinois have flatly rejected the rationale of the *Dickinson* case,[72] and courts in Arizona,[73] California,[74] Massachusetts[75] and Alabama[76] have considered the matter but have issued ambiguous rulings.

SUMMARY

The power of a judge to punish for contempt of court is a remnant of the power of English royalty. Today, courts have broad powers to punish people who offend the court, interfere with legal proceedings or disobey court orders. Contempt is used both to protect the rights of private persons who are litigating matters in the courts and to punish a wrong committed against the court itself.

Some limits have been placed on the contempt power. Legislatures often restrict the kinds of sentences judges may impose for contempt or require a jury trial before a contempt conviction. The Supreme Court has ruled that before criticism of a court may be punished by contempt, it must be shown that the criticism created a clear and present danger of the likelihood of interference with the administration of justice. In some jurisdictions appellate courts have ruled that people must obey even unconstitutional contempt orders (the *Dickinson* rule).

BIBLIOGRAPHY

Agents of Discovery. Washington, D.C.: Reporters Committee for Freedom of the Press, 2003.

Associated Press. "Judge: Shield Law Protects Anonymous Commentators." 4 September 2008.

Belluck, Pam. "Reporter Is Found Guilty for Refusal to Name Source." *The New York Times*, 19 November 2004, A24.

——. "Reporter Who Shielded Source Will Serve Sentence at Home." *The New York Times*, 10 December 2004, A28.

Calvert, Clay. "And You Call Yourself a Journalist? Wrestling With a Definition of 'Journalist' in the Law." *Dickinson Law Review* 103 (1999): 411.

Confidential Sources and Information. Washington, D.C.: Reporters Committee for Freedom of the Press, 1993.

Glaberson, William. "Wrestling Insults Fuel Free Speech Case." *The New York Times*, 24 October 1998, A10.

Lambert, Michael. "Stopping an End-run Around the Reporter's Privilege." *The News Media and The Law*, Winter 2016.

Utevsky, David. "Protection of Sources and Unpublished Information." Paper presented at the meeting of Washington Volunteer Lawyers for the Arts, Seattle, Wash., 27 January 1989.

Wigmore, John H. *A Treatise on the Anglo-American System of Evidence in Trials at Common Law*. 2nd ed. Boston: Little, Brown, 1934.

72. *State ex rel Superior Court* v. *Sperry*, 483 P. 2d 609 (1971); and *Cooper* v. *Rockford Newspapers*, 365 N.E. 2d 746 (1977).
73. *Phoenix Newspapers* v. *Superior Court*, 418 P. 2d 594 (1966); and *State* v. *Chavez*, 601 P. 2d 301 (1979).
74. *In re Berry*, 493 P. 2d 273 (1968).
75. *Fitchburg* v. *707 Main Corp.*, 343 N.E. 2d 149 (1976).
76. *Ex parte Purvis*, 382 So. 2d 512 (1980).

Free Press–Fair Trial

TRIAL-LEVEL REMEDIES AND RESTRICTIVE ORDERS

©McGraw-Hill Education/Jill Braaten

Legal problems often arise when the press and the criminal justice system intersect. These problems are the result of two seemingly conflicting constitutional rights: the right to a free press guaranteed by the First Amendment and the right to a fair trial by an impartial jury guaranteed by the Sixth Amendment. If the press publishes and broadcasts anything it chooses about a crime or a criminal suspect, isn't it possible readers and viewers will make up their minds about the guilt or innocence of the accused? And if they do, won't the members of the jury (who are also readers and viewers) approach the case with prejudice either for or against the defendant? What will happen to the guarantee of a fair trial? But if the court moves to restrict this publicity by the mass media to protect the integrity of the trial process, won't this interfere with the rights of the press? What about the First Amendment? We explore these issues in this chapter and in Chapter 12. Included is a discussion of the kinds of publicity that may damage the right to a fair trial, and the various schemes adopted by the courts to try to minimize the impact of this publicity or restrict the flow of this kind of information.

PREJUDICIAL CRIME REPORTING

Americans' fascination with news about crime is not a recent fetish. Indeed, the people of this nation have always found stories about crime and criminals alluring. In the 19th century, hangings were public spectacles with a carnival-like atmosphere and were usually well attended. In the 1920s and 1930s, state prisons would sometimes hold lotteries to distribute tickets to those who wanted to attend an execution. Today so-called true crime and mystery novels are among the most popular print genres, and dramas about crime and criminals, such as the various versions of "Law and Order" and "CSI," usually rank among the most popular TV shows. In addition, the recent success of the "Serial" podcast demonstrates that the public's fascination with crime and the justice system continues.

The news media, especially television news, are also saturated with stories about crime and the administration of criminal justice. Many television news producers salivate at the prospect of yet another celebrity trial. Five hundred or so print and broadcast reporters were on hand for the first day of the Michael Jackson trial in California in early 2005. That is clearly more coverage than most institutions of the federal government or major political events receive. And, in vying for the short attention span of many Americans, some members of the press have few qualms about reporting stories that go beyond the facts of the case to include rumors, their own opinions about guilt or innocence and speculations from scores of so called experts who dwell beyond the boundaries of the actual courthouse proceedings.

This quasi–news reporting of crime and the criminal justice system is at the heart of the long-standing matter that journalists and lawyers alike call the free press–fair trial controversy. This controversy—like the news coverage of crime—also dates to the early years of the republic. Many lawyers and judges argue that it is extremely difficult or even impossible for a defendant to get a fair trial—a right guaranteed by the Sixth Amendment—when important segments of the press have already decided the individual is guilty. This kind of publicity, they say, will surely influence members of the community who will ultimately sit on the jury that decides the defendant's guilt or innocence. Reporters and editors argue that the influence of the press is seriously exaggerated in such arguments, and regardless, the First Amendment protects the press from government interference, even if it occasionally acts irresponsibly.

No one claims that all reporting about crime or criminals is a problem. While the heavy emphasis by the press on reporting crime is regarded as misplaced by most observers, even the severest critics agree that most stories are straightforward and fair. But potential problems arise in those instances when the press saturates a community with stories about a particular crime or criminal defendant. Recent high-profile murder cases involving saturation news coverage include the 2015 conviction of football player Aaron Hernandez and the 2013 conviction of Jodi Arias. Both the Hernandez and Arias trials were broadcast and streamed live on the Internet. In fact, there were more than 2,400 television news reports on the Arias trial in the Phoenix area alone where it occurred. A site called Court Chatter offers live streaming of trials across the country. And when celebrities like Bill Cosby face sexual assault charges, the publicity can be even greater,

NFL American football player Aaron Hernandez enters courtroom to be arraigned on homicide charges. Hernandez' trial is an example of the type of trial that can produce extensive media coverage and cause concerns over the ability of a defendant to receive a fair trial. Hernandez hanged himself in prison in April 2017.

©Reuters/Alamy Stock Photo

featuring a sensational combination of rape and celebrity. What kind of news creates the greatest danger of prejudice? Here is a list of some of the more common kinds of stories that critics say can endanger the defendant's rights by causing prejudicial publicity either before a jury is impaneled or while a trial is in process:

1. **Confessions or stories about the confession that a defendant is said to have made, which include even alluding to the fact that there may be a confession.** The Fifth Amendment says that a person does not have to testify against himself or herself. A confession given to police can sometimes be retracted before the trial. People who are innocent sometimes confess to the crime they are accused of committing. In 2010 a man named Eddie Lowery was released from prison in Kansas after spending 10 years in jail for a rape he did not commit. DNA evidence revealed that another man committed the crime. Lowery's case is not unique. In 2012, *The New York Times* reported that the Innocence Project said false confessions figured in 24 percent or 70 of the 289 convictions overturned by DNA evidence. The organization noted that since DNA is available in just a fraction of all crimes, a much larger universe of erroneous convictions—and false convictions—surely exists. People who are mentally impaired, mentally ill, young or easily led are the likeliest to be induced by police to confess, according to research. Lowery told reporters he

was just pressed beyond endurance by persistent interrogators.[1] In 2006 John Mark Karr confessed to killing 6-year-old JonBenet Ramsey in 1996. Only after he was extradited from Thailand did authorities conclude the confession was a lie.

2. **Stories about the defendant's performance on a test, such as a polygraph, lie detector or similar device, and about the defendant's refusal to take such a test.** Many kinds of so-called scientific or forensic evidence, which may help police identify a suspect, are not admissible as evidence at a trial, often because they are not completely reliable. Even DNA evidence is not always 100 percent conclusive if the DNA materials were not properly gathered or processed.

3. **Stories about the defendant's past criminal record or that describe the defendant as a former convict.** This information is not permitted at the trial. Such "character" evidence is generally ruled inadmissible. It may seem entirely logical to some people that when someone has committed 99 robberies and is again arrested for robbery, the accused probably did commit the crime. As a matter of fact, past behavior is immaterial in the current trial for robbery. The state must prove that the defendant committed *this* robbery.

4. **Stories that question the credibility of witnesses and that contain the personal feelings of witnesses about prosecutors, police, victims or even judges.**

5. **Stories about the defendant's character** (he or she loves to party), **associates** (he or she hangs around with known syndicate mobsters) **and personality** (he or she attacks people on the slightest provocation and acts in highly erratic ways).

6. **Stories that tend to inflame the public mood against the defendant.** Such stories include editorial campaigns that demand the arrest of a suspect before sufficient evidence has been collected; person-on-the-street interviews concerning the guilt of the defendant or the kind of punishment that should be meted out after the accused is convicted; televised debates about the evidence of the guilt or innocence of the defendant. All these kinds of stories put the jury in the hot seat as well as circulate vast quantities of misinformation.

7. **Stories that are published or broadcast before a trial that suggest, imply or flatly declare that the defendant is guilty.** In 2008, Casey Anthony was charged with first-degree murder in the death of her 2-year-old daughter. Before the trial, many people, including those in the mass media (especially some television commentators), opined that she was guilty of the charge. But a jury found her not guilty of murder. The jury did find her guilty of four misdemeanors, such as lying to the police, but an appellate court in 2012 reversed two of these convictions.

---

1. Shipler, "Why Do Innocent"; Schwartz, "Confessing to Crime."

IMPACT ON JURORS

That intensive press coverage of a criminal case *might* jeopardize the rights of the defendant is generally assumed. But whether it *will* in fact harm the defendant's Sixth Amendment rights remains more of an open question. There are those who argue vigorously that any publicity can result in a jury biased for or against the defendant.

In fact, there is a serious lack of evidence that even intensive press coverage of a particular case can have a negative impact on the defendant. For nearly 60 years social scientists have attempted to prove or disprove this assumption with less than great success. The law prohibits the use of real jurors in actual trials as subjects for this research. Complicating the resolution of this problem is the fact that many social scientists are beginning to believe that people tend to remember far less about what they read or watch on television or blogs than has been traditionally assumed. Social scientists, then, have failed to firmly establish the validity of the assumption that prejudicial publicity will seriously damage the defendant's fair trial rights.

The Supreme Court of the United States weighed in on this question in 2010 in ruling on an appeal by Jeffrey K. Skilling, the former chief executive of Enron, after his conviction for fraud. When the Houston energy company failed, thousands of people in the community lost their jobs. Skilling's attorneys argued that the conviction should be reversed; the jury in the trial was certainly prejudiced because of what they called "pervasive community bias against those who oversaw Enron's collapse." The Supreme Court disagreed. Justice Ruth Bader Ginsburg wrote that the presumption of juror prejudice only arises in extreme cases. While there was certainly widespread negative publicity in Houston, Ginsburg made the following points:

- Four years elapsed between the time Enron collapsed and the trial. The shrillness of publicity had waned.
- There were four million potential jurors in the Houston area. "Given this large, diverse pool of potential jurors, the suggestion that 12 impartial individuals could not be empanelled is hard to sustain."
- The jury that convicted him also acquitted him of nine related counts of insider trading.
- Jurors had to fill out a lengthy questionnaire, drafted largely by Skilling's attorneys, and were then questioned individually.

Ginsburg added, "Appellate courts making after-the-fact assessments of the media's impact on jurors should be mindful that their judgments lack on-the-spot comprehensions of the situations possessed by the trial judges."

Justice Ginsburg's ruling in *United States* v. *Skilling*[2] plays a critical role today in cases involving pretrial publicity. For example, the Supreme Court of Kansas in 2015 in the murder case of *Kansas* v. *Longoria* considered whether a trial court's denial of the defendant's motion for a change of venue (see later in this chapter for more on changes of venue) due to extensive pretrial publicity in the small-population Kansas county of Barton violated the defendant's Sixth Amendment right to a fair trial by an impartial jury.[3] The Kansas high

2. 561 U.S. 358 (2010).
3. 343 P. 3d 1128 (Kan. 2015).

court wrote that "defendants face a high burden under the *Skilling* test—generally a defendant can obtain a change of venue only upon showing that publicity has displaced the judicial process entirely or that the courtroom proceedings more resemble a circus or a lynch mob." The court identified seven factors under the so-called *Skilling* test that courts should use to evaluate whether there is a presumption of prejudice caused by pretrial publicity:

1. Media interference with actual courtroom proceedings.
2. The magnitude and tone of the media coverage (factual coverage versus inflammatory coverage).
3. The size and characteristics of the community in which the crime occurred (smaller populations may make it less likely to receive an impartial trial since there are fewer potential jurors from which to choose).
4. The amount of time elapsed between the crime and the trial.
5. The jury's verdict.
6. The impact of the crime on the community.
7. The effect, if any, of publicity given to a confession or other "smoking-gun type of information," such as a co-defendant's publicized decision to plead guilty to the same crime.

Applying these factors in *Longoria*, the Supreme Court of Kansas concluded that although the defendant "established extensive media coverage and a high level of community familiarity," this was not enough "to give rise to a presumption that he would not receive a fair trial. He must present evidence of a lynch-mob mentality, and he failed to do so." Some courts, it should be noted, concentrate on a shorter list of four criteria from *Skilling*, namely: 1) the size and characteristics of the community in which the crime occurred; 2) the content of the media coverage; 3) the timing of the media coverage (i.e., the amount of time elapsed between the crime and the trial); and 4) the existence of media interference with court proceedings.[4]

THE LAW AND PREJUDICIAL NEWS

The U.S. Constitution guarantees both criminal and civil litigants a right to a fair trial by an impartial jury, with the Sixth Amendment safeguarding this right in criminal cases. An impartial juror is one who is capable and willing to decide the case solely on the evidence admitted into court. This definition is over 200 years old and comes from the famous trial of former U.S. Vice President Aaron Burr for treason.[5] Put slightly differently, an impartial juror is a person who can disregard his pre-existing opinions and knowledge and, in their place, render a verdict based only on the evidence and rules of law presented in court.

The fact that a juror may have prior knowledge of the facts of a case or preexisting opinions about it before being impaneled as a juror does not disqualify him or her from jury service. The keys are the ability and willingness "to set aside out-of-court information and to decide the case upon the evidence presented at trial."[6]

4. *United States* v. *Matusiewicz*, 2015 U.S. Dist. LEXIS 28906 (D. Del. Mar. 10, 2015).
5. *U.S.* v. *Burr*, 24 Fed. Cas. 49 No. 1492 (1807).
6. *Gentile* v. *State Bar of Nevada*, 501 U.S. 1030, 1055 (1991).

SUMMARY

The First Amendment to the U.S. Constitution guarantees freedom of the press; the Sixth Amendment guarantees every criminal defendant a fair trial. Many people believe these two amendments are in conflict because, often, publicity about a criminal case can prejudice a community against a defendant and make it impossible to find a fair and impartial jury in the case. The kinds of publicity that can be most damaging to a defendant include material about confessions or alleged confessions, stories about a past criminal record, statements about the defendant's character, comments about the defendant's performance on scientific tests or refusal to take such tests, and statements made before a trial suggesting the defendant's guilt.

Social science has not yet proved that such publicity does in fact create prejudice or that people cannot set aside their beliefs about a case and render a verdict based on the facts presented at the trial. An impartial juror is not required to be free of all knowledge or impressions about a case; the juror must be able to set aside his or her pre-existing knowledge and opinions and, instead, decide the case based only on the evidence admitted in court.

TRADITIONAL JUDICIAL REMEDIES

For more than 200 years American judges have had tools at their disposal to try to mitigate or lessen the impact that pretrial publicity might have on a trial. These tools range from carefully examining potential jurors about their knowledge of the case, to moving the trial, to delaying a hearing while publicity abates. As a last resort a criminal conviction can be reversed if there is evidence that the trial was tainted by publicity.* But this last resort is costly because it usually involves a retrial, resulting in added expense and inconvenience for all parties involved. These traditional judicial tools, sometimes called trial-level remedies, permit the court to reduce the impact of the publicity on the trial without inhibiting the press in any way.

As a last resort a criminal conviction can be reversed if there is evidence that the trial was tainted by publicity.

TRIAL-LEVEL REMEDIES FOR PRETRIAL PUBLICITY

1. Voir dire
2. Change of venue
3. Change of veniremen
4. Continuance
5. Admonition
6. Sequestration

---

* For example, a Kansas judge declared a mistrial in a 2008 rape case when a local newspaper published a story that possibly violated the fair-trial rights of the defendant. See "Judge Declares Mistrial, Faults Newspaper Story," http://www.rcfp.org/browse-media-law-resources/news/judge-declares-mistrial -faults-newspaper-story.

VOIR DIRE

Before prospective jurors finally make it to the jury box, they are questioned by the attorneys in the case and oftentimes the judge. These interviews are designed to protect the judicial process from jurors who have already made up their minds about the case or who have strong biases toward one party or the other. In a process called **voir dire** (French for to "tell the truth"), each prospective juror is questioned prior to being impaneled in an effort to discover bias. Pretrial publicity is only one source of juror prejudice. If the prospective juror is the mother of a police officer, she is likely to be biased if the defendant is on trial for shooting a police officer. Perhaps the juror is a business associate of the defendant. Possibly the juror says she doesn't believe in psychology or psychiatry, and the defendant intends to use an insanity defense.

When a pool of potential jurors (called the venire) is assembled, a preliminary screening may take place through the use of a written questionnaire. The jury selection process for the trial of James Holmes for the "Dark Knight" Aurora, Colorado theater shooting case was one of the longest and most complex on record. The court summoned 9,000 potential jurors, 403 of whom were asked face-to-face questions over 38 days.[7] After this initial screening, both sides in the case then question the remaining members of the venire, and either side can ask the court to excuse a potential juror. This procedure is called challenging a juror. There are two kinds of challenges: **challenges for cause** and **peremptory challenges.** To challenge a juror for cause, an attorney must convince the court that there is a good reason for this person not to sit on the jury. Deep-seated prejudice is one good reason. Being an acquaintance of one of the parties in the case is also a good reason. Any reason can be used to challenge a potential juror. All the attorney must do is to convince the judge that the reason is proper. There is no limit on the number of challenges for cause that both prosecutor and defense attorney may exercise.

A peremptory challenge is somewhat different. This challenge can be exercised without cause, and the judge has no power to refuse such a challenge.* There is a limit, however, on the number of such challenges that may be exercised. Sometimes there are as few as two or three and sometimes as many as 10 or 20, depending on the case, the kind of crime involved, the state statute and sometimes the judge. This kind of challenge is reserved for use against people whom the defense or the prosecution does not want on the jury but whom the judge refuses to excuse for cause. An attorney may have an intuitive hunch about a potential juror and want that person eliminated from the final panel. Or the juror's social or ethnic background may suggest a problem to the attorney.

---

7. John Ingold, "Aurora Theater Shooting Jury Pool."

* In 1986 the Supreme Court tried to place limits on the use of peremptory challenges to exclude people from a jury solely on the basis of their race (see *Batson* v. *Kentucky,* 476 U.S. 29 [1986]). But this ruling failed to live up to its promise, according to many defense attorneys, who argue that the use of peremptory challenges to remove black jurors continues. The high court tried again in 2008 when it reversed a conviction of a black man, who had been on death row for 12 years, because the prosecutor in the trial had used improper tactics to pick an all-white jury (see *Snyder* v. *Louisiana,* 522 U.S. 472 (2008)). The court has also indicated it is concerned about excluding potential jurors solely because of their gender in some cases (e.g., excluding women from juries in rape trials).

To select jury members for the typical criminal trial, attorneys rely on the answers to the questions they ask potential jurors and on their intuition. In the occasional high-profile trial it is not uncommon for attorneys on both sides to undertake a far deeper scrutiny of the panel of potential jurors.

Is voir dire a good way to screen prejudiced jurors? Most judges, including Supreme Court justices, place faith in the *voir dire* process and believe that, if correctly used, it can effectively weed out biased jurors. Most lawyers say they agree that voir dire can be effective, to a point. Still, it is difficult to argue with critics who say that voir dire uncovers only the prejudice that the prospective juror is aware of or is not too embarrassed to admit. Biased jurors can lie when questioned about their biases. They may not even know their mind is made up about the guilt or innocence of the defendant. And the prejudices may have nothing to do with pretrial news coverage of the crime. Potential jurors may be prejudiced against defendants because of their race, the kind of work they do or the neighborhood in which they live.

CHANGE OF VENUE

A serious crime that has been heavily publicized in one community might have received scant press coverage in another community in the state. The court can, in order to impanel a jury of citizens who know much less about the case, move the trial to the second community. This change of location of the trial is called a **change of venue.** If this relocation of the trial is ordered, all the participants in the trial—the prosecutor, defense attorney, judge, defendant, witnesses and others—go to this new location for the trial. The jury is selected from citizens in the new community. In 2016, for example, the criminal trial of Justin Ross Harris based on the "hot car" death of his 22-month-old son was moved from Cobb County, Ga., after the trial court judge determined that Harris had "carried the burden to make a substantive showing of a likelihood that prejudice exists because of extensive publicity, so it would not be just to try the case in Cobb County."

A trial in a state court can be moved to any other venue in the same state. A federal case can be moved to any other federal court, although keeping the trial as close as possible to the site of the crime is considered desirable. The federal trial in 1997 of the defendants charged with bombing of the federal building in Oklahoma City was moved to Denver, a city in the adjacent state of Colorado. In that case the move out of state rather than to another city in Oklahoma was prompted by the need to find courtroom facilities that could accommodate a trial of that magnitude.

Change of venue is costly. Witnesses, attorneys and others must be transported and housed and fed while the trial takes place in a distant city. The defendant must surrender the constitutional right to a trial in the district in which the crime was committed. Publicity about the case could appear in the media located in the community in which the trial is scheduled to be held, defeating the purpose of the change of venue. Often the effectiveness of the change of venue depends on how far the trial is moved from the city in which the crime was committed. A trial judge in Washington state who was concerned about newspaper coverage of a local murder case granted a change of venue. But he moved the trial to an adjoining county, the only other county in the state in which the "offending" newspaper had significant circulation. The move accomplished very little,

Often the effectiveness of the change of venue depends on how far the trial is moved from the city in which the crime was committed.

and the judge ultimately was forced to close portions of the proceedings to the press.[8] The concept that a change of venue might reduce the problem of a biased jury is constructed on the notion that publicity about a crime is, in all but rare instances, local in nature. The people of Jamesville may have made up their minds because of the intense publicity, but the publicity in Raymond Town, 250 miles away, was not as intense. But we are living in the age of the Internet, when high profile cases get gavel-to-gavel coverage on national cable news networks, and it is just as easy to spread a message across a state or region as it is to spread that message in a local venue. Whether this will have an impact on whether a change of venue remains a viable solution to the problem of potential juror prejudice remains an open question.

While a change of venue can reduce the risk of prejudicial publicity influencing a jury, other equally problematic factors may be introduced into the trial. The difference in the ethnic and racial composition of one community as opposed to another could possibly change the outcome of a trial. When the 1992 trial of four white police officers accused of beating Rodney King, a black man, was moved to the largely white distant suburbs of Los Angeles in a change of venue, three of the officers were acquitted of the charges and the jury failed to reach a verdict regarding the fourth officer. This occurred despite the fact that the beating was captured on videotape by a bystander. The officers' federal trial for violation of King's civil rights was held in the city of Los Angeles with a racially mixed jury, and all the officers were convicted.

In some states it is possible for the defense to seek a **change of veniremen** rather than a change of venue. Instead of moving the trial to another city, the court imports a jury panel from a distant community. In May 2011, the judge presiding over the highly publicized trial in Orlando, Fla., of Casey Anthony, who was charged with killing her 2-year-old daughter, brought in a jury from Clearwater, about 100 miles away, to hear the trial. A large segment of the population in Orlando had not only heard of the case, but scores had been protesting against the defendant, whose daughter was missing for about six months before her decomposed body was found near her home. When this procedure is employed, it usually means that the judge and attorneys visit the distant communities and select a jury panel, then transport the jurors to the community in which the trial will be held. This procedure costs the state less money, since all it must do is pay the expenses of the jurors for the duration of the trial.

CONTINUANCE

When a trial is continued, or a **continuance** is granted, the trial is delayed. By postponing a trial for weeks or even months, a judge expects that the people in the community will forget at least some of what has been written or broadcast about the case, and that expectation is probably legitimate. However, before a trial may be postponed, the defendant must sacrifice his or her right to a speedy trial, something guaranteed under the Constitution. Because courtrooms in America are clogged, there are few truly speedy trials today, but a continuance delays a trial even longer. The defendant may spend this additional time in jail if bail has not been posted. It is also possible, even likely, that when the trial is finally set to begin, publicity about the case will reappear in the mass media.

8. *Federated Publications* v. *Kurtz*, 94 Wash. 2d 51 (1980).

But a continuance is a perfect solution in some cases. One judge told of how, just as he was scheduled to begin hearing a medical malpractice suit on a Monday morning, the Sunday paper, quite innocently, carried a long feature story on the skyrocketing costs of physicians' malpractice insurance because of the large malpractice judgments handed down in courts. The article pointed out that physicians passed the additional insurance charges along to patients. The story was widely read. Jurors, who also pay doctors' bills, might hesitate to award a judgment to an injured patient knowing that it would raise insurance rates and ultimately cost patients more. The judge therefore continued the case for two months to let the story fade from the public mind.

ADMONITION TO THE JURY

Once a jury is impaneled, its members are instructed by the judge to render their verdict in the case solely on the basis of the evidence presented in the courtroom. Judges say they believe most jurors take this **admonition** quite seriously. In the single major study in which real jury deliberations were examined, researchers found that jurors listen carefully to and follow the cautionary instructions given to them by the judge. Failure to follow the orders can result in removal from the jury, citation for contempt of court or both. For example, in the Aurora theater shooting case, the judge released three jurors because one had discussed media coverage of the trial with the other two.[9] Jurors are also warned not to read newspaper stories or watch television broadcasts about the case while the trial is being held. But in this age of handheld electronic communication devices, many judges go further. Federal judges have been urged by the Judicial Conference of the United States to include these instructions as well:

> You may not communicate with anyone about the case on your cellphone, through e-mail, Blackberry, iPhone, text messaging, or on Twitter, through any blog or Website, through any Internet chat room, or by way of any other social networking Websites, including Facebook, MySpace, LinkedIn and YouTube.

Many judges feel admonitions are enough to discourage jurors from using social media. In 2014, nearly 500 federal judges were asked if admonitions to jurors against using social media during a trial were effective. Of the 494 judges who responded, only 33 reported any detectable instances of jurors using social media.[10]

State courts have adopted or will adopt their own rules. Judges have discovered that some jurors used their personal communication devices to gather outside information about the case during the trial and to communicate with people outside the trial.

In 2016, California considered a bill that would allow judges to fine jurors up to $1,500 for the use of social media and the Internet after evidence surfaced of jurors using Google to research details about cases. California juries are already admonished to consider only evidence presented in court and to not discuss the case until they are in the deliberating room after hearing all the evidence. In addition, a 2011 state law

---

9. Steffan and Ingold, *"Aurora Theater Shooting Judge Releases Three Jurors for Misconduct."*
10. "Survey Finds Infrequent Use of Social Media Use by Jurors."

makes improper electronic or wireless communications or research by a juror punishable by contempt charges. In the age of growing smartphone use supporters of the bill argue fines could further hold jurors accountable. Others, however, suggest that during the voir dire process judges should vet potential jurors to weed out social media and Internet addicts.[11] The Florida Supreme Court banned jurors from using electronic devices in 2012. During a criminal trial before jury instructions and again when a case is submitted to the jury for deliberations Florida judges must tell jurors they must not use "electronic devices or computer to talk about this case, including tweeting, texting, blogging, emailing, posting information on a website or chat room, or any other means at all."[12]

SEQUESTRATION OF THE JURY

Once a jury is selected, or impaneled, the problem of pretrial publicity diminishes. But other problems emerge. It is not uncommon for jurors to be removed from the courtroom during a trial while attorneys make arguments about the admissibility of evidence or the possible testimony of a witness. Except in extraordinary cases the public and press remain in the courtroom during these episodes, and what is discussed can and likely will be reported in newspapers and on television. Or prejudicial information may be generated by people outside the courtroom during the trial and, again, be reported by the news media. In some instances the aforementioned admonition to the jurors may be considered insufficient to shield them from this publicity, and so the members of the panel are isolated from outsiders during the trial. They are not allowed to go home each evening but are housed in a hotel. They eat their meals together, relax together, go to and from the courthouse together. Telephone calls and e-mail (if permitted) are screened by court personnel. Newspapers and television news broadcasts are also screened for stories about the trial. This process is called **sequestration of the jury** and is mandatory in some states for trials that last longer than a day, unless both the state and the defense agree to waive the procedure. In a few other states sequestration of the jury is required in all death penalty cases. In most jurisdictions, however, the jurors are isolated only if the judge specifically orders it.

Sequestration of the jury can have serious drawbacks for the state, the jurors and the criminal justice system. It costs the state a lot of money to house and feed the jurors. New York reportedly spent $2.5 million a year putting up jurors overnight until mandatory sequestration was abandoned in 2001.[13] It cost jurors both time and money. Staying in a hotel and eating in restaurants for two or three days may be considered a lark by some people, but the trials in which jurors are sequestered often last weeks or even months. Lives are seriously disrupted, and few jurors can afford a loss of income over such a prolonged period of time. In extremely long trials, some jury members suffering hardships will ask to be excused before the trial is completed. And many attorneys fear the criminal justice system may be compromised as well. Sequestration may keep jurors

---

11. Puente, "Jurors in California Could Be Fined for Using Internet, Social Media During Trials."
12. Zahorsky, "Florida Jurors Banned from Using Social Media to Discuss Criminal Cases."
13. Sengupta, "New York State."

free from unwanted prejudicial publicity about the case, but could generate a prejudice in jurors of a different kind, a prejudice against one party or the other for keeping them away from family and friends for an extended period. Defense attorneys express this fear most often, saying they believe jurors will blame the defendant for their hardships. But it was reported after the 1995 O.J. Simpson criminal trial, in which he was acquitted, that some jurors, who were sequestered for almost as long as Simpson was jailed, said they empathized with the defendant because of this.[14] The jurors in the second O.J. trial, the civil suit in which he was found guilty, were not sequestered.

SUMMARY

Trial courts have many ways to compensate for the prejudicial pretrial publicity in a criminal case. Each citizen is questioned by the attorneys and the judge before being accepted as a juror. During this voir dire examination, questions can be asked of the potential jurors about the kinds of information they already know about the case. People who have already made up their minds about the defendant's guilt or innocence can be excluded from the jury.

Courts have the power to move a trial to a distant county to find a jury that has not been exposed to the publicity about the case that has been generated by local mass media. While such a change of venue can be costly, it can also be an effective means of compensating for sensational publicity about a case.

A trial can be delayed until the publicity about the case dies down. The defendant must waive the right to a speedy trial, but, except in highly sensational cases, granting a continuance in a trial can thwart the impact of the massive publicity often generated in the wake of a serious crime.

Jurors are always admonished by the judge to base their decision on the facts presented in court and not to read or view any news stories about the case or use their personal handheld communication device while they are on the jury. There is evidence that they take these warnings quite seriously.

In important cases it is always possible to seclude, or sequester, the jury after it is chosen to shield it from publicity about the trial.

RESTRICTIVE ORDERS TO CONTROL PUBLICITY

Judges have been trying for many, many years to compensate for prejudicial pretrial publicity using the remedies outlined in the previous section. Some jurists and lawyers feel that these schemes are badly out-of-date. The mass media—especially cable TV channels and Internet blogs and other sites—have become far more ubiquitous in the past two decades. It costs the state more money to try a defendant when there is a change of venue or when an extensive voir dire is needed. These remedies don't always work, it is contended. There is a better solution to the problem: The court should control the kind

---

14. Labaton, "Lessons of Simpson Case."

and amount of information that is published or broadcast about the case. If this is done, it won't be necessary later on to compensate for any prejudicial publicity.

The Supreme Court gave trial judges guidance in adopting ways to limit the publication and broadcast of prejudicial information in a 1966 decision involving one of the most highly publicized criminal trials of the 20th century: the prosecution of Dr. Sam Sheppard for the murder of his pregnant wife, Marilyn. Mrs. Sheppard was killed early in the morning on July 4, 1954. Her husband, Sam, claimed she was bludgeoned to death by an intruder who attacked her in her bedroom as she slept. From the very beginning of the investigation local police thought Sheppard was the killer. The case, which had all the elements of a good murder mystery, caught the fancy of the nation's press and was front-page news in all parts of the country. Cleveland newspapers, like the *Cleveland Press*, demanded in front page headlines that Sheppard be charged and jailed. After three weeks of intense publicity, Sheppard was arrested and charged with murder. Publicity increased during the preliminary examination and trial, and few were surprised when the wealthy osteopath was convicted. Twelve years later, after several appeals had been denied, the U.S. Supreme Court reversed Sam Sheppard's conviction, ruling that he had been denied a fair trial because of pretrial and trial publicity about the case.[15]

The Supreme Court was critical of the press coverage of the case, noting that bedlam often reigned both before and during the trial. And while Justice Tom Clark did not excuse the journalists for their excesses, his sharpest criticism was aimed at the trial judge for allowing things to get so far out of hand. Clark said Judge Blythin and the other officers of the courts should have done more to control the use of the courtroom by the press; to control the release of information to the press by lawyers and police officers; and to even proscribe extrajudicial statements by lawyers, witnesses or other trial participants that divulged prejudicial matters. The Supreme Court made it quite clear that it would hold the trial judge responsible for ensuring that the defendant's rights were not jeopardized by prejudicial press publicity.

What the high court suggested, albeit obliquely, was that judges use court orders (called **restrictive orders**) to control the behavior of the participants in the trial. Limit what they can say, when they can say it and to whom they speak. If no prejudicial information is given to reporters, it cannot be published or broadcast. And that will go a long way in protecting the rights of the accused. The American Bar Association made a similar proposal two years later. Within a short time, restrictive orders became a popular way for judges to control the amount and kind of publicity about a pending criminal trial. But the judges went a step further than the high court proposed in 1966. Some orders were aimed not only at the participants in trials, but at the press as well. Some courts issued restrictive orders (or what journalists called **gag orders**) to the press, forbidding the publication or broadcast of specific kinds of information, or even barring journalists from commenting on some aspects of a pending trial. This latter kind of order raised distinct

---

15. *Sheppard* v. *Maxwell*, 384 U.S. 333 (1966). Sheppard was retried by the state of Ohio after the Supreme Court ruling. He was acquitted in this second trial. But his life was in ruins, and he died several years later of a liver disease. And yes, this case was the inspiration for both the television series and the movie called "The Fugitive."

and troubling First Amendment questions, for however the orders were structured, or whatever they were called, they amounted to the baldest form of prior censorship.

As we consider these restrictive orders in the following pages remember that they fall into two distinct categories:

- Orders that are aimed directly at the press, limiting what can be published or broadcast
- Orders that are aimed at the participants in the trial, limiting what they can tell the public and reporters about the pending legal matters

RESTRICTIVE ORDERS AIMED AT THE PRESS

There is no such thing as a typical restrictive order; in fact, that is one of the virtues seen in them by judges. Each order can be fashioned to fit the case at hand. They are often quite comprehensive. Orders aimed at the press usually limit the press coverage of certain specific details about a case; a defendant's confession or prior criminal record, for example. Orders aimed at the participants in a trial are usually much broader, forbidding comments by attorneys, witnesses and others about any aspect of the case. In 1975 another sensational murder case began, one that would ultimately bring the issue of pretrial publicity and gag orders before the Supreme Court.

Erwin Simants was arrested and charged in North Platte, Neb., with the murder of all six members of the Henry Kellie family. Like the *Sheppard* case, the arrest of Simants caught the eye of the national news media, and local judge Hugh Stuart had his hands full with scores of reporters from around the state and the nation. Stuart responded by issuing a restrictive order barring the publication or broadcast of a wide range of information that he said would be prejudicial to Simants. The order was later modified by the Nebraska Supreme Court to prohibit only the reporting of the existence and nature of any confessions or admissions Simants might have made to police or any third party and any other information "strongly implicative" of the accused. The order was to stand in effect until a jury was chosen.

The press in the state appealed the publication ban to the U.S. Supreme Court, and in June 1976 the high court ruled that Judge Stuart's order was an unconstitutional prior restraint on the press. All nine members of the court agreed that Judge Stuart's court order was a violation of the First Amendment. But is such a restrictive order aimed at the press a violation of the First Amendment in every case? This is where the high court split. Four justices—Potter Stewart, William Brennan, Thurgood Marshall and John Paul Stevens—said that this kind of restrictive order would never be permissible. Four other justices—Warren Burger, Harry Blackmun, William Rehnquist and Lewis Powell—said that such orders may be permissible in extraordinary circumstances. And the ninth justice—Byron White—said there was really no need in this case to decide whether this kind of restrictive order might be permissible in extreme cases, but concurred with Chief Justice Burger's opinion that became the court's opinion.

The chief justice wrote that a restrictive order levied against the press might be permissible where the "gravity of the evil, discounted by its improbability, justifies such an invasion of free speech as is necessary to avoid the danger."[16] Burger then outlined a

---

16. *Nebraska Press Association* v. *Stuart,* 427 U.S. 539 (1976).

three-part test to be used to evaluate whether a restrictive order that limited the press would pass First Amendment scrutiny. He said that such an order could be constitutionally justified only if these conditions are met:

1. Intense and pervasive publicity concerning the case is certain.
2. No other alternative measure might mitigate the effects of the pretrial publicity.
3. The restrictive order will in fact effectively prevent prejudicial material from reaching potential jurors.

Prior restraint is the exception, not the rule, Chief Justice Burger wrote. There must be a clear and present danger to the defendant's rights before such a restrictive order can be constitutionally permitted, he said. In Simants' case, Burger said, while there was heavy publicity about the matter, there was no evidence that Judge Stuart had considered the efficacy of other remedies to compensate for this publicity. Also, the small community was filled with rumors about Simants and what he had told the police. Burger expressed serious doubts whether the restrictive order would have in fact kept prejudicial information out of public hands.

NEBRASKA PRESS ASSOCIATION TEST FOR RESTRICTIVE ORDERS AIMED AT THE PRESS

1. There must be intense and pervasive publicity about the case.
2. No other alternative measure might mitigate the effects of the pretrial publicity.
3. The restrictive order will in fact effectively prevent prejudicial publicity from reaching potential jurors.

Please note, the Supreme Court did not declare restrictive orders aimed only at *trial participants* to be unconstitutional. This issue was not raised in the trial, but it was and still is assumed that courts have much broader power to limit what attorneys, police and other trial participants can say about a case out of court. "Guidelines on Fair Trial/Free Press," issued by the United States Judicial Conference, for example, specifically recommends that federal courts adopt rules that limit public discussion of criminal cases by attorneys and court personnel and suggests that courts issue special rules in sensational criminal cases to bar extrajudicial comments by all trial participants. But, in light of the ruling in *Nebraska Press Association* v. *Stuart,* the guidelines state:

> No rule of court or judicial order should be promulgated by a United States district court which would prohibit representatives of the news media from broadcasting or publishing any information in their possession relating to a criminal case.

In both 1978 and 1979 the Supreme Court issued opinions in cases that had the effect of reinforcing the rule from the *Nebraska Press Association* decision; that is, restrictions on what the press may publish are to be tolerated only in very rare circumstances.

In 1978 the high court prohibited the state of Virginia from punishing the *Virginian Pilot* newspaper for publishing an accurate story regarding the confidential proceedings of a state judicial review commission.[17] A Virginia state statute authorized the commission to hear complaints of a judge's disability or misconduct, and because of the sensitive nature of such hearings, the Virginia law closed the proceedings to the public and the press. The state argued that confidentiality was necessary to encourage the filing of complaints and the testimony of witnesses, to protect the judge from the injury that might result from the publication of unwarranted or unexamined charges, and to maintain confidence in the judiciary that might be undermined by the publication of groundless charges. Although acknowledging the desirability of confidentiality, the Supreme Court nevertheless ruled against the state. Chief Justice Burger, writing for a unanimous court, stated that the "publication Virginia seeks to punish under its statute lies near the core of the First Amendment, and the Commonwealth's interests advanced by the imposition of criminal sanctions are insufficient to justify the actual and potential encroachments on freedom of speech and of the press." The court did acknowledge that the state commission could certainly meet in secret and that its reports and materials could be kept confidential. But while the press has no right to gain access to such information, once it possesses the information, it cannot be punished for its publication. In this sense the court followed the *Nebraska Press Association* rule limiting restraints placed on the press's right to publish.

In 1979 the high court declared unconstitutional a West Virginia statute that made it a crime for a newspaper to publish, without the written approval of the juvenile court, the name of a youth charged as a juvenile offender.[18] Again Chief Justice Burger wrote the opinion for the court and stressed the fact that once the press has legally obtained truthful information, it may publish this information. In this case two Charleston, W. Va., newspapers published the name of a 14-year-old boy who was arrested for the shooting death of a 15-year-old student. Reporters for the newspapers got the name from people who had witnessed the shooting. "If the information is lawfully obtained," the chief justice wrote, "the state may not punish its publication except when necessary to further an interest more substantial than is present here."

"If the information is lawfully obtained, the state may not punish its publication except when necessary to further an interest more substantial than is present here."

The number of restrictive orders aimed at the press has dwindled substantially during the past three decades as a result of these three rulings. Most trial judges won't even bother to issue an order when it is requested. Examples of gag orders on the press are much rarer than attempts to close judicial proceedings and seal judicial records. These issues are discussed in Chapter 12.

Typical is the response of a U.S. District Court judge in New York state during the trial of a state legislator charged with failing to report $225,000 in income on his federal tax return and with lying to federal agents. The defendant asked the court to enjoin the press and the government prosecutors from issuing or publishing press releases, mug shots and photos and video taken during his so-called perp walk into the courthouse. The judge agreed there had been considerable publicity about the case, and that pictures of the defendant in handcuffs might interfere with his fair trial rights. But the judge pointed out there were seven million people in the federal court district and trial was

---

17. *Landmark Communications* v. *Virginia*, 435 U.S. 829 (1978).
18. *Smith* v. *Daily Mail Publishing Co.*, 443 U.S. 97 (1979).

not scheduled to start for six months. Surely with a jury pool this large, and by using a comprehensive voir dire, an impartial jury could be seated, the judge said. Request for the restrictive order was denied.[19] In 2012, in the case of James Holmes, the suspect accused of killing 12 people and wounding 58 in Aurora, Colo., Arapahoe County District Court Judge William Sylvester issued a gag order barring reporters from discussing certain aspects of the case and initially sealed all the documents related to the case. When asked to reconsider his order by more than 20 media organizations, the judge declined to overturn the gag order or unseal most documents related to the case.[20] An interesting motion that was filed in federal district court in 2016 sought to prevent prejudicial *advertising* that might taint a jury pool in a civil case involving claims that Tylenol caused liver damage. The plaintiffs, who were suing the makers of Tylenol, sought to prevent any marketing, advertising or publicity campaigns before a trial could take place, arguing such advertising could taint the jury pool. The makers of Tylenol argued that while they did not intend to engage in any advertising designed to influence potential jurors, they planned to continue normal advertising and marketing. Although the judge called the request "somewhat unprecedented," he acknowledged that pretrial publicity from advertising could affect the fairness of a civil trial. Although the order was not aimed at the press, the judge applied the Nebraska Press Association test and denied the motion, noting that other means were available to mitigate juror bias.[21]

When a trial court does issue such an order, it is typically overturned on appeal. For example, a newspaper photographer, with the permission of the court, snapped a photo of the defendant during the trial. After the photo was taken, the prosecutor told the judge that another judge had issued an order prohibiting the media from taking pictures of the defendant. The photo could improperly affect eyewitness identification issues. The court then ruled that no more photos could be taken, and that the picture that had been taken could not be published. The California Court of Appeals said the court order was a prior restraint and vacated it.[22] Although the order may have been issued to preserve the integrity of eyewitness identification, "the record does not demonstrate it is substantially probable that either the integrity of the identifications or the defendant's due process rights are at risk absent the prior restraint," the court ruled. The media already had a picture of the defendant in connection with charges being filed, and it was likely that witnesses had seen this picture. The Ohio Supreme Court overturned a restrictive order in 2010 that permitted the press to attend a trial, but barred it from reporting anything about it. A woman and her boyfriend, charged with involuntary manslaughter and child endangering, were to have separate trials. The trial court determined press reports about the woman's trial, which was to be held first, could taint the jury pool for the second trial. The Ohio Supreme Court noted that a restrictive order could not even be considered unless the circumstances were "imperative." While the court found the record supported the contention the man's right to a fair trial was in jeopardy, it ruled the trial court erred in issuing the restrictive order because it did not hold an evidentiary hearing to determine the extend of the danger. Instead, the judge based his decision on a speculative

19. *U.S.* v. *Corbin,* 37 M.L.R. 1840 (2009).
20. Simmons, "Colo. Judge Upholds Majority of Sealing and Gag Orders in Aurora Theater Shooting Case."
21. *In Re Tylenol Marketing, Sales Practices and Products Liability Litigation,* 2016 U.S. Dist. LEXIS 72774 (E.D. Penn. 2016).
22. *Los Angeles Times Communications LLC* v. *Superior Court,* 38 M.L.R. 2566 (2010).

assertion that other measures would not mitigate publicity. The judge only considered a change of venue to a large neighboring county, but ruled out this alternative because of the travel costs involved. The Ohio Supreme Court said avoiding additional travel costs was not enough to justify a prior restraint of the press.[23]

Are gag orders against the press ever affirmed by appellate courts? If there is good reason, such an order may be sustained. During the pretrial proceedings in the Kobe Bryant rape trial, an electronic transcript of an in-camera (nonpublic) hearing that would have revealed the rape victim's identity was accidentally disseminated to seven media outlets. The trial court issued an order barring the press from disseminating the information contained in this document. The Colorado Supreme Court upheld the trial court's order. While the court noted the U.S. Supreme Court rulings on permitting the publication of rape victims' identities (see pages 300–301), it also noted Justice Thurgood Marshall's statement that the state courts were not completely without the power to shield the identity of the victim of a sexual assault if such shielding were needed to protect an interest of the highest order, in this case the mandate of the Colorado rape shield statute.[24] The rape charges against the NBA star were subsequently dropped.

RESTRICTIVE ORDERS AIMED AT TRIAL PARTICIPANTS

While the law regarding restrictive orders aimed at the press is generally clear and has evolved swiftly since 1976, the law regarding restrictive orders barring participants from speaking or publishing about a case is less distinct and is still developing. The theory behind gagging the participants in the trial is simple: If attorneys, police officers, witnesses and others are forbidden from speaking about the case, reporters will be denied access to a considerable amount of material that might very well be prejudicial. Stories will not be written or broadcast, and potential jurors will not see or hear such information.

Gag orders aimed at the trial participants are not common, nor are they unusual, especially in high-profile cases involving celebrities or other high-visibility defendants. The judge in the 2005 Michael Jackson child molestation trial barred attorneys from discussing the case outside the courtroom. Lawyers, witnesses and police officers were barred from discussing the case against Scott Peterson for the murder of his wife and unborn child. These orders are often quite comprehensive. When the federal government prosecuted Richard Scrushy, the former corporate chairman and CEO of HealthSouth, a giant HMO, the case generated substantial publicity. A federal judge in Alabama issued a broad-based restrictive order to block extrajudicial statements by parties and the attorneys.[25] The order said:

■ No extrajudicial statements until the final verdict by any participant, including witnesses, concerning

1. materials provided in discovery in preparation for the case;
2. character, credibility, reputation or criminal record of a party or witness, or the expected testimony of a party or witness;

---

23. *State ex rel Toledo Blade* v. *Henry County Court of Common Pleas,* 926 N.E. 2d 634 (2010).
24. *Colorado* v. *Bryant,* 94 P. 3d 624 (2004).
25. *U.S.* v. *Scrushy,* 32 M.L.R. 1814 (2004).

3. matters that counsel should know would be inadmissible at the trial, and would create a substantial risk of prejudicing a trial jury; and

4. with the exception of Scrushy personally, any opinions as to the defendant's guilt or innocence.

▪ Participants must remove from their existing Web pages extrajudicial comments, allegations of prosecutorial misconduct and information discovered in the course of criminal discovery.

▪ Counsel for parties must avoid commenting in court papers that are not filed under seal on evidence that is irrelevant to legal matters involved in the case.

▪ All court personnel must not disclose any information relating to the case that is not part of the public record.

But sometimes judges will reject requests for such orders. The judges in the Trayvon Martin murder case in Florida refused requests from the prosecution to stop lawyers for defendant George Zimmerman from talking about the case outside the courtroom and from using a Web site that focused on legal issues, as well as using social media to comment about the case.

For many years trial judges were generally free to issue restrictive orders aimed at participants with little justification. In recent years, however, appellate courts are applying stricter rules that courts must follow.

In 2015, the 4th U.S. Circuit Court of Appeals overturned a gag order issued by a federal district court judge in the criminal trial against Donald Blankenship, former CEO of Massey Energy Co., who faced charges stemming from the Upper Big Branch mine explosion in 2010 that killed 29 people. The sweeping gag order, issued the day after a grand jury returned an indictment, prohibited both parties, their counsel, potential trial participants, court personnel and others from making any extrajudicial statements to any member of the media. None of the parties in the case sought the order. More than two dozen news organizations filed appeals. The 4th Circuit issued a short per curiam nonprecedential ruling overturning the injunction, stating "although we commend the district court's sincere and forthright proactive effort to ensure to the maximum extent possible that Blankenship's right to a fair trial before an impartial jury will be protected, we are constrained to conclude that the order here cannot be sustained."[26] That same year, the Michigan Court of Appeals overturned a gag order prohibiting prosecutors and defense lawyers from discussing a case involving criminal charges against two government employees related to the construction of a county jail in Wayne County, Mich. The Wayne County Jail Project, a 2010 project to construct a $300 million jail in downtown Detroit, came to a halt when construction was a quarter complete because of approximately $100 million in cost overruns. The failure of the project became the subject of public and media scrutiny. When a grand jury indicted former county chief financial officer Carla Sledge and county attorney Steven Collins on criminal charges related to the jail construction process, Wayne Circuit Judge Vonda Evans issued the gag order to preserve the defendants right to a fair trial. When the *Detroit Free Press* challenged the order, the

---

26. *In re The Wall Street Journal,* 43 Media L. Rep. 1349 (4th Cir. 2015).

Michigan Court of Appeals ruled the order was vague and overbroad because it applied to "all potential trial participants" and prevented "any extrajudicial statements" regarding the case, regardless of the content of the discussions. The court also held the gag order operated as a prior restraint on the freedom of the press. Although the gag order did not directly prohibit the media from discussing the case, it prohibited "the most meaningful sources of information from discussing the case with the media." Therefore, the court reasoned, the right of the media to obtain information was also impaired.[27]

The Alabama Supreme Court overturned a gag order focused on social media content and other online postings in 2014. The case involved two lawsuits against A-1 Exterminator Company for fraud, breach of warranty, negligence and breach of contract. After A-1 discovered the law firm representing the plaintiffs in the case featured the cases prominently on their Web site and Facebook page, the company sought a protective order banning extrajudicial statements by the firm. One of the trial court judges ordered the law firm to remove all mention of either case from their Web site, Facebook page, social media and "related web search engines." On appeal, the Alabama Supreme Court ruled that while it was important to make sure the jury pool remained untainted, the protective order issued by the trial judge was overbroad. The court concluded "the trial court should balance its interest in protecting A-1's right to a fair trial against the First Amendment rights of the plaintiffs and their attorneys" and that "any protective order . . . must be narrowly tailored so that it uses the least restrictive means necessary to protect A-1's right to a fair trial."[28] Similarly, in 2013 the California Court of Appeals overturned an order from a trial court for an attorney to remove two pages from her Web site discussing cases similar to one being tried in the court. The court concluded the order was more extensive than necessary to advance the government's interest and that there were other "adequate means of addressing the threat of jury contamination in th[e] case."[29]

When a judge in New York barred all parties from discussing *any* aspect of a criminal case, and threatened potential violators with a substantial fine, the 2nd U.S. Circuit Court of Appeals ruled that the order was inappropriate, even if needed. "The limitations on attorney speech should be not broader than necessary to protect the integrity of the judicial system and the defendant's right to a fair trial." The court said this order was too broad, and there was no determination that an alternative to this kind of blanket order would not work as well.[30] And the Ohio Court of Appeals ruled that a restrictive order that said "All parties to this action are hereby restrained from issueing any public comments about the pending status of this litigation" was not specific enough to block a litigant from writing a letter to a newspaper responding to an accusation published in the newspaper against his character. Barring comments about pending litigation did not cover comments made by the litigant in the newspaper, the court said.[31]

Finally, in a highly unusual case from New York, a trial court rejected a request for a gag order against a witness in a racketeering case, a witness who just happened

---

27. *State* v. *Sledge & Detroit Free Press,* No. 324680 (Mich. C. App. October 1, 2015).
28. Ex parte Jeffrey Wright, 166 So. 3d 618 (Ala. Sup. Ct. 2014).
29. *Steiner* v. *Superior Court of Santa Barbara County,* 220 Cal. App. 4th 1479 (Cal. App. 2013).
30. *U.S.* v. *Salameh,* 992 F. 2d 445 (1993).
31. *In re Contempt of Richard Scaldini,* 2008 Ohio 6154 (2008).

to be a member of the media. John A. Gotti Jr. was indicted for racketeering and other offenses that were related to the attempted murder in 1992 of Curtis Sliwa, the man who founded the Guardian Angels, a community-based anti-crime group. For years Sliwa insisted that Gotti ordered him killed, and he said so repeatedly on a talk radio program he aired on WABC-AM. The show has a large listenership. Gotti asked the court to bar Sliwa from making such extrajudicial statements, or talking in any way about the merits of the case since he would almost certainly be a witness at Gotti's trial. The court agreed that the comments could be prejudicial, but said a restrictive order would be less effective than a thorough voir dire and strong jury instructions. The court said it hoped that Sliwa would respect Gotti's right to a fair trial and refrain from making prejudicial comments on the radio, but that a gag order was a last resort it was not willing to impose at that time.[32]

Lawyers specifically may be barred under court rules or codes of conduct from making extrajudicial comments on a case, whether or not a restrictive order has been issued. The U.S. Supreme Court made that clear in a 1991 ruling that focused on an alleged violation of general court rules that applied to attorneys. A lawyer named Dominic Gentile, who represented a client charged with taking money and drugs from a safety deposit box rented by undercover police agents, held a press conference in which he claimed that police were using his client as a scapegoat. Gentile said his client was innocent, that a police officer was the likely thief who took the money and drugs, and described some of the witnesses for the prosecution in the case as drug dealers. Gentile's client was acquitted, but the Nevada Supreme Court ruled that the attorney's comments at the press conference violated a court rule that limits what an attorney can say about a pending case. The rule prohibited attorneys in a criminal case from making prejudicial statements about the character, credibility, reputation or criminal record of a party, suspect or witness. The rule did provide a so-called safe haven for lawyers who were permitted to "elaborate the general nature" of the defense.

The Supreme Court ruled by a 5-4 vote that states may prohibit out-of-court statements by attorneys if these statements have a substantial likelihood of materially prejudicing the proceeding.[33] But the court also ruled by the same 5-4 margin that the Nevada rule prohibiting extrajudicial comments by attorneys was a violation of Gentile's constitutional rights because it was too vague. The so-called safe-haven provisions contained terms that were so imprecise that they failed to give fair notice of what is permitted and what is forbidden, which could lead to discriminatory enforcement of the rule. What the court said, then, was that rules like these are permissible limits on free speech so long as they spell out specifically what can and cannot be said.

CONTACT WITH JURORS

It is common following the completion of a lawsuit for attorneys to talk with jurors to discover what factors led to the verdict the jurors reached. Today in highly publicized trials, reporters also want to talk with the jurors. It is not uncommon today for tabloid

It is not uncommon today for tabloid television programs and tabloid newspapers to offer jurors large sums of money if they will talk on the record about their deliberations.

32. *U.S.* v. *Gotti,* 33 M.L.R. 1083 (2004).
33. *Gentile* v. *Nevada State Bar,* 111 S. Ct. 2770 (1991).

television programs and tabloid newspapers to offer jurors large sums of money if they will talk on the record about their deliberations. A judge can certainly bar a juror from speaking with reporters while the trial is in progress or before the jury deliberations are completed. But once a jury has completed its work and is dismissed by the judge, the law becomes considerably murkier. Judges raise several concerns relating to the jury. One is to protect the jurors from harassment by the press. Both the verbal and sometimes physical pushing and shoving to get an interview can sometimes get intense. It is difficult enough these days to find people willing to serve on a jury. The prospect of facing harassment by the press after the trial does not help this situation. Another is to protect the sanctity of the deliberations. There are as many as 12 people on a jury. If one member speaks with reporters, it often reveals the actions and comments of other members of the panel. Finally, there are cases where subsequent trials of other defendants may involve the same crime, and juror comments about their deliberations could have an impact on these forthcoming hearings. And there is always the potential of a retrial following an appeal by the defendant who was found guilty by the jurors. In New Jersey in 2002 a jury was unable to reach a verdict in the trial of a former rabbi who was charged with killing his wife. The trial was extensively covered by the press and was televised by Court TV. Following the first trial the court forbade the press from contacting or attempting to interview the jurors. The New Jersey Supreme Court affirmed this order, ruling that interviews with jurors might reveal insights into the juror deliberative process, including the reaction to evidence presented in the trial. This would give the prosecution an advantage at the retrial, the court said.[34]

There are several means that a judge can use to limit communication between dismissed jurors and the press. Sometimes a court will simply set rules about how and when the press may contact jurors. Following a trial at a federal court in Massachusetts the judge delayed press access to the names and addresses of jurors for one day to permit jurors to recover from the stress of the trial and to think about what, if anything, they would say if contacted by the media. The court said there was a strong public interest in the case, since it involved charges of bribery against the former speaker of the Massachusetts House of Representatives, and access to juror's identities was appropriate.[35]

Some courts have tried to limit access to the names, addresses, phone numbers and other information that could be used to identify the jurors (see Chapter 12). The jurors are identified only by number throughout the trial. The use of these so-called anonymous juries is rare, but in recent years they have been used in the trial of the so-called Unabomber in 1996, and in the trials of both Oklahoma City federal building defendants, the trial of former government official Oliver North and the World Trade Center bombers.[36] Other judges have issued restrictive orders barring the news media from questioning jurors about their deliberations. But as a general rule, an order barring media access to jurors for an unlimited duration is unconstitutional. There have been exceptions.[37]

34. *State v. Neulander,* 30 M.L.R. 2281 (2002).
35. *United States v. DiMasi,* 39 M.L.R. 2191 (2011).
36. Kirtley, *The Privacy Paradox.*
37. *U.S. v. Cleveland,* 128 F. 3d 267 (1997).

Most state courts have their own rules regarding media access to jurors, and they vary. Federal judges are guided by *The Handbook for Jurors,* published by the U.S. Judicial Conference. *The Handbook* specifically says that it should be up to each juror to decide whether he or she talks to the press following a trial.

Some appellate courts have not permitted trial judges to ban such interviews. The 9th U.S. Circuit Court of Appeals struck down a lower-court order that prohibited anyone from interviewing jurors after a trial. The order was issued by the trial court to minimize harassment of jurors, according to the trial judge, but the Court of Appeals ruled that not all jurors might regard media interviews as harassing.[38] The Kentucky Supreme Court in 2000 overturned a trial court's order forbidding anyone to initiate contact with a juror even after the trial was completed. The order was needed, the trial judge said, to ensure jurors' personal safety and privacy. The state high court said the order was too broad. If a former juror doesn't want to talk with a reporter, he or she should refuse the interview. If the reporter persists, the former juror can complain to authorities about harassment or intimidation. He or she can even institute a civil suit against the reporter. But the court order barring anyone from contacting the former jurors after the trial went far beyond the court's jurisdiction, which ended when the trial ended.[39]

Finally, the U.S. Supreme Court ruled in 1990 that a Florida statute prohibiting witnesses who testified before a grand jury from revealing what they had said, even after the grand jury's term had expired, was unconstitutional.[40] Proceedings before grand juries are ultrasecret. Nothing but the true bill, or **indictment,** issued by a grand jury is a part of the public record. A reporter was working on a story when he uncovered information the prosecutor believed the grand jury should hear. The reporter was subpoenaed and testified before the grand jury. After he had given his testimony, he sought to write a news story about his investigation as well as his experiences before the grand jury. But the statute blocked his effort, so he sued in U.S. District Court to have the law declared to be unconstitutional. Ultimately, the Supreme Court did just that.

Chief Justice William Rehnquist wrote that traditionally courts have taken very seriously the need for secrecy in grand jury proceedings. But, he said, "we have recognized that the invocation of grand jury interests is not some talisman that dissolves all constitutional protections." In this case, the chief justice said, the situation involved a reporter's right to divulge information of which he was in possession before he testified before the grand jury, not information he had gained as a result of his participation in the grand jury proceeding. Citing the ruling in *Smith* v. *Daily Mail Publishing Co.*[41] (see page 445), Rehnquist said the state could not punish a journalist for publishing information that he or she had legally obtained. While important interests were at stake in maintaining a veil around the activities of a grand jury, these interests in this case were insufficient to outweigh the First Amendment interests.

Restrictive orders that bar the press from publishing information about a criminal case have ceased to be a serious problem for journalists. Orders that limit what

---

38. *U.S.* v. *Sherman,* 581 F. 2d 1358 (1978).
39. *Cape Publications Inc.* v. *Braden,* 39 S.W. 3d 823 (2001).
40. *Butterworth* v. *Smith,* 110 S. Ct. 1376 (1990).
41. *Smith* v. *Daily Mail Publishing Co.,* 443 U.S. 97 (1979).

trial participants can say remain a nuisance, however, and probably do not serve the judicial system as well as many observers might imagine. Rumors tend to thrive in an atmosphere in which the release of accurate information is stifled. It would be better perhaps to provide journalists determined to publish something about a case with accurate and truthful statements rather than push them to report what is ground out by a rumor mill.

SUMMARY

In some instances trial courts have attempted to limit the publication of prejudicial information about a case by issuing court orders restricting what the press may publish or what the trial participants may publicly say about a case. These restrictive orders grew out of a famous U.S. Supreme Court decision in the mid-1960s that ruled a trial judge is responsible for controlling the publicity about a case.

In 1976 the Supreme Court ruled that the press may not be prohibited from publishing information it has legally obtained about a criminal case unless these conditions are met:

1. Intense and pervasive publicity about the case is certain.
2. No other reasonable alternative is likely to mitigate the effects of the pretrial publicity.
3. The restrictive order will prevent prejudicial material from reaching the jurors.

In two subsequent rulings the high court reaffirmed its 1976 decision that confidential information legally obtained by the press may be published. These cases involved the name of a juvenile suspect in a murder case and the names of judges whose conduct had been reviewed by a confidential state judicial commission.

Although judges may still limit what trial participants say publicly about a case, even these restrictive orders have come under constitutional scrutiny in recent years. Press access to jurors following a trial is governed by various state and federal roles.

BIBLIOGRAPHY

Ingold, John. "Aurora Theater Shooting Jury Pool Cut Down to 115 Names." The Denver Post, 10 Apr. 2015.

Schwartz, John. "Confessing to Crimes but Innocent." The New York Times, 13 Sept. 2010.

Shipler, David K. "Why Do Innocent People Confess?" The New York Times, 23 Feb. 2012.

"Survey Finds Infrequent Use of Social Media Use by Jurors," Jul. 29, 2014, available at http://www .uscourts.gov/news/2014/07/29/survey-finds-infrequent-social-media-use-jurors."

Kirtley, Jane, ed. The Privacy Paradox. Arlington, Va.: Reporters Committee for Freedom of the Press, 1998.

Labaton, Stephen. "Lessons of Simpson Case Are Reshaping the Law." *The New York Times,* 6 October 1995, A1.

Puente, Kelly. "Jurors in California Could Be Fined for Using Internet, Social Media During Trials." *Orange County Register,* April 4, 2016.

Sengupta, Somini. "New York State Ends the Mandatory Sequestration of Jurors." *The New York Times,* 31 May 2001, A20.

Steffan, Jordan, and John Ingold. "Aurora Theater Shooting Judge Releases Three Jurors for Misconduct." The Denver Post, 9 June 2015.

Simmons, Amanda. "Colo. Judge Upholds Majority of Sealing and Gag Orders in Aurora Theater Shooting Case." AI.com, 14 Aug. 2012.

Zahorsky, Rachel M. "Florida Jurors Banned from Using Social Media to Discuss Criminal Cases." *ABA Journal,* 21 May 2012.

CHAPTER 12

Free Press–Fair Trial

CLOSED JUDICIAL PROCEEDINGS

Faced with Supreme Court rulings that blocked the use of restrictive orders to stop press coverage of the criminal justice system, judges in the 1980s began to close judicial proceedings and block access to records to deny reporters information they believed might be prejudicial to the defendant's fair trial rights. The press challenged these closures and, as with the restrictive orders, appellate courts found that such closures usually violated the First Amendment. This issue, as well as a discussion of the right to take photographs and use electronic recording equipment in the courtroom, is the focus of this chapter. Whether or not journalists and others who report on a trial can use computers and other texting devices in the courtroom is also discussed.

CLOSED PROCEEDINGS AND SEALED DOCUMENTS

When jurors were being selected in 2015 for the murder trial of James Holmes in Colorado, the process occurred in an open courtroom with members of the public and media present. Both the prosecution and defense attorneys representing Holmes, who was accused (and later convicted) of a mass shooting at a movie theater, had requested that the jury selection process be closed. They apparently feared that the media's presence would cause some jurors to provide dishonest answers during **voir dire**. Judge Carlos Samour Jr., however, rejected the motion to close the jury selection process. In doing so, he reasoned that "rather than hinder the effectiveness of jury selection, openness and the watchful eye of the media will increase scrutiny and enhance the reliability and fairness of the process. In the court's view, sunshine, not darkness, is the appropriate disinfectant here." In paraphrasing the late Supreme Court Justice Louis Brandeis' aphorism that "sunlight is said to be the best of disinfectants," Samour forcefully made the point that open access to judicial proceedings—as opposed to the closed-door courtrooms—helps to ensure fairness and integrity in the justice system, with the media playing a watchdog role on behalf of the public. Or to add another relevant maxim to the mix: "Justice must not only be done, it must be seen to be done. Without the appearance as well as the fact of justice, respect for the law vanishes in a democracy."[1]

This chapter explores the issue of access to the justice system. The Supreme Court first attempted to resolve the once-growing tendency of some trial court judges to close hearings and seal documents in 1980. Two other decisions followed in the middle of the decade. Today, a judge who is asked to close a judicial hearing or seal court documents faces a considerable hurdle if he or she agrees to bar the press and the public from the proceeding or deny access to documents. An outline of the judicial test that establishes this hurdle follows, along with an examination of how this test has been applied in a variety of situations.

OPEN COURTS AND THE CONSTITUTION

In 1980 the U.S. Supreme Court ruled that there was a right under both common law and the First Amendment to the U.S. Constitution for the public and the press to attend a criminal trial.[2] Six years later, the high court extended this right of access to other judicial proceedings and records. In its ruling in this case, *Press-Enterprise* v. *Riverside Superior Court,*[3] the justices fashioned a rather complicated test that a judge must apply before he or she can constitutionally close off access to the judicial process.

The first thing a judge must determine if the closure issue arises is whether the proceeding or document is presumptively open or closed. A hearing that is presumptively open, for example, is one that is normally open to the public and the press. To determine whether the proceeding or document is presumptively open, the judge must ask two questions:

1. **whether this kind of hearing (or document, if access to a court record is involved) has traditionally and historically been open to the press and public, or**
2. **whether public and press access to this hearing will play a positive role in the functioning of the judicial process.**

This two-part test for deciding if a proceeding or document is presumptively open is sometimes called the history-and-logic test or the experience-and-logic test. That's because the test asks courts to consider if there is an historical experience of openness

1. *In re Greenberg,* 280 A. 2d 370 (Pa. 1971).
2. *Richmond Newspapers v. Virginia,* 448 U.S. 555 (1980).
3. 478 U.S. 1 (1986).

surrounding the proceeding or document and whether the logic behind having it open relates to the positive functioning of the particular process in question.

While the question of the presumptiveness of access seems simple enough (Was the hearing or record historically open? Will access play a positive role in the functioning of the judicial process?), sometimes it is not. For example, in 2007 a U.S. District Court in Illinois ruled that there was no presumptive access to the names and addresses of jurors in a criminal trial because this information had not been historically or traditionally accessible, and access to this information was not tied to the proper functioning of the judicial process.[4] Twenty months later the 3rd U.S. Court of Appeals ruled in just the opposite way, saying that these names had been historically accessible. In an earlier era, the court said, when communities were small, everyone generally knew the names of jurors in a criminal trial. And for nearly a millennium before the 1970s, the withholding of jurors' names was "very rare."[5] If the judge determines that this kind of hearing has traditionally been open, *or* that allowing the press and the public to attend the hearing will have a positive impact on the judicial process, then he or she must declare the hearing to be presumptively open.

If the proceeding or document is presumptively open, then the burden shifts to the defendant or the government to convince the court there is a good reason to close the proceeding or seal the document. In doing this, the party seeking closure must

1. **advance an overriding interest that is likely to be harmed if the proceeding remains open or the court permits access to the court document.** Examples of such interests include the right to a fair trial for the defendant or protection of a witness's privacy. Then the advocate of closure must

2. **prove to the court that if the hearing or document is open to the press and public, there is a *substantial probability* that this interest will be harmed,** that the jury will be prejudiced or the privacy of the witness will be invaded, for example.

The words "substantial probability" are important; this is a high threshold for the advocate of closure to meet. A showing that there is a "chance" or even a "likelihood" of harm is insufficient to support a motion for closure.

If the advocate of closure proves that there is a substantial probability that such harm may occur, then the judge must

3. **consider whether there are reasonable alternatives to closure that might solve the problem.** Perhaps a thorough voir dire or change of venue would reduce the probability of prejudice. Closure of the hearing or the sealing of the document should be the last option, not the first option, considered by the court.

If there are no viable alternatives, then it is the responsibility of the judge to

4. **narrowly tailor the closure so there is an absolute minimum of interference with the rights of the press and public to attend the hearing or see the document.** A pretrial hearing on evidence might include many issues beyond the single issue that could harm the defendant. The court must close only that

4. *United States v. Black,* 483 F. Supp. 2d 618 (2007).
5. *United States v. Wecht,* 537 F. 3d 222 (2008).

portion of the hearing dealing with the single issue. Or the court must exclude the press and public from only that portion of a witness's testimony that might cause embarrassment or humiliation, not the entire testimony.

Finally, the trial judge must

5. **make evidentiary findings to support this decision and prepare a thorough factual record relating to the closure order, a record that can be evaluated by an appellate court.** This final element is important. Appellate courts want to be certain that the trial judge thoughtfully and carefully considered options other than closure as a solution to the problem. The Georgia Supreme Court voided an order closing the pretrial phase of a sensational murder trial because the judge had stated simply that alternatives to closure were considered and found to be insufficient. "A closure order must fully articulate the alternatives to closure and the reasons why the alternatives would not protect the movant's [the party seeking closure] rights," the court ruled.[6]

In summary, the right of access to a presumptively open judicial proceeding or document under the *Press-Enterprise* test is not absolute. Rather, it is only a qualified or limited right of access—one that can be overcome and denied if each of the five rigorous steps set forth immediately above is satisfied.

Let's look at an example of what a court must do before it may constitutionally close a proceeding. In 2002, singer R. Kelly was charged with multiple accounts of child pornography stemming from charges that he made a videotape of sexual acts between himself and a minor. After close to six years of continuances, Kelly's jury trial began in 2008. The trial ended in acquittal, when the jury found Kelly not guilty. Prior to the trial, a pretrial motion was made to allow evidence of other crimes, which was filed under seal. The trial court then held pretrial hearings, which were closed to the public. A number of media companies filed a motion to intervene in the case and obtain access to the pretrial hearings. On appeal, the appellate court used the history and logic test outlined above, ruling the pretrial hearings in question were "not ones that have been historically open to the public or which have a purpose and function that would be furthered by disclosure."[7]

This *Press-Enterprise* test applies to documents as well as to hearings. For example, in 2013, the Supreme Court of Virginia heard a case involving the sealing of exhibits during the criminal trials of Lillian Callender and her boyfriend, Michael Stoffa, for felony child neglect of Callender's 17-month-old and 27-month-old daughters and for second-degree murder of her 17-month-old daughter. Callender and Stoffa were tried separately. During Callender's trial, Ashley Kelly, a reporter for *The Daily Press*, requested permission to review photographs of and an autopsy report concerning the deceased daughter. The request was denied, and the court sealed the entire file from Callender's trial from public inspection until the conclusion of Stoffa's trial. *The Daily Press* and Kelly filed suit, asking the appellate court to unseal the records. The Supreme

6. *Rockdale Citizen Publishing Co. v. Georgia,* 463 S.E. 2d 864 (1995).
7. *Illinois v. Robert Kelly,* 397 Ill. App. 3d 232 (Ill. App. 2009).

> ### *PRESS-ENTERPRISE* TEST FOR THE CLOSURE OF PRESUMPTIVELY OPEN JUDICIAL PROCEEDINGS AND DOCUMENTS
>
> 1. The party seeking closure (either the defendant or the government, although sometimes it is both) must advance an overriding interest that is likely to be harmed if the proceeding or document is open.
> 2. Whoever seeks the closure must demonstrate that there is a "substantial probability" that this interest will be harmed if the proceeding or document remains open.
> 3. The trial court must consider reasonable alternatives to closure.
> 4. If the judge decides that closure is the only reasonable solution, the closure must be narrowly tailored to restrict no more access than is absolutely necessary.
> 5. The trial court must make adequate findings and put them into the record to support the closure decision.

Court of Virginia ruled in favor of the plaintiffs, holding the trial court failed to make "specific findings necessary to justify the sealing order." The court noted that while the trial court was concerned with potential pretrial prejudice from publication of information in the sealed documents and physical damage to the exhibits that would make them inadmissible in court, these rationales were "speculative and not supported by particularized factual findings." The court noted there was no evidence the information would prejudice Stoffa's right to a fair trial, and Stoffa was scheduled to be tried without a jury, anyway. In addition, the court ruled that making photocopies of the documents available to the public would protect both the original documents and the public's right of access.[8]

OPEN AND CLOSED TRIALS

With guidance from the Supreme Court, lower courts have applied the rules in the *Press-Enterprise* test to a wide variety of hearings and documents. Most of the cases expanding the open-access provisions have resulted from newspapers and broadcasting stations challenging court rulings to close the proceedings. But fewer and fewer access challenges are occurring today because the press is not raising this issue. Why? Partly because many of the small, medium and even some large media organizations are suffering financially, and don't have the resources to mount expensive litigation. As one media analyst described it, many in the press have shifted their emphasis from pursuing First Amendment principles to survival. And some large companies that have bought up

---

8. *The Daily Press* v. *Commonwealth of Virginia,* 285 Va. 447 (Sup. C. Vir. 2013).

hundreds of family-owned media operations in the past three decades as business ventures don't share the journalistic commitment to open government.*

Judges have an exceedingly difficult time closing off access to traditional criminal trials. The Supreme Court spoke unambiguously about such hearings in the 1980 ruling, *Richmond Newspapers* v. *Virginia.*[9] The case stemmed from a state court ruling in a Virginia trial. In March 1976 John Stevenson was indicted for murder. He was tried and convicted of second-degree murder, but his conviction was reversed. A second trial ended in a mistrial when a juror asked to be excused in the midst of the hearing. A third trial also resulted in a mistrial because a prospective juror told other prospective jurors about Stevenson's earlier conviction on the same charges. This exchange was not revealed until after the trial had started. As proceedings were about to begin for the fourth time in late 1978, the defense asked that the trial be closed. The prosecution did not object, and the court closed the trial. Richmond newspapers protested the closure to no avail. An appeal came before the U.S. Supreme Court in February 1980.

Chief Justice Burger wrote the court's opinion, noting that "through its evolution the trial has been open to all who cared to observe." A presumption of open hearings is the very nature of a criminal trial under our system of justice, the chief justice added. Although there is no specific provision in the Bill of Rights or the Constitution to support the open trial, the expressly guaranteed freedoms in the First Amendment "share a common core purpose of assuring freedom of communication on matters relating to the functioning of government," Burger wrote. "In guaranteeing freedoms such as those of speech and press the First Amendment can be read as protecting the right of everyone to attend trials so as to give meaning to those explicit guarantees," he added. The First Amendment, then, the chief justice noted, prohibits the government from summarily closing courtroom doors, which had been open to the public at the time that amendment was adopted.

The First Amendment, then, the chief justice noted, prohibits the government from summarily closing courtroom doors, which had been open to the public at the time that amendment was adopted.

But the chief justice refused to see the First Amendment as an absolute bar to closed trials. He noted that in some circumstances, which he explicitly declined to define at that time, a trial judge could bar the public and the press from a trial in the interest of the fair administration of justice. But, while the court did not outline such circumstances, it was clear from both the tone and the language of the chief justice's opinion that in his mind such circumstances would indeed be unusual. Justices White, Stevens, Brennan, Marshall, Stewart and Blackmun all concurred with the chief justice in five separate opinions. All but Stewart went further in guaranteeing access to trials than did Chief Justice Burger. Justice Rehnquist dissented.

The Supreme Court has not yet ruled that civil trials are open to the press and public, but lower federal and state courts have made such rulings. In 1984 the U.S. Court of Appeals for the 3rd Circuit ruled that civil proceedings are also presumptively open to the public and the press. In *Publicker Industries* v. *Cohen,*[10] a lawsuit involving a corporate proxy fight, the court noted that a "survey of authorities identifies as features of

---

* See Adam Liptak's report in *The New York Times,* "Shrinking Newsrooms Wage Fewer Battles for Public Access to Courtrooms," for a fuller discussion of this issue.
9. 448 U.S. 555 (1980).
10. 733 F. 2d 1059 (1984).

the civil justice system many of those attributes of the criminal justice system on which the Supreme Court relied in holding that the First Amendment guarantees to the public and to the press the right of access to criminal trials." The right is not absolute, the court said, but absent a clear showing that closing the trial serves an important governmental interest and that closing the trial is the only way to serve this interest, the civil proceeding should be open. In 1999 the California Supreme Court became the first state high court to make the same ruling, that the press and the public have a constitutional right of access to a civil proceeding.[11]

Some courts have based this right of access on the First Amendment, following the Supreme Court reasoning in Richmond Newspapers. Other courts have found there is a common-law or state constitutional basis for access to civil proceedings. In 2011, the Judicial Conference of the United States, which sets policy for the federal courts, adopted a national policy that encourages federal courts to limit instances in which they seal entire civil case files. The Conference, a body comprised of senior circuit court judges, concluded that federal judges should only seal civil case files when it is required by statutory law or justified by extraordinary circumstances.[12]

Frequently, neither party in a civil suit will fight an order to close a courtroom proceeding or to seal court records and it is left to the media to intervene. In 2011, for example, the Supreme Court of South Dakota ruled that a trial court judge improperly issued a gag order and an order closing a civil trial. The case involved a dispute over "Bear Country," a South Dakota family owned "unique drive-thru wildlife park featuring North American wildlife." The underlying action involved a civil suit among Bear Country's family-member shareholders concerning the management and control of the business. The shareholders asked a judge to determine Bear Country's value so that one faction could buy out the other. Before trial, the two parties submitted a motion to close the courtroom when financial information and testimony was to be presented to protect "confidential business information." The judge in the case imposed a gag order on both parties, closed the courtroom and sealed the court records. While both sides agreed to the motion, the *Rapid City Journal*, the Associated Press and the South Dakota Newspaper Association brought an action to remove the gag order and open the courtroom and documents. The South Dakota Supreme Court found a number of problems with the procedure and decision reached by the trial court judge. First, the court noted the judge did not correctly apply the First Amendment or common-law presumption of openness required. Second, he did not require either party to show that closure was necessary "to preserve higher values." Third, the judge did not articulate specific enough findings to allow an appellate court the ability to determine whether closure was proper. And, finally, the court ruled the order was not narrowly tailored. The court also found the judge did not have the authority to issue a gag order in the case.[13]

---

11. *NBC Subsidiary (KNBC-TV Inc.) v. Superior Court,* 980 P. 2d 337 (1999).
12. "Conference Approves Standards & Procedures for Sealing Civil Cases,"
13. *Rapid City Journal v. The Honorable John J. Delaney,* 804 N.W. 2d 388 (S. Dak. Sup. 2011).

There are, of course, exceptions to the rule that trials are open to the press and the public. Here are a few examples.

Juvenile Hearings. Traditionally, judicial hearings involving juveniles have been closed to the press and the public. Protecting both the victim and the accused is the common rationale that supports this policy. The victims are often juveniles as well, and the attempt to rehabilitate a juvenile offender is an underlying tenet of juvenile justice. Rehabilitation efforts might be much more difficult if the community is informed about the offender.

However, policies regarding the juvenile justice process have changed over the past two decades. Access to these proceedings is not commonplace, but not unusual either. There are at least a couple of reasons for this. First, many states have classified juvenile proceedings into two groups: those in which a juvenile is charged with a crime, and those in which the juvenile is the subject of a hearing related to child abuse, parental neglect, family reconciliation, dependency or some other similar concern. The law in many of the states that have instituted this two-tier system has made the first category of hearing (a criminal hearing) presumptively open to the press and the public, and the second kind of hearing (the kind concerned with social problems) presumptively closed. But at least a dozen states now regard this second kind of hearing presumptively open as well. In many instances juvenile court judges allow reporters to attend these hearings to get a sense of the problems with which the court is dealing, but grant access only if the journalists agree to refrain from identifying the parties in any story they publish or broadcast. Juvenile crime has taken on far more serious proportions in the past quarter century, and this is the second reason for increased openness. Whereas petty theft and assault were about the only charges placed against juveniles 50 years ago, robbery, rape and even murder charges are not uncommon today. Public concern has forced increased scrutiny of the juvenile justice process.

Despite the trend toward more access to juvenile hearings, the law is inconsistent from state to state, and case to case. The Ohio Supreme Court ruled in 2006 that in that state, juvenile proceedings are neither presumed open nor closed. The decision must be made by the court on a case-by-case basis, considering whether access to the proceeding could harm the child, whether this harm outweighs the benefits of public access and whether there are reasonable alternatives to closure.[14] Furthermore the 3rd U.S. Court of Appeals ruled in 1994 that the federal Juvenile Delinquency Act, a statute that governs the treatment of those under the age of 18 who are charged with violating the law, does not require that federal juvenile proceedings be open or closed. Rather, courts must make rulings regarding this issue on a case-by-case basis, balancing the interests of all parties involved.[15]

Here is a sampling of court decisions on juvenile hearings.

■ The New York Family Court ruled in 2006 that the privacy interests of a sibling of a 7-year-old who was beaten to death by her parents outweighed the public's interest to be privy to the workings of the court.[16]

---

14. *State ex rel Plain Dealer Publishing Co.* v. *Floyd,* 34 M.L.R. 2325 (2006).
15. *U.S.* v. *A. D.,* 28 F. 3d 1353 (1994); see also *U.S.* v. *Three Juveniles,* 61 F. 2d 86 (1995).
16. *In re S/B/B/R Children,* 34 M.L.R. 2147 (2006).

▪ In 2005 the Missouri Supreme Court ruled that the proceeding in which a juvenile was to be tried for a killing should be open because the charge would be first-degree murder if an adult were being tried for the same crime.[17]

Journalists and others concerned with reporting on juvenile proceedings should acquaint themselves with the law on this topic in their states or court district. Judges within a state may have varying interpretations of what is often ambiguous law. But for now and the foreseeable future, juvenile hearings remain an exception to the rule that criminal trials are normally open to the press and public.

Victim and Witness Protection.   The Supreme Court has ruled that it is permissible for a state to attempt to protect the victim of a sexual assault by permitting the closing of a trial during the victim's testimony or to protect the identity of witnesses such as undercover police officers. Laws exist in many states that provide for such closure. But these laws permit the court only to close the proceeding during the testimony; they cannot require that such a closure take place. A Massachusetts statute required closure of a trial during the testimony of a juvenile sex offense victim. The U.S. Supreme Court ruled that the law was unconstitutional. Justice William Brennan agreed that the state has a strong interest in protecting the victim in this kind of a case. The law was nevertheless flawed, he said, because it *required* closure of the proceeding.[18] Judges may still close trials, but they must provide a reason to close the trial and make sure the closure is narrowly tailored, or as brief as possible. For example, in 2008 a U.S. District Court in Idaho closed the courtroom during the testimony of a 12-year-old girl during a capital sentencing hearing regarding her suffering at the hands of a convicted sex offender and murderer. The defendant had killed several of the girl's family members, kidnapped her and her brother and then killed her brother. The judge ruled that there was a "compelling interest" in protecting the well-being of the surviving victim from embarrassment and psychological harm that outweighed the media's First Amendment right of access to that portion of the criminal judicial proceeding. Transcripts of the girl's testimony were provided to the press and public later.[19]

Traditional Military Courts.   Press and public access to military courts is generally open under both military law (Rules for Courts Martial 806 [b]) and the First Amendment.[20] There are exceptions. For example, when classified information is introduced at trial, closure will be permitted if the order is narrowly tailored—that is, no more of the hearing is closed than is necessary to protect the government's interest barring access to the classified material. But according to a report issued by the Reporters Committee for Freedom of the Press in the summer of 2013 public and press access to and information about both pretrial hearings and courts-martial of men and women in uniform has been routinely denied for years. The military has refused in many cases to provide any information about the pretrial hearing, declined to disclose

---

17. *State ex rel St. Louis Post-Dispatch LLC* v. *Garvey,* 179 S.W. 3d 899 (2005).
18. *Globe Newspapers* v. *Superior Court,* 457 U.S. 596 (1982).
19. *In re Spokesman-Review,* D. Idaho, No. MC 08-6420-5-EJL, 8/5/08; *United States* v. *Duncan,* No. 07-023-N-EJS, 8/5/08.
20. Cys and Mar, "Media Access to the New Special Tribunals."

courts-martial schedules and docketing information for both pretrials and courts-martial, and even withheld basic details such as the defendant's name and the criminal charge at issue.[21]

SUMMARY   American courtrooms traditionally have been open to the press and the public, but in the wake of the rejection of restrictive orders as a means to control publicity, some judges attempted to resolve this problem by closing off access to judicial proceedings and records. In the 1980s the Supreme Court fashioned a legal test, the *Press-Enterprise* test, for judges to use to determine if access to hearings and documents could be limited without violating the First Amendment. Since that time, courts have ruled that both criminal and civil trials must generally remain open. Exceptions have been granted for closure during the testimony of crime victims and some witnesses, and some juvenile proceedings.

CLOSURE OF OTHER HEARINGS

To laypeople, the judicial process generally means trials. But a surprisingly large percentage of the process takes place in hearings that are not trials, hearings that often resolve many of the issues formerly decided at trials. The growth of the wide array of especially pretrial hearings is the result of court decisions in the 1960s that substantially expanded defendants' rights in criminal cases, major changes in the way in which the criminal justice system works and attempts by members of the judiciary to work more closely with people who staff the penal institutions and social service agencies.

There are evidentiary or suppression hearings, pretrial detention hearings, plea hearings, presentence and postsentence hearings and so on. Many of these hearings take place long before the trial begins, weeks before the jury is even selected. Some focus on information that may be highly prejudicial to the defendant. At an evidentiary hearing, for example, the court may rule that a key piece of evidence, such as a weapon, is inadmissible at the trial because it was improperly seized by the police. The fact that the defendant had a weapon is certainly prejudicial. If this fact is publicized, some argue, it won't matter that the evidence is barred from trial because the members of the community, the jurors, will already know a weapon exists. Or the state may believe that the publicity about certain kinds of evidence may adversely affect the future prosecution of other defendants.

Since 1986 American courts have ruled that a wide range of judicial proceedings are presumptively open to the press and public.

Since 1986 American courts have ruled that a wide range of judicial proceedings are presumptively open to the press and public.* The Supreme Court has specifically ruled that both pretrial evidentiary hearings[22] (such as a hearing to consider motions to

---

* The Federal Judicial Center has published a guide to "Sealing Court Records and Proceedings." It is accessible through its Web site, www.fjc.gov.

21. Mackey, "Military Courts Continue to Stymie Public Access."

22. *Press-Enterprise* v. *Riverside Superior Court,* 478 U.S. 1 (1986).

suppress evidence) and voir dire proceedings[23] are presumptively open. These rulings apply to all courts, everywhere. Before such hearings can be closed, the trial judge must apply the rigid requirements of the *Press-Enterprise* test. This presents a high hurdle for a proponent of closure to cross. Lower courts have ruled that this applies to the content of the written jury questionnaires compiled by prospective jurors before the oral voir dire begins, but only with respect to the questionnaires completed by the jurors called for the oral voir dire. To close any portion of the voir dire the trial judge must apply the rigid requirements of the *Press-Enterprise* test, a high hurdle for the proponent of closure to cross. In 2010 the Supreme Court ruled that a Georgia trial court violated the constitution when it excluded the public during a voir dire. The court said that trial courts are obligated to take every reasonable measure to accommodate public attendance at criminal trials.[24] The court wrote there were circumstances where a judge could close voir dire, but in those cases the judge must articulate the reasons along with specific findings. Making a decision based simply on conclusory assertions, as happened in this case, is not sufficient. For example, a New Jersey trial judge closed a post-verdict jury voir dire to explore possible juror misconduct in a civil case. The judge said he wanted to talk with jurors about possible inappropriate behavior by one member of the jury. When the order was challenged, the appellate court agreed that there was no evidence that such hearings had been traditionally open. However, "Having the public observe the hearing would certainly discourage perjury and provide the public with evidence that juror actions are not unchecked," the court said. The hearing was presumptively open, and the judge failed to provide reasons to support closure, the court ruled.[25] In 2013, the Maine Supreme Judicial Court ruled that a generalized concern that juror candor might be reduced if the voir dire is conducted in public is insufficient to bar the public or media from the entirety of the proceeding.[26]

Other rulings on open hearings have come from U.S. Courts of Appeals and state appellate courts. Consequently, these rulings don't apply as broadly; they may, in fact, be confined to a single federal jurisdiction or a state. It is fair to say, however, that in most situations the following kinds of proceedings are regarded as open and can be closed only by a strong showing of the substantial probability of harm to some other compelling interest:

- Pretrial detention hearings
- Bail hearings
- Plea hearings
- Voir dire proceedings
- Sentencing hearings
- Attorney disciplinary hearings

But there are some kinds of proceedings that the courts have said are not presumptively open and generally remain closed to public scrutiny. The 6th U.S. Circuit Court

---

23. *Press-Enterprise* v. *Riverside Superior Court,* 464 U.S. 501 (1984).
24. *Presley* v. *Georgia,* 130 S. Ct. 721 (2010); see also *U.S.* v. *Bonds,* 39 M.L.R. 1507 (2011).
25. *Barber* v. *Shop-Rite of Englewood & Associates Inc.,* 923 A. 2d 286 (2007).
26. *Ex parte Hearst-Argyle Television Inc.,* 34 M.L.R. 1833 (2006); *State* v. *Strong,* 41 M.L.R. 1237 (2013).

of Appeals ruled that the press and public do not enjoy a presumptive right of access to what is called a summary jury trial, a rather unusual judicial proceeding sometimes used in civil cases. The **summary jury trial** is a device used by courts to attempt to get the parties in the case to settle their dispute before going to a full-blown jury trial. In such a case the attorneys present much-abbreviated arguments to jurors. There are no witnesses called, and objections to evidence or other matters are strongly discouraged. After hearing the arguments, the jurors issue an informal verdict that can then be used to settle the case. For example, if plaintiff Jones loses the verdict in the summary jury trial, she may be more willing to settle the case without a normal trial. The court said that there was no First Amendment right of access to such proceedings because such a right was not historically recognized and that permitting access might actually work against the purpose of the summary trial, that is, the settlement of the dispute.[27]

Grand jury proceedings are secret—and always have been. This is not an issue the press has disputed, but in two recent instances sensitive grand jury materials have been leaked to the press, much to the distress of defense lawyers, who argue that the release of this material violates the rights of defendants and can taint potential jurors. In December 2004 the *San Francisco Chronicle* published parts of federal grand jury testimony that suggested several major-league baseball players had used steroids. The following month both ABC News and a Web site called thesmokinggun.com carried substantial excerpts from grand jury proceedings in the Michael Jackson child molestation case. Under California law, grand jury transcripts are usually made public before the start of a trial, but in this case the judge had barred the release of the material because of the intense media coverage of the case. No penalties were exacted against the press in these cases,[28] but the mass media walk on very thin legal ice when they publish secret material generated by a grand jury hearing. The First Amendment provides little protection in such a case. (See pages 391–395 to see how the First Amendment rarely protects journalists who refuse to reveal the names of sources of such grand jury materials.) Rules that preserve the secrecy of grand jury proceedings apply equally to proceedings ancillary to grand jury proceedings.

ACCESSIBLE AND INACCESSIBLE DOCUMENTS

While a wide range of documents have been ruled presumptively open and hence potentially accessible by the press and public, sealing court records is a growing problem. Courts will agree to seal records to help the litigants avoid embarrassment, to encourage them to settle disputes and for a variety of other reasons. In the summer of 2008 the *The Oklahoman* newspaper reported that records in more than 2,000 court cases in Oklahoma were sealed between 2003 and 2007. These included divorce documents, wrongful death settlements and even name changes.[29] The problem has become so serious in some jurisdictions that in 2007, the state of Nevada created a committee to draft new rules governing the preservation, public access and sealing of civil court records.[30]

---

27. *Cincinnati Gas and Electric Co.* v. *General Electric,* 854 F. 2d 900 (1988).
28. Broder, "From Grand Jury Leaks."
29. "Courts Keeping Cases Secret."
30. *In re Creation of a Committee to Review the Preservation, Access and Sealing of Court Records,* 36 M.L.R. 1253 (2007).

Any party in a proceeding can ask that the records be sealed, but judges are supposed to apply the rules of the *Press-Enterprise* test (see pages 458–461) to determine whether such closure of records is permissible. In 2012, for example, the District of Columbia Court of Appeals ruled the right of access to the voir dire process established in *Press-Enterprise Co.* extended to questionnaires filled out by jurors in the murder trial of the man who was convicted of killing former congressional intern Chandra Levy.[31] This followed a similar decision to release the questionnaires of jurors administered during the trial of baseball player Barry Bonds for perjury and obstruction of justice.[32] In civil cases, courts have also found a right of access to pleadings, documents filed in connection with pretrial motions, summary judgment papers and settlement agreements. Some types of court records, however, are not generally available to the press and public. For example, as noted earlier, grand jury proceedings are closed, as are most grand jury records, including transcripts and evidence. However, when a grand jury hands down an indictment, it becomes a public record even though sometimes a court may seal an indictment until an arrest has been made. Patent trials are another area where documents are routinely filed under seal with no redacted versions available to the press or the public. As one court noted in a high-profile patent case, the result is that "many patent trials . . . contain mountains of sealed exhibits."[33] Over the past two decades a wide range of documents have been ruled to be presumptively open.

Evidence Introduced in Open Court. Evidence that is introduced in open court is generally accessible. In 2011 the Utah Supreme Court said the press was entitled to see a letter that revealed a criminal defendant's admissions. An inmate whose cell was adjacent to the defendant's cell sent the letter to the court. The court said most of the information in the letter was included in the defendant's brief to the court, which was a public document.[34] The Florida Court of Appeals ruled in 2005 that crime scene photos, crime scene videotapes and autopsy photos that were admitted into evidence in open court could be inspected by members of the press to determine whether the verbal descriptions of these materials provided by a witness were accurate. The court acknowledged the pictures were distressing to the family and friends of the victim, but that open justice was paramount in this case.[35] But this is not always the rule. A federal district court ruled in the trial of Zacarias Moussaoui that an audiotape of the cockpit voice recorder of Flight 93 (which crashed in Pennsylvania on Sept. 11, 2001) that was played for the jury should not be released to the press and public. Privacy rights of the victims and concerns of family members outweighed the right of the public to have access to the tape. A written transcript of the tape was made available, however.[36] And a federal court in Utah ruled in 2010 that copies of videotapes shown at a public competency hearing for David Mitchell,

---

31. *In re Access to Juror Questionnaires,* No. 10-SP-1612 (D.C. Cir. Jan. 19, 2012).
32. *Order re Access to Completed Juror Questionnaires, United States* v. *Bonds,* No. C07-0073251 (N.D. Cal. Mar. 14, 2011).
33. Order Granting-In-Part and Denying-In-Part Motions to Seal at 3, *Apple Inc.* v. *Samsung Electronics Co. et al.,* No. 11-CV-01846-LHK, 2012 WL 3536800.
34. *State* v. *Allgier,* 258 P. 3d 589 (2011).
35. *Sarasota Herald-Tribune* v. *State,* 924 So. 2d 8 (2005).
36. *United States* v. *Moussaoui,* 34 M.L.R. 1546 (2006).

who was accused (and later convicted) of kidnapping Elizabeth Smart in 2002 and holding her for nine months, should not be released. The judge said concerns about ensuring Mitchell had a fair trial and the privacy interests of the victim outweighed the presumption of access, even though the tapes had been played in open court during the hearing.[37]

Court Docket Sheet.   The 2nd U.S. Court of Appeals ruled in 2004 that there is a qualified First Amendment right to inspect these sheets that provide an index to judicial proceedings and documents.[38]

Documents Filed in Pretrial Proceedings.   The 9th U.S. Court of Appeals ruled that pretrial proceedings are open and "there is no reason to distinguish between pretrial proceedings and the documents filed in regard to them."[39]

Presentencing and Postsentencing Reports.   The U.S. Court of Appeals for the 9th Circuit ruled that unless a judge could demonstrate a compelling need to keep such records sealed, they should be open for public inspection.[40] But this isn't always the rule. In 2001 a federal court in Pennsylvania sealed a presentencing report on a former state senator who had pleaded guilty to charges of corruption. The court cited the defendant's right to privacy and the court's need for confidentiality to support its ruling.[41]

Plea Agreements.   These are written agreements between a prosecutor and a defendant in which the accused agrees to plead guilty, usually to a lesser charge than originally filed.

Information, Indictments, Search Warrants and Supporting Affidavits, Evidence and Other Materials Related to Sentencing.   The first four items all relate to materials generated in charging a suspect with a crime, or gathering material needed for prosecution. Sentencing materials may go beyond these kinds of documents and include items that are not admissible as evidence in determining an individual's guilt or innocence. A U.S. District Court in North Carolina ruled in 2005 that search warrant affidavits used during the course of an investigation of an FBI special agent accused of receiving gifts from a witness should be accessible. Any negative publicity before the trial could be addressed through voir dire, the court said.[42] But not all investigative records are necessarily open. When newspapers sought access to investigative records prepared by the police for the trial of Jared Loughner, who was charged in the killing of six people and the wounding of Congresswoman Gabrielle Giffords, the federal court denied the request. The court said such records are not judicial records under federal law, and the public has no right of access to them.[43]

But judges are often willing to draw a line if they feel that public interest will be harmed if some kinds of material are made public. A federal court in New York ruled in 2001 that while the press could have access to letters sent to the clerk of courts about a

---

37. *United States* v. *Mitchell,* 38 M.L.R. 2256 (2010).
38. *Hartford Courant* v. *Pellegrino,* 371 F. 3d 49 (2004).
39. *A.P.* v. *U.S. District Court,* 705 F. 2d 1143 (1983).
40. *U.S.* v. *Schlette,* 685 F. 2d 1574 (1988); *United States* v. *Langston,* 37 M.L.R. 1411 (2008).
41. *United States* v. *Loeper,* 132 F. Supp. 2d 337 (2001).
42. *U.S.* v. *Blowers,* 34 M.L.R. 1235 (2005).
43. *United States* v. *Loughner,* 39 M.L.R. 2155 (2011).

defendant who was about to be sentenced, similar letters that were sent to the court itself and used by the judge in the sentencing process were off-limits. The judge ruled that the people who sent those letters had an expectation of privacy about their comments, and there was a need for uninhibited commentary on the sentencing issue, something that might be deterred if citizens thought their ideas and opinions would be made public.[44] The Kentucky Supreme Court ruled in 2002 that a trial court could permanently seal some of the allegations of sexual abuse that were made against Roman Catholic priests in the diocese. The trial court said these particular allegations were a sham, immaterial, redundant and "scandalous." The state high court said it was difficult to see how access to such allegations would further the public's understanding of the judicial process and agreed that release of this material could cause irreparable harm to the diocese.[45]

Juror Records.　Access to information about jurors has become a sensitive issue during the past 15 to 20 years. As activity in the criminal courts has increased and fewer Americans seem willing to serve as jurors, judges have become increasingly protective of those citizens who are willing to perform this important public duty. In most trials the names and addresses of jurors are regarded as public records, open to inspection by the press and the public. But in some cases, judges have refused to reveal the names and addresses of the jurors, even after the trial has concluded. For example, in 2010 a U.S. District Court in Illinois refused to release the names of the jurors in the trial of former Illinois Governor Rod Blagojevich for lying to federal agents until after the trial was completed and a verdict rendered. The judge said he had promised jurors he would keep their identities confidential, and was worried about harassment of the members of the panel by the media and others because of the notoriety of the defendant. He said jurors receiving such contact might be distracted, disturbed or intimidated and be unable to do their duty. He added that he believed alternatives to the denial of access were impractical and burdensome.[46]

The appellate courts seem to be of two minds on whether such denial of access is permitted under the common law or the Constitution. The 3rd and 4th U.S. Court of Appeals, the Michigan Court of Appeals and the Pennsylvania Supreme Court have all ruled that there is at least a qualified right of access to these records.[47] The qualifications usually revolve around when and how the information is disseminated. The North Dakota Supreme Court ruled in 2008 that juror information was a public record, even if the trial court had promised jurors that the information they had provided on extensive jury questionnaires would be protected.[48] However, the 5th U.S. Court of Appeals, the Oregon Supreme Court and the Massachusetts Supreme Judicial Court have ruled that juror information is not necessarily accessible.[49]

---

44. *U.S. v. Lawrence,* 29 M.L.R. 2294 (2001).
45. *Roman Catholic Diocese of Lexington v. Noble,* 92 S.W. 3d 724 (2002).
46. *U.S. v. Blagojevich,* 38 M.L.R. 2089 (2010).
47. *In re Baltimore Sun,* 14 M.L.R. 2378 (1998); *People v. Mitchell,* 592 N.W. 2d 798 (1999);
Commonwealth v. Long, 922 A. 2d 892 (2007); and *United States v. Wecht,* 3d Cir. No. 07-4767, 8/1/08.
48. *Forum Communications Co. v. Paulson,* 36 M.L.R. 1929 (2008); *Stephens Media LLC v. Eighth Judicial District Court of Nevada,* 221 P. 3d 1240 (2009).
49. *U.S. v. Edwards,* 823 F. 2d 111 (1987); *Jury Service Resource Center v. Muniz,* 34 M.L.R. 1727 (2006); and *Commonwealth v. Silva,* 864 N.E. 2d 1 (2007).

Out-of-Court Settlements. There are some areas in which public and press access to court documents is routinely denied. Civil lawsuits often end with an out-of-court settlement; that is, both parties agree to a settlement without completing the trial. In the past, cases involving defective tires on Ford Explorers, the dangers of silicone breast implants, exploding cigarette lighters and defective television receivers were all settled out of court, and the terms and nature of the settlements were shrouded under confidentiality orders. Oftentimes judges play an important role in generating such settlements. These settlement agreements have traditionally been considered a private matter between the parties in the lawsuit.[50] Today more and more of these agreements contain provisions that the terms of the settlement are to remain confidential. Defendants often seek confidentiality to avoid the disclosure of sensitive or potentially damaging information. Plaintiffs are willing to agree to confidentiality in order to obtain a higher amount of money in the settlement. Therefore, the sealing of out-of-court settlements has become somewhat commonplace. At first glance there seems little difficulty with such sealed agreements; after all, these are private agreements between private parties. But the public interest can be harmed in some instances. The confidential settlement of a malpractice suit against a doctor, for example, will provide compensation to the injured patient. But such a settlement denies other patients knowledge of the doctor's wrongdoing. If an auto manufacturer obtains a confidential settlement with a customer who was injured because of a faulty part in the car, other owners of the same vehicle may not be warned of the danger.

Journalists are increasingly seeking access to such sealed agreements. Their quest for information is somewhat compromised by the fact that newspapers and broadcasting stations sometimes will seek the confidential settlement of a libel or invasion-of-privacy action. Most judges have not been receptive to the arguments that the press and public should have access to sealed agreements. Many jurists believe that the secrecy clause in these agreements encourages the settlement of lawsuits, and with courts in America as crowded as they are, judges favor anything that will reduce their caseload.* In 1986 the 3rd U.S. Circuit Court of Appeals ruled that there is a right of public access to sealed settlement agreements, the first important court to make such a ruling.[51] Since then a few other courts have ordered that such agreements be open for inspection.[52] As a rule, however, these agreements remain beyond the reach of even First Amendment arguments. Reporters who expose the terms of such secret settlements can face severe consequences. A court clerk mistakenly gave reporter Kirsten Mitchell a file containing the details of a secret settlement between Conoco Inc. and residents of a mobile home park who alleged that Conoco had contaminated their water supply. When the Wilmington (N.C.) *Morning Star* published a story about the settlement, the court held both the reporter and the newspaper in contempt. They were jointly fined $500,000.[53]

Many jurists believe that the secrecy clause in these agreements encourages the settlement of lawsuits, and with courts in America as crowded as they are, judges favor anything that will reduce their caseload.

* In 1995 the Judicial Conference of the United States, a policy-making body for the federal courts, rejected a proposal that would have made the sealing of records almost automatic in civil cases.

50. See Bechamps, "Sealed Out-of-Court Settlements."

51. *Bank of America* v. *Hotel Rittenhouse Assoc.,* 800 F. 2d 339 (1986).

52. See *EEOC* v. *The Erection Co.,* 900 F. 3d 168 (1990); *Pansy* v. *Stroudsburg,* 22 F. 3d 772 (1994); *Des Moines School District* v. *Des Moines Register and Tribune Co.,* 487 N.W. 2d 667 (1992); and *CLB* v. *PHC,* 36 M.L.R. 1990 (2008).

53. *Ashcraft* v. *Conoco Inc.,* 26 M.L.R. 1620 (1998).

Protective Court Orders. Other documents normally closed to inspection are records provided by litigants to the opposing party in a lawsuit that are covered by a protective court order. During the discovery process, both sides in a legal dispute are permitted to explore the records and witnesses and other material held by the opposing party. The court can assist in this process by first compelling disclosure of the information, and second, by issuing an order forbidding the parties from revealing the information to outside parties.

In 1984 the Supreme Court ruled that protective orders like this are not the classic kind of prior restraint that requires "exacting First Amendment scrutiny."[54] This decision has given broad leeway for judges to routinely issue such orders. And most courts follow this high court precedent in ruling on whether the contents of materials under protective orders are accessible. When the City of Detroit was sued after a woman was murdered following a party at a mansion owned by the city, a U.S. District Court in Michigan ruled that the press could not have access to depositions and other materials developed during the discovery process before the trial. The court said it issued the protective order to prevent interference in an ongoing homicide investigation, and protect the privacy of witnesses and other non-parties to the case.[55]

Discovery Documents. Access to civil discovery is sometimes an area of controversy. Journalists not only have sought to be present during the actual taking of depositions but also have tried to obtain access to deposition transcripts and documents obtained as part of discovery. In 2009, the Connecticut Supreme Court issued a detailed ruling involving sealed documents filed in 23 actions alleging sexual abuse by Roman Catholic clergymen. The Court ruled that there was a presumptive right of public access to "judicial documents" or "any document filed that a court reasonably may rely on in support of its adjudicatory function."[56] Although the cases had been settled and withdrawn in 2001, in 2002 four newspapers filed motions seeking permission to intervene in the cases and an order vacating the sealing of the documents. Although the court recognized there was a split as to whether discovery-related documents should be considered public, the court concluded that because "discovery proceedings can have a significant impact on the eventual resolution of disputes" those documents should be public in order to advance the public interest in judicial monitoring.[57] The 6th U.S. Circuit Court of Appeals ruled that protecting the associational privacy rights of non-parties was sufficient cause to justify sealing a list of Ku Klux Klan members that had been obtained as part of discovery in a civil lawsuit resulting from the fire-bombing of a black couple's home.[58] In a 2001 lawsuit brought against Bridgestone/Firestone, Inc. for the death of an 18-year-old football player from West Virginia University, four media companies sued to unseal nine discovery documents and 10 pages excerpted from legal briefs. The 11th Circuit ruled that under the "good cause" standard, Bridgestone/Firestone's interest in keeping trade secrets confidential had to be balanced against the press' contention that disclosure would serve the public's interest in health and

54. *Seattle Times Co.* v. *Rhinehart,* 104 S. Ct. 2199 (1984).
55. *Flagg* v. *City of Detroit,* 38 M.L.R. 1916 (2010).
56. *Rosado et al.* v. *Bridgeport Roman Catholic Diocesan Corp.,* 970 A. 2d 656, 682 (Conn. 2009).
57. *Ibid.* at 683.
58. *Courier-Journal* v. *Marshall,* 828 F. 2d 361 (6th Cir. 1987).

safety.[59] The "good cause" standard is based on Rule 26(c) of the Federal Rules of Civil Procedure, which requires a party in a civil lawsuit to show good cause as to why documents should be sealed, and similar provisions in state rules of civil procedure.[60]

Courts have traditionally been reluctant to make records obtained through the criminal discovery process open to the media or the public. The criminal discovery process involves the exchange of materials the prosecution will use to secure a conviction and material the defense will use to achieve an acquittal. In criminal cases, prosecutors are not required by law to turn over all evidence gathered in a criminal investigation to the defense, although prosecutors must share with the defense evidence that may exonerate the defendant.[61] This material may or may not eventually be submitted as evidence at trial.

National Security.   The nation's fight against terrorism and terrorist acts has resulted in many instances of closed court records. In early 2007 *The New York Times* reported that the Bush administration was employing extraordinary secrecy in defending civil lawsuits filed against the National Security Agency because of its highly classified domestic surveillance program. "Plaintiffs and judges' clerks cannot see its secret filings. Judges have to make appointments to review them and are not allowed to keep copies," the newspaper reported.[62]

The case of accused terrorist Zacarias Moussaoui provides an example of the access difficulties presented by such cases. In this instance, the government not only sought to deny access to certain portions of the proceedings, it also successfully convinced the judge to seal most of the court records. The questions focused on whether Moussaoui, a French citizen, could have access to captured Al Qaeda witnesses who he contended would help him prove his innocence. In August 2002 Judge Leonie Brinkema sealed many of the proceedings when the government contended that Moussaoui could use the material he placed in the record to secretly communicate with co-conspirators or sympathizers with coded messages. At the time, Moussaoui, who was ostensibly defending himself, was filing great numbers of highly inflammatory pleadings. Judge Brinkema modified her order a month later and said materials would be unsealed 10 days after they were filed, giving the government time to challenge the release of individual documents.[63] In April 2003 several news organizations went to court to try to gain access to these materials.[64] The following day the judge announced that she had serious doubts whether the government could actually prosecute Moussaoui in a civilian court "under the shroud of secrecy under which it seeks to proceed."[65] The case, then, might have to be moved to a military tribunal, in which secrecy would be more readily tolerated (see pages 465-466). Moussaoui abruptly pleaded guilty in April 2005 to charges of conspiracy and the access issues became moot.

---

59. *Chicago Tribune Co.* v. *Bridgestone/Firestone, Inc.,* 263 F. 2d 1304, 1314-15 (11th Cir. 2001).
60. See also *In re Alexander Grant & Co. Litig.,* 820 F. 2d 352, 356 (11th Cir. 1987) (discussing the operation of umbrella protective orders that postpones the necessary showing of "good cause").
61. *Brady* v. *Maryland,* 373 U.S. 83 (1963).
62. Liptak, "Secrecy at Issue."
63. *United States* v. *Moussaoui,* 31 M.L.R. 1574 (2002).
64. Shenon, "News Groups Want Terror Case Files."
65. Shenon, "Judge Critical of Secrecy."

TIPS FOR REPORTERS WHEN JUDICIAL HEARING IS CLOSED

■ Call the editor immediately to get a lawyer on the job.
■ Make a formal objection to closure.
■ Ask the judge to delay the closure until the lawyer arrives.

ACCESS AND THE BROADCAST JOURNALIST

Access to the judicial process for the broadcast journalist involves two issues that normally don't concern reporters in the print media.

Access to the judicial process for the broadcast journalist involves two issues that normally don't concern reporters in the print media.

■ Is it possible to obtain copies of evidence contained on audio- or videotape, and then air these tapes?
■ Is it possible to broadcast or telecast the entire judicial proceeding?

Two Supreme Court rulings initially loomed as major stumbling blocks for broadcast journalists: a 1965 ruling (*Estes* v. *Texas*[66]) that generally supported the ban on the telecast or broadcast of judicial proceedings, and a 1978 ruling (*Nixon* v. *Warner Communications*[67]) in which the high court refused to recognize the right of the journalists to make copies of audiotaped evidence for broadcast on the news. *Estes* will be discussed shortly. The second case involved tapes made by President Richard Nixon at the White House that were used as evidence in many of the Watergate trials of the 1970s. Broadcasters wanted to make copies of these tapes and play them for radio listeners and television viewers. The Supreme Court agreed that there is a generally recognized right of access to inspect evidentiary records in a case but said that this right was not an absolute right. "The decision as to access is one best left to the sound discretion of the trial court, a discretion to be exercised in light of the relevant facts and circumstances of the particular case," the court ruled. Courts have come a long way in granting press access to judicial evidence since 1978. But because the Nixon case focused specifically on the broadcast of taped evidence, those judges who wish to resist the broadcasters' efforts to use taped evidence in their newscasts have a fairly strong precedent on their side.[68] This section first focuses on gaining access to audio- or videotape evidence, and then, the recording or televising of judicial proceedings.

Access to Evidence

Courts consider a variety of factors when considering a request to permit the broadcast of audio- or videotape evidence.

■ **Was the material introduced into evidence in open court, or have written transcripts of the material been provided?** If the answer is yes to either

---

66. 381 U.S. 532 (1965).
67. 434 U.S. 591 (1978).
68. See, for example, *Group W Television Inc.* v. *Maryland,* 626 A. 2d 1032 (1993).

question, it is more likely, but by no means certain, that the court will agree to the request. In one of the earliest cases involving such a request TV journalists sought to broadcast videotapes of an FBI sting operation that involved members of the U.S. House of Representatives and Senate. The tapes had been played to the jury in open court, and several of the defendants were convicted. The trial judge refused the request, saying that if the tapes were broadcast, it would be difficult to later empanel a jury should an appellate court order a retrial. The U.S. Court of Appeals reversed the decision, stating that the trial court must keep in mind the nation's strong tradition of access to judicial proceedings when it balanced the competing interests. And in balancing these interests, "the court must give appropriate weight and consideration to the presumption—however gauged—in favor of public access to judicial records." The appellate court admitted a retrial might be a problem, but the tapes contained only admissible evidence that had been introduced in open court.[69] If the material has not or will not be introduced into evidence, chances of airing it are slim. In the highly publicized trial of John Hinckley, who was accused of trying to assassinate President Ronald Reagan, the television networks sought to televise the videotaped deposition of actress Jodie Foster, but the tape was never admitted into evidence. It was simply a statement from a witness; it just happened to be videotaped. The request was refused.[70] (Hinckley, who was found innocent by reason of insanity, was apparently infatuated with Foster and this fantasy played a part in his motivation to shoot the president.)

- **Could broadcast of the material prejudice the fair trial rights of the defendant?** The Maryland Court of Special Appeals affirmed a lower-court ruling barring the broadcast of home videotape that was introduced as evidence in a murder trial. Pictured in the videotape were two men who were charged with the murder of the victim. The defendants were being tried separately, and the trial judge barred the telecast of the videotape until the trial of the second defendant was concluded. The fair trial rights of the second defendant took precedence over any common law or First Amendment right to gain access to and then broadcast the evidence, the court said.[71] Eight years later, however, the 2nd U.S. Court of Appeals ruled it was permissible for the broadcast media to air tapes presented as evidence by the government at a pretrial detention hearing. Defendants argued that the broadcast of the tapes could endanger their fair trial rights, but the appellate court said these concerns could be addressed by a thorough voir dire, or even a change of venue.[72]

- **What people are on the audio- or videotape?** Tapes of defendants or police officers are more likely to be released than tapes of victims or witnesses.

69. *In re Application of NBC,* 653 F. 2d 609 (1981).
70. *In re Application of ABC,* 537 F. Supp. 1168 (1982).
71. *Group W Television Inc. v. Maryland,* 626 A. 2d 1032 (1993).
72. *United States v. Graham,* 257 F. 3d 143 (2001).

Jodie Foster was an innocent third party who was inadvertently pulled into the Hinckley case. A U.S. District Court in Minnesota rejected requests from broadcasters for permission to air videotapes of a hostage recorded by her kidnapper. The court said airing the tape would cause severe hardship for the woman, and would not serve a useful public purpose.[73]

▪ **Will airing the tape result in serving a public purpose?** Will it help members of the community understand the workings of the court, or law enforcement operations or important aspects of a trial? A court is more likely to permit the airing of so-called electronic evidence if it accomplishes a useful public purpose, as opposed to simply titillating listeners and viewers.

RECORDING AND TELEVISING JUDICIAL PROCEEDINGS

In 1976, only about 50 years ago, cameras and other recording equipment were barred from courtrooms in all but two states, Texas and Colorado. Today, such equipment is permitted in at least some courtrooms in all 50 states. Mississippi and South Dakota became the final two states to join in this massive reversal of the older rules. The rules vary from state to state and are often complex. Here is a brief overview of some of the kinds of variations that exist:

▪ In nearly all states cameras and/or recording equipment are permitted in both trial and appellate courts. In a handful of states recording is permitted only in appellate courts. But these state rules tend to be fluid and change from time to time. The best source for information regarding what is permitted in an individual state is the Web site maintained by the Radio-Television Digital News Association, www.rtdna.org.

▪ In some states the right to use this equipment in a courtroom is presumed. In other states broadcasters and photographers must first get the permission of the judge or justices or even the parties. But in either case, a judge can bar electronic equipment if there is sufficient reason.

▪ In some instances parties involved in the legal proceeding must agree before they can be photographed. But their refusal to be photographed cannot totally block cameras from recording the rest of the participants or the proceedings in general.

▪ Jurors cannot be photographed in some states.

The reversal of the rules regarding the use of cameras and other recording devices in the courtroom came after a more than 40-year struggle by the press. Prohibitions against the use of cameras were instituted in the 1930s after the almost unbridled photography during the trial of Bruno Hauptmann, the man accused of kidnapping and killing the baby of Charles and Anne Lindbergh, generated a circus-like atmosphere during the proceeding. The American Bar Association instituted Canon 35, which called for banning the use of cameras and other electronic recording equipment during trials, and

At that time the press had conducted itself in an outrageous fashion in covering the trial of Bruno Hauptmann, who in 1934 was charged with kidnapping the baby of Charles and Anne Lindbergh.

---

73. *In re Application of KSTP,* 504 F. Supp. 360 (1980).

the vast majority of American courts adopted this rule.[74] As photographic technology improved in the 1940s and 1950s, and as broadcast journalism became a more important part of Americans' news diets, pressure to change the rules increased. But in 1965 the Supreme Court of the United States blunted the efforts to modify these limits when it ruled that the presence of cameras and recorders at a trial in Texas (one of the two states that did not adopt Canon 35 rules) prejudiced the rights of the defendant to a fair trial.[75] Despite this setback, efforts by the press to open courtrooms to recording equipment continued across the nation, and one by one, states abandoned the rules of Canon 35. In 1981 the Supreme Court gave its approval to these changes when it ruled in *Chandler* v. *Florida* that the mere presence of cameras in the courtroom in and of itself would not necessarily have an adverse effect on the trial process. In order to block the use of cameras and recorders at a trial, the court will have to find that the equipment will adversely affect the trial process. To overturn a conviction at a trial that has been televised, the defendant would need to show that the electronic equipment actually made a substantial difference in some material aspect of the proceeding.[76]

State Courts. *Chandler* v. *Florida* permits states to open their courtrooms to cameras. It does not require them to do so. The Supreme Court did *not* say that photographers have a First Amendment right to take their equipment into courtrooms. Instead it simply said that states were free to experiment with television coverage of trials. States have developed their own standards to assess when cameras can be barred from courtrooms. In California, for example, a trial judge has to make specific findings before he or she can prohibit the recording of court proceedings. In Florida, the trial court must hold an evidentiary hearing if a defendant or other participant protests the television coverage. Before cameras and recorders may be excluded, there must be a finding that the electronic coverage of the trial would have an important "qualitatively different effect" on the trial than would other types of coverage.[77] In 2005 the Mississippi Supreme Court ruled that a trial court could not bar a television station from televising a sentencing hearing unless the court could justify closing the proceeding to all mass media.[78] And the Georgia Supreme Court ruled in the same year that a trial court must cite a specific factual basis to deny a newspaper's request to take still photographs at a murder trial. Speculation regarding potential harm was not sufficient.[79]

All 50 states allow some camera coverage. However, the extent of coverage permitted, as well as the rules journalists must follow, differs greatly among the states. In some states cameras will not be permitted unless various key trial participants agree. In more states the cameras are allowed on the discretion of the judge. If a participant objects to the admission of cameras to the courtroom, the press must honor this objection and refrain from photographing or recording this individual. And judges can and do require cameras to be turned off during the presentation of certain kinds of evidence, such as

74. White, "Cameras in the Courtroom."
75. *Estes* v. *Texas,* 381 U.S. 532 (1965).
76. 449 U.S. 560 (1981).
77. *Florida* v. *Palm Beach Newspapers,* 395 So. 2d 544 (1981).
78. *In re WBLT Inc.,* 905 So. 2d 1196 (2005).
79. *Morris Communications LLC* v. *Griffin,* 33 M.L.R. 2394 (2005).

gory crime scene photos. Most states have adopted guidelines that establish the number of still and motion picture cameras permitted in the courtroom at any one time. Rules often specify where the cameras may be placed, require that all pictures be taken with available light and even set standards of dress for photographers and technicians. The press must often be willing to share the fruits of the photography through pooling agreements, since most states have guidelines limiting movement and placement of cameras to when the court is in recess only.

Federal Courts. Cameras are generally barred from the Supreme Court of the United States. In 2011 there was a push by the media to permit cameras to at least record the arguments over the constitutionality of President Obama's health care law.* The request was doomed, Adam Liptak wrote in *The New York Times*. Why? Most of the justices don't want the arguments to be televised or even recorded.[80] Liptak cited several reasons:

- Some justices say the public cannot be trusted to understand what goes on during the oral arguments.
- Some say they worry that the kind of public scrutiny televised hearings would bring would alter the behavior of the lawyers and even the justices for the worse.
- Some say they fear harm to their personal privacy or the court's prestige.

Liptak notes that an unspoken but real concern is the "sound bite" factor. While some broadcasters seek to televise entire hearings, there is no doubt most would simply show brief bits and pieces of the hearings.

The ban against the use of cameras and other recording equipment in lower federal court is not absolute, as it is in the high court, but the courtrooms are not nearly as open as they are in state courts. Experimental use of cameras in federal trial courts occurs now and then. In September 2010, the Judicial Conference authorized a three-year pilot project to evaluate the effect of cameras in district court courtrooms. The program only applied to civil cases. Under the program, proceedings may be recorded with the approval of the presiding judge and parties must consent to the recording of each proceeding in a case. Videos were then posted on www.uscourts.gov. Fourteen courts participated in the pilot, which began June 18, 2011, and ended July 18, 2015.† In March 2016, the 9th Circuit Judicial Council, in cooperation with the Judicial Conference, authorized the three districts in the 9th Circuit that participated in the cameras pilot (California Northern, Washington Western and Guam) to continue the pilot program under the same terms and conditions.

IN 2010, however, the Supreme Court barred a federal district court from broadcasting a nonjury trial in *Hollingsworth* v. *Perry,*[81] a case involving Proposition 8, which

---

* The high court did release audio recordings of the oral arguments in the case a few days following the hearing, and two years later did the same thing for the oral arguments in the same-sex marriage cases.

† The courts are: Middle District of Alabama, Northern District of California, Southern District of Florida, District of Guam, Northern District of Illinois, Southern District of Iowa, District of Kansas, District of Massachusetts, Eastern District of Missouri, District of Nebraska, Northern District of Ohio, Southern District of Ohio, Western District of Tennessee and Western District of Washington.

80. Liptak, "Supreme Court TV?"

81. 558 U.S. 183 (2010).

amended the California Constitution to include a section providing that the state would only recognize marriage between a man and a woman as valid. Earlier, the 9th Circuit Judicial Council had decided to begin a pilot program allowing the use of cameras in federal district courts. Cases would be selected for participation by the chief judge of the district court in consultation with the chief circuit judge. Judge Vaughn R. Walker of the District Court for the Northern District of California announced that under the pilot program oral arguments in *Hollingsworth* would be streamed live to courthouses in other cities and recorded for broadcast on the Internet. Wishing to block the recording and broadcasting of their testimony, supporters of the proposition filed an application for a stay of the decision with the Supreme Court. In a per curiam opinion, the Court held that, while it was not "expressing any views on the propriety of broadcasting court proceedings generally," the district court had not properly amended its rules.[82]

Outside of the these isolated pilot programs, in some instances, cameras are allowed in federal courts on a very limited basis and typically only when if acceptable to the judges in a particular circuit. Currently, cameras are permitted in only the 2nd Circuit and the 9th Circuit.

The federal courts have revised rules regarding audio taping over the last decade. In March 2010 the Judicial Conference announced that federal courts could provide the public with digital audio recordings of court hearings. The recordings would be available online and cost $2.40. The presiding judge in each district would make the decision whether to make the recording available, largely based on security concerns. In September of the same year, the Supreme Court said it would post on its Web site audio recordings of the oral arguments presented to the court a few days after they take place. In the past the high court has released a small number of audio recordings of "notable" arguments on the same day they took place. Recordings of all arguments were released, but not until the beginning of the next court term. Most court observers applauded the change, noting it would take the court out of the business of deciding which arguments were notable or newsworthy, a practice that raised First Amendment considerations to some.

Cell Phones, Laptops, Tweets and Texts.   A section of Chapter 11 focuses on the use by jurors of personal, handheld communication devices. What about their use by others in the courtroom? Reporters, bloggers, spectators? These legal questions are just beginning to be asked and unfortunately, many of the answers are tentative.

Many, but not all, courts—state and federal—allow cell phones. The rules on using laptop computers vary greatly. Most federal courts have not addressed the issue of Twitter, although some have begun to confront the issue—with differing results. In 2009, U.S. District Judge J. Thomas Marten allowed a journalist to use a Blackberry device to update his Twitter account to cover a federal racketeering trial. While the reporter had been tweeting from the courtroom since 2007, Marten's decision was the first official order from a federal judge allowing this form of coverage.[83] Not long after Marten's

---

82. *Ibid.* at 184.
83. Rushmann, "Courtroom Coverage in 140 Characters."

order, however, U.S. District Judge Clay Land wrote that Rule 53 of the Federal Rules of Criminal Procedure should be interpreted as banning tweeting. According to Judge Land, the rule's prohibition on the "broadcasting of judicial proceedings" included "sending electronic messages from a courtroom that contemporaneously describe the trial proceedings and are instantaneously available for public viewing."[84] To date, the U.S. Circuit Courts of Appeals have remained silent on the issue of tweeting or using wireless communication devices.

In addition, many states have yet to consider the question of whether updating a Twitter feed is "broadcasting." However, even states that have traditionally been camera friendly may have trouble adjusting to new media such as Twitter. For example, in Florida, as mentioned earlier, electronic media and still photography coverage of proceedings is allowed. In early 2010, however, the Standing Committee on Rules of Practices and Procedures considered a statewide ban on electronic devices in courthouses, although the proposal was voted down.[85] The Florida District Court of Appeals ruled later that year that the use of laptop computers to transmit information outside the courtroom was permitted, unless it caused a disruption.[86]

While some courts are allowing Twitter, others have banned it—particularly in high-profile cases. In 2012, for example, Judge Charles Burns of Illinois banned all spectators, including journalists, from tweeting during the trial of William Balfour, who was charged with the murder of singer Jennifer Hudson's mother.[87] The same year, Judge John Cleland banned all "electronic-based communications from the courtroom during the trial of former Penn State football coach Jerry Sandusky for sex abuse."[88] Cleland interpreted Pennsylvania state court laws that ban broadcasting of court proceedings to prohibit live tweeting from the trial. Although Cleland originally interpreted the rule to only prohibit the tweeting of direct quotes, when members of the media including the Associated Press and ESPN filed a motion seeking clarification, he modified his ruling to ban all tweeting from the trial.[89]

These rulings and others indicate most courts appear to be taking an ad hoc approach and there is no broad consensus about whether to let journalists use portable electronic devices to do live updates during trails, with many jurisdictions considering the issue on a case-by-case basis. The best advice is to ask a court official if it is permissible to use any of these devices during a trial. In most instances, the question of whether a journalist is allowed to use social media will depend on the judge's sensibilities. Don't assume it is permitted.

Executions. Courts have barred the televising of executions in the United States, most recently in the summer of 2004 when the 8th U.S. Court of Appeals ruled that there was no First Amendment right to videotape an execution. The decision upheld a Missouri

---

84. *United States* v. *Shelnutt,* 2009 U.S. Dist. LEXIS 101427, *4 (M.D. Ga., Nov. 2, 2009).

85. Bishop, "New Rules Could End Tweets from Trials Statewide."

86. *Morris Publishing, LLC* v. *State of Florida,* 38 M.L.R. 1245 (2010).

87. Sachdev, "Judge Bans Tweets from Reporters in Hudson Trial."

88. Court Order, *Commonwealth of Pennsylvania* v. *Gerald A. Sandusky,* No. Cp-14-CR-24212011 (Penn. Ct. Com. Pl. June 4, 2012).

89. Miller, *"Judge Changes Mind, Prohibits Tweeting and Other Electronic Communication in Sandusky Trial."*

corrections department policy barring all cameras and recording devices from execution chambers.[90] Similar decisions have been rendered for the past 15 years.[91]

Broadcasters have also failed in their attempts to get cameras and other recording equipment into the jury room. In November 2002 a trial judge in Houston said he would allow the PBS documentary series "Frontline" to film the jury deliberations in a death penalty case. The 17-year-old defendant and his mother agreed to the filming, as did the young man's attorney. "If the State of Texas wants to execute a 17-year-old, the whole world should be watching to make sure it is done right," attorney Ricardo Rodriquez said. But the state argued against the filming, claiming the process would turn the deliberations into a "Survivor"-style reality program. Scholars who study juries tended to agree, calling the comparison with the popular TV program correct. "Conscripting citizens for a reality television program strikes me as a bad idea," Shari Diamond, a law professor at Northwestern University told *New York Times* reporter Adam Liptak.[92] "It involves jurors in signing on for a national public performance. The potential for that having a distorting effect on their work is palpable," she added.

Three months later the Texas Criminal Court of Appeals, the state's highest criminal appeals court, rejected the judge's plan. The court cited a state statute that said, "No person shall be permitted to be with a jury while it is deliberating." This prohibits the taping, the court said, adding that it believed that the filming would introduce "outside influence and pressure" on the jury.[93]

Some state courts have on occasion permitted the filming of jury deliberations in criminal cases. The taping of jury deliberations in civil cases for research or educational purposes has also taken place.[94] But as a general rule, cameras and audio recording equipment are barred from the jury room, and it is unlikely that this prohibition will change anytime soon.

SUMMARY The right of access to pretrial proceedings and documents is qualified. The presumption that these hearings are open can be overcome only by a showing that there is an overriding interest that must be protected, that there is a "substantial probability" that an open hearing will damage this right, that the closure is narrowly tailored to deny access to no more of the hearing than is necessary to protect this interest, that the court has considered reasonable alternatives to closure, that closure of the hearing would in fact protect the interest that has been raised and that the trial judge has articulated findings—which may be reviewed by an appellate court—that support these four points.

Broadcast journalists are given somewhat less access when they seek to obtain copies of audio- or videotaped evidence or seek to record or televise a judicial proceeding. Access to the taped evidence is developing through a case-by-case approach, and courts have granted journalists increasing rights to make copies of this material for later

---

90. *Rice* v. *Kempker,* 374 F. 3d 675 (2004).

91. See *KQED, Inc.* v. *Vasquez,* 18 M.L.R. 2323 (1991). See also *Campbell* v. *Blodgett,* 982 F. 2d 1356 (1993); *California First Amendment Coalition* v. *Calderon,* 130 F. 3d 976 (1998); and *Entertainment Network Inc.* v. *Lappin,* 134 F. Supp. 2d 1002 (2001).

92. Liptak, "Inviting TV into Jury Room."

93. *State ex rel Rosenthal* v. *Poe,* Tex. Crim. App., No. 74, 515, 2/13/03.

94. Liptak, "Inviting TV into Jury Room."

broadcast. The Supreme Court has ruled that the mere presence of such devices does not in and of itself prejudice a defendant's right to a fair trial. The federal courts have generally refused to permit cameras in the courtroom. Cameras are barred from executions, and the filming of jury deliberations is generally prohibited.

BENCH-BAR-PRESS GUIDELINES

Both restrictive orders and the closure of court proceedings are admittedly effective ways of stopping publicity from reaching the hands of potential jurors, but they are equally dangerous in a representative democracy where information about how well government is operating is fundamental to the success of the political system. The bench, the bar and the press in many states have found that cooperation, restraint and mutual trust can be equally effective in protecting the rights of a defendant, while at the same time far less damaging to rights of the people.

Judges, lawyers and journalists have tried to reach a common understanding of the problems of pretrial news coverage and have offered suggestions as to how most of these problems might be resolved. These suggestions are usually offered in the form of guidelines or recommendations to the press and to participants in the criminal justice system. **Bench-bar-press guidelines** normally suggest to law enforcement officers that certain kinds of information about a criminal suspect and a crime can be released and published with little danger of harm to the trial process. The guidelines also suggest to journalists that the publication of certain kinds of information about a case (see the list of damaging kinds of statements on pages 431–432) can be harmful to the defendant's chances for a fair trial without providing the public with useful or important information. The guidelines are often presented in a very brief form; at other times they encompass several pages of text.

Bench-bar-press guidelines have existed in some states for more than 50 years. In some communities these guidelines work very well in managing the problems surrounding the free press–fair trial dilemma. A spirit of cooperation exists between press, courts, attorneys and law enforcement personnel. In such communities it is rare to find a restrictive order or a closed courtroom. But most communities and states have found it takes considerable effort to make the guidelines work. Drafting the guidelines is only the first step. If, after agreement is reached on the recommendations, the bench, the bar and the press go their separate ways, the guidelines usually fail as a means of resolving the free press–fair trial problems.

Most communities and states have found it takes considerable effort to make the guidelines work.

Crime, especially violent crime, has become the focus of many segments of the American press. Television news is especially afflicted by this trend. But serious reporting on the criminal justice system remains in short supply, despite the importance to society of the tasks undertaken by the police, the prosecutors and the courts. Reporters dealing with the courts and the court system must be aware of legal issues pertaining to covering trials. They should not be blinded to the sensitive mechanisms that operate in the courts to provide justice and fairness as they clamor for news. At the same time they should not let the authoritarian aspects of the judicial system block their efforts to provide the information essential to the functioning of democracy.

SUMMARY In some states the press, attorneys and judges have agreed to try to solve the problems surrounding the free press–fair trial controversy through voluntary bench-bar-press agreements. Such agreements usually contain suggestions to all parties as to what information should and should not be publicized about criminal cases. When the guidelines work, there is usually a cooperative, rather than a combative, spirit among the members of the press, the judiciary and the bar. These guidelines often reduce or eliminate the need for restrictive orders or closed hearings.

BIBLIOGRAPHY

Aaron Mackey, "Military Courts Continue to Stymie Public Access." The News Media and the Law. Summer 2013.

Bechamps, Anne T. "Sealed Out-of-Court Settlements: When Does the Public Have a Right to Know?" *Notre Dame Law Review* 66 (1990): 117.

Bishop, Tricia. "New Rules Could End Tweets from Trials Statewide." *Baltimore Sun*, 22 February 2010.

Broder, John M. "From Grand Jury Leaks Comes a Clash of Rights." *The New York Times*, 15 January 2005, A8.

"Courts Keeping Cases Secret." The Oklahoman, 11 Aug 2008.

Cys, Richard L., and Andrew M. Mar. "Media Access to the New Special Tribunals: Lessons Learned from History and the Military Courts." *First Amendment Law Letter*, Winter 2002, 1.

Liptak, Adam. "Inviting TV into Jury Room in Capital Case." *The New York Times*, 11 November 2002, A1.

Liptak, Adam. "Secrecy at Issue in Suits Opposing Domestic Spying." The New York Times, 26 January 2007, A1.

——. "Shrinking Newsrooms Wage Fewer Battles for Public Access to Courtrooms." *The New York Times*, 1 September 2009, A10.

——. "Supreme Court TV? Nice Idea but Still Not Likely." *The New York Times*, 29 November 2011, A16.

Miller, Emily. "Judge Changes Mind, Prohibits Tweeting and Other Electronic Communication in Sandusky Trial." Reporters Committee for Freedom of the Press, June 4, 2012.

Rushmann, Ahnalese. "Courtroom Coverage in 140 Characters." *News Media & L.*, Spring 2009.

Sachdev, Ameet. "Judge Bans Tweets from Reporters in Hudson Trial." *Chicago Tribune*, 26 April 2012.

See "Conference Approves Standards & Procedures for Sealing Civil Cases," Third Branch News (Sept. 13, 2011), http://www.uscourts.gov/News/NewsView/11-09-13/Conference_Approves_Standards _Procedures_for_Sealing_Civil_Cases.aspx.

Shenon, Philip. "Judge Critical of Secrecy in Terror Case Prosecution." The New York Times, 5 April 2003, B13.

——. "News Groups Want Terror Case Files." The New York Times, 4 April 2003, B13.

White, Frank W. "Cameras in the Courtroom: A U.S. Survey." Journalism Monographs 60 (1979).

CHAPTER 13

Regulation of Obscene and Other Erotic Material

In 2012, a federal jury in Los Angeles convicted adult filmmaker Ira Isaacs on multiple counts of obscenity for distributing on his Web site fetish films that featured scatology and bestiality. The videos, with titles such as "Hollywood Scat Amateurs 7," went far beyond the type of content found in mainstream adult content produced by the likes of Wicked Pictures and Vivid Entertainment. As described by the U.S. Department of Justice in a press release trumpeting the conviction of Isaacs, "the obscene videos included a video approximately two hours in length of a female engaging in sex acts involving human bodily waste and a video one hour and 37 minutes in length of a female engaged in sex acts with animals." Isaacs, in contrast, had testified that his movies were a form of "shock art" that merely "explored the darker side of the human condition." In 2013, the 61-year-old Isaacs was sentenced to serve four years in federal prison.

By August 2017, however, the Ira Isaacs case was the last major federal obscenity prosecution in the United States. That's partly due to a combination of: (1) the mainstreaming popularity of adult content, which makes it harder to win an obscenity conviction (unless the content features bestiality and scatology, such as that depicted in Isaacs' movies, or appears to portray violence); (2) the Obama administration's decision to focus its resources on prosecuting child pornography rather than obscenity cases (as this chapter illustrates, child pornography and obscenity are very different concepts and should not be confused with each other); and (3) the fact that large-scale producers of adult content in the United States (e.g., Wicked Pictures, Hustler, Brazzers, Evil Angel) know what kind of content not to show to avoid prosecutions.

Whether the Justice Department under the administration of Donald Trump rekindles the type of obscenity prosecutions that were the norm under President George W. Bush, but were absent during Barack Obama's presidential tenure, remains to be seen. Obscenity prosecutions often are driven by political motives. It might be that President Trump attempts to pander to the cultural-conservative wing of the Republican Party by instructing his attorney general to bring obscenity prosecutions in states with heavy conservative bases (and where they are more likely to win convictions under the *Miller* test for obscenity with its local community standards consideration, as discussed later in this chapter). On the other hand, Trump's pro-business attitude and anti-regulation stance might suggest otherwise. By August 2017, the Justice Department, under attorney general Jeff Sessions' leadership, had not filed any obscenity prosecutions. Instead, it was focusing on child pornography cases and the sexual exploitation of minors.

Despite the recent paucity of obscenity prosecutions, sexually explicit content remains highly controversial in some quarters. It is criticized by religious conservatives, anti-pornography feminists and by some lawmakers. In early 2017, for instance, a state senator in Utah proposed a bill in that state that would give people the ability to sue pornography makers in an attempt to prove that watching pornography causes emotional and psychological damage. (Ironically, a 2009 study found that conservative-leaning

Utah led the nation in subscriptions to online pornography sites.) Additionally, municipalities across the country continue to zone adult bookstores and strip clubs to a few tiny areas of the community and far away from parks, schools and private residences. And First Amendment defense attorney Lawrence Walters observed in 2016 that the "war on porn" simply has shifted and been rebranded as a "war on sex trafficking," with sites such as Backpage drawing lawmakers' wrath for supposedly promoting minors in prostitution through "escort" ads. This chapter thus examines contemporary obscenity law, child pornography (including "sexting" by minors) and the regulation of sexually oriented business (known, perhaps fittingly, by the acronym "SOBs").

THE LAW OF OBSCENITY

An "intractable problem"—that's how U.S. Supreme Court Justice John Harlan described regulation of sexually explicit speech in 1966.[1] Sadly, it remains equally problematic today, despite two important facts:

1. The nation's high court made it clear more than 60 years ago in *Roth* v. *United States*[2] that a narrow category of sexually explicit speech called "obscenity" is not protected by the First Amendment freedoms of speech and press.
2. The Supreme Court articulated in 1973 in *Miller* v. *California*[3] a test still used by all courts for determining when speech is obscene.

Problems exist today for many reasons. First, the *Miller* obscenity test (see later in this chapter) leaves much wiggle room for interpretation in its actual application by judges and juries. The test also embraces the use of contemporary community standards that vary from state to state, leading to the anomalous result that any given adult DVD might be protected by the First Amendment in one state but not in another.

Second, technologies like the Web and smartphones, as well as cable and satellite television services such as video-on-demand and pay-per-view movies, have made adult content readily accessible. That's good news for consenting adults who want to view it in the privacy of their homes where no one else in the community needs to see or be offended by it,[4] but it is unfortunate news for parents of minors, as young children

---

1. *A Book Named "John Cleland's Memoirs of a Woman of Pleasure"* v. *Massachusetts*, 383 U.S. 413, 455 (1966) (Harlan, J., dissenting).
2. 354 U.S. 476 (1957).
3. 413 U.S. 15 (1973).
4. The argument that obscenity laws violate an adult's constitutional right to privacy—not simply the First Amendment protection of speech—to watch sexual content in the privacy of his or her home was made successfully in 2005 before a federal court in Pittsburgh, Pa., in *United States* v. *Extreme Associates, Inc.*, 352 F. Supp. 2d 578 (W.D. Pa. 2005). The decision, however, was reversed by an appellate court, and the Supreme Court refused to hear the case, thus sending it back to a trial court. *United States* v. *Extreme Associates, Inc.*, 431 F. 3d 150 (3d Cir. 2005), cert. den., 126 S. Ct. 2048 (2006).

©Jeff Koga

*Casey Calvert,
a current adult
industry star who was
nominated for a 2016
AVN (Adult Video
News) Award as female
performer of the year,
graduated magna cum
laude from the College
of Journalism and
Communications at the
University of Florida
(and took her stage
name after a certain
co-author of this book).*

may come across it (either intentionally or unexpectedly) with greater ease. Third, some people feel that speech considered obscene under *Miller* nonetheless deserves First Amendment protection. Not only is sexually explicit content an incredibly popular form of entertainment enjoyed by many adults, but evidence is inconsistent and conflicting about whether viewing it really causes harm.

Feminist legal scholars like Catharine MacKinnon claim pornography objectifies women and represents "the power of men over women, expressed through unequal sex, sanctioned both through and prior to state power."[5] Others feel equally as strongly, coming from a conservative, religious-based perspective, that pornography harms family values, erodes marriages and leads to addiction that destroys users' lives. Although the arguments of both anti-porn feminists and religious conservatives certainly deserve study, it must be emphasized that the term "pornography" is not the same thing as obscenity. In fact, while obscenity has a legal definition under the *Miller* test, the term "pornography" is without legal significance in the United States and instead is commonly used (and misused) as a catch-all term by laypeople to describe anything sexually explicit they find offensive or believe is harmful.

Beyond this, some women in the adult industry contradict certain negative stereotypes about the kind of women who perform in adult movies. In 2015, a Duke University student who performed under the name Belle Knox received an AVN (Adult Video News) Award nomination as best new starlet. Casey Calvert, a magna cum laude graduate of the College of Journalism and Communications at the University of Florida, earned a 2016 AVN Award nomination as female performer of the year. In 2017, Calvert received several more AVN nominations. She has written columns about sex and the adult industry for the *Huffington Post*. Additionally, veteran female stars like Stormy Daniels and Nina Hartley also work as writers and directors. This is not to say that exploitation does not exist today in the adult movie industry (it does in almost all industries), but simply that some female performers are indeed smart and control the content in which they and others appear.

Fourth, there is the question of the inefficient use of scarce government monetary resources in prosecuting obscenity cases today when the content involves adults who freely consented to take part in the activities shown. Many people feel there are greater problems to worry about, such as child pornography—a distinct category of sexually explicit speech that, like obscenity, is not protected by the First Amendment (see later in this chapter)—and terrorism and global warming.

Finally, there is the problem of dealing with sexually explicit content that may not quite rise to the level of obscenity under *Miller* (in other words, it may not be quite as "bad" as obscenity), but that nonetheless is sexual and is broadcast over the nation's television and radio airwaves. As Chapter 16 discusses, the Federal Communications Commission restricts such nonobscene sexual content if it satisfies the FCC's definition of indecency (another legal definition that, like obscenity under the *Miller* test, is extremely problematic in its real-world application).

5. MacKinnon, *Only Words*, 40.

COMMON TERMS

Obscenity—A narrow class of material defined by the Supreme Court in the *Miller* test. Material that is obscene is not protected by the First Amendment. Obscene material is sometimes referred to as hard-core pornography.

Indecent Material—Material that may be sexually graphic; often referred to as adult material or sexually explicit material. This material is protected under the First Amendment. However, such material may be barred in works available to children (variable obscenity laws) and in over-the-air (as opposed to cable or satellite-generated) radio and television broadcasts. (See Chapter 16 for a full discussion of broadcast indecency and its regulation by the FCC.)

Pornography—This term has no legal significance but is often used by laypeople and politicians to describe anything from real obscenity to material such as a passionate love scene that is simply offensive to the viewer. The overuse (and misuse) of this imprecise term adds more confusion to an already muddled legal landscape.

EARLY OBSCENITY LAW

The first obscenity prosecution in the United States occurred in 1815, when Jesse Sharpless was fined for exhibiting a painting of a man "in an imprudent posture with a woman." There are on record earlier convictions for offenses tied to obscenity; these were prosecutions under common law for crimes against God, not for merely displaying erotic pictures. In 1821 Peter Holmes was convicted for publishing an erotically enhanced version of John Cleland's *Memoirs of a Woman of Pleasure*.

As the 19th century progressed, obscenity laws and prosecutions became more common, ebbing and flowing with major reform movements in the 1820s and 1830s and in the wake of the Civil War. The first federal obscenity statute, a customs law regulating the importation of obscene articles, was adopted in 1842. The most comprehensive federal statute adopted during the century became law in 1873. Known as the Comstock Act because of the intense pressure applied on Congress by Anthony Comstock, the law declared that all obscene books, pamphlets, pictures and other materials were nonmailable. No definition of obscenity was provided by Congress, however. The Comstock law, as amended, remains the federal law today.

Federal agencies such as the Bureau of Customs and the U.S. Postal Service were the nation's most vigilant obscenity fighters during the late 19th and first half of the 20th centuries. These agencies banned, burned and confiscated huge amounts of erotic materials, including religious objects, pieces of art, books (including some of the best written during that era), magazines (including science and diving publications) and a wide array of material on birth control. When the motion picture industry began to grow in the early part of this century, local and state censors went after films that they believed to be obscene as well. The courts, especially the federal courts, became inundated with obscenity prosecutions and appeals. The U.S. Supreme Court seemed especially drawn to such litigation. Between 1957 and 1977, for example, the high court heard arguments in almost 90 obscenity cases and wrote opinions in nearly 40 of those cases. In stark contrast, as of the start of 2018, the Supreme Court had not heard a single obscenity case in the 21st century involving whether or not a particular movie, book, magazine, Web site or other media product was obscene. It has, instead, considered other issues since the year 2000, such as the constitutionality of statutes regulating child pornography, virtual (computer-generated) child pornography and nonobscene sexual content on the Internet.

DEFINING OBSCENITY

Outlawing obscenity is one thing; defining it is something else. When American courts, in the wake of the adoption of the Comstock Act in 1873, first began considering what is and what is not obscenity, they borrowed a British definition called the *Hicklin* rule.[6] Under this rule a work is obscene if **it has a tendency to deprave and corrupt those whose minds are open to such immoral influences and into whose hands it might fall.** If something might influence the mind of a child, it was regarded as obscene for everyone, under this definition. In addition, if any part of the work, regardless of how small, met this definition, the entire work was regarded as obscene. This very broad and loose definition made it possible for both federal and state authorities to wage an aggressive and highly successful war against erotic materials in the first half of the 20th century.

In 1957, the Supreme Court abandoned the *Hicklin* rule, declaring that because of this rule American adults were permitted to read or watch only what was fit for children. "Surely this is to burn the house, to roast the pig," Justice Felix Frankfurter noted.[7] In abandoning the *Hicklin* rule, the high court was forced to fashion a new definition of obscenity, beginning with the case of *Roth* v. *U.S.*[8] in 1957. Over the next nine years, in a variety of obscenity rulings, the *Roth-Memoirs* test was developed by the Court.[9] The test had three parts.

First, the dominant theme of the material taken as a whole must appeal to prurient interest in sex.

Second, a court must find that the material is patently offensive because it affronts contemporary community standards relating to the description or representation of sexual matters.

Third, before something can be found to be obscene, it must be utterly without redeeming social value.

While this entire test was far narrower than the *Hicklin* rule, it was the third part of the test that continually bedeviled government prosecutors. If a work had even the slightest social value, it could not be deemed to be obscene.

---

6. *Regina* v. *Hicklin,* L.R. 3 Q.B. 360 (1868).
7. *Butler* v. *Michigan,* 352 U.S. 380 (1957).
8. 354 U.S. 476 (1957).
9. See *Manual Enterprises, Inc.* v. *J. Edward Day,* 370 U.S. 478 (1962); *Jacobellis* v. *Ohio,* 378 U.S. 184 (1964); and *Memoirs of a Woman of Pleasure* v. *Massachusetts,* 383 U.S. 413 (1966).

SUMMARY

Prosecutions for obscenity did not occur in this nation until the early 19th century. In the 1820s and 1830s, many states adopted their first obscenity laws. The first federal law was passed in 1842. The government actively prosecuted obscenity in the wake of the Civil War, and in 1873 Congress adopted a strict new obscenity law. Obscenity was defined as being anything that had a tendency to deprave and corrupt those whose minds might be open to such immoral influences and into whose hands it might happen to fall. This rule, called the *Hicklin* rule, meant that if any part of a book or other work had the tendency to deprave or corrupt any person (such as a child or overly sensitive individual) who might happen to see the work, the material was obscene and no person could buy it or see it. This definition facilitated government censorship of a wide range of materials.

In the 1950s and early 1960s, the Supreme Court adopted a new three-part definition or test for obscenity, the *Roth-Memoirs* test.

CONTEMPORARY OBSCENITY LAW

The Supreme Court abandoned the *Roth-Memoirs* test and created a new test for obscenity in 1973 in a case called *Miller* v. *California*.[10] Today, some 45 years later, the three-part test for obscenity adopted in *Miller*, which is known simply as the *Miller* test, provides the current standard for obscenity that all courts in the United States must apply.

THE *MILLER* TEST

Marvin Miller was convicted of violating the California Penal Code for sending five unsolicited brochures to a restaurant in Newport Beach. The brochures, which advertised four erotic books and one film, contained pictures and drawings of men and women engaging in a variety of sexual activities. The recipient of the mailing complained to police, and Miller was prosecuted by state authorities.

In *Miller*, for the first time since 1957, a majority of the Supreme Court reached agreement on a definition of obscenity. Chief Justice Warren Burger and four other members of the high court agreed that material is obscene if the following standards are met:

1. **An average person, applying contemporary local community standards, finds that the work, taken as a whole, appeals to a prurient interest in sex.**
2. **The work depicts in a patently offensive way sexual conduct specifically defined by applicable state law.**
3. **The work in question lacks serious literary, artistic, political or scientific value.**

The implications and ambiguities in these three elements create the need for fuller explanation. As a result of the *Miller* ruling and subsequent obscenity decisions handed down by the court since 1973, some guidelines have emerged.

In Miller, *for the first time since 1957, a majority of the Supreme Court reached agreement on a definition of obscenity.*

10. 413 U.S. 15 (1973).

An Average Person

The first element of the *Miller* test asks if an average person, applying contemporary community standards, would find that the work, taken as a whole, appeals to a prurient interest in sex. It is the trier of fact who makes this determination. This can be the trial judge, but more commonly it is the jury. The Supreme Court expects the trier of fact to rely on knowledge of the standards of the residents of the community to decide whether the work appeals to a prurient interest. The juror is not supposed to use his or her own standards in this decision. The Supreme Court noted in 1974:

> This Court has emphasized on more than one occasion that a principal concern in requiring that a judgment be made on the basis of contemporary community standards is to assure that the material is judged neither on the basis of each juror's personal opinion nor by its effect on a particular sensitive or insensitive person or group.[11]

Note the last phrase in this quote. The court expects the standards of an average person to be applied in making this critical determination. The Supreme Court has made it clear that only adults—not children and minors—are to be considered under the "average person" aspect of the first part of the *Miller* test.

Prurient interest has been defined by courts to mean a shameful or morbid interest in nudity, sex or excretion.

Prurient interest has been defined by courts to mean a shameful or morbid interest in nudity, sex or excretion. Two things are key here. First, in determining if material appeals to a prurient interest, the work must be taken as a whole (a single scene from a DVD cannot be considered in isolation or standing alone; all of the contents of the DVD must be viewed in the aggregate). Second, the definition of prurient interest focuses only on nudity, sex and excretion; it has nothing to do with violence. Thus obscenity law deals only with sexually oriented content, not violent stories or violent images.

Community Standards

The definition of community standards is a key to the first part of the *Miller* test. Chief Justice Burger made it clear in the *Miller* decision that local standards were to be applied. In most jurisdictions the term "local standards" has been translated to mean "state standards." All communities within the same state share the same standards. The question of applicable community standards becomes an important factor in cases that involve the shipment of erotic material over long distances within the United States and in cases involving the importation of sexually explicit material from outside the United States.

When imported erotic material is seized, the standards of the state in which the material is seized are applied at trial.

In prosecutions initiated by the U.S. Postal Service, the government is free to choose the venue in which to try the case. This might be the city from which the material was sent; it might be the city in which it was received; or it might be any city through which the material passed during its transit. For example, a trial involving a magazine sent from Boston to Dallas might be held in Boston, Dallas or anywhere in between. So Massachusetts standards might apply at the trial, or Texas standards, or even Pennsylvania or Kentucky standards if the publication passed through or over those states during its shipment. This government practice is called "venue shopping," or selecting a site where a conviction is most easily obtained.

11. *Hamling* v. *United States*, 418 U.S. 87 (1974).

Venue shopping thus favors the prosecution. Simply put, law enforcement officials will purchase and order adult content in conservative communities (typically today by logging on to a Web site while situated in a conservative community) in order to drag defendants located in more liberal venues into those conservative communities to stand trial. For example, Los Angeles-based adult filmmaker Paul Little (a.k.a. Max Hardcore) was dragged across country and prosecuted for obscenity in 2008 in Tampa, Fla. Why Tampa? First, because that's where law enforcement officials purchased his content from a Web site. Second, because the community standards that applied were local ones in Florida, including a large swath of conservative areas stretching well outside of Tampa (Florida does not use statewide community standards in obscenity cases, but rather more local ones, in this case the U.S. Middle District of Florida that includes some very conservative counties). Why not Los Angeles? Because it is the capital of the adult industry in the United States, with the nearby San Fernando Valley known as Porn Valley. The strategy worked. Little was convicted on multiple counts of transporting obscene matter by use of an interactive computer service and of mailing obscene matter into Florida. He was sentenced to more than three years in prison.

The notion that local standards should apply to Internet-transmitted adult content received some legal pushback, however, in 2009 when the 9th U.S. Circuit Court of Appeals held in *United States* v. *Kilbride*[12] that a "national community standard must be applied in regulating obscene speech on the Internet, including obscenity disseminated via email." This decision applies, however, only within the 9th Circuit, and so far other courts seem reluctant to adopt it. For instance, the 11th U.S. Circuit Court of Appeals rejected the use of a national community standard for Internet-transmitted materials in *United States* v. *Little*.[13] Similarly, a district court within the U.S. Court of Appeals for the District of Columbia rejected the use of a national community standard for the Internet in 2010 in *United States* v. *Stagliano*.[14]

How does one prove what contemporary community standards are when it comes to sexually explicit content? It is not easy. First, it is for the jury (or the judge if there is no jury) to decide what the community standards are. Jurors must speculate about what other adults in their community would accept and tolerate. Most people, of course, don't talk with their neighbors about what, if any, adult DVDs they watch or what adult Web sites they visit. Imagine, then, the difficulty in guessing what the standard is in a city with hundreds of thousands of people or a state with millions. Second, the government is not required to present any evidence about community standards. An obscenity defendant, however, may put on evidence of what the community standards allegedly are. One way to try to demonstrate this is a "comparables" argument. In particular, a defense attorney will demonstrate that sexually explicit material that is exactly comparable to that being targeted for prosecution is freely sold at stores in the community and, by extension, the community tolerates the material being prosecuted. Thus, if *Barely Legal* magazine is prosecuted in a community but comparable magazines that also focus on young women are freely sold, this would be relevant for determining the community's tolerance of the content in *Barely Legal*. Today, defense attorneys are using in-court, search-engine demonstrations to prove

One way to try to demonstrate this is a "comparables" argument.

12. 584 F. 3d 1240 (9th Cir. 2009).
13. 2010 U.S. App. LEXIS 2320 (11th Cir. 2010).
14. 693 F. Supp. 2d 25 (D. D.C. 2010).

either that many people in the community regularly search online for sexually explicit content exactly like that being prosecuted or to show that there are places online (and thus within their virtual community) where they can purchase material similar to that being prosecuted. Such Internet searches using the likes of Google Trends may provide accurate measures of the type of content people are willing to view in privacy and at home.

Patent Offensiveness

The second element of the *Miller* test says that a work is obscene if it depicts in a patently offensive way sexual conduct specifically defined by applicable state law. Patent offensiveness is also to be judged by the trier of fact, using contemporary community standards. But the Supreme Court has put limits on this judgment, ruling that only what it calls hard-core sexual material meets the patently offensive standard. Georgia courts ruled that the motion picture "Carnal Knowledge," an R-rated film starring Jack Nicholson and Candice Bergen, was patently offensive. The Supreme Court reversed this ruling, saying that the Georgia courts misunderstood this second part of the *Miller* test.[15] Material that was patently offensive, Justice Rehnquist wrote, included "representations or descriptions of ultimate sexual acts, normal or perverted, actual or simulated" and "representations or descriptions of masturbation, excretory functions, and lewd exhibition of genitals." Rehnquist acknowledged that this catalog of descriptions was not exhaustive, but that only material like this qualifies as patently offensive material. The second part of the *Miller* test was "intended to fix substantive constitutional limitations . . . on the type of material . . . subject to a determination of obscenity," he added.

State laws are supposed to define the kinds of material or conduct that are prohibited as obscene.

State laws are supposed to define the kinds of material or conduct that are prohibited as obscene. Many state obscenity statutes contain Rehnquist's descriptions as their definition of obscenity. Other state laws are less precise.

Serious Value

To be obscene a work must lack serious literary, artistic, political or scientific value. While not as broad as the "utterly without redeeming social value" element in the *Roth-Memoirs* test, this third criterion in the *Miller* test nevertheless acts as a brake on judges and juries eager to convict on the basis of the first two parts of the test. The judge is supposed to play a pronounced role in deciding whether a work has serious value. The serious value element is not judged by the tastes or standards of the average person. The test is not whether an ordinary person in the community would find serious literary, artistic, political or scientific value, but whether a reasonable person *could* find such value in the material.[16] Jurors are supposed to determine whether a reasonable person would see a serious value in the work. Both the state and the defense will frequently introduce expert testimony to try to "educate" the jury on the relative merit of the material in question.

For instance, when the Cincinnati Contemporary Arts Center was prosecuted for obscenity in 1990 for a display of photographs by Robert Mapplethorpe (some photos featured homoerotic and sadomasochistic images), defense attorney Lou Sirkin used

15. *Jenkins v. Georgia*, 418 U.S. 153 (1974).
16. *Pope v. Illinois*, 481 U.S. 497 (1987).

experts from the art world (museum directors/curators) to testify before the jury about the serious artistic value of the photos. The testimony was pivotal in gaining an acquittal for the museum.[17] Today, when adult DVDs and videos are prosecuted as obscene, defense attorneys often call sex therapists and experts from places like the Kinsey Institute for Research in Sex, Gender and Reproduction to describe how the content is used by normal couples to stimulate their own sex lives, learn about different sexual practices and open up discussion about their sexual habits. In other words, adult DVDs and videos can have educational value. Such was the case in 2000 when a jury of 12 women near St. Louis, Mo., found two adult videos featuring anal, oral and vaginal sex among women and between men and women were not obscene after hearing testimony from sex therapist Dr. Mark F. Schwartz of the Masters and Johnson clinic.[18]

THE *MILLER* TEST

1. An average person, applying contemporary local community standards, finds that the work, taken as a whole, appeals to a prurient interest in sex.
2. The work depicts in a patently offensive way sexual conduct specifically defined by applicable state law.
3. The work in question lacks serious literary, artistic, political or scientific value.

OTHER STANDARDS

The three-part test developed in *Miller* v. *California* is the legal test for obscenity in the United States today. But the Supreme Court, lower courts and other elements of the government have with varying degrees of success attempted to raise additional standards by which to judge erotic material. Here is a brief outline of some of these standards.

Variable Obscenity

The Supreme Court has ruled it is permissible for states to adopt what are known as **variable obscenity statutes.** Material that may be legally distributed and sold to adults may be banned for distribution or sale to juveniles, usually anyone under the age of 18. In other words, variable obscenity laws allow *Hustler* to be sold to adults but not to minors. This concept emerged from *Ginsberg* v. *New York* in 1968.[19] In *Ginsberg* the Supreme Court ruled that the First Amendment did not bar New York state from prosecuting the owner of a Long Island luncheonette who sold four so-called girlie magazines to a 16-year-old boy. The magazines, which contained female nudity, could have been legally sold to an adult. Justice Brennan said the state could maintain one definition of obscenity for adults and another for juveniles because the Supreme Court recognized the important

17. Wilkerson, "Obscenity Jurors Were Pulled 2 Ways."
18. Munz, "Jury Finds Explicit Videos from Store Are Not Obscene."
19. 390 U.S. 51 (1968).

state interest in protecting the welfare of children. But even variable obscenity statutes are not without constitutional limits. In 1975 the Supreme Court struck down such a law in *Erznoznik* v. *City of Jacksonville*[20] because the definition of material that could not be distributed to juveniles was not specific enough. A city ordinance barred drive-in theaters from showing films in which either female breasts or buttocks were exposed if the theater screen was visible from the street. The ordinance was justified as a means of protecting young people from exposure to such material. "Only in relatively narrow and well-defined circumstances may government bar dissemination of protected material to children," Justice Lewis Powell wrote. Banning the exhibition of nudity is simply not narrow enough; only materials that have significant erotic appeal to juveniles may be suppressed under such a statute, he added. A simple ban on all nudity, regardless of context, justification or other factors, violates the First Amendment.

Although states and cities may adopt variable obscenity laws, these regulations cannot in any way interfere with the flow of constitutionally protected material to adults. One permissible way of striking the balance between allowing adults to see sexual content but shielding minors from it is the use of so-called blinder racks (opaque covers) where magazines are sold. Blinder racks cover up all but the very top part of magazines, thus allowing adults to view the magazines' titles but covering up the sexual images below them that minors should not see. Ordinances that require the use of blinder racks to cover up the lower two-thirds of magazines are perfectly legal. Another permissible way of striking the balance is to require a store that rents or sells adult DVDs to segregate those DVDs into a separate section of the store that only adults can enter.

Ordinances that require the use of blinder racks are perfectly legal.

The tricky issue is how to define the material that minors cannot purchase. The material is not obscene under *Miller* (adults thus can purchase it), but any definition cannot be drafted so broadly as to prohibit the sale of all images of nudity to minors (that would sweep up biology textbooks). Many states use the phrase "harmful to minors" to describe sexual material that is permissible for adults to purchase but that minors may not buy. These definitions often are tweaked or modified versions of the *Miller* test. For instance, Florida uses the term "harmful to minors" and defines it as any image "depicting nudity, sexual conduct, or sexual excitement when it: (a) predominantly appeals to a prurient, shameful, or morbid interest; (b) is patently offensive to prevailing standards in the adult community as a whole with respect to what is suitable material or conduct for minors; and (c) taken as a whole, is without serious literary, artistic, political, or scientific value for minors."[21]

Child Pornography

Child pornography is one of the most reviled forms of expression in the United States today, yet convictions for distributing and possessing it via the Internet and on smartphones are common. In 2016, for example, Erick Fernando Duarte of Garland, Tex., was sentenced to 15 years in federal prison after a search of his phone and other media revealed more than 1,200 images of child pornography, including ones of prepubescent children involved in sex acts. And in May 2017, Roy Harvender Jr. of Wilmington, Del., was

20. 422 U.S. 205 (1975).
21. Florida Statute § 847.001 (2017).

sentenced to 13 years in federal prison for posting child pornography to a Web site dedicated to the sexual exploitation of children; Harvender Jr. admitted that he uploaded child pornography to the site and that he owned devices at his home that contained the images.

The production, distribution and possession of child pornography is not protected by the First Amendment. Federal statutes outlaw images of minors—people under age 18—engaged in "sexually explicit conduct," including sexual intercourse, bestiality and masturbation, as well as images depicting a "lascivious exhibition of the genitals or pubic area."[22] Laws against child pornography are justified by both the physical and emotional harm minors incur during its creation, as well as by the fact that the images are a permanent record of participation and exploitation that could haunt the children when they grow up if discovered by others.

The production, distribution and possession of child pornography is not protected by the First Amendment.

It is important to note that the kind of material outlawed does not have to meet the test for obscenity outlined in the *Miller* ruling. In other words, images of minors engaged in sexually explicit conduct do not need to rise to the level of obscenity under *Miller* in order for them to constitute child pornography—an illegal product—and fall outside the scope of First Amendment protection.

A nude image of a child does not always constitute child pornography. There must be a lascivious exhibition of the genitals or pubic area to constitute child pornography, such as a tightly focused or unnaturally zoomed-in view of those areas. Thus, a naked picture of you as a baby or toddler being washed in a bathtub does not constitute child pornography. Courts often weigh six factors, known as the *Dost* factors (based on a case by that name), to determine if an exhibition is lascivious, including whether the (1) focal point of the depiction is on the child's genitalia or pubic area; (2) setting for the image is sexually suggestive, that is, a place or pose generally associated with sexual activity; (3) child is depicted in an unnatural pose or in inappropriate attire, considering the child's age; (4) child is fully or partially clothed or nude; (5) image suggests sexual coyness or a willingness to engage in sexual activity; and (6) image is intended to elicit a sexual response from a viewer. Not all the factors need to be present to constitute a lascivious exhibition; rather, the factors are considered holistically in what courts sometime call a "totality of the circumstances" approach.

In 1996 Congress adopted an amendment to the original federal child pornography law that barred the sale and distribution of any images that "appear" to depict minors performing sexually explicit acts. Under this statute child pornography is defined to include not only actual images (photos, videotapes, films) of children but also computer-generated images and other pictures that are generated by electronic, mechanical or other means in which "such visual depiction is, or appears to be, a minor engaging in sexually explicit conduct." Whereas the original child pornography laws were justified as a means to protect children from being exploited, the 1996 Child Pornography Prevention Act (CPPA) was justified as a means to protect children from pedophiles and child molesters, people whose criminal behavior may be stimulated by such images. The law specifically stated that no prosecution can be maintained if the material was produced by adults and was not advertised, promoted, described or presented in such a way as to suggest children were in fact depicted in the images. In 2002 the Supreme Court ruled that

22. 18 U.S.C. § 2256 (2017).

important segments of the law violated the First Amendment. Justice Anthony Kennedy wrote that the CPPA "prohibits speech that records no crime and creates no victims by its production." Instead, he said, "the statute prohibits the visual depiction of an idea—that of teenagers engaging in sexual activity—that is a fact of modern society and has been a theme in art and literature throughout the ages." The court also ruled that the justification for the law was insufficient since Congress failed to produce any evidence of more than a remote connection between speech that might encourage thoughts or impulses and any resulting child abuse. "The mere tendency of speech to encourage unlawful acts is not a sufficient reason for banning it," Kennedy added.[23]

After the Supreme Court struck down the CPPA, Congress passed the PROTECT Act (short for Prosecutorial Remedies and Other Tools to End the Exploitation of Children Today Act of 2003) which was, in part, aimed at curbing the promotion (or "pandering") of child pornography. By its terms, the PROTECT Act prohibits a person from knowingly advertising, promoting or soliciting material "in a manner that reflects the belief, or that is intended to cause another to believe" that the advertised material is child pornography involving real minors, even if the underlying material does not, in fact, include real minors or is otherwise completely innocuous. In 2008 the U.S. Supreme Court in *United States* v. *Williams* upheld the PROTECT Act, concluding that it was neither overbroad nor vague (see Chapter 1 discussing the vagueness and overbreadth doctrines) and finding that a crime is committed under the act "only when the speaker believes or intends the listener to believe that the subject of the proposed transaction depicts *real* children."[24] Writing the majority opinion, Justice Antonin Scalia made it clear the high court was not overruling its 2002 decision in *Ashcroft* v. *Free Speech Coalition* involving the CPPA. "Simulated child pornography will be as available as ever, so long as it is offered and sought as such, and not as real child pornography," Scalia wrote. Although one can be convicted under the PROTECT Act even if the advertised material is not real child pornography, Scalia interpreted the act as requiring, for conviction, "that the defendant hold, and make a statement that reflects, the belief that the material is child pornography; or that he communicate in a manner intended to cause another so to believe." In what situations, then, does the PROTECT Act apply? Scalia observed that "an Internet user who solicits child pornography from an undercover agent violates the statute, even if the officer possesses no child pornography. Likewise, a person who advertises virtual child pornography as depicting actual children also falls within the reach of the statute."

In an interesting twist on the U.S. Supreme Court's 2002 ruling involving the CPPA and "virtual" child pornography, the Ohio Supreme Court in 2007 in *Ohio* v. *Tooley* upheld a state statute prohibiting blended or "morphed" images that digitally combine and graft separate photos of actual adults and real children in order to create the appearance of sexual acts.[25] In brief, under the Ohio statute, prosecutors in that state must still prove beyond a reasonable doubt (the standard of proof in a criminal case) that a real child is pictured in the morphed photograph in order to gain a conviction while, consistent with

---

23. *Ashcroft* v. *Free Speech Coalition,* 535 U.S. 234 (2002).
24. 553 U.S. 285 (2008) (emphasis added).
25. 872 N.E. 2d 894 (Ohio 2007), cert. den., 128 S. Ct. 912 (2008).

the U.S. Supreme Court's ruling in the *Free Speech Coalition* case involving the CPPA described earlier, images that involve only computer-generated and completely fictitious images of children remain protected under the First Amendment. The Ohio Supreme Court thus drew a critical distinction between

- *virtual child pornography* (images that are either entirely computer-generated or that are created using only adults) protected by the First Amendment; and
- *morphed child pornography* (images that are created by altering a real child's image to make it appear that the child is engaged in some type of sexual activity) not protected by the First Amendment.

In 2008 the U.S. Supreme Court chose not to disturb the Ohio Supreme Court's ruling in *Tooley* when it denied the defendant's petition for a writ of certiorari in the case.

Children as Child Pornographers and Sexting

A new issue regarding child pornography involves minors who create their own sexual content and then post the images on online social networks or trade them via cell phones, the latter process known as "sexting." In other words, what happens when a child is a child pornographer?

What happens when a child is a child pornographer?

Sexting among minors first gained national attention around 2008 and 2009 when some prosecutors began charging 14- and 15-year-olds with creating, distributing and possessing child pornography after they were caught trading sexually explicit images of themselves on cell phones. But the problems with sexting continue today. For example, in 2016 five students at Newtown High School in Connecticut were arrested on felony child pornography charges for transmitting sexually explicit images and videos of classmates and other students via smartphone messaging apps such as Snapchat and Kik.

It is important here to remember from the discussion just a few pages ago that a picture or video showing a "lascivious exhibition of the genitals or pubic area" of a person under age 18 constitutes child pornography, as well as images of masturbation. Minors who take, possess and/or distribute such photos or videos of themselves or other minors are not exempt from child pornography statutes. Starting in 2010 and 2011, some states began adopting new statutes to address sexting between minors because the application of traditional child pornography laws seemed far too harsh, especially when the sexting was consensual and confined between two willing minors. Why? Because a minor convicted on child pornography charges for engaging in sexting is guilty of a felony, can serve five years in prison for a single count of transmitting or possessing child pornography and must register as a sex offender, a stigma that will haunt him or her for life. In 2011, Florida adopted a sexting statute, and by 2018 more than 20 states had adopted some form of sexting legislation. Louisiana's sexting law, for instance, provides that "no person under the age of seventeen years shall knowingly and voluntarily use a computer or telecommunication device to transmit an indecent visual depiction of himself to another person." Most of the new legislation either reduces consensual sexting committed by minors of a certain age to only a misdemeanor offense, rather than a felony, or treats it (at least on the first occasion for a minor) as a noncriminal offense subject only to monetary fines and/or community service obligations.

Obscenity and Women

Some feminist scholars assert that sexually explicit content subordinates women to men.

Some feminist scholars assert that sexually explicit content subordinates women to men, objectifies and exploits women as sex objects for men's pleasure and leads to violence.[26] In 1984 Indianapolis adopted a statute, based on such arguments, banning "pornography"—not obscenity. It defined pornography as "the graphic sexually explicit subordination of women, whether in pictures or in words" that also includes such things as women being presented "as sexual objects who enjoy pain or humiliation" or "as sexual objects for domination, conquest, violation, exploitation, possession, or use, or through postures or positions of servility or submission or display." In 1985 an appellate court declared the law unconstitutional in *American Booksellers Association, Inc.* v. *Hudnut*,[27] noting it went far beyond regulating obscenity under the *Miller* test. The court found the statute constituted **viewpoint-based discrimination** (see Chapter 3) on speech. It wrote that, under the statute, "speech that 'subordinates' women and also, for example . . . presents women in 'positions of servility or submission or display' is forbidden, no matter how great the literary or political value of the work taken as a whole. [Conversely,] speech that portrays women in positions of equality is lawful, no matter how graphic the sexual content. This is thought control. It establishes an 'approved' view of women." The decision ended adoption of similar laws in the United States.

SUMMARY   The *Miller* test is used today by American courts to determine whether something is obscene. It has three parts. Material is obscene under the following conditions:

1. An average person, applying contemporary local community standards, finds that the work, taken as a whole, appeals to a prurient interest in sex. This requires the fact finder to apply local (usually state) standards rather than a national standard.
2. The work depicts in a patently offensive way sexual conduct specifically defined by applicable state law. Again, the fact finder in the case determines patent offensiveness, based on local community standards. But the Supreme Court has ruled that only so-called hard-core pornography can be found to be patently offensive. Also, either the legislature or the state Supreme Court must specifically define the kind of offensive material that may be declared to be obscene.
3. The material lacks serious literary, artistic, political or scientific value.

The Supreme Court has ruled that states may use a broader definition of obscenity when they attempt to block the sale or distribution of erotic material to children or when they attempt to stop the exploitation of children who are forced to engage in sexual conduct by filmmakers. But such laws must be careful so as not to unconstitutionally ban legal material as well. Laws aimed at stopping the use of children in preparing sexually explicit material have also been permitted by the high court.

26. See MacKinnon, *Only Words;* and Stark and Whisnant, *Not for Sale.*
27. 771 F. 2d 323 (7th Cir. 1985).

REGULATION OF NONOBSCENE EROTIC MATERIAL

Battles over obscenity have gone on for more than a century. But as the Supreme Court narrowed its definition of legal obscenity during the past 50 years, more and more pressure has been applied by advocacy groups and even some government agencies to stop the flow of nonobscene, adult material that would probably have been considered legally obscene half a century ago, but is protected by the First Amendment today. In fact, in many respects, this has become the primary battleground in the fight over the distribution and exhibition of adult, sexually explicit material. Magazines like *Hustler* and *Barely Legal*, rap music, homoerotic art exhibits, adult videos and sexually oriented sites on the Internet are among a wide variety of mass media targeted for control and even censorship in various parts of the nation. Although this material is certainly offensive to some people, it generally enjoys the full protection of the First Amendment because it does not qualify as obscenity under the *Miller* test. Here is an outline of some of these legal skirmishes.

SEXUALLY ORIENTED BUSINESSES

Sexually oriented businesses (SOBs)—strip clubs, adult video stores and adult theaters—are subject to two types of local laws:

1. *Zoning regulations*
2. *Expressive conduct regulations*

To the extent speech products (DVDs, videos and magazines) sold in these establishments are not obscene under the *Miller* test,[28] and to the extent that the U.S. Supreme Court has held that nude dancing "is expressive conduct that is entitled to some quantum of protection under the First Amendment,"[29] the zoning of SOBs and the regulation of activities inside them raise constitutional issues of free expression. In fact, federal and state courts hear at least a dozen challenges each year to these laws, despite the fact that many municipalities hire consulting firms like Duncan Associates to help them when crafting such laws (see http://www.duncanassociates.com).

When cities zone SOBs, they use one of two approaches—clustering the businesses into a single area (called a red-light district or combat zone), or dispersing them across

When cities zone SOBs, they use one of two approaches.

---

28. Although hard to believe, a few states today consider sex toys like vibrators to be "obscene" sexual devices and thus outlaw their sale and distribution. For example, the 11th U.S. Circuit Court of Appeals in 2007 upheld an Alabama statute that prohibits the commercial distribution of devices "primarily for the stimulation of human genital organs." *Williams* v. *Morgan,* 478 F. 3d 1316 (11th Cir. 2007), cert. den., 128 S. Ct. 77 (2007). The 11th Circuit found that protecting "public morality" was a sufficient reason to justify and uphold the Alabama law. In 2008, however, the 5th U.S. Circuit Court of Appeals struck down a similar Texas statute that made it a crime to promote, sell, give or lend a sexual device unless done so "for a bona fide medical" purpose. *Reliable Consultants* v. *Earle,* 517 F. 3d 738 (5th Cir. 2008). The 5th Circuit, citing the U.S. Supreme Court's 2003 ruling in *Lawrence* v. *Texas* (see Chapter 1), rejected Texas' public morality justification and found, instead, that the statute "impermissibly burdens the individual's substantive due process right to engage in private intimate conduct of his or her choosing."
29. *City of Erie* v. *Pap's A.M.,* 529 U.S. 277 (2000).

the community, usually to remote industrial areas away from schools and most residential areas. These zoning tactics are OK if certain criteria are met. For instance, the Supreme Court in *Renton* v. *Playtime Theatres, Inc.* upheld a municipal ordinance in Washington state prohibiting adult theaters from locating within 1,000 feet of any residential zone, family dwelling, church, park or school.[30] The high court allows such zoning laws and subjects them to a relatively relaxed form of judicial scrutiny if they are designed to decrease and reduce so-called *secondary effects* of SOBs. Secondary effects of SOBs typically are problems that may go on outside an SOB such as increased crime rates, decreased property values and decreased quality of life. Other secondary effects may include the spread of sexually transmitted diseases inside an SOB that might result from direct contact between dancers and patrons. If a municipality proves that it is targeting such negative secondary effects ostensibly caused by SOBs and, conversely, is not targeting the actual speech inside the SOB, then the ordinance is considered content neutral and the municipality simply must prove that the zoning law

1. serves a substantial government interest, and
2. does not completely ban all SOBs in the municipality and unreasonably limit alternative avenues of communications.

Notice how this approximates the intermediate scrutiny standard of review for content-neutral time, place and manner regulations (see Chapter 3). As the 7th Circuit U.S. Court of Appeals observed in 2015, "regulations on sexually oriented businesses are nearly always reviewed under intermediate scrutiny as content-neutral regulations."[31] The 7th Circuit added in the same opinion that "it's no surprise that regulations on businesses offering sexually oriented entertainment are rarely subject to strict judicial scrutiny. Local governments are usually smart enough to invoke 'secondary effects' in their regulation of adult businesses." In applying this test, courts generally give vast deference to municipalities. While municipalities are required to rely on some pre-enactment evidence of negative secondary effects that "must fairly support the municipality's rationale for its ordinance,"[32] this often is not a burdensome task. For instance, they are not required to conduct their own studies about negative secondary effects in their communities and they are not required to submit empirical data of alleged harms caused by SOBs. As the Supreme Court of Georgia observed in 2015, "it is not necessary for a local government to prove that the negative secondary effects it reasonably fears, based on evidence of problems experienced elsewhere, have already been experienced locally."[33] It added that "the Constitution does not require governments to forestall reasonable regulation until the mess meant to be avoided is proved to have arrived and now needs to be cleaned up." The Supreme Judicial Court of Massachusetts in 2015 similarly pointed out that although a "municipality cannot rationalize the restriction post hoc" (that is, after the adoption of a zoning regulation), it is not "necessary that the municipality demonstrate these secondary effects by evidence specifically studying its own unique

30. 475 U.S. 41 (1986).
31. *BBL, Inc.* v. *City of Angola*, 809 F. 3d 317 (7th Cir. 2015).
32. *City of Los Angeles* v. *Alameda Books, Inc.*, 535 U.S. 425, 438 (2002).
33. *Oasis Goodtime Emporium I, Inc.* v. *City of Doraville*, 773 S.E. 2d 728 (Ga. 2015).

circumstances."[34] Furthermore, the 7th U.S. Circuit Court of Appeals wrote in 2015 that municipalities have "considerable flexibility in identifying evidentiary support" and are "not required to conduct independent studies regarding undesirable secondary effects."[35]

Although owners of SOBs may counter such evidence and have done so success-fully in some recent cases as courts grow more skeptical of alleged secondary effects,[36] this is a time-consuming and expensive task in terms of hiring expert witnesses and com-missioning their own studies, and the evidence SOBs produce must cast direct doubt on that offered by the municipality.

When it comes to proving a substantial interest, courts usually find with no hesita-tion that municipalities have a substantial interest in curbing the secondary effects associ-ated with adult entertainment establishments. In 2006, however, a federal court issued a restraining order against a Duluth, Minn., ordinance that limited the hours of operation of SOBs. The court noted that Duluth "presented no legislative history indicating that the hours of operation restriction is necessary to combat adverse secondary effects," and concluded that the plaintiff-SOB was "likely to succeed on its claim that the statute was not designed to promote the substantial governmental interest of combating negative secondary effects."[37]

On the requirement of not completely banning all SOBs and not unreasonably limiting the space in the community in which they can be located, courts are clear that the land available for SOBs does not need to be the most commercially favorable and that there does not, in fact, need to be much space available. For instance, the ordinance of Renton, Wash., was upheld by the Supreme Court even though it left open just 5 percent (520 acres) of all land for SOB use. However, a municipality cannot enact a zoning law that provides for fewer available locations than there are presently operating SOBs in the municipality, and an SOB forced to move by a new zoning law must have ample oppor-tunity for relocation.[38]

In addition to zoning SOBs, many municipalities enact laws affecting the expressive conduct that takes place inside these businesses. As noted earlier, nude dancing is con-sidered speech by the U.S. Supreme Court, yet it and other courts have allowed cities to adopt minimal clothing requirements (G-strings, thongs and pasties) since these interfere in a very minor way with the erotic message conveyed by dancing. As the Supreme Court stated in 2000 in upholding an Erie, Pa., ban on public nudity against a lawsuit filed by a nude dancing establishment, "any effect [of wearing G-strings and pasties] on the overall

---

34. *Showtime Entertainment LLC v. Town of Mendon*, 32 N.E. 3d 1259 (Mass. 2015).

35. *Foxxxy Ladyz Adult World, Inc. v. Village of Dix*, 779 F. 3d 706 (7th Cir. 2015).

36. See *Daytona Grand, Inc. v. City of Daytona Beach*, 2006 U.S. Dist. LEXIS 41164 (M.D. Fla. 2006), which struck down an ordinance prohibiting nude dancing in clubs that sell alcohol after the clubs introduced expert testimony and evidence refuting the municipality's claim of a link between secondary effects and the combination of drinking alcohol and viewing nude entertainment. Even this victory for an SOB was short-lived, however, as a federal appellate court in June 2007 reversed the district court's decision and held that the SOB's experts "failed to cast direct doubt on all of the evidence" that the City of Daytona Beach had relied on to show secondary effects. *Daytona Grand, Inc. v. City of Daytona Beach*, 490 F. 3d 860 (11th Cir. 2007).

37. *Northshore Experience, Inc. v. City of Duluth*, 442 F. Supp. 3d 713 (D. Minn. 2006).

38. *Fly Fish, Inc. v. City of Cocoa Beach*, 337 F. 3d 1301 (11th Cir. 2003).

expression is *de minimis*."[39] Municipalities also are allowed to adopt reasonable rules designed to prevent sexual conduct and contact such as lap dances between dancers and patrons. Typical efforts include:

- Minimum distance requirements between dancers and patrons
- Stage height requirements
- Railing requirements around stages
- Rules against direct tipping
- Minimum levels of lighting
- Rules prohibiting doors and partitions on booths and VIP rooms

Like zoning regulations, these restrictions affecting expressive conduct inside SOBs are subject to intermediate scrutiny review if they target negative secondary effects on public health and safety such as the spread of sexually transmitted diseases, lewdness and public indecency. Assuming that the authority to regulate SOBs rests with the government entity that is trying to regulate them, all the government needs to prove is that the regulations

1. serve a substantial government interest unrelated to the content of speech, and
2. are narrowly tailored (not substantially broader than necessary) to serve the interest.

In 2008 the 6th U.S. Circuit Court of Appeals applied this **intermediate scrutiny** standard and upheld a Kenton County, Ky., ordinance that requires dancers to stay at least five feet away from areas of an SOB occupied by customers for at least one hour after they perform seminude on stage.[40] This postperformance, anti-commingling ordinance was aimed at reducing the secondary effect of prostitution, which Kenton County contended sometimes arises in SOBs when performers sit down next to customers immediately after dancing and ask the customers to buy them "conversation drinks" that, in turn, sometimes lead to sex acts. Observing that the ordinance "restricts only those dancers performing on a particular night and restricts them only for an hour after their performances," the appellate court reasoned that Kenton County "has targeted contact between adult entertainers and customers that created a risk of prostitution. It has done so in a manner that substantially preserves the ability of those affected to communicate with each other, although in a less physical way than they could previously. We thus conclude that the provision satisfies intermediate scrutiny."

What about banning booze inside of SOBs? The 11th U.S. Circuit Court of Appeals in 2010 upheld a Fulton County, Ga., statute in *Flanigan's Enterprises, Inc.* v. *Fulton County*[41]

---

39. *City of Erie* v. *Pap's A.M.*, 529 U.S. 277, 294 (2000). Appellate courts have since noted that statutes requiring dancers to wear more than just G-strings, thongs and pasties may actually infringe too much on speech rights. *Peek-a-Boo Lounge* v. *Manatee County*, 337 F. 3d 1251 (11th Cir. 2003) held that a statute requiring clothing that covers "one-third of the buttocks" and "one-fourth of the female breast" area "effectively redraw[s] the boundary between nudity and non-nudity, thereby prohibiting erotic dancers from wearing the amount of body covering the [Supreme] Court found to be consistent with the First Amendment."

40. *729, Inc.* v. *Kenton County Fiscal Court*, 515 F. 3d 485 (6th Cir. 2008).

41. 596 F. 3d 1265 (11th Cir. 2010).

prohibiting the sale, possession and consumption of alcohol in SOBs. Fulton County claimed it was concerned about the secondary effects on its communities of the mixture of alcohol and live nude dancing, and it thus claimed the law should be subjected only to the **intermediate scrutiny** standard of review discussed earlier in this section. The appellate court agreed and found that the evidence offered by Fulton County in support of its law "certainly creates a vivid image of a County in which strip clubs that served alcohol played a prominent and unwelcome role. Sex and drug crimes occurred in and around the clubs and the neighborhood's cheap hotels, and required law enforcement and the judiciary (the juvenile court, at least) to invest resources in combating the secondary effects. Moreover, the neighborhoods themselves were dilapidated and in need of repair."

In 2011, the Supreme Court of Missouri upheld a comprehensive state law that: (1) bans nude dancing in public; (2) requires semi-nude dancers not to touch or come within six feet of customers; (3) prohibits alcohol in SOBs; (4) requires SOBs to close between midnight and 6:00 A.M.; and (5) requires SOB viewing booths to be visible from a central operating station.[42] In upholding the statute, the court applied the secondary effects doctrine, reasoning that "the restrictions are not content-based limitations on speech but rather are aimed at limiting the negative secondary effects of sexually oriented businesses on the health, welfare and safety of Missouri residents." It reached this conclusion, in part, because the preamble to the statute—the legislative intent, as it were—stated that the law was adopted "to promote the health, safety, and general welfare of the citizens of this state, and to establish reasonable and uniform regulations to prevent the deleterious secondary effects of sexually oriented businesses within the state."

As a content-neutral law, the Missouri statute was subject only to the **intermediate scrutiny** standard of judicial review. Applying this standard, the Supreme Court of Missouri found that the state had "reasonably relied on a plethora of evidence. While the businesses attacked and sought to undermine some of this evidence, they failed to cast direct doubt on other evidence or on the government's rationale of trying to limit the negative secondary effects within the establishments themselves." It thus concluded "that the government presented at least some evidence to support the legislature's reasonable belief that the restrictions in question are designed to serve the substantial government interest in minimizing the negative secondary effects caused by sexually oriented businesses." In October 2012, the U.S. Supreme Court denied the adult entertainment industry's petition for writ of certiorari to hear the case.

ATTACKS ON THE ARTS AND POPULAR CULTURE

Beyond sexually explicit magazines, DVDs and Web sites, other forms of American popular culture often are challenged, both in court and by advocacy groups, for sexual content. For instance, the fast-food chains Hardee's and Carl's Jr. drew criticism for their racy advertisements featuring scantily clad women suggestively eating food. Critics compared the ads to soft-core pornography, and the ads inspired boycotts. But Andrew Puzder, the then-CEO of Carl's Jr. and Hardee's parent company CKE Restaurants, defended the ads.

---

42. *Ocello v. Koster*, 354 S.W. 3d 187 (Mo. 2011).

He told *Entrepreneur* in 2015, "I like our ads. I like beautiful women eating burgers in bikinis. I think it's very American."

The rap group 2 Live Crew's "As Nasty As They Wanna Be" recording was declared obscene by a judge in 1990,[43] and the Cincinnati Contemporary Arts Center was unsuccessfully prosecuted for obscenity that same year for a display of photographs by Robert Mapplethorpe (see pages 492–493). In 1999 New York City Mayor Rudy Giuliani withheld funds already appropriated to the Brooklyn Museum after it opened a temporary exhibit the mayor called "sick" and "disgusting."[44] And when the National Endowment for the Arts doles out money today to artists, it is required under federal law to take "into consideration general standards of decency."[45]

The late comedian Lenny Bruce was twice convicted of obscenity in 1964.

Proving that censorship is no laughing matter, the late comedian Lenny Bruce was twice convicted of obscenity in 1964: once for a stand-up performance in Chicago[46] and once for a profane routine in New York City's Greenwich Village.[47] Showing how "contemporary community standards" (the phrase used in the *Miller* obscenity test) change, comedians today often "work blue," using the same words as Bruce but with little fear of obscenity prosecution. The 2005 movie "The Aristocrats" featuring multiple comedians telling "the dirtiest joke ever told" (it involves graphic descriptions of incest, bestiality and bodily excretions) was rented at video stores across the nation.

CLOSING THE DOORS ON JIM MORRISON: FLORIDA'S POSTHUMOUS PARDON OF MR. MOJO RISIN'

During a March 1969 concert in Miami, the lead singer for the Doors, Jim Morrison, was arrested and charged with "lewd and lascivious behavior in public by exposing his private parts and by simulating masturbation and oral copulation" while on stage. Morrison whipped it out, as it were, after allegedly asking the audience, "Do you want to see my cock?" He was convicted of two misdemeanor counts. More than 40 years later, in December 2010, the Florida Clemency Board pardoned Morrison at the request of outgoing Gov. Charlie Crist. It was far too late for Morrison, who died in 1971.

---

43. *Skyywalker Records, Inc.* v. *Navarro,* 739 F. Supp. 578 (S.D. Fla. 1990). The conviction was thrown out by a federal appellate court because the local sheriff "submitted no evidence to contradict the [expert] testimony [put on by 2 Live Crew] that the work had artistic value." *Luke Records* v. *Navarro,* 960 F. 2d 134 (11th Cir. 1992).
44. A federal judge held the mayor's defunding of the museum violated the First Amendment, noting that the museum cannot be penalized "because of the perceived viewpoint of the works in the exhibit" and adding there was no language in the lease or contract between the City of New York and the museum "that gives the Mayor or the City the right to veto works chosen for exhibition by the Museum." *Brooklyn Institute of Arts and Sciences* v. *City of New York,* 64 F. Supp. 2d 184 (E.D. N.Y. 1999).
45. 20 U.S.C. § 954 (2007).
46. See *Illinois* v. *Bruce,* 202 N.E. 2d 497 (Ill. 1964) (reversing the conviction).
47. Thirty-nine years later, in 2003, then New York Gov. George Pataki formally pardoned Bruce, long after his death of a drug overdose in 1966.

The words of the frat party anthem "Louie, Louie" by the Kingsmen are hard to decipher, even when listening in an otherwise quiet and keg-free room. For several months in 1964, in fact, the FBI launched an investigation to determine if the lyrics were obscene. A Florida resident filed a complaint that obscene lyrics were detectable when the album (yes, vinyl) was played at an abnormal speed. You can find the FBI's file on the song at http://vault.fbi.gov/louie-louie-the-song to see what the Feds determined!

EROTIC MATERIALS IN CYBERSPACE

Beginning in 1996 Congress passed a series of three federal statutes designed to control what Americans could see on the Internet. It should be noted that the transmission of obscene material over the Internet is clearly banned by federal law. Statutes that make it a crime to transport obscene material in interstate commerce, whether in a truck or car, via the U.S. Postal Service or UPS, or by television transmission or satellite relay, also bar the movement of such material over the Internet, even through e-mail.[48] Transmission of child pornography via computers is also banned under federal law.

The statutes adopted by Congress focused on nonobscene, adult-oriented, sexually explicit material—material that is protected by the First Amendment. The laws included:

- 1996 Communications Decency Act
- 1998 Child Online Protection Act
- 2001 Children's Internet Protection Act

What follows is a brief summary of these regulations, as well as the court rulings that focused on the laws.

The Communications Decency Act

The Communications Decency Act (CDA) was one part of a massive law that restructured telecommunication regulations. Among other things, the act made it a crime to transmit indecent material or allow indecent material to be transmitted over public computer networks to which minors have access. Fines of $250,000 and a jail sentence of five years were possible for those convicted of violating this measure. The law defined indecency as "any comment, request, suggestion, proposal, image or other communication that, in context, depicts or describes in terms patently offensive as measured by contemporary community standards, sexual or excretory activities or organs."

In 1997 in *Reno* v. *ACLU*[49] the U.S. Supreme Court held unconstitutional the CDA's provisions protecting minors from "indecent" and "patently offensive" Internet communications. Initially observing that Internet-conveyed speech deserves the same full First Amendment protection as speech transmitted in print (see Chapter 3), Justice John Paul Stevens wrote for the majority that the statute "places an unacceptably heavy burden on protected speech" and, by going far beyond restricting obscene speech under *Miller,* "threatens to torch a large segment of the Internet community." The court did not attack the congressional goal of protecting minors from potentially harmful materials, but it

48. 18 U.S.C. § 1465.
49. 521 U.S. 844 (1997).

criticized, on grounds of both void for vagueness and overbreadth (see Chapter 1 discussing these doctrines), the terms and language used in the CDA to carry out that goal. Not only were the terms "indecent" and "patently offensive" lacking precise definition, but the court held that the CDA, in attempting "to deny minors access to potentially harmful speech . . . effectively suppresses a large amount of speech that adults have a constitutional right to receive and to address to one another." Stevens noted that whereas the *Miller* obscenity test protects speech with serious literary, artistic, political or scientific value, the CDA lacked such a saving provision to protect socially redeeming speech that may be sexually explicit. The CDA thus could stop discussion of sexually frank but legitimate topics such as birth control practices, homosexuality and the consequences of rape.

The Child Online Protection Act

The following year Congress tried again when it adopted the Child Online Protection Act (COPA). The statute prohibits commercial Web sites from knowingly transmitting to minors (people under 17 years of age) material that is harmful to minors. Harmful material was defined as material that, with respect to minors, is specifically created to appeal to prurient interests, that graphically depicts lewd or sexual behavior and that lacks serious literary, artistic or scientific value. The law requires jurors to apply "contemporary community standards" when assessing material. A fine of $50,000 and a six-month jail sentence may be imposed for each violation. But the law includes provisions that bar any prosecution of a Web site operator who has restricted access to the site to those with credit cards, debit accounts, adult access codes or adult personal ID numbers. The idea of this provision is that only adults would have access to one of these items, and therefore the site operator could honestly believe he or she is communicating with an adult, not a minor.

In 2004, after the case bounced around the federal courts for five years, the U.S. Supreme Court upheld on First Amendment grounds a lower-court preliminary injunction against enforcement of COPA in *Ashcroft* v. *ACLU*.[50] Examining COPA as a content-based restriction on speech subject to **strict scrutiny** review (see Chapter 2), the high court noted that the government must prove that COPA restricts no more speech than is necessary to achieve the goal of making the Internet safe for minors. As part of this task, the government must show that any less restrictive alternatives proposed by the ACLU and the other plaintiffs would not be as effective as COPA in serving its goal. Justice Anthony Kennedy wrote for the five-justice majority that Internet filters that parents can purchase "are less restrictive than COPA. They impose selective restrictions on speech at the receiving end, not universal restrictions at the source." What's more, Kennedy noted that, in contrast to COPA, "promoting the use of filters does not condemn as criminal any category of speech, and so the potential chilling effect is eliminated, or at least much diminished." He added that filters "may well be more effective than COPA." Concluding that the government had not yet demonstrated that COPA is the least restrictive alternative available to protect minors, the majority sustained the preliminary injunction preventing enforcement of COPA and remanded the case for a trial on the merits.

50. 542 U.S. 656 (2004).

In late 2006, the government was back in federal court in Pennsylvania trying to resuscitate COPA, with the case now called *ACLU* v. *Gonzales* (because Alberto Gonzales replaced John Ashcroft as attorney general). But in March 2007, U.S. District Court Judge Lowell A. Reed Jr. again rebuffed the government, issuing a permanent injunction against the enforcement of COPA and holding, among other things, that COPA is "not narrowly tailored to Congress' compelling interest" in protecting minors and that "COPA is impermissibly vague and overbroad" (see Chapter 1 discussing the void for vagueness and overbreadth doctrines).[51]

Amazingly, the federal government did not give up on COPA; it went back to court in 2008 (a full decade after COPA became law) to ask the 3rd U.S. Circuit Court of Appeals in Philadelphia to overturn Judge Reed's March 2007 ruling that had permanently enjoined the measure. Predictably, the 3rd Circuit in July 2008 affirmed Reed's injunction and concluded that "COPA cannot withstand a strict scrutiny, vagueness, or overbreadth analysis and thus is unconstitutional."[52] The appellate court extolled the virtues of filtering software rather than government regulation, writing that "filters and the Government's promotion of filters are more effective than COPA." The case finally came to a close in January 2009 when the U.S. Supreme Court denied the government's petition for a writ of certiorari to revisit the 3rd Circuit's opinion. The bottom line? After more than a decade of litigation, the COPA never took effect and the First Amendment triumphed.

After more than a decade of litigation, the COPA never took effect.

The Children's Internet Protection Act

Congress made its third attempt at limiting access to the Internet in 2001 when it adopted the Children's Internet Protection Act (CIPA). The law requires public libraries to install anti-pornography filters on all their computers that provide Internet access in order to continue to receive federal funding (so-called e-rate funds) that subsidizes their Internet access. About 14 million Americans access the Web via library computers. The federal government provides about $200 million each year to pay for this access.

One problem with filters is they "overblock" and screen out innocent material and important information on topics such as safe sex, rape, breast cancer and sexually transmitted diseases. Some libraries today thus maintain two sets of computers—some with filters that minors must use (a children's section), and some without filters that adults may use (an adult section). Alternatively, public libraries in Houston, Tex., have filters on all computers, but adults may request the filter be disabled before their own computer sessions.[53] Other libraries choose not to filter sexually explicit online content at all, a fact exposed in 2006 in Connecticut when a registered sex offender "was caught looking at child pornography on a computer at the main branch of the Hartford Public Library."[54]

In 2003 the U.S. Supreme Court upheld CIPA in *United States* v. *American Library Association* against a challenge that the act violated the First Amendment rights of adult library patrons to receive speech.[55] The court made clear that adults must be allowed,

51. *ACLU* v. *Gonzales*, 478 F. Supp. 2d 775 (E.D. Pa. 2007).
52. *ACLU* v. *Mukasey*, 534 F. 3d 181 (3d Cir. 2008), cert. den., 2009 U.S. LEXIS 598 (Jan. 21, 2009).
53. Levine and Radcliffe, "Texas AG: Children Need to Be Protected."
54. Brown, "Sex Convict Charged Again."
55. 539 U.S. 194 (2003).

upon request, to have blocked sites unblocked and/or to have filtering software disabled during their sessions. This balances adults' rights to receive information with the interest in shielding minors from sexual expression. As Justice Kennedy wrote in concurrence, "[I]f, on the request of an adult user, a librarian will unblock filtered material or disable the Internet software filter without significant delay, there is little to this case."

Online Speech Rights of Sex Offenders: The Packingham Case

In June 2017, the U.S. Supreme Court struck down a North Carolina statute that made it a crime for a registered sex offender simply to access a commercial social networking site, such as Facebook and Twitter. In *Packingham* v. *North Carolina*,[56] the high court said that even assuming the law was a content-neutral restriction subject to intermediate scrutiny, it was not "narrowly tailored to serve a significant governmental interest." A more specific law—one that prohibited "a sex offender from engaging in conduct that often presages a sexual crime, like contacting a minor or using a website to gather information about a minor"—could pass muster, the Court said. But instead, Justice Anthony Kennedy wrote, the law here enacts "a prohibition unprecedented in the scope of First Amendment speech it burdens." He continued, "North Carolina with one broad stroke bars access to what for many are the principal sources for knowing current events, checking ads for employment, speaking and listening in the modern public square, and otherwise exploring the vast realms of human thought and knowledge."

SUMMARY Significant efforts are made to control nonobscene sexual expression. Many cities zone sexually oriented businesses (SOBs) and impose regulations on the sexual expression that is nude dancing inside SOBs. Museums, musicians and comedians all have faced the wrath of government officials for sexual content. The Internet is a key battleground for censorship of sexually explicit conduct, as evidenced by three major congressional efforts to regulate it since 1996: the Communications Decency Act, the Child Online Protection Act and the Children's Internet Protection Act.

BIBLIOGRAPHY

Brown, Tina. "Sex Convict Charged Again." *Hartford Courant,* 25 October 2006, B1.

Levine, Samantha, and Jennifer Radcliffe. "Texas AG: Children Need to Be Protected from Net Predators." *Houston Chronicle,* 12 July 2006, A4.

MacKinnon, Catharine A. *Only Words.* Cambridge, Mass.: Harvard University Press, 1993.

Munz, Michele. "Jury Finds Explicit Videos from Store Are Not Obscene." *St. Louis Post-Dispatch,* 27 October 2000, 1.

Stark, Christine, and Rebecca Whisnant. *Not for Sale: Feminists Resisting Prostitution and Pornography.* North Melbourne, Australia: Spinifex Press, 2004.

Wilkerson, Isabel. "Obscenity Jurors Were Pulled 2 Ways." *The New York Times,* 10 October 1990, A12.

56. 137 S. Ct. 1730 (2017).

CHAPTER 14

Copyright and Trademark

The law of copyright is almost 500 years old. British King Henry VIII issued the first royal grant of printing privilege, the forerunner of copyright law, in 1518. American copyright law springs from the U.S. Constitution and protects a wide variety of intellectual creations. While case law today still focuses on the rights of authors and artists who generate traditional creative compositions like books, photographs and poetry, the courtroom battles also involve the protection of motion pictures, videotapes, databases, e-books and CDs.

INTELLECTUAL PROPERTY LAW

Copyright law, along with trademark law, patent law and trade secret law, constitutes one aspect of a larger body of law known as intellectual property—intangible property that a person cannot touch, hold, or physically lock away for safekeeping. This concept is sometimes confusing to people; how can the law protect something you can't hold or touch? Consider that new paperback novel you just purchased at the bookstore. You own that book; you can do with it what you wish. After you read it you can sell it, donate it to Goodwill, give it to a friend to read or tear out the pages and use them to start a campfire. But you don't own the arrangement of the words in that book; whoever holds the copyright, the book publisher or author, owns that part of the book. Hence, you can't reprint the book or copy long sections of it without permission. The book thus consists of two pieces of property: the physical or material book, and the words and artwork printed on the pages. At first glance, intellectual property seems both esoteric and, well, a bit dull when compared with the law regulating students' rights of free speech, the distribution of adult material or using celebrities names or images without their permission in advertising. But as mass-mediated entertainment has grown as a part of our culture and our commerce, issues relating to intellectual property rights have become somewhat more complicated and a lot more interesting to those outside the legal system.

For example, who owns sports coverage? Do newspapers and magazines and television and radio stations and bloggers and others who publish (in the broadest sense) anything and everything about professional athletes and their teams own the rights to this coverage? Do the athletes own the rights to their images and accomplishments? Or do professional team owners control the rights to the pictures and stories about their businesses and their employees? This is complicated. Take, for example, a mythical major league baseball team, the Nashville Knights. The Knights have certainly assigned the rights to broadcast their games to a radio, a television station or a cable channel. So these broadcasters own some rights, and the Knights don't want to jeopardize these lucrative contracts by giving free coverage rights to others. Then the Knights have their own Web site, and Major League Baseball has its own Internet arm, which generates hundreds of millions of dollars in revenues each year. Those are revenue sources that might be diminished if the team and baseball generally cannot limit to some extent the content in the mainstream mass media.* Reporters who cover the team expect to have access to players; when the Knights limit interviews or photo coverage so they can have exclusive reports on their own Web site, the members of the press raise freedom of the press issues. The Knights are willing to work with the reporters from established newspapers or magazines or broadcast stations, but the teams expect these journalists to be disciplined and follow rules established for their behavior, both in the clubhouse and elsewhere (whom the reporters can talk to and what they can talk about). Recently, however, a large influx of bloggers have emerged, individuals who also want access to players and the clubhouse, cybernet journalists who may or may not be willing to play by the established rules. So what is the team to do? Who owns the rights to the players and the games? Questions like this are emerging rapidly, and involve elements of intellectual property law.[1]

This chapter concentrates on two aspects of intellectual property law, namely, trademark law and copyright law. A third facet of intellectual property law is called patent law, which focuses on the invention of useful goods and processes, and is described very briefly below. A fourth aspect of intellectual property law deals with trade secrets and is not covered in this textbook.

PATENTS

Patent protection serves as an important element in the technological development of the nation. Without patent law, it's doubtful that this society would have enjoyed the fruits of geniuses like Thomas Edison, Alexander Graham Bell and the Wright brothers. The Constitution gives Congress the right to promote the sciences and the useful arts by protecting the rights of inventors. Hence, as author James Gleick wrote in *The New York Times* Magazine, the patent office is charged with the enforcement of a Faustian bargain: "Inventors give up their secrets, publishing them for all to see and absorb, and in exchange they get 20-year government-sanctioned monopolies on their technologies."[2]

There are at least three different kinds of patent protections. One variety protects inventions that have utility, such as a machine or a process. A typewriter can be patented; so can a specific way of reducing the hiss or noise on a recording. Patent law also protects designs—the appearance of an article of manufacture. The design of a piece of furniture or a tire tread or a belt buckle can be patented. A variety of patents protect plants, but only those kinds that can be reproduced asexually through means other than seeds, like cuttings or grafting. Patent rights do not exist until the patent is issued by the

---

* Officials in some university sports conferences like the Southeastern Conference have issued rules barring fans from distributing photos or videos taken at games or team practices with camera phones or video recorders. They claim the distribution of these images online exploits the athletes, and could undermine the schools' own Web sites, causing financial harm. See Benson and Arango, "With Bloggers in the Bleachers."
1. For a more complete discussion of this issue see Arango's "Who Owns Sports Coverage?"
2. Gleick, "Patently Absurd."

U.S. government. Hence, the famous abbreviation on many items, "pat. pending," which means the patent has been applied for and is pending.

TRADEMARKS

A trademark is any word, name, symbol, device or any combination thereof that is used by a company (or an individual) to distinguish its goods and services from those produced by other companies. We thus commonly think of marks as brand names (Nike and McDonald's), brand logos (the Nike swoosh and McDonald's golden arches) and brand slogans (Nike's "Just Do It" and McDonald's "I'm Lovin' It").

But marks can also be: (1) colors that are distinctively associated with a brand (Tiffany's blue for its jewelry boxes and bags or Owens Corning's pink color on its insulation products); (2) sounds distinctively associated with a company (television network NBC's chimes or movie company MGM's roaring lion); and (3) the distinctive design and appearance or look of a product (the appearance of the front of an iPhone), a product's packaging (Tiffany's blue boxes tied with white ribbons or the red dripping wax on the top of Maker's Mark bourbon bottles), a store (Apple has a registered trademark for the appearance of its retail stores), or a restaurant (Chipotle has a registered trademark for the appearance of its restaurants). Marks relating to such distinctive looks and appearances are known as trade dress or dress marks, while marks used to identify the source of services (rather than products) are called service marks.

The key functions of all marks (trade, service or dress) are to clearly identify the source or origin of a product and service with a specific company and, in doing so, to prevent consumer confusion about whose goods and services one is buying. In other words, when you see Nike's swoosh logo—one of the most well recognized marks today—on a pair of running shorts, you know you are buying a genuine Nike product without even needing to see the word Nike on the shorts. If, in contrast, you saw three parallel stripes on a pair of running shorts or running shoes, you would know the product is from Adidas. Such famous marks thus serve other functions by allowing companies to tout the quality of their goods and to advertise with their marks, with the marks standing in for the goodwill and quality of the product or service.

Some marks are stronger than others. The strength of a trademark is based on its distinctiveness. The more distinctive a mark is, the easier it is to register with the U.S. Patent and Trademark Office (USPTO) (addressed later in this chapter) and the stronger it will stand up as protectable in a lawsuit for trademark infringement. (When a company believes that another company is using a mark—be it a name, logo or any other type of mark—that is too similar to its own mark and is likely to cause confusion among consumers about the origins of a product, it can sue the other company for trademark infringement). When it comes to a mark's distinctiveness, attorneys refer to a "spectrum of the distinctiveness." Proceeding from strongest to weakest categories of marks that can be registered with the USPTO, the spectrum of distinctiveness involves the following categories:

▪ **Fanciful.** These are the strongest types of marks. They consist of made-up or invented ("coined") words. Lexus is a made-up word for a car company. Exxon is a made-up word for a gasoline and oil company. Xerox is a fanciful name for a company known for copying machines. Most drug companies make up words for their products. Viagra, for example, is a made-up word.

- **Arbitrary.** This is the next strongest type of mark, second only to fanciful ones. In this category, an existing word (rather than a made-up one) is used as a mark for a good or service that is unrelated to the common or ordinary meaning of the existing word. Apple is an arbitrary mark for a computer company, as the fruit known as an apple has nothing to do with computers or iPhones. The connection, in other words, is arbitrary or random. Camel is an arbitrary mark for a cigarette company, and Pledge is an arbitrary name for a brand of furniture polish.

- **Suggestive.** Weaker than fanciful and arbitrary marks, suggestive marks suggest to consumers some attributes or qualities about the product in question, but do not clearly describe the product. In other words, consumers must do a little bit of thinking and use their imagination to understand what the product is. Coppertone is a suggestive mark for a suntan lotion, implying the shade of skin one achieves from using it. Microsoft is a suggestive mark for a company that makes computer software. Chicken of the Sea is a suggestive mark for the name of a brand of canned and packaged tuna products. (You may remember that Jessica Simpson famously had to think hard about this connection in her reality show "Newlyweds: Nick and Jessica.")

- **Descriptive.** This is the weakest type of mark. A descriptive mark directly describes features or qualities of the product in question without a consumer having to do any additional thinking. The company Arm & Hammer, for instance, makes a daily shower spray to prevent mildew and mold called "Clean Shower." That's about as descriptive as it can get. Unlike fanciful, arbitrary and suggestive marks, each of which is considered inherently distinctive, descriptive marks can only be registered with the U.S. Patent and Trademark Office after an extended period of continuous use (typically five years or more) in which they acquire a "secondary meaning" (also known as "acquired distinctiveness") such that they become associated exclusively with a particular company among members of the public that consume the product or use the service in question. In other words, consumers must come to directly associate the mark "Clean Shower" with Arm & Hammer as the source of those goods. The name "Holiday Inn" is an example of a descriptive mark that has, indeed, acquired distinctiveness and a secondary meaning over time in the eyes of hotel users such that the name is associated with a specific brand of hotel.

It is not always easy to determine whether a mark is suggestive or descriptive. The difference, however, is critical. Why? Because it is much easier to successfully register with the USPTO a suggestive mark, as there is no need to prove that a suggestive mark (or a fanciful or arbitrary mark, for that matter) has acquired a secondary meaning. Descriptive marks, in contrast, require a company to demonstrate the mark has obtained a secondary meaning in the minds of the consuming public. Attorneys thus sometimes think of this as the difference between marks that are inherently distinctive (fanciful, arbitrary and suggestive) and those that must acquire distinctiveness before they can be registered with the USPTO (descriptive).

Acquired distinctiveness also is necessary for a surname, such as Hilton or Hyatt, to be trademarked. The last name of the late hotel mogul Conrad Hilton (fans of "Mad Men" may recall him) has acquired a distinctive meaning among hotel customers such that they associate Hilton with a particular brand of hotel.

Finally, there is a fifth category of words or names that are considered generic. Generic words and terms describe broad categories or classes of products or services (rather than a specific company's product) and cannot be trademarked. In 2012, for instance, the 6th U.S. Circuit Court of Appeals held that "Texas Toast" could not be trademarked because it is a generic term for a type of oversized bread product. Similarly, the 1st Circuit Court of Appeals in 2008 held that "Duck Tours" was a generic term and could not be trademarked because it described a class of sightseeing tours that use amphibious vehicles that can function as both trucks and boats. Phrases like "pizza parlor" and "shoe store" are other examples of generics that cannot be trademarked. Apple is a generic word for a type of fruit and cannot be trademarked, unless it is used in an arbitrary way as described earlier as a brand of computer company.

THE FOUR MAIN FUNCTIONS OF TRADEMARKS AND SERVICE MARKS

- They identify one seller's goods and distinguish them from goods sold by others.
- They signify that all goods bearing the trademark or service mark come from a single source.
- They signify that all goods bearing the mark are of an equal level of quality.
- They serve as a prime instrument in advertising and selling goods.

While ownership of a trademark may exist perpetually, the ownership of a trademark or trade name can also be lost.

While ownership of a trademark may exist perpetually, the ownership of a trademark or trade name can also be lost. The Ford Motor Company in 2003 wanted to name one of its automobiles "Futura," a name it had used from 1959 to 1962 and in the late 1970s and early 1980s. But when it stopped using the name, Pep Boys, an auto parts retail chain, registered the name as a trademark. When the automaker tried to use "Futura" again, Pep Boys went to court to block Ford, and a federal court ruled in 2004 that the company had abandoned the trademark when it stopped using the name some 20 years earlier. Failure to use a name for as little as three years can constitute abandonment.

It is also possible that trademark protection can be lost if the owner of the mark allows others to use the mark in a generic way. For example, if the makers of Super Glue (a trade name) adhesive failed to try to stop other adhesive makers from referring to their products as super glues, the trademark protection could be lost. These generic words—nylon, dry ice, escalator, toasted corn flakes, raisin bran, aspirin, lanolin, mimeograph, cellophane, linoleum, shredded wheat, zipper, yo-yo and brassiere—were all at one time registered trademarks that slipped away from owners who failed to protect these names. This process of a once-trademarked term losing its trademark-protected status is known as "genericide." In brief, the trademark comes to represent an entire class of goods and no longer a specific brand within that class. And as trade names become more commonly used, there is a tendency for them to slip into a generic term. In July 2006 the owners of the search engine Google were thrilled to note that the word "google" was included in the new edition of Merriam-Webster's Collegiate Dictionary, the term going from a nonentity to common usage in less than eight years. But they were less thrilled to note that a great many people were using the term as a verb, without the capital letter G. ("John googled 'downtown car dealers' to find a used Honda.") What they want people to write or broadcast is that "John used the Google search engine to find a Honda at a downtown car dealer." Stern letters, threats of lawsuits, even legal action must be initiated to stop others from illegally using the name or phrase or mark. This responsibility falls on the owner of the mark; no government agency polices such misbehavior.

Trademark law is designed to reduce the likelihood of confusion in the marketplace. But courts have ruled that a parody of a trademarked item is not necessarily an infringement because it would not generate such confusion. Hence, when Haute Diggity Dog's toys marketed its "Chewy Vuiton" dog toys, it did not infringe on the trademark of luggage and fashion designer Louis Vuitton. "The furry little 'Chewy Vuiton' imitation, as something to be chewed by a dog, pokes fun at the elegance and expensiveness of a LOUIS VUITTON handbag, which must not be chewed by a dog," the 4th U.S. Court of Appeals ruled in 2007.[3]

For many years U.S. trademark law forbade only the use of a registered trademark or trade name on a product that was similar to the product produced by the owner of the trademark or trade name. A competitor to Apple could not call its tablet an iPad, but the manufacturer of exercise equipments could call its treadmill an iPad. In 1996 Congress, following the lead of the legislatures in 27 states, added more muscle to trademark protection when it adopted the Federal Trademark Dilution Act. This 1996 statute was later amended by the Trademark Dilution Revision Act of 2006. Viewed collectively, these federal trademark dilution statutes only apply to and protect "famous" trademarks, including names, slogans and logos. Specifically, famous marks are protected by dilution statutes from having their value weakened (i.e., diluted) by other marks *regardless* of whether or not the other marks are for similar products and *regardless* of whether consumers are actually confused as to who is producing the products. While proving a likelihood of confusion among consumers between similar or rival products generally is required in a trademark *infringement* lawsuit, it is not required in a trademark *dilution* lawsuit. Owners of famous marks thus are lucky in that they can sue the owners of offending marks not only for trademark infringement, but also for trademark dilution.

---

3. *Louis Vuitton Malletier S.A.* v. *Haute Diggity Dog LLC*, 507 F. 3d 252 (2007).

Two basic questions arise: (1) What is a famous mark? and (2) How is a famous mark diluted?

A famous mark, according to the relevant federal statute (15 U.S.C. §1125), is a mark "widely recognized by the general consuming public of the United States as a designation of source of the goods or services of the mark's owner." Among the factors considered in this determination of famousness are the "duration, extent, and geographic reach of advertising and publicity of the mark" in question, as well as the "amount, volume, and geographic extent of sales of goods or services offered under the mark."

In 2009, a federal court in Texas found the phrase "America's Team" was a famous mark controlled by the owners of the Dallas Cowboys football team. In 2011, the Trademark Trial and Appeal Board (TTAB), which is the branch of the U.S. Patent and Trademark Office that hears and decides certain kinds of trademark cases, concluded that "ROLEX" was a famous mark for a watchmaker and was protected from dilution against a company that wanted to use the mark "ROLL-X" for X-ray tables for medical and dental use. The TTAB also has found that "Just Do It" is a famous mark for Nike. More recently, luxury-clothing company Burberry in 2016 sued J.C. Penney for trademark dilution, with Burberry claiming that its ubiquitous check pattern found on coats, purses, scarves and umbrellas constitutes a famous mark. Burberry accused J.C. Penney of producing clothes that used this check pattern. Ultimately, determining whether a mark is famous is a rather subjective determination and not always easy to make.

As for the second question, a famous mark may be diluted in one of two ways under the federal statutes. In the first, known as dilution by blurring, the diluting mark "impairs the distinctiveness of the famous mark" primarily by the degree of similarity between the diluting mark and the famous mark and by whether the user of the diluting mark intended to create an association with the famous mark. This is rather hard to understand, but as one noted commentator put it, dilution by blurring is "the gradual whittling away or dispersion of the identity and hold upon the public mind of the [famous] mark or name." In brief, the famous mark's power is slowly weakened by other's use of it, even though the other's use is not on competing or similar goods.

In the second form of dilution, known as dilution by tarnishment, the diluting mark harms (i.e., tarnishes) the reputation of the famous mark by connecting the famous mark with something distasteful, negative or objectionable (think here about connecting a famous mark with illegal drugs or something sexually sordid). This category is much easier to understand than blurring.

For instance, the makers of Ben & Jerry's ice cream in 2012 sued Rodax Distributors and Caballero Videos for dilution by tarnishment based on a series of sexually explicit adult videos called "Ben & Cherry's" that featured titles such as "Peanut Butter D-Cups," "Boston Cream Thigh" and "Chocolate Fudge Babes." The parties settled the case in 2013, with Rodax and Caballero agreeing to discontinue the "Ben & Cherry's" series and the use of movie titles that play off of real Ben & Jerry's flavors.

The remedies for the owner of a famous mark that proves its case for trademark dilution are an injunction (a type of equitable remedy discussed in Chapter 1) prohibiting the use of the diluting mark, as well as monetary damages. Importantly, as the "Chewy Vuiton" example noted earlier illustrates, the federal trademark dilution laws provide a defense for "parodying, criticizing, or commenting upon the famous mark owner or the goods or services of the famous mark owner" and for "all forms of news reporting and news commentary." The "Ben & Cherry's" adult video example above likely would not count under the parody exception because the adult movies in question were not commenting on or criticizing Ben & Jerry's ice cream products, but rather were simply using names similar to those of Ben & Jerry's products to garner attention for the movies.

In 1998 Victor Moseley of Elizabethtown, Ky., opened Victor's Little Secret, a small shop in a strip mall that sells sex toys, lingerie and novelty items. Subsequently the owners of Victoria's Secret, the catalog and retail seller of lingerie and women's clothing, sued under the new law, claiming the store's name was causing dilution of the distinctive quality of their famous brand. The Supreme Court ruled in the spring of 2003 that Victoria's Secret did not have to prove actual economic harm from the appropriation of its name in its lawsuit against Moseley, but the company must show some kind of current harm (as opposed to future harm), such as a loss of its distinctive identity or a blurring of its image. But the court did not specifically outline what factors might be considered in proving such a case. The court said it would not be enough to show a mental association between the two trademarks, that consumers think of one when they see the other. It would have to be shown that consumers had a different impression of the Victoria's Secret trademark because of the competitor's branding.[4] The case was sent back to the lower court for resolution of the matter. In 2010 the 6th U.S. Court of Appeals ruled that Victor and Cathy Moseley could not use the names "Victor's Secret" or "Victor's Little Secret" on their adult novelty and lingerie shop. The court said that the use of those names cast an unflattering shadow on the Victoria's Secret chain and could potentially hurt its business.[5]

To register a trademark the applicant must submit a registration application to the Patent and Trademark Office in Washington, D.C. Before submitting the application a search should first be undertaken to determine whether someone else has already registered the trademark. This search can be done at the Patent and Trademark Office Library in Arlington, Va., or at about 60 regional sites (libraries) around the nation, or through the U.S. Trademark Electronic Search Systems via the Internet. It is also wise to hire an intellectual property attorney to help with this process. A registration fee of $275 to $375 must accompany the application. Although it is not mandatory to precede the application with a search, it is advisable. If the examiner discovers in his or her search that the mark or a very similar mark has been previously registered, the application fee is forfeited. Anyone who claims the right to a trademark can use the ™ designation with the mark to alert the public to the claim. It is not necessary to have a registration or even a pending application to use this designation. Under the law, it is the person who first uses the mark, not the person who first registers the mark, who holds the rights to the symbol or word or phrase.*

---

4. *Moseley* v. *V. Secret Catalogue, Inc.,* 537 U.S. 418 (2003). See also Greenhouse, "Ruling on *Victor* vs. *Victoria.*"
5. *V. Secret Catalogue, Inc.,* v. *Moseley,* 605 F. 3d 382 (2010).
* A booklet titled *Basic Facts About Trademarks* is available online at http://www.uspto.gov. Contact the Trademark Assistance Center at 1-800-986-9199 for a hard copy.

DISPARAGING TRADEMARKS AND VIEWPOINT-BASED CENSORSHIP

Trademark protection can promote expression, but it can also chill speech. Judges have long been skeptical about allowing private businesses to assert exclusive rights to words or phrases. More recently, courts have considered how the First Amendment is impacted by bans on disparaging trademarks. In 2017, an Asian-American rock band called "The Slants" took its legal fight over its name all the way to the U.S. Supreme Court in *Lee v. Tam*.

In 2011, Simon Tam tried to register "The Slants" as a trademark for his rock band. According to Tam, by choosing THE SLANTS as its name, the band was following the tradition of reappropriation, whereby members of minority groups reclaim slurs and epithets and turn the insults into badges of pride. The U.S. Patent and Trademark Office (USPTO) denied The Slants registration, however, under a section of trademark law that denies registration to "disparaging" marks. The U.S. Court of Appeals for the Federal Circuit, sitting *en banc*, struck down both the USPTO's decision about The Slants and ruled the entire section of the Lanham Act that bars "disparaging" trademarks as unconstitutional. The case garnered widespread attention because it was sure to have repercussions for other owners of controversial trademarks—most notably, the Washington Redskins, the NFL football team that was stripped of its trademark rights.

Section 2(a) of the Lanham Act bars registration of a mark that "[c]onsists of or comprises immoral, deceptive, or scandalous matter; or matter which may disparage or falsely suggest a connection with persons, living or dead, institutions, beliefs, or national symbols, or bring them into contempt or disrepute." In *Lee v. Tam*, the Federal Circuit ruled § 2(a) was a content-based and viewpoint-discriminatory regulation of speech, "created and applied in order to stifle the use of certain disfavored messages." Under USPTO rules, trademark examiners consider the "likely meaning" of the mark, and then determine if that meaning "may be disparaging to a substantial composite of the referenced group." Those rules led to puzzling and differing results, "rife with inconsistency," the court noted.

For instance, the USPTO denied the mark HAVE YOU HEARD SATAN IS A REPUBLICAN because it disparaged the Republican Party, but didn't find the mark THE DEVIL IS A DEMOCRAT disparaging. The office rejected registration for FAG FOREVER A GENIUS! and MARRIAGE IS FOR FAGS, but accepted the mark F*A*G FABULOUS AND GAY.

The appeal of the decision to cancel the Redskins trademark to the 4th Circuit is particularly interesting in that it contained an extensive list of terms that are potentially offensive, yet have received trademark registration. In their brief, lawyers for the team pointed out that the USPTO has registered "hundreds if not thousands" of racist, misogynistic, vulgar or otherwise offensive marks, including: Take Yo Panties Off clothing, Dangerous Negro shirts, SlutsSeeker dating services, Dago Swagg clothing, Dumb Blonde beer, Twatty Girl cartoons, Baked By a Negro bakery goods, Big Titty Blend coffee, Retardipedia Web site, Midget-Man condoms and inflatable sex dolls and Jizz underwear.

In defending the decision to not grant trademark protection in *Lee v. Tam*, the government argued denying trademark registration isn't equivalent to denying someone the right to speak. There is nothing that can stop Tam from calling his band "The Slants," the government argued. The government is simply refusing to register it as a trademark, which would give Tam the right to stop others from using the term "The Slants" for commercial purposes. The same can be said for the Redskins. The team is not barred from using the term. The government simply cancelled the team's registration. The team has argued, however, that a cancellation of its trademarks could taint its brand and remove legal benefits that would protect it against copycat entrepreneurs. The team, after all, sells everything from T-shirts to thong underwear emblazoned with its logo.

In 2017, the Supreme Court agreed to weigh in and heard oral argument in *Lee v. Tam*, now called *Matal v. Tam*. In an 8-0 decision, the Court held that section 1052(a) was a viewpoint based restriction on freedom of expression. The Court unanimously held the government could not deny registration that disparages persons, institutions, beliefs or symbols, while allowing registration for positive or benign words. The justices were not unanimous in their reasoning, however. Justices Samuel Alito, Jr., joined by Chief Justice John G. Roberts and Justices Clarence Thomas and Stephen G. Breyer wrote the law should be struck down using intermediate scrutiny, the level of scrutiny that is typically applied to commercial speech. Justices Anthony M. Kennedy, Sonia Sotomayor, Ruth Bader Ginsburg and Elena Kagan argued that the law should be struck down the using strict scrutiny because it was a viewpoint discrimination. Justice Neil M. Gorsuch did not participate in the decision because it was argued before he joined the Court.

ROOTS OF COPYRIGHT

Copyright protection was unneeded until the development of mechanical printing. The time and effort it took to hand-copy a manuscript made the theft of such work both tedious and unprofitable. But the printing press gave thieves the ability to reproduce multiple copies of a work relatively quickly and cheaply, and this capability changed things dramatically. Each subsequent technological development has put new stress and strain on copyright law. The development of motion pictures and the broadcast media, recorded music, audio- and then videotape, photocopying and most recently interactive computer-mediated communication have all required modifications or new interpretations in the law as the government has sought to protect the right to literary property.

The British were the first to attempt such protection. Copyright law developed in England in the 16th century as the government sanctioned and supported the grant of printing privileges to certain master printers in exchange for their loyalty and assistance in ferreting out anti-government writers and publishers. But the rights of authors, as opposed to printers, were not protected until the early 18th century when the British Parliament passed the nation's first copyright law. The law gave the legal claim of ownership of a piece of literary property to the person who created the work or to a person who acquired the rights to the work from the author. The statute was a recognition by

That is the real logic behind copyright law, the fostering of the creative spirit.

the Crown that in order to encourage the creation of books, plays and art, the creators of these works had to be assured that they would be rewarded for their labor. That is the real logic behind copyright law, the fostering of the creative spirit. If a dramatist knew, for example, that as soon as her play was published she would lose control of the work because others could freely copy it, there would be little incentive for the creation of plays. The muses of creativity are strong, but there must be some reward to pay the piper. Thus, copyright has been called the "engine of freedom of expression."

British copyright law was applied in the colonies until American independence. American copyright law derives directly from the U.S. Constitution. In Article I, Section 8, Clause 8, of that document lies the basic authority for modern United States copyright law:

> The Congress shall have Power . . . To promote the Progress of Science and useful Arts, by securing for limited Times to Authors and Inventors the exclusive Right to their respective Writings and Discoveries.

This provision gives Congress the power to legislate on both copyright and patent. The Congress did just that in 1790 by adopting a statute similar to British law. The law gave authors who were U.S. citizens the right to protect their books, maps and charts for a total of 28 years—a 14-year original grant plus a 14-year renewal if the author was still alive and wished to extend the copyright. In practical use, however, because little work was still economically profitable after 14 years, few authors renewed their copyright. In 1802 the law was amended to include prints as well as books, maps and charts. In 1831 the period of protection was expanded by 14 years. The original grant became 28 years with a 14-year renewal. Also, musical compositions were granted protection. Protection for photography, works of fine art and translations were added later in the 19th century.

A major revision of the law was enacted in 1909, and our current law was adopted in 1976. The 1976 federal law pre-empted virtually all state laws regarding the protection of writing, music and works of art. Hence, copyright law is essentially federal law and is governed by the federal statute and by court decisions interpreting this statute. In 1988 Congress finally approved U.S. participation in the 102-year-old Berne Convention, the world's pre-eminent international copyright treaty. The United States had been hesitant in the past to join the treaty because of significant differences between United States and international law, but after the 1976 revision of U.S. copyright law, the differences were minimal. American media companies, eager to expand their international business, sought to improve trade relations and strengthen U.S. influence on matters relating to international copyright law and therefore put pressure on the government to join the convention.

WHAT MAY BE COPYRIGHTED

The law of copyright gives to the author, or the owner of the copyright, the sole and exclusive right to reproduce the copyrighted work in any form for any reason. There are actually six exclusive rights recognized under the law, including the rights to:

- **Reproduce the work**
- **Prepare and create derivative works**

- **Publicly distribute the work**
- **Publicly perform the work**
- **Publicly display the work**
- **Publicly perform a digital sound recording**

These rights are fairly clear with regard to traditional mass media. If Bogus Publishing prints 1,000 copies of a copyrighted Stephen King novel and distributes them to bookstores, this is a violation of King's exclusive distribution rights under the law. But the rights are less clear when it comes to computers and the Internet. Is storing a copyrighted document on a hard disk or a diskette or even in the computer's RAM a violation of the exclusive right to reproduce a copyrighted item? Probably, the courts seem to indicate. Does transmitting a copyrighted work via the Internet constitute a public performance of the work? Most likely. The courts are still sorting out these questions. Several lower courts have ruled that it can be an infringement of copyright to download material off the Internet for unauthorized use or upload copyrighted material onto a Web site without the permission of the copyright holder.[6] A federal court in Texas ruled in December 1997 that an online service provider that provided subscribers unauthorized copies of copyrighted images infringed on the copyright holder's rights of reproduction, distribution and display and was liable for direct copyright infringement. The provider argued that it was merely a conduit between the subscription service that scanned the photos into the system and the subscribers who downloaded them. The defendant said that all it sold was access to the subscription service, not images. The court disagreed, ruling that "Webbworld didn't sell access—it sold images."[7] However, under a federal statute adopted in 1998 an online service provider that acts as merely a *conduit* during the infringement of copyrighted works will not be held liable for the illegal act in most instances (see page 555). A U.S. District Court in Nevada ruled in 1999 that scanning a copyrighted photo into a computer for graphic manipulation and insertion into a new work constitutes a copyright infringement. The court said that digitizing any copyrighted material may support an infringement finding—even if it has only the briefest existence in a computer's memory.

Before a copyrighted work may be printed, broadcast, dramatized or translated, the consent of the copyright owner must first be obtained. The law grants this individual exclusive monopoly over the use of that material. To quote the statute specifically, copyright extends to "original works of authorship fixed in any tangible medium of expression." Congress has defined *fixed in a tangible medium* as that work that is "sufficiently permanent or stable to permit it to be perceived, reproduced, or otherwise communicated for a period of more than a transitory duration." Under these standards such items as newspaper stories or entire newspapers, magazine articles, advertisements and almost anything else created for the mass media can be copyrighted. Material that is created in digital form and stored or transmitted electronically can also be protected by copyright.

---

6. See, for example, *Playboy Enterprises, Inc.* v. *Starware Publishers Corp.*, 900 F. Supp. 433 (1995).
7. *Playboy Enterprises, Inc.* v. *Webbworld Inc.*, D.C.N. Texas Civil No. 3196-CV-3222-H, 12/11/97. But see also *Rogers* v. *Better Business Bureau of Metropolitan Houston, Inc.* S.D. Tex., 4:10-3741 (8-15-12) where a federal court in Texas reached a different conclusion.

Extemporaneous performances and speeches, and improvised sketches are examples of materials that are not fixed in a tangible medium and are not protected by the federal copyright statute. But this lack of protection does not mean that someone can film or record a performer's act, for example, without the performer's permission. This action would also be forbidden by other laws, such as the right to publicity (see Chapter 7) and common-law copyright.*

The federal Copyright Act lists multiple items that can be copyrighted, but this list is only illustrative. It includes the following:

1. Literary works (including computer software)
2. Musical works, including any accompanying words
3. Dramatic works, including any accompanying music
4. Pantomimes and choreographic works
5. Pictorial, graphic and sculptural works
6. Motion pictures and other audiovisual works
7. Sound recordings

Copyright law is equally specific about what cannot be copyrighted:

1. Trivial materials cannot be copyrighted. Such things as titles, slogans and minor variations on works in the public domain are not protected by the law of literary property. A slogan such as Nike's "Just Do It" cannot be copyrighted, but it can be trademarked.

2. Ideas are not copyrightable. The law protects the literary or dramatic expression of an idea, such as a script, but does not protect the idea itself. "This long established principle is easier to state than to apply," notes law professor David E. Shipley. It is often difficult to separate expression from the ideas being expressed. That is because there is often only a subtle difference between an idea and the expression of that idea. A musician named Michael John Blake wrote and recorded a song based on the number Pi, 3.14, with

* Under the 1909 law the United States had two kinds of copyright protection: common-law copyright and statutory copyright. Much as it did in 18th-century England, common law protected any work that had not been published. Common-law protection was automatic; that is, the work was protected from the point of its creation. And it lasted forever—or until the work was published. In order to protect published works, the author, photographer or composer had to register the book or picture or song with the U.S. government and place a copyright notice on the work. The 1976 statute does away with common-law copyright for all practical purposes. The only kinds of works protected by common law are works like extemporaneous speeches and sketches that have not been fixed in a tangible medium. They are still protected from the point of their creation by common-law copyright. Once they are written down, recorded, filmed or fixed in a tangible medium in any way, they come under the protection of the new law.

additional digits that seem to go on indefinitely. The number Pi is the ratio of the circumference to the diameter of a circle. Many musicians have used these numbers to create songs, with each number representing a different note. Blake launched a music video—"What Pi Sounds Like"—that became popular on YouTube. He was soon faced with a copyright infringement suit brought by Lars Erickson, who had done something similar to this more than a decade earlier—and copyrighted the music. In 2012 U.S. District Judge Michael Simon ruled that Pi is not a copyrightable fact, and the transcription of Pi to music is a non-copyrightable idea. "The resulting pattern of notes is an expression that merges with the non-copyrightable idea of putting Pi to music: assigning digits to musical notes and playing these notes in the sequence of Pi is an idea that can only be expressed," Simon said. Erickson's copyright was valid, but he could not use his copyright to stop others from employing the same pattern of musical notes.[8]

3. Facts cannot be copyrighted. "The world is round" is a fact. An author cannot claim that statement as his or her own and protect it through copyright.

4. Utilitarian goods—things that exist to produce other things—are not protected by copyright law. Thus, useful articles, such as a lamp, a chair, a dress or a uniform, cannot be copyrighted. In addition, the articles' component features or elements cannot be copyrighted either, unless they are capable of being "identified separately from, and . . . existing independently of, the utilitarian aspects of the article." Thus, a design for a Tiffany lamp could be copyrighted because the unique aspects of that specific lamp have nothing to do with the utilitarian purpose of producing light. The design elements are purely decorative. What is the appropriate test to use to determine when a feature of a useful article is protectable under Section 101 of the Copyright Act? In 2016, the U.S. Supreme Court granted cert in *Star Athletica* v. *Varsity Brands*[9] to address the question. Since useful articles cannot be copyrighted, but the "design elements" on them can, the Court was asked to determine what test to use to determine when clothing designs can be copyrighted. Varsity received copyright protection for designs on its cheerleader uniforms for graphical elements such as stripes, chevrons, zigzags and colorblocks. Star Athletica advertised cheerleading uniforms that were strikingly similar in appearance to Varsity's designs. Varsity sued Star for copyright violation. The Court ruled that designs could achieve copyright protection if (1) the design can be perceived as a two- or three-dimensional work of art separate from the useful article and (2) the design would qualify as a protectable pictorial, graphic, or sculptural work on its own.

5. Methods, systems and mathematical principles, formulas and equations cannot be copyrighted. But a description, an explanation or an illustration of an idea or system can be copyrighted. In such an instance the law is

8. *Erickson* v. *Blake,* 839 F. Supp. 2d 1132 (2012).
9. 136 S.Ct. 1823 (2016)

protecting the particular literary or pictorial form in which an author chooses to express herself or himself, not the idea or plan or method itself. For example, an individual writes and publishes a book in which she outlines a new mathematical formula. Although the book itself may be protected by copyright, the formula cannot be, and others may use it freely. In other words, the copyright on an article or a book does not preclude the public from making use of what the book teaches.

Can all books and other creative works be copyrighted? No. The law specifically says that only "original" works can be copyrighted. What is an original work? In interpreting this term in the 1909 law, courts ruled that the word "original" means that the work must owe its origin to the author. To be copyrightable, a work must be created independently. It cannot be copied from another work.

In 1985 an organization called Production Contractors Inc., or PCI, tried to block Chicago television station WGN from televising a Christmas parade on Thanksgiving Sunday. PCI, which put on the parade, sold the exclusive right to televise it to another station, WLS. The plaintiff claimed the parade was copyrighted, and WGN would be in violation of the law by televising it. A federal district court disagreed and ruled that a Christmas parade is not something that can be copyrighted; it is a common idea, not an event of original authorship.[10]

The work must be original. It does not have to be novel (new), unique or even good. Even common and mundane works are copyrightable. Courts have consistently ruled that it is not the function of the legal system to act as literary or art critic when applying copyright law. In 1903 Justice Oliver Wendell Holmes wrote in *Bleistein* v. *Donaldson Lithographing Co.,* "It would be a dangerous undertaking for persons trained only to the law to constitute themselves final judges of the worth of pictorial illustrations, outside of the narrowest and most obvious limits."[11] Even the least pretentious picture can be an original, Holmes noted in reference to the posters involved in this case. Even basic (or ugly) selfies you take are copyrightable.

The 9th U.S. Circuit Court of Appeals echoed this statement in 1992 when it ruled that raw, unedited video footage of news events was sufficiently original to be protected by copyright.[12] The case involved the Los Angeles News Service and Audio Video Reporting Service. LANS records live news events on video and then sells the unedited but copyrighted footage to television stations. The TV stations take the raw footage, edit it any way they want and use it in newscasts. Audio Video Reporting Services videotapes newscasts and then sells clips of the newscasts to interested parties. A businesswoman who has been interviewed for a news story, for example, may want to buy a copy of the story from Audio Video. Or the parents of children featured in a news story on a school project might want to have a copy of that story.

LANS sued Audio Video, claiming that in selling these video clips, which were taken from the copyrighted raw footage LANS had provided to local television stations,

10. *Production Contractors* v. *WGN Continental Broadcasting,* 622 F. Supp. 1500 (1985).
11. 188 U.S. 239 (1903).
12. *Los Angeles News Service* v. *Tullo,* 973 F. 2d 791 (1992).

Audio Video was infringing on the copyright LANS held on the videotape. Audio Video attempted to defend the suits on several bases, including the argument that raw, unedited videotape was not sufficiently original to be protected by copyright; all the photographer did was switch on the camera and point it at the news event. No creativity or intellectual input was required. The Court of Appeals disagreed, noting that there were several creative decisions involved in producing a photograph. The photographer must select the subject, the background, the perspective, consider the lighting and the action and so on. The "requisite level of creativity [to qualify as an original work] is extremely low; even a slight amount will suffice," the court said. Likewise, novelty is not important to copyright: The author does not have to be the first person to say something in order to copyright it. "All that is needed to satisfy both the Constitution and the statute is that the 'author' contributed something more than a merely trivial variation, something recognizably his own," one court ruled.[13]

COPYRIGHT AND FACTS

Facts cannot be copyrighted. That the Denver Broncos won the 2016 Super Bowl, or that John Kennedy was killed in November 1963, or that George Washington was the nation's first president are all facts. No one can claim ownership of these facts; anyone can publish or broadcast them. But this simple concept can get a bit more complicated when someone works diligently to collect a set of facts and then seeks to copyright his or her work. This section focuses on three such areas: databases, news events and research findings.

Telephone Books and Databases

Long before the birth of the computer, most homes contained relatively sophisticated databases. These are called telephone directories—a listing of phone company customers' names, addresses and telephone numbers. In 1991 the Supreme Court decided a seemingly innocuous case involving copyright protection for a white-pages telephone book—by any measure a collection of thousands of facts. But the ruling would have a profound impact on other kinds of databases and generate problems that have not yet been completely resolved.

The case involved a small, rural telephone company (Rural Telephone Service) that issued a standard white-pages directory of its customers' names, addresses and phone numbers, and a company (Feist Publications) that publishes regional telephone directories, which include the names, addresses and phone numbers of the customers of numerous small telephone companies. Feist asked Rural for permission to include the names of its customers in a directory, but Rural said no. Feist used the information anyway, and Rural sued for copyright infringement. Feist argued that a telephone directory contains only facts, which can't be copyrighted. Rural disagreed and argued that the phone book was a collection of facts, and that a *collection* of facts can be copyrighted. Rural also raised a second argument, what some call "the sweat of the brow" doctrine. This is a legal proposition previously recognized by some courts that asserts that even though facts are

---

13. *Amsterdam v. Triangle Publishing Co.*, 189 F. 2d 104 (1951).

not copyrightable, someone who invests substantial time and energy in amassing these facts deserves a reward for the hard work. Collecting the information that goes into a telephone directory takes time and energy, and copyright law should protect the results of this effort, Rural argued.

In a unanimous decision the Supreme Court rejected both arguments. With regard to the latter, Justice Sandra Day O'Connor said the sweat-of-the-brow doctrine was a bogus argument. Quoting former justice William Brennan, she said, "The primary objective of copyright law is not to reward the labor of authors, but to promote the progress of science and the arts." O'Connor said that some compilations of facts can be protected by copyright. The key to determining whether protection is merited is whether there is *some novelty or originality in the manner in which the facts are organized or selected or coordinated.* An alphabetical listing of names—the organization of the Rural directory and indeed all white pages—is not novel enough to generate copyright protection for the directory.[14]

In a pre-digital era, this ruling would have little impact. But in the computer age, the creation of alphabetically ordered lists of facts, which are also called databases, is one of the fastest and most profitable uses for computer software and interactive Web sites. Because of the *Feist* ruling, only those databases in which factual items are selected or arranged in some *novel* or *artful manner* will be protected by copyright law. Even a massive alphabetical listing of all the certified public accountants in New York state or the names of all the massage parlors in California fails to meet the test laid down by the high court.[15]

Many states have misappropriation laws (see pages 528–530) that may be used to bar database piracy. Congress, under pressure from the owners of large, commercial databases, has tried several times to pass legislation to protect these collections of facts. But in every case the legislators have run into roadblocks. Organizations outside the database industry, notably libraries and some technology companies, have opposed such legislation, claiming that such laws would allow some companies to monopolize facts, and this would hamper research projects. And there of course is the constitutional issue. The Supreme Court ruled that the so-called sweat-of-the-brow doctrine was constitutionally invalid in 1991, and this doctrine is at the heart of such legislation. There was no resolution of this issue as of late 2017.

News Events

When the news is reported correctly, it is basically an account of facts. Can a news account be copyrighted? Can one journalist claim the exclusive right to report on a story? Suppose a TV reporter gets an exclusive interview with a reclusive public figure and then broadcasts the copyrighted interview on the evening news. Does the law of copyright

14. *Feist Publications, Inc. v. Rural Telephone Service Co., Inc.,* 111 S. Ct. 1282 (1991).

15. The same year the *Feist* case was decided, the 2nd U.S. Circuit Court of Appeals ruled that the creator of a directory of businesses in New York City had demonstrated novelty by arranging and selecting the businesses to be included in the directory in a creative fashion. See *Key Publications, Inc.* v. *Chinatown Today,* 945 F. 2d 509 (1991). And in 1997 the 7th U.S. Circuit Court of Appeals ruled that a taxonomy (a way of describing items in a body of knowledge or practice) of dental procedures was a creative work, far different from a simple compilation. *American Dental Association* v. *Delta Dental Plan Association,* CA-7, No. 96-4140, 9/30/97. See also *Warren Publishing Co. v. Microdos Data Corp.,* CA-11 en banc, No. 93-8474, 6/10/97.

"The primary objective of copyright law is not to reward the labor of authors, but to promote the progress of science and the arts."

prevent other journalists from relating the substance of what was revealed in that interview? The answer is no. Other stations cannot replay the same interview. Newspapers cannot publish a transcript of the interview. But both broadcast and print journalists can tell their viewers and readers what the public figure said in the interview. Copyright law doesn't even require the competitors to credit the TV journalist for the interview. Failing to give proper credit to the TV journalist who got the interview is grossly unethical but happens all too often.

Copyright law protects the expression of the story—the way it is told, the style and manner in which the facts are presented—but not the facts in the story. For many writers this concept is a difficult one to understand and to accept. After all, if one reporter works hard to uncover a story, shouldn't he or she have the exclusive right to tell that story? This argument again reflects the sweat-of-the-brow doctrine that has been rejected by the Supreme Court. Shouldn't hard work be rewarded? In this case the law is clear: Hard work must be its own reward. Copyright protects only the way a story is told, not the facts in the story.

Research Findings and History

Gene Miller, a Pulitzer Prize-winning reporter for the *Miami Herald,* wrote a book titled *83 Hours Till Dawn*, an account of the widely publicized kidnapping of Barbara Mackle. Miller said he had spent more than 2,500 hours on the book, and many aspects of the kidnapping case were uncovered by the journalist and reported only in his book. Universal Studios wanted to film a dramatization of the 1971 incident but was unable to come to terms with Miller on payment for the rights. The studio produced the so-called docudrama anyway, and Miller sued for infringement of copyright. The similarities between Miller's book and the Universal script were striking—even some of the errors Miller had made in preparing the book were found in the film. But Universal argued that it was simply telling a story of a news event, and as such the research that Miller had done in digging out the facts regarding the story was not protected by copyright law. A U.S. District Court agreed with Miller's contention. "The court views the labor and expense of the research involved in the obtaining of those uncopyrightable facts to be intellectually distinct from those facts, and more similar to the expression of the facts than the facts themselves," the court said. The judge ruled that it was necessary to reward the effort and ingenuity involved in giving expression to a fact.[16] But the U.S. Court of Appeals for the 5th Circuit reversed the lower-court ruling. "The valuable distinction in copyright law between facts and the expression of facts cannot be maintained if research is held to be copyrightable. There is no rational basis for distinguishing between facts and the research involved in obtaining the facts," the court said. To hold research copyrightable, the court said, is no more or less than to hold that the facts discovered as a result of research are entitled to copyright protection.[17] The court added: "A fact does not originate with the author of a book describing the fact. Neither does it originate with the one who 'discovers' the fact. The discoverer merely finds and records. He may not claim that the

---

16. *Miller v. Universal City Studios,* 460 F. Supp. 984 (1978).
17. *Miller v. Universal City Studios,* 650 F. 2d 1365 (1981).

facts are 'original' with him, although there may be originality and hence authorship in the manner of reporting, i.e., the 'expression' of the facts."

The dichotomy between historical fact and fiction that is fundamental to American copyright law likely would have doomed any lawsuit filed in the United States by the authors of the book *Holy Blood, Holy Grail* against Dan Brown and Random House, the author and publisher of *The Da Vinci Code*. Michael Baigent and Richard Leigh said they spent 10 years doing research before they published their book that argues, essentially, that Jesus was married, Mary Magdalene was his wife, they had children and the descendants of the children are still around. Baigent and Leigh also asserted that factions within the Roman Catholic Church have, for centuries, attempted to cover up these historical facts. Along came Dan Brown, who in 2003 wrote a fictional thriller (which just happened to sell 40 million hardback copies) that suggests the same story. Brown admitted he owed a debt to the Baigent/Leigh book, which was published in 1982, but he denied he infringed upon its copyright. The plaintiffs filed their infringement lawsuit in the United Kingdom, where the fact/fiction distinction is not as widely accepted. "What makes this case so interesting is that there is little clarity [in Great Britain] over the extent to which an author can use another person's research for either background or a direct influence on a book," noted British copyright attorney Antony Gold. Baigent and Leigh argued that Brown had stolen the central theme of their historical account, but lost the case when a London court ruled that they had failed to prove this point because they could not accurately state what that central theme was.[18]

MISAPPROPRIATION

Although this chapter focuses on copyright, an ancillary area of the law needs to be briefly mentioned, as it too guards against the theft of intangible property. **Misappropriation,** or **unfair competition,** is sometimes invoked as an additional legal remedy in suits for copyright infringement. Unlike copyright, which springs largely from federal statute today, misappropriation remains largely a creature of common law. One of the most important media-oriented misappropriation cases was decided by the Supreme Court more than 80 years ago and stemmed from a dispute between the Associated Press (AP) and the International News Service (INS), a rival press association owned by William Randolph Hearst.

AP charged that INS pirated its news, saying that INS officials bribed AP employees to gain access to news before it was sent to AP member newspapers. The press agency also charged that the Hearst wire service copied news from bulletin boards and early editions of newspapers that carried AP dispatches. Sometimes INS editors rewrote the news, and other times they sent the news out on the wire just as it had been written by AP reporters. Copyright was not the question, because AP did not copyright its material. The agency said it could not copyright all its dispatches because there were too many and

---

18. Lyall, "Idea for 'Da Vinci Code'"; and Lattman, "English Copyright Lawsuit." In 2006 the 2nd U.S. Court of Appeals affirmed a lower-court ruling granting a summary judgment to Brown in an infringement action brought by Lewis Perdue, who claimed *The Da Vinci Code* contained material stolen from two novels he had written. The court said Brown's book was not substantially similar to either *The Da Vinci Legacy* or *Daughter of God.*

they had to be transmitted too fast. INS argued that because the material was not copyrighted, it was in the public domain and could be used by anyone.

Justice Mahlon Pitney wrote the opinion in the 7-1 decision. He said there can be no property right in the news itself, the events, the happenings, which are publici juris, the common property of all, the history of the day. However, the jurist went on to say:

> Although we may and do assume that neither party [AP or INS] has any remaining property interest as against the public in uncopyrighted matter after the moment of its first publication, it by no means follows that there is no remaining property interest in it as between themselves.[19]

The law of appropriation is intended to stop

- **a person trying to pass off his or her work as the work of someone else, and**
- **a person trying to pass off the work of someone else as his or her work.**

If Joan Brown published a magazine called *Vanity Fare* with a cover design that mirrors that of *Vanity Fair* in an attempt to confuse readers, this is an example of her trying to pass off her work as that of someone else. Or if, during its news broadcasts, a radio station announcer simply reads stories from the local newspaper, pretending that they were original, this is an example of trying to pass off the work of someone else as its own. In either case a misappropriation action would succeed. The critical legal issue in a misappropriation or unfair competition suit is whether there is the likelihood that an appreciable number of ordinarily prudent persons will be misled or simply confused as to the source of the material.

In the wake of the *AP* v. *INS* ruling in 1919, misappropriation cases involving the media were relatively rare. But with the coming of the Internet and the easy access to so much material, litigation in this area has increased. For example, in 2009 the Associated Press brought suit for misappropriation against All Headline News Corp. The defendant employed people to search the Internet for news stories it could republish, sometimes after rewriting the text, more often using the entire story without editing. AP stories were a prime target for All Headline. The lawsuit was settled after the defendant admitted to many instances of improperly using AP's content and agreed to pay damages.[20] Individuals and companies that do this are called "aggregators" because they aggregate or bring together the work of others for their own use. And these third-party repackagers, especially of news, are becoming more common.

Some of this repackaging is defensible under the fair use doctrine in copyright law. For example, a federal court in Nevada ruled in 2010 that when a real estate company posted material on its blog that it had taken from an article in the *Las Vegas Review-Journal*, it was a fair use. (see pages 539–540.) But more and more lawsuits are founded on claims of misappropriation and something called the "hot news doctrine," which was inherent in the 1919 *AP* v. *INS* ruling. This doctrine provides for a legal claim that can be used by news gatherers to prevent competitors from free riding on their efforts by redistributing their breaking news. But while the law clearly protects a news gatherer like the AP when someone else republishes a substantial portion of an article, the courts are

19. *Associated Press* v. *International News Service,* 248 U.S. 215 (1919).
20. *Associated Press* v. *All Headline News Corp.,* 608 F. Supp. 2d 454 (2009).

still trying to determine how far the redistribution can legally go in merely reporting the basic substance of a report. For example, a group of banks sued a small Web site operator called theflyonthewall.com that was posting reports online about the banks equity research recommendations; in other words, advice on the future performance of stocks. The banks argued thefly was publishing these recommendations even before their own customers have a chance to consider them—a violation of the hot news doctrine. A U.S. district court agreed with the banks in 2010 that theflyonthewall was free riding on the work the banks had done. But in 2011 the 2nd U.S. Court of Appeals reversed this ruling. It is said that while traditional copyright law still protects the work done by the banks—theflyonthewall could not legally reprint the banks' analysts reports—the redistributors could legally report on the analysts' findings, such as Morgan Stanley's analysts upgrade shares of Ford or Microsoft. That's news, Judge Robert D. Sack wrote. "A firm's ability to make news—by issuing a recommendation that is likely to affect the market price of a security—does not give rise to a right for it to control who breaks that news and how," he added. The court said the viability of the hot news doctrine remained intact, but that the banks' case did not fall within this law.

What thefly did was akin to Google or CNN publishing online that *The New York Times* was reporting that the U.S. Attorney General was going to resign. While the ruling only directly affects cases in the Second Circuit—New York, Connecticut and Vermont—decisions by this court are regarded as very influential nationally and Judge Sack is considered a leading expert on copyright law.[21] As many newspapers, magazines and others in the mass media face growing economic pressure because of the growth of the Internet, these issues will undoubtedly be litigated more often. Established news organizations fear that emerging online services who ride free can decrease the demand for their often expensive newsgathering efforts. An incredible amount of time and money goes into creating news stories, they argue. The hot-news misappropriation doctrine is a creature of state law, but efforts were made to encourage the enactment of federal legislation. However, the call by news organizations for a federal hot news legislation has been unsuccessful. In addition, any such legislation would have to be limited to avoid a First Amendment challenge.

DURATION OF COPYRIGHT PROTECTION

The length of time that a copyright will protect a given work depends on when the work was created. The major revision of the copyright law in 1976 included a significant extension of the duration of copyright protection. In 1998 Congress adopted the Sonny Bono Copyright Extension Act, adding 20 more years to the protection of a copyrighted work. Any work created after January 1, 1978, will be protected for the life of the creator, plus 70 years. This rule allows creators to enjoy the fruits of their labor until death and then allows the heirs to profit from the work of their fathers, mothers, sisters or brothers for an additional length of time. After 70 years, the work goes into what is called the public domain. At that point it may be copied by any person for any reason without the payment of royalty to the original owner. The copyright on a work created by two or more authors extends through the life of the last author to die plus 70 years. What is called a "work for

21. *Barclays' Capitol Inc.* v. *Theflyonthewall.com,* 700 F. Supp. 310 (2010); 650. F. 3d 876 (2011). See also *National Basketball Association, Inc.* v. *Motorola Inc.,* 105 F. 3d 841 (1997).

hire" is protected for 95 years after publication. Works for hire include books written by an author for a publisher, which then holds the copyright. Also included are most motion pictures, sound recordings, television programs and so on that are created through a collaborative effort.* Works created before 1978 when the 1976 law went into effect are protected for a total of 95 years from the date of the original copyright.

HOW LONG DOES COPYRIGHT PROTECTION LAST?

Works Created After January 1, 1978
The life of the creator plus 70 years

Works Created by More Than One Person
The life of the last living creator plus 70 years

Works for Hire
Ninety-five years after publication

Works Created Before January 1, 1978
Ninety-five years

SUMMARY

American copyright law derives from rules and regulations established by the British government in the 16th and 17th centuries. The contemporary basis for the protection of intangible property is contained in the U.S. Constitution, and since 1789 the nation has had numerous federal copyright statutes. The current law, adopted in 1976, gives to the author or owner of a work the sole and exclusive right to reproduce the copyrighted work in any form for any reason. The statute protects all original works of authorship fixed in any tangible medium. Included are such creations as literary works, newspaper stories, magazine articles, television programs, films and even advertisements. Trivial items, utilitarian goods, ideas and methods or systems cannot be copyrighted.

News events cannot be copyrighted, but stories or broadcasts that describe or explain these events can be copyrighted. What is being protected is the author's style or manner of presentation of the news. Similarly, facts cannot be copyrighted, but works that relate these facts can be protected as expression. While news and facts cannot be copyrighted, anyone who attempts to present news or facts gathered by someone else as his or her own work may be guilty of breaking other laws, such as misappropriation, or unfair competition. In most cases copyrighted works are protected for the life of the author or creator plus 70 years. Different rules apply for works created before 1978 and for works made for hire.

---

* The U.S. Copyright Office has available information regarding all matters relating to copyright law, including duration of protection (http://www.copyright.gov/).

FAIR USE

*Owners of a copyright
are granted almost
exclusive monopoly
over the use of their
creations.*

Owners of a copyright are granted almost exclusive monopoly over the use of their creations. The word "almost" must be used, for there are really four limitations on this monopoly. Three of the limitations have been discussed already. First, the work must be something that can be copyrighted. There can be no legal monopoly on the use of something that cannot be protected by the law. Second, the monopoly protects only original authorship or creation. If the creation is not original, it cannot be protected. Third, copyright protection does not last forever. At some point the protection ceases and the work falls into the public domain.

The fourth limitation on exclusive monopoly is broader than the other three, is certainly more controversial and is concerned with limited copying of copyrighted material. This is the doctrine of **fair use,** which has been defined by one court as follows:

> A rule of reason . . . to balance the author's right to compensation for his work, on the one hand, against the public's interest in the widest possible dissemination of ideas and information on the other.[22]

This doctrine, then, permits limited copying of an original creation that is copyrighted and has not yet fallen into the public domain. But in many instances describing the fair use doctrine is easier than applying it to a particular case. As copyright attorney Michael D. Kuznetsky noted, the courts and many legal scholars have commented that fair use is the most difficult issue in copyright law. It is mixed inquiry of fact and law, which oftentimes can lead to differing opinions on how the factors weigh out. A court decision in 2012 bears this out.

Pop singer Noelia Lorenzo Monge and her producer Jorge Reynoso were married in a secret ceremony in Las Vegas in 2007. The couple hid their marriage to ostensibly preserve Monge's image as a young, single celebrity. Not even Reynoso's mother knew of the marriage. But a paparazzo who sometimes worked as a bodyguard for the pair found a memory chip from their personal camera used at the wedding. After being unsuccessful in trying to get the couple to pay him to return the photos, he sold them to a magazine called *TVNotas* in 2009. The couple had copyrighted most of the photos to protect themselves, including five of the six the magazine published. They sued for copyright infringement. The magazine raised the fair use doctrine in its defense, arguing correctly that copyrighted material may be published for the purpose of news reporting, among other things. The question, then, was, "Was the publication of the pictures a news report, informing fans that the couple were in fact married, proving that the speculation about their relationship was correct?"

A lower court dismissed the copyright challenge, but in 2012 the 9th U.S. Court of Appeals reversed this ruling, saying the fair use defense would not work and that this commercial use of previously unpublished works was not permitted under the law. "Waving the news reporting flag is not a get out of jail free card in the copyright arena," wrote Judge M. Margaret McKeown. If the magazine wanted to report that it had evidence that the couple was in fact married, it could have done so in other ways (e.g., publishing

---

22. *Triangle Publications* v. *Knight-Ridder,* 626 F. 2d 1171 (1980).

a copy of their marriage certificate) rather than publishing the copyrighted photos. In many fair use cases, the issues are as obtuse as these issues.[23]

More than 130 years ago all copying of a copyrighted work was against the law. This absolute prohibition on copying constituted a hardship for scholars, critics and teachers seeking to use small parts of copyrighted materials in their work. A judicial remedy for this problem was sought. It was argued that since the purpose of the original copyright statute was to promote art and science, the copyright law should not be administered in such a way as to frustrate artists and scientists who publish scholarly materials. In 1879 the U.S. Supreme Court ruled in *Baker* v. *Selden:*

> The very object of publishing a book on science or the useful arts is to communicate to the world the useful knowledge which it contains. But this object would be frustrated if the useful knowledge could not be used without incurring the guilt of piracy of the book.[24]

The doctrine of fair use emerged from the courts, and under this judicial doctrine small amounts of copying were permitted so long as the publication of the material advanced science, the arts, criticism and so forth.

In 1976 Congress included the judicial doctrine of fair use in the revision of the copyright law. Section 107 of the measure declares, "The fair use of a copyrighted work . . . for purposes such as criticism, comment, news reporting, teaching (including multiple copies for classroom use), scholarship or research is not an infringement of copyright."

In determining whether the use of a particular work is a fair use, the statute says that courts should consider the following factors:

1. **The purpose and character of the use**
2. **The nature of the copyrighted work**
3. **The amount and substantiality of the portion used in relation to the copyrighted work as a whole**
4. **The effect of the use on the potential market for or value of the copyrighted work**

Each factor on this list will be considered separately as the doctrine of fair use is explored. Interestingly, the fair use criteria included in the statute and just listed here (1 through 4) are very close to the criteria that courts used under the old common-law fair use doctrine. This similarity is no accident. In a report issued by committees in the House and the Senate on Section 107, the legislators said that the new law "endorses the purpose and general scope of the judicial doctrine of fair use" but did not intend that the law be frozen as it existed in 1976. "The courts must be free to adapt the doctrine to particular situations on a case-by-case basis. Section 107 is intended to restate the present judicial doctrine of fair use, not to change, narrow or enlarge it in any way."

PURPOSE AND CHARACTER OF USE

The purpose and character of the use of a work is the initial factor to be considered. A use is more likely to be considered a fair use if it is a noncommercial or nonprofit use. But

---

23. *Monge* v. *Maya Magazines,* No. 10-56710 (9th Cir. 2012).
24. *Baker* v. *Selden,* 101 U.S. 99 (1879).

simply because material is used in a commercial venture doesn't disqualify it as a fair use. The U.S. Court of Appeals for the 2nd Circuit noted that according to committee reports compiled when the new copyright law was adopted, Congress did not intend that only nonprofit educational uses of copyrighted works would qualify as fair use. The reports, said the court, are "an express recognition that . . . the commercial or nonprofit character of an activity, while not conclusive with respect to fair use, can and should be weighed along with other factors in fair use decisions."[25]

The law lists several categories of use that may be protected by fair use. These include

- criticism and comment,
- teaching, and
- scholarship and research.

Just because a use falls into one of these categories doesn't mean a fair use defense will automatically be successful. At the same time, uses that fall outside one of these categories may still qualify as a fair use. Here are some cases that illustrate these principles.

"The Daily Show" on Comedy Central used a video clip from a public access television show, "The Sandra Kane Blew Comedy Show," to introduce a segment called Public Excess. The segment features examples of public access television. Sandra Kane, a comedienne and former stripper, sings, dances and tells jokes on her show while wearing little or no clothing. She sued for copyright infringement, but the federal court said the use of the clip by Jon Stewart on "The Daily Show" was a fair use because it was used for critical purposes. "In presenting plaintiff's clip, defendant sought to critically examine the quality of plaintiff's public access television show," the court ruled.[26]

But a federal court in California rejected a fair use argument made by the operator of an Internet bulletin board who posted complete copyrighted articles from the *Los Angeles Times* and the *Washington Post* on the site so people could comment on the news and criticize the manner in which the news stories were reported. The court noted that adding commentary to a verbatim copy of a copyrighted work does not automatically protect it as a fair use. The court issued an injunction barring future postings and assessed $1 million in damages against the defendant.[27] How do you explain the seemingly opposite rulings? Surely the concepts "comment" and "criticism" are elusive and subject to interpretation. But a more obvious explanation involves the amount of copyrighted material used in these three instances. In the California case, the defendants used a great many copyrighted articles from the two newspapers. Significantly smaller amounts of copyrighted material were used in the other two cases. The comment and criticism element is more aptly applied to republishing small segments of a work.

Copyright law has traditionally regarded the limited use of copyrighted material for educational purposes as a fair use. The teacher who makes copies of a short article from *Newsweek* and distributes them to class members is normally considered an innocent infringer. But more substantial copying may not receive the same protection, especially when commercial interests are involved. This issue came up in the 1990s when

25. *Maxtone-Graham v. Burtchaell,* 803 F. 2d 1253 (1986).
26. *Kane v. Comedy Partners,* 32 M.L.R. 1113 (2003).
27. *Los Angeles Times v. Free Republic,* 29 M.L.R. 1028 (2000).

photocopy businesses worked with college and university faculty members to prepare so-called coursepaks. A faculty member would provide the copy center with a list of articles and book chapters for use in a class. The centers would then make photocopies of the material, loosely bind them and then sell these ad hoc anthologies to the students enrolled in the course for use as a text. Publishers and others who held the copyright on the material that was copied brought suit for infringement. The copy centers, like Kinko's, argued that these materials were being copied for educational purposes, an acceptable use under the law. The federal courts agreed that while the materials were ultimately being used for educational purposes, the copy centers were making the coursepaks for commercial reasons—something that did not qualify as a fair use.

Use of small amounts of copyrighted material in a news article or broadcast is usually regarded as a fair use. But this kind of use has become more problematic in recent years with the growth of content on the Internet. In 2009 the Associated Press—a news cooperative owned by 1,500 daily newspapers that provides written articles and broadcast materials to thousands of news organizations—announced that it would consider seeking legal remedies to stop Web sites, bloggers and search engines like Google and Yahoo! from using its work without first getting permission, and then sharing revenues earned by using the AP material. The news aggregators and search companies argued that such a use was a fair use. AP spokespeople said it was becoming all too common for bloggers to use direct quotations from AP stories, a use that sometimes went beyond a fair use. AP officials said it is more appropriate for the bloggers to use short summaries of the articles rather than the direct quotations from the stories. In July 2009 the AP announced it would henceforth attach software called metatags to its articles. The tags would explain what copyright rules apply to the reuse of the material, and alert the AP if and how the article is being revised.[28] (See pages 552–553 for more on this problem.)

On at least two occasions federal courts have ruled that a use that serves the public interest could qualify as a fair use. One case involved the use of copyrighted material in a biography of the reclusive multimillionaire Howard Hughes. A company owned by Hughes bought the rights to the copyrighted material when it discovered it was to be used in the biography, and then attempted to stop the publisher from using the material in the book. The 2nd U.S. Court of Appeals ruled that it would be contrary to the public interest to permit individuals to buy the rights of anything published about them to stop authors from using the material.[29] In another case a federal court ruled that it was in the public interest to permit the author of a book on the assassination of John F. Kennedy to use copyrighted frames of 8 mm motion picture film to illustrate his theory on the murder of the president. The film was shot by a spectator at the scene and was purchased by Time, Inc., which owned the copyright.[30] Please note, these are singularly uncommon rulings.

Today, many judges talk about "transformative uses" when they consider claims of fair use. What does this mean? Under the purpose and character factor, if an individual takes a portion of a copyrighted work and uses it for another purpose, in other words

---

28. Hansell, "The Associated Press to Set Guidelines"; and Pérez-Peña, "A.P. Seeks to Rein" and "A.P. Seeks to Block."
29. *Rosemont* v. *Random House*, 366 F. 2d 303 (1966).
30. *Time, Inc.* v. *Bernard Geis Associates*, 239 F. Supp. 130 (1968).

transforms it, it is much more likely to be regarded as a fair use. For example, when ABC broadcast a television news report about how the advocates of the legalization of marijuana have changed the image of the typical user from the long-haired pothead to a seriously ill medical patient, it used both the cover from a recent issue of *Newsweek* and a photo from a story in the issue to illustrate its video story. The magazine story had focused on the medical use of marijuana. The federal court said the use of the cover and the photo was a fair use because it was a transformative use.[31] The network had taken the original copyrighted art and transformed it into a story about the news coverage of a current issue.

A transformative use is also impacted by the fourth factor. If a work is truly transformed, there is most likely little chance it will steal the audience of the original work. For example, a court ruled that the re-creation of three scenes from the famous pornographic film "Deep Throat" was a fair use when used for a biographical film about actress Linda Lovelace. The biography, called *Lovelace*, was released in 2013 and documented Lovelace's marriage to her husband Chuck Traynor. The film presented a critical behind-the-scenes look at Traynor's abuse of Lovelace and the way he coerced her to participate in "Deep Throat." Lovelace contains no pornographic scenes or nudity. The court said the use illustrated a strong transformative purpose and the copyright owner of "Deep Throat" would be unlikely to lose revenue from this nonpornographic use.[32]

Questions regarding so-called transformative use were an issue in a copyright lawsuit between the Associated Press and controversial street artist Shepard Fairey. In April 2006, freelance photographer Mannie Garcia (working for the AP) took a picture of then Sen. Barack Obama at the National Press Club; a pensive Barack Obama looking upward, as if to the future, as one reporter described it. Using the photo as a starting point, Fairey created the now famous red, white and blue HOPE poster that became so popular during the presidential campaign. Hundreds of thousands of posters and stickers containing the poster image were sold; signed copies of the poster have been bought on eBay for thousands of dollars; and a stenciled collage version of the work has been added to the permanent collection of the National Portrait Gallery in Washington, D.C. In 2009 the AP claimed copyright infringement and said the use of the photo by Fairey required its permission. The news cooperative said it wanted credit and compensation. Attorneys for Fairey admitted that the artist used the photo as a reference, but argued the artist transformed it into a "stunning, abstracted and idealized visual image that created a powerful new meaning that conveys a radically different message" from the photo taken by Garcia.[33] The transformative issues were never played out in court because the parties settled the case in early 2011. The A said that Fairey agreed he will not use another A photo in his work without obtaining a license from the wire service, and that the two sides would "work together going forward with the 'Hope' image and share the rights to make the posters and merchandise bearing the 'Hope' image and to collaborate on a series of images that Fairey will create based on A.P. photographs."

31. *Morgenstein* v. *ABC Inc.*, 27 M.L.R. 1350 (1998).
32. *Arrow Productions, LTD* v. *The Weinstein Company LLC*, Case 1:13-cv-05488-TPG (D.C. S.D.N.Y. 8/25/14).
33. Italie, "Compensation for Use"; and Kennedy, "Artist Sues the A.P."

In an interesting case decided in 2015, the 2nd Circuit considered whether a parody of a pre-existing work could itself qualify for copyright protection. An individual created a parody of the classic Keanu Reeves surfer-thriller flick, "Point Break." The court found the work to be sufficiently transformative to justify fair use of the movie materials. At focus in this case, however, was the more novel issue of whether the resulting parody could itself be protected under copyright. The 2nd Circuit held that if an author of an unauthorized work provides enough original material and the resulting new work is protected under fair use rules, then the resulting new work is also eligible for copyright protection.[34]

Adding something to a copyrighted work can be considered a transformative use. But at least one court has ruled that removing something from such a work is not transformative. A company called Clean Flicks of Colorado was in the business of buying copies of films released on DVDs, and then editing them, taking out what the firm regarded as offensive content. These would then be sold to buyers who wanted a sanitized version of the film. A coalition of motion picture studios and film directors sued for copyright infringement. The company called its editing merely a transformative use; the court disagreed, ruling that transformative means adding something. Here the infringers added nothing, but merely deleted material from the original. Clean Flicks also argued it was not harming the filmmakers; it was simply exploiting a new market, a market not being served by Hollywood. After all, the company bought each DVD it altered before resale. But the court said the film studios have the right not to enter a market. "Whether these films should be edited in a manner that could make them acceptable to more of the public playing them on DVD in a home environment is more than merely a matter of marketing; it is a question of what audience the copyright owner wants to reach," wrote U.S. District Judge Richard Matsch.[35]

NATURE OF THE COPYRIGHTED WORK

Courts look at several considerations when applying this criterion of fair use.

- **Is the copyrighted work still available?** Using part of a work that is out of print is more likely to be considered a fair use than using a segment of a book that can be readily purchased at the local bookstore.
- **Is the copyrighted work what is called a consumable work?** A consumable work is something that is intended to be used just once: a workbook that accompanies a text, or a book of crossword puzzles. Consumables are usually cheaply priced and are intended to be used and then discarded. It would not be a fair use for a teacher to purchase a single copy of a biology workbook, make 30 photocopies of each page, and then pass out the photocopies for use by the students. But it would very likely be a fair use for the same teacher to make 30 copies of an article in *Science* magazine for class distribution.
- **Is the work an informational work or a creative work?** It is more likely to be a fair use if the copying involves a work like a newspaper or newsmagazine

---

34. *Keeling* v. *Hars*, No. 13-694 (2d Cir. 2015).
35. *Clean Flicks of Colorado* v. *Soderbergh*, 433 F. Supp. 2d 1236 (2006).

article or an item in an encyclopedia rather than a novel or play or poem. This doesn't mean that copying an informational work is always a fair use; just that it is more likely to be.

■ **Is the work published or unpublished?** Materials like manuscripts, letters and other works that have not yet been published are sometimes accessible by the public when they are stored in libraries or other places. The author's right to be the first to publish these works is regarded as a valuable right.

The question of the right of first publication came to the forefront more than 25 years ago when *The Nation* magazine pre-empted the publication of the late President Gerald Ford's memoirs by publishing a 2,250-word article that contained paraphrases and quotes from the unpublished manuscript. Only about 300 words in the article were legitimately protected by copyright, but these focused on the heart of the long memoir—Ford's discussion of why he chose to pardon former President Richard Nixon, who resigned in the face of impeachment proceedings. (Nixon was impeached, but resigned before he was tried by the Senate.) When Ford's publisher sued for copyright infringement, *The Nation* claimed its use of the 300 words was a fair use. The U.S. Supreme Court disagreed. The U.S. Supreme Court rejected the fair use claim and reversed the lower appellate court ruling. "In using generous verbatim excerpts of Mr. Ford's unpublished manuscript to lend authenticity to its account of the forthcoming memoirs, The Nation effectively arrogated to itself the right of first publication, an important marketable subsidiary right," Justice Sandra Day O'Connor wrote. The 1976 Copyright Act clearly recognizes the right of first publication for an author, O'Connor said. The scope of fair use is narrowed where unpublished works are concerned. Justice O'Connor concluded that "the unpublished nature of a work is a key, though not necessarily determinative, factor, tending to negate a defense of fair use."[36]

Mark Twain once noted that it is possible to get more out of a lesson than the teacher intended. A cat that sits on a hot stove will likely never sit on another hot stove, he noted. It is just as likely, he added, the cat won't sit on a cold stove either. Such was the case when some lower courts interpreted Justice O'Connor's opinion in the *Nation* decision. When judges read the sentence, "We conclude that the unpublished nature of a work is a key, *though not necessarily determinative* [emphasis added] factor, tending to negate a defense of fair use," they ignored the italicized phrase. In a series of increasingly restrictive rulings, judges on the 2nd U.S. Circuit Court of Appeals, a court with considerable national authority, ruled that the copying of an unpublished work *can never* be a fair use.[37]

Congress resolved the issue in the autumn of 1992 when it amended the federal copyright statute. The law now states that "the fact that a work is unpublished shall not itself bar a finding of fair use," if such a finding is justified based on the application of all

Justice O'Connor concluded that "the unpublished nature of a work is a key, though not necessarily determinative, factor, tending to negate a defense of fair use."

---

36. *Harper & Row Publishers* v. *Nation Enterprises,* 471 U.S. 539 (1985). A newspaper or television broadcast or Web site can surely summarize what it has learned from a copy of an unpublished memoir or book, but it cannot quote sentences, paragraphs or pages from the manuscript. This may be a fine line to some, but it is an important dividing line to the courts.
37. See *Salinger* v. *Random House,* 811 F. 2d 90 (1987); and *New Era Publications* v. *Henry Holt & Co., Inc.,* 873 F. 2d 576 (1990).

four fair use criteria. This change puts the law back to where it was immediately after the ruling in *Harper & Row Publishers* v. *Nation Enterprises,* before appellate courts began to misinterpret it. It remains exceedingly dangerous, though not necessarily fatal, to publish or broadcast material that has never before been published. Such a use will likely be sustained only if the user can make a strong case under the other three fair use criteria.

THE PORTION OR PERCENTAGE OF A WORK USED

The amount of a work used is not as important as the relative proportion of a work used. Word counts, for example, really don't mean as much as percentages. The use of 500 words from a 450-page book is far less damaging than the use of 20 words from a 40-word poem. How much of the work, in relation to the whole, was used? Courts will consider exact copying when looking at this question; but they will also often consider paraphrasing. Pirates will find little refuge in a dictionary of synonyms. For example, in the mid-1980s respected writer Ian Hamilton sought to publish a biography of reclusive novelist J.D. Salinger, the author of *Catcher in the Rye*. Lacking Salinger's cooperation in the endeavor, Hamilton sought to prepare the biography by using portions of numerous letters the novelist had written to friends and acquaintances. The letters had never been published. Salinger sued for copyright infringement, claiming the contents of the letters were his literary property. To avoid the lawsuit Hamilton reworked the manuscript, deleting most phrases and sentences copied directly from the letters. But he extensively paraphrased the contents of the correspondence in place of using Salinger's actual words. The 2nd U.S. Circuit Court of Appeals ruled that this use was an infringement of copyright, not a fair use. Paraphrasing Salinger's words did not protect Hamilton. "What is protected is the manner of expression, the author's analysis or interpretation of events—the way he structures his material and marshalls facts, his choice of words and the emphasis he gives to particular developments," wrote Judge Jon O. Newman.[38] The paraphrasing was too close to Salinger's own choice of words, to his creativity. The biographer had taken the "heart of the material" from the letters. Hamilton abandoned his initial effort and instead wrote *In Search of J.D. Salinger*, a book about Salinger's literary life (without the material from the letters) and his unsuccessful efforts to publish a biography of the reclusive author.

How much of the original work can be used can sometimes depend on what material is taken. A law firm representing the *Las Vegas Review-Journal* sued a realty company for using eight sentences from a 30-sentence article published in the paper. The defendant argued it was a fair use. The federal court agreed, noting that the part of the article republished on a blog was simply factual news about a new federal housing program. The court said that the use of even eight sentences, about a quarter of the article, was not enough in this case to negate the defense of fair use.[39] The same can be said of Web sites that take only a few factual statements from copyrighted news stories. For example, a court ruled it was fair use when a real estate blog copied the first eight sentences of

38. *Salinger* v. *Random House,* 811 F. 2d 90 (1987).
39. *Righthaven LLC* v. *Realty One Group Inc.,* 38 M.L.R. 2441 (2010). See also *Righthaven LLC* v. *Hoehm,* 39 M.L.R. 1956 (2011).

a newspaper article. Because the blogger had copied only eight sentences and not the "valuable" section of the original article, the commentary of the original author, the court ruled it was a fair use. The court also noted that the copying would not affect the market for the original article (the fourth fair use factor, discussed below).[40] As noted earlier, however, a Web site that takes an entire story is unlikely to be protected by fair use.

One of the toughest tasks facing a judge is measuring fair use when someone presents a parody of a copyrighted work. A parody is a critical and usually humorous effort to lampoon a creation. But in order to be a successful parody, the work must reflect the content of the original book or movie or song, not simply the style and presentation of the original creation. The question of parody was at the heart of one of the silliest legal actions in recent years when the Fox News Network tried to stop author Al Franken from calling his book, a critical evaluation of the conservative press in America, *Lies and the Lying Liars Who Tell Them: A Fair and Balanced Look at the Right*. Fox claimed that it owned the rights to the phrase "fair and balanced," a slogan it uses to identify its newscasts. Franken said the book was a social commentary on the network and others, and that the use of the phrase was a parody. A federal court agreed, saying the lawsuit was wholly without merit, both factually and legally. "Parody is a form of artistic expression protected by the First Amendment. The keystone to parody is imitation. Here, whether you agree with him or not in using the mark [fair and balanced], Mr. Franken is clearly mocking Fox," wrote judge Denny Chin.[41]

In 1992 the 6th U.S. Court of Appeals ruled that a commercial parody, whether a book or a movie or a song, could never be a fair use. Such a work was commercial and could not be regarded as artistic comment or criticism, something usually protected under the fair use doctrine.[42] The ruling, if widely accepted, would have had a devastating impact on an entire range of creative work. But the Supreme Court rejected this notion two years later in one of the most colorful and significant cases ever decided. The case focused on a rap music parody of the song "Oh, Pretty Woman," a 1964 rock/country hit written by Roy Orbison (who performed the song) and William Dees. Rapper Luther Campbell, leader and founder of the group 2 Live Crew, was rebuffed when he sought permission from the publisher of the song, Acuff-Rose Music, to record his version of "Oh, Pretty Woman." Campbell was sued by Acuff-Rose when he made the recording anyway with lyrics wildly divergent from the original. (A quick search on Youtube should lead students to both versions of the song.) A trial court called the 2 Live Crew version a parody and rejected the suit, but the Court of Appeals reversed, ruling that a commercial parody could never be a fair use. The Supreme Court sided with the trial court and sent the case back for trial, ruling that a jury trial was needed to determine whether the parody was a fair use. "The language of the statute," wrote Justice David Souter, "makes it clear that the commercial or nonprofit educational purpose of a work is only one element of the first factor enquiry into its purpose and character. . . . Accordingly, the mere fact that a use is educational and not for profit does not insulate it from a finding

40. *Righthaven LLC* v. *Realty One Group, Inc.*, No. 2:10-cv-LRH-PAL, 2010 WL 4115413 (D. Nev. October 19. 2010).
41. *Fox News Network LLC* v. *Penguin Group (USA) Inc.*, 31 M.L.R. 2254 (2003).
42. *Campbell* v. *Acuff-Rose Music, Inc.*, 92 F. 2d 1429 (1992).

of infringement, any more than the commercial character of a use bars a finding of fairness. If indeed, commerciality carried presumptive force against a finding of fairness, the presumption would swallow nearly all of the illustrative uses listed [in the statute] . . . including news reporting, comment, criticism, teaching, scholarship and research since these activities are generally conducted for profit in this country."[43]

Parody, Justice Souter said, springs from its allusion to the original. "Its art lies in the tension between a known original and its parodic twin." It is true the parody here took the opening lines and the musical signature. "But if quotation of the opening riff and the first line may be said to go to the 'heart' of the original, the heart is also what most readily conjures up the song for parody, and it is the heart at which parody takes aim. Copying does not become excessive in relation to parodic purpose merely because the portion taken was the original's heart." It was significant, Souter said, that after taking the first line, 2 Live Crew added its own lyrics. And while the bass riff was copied, other original sounds were added as well. The case is also noteworthy for giving rise to the transformative use consideration under the first fair use criterion, purpose and character of the use.

The ruling in the *Campbell* case failed to provide precise guidelines for parodists regarding how much original material can be used in a parody that can be defined as a fair use. Maybe such precise guidelines are impossible to fashion. But without them the matter of fair use and parody continues to bedevil the judiciary. Protection for parody was further complicated when some courts made the distinction between parody and satires. Parodies can be considered "transformative" works and are thus protected by fair use. The Court explained, however, that while a parody must mimic the original work to make its point, a satire uses the work to criticize something *else*, and therefore requires other justification for the very act of borrowing. As a result, lower courts interpreted this as the Court favoring parody under the fair use doctrine, while devaluing satire. Based on this distinction, lower courts focused on the dichotomy between a parody and satire, finding that if a new work comments or criticizes the original work, it is a parody and thus protected. If it instead focuses on commenting and criticizing something else, it is not a satire and therefore less likely to be protected.

Recently, however, at least one court has questioned this distinction. In *Cariou* v. *Prince*, the 2nd Circuit examined whether 30 works by "appropriation artist" Richard Prince that altered and incorporated various copyrighted photographs by Patrick Cariou qualified as fair use. Although the 2nd Circuit analyzed each of the Copyright Act's fair use factors, it particularly emphasized the purpose and character of Prince's use. Because Prince testified that he did not intend to transform or comment on Cariou's work, typically, this would have weighed against a finding of fair use. The 2nd Circuit, however, held that "[t]he law imposes no requirement that a work comment on the original or its author in order to be considered transformative." In addition, the court held it was not important whether the author of the new work intended to comment on or criticize the original work. Instead, the court held, the correct standard is whether the new work would be "reasonably perceived" by a "reasonable observer" to alter the original

43. *Campbell* v. *Acuff-Rose Music, Inc.,* 114 S. Ct. 1164 (1994).

with "new expression, meaning, or message." Applying this standard, the court found 25 of the 30 works in the case were transformative because they "manifest an entirely different aesthetic from Cariou's photographs. . . . Prince's composition, presentation, scale, color palette, and media are fundamentally different and new compared to the photographs, as is the expressive nature of Prince's work."[44] How this ruling affects future cases remains to be seen. For now, courts continue to struggle with the ambiguous nature of fair use, especially as the doctrine applies to new and emerging art forms.

EFFECT OF USE ON MARKET

The effect of the use on the potential market for, or value of, the copyrighted work is the fourth criterion. While a cautionary note should be sounded against assigning relative weight to the four criteria, this final one—harm to the plaintiff—is given greater weight by most courts than any of the other three. In a congressional committee report on the 1976 law, the legislators noted that "with certain special exceptions . . . a use that supplants any part of the normal market for a copyrighted work would ordinarily be considered an infringement." In the action by Harper & Row against The Nation, Justice Sandra Day O'Connor noted that "this last factor is undoubtedly the single most important element of fair use."[45] "More important," Justice O'Connor wrote, "to negate fair use one need only show that if the challenged use should become widespread, it would adversely affect the potential market for the copyright work."

The inability of the plaintiff to demonstrate an adverse economic impact from the copying can frequently in and of itself sustain a fair use ruling. In 1997 Warner Books published a book by Gerald Celente titled *Trends 2000: How to Prepare for and Profit from the Changes of the 21st Century.* In a chapter on power generation the author criticized the nuclear power industry and used a photo that was previously included in an advertisement published by the United States Council for Energy Awareness. The photo was a picture of a dairy farmer, Louise Ihlenfeldt, and a cow standing in a field of clover framed against a blue sky. A print message accompanying the photo in the ad described the harmonious relationship between the Ihlenfeldt family and a nuclear power plant located only a mile away. The book author belittled the message in the ad and criticized the industry. When a copyright action was brought against Warner Books for using the photo without permission, the publisher argued fair use. The use was for profit, and the entire picture was used, the court noted, but ruled that the black-and-white reprint of the color photo was unlikely to have a negative impact on the market for the original. "The idea that a thriving market for photographs of Louise Ihlenfeldt and the cow (however dramatically portrayed) actually exists is dubious to say the least," the court ruled.[46] In 1998 a federal judge in Washington state threw out a nearly $700,000 jury award to author Wade Cook after a trial where Cook asserted that motivational writer and speaker Tony Robbins had copied two phrases originated by Cook. The jury decided that Robbins had used the two phrases, "meter drop" and "rolling stocks," as many as 12 times in a

44. 714 F. 3d 694 (2d Cir. 2013).
45. *Harper & Row Publishers* v. *Nation Enterprises,* 471 U.S. 539 (1985).
46. *Baraban* v. *Time Warner Inc.,* 28 M.L.R. 2013 (2000).

workbook he (Robbins) distributed at financial seminars. But Judge Jack Tanner said there was not a scintilla of evidence that the use of these phrases caused any harm at all to plaintiff Cook.[47] In 2002 a federal court in New York ruled that when Web site operator Susan Pitt created a "Dungeon Doll" based on an altered head of a Barbie doll for a story about sexual slavery and torture, the use of Barbie was a fair use chiefly because the erotic dolls were unlikely to affect the market for the original Barbies.[48] And the 2nd U.S. Court of Appeals rejected the claim of negative economic impact made by a company that argued that when the defendant used some of the plaintiff's copyrighted materials to support his criticism of the company, which conducted executive training seminars, this would seriously reduce the demand for the company's service. "If criticisms on the defendants' web sites kill the demand for plaintiff's services, that is the price that, under the First Amendment, must be paid in the open marketplace of ideas," the court said.[49] Of course, if the defendant had used the plaintiff's materials to operate competing training seminars, the case would likely have ended differently.

In evaluating economic impact the court considers not only direct impact, but also the impact that using the copyrighted material might have on some derivative creation. For example, when a company published a book of trivia questions about the events and characters of the popular Seinfeld television series, a court ruled this was not protected by fair use. The book included questions based upon events and characters in 84 Seinfeld episodes and used actual dialogue from the show in 41 of the book's questions. The court ruled the book affected the ability of the copyright owner to make future derivative Seinfeld trivia books.[50]

FACTORS TO BE CONSIDERED IN DETERMINING FAIR USE

1. The purpose and character of the use
2. The nature of the copyrighted work
3. The amount and substantiality of the portion used in relation to the copyrighted work as a whole
4. The effect of the use on the potential market for or value of the copyrighted work

---

APPLICATION OF THE CRITERIA

When a court is faced with a defendant who claims a fair use, it must apply the four criteria to the facts in the case. Here are two cases that demonstrate how these criteria might be applied. Conservative talk-show host Michael Savage brought a copyright

47. "Jury Award for Wade Cook Overruled."
48. *Mattel Inc.* v. *P.H.*, 50 N.Y., No. 01 CIV. 1864 (LTS), 10/30/02.
49. *NXIVM Corp.* v. *Ross Inst.*, 2d Cir., No. 03-7952, 4/24/04.
50. *Castle Rock Entertainment, Inc.* v. *Carol Publ. Group*, 150 F. 3d 132 (2d Cir. 1998).

infringement suit against the Council on American-Islamic Relations for its use of a four-minute excerpt from a two-hour copyrighted Savage broadcast in which he made statements attacking both the council and the Islamic religion. The short segment was included in a critique of Savage comments that was posted on the council's Web site. The council argued that its use was a fair use.

- **Purpose and character of the use:** The clips were used for criticism and comment of Savage's views. It was not unusual to use the audio clips to authenticate Savage's critical statements. This factor favors the defendant.
- **Nature of the copyrighted work:** While the works appear to be more informational than creative, because the hearing was held on the defendant's motion for a summary judgment based on the pleadings, the plaintiff's allegations that the material was in fact a "creative performance" must be assumed at this point, the court said. This factor therefore favors the plaintiff.
- **Amount and substantiality of the material used:** Four minutes from a two-hour broadcast was a reasonable amount for the purposes of criticizing the plaintiff's views on the topics. This factor favors the defendant.
- **Effect on the market value of the original work:** If the use of the four-minute segment from the original show by the council led some potential listeners to reject Savage's subsequent programs, this might have an impact on Savage's future overall revenues. But the use of the clip in the council's critique would have no impact on the market for the original program that contained the four minutes of commentary. The plaintiff never even implied that there was any market for the copyrighted work outside its original airing. This factor favors the defendant. The use of the four minutes by the council was a fair use.[51]

In a second case, Gawker Media posted 21 pages of Sarah Palin's book, *America by Heart*, online, days before the book's release. Media outlets often publish reports about the contents of unreleased books, but usually paraphrase the contents and use direct quotations sparingly. Publisher HarperCollins brought suit and asked for a court order to force Gawker to remove the excerpts. Before it could issue the order, the court had to evaluate whether HarperCollins was likely to prevail in an infringement action, or whether the posting was a fair use.

- **Purpose and character of the use:** The court ruled that this was purely a commercial use; there was no criticism or commentary regarding the book posted on the Web site. This favored the plaintiff.
- **Nature of the copyrighted work:** This was an unpublished work. This favored the plaintiff.
- **Amount and substantiality of the material used:** Gawker had taken 21 pages from the unpublished book. This was a substantial amount, the court ruled. This favored the plaintiff.
- **Effect on the market value of the original work:** The court said it could only speculate on the effect the posting might have on the original work. But it did

---

51. *Savage v. Council on American-Islamic Relations Inc.,* 36 M.L.R. 2089 (2008).

note that the posting came during the home stretch of a carefully orchestrated promotional campaign for "America by Heart," and could mean that a commercial advantage the publisher might have had was lost. Still, this factor favored neither side.

These findings suggested that Gawker would lose an infringement case on the merits, and a court order was issued, ordering the blogger to remove the excerpts from its site.[52] Days after the decision there were reports that HarperCollins and Gawker settled the matter.[53]

Sofa Entertainment, which owns copyright in a library of film and television, sued the producers of the musical "Jersey Boys" for the use of a seven-second clip from "The Ed Sullivan Show" in the production. At one point in the show, which is a dramatization of the musical group, The Four Seasons, one of the actors used the clip to explain to the audience how the group was coming of age during the invasion of British musical groups in the Sixties. In the clip Sullivan introduces the group (the Seasons) to his audience and cues the group to perform.

- **Purpose and character of the use:** The court said the use was clearly transformative, showing the band's enduring prominence in the biographical production. This favors the defendant.
- **Nature of the copyrighted work:** The clip conveys mainly factual information. This favors the defendant.
- **Amount and substantiality of the material used:** The court said the clip used was "hardly qualitatively significant." This favors the defendant.
- **Effect on the market value of the original work:** The court said "Jersey Boys" was clearly not a substitute for "The Ed Sullivan Show" and would have little if any effect on Sofa's licensing of the variety series. This favors the defendant also.

This was a fair use, the court said.

SUMMARY

While the copyright statute gives the author or owner of a copyrighted work an exclusive monopoly over the use of that work, the law recognizes that in some instances other people ought to be able to copy portions of a protected work. No liability will attach to such copying if the use is what the law calls a fair use.

A court will consider four factors when determining whether a specific use is fair use:

1. What is the purpose and character of the use? Why was the material copied? Was it a commercial use or for nonprofit educational purpose? Was the use intended to further the public interest in some way? Is the original purpose and character transformed with a new meaning or a new purpose by the new use? Did the new use add to the value of the old use?

---

52. *HarperCollins Publishers LLC v. Gawker Media LLC,* 721 F. Supp. 2d 303 (2010).
53. Peters and Bosman, "Palin's Publishers."

2. What is the nature of the copyrighted work? Is it a consumable item such as a workbook, or is it a work more likely to be borrowed from, such as a newspaper or magazine article? Is the copyrighted work in print and available for sale? Has the work been previously published or is it unpublished?

3. How much of the copyrighted work was used in relation to the entire copyrighted work? Was it a small amount of a large work? Or was it a large portion of a small work?

4. What impact does the use have on the potential market or value of the copyrighted work? Has the use of the material diminished the chances for sale of the original work? Or is the use unrelated to the value or sale of the copyrighted material?

Although a court considers each of these items closely, most courts tend to give extra weight to item 4. In a close ruling the impact on the market or value of the copyrighted work often becomes the most crucial question.

COPYRIGHT PROTECTION AND INFRINGEMENT

Until 1989 when the provisions of the Berne Convention (see page 520) became applicable to American copyright law, a work would not be protected from infringement unless it contained a **copyright notice.** Failure to affix a notice meant the automatic loss of most copyright protection. Under international law, however, the affixing of a copyright notice is not required to protect a work. Once a work is created, it is protected. American law now states that a copyright notice "may" be placed on works that are publicly distributed. The U.S. Copyright office, however, still strongly urges creators to include notice on all their works. Copyright law protects the "innocent infringer" from liability for infringement. Someone who copies a work that does not contain a notice could claim an innocent infringement; that is, could argue that she did not realize the work she copied was actually protected by copyright. Although the absence of notice doesn't guarantee a finding of innocent infringement, putting notice on a work eliminates the possibility of an innocent infringement defense. Placing a proper notice on the work is simply prudent behavior.

COPYRIGHT NOTICE

A copyright notice should contain the word "Copyright," the abbreviation "Copr." or the symbol © (the letter C within a circle; the symbol ℗ is used on phonorecords). The year of publication must also be included in the notice. For periodicals the date supplied is the date of publication. For books the date is the year in which the book is first offered for sale (e.g., a book printed in November or December 2017 to go on sale January 2018 should carry a 2018 copyright). The notice must also contain the name of the copyright holder or owner. Most authorities recommend that both the word "Copyright" and the symbol © be used, since the use of the symbol is required to meet the standards of the international copyright agreements. The symbol © protects the work from piracy in most foreign countries. A copyright notice should look something like this:

> Copyright © 2018 by Jane Adams

The copyright notice can be placed anywhere that it "can be visually perceived" on all publicly distributed copies. (The rules are different for sound recordings, which by nature cannot be visually perceived.) The Copyright Office of the Library of Congress has issued rules that implement the statutory description that the notice be visually perceptible. For example, the rules list eight different places where a copyright notice might be put in a book, including the title page, the page immediately following the title page, either side of the front cover and so forth. For photographs, a copyright notice label can be affixed to the back or front of a picture or on any mounting or framing to which the photographs are *permanently* attached.*

The copyright notice can be placed anywhere that it "can be visually perceived" on all publicly distributed copies.

REGISTRATION

Under the law, once a work is created and fixed in a tangible medium it is protected by copyright. Putting notice on the work is not required, but strongly advised. The work is then protected for the life of the author plus 70 years. However, before a copyright holder can sue for infringement under the law, the copyrighted work must be registered with the federal government. To register a work the author or owner must do three things:

1. Fill out the proper registration form. The type of form varies, depending on the kind of work being registered. The forms are available from the Information and Publications Section, Copyright Office, Library of Congress, Washington, D.C. Registration forms for some kinds of material are available at http://copyrightregistry-online-form.com.

2. The fee varies, depending upon how the work is registered, and the nature of the work. The fee for the online registration of a book, for example, is $35. Other fees are higher.

3. Deposit two complete copies of the work with the Copyright Office. (One complete copy is all that is required for unpublished works.)

The statute gives an author or owner 90 days to register a work. What happens if the work is still not registered after 90 days and an infringement takes place? The owner can still register the work and bring suit. But a successful plaintiff in such a suit cannot win statutory damages (see pages 558–559) or win compensation for attorney fees. It is best to get into the habit of registering a work as soon as it is published or broadcast. Courts are of at least two minds regarding when a work is officially registered. Some courts have said a work is not registered—prohibiting a court from exercising jurisdiction in a case—until a certificate of registration is actually issued by the Copyright Office.[54]

* The U.S. Copyright Office has available information regarding all matters relating to copyright law, including how to affix a proper copyright notice (http://www.copyright.gov/).
54. See *Goebel* v. *Manis,* 39 F. Supp. 2d 1318 (1999), for example.

Other courts have ruled that official registration begins once the registration application has been mailed to the Copyright Office.[55]

INFRINGEMENT

Litigating intellectual property lawsuits has become a burgeoning cottage industry in the United States as the muses of the creators of books, films, songs, articles and photos are seemingly unable to keep up with the insatiable appetite of the mass media for new products. A careful newspaper reader will routinely see references to new infringement actions. Most of these lawsuits don't amount to much, but they all play havoc with film producers, book publishers and others. In 2015, copyright law made headlines when Robin Thicke, T.I. and Pharrell Williams were sued by the family of Marvin Gaye for the song "Blurred Lines."

People who believe their exclusive right to control the use of a copyrighted work has been violated will sue for infringement. The federal copyright statute does not actually define infringement. The law simply states that anyone who violates any of the "exclusive rights" of the copyright holder is guilty of an infringement of copyright. Courts that litigate copyright cases seem to focus most often on three criteria to determine whether a particular use is an infringement (see following boxed text). A brief outline of each of these three points follows.

- ▮ Is the copyright on the plaintiff's work valid? While this inquiry will look at matters such as the proper registration of the work, the heart of this examination is to determine whether the copyrighted work is an original work that can be protected by copyright.
- ▮ Did the defendant have access to the plaintiff's work prior to the alleged infringement?
- ▮ Are the two works substantially similar?

Originality of the Plaintiff's Work

The copyright on the plaintiff's work must be valid before a successful infringement suit can be maintained. As has been previously noted, a work that is not original cannot be protected by copyright. When a work is initially copyrighted, there is no government assessment of whether it is original and can be legitimately copyrighted. The question of originality arises only if a lawsuit ensues. A central question, then, in many infringement suits is whether the plaintiff's work is original, or if the plaintiff is attempting to bring suit on the basis of the theft of material that cannot be legally copyrighted because it lacks originality or novelty.

History, for example, exists for all to use in a book or a story. Margaret Alexander brought an infringement suit against Alex Haley, claiming that he had copied portions of

---

55. *Denenberg* v. *Berman,* D. Neb. No. 4: 02CV7, 7/23/02; and *Well-Made Toy Mfg. Corp.* v. *Goffa Intern Corp.,* 210 F. Supp. 2d 147 (2002), for example.

her novel *Jubilee* and her pamphlet "How I Wrote Jubilee" when he wrote and published his successful novel *Roots* in 1976. But the court noted that most of what Alexander claimed Haley had stolen was history—the story of the slave culture in the United States— or material in the public domain, such as folktales about early American black culture. "Where common sources exist for the alleged similarities, or the material that is similar is not original with the plaintiff, there is no infringement," the court ruled.[56]

Courts have also ruled that what are called "scènes à faire" are also uncopyrightable. These are situations and incidents in a story that flow naturally from the basic plot premise. For example, movies about spies frequently include elements like spy gadgets, hidden in watches or shoes. These ideas or expressions are standard or common in spy films, and thus can't be copyrighted.

Access

The second dimension of an infringement suit is access: The plaintiff must convince the court that the defendant had access to the copyrighted work. An opportunity to copy has to exist. If plaintiffs cannot prove that the so-called literary pirate had a chance to see and read the work, they are hard-pressed to prove piracy. As Judge Learned Hand once wrote:

> If by some magic a man who had never known it were to compose anew Keats's, "Ode on a Grecian Urn," he would be an 'author' and if he copyrighted it, others might not copy that poem, though they might of course copy Keats's.[57]

Translating Hand's reference to John Keats' early 19th-century poem into contemporary terms, consider this hypothetical situation. A young woman, who has lived all her life on a deserted island, with no exposure to outside influences, manages to write and then publish an exact duplicate of Robert Crais' novel *Suspect*. Crais would be hardpressed to win a copyright infringement case because he would be unable to show that the young writer had access to his work. Obviously, such a scenario is unlikely to occur. But it makes the point. The plaintiff must prove not simply that the two works are the same, but that the defendant stole his work. To do that there must be proof that the defendant had access to the stolen work.

There must be proof that the defendant had access to the stolen work.

In 1998 Marion Leon Bea sued Home Box Office (HBO), claiming it had infringed on his script for a film called "N and Out" when it made the HBO motion picture "First Time Felon." The similarities between the two scripts were thin, the court noted. But what killed the suit was the plaintiff's inability to prove that HBO had access to his script before "First Time Felon" was produced.[58] Cynthia Clay sued James Cameron for copyright infringement claiming he had stolen elements of her book, *Zollocco: a Story of Another Universe* when he made the movie "Avatar." There were similarities between the two works, but Clay's case failed because she could not prove that Cameron ever had access to *Zollocco*. Clay said she sent her book to publishers and agents, but that was not sufficient to prove Cameron had seen it. There must be proof that there was a reasonable

---

56. *Alexander* v. *Haley*, 460 F. Supp. 40 (1978).
57. *Sheldon* v. *Metro-Goldwyn-Mayer Pictures*, 81 F. 2d 49 (1939).
58. *Bea* v. *Home Box Office*, 26 M.L.R. 2373 (1998).

possibility that the defendant had access to the work, proof beyond the plaintiff's speculation that the director had seen the story, the U.S. District Court ruled.[59]

Copying and Substantial Similarity

The final factor a court will consider is whether the defendant copied the plaintiff's work. In some cases evidences of such copying is irrefutable. The defendant has dubbed copies of a DVD or CD, or has reprinted a short story or a song lyric, or simply used too much of the defendant's work in his or her work. In one of the most celebrated copyright disputes of the past decade, Harry Potter author J.K. Rowling sued the publisher of *The Harry Potter Lexicon* for copyright infringement. The lexicon stemmed from a Web site of the same name, the creation of a 50-year-old middle school librarian (and huge fan of the Potter books) named Stephen Jan Vander Ark. There are scores of Web sites and chat rooms devoted to the book series, and Rowling has supported most of them. But when RDR books announced plans to publish the lexicon—a kind of guidebook to the Potter stories—Rowling brought suit against the publisher. The plaintiffs in the case argued that the lexicon merely "compiles and repackages Ms. Rowling's fictional facts derived wholesale from the Harry Potter works without adding any new creativity, insight or criticism." RDR argued that the book provided a significant amount of original analysis and commentary concerning everything—the characters, relationships among them, the meaning of literary allusions and so on. The U.S. District Court in New York agreed with Rowling in September 2008, ruling that the works were substantially similar. There was too much of Rowling's work in the lexicon.[60] Initially RDR announced it would appeal the ruling, but dropped the appeal two months later. In January 2009, RDR published a second Potter book, *The Lexicon: An Unauthorized Guide to Harry Potter Fiction and Related Materials*, which contained far more commentary on the Potter books, and far less material from the series.

In other instances it is a bit more complicated. A photo looks a lot like a copyrighted picture, for example. In these cases judges must often take on the role of art critic to flesh out the differences between two seemingly identical works. In 1993 Random House commissioned Jack Leigh to photograph the Bird Girl statue in the Bonaventure Cemetery in Savannah, Ga., to use on the cover of a novel it was publishing called *Midnight in the Garden of Good and Evil*. The book was successful and the photo became famous. When Warner Brothers made the book into a film, it wanted to use a similar photo in its advertising for the motion picture. But the owner of the statue, which had become famous because of the Leigh photo, had removed the object from the cemetery. With the statue owner's permission, the film studio had a replica crafted, took it to the cemetery and had it photographed for promotion of the movie. When the movie came out, Leigh sued for copyright infringement. Warner Brothers had not used Leigh's picture, but it had generated a photo that was remarkably similar to the original. Judges at the 11th U.S. Circuit Court of Appeals had to analyze the similarities and differences between the two. There was a difference in the contrast of the lighting; the statue was smaller and more distant in the Warner Brothers photo; the movie poster picture had a green/orange tint; and there was a Celtic cross on the new statue. But both photos were

---

59. *Clay* v. *Cameron*, 39 M.L.R. 2720 (2011).
60. *Warner Bros Entertainment, Inc. and J.K. Rowling* v. *RDR Books*, 575 F. Supp. 513 (2008).

taken from the same low angle; hanging Spanish moss bordered both photos; the statue was in the center of both pictures; the light source is from above in both shots; and the remainder of the cemetery is obscured. In this case the court ruled that there were sufficient similarities to preclude a summary judgment for Warner Brothers and sent the case back for a jury trial.[61]

More often than not, however, direct or literal copying is not an issue. In these cases the defendant is not accused of taking a particular line or segment of a work, but of appropriating "the fundamental essence or structure of the work." There must be more than minor similarities between the two works; they must be *substantially similar*. But this is another instance in which it is easier to state a rule than to apply it. How can you determine whether two works are substantially similar? Courts use a variety of tests to determine substantial similarity, but virtually all the tests focus on two aspects of the work. The courts will first ask whether the general idea or general theme of the works is the same. If the general idea of the two works is not similar, there is no infringement and the courts usually insist that the similarities must be apparent to an average, lay observer, not an expert.

Daryl Murphy filmed a documentary about the tenants residing in Chicago Housing Authority Projects. The motion picture included interviews with people who lived or had lived in the projects, and video of scenery, buildings, family gatherings and so on. Nine months later the television cartoon series "PJs" aired. It was also set in an urban housing project. Murphy sued the producers of the program, including comedian Eddie Murphy, for infringement of copyright. The federal district court ruled that the two creations were not substantially similar. The plaintiff's film is a documentary about the lives of real people living in the projects. "PJs" is a cartoon comedy. The documentary consists of disconnected series of interviews with real people. The cartoon is fiction and has a plot line in each episode. The look and feel of the two are entirely different.[62]

If the general idea in the two works is substantially similar, the court must then take a second step and look to see how the idea or concept is expressed in the works. How is the theme carried out? Some examples can help make this point. Tommy Pino sued Viacom Inc. for infringement because, he said, the defendant's reality TV show, "Pros vs. Joes," was similar to a program he proposed in a script treatment and a screenplay he submitted to a variety of agents and TV networks—including CBS, which is owned by Viacom. Both the program and Pino's proposal focused on a sports reality show featuring contests between professional athletes and amateurs. The federal court acknowledged the similarity, but the manner in which the program and the proposal developed the idea was substantially different. The plots were different, the dialogue was different, the mood was different and the setting and pace were different. Outside of a few stock elements and the general idea, the two were not substantially similar.[63] A federal court in California reached the same conclusion when E.W. Scripps Co., which owned the Food Network, was sued for infringement by an individual who claimed the Rachael Ray program, "Inside Dish," infringed on his proposal for a celebrity chef cooking show called "Showbiz Chef." The concept behind the two shows, a talk show that features celebrity chefs as guests, was similar, but

---

61. *Leigh* v. *Warner Brothers Inc.,* 212 F. 3d 1210 (2000).
62. *Murphy* v. *Murphy,* 35 M.L.R. 1716 (2007).
63. *Pino* v. *Viacom Inc.,* 36 M.L.R. 1678 (2008).

these elements cannot be protected by copyright. There was no similarity in the way the basic elements were carried out. The plots were different (the plaintiff's program had no discernable plot), the dialogue was not the same, the mood and the setting were dissimilar ("Showbiz Chef " was to be telecast from a celebrity's home, whereas the Rachael Ray show was taped at a studio), the sequence of events in the shows was not the same. No reasonable jury could conclude the shows were substantially similar, the court said.[64]

Gwen O'Donnell sued Time Warner Entertainment for infringement claiming the HBO series "Six Feet Under" was a copy of a story she had drafted in the late 1990s called "The Funk Parlor." O'Donnell's story traces the lives of people who run a small, family-owned funeral parlor in Connecticut. The HBO series is also set in a funeral parlor, but in Los Angeles. Both O'Donnell's screenplay and "Six Feet Under" commence with the death of a father and the return of a prodigal son. But the U.S. Court of Appeals ruled that was about the only similarity between the two. The death of the father in "The Funk Parlor" sets the stage for a series of additional murders. The characters, moods, themes, pace, dialogue and sequence of events is different in "Six Feet Under," the court said. "'The Funk Parlor,' a murder mystery, is driven by a series of murders, which catalyze the salvation of the business. The use of death in 'Six Feet Under' is quite different; there, death provides the focal point for exploring relationships and existential meaning," the court said. The works are not substantially similar.[65]

It is not easy to prove infringement of copyright; yet surprisingly, a large number of suits are settled each year in favor of plaintiffs. Most of these cases are settled out of court. In such instances the obvious theft of the material would generally appall an honest person. An individual who works to be creative in fashioning a story or a play or a piece of art usually has little to fear. The best and simplest way to avoid a suit for infringement is simply to do your own work, to be original.

COPYRIGHT INFRINGEMENT AND THE INTERNET

The law regulating mass media has had to adapt to changes in media technology many times in the past 200 years. When the nation's first copyright law was adopted, printed material comprised the mass media. But since then, the law has been forced to cope with photography, radio, motion pictures, sound recordings, television, audio- and videotaping, photocopying, computer programs, CD-ROM and so on. But no technology has challenged the law to the extent the Internet has. By its very nature the new medium lends itself to the theft of the work of others. As one legal expert noted, digitized information can be copied quickly, easily and cheaply, and the copy is every bit as good as the original. Once the information is copied, it can be easily distributed via the Web to receivers who can make their own copies of the material and further distribute it: an almost endless chain. Copyright issues involving computer-generated communication are commonplace today. Stories regarding lawsuits appear almost daily in the press. And the owner of the copyright can be left out completely. Publishers and authors sued Google in 2009 after it announced a plan to scan all the books in the world; those in the public domain

---

64. *Zella* v. *E.W. Scripps Co.*, 36 M.L.R. 1353 (2007); see also *Rosenfeld* v. *Twentieth Century Fox Film Corp.*, 37 M.L.R. 1348 (2009).
65. *Funky Films Inc.* v. *Time Warner Entertainment Co.*, 34 M.L.R. 2345 (2006).

and those protected by copyright. The online giant settled the lawsuit by promising to charge customers who read the books, and share the revenues with the copyright holders. The copyright holder would also get a flat fee for the initial scanning, or could opt out of the scanning system.[66] But in March 2011 a federal court rejected the settlement, saying the terms go too far in giving Google an advantage over competitive and copyright holders. In 2012 Google and the major book publishers worked out a settlement. But that didn't completely settle the matter.

The ease of copying and distribution is only one problem. Many Internet users apparently don't believe that other people's works should enjoy copyright protection. When cartoonist Gary Larson pleaded with Web users to stop duplicating his "The Far Side" cartoons on the Internet, a substantial number of users replied that they would not cease the practice. "All this copyright infringement enforcing ticks me off," one user responded. "What is the Net for if we can't view a Far Side cartoon, or listen to a sound file from the Simpsons," the user asked rhetorically. There have always been people who disdained the notion that a writer or photographer should be able to protect his or her own work. But until the Internet, all that most of these people could do was steal it for themselves: illegally dub a CD or a movie, photocopy a series of short stories. Now it is possible for an individual not only to make the illegal copy, but to distribute it to 100,000 of his or her close friends in a matter of seconds.

The courts have been applying traditional copyright law to these new problems with some success. And some jurists say the application of existing law is all that is required to solve the problems. "New technologies—from television, to video cassette recorders, to digitized transmissions—have all been made to fit within the overall scheme of copyright law and to serve the ends to which copyright was intended to promote," wrote U.S. District Judge Leonie Brinkema. "The Internet is no exception."[67] Other observers say they believe that new laws are needed.

Digital Millennium Copyright Act

An international group, the World Intellectual Property Organization, framed new copyright rules in two treaties in the mid-1990s that give copyright protection to the owners of digitized works. The treaties also provide for the fair use defense in cyberspace.[68] The United States agreed to abide by these new rules in adopting the Digital Millennium Copyright Act (DMCA) in 1998. But this law went beyond the WIPO treaties and also prevents the circumvention of technological measures that control access to copyrighted works—so-called encryption codes—and outlaws the manufacture, importation or sale of devices used to circumvent such protections. In the summer of 2001, a 27-year-old Russian cryptographer named Dmitry Sklyarov was arrested in Las Vegas after giving a presentation to a convention of computer hackers on ways to decrypt the software used to protect electronic books. Six months later the government agreed to defer the prosecution of Sklyarov in return for his promise to testify against his employer, Elcomsoft, a Russian software company. A basic question in this case and others that spring from this

66. Cohen, "A Google Search."
67. *Religious Technology Center* v. *Lerma,* 24 M.L.R. 2473 (1996).
68. Schiesel, "Global Agreement Reached."

section of the 1998 act is this: *Can the government make it a crime to manufacture and sell a device that can be used to circumvent copyright protection if that device can be used for other, legal purposes as well?* In 1984 the Supreme Court was asked that question about another technological invention, the videocassette recorder (VCR). Hollywood television production companies sought to stop the sale of the new device in the United States because it could be used to make copies of the copyrighted programs broadcast on television. At that time the Supreme Court ruled that even though some people may use the device illegally, there were numerous legal purposes for the VCR as well. The manufacturer of the machine could not be held liable for those who used the device illegally.[69] But times have changed, people in the entertainment industry argue. Copying protected material has become too easy and can be done too rapidly for rights holders to catch up with the illegal users. It is time to ban the devices. This is a basic legal issue in any case to determine whether software or hardware violates the DMCA. Does the machine or the program that permits illegal activity have functions that are clearly legal as well? Federal courts have upheld the constitutionality of the DMCA.[70] The 2nd U.S. Court of Appeals agreed that computer code is protected by the First Amendment but said a narrowly drawn statute—like the DMCA—would not violate the Constitution. But the issue is far from resolved, as more litigation enters the halls of justice. The law carries criminal penalties, a possible $500,000 fine and a five-year jail sentence. The 1998 law also imposes a compulsory licensing and royalty scheme for the transmission of music on the Internet similar to the scheme used to collect royalties for music broadcast on radio or television and exempts Internet service providers (ISPs) from copyright liability for simply transmitting copyrighted material users have put on the Internet. This is referred to as a "safe harbor."

This last provision got a serious court test because of YouTube, the video-sharing Web site owned by Google. The site carries hundreds of thousands of video clips, many of them copyrighted material. In 2007, Viacom, the parent company of MTV and Comedy Central, demanded that YouTube remove more than 100,000 clips of video the company says it owns. Viacom also demanded that YouTube begin automatically filtering out material that is obviously copyrighted. After making the demand, Viacom filed a $1 billion copyright infringement suit against Google. YouTube began removing material owned by Viacom while it evaluated the merits of the lawsuit. Other companies like NBC Universal, the Walt Disney Company and News Corporation were also negotiating with the site, asking that YouTube either remove copyrighted material, or begin paying a licensing fee for the use of the material. YouTube contends that as long as it removes copyrighted material when asked to, it is immune from legal liability because of the DMCA. In May 2010 a federal court agreed with Google's YouTube, saying the company was shielded from Viacom's copyright claims by the safe harbor provisions of the DMCA. As long as YouTube takes down the material when notified by its rightful owner that it was uploaded without permission, the operator of the site is protected from liability. Judge Louis L. Stanton said that while the company certainly knew that copyrighted material had been uploaded to its site, it did not know which clips had been uploaded with permission and

69. *Sony Corp.* v. *Universal City Studios, Inc.,* 464 U.S. 417 (1984).
70. *Universal City Studios, Inc.* v. *Corley,* 2d Cir., No. 00-9185, 11/28/01. See also *Felten* v. *Recording Industry Association of America,* D.N.J., No. CV-01-2669 (GEB), 11/27/01.

which had not. Forcing companies to police every video uploaded to their sites "would contravene the structure and operation of the DMCA," Stanton wrote.[71] But in April of 2012 a federal appeals court reversed the lower court ruling. The 2nd U.S. Court of Appeals ruled "a reasonable jury could conclude that YouTube had knowledge or awareness" of the copyright infringement, "at least with respect to a handful of specific clips." On April 18, 2013, Judge Stanton issued another order granting summary judgment in favor of YouTube. The judged ruled that YouTube had no actual knowledge of any specific instance of infringement of Viacom's works. Before another appeal could be heard by the 2nd Circuit, the two companies reached a settlement.[72]

File Sharing

File sharing, or the ability of computer users to move files from one computer to another or a great many other computers, caused some of the most perplexing and widely publicized copyright problems during the past decade. But by late 2009 file sharing had ceased to be a primary issue in copyright litigation; not because the questions had been resolved, but because this was a problem that appeared to be intractable. Every time a legal solution was fashioned, new technology allowed file sharers to bypass the legal limits put in place. At some point, leaders of especially the recording industry concluded that there was little more they could do to stop the widespread sharing of music. As someone said, the genie was out of the bottle.

The theft of recorded music via the Internet wasn't a serious problem until the late 1990s because it took too long to download a song. But the development of inexpensive data compression technology solved this problem, and the introduction of MP3 players, which brought this technology within reach of music lovers, resulted in the dramatic growth of illegal music file sharing. The music industry tried to block the manufacture and sale of the MP3 players, but the courts ruled they were simply space shifters, not audio recording devices. "The player merely makes copies in order to render portable . . . files that already reside in a user's hard drive," the court said, comparing the new device to a home video recorder, which the Supreme Court had ruled was legal.[73]

File-sharing services like Napster, StreamCast Networks, Grokster and many others began to spring up, facilitating the free transfer of copyrighted music, giving music fans access to recorded music without having to purchase a CD. One by one these services were sued for abetting copyright infringement, and for the most part, the courts supported the recording industry in its attempts to stop the piracy.[74] But the litigation was costly, time-consuming and did not end the problems generated by file sharing, as new, slightly different services sprang up. The industry then began to attack the file sharers themselves, individuals who used the peer-to-peer music sharing systems. From 2003 to the end of 2008 the Recording Industry Association of America (RIAA), the trade group representing the recording industry, sued about 35,000 people for swapping songs

71. Helft, "Judge Sides with Google."
72. Stelter, "Viacom Suit."
73. *Recording Industry Association of America* v. *Diamond Multimedia Systems,* 9th Cir., No. 98-56727, 6/15/99.
74. *A&M Records Inc.* v. *Napster Inc.,* 239 F. 3d 1004 (2001); *Metro-Goldwyn-Mayer Studios Inc.* v. *Grokster Ltd.,* 125 S. Ct. 2264 (2005).

online. Judgments or settlements averaged about $3,500 in these cases—hardly worth the cost of the lawsuit.[75]

While this was happening, Apple introduced the iPod and later the iPhone, two new devices for downloading music. Coupled with iTunes and other Web sites where music could be legally purchased, access to legal downloads became relatively commonplace. The recording companies made deals with Apple (and other device makers like Microsoft which introduced the Zune) to provide access to their recorded music and waived their digital copyrights for a small per-song fee. Songs generally cost 99 cents, with the label getting 70 cents and Apple (or whomever) getting the rest. By 2009 Apple was the nation's largest marketer of recorded music. Today most music fans are either downloading songs or, more commonly, using music streaming sites like Spotify, Pandora, and YouTube.

The file-sharing dilemma is a scenario that is still playing out. And the law of copyright is rife with other problems related to the Internet as well. The uploading, distribution and downloading of copyrighted photographs is a serious matter—especially from publications like *Playboy* where the photos (as well as the serious articles and essays) entice most people to buy the magazine.[76] The question of whether ISPs are liable for infringement when they act as a passive conduit for photos posted by their customers is an emerging issue, with at least one court ruling that the ISPs were not liable under the federal copyright law.[77]

FILM AND TELEVISION

Both the film and television industries—in many cases the same companies produce products for both—face problems similar to those experienced by the recording industry. At a time when DVD sales are shrinking, network television audiences are getting smaller and theater attendance is barely holding even, the video industry is losing billions of dollars to piracy. Illegal downloading of movies has been a problem for several years. In April 2009 a television comedian joked that during the previous weekend one million people had watched the movie "X-Men Origins: Wolverine." "Of course," he noted, "the film doesn't open until May 1." There were even some published reviews of the pirated film. "Avatar" was downloaded 500,000 times in the first two days of its release. Even e-books face piracy problems. Amazon.com sold more digital copies for its Kindle e-reader of Dan Brown's *The Last Symbol* in its first few days than hardback copies. But within days, the e-book had been illegally downloaded more than 100,000 times. The problem has gotten so serious for mass media industries that the U.S. Senate considered legislation in 2010 to combat illegal file sharing and counterfeiting. Under the legislation, which failed to even get a vote in the Senate, the Justice Department would have been authorized to file civil actions against Web sites that facilitated the piracy.

While downloading was the piracy method of choice, more recently the industry has had to face a new threat—streaming technology that makes TV shows and films instantly available. There are several legal sources for individuals to get instant access to

75. Nakashima, "Music Industry Desists."

76. *Playboy Enterprises, Inc.* v. *Starware Publishers Corp.,* 900 F. Supp. 433 (1995); and *Playboy Enterprises, Inc.* v. *George Frena,* 839 F. Supp. 1552 (1993).

77. *CoStar Group Inc.* v. *LoopNet Inc.,* 4th Cir., No. 03-1911, 6/21/04.

movies and television shows. But rarely are these just released films or new programs. Illegal sites offer access to pirated copies. The video industry is trying to control this streaming with lawsuits. For example, in early 2011 a federal court ordered a company called Ivi to stop streaming Web broadcasts of programming copyrighted by the television networks. The networks said that Ivi was capturing broadcast signals in four large cities including New York, and charging consumers a subscription fee for streaming the programming over the Internet without authorization. Subscribers needed a media player to download the programming to their computers and paid Ivi $4.99 a month. The television stations argued that by diverting customers from the over-the-air and cable broadcasts, Ivi compromised their ability to earn revenue from advertisers.[78]

The use of camcorders in theaters accounts for most piracy, but many video products are stolen or copied during the production process. To combat the problem, many studios are releasing both older and new TV shows for free viewing online. And contrary to previous practice, many major feature films are being released on the same day worldwide, not on staggered dates. The industry believes most people would rather pay to see a high-quality copy of a film, so long as they can see it as soon as it is released for commercial distribution.

SUMMARY

To protect the copyright of a work, the author or owner should give proper notice and register the work with the government. A proper copyright notice looks like this:

Copyright © 2018 by Jane Adams (use the symbol Ⓟ for phonorecords)

Notice must be placed where it can be visually perceived. To gain the full benefits of the law, a work must be registered with the Copyright Office in the Library of Congress as well. The proper registration form along with two complete copies of the work and the proper fee must be sent to the Register of Copyrights.

When a plaintiff sues for infringement of copyright, the court will consider three important criteria. First, is the plaintiff's work original? If the plaintiff has attempted to copyright material that legitimately belongs in the public domain, the plaintiff cannot sue for infringement of copyright. Second, did the defendant have access to the plaintiff's work? There must be some evidence that the defendant viewed or heard the copyrighted work before the alleged infringement took place. Finally, is there evidence that the defendant actually copied the plaintiff's work? If no such evidence exists, are the two works substantially similar? In examining this last issue, the court seeks to determine whether the ideas in the two works are similar. If the general idea of the two works is similar, is the expression of these ideas similar as well? Problems of copyright infringement via the Internet are just beginning to be litigated, with both traditional copyright law and new statutes being applied by the courts.

Litigation on the breadth and meaning of the Digital Millennium Copyright Act is just beginning, while the recording industry's battle with peer-to-peer file sharers appears to be coming to an end. The film and TV industries, however, are facing new challenges with video pirates.

---

78. Jeffrey and Van Voris, "Ivi Must Halt."

FREELANCING AND COPYRIGHT

What rights does a freelance journalist, author or photographer hold with regard to stories or pictures that are sold to publishers? The writer or photographer is the creator of the work; he or she owns the story or the photograph. Consequently, as many rights as such freelancers choose to relinquish can be sold or given to a publisher. Beginning writers and photographers often do not have much choice but to follow the policy of the book or magazine publisher. Authors whose works are in demand, however, can retain most rights to the material for their future benefit. Most publishers have established policies on exactly what rights they purchase when they decide to buy a story or photograph or drawing. The annual edition of *The Writer's Market* is the best reference guide for the freelancer. The boxed text lists some of the rights that publishers might buy.

1. *All rights:* The creator sells complete ownership of the story or photograph.
2. *First serial rights:* The buyer has the right to use the piece of writing or picture for the first time in a periodical published anywhere in the world. But the publisher can use it only once, and then the creator can sell it to someone else.
3. *First North American serial rights:* The rights are the same as those provided in number 2, except the publisher buys the right to publish the material first in North America, not anywhere in the world.
4. *Simultaneous rights:* The publisher buys the right to print the material at the same time other periodicals print the material. All the publishers, however, must be aware that simultaneous publication will occur.
5. *One-time rights:* The publisher purchases the right to use a piece just one time, and there is no guarantee that it has not been published elsewhere first.

It is a common practice for publishers to buy all rights to a story or photograph but to agree to reassign the rights to the creator after publication. In such cases the burden of initiating the reassignment rests with the writer or photographer, who must request reassignment immediately following publication. The publisher signs a transfer of rights to the creator, and the creator should record this transfer of rights with the Copyright Office within two or three weeks. When this transaction has taken place, the creator can then resell the material.

DAMAGES

Plaintiffs in a copyright suit can ask the court to assess the defendant for any damage they have suffered, plus the profits made by the infringer from pirating the protected work. Damages can be a little bit or a lot. In each case the plaintiff must prove to the court the amount of the loss or the amount of the defendant's profit. But, rather than prove actual damage, the plaintiff can ask the court to assess what are called statutory damages, or damage amounts prescribed by the statute. The smallest statutory award is

$750 per infringement, although in the case of an innocent infringement, the court may use its discretion and lower the damage amount. The highest statutory award is $30,000 per infringement. However, if the plaintiff can prove that the infringement was committed willfully and repeatedly, the maximum damage award can be as much as $150,000 per infringement.

In addition, the courts have other powers in a copyright suit. A judge can restrain a defendant from continued infringement, can impound the material that contains the infringement and can order the destruction of these works. A defendant might also be charged with a criminal offense in a copyright infringement case. If the defendant infringed on a copyright "willfully and for purposes of commercial advantage or private financial gain," he or she could be fined and jailed for not more than one year.

The law of copyright is not difficult to understand and should not be a threat to most creative people in the mass media. The law simply says to do your own work and don't steal from the work of others. Some authorities argue that copyright is an infringement on freedom of the press. In a small way it probably is. Nevertheless most writers, authors and reporters—people who most often take advantage of freedom of the press—support copyright laws that protect their rights to property that they create. Judge Jerome Frank once attempted to explain this apparent contradiction by arguing that we are adept at concealing from ourselves the fact that we maintain and support "side by side as it were, beliefs which are inherently incompatible." Frank suggested that we keep these separate antagonistic beliefs in separate "logic-tight compartments."

The courts have recognized the needs of society as well as the needs of authors and have hence allowed considerable latitude for copying material that serves some public function. Because of this attitude, copyright law usually has little, or should have little, impact on the information-oriented mass media.

BIBLIOGRAPHY

Arango, Tim. "Who Owns Sports Coverage?" *The New York Times,* 21 April 2009, C1.

Cohen, Naomi. "A Google Search of a Distinctly Retro Kind." *The New York Times,* 4 March 2009, C1.

Gleick, James. "Patently Absurd." *The New York Times Magazine,* 12 March 2000, 44.

Greenhouse, Linda. "Ruling on *Victor* vs. *Victoria* Offers Split Victory of Sorts." *The New York Times,* 5 March 2003, A16.

Hansell, Saul. "McCain in Fight Over YouTube." *The New York Times,* 20 October 2008, B8.

Helft, Miguel. "Judge Sides with Google in Viacom Video Suit." *The New York Times,* 23 June 2010, B1.

Italie, Hillel. "Compensation for Use of Copyright Obama Image Sought by AP." *The Seattle Post-Intelligencer,* 5 February 2009, A4.

Jeffrey, Don, and Van Voris, Bob. "Ivi Must Halt Web-Streaming of TV Shows." *The Seattle Times,* 23 February 2011, A13.

"Jury Award for Wade Cook Overruled." *Seattle Post-Intelligencer,* 18 December 1998, E4.

Kennedy, Randy. "Court Rules in Artist's Favor." *The New York Times,* 26 April 2013, C-23.

Lattman, Peter. "English Copyright Lawsuit Against 'The Da Vinci Code' Kicks Off in London." *The Wall Street Journal Online,* 26 February 2006.

Lee, Jennifer. "U.S. Arrests Russian Cryptographer as Copyright Violator." *The New York Times,* 18 July 2001, C8.

Lyall, Sarah. "Idea for 'Da Vinci Code' Was Not Stolen, Judge Says." *The New York Times,* 8 April 2006, A15.

Nakashima, Ryan. "Music Industry Desists from Suing Swappers." *The Seattle Post-Intelligencer,* 20 December 2008, B2.

Pérez-Peña, Richard. "A.P. Seeks to Block Unpaid Use of Content." *The New York Times,* 24 July 2009, B3.

——. "A.P. Seeks to Rein in Sites Using Its Content." *The New York Times,* 6 April 2009, B1.

Peters, Jeremy, and Bosman, Julie. "Palin's Publishers and Gawker Settle Case." *The New York Times,* 25 January 2010, B5.

Schiesel, Seth. "Global Agreement Reached to Widen Law on Copyright." *The New York Times,* 21 December 1996, A1.

Stelter, Brain. "Viacom Suit vs YouTube is Restored." *The New York Times,* 6 April 2012, B1.

Thomas, Katie. "Sports Stars' Catchphrase: 'If I Say It, I Own It.'" *The New York Times,* 12 October 2010, B4.

Whitley, Angus. "Legal Downloads Soar in iPod World." *Seattle Post-Intelligencer,* 20 January 2005, C1.

CHAPTER 15

Regulation of Advertising

©McGraw-Hill Education/Jill Braaten

Advertising, as a form of expression subject to legal regulation and potential First Amendment protection, is the dominant cultural icon of our time. It also is a huge business. In 2017, a 30-second television commercial on the Super Bowl cost a record $5 million. In 2016, more than

$190 billion (yes, billion) was spent on advertising in the United States, according to eMarketer. That same company also predicted that by the year 2020, U.S. total media advertising spending (including television, radio, print and digital) would exceed a whopping $230 billion. Ad dollars make possible most of the media content that we consume; were it not for ads, network television and daily newspapers would not exist. Advertising is, then, a very important form of speech.

Advertising messages are regulated by the government; in fact, advertising is probably the most heavily regulated form of modern speech and press. Laws at every level—federal, state and local—control what businesses and institutions may claim about their products and services. This chapter outlines the most common kinds of regulations that affect advertising; it is not comprehensive. Thousands of laws regulate advertising. People who work in advertising, especially copywriters, need a comprehensive understanding of the law and should use this material only as a starting point.

ADVERTISING AND THE FIRST AMENDMENT

For many years, advertising was not protected by the First Amendment. It was not until 1975 that the U.S. Supreme Court first explicitly held that "commercial advertising enjoys a degree of First Amendment protection," reasoning at the time in *Bigelow* v. *Virginia* that "the relationship of speech to the marketplace of products or of services does not make it valueless in the marketplace of ideas"[1] (see Chapter 2 regarding the marketplace of ideas). Yet the court also was clear in *Bigelow* that advertising is "subject to reasonable regulation." Since then, courts have developed a **commercial speech doctrine** articulating just how much First Amendment protection advertising receives and the criteria the government must satisfy to permissibly regulate it. The doctrine evolved in a series of cases in the five years after *Bigelow*.

- In 1976 the Supreme Court ruled that a Virginia statute that forbade advertising the price of prescription drugs violated the First Amendment.[2]
- In 1977 the high court invalidated a township ordinance in New Jersey that banned the placement of "for sale" and "sold" signs on front lawns. Township authorities said the law was needed because such signs contributed to panic selling by white homeowners who feared that property values would decline because the township was becoming populated by black families. The Supreme Court rejected this "white flight" argument and ruled that the placement of such signs was protected by the First Amendment.[3]

1. 421 U.S. 809, 826 (1975).
2. *Virginia State Board of Pharmacy* v. *Virginia Citizens Consumer Council, Inc.,* 425 U.S. 748 (1976).
3. *Linmark Associates* v. *Township of Willingboro,* 431 U.S. 85 (1977).

■ In the 1980 case of *Central Hudson Gas & Electric Corp.* v. *Public Service Commission*—known today simply as *Central Hudson*—the Supreme Court held unconstitutional a New York regulation that completely banned promotional ads by electric utility companies.[4]

The high court has granted states fairly extensive authority to regulate advertising for professional services by individuals like doctors, lawyers, dentists and others. For instance, the Supreme Court in 2006 upheld the Florida Bar's reprimand of two attorneys who used a pit bull logo and the number 1-800-PIT-BULL in their firm's advertisements.[5] But even attorneys, reviled as they are by many, still possess a right to advertise some things. For example, the 3rd U.S. Circuit Court of Appeals in 2014 struck down as unconstitutional a New Jersey attorney-conduct guideline that barred attorney advertising from using excerpts or quotations from judicial opinions—even if they were accurate—to advertise legal services, unless the opinions appeared in full. In the case, an advertisement on attorney Andrew Dwyer's Web site featured compliments New Jersey judges had written about him in judicial opinions. Those compliments—including that Dwyer was "an exceptional lawyer" who was "tenacious" and "professional" in his presentation to the court—were made in the context of a state law's fee-shifting provisions, which require judges to assess the abilities and legal services of plaintiffs' attorneys. In response to Dwyer's advertisement, the New Jersey Supreme Court approved the following guideline: "An attorney or law firm may not include, on a website or other advertisement, a quotation or excerpt from a court opinion (oral or written) about the attorney's abilities or legal services. An attorney may, however, present the full text of opinions, including those that discuss the attorney's legal abilities, on a website or other advertisement." Dwyer immediately moved for an injunction to block enforcement of the guideline. In *Dwyer* v. *Cappell*,[6] the 3rd Circuit said a guideline barring advertising using accurate excerpts from judicial opinions was "unduly burdensome" and violated Dwyer's "First Amendment right to advertise his commercial services."

COMMERCIAL SPEECH DOCTRINE

The First Amendment does not protect either false or misleading ads or ads for unlawful goods or services.

Government may regulate truthful advertising for legal goods and services if the following conditions are met:

a. There is a substantial state interest to justify the regulation.

b. There is evidence that the regulation directly advances this interest.

c. There is a reasonable fit between the state interest and the government regulation.

---

4. 447 U.S. 557 (1980).
5. *Florida Bar* v. *Pape,* 918 So. 2d 240 (Fla. 2005), cert. den., *Pape* v. *Florida Bar,* 547 U.S. 1041 (2006).
6. 762 F. 3d 275 (3rd Cir. 2014).

COMMERCIAL SPEECH DOCTRINE

Although truthful advertising for lawful goods or services receives some First Amendment protection, the extent of that protection is more limited when compared with political speech. While political speech is at the top of a First Amendment hierarchy of expression and while speech that fits the Supreme Court's definition of obscenity falls completely without any First Amendment protection (see Chapter 13), commercial speech lies somewhere in between.[7]

Determining what constitutes commercial speech, however, is not easy. Courts still wrestle with this threshold issue, often defining it as expression that either

- *is related solely to the economic interests of the speaker and its audience,* or
- *proposes a commercial transaction.*

In some cases it is not easy to distinguish political speech from commercial speech, as courts recently have observed.[8] But the difference is critical because it is much easier for the government to justify a law regulating commercial speech under the *Central Hudson* test (as the commercial speech doctrine sometimes is known) than it is to regulate political speech under the strict scrutiny standard. In cases involving speech transpiring in the context of promotional materials and activities (a doctor, for instance, giving a talk or seminar about a new drug), courts sometimes weigh three factors to help determine if it is commercial: (1) whether the expression is an advertisement, (2) whether it refers to a specific product, and (3) whether the speaker has an economic motivation for speaking.[9]

Two types of commercial speech receive no protection whatsoever.

Whereas commercial speech typically receives limited First Amendment protection, two types of commercial speech receive no protection whatsoever:

- **The government may ban advertising that is false, misleading or deceptive.** Much of the rest of this chapter is devoted to defining and explaining such regulation.
- **The government may ban advertising for unlawful goods and services.** This broad exception to the protection of the First Amendment was established primarily to permit the government to bar discriminatory employment advertising. It is illegal for an employer to discriminate on the basis of race or religion or ancestry or even gender when hiring employees. Help-wanted ads that offer employment to "whites" or "men only," for example, are illegal.[10] Advertisements for prostitution (an illegal service) are not protected by the First Amendment, with the Web site Backpage.com today often fighting legal battles over its "escort" ads.

7. Although the First Amendment gives limited protection to commercial speech, the Oregon Supreme Court has ruled that the Oregon Constitution gives it full protection. *Outdoor Media Dimensions, Inc.* v. *Department of Transportation,* 132 P. 3d 5 (Ore. 2006).
8. See, e.g., *Bellsouth Telecommunications, Inc.* v. *Farris,* 542 F. 3d 499 (6th Cir. 2008) (involving a law that prohibited telecommunications companies from stating separately on their customers' bills a new tax imposed by Kentucky, observing that this law "facilitates keeping consumers (and voters) in the dark about the tax and its impact on their wallets," and providing that it is "difficult to pin down where the political nature of these speech restrictions ends and the commercial nature of the restrictions begins").
9. *United States* v. *Caronia,* 576 F. Supp. 2d 385, 396 (E.D. N.Y. 2008).
10. *Pittsburgh Press Co.* v. *Pittsburgh Commission on Human Relations,* 413 U.S. 376 (1973).

Even truthful advertising for legal goods and services can be regulated, provided that the government can satisfy the three requirements outlined here.

- **The government must assert a substantial state interest to justify the regulation.** States that seek to limit advertising by doctors and lawyers will argue that the public is not sophisticated enough to evaluate many claims that might be made by these professionals, and even perfectly truthful claims could be deceptive. Protecting the public from such deception is a substantial state interest.[11] In another example, in a 2017 case the 8th U.S. Circuit Court of Appeals held that promoting responsible drinking was a substantial state interest supporting regulation under a *Central Hudson* analysis.[12]

- **Next, the government must demonstrate that the ban on advertising it has instituted will directly advance the interest outlined in the previous paragraph.** Think of the interest as a kind of goal the state is seeking to reach. Will the ban on advertising help the state reach this goal? On this element, mere speculation and conjecture that a law directly advances the government's interests and alleviates the alleged harms in a material way won't cut it. Rather, as a federal appellate court wrote in 2009, "we independently evaluate [the government's] assertion that the advertising restrictions advance the state's interest, and we rely on the valid sources of history, consensus, and common sense."[13] A Baltimore ordinance that banned outdoor advertising for alcoholic beverages in areas in which children walk to school or neighborhoods in which children play was ruled permissible because it directly and materially advanced the city's interest in promoting the welfare and temperance of minors.[14]

- **Finally, the state must show that there is a "reasonable fit" between the state interest being asserted and the government regulation.** A reasonable fit means the regulation must be narrowly tailored to achieve the desired objective, but it doesn't have to be the least restrictive means available. In 2006 a federal appellate court held that a Missouri law banning, within one mile of highways, billboard ads for sexually oriented businesses (regardless of the words or images on the billboards) was not narrowly tailored to meet the state's substantial interest in eliminating secondary effects of adult businesses (see Chapter 13 regarding secondary effects).[15] Missouri believed that by eliminating billboard ads, fewer people would visit sexually oriented businesses, thus forcing closure due to lack of customers. Although the court found evidence the law would directly advance this substantial interest, it held the law was not narrowly tailored because it "threatens criminal prosecution for the mere inclusion of the name or address of an affected business" and thus bans "an intolerable amount of truthful speech about lawful conduct."

A reasonable fit means the regulation must be narrowly tailored to achieve the desired objective, but it doesn't have to be the least restrictive means available.

11. *Bates and Van O'Steen* v. *Arizona,* 433 U.S. 350 (1977).
12. *Missouri Broadcasters Ass'n* v. *Lacy,* 846 F. 3d 295 (8th Cir. 2017).
13. *WV Association of Club Owners & Fraternal Services, Inc.* v. *Musgrave,* 2009 U.S. App. LEXIS 545 (4th Cir. 2009).
14. *Anheuser-Busch Inc.* v. *Schmoke,* 101 F. 3d 325 (4th Cir. 1996).
15. *Passions Video, Inc.* v. *Nixon,* 458 F. 3d 837 (8th Cir. 2006), petition for rehearing denied, 2006 U.S. App. LEXIS 24092 (2006).

Importantly, the court added that Missouri failed to show that "a more limited speech regulation would not have adequately served the state's interest."

In 2009 a judge entered a preliminary injunction (see Chapter 1 on equity law) in *Abilene Retail No. 30, Inc.* v. *Six* that stopped Kansas from enforcing a similar law targeting ads and billboards for sexually oriented businesses (see Chapter 13 regarding restrictions on sexually oriented businesses) along that state's highways. In ruling against the statute, U.S. District Judge Julie Robinson wrote that it "broadly sweeps [up] any speech that is 'for' a sexually-oriented business, whether or not that speech is obscene or relates to the sale of constitutionally protected products such as books and magazines." In other words, there was not a reasonable fit. Kansas Attorney General Steve Six announced in August 2009 that he would not appeal the decision. That same month, a judge in South Carolina in *Carolina Pride, Inc.* v. *McMaster* issued a permanent injunction against a similar ordinance in that state that prohibited billboards for sexually oriented businesses within one mile of public roads. This lawsuit, like the one in Kansas, was filed by the owner of a Lion's Den Adult Superstore that had several highway billboards. In striking down the South Carolina statute, U.S. District Judge Cameron McGowan noted how it was not narrowly tailored because it prohibited any and all billboards advertising adult businesses, regardless of the billboards' content or the legality of the businesses advertised.

MISSOURI RESTRICTIONS ON ALCOHOL ADVERTISING TAKE ON *CENTRAL HUDSON*

Aiming to promote responsible drinking, Missouri enacted a law and two regulations that restricted the information alcohol manufacturers, wholesalers, distributers and retailers could include in their advertisements. The law required manufacturers and wholesalers, if they chose to list any retailer in an advertisement, to exclude the retail price of the alcohol product from the advertisements, to list multiple retail businesses not affiliated with one another and to make the listing inconspicuous. One of the two regulations barred retailers from advertising price discounts in any location outside of their premises. That regulation, in other words, would prohibit "retailers from advertising information such as a two-for-one special on beer at the local grocery store, a going-out-of-business sale at a specialty wine shop, or a coupon for one free drink with the purchase of an entree at a neighborhood bar and grill." The regulation did allow, however, advertising using generic descriptions (such as "Happy Hour") and advertising all sales, promotions and discounts *within* the retail establishment itself. The other regulation at issue prohibited retailers from advertising prices below cost.

Four plaintiffs—a broadcasting industry group, a corporation operating radio stations, a winery and a commercial food and drink establishment licensed to sell alcohol—joined to file suit against Missouri's state supervisor of liquor control and state attorney general, claiming that the law and regulations "prohibit truthful, non-misleading commercial speech and restrict the free flow of truthful information to potential customers." A district court judge dismissed their case. But in January 2017, the 8th U.S. Circuit Court of Appeals in *Missouri Broadcasters*

Association v. *Lacy*[16] reversed the district court's dismissal and ruled the plaintiff's claims should be heard.

As mentioned earlier (see page 565), the 8th Circuit agreed that promoting responsible drinking was a substantial state interest, but the court held that the facts the plaintiffs alleged were "more than sufficient" to state a plausible claim that the law and regulations failed the remaining prongs of the *Central Hudson* test, and the lawsuit should thus go forward. The court, for instance, said the plaintiffs' claims "make clear the challenged provisions do little, if anything, to advance the asserted state interest. The multiple inconsistencies within the regulations poke obvious holes in any potential advancement of the interest in promoting responsible drinking, to the point the regulations do not advance the interest at all." The regulations prevent retailers from luring customers to their places of business by advertising deals, the court said, yet the state apparently is "not as concerned with retailers baiting consumers to drink excessively once they arrive," since advertising within an establishment is allowed. The court also pointed out that advertisements for Happy Hour or Ladies Night could encourage irresponsible drinking, but the regulation didn't prohibit those statements.

Moreover, the 8th Circuit ruled that the plaintiffs "included more than sufficient information to plead the challenged restrictions are more extensive than necessary," which is the final *Central Hudson* prong. The court said there are likely reasonable alternatives Missouri could have enacted that would have been less intrusive to the plaintiffs' First Amendment rights.

The 8th Circuit's ruling didn't strike down the law and regulations completely—the court merely said that, at this stage, the plaintiffs' case should go forward. But the opinion suggests the court is skeptical that the law and regulations are capable of surviving the *Central Hudson* test.

In 1995 the Supreme Court struck down a federal law that forbade brewers from listing the alcohol content on labels attached to bottles and cans of beer and malt liquor. The government justified the rule by arguing that it sought to discourage young drinkers from buying a particular beer or malt liquor simply because it had the highest alcohol content. The government's interest in reducing the amount of alcohol consumed by young people is a laudable goal, a unanimous Supreme Court said, but added that there is really no evidence this rule advances that goal. There was no government ban on the disclosure of the alcohol content in advertising for these brews, Justice Clarence Thomas wrote. Nor were there limits on the words a brewer could use to describe these products. "To be sure," Thomas wrote, "the Government's interest in combating strength wars is a valid goal. But the irrationality of this unique and puzzling framework ensures that the labeling ban will fail to achieve that end."[17]

In 2001 the Supreme Court ruled that a Massachusetts law that banned both outdoor ads and point-of-sale ads for smokeless tobacco products and cigars within 1,000 feet of

16. 846 F. 3d 295 (8th Cir. 2017).
17. *Rubin* v. *Coors Brewing Co.*, 514 U.S. 476 (1995).

public playgrounds and schools was unconstitutional.[18] The high court conceded that the state had a substantial interest in reducing the use of such products by youngsters. A majority also agreed that there was substantial evidence that tobacco sellers had boosted the sale of these products by targeting young males in their advertising. But the rule went too far; it was not a reasonable fit. Coupled with pre-existing zoning laws in the state, the rule constituted a complete ban on the communication of truthful information about smokeless tobacco products and cigars to adult consumers, Justice Sandra Day O'Connor wrote. The law also failed to distinguish among the types of signs with respect to their appeal to children as opposed to adults, or even their size. The law was simply not tailored narrowly enough to advance the state's declared interest without impeding protected speech as well.

One other dimension of the relationship between the First Amendment and advertising needs to be briefly explored. Is it a violation of the First Amendment for a newspaper, magazine or broadcasting station to refuse to carry an advertisement? No. The long-standing legal doctrine is that the First Amendment is not even implicated; such a situation is one private entity, the mass medium, refusing to do business with another private entity.* In 1996 a U.S. District Court extended this doctrine to the Internet when it ruled that a private company called Cyber Promotions had no right under the First Amendment to e-mail unsolicited promotional advertisements to America Online subscribers. The court ruled that although the Internet provides the opportunity to disseminate vast amounts of information, the Internet does not have at the present time the means to police the dissemination of that information. "We therefore find that . . . the private online service has a right to prevent unsolicited e-mail solicitations from reaching its subscribers over the Internet," Judge Weiner wrote.[19]

COMPELLED DISCLOSURE OF FACTUAL INFORMATION: HOW MUCH DOES THAT AIRPLANE TICKET REALLY COST?

Can the government, in the name of protecting against consumer deception, compel companies to include certain facts in ads they might not otherwise want to disclose? Yes, as long as the disclosure requirements are reasonably related to the government's interest in preventing deception of consumers.[20]

In 2012, a federal appellate court upheld a Department of Transportation rule affecting the price of tickets advertised by airlines. Specifically, the rule requires that the most prominent ticket price displayed on print ads and on Web sites be the *total price*, including taxes. Under this rule, airlines are free to provide an itemized breakdown (displaying to the customer the amount of the base fare,

* Broadcasters do have certain obligations related to carrying political advertising. See Chapter 16. In addition, if the publication is not privately owned but rather is published by a government entity, such as a state university's alumni magazine, there may be some situations in which advertisements cannot be rejected. See *Rutgers 1000 Alumni Council v. Rutgers,* 803 A. 2d 679 (2002).
18. *Lorillard Tobacco Co. v. Reilly,* 533 U.S. 525 (2001).
19. *Cyber Promotions, Inc. v. America Online, Inc.,* 1 E.P.L.R. 756 (1996), 24 M.L.R. 2505 (1996).
20. *Zauderer v. Office of Disciplinary Council,* 471 U.S. 626, 651 (1985).

taxes and other charges), but they may not display such individualized price components "prominently" or "in the same or larger size as the total price."

Several airlines challenged the rule on First Amendment grounds in *Spirit Airlines* v. *U.S. Dep't of Transportation*.[21] The U.S. Court of Appeals for the District of Columbia Circuit upheld the rule, reasoning that "the rule aims to prevent consumer confusion about the total price they have to pay, and it goes without saying that requiring the total price to be the most prominent number is reasonably related to that interest." The court added that the rule imposes "no burden on speech other than requiring airlines to disclose the total price consumers will have to pay. This the First Amendment plainly permits." In 2013, the U.S. Supreme Court declined to hear the airlines' appeal in the case.

COMPELLED ADVERTISING SUBSIDIES AND GOVERNMENT SPEECH

Almost anyone who has watched television advertisements during the past decade or so is familiar with trademarked slogans such as "Beef. It's What's for Dinner" and "Got Milk?" The former phrase played a pivotal role in a case decided by the U.S. Supreme Court in 2005. The case did not involve the just-discussed commercial speech test from *Central Hudson* but, instead, addressed "whether a federal program that finances generic advertising to promote an agricultural product violates the First Amendment."[22] In particular, *Johanns* v. *Livestock Marketing Association* centered on a federal statute and related order adopted in the 1980s under which the U.S. secretary of agriculture imposes a $1-per-head assessment, known as a checkoff, on all sales of cattle in the United States. Although $1 taken alone may seem small for each sale, the program has collected more than $1 billion since 1988. A large portion of that money, under the federal Beef Promotion and Research Act, has gone to finance generic advertising for the beef industry, including the "Beef. It's What's for Dinner" campaign.

Although that slogan at first may seem to benefit the entire beef and cattle industry, a number of cattle producers objected to it because, as the Supreme Court put it, "the advertising promotes beef as a generic commodity, which, they contended, impedes their efforts to promote the superiority of, *inter alia,* American beef, grain-fed beef, or certified Angus or Hereford beef." In other words, the Livestock Marketing Association and the other plaintiff in the case objected to the fact that they were compelled to subsidize speech—the generic beef advertising campaign—to which they objected. They would, instead, rather spend their own money on distinctive advertising for a particular niche or premium variety of beef, such as organically fed. The plaintiffs thus alleged a violation of their First Amendment right not to be compelled to fund speech—an unenumerated right to remain silent, as it were—with which they disagreed.

---

21. 687 F. 3d 403 (D.C. Cir. 2012), *cert. denied,* 133 S.Ct. 1723 (2013).
22. *Johanns* v. *Livestock Marketing Association,* 544 U.S. 550 (2005).

*A First Amendment
right not to be
compelled by the
government to speak
has been recognized by
the Supreme Court in
some situations.*

A First Amendment right not to be compelled by the government to speak has been recognized by the Supreme Court in some situations. For instance, in the seminal 1943 opinion in *West Virginia Board of Education* v. *Barnette,* the court held that children in public schools could not be forced or compelled to recite the Pledge of Allegiance or salute the American flag.[23] The students had a right, in other words, to not speak. The majority of the court in *Livestock Marketing Association,* however, distinguished that case and others like it on the ground that the beef situation was a compelled-subsidy case—not a true compelled-speech case—and, more important, the advertising campaign itself represented "government speech," not speech by a private person against his or her wishes. Writing for a six-justice majority, Justice Antonin Scalia wrote that "the message set out in the beef promotions is from beginning to end the message established by the Federal Government" and that the secretary of agriculture "exercises final approval authority over every word used in every promotional campaign." The majority concluded that while "citizens may challenge compelled support of private speech" they "have no First Amendment right not to fund government speech." To illustrate his point, Scalia noted that a person may not opt out of paying income taxes just because he or she doesn't agree with how the government is spending the money. In brief, the majority of the court concluded that the beef advertising is the government's own speech and, as such, does not raise First Amendment problems. The court thus ruled in favor of the federal beef promotion program and its compelled subsidization of advertising to which some cattle ranchers and farmers object.

SUMMARY American advertising is regulated by laws adopted by all levels of government. People who work in advertising must be aware of such rules as well as all other regulations (libel, invasion of privacy, obscenity) that restrict the content and flow of printed and broadcast material. Since the mid-1970s commercial advertising has been given the qualified protection of the First Amendment because much advertising contains information that is valuable to consumers. Under the commercial speech doctrine and the *Central Hudson* test, the government may prohibit advertising (1) that promotes an unlawful activity or (2) that is misleading or untruthful. It may also regulate truthful advertising for lawful activities and goods if it can prove (1) there is a substantial state interest to justify the regulation, (2) that such regulation directly advances this interest and (3) that there is a reasonable fit between the interest asserted and the governmental regulation. Advertising by professionals (attorneys and physicians) may be regulated in a more restrictive fashion.

THE REGULATION OF ADVERTISING

The regulation of deceptive or untruthful advertising is a large and difficult task policed by the advertising industry itself, the mass media and various governmental agencies. Let's briefly examine the current process of regulation.

23. 319 U.S. 624 (1943).

SELF-REGULATION

Newspapers, magazines, broadcasting stations, online service providers and other mass media all have rules that more or less regulate the kind of advertising they will carry. These guidelines spring from a variety of concerns. Sometimes the owner of the medium thinks the product that is being advertised is offensive, like NC-17 or adult movies, or condoms. Other times the ads themselves might be regarded as tasteless, like an advertisement for clothing in which the models are scantily dressed or posed erotically. It is not uncommon that an advertisement is rejected because of economic interests. A television station won't advertise a sporting event that will be telecast on a competing channel. Ads that promote illegal goods and services, that contain claims that appear to be deceptive or are not substantiated, or that unfairly trash a competitor's products might also be rejected. A Chattanooga TV station, NBC-affiliate WRCB-TV, drew criticism in June 2015 when it decided not to air a 30-second advertising spot made by Freedom to Marry, a national pro-marriage equality group. The station's president and general manager told Buzzfeed that the station turned down the ad because "it's just a very controversial and personal issue, and we just choose to not air a commercial on either side of that debate." Remember, a mass medium is permitted to reject any content it chooses, with or without a reason.

There are two key divisions of the Better Business Bureau's Advertising Self-Regulatory Council (ASRC), which was known until 2012 as the National Advertising Review Council, that provide both advice to advertisers and out-of-court methods for resolving disputes about advertisements. They are:

- **National Advertising Division (NAD):** This organization, a self-regulatory forum for the advertising industry, reviews national advertising for truthfulness and accuracy, and it provides a form of alternative dispute resolution for companies that is cheaper than litigation. For instance, in January 2017, NAD recommended that the Procter & Gamble Company modify or discontinue certain advertising claims for its "Easy Ups" training pants, including claims that Easy Ups are "the best way to potty-train" and "the easiest way to underwear." The challenge was filed with NAD by a competitor—the maker of Huggies Pull-Up training pants. NAD said that, in the absence of any supporting evidence that substantiated, or proved, the claims, NAD recommended that the claims "the best way to potty-train" and "the easiest way to underwear" "be discontinued and that the advertiser modify its advertising to avoid conveying the unsupported message that potty training is easier, and children will transition to underwear faster, with Easy Ups compared to using Pull-Ups or other brands." Proctor & Gamble announced that it would appeal NAD's finding to the National Advertising Review Board. Learn more about NAD online at http://www.asrcreviews.org/category/nad/about_nad.
- **Child Advertising Review Unit (CARU):** This agency describes itself as the children's arm of the advertising industry's self-regulation program, and it evaluates child-directed advertising and promotional material in all media to advance truthfulness, accuracy and consistency with its "Self-Regulatory Guidelines for Children's Advertising" and relevant laws. For instance, in

November 2016, CARU recommended that Dave & Buster's Entertainment, Inc., discontinue claims that children could play two video games for free—given that the offer actually required consumers to make a $10 purchase. In the commercial, while children were playing video games, a voiceover stated, "Play Luigi's Mansion and Mario Kart Arcade Grand Prix free!" A second voiceover stated, "Mario and Luigi have never been bigger or better. Play Luigi's Mansion and Mario Kart Arcade Grand Prix free!" The message "Play Both Free" even appeared in large font that covered the entire screen. But a message in small text contradicted those claims and revealed that the offer to play for "free" was valid only with a $10 Power Card purchase. CARU determined that "$10 is a substantial charge and neither the child nor an accompanying adult would consider it 'free.'" In response to CARU's finding, Dave & Buster's said that it would not run the commercial again. Read more about CARU online at http://www.asrcreviews.org/category/caru/about_caru.

As the earlier Proctor & Gamble example demonstrates, if an advertiser disagrees with a NAD or CARU decision, it can appeal to the **National Advertising Review Board (NARB).** Its Web site is found at http://www.asrcreviews.org/category/narb.

LAWSUITS BY COMPETITORS AND CONSUMERS

Yogurt-maker Chobani found itself embroiled in a legal dispute over its advertisements in 2016. Chobani's campaign highlighted the use of "bad stuff" in the yogurts of rivals Dannon and General Mills and suggested that Chobani's product—Simply 100 Greek yogurt—was a natural, healthier choice. The advertising campaign included television, print and online ads. As one example, a print ad featured pictures of Dannon Light & Fit Greek yogurt and Yoplait Greek 100 (made by General Mills) and opened with the question: "Did you know not all yogurts are equally good for you? You think you are doing something good for yourself and your family . . . by buying yogurt instead of bad stuff . . . And then you find that the bad stuff . . . is in your yogurt!" Next to a picture of Dannon Light & Fit Greek yogurt, the ad said: "There's sucralose used as a sweetener in Dannon Light & Fit Greek! Sucralose? Why? That stuff has chlorine added to it." And next to a picture of Yoplait Greek 100, the ad said: "Look, there's potassium sorbate as a preservative in Yoplait Greek 100. Potassium sorbate? Really? That stuff is used to kill bugs."

Dannon and General Mills contended Chobani's ads made false and misleading claims about their products in violation of the federal Lanham Act. They also moved for a preliminary injunction to stop Chobani from continuing the Simply 100 campaign. In January 2016, a federal judge in New York granted the injunction. Judge David Hurd said potassium sorbate is a widely used preservative that is considered safe for use in foods by the Food and Drug Administration (FDA). "It has been found to be nontoxic even in large quantities," he wrote. And he said that sucralose is a popular artificial sweetener that the FDA has determined is safe to consume and that the chlorine used to make sucralose is "distinct both chemically and practically" from the chlorine used in swimming pools. The judge ruled that Chobani is "free to continue to spread its message about the value of selecting natural ingredients. It is not, however, free to disseminate the false message that sucralose renders Dannon's products unsafe to consume . . . or that potassium sorbate renders Yoplait Greek 100 unsafe to consume."

Lawsuits for false advertising claims were relatively rare until the last quarter of the 20th century. With the rapid growth of comparative advertising (in which the advertised product is compared to a competitor's product), more and more advertisers have taken competitors to court over what they claim is deceptive and false advertising.

A SNIFF TEST FOR FALSE ADS & UNRELIABLE EVIDENCE? CAT LITTER, THE LAW AND A SMELLY SITUATION!

In 2012 a federal court in *Church & Dwight Co.* v. *Clorox Co.* issued an injunction prohibiting Clorox, the maker of Fresh Step cat litter, from airing a commercial that impliedly claimed its carbon-based litter better eliminated cat malodor than baking soda-based litter, which is sold by rival brand Arm & Hammer Double Duty Clumping Litter. The TV ad asserted "[W]e make Fresh Step scoopable litter with *carbon, which is more effective at absorbing odors than baking soda*" [emphasis added]. The ad's visuals featured two beakers, one labeled "carbon" that represented Fresh Step and the other labeled "baking soda." Each beaker, in turn, initially was shown filled with floating green gas, but the gas in the Fresh Step beaker rapidly evaporated while the gas level in the baking soda beaker barely changed. Although the ad never mentioned Arm & Hammer by name, Arm & Hammer is the only major litter brand that uses baking soda.

Church & Dwight Co. (C & D), the maker of the Arm & Hammer litter, sued Clorox under the Lanham Act, alleging the Fresh Step ad contained several misleading claims—namely, that cat litter products made with baking soda do not eliminate odors well and that cat litter products made with baking soda are less effective at eliminating odors than Clorox's Fresh Step cat litter. Clorox responded that a so-called sensory evaluation "Jar Test" it conducted proved that carbon better eliminates cat-box smells than baking soda. The test involved 11 people who sniffed different jars, some containing cat excrement (urine or feces) covered with carbon and others holding cat excrement covered with baking soda. The people repeated their sniff tests four times, and Clorox claimed that all 11 gave a malodor rating of zero (no odor) whenever cat excrement was treated with carbon.

Under the Lanham Act, a plaintiff like C & D can prove an ad is literally false if the test used to prove a claim for a product either is: (1) *not sufficiently reliable to permit a conclusion*; or (2) *simply irrelevant*. Importantly, under the doctrine of "falsity by necessary implication," a company's claims about particular aspects of its product may necessarily imply more sweeping claims about that product, and these implied claims also may be literally false within the meaning of the Lanham Act. In other words, the creators of ads should be wary of creating false implications.

United States District Judge Jed S. Rakoff concluded that Clorox's Jar Test was unreliable and, even if it were reliable, that it could not possibly support Clorox's implied claims in the Fresh Step ad about the relative merits of carbon and baking soda in cat litter. He wrote that "Clorox sealed the jars of cat waste for 22 to 26 hours before subjecting them to testing. In actual practice, however, cats do not seal their waste, and smells offend as much during the first twenty-two hours as they do afterwards. Thus, the Jar Test's unrealistic conditions say little, if anything, about how carbon performs in cat litter in circumstances highly relevant to a reasonable consumer." He added that because "the Jar Test says little about how substances perform in litter as opposed to jars, it cannot possibly support Clorox's very specific claims with regard to litter. Consequently, the necessarily contrary implication of Clorox's commercials is literally false." Furthermore, Rakoff wrote that "Clorox's own evidence acknowledges that humans, even trained panelists, report smells even when none are present. Thus, the Court agrees with C & D's expert that it is highly implausible that eleven panelists would stick their noses in jars of excrement and report forty-four independent times that they smelled nothing unpleasant."

The bottom line? The Fresh Step ad was literally false and the evidence upon which it was based was unreliable. As Judge Rakoff concluded in a parting salvo, "Clorox, cloaking itself in the authority of 'a lab test,' made literally false claims going to the heart of one of the main reasons for purchasing cat litter."

The federal Lanham Act was adopted more than 60 years ago by Congress to stop unfair competition in the marketplace. Section 43(a) creates a legal cause of action for false advertising. The statute, set forth at 15 U.S.C. § 1125, provides that a person who generates "any false designation of origin, false or misleading description of fact, or false or misleading representation of fact, which . . . in commercial advertising or promotion, misrepresents the nature, characteristics, qualities, or geographic origin of his or another person's goods, services, or commercial activities" is liable for civil damages. As originally written, the law prevented only one advertiser from making false statements about his or her own goods ("The new Escalade will get 60 miles to the gallon in city driving"). But Congress amended the act in 1989, and now the law also prohibits an advertiser from making false claims about a competitor's product as well ("The new Escalade will get 26 miles per gallon in city driving, while the Ford Focus gets only 5 miles to the gallon"). This provision of the Lanham Act was seldom used by advertisers until the 1970s. Between 1946 and 1968 the courts heard fewer than 30 false advertising cases.[24] Several developments propelled the growth of Lanham Act false advertising activity:

▪ Comparative advertising, in which an advertiser not only promotes his or her own goods but tends to disparage the product made by a competitor, became more common. Television networks had arbitrarily refused to air such commercials until urged to do so by the Federal Trade Commission, which suggested that such advertising would enhance the competitive nature of the marketplace.

24. Pompeo, "To Tell the Truth," 565.

- Advertising, as a part of the marketing mix for all products, took on more importance in the past 50 years. Sellers invested huge sums in building product images and establishing product claims. Attempts by competitors to undermine or dilute these images or claims were regarded more seriously than in the past.

- It became somewhat easier for plaintiffs to win Lanham Act false advertising suits.[25] The test of false advertising, for years a complex configuration of criteria, was reduced to basically three parts:

  1. What message, either explicitly or implicitly, does the ad convey?
  2. Is this message false or misleading?
  3. Does this message injure the plaintiff?

- The size of damage awards skyrocketed. Plaintiffs in Lanham Act cases had traditionally sought only to stop the competitor's advertising claims. It was easier to block a competitor's claims than to win damages, because in order to gain a monetary award the plaintiff had to show specific monetary loss, something that is often difficult to do given the nebulous nature of advertising claims and the forces that motivate a consumer to buy a specific brand of a product. But courts began to ease this standard at about the same time that they began to increase the size of damage awards.[26] Not only is it now possible for plaintiffs to win actual damages and court costs from the defendant, but they can also tap into any profit made by the competitor through the use of a bogus advertising campaign. On top of this, the judge can double or triple the damage award in cases of especially flagrant falsity.

In summary, competitor-versus-competitor lawsuits are now common. For instance, in March 2016, a California jury ruled in favor of Coca-Cola in a legal battle over one of its juice products. POM Wonderful LLC, a manufacturer and seller of pomegranate-blueberry juice products, sued Coca-Cola under the Lanham Act, alleging that Coca-Cola had unfairly misled consumers by marketing a pomegranate juice that actually contained hardly any pomegranate. POM Wonderful maintained that the labeling for Coca-Cola's pomegranate-blueberry juice blend—which included a pomegranate picture and the words "Pomegranate Blueberry" on the label—was misleading (even though it complied with FDA labeling requirements) because the juice contained only 0.5% pomegranate and blueberry juices and instead mostly consisted of apple and grape juice. But a unanimous jury ruled in favor of Coca-Cola, deciding that POM had not proved that the label or packaging of Coca-Cola's product misled a substantial portion of consumers.

Consumers, as opposed to competitors, have a much more difficult time in maintaining an action for false advertising. Part of the reason for this is that the Lanham Act's rules against false advertising, which are designed to remedy unfair competition, generally allow only economic competitors to sue. It is very difficult for noncompetitors to gain standing to sue for false advertising under the Lanham Act.

Consumers, as opposed to competitors, have a much more difficult time in maintaining an action for false advertising.

25. Singdahlsen, "The Risk of Chill," 339.
26. See *PPX Enterprises* v. *Audio! delity Enterprises,* 818 F. 2d 266 (1987); and *U-Haul International* v. *Jartran, Inc.,* 793 F. 2d 1034 (1986).

> ## WHO COUNTS AS A COMPETITOR IN THE LANHAM ACT RING?
>
> Lanham Act claims need to be filed by a competitor, but who counts as a competitor?
>
> The U.S. Supreme Court wrestled with who has standing (in other words, who is a competitor) to bring a false advertising claim under the Lanham Act in a 2014 case. In *Lexmark International, Inc. v. Static Control Components*,[27] the Court held that standing is determined by two factors: (1) Courts should apply a "zone-of-interests test," ensuring the law protects only those who fall within the "zone of interests" the law was intended to protect. The test in this context requires a plaintiff to allege a business or commercial injury, more specifically "an injury to a commercial interest in reputation or sales." (2) Plaintiffs must show the injury is "proximately caused" by the defendant's (the competitor's) false statements. This means that a plaintiff suing under the Lanham Act "must show economic or reputational injury flowing directly from the deception wrought by the defendant's advertising."

There is no common-law tort for deceptive advertising. As George and Peter Rosden point out in their massive compendium *The Law of Advertising,* historically, common-law courts have not been receptive to protecting consumers. "During the most formative period of common law," they write, "only a few goods in the marketplace were manufactured products so that the buyer was in an excellent position to judge for himself goods offered to him."[28] The basic slogan in those days was caveat emptor, or buyer beware.

Recently some consumer class-action lawsuits have netted huge settlements.

Recently some consumer class-action lawsuits have netted huge settlements. For instance, in February 2017, a California judge preliminarily approved a settlement of a false advertising class-action lawsuit against Guthy-Renker, the company that sells Proactiv skin care products. The lawsuit alleged that the company failed to adequately disclose the terms of Proactiv's auto-renewal subscription, did not require consumers to affirmatively agree to them and consumers were thus charged for additional products and shipments beyond their initial purchase. According to the settlement, class members—those who unknowingly agreed to Proactiv's auto-renewal subscription during a specified time frame, which amounted to more than 760,000 people—had the option to receive a cash payment or free skin care products worth at least $75. The company also agreed to more clearly and conspicuously disclose the terms of its automatic renewal or continuous service offers going forward and to require a consumer's "affirmative consent" before charging a consumer for such a service.

STATE AND LOCAL LAWS

State regulation of advertising predates federal regulation by several years. This fact is not surprising when you consider that at the time the public became interested in advertising regulation—around the early 1900s—the federal government was a minuscule creature

---

27. 134 S. Ct. 1377 (2014).
28. Rosden and Rosden, *The Law of Advertising.*

relative to its present size. Harry Nims, a New York lawyer, drafted a model law called the **Printers' Ink statute** (it was *Printers' Ink* magazine that urged passage of the law) in 1911. Most states today have such laws. In addition, many states have what are called unfair and deceptive acts and practices statutes, which give consumers the right to seek a judicial remedy in false advertising cases. These acts are often called "Little FTC Acts," and the guidelines developed by the FTC in applying federal advertising law (discussed shortly) are used by the state courts in administering these state regulations.[29] In addition, many local governments have consumer protection laws that apply broadly to false advertising.

State laws, for instance, were at the center of a class-action lawsuit in 2010 alleging that the Coca-Cola Company engaged in deceptive practices in describing the dietary benefits of VitaminWater on the label of that product. The plaintiffs filed claims under California, New York and New Jersey consumer protection statutes that broadly prohibit the misbranding of food in language that is largely identical to that found in the federal Food, Drug and Cosmetic Act (FDCA). The FDCA empowers the Food and Drug Administration (FDA) to protect the public health by ensuring that "foods are safe, wholesome, sanitary, and properly labeled" and deems a food as "misbranded" if its labeling "is false or misleading in any particular." There is, however, no right to a private cause of action under the FDCA, as the FDA is charged with enforcing it. The plaintiffs in *Ackerman* v. *Coca-Cola Company*[30] thus turned to state laws of California, New York and New Jersey to challenge claims for VitaminWater such as the phrase "vitamins + water = all you need" on the product label and the statement "specially formulated to support optimal metabolic function with antioxidants that may reduce the risk of chronic diseases, and vitamins necessary for the generation and utilization of energy from food" on the label of VitaminWater's "Rescue" flavor. U.S. District Judge John Gleeson in July 2010 refused to dismiss the majority of the plaintiffs' allegations, thus handing a victory to the Center for Science in the Public Interest in Washington, which had organized the lawsuit. In April 2016, Coca-Cola settled the lawsuit, agreeing to stop making health claims about the drink and to advertise on the labels that VitaminWater contains sweeteners. Jeff Cronin, the director of communications for the Center for Science in the Public Interest, said, "This VitaminWater settlement is good news for consumers. Coca-Cola was making all kinds of health claims on VitaminWater."

FEDERAL REGULATION

A variety of federal agencies are empowered to enforce consumer protection laws. The Federal Trade Commission (FTC) is the primary agent of the government, but clearly not the only agent. Beginning in the 1990s the Food and Drug Administration (FDA) began an aggressive campaign against a variety of companies to force them to change their labeling and promotional practices.

For instance, in 2014 the FDA issued a warning letter to Middle East Bakery, which is located in Massachusetts. After an inspection of the firm's manufacturing operations, the FDA found the bakery committed "significant" labeling violations for two of its

29. Kertz and Ohanian, "Recent Trends," 603.
30. *Ackerman* v. *Coca-Cola Co.,* 2010 U.S. Dist. LEXIS 73156 (E.D. N.Y. 2010).

products: the Market Basket brand Dairy-Free Gluten-Free Pancakes and the liveGfree brand Blueberry Pancakes. The FDA said the labeling for the Dairy-Free Gluten-Free Pancakes was false or misleading because batches of the product contained milk and therefore were not dairy-free. And the liveGfree brand Blueberry Pancakes were misbranded because although the label bore the claim "All Natural," the pancakes contained sodium acid pyrophosphate, which is a synthetic substance. Both products also failed on their labels to declare the presence of major food allergens in them. The warning letter gave the bakery 15 working days to inform the FDA of the steps it was or would be taking to correct the labels.

The FTC was created by Congress in 1914 to police unfair methods of business competition. Nearly a century later, the FTC today is the only federal agency with jurisdiction to protect consumers and maintain competition in broad sectors of the economy. It enforces the laws that prohibit business practices that are anticompetitive, deceptive or unfair to consumers, and it seeks to do so without impeding legitimate business activity. The FTC has more than 1,000 full-time employees and a budget of more than $300 million. Five commissioners, each of whom is nominated by the president of the United States to serve a seven-year term, head the FTC. One commissioner is chosen by the president to be the chairperson of the FTC. As with the structure of the Federal Communications Commission described in Chapter 16, no more than three of the five commissioners can be from the same political party. In 2015, the FTC filed 52 actions in federal court and obtained 118 orders for redress, disgorgement of profits and permanent injunctions against individuals and businesses. It also obtained 12 civil penalties in 2015. What's more, the FTC made sure in 2015 that more than 844,000 consumers received monetary redress totaling $22.3 million. For example, the FTC and the Consumer Financial Protection Bureau alleged that Green Tree Servicing, a national mortgage servicing company, harmed homeowners with illegal loan servicing and debt collection practices that involved making illegal and abusive debt collection calls to consumers and misrepresenting the amounts people owed, among other charges. The company settled the charges in 2015, agreeing to pay $63 million, with $48 million of the settlement going to affected consumers. In addition to such legal action, the FTC also educates consumers and businesses to encourage informed consumer choices, compliance with the law and public understanding of the competitive process.

In 1938 Congress adopted the Wheeler-Lea Amendment to the Trade Commission Act, which gave the FTC the power to proceed against all unfair and deceptive acts or practices in commerce, regardless of whether they affect competition. Since that time, the commission has developed into one of the nation's largest independent regulatory agencies. In addition to policing false advertising, the FTC is charged with enforcing the nation's antitrust laws and several federal statutes such as the Truth in Lending Law and the Fair Credit Reporting Act. Although the agency is located in Washington, D.C., it has 11 regional offices throughout the nation.

The history of the agency reveals that it has often been swept by the political winds of the time. For years it was known as the "Little Gray Lady on Pennsylvania Avenue" because of its timid performance. During the late 1960s and 1970s, in an era of consumer concern, the FTC showed new muscle and attacked some of the nation's largest advertisers, such as Coca-Cola and ITT Continental Baking. In the 1980s the FTC reflected the spirit of deregulation that ran throughout Washington, D.C., as Ronald Reagan entered the White House.

In the 1990s the agency renewed its aggressive efforts, instituting false advertising actions against several national advertisers, including Kraft General Foods, and bringing charges against a group of companies that were using program-length TV ads called infomercials to sell a variety of goods and services, including diet plans and treatments for cellulite buildup and baldness. The agency also brought a complaint against the tobacco industry that ultimately ended the career of Joe Camel and other cigarette advertising designed to appeal to children.

On the antitrust front, the FTC has been very active in recent years. For instance, in December 2015, the FTC challenged Staples, Inc.'s proposed acquisition of Office Depot. The FTC alleged the proposed merger would violate antitrust laws since Staples and Office Depot are the two primary competitors for large business customers buying consumable office supplies. In May 2016, the U.S. District Court for the District of Columbia granted the FTC's request for a preliminary injunction that would block the merger. And shortly thereafter, the companies announced that the merger would be abandoned. FTC Chairwoman Edith Ramirez said, "This outcome bodes well for business customers in the market for office supplies. These customers will continue to reap the benefits of direct competition between Staples and Office Depot, which would have been eliminated if the top two suppliers had been allowed to merge."

On the antitrust front, the FTC has been very active in recent years.

Privacy on the Internet—in particular, companies and advertisers tracking and monitoring the Web sites consumers visit—is now a major concern of the FTC. In 2011, the FTC considered a preliminary staff report called "Protecting Consumer Privacy in an Era of Rapid Change: a Proposed Framework for Businesses and Policy Makers." The report proposed a framework to balance the privacy interests of consumers with innovation that relies on consumer information to develop beneficial new products and services. It suggested implementation of a "Do Not Track" mechanism—likely a persistent setting on consumers' browsers—so consumers can choose whether to allow the collection of data regarding their online searching and browsing activities. The report also criticized industry efforts to address privacy through self-regulation as too slow and having failed to provide adequate and meaningful protection.

Social media networks, online search engines and Web sites increasingly find themselves caught in the crosshairs of the FTC's efforts to protect online privacy, particularly when they make false promises. In December 2014, for instance, Snapchat settled FTC charges that the service deceived consumers (1) with promises about the disappearing nature of messages sent through the service and (2) over the amount of personal data it collected and the security measures taken to protect that data from misuse and unauthorized disclosure. In an official statement, the FTC said the settlement with Snapchat "is part of the FTC's ongoing effort to ensure that companies market their apps truthfully and keep their privacy promises to consumers." In 2012, the FTC accepted a final settlement with Facebook that centered on allegations that the social network deceived users by telling them their information on Facebook could be kept private, yet Facebook repeatedly allowed it to be shared and made public. Among other charges, the FTC alleged that Facebook: (1) promised users it would not share personal information with advertisers when, in fact, it did share such information; (2) claimed that when users deactivated or deleted their accounts, their photos and videos would be inaccessible when, in fact, Facebook allowed access to the content; (3) represented that the third-party apps that users installed would have access only to user information that they needed to operate when, in fact, the apps could access nearly all of users' personal data, including data the apps did not need; and (4) made important, retroactive changes to its privacy practices without obtaining users' consent.

The final agreement and consent order between the FTC and Facebook required Facebook to: (1) provide consumers with clear and prominent notice and obtain their express consent before sharing their information beyond their privacy settings; (2) maintain a comprehensive privacy program to protect consumers' information; and (3) have biennial privacy audits conducted of its practices by an independent third party, with those reports being provided to the FTC. The consent order prohibited Facebook from misrepresenting in any manner the extent to which it maintains the privacy or security of any information it collects from or about consumers. In addition, Facebook now is subject to civil penalties of up to $16,000 for each violation of the order.

In December 2016, the operators of the AshleyMadison.com dating site agreed to settle FTC charges that the site deceived consumers and failed to protect users' account and profile information. The site has members from almost 50 countries around the world. The FTC alleged that the site lured customers, including almost 20 million Americans, with fake profiles of women in an attempt to convert those customers into paid members. Only paying members can use all of the site's features, such as sending messages and virtual gifts. The site also ensured users that their personal information was private and securely protected. But it turns out the site's security was sloppy, and in August 2015, hackers who had breached the site's network published profile, account security and billing information for millions of users, including those who had previously paid $19 for a service the site said was supposed to have deleted their data from the network. "This case represents one of the largest data breaches that the FTC has investigated to date, implicating 36 million individuals worldwide," the FTC chairwoman said. The FTC settlement required the operators of the site to implement a comprehensive data-security program and to pay a total of $1.6 million.

FACIAL RECOGNITION, PRIVACY AND THE FTC: GET YOUR DIGITAL HANDS OFF OF MY FACE!

Illustrating the FTC's interests in both the Internet and online privacy, the commission in 2012 released a report called "Facing Facts: Best Practices for Common Uses of Facial Recognition Technologies." Facial recognition technology is used in things such as "tagging" individuals in online photographs. Perhaps more sinisterly, the report notes that "companies can use the technology to compare individuals' facial characteristics across different images in order to identify them. In this application, an image of an individual is matched with another image of the same individual. If the face in either of the two images is identified—that is, the name of the individual is known—then, in addition to being able to demonstrate a match between two faces, the technology can be used to identify previously anonymous faces."

Although only setting forth voluntary recommendations (rather than binding laws), the 2012 report suggests, among other things, that companies using facial recognition technology "maintain reasonable data security protections for consumers' images and the biometric information collected from those images to enable facial recognition" and that they "establish and maintain appropriate retention and disposal practices for the consumer images and biometric data that they collect." The complete report is online at http://www.ftc.gov /os/2012/10/121022facialtechrpt.pdf.

Telemarketing

The FTC initiated in 2003 one of its most popular and well-used programs—the National Do Not Call Registry that allows people to block the calls of telemarketers. The registry, however, would also prove controversial. In particular, several telemarketing agencies filed lawsuits in 2003 against the FTC, alleging that it was beyond the scope of the FTC's jurisdiction to adopt the National Do Not Call Registry and claiming that the registry violated the First Amendment right of free speech of advertisers who use telemarketing.

In 2004 the U.S. Court of Appeals for the 10th Circuit upheld the National Do Not Call Registry in *Mainstream Marketing Services, Inc.* v. *Federal Trade Commission.*[31] In concluding that the registry did not violate the First Amendment free speech rights of telemarketers, the appellate court applied the commercial speech doctrine and *Central Hudson* test (see earlier in this chapter). In a unanimous opinion, the appellate court wrote that

> the government has asserted substantial interests to be served by the do-not-call registry (privacy and consumer protection), the do-not-call registry will directly advance those interests by banning a substantial amount of unwanted telemarketing calls, and the regulation is narrowly tailored because its opt-in feature ensures that it does not restrict any speech directed at a willing listener. In other words, the do-not-call registry bears a reasonable fit with the purposes the government sought to advance. Therefore, it is consistent with the limits the First Amendment imposes on laws restricting commercial speech.

The FTC contended that the registry, which is a list containing the personal telephone numbers of telephone subscribers who have voluntarily indicated that they do not wish to receive unsolicited calls from commercial telemarketers, was necessary to reduce both intrusions upon consumer privacy in the home and the risk of fraudulent or abusive solicitations from telemarketers. The government had specifically limited the reach of the National Do Not Call Registry, which already had more than 50 million phone numbers by the time the appellate court issued its February 2004 opinion, only to telemarketing calls made by or on behalf of sellers of goods or services, and not to charitable or political fund-raising calls. The telemarketers, however, argued that the exemptions for

31. 358 F. 3d 1228 (2004), cert. den., 543 U.S. 812 (2004).

political and charitable calls made the statute "underinclusive"—that to effectively serve the interests of protecting privacy and preventing fraud, the registry should also apply to political and charitable solicitations, not just to commercial sales calls. The appellate court, however, rejected the underinclusiveness argument, writing that "First Amendment challenges based on underinclusiveness face an uphill battle in the commercial speech context. As a general rule, the First Amendment does not require that the government regulate all aspects of a problem before it can make progress on any front." In other words, the government could focus its attention with the registry only on the problems caused by commercial sales calls without having to also sweep up and control problems caused by political and charitable calls.

The decision marked a victory for privacy advocates but can be seen as a blow to the free speech rights of telemarketers.

The decision marked a victory for privacy advocates but can be seen as a blow to the free speech rights of telemarketers. The U.S. Supreme Court turned back a challenge to the appellate court's ruling, thus bringing an end (at least for the time being) to telemarketers' efforts to invoke free speech arguments to have the popular ban on unwanted phone solicitations declared unconstitutional. In addition to the national registry, courts have upheld state do-not-call registries, paying favorable attention to the voluntary "opt-in" nature of the state laws (in other words, the registries apply only to individuals who sign up for them, rather than automatically applying to everyone).[32]

In 2008 legislation was signed under which numbers placed on the list remain on it permanently unless consumers specifically request a number's removal by calling 1-888-382-1222. The law originally required consumers to re-register their numbers every five years to remain on the registry. By December 2016, the Do Not Call Registry included more than 226 million active phone numbers, including both landline and wireless phones. But the system was not necessarily working well. During fiscal year 2016, the FTC received more than 5.3 million complaints regarding alleged violations of the registry, up from about 3.6 million in 2015.

There is an "established business relationship" (EBR) exception to the do-not-call provisions.

There is an "established business relationship" (EBR) exception to the do-not-call provisions that allows a company to call a consumer with whom it has such a relationship, even if the consumer's number is on the registry. An EBR exists when a consumer has purchased, rented or leased the company's goods or services within 18 months preceding a telemarketing call.

Finally, under the FTC's rules, telemarketers cannot call a person between the hours of 9:00 p.m. and 8:00 a.m. unless the person has given prior consent to such late-night, early-morning calls. Learn more about the National Do Not Call Registry by visiting the FTC's Web site at http://www.consumer.ftc.gov/articles/0108-national-do-not-call -registry. Rules governing the conduct of telemarketers are found at https://donotcall.gov /faq/faqbusiness.aspx.

The FTC, with the help of the Department of Justice, actively enforces the do-not-call rules. Businesses that violate the do-not-call regulations are subject to civil penalties

---

32. *National Coalition of Prayer, Inc.* v. *Carter,* 455 F. 3d 783 (7th Cir. 2006), which upheld Indiana's do-not-call list that allows Indiana telephone customers to add themselves to the list, and wrote that "the state's interest in protecting residents' right not to endure unwanted speech in their own homes outweighs any First Amendment interests"; and *Fraternal Order of Police* v. *Stenehjem,* 431 F. 3d 591 (8th Cir. 2005), which upheld North Dakota's do-not-call registry as a statute that "significantly furthers the state's interest in residential privacy."

of up to $16,000 per individual violation. By 2010, the FTC had brought more than 60 telemarketing cases alleging do-not-call violations. Forty-eight of those cases were resolved with court orders that cumulatively required payment of nearly $21 million in civil penalties and $12 million in redress or disgorgement of profits.

In 2009 the FTC banned so-called robocalls (those annoying prerecorded commercial telemarketing calls to consumers) unless the telemarketing company has obtained written permission from a consumer to receive such calls. Sellers and telemarketers that transmit such messages to consumers that haven't granted permission to accept them face penalties of up to $16,000 per call.

In 2009, the FTC banned so-called robocalls.

Robocalls are illegal even if the number dialed is not on the Do Not Call Registry. In fact, the only lawful sales robocalls are ones where consumers have stated in writing that they want to receive them from the company in question. In addition, political robocalls and those from charities seeking donations are permissible.

In March 2016, the FTC went after an Orlando-based telemarketing company that the FTC found was making millions of illegal robocalls and calls to numbers on the National Do Not Call Registry to pitch vacation packages. The company had used automated dialing machines to place millions of calls that played pre-recorded messages. The FTC permanently banned the company from robocalling consumers and also imposed a $1.2 million penalty—though the company claimed it was only able to pay $19,000. The FTC said if the company was later found to have misrepresented its financial condition, then it would have to pay more.

Finally, the FTC has offered this sage but simple piece of advice to anyone receiving a robocall: "Hang up the phone. Don't press 1 to speak to a live operator and don't press any other number to get your number off the list. If you respond by pressing any number, it will probably just lead to more robocalls."

REGULATING JUNK E-MAIL AND SPAM

One of the most pervasive and annoying forms of advertising today is on the Internet. Almost everyone who uses electronic mail has received unsolicited commercial advertising known as "spam." Without a filter or other form of protection on one's computer or e-mail system, spam can clutter an online mailbox. What's more, spam frequently takes the form of sexually explicit advertisements that may be both unwanted by, and offensive to, its recipients. On the other hand, to the extent that spam pertains to a lawful product and is neither false nor deceptive, it constitutes commercial speech protected by the First Amendment. Spam also represents an economically efficient and inexpensive way of marketing one's product or service.

To address the negative aspects of spam, Congress passed and President George W. Bush signed into law in 2003 the CAN-SPAM Act.[33] The act's title represents a tortured acronym for a bill officially called the "Controlling the Assault of Non-Solicited Pornography and Marketing Act of 2003." It applies to "commercial electronic mail messages" that have as their "primary purpose" the "commercial advertisement or promotion of a commercial product or service."

33. 15 U.S.C. § 7701 et seq. (2004).

In an excellent article on the CAN-SPAM Act,[34] attorneys Glenn B. Manishin and Stephanie A. Joyce identify five specific components of the law:

1. **False/Misleading Messages:** Commercial e-mail messages that include "materially false or misleading" header information or deceptive subject lines are prohibited.

2. **Functioning Return Address and Opt-Out Mechanism:** All commercial e-mail messages must contain either a functioning return address or an Internet-based reply "opt-out" mechanism for at least 30 days after transmission of a message.

3. **10-Day Prohibition Period:** Spam senders are barred from transmitting commercial e-mail messages to any recipient after 10 business days following the exercise by the recipient of his or her right to opt out of future commercial e-mail messages.

4. **Disclosure Requirements:** All commercial e-mail messages must disclose three specific items of content: (a) a clear and conspicuous identification of the message as an "advertisement or solicitation," (b) a notice of the "opt-out" mechanism and (c) a "valid physical postal address." All commercial e-mail "that includes sexually oriented material" must also include a warning label on the subject line. To implement this provision, the FTC in 2004 adopted a rule requiring spammers who send sexually oriented material to include the warning "SEXUALLY-EXPLICIT:" in the e-mail subject line or face fines for violations of federal law.[35] In addition, the matter in the spam e-mail message that is initially viewable when it is opened cannot include any sexually oriented material.

5. **Aggravated Violations:** The act proscribes as "aggravated violations," warranting additional civil and commercial penalties, (a) e-mail "harvesting" or the knowing use of harvested addresses, (b) the automated creation of multiple e-mail accounts used for commercial e-mail and (c) the use of unauthorized relays for commercial e-mail messages.

In 2008 the FTC clarified that the "valid physical postal address" that must be disclosed by the sender of commercial e-mail messages can be either a registered post office box or a private mailbox established under U.S. Postal Service regulations. In addition, the FTC made it clear that the "opt-out" mechanism used by a commercial sender cannot require a recipient to take any steps other than sending a reply e-mail message or visiting a single Internet Web page to opt out of receiving future e-mail from that sender.

The CAN-SPAM Act does not provide for a private legal cause of action.

The CAN-SPAM Act does not provide for a private legal cause of action or remedy for spam recipients. Instead, the FTC enforces the law, with help from the Justice Department and the FBI. For instance, in 2011 the FTC filed a complaint in federal court in California against Phillip A. Flora alleging that Flora, of Huntington Beach, Calif., had sent more than five million unauthorized and unsolicited commercial electronic text messages (text message spam) advertising loan modification and debt relief programs to the mobile tele-

---

34. Manishin and Joyce, "Current Spam Law & Policy."
35. 16 C.F.R. 316 (2004).

phones and other wireless devices of consumers throughout the United States. The texts were designed to misleadingly appear as if they had been sent by a federal government agency, as they included a Web address of "loanmod-gov.net" where people could respond (the term "gov," when used in the suffix, or "top-level" domain part of a Web site address, indicates that the Web site is operated by a federal, state or local governmental entity). Flora ignored an FTC order banning him from sending spam text messages, and he instead got involved in a different text message spamming operation, sending more than 29 million text messages to consumers promising "free" $1,000 Walmart and Best Buy gift cards. In May 2014, the FTC found him in contempt for violating the first order and ordered him to pay almost $150,000 for his involvement in the gift card scam.

In another example, in June 2016, the FTC charged a Florida-based marketing operation with sending consumers illegal spam e-mail in an attempt to sell "bogus" weight-loss products that used false celebrity endorsements. The FTC said the e-mails were sent from hacked e-mail accounts, which made it appear to consumers that the e-mails came from family members, friends or other familiar contacts. The messages then tried to lure consumers into clicking on links to Web sites that deceptively promoted "unproven weight-loss products," the FTC said, such as Original White Kidney Bean. The e-mails linked to fake Web sites designed to make it look as if a consumer reporter had endorsed the products. The sites also claimed, falsely, that the products had been endorsed by celebrities such as Oprah Winfrey. The director of the FTC's Bureau of Consumer Protection said the spammers "used a variety of deceptive tactics to sell their bogus diet pills. But we have a clear message for them—we want their illegal practices to stop and we want to give people back the money they took."

Although CAN-SPAM does not provide a civil remedy for those of us who receive spam, a provider of Internet access service that is adversely affected by spamming activities on its service may bring a civil lawsuit against the spammer in any federal court in the United States seeking both a permanent injunction to stop the spamming and monetary damages for harm caused by the spam. In 2009, Facebook was granted a permanent injunction and more than $711 million against Sanford Wallace, who allegedly engaged in a spamming scheme that compromised the accounts of a substantial number of Facebook users.

Under the terms of the CAN-SPAM Act, each separate e-mail in violation of the law is subject to penalties of up to $16,000, and more than one person may be held responsible for violations. That obviously can add up very fast.

In addition to the federal CAN-SPAM Act, some states have their own statutes targeting such e-mails. In 2008, however, Virginia's law restricting unsolicited bulk e-mails was declared unconstitutional by that state's highest court, thus allowing a notorious spammer named Jeremy Jaynes, who was convicted under it, to go free (Jaynes sent more than 10,000 spam messages in 24 hours on at least three occasions).[36] The Virginia Supreme Court concluded the law was "unconstitutionally overbroad . . . because it prohibits the anonymous transmission of all unsolicited bulk e-mails including those containing political, religious or other speech protected by the First Amendment to the United States Constitution" (see Chapter 1 regarding the overbreadth doctrine). The

Some states have their own statutes targeting such e-mails.

36. *Jaynes* v. *Virginia*, 666 S.E. 2d 303 (Va. 2008).

problem with Virginia's law, in brief, was that it was not limited in scope to only commercial or fraudulent e-mails. In describing the importance of protecting anonymous noncommercial e-mails with political content, the Virginia Supreme Court cited as precedent the U.S. Supreme Court's ruling in *McIntyre* v. *Ohio Elections Commission* (see Chapter 3). The Virginia decision does not impact the federal CAN-SPAM Act, and the U.S. Supreme Court declined in 2009 to review the Virginia Supreme Court's ruling.

In addition to tackling the problem of spam, the federal government is increasingly involved in taking on another pesky form of advertising—unsolicited commercial facsimile messages. The Junk Fax Prevention Act of 2005 bans unsolicited advertisement faxes unless there is an "established business relationship" between the sender and recipient, known as an EBR exemption. If an EBR exists, then express consent of the fax recipient is not needed before a commercial fax may be sent, provided that the fax number was voluntarily given by the recipient. In 2008 the Federal Communications Commission (FCC) clarified that facsimile numbers compiled on behalf of a fax sender are presumed to be voluntarily available for public distribution if they are obtained from the recipient's own directory, advertisement or Internet site. The Junk Fax Prevention Act of 2005 also imposes an opt-out provision requirement somewhat akin to that in the CAN-SPAM Act. In particular, the first page or cover sheet of all unsolicited fax ads must include a cost-free, opt-out provision allowing the recipient to be removed from the distribution list. In 2015, the FCC clarified that the law also applies to an efax, a document sent as a conventional fax and then converted to and delivered to a consumer as an electronic mail attachment.

In February 2016, the FCC imposed a fine of more than $1.8 million against Scott Malcolm, DSM Supply and Somaticare—which the FCC collectively referred to as "the DSM Parties"—for sending 115 unsolicited advertisements to the fax machines of 26 consumers. The FCC said the junk faxes were directed primarily to health-care practitioners, "many of whom repeatedly attempted to stop the relentless barrage of unwanted and unsolicited advertisements for chiropractic products" the company was sending. The FCC imposed the maximum fine of $16,000 per junk fax for each of the 115 violations, resulting in the total fine of close to $2 million.

SUMMARY   Self-regulation by the advertising industry has increased in recent years, especially with the growth of comparative advertising. The National Advertising Division and the Child Advertising Review Unit, divisions within the Better Business Bureau, are the primary agents for this self-regulation. Such regulation is geared toward satisfying the interests of advertisers rather than consumers, however. There has also been a rapid increase in lawsuits brought by advertisers against one another under Section 43(a) of the Lanham Act. An advertiser seeking redress under this federal law can seek to stop the misleading practice and/or win money damages. Again, this law provides little relief for consumers. Laws banning false advertising exist at both the state and local levels, but tend to be applied half-heartedly. The Federal Trade Commission remains the nation's most potent weapon against false or misleading advertising.

FEDERAL TRADE COMMISSION

One of the FTC's most important responsibilities is to ensure that Americans are not victimized by unfair, misleading or deceptive advertising. Through custom and practice, the agency has defined advertising as any action, method or device intended to draw the attention of the public to merchandise, to services, to people and to organizations. Trading stamps, contests, freebies, premiums and even product labels are included in this definition, in addition to the more common categories of product and service advertising. At times a business has challenged the FTC by arguing that its particular exposition is not an advertisement but an essay or a statement of business philosophy. Rarely have these challenges been successful. Normally, what the FTC says is an advertisement is considered to be an advertisement for purposes of regulation.[37]

Normally, what the FTC says is an advertisement is considered to be an advertisement for purposes of regulation.

Does the FTC regulate all advertising? Legally, no, it cannot. But practically, it can regulate almost all advertising. Because the agency was created under the authority of Congress to regulate interstate commerce, products or services must be sold in interstate commerce or the advertising medium must be somehow affected by interstate commerce before the FTC can intervene. Although many products and services are sold locally only, nearly every conceivable advertising medium is somehow affected by or affects interstate commerce. All broadcasting stations are considered to affect interstate commerce. Most newspapers ship at least a few copies across state lines. And importantly today, the FTC's prohibition against unfair or deceptive advertising and fraudulent marketing in any medium includes the Internet, allowing the FTC to crack down on misleading online advertising.

In a nutshell, the FTC's rules against deceptive advertising break down into two critical components:

The FTC's rules against deceptive advertising break down into two critical components.

1. Advertising must be truthful and not misleading, with misleading ads sweeping up those in which relevant information is omitted, those that imply something that's not true and those in which any disclaimers or disclosures are not clear and not prominent enough for reasonable consumers to see, hear and understand them.

2. All claims made in advertisements must be substantiated such that, before disseminating an ad, advertisers must have a reasonable basis for any and all express and/or implied product claims, with claims relating to health and safety coming under even closer FTC scrutiny that typically requires proof by competent and reliable scientific evidence.

---

37. The courts are not quite this consistent in defining advertising. For instance, judges in both New York and California were asked whether statements taken from the text of a book and reprinted on promotional blurbs on the cover of the book were ads for the book or part of the text of the book. The publication involved was the *Beardstown Ladies' Common-Sense Investment Guide,* a volume that contained highly exaggerated claims for the success of a particular investing scheme. All sides agreed that the false claims in the book were fully protected by the First Amendment, but the plaintiffs in both cases argued that when the claims were reprinted on the cover of the book (and the outside of a videotape cassette box) they were advertising or commercial speech and did not enjoy the full protection of the First Amendment. The court in California said the comments were commercial speech and not fully protected. The court in New York came to the opposite conclusion. See *Keimer* v. *Buena Vista Books,* 89 Cal. Rptr. 2d 781 (1999); and *Lacoff* v. *Buena Vista Publishing Inc.,* 705 N.Y.S. 2d 183 (2000).

Undergraduate advertising majors thus are well advised when they enter the profession to remember a few simple things: Ads must tell the truth, not mislead (either by sins of omission or sins of express or implied misrepresentation) and be backed up with prior substantiation.

In the actual implementation and application of the two critical components of the FTC's rules against deceptive advertising, three key considerations emerge that are set forth in the following box and then described in greater detail.

FTC DEFINITION OF FALSE OR DECEPTIVE ADVERTISING

1. There must be a representation, omission or practice that is likely to mislead the consumer.
2. The act or practice must be considered from the perspective of a consumer who is acting reasonably.
3. The representation, omission or practice must be material.

FALSE ADVERTISING DEFINED

The court must look to the advertisement's overall, net impression.

1. **There must be a representation, omission or practice that is likely to mislead the consumer.** The commission considers the entire advertisement as well as all other elements of a transaction when making this determination. As one federal court observed in 2008, "when assessing the meaning and representations conveyed by an advertisement, the court must look to the advertisement's overall, net impression rather than the literal truth or falsity of the words in the advertisement."[38] The same court noted that an ad's meaning "may be resolved by the terms of the advertisement itself or by evidence of what consumers interpreted the advertisement to convey." It also is important to remember that an ad may mislead because it omits material information.

2. **The act or practice must be considered from the perspective of a consumer who is acting reasonably.** The test is whether the consumer's interpretation or reaction is reasonable. When advertisements or sales practices are targeted to a specific audience, such as those aimed at children or people who are elderly or terminally ill, they will be viewed from the perspective of a reasonable member of that group. Also, advertising aimed at a special vocational group, such as physicians, will be evaluated from the perspective of a reasonable member of that group. A well-educated physician might be better able to understand a complicated pharmaceutical ad than the average individual can.

   The advertiser is not responsible for every interpretation or behavior by a consumer. The law is not designed to protect the foolish or the "feeble minded," the commission has noted. "Some people, because of ignorance or incomprehension, may be misled by even a scrupulously honest claim," one commissioner noted. "Perhaps a few misguided souls believe, for example, that all Danish pastry is made in Denmark. Is it therefore an actionable deception to advertise Danish

---

38. *FTC v. National Urological Group,* 2008 U.S. Dist. LEXIS 44145 (N.D. Ga. June 4, 2008).

pastry when it is made in this country? Of course not," the commissioner noted.[39] But when an advertisement conveys more than one meaning to a reasonable consumer, one of which is false, the seller is liable for the misleading interpretation.

The commission evaluates the entire advertisement when examining it for misrepresentation. Accurate information in the text may not remedy a false headline, because a reasonable consumer may only glance at the headline. If a television announcer proclaims that a watch is 100 percent waterproof, the advertiser cannot qualify this claim in a long printed message in small type that crawls across the bottom of the TV screen while the announcer tries to sell the product.[40] Nissan Motor Corporation agreed to stop its "Nissan Challenge" promotional advertising campaign. On its face the advertising said that Nissan would give consumers $100 if they bought a Honda Accord or Toyota Camry after test-driving a Nissan Stanza. But in order to get the $100 consumers had to meet several conditions, which were not prominently noted in the advertising. Consumers had to actually buy a Honda or Toyota, take delivery of it and submit proof of purchase to Nissan within seven days of the test drive—but not on the same day as the test drive.[41] Similarly, an advertiser cannot correct a misrepresentation in an advertisement with point-of-sale information. A seller cannot advertise a vacuum cleaner as having a 100 percent money-back guarantee and then expect to qualify that claim in a tag that is attached to the product as it is displayed for sale in a store. Qualifying disclosures must be legible and understandable, the FTC has ruled.

Accurate information in the text may not remedy a false headline.

"The commission generally will not bring advertising cases based on subjective claims (taste, feel, appearance, smell)," according to the guidelines. The agency believes the typical reasonable consumer does not take such claims seriously and thus they are unlikely to be deceptive. Such claims are referred to as **puffery** and include representations that a store sells "the most fashionable shoes in town" or a cola drink is "the most refreshing drink around."

Qualifying disclosures must be legible and understandable, the FTC has ruled.

Finally, the commission has stated that when consumers can easily evaluate the product or service, when it is inexpensive and when it is frequently purchased, the commission scrutinizes the advertisement or representation in a less critical manner. "There is little incentive for sellers to misrepresent . . . in these circumstances since they normally would seek to encourage repeat purchases," a 1983 statement proclaims.

3. **The representation, omission or practice must be material.** A material misrepresentation or practice is one that is likely to affect a consumer's choice of a product. In other words, according to the commission policy statement, "it is information that is important to the consumer." The FTC considers certain categories of information to be more important than others when deciding whether a claim is material. Express claims as to the attributes of a product are always considered material. Advertising claims that significantly involve health

---

39. *In re Kirchner,* 63 F.T.C. 1282 (1963), aff'd 337 F. 2d 751 (1964).
40. *Giant Food, Inc.* v. *FTC,* 322 F. 2d 977 (1963).
41. "A Nissan Unit Will Pull Ads."

and safety are usually presumed to be material. Information pertaining to the "central characteristics of the product or service" is usually considered to be material. Information has also been found to be material where it concerns the purpose, efficacy or cost of the product or service. Claims about durability, performance, warranties or quality have also been considered material.

A STICKY SITUATION: GLUE MANUFACTURER MISLEADS WHEN IT CLAIMS PRODUCTS ARE AMERICAN MADE

In October 2016, the specialty chemical company Chemence, Inc., the manufacturer of Kwik Fix, Hammer-Tite and Krylex glue products, agreed to pay $220,000 and to stop making misleading claims that its fast-acting glues were made in the United States. The FTC alleged that the company deceived consumers by claiming on the label of the products that they were "Made in USA" or "Proudly Made in USA." The company also assisted others in deceiving consumers by distributing its marketing materials to third-party Web sites and storefronts.

The FTC found that about 55 percent of the costs of the chemical inputs to the glues were from imported chemicals. Under the company's settlement with the FTC, Chemence is prohibited from making unqualified "Made in USA" claims "for any product unless it can show that the product's final assembly or processing—and all significant processing—take place in the United States, and that all or virtually all ingredients or components of the product are made and sourced in the United States." The upshot? The FTC said that if you claim your product is made in the USA, it better actually be made here!

Demonstrations or mock-ups often become the subject of FTC inquiries, and the question of materiality is often raised. For many years a shaving cream manufacturer claimed that its product was so good that it could be used to shave sandpaper. In a TV demonstration, Rapid Shave was spread on sandpaper and then, a few moments later, the sand was shaved off. The demonstration was phony. What the demonstrator shaved was not sandpaper, but sand sprinkled on glass. The FTC argued that this advertisement was deceptive and that the claim that Rapid Shave could be used to shave sandpaper was a material representation. The Supreme Court agreed, despite the plea from Colgate-Palmolive that the product really could shave sandpaper if it was left on the paper long enough, but because the sand and the paper were the same color, a TV demonstration did not work. Hence the company had to use sand on glass.[42] The FTC also found that two demonstrations used to advertise an immersion-style kitchen mixer in a 30-minute info-mercial called "Amazing Discoveries: Magic Wand" were phony and hence misleading. The advertiser used a pineapple with the center core removed and precrushed to create the impression that Magic Wand could crush a whole fresh pineapple. The marketers also claimed Magic Wand would whip up skim milk, but they actually used a commercial dairy topping in their demonstration, the FTC said.[43]

42. *FTC v. Colgate-Palmolive Co.,* 380 U.S. 374 (1965).
43. Tewkesbury, "FTC Restricts Claims."

BUY OUR FOOD SO YOUR DOG WILL LIVE LONGER—BUT WE CAN'T PROVE IT!

In August 2016, the FTC announced that it had settled charges with Mars Petcare U.S., Inc. The FTC alleged that the company had falsely advertised the health benefits of its Eukanuba brand dog food. According to the FTC, in ads that ran on television, in print and online, the company claimed, but could not prove, that a 10-year study found that dogs could extend their lifespan by 30 percent or more if they were fed Eukanuba.

The FTC order settling the charges prohibited Mars Petcare from employing similar deceptive ads in the future. The order barred the company from making misleading or unsubstantiated claims about the health benefits of any pet food and "requires the company to have competent and reliable scientific evidence to back up any such claims." The FTC also barred the company from misrepresenting "the existence, results, conclusions, or interpretations of any study, or falsely stating that the health benefits claimed are scientifically proven."

The FTC's director of the Bureau of Consumer Protection noted that Americans spend billions of dollars on pet food. "Pet owners count on ads to be truthful and not to misrepresent health-related benefits," she said. "In this case, Mars Petcare simply did not have the evidence to back up the life-extending claims it made about its Eukanuba dog food."

MEANS TO POLICE DECEPTIVE ADVERTISING

In dealing with false advertising, the FTC's greatest enemy is the time needed to bring an action against an advertiser. Since advertising campaigns are ephemeral, the FTC often has difficulty in catching up with the advertiser before the short-lived campaign has been replaced with something else. But if time is the greatest enemy, publicity is the FTC's strongest ally. Advertisers don't like the publicity that accompanies a charge of false advertising. Bad publicity can cost a company millions of dollars. In addition, consumer reaction to the charges often results in lost sales as well.

In addition to the informal sanction of publicity, the FTC has a wide range of remedies to deal with advertising. Let's briefly look at this arsenal.

FTC TOOLS OR REMEDIES TO STOP FALSE ADVERTISING

- Guides and the Child Online Privacy Protection Act
- Voluntary compliance
- Consent agreement
- Litigated orders
- Substantiation
- Corrective advertising
- Injunctions
- Trade regulation rules

Guides and the Children's Online Privacy Protection Act

The FTC issues industry guides for a variety of products, services and marketing practices. These guides are policy statements that alert businesses to what the agency believes are permissible advertising claims or practices. For instance, in 2012, and again in 2016, the FTC sought public input on possible revisions to its "Guides for the Jewelry, Precious Metals, and Pewter Industries." These particular guides explain how to avoid making deceptive claims and, for certain products, discuss when disclosures should be made to avoid unfair or deceptive trade practices. Hundreds of such guides have been issued, including a guide on when the word "free" can and cannot be used in advertising, and guides for advertising private vocational schools, home study courses and environmental claims. The FTC's Guides, Reports and Policy Statements can be found on the FTC's Web site.

In 1997 the FTC issued a statement that laid down principles by which it would evaluate the propriety of information collection and endorsement practices on Web sites used by children. The statement says, for example, that it is deceptive for a Web site operator to represent that the personally identifiable information it collects from a child will be used for one purpose if the information will really be used for another purpose. The guide also says it is improper for Web site operators to collect personally identifiable information about children and sell or disclose this information to third parties without the consent of the parents. In 1998 those guidelines were transformed into law after Congress passed the Children's Online Privacy Protection Act (COPPA), which the FTC now actively enforces as the "COPPA Rule" to protect the privacy of children online. The FTC maintains a Web site with details about COPPA at https://www.ftc.gov/tips-advice/business-center/privacy-and-security /children%27s-privacy. One must understand that COPPA applies to Web sites directed at children and that collect personal information from them. COPPA imposes requirements on operators of Web sites or online services that are aimed at children under 13 years of age, or that knowingly collect personal information from children under 13. Among other things, COPPA requires that online operators notify parents and get their permission before collecting, using or disclosing personal information from children. It also mandates that the operators keep the information they collect from children secure, and prohibits them from requiring children to turn over any more personal information than is reasonably necessary to participate in activities on their Web sites.

COPPA applies to Web sites directed at children and that collect personal information from them.

As noted above, COPPA was adopted in 1998. Much has changed since that time in the way that digital technology can capture personal information from children under 13 years of age. Thus, in December 2012 the FTC adopted amendments to its COPPA rules to bring them up to date with mobile applications that collect "personal information" from minors on smartphones and iPads. The amendments took effect on July 1, 2013.

Among other things, the FTC updated the definition of "personal information" to go beyond traditional items (names, home addresses, screen names, telephone numbers and Social Security numbers). Personal information now also includes photos, videos and audio files that contain a child's image or voice, as well as certain types of "persistent identifiers." Persistent identifiers include things such as Internet Protocol (IP) addresses and customer numbers held in cookies that: (1) can be deployed by a Web site operator or online service to recognize a user either over time or across different Web sites and online services; and (2) are used for functions other than or in addition to supporting internal operations of the Web site or online service. Valid internal operations for which persistent identifiers permissibly may be used include things such as authenticating users and protecting their security.

As described on the FTC's Web site, the 2012 amendments also expanded the definition of an "operator" subject to COPPA to include "a child-directed site or service that integrates outside services, such as plug-ins or advertising networks, that collect personal information from its visitors." In addition, the amendments updated the definition of a "website or online service directed to children" to encompass plug-ins or ad networks that have actual knowledge that they are collecting personal information through a child-directed Web site or online service.

In addition, "verifiable parental consent" to collect a minor's personal information can now be obtained using electronic scans of signed parental consent forms; video-conferencing; government-issued identification; and alternative payment systems like debit cards and electronic payment systems that meet certain criteria.

The FTC also issued a report in early 2012 called "Mobile Apps for Kids: Current Privacy Disclosures Are Disappointing." The report was based on a survey that focused on the largest app stores, the Apple App Store and the Android Market. It evaluated the types of apps offered to children, the disclosures provided to users, interactive features such as connectivity with social media and the ratings and parental controls offered for such apps. As the title of the report suggests, the FTC was not impressed by what it found. While the survey revealed a diverse pool of apps for children that were created by hundreds of different developers, there was almost no information about the data collection and sharing on the Apple App store promotion pages and little information beyond general permission statements on the Android Market promotion pages. The report called on all members of the "kids app ecosystem"—stores, developers and third parties providing services—to play an active role in providing key information to parents. A follow-up report by the FTC released in December 2012 concluded that "little or no progress has been made" and that "parents still are not given basic information about the privacy practices and interactive features of mobile apps aimed at kids." The FTC conducted a new survey in 2015 and found that app developers were doing a somewhat better job, with more than 45 percent including a direct link to their privacy policy on their app store page (only 20 percent included a link in 2012). Nonetheless, the FTC concluded that for many kids' apps "parents still don't have an easy way to learn about their data collection and usage practices."

The FTC actively enforces COPPA. For instance, in June 2016 the mobile advertising company InMobi agreed to pay $950,000 and implement a comprehensive privacy program, which will be audited every two years for 20 years, to settle FTC charges alleging that the company "deceptively tracked the locations of hundreds of millions of consumers—including children—without their knowledge or consent to serve them geotargeted advertising." The FTC said the company was tracking consumers' locations even when consumers had denied permission to access that information. And the company violated COPPA, the FTC alleged, by collecting geolocation information from apps that were clearly directed at children—in spite of promising that it did not do that. The company's software in fact tracked location in thousands of child-directed apps without following the requirements from COPPA to get a parent or guardian's consent to collect and use a child's personal information. Under the terms of the settlement, InMobi is required to delete all information it collected from children. The InMobi case shows how the recent amendments to the law are vital in moving COPPA beyond the mere collection of information in the "old days"—where a child on a computer typed in information on a Web site directed at kids—to the mobile device era.

APPS, PERSONAL INFORMATION AND CHILDREN: A SURE PATH LEADING TO TROUBLE WITH THE FTC

In 2013 the operator of the Path social networking app agreed to pay the FTC $800,000 to settle charges; it violated the Child Online Privacy Protection Act (COPPA) by collecting personal information from about 3,000 children without obtaining their parents' verifiable consent. According to an FTC press release, Path enabled children through its apps and its Web site "to create personal journals and upload, store and share photos, written 'thoughts,' their precise location, and the names of songs" to which the child was listening. Path version 2.0 also collected personal information from a child's address book, including full names, addresses, phone numbers, e-mail addresses, dates of birth and other information, where available.

Path was also required to delete the information it had collected from children under age 13.

In 2012 the FTC updated and strengthened its COPPA rules to keep pace with evolving mobile and digital technologies. Among other things, the amendments: (1) clarified that minors' "personal information" encompasses geolocation information, photos, videos and audio files that include their images or voices; and (2) expanded the definition of a "website or online service directed to children" under the age of 13 years to sweep up outside services such as plug-ins and ad networks that have actual knowledge they are collecting personal information through a child-directed Web site or online service. This second change closed a loophole that previously had allowed child-directed apps and Web sites to permit third parties to collect personal information from children through plug-ins without parental notice and consent.

The 2012-approved changes also update the ways in which "verifiable parental consent" may be obtained to include electronic scans of signed consent forms and video-conferencing.

The FTC's guides don't have the force of law; in other words, a business that violates a provision of a guide is not automatically guilty of false advertising. The FTC usually requires an advertiser to substantiate claims that go beyond those permitted by the guides or may even bring a false advertising action against the business. The guides are of great benefit, however, to honest advertisers who seek to stay within the boundaries of what is allowable under the law.

Voluntary Compliance

Industry guides apply only to prospective advertising campaigns, events that have not yet occurred. The next remedy on the ladder is voluntary compliance and is used for advertising campaigns that are over or nearly over. Imagine that a company is nearing the end of an advertising campaign in which it has advertised that its mouthwash can prevent a consumer from getting a common cold. The FTC believes that the claim is deceptive. If the advertiser has had a good record in the past and if the offense is not too great, the company can voluntarily agree to terminate the advertisement and never use the claim again. In doing this, the advertiser makes no admission and the agency no determination that the claim is deceptive. There is just an agreement not to repeat that particular claim in future advertising campaigns. Such an agreement saves the advertiser considerable legal hassle, publicity and money, all especially desirable since the advertising campaign is over or almost over. This remedy is infrequently used.

Consent Agreement

The most commonly used FTC remedy is the consent agreement, or **consent order or decree.** This is a written agreement between the commission and the advertiser in which the advertiser agrees to refrain from making specific product claims in future advertising. The advertiser admits no wrongdoing by signing such an order, so there is no liability involved. The consent agreement is merely a promise not to do something in the future. Sometimes the misleading statements are minor errors, but other times they represent a major attempt at deception. In 2009 Kellogg entered into a consent agreement with the FTC to settle charges that ads touting a breakfast of Frosted Mini-Wheats as "clinically shown to improve kids' attentiveness by nearly 20%" were false and violated federal law. The settlement bars deceptive or misleading cognitive health claims for Kellogg's breakfast foods and snack foods and prohibits it from misrepresenting any tests or studies. In 2010, the FTC expanded the consent agreement with Kellogg to prohibit the company from making claims about any health benefit of any food unless the claims are backed by scientific evidence and not misleading. Why did the FTC take this step? Because around the same time Kellogg agreed to stop making false claims for Frosted Mini-Wheats, it began a new ad campaign promoting the purported health benefits of Rice Krispies. On product packaging, Kellogg claimed that Rice Krispies cereal "now helps support your child's immunity," with "25 percent Daily Value of Antioxidants and Nutrients—Vitamins A, B, C, and E." The back of the cereal box stated that "Kellogg's Rice Krispies has been improved to include antioxidants and nutrients that your family needs to help them stay healthy." Then-FTC Chairman Jon Leibowitz remarked in a press release that "we expect more from a great American company than making dubious claims—not once, but twice—that its cereals improve children's health. Next time, Kellogg needs to stop and think twice about the claims it's making before rolling out a new ad campaign, so parents can make the best choices for their children."

Considerable pressure is placed on the advertiser to agree to a consent order. Refusing to sign the agreement will result in litigation and publicity. The publicity can do more harm to the advertiser than a monetary fine. Also, the time factor works in the advertiser's favor. Typically the advertising campaign is already over.

Considerable pressure is placed on the advertiser to agree to a consent order.

What happens to an advertiser who signs a consent decree, and then violates the provisions of the decree? When the FTC issues a consent order on a final basis, it carries the force of law with respect to future actions. Each violation of such an order may result in a civil penalty of up to $16,000.

SHOW ME THE MONEY!

When the FTC recovers money against a company for false or misleading advertisements, who gets to keep it? The good news for consumers is that they sometimes get part of their money back. For instance, in February 2017, the FTC announced that it was distributing $88 million in refunds to AT&T customers. More than 2.7 million AT&T customers were charged $9.99 per month for "premium text message services" without their consent. More than 2 million customers received bill credits from the company, and more than 660,000 former customers were mailed a check. The average refund amount was $31. Also in 2017, the FTC mailed refunds that totaled almost $2.6 million to more than 1,300 people who bought Mercola indoor tanning systems. The FTC alleged that Mercola.com made false and unsupported claims that its indoor tanning systems are safe, that they don't increase the risk of skin cancer and that they can reverse the appearance of aging. The FTC said those claims were not supported by science. As part of its settlement with the FTC, the company is also banned from selling indoor tanning systems going forward.

Litigated Order

Sometimes an advertiser doesn't want to sign a consent agreement. It may believe that the advertising claim is truthful or may simply want to hold off any FTC ban on certain kinds of product claims. In this case the commission can issue an order, usually called a **litigated order,** to stop the particular advertising claim. Staff attorneys at the FTC will issue a complaint against the advertiser, and a hearing will be held before an administrative law judge. The judge can uphold the complaint or reject it. In either case, the losing side can appeal to the federal trade commissioners for a final ruling. If the advertiser loses this final appeal before the commissioners, he or she can appeal the litigated order in federal court. Failure to abide by the provisions of a litigated order can result in the advertiser facing a severe civil penalty, as much as $10,000 per day. In the long-running (11 years) Geritol case, for example, the commission issued an order in 1965 prohibiting the J.B. Williams Company from implying in its advertising for Geritol that its product could be helpful to people who complained that they were tired and run-down.[44] The commission contended that medical evidence demonstrated that Geritol, a vitamin-and-iron tonic, helps only a small percentage of people who are tired and that in most people tiredness is a symptom of ailments for which Geritol has no therapeutic value. The J.B. Williams Co. violated the cease and desist order (at least, that is what the commission alleged) and in 1973 was fined more than $800,000. A court of appeals threw out the fine in 1974 and sent the case back to district court for a jury trial, which the advertisers had been denied the first time around.[45] The jury was to decide whether the Geritol advertisements did in fact violate the cease and desist order. At a second hearing in 1976, the FTC won a $280,000 judgment against the patent medicine manufacturer.

In 2010, LifeLock, Inc. agreed to pay the FTC $11 million to settle a federal lawsuit charging that it used false claims to promote its identity theft protection services, which

44. *J.B. Williams v. FTC,* 381 F. 2d 884 (6th Cir. 1967).
45. *U.S. v. Williams Co.,* 498 F. 2d 414 (2nd Cir. 1974).

it widely advertised by displaying the CEO's Social Security number on the side of a truck driving through the streets of a major city. The company's ads made statements such as, "By now you've heard about individuals whose identities have been stolen by identity thieves. . . . LifeLock protects against this ever happening to you. Guaranteed." As part of the settlement, LifeLock also was barred by a permanent injunction from making deceptive claims and prohibited from misrepresenting the means, methods, procedures and effectiveness of any identity theft protection service.

Sometimes filing a lawsuit is the only effective way for the FTC to pressure some companies. In 2010, the FTC filed a complaint in federal court against a Florida-based company called Alcoholism Cure Corporation alleging that it touted a phony "Permanent Cure" program for alcoholism and tricked hundreds of problem drinkers into spending thousands of dollars for a service prescribing ineffective concoctions of natural supplements, and then threatened to reveal their alcohol problems if they canceled their memberships. According to the FTC, the ads falsely boasted that the company had a "team of doctors" with expertise in addictive diseases and that the doctors would create customized cures for members. The FTC's complaint sought a permanent injunction (see Chapter 1 regarding equity law) ordering the company to stop making such claims.

Substantiation

Advertising **substantiation** has been an important part of the FTC regulatory scheme since 1972. The basis of the program is simple: The commission asks advertisers to substantiate claims made in their advertisements. The FTC does not presume that the claims are false or misleading. The advertiser is simply asked to prove the claims are truthful. The substantiation process today involves panels of experts who scrutinize advertisements and target for documentation those claims that seem most suspect. The most recent commission policy statement on substantiation was issued in 1984. Under this policy, express substantiation claims, such as "doctors recommend" and "specific tests prove," require the level of proof advertised. Otherwise, advertisers will be expected to have at least a "reasonable basis" for claims in their advertising, wrote attorney Thomas J. McGrew in the *Los Angeles Daily Journal*.[46] The degree of substantiation that will be deemed reasonable varies with "the type of claim, the product, the consequences of a false claim, the benefits of a truthful claim, the cost of developing substantiation . . . and the amount of substantiation experts in the field believe is reasonable," the policy statement said. Claims for health-related products like dietary supplements and weight-loss pills require substantiation, before the claims are made, by what the FTC calls "competent and reliable scientific evidence."

Corrective Advertising

Corrective advertising is a highly controversial scheme based on the premise that to merely stop an advertisement is in some instances insufficient. If the advertising campaign is successful and long running, a residue of misleading information remains in the mind of the public after the offensive advertisements have been removed. Under the corrective advertising scheme, the FTC forces the advertiser to inform the public that in the past it has not been honest or has been misleading.

46. McGrew, "Advertising Law."

The corrective advertising sanction was first used by the FTC in 1971 and was applied frequently during the heady consumer protection years of the 1970s. The agency has never outlined a hard-and-fast policy regarding when corrective advertising will be used. In response to a request from the Institute for Public Representation for such a policy statement, the FTC said corrective advertising may be applied:

> If a deceptive advertisement has played a substantial role in creating or reinforcing in the public's mind a false and material belief which lives on after the false advertising ceases, there is clear and continuing injury to competition, and to the consuming public as consumers continue to make purchasing decisions based on the false belief.

Since the early 1980s the corrective advertising sanction has been used sparingly by the agency. But it does still exist as a policy choice. In May 1999 the FTC ordered a giant pharmaceutical company, Novartis A.G., to run advertising correcting earlier statements that called its Doan's back-pain relievers superior to other analgesics. The agency said the company had to spend $8 million on advertising messages that include the words, "Although Doan's is an effective pain reliever, there is no evidence that Doan's is more effective than other pain relievers for back pain." The company had to make similar disclosures on its packaging for one year.[47]

Injunctions

Attorneys for the FTC can seek these restraining orders in federal court.

When Congress passed the Trans-Alaska Pipeline Authorization Act in 1973, attached to that piece of legislation was a bill that authorized the FTC to seek an injunction to stop advertisements that it believed violated the law. Attorneys for the FTC can seek these restraining orders in federal court. An injunction is clearly a drastic remedy and one that the agency has said it will not use often. Spokespersons for the FTC have said that the agency will use the power only in those instances in which the advertising can cause harm, in those cases that contain a clear law violation and in those cases in which there is no prospect that the advertising practice will end soon.

In 2004 the FTC reached a massive settlement, including a permanent injunction, in federal court with Kevin Trudeau, a prolific marketer who had either appeared in or produced hundreds of infomercials. The settlement enjoined Trudeau from appearing in, producing or disseminating future infomercials that advertise any type of product, service or program to the public, except for truthful infomercials for informational publications.[48] Trudeau agreed to these prohibitions and to pay the FTC $2 million to settle charges that he falsely claimed in nationally televised infomercials that a coral calcium product called Coral Calcium Supreme can cure cancer and other serious diseases and that a purported analgesic called Biotape can permanently cure or relieve severe pain. Lydia Parnes, then-acting director of the FTC's Bureau of Consumer Protection, said the permanent injunction "is meant to shut down an infomercial empire that has misled American consumers for years. Other habitual false advertisers should take a lesson; mend your ways or face serious consequences."

47. "Novartis Is Ordered to Fix Doan's Ads."
48. *FTC* v. *Trudeau,* Stipulated Final Order for Permanent Injunction and Settlement of Claims for Monetary Relief, Case Nos. 03-C-3904 and 98-C-016 (N.D. Ill. 2004).

To no one's surprise, a federal judge in November 2007 found Trudeau in contempt for violating the 2004 permanent injunction by misrepresenting, during yet more infomercials, the content of his book, *The Weight Loss Cure 'They' Don't Want You to Know About.*[49] Trudeau repeatedly claimed during the infomercials, which were staged to look like interviews conducted by a talk-show host with Trudeau about his book, that his diet was "easy." In fact, as U.S. District Judge Robert W. Gettleman pointed out in an opinion that called Trudeau both "one heck of a salesman" and "an ex-felon" (he had two felony convictions in the 1990s related to bad checks and credit card fraud), the diet's regimen was very complex and difficult.

In August 2008 Judge Gettleman rejected Trudeau's motion for reconsideration of the 2007 contempt finding, once again determining the infomercials violated the terms of the 2004 injunction.[50] As punishment for violating the 2004 injunction, the judge ultimately found against Trudeau in the amount of a whopping $37,616,161—the approximate amount consumers paid in response to Trudeau's deceptive infomercials. Judge Gettleman also banned Trudeau for three years from producing, broadcasting or participating in the production or broadcast of any infomercials for products, including books, in which Trudeau has any interest.

In November 2011, the U.S. Court of Appeals for the 7th Circuit in *Federal Trade Commission* v. *Trudeau*[51] upheld Judge Gettleman's $37.6 million fine. It reasoned that Gettleman had sufficiently explained how he reached that sum by multiplying the price of the book *The Weight Loss Cure 'They' Don't Want You to Know About* by the number of orders placed for it via an 800-number shown during infomercials for the book, plus the cost of shipping, less returns.

In addition, the appellate court upheld a $2 million performance bond imposed on Trudeau by Judge Gettleman. A performance bond is a sum of money that Trudeau must first post with the court before he is allowed to participate in any future infomercials promoting books or other informational publications about the benefits or performance of any product, program or service referenced in any such publication. Other courts also have upheld the imposition of such performance bonds as an acceptable method of deterring additional instances of unlawful commercial speech.

Judge Gettleman held Trudeau in civil contempt and jailed him for a year after Trudeau failed to pay any of the $37.6 million fine—even though he continued to live lavishly. Ultimately, a court-appointed receiver was able to find millions of dollars Trudeau had hidden, allowing the FTC to send partial refunds to hundreds of thousands of consumers who had bought Trudeau's book. Then in 2013 a federal jury found Trudeau guilty of criminal contempt for violating the 2004 injunction. In 2014, U.S. District Judge Ronald Guzman sentenced Trudeau to 10 years in prison for the criminal contempt charge. Judge Guzman said Trudeau had treated federal court orders "as if they were mere suggestions . . . or impediments to be sidestepped, outmaneuvered or just ignored."

Writing about Trudeau in July 2016, FTC attorney Lesley Fair said: "What's the one truth advertisers should take from the Trudeau story? That the heart and soul of the FTC's

To no one's surprise, a federal judge in November 2007 found Trudeau in contempt.

---

49. *FTC* v. *Trudeau,* 2007 U.S. Dist. LEXIS 85214 (N.D. Ill. Nov. 16, 2007).
50. *FTC* v. *Trudeau,* 2008 U.S. Dist. LEXIS 59675 (N.D. Ill. Aug. 7, 2008).
51. 662 F. 3d 947 (7th Cir. 2011).

mission is effective order enforcement. In most cases, people and companies under order implement in-house changes to prevent a repeat performance. But for those who don't, the FTC will take the steps necessary to protect consumers from recidivists. And as the Trudeau case suggests, we're in it for the long haul."

Trade Regulation Rules

In January 1975 President Ford signed the Magnuson-Moss Warranty–Federal Trade Commission Improvement Act, the most significant piece of trade regulation legislation since the Wheeler-Lea Amendment in 1938. The new law did many things, but basically it greatly enlarged both the power and the jurisdiction of the FTC. Until the bill was signed, the FTC was limited to dealing with unfair and deceptive practices that were "in commerce." The new law expanded the jurisdiction to practices "affecting commerce." The change of a single word gave the FTC broad new areas to regulate. The law also gave the agency important new power.

Three sections of the act expanded the remedies the FTC can use against deceptive advertising. First, the agency was given the power to issue trade regulation rules defining and outlawing unfair and deceptive acts or practices. The importance of this power alone cannot be overestimated. In the past the agency had to pursue deceptive advertisements one at a time. Imagine, for example, that four or five different breakfast cereals all advertise that they are good for children because they contain nine times the recommended daily allowance of vitamins and minerals. Medical experts argue that any vitamins in excess of 100 percent of the recommended daily allowance are useless; therefore, these advertisements are probably deceptive or misleading. In the past the FTC would have had to issue a complaint against each advertiser and in each case prove that the statement was a violation of the law. Under the new rules, the agency can issue a trade regulation rule—as it had done for nutritional claims—that declares that claims of product superiority based on excessive dosage of vitamins and minerals are false and misleading. If advertisers make such claims, they are in violation of the law. All the commission must prove is that the advertiser had actual knowledge of the trade regulation rule, or "knowledge fairly implied from the objective circumstances."

The advantages of the **trade regulation rules (TRRs)** are numerous. They speed up and simplify the process of enforcement. Advertisers can still litigate the question, challenge the trade regulation rule, seek an appeal in court and so forth. In most cases they probably will not go to that expense. Trade regulation rules have had a great deterrent effect, as they comprehensively delimit what constitutes an illegal practice. In the past, after the commission issued a cease and desist order, businesses frequently attempted to undertake practices that fell just outside the narrow boundaries of the order. The TRRs are much broader and make it much harder for advertisers to skirt the limitations. Finally, via TRRs the FTC is able to deal with problems more evenhandedly. An entire industry can be treated similarly, and just one or two businesses are not picked out for complaint.

The second aspect of the law that improved FTC remedies allowed the FTC to seek civil penalties against anyone who knowingly violates the provisions of a litigated order, even if that person was not originally the subject of the order. To wit: Chemical company A sells a spray paint that is toxic if used in a closed area, but the product is advertised as being completely harmless. The FTC moves against the company and issues a cease and desist order stating that in the future the firm must not advertise the product as being completely harmless. Chemical company B also sells a spray paint that has the same toxicity and is advertised the same way. If it can be shown that company B was aware of the provisions of the order against company A and continued to advertise its product as being completely safe, B can be fined up to $10,000 per day for violating the order, even though the order is not directed against B.

The third section of the law gave the FTC the right to sue in federal court on behalf of consumers victimized by practices that are in violation of a cease and desist order or by practices that are in violation of a TRR, a right that the agency has been reluctant to use.

SUMMARY

The Federal Trade Commission has the power to regulate virtually all advertising that is deceptive or misleading. To be deceptive an advertisement must contain a representation, omission or practice that is likely to mislead the consumer; the advertisement or practice must be considered from the perspective of a reasonable consumer; and the representation, omission or practice must be material. The FTC has many remedies to regulate deceptive or untruthful advertising:

1. Guides or advisory opinions that attempt to outline in advance what advertisers may say about a product
2. Voluntary agreements by advertisers to terminate a deceptive advertisement
3. Consent agreements or consent orders signed by advertisers promising to terminate a deceptive advertisement
4. Litigated orders to advertisers to terminate a particular advertising claim, failure to comply with which can result in severe penalty
5. Substantiation of advertisements, in which the advertiser must prove all claims made in an advertisement
6. Corrective advertising, in which an advertiser must admit in future advertisements that past advertisements have been incorrect
7. Injunctive power to immediately halt advertising campaigns that could cause harm to consumers
8. Trade regulation rules that can be issued to regulate advertising throughout an entire industry

THE REGULATORY PROCESS

To understand the importance of the regulatory process, students should be familiar with procedures followed in a deceptive advertising case, be aware of the kinds of advertising that can be considered deceptive and be familiar with the defenses to a charge of deceptive advertising.

PROCEDURES

The FTC does not attempt to scrutinize every advertisement that is published or broadcast. Most cases come to the attention of the agency from letters written by either consumers or competitors. Today, an individual can file a complaint online from the FTC's Web site at http://www.ftc.gov. When a complaint is received, FTC staff attorneys examine it to see if it has merit. If they can find none, the case ends. If the staff members believe there is a provable violation, then a proposed complaint, a proposed consent agreement and a memorandum are prepared for the commissioners. The commissioners then vote on whether to issue a complaint.

If the commissioners agree that the advertisement is in violation of the law, the advertiser is notified and given the opportunity to either sign the consent agreement that has been drafted or negotiate with the agency for a more favorable order. At this point one of three things can happen:

1. The advertiser can agree to sign the agreement, and the commissioners vote to accept this agreement. If this happens, the order is published and made final in 60 days.
2. The advertiser can agree to sign the agreement, but the commissioners reject it.
3. The advertiser can refuse to sign the agreement.

If either of the latter two events occurs, a complaint is issued against the advertiser, and a hearing is scheduled before an administrative law judge. The judge works within the FTC and officiates at these hearings. The hearing is a lot like a trial, only more informal. If the judge believes that there is substantial evidence that the advertisement violates the law, he or she will issue an order telling the advertiser to stop this illegal practice (this is the litigated order). The judge also has the authority to dismiss the case. At this point either side can appeal to the commissioners to overturn the ruling of the judge.

If the commissioners agree that the advertisement is not misleading or deceptive, the case ends. But if the commissioners support an administrative law judge's ruling against an advertiser, the order becomes law after it is finalized by an appellate court. The advertiser may appeal this decision in a federal court.

There are only a handful of reasons that a judge can use to overturn the commission decision.

It is difficult for courts to reverse an FTC ruling. There are only a handful of reasons that a judge can use to overturn the commission decision. The case goes to an appeals court, and there is no new finding of fact: What the FTC says is fact, is fact. The following are all instances in which a court can overturn an FTC ruling: (1) "convincing evidence" that the agency made an error in the proceedings; (2) no evidence to support the commission's findings; (3) violation of the Constitution—for example, the agency did not provide due process of law; (4) the action goes beyond the agency's powers; (5) facts relied on in making the ruling are not supported by sufficient evidence; and (6) arbitrary or capricious acts by the commission. An appeal of an adverse ruling by a circuit court can be taken to the Supreme Court, but only if certiorari is granted.

SPECIAL CASES OF DECEPTIVE ADVERTISING

A few special problems regarding deceptive advertising deserve special mention before we leave this topic.

TESTIMONIALS

All TV viewers have seen famous athletes and celebrities, as well as experts and ordinary consumers, on commercials making claims about products they supposedly use or in which they otherwise believe. The issue of truth and deception in such ads gained both public and congressional attention in 2008 when Pfizer, Inc. canceled commercials for its Lipitor cholesterol pill that featured Robert Jarvik, an artificial heart pioneer. As the *Los Angeles Times* reported, "the ads conveyed the impression that Jarvik was imparting medical advice, although in reality he's not licensed to practice medicine. They also used a body double to depict Jarvik robustly rowing across a mountain lake."[52] *USA Today* noted that although "Jarvik graduated from medical school, he's not licensed to practice medicine or to write prescriptions. He doesn't see patients. He was a consultant to Lipitor-maker Pfizer, under contract for $1.35 million. And he didn't start taking Lipitor until a month after he started doing the ads."[53] Congress held hearings on the matter.

Pfizer, Inc. canceled commercials for its Lipitor cholesterol pill.

The FTC enforces rules regarding endorsements of products and services by consumers, celebrities, experts and organizations. It defines an endorsement as any advertising message (including things such as verbal statements, demonstrations and depictions of the name of an individual or the name or seal of an organization) that consumers likely are to believe reflects the opinions, beliefs, findings or experiences of a party other than the sponsoring advertiser.[54] Under the FTC's rules, several key points emerge that must be understood by advertising students:

- Endorsements must reflect the honest opinions, findings, beliefs or experiences of the endorser and may not contain any representations that would be deceptive or could not be substantiated if made directly by the advertiser.[55]
- An advertiser may use an endorsement of an expert or celebrity only as long as it has good reason to believe that the endorser continues to subscribe to the views presented.[56]
- If an ad represents that an endorser uses the product, then the endorser must have been a bona fide user of it at the time the endorsement was given and, in addition, the advertiser may continue to run the ad only so long as it has good reason to believe that the endorser remains a user of the product.
- Ads presenting endorsements by individuals who are represented, either directly or by implication, to be "actual consumers" must use actual consumers, in both the audio and video, or else they must clearly and

52. Lazarus, "Drug Ads a Test of Doctors' Patience."
53. Editorial, "Can You Believe What You See on TV? Ask Your Doctor."
54. 16 C.F.R. § 255.0 (2008).
55. 16 C.F.R. § 255.1 (2008).
56. 16 C.F.R. § 255.1 (2008).

conspicuously disclose that the people in such ads are not actual consumers of the advertised product.[57]

▮ If an ad represents, either directly or by implication, that the endorser is an expert, then the endorser's qualifications must in fact give him or her the expertise that he or she is represented as possessing with respect to the endorsement.[58]

In 2007 the FTC requested public comment on its *Guides Concerning the Use of Endorsements and Testimonials in Advertising*, which had not been revised since 1980. In November 2008, in response to feedback, the FTC proposed several minor revisions to its guides, including, among others, clarification that when determining whether statements in an ad constitute an endorsement, it does not matter whether the statements made by an endorser are identical to or different from those made by the sponsoring advertiser. One significant change by the FTC in November 2008 was to amend its guides to make explicit

> two principles that the Commission's law enforcement activities have already made clear. The first is that advertisers are subject to liability for false or unsubstantiated statements made through endorsements, or for failing to disclose material connections between themselves and their endorsers. The second is that endorsers may also be subject to liability for their statements.[59]

The most controversial change, primarily affecting companies that advertise products, pills and diets designed to reduce weight, relates to commercials in which a real person (an endorser) claims to have lost a huge sum of weight ("I lost 40 pounds in just two weeks") and the advertiser runs a so-called disclaimer of typicality at the bottom of the commercial stating something like "Individual Results May Vary" or "Results Not Typical." Under the new guides, such disclaimers indicating that the results of the endorser are unusual or out of the ordinary would not be enough to protect the advertiser from potential liability. Instead, the FTC's revised guides say that testimonials that do not depict typical consumer experiences should be accompanied by a clear and conspicuous disclosure of the results consumers can generally expect to achieve from the advertised product or program. In other words, commercials should make clear what the typical results are (and, of course, have prior substantiation for such claims); merely stating that the results of the endorser are not typical will not cut it.

In December 2015, the FTC issued an enforcement policy pertaining to so-called "native" ads—ads that look like surrounding nonadvertising content. The FTC's policy explains that an advertisement is deceptive if it materially misleads consumers about the commercial nature of the ad. An ad cannot suggest, for instance, that it comes from a party other than the sponsoring advertiser. "The FTC's policy applies time-tested truth-in-advertising principles to modern media," said Jessica Rich, the director of the Bureau of Consumer Protection, in a press release. "People browsing the Web, using social media, or watching videos have a right to know if they're seeing editorial content or an ad."

57. 16 C.F.R. § 255.2 (2008).
58. 16 C.F.R. § 255.3 (2008).
59. Notice of Proposed Changes to the Guides and Request for Public Comments, 16 C.F.R. Part 255: *Guides Concerning the Use of Endorsements and Testimonials in Advertising*, November 2008.

BLOGGING, TESTIMONIALS AND ONLINE REVIEWS: THE FTC CRACKS DOWN

The FTC's revised 2009 guides on endorsements and testimonials make it clear that bloggers who receive cash or other in-kind payments to review a product or service must disclose the material connections they share with the seller of the product or service. The revised guides provide the following example to illustrate such a situation when disclosure by a blogger is required, as well as the obligations imposed on the advertiser who sought the blogger's endorsement.

> A college student who has earned a reputation as a video game expert maintains a personal blog where he posts entries about his gaming experiences. Readers of his blog frequently seek his opinions about video game hardware and software. As it has done in the past, the manufacturer of a newly released video game system sends the student a free copy of the system and asks him to write about it on his blog. He tests the new gaming system and writes a favorable review. Because his review is disseminated via a form of consumer-generated media in which his relationship to the advertiser is not inherently obvious, readers are unlikely to know that he has received the video game system free of charge in exchange for his review of the product, and given the value of the video game system, this fact likely would materially affect the credibility they attach to his endorsement. Accordingly, the blogger should clearly and conspicuously disclose that he received the gaming system free of charge. The manufacturer should advise him at the time it provides the gaming system that this connection should be disclosed, and it should have procedures in place to try to monitor his postings for compliance.

The bottom line, according to Lesley Fair, an FTC attorney, is that when there is a relationship between a blogger and an advertiser that would affect the credibility of the review in the eyes of consumers, the relationship should be clearly disclosed. Bloggers that receive free products or other perks with the understanding that they will promote an advertiser's product in their blogs thus fall within the purview of the revised guides, as do bloggers who are part of network marketing programs where they sign up to receive free product samples in exchange for writing about them or working for network advertising agencies.

BAIT-AND-SWITCH ADVERTISING

The FTC prohibits **bait-and-switch advertising,** which it defines as "an alluring but insincere offer to sell a product or service which the advertiser in truth does not intend or want to sell. Its purpose is to switch consumers from buying the advertised merchandise, in order to sell something else, usually at a higher price or on a basis more advantageous to the advertiser."[60] The FTC's rules state, among other things, the following:

- No ad containing an offer to sell a product should be published if the offer is not a bona fide effort to sell that product.[61]
- Advertisers cannot engage in practices that discourage purchase of advertised merchandise as part of a bait scheme to sell other merchandise, such as refusing to show or sell the product offered in accordance with the terms of the offer.[62]

In 2010, the FTC went after a high-tech form of bait-and-switch advertising when it settled charges that Ticketmaster and its affiliates used deceptive bait-and-switch tactics to sell concert tickets to consumers. The FTC alleged that when tickets went on sale February 2, 2009, for Bruce Springsteen concerts in May and June that year, Ticketmaster displayed a "No Tickets Found" message on its Web page to consumers to indicate that no tickets were available at that moment to fulfill their request. The FTC charged that Ticketmaster used this Web page to steer unknowing consumers to TicketsNow, where tickets were offered at much higher prices—in some cases double, triple or quadruple the face value. To settle the issue, Ticketmaster agreed to pay refunds to consumers who bought tickets for 14 Bruce Springsteen concerts through its ticket resale Web site TicketsNow, and to be clear about the costs and risks of buying through its reseller sites.

DEFENSES

The basic defense against any false advertising complaint is truth—that is, proving that a product does what the advertiser claims it does, that it is made where the advertiser says it is made, or that it is as beneficial as it is advertised to be. Although the burden is on the government to disprove the advertiser's claim, it is always helpful for an advertiser to offer proof to substantiate advertising copy.

Another angle that advertisers can pursue is to attack a different aspect of the government's case rather than try to prove the statement true. For example, an advertiser can argue that the deceptive statement is not material to the advertisement as a whole (that is, it will not influence the purchasing decision) or that the advertisement does not imply what the government thinks it implies. For example, to say, as Dry Ban did, that a deodorant "goes on dry" does not mean that it is dry when it is applied, merely that its application is drier than that of other antiperspirants.

ADVERTISING AGENCY/PUBLISHER LIABILITY

If you go to work at an advertising agency, you must understand that your agency may be held liable if it is an active participant in preparing a deceptive advertisement or if it knows or should know that an ad is either false or lacks substantiation. In fact, the FTC

---

60. 16 C.F.R. § 238.0 (2008).
61. 16 C.F.R. § 238.1 (2008).
62. 16 C.F.R. § 238.3 (2008).

makes it clear that an agency has "a duty to ascertain the existence of substantiation for the claims which it makes."[63]

A timely issue is the potential liability for Web sites such as Craigslist and Roommates.com for posting ads by other individuals who make statements that violate federal or state laws. In 2008 the 7th U.S. Circuit Court of Appeals held that Craigslist was protected from liability by Section 230 of the Communications Decency Act (CDA) (see Chapter 4) after it posted rental ads with discriminatory statements such as "no minorities" and "no children" that violate the federal Fair Housing Act.[64] The Fair Housing Act is regularly enforced against print newspapers that run such discriminatory ads. The 7th Circuit, however, held that Craigslist was protected by Section 230 of the CDA, which generally shields online service providers from liability when they are mere conduits (rather than publishers or speakers) for information posted by third parties. The appellate court reasoned that Craigslist "is not the author of the ads and could not be treated as the 'speaker' of the posters' words." But another 2008 opinion, this one before the 9th U.S. Circuit Court of Appeals and involving Roommates.com, reached the opposite conclusion. It held that an online roommate-matching service was not immune to liability under Section 230 of the CDA for posting information by others that violated the Fair Housing Act and California housing discrimination laws.[65] The problem for Roommates.com was that it solicited specific content from users and forced them to use pull-down menus with questions featuring specific answer options in which they could express illegal and discriminatory views. As Judge Alex Kozinski wrote for the majority of the 9th Circuit:

> Roommate both elicits the allegedly illegal content and makes aggressive use of it in conducting its business. Roommate does not merely provide a framework that could be utilized for proper or improper purposes; rather, Roommate's work in developing the discriminatory questions, discriminatory answers and discriminatory search mechanism is directly related to the alleged illegality of the site.

In brief, Roommates.com was more akin to a publisher or speaker rather than a mere conduit for the information that it posts. Craigslist, in contrast, did not solicit any content but merely provided a forum for ads.

A related issue is online classified advertising for sexual services. Several states, including Washington and Tennessee, have adopted laws targeting Web sites like Backpage.com that feature classified ads for escort services and massages that sometimes are fronts for illegal prostitution activity or for sex with minors. Tennessee's statute (Tennessee Code Ann. § 39-13-315) provided that "a person commits the offense of advertising commercial sexual abuse of a minor if the person knowingly sells or offers to sell an advertisement that would appear to a reasonable person to be for the purpose of engaging in what would be a commercial sex act." The Tennessee law made it clear that "it is not a defense that the defendant did not know the age of the minor depicted in the advertisement."

Backpage.com sued Tennessee, claiming the law would have a chilling effect on speech and that the CDA provides immunity for illegal content posted by others. In

63. *Bristol-Myers Co.,* 102 F.T.C. 21, 366 (1983).
64. *Chicago Lawyers' Committee v. Craigslist, Inc.,* 519 F. 3d 666 (7th Cir. 2008).
65. *Fair Housing Council of San Fernando Valley v. Roommates.com, LLC,* 521 F. 3d 1157 (9th Cir. 2008).

January 2013, a federal judge granted Backpage.com a preliminary injunction (see Chapter 1 regarding equity law) stopping Tennessee from enforcing the law. Judge John Nixon reasoned that "the Constitution tells us that—when freedom of speech hangs in the balance—the state may not use a butcher knife on a problem that requires a scalpel to fix." In March 2013, the judge converted the preliminary injunction into a permanent one, thus chalking up a victory for Backpage.com in *Backpage.com, LLC* v. *Cooper.*

Washington State adopted a similar law in 2012, and it also was challenged successfully by Backpage.com. In fact, Washington agreed in December 2012 to settle the case by repealing the law and to pay Backpage.com $200,000 in attorneys' fees. In announcing the settlement, Washington Attorney General Rob McKenna said that "Congress must revisit the CDA in order to close a loophole that allows companies such as Backpage to make millions advertising an illegal service that takes a particularly devastating toll on children."

The legal fights involving Backpage.com continued. In September 2015, the Washington Supreme Court refused to dismiss a case brought by three underage girls who alleged they were raped by Backpage.com customers. The girls sued the operators of Backpage.com, arguing that the site designs its advertising content to facilitate sex trafficking. In *J.S.* v. *Village Voice Media Holdings,* the Washington Supreme Court ruled the case should go forward (the site had moved to dismiss the case). The state Supreme Court said that, if the facts the plaintiffs alleged were proven true, it would show that Backpage.com (and its parent company, Village Voice Media Holdings) helped develop illegal content, which would thus make the site ineligible for CDA protection. "It is important to ascertain whether in fact Backpage designed its posting rules to induce sex trafficking to determine whether Backpage is subject to suit under the CDA," the court ruled.

But in March 2016, the 1st U.S. Circuit Court of Appeals ruled Backpage.com *did* have immunity under the CDA in a different lawsuit brought by three different plaintiffs (again, underage girls) against the site. In *Doe v. Backpage.com,*[66] the court said the plaintiffs' claims treated Backpage.com as the publisher or speaker of third-party content, which the CDA forbids. The court also said the site was not liable for failing to provide sufficient protections to users from harmful content created by others. In January 2017, the U.S. Supreme Court declined to review the 1st Circuit's decision.

Pressure on Backpage.com continued. And in January 2017, hours after the release of a critical report produced by a U.S. Senate subcommittee that had been investigating the site and alleged the site was knowingly profiting from illegal activity, Backpage.com shut down the "adult" section of its site, blaming "unconstitutional government censorship." For a time, the site put "censored" in red letters next to all of the entries in its "adult" section. "For years, the legal system protecting freedom of speech prevailed, but new government tactics, including pressuring credit card companies to cease doing business with Backpage, have left the company with no other choice but to remove the content in the United States," Backpage said in a statement. Critics, though, contend the controversial ads for sexual services instead just moved to the "dating" section of the site. In July 2017, a U.S. congresswoman referred to Backpage.com as "an awful, dark, underbelly of the world."

---

66. 817 F.3d 12 (1st Cir. 2016).

SUMMARY

Complaints against advertisers are prepared by the FTC staff and approved by a vote of the commission. Administrative law judges can hold hearings, which are somewhat like trials, to determine whether the FTC charges are valid. A U.S. Court of Appeals can review all commission orders. Advertisers need to take special care when dealing with testimonials and endorsements. The law outlaws bait-and-switch advertising, in which customers are lured to a store with promises of low prices but then are pushed by salespeople to buy more expensive products. Although ad agencies and publishers/broadcasters are generally not held liable in cases of false or harmful advertising, there are signs that the law is changing.

BIBLIOGRAPHY

Editorial. "Can You Believe What You See on TV? Ask Your Doctor." *USA Today,* 15 May 2008, 10A.

Kertz, Consuelo L., and Ohanian, Roobina. "Recent Trends in the Law of Endorsement Advertising: Infomercials, Celebrity Endorsers and Nontraditional Defendants in Deceptive Advertising Cases." *Hofstra Law Review* 19 (1991): 603.

Lazarus, David. "Drug Ads a Test of Doctors' Patience." *Los Angeles Times,* 14 May 2008, C1.

Manishin, Glenn B., and Stephanie A. Joyce. "Current Spam Law & Policy: An Overview and Update." *Computer & Internet Lawyer,* September 2004, 1.

McGrew, Thomas J. "Advertising Law: Inactive FTC, Activism in Courts." *Los Angeles Daily Journal,* 17 January 1985.

"A Nissan Unit Will Pull Ads." *The New York Times,* 10 March 1993.

"Novartis Is Ordered to Fix Doan's Ads." *The New York Times,* 28 May 1999, C16.

Pompeo, Paul E. "To Tell the Truth: Comparative Advertising and Lanham Act Section 43(a)." *Catholic University Law Review* 36 (1987): 565.

Rosden, George E., and Peter E. Rosden. *The Law of Advertising.* New York: Matthew Bender, 1986.

Singdahlsen, Jeffrey P. "The Risk of Chill: A Cost of the Standards Governing the Regulation of False Advertising under Section 43(a) of the Lanham Act." *Virginia Law Review* 77 (1991): 339.

Tewkesbury, Don. "FTC Restricts Claims by Infomercial Producers." *Seattle Post-Intelligencer,* 8 July 1993.

CHAPTER 16

Telecommunications Regulation

Volumes of federal rules govern telecommunications in the United States. A substantial number of them focus on technical rules; for example, regulations on the height of broadcast towers or the power of transmitters. This chapter focuses on two other kinds of rules: those that govern who can own and operate telecommunications facilities and those that regulate content carried over these facilities. In addition, this chapter addresses the FCC's recent efforts to regulate the Internet and broadband providers.

A PROLOGUE TO THE PRESENT

In the area of telecommunications regulation the past is an important prologue to the present. The past three-plus decades witnessed a revolution in the governance of broadcasting and cablecasting, a revolution not yet over. The changes were wrought by Congress and the Federal Communications Commission, under pressure from both the telecommunications industry and the federal courts. They are the result of a fundamental change in the way the industry is viewed, as less of a publicly oriented entity designed to serve society and more of a private business whose primary responsibilities lie with its customers (primarily advertisers) and its stockholders. To understand telecommunications regulations today it is necessary to spend a few paragraphs discussing the development of both the telecommunications industry and the government rules that shaped it.

HISTORY OF REGULATION

The regulation of telecommunications in the United States dates from 1910, shortly after radio was developed. Congress passed a law that required all U.S. passenger ships to have a radio. Two years later the federal legislature adopted the **Radio Act of 1912,** which required that all radio transmitters be licensed by the federal government and that radio operators be licensed by the government as well. In the 1920s radio grew far faster than most observers had thought possible. There were millions of listeners and far too many stations. The electromagnetic spectrum, or the airwaves, through which radio signals travel is a finite medium. As a modern freeway can hold only so many vehicles, the airwaves can hold only so many radio signals. Too many cars on the highway cause accidents and gridlock. Too many radio signals meeting in the spectrum cause similar chaos. Signals overlap and block each other. To listeners the result is gibberish. Near the end of the 1920s a reluctant Congress was forced to act once again; it adopted the **Radio Act of 1927,** a comprehensive set of rules aimed at creating order from the problem caused by too many people trying to broadcast radio signals at the same time. The new law governed who could and could not broadcast, and when they could broadcast. But it focused on the content of radio programs as well. Both the licensing and the content regulations implicated the First Amendment. Radio

The electromagnetic spectrum . . . through which radio signals travel is a finite medium.

broadcasting surely amounted to speech and press, rights guaranteed under the Bill of Rights. Surprisingly, the issue hardly arose.

The 1927 statute was substantially amended and revised seven years later when Congress adopted the **Federal Communications Act** in 1934. This law remains as the base for all telecommunications regulation today. It expanded the earlier statute to include telephones and the telegraph as well as radio. And it provided for the appointment of the Federal Communications Commission, or FCC, to regulate all these telecommunications media—the same FCC that years later was the bane of Eminem and Howard Stern's existence.

Although it is not the focus of this chapter, the FCC still regulates telephony (telephones) today. For instance, in 2014 and 2015 the FCC worked together with the Federal Trade Commission (FTC), the Consumer Financial Protection Bureau (CFPB) and states' attorneys general to go after the United States' four largest wireless companies for "cramming"—the illegal act of placing unauthorized charges on bills. The FCC estimated that cramming harmed tens of millions of households, with wireless companies billing customers for unauthorized third-party premium text messaging services. Through these cramming cases, the FCC, FTC, CFPB and states' attorneys general brought a total of $353 million in penalties and restitution against AT&T, Sprint, T-Mobile and Verizon. Almost $270 million of that total was returned to affected customers.

THE BLACKOUT RULE IS BLACKED OUT: AN OLD FCC RULE IS ELIMINATED

For almost 40 years, the FCC enforced a rule that prohibited cable operators and satellite companies (known collectively in FCC lingo as "multichannel video programming distributors" or MVPDs for short) from carrying a sporting event in a community if it was "blacked out" (i.e., not carried) by a local broadcast TV station.

Why would a game be blacked out in the first place? It all related to ticket sales or, more precisely, the lack thereof. Blackout rules were originally adopted by professional sports leagues to prohibit local TV broadcasts of home games that did not sell out. By 2014, only the National Football League continued to enforce a policy under which games could be blacked out locally if tickets were not sold out 72 hours prior to kickoff.

In September 2014, the FCC announced that it was eliminating the sports blackout rules. The agency said the rules were no longer justified in light of the significant changes in the sports industry and media landscape since the rules were first adopted. Then, ticket sales were the primary source of revenue for the NFL and most games failed to sell out. But now, the NFL is the most profitable sports league in the country, and television revenue provides the league's main source of income. Indeed, the NFL now brings in about $6 billion in television revenue per year!

THE CHANGING PHILOSOPHY
OF BROADCAST REGULATION

The broadcast spectrum is a limited transmission pathway. Not all who want to transmit radio signals can do so.

Although debate over First Amendment protection of broadcasting was never truly joined, a philosophy that justified a substantial regulation of broadcasting nevertheless existed, anchored by two seemingly immutable propositions. First, the broadcast spectrum is a limited transmission pathway. Not all who want to transmit radio signals can do so. The notion that there are a finite number of frequencies on which to broadcast and, in turn, that there are more people who want to broadcast than there are available frequencies is known as **spectrum scarcity.** Second, while private individuals might own the transmitters, the towers, the microphones and all the other paraphernalia that allow radio signals to be transmitted, the American people own the transmission path, the radio spectrum, through which the signals travel to the listener's radio set. As such, those who *use* the spectrum are bound to serve the needs of those who *own* the spectrum. So somebody had to decide who, among all those who sought to broadcast, should have that privilege. Rules were also needed to ensure that broadcasters met the needs of the spectrum owners. That is when the government stepped in, deciding who could and who could not broadcast, and establishing rules to ensure that those who did broadcast met their responsibilities to the people. The government called these responsibilities "meeting the public interest, convenience or necessity," or PICON, an acronym that became the code word to justify all the rules relating to broadcasting. And within PICON's critical concept of "public interest," the FCC traditionally has identified three major policy objectives that allegedly lead to its promotion:

PICON is the acronym that became the code word to justify all the rules relating to broadcasting.

- Competition
- Diversity
- Localism

Broadcasters who fulfill the public interest mandate are permitted to use the airwaves to reap power and wealth; those who do not are punished by fines or loss of the privilege of broadcasting. Both Congress and the Federal Communications Commission fashioned a wide range of rules to ensure the fidelity of broadcasters between the late 1920s and the 1960s. Some of the issues that were dealt with were

- who could and could not broadcast, and how long a broadcast license could be held without being renewed;
- the number of broadcast properties and other media properties, like newspapers, a single individual or company could own;
- the responsibility of broadcasters to try to divine the needs and interests of the public they served;
- rules that required license holders to broadcast information about important community issues and to make certain that all sides of these issues were represented in the broadcasts;
- rules that ensured that political candidates would have access to radio and television stations to communicate with the voters; and
- rules that limited the number of commercial minutes that could be contained in each broadcast hour.

The thrust of these rules was simple. It was thought that the broadcast industry could best serve the nation if as many different individuals as possible owned the limited number of broadcast stations and if those who were permitted to broadcast provided a broad range of material to entertain, educate and inform the listeners and viewers. The government, primarily the FCC, would ensure that these rules were followed.

But the two propositions that provided the underpinning for this regulatory philosophy turned out to be less immutable than first imagined, and the rationale for regulation began to unravel. True, the broadcast spectrum is limited. But new media forms, like cable television and the Internet, promised new pathways with unlimited transmission space. The notion that broadcasters must serve the public interest began to erode under pressure from the new economic liberalism that grew in the last 25 years of the 20th century. The idea of serving the interests of the market as opposed to serving the needs of the public developed as a dominant theme in the industry. The large corporations that owned much of the telecommunications media argued that giving listeners and viewers what they wanted to hear and watch made more sense than giving them what the government thought they should hear and see. It was also more lucrative for station owners. So capitalism and market-driven theories were in; paternalism and PICON were put on the back burner. There became a heated battle over the meaning of the term "public interest" in the PICON acronym that still exists today. Is the public interest

The notion that broadcasters must serve the public interest began to erode . . . in the last 25 years of the 20th century.

- whatever the public *wants* (whatever the public is interested in watching)?
- whatever the public *needs* (even if it is not interested in watching it)?

In addition, didn't the First Amendment bar just the sort of meddling that the government was undertaking with its myriad regulations? Ultimately the regulators, courts and even Congress bought into these ideas.

The incremental application of this new philosophy resulted in a general dismantling of broadcast regulations. These changes occurred over the past 35 or so years. In December 2007, for instance, the FCC narrowly approved the relaxation of a long-standing ban against a single company owning both a newspaper and a television station in the same city or market.[1] The new cross-ownership rule would have allowed a company to own one newspaper and one television station in the same city if (1) the city is in one of the 20 largest media markets, (2) the television station is not ranked among the top four stations in the market and (3) at least eight independent "major media voices" remain in the market. In 2011, however, the 3rd U.S. Circuit Court of Appeals threw out this relaxation of the cross-ownership rule on technical grounds because the FCC failed to meet public notice and comment requirements on the changes. In August 2016, the FCC under the administration of President Barack Obama voted to keep the cross-ownership rule in place after all.

But the FCC has modified other long-standing rules affecting ownership too, including controversial efforts in 2003 at relaxing ownership rules that also were rebuffed by a federal appellate court. Those 2003 efforts are described in the next section on the *Prometheus*

---

1. Although the outright ban on cross-ownership of a newspaper and television station in the same city had existed since 1975, the FCC had granted several waivers to companies allowing for cross-ownership on a case-by-case basis.

Radio Project case. Rules regarding the number of radio and/or television stations a single broadcaster could own and rules limiting the number of customers a multiple-system cable operator could serve were relaxed. The length of time a broadcast license can be held without being renewed was substantially lengthened. Details about most of the modified rules are outlined in subsequent sections of this chapter, but a great many regulations have simply been abandoned. Included were the following:

- Rules that restricted the major television networks from owning and syndicating television programs
- Rules that required broadcasters to formally ascertain the needs and interests of listeners and viewers so they could devise programming that best served these needs
- Rules that required broadcasters to report all sides of important public controversies in their community, the so-called fairness doctrine
- Rules that indirectly limited the number of commercial minutes that could be broadcast every hour
- Rules that barred one individual from owning both a radio and television station in one of the top 50 markets
- Rules that limited the rates a cable television provider could charge subscribers
- Rules that prohibited a television station from owning a cable system and a television station in the same market, or vice versa
- Rules that prohibited a television network from owning another television network
- Rules that required television stations to provide free reply time for opponents of political candidates endorsed by the station, and for people whose reputation or integrity was attacked by someone using the station
- Rules that prohibit a cable television system from carrying the signal of any broadcast station if the system owns a broadcast station in the same local market

THE *PROMETHEUS* DECISION AND CONTINUING FALLOUT

The FCC's 2003 attempt to loosen up ownership restrictions met with stiff judicial resistance when the new rules were challenged in 2004 before the 3rd U.S. Circuit Court of Appeals by a number of citizen-activist groups.

The case *Prometheus Radio Project* v. *FCC*[2] affirmed the power of the FCC to regulate media ownership. But, more important, it also held that "the Commission has not sufficiently justified its particular chosen numerical limits for local television ownership, local radio ownership, and cross-ownership of media within local markets." For instance, the appellate court held that while the FCC has the authority and power to repeal its ban that prohibits common ownership of a full-service television broadcast station and a daily public newspaper in the same media community (known as the television/newspaper

---

2. 373 F. 3d 372 (3d Cir. 2004), cert. den., 545 U.S. 1123 (2005).

cross-ownership rule), the numerical limits that the FCC adopted in its place in 2003 on matters such as cross-ownership of newspapers, radio stations and television stations (see pages 624–625) were not sufficiently justified by the FCC.

The appellate court instructed the FCC either to come up with additional justifications for its efforts to relax media ownership rules or to modify them. Until that time, the appellate court continued to stay the enforcement of the new rules (to put them on hold, as it were)—it previously had issued an emergency order in September 2003 preventing the FCC from enforcing the rules. As Bill Carter wrote in *The New York Times*, "frustration was the dominant emotion among media company executives" when they read the decision.[3] Those enjoined rules, for instance, would have allowed a media conglomerate to own a daily newspaper, three TV stations, eight radio stations and a cable system in the same city.

The *Prometheus Radio Project* decision, however, left intact the 39 percent "national audience reach" limit (see later this chapter) on television ownership adopted by Congress in 2004, thus allowing Viacom and News Corp., both of which already owned enough stations in 2004 to reach that cap, not to have to worry about selling off or divesting themselves of any stations. The term "national audience reach" is defined as the total number of television households reached by a single entity's stations, with UHF stations attributed with only 50 percent of the television households reached (known as a "50 percent UHF discount"). In addition to this 39 percent rule for national audience reach remaining in effect in the realm of television, there continues to be no limit on the total number of radio stations that a single entity/licensee can own on a national basis.

In 2005 the U.S. Supreme Court declined, without comment, to review the 3rd Circuit's opinion in *Prometheus Radio Project*. This meant that the 2003 changes enjoined by the 3rd Circuit would stay enjoined and thus not go into effect.

As mentioned above, in 2011 the 3rd Circuit in another *Prometheus Radio Project* case (known as *Prometheus II*) rejected the FCC's relaxation of the newspaper/broadcast cross-ownership rule in 2007 because the FCC had failed to give adequate public notice when it tried to make the change that time. In June 2012, the U.S. Supreme Court denied several petitions for writs of certiorari filed by large media companies and organizations—Tribune Co., Media General, Inc. and the National Association of Broadcasters (NAB)—asking the Court to revisit the 3rd Circuit's 2011 opinion.

The denials marked another blow to broadcasters' efforts to loosen the FCC's ownership limits and, in particular, the newspaper/broadcast cross-ownership rule that generally prohibits common ownership of a full-service broadcast station and a daily newspaper in the same market. That rule dates back to 1975 and a very different media marketplace, long before the proliferation of cable, satellite TV and the Internet.

In response to the high court's decision, an NAB representative said it was "disappointed the Supreme Court declined to review rules that limit local broadcasters' ability to compete with our national and multinational pay programming competitors." In brief, broadcasters claim the old rules make no sense in the Internet era and when new technologies allow access to news content across multiple platforms.

---

3. Carter, "Media Ruling Merely Irritates Big Owners."

The saga continued when the 3rd Circuit issued yet another opinion in *Prometheus Radio Project* v. *FCC*[4] (known as *Prometheus III*) in May 2016. This time, the plaintiffs—which included, among others, Prometheus Radio Project and the NAB—challenged the FCC's "eligible entity" definition, its 2014 rule on television joint sales agreements and its general inattention to the quadrennial review process.

In line with its obligation to promote minority and female broadcast ownership, the FCC has attempted to give preferences (including financing preferences) to certain "eligible entities"—though the FCC's definition of who counts as an eligible entity has been the cause of much consternation. The FCC has employed a revenue-based definition used by the Small Business Administration, but critics argue that definition fails to enhance minority and female ownership and have urged the FCC to adopt a new definition instead. In the first *Prometheus Radio Project* decision back in 2004, the 3rd Circuit had told the FCC it anticipated that the agency would experiment with a new definition. But, seeming exasperated, the 3rd Circuit noted in its 2016 decision that "to date the Commission still has not employed any alternative definitions for eligible entities." The court ordered the FCC "to act promptly to bring the eligible entity definition to a close."

As for the television joint sales agreements, in 2014 the FCC determined that companies were evading its ownership limits on television stations through the influence exerted by advertising contracts known as joint sales agreements. These agreements involve a contract that would allow "one station (the brokering station) to sell advertising (but not programming) on a second station (the brokered station)," the 3rd Circuit described. Arguing that the agreements allowed companies to effectively control, or have influence over, more television stations than the FCC otherwise allowed, the FCC banned joint sales agreements in 2014. But in its 2016 *Prometheus III* decision, the 3rd Circuit concluded that the FCC improperly enacted that rule without first justifying it.

Finally, as for the quadrennial review process, federal law requires the FCC to conduct a review of its rules every four years, but in its 2016 decision the 3rd Circuit said that 2006 was the last time the FCC had comprehensively reviewed all of its ownership rules, a situation the appellate court said was "troubling." The court said if the FCC did not "act quickly," wiping all of the FCC's ownership rules off the books might be justified.

In August 2016, shortly after the *Prometheus III* decision, the FCC completed a quadrennial review. A narrowly divided FCC (pitting the, at the time, three Democratic commissioners against the two Republican ones) voted to keep the existing ownership restrictions in place after all, including the cross-ownership rule (the FCC did make a minor modification to that rule by allowing an exception in the case of a "failing" newspaper). But with FCC Chairman Ajit Pai—who was appointed chairman by President Trump in early 2017—now leading an FCC where the majority of the commissioners are again Republicans, more deregulation efforts appear on the horizon. In May 2017, the FCC launched another review of its media ownership rules. In a statement announcing the review, the FCC said it was seeking "to reduce regulations that can stand in the way of competition, innovation, and investment in the media marketplace."

4. 824 F. 3d 33 (3rd Cir. 2016).

SUMMARY

Radio, the original electronic medium, was regulated almost from its inception. But until 1927 the regulation was minimal and failed to control the growing number of competitive broadcasters in a way that served the needs of the listeners. Congress passed comprehensive broadcasting rules in 1927, rules based on the assumption that because broadcasters used a valuable public resource, the radio spectrum or airwaves, they should be required to serve the public interest. This philosophy engendered the growth of broadcast regulation until the 1980s, when a competing philosophy constructed on free market economic theory began to dominate Congress and the government regulatory agencies. Under the new scheme, traditional market forces are seen as the best regulator of any industry.

BASIC BROADCAST REGULATION

FEDERAL COMMUNICATIONS COMMISSION

The 1934 Federal Communications Act provided that a seven-member **Federal Communications Commission (FCC)** regulate the broadcast industry. In 1982 Congress reduced the size of the commission to five members. Members of the FCC are appointed by the president, with the approval of the Senate, to serve a five-year term. One member is selected by the president to be chairperson. No more than a simple majority of the commission (three members) can be from the same political party. Under President Obama's watch, there were three Democrats and two Republicans serving as the five FCC commissioners. But under President Trump, the majority of the commissioners are Republicans. As was just discussed, the FCC under Chairman Ajit Pai appears set to push an agenda that favors deregulation.

BROADCAST TV CHANNELS ON THE INTERNET AND iPADS: A FAILED "AEREO" TO THE HEART OF A BUSINESS MODEL

Technological developments today are bringing immense changes to telecommunications regulation, how we watch TV and the business models upon which TV viewing was built.

In 2013, the leading over-the-air broadcast networks—ABC, CBS, NBC and FOX—fought efforts by a company called Aereo to send their broadcast signals and TV programs live to Aereo's customers to be watched on the mobile Internet devices of their choice. Consider it streamed broadcast TV on the go!

Aereo customers, who did not need a cable subscription, paid about $8 per month for the service. Customers were assigned their own private and remote miniature broadcast antenna (about the size of a dime and housed at an Aereo data center). Those antennas, in turn, were connected to the Internet so that

---

customers could watch live broadcast TV programs from the networks on their tablets, smartphones and computers. Customers also received their own remote DVR to record broadcast programs. Although initially only available in New York City, Aereo planned to expand in 2013 and 2014 to more than 20 cities.

The broadcast networks, however, asserted that the live retransmission by Aereo of their content—without their consent and without payment to them—violated their copyright interests in their programs. Typically, cable companies pay retransmission fees to broadcasters to air their content.

In 2013, the 2nd U.S. Circuit Court of Appeals ruled in favor of Aereo by a 2-1 vote in *WNET* v. *Aereo*, thus allowing Aereo to continue its business. The broadcasters, however, appealed the decision to the U.S. Supreme Court.

And in June 2014, the Supreme Court ruled in favor of the broadcasters in *ABC, Inc.* v. *Aereo*.[5] In a 6-3 decision, the Court ruled that Aereo had violated copyright laws. Writing for the majority, Justice Stephen Breyer said Aereo was "not simply an equipment provider," but it instead was acting like a cable system in that it retransmitted copyrighted content. Unlike Aereo, however, cable systems have to pay large fees to retransmit broadcast programming. Aereo would thus have to do that too.

The ruling was a deadly blow to Aereo's business model. The company filed for bankruptcy in November 2014, and Aereo's assets were pieced out and sold to the highest bidders. In March 2015, DVR maker TiVo bought Aereo's customer lists, names and other trademarks for $1 million.

Like all administrative agencies, the FCC is guided by broad congressional mandate—in this case the Federal Communications Act. The agency has the power to make rules and regulations within the broad framework of the act, and these regulations carry the force of the law. With regard to some matters, the 1934 law is very specific. For example, Section 315—the equal opportunity provision (or equal time rule)—details regulations concerning the use of the broadcast media by political candidates. But in other areas, Congress was eloquently vague. The mandate that broadcasters operate their stations in "the public interest, convenience or necessity" can mean almost anything a person wants it to mean.

A SPECTRUM SHORTAGE: CHANNEL SHARING AND REPURPOSING THE SPECTRUM

The United States faces a so-called spectrum crunch as more and more people use smartphones, iPads and other mobile wireless devices to communicate. Part of the massive Middle Class Tax Relief and Job Creation Act of 2012 was called the Spectrum Act, and it was designed to address the spectrum crunch. In particular, the Spectrum Act gave the FCC the authority to conduct incentive-based spectrum

---

5. 134 S. Ct. 2498 (2014).

auctions and required the FCC to undertake such an auction for a portion of the UHF and VHF frequency bands. As defined by the FCC, "incentive auctions are a voluntary, market-based means of repurposing spectrum by encouraging licensees to voluntarily relinquish spectrum usage rights in exchange for a share of the proceeds from an auction of new licenses to use the repurposed spectrum." The goals are to repurpose spectrum currently used for broadcast TV stations in order to: (1) address the growing demand for wireless broadband services; (2) promote innovation and investment in mobile communications; and (3) ensure the United States keeps pace with the global wireless revolution.

The auction began in March 2016, with the final rounds of bidding taking place in March 2017. The auction yielded $19.8 billion in revenue. The FCC said the auction would allow it to repurpose 84 MHz of low-band spectrum. [Megahertz (MHz) is a unit of measurement for the wireless spectrum.]

Now that the auction has ended, a 39-month post-auction transition period has begun, where some TV stations will be reassigned (what the FCC is calling "repacked") to new channels.

Powers

Congress approved the 1934 law under the authority of the commerce clause of the U.S. Constitution. States, counties and cities have no regulatory power over broadcasting stations. The federal government has *pre-empted* the law in this area (state and local authorities have retained some jurisdiction to regulate cable television and other telecommunication industries such as common carriers). Under the 1927 act, the question had arisen whether this clause meant that the federal government lacked power to regulate broadcasters whose signals did not cross state lines, stations that were not engaged in interstate commerce. In 1933 in *FRC* v. *Nelson Brothers*,[6] the U.S. Supreme Court ruled that state lines did not divide radio waves and that national regulation of broadcasting was not only appropriate but also essential to the efficient use of radio facilities.

States, counties and cities have no regulatory power over broadcasting stations.

Some communications businesses—telephone and telegraph companies, for example—have been designated common carriers by the government. A common carrier must do business with any customer who wishes to use its service. Broadcasting stations are not common carriers. They may refuse to do business with whomever they please. In addition, the commission lacks the power to set rates for the sale of broadcasting time. Broadcasting is founded on the basis of free competition among holders of broadcast licenses.

Broadcasting stations are not common carriers.

The FCC, along with the Department of Justice, also has the power to review mergers between media entities that may create powerful entities that control consumers' access to, and cost of, content. For instance, in May 2016 the FCC approved Charter Communications Inc.'s acquisition of Time Warner Cable, Inc. and Bright House Networks. Charter valued its deal for Time Warner Cable at $56.7 billion, excluding

6. 289 U.S. 266 (1933).

debt, and its acquisition of Bright House at $10.4 billion. The merger—resulting in a new company officially called New Charter—created a behemoth, turning Charter into the second-biggest broadband Internet provider in the country (after Comcast Corp.) and the third-largest pay-TV company (trailing only AT&T and Comcast). New Charter serves more than 25 million customers in 41 states.

Consumer groups criticized the merger and expressed worry that it would harm customers. But in its order approving the merger, the FCC said it "engaged in a rigorous analysis of the potential harms and benefits to ensure that the proposed transaction serves the public interest, convenience, and necessity." In the end, the FCC approved the merger with the adoption of "certain conditions" it said New Charter had to meet, including (1) that, for seven years, Charter is barred from imposing data caps or charging usage-based pricing for its residential broadband Internet service, (2) Charter agreed to refrain from telling its content providers that they cannot also sell shows online and (3) the FCC required New Charter "to undertake a build out program that will deploy high-speed broadband to 2 million more homes and a low-income broadband program for eligible households."

TURNING DOWN THE VOLUME ON LOUD TV COMMERCIALS

In December 2012, new rules took effect that require commercials to have the same average volume as the television programs they accompany, either before, during or after the programs. In brief, there can be no more volume spikes for commercials, which were commonplace (in other words, commercials were louder than the programs themselves). The rules were mandated by Congress as part of the Commercial Advertisement Loudness Mitigation Act (that's the CALM Act for those who love acronyms as much as lawmakers). The FCC adopted the rules back in December 2011, but broadcast television stations and pay TV providers were given one year to come into compliance with the law. The CALM Act allowed for smaller broadcasters to seek a one-year waiver if they could demonstrate a financial hardship in obtaining equipment necessary to comply with the rules.

Censorship Powers

Technically, the FCC lacks the power to censor broadcasters. Section 326 of the act states:

> Nothing in this act shall be understood or construed to give the commission the power of censorship over radio communications or signals transmitted by any radio station, or condition shall be promulgated or fixed by the commission which shall interfere with the right of free speech by means of radio communication.

In some instances the prohibition against censorship is applied literally, but the FCC can punish a broadcaster through a fine (called a forfeiture) or the refusal to renew a license if the broadcaster carries programming that in some way violates the law. The Supreme Court adopted this understanding of Section 326 in 1978 when it affirmed the agency's censure of radio station WBAI in New York for airing a monologue by comedian George Carlin that contained what the FCC said was indecent language.[7] Most people would call this censorship. Section 326, then, has limited meaning and is of limited value to broadcasters.

The commission has broad-ranging powers in dealing with American broadcasters. (These include the power to regulate the activities of the American broadcast networks. See *National Broadcasting Co. v. U.S.*)[8] Section 303 of the act outlines some of the basic responsibilities of the agency, which include classification of stations, determination of the power and technical facilities licensees must use and specification of hours during the day and night that stations can broadcast. The FCC also regulates the location of stations, the area each station can serve, the assignment of frequency or wavelength and even the designation of call letters. There are not many things that broadcasters can do without first seeking the approval or consent of the FCC.

Perhaps nothing better illustrates the sheer power of the FCC than the following example: In 2009 the FCC oversaw the massive switch and conversion of TV broadcasters in the United States from analog signals to digital signals.

The key powers held by the FCC, however, focus on licensing, renewal of licenses and the authority to regulate programming and program content. It is toward these powers that primary consideration is directed in the remainder of this chapter.

LICENSING

Licensing broadcasters is one of the most important functions of the FCC. In addition to getting a license for a new station, the broadcaster must also seek FCC approval for most operational changes, such as increasing power, changing the antenna height or location, selling the station, transferring ownership and so forth. For instance, Charter's aforementioned May 2016 acquisition of Time Warner Cable and Bright House Networks meant that those companies' FCC licenses had to be transferred to New Charter. Broadcasting licenses are granted to radio and television stations for eight years.

The FCC's Media Bureau is responsible for licensing radio and television broadcast services in the United States. In December 2016, the FCC announced the following totals for the number of licensed broadcast stations in each of these categories:

- 4,669 licensed AM radio stations
- 6,746 licensed commercial FM radio stations
- 4,101 licensed educational FM radio stations
- 1,384 full-power commercial (UHF and VHF) TV stations

In addition to these types of stations, the FCC grants licenses for things such as translators and boosters, as well as low-power TV stations.

Unauthorized and unlicensed stations, often known as pirate radio stations, still exist today. They are subject to a variety of enforcement actions by the FCC's Enforcement Bureau, including the seizure of equipment, imposition of monetary fines and ineligibility to hold any FCC license and criminal penalties.

7. *FCC v. Pacifica Foundation,* 438 U.S. 726 (1978).
8. 319 U.S. 190 (1943).

For instance, in 2015 the FCC fined Andrew O. Turner $15,000 for operating an unlicensed radio station on frequency 95.9 MHz, which Turner identified as "Big Station 95.9," in Broward County, Fla. Also in 2015, the FCC fined Jose Luis Hernandez $10,000 for operating an unlicensed radio station on frequency 95.9 MHz in Passaic, N.J. The FCC said it had previously warned Hernandez that operating an unlicensed station was illegal. The FCC says unlicensed radio stations create a danger of interference with licensed stations and also undermine the FCC's authority over broadcast radio operations. In such cases, officials from the FCC Enforcement Bureau use direction-finding techniques to locate the source of radio frequency transmissions.

An applicant for a broadcast license may seek a license to operate a new station or an existing station that he or she wishes to purchase. In either case the process is extremely complicated. Attorneys familiar with FCC rules guide the applicant throughout the process. Someone seeking a license for a new station, more and more a rarity as the broadcast spectrum is being filled up, must first obtain what is called a construction permit. Obtaining this permit is actually the biggest hurdle. If the permit is granted, if construction of the station conforms to technical requirements and if the work is completed within the time specified by the permit, the license is routinely issued.

The prospective licensee must meet several qualifications:

1. The applicant must be a citizen of the United States. Companies with less than 25 percent foreign ownership also qualify.*

2. The applicant must have sufficient funds to build and operate the station for at least three months without earning any advertising revenue.

3. The applicant must either possess or be able to hire people who possess the technical qualifications to operate a broadcasting station.

4. The applicant must be honest and open in dealing with the commission and must have good character. Making fraudulent statements on the application can doom the applicant to failure. The character matter relates to violation of FCC rules and regulations as well as felony convictions of the owners or managers.

Multiple Ownership Rules

The government has always placed a cap on the number of broadcast properties any single individual or company could own. As recently as 1984 that number was 21—seven TV, seven AM radio and seven FM radio stations. The rule represented classical libertarian First Amendment theory; that is, the more voices that are capable of speaking in the marketplace, the more likely truth will be discovered. These rules have been whittled away in the past quarter century under pressure from the industry and from Congress. In addition, the federal courts ruled that unless the government could show specifically how these rules served the public interest, they would have to be abandoned. Simply arguing that a diversity of broadcast voices was better for the nation could not carry the day.

* The FCC in 1995 granted Rupert Murdoch, owner of the Fox Network and eight television stations, a waiver of this rule. Although Murdoch is a naturalized U.S. citizen, News Corp., Murdoch's parent company, which owns a 99 percent share in the broadcast properties, is an Australian company.

In 2017 some of the key federal rules in effect related to ownership issues included:

■ **Television/newspaper cross-ownership ban:** As discussed earlier, this rule generally prohibits common ownership of a full-service broadcast station (television or radio) and a daily newspaper in the same market.[9]

■ **National television ownership rule:** A single entity may own any number of television stations on a nationwide basis as long as the station group collectively reaches no more than 39 percent of the total national TV viewing audience.

■ **National radio ownership rule:** There is no limit on the number of radio stations nationally that a single entity like iHeartMedia, formally known as Clear Channel Communications, can own. (In 2017, Texas-based iHeartMedia operated 850 radio stations with an audience of almost 250 million listeners each month while serving approximately 150 U.S. markets.)

■ **Local television ownership limit:** A single entity may own two TV stations in the same local market (known as a "designated market area" or "DMA" in FCC lingo) if (1) the contours of the stations do not overlap; or (2) at least one of the two stations is not ranked among the top four stations in terms of audience share and at least eight independently owned and operating commercial or noncommercial full-power broadcast television stations would remain in the market after the combination of the two jointly owned stations.

■ **Local radio ownership limit:** The limits are based on a sliding scale related to the size of the local market. In general, one entity may own (a) up to five commercial radio stations, not more than three of which are in the same service (i.e., AM or FM), in a market with 14 or fewer radio stations; (b) up to six commercial radio stations, not more than four of which are in the same service, in a market with between 15 and 29 radio stations; (c) up to seven commercial radio stations, not more than four of which are in the same service, in a radio market with between 30 and 44 (inclusive) radio stations; and (d) up to eight commercial radio stations, not more than five of which are in the same service, in a radio market with 45 or more radio stations.

■ **Dual network ban:** Common ownership of multiple broadcast networks generally is permitted, with the exception that mergers are prohibited between or among the "top four" networks (ABC, CBS, Fox and NBC).

The government has also attempted to ensure racial and gender diversity in the ownership of telecommunications properties. From time to time, the FCC has instituted numerous programs to try to make it easier for blacks, Hispanics and other ethnic minorities as well as women to own radio and television stations and hold jobs in

9. Although there is a presumption against waiving the cross-ownership rule, the FCC applies four factors when reviewing any proposed combination: (1) the extent to which cross-ownership will serve to increase the amount of local news disseminated through the affected media outlets in the combination; (2) whether each affected media outlet in the combination will exercise its own independent news judgment; (3) the level of concentration in the market area; and (4) the financial condition of the newspaper or broadcast station, and if the newspaper or broadcast station is in financial distress, the owner's commitment to invest significantly in newsroom operations.

broadcasting. The courts have viewed such efforts with suspicion for the most part. The Supreme Court in 1990 upheld the constitutionality of these preferential programs, with Justice William Brennan writing that the federal government has the power to devise what he called "benign race conscious" measures to the extent they serve important governmental objectives. Enhancing diversity in broadcast ownership was an important governmental objective, Brennan said.[10] But by 1995 many affirmative action programs in the United States were under attack. Not surprisingly, the high court reversed its earlier stance in a 1995 ruling and said that government set-aside programs that benefited minorities were illegal.[11] In 2002 the FCC tried once again to increase racial diversity in broadcasting with a new set of rules that in effect required intensive recruiting for vacancies within a station and longer-term recruitment initiatives by broadcasters designed to inform all members of the community about employment opportunities in broadcasting. Substantial record-keeping requirements were included. These records are scrutinized by the government during the licensing and relicensing processes, but the new system appeared to many observers to be less "coercive" than the previous attempts.

The lack of diversity of ownership remains a problem today. One recent FCC report, for instance, showed that men own more than 72 percent of the commercial TV stations in the United States and more than 77 percent of commercial TV station owners are white.

Often more than one applicant seeks a single broadcast license. In the past the FCC used an elaborate formula that contained a variety of criteria to determine which applicant deserved to get the license. But in 1993 a federal court ruled that this so-called comparative-hearing process was capricious and arbitrary and had little relevance to whether the operation of a broadcasting station by a particular license applicant would serve the public interest.[12] While the FCC struggled to develop new criteria for its hearing process, Congress stepped in and told the agency that in the future it should award the license to the qualified applicant who was willing to pay the most money for it to the current owner. In other words, the agency should use an auction system. That is the way in which most licenses that are contested are awarded today.

A licensee doesn't have to pay the government for the license, but it must pay an annual licensing fee to hold the license. The fee is based on whether the license is for a television or radio station, and the size of the market served by the station.

License Renewal

The current renewal process is certainly not automatic, but it is very close.

Broadcasting licenses must be renewed every eight years. The current renewal process is certainly not automatic, but it is very close. Unless the license holder has seriously fouled up in the preceding eight years, the FCC will not even consider other applicants for the license. Congress has instructed the FCC to renew a broadcaster's license as long as

1. the station has served the public interest, convenience and necessity;
2. the licensee has not committed any *serious* violations of the Communications Act or commission rules and regulations; and

10. *Metro Broadcasting, Inc.* v. *FCC,* 497 U.S. 547 (1990).
11. *Adarand Constructors, Inc.* v. *Pena,* 515 U.S. 200 (1995).
12. *Bechtel* v. *Federal Communications Commission,* 10 F. 3d 875 (D.C. Cir. 1993).

3. the licensee has not committed any other violations of the Communications Act or the rules and regulations of the commission that, taken together, would constitute a pattern of abuse.

The act specifically states that the commission cannot even consider whether the public interest might be better served by granting the license to someone other than the license holder. If the commission determines that the license holder has in fact failed to meet the requirements listed here, the license renewal must be denied. Only after the renewal is denied can the commission consider other applicants for the license.

Only after the renewal is denied can the commission consider other applicants for the license.

What kinds of law violations is the FCC sensitive about? Stations that broadcast fraudulent advertising have been denied the renewal of their licenses.[13] The renewal of a license for a station that was used solely to promote the causes of its owner was denied.[14] If a station does not adequately supervise the programming it carries, its license may not be renewed.[15] Today, most nonrenewals result from the applicant lying on the renewal application. Federal courts have ruled that denial of a license renewal does not violate the First Amendment. Acknowledging that a First Amendment issue might arise when a licensee is stripped of the power to broadcast, the U.S. Court of Appeals for the District of Columbia Circuit nevertheless ruled more than 85 years ago:

> This does not mean that the government, through agencies established by Congress, may not refuse a renewal of license to one who has abused it to broadcast defamatory or untrue matter. In that case there is not a denial of freedom of speech, but merely the application of the regulatory power of Congress in a field within the scope of its legislative authority.[16]

The previous year another U.S. Court of Appeals judge had ruled that the commission had a perfect right to look at past programming practices of a renewal applicant to determine whether the license should be renewed.

THE UNLICENSED USE OF WHITE SPACES: FILLING IN EMPTY SPECTRUM

The FCC in 2008 adopted rules that allow sophisticated new wireless and mobile devices to operate without a license on previously unused portions of the broadcast television spectrum known as "white spaces." These are the spaces that fall in between TV channels and previously were used by older technologies such as wireless microphones worn by on-stage performers and football referees and coaches. The new rules continue to allow wireless microphones to use the white spaces, but now also permit new devices that transmit broadband data to use the spaces, provided those devices do not interfere with TV channels or wireless microphones (the latter situation would give new meaning to a

---

13. *May Seed and Nursery,* 2 F.C.C. 559 (1936).
14. *Young People's Association for the Propagation of the Gospel,* 6 F.C.C. 178 (1936).
15. *Cosmopolitan Broadcasting Corp.,* 59 F.C.C. 2d 558 (1976).
16. *Trinity Methodist Church, South* v. *FRC,* 62 F. 2d 650 (D.C. Cir. 1932).

referee calling interference). The new devices are subject both to equipment certification by the FCC's laboratory and removal from the market if they cause harmful interference. A government database exists to track devices using the white spaces, but reports in 2015 revealed that up to a third of the information in the database may be either inaccurate or made up. For instance, the database included numerous entries under the names "John Doe" and "John Smith," and the National Association of Broadcasters (NAB) found that more than 80 devices were registered in the database under the name "Meld test." The NAB has been frustrated that the FCC hasn't acted quickly to clean up the database.

The NAB was also frustrated with Google in May 2016. Google had claimed that it was burdensome to require devices using white spaces to frequently briefly check all channels in the FCC database to make sure the devices are using vacant channels. But the NAB told the FCC that frequent checking—NAB suggests every 20 minutes—is necessary to ensure unlicensed devices won't interfere with wireless microphones.

The Public's Role and Online Public Inspection Files

Although it is rare, a renewal applicant can also face a challenge from listeners and viewers. In particular, either a formal petition to deny or an informal objection to a radio or television license renewal application may be filed with the FCC after the filing of the license renewal application by a station. The last day for filing a petition to deny is one month before the license expiration date. In addition to filing a formal petition, anyone can file an informal complaint with the FCC about a station at http://www.fcc.gov/complaints.

Each broadcast station must maintain files that are open for public inspection. These files must contain, as the FCC states on its Web site, "a variety of information about each station's operations and service to its community of license, including information about political time sold or given away by each station, quarterly lists of the most significant programs each station aired concerning issues of importance to its community, data on ownership of each station and active applications each station has filed with the Commission."

In 2012, the FCC amended its public file rules to require television stations to post their files online in a central FCC-hosted Internet database rather than maintaining paper records locally at their studios. Although the change enhanced public access to information—no longer does one need to travel to a station's main studio to inspect and make copies of a station's record—there was stiff opposition from broadcasters who objected to having to put the rates they charge political candidates for commercials online.

Why was this controversial? Because television stations are required by law to offer political candidates their lowest available ad rates. The stations contended that disclosing this information in such a publicly accessible manner would allow business advertisers to demand lower rates, more in line with what stations charge candidates and political interest groups. "By forcing broadcasters to be the only medium to disclose on the Internet our political advertising rates, the FCC jeopardizes the competitive standing of stations that provide local news, entertainment, sports and life-saving weather information free of charge to tens of millions of Americans daily," asserted the National Association of Broadcasters in an April 2012 press release. The flipside, however, is that the change makes it much easier for the public to discover how much candidates are spending on ads and how many ads they are purchasing.

In August 2012, the FCC's online public-inspection file interface became active and is found at https://publicfiles.fcc.gov/. All public file documents generated by broadcasters after that date must be posted online, and broadcasters were given six months to upload public file documents that already existed in their records.

In January 2016, the FCC announced that it would start requiring cable operators, satellite TV providers, broadcast radio licensees and satellite radio licensees to post their public file documents to the FCC-hosted online database as well. "By including these services in our transition to an online public file, we continue our effort to harness the efficiencies made possible by digital technology to make public file information more readily available to the public," the FCC said. Cable systems with 1,000 or more subscribers, satellite TV providers, satellite radio licensees and commercial radio stations in the top-50 Nielsen Audio radio markets with five or more full-time employees had to begin uploading their new public inspection file documents in the online public file database starting on June 24, 2016. Commercial radio broadcast stations in the top-50 Nielsen Audio markets with fewer than five full-time employees and all commercial radio broadcast stations in markets below the top 50 start using the online database on March 1, 2018.

SUMMARY

The five-member Federal Communications Commission was established to regulate the broadcasting industry. The agency has the responsibility to supervise all over-the-air broadcasting, as well as any other electronic communication that has an impact on over-the-air communications. Although the FCC is forbidden by law from censoring the content of broadcast programming, the agency nevertheless has considerable control over what is broadcast by radio and television. By licensing and relicensing broadcasting stations, the FCC can ensure that broadcasters meet certain standards, including programming standards.

Broadcast stations are licensed for eight years. To gain a license to broadcast, an applicant must meet several important criteria established by Congress and the FCC. When two or more people seek the same license, the FCC uses an auction process to select who will get the license. The auction replaces a comparative hearing process that was based on applicant merit. This latter process was costly and time-consuming, and courts ruled that at least one criterion used in the process was unenforceable. Listeners and viewers can challenge a renewal. Public participation in this process is relatively rare, and recent rule changes have made it even harder for citizens to mount an effective license challenge.

REGULATION OF PROGRAM CONTENT

SANCTIONS

Failure to abide by programming rules can cost a broadcast license at renewal time. But this sanction is rarely imposed by the FCC. The agency has a wide range of other kinds of sanctions, however, which are frequently levied against those who transgress the regulations (see boxed text).

FCC REMEDIES AGAINST BROADCASTERS FOR CONTENT VIOLATIONS

1. Issue a warning notice.
2. Impose a monetary fine (a "forfeiture," an increasingly common remedy).
3. Place conditions on renewal of a broadcast license.
4. Revoke a broadcaster's license entirely (very rarely used).

Broadcasters have myriad programming responsibilities that range from the very broad, such as serving the public interest in the community in which it is licensed, to the very small, such as airing a proper station break at prescribed times of the day or night. Like the rules related to licensing, rules related to program content are also evolving quickly in this new century. The FCC itself has made changes, but oftentimes it has been the courts that have insisted on the abandonment or modification of rules. Rules related to the broadcast of information and advertising of lotteries were deemed unconstitutional by the U.S. Supreme Court,[17] as noted in Chapter 15.

Can the FCC control a broadcast station's format as part of its regulation of programming content?

Can the FCC control a broadcast station's format as part of its regulation of programming content? For many years the FCC resisted efforts by citizens' groups to force the agency to get involved when a radio station dropped one kind of music format—classical, for example—and adopted another format, such as rock. But listeners went to federal court, and the FCC was ordered in 1970 to *review* a format change by a station when the abandonment of a unique format produced community protests.[18] The U.S. Court of Appeals for the District of Columbia Circuit went one step further in 1974 and ordered the FCC to *hold a hearing* whenever a unique format was being abandoned by a radio station and people in the community objected.[19] A unique format would be one that no other station in the market used. The loss of this format would deny the citizens in the community access to a particular kind of music or programming. Normally it has been supporters of classical music who have protested when a local station drops the classical format. But in Seattle in 1981, New Wave rock fans mounted a protest when the

---

17. *Greater New Orleans Broadcasting Association* v. *United States,* 527 U.S. 173 (1999).
18. *Citizens' Committee to Preserve the Voice of the Arts in Atlanta* v. *FCC,* 436 F. 2d 263 (D.C. Cir. 1970).
19. *Citizens' Committee to Save WEFM* v. *FCC,* 506 F. 2d 246 (D.C. Cir. 1974).

community's only (at that time) New Wave music station abandoned that format. Despite the earlier court rulings, the FCC continued to argue through the late 1970s that the marketplace should determine the broadcaster's format; the government should not get involved. And in 1981 the Supreme Court of the United States supported the agency and overturned a lower federal court decision calling for a hearing on a format change. Justice Byron White, writing for the majority, stated, "We decline to overturn the commission's policy statement which prefers reliance on market forces to its own attempt to oversee format changes at the behest of disaffected listeners." Justice White warned the agency, however, to be alert to the consequences of its policies and stand ready to change its rules if necessary to serve the public interest more fully.[20]

REGULATION OF CHILDREN'S PROGRAMMING

There are two key aspects to the FCC's regulation of children's television programming:

1. Limitations on commercials during programming targeting children
2. Requirements regarding educational programming that must be carried

With regard to limits on commercials, the FCC mandates that in an hour-long program aired primarily for an audience of children 12 years old and younger, advertisements must not exceed 10.5 minutes on the weekends and 12 minutes during the week. The commercial time limits, however, are not applicable to noncommercial educational stations that are prohibited from airing commercials. The FCC also bars what it calls "program-length commercials" targeting children. What does this term mean? When an advertisement for a product is aired in a program associated with that product, the entire program is counted as commercial time. An example is a cartoon program that airs a commercial for the dolls of its characters during the program broadcast. Children's programs must also be separated by either buffers or substantial pauses from commercials to help minors distinguish between shows and ads.

The FCC also bars what it calls "program-length commercials" targeting children.

In terms of educational programming, the FCC today, under guidelines it adopted in 1996 to comply with the Children's Television Act of 1990, mandates that broadcasters carry a minimum of three hours per week (averaged over a six-month period in order to provide broadcasters with scheduling flexibility) of "core educational programming." Such programming must be specifically designed to serve the educational and informational needs of children ages 16 years and under. It must be

- at least 30 minutes long;
- aired between 7:00 a.m. and 10:00 p.m.; and
- a regularly scheduled weekly program not pre-empted more than 10 percent of the time.

Complete and current information on children's television programming rules and requirements can be found on the FCC's Web site at https://www.fcc.gov/consumers/guides /childrens-educational-television.

---

20. *FCC v. WNCN Listeners Guild,* 101 S. Ct. 1266 (1981).

In a very different effort to protect children when watching television, the FCC in 2009 implemented the Child Safe Viewing Act of 2007, which was adopted December 2008 and directed the FCC to initiate a proceeding to examine "the existence and availability of advanced blocking technologies that are compatible with various communications devices or platforms." In particular, the proceeding was designed to examine blocking technologies that (1) may be appropriate across a wide variety of distribution platforms and devices; (2) can filter language based upon information in closed captioning; (3) can operate independently of preassigned ratings; and (4) may be effective in enhancing a parent's ability to protect his or her child from indecent or objectionable programming, as determined by the parent. Such technologies would be in addition to or otherwise enhance the V-chip that has been installed on all TV sets with screens of 13 inches or larger sold in the United States since 2000. As described later in this chapter, the V-chip works in conjunction with the TV Parental Guidelines that include both age- and content-based ratings for television programs.

The FCC's rules on children's programming apply not only to television broadcasters, but also to cable operators and direct broadcast satellite systems. Do cable and satellite providers comply with them? In July 2012, the FCC's Enforcement Bureau issued a report after its field agents and employees recorded and reviewed programming from several children's programming networks on numerous cable and satellite systems, focusing on programs aimed at children age 12 years and under. The Bureau concluded "that cable and satellite compliance with the CTA (Children's Television Act) requirements was generally good. The Bureau's review of children's programming material revealed no violations of the limits on commercial matter."

OBSCENE, INDECENT AND PROFANE MATERIAL

"The only thing [Trump's] mouth is good for is being Vladimir Putin's cock holster," comedian Stephen Colbert quipped during the opening monologue of his "Late Show" on CBS in May 2017. Although CBS bleeped out the word "cock holster" on the broadcast, the FCC said it received thousands of complaints about Colbert's crude joke. Later that month the FCC said in a statement that it had reviewed the complaints and the monologue and determined "there was nothing actionable under the FCC's rules" regulating indecency. This was not surprising since Colbert's show aired during what is known as the **safe-harbor time period** when indecent material is protected from FCC regulation (see below for more information about the safe harbor). But if the show had aired earlier in the night, the FCC might have penalized CBS. This section addresses the FCC's power to regulate indecent content on over-the-air broadcast television and radio during certain times of the day.

Obscenity is not protected by the First Amendment.

The sale, distribution or publication of obscenity is illegal by virtue of myriad federal, state and local laws. Obscenity is not protected by the First Amendment, as noted in Chapter 13. Similarly, the broadcast of obscenity over television or radio is illegal under the Federal Communications Act. But federal law also makes it illegal to broadcast what is called indecent material via radio and over-the-air television (cable is treated differently and is discussed later in the chapter). The courts have defined obscenity. The struggle to find a workable definition for indecency has been much more difficult.

BOSTON, DAVID ORTIZ AND THE FCC: "THIS IS OUR FUCKING CITY"

Shortly after the capture of the Boston Marathon terrorists in April 2013, then–Boston Red Sox slugger David "Big Papi" Ortiz delivered an emotional speech to the fans at Fenway Park. "This is our fucking city and nobody gonna dictate our freedom," Ortiz said. The speech was broadcast live on television and radio stations. Would the FCC, under its power to target broadcast indecency, go after those stations for airing this fleeting use of an expletive?

The answer was no, and it came almost immediately from then–FCC Chairman Julius Genachowski in the form of a tweet: "David Ortiz spoke from the heart at today's Red Sox game. I stand with Big Papi and the people of Boston."

The incident illustrates not only the subjectivity in determining what is or is not indecent, but also the FCC's recent decision to target only the most "egregious" incidents of broadcast indecency.

The broadcast of obscenity over the airwaves has never been a serious problem. Indecency was not a problem either, until more recent times. In television the issue first reached national prominence in 1975 when ABC, CBS and NBC, with the cooperation of the National Association of Broadcasters and the FCC, instituted what they called "the family hour" in prime time.[21] Stations that subscribed to programming policies established by the NAB, and most of them did, were told to set aside the hours from 7 to 9 each evening for family viewing; programs with sexual overtones and excessive violence were taboo in this period. The result was a few months of silly self-censorship (e.g., the word "virgin" was cut from one program, and performers on programs starring Cher and Cloris Leachman were recostumed in a more modest fashion) before a federal court ruled that the constraints constituted a violation of the First Amendment because they had been motivated by the FCC.[22]

Until recently, over-the-air television, as opposed to cable channels like HBO or MTV which are governed by far more relaxed standards, rarely generated indecency complaints because it sought to appeal to a large, heterogeneous audience. Radio stations, on the other hand, were more brazen and frequently subject to fines for broadcasting indecent material. But TV broadcasters began to push vigorously at the legal boundaries in recent years. When CBS telecast a salacious Super Bowl halftime show in 2004 that included a very fleeting glimpse of singer Janet Jackson's breast, it ignited a firestorm of criticism that included angry congressional hearings. Mea culpas by industry officials did little to quiet the anger. Action against the Super Bowl broadcast came in September 2004 (see pages 637–638). Congress showed its resolve in 2006 to

---

21. Cowan, *See No Evil.*
22. *Writers Guild* v. *FCC,* 423 F. Supp. 1064 (C.D. Cal. 1976). A U.S. Court of Appeals later overturned the lower-court ruling on the grounds that the U.S. District Court lacked jurisdiction in the case, that the issue should have first gone to the FCC for resolution. See *Writers Guild* v. *ABC,* 609 F. 2d 355 (9th Cir. 1979). The networks made no effort to re-establish the policy.

A fleeting glimpse of Janet Jackson's right breast during the 2004 Super Bowl halftime show sparked an FCC crackdown on broadcast indecency. Jackson is shown here with singer Justin Timberlake.

©AP Photo/David Phillip

punish indecent broadcasts when it increased tenfold the maximum fine the FCC can mete out against a station for a single instance of indecent or profane content, raising the amount from $32,500 to a whopping $325,000. The dramatic increase may make broadcasters think twice before airing potentially indecent content. Many broadcasters responded in 2004 after the Janet Jackson incident to the political pressures placed by Congress and the FCC by engaging in self-censorship—NBC, for example, eliminated "a glimpse of an 80-year-old patient's breast" from an episode of "ER,"[23] and several ABC affiliates in November 2004 chose not to carry the network's showing of Steven Spielberg's movie "Saving Private Ryan" because of its coarse language and intense violence[24]—and quickly settling indecency actions for massive amounts of money. For instance, Clear Channel Communications, now known as iHeartMedia, paid the FCC a record $1.75 million to settle a slew of pending indecency complaints filed by listeners against its stations, as well as $800,000 in outstanding fines, based on broadcasts by Howard Stern and other radio personalities. Stern later announced in 2004 that he was leaving broadcast radio and escaping the reach of both the FCC's fines and Clear

23. Collins, "The Decency Debate."
24. Huff, "Fear Over 'Private' Parts."

Channel's self-censorship by moving in 2006 to Sirius Satellite Radio. Satellite radio currently is not subject to the FCC's indecency regulations.

Satellite radio currently is not subject to the FCC's indecency regulations.

How did it come to this point? It began about 35 years ago with a case called *FCC v. Pacifica Foundation*. The Supreme Court ruled in 1978 that it was not a violation of the First Amendment to bar indecency during certain times of the day from the airwaves. The high court upheld an FCC ruling that radio station WBAI in New York City had violated the law when it broadcast during the afternoon a recorded monologue by comedian George Carlin.[25] The monologue, called "Seven Dirty Words," was broadcast on the listener-supported station during a long discussion on the English language. The FCC said it was impermissible to broadcast "language that describes in terms patently offensive as measured by contemporary community standards for the broadcast medium, sexual or excretory activities and organs, *at times when there is a reasonable risk children may be in the audience* [emphasis added]." The agency said it was unlikely children would be listening or watching after 10 p.m. and before 6 a.m., and it later designated this eight-hour block of time a safe harbor for the broadcast of adult material. Although Carlin died in 2008, his legacy with the FCC lives on today, haunting broadcasters that air indecent content.

In the years following this high court ruling, the FCC refined its policies on indecent broadcasts. It was consistently challenged in court, but generally the agency's policy weathered these challenges.[26] Then in 2001 the commission published a new and fairly comprehensive policy statement relating to the broadcast of indecent matter.[27]

The commission's definition of indecency remains the standard: language or material that, in context, depicts or describes, in terms patently offensive as measured by contemporary community standards for the broadcast medium, sexual or excretory activities or organs. Before finding a broadcast indecent, the FCC must make two determinations. First, the material must fall within the subject matter scope of indecency; that is, it must depict or describe sexual or excretory organs or activities. Second, it must be patently offensive as measured by contemporary community standards for the broadcast medium. The standards are not local and do not encompass any particular geographic area. The standard is that of an average broadcast viewer or listener.

Before finding a broadcast indecent, the FCC must make two determinations.

Notice that speech must relate to sexual or excretory activities or organs in order for it to fall within the FCC's definition of indecency. Thus, when radio host Don Imus in 2007 referred to members of the Rutgers women's basketball team as "nappy-headed hos," the language did not fall within the scope of indecency. The language certainly was racist, offensive and disagreeable, but it did not depict sexual or excretory organs and activities. The firing of Imus by CBS Radio thus was an act of community censorship (see Chapter 2 regarding community censorship)—in this case, corporate censorship—rather than government censorship.

Although this definition of indecency and the two-step determination process remains intact today, the commission issued a controversial order in 2004 that radically changed how the FCC interprets and applies its own standards. In particular, the FCC

25. *FCC v. Pacifica Foundation*, 438 U.S. 726 (1978).
26. *Action for Children's Television* v. *FCC*, 58 F. 3d 654 (D.C. Cir. 1995); *Action for Children's Television* v. *FCC*, U.S. Sup. Ct. No. 95-520, cert. den.; and *Pacifica Foundation* v. *FCC*, U.S. S. Ct. No. 95-509, cert. den.
27. *In re Industry Guidelines on the Commission's Case Law Interpreting 18 U.S.C. §1464 and Enforcement Policies Regarding Broadcast Indecency*, FCC, File No. EB-00-1H-0089, April 6, 2001.

ruled that the use of the phrase "this is really, really fucking brilliant" by Bono, lead singer for the Irish rock group U2, during an acceptance speech at the 2003 Golden Globe Awards television program and broadcast by NBC outside the FCC's safe-harbor time period, constituted "material in violation of the applicable indecency and profanity prohibitions."[28] The decision stunned many legal observers. Why? Because Bono's use of the word "fucking" was both isolated and fleeting—it was not repeated or dwelled upon, a factor that traditionally is important for the FCC in determining whether or not speech is patently offensive—and because it was not used in a sexual sense, but rather as a modifier for emphasis of how "brilliant" it was that U2 had won for Best Original Song. Furthermore, officials at NBC had no advance knowledge that Bono was going to use the expletive in question, and the network was able to "bleep" the language for its West Coast airing of the program (the program was aired live to the East Coast).

Bono's use of the word "fucking" was both isolated and fleeting.

Despite these facts, the FCC concluded that Bono's language, as used in context, was both indecent and profane. As to why the program was indecent, the FCC began its analysis by rearticulating its two-step process for indecency determinations, writing that "indecency findings involve at least two fundamental determinations. First, the material alleged to be indecent must fall within the subject matter scope of our indecency definition; that is, the material must describe or depict sexual or excretory organs or activities. . . . Second, the broadcast must be patently offensive as measured by contemporary community standards for the broadcast medium."

With respect to the first step, the FCC found that "given the core meaning of the 'F-Word,' any use of that word or a variation, in any context, inherently has a sexual connotation, and therefore falls within the first prong of our indecency definition." Turning to the second step of its indecency analysis—whether the broadcast of Bono's speech was patently offensive under contemporary community standards for the television medium—the FCC wrote:

> The "F-Word" is one of the most vulgar, graphic and explicit descriptions of sexual activity in the English language. Its use invariably invokes a coarse sexual image. The use of the "F-Word" here, on a nationally telecast awards ceremony, was shocking and gratuitous. In this regard, NBC does not claim that there was any political, scientific or other independent value of use of the word here, or any other factors to mitigate its offensiveness.

The FCC thus concluded that the Golden Globes broadcast was indecent. Importantly, the commission suggested that NBC could have prevented the entire problem, writing that the network "and other licensees could have easily avoided the indecency violation here by delaying the broadcast for a period of time sufficient for them to effectively bleep the offending word." The FCC then added a new element to its indecency calculus, holding that the "ease with which broadcasters today can block even fleeting words in a live broadcast is an element in our decision to act upon a single and gratuitous use of a vulgar expletive." In addition, the commission wrote that "the mere fact that specific words or phrases are not sustained or repeated does not mandate a finding that

---

28. *In re Complaints Against Various Broadcast Licensees Regarding Their Airing of the "Golden Globe Award" Program,* Memorandum Opinion and Order, File No. EB-03-IH-0110 (March 18, 2004).

material that is otherwise patently offensive to the broadcast medium is not indecent." What's more, the commission held that it made no difference whatsoever that NBC did not intend for the offensive language to occur.

The FCC did much more, however, than just hold the broadcast to be indecent; it also concluded that the broadcast was profane. Federal law provides: "Whoever utters any obscene, indecent, or *profane language* by means of radio communication shall be fined under this title or imprisoned not more than two years, or both."[29] Prior to the dispute over Bono's language during the Golden Globes ceremony, however, the FCC narrowly had limited the statutory meaning of the term "profane language" to "blasphemy or divine imprecation." It completely reversed course, however, in March 2004 and concluded that Bono's acceptance speech was profane. The FCC wrote:

The FCC did much more, however, than just hold the broadcast to be indecent; it also concluded that the broadcast was profane.

> Broadcasters are on notice that the Commission in the future will not limit its definition of profane speech to only those words and phrases that contain an element of blasphemy or divine imprecation, but, depending on the context, will also consider under the definition of "profanity" the "F-Word" and those words (or variants thereof) that are as highly offensive as the "F-Word," to the extent such language is broadcast between 6 a.m. and 10 p.m. We will analyze other potentially profane words or phrases on a case-by-case basis.

In summary, the FCC's 2004 opinion regarding Bono's speech marked an aggressive new approach to clean up language on the public airwaves. The FCC not only concluded that Bono's speech was indecent, but it also opened up a second avenue of attack, under the guise of profane language, for regulating broadcast content. The FCC in 2014 defined profane language as language that is "so grossly offensive to members of the public who actually hear it as to amount to a nuisance."

The FCC in 2014 defined profane language as language that is "so grossly offensive to members of the public who actually hear it as to amount to a nuisance."

ADELE'S GRAMMY PROFANITY DOESN'T MAKE THE AIRWAVES

During a tribute performance for the late George Michael during the 2017 Grammy Awards, which aired on CBS, superstar Adele stopped mid-song, said she "fucked up" (her vocals were off key) and asked to start over.

A frazzled Adele said, "I'm sorry for swearing, and I'm sorry for starting again. Can we please start it again?"

The audience watching on television heard her apology, but only the live audience in the arena heard her say she "fucked up." That's because CBS bleeped out the expletive on its broadcast. The incident shows how broadcasters are adopting technological answers to indecency issues—in this case airing the live broadcast using a seven-second delay that enabled CBS to catch Adele's slipup.

In September 2004 the FCC once again vigorously applied its indecency standard when it released a Notice of Apparent Liability (NAL) for a whopping aggregate sum of $550,000 against various television licensees concerning their February 1, 2004,

---

29. 18 U.S.C. § 1464 (2004).

broadcast of the Super Bowl XXXVIII halftime show.[30] The amount was, at the time, the largest indecency fine ever levied against a television broadcaster, namely CBS affiliates. The FCC focused its inquiry on Janet Jackson and Justin Timberlake's performance of the song "Rock Your Body." The raunchy duet infamously concluded with Timberlake's removal of a portion of Jackson's leather bustier, briefly exposing her breast to the camera, at the precise moment when Timberlake finished the song's lecherous last lyric, "gonna have you naked by the end of this song."

The FCC applied its two-step indecency analysis to this performance, considering first whether the broadcast described or depicted sexual or excretory organs or activities, and then, second, whether it was patently offensive as measured by contemporary community standards for the broadcast medium. The first step was easily satisfied, as the FCC wrote that the broadcast culminated in on-camera partial nudity with Jackson's exposed breast, thus constituting a depiction of a sexual organ. As to the second step—whether the broadcast was patently offensive—the FCC initially set forth three factors that it often considers to determine patent offensiveness:

The FCC initially set forth three factors that it often considers to determine patent offensiveness.

1. The explicitness or graphic nature of the description
2. Whether the material dwells on or repeats at length descriptions of sexual or excretory organs or activities
3. Whether the material is used to shock, titillate or pander

Applying these three factors in a totality-of-the-circumstances approach in which they are weighed and balanced with each other, the FCC concluded that the broadcast was indeed patently offensive. It initially found that the videotape of the performance "leaves no doubt that the Jackson/Timberlake segment is both explicit and graphic. The joint performance by Ms. Jackson and Mr. Timberlake culminated in Mr. Timberlake pulling off part of Ms. Jackson's bustier and exposing her bare breast. CBS admits that the CBS Network Stations broadcast this material, including the image of Ms. Jackson's bared breast." The FCC then reasoned that the "nudity here was designed to pander to, titillate and shock the viewing audience. The fact that the exposure of Ms. Jackson's breast was brief is thus not dispositive."

The Super Bowl decision did not mark the end of the FCC's crackdown on broadcast indecency in 2004. In fact, the commission issued a proposed fine totaling more than $1.18 million—more than double the amount of the Super Bowl fine, and a new record-level fine for indecency on a television program—against 169 Fox Television Network stations for airing an April 2003 episode of a program called "Married by America." The episode included scenes in which party-goers licked whipped cream from strippers' bodies in a sexually suggestive manner. Although the program electronically obscured any nudity, the FCC nonetheless held that the broadcast was indecent, in part because it believed that "the sexual nature of the scenes is inescapable, as the strippers attempt to lure party-goers into sexually compromising positions."[31] In September 2012—more than nine years after the

30. *In re Complaints Against Various Television Licensees Concerning Their February 1, 2004, Broadcast of the Super Bowl XXXVIII Halftime Show,* Notice of Apparent Liability for Forfeiture, File No. EB-04-IH-0011 (Sept. 22, 2004).

31. *In re Complaints Against Various Licensees Regarding Their Broadcast of the Fox Television Network Program "Married by America" on April 7, 2003,* Notice of Apparent Liability for Forfeiture, File No. EB-03-IH-0162 (Oct. 12, 2004).

episode in question aired—the FCC dropped its case against Fox for "Married by America." The decision not to continue to go after Fox came in light of the U.S. Supreme Court's June 2012 ruling in a case called *FCC v. Fox Television Stations* described later in this unit. In choosing not to pursue the "Married by America" case further, FCC Chair Julius Genachowski signaled the FCC might loosen up its enforcement of indecency and target only the worst possible cases. "I have directed the Enforcement Bureau to focus its resources on the strongest cases that involve egregious indecency violations," Genachowski said in September 2012.

While the FCC began its vigorous approach to both indecency and profanity in 2004 with decisions affecting the Golden Globes, the Super Bowl and "Married by America," one thing did not change: the **safe-harbor time period** when such content is protected from the FCC's regulation. The safe-harbor period today remains in effect from 10 p.m. to 6 a.m.—an eight-hour window during which both indecent and profane language may be broadcast. Obscene speech, however, falls completely outside the scope of First Amendment protection (see Chapter 13) and is not protected at any time of day. In other words, there is no safe-harbor period for obscenity on the public airwaves.

The safe-harbor period today remains in effect from 10 p.m. to 6 a.m.

The FCC rejected a complaint in 2005 filed by the American Family Association that claimed that an ABC broadcast of the award-winning World War II movie "Saving Private Ryan" was both indecent and profane.[32] The film's dialogue contains a number of expletives that are repeated over and over, including variations of the same word ("fuck") that landed Bono and NBC in trouble. Although the FCC once again found that this word has an inherently sexual meaning, it nonetheless found that, as used in the context of the movie "Saving Private Ryan," it was not patently offensive. The FCC wrote:

> We do not find indecent every depiction or description of sexual or excretory organs or activities. Rather . . . we find material indecent only if it is patently offensive based on an examination of the material's explicit or graphic nature, whether it is dwelled upon or repeated, and whether it appears to pander or is intended to titillate or shock the audience. In connection with the third factor, we consider whether the material has any social, scientific or artistic value, as finding that material has such value may militate against finding that it was intended to pander, titillate or shock.

Applying this approach to the ABC broadcast of "Saving Private Ryan," the FCC found that, although the language was repeated and dwelled upon, "the complained-of material, in context, is not pandering and is not used to titillate or shock." This factor was key to its decision. The commission added that the language in question "is integral to the film's objective of conveying the horrors of war through the eyes of these soldiers, ordinary Americans placed in extraordinary situations. Deleting all of such language or inserting milder language . . . would have altered the nature of the artistic work and diminished the power, realism and immediacy of the film experience for viewers." The FCC's opinion rejecting the indecency and profanity complaints against the movie thus

32. *In re Complaints Against Various Television Licensees Regarding Their Broadcast on November 11, 2004, of the ABC Television Network's Presentation of the Film "Saving Private Ryan,"* Memorandum Opinion and Order, File No. EB-04-IH-0589 (Feb. 28, 2005).

represents a major victory for the First Amendment rights of both broadcasters and their audiences—in particular the audience's right to receive and view important films.

Perhaps more significantly, the FCC issued a record Notice of Apparent Liability of more than $3.6 million in 2006 against CBS affiliates in the Central and Mountain time zones for airing an episode of "Without a Trace" outside the safe-harbor zone that featured "material graphically depicting teenage boys and girls participating in a sexual orgy."[33] Although the episode never showed any actual nudity or real sex, the FCC reasoned that the material

> does depict male and female teenagers in various stages of undress. The scene also includes at least three shots depicting intercourse, two between couples and one "group sex" shot. In the culminating shot of the scene, the witness exclaims to the others in the party that the victim is a "porn star."

With this in mind, the FCC noted that "the material is particularly egregious because it focuses on sex among children," and it reasoned that "the complained-of material is pandering, titillating and shocking to the audience. The explicit and lengthy nature of the depictions of sexual activity, including apparent intercourse, goes well beyond what the story line could reasonably be said to require." The FCC thus seemed to go beyond the scope of its authority to take on the role of producer and director, somehow knowing what scripts, plots and story lines are required to convey a message. The commission added that the content in question was "portrayed in such a manner that a child watching the program could easily discern that the teenagers shown in the scene were engaging in sexual activities, including apparent intercourse."

Between 2006 and 2011, several cases challenging the FCC's ramped-up indecency enforcement efforts, including its crackdown on fleeting expletives and brief instances of nudity such as the Janet Jackson Super Bowl incident, worked their way through the federal courts. The cases ultimately came to a head—and a somewhat anticlimactic conclusion—in 2012.

In June 2012, the U.S. Supreme Court in *FCC* v. *Fox Televisions Stations, Inc.*[34] dealt the FCC a relatively minor blow when the Court threw out fines the FCC had imposed on both Fox and ABC for airing allegedly indecent content during 2002 and 2003. The Fox controversies involved two incidents of so-called fleeting expletives—celebrities briefly swearing during unscripted remarks at the Billboard Music Awards. In one case, Cher exclaimed during an acceptance speech that "I've also had my critics for the last 40 years saying that I was on my way out every year. Right. So fuck 'em." In the other, Nicole Richie said, "Have you ever tried to get cow shit out of a Prada purse? It's not so fucking simple." The ABC controversy, however, did not involve expletives or words, but rather fleeting images—namely, the nude buttocks of an adult female (Charlotte Ross) on an episode of *NYPD Blue* for approximately seven seconds and, for an even briefer moment, the side of her breast.

---

33. *In re Complaints Against Various Television Licensees Concerning Their Dec. 31, 2004, Broadcast of the Program "Without a Trace,"* Notice of Apparent Liability for Forfeiture, File No. EB-05-IH-0035 (Mar. 15, 2006).
34. 132 S. Ct. 2307 (2012).

Importantly, all three incidents occurred *before* the FCC issued its 2004 order in the Bono case in which the FCC held it would start punishing broadcasters for even isolated and fleeting uses of unscripted expletives, such as Bono's use of the word "fucking" during a speech at the Golden Globe Awards. In brief, with its 2004 order in the Bono/Golden Globes case, the FCC adopted a new policy of targeting isolated and brief instances of expletives and nudity. Prior to this ruling, the FCC had not punished broadcasters for such content.

This timing proved pivotal for the Supreme Court in *Fox Television Stations*, as Justice Anthony Kennedy concluded that neither Fox nor ABC had "fair notice" of the FCC's new policy because the Fox and ABC broadcasts took place *prior* to the new policy's adoption. Kennedy wrote:

> In the challenged orders now under review, the [FCC] applied the new principle promulgated in the *Golden Globes* [Bono] Order and determined fleeting expletives and a brief moment of indecency were actionably indecent. This regulatory history, however, makes it apparent that the [FCC] policy in place at the time of the broadcasts gave no notice to Fox or ABC that a fleeting expletive or a brief shot of nudity could be actionably indecent; yet Fox and ABC were found to be in violation.

The decision thus was very narrow—the Court only tossed out the fines because the FCC failed to give Fox and ABC fair notice (as required by the Due Process Clause of the Fourteenth Amendment) prior to the broadcasts in question that fleeting expletives and momentary nudity could be found indecent.

The 2012 *Fox Television Stations* ruling thus is equally as important for what the Court did *not* do and what it did *not* decide. Specifically, the Court did not: (1) address the First Amendment implications of the FCC's current indecency policy, including its 2004 decision to suddenly target fleeting expletives; and (2) overrule its 1978 precedent in *FCC v. Pacifica Foundation* (the George Carlin case described earlier) that upheld the FCC's power to regulate broadcast indecency during times of the day when children are likely to be in the audience. Furthermore, the Court specifically said the FCC was free to modify its current indecency policy in light of the key "public interest" mandate described earlier in the chapter. In the mean time, Justice Kennedy wrote, lower courts are "free to review the current policy or any modified policy in light of its content and application."

The bottom line is this: the Supreme Court in 2012 dodged a great opportunity in *Fox Television Stations* to revisit both the First Amendment issues surrounding the FCC's regulation of broadcast indecency (including fleeting expletives) and the Court's seminal ruling in *Pacifica Foundation*. The case thus represents an instance of judicial minimalism— a characteristic of the Court under the leadership of Chief Justice John Roberts in which its rulings are very narrowly drawn to address only the smallest possible issues necessary to deal with a case. In a lone concurring opinion (there were no dissents), Justice Ruth Bader Ginsburg suggested that she would overrule *Pacifica Foundation* if given the chance.

Less than a week after its ruling in *Fox Television Stations*, the Supreme Court delivered another blow to the FCC when it denied the FCC's petition for a writ of certiorari in *FCC v. CBS, Corp.* That denial left intact a 2011 opinion by the 3rd Circuit Court of Appeals that struck down the FCC-imposed fines on CBS for airing the fleeting nudity of

Janet Jackson's breast during the 2004 Super Bowl halftime show. The 3rd Circuit struck down the fines because it found that the FCC, in punishing CBS, had arbitrarily and capriciously departed from its longstanding prior policy of exempting fleeting broadcast material from the scope of actionable indecency. Thus, eight years after the infamous "wardrobe malfunction" spawned a national ruckus, the case came to a rather quiet close, with CBS avoiding all liability. But broadcasters like CBS, Fox and ABC also now have plenty of notice that the FCC might punish them for airing both fleeting expletives and images of nudity if it so chooses.

STORY ABOUT PORN-STAR-TURNED-EMT LEADS TO STRIKING FCC FINE

In March 2015, the FCC announced that it was going to fine a Roanoke, Va., TV station $325,000 for broadcasting "graphic and sexually explicit material" during an evening newscast. It marked the highest fine the FCC had ever issued for a single indecent broadcast on one station.

What did the station do that could warrant such a fine? On a 6 p.m. newscast in July 2012, the station, WDBJ, aired a story about a former porn actress—Tracy Rolan, whose screen name was Harmony Rose—who was now working for a local rescue squad as a volunteer emergency medical technician (EMT). Rolan's new job was newsworthy, as some Roanoke County officials had questioned whether it was appropriate for her to train with the rescue squad. The station produced a story, which was more than three minutes long, that included interviews with Rolan's EMT colleagues, people she had assisted as an EMT and also those who had questioned her appropriateness to serve in the role. At one point, the story featured a screen grab, taken from the Web site of a distributor of Rolan's adult films, that showed Rolan in a suggestive but nonexplicit way.

During that part of the story, however, a graphic sexual image—"a video image of a hand stroking an erect penis," as the FCC described it—from the adult Web site was inadvertently also visible on the screen grab for about three seconds.

That offending image was located on the far edge of the Web page from which it was taken. The station told the FCC the image was not visible on the monitor screens that the station used when the story was edited, which is why the news director and reporter did not see it. The image occupied only about 1.7 percent of the entire TV viewing area. "The picture in question was small and outside the viewing area of the video editing screen. It was visible only on some televisions and for less than three seconds," said Jeff Marks, the station's president and general manager. He said the inclusion of the image "was purely unintentional." The station quickly deleted the story from its Web site and did not air the story in any other newscasts.

Nevertheless, the FCC determined that the station had violated federal law by airing indecent material. The FCC concluded that the three-second duration of the image "was sufficient to attract and hold viewers' attention" and that "the stroking of an erect penis on a broadcast program is shocking." The chief of the FCC's Enforcement Bureau said, "Our action here sends a clear signal that there are severe consequences for TV stations that air sexually explicit images when children are likely to be watching."

Industry groups quickly criticized the FCC. The National Association of Broadcasters and the Radio Television Digital News Association (RTDNA) told the FCC in a joint filing that "[l]evying the maximum possible fine under the law in a case where the broadcast station indisputably did not purposefully air the image at issue is tantamount to imposing a sentence of life imprisonment for petty theft." The RTDNA has also argued elsewhere that bona fide newscasts—which WDBJ's broadcast clearly was—should be exempt from indecency sanctions (though the FCC has said previously it does not have a "news exception" for indecency cases).

The Roanoke station initially vowed to fight the fine, but in early 2016 the station was sold to Gray Television, an Atlanta-based media company. As part of the sale, the fine was paid off—making for an anticlimactic ending to an otherwise stimulating story.

What, then, does it take to file a complaint with the FCC alleging that particular broadcast material is indecent? Three things are required by the FCC before it will investigate a viewer's or listener's complaint. In particular, so-called complainants must provide the FCC with

Three things are required by the FCC before it will investigate a viewer's or listener's complaint.

1. the date and time of the broadcast in question;
2. the call sign and letters of the station that aired the content; and
3. a significant excerpt of the program.

The first requirement is important because, if the broadcast occurred during the safe-harbor period of 10:00 p.m. to 6:00 a.m., then any complaint for indecent content or profane language will be dismissed. That eight-hour window is when indecent and profane content (although not obscene speech) is protected from the FCC's wrath.

The second requirement is important because the FCC must know the particular station—the particular broadcast licensee—that carried the content. That station will, in turn, be named and investigated by the FCC.

Finally, the third requirement—that a significant excerpt of the program be provided to the FCC by the complainant—can be satisfied in several different ways. For instance, the complaining viewer may provide a full or partial tape or transcript of not only *what* was said but the *context* in which it was said. It is not enough for the complainant simply to state that "there was a broadcast involving sexual dialogue." That won't cut it. More details showing what was actually said (the precise language used or images shown) and the context in which it was said are key.

AFTERMATH OF THE *FOX TELEVISION STATIONS* CASE: DOES AN "EGREGIOUS" NEW APPROACH LIE AHEAD?

What has the FCC done about broadcast indecency since the 2012 ruling by the Supreme Court described earlier in *FCC* v. *Fox Television Stations*? The just-discussed $325,000 fine against the Roanoke TV station in 2015 was an outlier in what has otherwise been a fairly dormant period of indecency regulation under the FCC. In fact, in a six-month period in 2012 and 2013 the FCC dismissed more than one million indecency complaints filed by members of the public that had languished in its files without action. Many complaints, in fact, were several years old.

What does the future hold for indecency regulation? In an April 2013 "Public Notice," the FCC sought comment on whether it "should make changes to its current broadcast indecency policies or maintain them as they are." The notice specifically asked the public to consider if the FCC should stand by its decision in the Bono case (described earlier) to target broadcasters for airing isolated and fleeting expletives.

While seeking such input, the FCC added it would still actively investigate only what it called "egregious indecency" cases. The FCC did not, however, explain what it meant by the vague phrase egregious indecency.

As of August 2017, more than four years after the FCC issued that "Public Notice," the FCC had failed to release any kind of response to the public comments it solicited, failed to propose a new indecency policy and failed to clarify what it meant by "egregious." The FCC's silence frustrates broadcasters, who say they need better guidance.

The number of complaints to the FCC about indecency has actually dropped dramatically in recent years, from 1.4 million in the year of the infamous wardrobe malfunction in 2004 to around a thousand in one recent year. It still remains to be seen how the FCC will treat indecency regulation under President Trump's administration. FCC Chairman Ajit Pai said in a February 2017 interview that "the law that is on the books today requires that broadcasters keep it clean so to speak," and he said he took that FCC obligation seriously.

VIOLENCE ON TELEVISION

The first thing to note is that violent content is not included in the FCC's definition of indecency discussed in the last section. Broadcast indecency currently focuses only on sexual or excretory organs or activities, *not* on violent images or story lines. Parsed differently, violence and sex simply are not the same thing in the FCC's regulatory universe.

Violence and sex simply are not the same thing in the FCC's regulatory universe.

Congress added new rules to the broad array of broadcast regulations when it adopted legislation in the Telecommunications Act of 1996 to regulate violence on television. The law required the manufacturers of television sets to include a microchip—nicknamed the V-chip—in television receivers manufactured after January 1, 2000. Sets with screens smaller than 13 inches are exempt from the regulation. This chip, along with a programming rating system imposed on broadcasters, permits viewers to block out violent television programming. The V-chip is activated by a signal contained in each television broadcast. The signal tells the receiver that a program with a certain rating is being transmitted. If the receiver is programmed to reject such a broadcast, reception of the show will be blocked. Two years after the law was passed, the broadcast industry, children's advocacy groups, the motion picture industry and the FCC agreed on a rating system. The ratings appear in the corner of the TV screen for the first 15 seconds of a program. They also are included in many magazine and newspaper listings for programs. Ratings are given to all TV programs except news, sports and unedited movies on premium cable channels. There are seven possible ratings: TV-Y; TV-Y7; TV-Y7-FV; TV-G; TV-PG; TV-14; and TV-MA. Descriptions of each are available at the FCC's Web site at http://www.fcc.gov/cgb/consumerfacts/vchip.html. In addition to the ratings, there are content descriptors designated by letters, including *V* (violence); *S* (sexual situations); *L* (coarse or crude language); and *D* (suggestive dialogue).

Most over-the-air and cable broadcasters have adopted the system. A few have not. But the industry's acceptance of the V-chip ratings seems far more enthusiastic than that of television set owners. A 2004 survey by the Kaiser Family Foundation found that "just 24% of parents used TV ratings often and only 15% used the V-chip."[35]

In 2007 the FCC issued a massive report in which it asked Congress to give it the power to regulate "excessively violent programming" on both broadcast and cable television, such as time-channeling such content away from hours when children are likely to be watching TV. By August 2017, however, Congress had not expanded the FCC's authority over violent content on TV.

SUMMARY

The FCC has broad control over the content of broadcast programming. To enforce this control, the agency has a wide variety of sanctions, which include letters of reprimand, fine or forfeiture, and nonrenewal or revocation of broadcast licenses. Content regulations involve a wide range of broadcast programming. In the broadest sense, the broadcaster must program to meet the needs of the community. But programming rules also involve simple regulations, such as the requirement to present station identification at various times of the broadcast day.

The FCC has chosen not to attempt to control the selection of format by a broadcaster. Citizens groups have urged the FCC to hold hearings when a radio station drops one program format and adopts a new one. In the early 1970s federal courts supported these citizen protests, but in 1981 the U.S. Supreme Court ruled that the government need not get involved when a broadcaster decides to switch from one format to another. In the mid-1980s the FCC attempted to remove rules dictating programming standards

35. Puzzanghera, "A Campaign to Head Off New Decency Rules."

for children's broadcasting. Congress resisted these changes and forced the agency to reinstate rules regarding both the number of commercial minutes permitted per hour in children's programming and minimum service standards for the younger viewers.

Federal law prohibits the broadcast of any obscene or indecent material. In 1978 the Supreme Court ruled that a radio or television station could be punished for broadcasting material that is not obscene but merely indecent. The court based its ruling on the premise that children might be present during the broadcast. In 2004 the FCC began an all-out crackdown on indecent content that has since subsided. In 2007 the FCC asked Congress to give it power to regulate violent content, much like it regulates indecent content, but by August 2017 Congress had not given the FCC such power.

REGULATION OF POLITICAL PROGRAMMING

The guarantees of free speech and press were added to the Constitution largely to protect political debate in the nation from government interference. In recent years the courts and the FCC have voided two important content regulations that were related in many instances to political discussion, the Fairness Doctrine and rules that focused on personal attacks and political editorials. The Fairness Doctrine, generated by the FCC in the late 1940s, stipulated that all broadcasters had a responsibility to provide coverage of important public issues that arose in their communities. In providing such coverage the broadcasters had the additional obligation of ensuring that all significant viewpoints on these issues were represented. In the late 1980s the FCC said it would no longer enforce the Fairness Doctrine and a U.S. Court of Appeals subsequently ruled that the agency was within its rights to abandon the doctrine.[36] The personal attack rules stipulated that when broadcasters air what amounts to a personal attack on an individual or group, they must also notify the target of the broadcast attack and offer free time for the target to reply. The rules on political editorials were similar. If a broadcaster endorsed a candidate for political office, the opposing candidate had to be notified about the endorsement and given an opportunity to respond. In October 2000 a U.S. Court of Appeals ordered the FCC to repeal these rules because of, among other reasons, First Amendment concerns.[37] Other rules remain, however.

The FCC stopped enforcing the Fairness Doctrine in 1987.

Although the FCC stopped enforcing the Fairness Doctrine in 1987, there were concerns among many Republicans and, in particular, conservative radio talk-show hosts that it would be resurrected by President Barack Obama and a Democratic-controlled Congress. Calling it the "Hush Rush" doctrine because the Fairness Doctrine ostensibly would require a radio station playing three hours of programming by conservative Rush

---

36. *Syracuse Peace Council* v. *FCC,* 867 F. 2d 654 (D.C. Cir. 1989). See also *Arkansas AFL-CIO* v. *FCC,* 11 F. 3d 1430 (8th Cir. 1993).
37. *Radio-Television News Directors Association* v. *FCC,* 229 F. 3d 269 (D.C. Cir. 2000).

Limbaugh each day to also put on three hours of programming by a liberal talk-show host in order to balance out viewpoints and thus be fair to all sides, Republicans introduced several "pre-emptive strike" bills, such as the Broadcaster Freedom Act of 2009. By 2017, however, the Fairness Doctrine had not been resurrected.

The FCC has a Web page (https://www.fcc.gov/media/policy/statutes-and-rules-candidate-appearances-advertising) devoted exclusively to statutes and rules on candidate appearances and candidate advertising. What follows is a brief discussion of two of those rules: the candidate access rule and the equal opportunity/equal time rule. You are encouraged to visit the FCC's Web page referenced in this paragraph for more detailed information.

CANDIDATE ACCESS RULE

Broadcasters cannot completely block candidates for *federal* office from buying airtime on the station to promote their candidacies because of the existence of the **candidate access rule. Section 312**(a)(7) of the Federal Communications Act, adopted in 1971 by Congress, states that a broadcast license can be revoked for willful and repeated failure "to allow reasonable access to or to permit the purchase of reasonable amounts of time for the use of a broadcasting station by a legally qualified candidate for federal elective office on behalf of his candidacy." This statute applies only to candidates for federal office: presidents and vice presidents and U.S. senators and representatives.

EQUAL OPPORTUNITY/EQUAL TIME RULE

Section 315 of the Communications Act outlines what are called the equal opportunity or **equal time rules.** These rules have been a part of the law since it was passed in 1934, although this section was substantially amended in 1959. The rules are quite simple. If a broadcasting station permits one legally qualified candidate for any elective public office to use its facilities, it must afford an equal opportunity for all other legally qualified candidates for the same office.

What does equal opportunity mean? It means equal time, equal facilities and comparable costs. If John Smith buys one-half hour of television time on station WKTL to campaign for the office of mayor, other legally qualified candidates for that office must be allowed to purchase one-half hour of time as well. If Smith is able to use the station's equipment to prerecord his talk, other candidates must have the same opportunity. If the station charges Smith $100 for the one-half hour of time, the station must charge his opponents $100.

The station does not have to solicit appearances by the other candidates; it merely must give them the opportunity to use the facilities if they request such use within one week of Smith's appearance. Finally, Section 315 does not provide a right of access to any candidate to use a station's facilities. Section 315 applies only if the station first chooses to permit one candidate to appear on the station. However, remember the earlier discussion about requirements that exist under Section 312 and the general public interest standards that govern station operation.

Section 315 specifically bars the station from censoring material in broadcasts made by political candidates, and the courts interpret this provision quite strictly.

Use of the Airwaves

Under Section 315 if one candidate gets the use of a broadcast facility, his or her opponents get to use the facility as well. What is a "use" under the law? Any presentation or appearance that features a candidate's voice or image is regarded as a "use" by the FCC. It is not a use if, for example, in a political advertisement an announcer simply recites the candidate's record or his or her position on an issue. Similarly, it is not a use if the candidate's voice or image is used by an opponent in one of his or her ads. But short of these exceptions most other appearances count, including appearances on TV entertainment programs like a situation comedy, and even appearances in televised feature films. For example, during his campaign to be the Republican nominee for president, eventual winner Donald Trump guest-hosted the NBC comedy show "Saturday Night Live" (SNL) in November 2015. Shortly after the SNL episode aired, WNBC, NBC's New York affiliate, filed this notice with the FCC: "Donald Trump, a candidate for the Republican nomination for President in the 2016 national election, appeared without charge on NBC's 'Saturday Night Live' for a total period of 12:05 (12 minutes and 5 seconds) commencing at 11:39:11 PM ET on Nov. 7 and ending at 1:01:01 AM ET on Nov. 8, 2015." Since Trump was a legally qualified candidate when he hosted, his appearance triggered a seven-day window in which his rival Republican candidates for the nomination could request equal time. NBC didn't have to guarantee those candidates slots on SNL (as the candidates are not entitled to the same platform), but the station did have to guarantee equal time (12 minutes and 5 seconds) and cost (in this case free). Four GOP candidates subsequently reached agreements with NBC that allowed them to broadcast campaign advertisements, at no cost, on NBC-affiliated stations in Iowa, New Hampshire and South Carolina over Thanksgiving weekend in 2015. Their advertisements, which appeared on 18 stations in those three states, aired during primetime on Friday and Saturday and during that weekend's telecast of SNL (which was a rebroadcast of an earlier episode).

In another example, during the 2008 Democratic primary race for a state representative position in Massachusetts, candidate Brian Ashe was granted 20 free commercial spots, each 30 seconds long, and four 15-second commercial spots by a radio station in Springfield, Mass.[38] Why? Because his opponent, Kateri B. Walsh, had continued to host a radio program on that same station after she announced her candidacy. The station, WHYN-AM 560 radio, also agreed not to continue to carry Walsh's show as long as she remained a candidate.

In 1959 Congress amended Section 315 and carved out four rather broad exceptions to the meaning of the term "use." Since 1959 the FCC has liberally interpreted these exceptions to broaden them even more. The following appearances by a candidate do not constitute a use under the law. That is, an opponent cannot use one of these appearances as a justification for equal time from the station.

---

38. Goonan, "Brian Ashe, Candidate for 2nd Hampden District, Says He Has Reached Accord with Radio Station Over Opponent's Program."

APPEARANCES BY A POLITICAL CANDIDATE THAT ARE NOT GOVERNED BY EQUAL OPPORTUNITY RULE

- Appearance in a bona fide newscast
- Appearance in a bona fide news interview
- Appearance in the spot news coverage of a bona fide news event
- Incidental appearance in a news documentary

---

1. **The appearance by a candidate in a bona fide or legitimate newscast does not constitute use of the facility in the eyes of the law.** Section 315 will not be triggered. This exemption is expansive. The FCC has ruled that "Entertainment Tonight" constitutes a bona fide newscast and that appearances by legally qualified candidates for public office on "Access Hollywood" should be accorded the bona fide newscast exemption from the equal opportunity provision. In another example, in August 2015, the FCC declared that the then-new program "Crime Watch Daily" qualified as a bona fide newscast and thus was exempt from the equal opportunities requirements. The FCC's principal consideration is whether the program reports news of some area of current events in a manner similar to more traditional newscasts, and it declines to evaluate the relative quality or significance of the topics and stories selected for newscast coverage. The FCC ruled that an appearance in a news clip broadcast as a part of the program "McLaughlin Group" constitutes an appearance in a newscast.[39] But a candidate appearance during the panel discussion part of the program would not fall under the newscast exemption. If the newscaster or reporter who reads the news is a candidate for public office, this exemption does not apply to that candidacy.

   The FCC has ruled that "Entertainment Tonight" constitutes a bona fide newscast.

2. **The appearance of a candidate in a bona fide news interview does not constitute a use.** The FCC has defined a bona fide news interview program as one that is regularly scheduled, within the journalistic control of the producers and is produced as a newsworthy and good faith journalistic exercise, not an attempt to advance a particular candidacy. This exemption is quite broad. The FCC concluded that an October 2006 interview by Jay Leno on "The Tonight Show" with California Gov. Arnold Schwarzenegger—then running for re-election—was a bona fide news interview, noting that "the fact that many interviews on the program concern entertainment is irrelevant" and adding that Leno's lack of journalistic credentials was not controlling.[40] The FCC has held that interviews conducted on the "Sally Jessy Raphael

39. *Telecommunications Research and Action Center* v. *FCC*, 26 F. 3d 185 (D.C. Cir. 1994).
40. *In re Equal Opportunities Complaint Filed by Angelides for Governor Campaign Against 11 California Stations*, DA 06-2098 (Oct. 26, 2006).

Show," "Jerry Springer," "Politically Incorrect" and "Howard Stern" also fall within the bona fide news interview exemption.

3. **The appearance of a candidate in the spot news coverage of a bona fide news event is not use.** When candidate Smith is interviewed at the scene of a warehouse fire about the problems of arson in the city, this is not use in terms of Section 315. Political conventions are considered bona fide news events; therefore an appearance by a candidate at the convention can be broadcast without invoking Section 315.

4. **The appearance of a candidate in a news documentary is not a use if the appearance is incidental to the presentation of the subject of the program.** Imagine that during a 2018 election campaign for a U.S. Senate seat from Washington, a Seattle television station broadcasts a documentary on the 1991 Persian Gulf War and the role played by a particular U.S. Air Force unit that before the war was stationed at an air base in the state. One segment focuses on the wartime experiences of Luis Sanchez, a fighter pilot who was shot down over Iraq during the war but managed to elude the enemy for 10 days before reaching safety in Saudi Arabia. Sanchez is a candidate for the Senate seat. Would his appearance in this documentary trigger Section 315? Would the TV station be required to give time to his opponent? No. Because Sanchez's appearance focuses exclusively on his experiences during the war and not his political candidacy, his appearance in the documentary is regarded as an incidental appearance.

Debates between political candidates are considered bona fide news events, and the broadcast of these events will not initiate use of Section 315. This is true even if the broadcaster sponsors the debate.

Press conferences held by political candidates are also normally considered bona fide news events and are exempt from the provisions of Section 315. The FCC considers three criteria to determine if a candidate's press conference is exempt from the equal opportunity provision. They are:

1. Whether the conference is broadcast live
2. Whether, in the good faith determination of the broadcaster, it is a bona fide news event
3. Whether there is evidence of broadcaster favoritism or bias toward a candidate

Legally Qualified Candidates

The FCC has attempted to define who is and who is not a legally qualified candidate as precisely as possible (see boxed text on the next page).

In primary elections, Section 315 applies to intraparty elections, not interparty elections.

In primary elections, Section 315 applies to intraparty elections, not interparty elections. In a primary election Democrats run against Democrats, Republicans run against Republicans, Libertarians run against Libertarians. If there is an appearance by a Democrat, the other Democratic candidates for the same office must be afforded an equal opportunity. The station does not have to give Republicans or Libertarians or even independents the opportunity to make an appearance. During general elections, Section 315 applies across party lines since at this point all candidates are running against each other for the same office.

A LEGALLY QUALIFIED CANDIDATE IS ANY PERSON

▮ who publicly announces that he or she is a candidate for nomination or election to any local, county, state or federal office, *and*

▮ who meets the qualifications prescribed by law for that office, *and*

▮ who qualifies for a place on the ballot or is eligible to be voted for by sticker or write-in methods, *and*

▮ who was duly nominated by a political party that is commonly known and regarded as such or makes a substantial showing that he or she is a bona fide candidate.

FORMER WHITE PATRIOT PARTY LEADER NOT A BONA FIDE CANDIDATE FOR FCC PURPOSES

In June 2010 the FCC's Media Bureau Policy Division offered informal, oral advice to the Missouri Broadcasters Association that Frazier Glenn Miller Jr., a former leader of the White Patriot Party, was likely not a bona fide candidate for a U.S. Senate seat in Missouri and thus was not entitled to mandatory access to Missouri's broadcast airwaves to run anti-Semitic campaign ads urging Caucasians to "take back our country." The Missouri Broadcasters Association, along with Missouri Attorney General Chris Koster, had petitioned the FCC contending that bona fide candidates must, per step number four in the previous gray-shaded textbox, make a "substantial showing" of engaging in activities like making speeches, distributing campaign literature, issuing press releases, having a campaign committee and a campaign headquarters, and they argued Miller had failed to make such efforts. Miller, a write-in candidate for the Republican nomination, still was able to spew his racist beliefs online.

Miller was back in the news again in 2014 when he was arrested for killing three people at two Jewish sites in Kansas. In November 2015, he was convicted and sentenced to the death penalty.

Whereas only an appearance by the candidate himself or herself can trigger Section 315, for more than 40 years appearances by supporters of the candidate triggered another regulation called the Zapple Rule. This rule was formulated by the FCC in 1970 in response to a letter from Nicholas Zapple, who was a staff member on the Senate Subcommittee on Communications. The rule or doctrine stated that if a broadcaster permits the supporter of a candidate to make an appearance on the station, then the station must provide an equal opportunity for an appearance by supporters of other legally qualified candidates for the same office. In May 2014, however, the FCC announced that it would no longer enforce the Zapple Rule. The FCC said the rule was an outgrowth of the fairness doctrine, which the FCC had long ago abandoned. "Given the fact that the Zapple Doctrine was based on an interpretation of the fairness doctrine, which has no current legal effect, we conclude that the Zapple Doctrine similarly has no current legal effect," wrote William Lake, the chief of the FCC's Media Bureau.

Two last points need to be made about Section 315. First, since broadcasters are not permitted to censor the remarks of a political candidate, they are immune from libel suits based on those remarks. In 1959 the Supreme Court ruled that because stations cannot control what candidates say over the air, they should not be held responsible for the remarks. The candidate, however, can still be sued.[41] Second, ballot issues like school bond levies, initiatives and referendums do not fall under Section 315.

Do these rules apply to the Internet? No Supreme Court or federal appellate court ruling has focused specifically on that question. But clearly, since the Supreme Court ruled in 1997[42] that communication on the Internet enjoys the same First Amendment protection as communication in the printed press, it would seem highly improbable that the candidate access rule, the equal opportunity rule or any broadcast regulation could be applied to the Internet.

SUMMARY   Several rules govern political broadcasts carried by radio and television broadcasters. Section 312 of the Federal Communications Act states that broadcasters cannot have an across-the-board policy rejecting all paid and nonpaid appearances by candidates for federal office. A candidate's request must be evaluated and can be rejected only if it could cause serious disruption of program schedules or might prompt an excessive number of equal time requests. Although this rule applies only to requests from candidates for federal office, the government's mandate that broadcasters operate their stations in the public interest may very well include similar standards for the treatment by broadcasters of requests for access to airtime from state and local candidates.

Section 315 states that if a broadcaster provides one candidate for office with the opportunity to use a station's broadcast facilities, all other legally qualified candidates for the same office must be given the same opportunity. The use of the station's facilities includes all appearances on the station with the exception of the following:

1. Bona fide newscasts
2. Bona fide news interviews
3. Spot news coverage
4. Incidental appearance in a news documentary

Candidate press conferences and debates between candidates are considered spot news events. During primary elections, Section 315 applies only to candidates from the same political party running against each other to win the party's nomination to run in the general election.

---

41. *Farmers Educational and Cooperative Union of America* v. *WDAY,* 360 U.S. 525 (1959).
42. *Reno* v. *American Civil Liberties Union,* 521 U.S. 844 (1997).

NEWS AND PUBLIC AFFAIRS

While the FCC has been quite willing to impose content regulations on entertainment programming, the agency has purposely steered away from making similar rules regarding broadcast news. The violence ratings do not apply to television news, for example. The agency reinforced this position in 1998 when it rejected a petition to strip four Denver television station licenses on the grounds that the news programs on the stations are heavily saturated with violent content. A group called Media Watch asked the FCC to deny the station's license renewals because the news programming contained "toxic" levels of television violence, which in turn leads to "fear, disrespect, imitative behavior, desensitization and increased violent behavior." The agency responded by saying that "journalistic or editorial discretion in the presentation of news and public information is the core concept of the First Amendment free press guarantee."[43]

Although the FCC takes action when it has documented evidence that a station has engaged in deliberate distortion of the news, the agency generally defers to the judgment of broadcasters, due to First Amendment free press concerns. As the FCC provided in 2013 on its Web page titled Complaints About Broadcast Journalism:

> As public trustees, broadcasters may not intentionally distort the news. Broadcasters are responsible for deciding what their stations present to the public. The FCC has stated publicly that "rigging or slanting the news is a most heinous act against the public interest." The FCC does act to protect the public interest where it has received documented evidence of such rigging or slanting. This kind of evidence could include testimony, in writing or otherwise, from "insiders" or persons who have direct personal knowledge of an intentional falsification of the news. Of particular concern would be evidence about orders from station management to falsify the news. In the absence of such documented evidence, the FCC has stressed that it cannot intervene.[44]

Broadcasters may not intentionally distort the news.

In addition to taking action against deliberate and documented news distortions, the FCC enforces a separate provision that targets news hoaxes. In particular, the FCC prohibits broadcast licensees from broadcasting false information concerning crimes and catastrophes if three things exist:

The FCC enforces a separate provision that targets news hoaxes.

1. the licensee knows the information is false;
2. it is foreseeable that broadcast of the information will cause substantial public harm; and
3. broadcast of the information does in fact directly cause substantial public harm.

On April Fool's Day in 2013, two disc jockeys at a radio station in Bonita Springs, Fla., told listeners that "dihydrogen monoxide" was coming out of local residents' water faucets. Although it may sound dangerous and sort of like carbon monoxide, "dihydrogen monoxide" simply means H_2O—the chemical name for water. Some listeners, not getting

---

43. Brooke, "FCC Supports TV News."
44. *"FCC Consumer Facts: Complaints About Broadcast Journalism,"* available online at http://www.fcc.gov /guides/broadcast-journalism-complaints.

the joke, panicked and called the local water company, prompting it to release a statement making it clear there was no problem with the water. The disc jockeys were suspended for one day, and the radio station (Gator Country 101.9) apologized. The station's general manager told the Fort Myers *News-Press*, "We take this very seriously. We take our FCC license very seriously." That's because it is precisely the type of hoax the FCC prohibits and for which a station can be fined and/or lose its license.

A related issue involves recent fines the FCC has imposed on stations for improperly broadcasting emergency alert system (EAS) tones when there is no emergency. The EAS' purpose is to provide timely warnings so that in an emergency the public may act quickly to protect themselves and their families. In January 2015, the FCC fined Viacom and ESPN $1.4 million for misusing the tones. A trailer for the movie "Olympus Has Fallen" included simulated EAS tones (the movie portrayed a fictional terrorist attack on Washington, D.C.), and the FCC said those cable networks had thus transmitted EAS tones outside of an emergency for several days when they aired the trailer. The cable networks were fined even though they didn't produce the trailer themselves (the movie company did) and even though the networks said they didn't intend to deceive anyone. The FCC concluded that airing the trailer violated "laws protecting the integrity of the [EAS] system," which prohibit the transmission of EAS tones in "any circumstance except when an actual emergency or authorized test warrants their use." The FCC pointed out that it had evidence that some viewers actually *were* confused "because they associated the tones in the [trailer] with emergencies that did not exist."

VIDEO NEWS RELEASES, SPONSORSHIP IDENTIFICATION AND THE FCC

Video news releases (VNRs) are the broadcast equivalent of written press releases that masquerade as news but, in reality, are created by public relations firms or government agencies. They often involve video clips that feature a person who appears to be a reporter covering a real story, when in fact the person is an actor, or they come with a script that can be read as a voice-over by a local news anchor. Groups like the Center for Media and Democracy[45] claim that VNRs, which are virtually indistinguishable today from real news clips, amount to fake news and press release journalism, especially when local television stations run them unedited as if they really were news and fail to disclose their origin. Several federal government agencies under the administration of President George W. Bush used VNRs to convey their messages.

VNRs raise obvious ethical issues for the broadcast news stations that air them because they blur the line between objective news content and commercials or propaganda. But VNRs also raise legal issues of sponsorship identification that the FCC addresses. In particular, the FCC in 2006 launched a major investigation of 77 broadcast licensees to determine whether the sources of the VNRs they aired were properly disclosed to viewers during news broadcasts. This followed on the heels of a Public Notice issued by the FCC in 2005 under which the agency made it clear that "whenever broadcast stations and cable operators air VNRs, licensees and operators generally must

45. The Web site for this organization is available online at http://www.prwatch.org.

clearly disclose to members of their audiences the nature, source and sponsorship of the material that they are viewing. We will take appropriate enforcement action against entities that do not comply with these rules." The FCC can impose monetary fines of $32,500 per violation when a station fails to label a VNR.

The FCC's rules on sponsorship identification and disclosure provide in key part that "all matter broadcast by any radio [or TV] station for which any money, service or other valuable consideration is directly or indirectly paid, or promised to or charged or accepted by, the station so broadcasting, from any person, shall, at the time the same is so broadcast, be announced as paid for or furnished, as the case may be, by such person." The FCC permits newscasts to use VNRs without sponsorship identification only if the identification of a product within them is fleeting and is reasonably related to the subject matter of the programming at issue.

How does this work in real life? In 2011, the FCC issued a proposed fine of $4,000 against the owner of station WMGM-TV in Wildwood, N.J. The fine was based upon the airing of a VNR produced for Matrixx Initiatives—the makers of the Zicam cold remedy—without also airing a sponsorship identification announcement. Although the subject matter of the VNR was how to treat the common cold, the identification of Zicam was far more than fleeting. As the FCC wrote, "The VNR focuses almost exclusively on Matrixx's Zicam product in its visual depictions or verbal identifications of products, and the VNR contained extensive images of Zicam—a total of four different shots, some of them close-up and some of them extended."

RADIO CONTESTS: THE FCC'S RULES FOR THE ON-AIR ROAD

Ever called in to a radio station to enter a contest? The FCC enforces rules on contests, which it defines as schemes "in which a prize is offered or awarded, based upon chance, diligence, knowledge or skill, to members of the public."

The FCC's contest rules have two main parts. First, the FCC requires stations to "fully and accurately disclose the material terms of a contest." Material terms include things such as: (1) eligibility restrictions; (2) entry deadlines; (3) the means of selecting winners; and (4) the extent, nature and value of prizes. The descriptions of these items must not be false, misleading or deceptive. In 2015, the FCC updated its contest rules and now allows stations to disclose contest terms either by broadcasting those terms over the air or by making them available on a publicly accessible Web site. If a station chooses to disclose the terms online, the FCC said the station must broadcast the relevant Web site periodically, providing enough information for a consumer to easily find the terms online; the station must establish a link or tab to the contest terms on the Web site's home page; and the station must maintain contest terms online for at least 30 days after the contest has ended.

Second, stations must conduct their contests substantially as announced or advertised. In other words, the FCC will examine how a contest actually was carried out.

Does the FCC enforce these rules? Yes. In February 2013 the FCC fined a Boston radio station (WMJX) $4,000 for "broadcasting information about a contest

> without fully and accurately disclosing all material terms thereof and by failing to conduct the contest substantially as announced or advertised." The station's promotion of its "Cool, Hot or Green" contest advertised that the winner would receive the choice of one of three new cars. That was misleading, however, as the actual prize turned out to be a two-year lease of a car, not permanent ownership, and the lease was only valid if the winner passed a credit check. The station's violation of the FCC's contest rules was "fundamental and serious," the FCC wrote in its order assessing the fine.

THE FIRST AMENDMENT

Broadcasting stations are not common carriers; that is, they have the right to refuse to do business with anyone they choose. During 1969 and 1970 two groups, the Democratic National Committee and a Washington, D.C., organization known as Business Executives Movement for Peace, sought to buy time from television stations and networks to solicit funds for their protest of the Vietnam War and to voice their objections to the way the war was being waged by the government. Broadcasters rebuffed these groups on the grounds that airing such controversial advertisements and programming would evoke the fairness doctrine, and they would then be obligated to ensure that all sides of the controversy were aired. Such action was a nuisance and could be costly. The broadcasters told the Democratic committee and the business executives that one of their basic policies was not to sell time to any individual or group seeking to set forth views on controversial issues.

When this policy was challenged before the FCC, the commission sided with the broadcasters, noting that it was up to each individual licensee to determine how best to fulfill fairness doctrine obligations. But the U.S. Court of Appeals for the District of Columbia Circuit reversed the FCC ruling, stating that the right of the public to receive information is deeply rooted in the First Amendment. A ban on editorial advertising, the court ruled, "leaves a paternalistic structure in which licensees and bureaucrats decide what issues are important, whether to fully cover them, and the format, time and style of coverage." This kind of system, the court ruled, is inimical to the First Amendment.[46]

The victory of the business organization and the Democrats was short-lived, for by a 7-2 vote, the U.S. Supreme Court overturned the appellate court ruling. Stations have an absolute right to refuse to sell time for advertising dealing with political campaigns and controversial issues, the court ruled. To give the FCC the power over such advertising runs the risk of enlarging government control over the content of broadcast discussion of public issues.

In response to the argument that by permitting broadcasters to refuse such advertising, we place in their hands the power to decide what the people shall see or hear on important public issues, Justice Burger wrote:

---

46. *In re Business Executives Movement for Peace* v. *FCC,* 450 F. 2d 642 (D.C. Cir. 1971).

For better or worse, editing is what editors are for; and editing is the selection and choice of material. That editors—newspaper or broadcast—can and do abuse this power is beyond doubt, but that is no reason to deny the discretion Congress provided. Calculated risks of abuse are taken in order to preserve high values.[47]

"For better or worse, editing is what editors are for."

The court was badly fractured on this case, and Justices Brennan and Marshall dissented. Only two other justices—Stewart and Rehnquist—joined the chief justice in his opinion. The remainder joined in overturning the appeals court ruling, but for their own reasons.

Finally, the high court used the First Amendment to strike down a congressional statute forbidding all noncommercial educational broadcasting stations that receive money from the Corporation for Public Broadcasting from editorializing on any subject at all.[48] The ban on all editorials by every station that receives CPB funds was too broad and far exceeded what is necessary to protect against the risk of governmental interference or to prevent the public from assuming that editorials by public broadcasting stations represent the official views of government.

SUMMARY

The government exercises limited control over the content of public affairs broadcasts. The FCC has thus far rejected all complaints that television news coverage was slanted or staged and has made it difficult for those who seek to pursue this cause with the agency. The Supreme Court has given broadcasters the right to determine whether to air specific editorial advertising and has struck down a statute that forbade public broadcasting stations from telecasting editorial opinions.

REGULATION OF NEW TECHNOLOGY

Over-the-air broadcasting has been the primary focus of government attempts to regulate the electronic communications media, but as new technologies have emerged, the Federal Communications Commission and the Congress have moved to pass rules to govern their operation as well. Cable television has been the subject of numerous FCC rule-making efforts and two comprehensive federal statutes. Rules regulating low-power television, multipoint distribution services, satellite master antenna television and direct satellite broadcasting have also been promulgated. The deregulatory waves that have swept away many broadcast rules have also hit cable regulation. In 2001 a federal court ordered the FCC to reconsider and justify rules that limited both the size and program content of cable systems. Congress had given the FCC the authority to limit the number of cable subscribers one multiple system operator could reach—30 percent of all cable subscribers—and to

47. *CBS* v. *Democratic National Committee,* 412 U.S. 94 (1973).
48. *FCC* v. *League of Women Voters,* 468 U.S. 912 (1984).

prevent a cable operator, like AOL Time Warner for example, from filling the cable package it offered subscribers with programs created only by its affiliated companies. Only 40 percent of the programming could be produced by affiliated companies. The U.S. Court of Appeals ruled that both rules implicated the First Amendment and could be sustained only if it was shown they advanced important government interests unrelated to the suppression of speech and did not impact or limit more speech than necessary to further those interests. The court said in imposing the rules that the FCC had not adequately justified the need for the 30 percent cap on subscribers or the 40 percent cap on programming.[49]

SATELLITE RADIO

Just as air-conditioning once was a fancy option on the automobile that now is taken for granted by many buyers, today a prized option on a car or SUV is satellite radio—something that likely will become a standard vehicle feature in the not-so-distant future. Satellite radio stands in contrast to the free, over-the-air terrestrial radio to which we are accustomed. Sirius Satellite Radio was initially helped by the well-publicized $500 million signing of talk-show host and self-proclaimed "King of All Media" Howard Stern.[50]

Howard Stern's switch to satellite radio is important for media law students to understand. While free, over-the-air radio broadcasting is subject to the FCC's rules governing indecency and profanity discussed earlier in this chapter, satellite radio is—at least at the time this book went to press—exempt from similar content-based rules. Thus shock jocks like Stern can freely use profanity and expletives at any time of the day on satellite radio with no need to fear the wrath of the FCC.

Although the FCC does not yet control indecent content on either satellite radio or cable television, it does regulate other aspects of the relatively new medium of satellite radio. For example, Sirius, which was founded in 1990 (two years before former rival XM Satellite Radio), had to apply to the FCC to launch its three current satellites that were operating by 2000. The FCC also regulates power levels and emissions from satellite radio devices and modulators, as well as the land antennas that transmit signals from satellites used by Sirius and XM to local devices.

The FCC approved by a 3-2 vote the merger of Sirius and XM.

In 2008, with both companies struggling financially, the FCC approved by a 3-2 vote the merger of Sirius and XM (the new company is Sirius XM Radio Inc.). FCC approval came only after the two companies agreed to pay almost $20 million in combined fines for using some ground-based repeaters (signal towers) for their satellite signals that were not authorized by the FCC and for selling receiving devices that exceeded FCC-established power limits and thus interfered with reception of FM radio signals (indeed, Howard Stern's program on Sirius had bled onto National Public Radio's FM signal in some cases!). In addition, the combined companies agreed to cap prices on some services for three years after the merger and to set aside a portion of their channels (4 percent of the full-time audio channels on the Sirius platform and 4 percent of the full-time channels on the XM platform) for minority-owned entities. They also agreed to offer new packages of

---

49. Labaton and Fabrikant, "U.S. Court Ruling Lets Cable Giants." See also *Time Warner Entertainment Co.* v. *FCC,* 240 F. 3d 1126 (D.C. Cir. 2001).
50. Semuels, "Sirius Gives Stern, Agent $83-million Stock Bonus."

programs, including two á la carte options. In brief, the FCC used the merger review as an opportunity to impose burdens on and extract concessions from the new company. The Justice Department declared the merger would not violate antitrust laws.

Whether the cost-saving synergies created by the merger ultimately benefit the public interest—the critical concept for FCC regulation (see earlier in this chapter)—or whether the monopoly harms consumers remains to be seen.

By 2017, Sirius XM offered subscribers more than 175 channels of satellite radio, including more than 70 commercial-free music channels. It also followed through on the FCC's merger requirement that it offer multiple packages to customers. By 2017, the company had more than 30 million subscribers. In 2016, it had revenue of $5 billion, up 10 percent from the year before.

INTERNET AND BROADBAND

In 2009 the FCC began developing a national broadband plan designed to ensure that every American has access to broadband capability. The move came as part of the massive federal stimulus package, known as the American Recovery and Reinvestment Act of 2009, in which Congress charged the FCC with creating a national broadband plan by February 17, 2010.

Reflecting advances in technology, market offerings by broadband providers and consumer demand, in 2015 the FCC updated what it considers its broadband benchmark speeds to 25 megabits per second (Mbps) for downloads and 3 Mbps for uploads. In 2016, the FCC's Broadband Progress Report revealed that 34 million Americans (about 10 percent of the population) lacked access to fixed broadband service at those benchmark speeds. In rural areas, nearly 40 percent of the population (23 million people) lacked access to it.

The term broadband refers to high-speed Internet access that is always on, is faster than dial-up access and allows more content, such as streaming media (watching Netflix movies on your computer) and VoIP (Internet phone), to be transmitted. The FCC hosts a Web site regarding its implementation of the National Broadband Plan, which was adopted in 2010, at https://www.fcc.gov/general/national-broadband-plan.

Four key aspects of the National Broadband Plan are:

1. Designing policies to ensure robust competition and, as a result, to maximize consumer welfare, innovation and investment.
2. Ensuring efficient allocation and management of assets that the government controls or influences, such as spectrum, poles and rights-of-way, and to encourage network upgrades and competitive entry.
3. Reforming current universal service mechanisms to support deployment of broadband and voice in high-cost areas; ensuring that low-income Americans can afford broadband; and supporting efforts to boost adoption and utilization.
4. Reforming laws, policies, standards and incentives to maximize the benefits of broadband in sectors that the government significantly influences, such as public education, health care and government operations.

As discussed in Chapter 3, the FCC has also regulated the issue of net neutrality. In March 2015, the FCC released an Open Internet Order meant, it said, to "enact strong, sustainable rules . . . to protect the open Internet and ensure that Americans reap the economic, social, and civic benefits of an open Internet today and into the future." In the order, the FCC reclassified broadband Internet service as a telecommunications service, subject to common carrier regulation under Title II of the Communications Act of 1934. In effect, the FCC classified the Internet as a public utility, with the goal of ensuring an open Internet for all content.

The FCC's order banned three specific practices that it said invariably harm the principle of an open Internet—blocking, throttling and paid prioritization (see page 143 of Chapter 3 for more information about them).

The FCC passed the order along party lines, with the three Democratic commissioners voting for the order and the two Republican commissioners voting against it. The order frustrated broadband providers, who have fought against rules that mandate net neutrality.

In June 2016, the U.S. Circuit Court of Appeals for the District of Columbia voted to uphold the net neutrality rules as well as the FCC's classification of broadband Internet access as a public utility. But under the Trump administration, the majority of the FCC commissioners are now Republicans, and the Republican commissioners have indicated that they hope to roll back the net neutrality efforts launched under the Obama administration. In May 2017, the FCC voted to start a process aimed at reversing the 2015 order's classification of the Internet as a telecommunications service. So the net neutrality issue is far from settled.

CABLE TELEVISION

Cable television first appeared in the 1940s. It was called community antenna television (CATV). In rural communities where television reception was poor because of distance or topography, entrepreneurs installed large antennas on hilltops to receive the incoming television signals and then transmitted these signals (for a small price) to local homeowners via coaxial cable. The FCC first asserted its jurisdiction of cable or CATV in the early 1960s. But the agency had to move tenuously at first because its right to regulate cable television was not clearly established. Cable is not broadcast; signals travel through wires, not the airwaves. There is no scarcity of spectrum space, that important factor that justifies government regulation of broadcasting. Cable is not a common carrier, as are telephone and telegraph. The FCC authority to regulate these point-to-point services does not establish its right to regulate cable. It took more than 20 years, with the adoption of the Cable Communications Policy Act of 1984, before FCC jurisdiction over cable was firmly established.

FEDERAL LEGISLATION REGULATING CABLE TELEVISION

Two federal laws provide the foundation of the regulation of cable television. The first measure, the comprehensive Cable Communications Policy Act of 1984, was a cable-friendly measure designed to foster the orderly growth of this new medium. Cable flourished under this law. By the 1990s nearly all American homes had access to cable television, and more than 60 percent of all Americans received their television via cable. But viewers, and then members of Congress, became angry at many heavy-handed policies adopted by the cable industry using the freedom it had been granted under the 1984 legislation. Viewers complained about escalating cable rates among other things. In 1992 Congress adopted the Cable Television Consumer Protection and Competition Act, a decidedly not cable-friendly measure that imposed rate regulations on most cable systems, directed the FCC to develop mandatory service standards for cable television and greatly strengthened the competitive position of local, over-the-air television stations vis-à-vis cable. The 1984 law remains the basic regulatory measure. Its most important provisions are outlined on the following pages. It will be noted where the 1992 law has modified this legislation.

Viewers complained about escalating cable rates among other things.

In 2007 the FCC voted to retain its 30 percent cap on cable ownership. This rule, known as a horizontal ownership limit, sets the maximum number of subscribers that a single cable operator may serve at 30 percent of households nationwide. The 30 percent limit, first established in 1993 and modified in 1999, was challenged in federal court by Time Warner in 2001. The court determined that the FCC lacked a sufficient evidentiary basis for the 30 percent cap, and it sent the rule back to the FCC to further justify its existence. In justifying the 30 percent cap in 2007, the FCC contended the limit was necessary to ensure that no single cable operator would create a barrier to a video programming network's entry into the market or cause a video programming network to exit the market simply by declining to carry the network. But in August 2009 in *Comcast Corp.* v. *FCC*, the U.S. Court of Appeals for the District of Columbia struck down the FCC's 30 percent cap limiting the number of U.S. cable subscribers that any one cable company can have. The court held the FCC's decision to adopt the 30 percent figure was "arbitrary and capricious."

The Cable Communications Policy Act of 1984 (hereafter Cable Act) was adopted after decades of crazy-quilt regulation at the federal, state and local levels. The act was needed because some state and local governments were attempting to assert increased control over an industry that had become increasingly national in scope. In the summer of 1988, in a decision regarding the right of the FCC to establish certain technical standards for cable television, the Supreme Court read the new Cable Act in an expansive fashion, giving the FCC assurances that its regulation of the medium would be supported under the law.[51]

Purpose of the Law

The purposes of this legislation are enumerated in Section 601 of the Cable Act itself. They are as follows:

1. To establish a national policy concerning cable communications
2. To establish franchise procedures and standards that encourage the growth and development of cable systems and that ensure that cable systems are responsive to the needs and interests of the local community
3. To establish guidelines for the exercise of federal, state and local authority with respect to the regulation of cable systems

---

51. *New York City* v. *FCC,* 486 U.S. 57 (1988).

4. To ensure and encourage that cable communications provide the widest possible diversity of information sources and services to the public

5. To establish a process that protects cable operators against unfair denials of renewal by franchising authorities and that provides for an orderly process for consideration of renewal proposals

Jurisdiction and Franchises

The federal government has jurisdiction to regulate cable television, but has given local governments the power to impose a variety of obligations on cable operators. The local government is what is called the "franchising authority"; it is given the power to grant the cable system the right to operate in a particular area. This right is contained in a franchise agreement, which gives the cable operator the right to serve customers in a particular area in exchange for the promise to provide certain standards of service. Until about 25 years ago, this was an exclusive right. This means that only a single operator served a particular community. Cable companies often had to bid against one another to win this exclusive right. These exclusive agreements were challenged on constitutional grounds, but the Supreme Court did not outlaw their use.[52] Congress did, however, in 1992. Economics, even more than government policy, makes it unlikely that more than a single operator will serve the cable customers in a community. The cost of wiring a community is simply prohibitive without the promise of exclusivity. If, as some predict, the day comes when a single wire carries all telephone, television and Internet traffic in a community, and the use of that wire is open to anyone who seeks to send a signal, competition for cable customers within a city or even a neighborhood may become a reality.

Rate regulation has consistently been a bone of contention between cable operators and government regulatory bodies, both federal and local. The 1984 and 1992 cable laws gave the FCC substantial power to control what cable companies charge their customers. But the 1996 Telecommunications Act reversed this policy and immediately abolished the FCC's power to regulate the rates for small cable systems and ordered the agency to phase out rate regulation for larger systems by March 1999. The marketplace model was the justification for this change in policy, and supporters of deregulation argued that the delivery of television programming through telephone lines and by direct broadcast satellite (DBS) would force cable operators to keep their rates competitive. But the competition to cable did not develop.[53] The telephone companies lost interest in carrying television programming when they discovered they could make more money providing homeowners and businesses with hookups to the Internet. And television viewers resisted direct broadcast satellite services because these providers were not permitted to transmit programming from local television stations. In 1999 Congress changed the law and required DBS operators whose systems carried even one local channel to carry all the local channels.[54] The satellite operators didn't like this, but their challenge of the law on

52. *Los Angeles* v. *Preferred Communications,* 476 U.S. 488 (1986).
53. Gomery, "Cable TV Rates"; and "Cable Rates Rising."
54. The Satellite Home Viewer Improvement Act of 1999; see also Clausing, "Satellite TV Is Poised."

First Amendment grounds failed.[55] The change actually spurred the growth of DBS home receiving systems, but this seemed to have little impact on higher-than-ever cable rates in most communities.

Must-Carry Rules

Historically the government required all cable operators to retransmit the signals of all local television stations. These requirements were called the "must-carry rules" and were instituted to protect local broadcasters. By the 1980s, when cable networks proliferated, many cable operators found the rules to be onerous because they required operators to carry local over-the-air stations in preference to the more attractive (and lucrative for them) cable networks. Despite the so-called lack of scarcity in cable at the time, most systems were limited to 36 channels. The must-carry rules were challenged, and in 1985 a U.S. Court of Appeals ruled them to be a violation of the First Amendment.[56] By forcing a cable operator to carry a local station, the government denied the cable operator his or her First Amendment rights to communicate some other kind of programming. In other words, the court saw the must-carry rules as a content-based regulation. Attempts by the government to recast the rules failed to win court approval.[57] The 1992 cable law attempted to strengthen the position of the local broadcaster and contained substantially modified must-carry rules. Under this law the local broadcaster could either insist that the cable operator retransmit the station's signal to subscribers or forbid the cable operator from retransmitting the signal unless he or she paid what is called a retransmission fee. The application of the must-carry provisions varied with the channel capacity of the cable system. Small systems with less than 12 channels, for example, had to carry only three local commercial stations and one noncommercial station. Larger cable systems had to carry most or all local stations. Independent local stations with limited popularity insisted on cable carriage; popular network-affiliated stations often sought the retransmission fee.

Congress justified the new rules with the argument that 60 percent of Americans receive their television signals via cable. The heart of the American broadcasting system has consistently been local broadcasting. If cable operators are free to refuse to carry local broadcasters on their cable systems, this action could cause serious harm to the local stations. Cable operators said this fear was groundless, that it would be imprudent of them to drop the retransmission of popular local stations. But many local stations are not that popular, the broadcasters said, and the cable operator earns substantially more revenue by carrying a cable channel than by retransmitting a local broadcast signal. Many of the less popular over-the-air channels could be abandoned and ultimately die.

Turner Broadcasting, which owned several cable channels that might be displaced by the addition of local channels to the limited cable mix, challenged the new rules and a

---

55. *Satellite Broadcasting and Communications Association* v. *Federal Communications Commission,* 275 F. 3d 337 (4th Cir. 2001).
56. *Quincy Cable* v. *FCC,* 768 F. 2d 1434 (D.C. Cir. 1985).
57. *Century Communications* v. *FCC,* 835 F. 2d 292 (D.C. Cir. 1987).

protracted legal battle ensued.[58] In two separate decisions the Supreme Court ultimately approved the new rules. Opponents of the rules challenged them on the grounds that by forcing a cable operator to carry one channel rather than another, the government was imposing decisions regarding the content of cable television on a system operator and that this content regulation violated the First Amendment. Justice Anthony Kennedy agreed that the rules do impact content because they determine who is allowed to speak in a given cable market. "But they do so based only upon the manner in which the speakers transmit their messages to viewers, not upon the messages they carry," he said.[59] The justification for the rules—the protection of local over-the-air broadcasting, the promotion of a diversity of programming sources and the maintenance of fair competition in the TV market—is sufficient, the court said, inasmuch as in the end the rules are content neutral.[60] The issue of carrying local signals has receded with the growth of the capacity of most cable systems, yet the competition among cable channels to gain access to cable systems is as heated as ever.

In 2010 the must-carry rules were back in the legal limelight. That's when the U.S. Supreme Court let stand an appellate court ruling supporting the FCC's decision to use the rules to order Cablevision, at the time a major cable television operator, to carry TV station WRNN on Cablevision's Long Island, N.Y., cable system. The dispute in *Cablevision Systems Corp.* v. *FCC* [61] arose after the FCC engaged in what is known as a market modification. In particular, the market modification provision of the must-carry statute provides that the FCC may add or remove communities from a local broadcast station's designated market area "to better effectuate the purposes" of the must-carry rules. If a given community is excluded from a television station's designated market area, then cable operators in that community are no longer required to carry that station (the must-carry rules don't apply). If, however, a given community is added to the market area, then cable operators in that community must commence carriage of that station's signal, unless they already have devoted one-third of their channels to local, over-the-air broadcast stations, as is required by the must-carry rules. In this case, the FCC modified the market area of WRNN to include the Long Island communities covered by Cablevision, and Cablevision protested the move. In ruling against Cablevision, the 2nd U.S. Circuit Court of Appeals initially determined that the FCC's order requiring Cablevision to carry WRNN was content-neutral. It thus was subject only to an intermediate scrutiny standard of judicial review, just as Justice Kennedy had found was applicable to the must-carry rules in *Turner,* as noted earlier. The 2nd Circuit then reasoned that the "burden imposed by the [FCC's] order—the loss of control over one channel—is no greater than necessary to further the government's interest in preserving a single broadcast channel it found serves the local community." In brief, there was no violation of the First Amendment in requiring Cablevision to carry WRNN.

58. *Turner Broadcasting System, Inc.* v. *FCC,* 819 F. Supp. 32 (1993).
59. *Turner Broadcasting System, Inc.* v. *FCC,* 114 S. Ct. 2445 (1994).
60. *Turner Broadcasting System, Inc.* v. *FCC,* 117 S. Ct. 1174 (1997).
61. 570 F. 3d 83 (2d Cir. 2009), cert. den., 130 S. Ct. 3275 (2010).

Programming and Freedom of Expression

The FCC has imposed on cable systems that originate programming many of the same content rules that govern over-the-air television. The equal time rules, the "lowest unit rate" rule for political advertising, the candidate access rules, the sponsor identification rule and many others apply to cable-originated programs. Federal rules prohibit the broadcast of obscenity on over-the-air television; similar rules apply to cable. The FCC has also ruled that over-the-air broadcasters must limit their broadcast of indecent material to those hours when children are not likely to be in the television viewing audience, between 10 p.m. and 6 a.m. (see page 639). But Congress and the courts have, in the past, given cable television operators far greater leeway in the broadcast of indecency. Federal courts, for example, have consistently struck down attempts by the states to bar cable companies from transmitting indecent or adult programming but denied cable operators any right to censor programming.[62] The 1984 Cable Act required that every cable operator provide, on request from a subscriber, a lock box device that permits the subscriber to block out the reception of specific channels. The 1992 law contained hastily drafted provisions that *permitted* cable operators to prohibit indecent programming on the commercial leased-access channels and on the public access channels available to government and public schools. If the operator decided to permit indecent programming on the commercially leased channels, these signals had to be scrambled and subscribers could only view these channels by requesting access in writing 30 days in advance of the viewing. In 1995 the U.S. Court of Appeals for the District of Columbia Circuit ruled that the provisions that *permitted* the cable operator to ban indecent programming from the access channels didn't involve any action by the government. The censorship is the result of an action by the cable system operator, a private party. Hence there were no First Amendment implications to these provisions.[63] In June 1996 a badly splintered Supreme Court voided some of these new cable rules but sustained other portions of the law. The court sustained the portion of the law that allowed the cable operator to ban patently offensive programming from the leased-access channels but struck down the regulation that required cable operators to scramble such programming and force subscribers to ask for access in writing. This latter rule limited what subscribers could see and constituted an invasion of their privacy by forcing them to acknowledge in writing that they wanted to see such programming, the court said. At the same time, the high court struck down that portion of the law that gave cable operators the right to ban indecent programming from the government access channels. The court said there was no history of problems of the transmission of indecency on such channels and indicated a concern that conservative cable operators might try to control the kind of programming telecast on public access channels, traditionally the haven of nonprofit organizations who seek to communicate with the larger audience.[64]

---

62. See, for example, *Home Box Office* v. *Wilkinson,* 531 F. Supp. 987 (1982); and *Jones* v. *Wilkinson,* 800 F. 2d 989 (10th Cir. 1986), aff'd 480 U.S. 926 (1987).
63. *Alliance for Community Media* v. *FCC,* 56 F. 3d 105 (D.C. Cir. 1995).
64. *Denver Area Educational Telecommunications Consortium Inc.* v. *FCC; Alliance for Community Media* v. *FCC,* 1 E.P.L.R. 331 (1996).

In December 1998 a special three-judge panel of the U.S. District Court for Delaware struck down Section 505 of the 1996 Communications Decency Act, which required the distributors of adult programming over cable television to completely scramble both the video and audio signals, regardless of whether customers requested the programming to be scrambled. The law was aimed at protecting children from what is called "signal bleed," or incomplete scrambling. When signal bleed occurs, viewers can see and hear portions of the scrambled program. Programming distributors who could not fulfill this obligation were told to confine the transmission of this adult programming to the hours between 10 p.m. and 6 a.m. Playboy Entertainment challenged the provision, arguing that cable operators who could not afford the expensive scrambling technology would simply stop carrying this kind of programming rather than risk violating the law. The court ruled that while the government had a legitimate interest in attempting to shield young people from the adult programming, Section 505 was not the least restrictive means to fulfill this interest. The court said another provision in the CDA, which requires cable operators to supply blocking devices to subscribers who want them to screen out such channels, accomplishes the same goal without substantially interfering with the program distributors' First Amendment rights.[65] Two years later the Supreme Court affirmed the lower-court decision by a 5-4 vote. Justice Anthony Kennedy wrote that because signal-scrambling technology is imperfect, the "only reasonable way for a substantial number of cable operators to comply with the letter of §505 is to 'time channel,' which silences protected speech for two-thirds of the day in every home in a cable service area, regardless of the presence or likely presence of children or the wishes of the viewer." This requirement is a significant restriction on First Amendment protected speech, he wrote. The capacity required in cable systems to allow subscribers to block unwanted channels is a far narrower and less restrictive alternative that would still serve the government's interest.[66]

The Cable Act has established that third parties—that is, people other than the cable operator or the local government—must have access to the cable system. Several means are provided for such access. The local franchising authorities are permitted to require that the cable operator provide public access and government and educational access channels. A public access channel is set aside for free public use on a nondiscriminatory, first-come, first-served basis. Neither the cable operator nor the government can censor what appears on such a channel (with the exception that the cable operator may refuse to transmit a public access program that the cable operator reasonably believes contains obscenity). The franchising authority can prescribe limited (content-neutral) time, place and manner rules for the public access channel, such as deciding that the access channel will give each user 30 minutes of time or that they must sign up three days before the date they wish to use the channel. But these are about the only limits. The government and educational channels are used either by schools or to broadcast public hearings or city council meetings. These channels are to be programmed as the government sees fit.

---

65. *Playboy Entertainment Group, Inc. v. U.S.,* 30 F. Supp. 2d 702 (1998).
66. *United States* v. *Playboy Entertainment Group, Inc.,* 529 U.S. 803 (2000); the FCC repealed these rules in November 2001.

Commercial access channels must also be provided by the cable operator. The law provides that a certain number of channels must be set aside for use by "unaffiliated programmers" at reasonable rates. The cable operator cannot control the content of these programs. The number of channels that must be set aside for commercial access depends on the number of activated channels in the cable system. An activated channel is one that is being used or is available for use. The cable operator can set the price and conditions of use for these channels, so long as they are "reasonable." Costs cannot have anything to do with content; that is, a cable operator cannot charge someone who puts on a conservative talk show $100 per hour and someone who puts on a liberal talk show $500. However, the cable operator can set different rates for different categories of program; for example, news programs cost $50 per hour, movies $100 per hour.

Commercial access channels must also be provided by the cable operator.

SUMMARY

The power of the FCC to regulate cable television was a clouded issue for many years. Slowly but surely, the commission, with the permission of the courts, moved to regulate this new technology. In 1984 both the Supreme Court and Congress gave the FCC what seemed to be clear jurisdiction to set broad rules for governing cable television.

The Cable Communications Policy Act of 1984 is a comprehensive measure setting policies and standards for the regulation of cable television. The 1992 Cable Television Consumer Protection and Competition Act made some modifications in the earlier law. Local governments are given the primary responsibility under this measure to regulate the cable systems in their communities. They may issue franchises, collect franchise fees and renew franchises. The Cable Act also provides for the inclusion of public, government and commercial access channels.

BIBLIOGRAPHY

Brooke, James. "The FCC Supports TV News as Free Speech." *The New York Times,* 3 May 1998, A13.
Carter, Bill. "Media Ruling Merely Irritates Big Owners." *The New York Times,* 25 June 2004, C1.
Clausing, Jeri. "Satellite TV Is Poised for New Growth." *The New York Times,* 26 November 1999, C1.
Collins, Scott. "The Decency Debate; Pulled Into a Very Wide Net: Unusual Suspects Have Joined the Censor's Target List, Making for Strange Bedfellows (Wait Can We Say That?)." *Los Angeles Times,* 28 March 2004, E26.
Cowan, Geoffrey. *See No Evil.* New York: Simon & Schuster, 1979.
Gomery, Douglas. "Cable TV Rates: Not a Pretty Picture." *American Journalism Review,* July/August 1998, 66.

Goonan, Peter. "Brian Ashe, Candidate for 2nd Hampden District, Says He Has Reached Accord with Radio Station Over Opponent's Program." *The Republican* (Springfield, Mass.), 11 September 2008, B1.

Huff, Richard. "Fear Over 'Private' Parts." *Daily News* (New York), 11 November 2004, 111.

Labaton, Stephen. "Cable Rates Rising as Industry Nears End of Regulation." *The New York Times,* 3 March 1999, A1.

——, and Geraldine Fabrikant. "U.S. Court Ruling Lets Cable Giants Widen Their Reach." *The New York Times,* 31 March 2001, A1.

Puzzanghera, Jim. "A Campaign to Head Off New Decency Rules." *Los Angeles Times*, 26 July 2006, C3.

Semuels, Alana. "Sirius Gives Stern, Agent $83-million Stock Bonus." *Los Angeles Times,* 10 January 2007, C1.

GLOSSARY

A

absolute privilege An immunity from libel suits granted to government officials and others based on remarks uttered or written as part of their official duties.

absolutist theory The proposition that the First Amendment is an absolute, and that government may adopt no laws whatsoever that abridge freedom of expression.

actual damages Damages awarded to a plaintiff in a lawsuit based on proof of actual harm to the plaintiff.

actual malice A fault standard in libel law: knowledge before publication that the libelous material was false or reckless disregard of the truth or falsity of the libelous matter.

administrative agency An agency, created and funded by Congress, whose members are appointed by the president and whose function is to administer specific legislation, such as law regulating broadcasting and advertising.

admonition to a jury Instructions from a judge to a trial jury to avoid talking to other people about the trial they are hearing and to avoid news broadcasts and newspaper or magazine stories that discuss the case or issues in the case.

Alien and Sedition Acts of 1798 Laws adopted by the Federalist Congress aimed at stopping criticism of the national government by Republican or Jeffersonian editors and politicians.

amici curiae "Friends of the court"; people who have no specific legal stake in a lawsuit but are allowed to appear on behalf of one of the parties in a case.

answer A document often filed by a defendant in response to a civil complaint that denies allegations and factual assertions.

appellant The party who initiates or takes the appeal of a case from one court to another.

appellate court A court that has both original and appellate jurisdiction; a court to which cases are removed for an appeal.

appellee The person in a case against whom the appeal is taken; that is, the party in the suit who is not making the appeal.

appropriation In the law of privacy, use of a person's name or likeness without consent for advertising or trade purposes.

arraignment The first official court appearance made by a criminal defendant at which he or she is formally charged with an offense and called on to plead guilty or not guilty

to the charges contained in the state's indictment or information.

B

bait-and-switch advertising An illegal advertising strategy in which the seller baits customers by an advertisement with a low-priced model of a product but then switches customers who seek to buy the product to a much higher-priced model by telling them that the cheaper model does not work well or is no longer in stock.

bench-bar-press guidelines Informal agreements among lawyers, judges, police officials and journalists about what should and should not be published or broadcast about a criminal suspect or criminal case before a trial is held.

bond; bonding A large sum of money given by a publisher to a government to be held to ensure good behavior. Should the publisher violate a government rule, the bond is forfeited to the government, and the newspaper or magazine cannot be published again until a new bond is posted.

C

California Plan See *Missouri Plan*.

candidate access rule Section 312 of the Federal Communications Act, which forbids a broadcaster from instituting an across-the-board policy that denies all candidates for federal office the opportunity to use the station to further a political campaign.

case reporter A book containing a chronological collection of the opinions rendered by a particular court for cases that were decided by the court.

challenge for cause The request by a litigant in a criminal or civil case that a juror be dismissed for a specific reason.

change of veniremen Drawing a jury from a distant community in order to find jurors who have heard little or nothing about a criminal case or criminal defendant.

change of venue Moving a trial to a distant community in order to find jurors who have not read or viewed prejudicial publicity about the defendant.

Child Advertising Review Unit (CARU) The children's branch of the advertising industry's self-regulation program that evaluates child-directed advertising and promotional material in all media in order to advance truthfulness and accuracy and to protect minors' online privacy while visiting advertisers' Web sites.

citation The reference to a legal opinion contained in a case reporter that gives the name, volume number and page number where the opinion can be found. The year the opinion was rendered is also included in the citation.

civil complaint A written statement of the plaintiff's legal grievance, which normally initiates a civil suit.

Classified Information Procedures Act (CIPA) This federal law gives procedures for courts to apply in determining whether to protect and seal classified information that could jeopardize national security from unnecessary public disclosure at any stage of a criminal trial.

collateral bar rule A rule that bars someone who violates a court order from trying to defend this action by arguing that the court order was unconstitutional.

commercial speech doctrine The legal doctrine that states that truthful advertising for products and services that are not illegal is normally protected by the First Amendment to the U.S. Constitution.

common law Principles and rules of law that derive their authority not from legislation but from community usage and custom.

concurring opinion A written opinion by an appellate judge or justice in which the author agrees with the decision of the court but normally states reasons different from those in the court opinion as the basis for his or her decision.

consent A defense in both libel and invasion of privacy cases that provides that individuals who agree to the publication of a libelous story or the appropriation of their name cannot then maintain a lawsuit based on the libel or the appropriation.

consent order or decree A document in which an individual agrees to terminate a specific behavior, such as an advertising campaign, or to refrain from a specific action, such as making a certain advertising claim.

constitution A written outline of the organization of a government that provides for both the rights and responsibilities of various branches of the government and the limits of the power of the government.

contempt of court An act of disobedience or disrespect to a judge, which may be punished by a fine or jail sentence.

continuance The delay of a trial or hearing; that is, the trial is postponed.

copyright That body of law that protects the works created by writers, painters, photographers, performing artists, inventors and others who create intangible property.

copyright notice The words "Copyright © 2018 by Don R. Pember," for example, which indicate to a user that a work is copyrighted by the author or creator.

corrective advertising Rules established by the Federal Trade Commission that require an advertiser to correct the false impressions left by deceptive advertising in a certain percentage of future advertisements.

counterspeech The preferred remedy for speech that we disagree with is not censorship, but to add more speech to the marketplace of ideas in order to counter it or to rebut it.

court's opinion The official opinion of an appellate court that states the reasons or rationale for a decision.

criminal libel A libel against the state, against the dead, or against a large, ill-defined group (such as a race) in which the state prosecutes the libel on behalf of the injured parties.

criminal prosecution; criminal action A legal action brought by the state against an individual or group of individuals for violating state criminal laws.

criminal syndicalism laws Laws that outlaw advocacy, planning or processes aimed at establishing the control over industry by workers or trade unions.

D

damages Money awarded to the winning party in a civil lawsuit.

defamation Any communication that holds a person up to contempt, hatred, ridicule or scorn and lowers the reputation of the individual defamed.

defendant The person against whom relief or recovery is sought in a civil lawsuit; the individual against whom a state criminal action is brought.

demurrer An allegation made by the defendant in a lawsuit that even if the facts as stated by the plaintiff are true, they do not state a sufficient cause for action.

de novo "New or fresh." In some instances a court of general jurisdiction will hear an appeal from a case from a lower court and simply retry the case. This is a de novo hearing.

dicta Remarks in a court opinion that do not speak directly to the legal point in question.

direct appeal The statutorily granted right of an aggrieved party to carry the appeal of a case to the U.S. Supreme Court. The high court can deny this right if the appeal lacks a substantial federal question.

dissenting opinion A written opinion by a judge or justice who disagrees with the appellate court's decision in a case.

E

en banc A French term to describe all or most of the justices or judges of an appellate court sitting together to hear a case. This situation is the opposite of the more typical situation in which a small group (called a panel) of judges or justices in a particular court hears a case.

equal time rules Section 315 of the Federal Communications Act, which states that when broadcasters permit a legally qualified candidate for elective office to use their broadcasting facilities, all other legally qualified candidates for the same elective office must be given similar opportunity.

equity A system of jurisprudence, distinct from common law, in which courts are empowered to decide cases on the basis of equity or fairness and are not bound by the rigid precedents that often exist in common law.

Espionage Act A law adopted by Congress in 1917 that outlawed criticism of the U.S. government and its participation in World War I in Europe.

executive privilege An asserted common-law privilege of the president and other executives to keep presidential papers, records and other documents secret, even from Congress.

executive session A popular euphemism for a closed meeting held by a government body such as a city council or school board.

F

fair comment A libel defense that protects the publication of libelous opinion that focuses on the public activities of a person acting in a public sphere.

fair use A provision of the copyright law that permits a limited amount of copying of material that has been properly copyrighted.

false light That portion of privacy law that prohibits all publications or broadcasts that falsely portray an individual in an offensive manner.

Federal Communications Act The law, adopted in 1934, that is the foundation for the regulation of broadcasting in the United States.

Federal Communications Commission (FCC) A five-member body appointed by the president whose function is to administer the federal broadcasting and communications laws.

federal open-meetings law (Government in Sunshine Act) A federal law that requires approximately 50 federal agencies and bureaus to hold all their meetings in public, unless a subject under discussion is included within one of the 10 exemptions contained in the statute.

Federal Trade Commission (FTC) A five-member body appointed by the president whose function is to administer the federal laws relating to advertising, antitrust and many other business matters.

fighting words doctrine A legal doctrine that permits prior censorship of words that create a clear and present danger of inciting an audience to disorder or violence.

FOIA See *Freedom of Information Act.*

Freedom of Information Act (FOIA) A federal law that mandates that all the records created and kept by federal agencies in the executive branch of government must be open for public inspection and copying, except those records that fall into one of nine exempted categories listed in the statute.

FTC See *Federal Trade Commission.*

G

gag order A restrictive court order that prohibits all or some participants in a trial from speaking about a case or that stops publications and broadcasting stations from reporting on certain aspects of a case.

Government in Sunshine Act See *federal open-meetings law.*

grand jury A jury whose function is to determine whether sufficient evidence exists to issue an indictment or true bill charging an individual or individuals with a crime and to take such persons to trial. It is called a grand jury because it has more members than a petit, or trial, jury.

H

heckler's veto A situation that occurs when the audience's negative, adverse and sometimes violent reaction to the message conveyed by a peaceful speaker is allowed to control and silence the speaker. The duty, instead, should be on the government to protect the speaker rather than to allow a "veto" of the speech by the audience.

I

identification As used in a libel suit, the requirement that the plaintiff prove that at least one person believes that the subject of the libelous remarks is the plaintiff and not some other person.

impeachment A criminal proceeding against a public officer that is started by written "articles of impeachment" and followed by a trial. The House of Representatives, for example, can issue articles of impeachment against the president, who is then tried by the Senate.

indictment A written accusation issued by a grand jury charging that an individual or individuals have committed a specific crime and should be taken to trial.

information A written accusation issued by a public officer rather than by a grand jury charging that an individual or individuals have committed a specific crime and should be taken to trial.

intermediate scrutiny The standard of judicial review for content-neutral laws, such as time, place and manner regulations, that requires the government to prove that the regulation is content neutral; justified by a substantial interest; not a complete ban on communication; and narrowly tailored.

intrusion An invasion of privacy committed when one individual intrudes upon or invades the solitude of another individual.

invasion of privacy A civil tort that emerged in the early 20th century and contains four distinct categories of legal wrongs: appropriation, intrusion, publication of private facts and false light.

J

judgment of the court The final ruling of a court, which determines the outcome of a lawsuit. It is different from the verdict, which is the decision of the jury in a trial.

judicial decree A judgment of a court of equity; a declaration of the court announcing the legal consequences of the facts found to be true by the court.

judicial instructions A statement (often written) made by a judge to the members of a jury informing them about the law (as distinguished from the facts) in a case.

judicial review The power of a court to declare void and unenforceable any statute, rule or executive order that conflicts with an appropriate state constitution or the federal constitution.

jury A group of men and women called together in a trial court to determine the facts in a civil or criminal lawsuit. It is sometimes called a petit jury to distinguish it from a grand jury.

jury nullification The controversial power of a jury, despite its sworn duty under oath to apply a law as interpreted and instructed by a judge, to instead ignore (and thereby to "nullify") a law and decide a case according to its own conscience and sensibilities or, as the U.S. Supreme Court once put it, the ability of a jury to acquit "in the teeth of both law and facts."

L

legal brief; brief Written legal argument presented to the court by one or both parties in a lawsuit.

libel Published or broadcast communication that lowers the reputation of an individual by holding him or her up to contempt, ridicule or scorn.

licensing process The process by which a government gives a publisher or a broadcaster prior permission to print a newspaper or operate a broadcasting station. Revocation of a license can be used as punishment for failing to comply with the law or the wishes of the government. Licensing of the printed press in the United States ended in the 1720s.

litigant A party in a lawsuit; a participant in litigation.

litigated order An order issued by a government agency, like the FTC, requiring that a particular practice, such as a certain advertisement, be stopped.

M

memorandum order The announcement by an appellate court of a decision in a case that does not include a written opinion containing the rationale or reasons for the ruling.

misappropriation Taking what belongs to someone else and using it unfairly for one's own gain; for example, attempting to pass off a novel as part of a popular series of novels written and published by someone else. It is often called unfair competition.

Missouri Plan A system used in some states by which judges are appointed to the bench initially and then must stand for re-election on a ballot that permits citizens to vote to retain or not retain the judge.

N

National Advertising Division (NAD) Part of the Council of Better Business Bureaus, this industry organization evaluates and rules on the truthfulness of advertising claims. Complaints are normally brought to the NAD by competing advertisers.

National Advertising Review Board (NARB) The appeals body of a two-tier system created by the advertising community in 1971 for self-regulation that works closely with the National Advertising Division, the investigative body, in affiliation with the Better Business Bureau.

negligence A fault standard in libel and other tort law. Negligent behavior is normally described as an act or action that a reasonably prudent person or a reasonable individual would not have committed. In libel law, courts often measure negligence by asking whether the allegedly libelous material was the work of a person who exercised reasonable care in preparation of the story.

neutral reportage An emerging libel defense or privilege that states that it is permissible to publish or broadcast an accurate account of information about a public figure from a reliable source even when the reporter doubts the truth of the libelous assertion. The defense is not widely accepted.

nonjusticiable matter An issue that is inappropriate for a court to decide because the jurists lack the knowledge to make the ruling, because another branch of government has the responsibility to answer such questions, or because a court order in the matter would not likely be enforceable or enforced.

O

open-meetings laws State and federal statutes that require that certain meetings of public agencies—normally in the executive branch of government—be open to the public and the press.

open-records laws State and federal statutes that require that certain records of public agencies—normally in the executive branch of government—be open for inspection and copying by the public and the press.

opinion The written statement issued by a court that explains the reasons for a judgment and states the rule of law in the case.

oral argument An oral presentation made to a judge or justices in which the litigants argue the merits of their case.

original jurisdiction Jurisdiction in the first instance, as distinguished from appellate jurisdiction. A court exercising original jurisdiction determines both the facts and the law in the case; courts exercising appellate jurisdiction may rule only on the law and the sufficiency of the facts as determined by a trial court.

overbreadth doctrine A statute or regulation will be declared unconstitutional if it sweeps up and bans a substantial amount of protected speech in the process of targeting unprotected speech; in other words, the doctrine prohibits the government from banning unprotected speech if a substantial amount of protected speech is prohibited or chilled in the same process.

P

per curiam opinion An unsigned court opinion. The author of the opinion is not known outside the court.

peremptory challenge A challenge without stated cause to remove a juror from a panel. Litigants are given a small number of such challenges in a lawsuit.

petitioner One who petitions a court to take an action; someone who starts a lawsuit, or carries an appeal to a higher court (appellant). This person is the opposite of a respondent, one who responds to a petition.

plaintiff An individual who initiates a civil lawsuit.

pleadings The written statements of the parties in a lawsuit that contain their allegations, denials and defenses.

plurality opinion A Supreme Court opinion in which five justices cannot agree on a single majority opinion—there is no opinion of the court—but that is joined by more justices than any other opinion in the case.

precedent An established rule of law set by a previous case. Courts should follow precedent when it is advisable and possible.

presumed damages Damages a plaintiff can get without proof of injury or harm.

pretrial hearing A meeting prior to a criminal trial at which attorneys for the state and for the defense make arguments before a judge on evidentiary questions—for example, whether a confession made by the defendant should be admitted as evidence at the trial. This type of hearing is sometimes called a suppression hearing.

Printers' Ink statute A model law drafted in 1911 to control false or misleading advertising. Most states adopted some version of this model in the early 20th century. Such laws are largely ineffective because they are not normally enforced.

prior restraint Prepublication censorship that forbids publication or broadcast of certain objectionable material, as opposed to punishment of a perpetrator after the material has been published or broadcast.

Privacy Act A federal statute that forbids the disclosure of specific material held by federal agencies on the grounds that its release could invade the privacy of the subject of the report or document.

public figure The designation for a plaintiff in a libel suit who has voluntarily entered a public controversy in an effort to influence public opinion in order to generate a resolution of the issue.

public official The designation of a plaintiff in a libel suit who is an elected public officer or is an appointed public officer who has or appears to have considerable responsibility for or control over the conduct of governmental affairs.

publication In libel law, exposing an allegedly libelous statement to one person in addition to the subject of the libel.

publication of private information In privacy law, publicizing embarrassing private information about an individual that is not of legitimate public concern. More than one person must see or hear this information.

puffery Often expansive hyperbole about a product that does not contain factual claims of merit. Normally, puffery is permitted by the law (e.g., "This is the best-looking automobile on the market today").

punitive damages Money damages awarded to a plaintiff in a lawsuit aimed not to compensate for harm to the injured party but to punish the defendant for his or her illegal conduct.

Q

qualified privilege In libel law, the privilege of the reporter (or any person) to publish a fair and accurate report of the proceedings of a public meeting or public document and be immune from lawsuit for the publication of libel uttered at the meeting or contained in the document.

R

Radio Act of 1912 The first federal broadcast law, which imposed only minimal regulation on the fledgling broadcast industry. Radio operators were required to have a license under this statute.

Radio Act of 1927 The first comprehensive national broadcast law, which provided the basic framework for the regulation of broadcast that was later adopted in the Federal Communications Act of 1934.

respondent The person who responds to a petition placed before a court by another person; the opposite of the petitioner. At the appellate level, the respondent is often called the appellee.

restrictive order A court order limiting the discussion of the facts in a criminal case both by participants in the case and by the press. See also *gag order*.

retraction In libel law, a statement published or broadcast that attempts to retract or correct previously published or broadcast libelous matter. A timely retraction will usually mitigate damages, and in some states that have retraction laws, plaintiffs must seek a retraction before beginning a lawsuit or they lose the opportunity to collect anything but special damages.

right of publicity An offshoot of privacy law that protects the right of persons to capitalize on their fame or notoriety for commercial or advertising purposes.

right of reply A little-used libel defense that declares as immune from a lawsuit a libelous remark made against an individual in reply to a previously published libelous remark made by that individual.

rule of four At least four justices of the U.S. Supreme Court must agree to hear a case before a petition for a writ of certiorari will be granted.

S

safe-harbor time period The window of time from 10 p.m. to 6 a.m. when indecent and profane material is protected from FCC regulation on over-the-air broadcast television and radio.

scienter Guilty knowledge. In many criminal prosecutions, the state must prove that the accused was aware of the nature of his or her behavior. In an obscenity case, for example, the state must normally show that the defendant was aware of the contents of the book he or she sold.

secret dockets The practice by some courts of keeping private and out of the view of both reporters and the general public the names and docket numbers of cases, thus keeping secret the very existence of the cases themselves.

Section 312 See *candidate access rule*.

Section 315 See *equal time rules*.

Sedition Act of 1918 An amendment to the Espionage Act adopted in the midst of World War I that severely limited criticism of the government and criticism of U.S. participation in the European war.

seditious libel Libeling the government; criticizing the government or government officers. It is sometimes called sedition.

sequestration of the jury Separating the jury from the community during a trial. Usually a jury is lodged at a hotel and members are required to eat together. In general, sequestration means to keep jurors away from other people. Exposure to news reports is also screened to shield jurors from information about the trial.

shield laws State statutes that permit reporters in some circumstances to shield the name of a confidential news source when questioned by a grand jury or in another legal forum.

single mistake rule In libel law, a rule that states that it is not libelous to accuse a professional person or businessperson of making a single mistake (e.g., "Dr. Pat Jones incorrectly diagnosed the patient's illness").

sitting en banc See *en banc*.

slander Oral defamation.

Smith Act A federal law adopted in 1940 that makes it illegal to advocate the violent overthrow of the government.

special damages Damages that can be awarded to a plaintiff in a lawsuit upon proof of specific monetary loss.

spectrum scarcity The notion, in the realm of the FCC's regulation of over-the-air broadcasting, that there are a finite number of frequencies on which to broadcast and that, in turn, there are more people who want to broadcast than there are available frequencies.

split of authority A disagreement among lower courts on the same legal issue.

stare decisis "Let the decision stand." This concept is the operating principle in the common-law system and requires that judges follow precedent case law when making judgments.

state secrets privilege An executive branch privilege, often asserted during wartime, that allows the government to block a lawsuit if any information disclosed during it would adversely affect national security. Under this doctrine, the United States may prevent disclosure of information during a judicial proceeding if there is a "reasonable danger" the disclosure would expose military matters that, in the interest of national security, should not be divulged.

statute of limitations A law that requires that a legal action must begin within a specified period of time (usually one to three years for a civil case) after the legal wrong was committed.

statutes Laws adopted by legislative bodies.

statutory construction The process undertaken by courts to interpret or construe the meaning of statutes.

strict scrutiny The standard of judicial review for content-based statutes, requiring the government to prove that it has a compelling interest (an interest of the highest order) in regulating the speech at issue and that the means of serving that interest are narrowly tailored such that no more speech is restricted than is necessary to serve the allegedly compelling interest.

subpoena A court document that requires a witness to appear and testify or to produce documents or papers pertinent to a pending controversy.

substantiation A Federal Trade Commission rule that requires an advertiser to prove the truth of advertising claims made about a product or service.

summary judgment A judgment granted to a party in a lawsuit when the pleadings and other materials in the case disclose no material issue of fact between the parties, making it possible for the case to be decided on the basis of the law by the court. A summary judgment avoids a costly jury trial.

summary jury trial An abbreviated jury trial where jurors hear arguments but no witnesses are called and little evidence is presented. The jurors can issue an informal verdict, which can be used as the basis for a settlement of the case, thus avoiding a full-blown and costly trial.

survival statute A statute that permits an heir to continue to maintain a lawsuit if the plaintiff died after the suit was filed but before it was resolved.

symbolic speech doctrine The two-part judicial test used to determine when conduct rises to the level of "speech" within the meaning of the First Amendment. The person engaging in the conduct must intend to convey a particularized message with his or her conduct, and there must be a substantial likelihood, under the circumstances in which the conduct takes place, that some members of the audience will understand the meaning that was intended.

T

time, place and manner restrictions or rules Rules, when justified by a substantial government interest, that can regulate the time, place and manner of speaking or publishing and the distribution of printed material.

tort A civil wrong not based on a contract, against the person or property of another. Typical torts are libel, invasion of privacy, trespass and assault.

trade libel Product disparagement, and not considered true libel; disparaging a product as opposed to the manufacturer or maker of the product.

trade regulation rules (TRRs) Rules adopted by the Federal Trade Commission that prohibit specific advertising claims about an entire class of products. For example, makers of fruit drinks that contain less than 10 percent fruit juice cannot advertise these products as fruit juice.

trespass Unlawful entry on another person's land or property.

trial court Normally the first court to hear a lawsuit. This court is the forum in which the facts are determined and the law is initially applied, as opposed to an appellate court, to which decisions are appealed.

true threats A category of speech that is not protected by the First Amendment. Statements where the speaker means to communicate a serious expression of an intent to commit an act of unlawful violence to a particular person or group of people.

U

unfair competition See *misappropriation*.

V

variable obscenity statutes A Supreme Court doctrine that permits states to prohibit the sale, distribution or exhibition of certain kinds of nonobscene matter to children, so long as these laws do not interfere with the accessibility of this material to adults.

verdict The decision of a trial jury based on the instructions given to it by the judge.

viewpoint-based discrimination The worst form of content-based regulation that exists when the government censors or regulates one particular viewpoint or side on a given topic or issue but does not censor or regulate another viewpoint or side on the same topic or issue. For instance, if the government censored pro-life speech on the topic of abortion but did not censor pro-choice speech on the topic of abortion, that would constitute viewpoint-based discrimination. Viewpoint-based discrimination by the government on speech is always unconstitutional.

void for vagueness doctrine A statute or regulation is unconstitutional if it is so vague that a person of reasonable and ordinary intelligence would not know, from looking at its terms, what speech is allowed and what speech is prohibited.

voir dire A preliminary examination the court makes of people chosen to serve as jurors in a trial. People can be challenged for cause or on the basis of a peremptory challenge by either side in the legal dispute.

W

warrant A written order, signed by a judge or magistrate, that may take many varieties, such as a search warrant that allows a law enforcement officer to search for and seize property or possessions that constitute evidence of the commission of a crime.

writ of certiorari A writ by which an appellant seeks the review of a case by the U.S. Supreme Court. When the writ is granted, the court will order the lower court to send up the record of the case for review.

INDEX

Index

Index